INTERNATIONAL HUMAN RIGHTS LAW

INTERNATIONAL HUMAN RIGHTS LAW

Third Edition

EDITED BY

DANIEL MOECKLI
University of Zurich

SANGEETA SHAH
University of Nottingham

SANDESH SIVAKUMARAN
University of Nottingham

CONSULTANT EDITOR:

DAVID HARRIS
*Professor Emeritus and Co-Director, Human Rights
Law Centre, University of Nottingham*

Great Clarendon Street, Oxford, OX2 6DP,
United Kingdom

Oxford University Press is a department of the University of Oxford.
It furthers the University's objective of excellence in research, scholarship,
and education by publishing worldwide. Oxford is a registered trade mark of
Oxford University Press in the UK and in certain other countries

Published in the United States of America by Oxford University Press
198 Madison Avenue, New York, NY 10016, United States of America

British Library Cataloguing in Publication Data

Data available

Library of Congress Control Number: 2017948019

ISBN 978-0-19-876723-7

Printed in Great Britain by
Bell & Bain Ltd., Glasgow

OUTLINE CONTENTS

PART IV PROTECTION

PART V LINKAGES

PART VI CHALLENGES

DETAILED CONTENTS

PART II INTERNATIONAL LAW

PART III SUBSTANTIVE RIGHTS

PART V LINKAGES

PART VI CHALLENGES

PREFACE

Human rights mean different things to different people. From the woman on the street to the UN High Commissioner for Human Rights, from the local human rights activist to the government official, each of us has a different conception of the origin, purpose, and function of human rights. To reflect this diversity of views, we have invited a range of practitioners and academics with different regional, theoretical, and professional backgrounds to contribute chapters to this textbook on their respective fields of expertise.

The book covers the key elements of a typical international human rights law course. It follows the same format as the first two editions. Part I seeks to show how human rights have developed over time, how they can be justified, and on what basis they may be criticized. Today, human rights are firmly located in international law and Part II explores the key international law aspects of human rights. Part III considers some of the rights guaranteed to individuals and groups by international human rights law. Part IV addresses the systems of human rights protection at the UN, regional, and national levels. Part V examines the linkages between international human rights law and three other areas of international law: international humanitarian law, international criminal law, and international refugee law. Finally, the book concludes, in Part VI, with a consideration of some of the major challenges to the protection of human rights. For want of space, it is impossible to cover all substantive rights, protected groups, systems of protection, linkages, and challenges. This is not meant to reflect in any way the importance, or lack thereof, of the omitted issues.

There are some changes to the book for this third edition. The most obvious is the addition of chapters on Children's Rights by Geraldine Van Bueren and on Regional Protection by Başak Çalı. All other chapters have been thoroughly updated to take account of developments since the publication of the second edition in 2013. Many chapters have also been expanded or elaborated in response to helpful comments received about the second edition. We are grateful to friends and colleagues for these comments. There have also been some changes in authors. Sadly, Sir Nigel Rodley passed away in January 2017 and we wish to thank Dr Lyn Rodley for her agreement that we may continue to use his chapter. We are grateful to Raffael Fasel for updating this chapter. Dominic McGoldrick has updated the chapter on Thought, Expression, Association, and Assembly; Thomas Antkowiak has updated the chapter on the Americas; and Sarah Joseph has been joined by Sam Dipnall in the update of her chapter on Scope of Application. The chapters take into account developments as far as July 2017. Where it has been possible, some later developments have been added at the proof stage.

Many people have supported us in various ways throughout the process of producing this textbook. We are particularly grateful to the contributors to the book for their enthusiasm and support, to our consulting editor, David Harris, for his guidance throughout the process, to Christine Tramontano and Olivia Salmon for their editorial assistance, and to the team at Oxford University Press for steering us through the various editorial stages.

DM/SS/SS
Zurich/Nottingham, September 2017

NOTES ON CONTRIBUTORS

Thomas M Antkowiak is Associate Professor of Law and Director of the International Human Rights Clinic at Seattle University School of Law, United States. He has handled numerous cases in the Inter-American Human Rights System and is the co-author of *The American Convention on Human Rights: Essential Rights* (OUP, 2017).

Ed Bates, PhD, is an Associate Professor in Law at the University of Leicester. His recent work includes 'Activism and Self-Restraint: The Margin of Appreciation's Strasbourg Career … Its "Coming of Age"?', in Symposium in Honour of Judge Paul Mahoney 36 (2016) No. 7–12 *Human Rights Law Journal* (forthcoming); 'Democratic Override (or Rejection) and the Authority of the Strasbourg Court: The UK Parliament and Prisoner Voting', in Saul, Follesdal, and Ulfstein, *The International Human Rights Judiciary and National Parliaments: Europe and Beyond* (Cambridge University Press 2017, forthcoming); 'Analysing the Prisoner Voting Saga and the British Challenge to Strasbourg' (2014) 14 *Human Rights Law Review* 503. He is a co-author of Harris, O'Boyle, and Warbrick, *The Law of the European Convention on Human Rights* (Oxford University Press, 2014; 2018 edition forthcoming) and the author of *The Evolution of the European Convention on Human Rights* (Oxford University Press, 2010). Ed runs the blog UKStrasbourgspotlight (<https://ukstrasbourgspotlight.wordpress.com/>). He can be found on twitter: @ed_epb3.

Samantha Besson is Professor of Public International Law and European Law and Co-Director of the European Law Institute at the University of Fribourg, Switzerland.

Andrew Byrnes is Professor of International Law at the Faculty of Law, The University of New South Wales (UNSW), and Chair of the Steering Committee of the Australian Human Rights Centre, UNSW from 2006 until 2017. He served as external legal adviser to the Australian Parliamentary Joint Committee on Human Rights from 2012 to 2014. His chapter with Catherine Renshaw draws on research conducted under two Australian Research Council-funded Linkage projects (LP0776639 and LP0989167) on national human rights institutions in the Asia Pacific, and economic, social, and cultural rights, respectively.

Başak Çalı is Professor of International Law at Hertie School of Governance, Berlin and Director of Center for Global Public Law at Koç University, Istanbul. She has written extensively on international human rights law, with an emphasis on its purpose, legitimacy, and domestic impact. Her work treats international human rights law in its broader normative, comparative and political context. She is the inaugural Chair of the European Implementation Network and editor in chief of Oxford Reports on United Nations Human Rights Body Case-Law. She is a fellow of the Human Rights Centre of the University of Essex, and a senior fellow of Pluri-Courts Center at the University of Oslo. She has been a Council of Europe expert on the European Convention on Human Rights since 2002.

Christine Chinkin, FBA, is Director of the Centre for Women, Peace and Security and Emerita Professor of International Law, London School of Economics and Political Science, and William W. Cook Global Law Professor, University of Michigan Law School.

Andrew Clapham is a Professor of International Law at the Graduate Institute of International and Development Studies in Geneva. He is currently a member of the Executive Committee of the International Commission of Jurists. His publications include *Brierly's Law of Nations: An Introduction to the Role of International Law in International Relations* (7th ed, 2012), *The Oxford Handbook of International Law in Armed Conflict* co-edited with Paola Gaeta (2014), and *The 1949 Geneva Conventions: A Commentary* co-edited with Paola Gaeta and Marco Sassòli (2015).

Jane Connors is the International Advocacy Director (Law and Policy) of Amnesty International, based in Geneva. From 1996 to 2015 she worked in various positions at the United Nations, including at the Office of the High Commissioner for Human Rights. Before joining the United Nations, she held academic posts in the UK and Australia, including 14 years at the School of Oriental and African Studies in London. She has published widely on United Nations human rights mechanisms, the human rights of women, and violence against women and children.

Fons Coomans holds the UNESCO Chair in Human Rights and Peace at the Department of International and European Law of Maastricht University. He is also the Director of the Maastricht Centre for Human Rights, Senior Researcher at the Netherlands Network for Human Rights Research, and Visiting Professor at the University of Cape Town. His research focuses on economic, social, and cultural rights and international human rights monitoring procedures.

Robert Cryer is Professor of International and Criminal Law at the University of Birmingham. He teaches international law, criminal law, transnational criminal law, and international criminal law. He is one of the authors of Cryer, Friman, Robinson, and Wilmshurst, *An Introduction to International Criminal Law and Procedure* (Cambridge: CUP, 3rd ed 2014), and co-editor of the *Journal of Conflict and Security Law*.

Marie-Bénédicte Dembour is Professor of Law and Anthropology at the University of Brighton. She was educated at Brussels (ULB) and Oxford. Her latest monograph *When Humans Become Migrants: Study of the European Court of Human Rights with an Inter-American Counterpoint* (Oxford University Press, 2015) received the Odysseus Prize for outstanding academic research. Although her many distinguished publications cover various fields, she has developed a particular expertise in human rights. Her monograph *Who Believes in Human Rights? Reflections on the European Convention* (Cambridge University Press, 2006) continues to attract high praise; her paper 'What are human rights? Four schools of thought' has counted amongst *Human Rights Quarterly*'s most downloaded articles since its publication in 2010. She has been a visiting professor in many institutions, including most recently at the Free University Amsterdam and the University of Caen Normandy. She has been invited to give talks throughout the world.

Sam Dipnall, BA/LLB(Hons), is a human rights lawyer. He is a current postgraduate candidate in the Masters of Human Rights Law programme at Monash University, Australia. He is a current member of the Law Institute of Victoria Human Rights & Charter of Rights Committee, and has previously held positions with Justice Connect, the Victorian Law Reform Commission, the Castan Centre for Human Rights, as well as the International Service for Human Rights (ISHR).

Alice Edwards, PhD, is Head of the Secretariat for the Convention against Torture Initiative, <http://www.cti2024.org/>, a ten-year initiative of the Governments of Chile, Denmark, Ghana, Indonesia and Morocco, to achieve universal ratification and better implementation of the UN Convention against Torture by 2024. She has previously held positions at UNHCR, Amnesty International, and the Universities of Oxford and Nottingham, and has advised governments and organizations in all regions of the world on human rights and refugee matters. She is the author of inter alia *Violence against Women under International Human Rights Law* (Cambridge University Press, 2011) and teaches part time at the University of London.

Asbjørn Eide is former Director and presently Professor Emeritus at the Norwegian Center for Human Rights at the University of Oslo. He has been Torgny Segerstedt Professor at the University of Gothenburg, Sweden, visiting professor at the University of Lund, and was for several years adjunct professor at the College of Law, American University in Washington.

He is author and editor of several books and numerous articles on human rights, and was for 20 years an expert member of the UN Sub-Commission on Promotion and Protection of Human Rights.

Steven Greer, FAcSS FRSA, is Professor of Human Rights at the University of Bristol Law School. He studied Law at the University of Oxford, Sociology at the London School of Economics, and has a PhD in Law from the Queen's University of Belfast. He has taught in the UK, the US, Germany, France, and Australia, acted as consultant/adviser to various organizations including the Council of Europe and others in Northern Ireland, Palestine, and Nepal, and lectured and given conference and other papers all over the world including China. He has been Nuffield Foundation Visiting Research Fellow at the Oñati International Institute for the Sociology of Law (Spain) and British Academy Research Fellow at the University of Bristol, and has published widely, particularly in the fields of criminal justice, human rights, and law and terrorism. Two of his books have been shortlisted for prizes, and some of his published and other work has been translated into half a dozen languages. His most recent book, *Human Rights in the Council of Europe and the European Union: Achievements, Trends and Challenges* (co-authored by Janneke Gerards and Rosie Slowe), was published by Cambridge University Press in 2017.

Christof Heyns is Professor of Human Rights Law at the University of Pretoria and a member of the UN Human Rights Committee. He teaches human rights law in the Masters' programme at Oxford University, is an adjunct professor at the American University in Washington DC, and was a visiting professor at the University of Geneva in 2016. He was UN Special Rapporteur on extrajudicial, summary or arbitrary executions 2010–2016. During 2016 he chaired the UN Independent Investigation on Burundi. He holds degrees in law and philosophy from the Universities of Pretoria, the Witwatersrand and Yale Law School. He has been a Humboldt Fellow at the Max Planck Institute in Heidelberg and a Fulbright Fellow at Harvard Law School.

Sarah Joseph is a Professor of International Human Rights Law and, since 2005, the Director of the Castan Centre for Human Rights Law at Monash University, Melbourne. She has written extensively in the area of human rights, including in relation to global trade and investment, multinational corporations, and terrorism. She is the main author of *The International Covenant on Civil and Political Rights: Cases, Materials, and Commentary* (Oxford University Press, 3rd ed, 2013). Her latest research is on the intersections between human rights and media, art, and sport.

Magnus Killander is Associate Professor and Head of Research at the Centre for Human Rights at the University of Pretoria Faculty of Law.

Stephen P Marks is the François-Xavier Bagnoud Professor of Health and Human Rights at the Harvard T.H. Chan School of Public Health, where he directs the Program on Human Rights in Development. He also teaches human rights in the Faculty of Arts and Sciences at Harvard University. He served in the United Nations system for 12 years, including in Unesco, in peacekeeping operations, and as member and chair of the UN High-level Task Force on the Implementation of the Right to Development (2004–2010). Among his recent publications as editor or co-editor are *Development as a Human Right: Legal, Political and Economic Dimensions* (2nd ed, 2010), *Health and Human Rights: Basic International Documents* (3rd ed, 2012), *Achieving the Human Right to Health* (2013), *Realizing the Right to Development: Essays in Commemoration of 25 Years of the United Nations Declaration on the Right to Development* (2013, as editorial consultant to the OHCHR), and *Research Handbook on Human Rights and Development* (in preparation for 2018).

Robert McCorquodale is the Director of the British Institute of International and Comparative Law in London and a barrister at Brick Court Chambers. He is also Professor of International

Law and Human Rights, School of Law, University of Nottingham. Previously he was a Fellow and Lecturer in Law at St John's College, University of Cambridge and at the Australian National University in Canberra. Before embarking on an academic career, he worked as a qualified lawyer in commercial litigation in Sydney and London. Robert's research and teaching interests are in the areas of public international law and human rights law, including the role of non-state actors. He has published widely on these areas, including being co-author of *Cases and Materials on International Law* (Oxford University Press, 5th ed, 2011), and has provided advice to governments, corporations, international organizations, non-governmental organizations, and peoples concerning international law and human rights issues, including advising on the drafting of new constitutions and conducting human rights training courses.

Dominic McGoldrick is Professor of International Human Rights Law and Co-Director of the Human Rights Law Centre, University of Nottingham. He teaches and researches on UK human rights, European human rights, and international human rights. He has been a Fulbright Distinguished Scholar and a Human Rights Fellow at the Harvard Law School. His publications include *The Human Rights Committee* (Oxford University Press, 1994), *International Relations Law of the European Union* (Longman, 1997), *From 9-11 to the Iraq War 2003* (Hart, 2004) and *Human Rights and Religion—The Islamic Headscarf Debate in Europe* (Hart, 2006). He was a major contributor to and co-editor of *The Permanent International Criminal Court* (Hart, 2004). Recent articles have concerned sexual orientation discrimination, religious symbols, and the margin of appreciation.

Frédéric Mégret is an Associate Professor and Dawson Scholar at McGill University's Faculty of Law. He holds a PhD from the Université de Paris I and the Geneva Graduate Institute of International Studies.

Daniel Moeckli is Assistant Professor of Public International Law and Constitutional Law at the University of Zurich and a Fellow of the University of Nottingham Human Rights Law Centre. He is the author of *Human Rights and Non-discrimination in the 'War on Terror'* (Oxford University Press, 2008) and *Exclusion from Public Space: A Comparative Constitutional Analysis* (Cambridge University Press, 2016).

Michael O'Flaherty is Director of the European Union Agency for Fundamental Rights. Previously he has been Established Professor of Human Rights Law and Director of the Irish Centre for Human Rights at the National University of Ireland, Galway and Professor of Applied Human Rights at the University of Nottingham. He has also served as Chief Commissioner of the Northern Ireland Human Rights Commission. From 2004–2012 he was a member, latterly Vice Chair, of the United Nations Human Rights Committee. He was Rapporteur for the 2007 Yogyakarta Principles on the Application of International Human Rights Law Regarding Sexual Orientation and Gender Identity.

Dianne Otto is Professorial Fellow at Melbourne Law School where she held the Francine V. McNiff Chair in Human Rights Law from 2013–2016. Her research examines gender, sexuality, and race inequalities in the context of international human rights law, the UN Security Council's peacekeeping work, the technologies of global 'crisis governance', threats to economic, social and cultural rights, and the transformative potential of people's tribunals and other NGO initiatives. Recent publications include the ground-breaking collection, which she edited, *Queering International Law: Possibilities, Alliances, Complicities, Risks* (Routledge 2017), an article on people's tribunals in the *London Review of International Law* (2017) and 'Feminist Approaches to International Law' in Anne Orford and Florian Hoffman (eds), *Oxford Handbook of International Legal Theory* (2016).

Catherine Renshaw, PhD, is Associate Professor and Deputy Head of the Thomas More Law School at Australian Catholic University, where she teaches international human rights law.

Julie Ringelheim is Senior Researcher with the Belgian National Fund for Scientific Research (FNRS) and with the Centre for Philosophy of Law of Louvain University (Belgium). She teaches International Human Rights Law and Sociology of Law at Louvain University. She holds a PhD from the European University Institute (Florence) and an LLM from Cambridge University (UK).

Sir Nigel S Rodley was Professor of Law and Chair of the Human Rights Centre at the University of Essex. From 1992 to 2001 he served as UN Commission on Human Rights Special Rapporteur on the question of torture. He was a member of the UN Human Rights Committee from 2001 to 2016 and also served as its Chair. He was also President of the International Commission of Jurists.

Martin Scheinin is, since 2008, Professor of International Law and Human Rights at the European University Institute in Florence. He served as the UN Special Rapporteur on human rights and counter-terrorism (2005–2011). He has a doctorate in law from the University of Helsinki (1991) and was in 1997–2004 a member of the UN Human Rights Committee and in 1998–2008 Director of the Institute for Human Rights at Åbo Akademi University.

Sangeeta Shah is Associate Professor in the School of Law, University of Nottingham and Member of the Human Rights Law Centre, University of Nottingham. She is the co-editor of the Recent Developments Section of the *Human Rights Law Review*.

Sandesh Sivakumaran is Professor of Public International Law at the University of Nottingham. He is a non-resident research scholar at the United States Naval War College Stockton Center for International Law, a member of the advisory board of Geneva Call, and a member of the working group on non-state armed groups at the Centre of Competence on Humanitarian Negotiation. He is the author of *The Law of Non-International Armed Conflict* (OUP, 2012) and co-author of *Oppenheim's International Law: United Nations* (OUP, 2017) with Dame Rosalyn Higgins, Philippa Webb, Dapo Akande, and James Sloan and *Cases and Materials on International Law* (Sweet and Maxwell, 8th ed, 2015) with David Harris.

Theo van Boven is Professor Emeritus of International Law at Maastricht University, the Netherlands. Over the years he has been closely associated with the human rights programme of the UN, notably as Director of Human Rights, member of the Commission and the Sub-Commission for Human Rights, member of the Committee on the Elimination of Racial Discrimination, and Special Rapporteur on Torture.

Geraldine Van Bueren QC helped draft the UN Convention on the Rights of the Child and other international instruments. She is Professor of International Human Rights Law at Queen Mary University of London and Visiting Fellow, Kellogg College, Oxford. She is a former Commissioner on the Equality and Human Rights Commission and a barrister and member of Doughty Street Chambers.

ABBREVIATIONS

AAA	American Anthropological Association
ACHPR	African Charter on Human and Peoples' Rights
ACHR	American Convention on Human Rights
ACommHPR	African Commission on Human and Peoples' Rights
ADHR	American Declaration of the Rights and Duties of Man
AICHR	ASEAN Inter-governmental Commission on Human Rights
AIDS	Acquired Immunodeficiency Syndrome
AJIL	American Journal of International Law
APRM	African Peer Review Mechanism
ASEAN	Association of Southeast Asian Nations
ASIL	American Society of International Law
AU	African Union
BBC	British Broadcasting Corporation
BC	Before Christ
BGE	Bundesgerichtsentscheid (Swiss Federal Supreme Court decision)
BYIL	British Year Book of International Law
CAT	Committee Against Torture
CDDH	Steering Committee for Human Rights
CEDAW	Convention on the Elimination of All Forms of Discrimination Against Women
CEDAW-OP	Optional Protocol to the CEDAW
CEJIL	Center for Justice and International Law
CERD	Committee on the Elimination of Racial Discrimination
CESCR	Committee on Economic, Social and Cultural Rights
CFI	Court of First Instance
CHR	UN Commission on Human Rights
CIDA	Canadian International Development Agency
CJEU	Court of Justice of the European Union
CLP	Current Legal Problems
CPED	International Convention for the Protection of all Persons from Enforced Disappearance
CRC	Convention on the Rights of the Child
CRC-OP3	Optional Protocol to the Convention on the Rights of the Child on a Communications Procedure
CRNZ	Criminal Reports of New Zealand
CRPD	Convention on the Rights of Persons with Disabilities
CRPD-OP	Optional Protocol to the CRPD
CSCE	Conference on Security and Cooperation in Europe
CTC	Counter-Terrorism Committee
CUP	Cambridge University Press
DANIDA	Danish International Development Agency
Dec	Decision
DFID	UK Department for International Development

DPKO	UN Department of Peacekeeping Operations
DRC	Democratic Republic of Congo
EACJ	East African Court of Justice
EC	European Community
ECHR	European Convention on Human Rights
ECJ	European Court of Justice
ECommHR	European Commission on Human Rights
ECOMOG	Economic Community of West African States Monitoring Group
ECOSOC	UN Economic and Social Council
ECOSOCC	Economic, Social and Cultural Council of the African Union
ECOWAS	Economic Community of West African States
ECPT	European Convention for the Prevention of Torture and Inhuman or Degrading Treatment or Punishment
ECSR	European Committee of Social Rights
EEC	European Economic Community
EHRLR	European Human Rights Law Review
EHRR	European Human Rights Reports
EJ	European Journal
EJIL	European Journal of International Law
ELJ	European Law Journal
ELR	European Law Review
EPO	European Patent Office
EU	European Union
EWCA	England and Wales Court of Appeal
EWHC	England and Wales High Court
FAO	UN Food and Agriculture Organization
FARC	Revolutionary Armed Forces of Colombia
FRA	Fundamental Rights Agency
FRY	Federal Republic of Yugoslavia
G-20	The Group of Twenty
GA	UN General Assembly
GDR	German Democratic Republic
HDCA	Human Development and Capability Association
HHRJ	Harvard Human Rights Journal
HIPC	Highly Indebted Poor Countries
HIV	Human Immunodeficiency Virus
HLR	Harvard Law Review
HMSO	Her Majesty's Stationery Office
HRAP	Human Rights Advisory Panel
HRBA	Human Rights-Based Approach
HRC	Human Rights Committee
HR Council	UN Human Rights Council
HRLJ	Human Rights Law Journal
HRLR	Human Rights Law Review
HRQ	Human Rights Quarterly
IACtHR	Inter-American Court of Human Rights
IACommHR	Inter-American Commission on Human Rights
ICC	International Criminal Court
ICCPR	International Covenant on Civil and Political Rights
ICCPR-OP1	First Optional Protocol to the ICCPR

ICCPR-OP2	Second Optional Protocol to the ICCPR
ICERD	International Convention on the Elimination of All Forms of Racial Discrimination
ICESCR	International Covenant on Economic, Social and Cultural Rights
ICESCR-OP	Optional Protocol to the ICESCR
ICLQ	International and Comparative Law Quarterly
ICJ	International Court of Justice
ICRC	International Committee of the Red Cross
ICRMW	International Convention on the Protection of the Rights of All Migrant Workers and Members of Their Families
ICTR	International Criminal Tribunal for Rwanda
ICTY	International Criminal Tribunal for the former Yugoslavia
IDC	International Disability Caucus
IDEA	International Development Ethics Association
IJHR	International Journal of Human Rights
IJRL	International Journal of Refugee Law
ILC	International Law Commission
ILM	International Legal Materials
ILO	International Labour Organization
IMF	International Monetary Fund
INSC	Supreme Court of India
IR	International Relations
IRA	Irish Republican Army
IRRC	International Review of the Red Cross
JCHR	Joint Committee on Human Rights (UK)
JCSL	Journal of Conflict and Security Law
JHR	Journal of Human Rights
JICJ	Journal of International Criminal Justice
KFOR	Kosovo Force
KLA	Kosovo Liberation Army
LGBT	Lesbian, Gay, Bisexual, and Transgender
LGBTI	Lesbian, Gay, Bisexual, Transgender, and Intersex
LJIL	Leiden Journal of International Law
LNOJ	League of Nations Official Journal
LTTE	Liberation Tigers of Tamil Eelam
LQR	Law Quarterly Review
MCC	Millennium Challenge Corporation
MDGs	Millennium Development Goals
MLR	Modern Law Review
NAACP	National Association for the Advancement of Colored People
NATO	North Atlantic Treaty Organization
NEPAD	New Partnership for Africa's Development
NGO	Non-Governmental Organization
NHRI	National Human Rights Institution
NJIL	Nordic Journal of International Law
NPMs	National Preventive Mechanisms
NQHR	Netherlands Quarterly of Human Rights
Nuremberg IMT	Nuremberg International Military Tribunal
NYU	New York University
NYUJILP	New York University Journal of International Law and Politics

OAS	Organization of American States
OAU	Organization of African Unity
ODIHR	Office for Democratic Institutions and Human Rights
OECD	Organization for Economic Co-operation and Development
OHCHR	Office of the UN High Commissioner for Human Rights
OIC	Organisation of the Islamic Conference
OJLS	Oxford Journal of Legal Studies
OPT	Occupied Palestinian Territory
OSCE	Organization of Security and Co-operation in Europe
OUP	Oxford University Press
PACE	Parliamentary Assembly of the Council of Europe
PAP	Pan-African Parliament
PCIJ	Permanent Court of International Justice
PKK	Kurdistan Workers' Party
PL	Public Law
PLD	Pakistan Legal Decisions
PRSPs	Poverty Reduction Strategy Papers
PSC	Peace and Security Council
Rec des Cours	Recueil des Cours de l'Académie de Droit International
RECs	Regional Economic Communities
Res	Resolution
SADC	Southern African Development Community
SC	UN Security Council
SCSL	Special Court for Sierra Leone
SDG	Sustainable Development Goals
SGBV	Sexual and Gender-Based Violence
SSR	Soviet Socialist Republic
Tokyo IMT	Tokyo International Military Tribunal
UDHR	Universal Declaration of Human Rights
UK	United Kingdom
UKHL	United Kingdom House of Lords
UN	United Nations
UNCAT	Convention against Torture and Other Cruel, Inhuman or Degrading Treatment or Punishment
UNCAT-OP	Optional Protocol to the UNCAT
UNDAT	UN Declaration against Torture
UNDG	UN Development Group
UNDG-HRM	UN Development Group Human Rights Mainstreaming Mechanism
UNDP	UN Development Programme
UNESCO	UN Educational, Scientific and Cultural Organization
UNHCR	UN High Commissioner for Refugees
UNICEF	UN Children's Fund
UNIFEM	UN Development Fund for Women
UNMIK	UN Interim Administration Mission in Kosovo
UNMISS	UN Mission in South Sudan
UNRWA	UN Relief and Works Agency for Palestine Refugees in the New East
UP	University Press
UPR	Universal Periodic Review
USA	United States of America
USC	United States Code

USSR	Union of Soviet Socialist Republics
VCLT	Vienna Convention on the Law of Treaties
WGC	Working Group on Communications
WGS	Working Group on Situations
WHO	World Health Organization
WLR	Weekly Law Reports
WTO	World Trade Organization
YB	Year Book
YJIL	Yale Journal of International Law

TABLE OF INTERNATIONAL INSTRUMENTS

TABLE OF CASES

INTERNATIONAL

PART I

FOUNDATIONS

1

HISTORY

Ed Bates

SUMMARY

This chapter tells the story of the historical development of the concept of human rights and their status in international law. It is divided into three main sections. As the human rights story began on the domestic plane, the chapter starts by considering this. The focus is on the key developments since the seventeenth century, but in particular since the late eighteenth century. The chapter then turns to international law, examining it from the perspective of human rights over the period up to the Second World War. Finally, it focuses on the efforts to create international human rights law in the 1940s, culminating with the proclamation of the Universal Declaration of Human Rights in 1948.

1 INTRODUCTION

As an esteemed professor of international law and (later) international judge, Hersch Lauterpacht wrote in 1945: 'any attempt to translate the idea of an International Bill of the Rights of Man into a working rule of law is fraught with difficulties which disturb orthodox thought to the point of utter discouragement'.[1] The transformation of relations between a state and its nationals into international legal obligations by which the international community could derive a respectable and meaningful level of control and censure would, Lauterpacht argued, engender 'restrictions on sovereignty more far-reaching in their implications than any yet propounded in the annals of international utopias'.[2]

To be clear, Lauterpacht was firmly committed to the establishment of international human rights law, as his books of 1945 and 1950,[3] and his other work,[4] revealed. His 1945 study was published at a time when hopes were high that there would soon be established an International Bill of Rights. It was a pioneering work as not only did it address the substance of a proposed International Bill, but it also provided a detailed discussion of how it might be implemented and enforced at the international level. The dramatic quotations above were not intended to strike a pessimistic chord. Instead, the aim was to emphasize the extent of the task ahead for the international community. Lauterpacht was calling

---

[1] Lauterpacht, *An International Bill of Rights of Man* (Columbia University Press, 1945) 9–10.
[2] Lauterpacht (1945), 14.
[3] Lauterpacht, *International Law and Human Rights* (Stevens and Sons, 1950).
[4] See Simpson, 'Hersch Lauterpacht and the Genesis of the Age of Human Rights' (2004) 120 *LQR* 49.

upon the international community, and leading states in particular, to face up to that task as the Second World War came to an end and plans for a 'new world order' started to take shape.

We will return to the successes and failures of the immediate post-war effort as regards international human rights law in Section 4. However, in order to obtain a better perspective on this, and the other chapters in this book, we should trace the story of the protection of human rights, first, in domestic law and then in international law prior to 1945.

2 HUMAN RIGHTS ON THE DOMESTIC PLANE

Where should an analysis of the history of human rights begin?[5] One could go back several thousand years and find concepts related to human rights in ancient civilizations across the world, as with the Law Code of Hammurabi, created by the Babylonian king Hammurabi in the eighteenth century BC. The origins of human rights might also be traced back to various religious codes through the ages. By contrast, if the point of departure is the idea that human beings have natural rights, then the story commences at least as far back as the time of the Greek city states and the thinking of the Stoics.[6]

Finding a precise point of departure for 'a history of human rights' is an inherently controversial matter. It is probably quite unrealistic to credit any one culture, religion, or region of the world with the origins of human rights. Moreover, as a leading expert has put it, an attempt to do so would be 'politically charged'.[7] It inevitably risks privileging 'a particular world view' of human rights; it might be viewed as 'a way either to defend a specific status quo or value system against possible challenges'.[8] Two points must therefore be made at the outset. First, there are many different threads to the human rights idea as it exists today, and it is invidious to locate any one specific thread as *the* beginning. Second, the account that follows focuses especially on the origins of legal measures in the field of human rights. In that regard the first part of this chapter looks to the early developments in the Western world in particular, and to the extent that it might convey a Western bias, this is not the author's intention.[9]

From the perspective of legal measures championing the rights of the common person against the state, the starting point of the history of human rights is typically taken to be the Magna Carta of 1215. Yet this is somewhat erroneous. The Magna Carta resounds with statements that have since come to be celebrated: 'To none will we sell, to none deny or delay, right or justice'; and 'No freeman shall be taken, or imprisoned, or disseized, or outlawed, or exiled, or in any way harmed . . . save by the lawful judgment of his peers or by the law of the land.' But the rights to trial by jury and of habeas corpus for all were hardly established by the Magna Carta. It had little to do with the rights of the common man, and much to do with securing rights for powerful barons against an overbearing king of England. The enduring significance of the Magna Carta, and other similar documents of this age,[10] for the history of human rights lies in the fact that it has come to be seen as a starting point—the beginning of the limitation of absolute and arbitrary power of the sovereign. It therefore earns its place as the traditional point of

---

[5] See Ishay, *The History of Human Rights: From Ancient Times to the Globalization Era* (University of California Press, 2004) ch 1; Ishay, *The Human Rights Reader* (Routledge, 2007) chs 1–4.

[6] See Lauterpacht (1950), ch 5.   [7] Ishay (2004), xxii.   [8] Ishay (2004), xxii.

[9] For much broader perspectives on the history of human rights, see Ishay (2004).

[10] eg the King's agreement with the Cortes of Leon (1188, Spain) and the Magnus Lagaboters Landslov (1275, Norway).

departure in the story of how domestic law has addressed the enduring struggle of the individual against the tyranny and oppression of the state. This is a story that has lasted many centuries for some states and is still very much continuing in others.

We advance to the latter half of the seventeenth century for the next chapter in the overall story. The context was the English Civil War and the so-called 'Glorious Revolution', culminating in the Bill of Rights of 1689. Despite its name, that document was really a constitutional settlement that championed the sovereignty of Parliament. It set the seal on the absolute power of the Stuart kings after the myth of their 'divine power' had been debunked—in England at least, for it would last many more decades in France. So the bill of 1689 was no bill of rights in the sense that would be understood in modern democratic societies today.[11] Nonetheless it was the source of a limited number of defined rights, for example that 'cruel and unusual punishments [should not be] inflicted', which were applicable to all, at least in theory. Moreover, there were other important developments in this era such as the eradication of the practice of torture from the legal system of England in 1641 and the Habeas Corpus Act of 1679. The Bill of Rights of 1689 therefore saw the assertion of human liberty progress a stage further but, above all, its significance lay in its confirmation of a fundamental idea: that the absolute power of the state should be limited *for the sake of the individuals within it.* This idea had been prevalent in the contemporary writing of Thomas Hobbes and especially John Locke. And it deserves special emphasis since it is arguably the foundation stone upon which all progress in the field of human rights has been built.

2.1 THE ENLIGHTENMENT THINKERS

Hobbes' *Leviathan*,[12] published in 1651, soon after the beheading of Charles I, spoke of a world in which there was an imperative for absolute power; it was needed to keep society from the very type of disorder that had afflicted England in the 1640s. The *Leviathan* world did not accept the idea of formal restraints on power. It envisaged few if any natural rights for the individual, for all were subservient to the ruler. A level of abuse on the part of the ruler vis-à-vis his subjects might almost be expected; it was the price to be paid for the greater collective gain for a society that was protected from the much greater evil of mass disorder. Having said this, the ruler was expected to exercise his authority responsibly, and in accordance with the laws of God and of nature, and in turn this placed theoretical restraints on his authority. Hobbes' *Leviathan* is therefore credited with introducing the concept of the 'social contract', that is, the idea that power to govern is to some extent derived from the consent of the governed.

However, it was Locke who carried this concept very much further, above all in his *Two Treatises of Government*,[13] published in 1690, shortly after the overthrowing of another English king in 1688 (James II) and the approval of the Bill of Rights by Parliament in 1689. Locke advocated the natural liberty and equality of human beings: '[m]an' was *born* with 'a title to perfect freedom, and an uncontrolled enjoyment of all the rights and privileges of the law of nature, equally with any other man, or number of men in the world'; he had '*by nature* a power . . . to preserve his property, that is,

---

[11] For modern bills of rights, see Chapter 24. For a highly readable account of events and legal milestones related to this period, from the perspective of human rights and the rule of law, see Bingham, *The Rule of Law* (Penguin, 2010) ch 2.

[12] Many modern versions of the text are available, see eg Hobbes, *Leviathan* (OUP, 2009).

[13] eg Laslett (ed), *Locke: Two Treatises of Government* (CUP, 1988).

his life, liberty and estate, against the injuries and attempts of other men'.[14] Locke was therefore a strong advocate of natural rights, and in particular the right to property in the broad sense identified here, and, as he saw things, it was the state's duty to provide an environment in which such rights could flourish. His enduring contribution to the ideas that fuelled human rights thinking, however, lay in his theory of government, for it is in Locke that we see the origins of the idea of limited constitutional government and the fuller development of the idea of government by consent. Locke wrote that the 'end of government is the good of mankind', so rulers 'should be sometimes liable to be opposed, when they grow exorbitant in the use of their power, and employ it for the destruction, and not the preservation of the properties of their people'.[15] Within Locke's writing therefore were the seeds to the idea of modern democratic governance, although how much Locke expounded the democratic ideal through the idea of government by consent should not be exaggerated. He did not advocate universal suffrage and was, after all, writing in the seventeenth century when the right to vote remained a privilege of very few in England. But it is surely Locke we recall first when we read from the preamble to the Universal Declaration of Human Rights (UDHR) of almost three hundred years later: 'Whereas it is essential, if man is not to be compelled to have recourse, as a last resort, to rebellion against tyranny and oppression, that human rights should be protected by the rule of law'.

On the continent of Europe, the major historical contribution to ideas concerning the state and its relationship with the individual came in the eighteenth century. Authors such as Baron de Montesquieu (*The Spirit of Laws*, 1748), Jean-Jacques Rousseau (*The Social Contract*, 1762), Voltaire (*Philosophical Dictionary*, 1769), and Immanuel Kant (*On the Relationship of Theory to Practice in Political Right*, 1792) were leading figures in a movement which was later called 'the Enlightenment'. Montesquieu's contribution remains best known for his thoughts on the structures of government and his emphasis on the separation of powers. Rousseau advanced the theory of the 'social contract', but justice cannot be done in a few sentences here to the immense contribution made by him and others. It must suffice to say that the essence of all these philosophers' thinking was to place a new importance on the intrinsic value of man in society. There was thus further emphasis on the idea that everyone was born with certain natural rights which no authority could take away. This thinking was the intellectual force behind the French Declaration of the Rights of Man and Citizen (1789), but of course its impact was felt far beyond France. Indeed as one author has neatly put it:

> Natural rights were the cutting edge of the ax of rationalization that toppled many of the inherited medieval traditions of eighteenth-century Europe. They were part of that general aspiration toward bringing peace and order to the world that led Immanuel Kant to think that royal dynasties were the cause of war, and that a world of republics would bring a peaceful era to mankind.[16]

2.2 HUMAN RIGHTS TRANSFORMED INTO POSITIVE LAW

It was, however, in the 'new world' where the 'ax of rationalization' first achieved practical effect in a constitutional document. Locke's influence was unmistakable, and immortalized, in the US Declaration of Independence of 1776. That document listed grievances against

---

[14] Laslett (ed), ch VII, para 87 (emphasis added).   [15] Laslett (ed), ch XIX, para 229.
[16] Minogue, 'The History of the Idea of Human Rights' in Laqueur and Rubin (eds), *The Human Rights Reader* (Meridian, 1977) 11.

George III and inspired the successful prosecution of the American War of Independence. Its opening words are now infamous:

> We hold these truths to be self-evident, that all men are created equal, that they are endowed by their Creator with certain unalienable Rights; that among these are Life, Liberty and the Pursuit of Happiness. That to secure these rights, governments are instituted among men, deriving their just powers from the consent of the governed; that whenever any form of government becomes destructive of these ends, it is the right of the people to alter or to abolish it, and to institute new government, laying its foundation on such principles and organizing its powers in such form, as to them shall seem most likely to effect their safety and happiness.

Even before Thomas Jefferson and others penned these words on 4 July 1776, the process of drafting the constitutions of the newly independent individual states in what would become the United States of America was well underway. In 1776, five would be drafted so as to enshrine the protection of human rights, and by 1783 all states would have done so in one form or another. Probably the most celebrated example was the Virginia Declaration of Rights of 12 June 1776, regarded by many as the first 'proper' bill of rights. Its first article proclaimed that:

> all men are by nature equally free and independent, and have certain inherent rights, of which, when they enter into a state of society, they cannot, by any compact, deprive or divest their posterity; namely, the enjoyment of life and liberty, with the means of acquiring and possessing property, and pursuing and obtaining happiness and safety.

The Virginia Declaration then set out the idea of government by consent ('all power is vested in, and consequently derived from, the people') and separation of powers ('the legislative and executive powers of the state should be separate and distinct from the judicative'), before listing a number of human rights including, for example, basic due process rights and freedom of expression ('the freedom of the press is one of the greatest bulwarks of liberty and can never be restrained but by despotic governments').

Events in France would help to ensure that the end of the eighteenth century was a defining time in the history of human rights. The years 1789–91 stand out above all. The French Revolution swept away any notions of absolute monarchical power, replacing it with the philosophy of the French Declaration of the Rights of Man and Citizen. With this Declaration on 26 August 1789, the French National Assembly pronounced that 'ignorance, forgetfulness, or contempt of the rights of man' were 'the sole causes of public misfortunes and of the corruption of governments'. It therefore:

> resolved to set forth in a solemn declaration the natural, inalienable, and sacred rights of man, in order that such declaration, continually before all members of the social body, may be a perpetual reminder of their rights and duties; in order that the acts of the legislative power and those of the executive power may constantly be compared with the aim of every political institution and may accordingly be more respected; in order that the demands of the citizens, founded henceforth upon simple and incontestable principles, may always be directed towards the maintenance of the Constitution and welfare of all.

Article 16 French Declaration provided a classic formulation of the link between institutional limitations on state power and protecting human rights: 'Any society', it proclaimed, 'in which no provision is made for guaranteeing rights or for the separation of powers, has no Constitution.'[17]

---

[17] See also the French Declaration of the Right of Man and Citizen of 1793, a redraft of the 1789 text with an added emphasis on the principle of equality.

Today, a study of the French Declaration would form a good starting point for any course on human rights and, no doubt, stimulate much debate. The Declaration defined 'liberty' as 'the power to do whatever is not injurious to others'. It followed that 'the enjoyment of the natural rights of every man has for its limits only those that assure other members of society the enjoyment of those same rights'. According to the Declaration 'such limits may be determined only by law'. A flavour of what followed may be gleaned from paragraphs in the Declaration setting out due process rights such as the presumption of innocence and to the effect that free speech was 'one of the most precious of the rights of man', so 'every citizen may speak, write, and print freely', 'subject to responsibility for the abuse of such liberty in cases determined by law'. More generally the Declaration profoundly announced that: 'The law has the right to forbid only actions which are injurious to society. Whatever is not forbidden by law may not be prevented, and no one may be constrained to do what it does not prescribe.'

Against this background, the US Constitution of 1789 might, at first sight, have been regarded as a disappointment. There was no grand statement about the theory of government along the lines of the Declaration of Independence. Moreover, it provided for the protection of just a few rights; for example, the right to trial by jury (Article III, Section 2) and a right of habeas corpus, not to be suspended unless 'in cases of rebellion or invasion the public safety may require it' (Article I, Section 9). However, in 1791 the first ten amendments to the Constitution came into force having been ratified by three-quarters of the states. The (US) Bill of Rights, as it became known, began in now celebrated tones: 'Congress shall make no law respecting an establishment of religion, or prohibiting the free exercise thereof; or abridging the freedom of speech, or of the press; or the right of the people peaceably to assemble and to petition the government for a redress of grievances.' Among other things, the bill included the famous right to bear arms (Amendment II), protection from unreasonable search and seizure (Amendment IV), various protections relating to due process and fair trial (Amendments V and VI), and a prohibition on 'cruel and unusual punishments' (Amendment VIII). It should be added, however, that at this stage such rights were to be protected only at the federal level. It was in the individual constitutions of the states, with their own bills of rights, that the expression of the rights of man was really seen in the USA in the late eighteenth century.

These comments on the French and US experiences would not be complete without paying tribute to the work of Thomas Paine. Paine's 1776 work *Common Sense* set out the case for US democracy in the lead up to 4 July 1776. In 1791–2 he published *The Rights of Man*, which was in part a response to Edmund Burke's attack on the French Revolution. But he also subjected England's constitutional arrangements to severe criticism: 'government without constitution, is power without a right'. *The Rights of Man*, perhaps the first book ever to use the phrase 'human rights',[18] is said to have sold over 250,000 copies, making it a huge bestseller in today's terms. Paine did not invent the human rights thinking that was distilled into the landmark documents referred to here. But, as Louis Henkin has observed, his writing 'did much to spread and root' the idea of human rights: 'he provided us a theology and a terminology, guiding principles as well as blueprints'.[19] Paine remains revered in the USA, as was evidenced when he was quoted by former President Obama in his inauguration speech in 2009. But he remains little known in his native England where, in his lifetime, he was considered as a dangerous revolutionary and convicted of seditious libel.[20]

---

[18] See Lauren, *The Evolution of International Human Rights: Visions Seen* (University of Pennsylvania Press, 1998) 20.

[19] Henkin, *The Rights of Man Today* (Stevens and Sons, 1978) 135.   [20] Lauren (1998), 21.

2.3 NINETEENTH-CENTURY CHALLENGES TO NATURAL RIGHTS

The French Declaration and the US Bill of Rights were landmarks in the history of human rights for they transformed the philosophy espoused by the likes of Locke and Rousseau, and the thinking behind natural rights, into positive law. Nonetheless, during the nineteenth century the idea of natural rights came under attack from a new generation of philosophers.

The critics were led by Jeremy Bentham who famously criticized the idea of natural, God-given rights obtained by virtue of birth as 'nonsense upon stilts'.[21] His point was that natural rights counted for nothing on their own. To mean something, they required the protection of the law; so the real issue for Bentham, expounding a very British 'rights and remedy' approach to things, was what the law actually protected. As he famously put it: 'from real law come real rights; but from imaginary laws, from laws of nature, fancied and invented by poets, rhetoricians, and dealers in moral and intellectual poisons, come imaginary rights'.[22] For Bentham natural rights were dangerous since they fuelled revolutions such as those in France and so ultimately caused great social damage, hence the title of his famous work *The Anarchical Fallacies* (1843). Criticism of this type had already been made by another Englishman at the very time of the French Revolution. In his *Reflections on the Revolution of France*, Burke attacked the French Declaration as a 'monstrous fiction'. It inspired 'false ideas and vain expectations into men destined to travel in the obscure walk of laborious life' and had 'serve[d] to exaggerate and embitter that real inequality, which it can never remove'.[23]

The nineteenth century also saw an altogether different type of opposition to natural rights in the writing of Karl Marx. His 1844 work *On the Jewish Question* asked what use the French Declaration would be for Jews such as himself. As he saw it, it was found completely wanting for in reality the rights of man were the privileged rights of the bourgeoisie. According to Marx, rights were for egotistical men; they did not truly free the individual at all.[24]

As shown in Chapter 3, the longer term legacy of Bentham's and Marx's attacks on natural rights and the perspective they offer to contemporary thinking on human rights is still keenly debated today.

2.4 DOMESTIC PROTECTION OF HUMAN RIGHTS TODAY

We have seen, then, that for domestic law the human rights story really began in the seventeenth and eighteenth centuries. History will record the tribute to be paid to the visionaries of that age, such as Locke and Rousseau, many of whom were treated as dissidents at the time. The Bill of Rights of 1689, and in particular the American Declaration of Independence (1776), the French Declaration of the Rights of Man and Citizen (1789), and the US Bill of Rights (1791) were milestones in constitutional history, curtailing the sovereign power of the state in various ways, including by reference to the basic rights of the individual. This constitutional model certainly caught on as was evident by the constitutional arrangements secured in the Netherlands in 1798, Sweden in 1809, Spain in 1812, Norway in 1814, Belgium in 1831, Liberia in 1847, Sardinia in 1848, Denmark in 1849, and Prussia in 1850. In fact, it has been suggested that over 80 per cent of national

---

[21] See Chapter 3.
[22] Waldron (ed), *Nonsense upon Stilts: Bentham, Burke and Marx on the Rights of Man* (Routledge, 1987) 69.
[23] Burke, *Reflections on the Revolution in France* (Rivington, 1868) 46.   [24] See Chapter 3.

constitutions adopted between 1778 and 1948 provided a human rights guarantee in one form or another, and that between 1949 and 1975 the figure was 93 per cent.[25] That this upward trend continued was evident in the 1990s with the new constitutions of those states which were formerly part of the Soviet Union.

As we look back on the achievements secured in the eighteenth century via the French and US settlements, one should be careful to keep them in perspective. They were certainly landmarks, but it would be wrong to exaggerate the practical effects that they had at the time. Indeed one does not have to look far in French and US history to see that in practical terms the idea of human rights had made only relatively limited headway at this stage—at least, that is, compared to how we would view things today. The inferior position of women both in society generally and in law stirred women's rights campaigners such as Mary Wollstonecraft (*Vindication of the Rights of Women*, 1792). Moreover, at this stage the idea of judicial protection of human rights was virtually non-existent. The French Declaration had been incorporated as the first part of the formal French Constitution in 1791, but it was not enforceable by the courts at that time. As Lauren has observed, the French Declaration, 'reflected far more vision than reality'. It 'emerged not out of long tradition or wide-spread experience or inclusive election, but rather out of . . . revolution and had to be nurtured in the face of overwhelming opposition'.[26]

The USA was quite exceptional in that judicial protection of constitutional safeguards came in 1803 with the US Supreme Court's watershed decision in *Marbury v Madison*, holding that it had an inherent power of judicial review by which it could even declare acts of Congress unconstitutional.[27] Nonetheless, this was of limited use for individuals in human rights terms, for at this stage the Bill of Rights was an instrument that applied overwhelmingly at the federal, not the individual state, level. Of course, the individual state constitutions guaranteed rights, as noted already, but slavery was flourishing in many such states in the late eighteenth century and would continue to do so for decades into the nineteenth century. In fact, when the controversy about slavery was reaching its peak the contribution made by the US Supreme Court served to perpetuate the practice. In *Dred Scott v Sandford* in 1857, it ruled that the Bill of Rights protected the right of slaveholders to their property, which included slaves, and that, in effect, Congress had acted illegally by outlawing slavery in Northern states.[28] Neither slaves 'nor their descendants, were embraced . . . [by] the Constitution',[29] the Court held. That is, they had no protection under the Bill of Rights. It would take a civil war and further amendments to the Constitution to secure the abolition of slavery in the 1860s. And it would take the better part of the next century for the Supreme Court to finally start to use the Bill of Rights to attack grossly unfair and discriminatory practices suffered by the black population of certain states. The breakthrough case was *Brown v Board of Education*[30] of 1954 bringing an end to the 'separate but equal' doctrine previously upheld by the Court in *Plessy v Ferguson*.[31]

The point of this digression is not to single out the practice of the USA in any way. If this chapter were to attempt to provide even the broadest of overviews of the failures of other states to protect human rights over the same timeframe, it would no doubt run into dozens of pages. What has been said here, however, provides a very useful perspective on Section 3, which looks at the international protection of human rights. It helps us to understand how very recent the protection of human rights is by domestic courts (see Table 1.1) and by reference to bills of rights in the overall story of the history of human rights. In the

---

[25] Van Maarseveen and van der Tang, *Written Constitutions: A Computerized Comparative Study* (Oceana, 1978) 191–5.

[26] Lauren (1998), 32.   [27] 1 Cranch 137 (1803).   [28] 60 US 353 (1857).

[29] 60 US 353 (1857), Taney, J.   [30] 347 US 483 (1954).   [31] 163 US 537 (1896).

Table 1.1 Human rights on the domestic plane: key dates

1215	Magna Carta
1689	English Bill of Rights
1776	US Declaration of Independence
	Virginia Declaration of Rights
1789	French Declaration of the Rights of Man and Citizen
	US Constitution
1791	US Bill of Rights

UK, for example, there existed a long tradition of Parliament and the courts protecting the rights of individuals by various statutes and under the common law. But only in 2000, with the entry into force of the Human Rights Act 1998, did the UK obtain something akin to a modern bill of rights encompassing judicial protection of a select number of human rights against the acts of public authorities, albeit not against parliamentary acts.[32] In France, the 1958 Constitution refers in its preamble to the French people's commitment to the Declaration of 1789, but only a limited challenge to the authority of the legislature is possible via the *Conseil constitutionnel*.[33] Finally, the USA is without doubt the most celebrated exponent of the judicial protection of human rights. Yet only since around 1925 has the Supreme Court begun to use the Bill of Rights more widely to protect the rights of individuals against encroachments by the individual states themselves. Indeed, the story of human rights protection by the Supreme Court is overwhelmingly a post-Second World War phenomenon.[34]

The perspective we might take with us as we turn to the story of the *international* protection of human rights is therefore this: how incredibly grand the idea of an International Bill of Rights must have been in the 1940s when it was first proposed.

3 HUMAN RIGHTS ON THE INTERNATIONAL PLANE BEFORE THE SECOND WORLD WAR

Even if within domestic law there was a greater recognition of individual human rights by the start of the twentieth century, this was certainly not the case for international law. Prior to the 1940s there was no real conception in international law of the idea that one state had a right to interfere in the sovereign affairs of another state as regards how it treated its own citizens. International law was virtually a blank canvas as far as the protection of human rights was concerned. We say this from the perspective of a basic definition of human rights as the rights owing to human beings by nature of their humanity. Historically, international law could touch on or address the plight of human beings only in very limited ways.

---

[32] See Human Rights Act 1998, ss 3 and 4.

[33] For important recent developments see Hunter-Henin, 'Constitutional Developments and Human Rights in France: One Step Forward, Two Steps Back' (2011) 60 *ICLQ* 167.

[34] In 1935–6 only two of the 160 signed written opinions of the Supreme Court covered 'basic human freedoms', but by 1979–80 the ratio had increased to 80 out of 149. See Abraham and Perry, *Freedom and the Court* (OUP, 1998) 5.

For example, the inkling of the idea of certain minimal rights for certain human be-ings was present in customary international law in the guise of the doctrine of 'diplomatic protection', or the treatment of aliens. This doctrine has deep historical roots. It basically requires a state to treat foreigners in accordance with an 'international minimum stan-dard' of protection,[35] at least as regards life, liberty, property, and protection from manifest denial of justice, regardless of how the state treats its own nationals. The point to note, then, is that the protection concerned is not afforded to the individuals as human beings, but because they are nationals of a foreign state. Moreover, it falls to that foreign state, not the individual, to pursue the enforcement of any claims. In the absence of such support, historically the foreigners concerned had no one to speak for them. As such they were placed in the same position as the nationals of the host state, for the traditional, pre-war position of customary international law was that it simply had nothing to say about the way that a state could treat its own nationals.

3.1 INTERNATIONAL HUMANITARIAN LAW AND THE ABOLITION OF THE SLAVE TRADE

Of course, states could enter into legal relations with each other motivated by a desire to relieve human suffering in certain ways. In this regard an apparently compassionate dimen-sion to international law had been evident in the nineteenth century, first with the move-ment towards the abolition of the slave trade and, second, with the first steps that were taken in the field of international humanitarian law.

The second of these is addressed in Chapter 25 and all that need be said here is that the nineteenth century saw increasing international activity which expressed a concern with the plight of the individual subjected to the ravages of war—prisoners of war and wounded soldiers above all. The founding father of this movement was Henry Dunant, who was so shocked by scenes of the wounded and vanquished he witnessed at the Battle of Solferino (1859) that he later helped to establish the International Committee of the Red Cross. The Geneva Convention of 1864 soon followed, while the Hague Conventions were adopted in 1899 and 1907. Perhaps the most significant achievements of this sector of interna-tional law from the perspective of human rights, however, were secured with the Geneva Conventions of 1949 and the Additional Protocols thereto.

The nineteenth century also saw remarkable progress in the abolition of the slave trade. Slavery became illegal in England in 1771 after *Somersett's case*.[36] The UK and the USA subsequently passed legislation at the start of the nineteenth century to outlaw the trade of slaves within their own jurisdictions, which included the British colonies. Yet inter-national action was required to abolish the trade altogether, and here progress was slow. Despite the campaigning efforts of figures such as William Wilberforce, the best that could be achieved by the major European states at the Congress of Vienna (1815) was a mere declaration expressing a commitment to the abolition of the slave trade. There then followed more than half a century in which the British made great diplomatic efforts to secure dozens of bilateral treaties with trading nations principally in the European and Latin American regions, and other agreements with native chiefs from the African coast. In each instance there was an agreement to abolish the slave trade but also, where relevant, various measures of enforcement were provided for. Typically, the treaties provided for the inspection of ships if there was a suspicion that a merchant vessel was engaging in illicit activity. The abolition of the slave trade was therefore one of the earliest, if not the first, human rights related British foreign policy initiatives. This period also witnessed the

---

[35] See Shaw, *International Law* (CUP, 2014) 599.   [36] 20 State Trials 1.

establishment of Anti-Slavery International, the oldest human rights NGO in the world; its origins go back to 1839.[37]

The list of states committed to abolishing the trade slowly grew, but a sufficient global consensus on abolition of the slave trade did not emerge until the last decades of the nineteenth century. Only in 1885 did the Conference on Central Africa, held in Berlin, see in its General Act a commitment by states 'to help in suppressing slavery, and especially the slave trade' and their recognition that 'trading in slaves is forbidden in conformity with the principles of international law as recognized by the Signatory Powers'. Five years later, negotiations in Brussels saw the conclusion of the 1890 General Act, which included an Anti-Slavery Act ratified by 18 states stipulating specific measures for countering slavery and the slave trade. By this stage the great majority of states had made slavery illegal in their own jurisdictions. The experience of the USA, with President Lincoln's Emancipation Proclamation of 1863, is known best. Yet even after the US Civil War, Cuba and Brazil maintained domestic slavery into the 1880s.

In the twentieth century, the international abolition of the slave trade and slavery was taken up by the League of Nations, the key international organization established after the First World War with the principal objective of maintaining peace and stability in the world. There followed the International Convention on the Abolition of Slavery and the Slave Trade of 1926. The declared aim of this treaty was 'the complete suppression of slavery in all its forms and of the slave trade by land and sea'. There have been further international agreements since.

The international effort toward the abolition of the slave trade and slavery provides some interesting general lessons for students of international human rights law. The abolition of the trade evidenced why international law, in the form of bilateral treaties, was needed to improve the protection of individuals when the activities of more than one state were involved. But it also demonstrated that general international agreements may only follow a consensus being reached across a sufficient number of states, and that this may take a considerable time to achieve. The abolition of slavery itself inevitably required action on the part of the individual states—in some cases prompted, no doubt, by the growing body of international opinion encouraging them to do so. State practice in this field became so clearly defined that the prohibition of slavery became part of customary international law. Hence an absolute prohibition on 'slavery and servitude' passed without controversy into the main post-Second World War human rights documents, with images of Nazi concentration camps still fresh in the mind.[38] Finally, however, it would be wrong to assume that such documents have in themselves magically abolished slavery and servitude (and forced labour) in all its forms.[39] The creation of international standards for the protection of human rights may be one thing; their actual implementation and enforcement is another.

3.2 THE PROTECTION OF MINORITIES AND THE LEAGUE OF NATIONS

Resuming our analysis of the position of international law with respect to human rights before 1945, the protection of minorities should now be discussed. Here we need to recall the pre-Second World War stance of international law whereby, in effect, states had free

---

[37] For further details see <http://www.antislavery.org>.

[38] See UDHR, Art 4. See also International Covenant on Civil and Political Rights, Art 8; European Convention on Human Rights, Art 4; American Convention on Human Rights, Art 6; African Charter on Human and Peoples' Rights, Art 5.

[39] Slavery persists today, in modern forms, see <http://www.antislavery.org>, including in connection with human trafficking. On 'slavery' and 'forced and compulsory labour' see Chapter 12.

rein to abuse their own citizens behind their own borders. Indeed, stories of oppression directed toward national and religious minorities in particular fill many pages of our history books.

The first, rather sporadic, efforts to provide a level of protection for religious minorities may be traced back to the end of the Thirty Years War with the Treaty of Westphalia (1648) and, subsequently, those of Utrecht (1713) and Berlin (1878).[40] But it was not until the early twentieth century that international law saw a much more organized, institutionalized approach to the minorities issue. It was prompted by the end of the First World War and in particular the significant redrawing of the political map of parts of Europe. This involved, for example, the restoration of Poland and for some states, Germany in particular, a rather radical redrawing of their boundaries. Given how mixed the population was in parts of Europe, no matter how those boundaries were (re)shaped, the result was that a significant number of minorities found themselves displaced. As Tomuschat has described it, 'ethnic Hungarians suddenly found themselves in Romania or Czechoslovakia, ethnic Germans became Polish citizens, and ethnic Poles continued to live in Germany'.[41]

President Wilson is reported to have said at the Paris Peace Conference of 1919, '[n]othing . . . is more likely to disturb the peace of the world, than the treatment which might in certain circumstances be meted out to the minorities'.[42] It being recognized then that Europe's peaceful future could be jeopardized by the abuse of minorities by the dominant majority, arrangements were made to try to safeguard against this. As part of the various peace settlements ending the First World War, nine states[43] were required to enter into specific treaty obligations for the protection of minorities and, between 1921 and 1923, a further five[44] were required to settle upon similar arrangements as a condition of their membership of the League of Nations. The arrangements were complex and here we will identify only three main aspects.[45]

First, the individual peace treaties required that as part of their constitutional arrangements respective states should provide basic guarantees of protection as to life, liberty, and equality before the law for all inhabitants within their borders. There were also more specific guarantees which were particularly relevant for minorities including, for example, provisions guaranteeing the enjoyment of freedom of religion, use and recognition of minority languages, and various freedoms in the field of education. Second, when the League of Nations was set up, the Council of the League of Nations was mandated to make arrangements for the supervision of the aforementioned obligations at the international level. The states which were subjected to the treaty arrangements acknowledged that the guarantees constituted 'obligations of international concern' for the League of Nations, albeit only insofar as they affected persons belonging to racial, religious, or linguistic minorities, and therefore not for individuals forming part of the majority population. Third, oversight and possible measures of implementation with respect to the aforementioned obligations

[40] See Ezejiofor, *Protection of Human Rights under the Law* (Butterworths, 1964) 35–8.

[41] Tomuschat, *Human Rights: Between Idealism and Realism* (OUP, 2014) 24.

[42] Ezejiofor (1964), 38.

[43] The treaties were concluded between 1919 and 1923. Czechoslovakia, Greece, Poland, Romania, and Yugoslavia entered into specific minority treaty arrangements with the Principal and Allied Powers. For Austria, Bulgaria, Hungary, and Turkey special chapters were inserted into the General Peace Treaties. Additionally special chapters were inserted into the German Polish Convention concerning Upper Silesia, and for the Memel Territory.

[44] Declarations undertaking to protect the rights of minorities were made by Albania, Estonia, Finland, Latvia, and Lithuania.

[45] The classic account is De Azcarate, *League of Nations and National Minorities* (trans Broke) (Carnegie, 1945). See also Simpson, *Human Rights and the End of Empire* (OUP, 2001) 121–45.

were envisaged. Arrangements were put in place to allow members of the minorities to directly petition the Council of the League about actual or potential infractions of the obligations.[46] If a petition was not settled, then the Permanent Court of International Justice was given competence to adjudicate upon the dispute. In fact, this occurred on only one occasion in a dispute concerning Germany and Poland regarding minority schools in Upper Silesia.[47] However, the Court could also deliver advisory opinions upon a request from the Council, and there were a small number of these, the most well-known of which concerned the treatment of Greek minorities in Albania.[48]

Details of the successes and failures of these minority treaties can be found elsewhere.[49] Our concern here is to reflect on their significance from an historical perspective. So what should we say about these treaties today?

An extreme view might be that the treaties were not really about human rights at all, given that they applied only to certain geographical areas and that the petitions system developed by the League of Nations depended on status (belonging to a national minority). A sceptic would also point out that the motive for the creation of the treaties was not so much the protection of the minorities for humane reasons, but for the broader aim of regional stability.

A less cynical perspective would point to the significant advances made by the treaties. For the first time, international law imposed on the sovereign states concerned certain obligations to treat their inhabitants in certain ways—a stark contrast to the 'blank canvas' position noted already. Equally radical for its time was the idea of institutionalized oversight of such obligations, especially the notion that individuals could petition international organs, potentially challenging the actions of their own national authorities. In this way the treaties started to challenge the orthodox view that individuals simply could not be the subjects of international law. Such notions had underpinned Oppenheim's confident dismissal, in 1905, of the contention that 'the law of nations' guaranteed individuals 'at home and abroad the so-called rights of mankind' (alleged to be 'the right of existence, the right to protection of honour, life, health, liberty and property, the right of practicing [sic] any religion one likes, the right of emigration, and the like'). Such rights, it had been argued, 'cannot enjoy such guarantee, *since the Law of Nations is a law between States, and since individuals cannot be subjects of this Law*'.[50]

Such a view had prevailed as far as most states were concerned when the Covenant of the League of Nations was concluded in 1919. As its preamble recited, the main aim of that organization was 'to promote international co-operation and to achieve international peace and security'. Talk that all states should protect minorities along the lines of the minority treaties was quickly dismissed; therefore no guarantees for the protection of individuals generally were imposed on states after the First World War. Quite simply, outside the discrete context of the minority treaties, the notion that international bodies could or should have an influence on how the state treated its own nationals was not developed at the general level at this stage. Hence, governments and the League of Nations made little attempt to intervene in what would today be seen as the human rights abuses that

---

[46] Such arrangements were the product of procedures settled upon by the League itself. Only the treaty concerning Upper Silesia actually conferred a right of petition, although Finland was also obliged to forward petitions in relation to the Aaland Islands.

[47] *Rights of Minorities in Upper Silesia*, PCIJ Rep Series A No 15 (1928).

[48] *Minority Schools in Albania case*, PCIJ Rep Series A/B No 64 (1935).

[49] See De Azcarate (1945) and Simpson (2001) and MacCartney, 'League of Nations' Protection of Minority Rights' in Luard (ed), *The International Protection of Human Rights* (Thames and Hudson, 1967) 22, 34–7.

[50] Oppenheim, *Treatise on International Law, Vol I, Peace* (1905) 346 (emphasis added).

occurred in countries such as Germany, the Soviet Union, and Italy in the lead up to the Second World War. As Luard once put it, this was not because people did not care, rather:

> The assumptions of national sovereignty were almost everywhere still accepted. Regulations restricting freedom of the press, of speech and assembly, imprisonment for political offences, persecution on racial grounds, all these things were deplored and denounced. But it was widely accepted that they were ultimately the sole responsibility of the legal government of the territory in question: and not therefore matters over which foreign individuals or governments could legitimately take action.[51]

4 HUMAN RIGHTS ON THE INTERNATIONAL PLANE AFTER THE SECOND WORLD WAR

> And here, over an acre of ground, lay dead and dying people. You could not see which was which, except perhaps by a convulsive movement, or the last quiver of a sigh from a living skeleton, too weak to move. The living lay with their heads against the corpses, and around them moved the awful ghostly procession of emaciated, aimless people, with nothing to do, and no hope of life, unable to move out of your way, unable to look at the terrible sights around them . . . Babies had been born here, tiny wizened things that could not live. A mother, driven mad, screamed at a British sentry to give her milk for her child, and thrust the tiny mite into his arms and ran off, crying terribly. He opened the bundle, and found the baby had been dead for days. This day at Belsen was the most horrible of my life.[52]

These were the words of Richard Dimbleby reporting for the BBC at the time of the liberation of the Nazi concentration camp in Belsen. Such human rights atrocities, and countless others committed during the Second World War, were a galvanizing force that would help to ensure a new approach for international law after 1945 as regards the rights of the individual. They would prompt the first steps towards a modern international law of human rights.

The first proposals for an international code of human rights can be traced at least as far back as 1929, when in New York the Institute of International Law adopted 'An International Declaration of the Rights of Man'. Soon after the outbreak of war, the British author HG Wells campaigned for a Declaration of Rights; his book *HG Wells on the Rights of Man* sold well in the UK and 'in an act of utter optimism'[53] the war ministry had German translations dropped on the advancing German forces on the continent. Also dropped were leaflets from the White Rose Movement—a body made up of a small group of students and some academics at the University of Munich. In 1942–3 they courageously produced and distributed a series of leaflets in defiance of the Nazi regime, calling for democracy in Germany and for the protection of certain fundamental rights in a new Europe. Six of the student authors and one academic were captured by the Gestapo in 1943; they were summarily tried and executed.[54]

Back in January 1941, in his message to Congress, US President Roosevelt spoke of a world founded on 'four essential human freedoms' ('freedom of speech and expression',

---

[51] Luard, 'The Origins of International Concern over Human Rights' in Luard (1967), 21. The League of Nations did take some notable steps in the fields of anti-slavery law, refugee law, and trafficking in drugs.

[52] Richard Dimbleby, BBC News (13 May 1945), available at: <http://news.bbc.co.uk/1/hi/in_depth/4445811.stm>.   [53] Robertson, *Crimes Against Humanity* (Penguin, 2006) 28.

[54] See Dumbach and Newborn, *Sophie Scholl and the White Rose* (Oneworld, 2006).

'freedom of every person to worship God in his own way', 'freedom from want', and 'freedom from fear'). Later that year, on 14 August, Roosevelt and the British Prime Minister Winston Churchill proclaimed the Atlantic Declaration; they hoped to see a world where 'the men *in all lands* may live out their lives in freedom of fear and want'.[55] This was followed in 1942 by the Declaration of the United Nations (UN). Not to be confused with the UN Charter of some three years later, the Declaration of 1942 was signed by 47 alliance states all prepared to subscribe to the principle that 'complete victory over their enemies [was] essential to defend life, liberty, independence and religious freedom, and to preserve human rights and justice in their own lands as well as in other lands'. 'Human rights' and democracy therefore became one of the moral bases upon which the Second World War was fought; Churchill even spoke of a time when the world's struggle ended with 'the enthronement of human rights'.[56] Passages such as these were quoted by Lauterpacht in his 1945 book, referred to in Section 1, as he looked forward to the post-war world.

So what happened when the conflict finally ended? To what extent were these lofty ambitions realized in the war-shattered world?

4.1 CRIMES AGAINST HUMANITY

A very important step was taken in 1945 when the victorious powers decided that the major war criminals of the German Third Reich should be brought to justice. The Four-Power Agreement of 8 August 1945 provided for the establishment of the International Military Tribunal for the Prosecution and Punishment of Major War Criminals of the European Axis (Nuremberg Tribunal). The crimes in question were primarily those of planning and waging a war of aggression and the committal of war crimes, but they also included 'crimes against humanity'. The Nuremberg Tribunal eventually interpreted these crimes in a rather restrictive way. Nonetheless, the concept of such crimes was very significant for international human rights law, for it realized the possibility of international accountability and punishment for appalling crimes committed against individuals. More detailed discussion of the Nuremberg Tribunal can be found in Chapter 26.

4.2 THE UN CHARTER

The main focus of the immediate post-war story for international human rights law concerned the attempts made to create legal instruments protecting human rights. Of course, this meant securing agreement on what that concept actually covered. The framing of the UN Charter in San Francisco in 1945 was the obvious starting point in this endeavor. Its preamble stated that the peoples of the UN were:

> determined to save succeeding generations from the scourge of war, which twice in our lifetime has brought untold sorrow to mankind, and to reaffirm faith in fundamental human rights, in the dignity and worth of the human person, in the equal rights of men and women and of nations large and small.

Therefore, with the framing of the UN Charter human rights had finally become a subject of official concern for the international community. Nonetheless, Article 2(7) UN Charter, the 'domestic jurisdiction' clause,[57] cast something of a shadow over this, while the six references

---

[55] 35 AJIL (1941), Supplement, 191, principle six (emphasis added).

[56] *The Times* (30 October 1942), quoted by Lauterpacht (1945), 6.

[57] Art 2(7) reads (in part): 'Nothing contained in the present Charter shall authorize the United Nations to intervene in matters that are essentially within the domestic jurisdiction of any state'.

to 'human rights' in the main body of the Charter itself did not appear to commit member states to very much.[58] At most, members of the UN would be required to 'promote' human rights in accordance with Article 55(c) read with Article 56. There had been proposals to go further than this; Chile and Cuba, for example, had been prepared to accept provisions in the Charter to guarantee *specified* rights, and there had been a Panamanian proposal to include a bill of rights in the Charter. But this was all far too ambitious for the majority of states, which thwarted such proposals given the radical implications they had for state sovereignty. This was an inauspicious beginning. However, there remained hope that a more faithful consummation of the place of human rights in the new world order would follow. After all, President Truman's address to the San Francisco conference, which had concluded the Charter, had spoken of an International Bill of Rights 'acceptable to all the nations involved' to follow soon, one which would be 'as much part of international life as our own Bill of Rights is a part of our Constitution'.[59]

4.3 THE UNIVERSAL DECLARATION OF HUMAN RIGHTS

In 1946 the UN Commission on Human Rights was instituted and given the task of working on an International Bill of Rights. The task, to create a human rights instrument applicable to all states and peoples across the globe, threw up a series of difficult philosophical and political questions.[60]

Even before the Commission began its work, the politics of international human rights protection had become apparent, but by 1947 'human rights' was rapidly becoming an ideological weapon in the war of words between East and West.[61] So the idea of an International Bill of Rights was an attractive one in principle, but there were major difficulties when it came to putting in place concrete measures, especially international legal obligations.

The Commission quickly decided that the International Bill should have three parts: a declaration, a convention containing legal obligations, and 'measures of implementation', that is, a system of supervision and control. A drafting committee of eight members (from Australia, Chile, China, France, Lebanon, the UK, the USA, and the Soviet Union) was appointed to formulate the declaration. Its chair was Eleanor Roosevelt. The Universal Declaration of Human Rights (UDHR) was subsequently formulated from an initial outline produced by John Humphrey, as well as a British draft.[62] Following many sessions of the drafting committee and approval by the plenary Commission, on 10 December 1948, the UDHR was proclaimed by 48 states in the UN General Assembly. Indeed, the years 1948–9 proved to be remarkable ones for human rights standard-setting (see Table 1.2 for key dates). The Convention on the Prevention and Punishment of the Crime of Genocide[63] was opened for signature on 11 December 1948 and the four Geneva Conventions in 1949.

The UDHR had been accepted by the General Assembly without any dissenting votes, although there had been eight abstentions from the six communist states which were then members of the UN (Byelorussian SSR, Czechoslovakia, Poland, Ukrainian SSR, USSR, and Yugoslavia), plus Saudi Arabia and South Africa. The 48 states had nevertheless backed the UDHR as a 'common standard of achievement for all peoples and all nations'.

---

[58] See Arts 1, 13, 55, 62(2), 68, and 76. See also the preamble to the Charter.

[59] UN Information Organisation, Documents of the UN Conference on International Organisation (1945), Vol I, 717, cited by Sohn, *The United Nations and Human Rights* (Oceana Publications, 1968) 55.

[60] Lauren (1998), 219.   [61] Lauren (1998), 228.

[62] See Humphrey, *Human Rights and the United Nations: A Great Adventure* (Transnational Publishers, 1984) 42–3.   [63] See Chapter 26.

Table 1.2 Human rights on the international plane: key dates

1941	Roosevelt's Four Freedoms speech
1942	Declaration of the UN
1945	UN Charter
1948	Universal Declaration of Human Rights
	Convention on the Prevention and Punishment of the Crime of Genocide
1949	Four Geneva Conventions
1966	ICCPR and ICESCR opened for signature
1976	ICCPR and ICESCR enter into force

Eleanor Roosevelt famously told the General Assembly that the Declaration 'might well become the *Magna Carta* of all mankind'. Yet as she herself was quick to acknowledge, in her capacity as a US representative, the basic character of the UDHR had to be kept in mind. It was not, she stressed, a treaty; it did not 'purport to be a statement of law or of legal obligations'. Similarly, most of the delegates at the General Assembly were ready to applaud the UDHR, but quick to deny that it had legal force. In fact the emphatic and repeated denials that the UDHR had legal force were probably part of the efforts that were necessary for its acceptance by the 48 states in the first place.[64]

Writing less than two years after the UDHR had been proclaimed, Lauterpacht dismissed it as being of 'controversial moral authority'.[65] He was not alone in his criticism of the Declaration. Events, it seemed, had confirmed that states had failed to rise to the challenge foreseen by Lauterpacht in his 1945 book. From the perspective of 1950, Lauterpacht's disappointment can be appreciated. No International Bill of Rights was secured in the 1940s. Moreover, in 1950 the prospects for the remainder of the bill looked bleak. It took until 1954 for the UN Commission to complete the drafts of what would become the International Covenant on Civil and Political Rights (ICCPR) and the International Covenant on Economic, Social and Cultural Rights (ICESCR). However, they would not be opened for signature until 1966 and it would take until 1976 before they entered into force for the 35 states that were prepared to ratify them. The drafting history of the two Covenants reveals the many compromises and amendments that were necessary to secure their acceptability to the members of the UN, especially as the size of that organization grew significantly in the post-colonial era. A similar point may be made about the relatively weak enforcement regimes that were eventually agreed for both treaties. They revealed how unrealistic it had been in the mid-1940s to assume that classic features of state sovereignty could be pushed aside easily when it came to establishing an effective International Bill of Rights.

5 CONCLUSION

Nearly 70 years on from when Eleanor Roosevelt unveiled the UDHR, it seems that her description of it as a possible Magna Carta for mankind was most apt. After all, as already noted, the document of 1215 was but the start of the story of the domestic protection of

---

[64] Moskowitz, *Human Rights and World Order* (Stevens and Sons, 1959) 79.

[65] Lauterpacht (1950), 279. He was highly critical of the leading nations for their limited achievements. See Lauterpacht, 397–408.

human rights. Can the same comment not be made for the UDHR today with respect to the international protection of human rights?

As the subsequent chapters in this book will reveal, the rights protected by the UDHR, and the two Covenants more generally, which today have been ratified by a large majority of states, have become part of a body of international law the scope, breadth, and general significance of which would have been impossible to predict in the late 1940s. And if these are the achievements of only the last 70 years,[66] then what further progress can we expect in this century and beyond?

Of course, none of this is to suggest that things are anywhere near perfect today. We know that serious human rights violations occur across the globe every day. We may nevertheless compare the situation now with that existing before 1945. Today, there are international legal obligations that restrain how a sovereign state may treat individuals within its jurisdiction. This is now a matter for legitimate international concern, and international human rights law represents the standard by which the conduct of states may be judged. Today, even the most authoritarian of regimes would not publicly oppose the principle that their citizens have certain fundamental rights, even though the actions of many such governments may not always faithfully uphold such ideals. Certainly much more needs to be done to see the proper enforcement of the international standards that have been created. But here we may recall the words of Lauterpacht; the history of human rights law, both at the domestic and the international level, confirms that '[t]he vindication of human liberties does not begin with their complete and triumphant assertion at the very outset'. Rather, 'it commences with their recognition in *some* matters, to *some* extent, for *some* people, against *some* organ of the State'.[67] The story of the history of human rights is, therefore, most certainly an ongoing one.

FURTHER READING

BINGHAM, *The Rule of Law* (Penguin, 2010) (esp ch 2).

HENKIN, *The Rights of Man Today* (Stevens and Sons, 1978).

HOFFMANN (ed), *Human Rights in the Twentieth Century* (Cambridge University Press, 2011).

HUMPHREY, *Human Rights and the United Nations: A Great Adventure* (Transnational Publishers, 1984).

ISHAY, *The History of Human Rights: From Ancient Times to the Globalization Era* (University of California Press, 2004).

ISHAY, *The Human Rights Reader* (Routledge, 2007).

LAUREN, *The Evolution of International Human Rights: Visions Seen* (University of Pennsylvania Press, 2003).

MOYN, *The Last Utopia: Human Rights in History* (Harvard University Press, 2010).

ROBERTSON, *Crimes Against Humanity* (Penguin, 2006).

ROBERTSON and MERRILLS, *Human Rights in the World* (Manchester University Press, 1996) ch 1.

---

[66] In particular since the late 1970s: see Moyn, *The Last Utopia: Human Rights in History* (Harvard University Press, 2010) ch 5. For debate and discussion on when human rights became a central concept in the twentieth century, see Hoffmann, 'Human Rights and History' (2016) 232 *Past and Present* 279; Moyn, 'The End of Human Rights History' (2016) 233 *Past and Present* 307; and Hunt, 'The Long and the Short of the History of Human Rights' (2016) 233 *Past and Present* 323.   [67] Lauterpacht (1945).

SIMPSON, *Human Rights and the End of Empire* (Oxford University Press, 2001) especially chs 2–5.

TOMUSCHAT, *Human Rights: Between Idealism and Realism* (Oxford University Press, 2014) ch 2.

USEFUL WEBSITES

Avalon Project: Documents in Law, History and Diplomacy (many of the 'constitutional' documents referred to in this chapter are available on this site): <http://avalon.law.yale.edu>

Official UN website on the UDHR, with links to audiovisual materials on the UDHR: <http://www.ohchr.org/EN/UDHR/Pages/UDHRIndex.aspx>

A useful 'timeline' on the history of human rights: <http://www.facinghistory.org/udhr-timeline>

2

JUSTIFICATIONS

Samantha Besson

SUMMARY

International human rights are often criticized. Proponents of human rights usually have a hard time responding to critiques that bear on their justifications. They may say that human rights are self-justificatory or justified by being themselves justifications (for example, of the authority of domestic or international law), and hence do not regard them as being in need of justification. Human rights theorists do not necessarily fare any better: some human rights theories do not include the justification of human rights among their aims, while others justify human rights albeit without clarifying why justifications are needed in the first place or what they are actually justifying, thereby often talking at cross purposes with each other. This chapter purports to explain: first, why we need to justify human rights; second, what it means to justify them; third, what the different justifications for human rights may be; and, finally, what some of the implications of the justifications of human rights could be.

1 INTRODUCTION

International human rights law[1] has come under critique for quite some time now.[2] Curiously, however, proponents of human rights have not, by and large, responded to those critiques. Nor, more importantly, have they tried to justify human rights in the first place. This may be because they think human rights are self-justificatory,[3] an irreducible value that is not in need of further justification, justified by being themselves justifications (for example, of the authority of domestic or international law), or justified by reference to another value that does not itself need justification (for example, dignity or equality).

---

[1] This chapter pertains to the justification of *international* human rights *law*. See on those two dimensions of human rights: Besson, 'The Law in Human Rights Theory' (2013) 7 *Zeitschrift für Menschenrechte—Journal for Human Rights* 120; Besson, 'Human Rights and Constitutional Law—Patterns of Mutual Validation and Legitimation' in Cruft, Liao, and Renzo (eds), *The Philosophical Foundations of Human Rights* (OUP, 2015) 279; Besson, 'Human Rights and Justification—A Reply to Mattias Kumm' in Etinson (ed), *Human Rights: Moral or Political?* (OUP, 2018).   [2] See Chapter 3.

[3] This could be, for instance, because they are rights human beings have by virtue of their human nature and they hence find their justification in human nature itself. On the dangers of the naturalistic fallacy (that is, deriving an 'ought' from an 'is') in the human rights context, see, however, Beitz, *The Idea of Human Rights* (OUP, 2009) 49 ff.

Others have hinted at the need to agree on human rights without even asking why.[4] These various positions come close to making human rights a matter of faith rather than of reason.[5] And this in turn may explain why many human rights activists tend to see inquiries into the justification of human rights as quasi-blasphematory or, at the least, a waste of time and energy that would be better channelled towards working for and enforcing human rights in practice.

International human rights law is itself of no avail in this respect. It cannot provide justifications external to the law. Generally speaking, the law provides reasons for action that are independent of its content. Therefore, the justifications for its authority should not be identified with moral justifications for the content of legal norms. True, the justifications for the law's authority depend on those moral justifications and thus presume their existence. International human rights law is no exception. As a result, legal reasoning on human rights, like legal reasoning in general, is a special kind of moral reasoning. Human rights justifications and critiques are inherent to human rights legal reasoning just as justification and critique are inherent to the law in general. Interestingly, international human rights law does more than other international law in this respect as it refers expressly to the independent existence of various moral justifications for human rights. In particular, preambles to human rights instruments refer to concepts such as dignity, equality, or autonomy,[6] and use foundational or derivational language.[7] In short, international human rights law does not, itself, morally justify human rights and one should not expect it to do so. However, the way human rights law works and the manner in which its authority is justified do not only confirm the need to justify such rights, but also provide the institutional and deliberative space to do so.

The obvious place to turn to for justification then is human rights philosophy or theory. After all, justifying is what moral philosophers and philosophers of law do. Curiously, however, human rights theorists do not necessarily fare much better on this count.[8] Of course, they disagree about the justifications of human rights, but that is not the problem. On the contrary, human rights are essentially contestable concepts, and so should their justifications be. Rather, the concern is that, while the majority of human rights theorists do justify human rights, they do so without clarifying why justifications are needed in the first place or what exactly they are justifying (for example, human rights *law* or human rights as either legal or moral rights or both),[9] thereby often talking at cross purposes.[10] This is a shame as a lot in human rights theory depends on the justification(s) given to human rights. For instance, their justification(s) affect the kind of guidance human rights

---

[4] In 1949, after the adoption of the Universal Declaration on Human Rights, Jacques Maritain wrote: 'We agree about the rights but on condition that no one asks us why.' Maritain, *Man and the State* (Hollis and Carter, 1954) 70.

[5] See Ignatieff, 'Human Rights: The Midlife Crisis' (1999) 46 *NY Review of Books* 58.

[6] eg UDHR, ICCPR, and ICESCR, preambles.

[7] eg ICESCR and ICCPR, preambles: '... *recognition* of the inherent dignity and of the equal and inalienable rights of all members of the human family is the *foundation* of freedom, justice and peace in the world' [emphases added].

[8] There are important exceptions. See eg Buchanan, 'Why International Legal Human Rights?' in Cruft, Liao, and Renzo (2015), 244 ff; Waldron, 'Is Dignity the Foundation of Human Rights?' (2013) *NYU School of Law, Public Law Research Paper No 12–73*.

[9] eg Griffin, *On Human Rights* (OUP, 2008); Tasioulas, 'Are Human Rights Essentially Triggers for Intervention?' (2009) 4 *Philosophical Compass* 938; Wellman, *The Moral Dimensions of Human Rights* (OUP, 2011).

[10] See Buchanan (2015); Buchanan and Sreenivasan, 'Taking International Legality Seriously: A Methodology for Human Rights' in Etinson (2017).

theory may give to human rights practice with respect to difficult questions such as the stringency of specific human rights duties, the resolution of conflicts between human rights or between human rights and other moral considerations, the allocation of human rights duties, or the prioritization among human rights duties.

Despite the importance of justification in human rights theory, it is important not to be too disappointed by the indeterminate state of the debate. One should not lose sight of the reverse impact of one's respective theoretical approach to the nature, object, or scope of human rights on their justification. Justifications may engage with human rights at very different levels depending on what one understands their nature and content to be. And those features of human rights work as constraints on potential justifications in return. For instance, endorsing the universality or generality of human rights conditions the kind of justifications that may be given to those rights if their scope is to be sufficiently universal or general. Furthermore, human rights are usually understood as giving rise to strong, if not exclusionary, duties, and this in turn affects the kind of justifications that may warrant such correlative duties. As a result, if it is true that the justifications of human rights and their role are indeterminate and contested, it should be a consolation to realize that so is the rest of human rights theory. All aspects of human rights need to be worked on at the same time to identify the right justifications of human rights.

As a matter of fact, and more generally, the way in which one approaches the nature and role of human rights *theory* itself also affects one's understanding of the *justification* of human rights, and vice-versa.[11] For instance, since arguably the best human rights theory ought to attempt to account for our contemporary human rights practice, the justification of human rights should also be about the point of our human rights practice. This in turn means looking for human rights justifications in the normative practice of human rights themselves, and in particular in human rights legal reasoning.

In the light of these preliminary observations, this chapter explains why we need to justify human rights (Section 2), what it means to justify them (Section 3), what the different justifications for human rights may be (Section 4), and, finally, what some of the implications of the justifications of human rights may be for other key issues in human rights theory (Section 5).

2 WHY JUSTIFY HUMAN RIGHTS

2.1 EXPLAINING JUSTIFICATION

Moral justification amounts to giving moral reasons for action or belief. In the legal context, moral justification is about understanding the point of the legal norms we have.[12]

Depending on one's moral theory, justifying may equate with 'founding', 'basing', 'deriving', or 'grounding'. As a matter of fact, those terms are used interchangeably by many authors.[13] It is important to be cautious, however, especially if one wants to distance oneself from foundationalist approaches to morality. In short, foundationalism is a characteristic of those moral theories that claim there are foundations in morality and that hence attempt to derive moral values or entities from other foundational ones that are non-derivative.[14]

---

[11] Contrast Beitz (2009), or Raz, 'Human Rights in the Emerging World Order' (2010) 1 *Transnational Legal Theory* 31 with Griffin (2008), or Tasioulas, 'Towards a Philosophy of Human Rights' (2012) 65 *CLP* 1.

[12] eg Waldron (2013), on human rights; Waldron, *Dignity, Rank and Rights* (OUP, 2012) on dignity.

[13] eg Tasioulas, 'The Moral Reality of Human Rights' in Pogge (ed), *Freedom from Poverty as a Human Right: Who Owes What to the Very Poor?* (OUP, 2007) 75; Griffin (2008).

[14] See Nickel, *Making Sense of Human Rights* (Blackwell, 2007) ch 4; Waldron (2013).

There is nothing, however, in the enquiry into the justifications of human rights that necessarily implies foundationalism.

In the case of human rights, justifying implies giving reasons for human rights. Because human rights are grounds for duties in concrete circumstances, and hence reasons for action, justifying human rights comes close to providing an abstract justification for a further concrete justification. Abstract justifications of human rights may themselves be general or specific, depending on whether they pertain to all human rights or to some in particular. Considerations about the abstract justification of human rights as justifications for concrete duties that correspond to concrete human rights enable us to draw two key distinctions.

First, the justification of human rights should not be conflated with the *object* of human rights. It often is, however. This may be because the object of human rights is generally perceived as a normatively loaded question. Not everything can be protected by a human right, precisely because human rights justify duties. However, the object of a human right, that is, the concrete content of the duties corresponding to a specific human right, is identified by reference to the threats against which the right protects the interests of its holder in concrete circumstances and not abstractly. All the same, the equation of the justification and object is often made in pluralistic accounts of the justifications of human rights.[15] Those authors argue for a plurality of justifications in order to match the plurality of objects of human rights. However, the reading proposed here is equally reconcilable with a monist approach to the justification of human rights. This would be the case in particular with an account that justifies human rights by reference to one single value such as dignity, but also understands that every particular right protects, and hence has as an object, something specifically required by dignity in a particular area. The loose relationship between the object and the justification of human rights also means that the correlation often made between the justification of human rights and their fundamental or intangible core (duties) is not a direct one. They are related, of course, and it will be explained how in this chapter, but not directly, and certainly not by reference to the object of the human right in question.

Second, and more generally, the justification of human rights should be carefully distinguished from other elements in the *moral structure* of human rights. Those elements are constitutive of any given human right in general and necessary for the recognition of a specific human right. They are, in a nutshell: the existence of an interest equally fundamental to all people, the existence of standard threats to that interest, the fair burden of the protection of the interest against those threats, and the abstract feasibility of that protection. Often, human rights theorists conflate some elements in the structure of human rights with their justification.[16] This is particularly the case with interest-based accounts of human rights. In the interest-based approach, as opposed to the choice-based or will-based approach,[17] human rights protect fundamental human interests that all human beings have. More precisely, a human right exists when a fundamental and general human interest is a sufficient reason to hold someone else (the duty-bearer) under a duty to respect that interest vis-à-vis the right-holder. Just as the choice-based approach does not necessarily mean that human rights are justified by autonomy, the interest-based approach does not imply that they are justified by reference to well-being. Of course, identifying interests as fundamental and general, threats as standard, and burdens as fair are matters of specific justification as well, but they are distinct from the general justification of human rights and can be established by analysis at a general level.

---

[15] See eg Tasioulas (2009), critique of Griffin's autonomy-based account of human rights.

[16] See eg Tasioulas (2012), on the dual root of human rights (interests and dignity).

[17] See Waldron, 'Introduction' in Waldron (ed), *Theories of Rights* (OUP, 1984) 1, 9–12.

Furthermore, it is important not to conflate the justification of human rights with other connected endeavours.

First, the justification of human rights does not equate with their *history*. The former is normative, whereas the latter is descriptive. Of course, human rights theory and human rights history ought to inform each other to be successful in their respective projects.[18] Not only because human rights history is also a kind of intellectual history, and hence the history of justifications, but also because human rights theory contributes to determining the object of human rights history and vice-versa. However, their aims and methods are clearly different.

Second, justifying human rights does not amount to explaining the *sources* of human rights. Their sources as legal norms are the sources of international human rights law, that is, treaties, customary international law, and general principles, as identified, specified, and interpreted by international judicial decisions.[19] Of course, those law-making processes and their normative outcome may themselves be morally justified, and often will be, as their content may correspond to that of universal moral rights. However, this is not a condition for the validity of the corresponding legal norms. True, this is a resolutely legal positivist take on international human rights. Some, albeit presumably very few, natural law accounts of international human rights law may condition the legal validity of human rights on their moral justification.

Finally, justifying human rights does not amount to accounting for their *legitimacy*, and hence to justifying their authority. Admittedly, their legitimacy is not entirely distinct from their moral justification, to the extent that the reasons given by a legal norm should match pre-existing reasons of those subject to the law and depend on these pre-existing reasons. The search for the moral justification of human rights remains distinct from that of the legitimacy of international human rights law, however, even if the former will eventually inform the latter.

2.2 JUSTIFYING JUSTIFICATION

The next question is why we should care about justifying human rights.

The first argument lies in the nature of human rights as rights. Rights protect interests that are recognized as sufficiently important to give rise to duties. As normative relationships, they are grounds for reasons for action and are in themselves justifications as a result. Every time a right gives rise to specific duties in concrete circumstances, a justification is provided. This turns the law into a forum of justification for human rights duties. And this in turn requires a justification: the justification of abstract human rights themselves.

Second, the legality of human rights also explains why we should justify them. International human rights law does not provide external justifications of human rights, but makes it clear that we need to justify them. This is because of the relationship between law and morality generally, and in particular between the justifications for the law's authority and moral justifications. The justifications for the law's authority are content-independent and do not amount to moral justifications of the content of any given legal norm, but the reasons for action it gives have to match pre-existing moral reasons of those

---

[18] Besson and Zysset, 'Human Rights History and Human Rights Theory: A Tale of Two Odd Bedfellows' (2012) *Ancilla Juris*, available at: <http://www.anci.ch/_media/beitrag/ancilla2012_204_besson.pdf>.

[19] See Chapter 4. See also Besson, 'The Sources of International Human Rights Law' in Besson and d'Aspremont (eds), *Oxford Handbook on the Sources of International Law* (OUP, 2017) 837.

bound by it. This so-called dependence condition of legitimacy in turn implies that the law's content be also justified morally, not so much to be valid law but for the authority it claims ever to be justifiable.

Finally, international human rights law refers expressly to the independent existence of various moral justifications for human rights. It does so mostly in preambles to human rights instruments.[20] International human rights law invites us, therefore, to explore those justifications further.

Of course, justifications may themselves call for further justifications. Thus, one value may be given as a justification for something and itself be regarded as having to be justified. Usually, at this stage, alternatives for 'justifications of justifications' are suggested. The choice lies between either a metaphysical[21] or religious[22] route.[23] They are indeed the only ones able to provide these kinds of bedrock foundations. If neither approach is taken, however, there is no reason why the search for justification should be one for ultimate foundations and why a failure to identify those ultimate foundations should be a problem. The regress in the search for justifications has to halt at some stage. One may be satisfied with pausing at, for instance, equality or dignity without further justification and without searching for a master-justification or master-value. This may be because those moral values and principles are so widely accepted as part of people's moralities that one does not have to argue for them before using them to argue for human rights.[24]

3 HOW TO JUSTIFY HUMAN RIGHTS

3.1 JUSTIFICATIONS OF MORAL AND LEGAL RIGHTS

Human rights mean different things to different people. Some regard human rights as rights in the strict sense, while others do not see them as rights beyond their name. And those who understand them as rights may conceive them as legal rights, as moral rights, or as both.

The moral justifications of human rights will differ significantly depending on how one understands them. For instance, there may be moral justifications of legal human rights that are distinct from the moral justifications of corresponding moral rights. One may consider that international human rights law is justified by reference to peace, independently of whether it entails rights in the strict sense, whether those are also moral rights, and whether they have separate justifications as such. Or one may justify international human rights law by reference to their specifying role of universal moral rights or to their entrenching a canonical version of them.[25]

It is submitted here that we should understand the justification of human rights as a justification of rights, and of legal and moral rights at the same time. Further, as rights, human rights should also be regarded as grounds for duties, and hence their justification as a justification of a justification.

---

[20] eg UDHR, ICCPR, and ICESCR, preambles.
[21] eg Habermas, 'The Concept of Human Dignity and the Realistic Utopia of Human Rights' (2010) 41 *Metaphilosophy* 464.
[22] eg Waldron, *God, Locke, and Equality: Christian Foundations in Locke's Political Thought* (CUP, 2002) ch 3.
[23] See Tasioulas, 'Justice, Equality and Rights' in Crisp (ed), *The Oxford Handbook of the History of Ethics* (OUP, 2013) 768.   [24] See Nickel (2007), 61.
[25] eg Buchanan and Sreenivasan (2017); Buchanan (2015). See also Buchanan, *The Heart of Human Rights* (OUP, 2013) ch 2. For a discussion, see Luban, 'Response to Buchanan' in Cruft, Liao, and Renzo (2015), 263 ff.

First, human rights understood as *rights*. The practice of international human rights law treats human rights as rights. Of course, sometimes they go by other names such as principles or, at least, are applied as principles and not as subjective and claimable rights. In most cases, however, human rights legal, and especially judicial, reasoning is rights-based reasoning. In a practice-sensitive human rights theory like the proposed one, human rights ought, therefore, to be understood as rights.

Second, human rights understood as *legal and moral rights*. As rights guaranteed by legal norms, international human rights are clearly legal rights. The question is whether they also correspond to moral rights. Just as moral rights are moral propositions and sources of moral duties, legal rights are legal propositions and sources of legal duties. They are moral interests recognized by the law as sufficiently important to generate moral duties.[26] The same may be said of legal *human* rights: legal human rights are fundamental and general moral interests recognized by the law as sufficiently important to generate moral duties. Generally speaking, moral rights can exist independently from legal rights, but legal rights recognize, modify, or even create moral rights by recognizing certain moral interests as sufficiently important to generate moral duties. As such, legal rights are always also moral rights, whether by recognition (as such or with specification) of pre-existing moral rights or by creation of moral rights. Of course, there may be ways of protecting moral interests or even independent moral rights legally without recognizing them as legal rights. Conversely, some legal rights may not actually protect pre-existing moral rights or create moral rights, thus only bearing the name of rights and generating legal duties at the most. However, the same cannot be said of human rights. The universal moral rights that will become human rights create moral duties for institutions, and hence for the law as well, to recognize and protect human rights.[27] This is the only way to give them their central egalitarian dimension, and to assess, for instance, whether the interests and threats at stake are general and to specify and allocate the corresponding duties in an egalitarian fashion. In other words, human rights as a subset of universal moral rights are also of an inherently legal nature. The law makes universal moral rights human rights, either by recognizing them as legal rights or by creating them in recognition of certain fundamental universal moral interests. This understanding of the relationship between moral and legal human rights is one of mutuality. It goes beyond the traditional understanding of a one-way relationship of translation or enforcement of moral rights through legal rights.

Finally, human rights understood as *grounds for duties*. As normative relationships, human rights imply duties. There are three remarks one should make about the correlativity between human rights and duties. First, while human rights can be abstract, there can be no abstract human rights duties; since they may only be specified by reference to a concrete threat to the protected interest, they are always context-specific and concrete. As a result, a human right may be justified, recognized, and protected before specifying which duties correspond to it. This is what one may refer to as the justificatory priority of rights over duties.[28] Once a duty is specified, however, it will be correlative to the (specific) right. Second, a human right is a sufficient ground for holding duty-bearers under all the duties necessary to protect the interest against standard threats. It follows that a right might

---

[26] Raz, 'Legal Rights' (1984) 4 *OJLS* 1, 12; Raz (2010).

[27] See Raz, 'Human Rights without Foundations' in Besson and Tasioulas (eds), *The Philosophy of International Law* (OUP, 2010) 321.

[28] See MacCormick, 'Rights in Legislation' in Hacker and Raz (eds), *Law, Morality and Society: Essays in Honour of HLA Hart* (OUP, 1977) 189, 199–202; Raz, 'On the Nature of Rights' (1984) 93 *Mind* 194, 196, and 200.

provide for the imposition of many duties and not only one. This is what one refers to as the pluralism of human rights duties. Importantly, those duties will also evolve with time and place.[29] Third, therefore, human rights have a dynamic nature. As such, successive specific duties can be grounded on the same right depending on the circumstances. This application indeterminacy of rights also implies that rights need to be localized to be fully effective; it is only in local circumstances that the allocation and specification of duties can take place.

3.2 MORAL AND LEGAL JUSTIFICATIONS OF MORAL AND LEGAL RIGHTS

Moral justifications of human rights ought to be distinguished from legal justifications of human rights as legal rights, that is, justifications entirely internal to the law.

Moral justifications of human rights are moral justifications of those rights as moral and/or legal rights. Depending on whether it is the moral or the legal dimension of human rights that is justified, different moral justifications may be proposed. The justifications of human rights that matter are those that pertain to human rights in general, that is, human rights as moral *and* legal rights.

Moral justifications of human rights as moral and legal rights may be articulated, in an ideal fashion, as external moral justifications. This is what most human rights theorists have done so far.[30] They treat justifications as a basis for the 'top-down' derivation of human rights. However, in a theory of human rights that takes their legal dimension seriously it is important to assess the moral justifications that one finds embedded in the legal practice of human rights. As explained in the introduction to this chapter, moral justifications and critiques of human rights are inherent to human rights law and legal reasoning. It is this kind of law-immanent and internal moral justification that is relevant to accounting for human rights practice and explaining its point from within.

The best way to capture the moral justifications of human rights present in legal practice in a 'bottom-up' fashion is to focus on human rights legal reasoning and in particular on the interpretation, especially judicial interpretation, of human rights. This kind of justification of human rights is normative in kind and cannot be reduced to some kind of descriptive account of human rights practice. The legal practice of moral justification of human rights is considered in this section with respect to two main justifications that are brought forward, namely equality and dignity.

Last but not least, one should emphasize that human rights do not exhaust morality. As a result, their justifications do not either. They may, therefore, conflict with those of other moral and legal norms. One may think of considerations of justice or democracy that often conflict with human rights whatever their justifications. For instance, the protection of specific human rights, such as the right to property, may conflict with concerns of distributive equality in practice. This explains how human rights are wrongly accused of epitomizing moral individualism at any price. It is quite the contrary actually, as they have to be interpreted in the broad context of morality, including by reference to the collective dimensions of morality.

---

[29] See Beitz and Goodin (eds), *Global Basic Rights* (OUP, 2009) 10.

[30] eg Nickel (2007); Griffin (2009); Tasioulas (2012); Wellman (2011). Note that some have done so taking as their object human rights as moral rights, as legal rights, or as both.

4 WHICH JUSTIFICATIONS FOR HUMAN RIGHTS

4.1 A PLURALITY OF JUSTIFICATIONS

Moral justifications of human rights may be of various types, and a few clarifying distinctions are in order.

The first distinction is between *religious* and *non-religious* justifications of human rights. It follows from the structure of human rights presented in Section 2 that human rights protect fundamental human interests. Of course, this does not exclude providing religious justifications of human rights.[31] As a matter of fact, religious approaches often converge on the same list of rights as secular ones. It suffices to think here of the right to life or freedom of religion. It is key, however, that the interests protected be humanistic interests, that is, interests that individuals have as human beings, and not extra-human concerns including the will of God.[32] In this section, and for reasons that pertain to the antecedence of morality over religion,[33] the focus will be on non-religious justifications of human rights.

A second distinction opposes *prudential* justifications of human rights to *objective* ones. Prudential reasons are reasons relating to a person's own prospects for a good life and what is in his or her subjective interest as a result. Prudential reasons for human rights may be, for instance, that human rights contribute to making society safer both for individuals and for the group. Focusing on prudential reasons for human rights is attractive because their existence confirms that the feasibility of human rights ought to matter for their justification, and that their cost is not too high for our societies. In addition, they confirm that there are psychological patterns in place to support those rights in practice. Those reasons also demonstrate the importance of the collective dimension of human rights, and that it is necessary to factor this into any justification of human rights whether prudential or not. However, there are various difficulties with prudential justifications of human rights. One is their relativity, and the problem this creates when accounting for the universality of human rights. Another one is the instability of these justifications when majorities and power shift. In the remainder of this chapter, I will focus on objective justifications of human rights, that is, those arguments that appeal directly to what is reasonable from the interpersonal moral point of view. Again, of course, many prudential reasons for human rights may correspond to those objective justifications.

Third, among objective justifications of human rights, it is useful to distinguish *consequentialist* justifications from *non-consequentialist* ones. Consequentialist justifications refer to results and support human rights because they make the societies that respect them more peaceful or prosperous. A common example may be utilitarian justifications, according to which human rights are justified by reference to their consequences for the general welfare.[34] The main difficulty with utilitarian justifications of human rights lies in their quantitative approach: human rights, and their corresponding duties, are regarded as commensurable and as having to be balanced against considerations of utility or other human rights, with the potential consequence of justifying grave restrictions to certain human rights or even emptying them of their whole purpose by reference to the general welfare. This contradicts an important dimension of human rights in practice: their

---

[31] eg Perry, *Toward a Theory of Human Rights: Religion, Law, Courts* (CUP, 2006).

[32] See Buchanan, *Justice, Legitimacy, and Self-determination: Moral Foundations for International Law* (OUP, 2004) 130–1, 141–2.

[33] See Dworkin, 'Religion without God' (2013) 60 *NY Review of Books*.

[34] eg Talbott, *Human Rights and Human Well-Being* (OUP, 2010).

demanding normative nature and their alleged resistance to trade-offs. In this section, therefore, the focus will be on non-consequentialist, that is deontological, justifications of human rights. Of course, this does not exclude convergence with consequentialist considerations, and in particular the importance of paying due attention to the egalitarian, and hence collective, dimension of human rights.

Finally, among non-consequentialist justifications, one may distinguish between *instrumental* and *inherent* justifications. Instrumental justifications account for one human right by reference to its relationship to others, thus making the former a more fundamental right. Certain human rights are regarded as being instrumental to others when they are necessary to their effective implementation or enjoyment. One may think here of the human rights to security and subsistence and their necessity to the enjoyment of other human rights.[35] This is sometimes referred to as a linkage argument or a derivative justification for human rights. The supportive relationship between human rights may be unilateral or mutual.[36] Either way, it may be more or less strong depending on how important it is to the effective implementation of other rights in practice. Importantly, the instrumental justification needs to be assessed in the abstract when first justifying another human right. However, there are difficulties with the idea of instrumental justification of some human rights. One may mention, for instance, its all or nothing consequences for every given human right, and the indeterminacy of instrumental justifications at the abstract level of rights. In any case, no further conclusions may be drawn as to the abstract priority of non-instrumentally justified rights over instrumental ones.[37] Indeed, all human rights are equal and relationships among their justifications should not affect their relationships. This argument will be returned to in the context of the discussion of the stringency of human rights, but for now the focus should be on inherent justifications of human rights.

The next question is whether one should try to identify a single justification and defend a monist account of the justification of human rights or whether a pluralistic account is more plausible. Among the arguments put forward in favour of a single justification, one may mention the holistic approach to humanity or, better, moral personhood, and in particular the indivisibility of that basic moral status. In reply, one may stress not only the pluralism that characterizes morality, but also the plurality of the corresponding dimensions of moral personhood and hence presumably of moral justifications of the rights that correspond to those dimensions of personhood. Furthermore, the more justifications for human rights are identified, the more one enhances their potential subjective or psychological legitimacy or acceptance. It is important to emphasize that one should differentiate between justifications articulated as such and those reached through overlapping consensus.[38] Not endorsing the latter and focusing on the former kind of justifications does not mean, however, that we should not be concerned with the degree of subjective recognition of the proposed objective justifications of human rights.

---

[35] See Nickel (2007), 87–90; Shue, *Basic Rights: Subsistence, Affluence and US Foreign Policy* (Princeton UP, 1996) 11.

[36] When the linkage between human rights is strong and mutual, one may speak of indivisibility of human rights: eg Nickel, 'Rethinking Indivisibility: Towards a Theory of Supporting Relations between Human Rights' (2008) 30 *HRQ* 984.

[37] See Waldron, 'Security as a Basic Right (After 9/11)' in Beitz and Goodin (eds), *Global Basic Rights* (OUP, 2009) 207.

[38] eg Cohen, 'Minimalism about Human Rights: The Most We Can Hope For?' (2004) 12 *J of Political Philosophy* 190. For a critique, eg Beitz (2009); Forst, 'The Justification of Human Rights and the Basic Right to Justification: A Reflexive Approach' (2010) 120 *Ethics* 711.

Of course, defending a pluralist account of the justification of human rights means that there could be conflicts between those justifications themselves, and not only between human rights duties. The connection between the two issues is discussed in Section 4.2. It suffices here to recognize that pluralism and the possibility of conflict in justifications of human rights are a quality of one's human rights theory, and in particular of its ability to account for the pluralist practice of human rights.

4.2 TWO POTENTIAL JUSTIFICATIONS

The two moral grounds most commonly advanced for human rights are equality and dignity. Many other potential justifications could be mentioned, in particular autonomy and fairness. As pluralistic approaches to the justification of human rights are more promising, I will not address equality and dignity's virtues as monistic or sole justifications of human rights.

Equality and dignity constitute status-related justifications of human rights. This focus on status-related justifications should not be mistaken for a rejection of an interest-based approach to human rights. A basis in interests or status does not imply a justification only in interests or status. The moral structure of human rights endorsed in Section 2 regards human rights as based on objective interests. However, interests are part of the moral structure of human rights and do not justify them. Even if human rights are not status-based, they may be justified by reference to status. Human rights are constitutive of a status and that status amounts to those human rights in return. Human rights cannot, therefore, be based on that status, even though they are justified by reference to that status. It is the underlying idea informing that status and explaining how different rights constitute that status, and not the status itself, that justifies the rights constitutive of the status, whether it is equality or dignity.[39]

4.2.1 Equality

Human rights are sometimes justified by reference to equality, and in particular thin or basic moral equality. Basic moral equality is usually referred to as equal moral status.

The concept of equal moral status is best explained by distinguishing the notion of moral status from that of *equal* moral status. In a nutshell, *moral status* pertains to the way in which a being is subject to moral evaluation, how it ought to be treated, whether it has rights, and what kind of rights it has.[40] Moral status goes further, therefore, than mere moral considerability: the latter is a standing that may be shared with many other sentient animals and even with things, whereas moral status only belongs to human beings. *Equal moral status* refers to the idea that 'all people are of equal worth and that there are some claims people are entitled to make on one another simply by virtue of their status as persons'.[41]

There are two, inseparable core ideas in this understanding of equal moral status: the idea that all persons should be regarded as having the same moral worth, and the idea that this equal moral worth is relational and the basis for mutual moral claims. The first core idea in equal moral status pertains to the inherent and non-instrumental value of personhood. According to that idea, no person may be deemed as morally inferior to another: all those who have the characteristics that are sufficient for being a person, and hence the capacity for rational and moral agency, have the same moral status.[42] Equal moral status is of course compatible with important inequalities on other counts such as health, beauty,

---

[39] See Waldron (2013).
[40] See Buchanan, 'Moral Status and Human Enhancement' (2009) 37 *Philosophy and Public Affairs* 346.
[41] Scheffler, 'What is Egalitarianism?' (2003) 31 *Philosophy and Public Affairs* 5, 22.
[42] See Buchanan (2009), 347.

luck, etc. It is important to stress that what matters here is personhood and not human nature. The former captures what ought to be protected morally in human beings as moral agents, and it escapes the naturalistic fallacy and many other misconceptions that come with the notion of human nature. The second core idea in equal moral status pertains to its relational dimension. One is at once a person valuable in him- or herself and a person equal to others, that is, a person whose status and moral worth is defined by one's moral relations to others. The relational or social nature of equal moral status explains why the latter amounts to more than mere autonomy or rational capacity that is covered by the first core idea.[43] The denial of equal moral status amounts to a judgment of exclusion and inferiority *to others* where this kind of judgment is 'thought to disqualify one from participation as an equal in important social practices or roles'.[44]

As a result, equal moral status does more than simply entitle persons to mutual claims. It is *defined* by reference to those mutual claims. The mutual entitlements inherent in equal moral status are usually described as mutual basic moral rights.[45] Human rights are among the mutual basic moral rights that constitute one's equal moral status, although they may not exhaust them. What these basic moral rights or entitlements amount to are rights or entitlements to equal treatment or respect in a broad sense. This relationship between equal status and rights explains how human rights protect only those interests that can give rise to mutual entitlements that are themselves constitutive of equal moral status, with that status itself amounting to those mutual entitlements in return. This is why human rights cannot be said to be 'grounded' in (political) equality, even though the latter can be a 'ground' or justification for the recognition of human rights[46] and human rights a 'ground' for the recognition of equal (political) status.

Political equality is indeed the kind of equality that matters in a legal order and, accordingly, in the context of human rights law. The passage from equality to political equality corresponds to that from basic moral rights to human rights. The relational or social nature of equal moral status alluded to before implies that 'the proper acknowledgement of a person's moral status requires some sort of fundamental public recognition of equality'.[47] Political, or public, equality implies that people can see that they are being treated as equals and takes the form of its recognition by the law and institutions. The political dimension of equal moral status leads to a further process: the struggle for equal participation rights. And this in turn implies struggling for the establishment of a democratic regime that includes all those subjected to a decision into the decision-making process. Democracy is indeed the way 'of publicly realizing equality when persons who have diverse interests need to establish rules and institutions for the common world in which they live',[48] in spite of persistent and widespread reasonable disagreement.

It is precisely in the equal political status of each individual as an equal member of the moral-political community that the threshold of importance and point of passage from a general and fundamental interest to a human right may be found. Only those interests that are recognized as sufficiently important by members of the community can

---

[43] See Anderson, 'What is the Point of Equality?' (1999) 109 *Ethics* 287, 288–9 and 313.

[44] Buchanan, 'The Egalitarianism of Human Rights' (2010) 120 *Ethics* 679, 708–10.

[45] See Buchanan, *Beyond Humanity?* (OUP, 2011) 233.

[46] See on dignity, Waldron (2013). See also Besson, 'The Egalitarian Dimension of Human Rights' (2013) 136 *Archiv für Sozial- und Rechtsphilosophie Beiheft* 19.

[47] Buchanan (2009), 379.

[48] Christiano, 'Democratic Legitimacy and International Institutions' in Besson and Tasioulas (2010), 119, 121–2.

be recognized as giving rise to duties and hence human rights. Each person's interests deserve equal respect by virtue of his or her status as member of the community and of his or her mutual relations to other members of the community. As a result, the recognition of human rights does not occur in a top-down fashion; they are not externally promulgated but mutually granted by members of a given political community.[49] This is particularly important as it allows for the mutual assessment of the general and standard nature of the threats to certain interests that, therefore, deserve protection, on the one hand, and of the burdens and costs of the recognition of the corresponding rights and duties, on the other. As a matter of fact, human rights are not a consequence of individuals' equal political status, but a way of earning that equal status and consolidating it. Without human rights, political equality would remain an abstract guarantee; through mutual human rights, individuals become actors of their own equality and members of their political community. Borrowing Hannah Arendt's words: 'we are not born equal; we become equal as members of a group on the strength of our decision to guarantee ourselves mutually equal rights.'[50]

Evidence of the egalitarian dimension and justification of human rights may be found in practice. One may think, for instance, of the non-inherently individualistic nature of human rights that protect basic individual interests deemed comparatively important within the political community. Some human rights, like freedom of expression, protect individual interests in collective goods or individual interests whose social importance is part of the reason to protect them as individual rights. The egalitarian dimension of human rights is also echoed in the idea of an inviolable core of human rights as a limit on restrictions to the enjoyment of human rights. Contrary to the standard inviolability approach to that core,[51] on the proposed account, each human right is based on an interest (rather than a status) that is deemed, when protected as a right, as fundamental and constitutive of one's political equality, and, as a result, status. What is inviolable is not the interest, but the fact that everyone ought to benefit from its protection and hence from the right to have rights that protect it.

4.2.2 Dignity

Dignity is sometimes invoked as another way of justifying human rights.[52] The problem is that dignity is an extremely indeterminate and historically complex concept, often used as placeholder in morality.[53]

It remains unclear, for instance, whether dignity does some work in the human rights context that equal moral status cannot do. To start with, authors use dignity to refer to what is unique in human beings and shared by all of them: their personhood and capacity for rational and moral agency. This is, however, the very idea captured by the concept of equal moral status.[54] Another important element about dignity as it is used in the human rights context is its comparative or relational dimension. However, the fact that authors usually use the term 'equal dignity'[55] to describe this dimension shows how the question

---

[49] See Forst (2010).   [50] Arendt, *The Origins of Totalitarianism* (Penguin, 1951) 147.

[51] eg Kamm, 'Rights' in Coleman and Shapiro (eds), *The Oxford Handbook of Jurisprudence and Philosophy of Law* (OUP, 2002) 476; Nagel, 'La valeur de l'inviolabilité' (1994) 99 *Revue de métaphysique et de morale* 149.

[52] eg Waldron (2012); Habermas (2010); Forst (2010); Habermas, *Zur Verfassung Europas: Ein Essay* (Suhrkamp, 2011); Tasioulas (2012).

[53] eg Pinker, 'The Stupidity of Dignity', *The New Republic* (28 May 2008).

[54] This becomes clear when one looks at Habermas (2010), 468–9 and 472.

[55] eg Gosepath, 'The Place of Equality in Habermas' and Dworkin's Theories of Justice' (1995) 3 *EJ of Philosophy* 2, 27.

of equality cannot be escaped by gesturing to dignity. Confirmation that 'equal dignity' is redundant if one adopts the proposed approach to equal moral status as equal universal moral rights may be found in Article 1 of the Universal Declaration of Human Rights that refers to human beings being born 'equal in dignity *and* rights'.[56]

If this argument against dignity as a foundation of human rights holds, one still needs to explain why dignity has been a key feature within major international and domestic human rights law instruments since 1945.[57]

An historical explanation is the post-Second World War political convergence of two extremely powerful traditions: Christian theology and Kantian philosophy.[58] Yet historical compromises do not necessarily make for good moral interpretations of law, and historical understandings do not necessarily stick in judicial interpretations of legal norms. As to the resurgence of interest in dignity these days, explanations are easy to find. Legal reasons may lie in the development of comparative constitutional law, and the influence of German constitutional law (where dignity is a central concept) in that context, but also within EU fundamental rights law and international human rights law. Morally, one may find explanations in the return of the religious or at least of the sacred, but also in the coming under threat of Kantian moral philosophy within moral philosophy in general. Those debates within morality ensure that the fascination for dignity can endure. And this may not necessarily be a regrettable state of affairs given the role such essentially contestable concepts play in a democratic legal order. Besides, if dignity works as a moral placeholder and 'status-indicator',[59] then its resilience may be good news for the protection of equal moral status and human rights.

All of this is not to say, of course, that dignity does not have a moral existence of its own besides equal moral status, but merely that it is redundant to equal moral status in its relationship to human rights. Dignity is a way to be treated. That meaning of dignity corresponds to the idea of being treated with dignity or dignified respect. It usually takes the shape of a duty to dignified treatment, as opposed to a right.

5 WHAT FOLLOWS FROM THE JUSTIFICATION OF HUMAN RIGHTS

5.1 HUMAN RIGHTS JUSTIFICATIONS AND THE UNIVERSALITY OF HUMAN RIGHTS

The justifications of human rights have to be such that they can account for the claim to universality of human rights, or, at least, provide an explanation of why that claim is made in practice.

A well-known challenge to the legitimacy, but also to the moral justification, of the universality of international human rights law is based on a brand of moral relativism. In

---

[56] Emphasis added.

[57] eg McCrudden, 'Dignity and Judicial Interpretation of Human Rights' (2008) 19 *EJIL* 655; McCrudden, 'In Pursuit of Human Dignity: An Introduction to Current Debates' in McCrudden (ed), *Understanding Human Dignity* (OUP, 2013). Of course, there are also counter-arguments in international and domestic human rights practice, as not all constitutional traditions know dignity, and some have now abandoned it.

[58] See Rosen, *Dignity: Its History and Meaning* (Harvard UP, 2012) 53, 80 ff and 90 ff. See also Moyn, *Christian Human Rights* (UPenn Press, 2015).

[59] Ladwig, 'Menschenwürde als Grund der Menschenrechte' (2010) 1 *Zeitschrift für Politische Theorie* 51, 65. See also Habermas (2010), 26; Beitz, 'Human Dignity in the Theory of Human Rights: Nothing But a Phrase?' (2013) 41 *Philosophy & Public Affairs* 259, 288.

short, the objection is that international human rights law embodies a 'parochial' (that is, limited or narrow) set of values (or ordering of such values) that it unjustifiably imposes through its claim to a universal personal scope, on people and societies who do not share it. If one refers to the conditions of justified authority or legitimacy in Joseph Raz's conception of authority (that is, the dependence condition and the normal justification condition),[60] the claim made by parochialism is that international law does not have legitimate authority over certain subjects of international law. The parochialist complaint can be read as denying that international law facilitates conformity with pre-existing objective reasons, as opposed to the reasons asserted by certain dominant groups. In other words, parochialism denounces the legitimacy of international law for disregarding the dependence condition.

There are three ways of understanding the moral relativist challenge: moral relativism in the strict sense, epistemological relativism, and social relativism. One may assume here that the parochialism objection is not based on a sceptical view of morality.[61] In respect of the first challenge, *moral relativism in the strict sense*, it may be pointed out that adopting an objective view of morality does not equate with adhering to a single conception of morality. The background to the present analysis is an objective, albeit pluralist, account of morality that can accommodate conflicts of values and different orderings between them. As to the second challenge, *epistemological relativism*, one may legitimately contend that the institutionalized intercultural dialogue and mutual adjustment promoted by democratic coordination in international human rights law-making, and international human rights decision-making generally, could pay sufficient attention to the issue of the diversity of perspectives and understandings when adopting or applying international human rights law.[62] Finally, with regard to the third challenge, that of *social relativism*, it should be emphasized that holding to moral objectivity does not mean denying the importance of the contextualization of moral values recognized by international human rights law at the domestic level, nor the possibility of the historical national localization of objective values and of historical changes in that localization over the course of time.[63] This is particularly appropriate in the context of human rights where duties can only be specified in a concrete political and, in particular, democratic context. In short, parochialism is a necessary component of human rights enforcement that requires contextualization and hence some form of vernacularization or adaptation to the local circumstances.[64]

It seems, therefore, that the difficulties raised by moral, epistemological, and social relativism can be adequately met. However, the critique based on moral relativism retains some of its original bite when it is understood as based on moral pluralism. This version of the challenge relies on the absence of correspondence between the basic values or reasons or, more often, their orderings or rankings imposed by international human rights norms, and those applying

[60] Raz, *The Morality of Freedom* (Clarendon, 1986); Raz, *Ethics in the Public Domain* (Clarendon, 1995).

[61] Defeating a moral relativist objection would take us beyond the scope of this chapter. It is clear, however, that reasonable moral disagreement does not validate a moral relativist argument (see Griffin (2009), 128–32). Nor actually does reasonable moral agreement validate a moral realist one. Acceptability and acceptation are deeply parochial. This is why, for instance, the legal universality of human rights may not be proposed as a solution to the problem of human rights parochialism, but is at its source.

[62] See Buchanan (2004); Buchanan, 'Human Rights and the Legitimacy of the International Legal Order' (2008) 14 *Legal Theory* 39.

[63] See Williams, *In the Beginning was the Deed: Realism and Moralism in Political Argument* (Princeton UP, 2005) 62, 66.

[64] See also Buchanan (2004); Merry, *Human Rights and Gender Violence: Translating International Law into Local Justice* (University of Chicago Press, 2006); Benhabib, 'The Legitimacy of Human Rights' (2008) 137 *Daedalus* 94.

within any given political community. One may think, for instance, of collectivist moralities that give the group priority over the individual. This objection affects the plausibility of universal moral justification of international human rights law and cannot simply be put at rest by reference to the piecemeal or fragmented nature of the legitimate authority of international law. If successful, the challenge would preclude a whole set of international human rights, albeit abstract rights, from applying to a whole range of cultures (regions and countries).

Despite appearances, the moral pluralism objection can also be met. The situation differs, however, depending on the state and its existing level of human rights protection.

Those states that do not have domestic human rights norms do not yet have the duties that correspond to those rights. What they have, however, is a moral duty to protect fundamental universal interests and this ought to be done by recognizing those interests as human rights. In such cases, the dependence condition is met because the reason corresponding at least to the right to have rights is pre-existing. However, the other reasons corresponding to international human rights duties cannot match pre-existing state reasons. Thus, the inescapable parochialism of political equality that only exists within the bound of a given political community and that is hence ingrained in human rights defeats the universal justification and legitimacy of international human rights law, just as it conditions their very legalization as human rights in the first place. With respect to the right to have rights, in any case, it is important to work on substantive and institutional mechanisms of deliberation and inclusive transcultural dialogue that increase the epistemic virtues of international human rights law-making and can, therefore, minimize the discrepancies in the ordering of interests and of reasons between international human rights norms and domestic ones.

If, by contrast, a state already has a set of corresponding domestic human rights norms, the reasons stemming from those human rights duties can be matched by the reasons given by international human rights norms. It is the specific ordering of interests and reasons that may differ, however, in circumstances of moral pluralism. Given what was said before about the interdependence between human rights and political equality and given the role of the political community and hence of domestic law in identifying the egalitarian threshold of importance of those interests that need to be protected as human rights, international human rights norms are drafted as minimal and abstract legal norms. Their threshold may then be set higher by domestic law. Their ordering with other interests that is necessary to further specify the rights and identify the corresponding duties may depend on the contextualization made by domestic authorities. Since most of the legalization of human rights takes place at domestic level, this also makes domestic law the locus of justification and hence legitimization of international human rights norms.

International human rights law accommodates moral pluralism, in other words, by not forcing complete orderings of the same values. This minimizes the chances of disconnect between the ordering of interests in international human rights norms and states' pre-existing reasons for action. It should be added that the egalitarian justification of human rights proposed before grants human rights a relational and collective dimension that goes part of the way in accommodating collectivist and non-individualistic moralities and hence moral pluralism within human rights.

5.2 HUMAN RIGHTS JUSTIFICATIONS AND THE STRINGENCY OF HUMAN RIGHTS

The justifications of human rights have to be such that they can account for the special stringency and demanding normative nature of human rights in practice, but also provide an explanation of why and how they are being restricted in case of conflict with other moral considerations or other human rights.

It is commonly expected that human rights weigh as much as their justification and thus that conflicts between rights should be resolved by reference to that weight. This is, for instance, what many status-based approaches to the justification of human rights claim.[65] Those who defend the idea of a minimal core in every human right that is resistant to trade-offs also usually relate its special stringency to that of the justification of the human right (for example dignity). Other accounts that endorse linkage approaches to the justification of certain human rights see their priority in case of conflict as conditioned by whether they are instrumental rights or not.[66]

Things are not that straightforward, however. Human rights do not have a certain weight that may be quantitatively balanced and traded off like utility, but are described and relate by reference to their moral stringency. Actually, it is the concrete duties that have that stringency and not the abstract rights. And the different duties corresponding to any given human right may have very different stringencies depending on the threats against which they are shielding the protected interest. As a result, human rights should not be weighed and balanced quantitatively when they conflict with other rights or moral considerations, but their duties' respective and variable stringency should be assessed to reach a qualitative trade-off.

No wonder then that the stringency of human rights is only indirectly related to their moral justification. This dispels the apparent paradox that besets human rights theory according to which it is hard to understand why human rights justified by reference to extremely stringent values can be restricted on the basis of conflicting public interests and less stringent moral considerations, on the one hand, or how human rights that are equal in justification may have to be weighed and balanced against each other, on the other.[67] It is true that all equally justified human rights are equal in the abstract and have very stringent justifications, but this does not mean that their corresponding duties are of equal stringency and may not be restricted in a differentiated fashion. Nor does it mean that they may be restricted to any degree, however. They may be restricted, but in a manner that is justified by reference to the underlying justification of human rights.

The specific stringency of human rights pertains to the ranking or priority of human rights when they conflict with other moral considerations. It is part of the meaning of human rights that they should have a relationship of priority over certain other moral considerations. Human rights are often portrayed as resistant to 'changes on the scale of social costs'.[68] This was famously captured by Ronald Dworkin's idea of rights as trumps,[69] Robert Nozick's conception of rights as side-constraints,[70] or John Rawls' idea of lexical priority.[71]

The first question, however, is whether human rights should take priority over any other moral considerations or just some of them. Other moral considerations may include, depending on the accounts, moral interests, values, interests, goods, welfare, justice, utility, security, and so on. It may be useful to refer to Dworkin's idea of rights as trumps, as he is very careful when identifying the considerations he has in mind. His idea is to exclude merely external preferences, that is, others' preferences about how one should lead one's own life.[72] His argument for that exclusion is egalitarian. Rights should be invoked in cases

---

[65] eg Kamm (2002); Nagel (1994).

[66] eg Shue (1996); and a critique by Waldron (2009).

[67] eg Griffin (2009), 76: 'Human rights are resistant to trade-offs, but not completely so'.

[68] See Waldron, 'Security and Liberty: The Image of Balance' (2003) 11 *J of Political Philosophy* 191, 196.

[69] Dworkin, *Taking Rights Seriously* (Harvard UP, 1977) 190 ff.

[70] Nozick, *Anarchy, State and Utopia* (Basic Books, 1974) 28 ff.

[71] Rawls, *The Law of Peoples* (Harvard UP, 1999) 36 ff.

[72] See Dworkin, 'Rights as Trumps' in Waldron (ed), *Theories of Rights* (OUP, 1984) 153, 165. See also Waldron, 'Rights in Conflict' in *Liberal Rights: Collected Papers* (CUP, 1993) 203, 220–1.

where invocations of the common good or the general interest of the community are likely to have been contaminated by those external preferences and the latter granted more importance than they should as a result.

The next question pertains to the degree of stringency of human rights duties when they enter in relation with other moral considerations and to whether their stringency is absolute or not. Here again, Dworkin's account is helpful as he does not preclude that, in some cases, some of the considerations *a priori* excluded from restricting human rights may be allowed to restrict them.[73] This is why some authors have referred to Dworkin's account as one that treats rights as 'shields' rather than trumps.[74] There are two ways in which this conclusion seems plausible. The first one pertains to the plurality of human rights duties at any given time and over time. Depending on the circumstances and the kinds of threats to the interest protected by the human right, different duties corresponding to the same right may be of different stringency, at least relatively to one another. The second one is that not all moral considerations that may be conflicting with human rights duties are of the same stringency. Some may be more stringent than others, depending on the circumstances.

The question, however, is how to structure the relationship between those moral considerations that are not trumped by human rights and the idea of human rights that work as trumps over moral considerations. As Jeremy Waldron argues, the answer cannot lie in any quantitative assessment of the interest protected as this would bring back the dangers of the utilitarian weighing and balancing of interests.[75] The same may be said of any quantitative measurement of the degree of threat to the interest protected. The logic of the idea of weight would indeed suggest that ultimately any human rights duty associated with that interest may be dealt with in that way.

The answer to this dilemma lies arguably in the collective dimension of the interests protected by human rights and, more specifically, their egalitarian dimension. These two features are internal to human rights as rights and enable them to relate to other interests and moral considerations in their own way and within their specific moral category without threatening the special stringency of that moral category in general.[76]

First, the collective dimension of some of the individual interests protected by human rights provides guidance as to how qualitative trade-offs may be operated and this within the rights themselves. Human rights are normative relations and have a socio-comparative dimension that incorporates a given relationship between the individual and the group. Thus, one may imagine that the collective dimension of the interest protected by freedom of expression in a democracy, that is, its contribution to political life, may allow for justified restrictions of some of its corresponding duties in circumstances where that collective dimension requires them. The role of the collective dimension of any given human right is precisely to help draw the line between what is collectively necessary in the protection of a right and what is not.

Second, the egalitarian idea underlying all human rights calls for egalitarian justifications of restrictions to human rights duties. All restrictions of human rights should be egalitarian, implying, for instance, that attention is paid to the distributive consequences of restrictions: the losers should not always be on the same side. The egalitarian justification of human rights also explains why the restriction of human rights duties by reference to other moral considerations may never lead to the complete erosion of any one of them or to the restriction of their fundamental core.[77] This would amount to denying equal rights-holders their

---

[73] See Dworkin (1984), 191.

[74] See Schauer, 'A Comment on the Structure of Rights' (1993) 27 *Georgia LR* 415, 429.

[75] Waldron (1993), 216 ff.

[76] See Besson, 'Human Rights in Relation' in Smet and Brems (eds), *Human Rights Conflicts* (OUP, 2017) 23.

[77] See Waldron (2009), 224–6; Shue (1996), 114, 166.

equal rights and their equal moral status as members of the political community. Finally, in institutional terms, this egalitarian requirement of human rights restrictions also implies that democratic procedures are the adequate procedures in which to justify human rights restrictions. This is why most international and regional human rights instruments include a reference to democracy in the justification test they apply to human rights restrictions.

6 CONCLUSION

Human rights need to be justified, not least because they have been under critique lately. The purpose of this chapter was to explain what the justification of human rights amounts to, why it is necessary, how we should go about it, and what its implications are.

Of course, as it should have become clear in the course of the argument, the justification of human rights is so central to human rights theory that it is conditioned by, and conditions in return, other key issues in human rights theory. Those are not only the nature, object, scope, rights-holders, and duty-bearers of human rights, but also what we understand the project of human rights theorizing itself to be.

FURTHER READING

BEITZ, *The Idea of Human Rights* (Oxford University Press, 2009).

BEITZ, 'Human Dignity in the Theory of Human Rights: Nothing But a Phrase?' (2013) 41 *Philosophy & Public Affairs* 259–90.

BUCHANAN, 'The Egalitarianism of Human Rights' (2010) 120 *Ethics* 679–710.

BUCHANAN, 'Why International Legal Human Rights?' in Cruft, Liao, and Renzo (eds), *The Philosophical Foundations of Human Rights* (Oxford University Press, 2015) 244–62.

BUCHANAN, *The Heart of Human Rights* (Oxford University Press, 2013).

FORST, 'The Justification of Human Rights and the Basic Right to Justification: A Reflexive Approach' (2010) 120 *Ethics* 711–40.

GRIFFIN, *On Human Rights* (Oxford University Press, 2008).

HABERMAS, 'The Concept of Human Dignity and the Realistic Utopia of Human Rights' (2010) 41 *Metaphilosophy* 464–80.

NICKEL, *Making Sense of Human Rights* (Blackwell, 2007).

RAZ, 'Human Rights without Foundations' in Besson and Tasioulas (eds), *The Philosophy of International Law* (Oxford University Press, 2010) 321–37.

ROSEN, *Dignity: Its History and Meaning* (Harvard University Press, 2012).

TALBOTT, *Human Rights and Human Well-being* (Oxford University Press, 2010).

TASIOULAS, 'Towards a Philosophy of Human Rights' (2012) 65 *CLP* 1–30.

WALDRON, 'Is Dignity the Foundation of Human Rights?' (2013) *NYU School of Law, Public Law Research Paper No 12–73*.

USEFUL WEBSITES

Stanford Encyclopedia of Philosophy: <http://plato.stanford.edu>
Routledge Encyclopedia of Philosophy: <http://www.rep.routledge.com/>

3

CRITIQUES

Marie-Bénédicte Dembour

SUMMARY

Whether they are conceived as the rights that every human being has, thus 'naturally' setting limits to the legitimate action of states and others, or as principles of good political action which society agrees to adopt and follow, human rights have always been subjected to intense and perceptive critiques. This chapter reviews six such critiques, deriving from realist, utilitarian, Marxist, particularist (cultural relativist), feminist, and post-colonial theoretical perspectives. The first three critiques emerged in reaction to the (successive) French Declarations of the Rights of Man of the late eighteenth century; the last three were fully developed in reaction to the International Bill of Rights enacted after the Second World War. Each of these critiques reveals a gap between what human rights claim to be or achieve, on the one hand, and what human rights are or do in practice, on the other. The question arises as to whether this gap is bridgeable. The critiques answer this question in various ways.[1]

1 INTRODUCTION

Human rights, for those who believe in them, embody the promise of a better world. They are, in Samuel Moyn's words, the current 'last utopia'.[2] From the late 1970s, they became the language in which to articulate high moral precepts in the political sphere, and they displaced alternative utopias. However, the concept of human rights —and of its antecedent, natural rights—has always attracted persuasive critiques. This chapter reviews six critiques, emanating respectively from realist, utilitarian, Marxist, particularist (cultural relativist), feminist, and, finally, post-colonial theoretical perspectives.

Before understanding a critique, the concept it is critiquing first needs to be understood. This is not the context, however, to discuss in detail what human rights are.[3] Suffice it to say here that this chapter is written with the understanding that human rights orthodoxy has been moving from conceiving human rights as a given ('natural school') to conceiving them as values and principles which are agreed upon ('deliberative school'). For ease of terms, the natural school will be referred to as the 'old orthodoxy' and the deliberative

---

[1] Parts of this chapter draw upon *Who Believes in Human Rights?: Reflections on the European Convention* © Marie-Bénédicte Dembour (CUP, 2006) extracts reproduced with permission.

[2] Moyn, *The Last Utopia: Human Rights in History* (Harvard UP, 2010).   [3] But see Chapter 2.

school as the 'new orthodoxy', even though this terminology may suggest that the understanding of human rights at any one time is clearly set. It is not. Human rights are a highly contested concept.[4]

In one way or another, each of the six critiques reviewed in this chapter points to a gap between the promise that every human being enjoys a number of fundamental rights and a world where human rights violations abound and many people are excluded from the enjoyment of human rights; that is, a gap between the human rights ideal and practice. Why is there such a gap? Two rather different answers are possible. The gap can be thought to exist *either* because the practice has, so far, failed to live up to the theory, but without this affecting the validity of the concept of human rights, *or* because human rights cannot be what they are said to be, making the concept invalid. In other words, critiques of human rights can either require human rights to be true to their word or reject them as constructed on unsound premises. These two positions correspond to what will be called in this chapter the practical and the conceptual critiques of human rights.

Practical critiques conceive of problems with human rights as demanding that a better practice be elaborated. The problems that such critiques identify are various and include, in a non-exhaustive list, the existence of double standards in the application of human rights, the fact that powerful non-state actors largely remain outside the human rights compass, the relative neglect of economic and social rights, the status of collective rights, overzealous responses to the terrorist threat, and so on.[5] Practical critiques accept the idea of human rights, but demand that human rights be made to work better in the face of challenges. Crucially, they do not suggest that the concept is irretrievably defective. They 'simply' ask for the gap between what the concept promises and what it delivers to be closed, believing that human rights must and *can* be improved.

In contrast, conceptual critiques conceive of the concept of human rights as fundamentally flawed. They regard problems of bad governance as requiring a solution that lies outside the human rights logic. For them, human rights are not the best way to try to implement the ideas of justice, equality, and humanity which human rights supposedly stand for; better ways have to be found. Obviously those who embrace these views are not *against* human rights in the sense that their aim is not to call for the supposed binary opposite of human rights, namely, violations of human rights. Rather, their view is that the route towards emancipation need not, or even, *should not*, take the form of human rights.

The critiques reviewed in this chapter have both conceptual and practical variants. To complicate matters further, they often overlap. At the risk of caricature, but in order to introduce them, an attempt can be made to encapsulate each of them in one sentence. Realists reject the idea that human rights are natural, simply existing out there to be recognized and implemented; they argue that human rights cannot be 'above' or 'beyond' the state but necessarily originate from and are enmeshed within the state. Utilitarians, seeking the common good, oppose the granting of individual rights regardless of the consequences for the common good; they think it is impossible for human rights to be absolute and/or inalienable. Marxists view rights as sustaining the bourgeois order and thus feeding oppression by privileging a particular class to the detriment of the oppressed majority. Particularists object to the idea that moral judgments can be made that hold true across cultures; they call for tolerance of practices that are not comprehensible within the dominant perspective and denounce what they see as the inherent imperialism of human rights, which are not universal but the product of the society which has created them. Feminists

---

[4] See further Dembour, 'What are Human Rights? Four Schools of Thought' (2010) 32 *HRQ* 1.
[5] Some of these problems are discussed in Chapters 28–30.

dispute the idea that human rights are gender-neutral; they attack human rights' pretence of equality and neutrality by observing that rights, which have generally been defined by men, tend to regulate the so-perceived public sphere, thereby bypassing the interests and concerns of women, typically associated with the private sphere. Post-colonial theorists link human rights to imperialism; they observe that the International Bill of Rights was developed outside any concern for the inequities arising from the colonial situation and that the rise of human rights in political discourse has not signalled an end to inequality.

These critiques encompass variants which dismiss the concept of human rights altogether. When they are conceptual, the critiques tend to hold the human rights logic to be defective in at least four respects. First, the human rights logic is said to present the concept as universal, while the claim that human rights are relevant to all human beings across time and space is not credible in the face of human history. Second, the logic is criticized for celebrating the individual to the neglect of solidarity and other social values. Third, the human rights logic is found to be derived from an abstract reasoning about 'man' which is ill-equipped to assess both the reality of political life and the requirements of social justice. Fourth, the human rights logic is denounced for being oblivious to the way it directly participates in sustaining power relationships and thus fails to produce equality.

For some thinkers, there is a very close connection—almost a conflation—between human rights and liberalism, understood as the political philosophy that either holds that government should interfere as little as possible in the lives of its citizens or signifies, more broadly, 'an order in which the state exists to secure the freedom of individuals on a formally egalitarian basis'.[6] For example, Jack Donnelly refuses to say of the US that they are a liberal society because they do not realize the very high human rights benchmarks he associates with a liberal society.[7] At the opposite end of such a conflation, it is increasingly common for scholars to bemoan the 'hijacking' of human rights by liberalism.[8] This position might suggest that conceptual critiques of human rights necessarily stand opposed to or outside liberalism. However, it is possible to oppose the concept of human rights (as understood under the old orthodoxy) on liberal grounds. A resounding illustration is provided by Jeremy Bentham, a utilitarian firmly belonging to the liberal tradition, who, as we shall see in Section 2, famously qualified human rights as 'nonsense upon stilts'.[9]

2 EARLY CRITIQUES

2.1 THE REALIST CRITIQUE

Considering the old orthodoxy, which viewed human rights as a given, it is not surprising that human rights have typically first been *declared* before being turned into conventional law. This practice can be traced back to the two French Declarations of the Rights of Man and the Citizen of the eighteenth century (French Declarations) and, in the contemporary era, the 1948 Universal Declaration of Human Rights (UDHR) (which was directly

---

[6] In a definition borrowed from Brown, 'Neo-Liberalism and the End of Liberal Democracy' (2003) 7 *Theory & Event* 6.

[7] Donnelly, *Universal Human Rights in Theory and Practice* (Cornell UP, 1989) 68 and 73.

[8] eg Douzinas, *Human Rights and Empire: The Political Philosophy of Cosmopolitanism* (Routledge-Cavendish, 2007) 24; Stammers, *Human Rights and Social Movements* (Pluto, 2009).

[9] Bentham, 'Anarchical Fallacies: An Examination of the Declaration of the Rights of the Man and the Citizen Decreed by the Constituent Assembly in France' in Bentham, *Selected Writings on Utilitarianism* (Wordsworth, 2000) 381, 405.

inspired by the French Declarations). Why is there this tradition of 'declaring' rights? In contemporary international law it is, of course, important to distinguish between a declaration, which has no binding force, and a convention, which has binding force for those states that have ratified it. This crucial distinction, however, cannot have been the reason why the French National Assembly entitled the document it adopted in 1789 'Declaration'. The preamble of the Declaration spoke of the need to 'set forth in a solemn declaration, the natural, inalienable, and sacred rights of man'. It purported to have done this 'in the presence and under the auspices of the Supreme Being'. Clearly, the intention was to spell out the belief that human rights were being *declared* rather than created. This idea is also found in the UDHR, albeit more implicitly, in line with the fact that an exact convergence on the foundations of human rights was lacking, in the more plural context of the United Nations (UN). The UDHR laconically refers to a 'faith in fundamental human rights'.[10]

The implications of believing that human rights pre-exist any legislative or social recognition have been helpfully spelled out by Louis Henkin: 'Implied in one's humanity, human rights are inalienable and imprescriptible: they cannot be transferred, forfeited, or waived; they cannot be lost by having been usurped, or by one's failure to exercise or assert them.'[11] This is another way of saying that human rights are 'natural', existing irrespective of social recognition and so discoverable through reason. These assumptions were at the core of the old human rights orthodoxy. But they have not been without their detractors. Among these is what is referred to here as the realist critique of human rights, which stresses the man-made origin of human rights and argues that they are not obvious at all.

For present purposes, Jeremy Bentham, popularly known as the father of utilitarianism, can be qualified as a realist. His virulent critique of the 1789 French Declaration argued:

> [F]rom *real* laws come real rights; but from *imaginary* laws, from laws of nature, fancied by poets, rhetoricians, and dealers in moral and intellectual poisons, come *imaginary* rights, a bastard brood of monsters, 'gorgons and chimeras dire'.[12]

For Bentham, it was clear that the French Declaration was 'nonsense upon stilts' and the rights it declared imaginary. Not only did these rights not exist, but making people believe they existed was dangerous, for their inevitable disrespect would lead to discontent, and possibly in turn, insurrection. Bentham's critique was published under the title 'Anarchical Fallacies', which said it all. The Declaration was *conceptually* fallacious—a nonsensical flow of words amounting to nothing more than a bundle of contradictions. It also presented a *practical* problem as the promise of rights that could not be respected in practice invited a perpetual overthrowing of political institutions. As far as Bentham was concerned, the rights proclaimed in the Declaration were a 'mere effusion of imbecility'.[13] For him, the way to deal with abusive government was to induce the legislator to change the law, not to call for its abandonment in the name of non-existent natural rights.

Bentham argued that the rights of the French Declaration, if taken literally, meant nothing. For example, he noted that, contrary to what the Declaration stated, human beings are obviously not born equal. In Bentham's opinion, the drafters of the Declaration were constantly oscillating between a utopian world, where all men would be equal, and the real world, where they clearly were not. This led them to use ambiguous wording, for example, 'can' instead of 'ought' (as in 'every man can do this' instead of 'every man ought to be able to do this').[14] If the rights of the Declaration were not to be taken literally, then they still

---

[10] Preambular para 5.
[12] Bentham (2000), 458 [original emphases].
[14] Bentham (2000), 402 and 393.

[11] Henkin, *The Age of Rights* (Columbia UP, 1990) 2.
[13] Bentham (2000), 441.

meant nothing as they would need to be given limits. For example, Article 10 guaranteed freedom of expression and religion. However, it accepted exceptions governed by public order considerations. Bentham derided: 'Disturb the public order?—what does that mean? Louis XIV need not have hesitated about receiving an article thus worded into his code.'[15] Of liberty, he said:

> Suppose a declaration to this effect—no man's liberty shall be abridged in any point. This, it is evident, would be an useless extravagance, which must be contradicted by every law that came to be made. Suppose it to say—no man's liberty shall be abridged, but in such points as it shall be abridged in, by the law. This, we see, is saying nothing: it leaves the law just as free and unfettered as it found it.[16]

Giving or recognizing supposedly 'natural', 'superior', 'inalienable', 'fundamental' rights which can then be defeated through legislation amounts to *nothing*. Bentham concluded: 'Look to the letter, you find nonsense—look beyond the letter, you find nothing.'[17]

Bentham's critique was very much directed at the old human rights orthodoxy, which regarded human rights as natural—a given. For a realist critique of human rights in their new, increasingly dominant conception—as agreed upon through a deliberative process—one can turn to International Relations (IR). IR realism holds the state as the key actor on the international scene, and one which always follows its own interests.[18] According to one of its long dominant variants, the state does whatever is required to ensure its own survival and, what is more, acts morally when it does as, in this pursuit, it should not be guided by private morality. The idea that political ethics should be brought into line with private ethics is thought 'not only ill-advised but also irresponsible . . . not only mistaken intellectually but also fundamentally wrong morally'.[19] In this perspective, given the ill-advisability of cooperation with other states that by definition also follow their own interests and cannot be trusted, *raison d'état* (literally, reason of state, an idea linked to realpolitik) is a fundamental concept and state sovereignty a chief concern. Human rights have no real place.

Not all IR realist scholars are of the persuasion described here. For some, that states are unwilling to act in ways which restrict their power is an empirical fact, but not a moral precept. Starting from the observation that states cling to power as much and as long as they can, these scholars argue that if states act in apparently immoral ways, it is because it is in their interests to do so, not because they (should) follow a public morality different from the one governing relations between individuals. Realism, in this variant, is not a moral vision but an inescapable fact. These realists are wary of the idea that states might ever truly approach a document such as the UDHR as 'a common standard of achievement for all peoples and all nations'—whatever its preamble asserts. They would be quick to point out how human rights law is yet another sphere where states play their power games, as evidenced by reservation clauses and derogations which let them off the hook or the double standards they apply.[20] At best, then, human rights provide protection akin to a sandbag, holding back the bulk of the water/government's arbitrariness and oppression—for as long as the tide/repressive impulse is not too strong.

Like all 'isms', realism can mean many things. What the realisms of Bentham and IR have in common is that, taking a realistic look at the world, they reject the idea that human rights could somehow exist 'above' or 'aside from' the state. For them, human rights belong

---

[15] Bentham (2000), 435.   [16] Bentham (2000), 387.   [17] Bentham (2000), 397.

[18] Jackson and Sørensen, *Introduction to International Relations* (OUP, 1999) 96.

[19] Jackson and Sørensen (1999), 77.

[20] eg Mertus, *Bait and Switch: Human Rights and US Foreign Policy* (Routledge, 2004).

to the imagination of utopian dreamers. In Bentham's case, this is because the French Declaration did not provide a positive legal framework which made the declared rights real. In the case of today's realists, it is because they do not believe that states wish to submit to either the spirit or the letter of the human rights declarations and conventions that are supposedly now guiding the international community.

2.2 THE UTILITARIAN CRITIQUE

Bentham, a towering figure of the utilitarian movement, dismissed the predecessor of human rights (the rights of man) as 'nonsense upon stilts'. Does this mean that utilitarianism is irretrievably opposed to human rights? Yes and no. On the one hand, the logic of utilitarianism is such that it cannot accept the idea of absolute and inalienable rights, which at first sight seems central to human rights orthodoxy—at least in its old version. On the other hand, individual rights being obviously conducive to the happiness of a great number of individuals, utilitarianism can act as a strident defender of human rights. Appreciating why these two apparently contradictory positions coexist requires understanding the nature of both utilitarianism and human rights orthodoxy.

Utilitarianism is the ethical philosophy that posits that an action must be judged morally by reference to the welfare (utility) it produces. It holds that the good act is the one that maximizes happiness. Such a philosophy is consequentialist: it judges actions by reference to their consequences. Before deciding on a course of action, utilitarianism demands that the action's likely effects on various interests be considered and weighed. In other words, it does not believe in *a priori* judgments as to the value of some good (in the sense of an interest worthy of protection) over other goods.

The trade-offs that utilitarianism never rules out have led its detractors to intimate that it allows the individual to be sacrificed to the collective interest. One healthy person, so the argument goes, could be killed under utilitarianism for the benefit of a number of people who depend for their survival on the transplant of various organs. In a similar vein, an innocent could be found guilty in order to defuse a riotous situation when his condemnation would appear to facilitate a return to peace and order. These kinds of scenarios, however, are more often than not put forward by thinkers who oppose utilitarianism. Self-declared utilitarians observe that they are unlikely to present themselves in the clear-cut form imagined by their detractors.[21] Utilitarians are quick to note that repeated sacrifices of individuals would immediately generate a substantial decrease in general happiness because of the sense of insecurity it would foster across the population.

Many utilitarians are thus wary of the concept of individual sacrifice for the collective good which utilitarianism supposedly supports. Nonetheless, it remains that utilitarianism does not accept the idea that some rights are absolute and inalienable. By contrast, this idea is at the core of (the old) human rights orthodoxy. To understand the crucial difference between these two positions, one must understand what makes a right absolute.

For a right to be absolute, the corresponding duty to which it gives rise must be expressed in a negative form. Let us take the example of the right to be free from torture, one of the few rights to be considered absolute in human rights orthodoxy. To respect this right, it might be thought that governments must do one thing and one thing only: *refrain from* inflicting torture. Clearly, this is a negative duty: that of *not acting* in a certain way. If this reasoning is followed, there is only one way to respect the right not to

---

[21] Häyri, *Liberal Utilitarianism and Applied Ethics* (Routledge, 1994) 80.

be tortured; hence its infringement is easy to establish (at least in principle). Now, rights which are not absolute are relative. Their respect is relative to many things; it is never easy, in the sense of clear-cut, to establish when they are, in fact, respected. A standard example of relative rights is economic and social rights. Their respect requires the state to provide education, healthcare, and so on, that is, *to act* in a certain way. Endless discussions can be had as to whether a state has done enough to fulfil its positive obligations in that respect. A positive obligation is by nature unclear, in the sense of never strictly defined.

Logically, only a negative obligation can give rise to an absolute right. In turn, thinking in these terms entails categorical reasoning. To return to the example of the prohibition of torture, human rights orthodoxy considers torture to be intrinsically wrong: it considers that torture is and always will be wrong, whatever the circumstances. This is based on deontological philosophy, which holds that some things have an intrinsic, categorical, non-consequential value.[22]

By contrast, utilitarianism is a consequentialist theory which evaluates the morality of an action by reference to its consequences. Utilitarianism does not ask, 'Is this wrong?' but, 'Is this *causing* wrong?' It does not hold anything to have intrinsic value as such. A utilitarian cannot rule out, once and for all, the possibility that one day utility will require a right to be set aside in order to further the collective good. This is true in particular of the right to be free from torture, even though it is difficult to imagine *sound* utilitarian reasoning justifying it easily. It is worth stressing in this respect that the would-be convincing scenario of the ticking bomb is not very convincing at all: the police would know everything, including who has the vital information, except for the single element of where the bomb is—how likely is this? Even if this unlikely scenario were to happen in practice, there would still be strong utilitarian arguments against the use of torture, including the corrupting effect of having to train officials to inflict it.[23] Having said this, it remains that the consequential logic of utilitarianism makes it ill-fitted to defend human rights in all cases. Does this mean that there is an unbridgeable divide between utilitarianism and human rights orthodoxy?

In many ways, utilitarianism and human rights have in practice always been largely compatible. A long tradition within utilitarianism, going back to John Stuart Mill, has never stopped to defend human rights for being conducive to the common good. Allan Gibbard argues, from a self-avowed utilitarian perspective, that rights contribute to good institutional design.[24] Conversely, starting from the other end of the relationship, the human rights orthodoxy has always been replete with utilitarian considerations, as the numerous possible limitations of human rights in the name of public considerations (such as public order, health, or morality) and the concept of proportionality (requiring different interests to be balanced), central to human rights law, readily demonstrate.[25] More generally, the old human rights orthodoxy has had to give way: while its emphasis on clear-cut negative rights should have generated a relatively well-delimited list of 'core' rights,[26] what has happened instead is a continual identification of 'new' rights as well as a recognition that positive obligations attach to *all* rights—including the right to be free from torture, which also entails action by the state, such as appropriate training of the police force, for its full implementation.[27]

---

[22] See Chapter 2.   [23] Brecher, *Torture and the Ticking Bomb* (Blackwell, 2007) ch 2.

[24] Gibbard, 'Utilitarianism and Human Rights' in Paul, Miller Jr, and Paul (eds), *Human Rights* (Blackwell, 1984) 92.   [25] See Chapter 5.

[26] Dembour, *Who Believes in Human Rights? Reflections on the European Convention* (CUP, 2006) 87. See also Chapter 7.   [27] See Chapter 9.

The compatibility between human rights and utilitarianism is arguably deepening today as human rights orthodoxy increasingly slides from 'natural' logic into 'deliberative' mode. The latter tends to regard human rights as guiding principles of good governance (rather than firm entitlements). It conceives of human rights as being agreed upon, the result of a consensus most evident in the development of international human rights law, rather than constituted as a universal given that exists outside social recognition. The 'deliberative' orientation of the new orthodoxy makes it possible for some thinkers to refer explicitly to utilitarian considerations (admittedly alongside other ones) in order to justify human rights.[28] This would have been unthinkable under the old orthodoxy. The divide between utilitarianism and human rights is ceasing to be the great chasm once intimated both by 'the father of utilitarianism' (as Bentham came to be known) and by human rights defenders. Having said this, it remains relatively rare for human rights to be defended today from a perspective which is conspicuously utilitarian in its inspiration.

2.3 THE MARXIST CRITIQUE

For Karl Marx, far from being nonsense, the French Declaration was problematic because it made too much sense in the political order of the so-called 'free state' which had followed the French Revolution but had not succeeded in emancipating man. (Marx did not think much about women.)

Marx's essay 'On the Jewish Question', written at the tender age of 23, was implacable in its critique of the French Declaration of the Rights of Man and the Citizen of 1791. The essay denounced the rights of man as being 'nothing but the rights of the member of civil society, i.e. egoistic man, man separated from other men and the community'.[29] The right to liberty, the young Marx argued, was the right to do anything which does not harm others, that is, the liberty of man 'as an isolated monad . . . withdrawn into himself'; the right to private property was the right to enjoy and dispose of one's possessions 'arbitrarily, without regard for other men, independently from society, the right of selfishness'. The right to equality represented nothing else but access to liberty as described already; the right to security provided the guarantee of egoism.[30] Marx concluded:

> Thus none of the so-called rights of man goes beyond egoistic man, man as he is in civil society, namely an individual withdrawn behind his private interests and whims and separated from the community. Far from the rights of man conceiving of man as a species-being, species-life itself, society, appears as a framework exterior to individuals.[31]

A question mark has been raised on the value to be assigned to Marx's initial writings in Marxist theory. Marx's early work grappled with philosophy and was explicitly interested in discussing the nature of man; his mature work was devoted to the 'scientific' study of material conditions, leading him to identify the 'laws of motion' of capitalism and to elaborate a theory of history as progress through stages conditioned by society's attained level of productivity and the requirements of increase. While Louis Althusser forcefully rejected the relevance of Marx's 'pre-scientific' writings, Erich Fromm relied on these early works to develop a humanist interpretation of Marxism and denounce the claims of 'scientific Marxism', especially as propounded in the Soviet Union.

---

[28] Nickel, *Making Sense of Human Rights* (Blackwell, 2007) 58–61.
[29] 'On the Jewish Question', reproduced in McLellan, *Karl Marx: Selected Writings* (OUP, 2000) 46, 60.
[30] 'On the Jewish Question' (2000), 46, 60.   [31] 'On the Jewish Question' (2000), 61.

If the absence of a break in Marx's works is accepted, 'On the Jewish Question' appears recognizably Marxian in its denunciation of human alienation. The essay cautions that man is not yet free in the free state.[32] While it recognizes that political emancipation may have been achieved, it argues that this falls short of human emancipation. The rights granted in the political state newly created in France supposedly endow man with freedom; but, in fact, they alienate him. Why? Because they split the 'citizen' from the 'bourgeois' in the individual. The 'citizen' part of man corresponds to the public self and belongs to the political state; the 'bourgeois' part corresponds to the private self and belongs to civil society.[33] In the political state, Marx argues, man is condemned to lead a double life. This is the more serious since the citizen (the part where man regards himself as a communal being) is put at the service of the bourgeois (the part where man acts as a private individual and leads an egoistic life). Man is thus alienated from his true self which is to be a species-being where the individual interest corresponds to everyone else's interest.

'On the Jewish Question' can also be read in the light of the concept of ideology which Marx developed fully in his later work. As an ideology, the rights declared in France announce and guarantee man's liberty. However, what they really do is to mask and sustain the inequality and oppression characteristic of capitalist society. Applying this reading to the contemporary era, the anthropologist Talal Asad urges us to 'examine critically the assumption that . . . human rights always lead in an emancipatory direction, that they enable subjects to move beyond controlling power into the realm of freedom'.[34] In Asad's view, the language of human rights 'articulates inequalities in social life'.[35] It is therefore doubtful that the human rights project could bring about 'practical equality and an end to all suffering'.[36]

That real emancipation cannot be expected through human rights is an idea that was explicitly stated in 'On the Jewish Question'. Marx believed that true emancipation would come through the establishment of a society where man would be able to 'take the abstract citizen back into himself and . . . become a species-being', recognizing his own forces as social forces.[37] Under communism, he believed, the institutions of state, law, and property would have withered away. The political state—and its declaration of the rights of man and citizen—represented a necessary stage in the progression towards communism. But it was only a step. In Marx's words: 'Political emancipation is of course a great progress. Although it is not the final form of human emancipation in general, it is nevertheless the final form of human emancipation inside the present world order'.[38]

History has shown that Marx's belief in the establishment of a communist society true to his words was ridiculously naive. Not surprisingly perhaps given the utopian character of his project, Marx failed to indicate anywhere in his work how the transformation from bourgeois man to species-being would be achieved. He did mention 'a political transition period in which the state [could] be nothing but the revolutionary dictatorship of the proletariat',[39] but without working out its details. Taken as a political programme, Marx's writings were at best hollow, at worst dangerous. Had they had little impact, this would not have mattered much. But Marx, who died in 1883, inspired revolutions and dictatorships throughout the world, starting in 1917 in what became the Soviet Union. The most

---

[32] 'On the Jewish Question' (2000), 51.   [33] 'On the Jewish Question' (2000), 53; see also 57.

[34] Asad, 'What Do Human Rights Do? An Anthropological Enquiry' (2000) 27 *Theory and Event* 40.

[35] Asad (2000), 43.   [36] Asad (2000), 57.   [37] 'On the Jewish Question' (2000), 64.

[38] 'On the Jewish Question' (2000), 54.

[39] Marx, 'Critique of the Gotha Programme' reproduced in McLellan (2000) 610, 611.

appalling acts were committed in the twentieth century in the name of Marxism and communism. It is probably disingenuous to criticize a thinker for ideas that have been used in a way that he could not have imagined and to hold him partly, if unwillingly, responsible for the Stalinist gulag. But many did exactly that. At the same time, during the Cold War, others continued to profess their faith in Marxism, refusing to acknowledge the terror which Marxist ideas, taken to a logical extreme, could inspire.

There were exceptions. For example, the British Marxist historian EP Thompson did not end *Whigs and Hunters*, his study of the eighteenth-century 'Black Act',[40] with a conventional Marxian conclusion. This would have been that 'law is an instrument of brute force by which the ruling class consolidates and reinforces its hegemony'.[41] In an afterword, which made him controversial in Marxist circles, Thompson stated instead that the rule of law is an 'unqualified human good'.[42] This qualification was spurred by his disturbing experience of the Soviet regime which had led him to resign his membership of the Communist Party in 1956. Thompson wanted to stress the 'very large difference . . . between arbitrary extra-legal power and the rule of law [which] may disguise the true realities of power, but, at the same time, . . . may curb that power and check its intrusions'.[43] He declared the rule of law—to which he would likely have readily associated human rights law—'a cultural achievement of universal significance'.[44] This attracted the ire of many fellow Marxist thinkers.

It could be asked, 'Who were/are the true Marxists?' This question is controversial, with one person often accusing another of abusing Marxism. What is not disputed, however, is that the way Marx analysed power relationships and examined how things are not as they seem left a mark on all the social sciences. This is clear, in particular, in respect of the human rights critiques reviewed in Section 3.

3 MORE RECENT CRITIQUES

3.1 THE CULTURAL RELATIVIST OR PARTICULARIST CRITIQUE

The universal versus cultural relativist debate can be said to have been spurred by discussions generated by the UDHR. In 1947, the year before the UDHR was adopted, the American Anthropological Association (AAA) addressed a 'Statement on Human Rights' to the UN Commission on Human Rights, which was drafting the Universal Declaration.[45] The Statement asked: 'How can the proposed Declaration be applicable to all human beings, and not be a statement of rights conceived only in terms of the values prevalent in the countries of Western Europe and America?'[46] It argued for the need to seek respect for the individual both as individual and as member of 'his' society (at a time when feminist concerns were still very much out of public consciousness). Bearing in mind the cultural destruction heralded by colonialism, imperialism, and the very establishment of the USA (not least in respect of native Americans), it called for 'respect for the cultures of differing human groups'.

The AAA Statement was right in arguing that the formulation of human rights cannot but derive from a particular culture. The UDHR is replete with concepts, such

---

[40] Thompson, *Whigs and Hunters: The Origins of the Black Act* (Allen Lane, 1975).
[41] Cole, ' "An Unqualified Human Good": EP Thompson and the Rule of Law' (2001) 28 *J Law & Soc* 177, 181.   [42] Thompson (1975), 266.
[43] Thompson (1975), 265.   [44] Thompson (1975), 265.
[45] 'Statement on Human Rights' (1947) 49 *American Anthropologist* 539.
[46] 'Statement on Human Rights'.

as legal personality (Article 6), nationality (Article 15), and protection against unemployment (Article 23), which are simply not known to most human societies. The concept of human rights itself is not incontrovertible in humankind's repertoire. If the Statement rightly cautioned that no declaration could ever manage to identify universal human rights valid for all humankind across time and space, it was nonetheless problematic in other respects. It treated culture as a static and homogeneous 'thing' rather than the dynamic and contested process that anthropologists have now demonstrated culture always is.[47] Moreover, it lent itself to be taken to call for the respect of any cultural trait, simply because of its cultural nature; which is ethically unacceptable. In other words, the Statement bore the mark of cultural relativism, the core tenet of US anthropology in the 1920s and 1930s which, with time, increasingly came to appear untenable.

But what do we mean by 'cultural relativism'? The theory is founded on the double observation that moral systems are embedded in culture and that different cultures produce different moralities. However, to become an 'ism', ethical inferences must be derived from these (assuredly sound) empirical observations. What are these inferences? According to its detractors, cultural relativism would dictate tolerance of any culturally embedded moral system on earth, perhaps even any morality. However, whether self-declared cultural relativists hold this position is doubtful.[48]

Recognizing that different societies hold different values need not logically lead to the conclusion that all these different values and practices must be tolerated. The observation that cultures produce different moral norms does not say anything about the respective value of these norms.[49] Despite this, and no doubt also due to excessive formulations by its proponents, cultural relativism came to be denigrated for demanding that the intolerable be tolerated. The doctrine is even said to have been an embarrassment to anthropologists, because of the indifference and/or inaction which it advocated.[50] It has also been criticized for lending itself to abuse, allowing those in power to make spurious or disingenuous cultural arguments in pursuit of their own political ends.[51] Undoubtedly, cultural relativism, like other theories, has been abused, and the last point must indeed be conceded. This, however, should not detract from appreciating what the doctrine offers.

In the words of anthropologist Elvin Hatch, the 'good side' of relativism is that it highlights the difficulty of 'establishing reasonable and general grounds for making moral judgments about the actions of others' and the 'strong tendency among the more powerful peoples of the world to use their own standards, or standards favourable to them, in their relations with others'.[52] Put more simply, the doctrine acts as a counterpart to the arrogance and abusive effect of universalism. This is vital, given the imperialism which has accompanied and still accompanies human rights enunciation and practice.

The universality of human rights is *not* a fact. At best, human rights universal*ism* is a theory. It is a worthwhile project, directed at discussing, agreeing upon, and practising principles of governance which should benefit all individuals equally, but which also has a

---

[47] Cowan, Dembour, and Wilson (eds), *Culture and Rights: Anthropological Perspectives* (CUP, 2001).

[48] eg Herskovits, *Cultural Relativism: Perspectives in Cultural Pluralism* (Random House, 1972) 64.

[49] Renteln, 'Relativism and the Search for Human Rights' (1988) 90 *American Anthropologist* 56, 64.

[50] Engle, 'From Skepticism to Embrace: Human Rights and the American Anthropological Association from 1947–1999' (2001) 23 *HRQ* 536. For a more nuanced view, see Goodale, *Surrendering to Utopia: An Anthropology of Human Rights* (Stanford UP, 2009) ch 2.

[51] Pollis, 'Cultural Relativism Revisited: Through a State Prism' (1996) 18 *HRQ* 316.

[52] Hatch, 'The Good Side of Relativism' (1997) 53 *J Anthropological Research* 371, 372.

dark side which it would be either disingenuous or naive not to recognize. This dark side includes the inherent danger not to respect the ways of others, if not an active collusion in their destruction. Universalists too often assume that they are on firm ground in making judgments about others. They can easily end up imposing their ways on others for no other reason than sheer dominant position, without even realizing it, so full are they of their good intentions. By contrast, instead of saying 'we know best' or 'we know', relativism poses the question, 'What do we know?'

Universalism has a good side—the elaboration of minimal common standards—but it also has a bad side—arrogance. Similarly, relativism has a good side—respect for different ways—but it also has a bad side—inaction or indifference. Let us think about the implications of this conceptual matrix with a concrete example. In 1994, an 18-year-old US citizen was sentenced in Singapore to six lashes for spray-painting parked cars.[53] Let us first judge the caning abhorrent, assaulting the dignity of the young man. If so, universalism should be applauded for making it possible to condemn the punishment, while relativism would show only its bad side by calling for inaction when resistance is needed. Another assessment, however, is to say that the caning is a legitimate element in the disciplinary framework put in place in the context of a particular society. If so, universalism would be showing its bad side by condemning the practice while it is relativism which should be welcome for letting the punishment be. What some regard as an expression of the good side of relativism is *always* regarded by others as an expression of its bad side, and the same is true of universalism (see Table 3.1). Applying the conceptual matrix to concrete situations and deciding which position is which is rarely easy; nor is it uncontroversial.

Wishing the controversy away will not do. It arises *every time* common standards are predicated, whatever the limits of the constituency—the whole world, a regional system, a nation, a village. Establishing common standards is never completely unproblematic because minimal common standards are never entirely common. However small the relevant constituency, it always stands in the way of more peculiar, or particular, norms.

Universalism cannot exist independently of its opposite, most aptly named 'particularism'. (Etymologically, what is not universal is special, specific, or particular; what is not relative is absolute. Using the word 'particularism' presents the further advantage of avoiding both the possibly reifying tone of the reference to 'culture' and the embarrassment of the faint moral position commonly associated with 'cultural relativism'.) It is in opposition to practices that appear abhorrent that universal norms are being set, and it is by reference to local particularities that these universal norms are implemented. The reverse is true. Particularism does not exist independently of universalism. As moral beings concerned with ethics, we are not just beings of culture but respond to what could be termed the call of universalism. This is to say that we are always somewhere between the ideal represented by universalism (which should be recognized as an ideal) and the reality of our being embedded in culture (which is inescapable). We are bound to oscillate between the two positions in a pendulum-like motion.[54]

Contrary to a commonly held assumption, the debate between universalism and particularism is not primarily concerned with the reaction by the rest of the world to something which originated in the West. Its essence is to capture the difficult and always controversial accommodation of unity and diversity in mankind. While the debate was

---

[53] Hubbard, 'Singapore shrugs off uproar over "barbaric" flogging', *The Independent*, 2 April 1994.
[54] Dembour, 'Following the Movement of the Pendulum: Between Universalism and Relativism' in Cowan *et al.* (2001), 56.

Table 3.1 The universalism vs relativism matrix

	Universalism	Relativism
Good side	Respect for common standards (*caning is abhorrent*)	Respect for difference (*caning is OK*)
Bad side	Arrogance (*caning is abhorrent*)	Indifference (*caning is OK*)

obviously pertinent under the old orthodoxy where human rights were conceived as a given, it remains relevant under the new orthodoxy. The reason why the debate cannot be put to rest once and for all is that we do not have a choice between being either universalists or particularists: we must be both at the same time. Similarly, human rights law must accommodate both positions—whether it does so explicitly or not. (This contributes to an explanation of, for example, the development of the doctrine of the margin of appreciation in the European Convention system whereby the European Court of Human Rights often asserts that local authorities are in principle in a better position than an international court to assess local requirements.) Properly understood, the particularist critique is less a critique than a corrective to the ever-possible excesses of universalism. These excesses remain a danger under the new human rights orthodoxy, for the human rights values supposedly agreed upon at any given level (international, regional, or national) rarely derive from a consensus as broad as believed by those who unreservedly declare their commitment to them.

3.2 THE FEMINIST CRITIQUE

In 1789, the first article of the French Declaration proudly stated: 'Men are born and remain free and equal in rights.' One year later, Olympe de Gouges asserted in a 'Declaration of the Rights of Woman', of her own making: 'Women are born free and remain equal to men in rights.'[55] This stance did not go down well. On 3 November 1793, de Gouges was guillotined—like a man—for having forgotten the virtues of her sex and inappropriately sought to become a statesman. A feminist critique of human rights was then largely silenced, but it has now become vigorous. Can the argument that human rights remain predominantly male in their conception and implementation be dismissed in an age when women, especially in the West, have successfully fought for the rights to vote, be educated, manage their property, open a bank account, exercise a profession, keep their nationality upon marriage with a foreign man, claim equal pay for equal work, and so on? The answer is a resounding no. The affirmation in law of women's entitlement to equal rights is assuredly a momentous achievement. While it must be celebrated, it should not lead to complacency. Feminist analyses demonstrate human rights law to have been and continue to be male-oriented.

Before turning to these analyses, it is worth pondering what feminism is. As noted in Section 2.1, virtually all 'isms' have more than one variant. This is certainly the case with feminism, of which the variants are so pronounced that for someone to declare herself—and possibly, though more rarely, himself—a feminist does not say much about her

---

[55] De Gouges's Declaration is reproduced in Ishay (ed), *The Human Rights Reader: Major Political Writings, Essays, Speeches and Documents. From the Bible to the Present* (Routledge, 1997) 140–7. My translation of Art 1 is slightly different from that of Ishay, who offers: 'Woman is born free and lives equal to man in her rights.'

position. One can nonetheless tentatively speak of feminism in the singular. Janet Halley has identified its components as follows:

> First, to be feminism, a position must make a distinction between *m* and *f*. Different feminisms do this differently: some see men and women; some see male and female; some see masculine and feminine. . . And secondly, to be a feminism . . ., a position must posit some kind of subordination as between *m* and *f*, in which *f* is the disadvantaged or subordinated element. At this point feminism is both descriptive and normative . . . Feminism is feminism because, as between *m* and *f*, it carries a brief for *f*.[56]

Feminism is a way of looking at the world, seeing it as organized along gendered lines which benefit men, and trying to change it so that women are empowered. In the human rights field, feminist critique has taken a long time to be expressed—or, perhaps more accurately, to be heard. For two centuries, the vibrant and clear message sent by Olympe de Gouges in her Declaration of 1790 remained dormant in human rights scholarship. In the last 30 years, however, feminist critiques of human rights have become inescapable. In 1989, a working bibliography on women's international human rights contained a mere 142 publications and a list of 15 international governmental and NGOs and other sources of information; by 2003, it included approximately 700 articles and 246 links to websites.[57] No doubt the increase has continued to be exponential.

The feminist critique to which human rights have increasingly been subjected does not mean that an agreement has emerged as to what constitutes, and what should be done in respect of, a human rights situation analysed as problematic for women. This is because there are many different ways of being a feminist. Following an admittedly limited, but nonetheless useful, classification adopted in various synthesizing works, this section first discusses the liberal, cultural, and radical strands of feminism before highlighting more recent (post-modern) trends.

At the core of the *liberal* feminist strand is the assumption that women are equal to men, with the consequence that women must not in principle be excluded from the rights enjoyed by men—and vice versa. In other words, liberal feminism asks for liberalism to be true to its fundamental intuition that everyone must have their rights guaranteed. Laws that explicitly guarantee, or implicitly endorse, the principle of sex and gender equality constitute its great achievement. Today, this principle is for the most part accepted. However, assessing what it requires in the practice of actual rights is riddled with difficulties. The implementation of a feminist liberal agenda is far from a straightforward matter, the more so since liberal feminism is concerned not simply with the formal allocation of rights but also with the under-representation of women in politically and socially significant positions, as well as their over-representation among the poor.

'But why should a woman want to be treated like a man?', asks a second strand of feminism. In 1982, the book *In a Different Voice* contrasted the logical, abstract, deductive reasoning favoured by boys to the emotional, concrete, and contextual reasoning favoured by girls.[58] Its author, the social psychologist Carol Gilligan, concluded that the masculine model of an 'ethic of rights' is not universal and called for the feminine model of an 'ethic of care' to be valued. Her book established the feminist strand generally known as *cultural* feminism, in recognition of the fact that men and women develop different patterns of thinking and acting

---

[56] Halley, 'Take a Break from Feminism?' in Knop (ed), *Gender and Human Rights* (OUP, 2004) 57, 61.
[57] Knop, 'Introduction' in Knop (ed), *Gender and Human Rights* (OUP, 2004), 1.
[58] Gilligan, *In a Different Voice: Psychologist Theory and Women's Development* (Harvard UP, 1982).

due to being educated into different social roles which are culturally evolved. This strand of feminism has clear implications for human rights. As with other areas of law, human rights law tends to look at individuals as individuals, to decontextualize situations, and to be confrontational; it accordingly has—so the cultural feminist argument goes—nothing or little to offer to women who are 'naturally'/'culturally' inclined to think their problems through contextually, for example by assessing the implications of any possible solution for the people for whom they care (including, but not only, their children). Human rights law should either be rejected, or at the very least transformed, in order to accommodate the female way of thinking and acting.[59]

For the leading *radical* feminist Catharine MacKinnon, however, getting women to think of themselves as carers is, in itself, a male trick. The problem is not whether women are equal or different to men; the problem is that men subordinate women. The key issue is women's oppression, whereby men reduce women to their sexuality and use them as sexual objects. In MacKinnon's phrase, 'Man fucks woman: subject, verb, object.'[60] The aim of the radical feminist movement, led in law by MacKinnon, is therefore the empowerment of women—even those who are not aware of the continual sexual oppression to which men subject them because of 'false consciousness'. MacKinnon asks that women become women on their own terms: feminism 'unmodified'. One can again immediately see the implications of this strand of feminism for our subject. Far from being neutral, human rights theory and law are on the whole made by men for men. They do not adequately address women's concerns, such as sexual violence in the home, and rely on concepts, such as the public–private dichotomy, which tend to perpetuate men's sexual subordination of women.

With the *post-modern* turn of the late 1980s and early 1990s in the social sciences, the failure by the feminist strands discussed above to acknowledge that the situation of one woman was not that of another became glaringly obvious: clearly, no woman could speak for all women.[61] Post-modern feminists deconstructed the categories of 'woman' and 'gender'. Listening to the 'Other', they explored rather than explained. As meta-narratives were distrusted, myths debunked, basic concepts questioned, post-modern feminism did not produce a definite political agenda. Its resistance to claims of universal truths was critiqued for being relativist. On the positive side, however, its insights generated new awareness, including the obvious fact that various factors of marginality intersect. Put in simple terms, the situation and experiences of a white middle-class woman are hardly comparable to those of a black poor woman; other factors, such as sexual orientation, nationality, disability, and so on, come to play a role, too. In the wake of intersectionality, current directions in feminist critiques of human rights—sometimes called 'black' or 'Third World'—are at the forefront of arguing for 'the transformative potential of a feminist human rights praxis' that embraces collective justice.[62]

The theoretical framework presented here is simplistic. Feminist scholars are not necessarily encompassed by it nor do they all fit neatly within the reviewed categories. Nonetheless, this section should have indicated that there are many ways in which feminists will wish to challenge the human rights orthodoxy, both in its old and new guises.

---

[59] eg Hardwig, 'Should Women Think in Terms of Rights?' (1984) 94 *Ethics* 441.

[60] MacKinnon, *Feminism Unmodified: Discourses on Life and Law* (Harvard UP, 1987) 71. See also her *Toward a Feminist Theory of the State* (Harvard UP, 1989).

[61] eg Mohanty, 'Under Western Eyes: Feminist Scholarship and Colonial Discourses' (1988) 30 *Feminist Review* 61.

[62] Collins, Falcón, Lodhia, and Talcott, 'New Directions in Feminism and Human Rights: An Introduction' (2010) 12 *International Feminist Journal of Politics* 298.

3.3 THE POST-COLONIAL CRITIQUE

It is often remarked that it was the atrocities of the Second World War that brought into being the International Human Rights Bill. Some would be ready to thank, admittedly not without irony, Hitler and Stalin for this gift.[63] Others bitterly note that it took the suffering of whites to force the powers that be into action; by comparison, slavery and colonialism left the world indifferent.[64] The post-colonial critique teases out the implications of this observation. At its core is the argument that there were, and continue to be, direct connections between the Enlightenment universalizing project and the history of European and Western conquest. A mild post-colonial critique of human rights shows human rights, as a child of the Enlightenment, not to have been completely immune to the colonial logic which long governed the world. Deeper critiques go further than this and argue that human rights are, to this day, irretrievably entrenched in a colonial logic.

The term 'post-colonial' has been used in many different ways. It emerged first to denote the condition that succeeded the formal passing of colonial rule, but soon came to denote a variety of theoretical perspectives. The three towering figures of post-colonialism in its theoretical form are commonly recognized to be the late Edward Said, Gayatri Spivak, and Homi Bhabha, three scholars of southern origin who have pursued an academic career in the West and grappled with the question of how the post-colonial subject can understand and overcome the condition of having been born into the abjection of colonialism. Said forever changed the way we look at representation with the publication in 1978 of *Orientalism*: after this book, the way we (academics, journalists, novelists, film makers, and common people) represent (study, report, discuss, portray, and talk about) the 'Other' could never again appear as a neutral exercise.[65] Spivak asked: 'Can the Subaltern Speak?', directly pointing at the muteness suffered by those who are not in a position to speak or be heard.[66] More optimistically, Bhabha's development of the concept of 'hybridity' (meaning mixture) seems to promise the possibility of finding a space where we shall be able to speak of Ourselves and Others.[67]

Post-colonialism is many different things. What these things have in common is a commitment 'to critique, expose, deconstruct, counter and (in some claims) to transcend, the cultural and broader ideological legacies and presences of imperialism'.[68] In this phrasing, imperialism is understood as the source of power at the receiving end of which are the colonized, in their physical but also cultural and mental self; colonialism is not understood as pertaining exclusively to the formal colonial era—it existed in the past and continues to exist today under many guises. Post-colonialism is committed to a double task: revealing how the colonial logic imbibes ideas and behaviours, even ones which seemingly have nothing to do with colonialism, and trying to make it possible to hear the experiences of the colonized.

How does this relate to human rights? Listen to Makau Mutua, born 'in a part of colonial Africa that the British had named Kenya'.[69] Mutua recalls how colonialism stripped him of his identity, forcing him to take a Christian name to enter the Church, and then argues:

---

[63] Sieghart, *The Lawful Rights of Mankind: An Introduction to the International Legal Code of Human Rights* (OUP, 1985) 38.

[64] Mutua, *Human Rights: A Political and Cultural Critique* (University of Pennsylvania Press, 2002) 16.

[65] Said, *Orientalism* (Routledge and Kegan Paul, 1978).

[66] Spivak, 'Can the Subaltern Speak?' in Nelson and Grossberg (eds), *Marxism and the Interpretation of Culture* (University of Illinois Press, 1998).

[67] Bhabha, *The Location of Culture* (Routledge, 1994).

[68] In a formulation borrowed from Sidaway, 'Postcolonial Geographies: An Exploratory Essay' (2000) 24 *Progress in Human Geography* 591, 594.   [69] Mutua (2002), x.

There was a basic assumption that Christianity was *superior* to, and better than, any African spirituality. It was presented as a cultural package. What is interesting are the parallels between Christianity's violent conquest of Africa and the modern human rights crusade. The same methods are at work and similar cultural dispossessions are taking place, without dialogue or conversation. The official human corpus, which issues from European predicates, seeks to supplant all other traditions, while rejecting them. It claims to be the only genius of the good society.[70]

Contrary to its claims of being inclusive, the idea of human rights was always an exclusionary concept—as Marx and feminists such as de Gouges had perceived from the start. Post-colonial perspectives broaden these early critiques by showing how the supposedly universal and all-encompassing liberal tradition in which human rights were developed nurtured stark differences between 'us' and 'them' on the basis of arguments about civilization, cultural backwardness, and racial superiority. The Enlightenment figure of 'the individual', bearer of human rights, suddenly appears to be full of the arrogance of the West, rather than neutral and innocent. Moreover, even if the presumed existence of an essential difference between us and them is no longer referred to in the explicit language used in the formal colonial era, this arrogance is not something of the past but something which carries on, albeit in new forms. The conduct of international relations in the post-Cold War era has been characterized as follows:

> 'We' of the West are not inefficient, corrupt or dependent on a benevolent international society for our existence. 'We' are the unquestioned upholders of human rights. 'We' attained positions of privilege and authority as a result of our capacities. 'We' of the West are different from 'them'. 'Their' fate could not befall 'us'. 'They' can succeed only if 'they' become more like 'us' . . .. The North is constituted vis-à-vis the South as modern, efficient, competent. The South is constituted as its lack, its other. . .. The incapacity to exercise agency in the same manner as the Western 'self' is repeatedly inscribed in the identity of non-Western 'other'.[71]

The 'civilizing mission' was at the very heart of colonialism's justification and remains so in the deployment of new imperial forms. The bringing of law, and rights, and gender equality are some of its key elements. But the overall achievements of human rights are dubious in the face of continual oppression, hurry for wars, rampant poverty, persistent inequalities in trade, lack of attention to the consequences of global warming, and, more generally, rejection of the 'Other'. In this light, trumpeting the rise of human rights as 'one of the great civilising achievements of the modern era'[72] appears problematic. Post-colonialism asks, 'Is there a sense in which human rights have been "civilizing?"'

A post-colonial critique intimates that the human rights logic has all too often led to the annihilation of the 'Other'. This has occurred not only in respect of their identity—for example, through 'assimilation' and the imposition of a Christian name as in Mutua's experience—but also in their physicality—still holding true when, among other current atrocities taking place in the world, wars conducted in the name of human rights entail 'collateral damage' which refer to the death of the 'Other'. There is also a whole spectrum of exclusionary discourse and practices, which the treatment of the deemed illegal or

---

[70] Mutua (2002), xi (original emphasis).
[71] Doty, *Imperial Encounters: The Politics of Representation in North-South Relations* (University of Minnesota Press, 1996) 162.   [72] Gearty, *Can Human Rights Survive?* (CUP, 2006) 1.

suspected terrorist migrant—barred from entry, detained, deported, subjected to extraordinary rendition, tortured, or simply left to die—exemplifies today.

The crucial question for post-colonial critiques therefore is, 'Can human rights be redeemed?' Most seem unwilling to reject human rights outright. In the words of Ratna Kapur: 'We "cannot not want" human rights. Rights are radical tools for those who have never had them. Human rights seems a preferable, though a flawed ideal, to no rights at all.'[73] According to her, 'the centering of excluded subjects, excluded zones and excluded histories can bring the project back to a space of greater optimism and lesser despair'.[74] This, however, is easier said than done. This is to say that the post-colonial critique hits at the new—not to mention the old—human rights orthodoxy very hard. Those ready to see that a colonial logic remains pertinent in understanding today's world would all agree that managing 'to give the human rights body a soul'[75] is a challenge which, if at all successful, will need to be taken up over and over again, rather than being met once and for all.

4 CONCLUSION

Human rights accounts are generally celebratory and triumphalist. This is so much the case that a student can take a course entirely devoted to human rights without ever being introduced to some of the critiques reviewed in this chapter. Admittedly, it has become politically incorrect for human rights tutors not to refer, at least in passing, to the feminist critique. A lack of formal reference to the IR realist critique is not very damaging, given that most students are attuned to its suggestions. This may also largely be true of the utilitarian perspective: students perceive immediately, especially in the context of the war on terror, its relevance (and difficulties). Grasping the implications of the Marxist critique is already more difficult. And is it not irresponsible to relegate the particularist (cultural relativist) critique to something worthy of discussion only if time allows, which it apparently most often does not (in a manifestation of what I have called elsewhere 'the footnote 10 phenomenon')?[76] As for the post-colonial critique, its neglect is even more staggering: this critique is hardly mentioned in human rights courses, leaving not only the 'Other' but also those in the privileged world moved by the idea of a social justice project more disempowered than if they had been made aware of the critique.

Such silences are unfortunate because all the critiques reviewed in this chapter (as well as others) are worth pondering. They each make important points. Some critiques are more profound than others that can be, and indeed have already been, absorbed in human rights theory. Bentham's objection to the rights of man as 'imaginary' falls in the face of the new orthodoxy and the constant definition, re-definition, and implementation of 'real' rights. The utilitarian perspective is capable of being accommodated in the new orthodoxy—as has already started to happen.[77] In a different mode, this is also the case of the particularist (cultural relativist) critique, which this chapter has argued is in need of being constantly considered by human rights theory and practice, thus hopefully making it possible to keep in check the possible excesses of universalism.

The other human rights critiques that have been reviewed are less easily absorbed. The Marxist critique remains as pertinent as ever, pointing as it does to the exclusion that the human rights discourse continues to encompass. This insight penetrates the critiques that

---

[73] Kapur, 'Human Rights in the 21st Century: Take a Walk on the Dark Side' (2006) 28 *Sydney LR* 665, 682.
[74] Kapur (2006), 687.   [75] In a paraphrase of Kapur's concluding sentence, in Kapur (2006), 687.
[76] Dembour (2001), 72.   [77] eg Nickel (2007).

have been developed in the last decades. Radical feminists, some IR realists, and some post-colonial theorists posit that human rights will *never* be able to live up to the promises it makes, so that it is hardly a project worth pursuing.[78] Others, again found across a broad theoretical spectrum that includes realism, feminism, and post-colonialism, are less extreme in their critique and argue that human rights has contradictory effects, which make it an inherently ambiguous project or discourse, sometimes worth pursuing and sometimes not.[79] Still others believe in the intrinsic value of human rights but call for them to be, or to become, true to themselves, which in their view means doing the protest work that brought them into being in the first place.[80] What is nonetheless clear is that recent important grassroots protests such as the Occupy movement against neo-liberalism have not relied much on human rights.

FURTHER READING

BAXI, *The Future of Human Rights* (Oxford University Press, 2006).

BHAMBRA and SHILLIAM (eds), *Silencing Human Rights: Critical Engagements with a Contested Project* (Palgrave, 2009).

BREMS, 'Human Rights: Minimum and Maximum Perspectives' (2009) *HRLR* 349.

BROWN, '"The Most We Can Hope For . . . ": Human Rights and the Politics of Fatalism' (2004) 103 *South Atlantic Quarterly* 451.

CAMPBELL, *Rights: A Critical Introduction* (Routledge, 2006).

COLLINS, FALCÓN, LODHIA, and TALCOTT, 'New Directions in Feminism and Human Rights: An Introduction' (2010) 12 *International Feminist Journal of Politics* 298.

DEMBOUR, *Who Believes in Human Rights? Reflections on the European Convention* (Cambridge University Press, 2006).

DOUZINAS, *Human Rights and Empire: The Political Philosophy of Cosmopolitanism* (Routledge, 2007).

KAPUR, 'Human Rights in the 21st Century: Take a Walk on the Dark Side' (2006) 28 *Sydney LR* 665.

LANGLOIS, 'Human Rights in Crisis? A Critical Polemic Against Polemical Critics' (2012) 11 *J of HR* 558.

MERTUS, *Bait and Switch: Human Rights and US Foreign Policy* (Routledge, 2004).

MOYN, 'The First Historian of Human Rights' (2011) 116 *American Historical Review* 58.

MUTUA, *Human Rights: A Political and Cultural Critique* (University of Pennsylvania Press, 2002).

NASH, *The Cultural Politics of Human Rights: Comparing the US and UK* (Cambridge University Press, 2009).

STAMMERS, *Human Rights and Social Movements* (Pluto Press, 2009).

WALDRON (ed), 'Nonsense upon Stilts': *Bentham, Burke and Marx on the Rights of Man* (Methuen, 1987).

---

[78] See Brown, '"The Most We Can Hope For . . . ": Human Rights and the Politics of Fatalism' (2004) 103 *South Atlantic Quarterly* 451.

[79] eg Cowan, 'Ambiguities of an Emancipatory Discourse: The Making of a Macedonian Minority in Greece' in Cowan *et al.* (2001), 152; Bhambra and Shilliam, 'Introduction: "Silence" and Human Rights' in Bhambra and Shilliam (eds), *Silencing Human Rights: Critical Engagements with a Contested Project* (Palgrave, 2009) 1, 9; Nash, *The Cultural Politics of Human Rights: Comparing the US and UK* (CUP, 2009) vii.

[80] See eg Douzinas (2007); Stammers (2009); Bowring, *The Degradation of the International Legal Order? The Rehabilitation of Law and the Possibility of Politics* (Routledge-Cavendish, 2009).

PART II

INTERNATIONAL LAW

4

SOURCES

Christine Chinkin

SUMMARY

This chapter outlines the sources of international human rights law that are listed in Article 38(1) Statute of the International Court of Justice: treaties, custom, general principles of law, and, as subsidiary means for determining the law, judicial decisions and the writings of jurists. The chapter also considers how so-called 'soft law' instruments, such as resolutions of the UN General Assembly and the work of human rights expert bodies, may also be regarded as sources of human rights law.

1 INTRODUCTION

A source of law identifies what constitutes law, that is, how decision-makers can determine what instruments, practices, or policies constitute legally binding obligations as opposed to moral, political, or other social commitments. Sources of law provide us with the basis of legal obligation: they are 'really all about the provenance of norms'.[1] In practical terms, the sources of law tell us how new rules are made and existing rules are repealed or abrogated. International human rights law is a specialist regime within general public international law. Its prescribed or *formal sources* are, therefore, the same as those for other subject areas of international law, such as international environmental law, trade law, or the law of the sea. Unlike national legal systems, international law lacks a central legislative body (comparable to a national parliament), an executive (a government), and a general court of compulsory jurisdiction. Nevertheless the International Court of Justice (ICJ) has reminded states 'that the absence of a court or tribunal with jurisdiction to resolve disputes about compliance with a particular obligation under international law does not affect the existence and binding force of that obligation. States are required to fulfil their obligations under international law, including ... international human rights law.'[2]

The sources of international law and hence human rights law are set out in Article 38(1) Statute of the ICJ. This provision directs the judges of the ICJ on where they should turn

---

[1] Higgins, *Problems and Process: International Law and How We Use it* (OUP, 1994) 17.

[2] *Application of the Convention on the Prevention and Punishment of the Crime of Genocide (Croatia v Serbia)* [2015] ICJ Rep 1, para 86.

when deciding a dispute brought before them. Article 38 is the starting point for any discussion of the sources of international law. It states that the Court shall apply:

a. international conventions, whether general or particular, establishing rules expressly recognized by the contesting states;

b. international custom, as evidence of a general practice accepted as law;

c. the general principles of law recognized by civilized nations;

d. subject to the provisions of Article 59, judicial decisions and the teachings of the most highly qualified publicists of the various nations, as subsidiary means for the determination of rules of law.

As well as stipulating the formal sources of international law, this statement contains elements of both law-making and what are often termed material sources of law. *Law-making* is the 'how' of international law, the methods adopted by the relevant participants in the international arena through which international law is made.[3] Under Article 38 the state-centric nature of international law and the pre-eminent role of states in law-making are evident. The *material sources* of international law are the 'where' of international law: where to look for evidence of the content of a rule—the words of a treaty, the resolution of an international organization, a statement by the Prime Minister or Foreign Secretary to Parliament or the UN General Assembly. Material sources are numerous and diverse.

Article 38(1) has remained unaltered since 1920 when it was first included in the Statute of the Permanent Court of International Justice, the predecessor of the ICJ. Unsurprisingly there has been much debate about its adequacy with respect to contemporary international law and it does not indicate the complexity or diversity of contemporary international human rights law, which are reflected in contestations about its content and sources. Like other areas of international law, in the decades since 1945 international human rights law has grown exponentially and on an essentially ad hoc basis. There has been no overarching plan or design; rather it has developed through a range of instruments and processes and in response to demands from numerous participants. Human rights offer a vision of the 'good life' and engender an almost messianic zeal among their proponents. People seek to ground claims in the language of human rights so as to gain the 'moral high ground' against governments, against corporations, against faceless bureaucrats, against anyone that they deem to have violated their rights. To this end, multiple actors operating within an array of institutions—civil society activists, legal advocates, the media, individual lobbyists—draw on material far beyond the formal sources listed in Article 38(1) ICJ Statute and engage a wide variety of instruments and statements as material sources to bolster their arguments that a particular matter can be cast as a binding rule of international human rights law.

Human rights generate claims and counterclaims. Those against whom claims are made—primarily governments—seek to contain their human rights obligations within the formal sources of law to which they have agreed, while claimants may receive support from the growing body of specialist human rights experts mandated to monitor human rights compliance. There is no 'litmus test'[4] for determining claims of new rights, nor any final, authoritative global decision-maker. As long ago as 1984 Alston expressed his concern about the lack of any 'quality control' in the creation of new rights and argued for

---

[3] Boyle and Chinkin, *The Making of International Law* (OUP, 2007).

[4] Koskenniemi, 'Human Rights Mainstreaming as a Strategy for Institutional Power' (2010) 1 *Humanity: An International Journal of Human Rights, Humanitarianism, and Development* 477.

a formal and rigorous process for the 'thoughtful consideration' of new rights.[5] This did not eventuate and the sources of international human rights law, and thus its substantive content, remain often hotly contested.

This chapter first discusses the formal sources of international human rights law as set out in Article 38(1) ICJ Statute. It then examines other, more disputed, sources so as to give a fuller picture of how contemporary international human rights law is made.

2 FORMAL SOURCES

What we now regard as the international human rights story largely dates from the adoption of the UN Charter in 1945,[6] although the underlying ideas are much older.[7] Since 1945 human rights have been legalized within global and regional institutional frameworks. Today, it is widely accepted that international human rights law is based on state consent as expressed through the forms outlined in Article 38(1) ICJ Statute.

This was not always the case. The idea of human rights derives its inspiration from multiple sources, including religious creed, natural law, and the nature of society. Natural law sources of rights have long been influential. They rest in the concept of a higher law than that made through human agency, although the content of such law must be mediated through the exercise of human reason.[8] A natural law basis for rights is incapable of empirical proof and its legitimacy rests upon societal agreement on what constitutes the common good, or on the exercise of power in its assertion. In the eighteenth century natural law theories evolved away from reliance on the state of nature through to concepts of the social contract, while in the nineteenth century positivist views based on state consent prevailed. Natural law was to some extent reinvigorated after the horrors of the Second World War and the judgments of the International Military Tribunals at Nuremberg and Tokyo revealed the potential moral abyss of excessive adherence to positivist law.

Nevertheless, although the UN Charter was adopted in a climate of revulsion at the extremism of some state law, the foundations of contemporary human rights law lie in positivist law, based on state consent. The principal way in which states express that consent is through the first instrumentality listed in Article 38(1), the negotiation and adoption of treaties.

3 TREATIES

International human rights law today primarily derives from international and regional treaties.[9] An agreement between states may be termed a treaty, convention, charter, covenant, protocol, pact, or even statute. The chosen term does not denote any legal difference. Generally only states can become parties to treaties, but exceptionally other actors may be authorized to become parties.[10] States are bound by the treaties to which they

---

[5] Alston, 'Conjuring Up New Human Rights: A Proposal for Quality Control' (1984) 78 *AJIL* 607, 620.

[6] Moyn argues that it was not until the late 1970s that human rights became a significant force in international relations: Moyn, *The Last Utopia* (Harvard University Press, 2010); for rebuttal of this view, see Alston, 'Does the Past Matter?: On the Origins of Human Rights' (2013) 126 *Harvard LR* 2043.   [7] See Chapter 1.

[8] See Chapter 2.   [9] Crawford, *Brownlie's Principles of Public International Law* (OUP, 2012) 638.

[10] Convention on the Rights of Persons with Disabilities, Art 43 provides for regional integration organizations to do so; European Convention for the Protection of Human Rights and Fundamental Freedoms (ECHR), Art 59(2), and Council of Europe Convention on Preventing and Combating Violence against Women and Domestic Violence (CPCVAW) (2011), Art 75, allow for the European Union to do so.

have given formal consent, generally through ratification or accession. This is done by the constitutionally appropriate state organ depositing an instrument of ratification with the body so designated within the treaty, in the case of UN human rights treaties generally the UN Secretary-General.[11] International human rights treaties are unlike many other treaties in that they do not provide for a reciprocal exchange of rights and duties between states parties.[12] Instead, by accepting the terms of such treaties, states accept legal constraints upon their treatment of individuals within their territory and subject to their jurisdiction.

3.1 THE PRINCIPAL TREATIES

The UN Charter provides the first guarantees of human rights and fundamental freedoms within a global treaty, albeit in general and indeterminate language.[13] The immediate follow up to the Charter was the adoption by the General Assembly of the non-binding Universal Declaration of Human Rights (UDHR), in 1948, eventually followed in 1966 by the adoption of two UN Covenants, the International Covenant on Civil and Political Rights (ICCPR) and its First Optional Protocol and the International Covenant on Economic, Social and Cultural Rights (ICESCR). These three instruments—the UDHR, ICCPR, and ICESCR—are often referred to as the International Bill of Rights.

There has since followed a large number of multilateral treaties that complement the International Bill of Rights by adding new rights, by identifying categories of people who are especially vulnerable to violations of their rights, and by refining the obligations of those first treaties. The multilateral treaties that share some common features are widely regarded as constituting the UN human rights treaty system. In addition to the ICCPR and ICESCR, in chronological order these treaties are: the International Convention on the Elimination of All Forms of Racial Discrimination (1965) (ICERD); the Convention on the Elimination of All Forms of Discrimination Against Women (1979) (CEDAW) and its Optional Protocol (1999); the Convention against Torture and Other Cruel, Inhuman or Degrading Treatment (1984) (UNCAT) and its Optional Protocol (2002); the International Convention on the Rights of the Child (1989) (CRC) and three Optional Protocols (on the Involvement of Children in Armed Conflict (2000); on the Sale of Children, Child Prostitution and Child Pornography (2000); and on a Communications Procedure (2011)); the International Convention on the Protection of the Rights of All Migrant Workers and Members of their Families (1990); the Convention on the Rights of Persons with Disabilities (2006) (CRPD) and its Optional Protocol (2006); and the International Convention for the Protection of All Persons from Enforced Disappearance (2006). A Second Optional Protocol (ICCPR-OP2) to the ICCPR was adopted by the General Assembly in 1989 and an Optional Protocol to the ICESCR (ICESCR-OP) was adopted by the General Assembly in 2008. NGOs have been the driving force in the negotiation of a number of these treaties (for example, the UNCAT, the CRC, and the CRPD) and their recommendations and monitoring activities may influence state acceptance.[14] The list is not closed and further UN human rights treaties may be negotiated. For instance

---

[11] Ratification is the name of the process where a state has previously signed the treaty text, while the same process is called accession in the case of a non-signatory state.   [12] See Chapter 5.

[13] UN Charter, Art 1(3) provides that one of the purposes of the UN is '[t]o achieve international co-operation in … promoting and encouraging respect for human rights and for fundamental freedoms for all without distinction as to race, sex, language, or religion'. See also Arts 55 and 56.

[14] For example, Amnesty International played an important role in the conclusion of the UNCAT.

there has been considerable advocacy for a binding instrument for the protection of the human rights of older persons and an Open-ended Working Group on Ageing has been established to consider the issues arising in this context.[15]

The most important of the common features shared by the treaties comprising the UN human rights system is the establishment of specialist committees ('treaty bodies') in accordance with their terms.[16] Each committee, whose members serve in their personal capacity, monitors implementation of the relevant treaty and their work has been central to the development of international human rights law. No account of the sources of human rights law at the global level is complete without taking the work of the treaty bodies into account.

There are many other multilateral treaties that include human rights obligations but which do not have such monitoring mechanisms. Other treaties adopted by the General Assembly include the Convention on the Prevention and Punishment of the Crime of Genocide (1948), the International Convention on the Suppression and Punishment of the Crime of Apartheid (1973), and the Convention relating to the Status of Refugees (1951). Specialist bodies within the UN system have adopted important human rights treaties, notably the International Labour Organization with respect to workers' rights and the UN Educational, Scientific and Cultural Organization (UNESCO) on rights to education and information.[17] Human rights obligations for particular states may also derive from peace agreements, which now almost routinely incorporate existing human rights treaties or set out specific rights. For example, the Dayton Peace Accords, which terminated the armed conflict in Bosnia-Herzegovina, gives the European Convention on Human Rights (ECHR) priority over all other domestic law, incorporates certain specific rights enumerated in the Convention, and requires the state to become (or to remain) a party to listed UN and regional human rights instruments.[18]

Regional institutions have developed their own human rights systems through the adoption of treaties that are limited to states within the region.[19] Today the ECHR, the American Convention on Human Rights (ACHR), and the African Charter on Human and Peoples' Rights are principal sources of human rights obligations for states parties.

3.2 THE IMPORTANCE OF TREATIES

Treaty law is indisputably the most significant source of international human rights law today. It has a number of advantages. Potentially a large number of states may become parties to a treaty, thereby accepting its provisions as binding legal obligations. After a somewhat slow start (the two UN Covenants each took ten years to receive the required number of parties to come into force), the objective of widespread—ideally universal—adherence to the human rights treaties has been largely successful. Widespread treaty adherence provides for a degree of uniformity between states in their understanding of the requirements of international human rights law, which undermines arguments of cultural or other specificity. Treaty ratification and accession also allow for certainty in identifying states parties and written texts set out the obligations accepted.

But there are also some downsides. The authority of a treaty as a source of law lies in states' consent to be bound. Some treaties may not be widely accepted; for example,

[15] Established pursuant to GA Res 65/182 (2010). [16] See Chapter 19.

[17] eg ILO Convention No 100, Equal Remuneration Convention, 1951; UNESCO Convention Against Discrimination in Education, 1960.

[18] Framework Agreement for Peace in Bosnia and Herzegovina, 1995.

[19] Exceptionally, the CPCVAW, Arts 75 and 76, allow non-member states of the Council of Europe to become parties.

the Migrant Workers Convention has in 2017, nearly 30 years after its adoption, only 50 states parties. Treaty language is open to differing interpretations, so states may agree to be bound by the same obligations but may differ on their precise meaning. Further, as an expression of their consent states may make reservations to their acceptance of a treaty. Allowing states to make reservations recognizes the many interests of over 190 states and that concessions may have been made during the negotiation process. But reservations also eat away at the integrity of the text and may undermine any serious obligation.[20]

3.3 REVITALIZING THE TREATY SYSTEM

It is evident that many human rights treaties are now relatively old. The International Bill of Rights was negotiated between 1945 and 1966 when the global, political, and economic environments were very different from those of today. There is a dilemma for the development of human rights law. On the one hand, the early conventions have acquired a significant authority and status but, on the other hand, they risk becoming outdated. While international law provides recognized procedures for treaty amendment,[21] the process risks dilution (or even rejection) of existing obligations. Other techniques have been sought for ensuring that the legal guarantees of human rights retain their relevance within a dynamic system. This entails the articulation of new rights as societal conditions demand them, the refinement and extension of existing rights through treaty interpretation,[22] and the enhancement of implementation mechanisms. A number of such techniques have been developed, which add to the richness of the sources of human rights law.

3.3.1 Additional protocols

One such technique comes directly within the ambit of treaty law and that is the adoption of additional protocols to an existing treaty. This has been done at both the UN and regional levels. An additional protocol is essentially a new treaty. States may select whether (and when) to become a party to a protocol in exactly the same way as they do for the main treaty. Protocols to the human rights treaties serve one of two functions: they either provide for rights not included within the original treaty or provide for new methods of enforcement.

An example of the former is ICCPR-OP2 aiming at the abolition of the death penalty. Abolition of the death penalty is controversial, with its proponents claiming that capital punishment is contrary to the right to life while those committed to its use deny that this is the case. Article 6 ICCPR recognizes the continued existence of the death penalty. The adoption of OP2 allows each state to choose its legal stance on the subject. For those states that become a party, the protocol is the formal source of a legal obligation not to execute any person within their jurisdiction. Other states can remain parties to the ICCPR without accepting this additional obligation. Similarly, states parties to the CRC have the choice whether to accept additional legal obligations relating to the recruitment and use of children in armed forces and hostilities and to the economic and sexual exploitation of children. An unusual situation is that of the US which has chosen to become a party to these two Optional Protocols to the CRC, but not to the 'parent' Convention.

---

[20] See Chapter 5.   [21] Vienna Convention on the Law of Treaties 1969, Arts 39–41.
[22] The regional human rights courts have often referred to human rights treaties as 'living', 'dynamic', or 'evolutive' instruments, eg *Gomez Paquiyauri Brothers v Peru*, IACtHR Series C No 110 (8 July 2004) para 165; *Loizidou v Turkey* (Preliminary Objections) (1995) 20 EHRR 99, para 71. See also *Ahmadou Sadio Diallo (Republic of Guinea v Democratic Republic of the Congo)* [2010] ICJ Rep, Separate Opinion of Judge Cancado Trindade, para 86.

An example of the latter is the ICESCR-OP, which entered into force in May 2013. It makes three new procedures available with respect to states parties to it: communications from an individual, or group of individuals, alleging violation of the ICESCR; inquiry into situations that appear to constitute a consistent pattern of gross or systematic violations of economic, social, and cultural rights within a state party; and inter-state complaints.

3.3.2 General comments or recommendations

Another technique through which states' treaty obligations have arguably evolved is the adoption of general comments or recommendations by the various treaty bodies, which set out their understanding of the scope, applicability, and content of the respective treaties. Other general comments (or statements) relate to the status of human rights treaties, such as their continuing validity following state succession or the effect of withdrawal from a treaty. The status of such general comments, of which there are now many,[23] as a source of human rights law is uncertain. While general comments are readily cited by advocates as sources of human rights law, and may be relied upon by decision-makers, any assertion of legally binding effect must depend upon states' consent to their terms. Thus Judge Weeramantry has noted that such statements are 'not authoritative in themselves' but nevertheless contribute to the understanding of the relevant principle. He was mindful of the fact that the treaty bodies 'are all committees with special experience of handling problems in the human rights area'.[24]

Where a general comment clarifies treaty provisions it might be seen as a form of secondary treaty law, deriving its authority from the binding nature of the treaty and the implied consent of states to it, or as indicative of subsequent agreement and practice for interpretation of the respective treaty as provided for in Article 31(3) Vienna Convention on the Law of Treaties. However, the treaty bodies have not been bestowed with law-making competence and in some instances states may consider a particular treaty body to have exceeded its competence. It must then be doubtful whether any such consent can be assumed.

Two examples illustrate the different possibilities. The CEDAW has no provision directly addressing gender-based violence against women as a violation of women's human rights. In its General Recommendation 19, the CEDAW Committee asserted that the Convention did indeed prohibit such violence as a form of discrimination against women within the terms of Article 1. The Committee required states to include the measures they had taken to combat violence against women in their reports. States have responded positively to this recommendation and have engaged in dialogue with the Committee on the issue, which is routinely addressed in the Committee's concluding observations. Through this practice it seems that they have consented to an interpretation of the CEDAW that includes violence against women.

In contrast is the response of at least some states to the Human Rights Committee's General Comment on treaty reservations. The Committee asserted that the special nature of human rights treaties and its need to be able to perform adequately its monitoring tasks mean that it 'necessarily falls to the Committee to determine whether a specific reservation is compatible with the object and purpose of the [ICCPR]'.[25] This assertion was challenged, in particular by the US, the UK, and France.[26] State consent to the Human Rights Committee's interpretation of its role is thus lacking, at least in the case of these

---

[23] The human rights treaty bodies' general comments and recommendations up to 2008 are compiled in UN Doc HRI/GEN/1/Rev.9 (Vol I) and (Vol II). More recent general comments and recommendations can be found at: <http://www.ohchr.org/EN/HRBodies/Pages/TBGeneralComments.aspx>.

[24] *Application of the Convention on the Prevention and Punishment of the Crime of Genocide (Bosnia and Herzegovina v Serbia and Montenegro)* [1996] ICJ Rep 595, 654 (Separate Opinion of Judge Weeramantry).

[25] HRC, General Comment 24, HRI/GEN/1/Rev.9 (Vol I) 210.

[26] See A/50/40, 126 (US), 130 (UK); A/51/40, 104 (France).

states. Nevertheless the General Comment formed part of the 'dialogue' on the effect of reservations, which was taken up by the International Law Commission (ILC) and culminated in the Guide to Practice on Reservations to Treaties.[27] In this sense it has contributed to the evolving law on reservations.

A general comment may be updated to reflect normative change since its adoption. In its Advisory Opinion regarding a *Complaint Filed against the International Fund for Agricultural Development*,[28] the ICJ turned to two General Comments adopted by the Human Rights Committee to underline the development of the principle equality in access to courts that had taken place in the 30 years between the adoption of the first general comment in 1984 and the second in 2007.[29] The Court implicitly accepted that the Committee's years of experience in the application of Article 14(1) ICCPR gave authority to its understanding of legal change. In 2017 the CEDAW Committee of updated its General Recommendation 19,[30] and the Human Rights Committee is preparing a new General Comment on the right to life revisiting and expanding its earlier general comments Nos 6 and 14 (from 1982 and 1984, respectively),[31] in both cases in light of normative developments and experience.

In addition to being seen as a form of secondary treaty law, a general comment may also become a resource for negotiation of a subsequent treaty[32] or generate state practice, which leads on to the next source of international human rights law—customary international law.

4 CUSTOMARY INTERNATIONAL LAW

The second source of international law, and, therefore, also international human rights law, listed in Article 38(1) ICJ Statute is customary international law. While treaties are binding only on states that have chosen to become parties, custom is binding upon all states with limited exceptions.[33] A treaty may codify customary international law or come to be accepted as customary international law. It is then binding on all states as custom. Customary international law is unwritten. Just as there are regional human rights treaties there may also be regional customary law.[34]

The ICJ has affirmed that customary international law—whether global or regional—comprises two components: an extensive and virtually uniform and consistent state practice and the belief that the practice is required by law (*opinio juris*),[35] rather than for some

---

[27] Report of the ILC on the work of its 63rd session, 2011, A/66/10, para 75.

[28] *Judgment No. 2867 of the Administrative Tribunal of the International Labour Organization upon a Complaint Filed against the International Fund for Agricultural Development* [2012] ICJ Rep 10, para 39.

[29] HRC, General Comment 13, HRI/GEN/1/Rev.9 (Vol I) 184; HRC, General Comment 32, HRI/GEN/1/Rev.9 (Vol I) 248.

[30] CEDAW Committee, General Recommendation 35, CEDAW/C/GC/35 (26 July 2017).

[31] Draft General Comment No. 36, Article 6: Right to life, Draft prepared by Yuval Shany and Nigel Rodley, Rapporteurs, CCPR/C/GC/R.36 (1 April 2015).

[32] eg, the preamble to the CPCVAW includes the CEDAW Committee's General Recommendation 19 as an instrument to which it had had regard.

[33] One exception is the so-called persistent objector rule. See Crawford, *Brownlie's Principles of Public International Law* (OUP, 2012) 28. The rule appears to have little application to human rights: eg, South Africa persistently objected to the designation of apartheid as contrary to customary international law but was nevertheless held to be in violation. [34] *Asylum Case (Columbia v Peru)* [1950] ICJ Rep 266.

[35] eg *North Sea Continental Shelf Cases (FRG v Denmark) (FRG v The Netherlands)* [1969] ICJ Rep 3, para 77; *Continental Shelf (Libyan Arab Jamahiriya v Malta)* [1985] ICJ Rep 29, para 27.

other reason such as diplomatic nicety or etiquette. But these two requirements are not easily applied, and determining the content of customary international law is strewn with practical and theoretical difficulties. The first problem is selecting from among the daily activities and statements made by states, those that constitute evidence of state practice. Places where one might look to discover evidence of custom include diplomatic correspondence, government policy statements, press releases, the opinions of government legal advisers, official manuals, and government comments on international drafting processes. In the context of human rights, other materials may be included such as the behaviours described in states' reports to the UN treaty bodies, material gathered for the Human Rights Council Universal Periodic Review (UPR) process, and the work and documentation of national human rights institutions. Unlike the state treaty reporting process, the UPR does not rest on any specific treaty but on states' general human rights obligations including, therefore, customary international law. As a peer (state) review process, both the reports and recommendations can provide evidence of practice and *opinio juris*.

Two examples illustrate how some decision-makers have approached the task of deciding whether a customary rule of international law exists and some of the theoretical quandaries in so deciding. In *Filartiga v Peña-Irala*, a US judge had to decide whether torture is contrary to customary international law. The case was in 1980, four years before the adoption of the UNCAT. Judge Kaufman sought to find international consensus on the prohibition of torture. He looked to General Assembly resolutions (including the UDHR), 'numerous international treaties and accords', and their reiteration in municipal law, including the constitutions of over 55 states. In sum, he found evidence of state practice in 'the usage of nations, judicial opinions and the work of jurists'.[36]

In *R v Jones*, the House of Lords determined the crime of aggression to be established under customary international law. Lord Bingham referred to what he called the 'major milestones along the road leading to this conclusion'.[37] These included a mix of treaties and statements: a draft Treaty of Mutual Assistance in 1923 (which never came into force); descriptions by the League of Nations Assembly; a resolution of the Pan-American Conference (1928); the Charter of the International Military Tribunal, Article 6; decisions of the International Military Tribunal; General Assembly Resolutions dating from 1946; the work of the International Law Commission; and the Rome Statute of the International Criminal Court (1998). In neither of these cases did the judge have to decide when the rule of custom had emerged; it was sufficient that it had done so by the time of the litigation.

Two further issues emerge from these examples. The first issue is that treaties, including treaties that never came into force, were drawn upon as evidence of state practice. It might be argued that a treaty that has not come into force is evidence of what states have not accepted, rather than of what they have. Further, the practice of states parties to treaties is not evidence of state practice for the purpose of establishing a rule of custom, because it must be assumed that such states are acting in accordance with their treaty obligations, not because they consider themselves bound by custom to do so.[38] They, therefore, lack the requisite *opinio juris*. States' reports to the treaty bodies are relevant as they provide a wealth of information about that state's policies, practices, and legislation, including changes that can be traced through the multiple rounds of reporting that many states have now undergone. If states have changed their practices in response to the concluding comments addressed to them by the relevant treaty bodies, this too must be viewed as action taken for treaty compliance, not as evidence of state practice for the purpose of establishing a rule of customary international law. Nevertheless, in terms of human rights

---

[36] (1980) 630 F2d 876.   [37] [2007] 1 AC 136.   [38] *North Sea Continental Shelf Cases*, para 76.

policy, changed behaviour towards implementation is precisely the desired objective and if consistency in state practice can be identified it seems artificial to discount it as evidence of customary international law.

The second issue is the problem caused by the divergence between what states do and what states say. In *Filartiga*, Judge Kaufman noted that he had not been 'directed to any assertion by any contemporary state of a right to torture its own or another nation's citizens'.[39] But this optimistic statement is contradicted by reports of torture evidenced by human rights organizations. In its 2015–6 Annual Report Amnesty International documented cases of torture and other ill-treatment across the world.[40] For evident policy reasons—the desire not to deny the existence of a rule of customary international law prohibiting torture—custom may be asserted by reference to states' words rather than the reality of their actions. As will be seen in this chapter, General Assembly resolutions are formally non-binding, but are often used as evidence of *opinio juris*, overriding inconsistent practice.[41] Both Judge Kaufman, and Lord Bingham in *R v Jones*, referred to General Assembly resolutions in determining customary international law. The desire to hold states to their words, particularly when pronounced in the formal setting of the General Assembly, is especially strong where the conduct is 'violative of the basic concept of human dignity', which is at the core of human rights.[42] Treaties and custom coexist and despite the wide adherence by states to human rights treaties, customary international law retains some considerable importance as a source of human rights law.[43] A claim of obligation under custom may be made against a state that has not become a party to a particular treaty, or which has made a reservation to a treaty provision as a state cannot reserve out of customary international law. A binding treaty may not yet have been concluded on the topic in question. Rules of customary international law (or 'general rules of international law'[44]) may be held to bind non-state actors that cannot be parties to treaties. In a number of states, including the UK, treaty law creates rights and obligations that can be relied on in national courts only if the treaty has been made part of national law through incorporating legislation. A state may thus become a party to a treaty but have failed to take the requisite action to allow it to be relied on within its own courts, as was the case in the UK before the passing of the Human Rights Act in 1998 to give domestic effect to the ECHR, which it had ratified in 1951. It has still not taken such action with respect to the ICCPR[45] or ICESCR. In contrast, customary international law may be accepted as the law of the land without any such act of incorporation.[46]

---

[39] *Filartiga*, 884.

[40] Amnesty International, *Annual Report 2015/2016*, available at <https://www.amnesty.org/en/latest/research/2016/02/annual-report-201516/>.

[41] In the *Nicaragua* case, the ICJ found that, despite numerous examples of armed conflict, there was sufficient evidence of contrary *opinio juris* in General Assembly resolutions to support principles of customary law prohibiting the use of force and wrongful intervention: *Military and Paramilitary Activities in and against Nicaragua (Nicaragua v US)* [1986] ICJ Rep 14, paras 186–90. However, in *Legality of the Threat or Use of Nuclear Weapons* the ICJ considered that 'although those [General Assembly] resolutions are a clear sign of deep concern regarding the problem of nuclear weapons, they still fall short of establishing the existence of an *opinio juris* on the illegality of the use of such weapons': [1996] ICJ Rep 226, para 71.

[42] Schachter, 'International Law in Theory and Practice: General Course in Public International Law' (1982) 178 *Rec des Cours* 21, 334–8. In such instances Schachter considered that 'statements of condemnation are sufficient evidence of its illegitimacy under customary international law'.

[43] See Clapham, *Human Rights Obligations of Non-State Actors* (OUP, 2006) 85–6.

[44] *Interpretation of the Agreement of 25 March 1951 between the WHO and Egypt* [1980] ICJ Rep 73, para 37.

[45] HRC, Concluding observations on the seventh periodic report of the United Kingdom of Great Britain and Northern Ireland CCPR/C/GBR/CO/7 (17 August 2015), para 5.

[46] See Chapter 24.

5 JUS COGENS

A *jus cogens* norm is a 'peremptory norm of general international law ... accepted and recognized by the international community of states as a whole as a norm from which no derogation is permitted and which can be modified only by a subsequent norm of general international law having the same character'.[47] *Jus cogens* norms or 'intransgressible principles of customary international law'[48] constitute the pinnacle of the hierarchy of sources of international law. They both limit states' freedom to enter into treaties by reference to fundamental values of the international community and bind all states regardless of whether they have ratified the treaties that contain them. They import notions of universally applicable norms into the international legal process.

Until the 1990s candidates for *jus cogens* norms were designated by commentators or scholars but had had relatively little application. Many of the norms most commonly asserted to have this status were those of human rights, including the prohibitions of genocide, slavery and the slave trade, murder/disappearances and torture, prolonged arbitrary detention, and systematic racial discrimination.[49] Indeed, it has been remarked that there is 'an almost intrinsic relationship between peremptory norms and human rights'.[50] Since the 1990s, international, regional, and national courts have recognized—albeit belatedly in the case of the ICJ[51]—certain norms as *jus cogens*, including the prohibitions of torture[52] and genocide,[53] and fundamental rules of humanitarian law.[54] Such judicial recognition has an important symbolic effect, signifying the seriousness with which the international community regards certain behaviours. It also has practical consequences, including making illegitimate any national legislative, administrative, or judicial act authorizing such acts, and forbidding their exclusion from extradition under any political offence exemption.

States are bound by *jus cogens* norms whether or not they have expressly consented to them. For example, the 36 states that are not party to the UNCAT remain subject to the prohibition of torture: they cannot derogate from it through international treaties, through local or special customs, or even 'through general customary rules not endowed with the same normative force'.[55] Although the grounding of *jus cogens* norms in fundamental interests of the wider international community overrides the requirement for individual state consent, the threshold is high. These norms must be accepted as such by the 'international community of states as a whole' indicating widespread general consent.

---

[47] Vienna Convention on the Law of Treaties, Art 53.

[48] *Legality of the Threat or Use of Nuclear Weapons*, para 79.

[49] American Law Institute, *Restatement (Third) of the Foreign Relations Law of the United States* (1987) para 702.   [50] Bianchi, 'Human Rights and the Magic of *Jus Cogens*' (2008) 19 *EJIL* 491.

[51] Judge Cançado Trindade noted that 'it has taken more than six decades for [the ICJ] to acknowledge its existence ..., in spite of its being one of the central features of contemporary international law'. *Questions relating to the Obligation to Prosecute or Extradite (Belgium v Senegal)* [2012] ICJ Rep, Separate Opinion of Judge Cançado Trindade, para 159.

[52] eg *A and others v Secretary of State for the Home Department (No 2)* [2005] UKHL 71; *Prosecutor v Furundžija*, Judgment, IT-95–17/1-T, 10 December 1998 (ICTY); *Ould Dah v France*, App no 13113/03, Decision of 30 March 2009 (European Court of Human Rights); *Questions relating to the Obligation to Prosecute or Extradite*, para 99.

[53] eg *Armed Activities on the Territory of the Congo* (New Application 2002) (*Democratic Republic of the Congo v Rwanda*) [2006] ICJ Rep 6, para 64.

[54] *Legality of the Threat or Use of Nuclear Weapons*, para 79; *Jurisdictional Immunities of the State* (*Germany v Italy: Greece intervening*) [2012] ICJ Rep, para 93 (with respect to 'rules of the law of armed conflict which prohibit the murder of civilians in occupied territory, the deportation of civilian inhabitants to slave labour and the deportation of prisoners of war to slave labour').   [55] *Furundžija*, para 153.

However, there remains controversy over which human rights norms have this status and over some of its implications. There is widespread agreement on the *jus cogens* quality of certain rights such as the prohibition of torture and genocide, but others that have been accepted by some bodies are more controversial; for example, all forms of discrimination,[56] the death penalty for those under 18,[57] and the right to property.[58] With respect to the legal consequences of a determination of *jus cogens*, it seems that it does not override jurisdictional requirements. On its detailed analysis of state practice as evidenced by national legislation and decisions of national courts, as well as the jurisprudence of the regional human rights courts, the ICJ has concluded that there is no rule of customary international law displacing state immunity for torts allegedly committed on the territory of another state by state organs during armed conflict, nor that this is changed by the status of the relevant norms as *jus cogens*.[59]

6 GENERAL PRINCIPLES OF LAW

The meaning of 'general principles of law' as listed in Article 38(1)(c) ICJ Statute remains controversial and has had little practical application. One view is that this expression refers to principles found in most, if not all, national legal systems, such as notions of procedural fairness or equity, while another view is that they include 'general principles applicable directly to international legal relations',[60] for example, the principle that treaties are binding upon states parties. In both cases, human rights are more likely to be applied as general principles rather than general principles constituting a source of human rights.[61]

Simma and Alston have argued for greater use of general principles as a contemporary source of human rights law and that general principles derived from the international plane should be expanded:

> Principles brought to the fore in this 'direct' way ... would (and should) then percolate down into domestic fora, instead of being elevated from the domestic level to that of international law by way of analogy.[62]

General principles drawn from international arenas may be found in statements of consensus, such as those expressed at global summits, and in the resolutions of UN organs. Simma and Alston reason that this would retain the consensual basis of international law while overcoming many of the conceptual and practical problems of customary international law, in particular the need to prove state practice and *opinio juris*. However, it does not seem that their position has influenced decision-makers.

---

[56] *Juridical Conditions and Rights of Undocumented Migrants*, IACtHR Series A No 18 (2003) paras 82–110.

[57] Case 12.240, *Douglas Christopher Thomas v United States*, IACommHR Report No 100/03, OEA/Ser./L/V/II.114 Doc.70 rev.1 (2003) 790, para 52.

[58] The European Court of First Instance suggested this in *Kadi v Council of the EU and Commission of the EC* (T-315/01) [2005] ECR II-3649, 293, at least where there is arbitrary deprivation.

[59] *Jurisdictional Immunities of the State*. See also *Stichting Mothers of Srebrenica and Others v the Netherlands* (2013) 57 EHRR SE10, paras 156–160.

[60] Thirlway, 'The Sources of International Law' in Evans (ed), *International Law* (OUP, 2006) 128.

[61] But see Capaldo, *The Pillars of Global Law* (Ashgate, 2008) ch 1.

[62] Simma and Alston, 'The Sources of Human Rights Law: Custom, *Jus Cogens* and General Principles' (1992) 12 *Australian YIL* 82, 102.

7 JUDICIAL DECISIONS

There is no dedicated international human rights court. However, a feature of the international legal system over the past few decades has been the proliferation of judicial bodies, many of which determine questions of human rights that arise before them. There is no hierarchy between these courts but their interaction has contributed to the dynamic quality of human rights law.

Article 38(1)(d) ICJ Statute provides that judicial decisions are 'subsidiary means' for determining rules of international law. The article does not clarify which courts it is referring to or the weight that should be given to judicial decisions. It does, however, refer to Article 59, which rejects any doctrine of precedent before the ICJ.[63] The formal position is that international courts do not make law and that their decisions are binding only on the parties to the particular case and can be discounted in subsequent cases. However, this ignores the reality that, through the interpretation and application of treaties and custom, judicial decisions elucidate and develop international law. In a decentralized legal system that lacks a legislature and where unwritten law is developed through the amorphous processes of state practice and *opinio juris*, judicial decision-making carries great weight through exposition of the law and accelerates the formation of customary international law.[64] At the national, regional, and international levels courts play an especially important role in developing and molding human rights law in accordance with changing social circumstances and understandings of rights. The ICJ has noted their relevance as evidence of customary international law.[65]

7.1 INTERACTION AT THE INTERNATIONAL AND REGIONAL LEVELS

The ICJ is the only international court with jurisdiction over all questions of international law, which includes issues relating to human rights.[66] It has, for example, asserted the applicability of human rights law in armed conflict and in occupied territories,[67] for instance that the ICCPR 'is applicable in respect of acts done by a State in the exercise of its jurisdiction outside its own territory.'[68] The Human Rights Committee (HRC) has adopted a similar approach in its General Comment 31,[69] and in its concluding observations to Israel's reports submitted under Article 40 ICCPR. It has reiterated that the ICCPR has extra-territorial effect with respect to the Occupied Territories and that this position is supported by the ICJ and state practice.[70] The Human Rights Committee did not refer to the Court's advisory opinion on the *Threat or Use of Nuclear Weapons* in its General Comment 31, which was adopted shortly before the advisory opinion on Israel's security wall, although it has since referred to the 'jurisprudence of the International Court of Justice.'[71] The ICJ did draw upon the Committee's practice and observations in that case. The consistency

---

[63] Art 59 states that '[t]he decision of the Court has no binding force except between the parties and in respect of that particular case'.

[64] Clapham, *Brierly's Law of Nations* (OUP, 2012) 65.   [65] *Jurisdictional Immunities of the State.*

[66] See Al-Khasawneh, 'The International Court of Justice and Human Rights', in Sheeran and Rodley (eds), *Routledge Handbook of International Human Rights Law* (Routledge, 2013) 353.

[67] *Legality of the Threat or Use of Nuclear Weapons*; *Legal Consequences of the Construction of a Wall in the Occupied Palestinian Territory* [2004] ICJ Rep 136.

[68] *Wall*, para 111.   [69] HRC, General Comment 31, HRI/GEN/1/Rev.9 (Vol I) 243, para 11.

[70] HRC, Concluding observations on the fourth periodic report of Israel, CCPR/C/ISR/CO/4 (21 November 2014), para 5.

[71] eg HRC, Concluding observations on Israel; see also HRC, Concluding observations on the fourth periodic report of the United States of America, CCPR/C/USA/CO/4 (23 April 2014), para 4.

between the two bodies strengthens and adds legitimacy to the emergent law. Decisions of the ICJ may also contribute to state practice where its decisions are followed by national courts, although there is no guarantee that this will be the case.

International human rights law and international criminal law are companion legal regimes and developments in one area may impact on the other, adding to the richness of the sources of each. Thus, international criminal courts may consider human rights law as a potential source of international criminal law.[72] For example, the sources of the prohibition of torture, as a human rights violation, are customary international law, the ICCPR, and the UNCAT. The human rights definition of torture can be found in Article 1 UNCAT. Torture is also an international crime and the International Criminal Tribunal for the former Yugoslavia (ICTY) has had to determine whether the international crime of torture has the same definition as the human rights violation. The ICTY first looked to human rights law and accepted the UNCAT definition as customary international law.[73] It subsequently changed its stance and adapted the definition to suit its own context—armed conflict—and the requirement that it apply international humanitarian law.[74] The ICTY Appeals Chamber affirmed that the UNCAT definition remains important as customary international law when considering state responsibility—the domain of human rights— but not for individual criminal responsibility—the domain of international criminal law.[75]

Similarly, decisions of international criminal tribunals may be turned to by human rights courts as a subsidiary source of human rights law. For example, in *MC v Bulgaria* the European Court of Human Rights noted the jurisprudence of the ICTY in determining that rape constitutes treatment incurring positive obligations under Article 3 ECHR. While accepting that the ICTY was dealing with the particular context of rape in armed conflict, the European Court considered that its jurisprudence 'reflected a universal trend' that was relevant to its own determination of rape as a human rights violation.[76] The decisions of international criminal courts may be a subsidiary source of human rights law, but their different legal focus means that there cannot be an automatic transposition between the two legal regimes.

7.2 INTERACTION BETWEEN NATIONAL COURTS

Domestic courts may also be influential in developing international human rights law: 'Development of the law by domestic courts feeds into the interpretation of human rights by supranational human rights courts and together they feed into, and inform, the development of international law.'[77] Many states have adopted international human rights standards into their constitutions and legislation, requiring national courts to interpret and apply the relevant provisions. In some cases international human rights treaties are incorporated into national law, while in others language is simply taken from them. In either event, judges in different jurisdictions must interpret and apply similarly worded provisions and may look to each other's decisions in doing so. The jurisprudence of regional and national courts is authoritative only within their own legal system, but careful judicial analysis can be influential in the decision-making by courts in other regions and states that

---

[72] Rome Statute of the International Criminal Court, Art 21(3) requires application and interpretation of the law to be 'consistent with internationally recognized human rights'.

[73] *Prosecutor v Mucić et al.*, Judgment, IT-96-21-T, 16 November 1998, para 459.

[74] *Prosecutor v Kunarac*, Judgment, IT-96-23-T and IT-96-23/1-T, 22 February 2001, paras 465 ff.

[75] *Prosecutor v Kunarac*, Judgment, IT-96-23 and IT-96-23/1-A, 12 June 2002, para 146.

[76] (2005) 40 EHRR 20.

[77] Arden, 'Water for All? Developing a Human Right to Water in National and International Law' (2016) 65 *ICLQ* 771, 784.

are faced with comparable problems and must apply similar language. Judicial decisions can carry persuasive weight across national and regional boundaries and it is becoming commonplace for judges in one jurisdiction 'to refer extensively to the decision of the courts of foreign jurisdictions when interpreting human rights guarantees'.[78] Especially when deciding a novel point, judges may feel that drawing on a decision, or reasoning, of other courts bestows legitimacy on their own judgment. Nevertheless, this process must not be taken for granted and research is required on specific issues to determine whether there is judicial consistency on a particular point and its extent. Where there is such consistency, it can be used as evidence of uniform state practice.

The reputation of certain courts, or the novelty of the point of human rights law under consideration, may give some decisions additional persuasive weight. They may also be used in advocacy and in writings and reports by human rights groups. For example, the decision of the House of Lords in the *Pinochet* case[79] has been widely cited and referred to by courts elsewhere, although subsequent decisions have narrowed its potential scope and limited its impact on the evolution of customary international law.[80] Similarly, the decisions of the South African Constitutional Court with respect to the understanding of economic and social rights have been influential.[81] The importance of this latter jurisprudence may have been enhanced because of the lack of judicial decision-making on these rights at the international and regional levels: the Committee on Economic, Social and Cultural Rights (CESCR) historically has not had the competence to hear individual complaints,[82] and the ECHR and ACHR are primarily focused on civil and political rights.

7.3 HUMAN RIGHTS LITIGATION

Human rights litigation is a comparatively new phenomenon but one that has rapidly evolved, thereby increasing the availability of argument, interpretation, and application of norms and enhancing the value of judicial decisions as a source of human rights law. Electronic information means that pleadings and decisions from numerous fora are readily available and accessible. Global networks of human rights activists devise litigation strategies, seek out test cases, submit amicus briefs and publicize successful claims so that similar arguments may be made elsewhere. There is now a body of judges and experts in global and regional institutions who regularly hear cases involving claims of violations of human rights. These are complemented by judges in national courts responsible for the judicial enforcement of human rights. They too form networks through bodies such as the International Bar Association, and can thus support and reinforce each other. They may attend training sessions on international human rights law. While they must all work within the constraints of their particular institution and legal framework, they face similar issues and may turn to the decisions of other bodies in determining their own approach. In all these ways judicial decision-making fleshes out and develops international human rights treaties and custom and, thus, has a greater influence than might be expected of a 'subsidiary means for the determination of rules' of human rights law.

---

[78] McCrudden, 'A Common Law of Human Rights? Transnational Judicial Conversations on Constitutional Rights' (2000) 20 *OJLS* 499, 506.

[79] *R v Bow Street Metropolitan Stipendiary Magistrate, ex parte Pinochet Ugarte (No 3)* [1999] 2 WLR 827.

[80] Wuerth, '*Pinochet's* Legacy Reassessed' (2012) 106 *AJIL* 731.

[81] eg *Government of the Republic of South Africa & Ors v Grootboom & Ors* 2000 (11) BCLR 1169; *Minister of Health v Treatment Action Campaign (TAC)* (2002) 5 SA 721 (CC).

[82] The ICESCR-OP means that this is no longer the case. In *IDG v Spain*, E/C.12/55/D/2/2014 (13 October 2015), the CESCR for the first time found a violation of the ICESCR.

8 WRITINGS OF JURISTS

Article 38(1)(d) ICJ Statute includes the 'teachings of the most highly qualified publicists' as another subsidiary means for determining the law. Within the international and regional human rights systems there are now a plethora of expert bodies and individuals who produce important reports and commentaries on a wide range of human rights issues. These include the UN Human Rights Council special procedures (Special Rapporteurs, fact-finding missions, working groups, expert meetings), the reports of the former Sub-Commission on Human Rights (now advisory council), reports of the UN High Commissioner for Human Rights, human rights work of UN specialized agencies, and NGO reports such as those of Human Rights Watch and Amnesty International. Such works are often scholarly, well researched, and analytical. They are compiled for many purposes: to expose a particular violative practice, to provide an academic analysis of an issue, or to gain media attention. They may also consciously seek to develop human rights law, by bringing together examples of state practice and *opinio juris* and arguing that these are sufficiently consistent to found a new rule of custom, or to demonstrate the need for a treaty on the subject. Writings of this type are not binding and do not constitute a formal source of human rights law, but may be relied upon by decision-makers as sources of information and for analysis.[83] The result is that there is a wealth of literature that may be understood as a subsidiary means for determining the law. The persuasiveness of any one piece of writing depends upon the quality of research and analysis and the authority of the relevant institution or author. There may be deliberate strategies to enhance the authority of a particular piece of work; for example, the growing practice of reports by multiple Special Rapporteurs,[84] or the joint General Recommendation between the CEDAW Committee and the Committee on the Rights of the Child.[85] As with judicial decisions, much depends on the use made of such works by states and other actors. Today, such works are more influential in developing human rights law than the writings of more traditional publicists referred to in Article 38(1)(d).

9 OTHER SOURCES

In addition to the formal sources of international law as spelled out in Article 38(1) ICJ Statute, other methods of developing human rights law must be identified. These are primarily located within the human rights institutions of the UN, which allow for scrutiny and analysis by independent experts of potential new rights,[86] as well as for political advocacy in favour of, or against, the acceptance of a new right.

---

[83] eg the European Court of Human Rights referred to reports of the European Commissioner for Human Rights and the Cypriot Ombudsman to highlight the nature of human trafficking in Cyprus: *Rantsev v Cyprus and Russia* (2010) 51 EHRR 1.

[84] eg Joint report of the Special Rapporteur on the rights to freedom of peaceful assembly and of association and the Special Rapporteur on extrajudicial, summary or arbitrary executions on the proper management of assemblies, A/HRC/31/66 (4 February 2016).

[85] Joint General Recommendation 31 of the CEDAW Committee/General Comment 18 of the Committee on the Rights of the Child on harmful practices, CEDAW/C/GC/31-CRC/C/GC/18 (14 November 2014).

[86] Bouwhuis, 'Revisiting Philip Alston's Human Rights and Quality Control' (2016) *EHRLR* 475, 483.

9.1 WORK OF TREATY BODIES

The role of the UN treaty bodies in developing human rights law has been mentioned.[87] The different activities of these bodies cut across the different sources. The treaty bodies elucidate and develop states' obligations under the various treaties through the adoption of general comments and concluding observations in response to states' reports. These might be described as secondary treaty law, in that state consent can be implied from their acceptance of the treaties and the authority of the expert committees. This is reinforced where states comply with the reporting requirements and are responsive to the concluding observations made by the various committees.

Repetition of itself does not transform a non-binding recommendation into a legally binding obligation. However a similar approach taken by a number of the treaty bodies may promote acquiescence and thus provide supporting evidence for state practice. One example is the now wide acceptance of the multi-layered state obligation to respect, protect, and fulfil human rights. Another more controversial example is extraterritorial applicability of human rights which has in some form been included in general comments by the Human Rights Committee,[88] the Committee against Torture,[89] the Committee on Economic, Social and Cultural Rights,[90] and the CEDAW Committee.[91] The argument is strengthened where there is a similar approach taken by regional human rights institutions and academic writings,[92] illustrative of the interaction of diverse sources of human rights law.

Some of the treaty bodies also have a form of quasi-judicial competence. This is the individual complaint or communication procedure, which is primarily a written procedure and concludes with views and recommendations by the relevant committee.[93] Can such opinions be regarded as judicial decisions under Article 38(1)(d)? On the one hand, they are non-binding and in many instances include only limited reasoning. On the other hand, the monitoring role accorded by treaty to the expert committees means that their opinions cannot be easily disregarded. The individual complaint procedure allows the treaty bodies to develop jurisprudence on the interpretation and application of the relevant convention and their opinions may be cited before decision-makers, used as supporting evidence of current human rights law, and cited in judicial proceedings. The Human Rights Committee has described its views as having some of the characteristics of judicial decisions in that they 'are arrived at in a judicial spirit, including the impartiality and independence of Committee members, the considered interpretation of the language of the Covenant, and the determinative character of the decisions' and as such provide 'an authoritative determination by the organ established under the Covenant itself charged with the interpretation of that instrument.'[94] This view appears to be accepted by the ICJ, which

---

[87] See Ulfstein, 'Law-making by Human Rights Treaty Bodies', in Liivoja and Petman (eds), *International Law-making* (Routledge, 2014) 249. [88] HRC, General Comment 31.

[89] CAT, General Comment 2, Implementation of article 2 by States parties, CAT/C/GC/2 (24 January 2008), para 16.

[90] General Comment on State Obligations under the International Covenant on Economic, Social and Cultural Rights in the Context of Business Activities, Draft prepared by Olivier De Schutter and Zdzislaw Kedzia, Rapporteurs, E/C.12/60/R.1 (17 October 2016), para 31.

[91] CEDAW Committee, General Recommendation 28 on the Core Obligations of States Parties under Article 2 of the Convention on the Elimination of All Forms of Discrimination against Women, CEDAW/C/2010/47/GC2 (19 October 2010), para 12.

[92] eg, Milanovic, *Extraterritorial Application of Human Rights Treaties: Law, Principles, and Policy* (OUP, 2011). [93] See Chapter 19.

[94] HRC, General Comment 33, CCPR/C/GC/33 (5 November 2008), paras 11–13.

has stated that the opinion of the Human Rights Committee—'an independent body established specifically to supervise the application of that treaty'—should be given 'great weight'.[95] The weight given to the output of treaty bodies varies according to the strength of the argument, the esteem accorded to the particular committee, and the extent to which their work is in tune with other developments in human rights law.

Another individual complaints mechanism is the Human Rights Advisory Panel (HRAP) in Kosovo. Its authority ultimately derives from Security Council Resolution 1244 (1999), which mandated the international civil presence in Kosovo (the UN Interim Administration Mission in Kosovo (UNMIK)) with, inter alia, 'protecting and promoting human rights'. The first Regulation promulgated by UNMIK affirmed that the Mission 'shall observe internationally recognized human rights standards'.[96] In 2006 UNMIK established the Panel 'to examine alleged violations of human rights by UNMIK' and to issue opinions in accordance with a list of applicable instruments, including UN human rights treaties, the ECHR, and the formally non-binding UDHR.[97] As an international organization the UN cannot become party to a human rights treaty (unless explicitly provided for), but in this way the treaties listed are made an applicable source of law for the performance of the mandate of a UN mission. The Panel's opinions largely follow the jurisprudence of the European Court of Human Rights, but its mandate allowed it to extend that jurisprudence, which it did on some occasions. For instance in a case involving the separation of women and men detainees, the Panel considered there to be an investigative duty under Article 5 ECHR (the right to liberty).[98] The reasoned opinions may be influential in developing the law, especially with respect to the human rights standards required of a UN mission in the field.

9.2 RESOLUTIONS OF INTERNATIONAL INSTITUTIONS

An important omission from Article 38(1) ICJ Statute is resolutions of international institutions. Of particular significance are the numerous resolutions of the General Assembly and Human Rights Council, which have widened the scope of human rights, set standards for states and non-state actors, and provided aspirations and goals. The status of the Human Rights Council as a subsidiary body of the General Assembly may add greater authoritative weight to its resolutions than those of its predecessor, the Commission on Human Rights. Indeed, the foundational document of international human rights law—the UDHR—is in the form of a General Assembly resolution. Such non-binding instruments (often termed 'soft law') may be the basis for binding norms where they are declaratory of custom, or are subsequently transformed by state practice into a treaty or custom. The UDHR was followed, albeit 18 years later, by the ICCPR and ICESCR, treaties binding on states parties. It is also regarded by many commentators as having become customary international law. This transformation into formal sources, however, fails to indicate its own abiding authority and status.

The same pattern—resolution followed by treaty—has occurred in many other instances: the Declaration on Torture was followed by the UNCAT; many resolutions on the rights of the child were followed eventually by the CRC; resolutions on the rights of persons with disabilities were followed by the CRPD. In other cases no treaty has been adopted on the subject matter addressed in a General Assembly resolution. There has been no global treaty on the rights of minorities following the General Assembly Declaration on the Rights of Persons belonging to National, Ethnic, Religious and Linguistic Minorities, or on those of indigenous peoples

---

[95] *Diallo*, para 66.   [96] UNMIK/REG/1999/1 (25 July 1999).
[97] UNMIK/REG/2006/12 (23 March 2006).
[98] *Bogoljub Kostić and Others v UNMIK*, HRAP Cases Nos 111/09 and others (23 October 2015).

following the General Assembly Declaration on the subject. Even where a treaty has followed a resolution, it is unlikely that all states will become parties. Individuals may, therefore, wish to argue that the resolution has crystallized into customary international law. Criteria for determining that a resolution has become customary international law have been put forward. They include adoption of the resolution by consensus, the inclusion of normative language, and follow-up procedures—all factors that indicate states' consent to be bound.

Another way in which a non-binding resolution may be understood as a source of human rights law is where it provides an authoritative interpretation of a treaty. This was the approach taken by the Inter-American Court of Human Rights in considering the status of the American Declaration of the Rights and Duties of Man. The Court considered that for:

> member states of the Organization, the Declaration is the text that defines the human rights referred to in the [OAS] Charter ... with the result that ... the American Declaration is for these States a source of international obligations related to the Charter of the Organization. ... That the Declaration is not a treaty does not, then, lead to the conclusion that it does not have legal effect.[99]

The Inter-American Commission has accordingly determined that the USA has human rights obligations under the Declaration despite it not having become a party to the ACHR.

Security Council resolutions adopted under Chapter VII of the UN Charter are binding on states parties. By specifying the human rights obligations of non-state actors (for instance armed groups) the Council has contributed to the expanding applicability of human rights law.[100] Through a series of thematic resolutions it has developed principles and institutional practices, for instance relating to the protection of children and women, and more generally civilians, in armed conflict. The eight resolutions following Resolution 1325 (2000) have become known as the Women, Peace and Security agenda, which forms 'part of the international tradition of human rights'. Although not adopted under Chapter VII of the Charter, these resolutions contribute to state and institutional practice (although not as fully or consistently as urged by the Council) and thus to further development of human rights.

9.3 OTHER FORMS OF SOFT LAW

There are multiple other forms of soft law. They include guidelines,[101] codes of conduct,[102] standards of behaviour,[103] and the final instruments of global summit meetings held under UN auspices. The last became noteworthy features of the international landscape since the 1990s. They have typically generated great energy through the establishment of a conference secretariat, wide participation, intensive preparations, lobbying, and intense (often heated) negotiations. They culminated in declarations and programmes of action directed to states, intergovernmental organizations, and NGOs.[104] There have been follow-up procedures, normally at five-year intervals.

---

[99] OC-10/89, *Interpretation of the American Declaration of the Rights and Duties of Man within the Framework of Article 64 of the American Convention on Human Rights*, Series A No 10 (1989), paras 45–7.

[100] Clapham, 'Human Rights Obligations of Non-state Actors in Conflict Situations' (2006) 88 *IRRC* 491.

[101] eg Basic Principles and Guidelines on the Right to a Remedy and Reparation for Victims of Gross Violations of International Human Rights Law and Serious Violations of International Humanitarian Law, GA Res 60/147 (16 December 2005); Guiding Principles on Business and Human Rights: Implementing the United Nations 'Protect, Respect and Remedy' Framework, A/HRC/17/31 (21 March 2011).

[102] eg Code of Conduct for Law Enforcement Officials, GA Res 34/169 (17 December 1979); Basic Principles on the Use of Force and Firearms by Law Enforcement Officials, 1990.

[103] eg Standard Minimum Rules for the Treatment of Prisoners, 1955.

[104] eg World Conference on Human Rights, Vienna, 1993; Fourth World Conference on Women, Beijing, 1995; and review conferences.

It is noticeable that many of these instruments are negotiated with as much care and attention to detail as binding texts and states also make reservations to them, undermining the formal position that they lack legal authority. The practical difference in impact between treaties and non-binding instruments may not be great, especially where treaty language is imprecise and seems to deny legal obligation. For example, under Article 2 ICESCR, each state party undertakes to 'take steps ... to the maximum of its available resources, with a view to achieving progressively the ... rights recognized ... by all appropriate means'. Phrases such as 'take steps', 'progressively', and 'appropriate means' lack precise legal content. As there was originally no right of individual complaint under the ICESCR, the treaty might be considered as imposing only a 'soft' obligation despite its legal form.[105] There are advantages to the 'soft' form: it may facilitate reaching a political consensus, bring an issue onto the international agenda, define the area of international concern, and provide guidelines for behaviour that may generate the requisite practice for a rule of customary international law. Judges and other decision-makers may turn to formally non-binding instruments in much the same way as treaties,[106] and there is often little distinction in terms of compliance.[107]

What might be termed a 'fusion' of soft law sources can lead to the emergence of new norms without input from 'formal' sources, for instance where negotiation of a convention remains politically contested. The example of violence against women illustrates how the multiple processes of a specialist UN human rights treaty body, the CEDAW Committee, in conjunction with other non-binding processes, may work together to produce binding norms. The Committee has used its General Recommendation 19 on violence against women, its concluding observations on states parties' reports, its inquiry procedure,[108] and its decisions in individual complaints of brutal domestic violence sustained over many years,[109] to develop the understanding that gender-based violence is discrimination within the terms of the CEDAW and that states have an obligation to exercise due diligence to protect women from such violence, prosecute it, and punish it. The concept of due diligence was embedded in the international law principle of state responsibility for wrongful treatment of aliens, formulated in an expert report on disappearances,[110]

---

[105] See Chapter 7.

[106] eg in *R v Immigration Officer at Prague Airport, ex parte European Roma Rights Centre and Others* [2005] 2 WLR 1, the UK House of Lords referred to a range of formally non-binding documents, including a UN High Commissioner for Refugees *Handbook on Procedures and Criteria for Determining Refugee Status*; the Declaration on Territorial Asylum, 1967; American Law Institute, *Restatement of the Foreign Relations Law of the United States (Third)*; resolutions of the Committee of Ministers of the Council of Europe; reports of the International Law Association; HRC, General Comment 31; reports by the Inter-American Commission for Human Rights and UN Committee on the Elimination of Racial Discrimination; and academic articles.

[107] Shelton (ed), *Commitment and Compliance: The Role of Non-Binding Norms in the International Legal System* (OUP, 2000).

[108] Report on Mexico produced by the CEDAW Committee under Art 8 of the Optional Protocol to the Convention, and reply from the Government of Mexico, CEDAW/C/2005/OP8/Mexico (27 January 2005); Report of the inquiry concerning Canada of the CEDAW under article 8 of the Optional Protocol to the Convention, CEDAW/C/OP.8/CAN/1 (30 March 2015).

[109] eg, *Ms AT v Hungary*, CEDAW/C/36/D/2/2003 (26 January 2005); *Şahide Goekce v Austria*, CEDAW/C/39/D/5/2005 (6 August 2007); *Fatma Yildirim (deceased) v Austria*, CEDAW/C/39/D/6/2005 (6 August 2007); *Vertido v Philippines*, CEDAW/C/46/D/18/2008 (22 September 2010); *Angela González Carreño v Spain*, CEDAW/C/58/D/47/2012 (16 July 2014).

[110] Report of the Special Rapporteur on extrajudicial, summary or arbitrary executions, E/CN.4/2005/7 (22 December 2004) para 73. Alston attributes the formulation in the human rights context to Abdoulaye Dieye of Senegal, in his capacity as an expert in relation to the situation in Chile, A/34/583/Add.1 (21 November 1979) para 124.

developed by the Inter-American Court of Human Rights (also in the context of disappearances),[111] conceptualized in the context of violence against women in two reports of the Special Rapporteur on violence against women,[112] and incorporated into jurisprudence of regional human rights courts[113] and treaty law within the OAS,[114] African Union,[115] and Council of Europe frameworks,[116] a trajectory that illustrates how diverse bodies draw upon and explicate concepts developed elsewhere. The Committee's work has been reinforced by General Assembly resolutions,[117] resolutions of the Commission on Human Rights (and now Council), including the adoption of a mandate for a Special Rapporteur on the causes and consequences of violence against women, the final instruments of global conferences, and ongoing work by the General Assembly, including commissioning the Secretary-General to prepare an 'In-Depth Study on Violence against Women' and an annual report on implementation of its recommendations. These non-binding processes taken together have strong accumulative effect in determining that violence against women violates human rights law. At the very least, these expressions by states, by experts, and by judicial bodies of the wrongfulness of failing to exercise due diligence to prevent and punish such behaviour constitute considerable evidence to ground an argument that there is the requisite *opinio juris* for an international norm prohibiting gender-based violence against women, despite its continuing prevalence. Another example is non-discrimination on the grounds of sexual and gender identity. The treaty bodies, and in particular the European Court of Human Rights, have found such discrimination to be in violation of the various conventions. Following a controversial resolution of the UN Human Rights Council,[118] the Office of the High Commissioner for Human Rights produced a detailed report entitled Discriminatory Laws and Practices and Acts of Violence against Individuals based on their Sexual Orientation and Gender Identity. This demonstrated the extent of harmful discriminatory practices and violence, analysed the practice of the treaty bodies in developing a coherent and consistent approach to condemnation of such discrimination, and generated a panel discussion at the Human Rights Council,[119] a further resolution,[120] and, over heated opposition, a mandate for a new special rapporteur.[121] These actions were bolstered by states' questioning and recommendations through the Council's UPR process and many references in concluding observations to states' reports. Although the issue continues to divide states, these steps indicate how multiple processes are engaged to further legal development.[122]

---

[111] *Velásquez Rodriguez v Honduras (Merits)*, IACtHR Series C No 4, 29 July 1988.

[112] Reports of the Special Rapporteur on violence against women, E/CN.4/2006/6 (20 January 2006) and A/HRC/23/49 (14 May 2013).

[113] *Opuz v Turkey*, App no 33401/02, Judgment of 9 June 2009; see also *Case of González et al. ('Cotton Field') v Mexico (Preliminary Objection, Merits, Reparations, and Costs)*, IACtHR Series C No 205, 16 November 2009.

[114] Inter-American Convention on Prevention, Punishment and Eradication of Violence against Women (1994) (Convention of Belém do Pará).

[115] Protocol to the African Charter on Human and Peoples' Rights on the Rights of Women in Africa (2003) (Maputo Protocol). [116] CPCVAW, Art 5.

[117] Most importantly the Declaration on the Elimination of Violence against Women, GA Res 48/104 (20 December 1993). [118] Res A/HRC/17/L.9/Rev.1.

[119] A/HRC/19/41 (17 November 2011). [120] A/HRC/27/32/L.27/Rev.I (24 September 2014).

[121] Protection against violence and discrimination based on sexual orientation and gender identity, A/HRC/32/L.2/Rev.1 (28 June 2016). See generally Chapter 15.

[122] CPCVAW, Art 4(3), is the first treaty provision prohibiting discrimination on the grounds of sexual orientation and gender identity with respect to the provisions of the Convention.

10 CONCLUSION

The formal sources of international human rights law derive from state consent: states negotiate and enter into treaties; custom is drawn from state behaviour and intent. However, this conclusion should be treated with some caution for two reasons. First, the requirement for state consent may be weakening through the turn to international community interests and values as in the concept of *jus cogens*. Long a theoretical concept that held little attraction for judges and decision-makers, *jus cogens* has been more widely appealed to since the 1990s. Second, human rights is a vibrant field engaging many and varied actors—activists, lawyers, states, and civil society organizations. Human rights law speaks to people who appeal to its standards against what they regard as unwarranted state (and increasingly non-state) intrusion into their lives. It provides a language, a methodology, and techniques for challenging state action. Working as individuals, through human rights NGOs, and institutional human rights bodies, they seek to influence the development of human rights law through a range of activities and processes. The practice and statements of these non-state actors do not constitute formal sources of human rights law but they cannot be ignored.

Contemporary human rights law is dynamic and evolving through claims for new rights, additional instruments, and practices. Decision-makers have a choice: they can be rigid and rely strictly on formal sources which they interpret narrowly; or they may interpret open-ended and indeterminate treaty language, or move beyond treaties to the range of other instruments that are out there to capture a wide range of behaviours and assert them to be contrary to international law.

FURTHER READING

ALVAREZ, *International Organizations as Law-Makers* (Oxford University Press, 2005).

ARDEN, 'Water for All? Developing a Human Right to Water in National and International Law' (2016) 65 *ICLQ* 771.

BOUWHUIS, 'Revisiting Philip Alston's Human Rights and Quality Control' (2016) 5 *EHRLR* 475.

BOYLE and CHINKIN, *The Making of International Law* (Oxford University Press, 2007).

CLAPHAM, 'Human Rights Obligations of Non-state Actors in Conflict Situations' (2006) 88 *IRRC* 491.

CRAWFORD, *Brownlie's Principles of Public International Law* (Oxford University Press, 8th edn 2012) ch 2.

INTERNATIONAL LAW ASSOCIATION, *Final Report of the Committee on Formation of Customary (General) International Law* (2000) available at <http://www.ila-hq.org/en/committees/index.cfm/cid/30>.

MECHLEM, 'Treaty Bodies and the Interpretation of Human Rights' (2009) 42 *Vanderbilt J Trans'l L* 905.

MOYN, *The Last Utopia* (Harvard University Press, 2010).

ORAKHELASHVILI, *Peremptory Norms in International Law* (Oxford University Press, 2008).

ROBERTS and SIVAKUMARAN, 'Lawmaking by Nonstate Actors: Engaging Armed Groups in the Creation of International Humanitarian Law' (2012) 37 *Yale JIL* 107.

SIMMA and ALSTON, 'The Sources of Human Rights Law: Custom, *Jus Cogens* and General Principles' (1992) 12 *Australian YIL* 82.

Teitel, *Humanity's Law* (Oxford University Press, 2011).

Ulfstein, 'Law-making by Human Rights Treaty Bodies', in Liivoja and Petman (eds)

International Law-making (Routledge, 2014) 249.

Wuerth, '*Pinochet's* Legacy Reassessed' (2012) 106 *AJIL* 731.

USEFUL WEBSITES

For the work of the UN treaty bodies, see the website of the Office of the High Commissioner for Human Rights, Human Rights bodies: **<http://www.ohchr.org/EN/HRBodies/Pages/ HumanRightsBodies.aspx>**

For the UN Human Rights Council, see: **<http://www.ohchr.org/EN/HRBodies/HRC/ Pages/HRCIndex.aspx>**

For human rights treaties, see the University of Minnesota human rights library: **<http:// www1.umn.edu/humanrts/>**

5

NATURE OF OBLIGATIONS

Frédéric Mégret

SUMMARY

Human rights obligations have a special status in international law because they are, in some ways, fundamentally different from other international law obligations. States that ratify international human rights treaties are not primarily committing to respect human rights vis-à-vis other states, but vis-à-vis persons within their jurisdiction. This is what is sometimes known as the 'special character' of international human rights obligations and it has concrete implications. States must implement human rights domestically in particular ways, even though they may have a 'margin of appreciation' in doing so. When ratifying human rights treaties, states must be particularly careful of what reservations they make, as many reservations have been found to be incompatible with the 'object and purpose' of such treaties. Human rights obligations can be limited on the basis of certain needs justifiable in a democratic society, and can even be derogated from in very exceptional circumstances, but it is likely that a state cannot withdraw entirely from a human rights treaty if the treaty does not contain a clause on denunciation.

1 INTRODUCTION

What is the fundamental nature of human rights obligations? What does it mean to be bound by international human rights law? Obligations can be defined in terms of their duty-holders and their beneficiaries, for example states and persons within their jurisdiction. In trying to assess the 'nature' of human rights obligations, however, this chapter will go beyond duty-holder/beneficiary analysis to understand what *sort* of obligations are involved. For example, are human rights obligations fundamentally unilateral or multilateral, reciprocal or non-reciprocal, temporal or eternal, conditional or unconditional, relative or absolute? The main idea is that human rights obligations are in some ways very distinct from other types of obligations existing under general international law.

The chapter first seeks to conceptualize the relationship of human rights to public international law, which is crucial to understanding the nature of human rights obligations (Section 2). It then introduces the basic idea of what it means for a legal obligation to be described as 'special' in nature in international law (Section 3). It will then identify several key consequences that can be said to flow from this character in terms of reservations (Section 4), implementing human rights obligations (Section 5), limitations and derogations (Section 6), enforcement (Section 7), and withdrawal (Section 8).

2 THE RELATIONSHIP OF HUMAN RIGHTS TO GENERAL INTERNATIONAL LAW

Why does this matter and why should general international law be the standard of comparison? First, international human rights law is a branch of public international law. When human rights lawyers sought to internationalize the human rights project in the middle of the twentieth century, they had no choice but to draw on the primary body of law existing at the global level.[1] Only public international law could bind states 'from above' and change domestic practices. However, international law as a legal system is far from neutral. It comes with its own legal assumptions, preferences, and logic, some of which, as will be seen, might be at odds with the very idea and purpose of human rights. It must be remembered that, classically, international law was a law created by, between, and for states. Its cardinal concept was state sovereignty, and the typical source of obligation was state voluntarism (that is, states are only bound by those obligations to which they have consented). International law was, in a sense, dedicated to ensuring that state sovereignty and state voluntarism would not be undermined. It would be surprising, therefore, if these origins did not lead to some tensions with the human rights project, the goal of which is very much geared towards redefining sovereignty.

Although the stark divide between public international law and international human rights law has lessened over time as the development of the former has been influenced by the growth of the latter, some tensions between these bodies of law remain. The problem can be analysed as one of tension between substance and form. Substantively, the projects of public international law and international human rights law could not be more at odds. Human rights law is concerned with proclaiming and enforcing certain fundamental guarantees for individuals against the state. As such, it is potentially at least both radical and revolutionary. The strict protection of sovereignty characteristic of international law is, in principle, largely incompatible with a strong stance in favour of human rights, in that human rights deal with issues that are essentially domestic and traditionally considered to be part of states' exclusive purview.

Formally, human rights law and general international law also differ very significantly. International law is the slow maturing of ancient customary practice. It emphasizes states' obligations, and it is marked by a high degree of flexibility. Human rights law, by contrast, emerges from the proclamation of rights, usually in declarations or constitutions. It outlines minimum rights with a strong principled component, and its focus is on the beneficiaries of obligations (individuals). At the same time, the two have converged formally, at least to the extent that human rights obligations are typically given their binding character internationally by being recognized in international sources, such as custom and treaty.

Inevitably, this creates a tension between the *substance* of human rights and the *form* they take, between the idea of rights as inherent to the human person and the fact that they only have traction internationally to the extent they are recognized in, especially, treaties. Historically, international law has been seen as neutral about political ends, essentially only offering states the means for a very basic interaction that safeguarded their sovereignty by allowing them to coexist. International norms emerged from consent between equals. The model for such obligations was the *contract*, that is, an obligation based on reciprocity. In other words, the obligations of each party are entered into in exchange for the other party undertaking similar obligations, and each party is bound to the extent that the other respects its own obligations.

---

[1] See Chapter 1.

Some of the implications of this included the fact that states could subscribe to whatever obligations they freely agreed to, modify the content of their obligations through consensus, and even under certain conditions cease to respect certain obligations. A further consequence was that international legal instruments only created obligations between states, at the expense of individuals who were considered mere 'objects' of international law, at best unintended and collateral beneficiaries of obligations undertaken by sovereigns. Although international law diversified substantively over time—regulating ever more areas of international life—it did and largely still does claim to lay the ground rules for all thematic branches of international law. For example, the Vienna Convention on the Law of Treaties (VCLT) is not interested in the particular content of treaties, whether they deal with trade, the environment, or diplomatic immunities; it lays down the same basic rules which apply to all treaties.

The problem is that the international law form—the particular expression international commitments take legally—is not substantively neutral and the substance of human rights does not always fit this form. The point has been made eloquently by Craven in the context of human rights treaties:

> [In human rights] treaties the two elements of 'form' and 'function' appear to be fundamentally at odds with one another. On the one hand, the form in which the rights are expressed—the treaty—supposes that human rights are merely the incidental subject of a contractual bargain between states. Individual 'right-holders' are therefore simply the fortuitous beneficiaries of a regime that is otherwise concerned with promoting the rights and interests of states. The teleology of the regime on the other hand—focused as it is on individual or group 'human rights'—supposes that the treaties are quasi-constitutional in character.[2]

Historically, this has created a very significant conceptual and practical challenge for human rights lawyers: how can we avoid the human rights project being stultified, or even absorbed, by the language of traditional international law? The answer generally has been to redefine human rights obligations, particularly treaty obligations, as having a 'special character'. Thus, human rights obligations are dependent on, and yet also crucially distinct from, the way in which international legal obligations typically operate. But this idea that human rights obligations are somehow 'special' needs to be grounded and explained, to understand exactly what its basis and implications are.

3 THE 'SPECIAL CHARACTER' OF HUMAN RIGHTS OBLIGATIONS

Defining in general terms the 'special character' of human rights obligations is a difficult exercise. The fundamental idea is that international human rights obligations differ from other international law obligations in that they deal with the obligations of states towards individuals rather than between states.

At a certain level, international human rights law is hardly a rejection of all the rules of public international law. As has been seen in Chapter 4, for example, there is no reason to think that the list of existing sources of the 'branch' that is international human rights law is entirely different from the 'trunk' of public international law. International human

---

[2] Craven, 'Legal Differentiation and the Concept of the Human Rights Treaty in International Law' (2000) 11 *EJIL* 489, 493.

rights treaties borrow much from the traditional law of treaties, including the way treaties come into existence, the simple idea that states are bound by treaties they ratify (the *pacta sunt servanda* rule), and that states should discharge their obligations in good faith. Many of the key aspects of state responsibility (that is, what happens when a state violates its obligation), moreover, are applicable in the field of human rights. There is no reason to think that any of these rules apply in markedly different ways simply because the subject matter of a treaty is human rights.

However, there are also clearly some ways in which human rights obligations are different. A traditional treaty is one that creates rights and obligations between states, to the broad exclusion of any other actor, even if that other actor may objectively benefit from or even be adversely affected by such arrangements. States typically *exchange* such rights and obligations, with a view to securing advantages commensurate with their costs. Moreover, treaties are often quite strictly relational: states enter into treaties only with those states with which they want to enter into such treaties. Finally, just as domestically states are not normally interested in the substantive content of contracts concluded between private parties (outside violations of public order), international law traditionally does not have a significant stake in the subject matter to which states commit (as opposed to the fact that they should honour whatever commitments they make).

Human rights treaties superficially borrow the idea of an agreement between states as the basis of international human rights obligations. But they are also strikingly different. They are agreements, typically between states, the beneficiaries of which are in fact third parties, namely 'all individuals within [the state's] territory'.[3] Indeed, human rights treaties create rights specifically for individuals, even though individuals are not normally subjects of international law generally or treaties specifically or indeed parties to the human rights treaties that recognize or grant them rights.

To describe human rights treaties as contractual, moreover, would be profoundly misleading. It is wrong to say that states commit to respecting certain human rights obligations in exchange for other states doing the same. Rather states are formally binding themselves to other states, whilst in fact mostly creating rights for individuals within their jurisdiction. From a practical point of view, international human rights obligations are not as dependent on the idea of reciprocity as most ordinary treaties, where the interest of incurring an obligation will very quickly lapse if the other party or parties do not comply with theirs. For example, one would hope that a state would not feel it is no longer bound by the obligation not to torture simply because other states party to the UN Convention against Torture engage in torture. Finally, human rights lawyers think that human rights treaties have a substance that is inherently of a high normative worth, above and beyond states' consent to be bound by them, which relativizes treaties as mechanisms for norm enforcement.

All these differences are crucial, because they have an impact on the way international human rights obligations are understood, administered, and interpreted. To capture what makes human rights different, human rights lawyers have forged the quite unique notion of the 'special character' of human rights obligations. At first, the meaning of 'special character' was unclear. It seemed to be one of those 'catch-all' phrases that merely seemed to imply that ordinary rules of international law did not apply when it came to human rights. However, human rights bodies have refined the idea over the years to reflect what is distinctive about human rights, and the idea now has a quite distinct doctrinal content.

The first reference to the special character of a human rights treaty occurred when the General Assembly sought an advisory opinion from the International Court of Justice

---

[3] ICCPR, Art 2.

(ICJ) on reservations to the Genocide Convention. The Court distinguished between ordinary treaties and those of a humanitarian or human rights character. In the case of the latter:

> [T]he contracting States do not have any interests of their own; they merely have, one and all, a common interest, namely, the accomplishment of those high purposes which are the *raison d'être* of the convention. Consequently, in a convention of this type one cannot speak of individual advantages or disadvantages to States, or of the maintenance of a perfect contractual balance between rights and duties.[4]

The idea was that the Genocide Convention created something greater than the sum of each party's will. Moreover, there was a certain vertical element involved: states were not so much bargaining between each other horizontally, as solemnly committing themselves to a certain supranational standard of behaviour.

A similar approach was taken by the European Commission of Human Rights in 1961, when it affirmed that:

> The obligations undertaken by the High Contracting Parties in the [European] Convention [on Human Rights] are essentially of an objective character, being designed rather to protect the fundamental rights of individual human beings from infringements by any of the High Contracting Parties than to create subjective and reciprocal rights for the High Contracting Parties themselves.[5]

In this context, 'objective' does not mean that the obligations in question are absolute or that they are scientifically proven. Rather, it should be understood in the legal meaning of not strictly dependent on the commitments of other states ('subjective'). Again, the idea is that, despite the appearance of a treaty being concluded with other states, there is something relatively unilateral about states' adherence to a treaty like the European Convention on Human Rights (ECHR). States are better understood as making a solemn promise to the international community, and indeed to individuals within their jurisdiction.

The Inter-American Court of Human Rights has added its own views on the idea of special character. As the Court put it in one of its advisory opinions:

> [M]odern human rights treaties in general, and the American Convention in particular, *are not multilateral treaties of the traditional type concluded to accomplish the reciprocal exchange of rights for the mutual benefit of the contracting States*. Their object and purpose is the protection of the basic rights of individual human beings irrespective of their nationality, both against the State of their nationality and all other contracting States. In concluding these human rights treaties, the States *can be deemed to submit themselves to a legal order within which they, for the common good, assume various obligations, not in relation to other States, but towards all individuals within their jurisdiction*.[6]

Taken to its extreme, the special character of human rights suggests that states' human rights obligations are in some ways independent of their consent to be bound by them. This is also linked to old claims about human rights pre-existing their legal recognition (the idea, for example, that rights exist 'in nature'). States are solemnly committing to something which they were already, at least morally or philosophically, obliged to recognize.

---

[4] *Reservations to the Genocide Convention* (Advisory Opinion) [1951] ICJ Rep 15, para 23.

[5] *Austria v Italy (Pfunders Case)* (1961) 4 YB 116, para 138.

[6] OC-2/82, *The Effect of Reservations on the Entry into Force of the American Convention (Arts 74 and 75)*, IACtHR Series A No 2 (24 September 1982), paras 29–30 (emphases added).

Another way of putting it would be to say that becoming a party to a human rights treaty is *declaratory* of states' obligations rather than *constitutive* of them.[7] Moreover, even once they have come into positive legal existence human rights continue to have a normative life of their own beyond the law.

The objective character of human rights obligations also points, for example, to their *erga omnes* status. The ICJ famously suggested that certain obligations may have an *erga omnes* character in that they are owed 'towards the international community as a whole' so that 'by their very nature, (they) are the concern of all States'.[8] What was a slightly puzzling obiter dictum in the general international law context, has become relatively mainstream in the human rights environment, where it is understood that, precisely as a result of the special character of human rights obligations, each and every state (that is a party to the human rights system) has an interest in their enforcement. Indeed, it could be said that international human rights obligations have become a typical example of *erga omnes* obligations. This, in turn, justifies routine scrutiny by states of the human rights record of others even though they have not directly suffered a prejudice, something that would be unthinkable in general international law.[9]

Another dimension of the 'special character' is the idea that human rights instruments are more like legislative, or even constitutional, norms than the treaties they are embedded in would suggest. The ECHR has been described by the European Court of Human Rights as a 'constitutional instrument of European public order'.[10] The reference to this constitutional character also underlines the extent to which international human rights treaties, perhaps especially regional ones, are part of governance structures and, beyond that, one of the normative foundations of particular political communities (for example, that of the Council of Europe in the case of the ECHR, or the entire international community in the case of the International Covenant on Economic, Social and Cultural Rights (ICESCR) and the International Covenant on Civil and Political Rights (ICCPR)). International human rights thus appear as the cement that binds groups of states together in a collective project that is both domestic and supranational, rather than international in the strict sense of the term.

Although the special nature of human rights obligations might at first appear to be a mere doctrinal construct, what is remarkable is the extent to which concrete consequences have flowed from this idea. In the following sections of this chapter we will see some of the manifestations of the special character of human rights obligations, and the considerable impact it has had on the implementation of human rights.

4 RESERVATIONS

States may modify their obligations under international human rights treaties by entering reservations but in conditions that differ from those normally laid out for general international law. Reservations are a particularly technical area of international law, but the study of this rather dry subject in the context of international human rights law is enlightening. A reservation is defined in Article 2 VCLT as a 'unilateral statement, however phrased or named, made by a State, when signing, ratifying, accepting, approving or acceding to a

---

[7] See Chapter 2.

[8] *Barcelona Traction, Light and Power Company, Limited* (*Belgium v Spain*) (New Application: 1962) [1970] ICJ Rep 3, para 33.

[9] See *Questions Relating to the Obligation to Prosecute or Extradite* (*Belgium v Senegal*) [2012] ICJ Rep, paras 68–69.   [10] *Loizidou v Turkey* (Preliminary Objections) (1995) 20 EHRR 99, para 75.

Treaty, whereby it purports to exclude or to modify the legal effect of certain provisions of the Treaty in their application to that State.' The aim of a reservation is to limit a state's obligations under a particular treaty. International law is not formalistic about what constitutes a reservation: it does not matter whether a state presents it as a 'general political statement' or a 'declaration of interpretation'. If the result is exclusion or modification of the legal effect of certain provisions, it will be considered a reservation.

In the international human rights context, states have availed themselves broadly of the possibility of reservations, both quantitatively and qualitatively. For example, as of May 2017, 51 of the 169 state parties to the ICCPR had, between them, entered more than 100 reservations. A typical reservation is one whereby a state purports to interpret an internationally protected right only in accordance with its domestic, often constitutional or religious, law. For example, the US has entered a reservation to the ICCPR that its obligations under Article 7, regarding the prohibition of torture and other cruel, inhuman, and degrading treatment, are to be interpreted in the light of its constitutional protections of rights.[11] A common reservation from some states has been to the effect that accession to a human rights treaty, such as the Convention on the Elimination of Discrimination against Women (CEDAW), is 'subject to the general reservation that such accession cannot conflict with the laws on personal status derived from Islamic Sharia'.[12]

There are, of course, valid reasons why a state may wish to enter reservations to human rights treaties. A state may generally be committed to human rights but have problems with one particular provision in a treaty, and therefore want to exclude or limit the application of that provision in order to be able to become a party to the instrument. The state may wish to inject a certain cultural understanding of a particular obligation, or guard against an expansive interpretation by international human rights bodies by pre-empting the meaning of a particular provision. States may know in advance that part of their domestic law is incompatible with a provision of a treaty and seek some temporary accommodation. This sort of international legal flexibility is something that human rights lawyers may want to allow, if only to encourage states to ratify treaties.

However, it is clear at the same time that reservations are problematic for international human rights law, perhaps even more so than they are for general international law.[13] Human rights are clearly more of a 'package' than most other international normative instruments. There is a very real tension between the idea of human rights and the notion that a state may, through reservations, 'pick and choose' the obligations by which it wishes to be bound or interpret them as it so wishes, at the risk of emptying some of their content. It is the very universality of human rights and the whole point of international human rights treaties that is threatened if states do not agree to honor the same rights. Moreover, there is a sense that some states may 'free ride' human rights treaties, by obtaining the benefits broadly associated with being a party to them, whilst subscribing only to an eviscerated set of obligations. Finally and crucially, reservations also create problems of legal certainty, making it difficult for individuals to ascertain the exact scope of the rights they have been guaranteed if those have to be scrutinized constantly through the lens of often vague reservations.

---

[11] See US reservations, declarations, and understandings, International Covenant on Civil and Political Rights, 138 Cong Rec S4781–01 (2 April 1992).

[12] Such is the wording of the Libyan reservation to the CEDAW.

[13] The ILC Guide to Practice on Reservations to Treaties suggests a certain wariness of reservations and reflects the evolution of international law towards a relatively narrow concept of permissible reservations. See ILC, Guide to Practice on Reservations to Treaties, 2011.

Accordingly, human rights supervisory bodies have frequently deplored the abundance and scope of reservations, and urged states to repeal them. This is in itself a departure from ordinary international treaties, where few bodies are authorized or would see fit to criticize a practice that is largely seen as within a state's prerogative. In fact, international human rights law has also evolved specific notions of what reservations are permissible, who may decide on their permissibility, and what consequences flow from reservations.

4.1 PERMISSIBILITY

The general regime under Article 19 VCLT is that states may formulate reservations to a treaty, unless a reservation is prohibited by the treaty or, more ambiguously, is incompatible with its object and purpose. Although Article 19 provides 'relevant guidance',[14] and some states have insisted that the general regime of international law is sufficient,[15] human rights bodies have nonetheless developed a quite specific approach to permissible reservations. Most human rights treaties neither allow nor specifically exclude reservations.[16] Therefore, most of the discussion has focused on whether certain reservations are compatible with the 'object and purpose' of the respective treaties.

One of the most important sources of guidance on the issue is the Human Rights Committee's general comment on reservations, General Comment 24, the very existence of which is an indication of how seriously the issue is taken by the UN treaty monitoring bodies. According to the Committee:

> In an instrument which articulates very many civil and political rights, each of the many articles, and indeed their interplay, secures the objectives of the Covenant. *The object and purpose of the Covenant is to create legally binding standards for human rights* by defining certain civil and political rights and placing them in a framework of obligations which are legally binding for those States which ratify; and to provide an efficacious supervisory machinery for the obligations undertaken.[17]

The Human Rights Committee defines the object and purpose of the ICCPR very broadly. Moreover, the sheer interdependence of rights suggests that it will be difficult to make reservations to one right without altering the entire content of the obligations contained in a treaty. The Committee has also specifically identified a number of reservations that it considered would be incompatible per se with the object and purpose of human rights treaties, such as those violating peremptory norms, customary international law, or nonderogable norms.

States may not make reservations relating to certain basic guarantees associated with the rights protected, such as the right to an effective remedy. Defined as 'supportive guarantees,' these provisions are seen to provide 'the necessary framework for securing the rights in the Covenant and are thus essential to its object and purpose.'[18] In fact, they 'are an integral part of the structure of the Covenant and underpin its efficacy' so that to limit them would defeat the purpose of the ICCPR.[19] Finally, states cannot make reservations to institutional arrangements designed to supervise the implementation of treaties. For example, a state cannot become a party to one of the universal human rights treaties and

---

[14] HRC, General Comment 24, HRI/GEN/1/Rev.9 (Vol I) 210, para 6.

[15] eg Observations on General Comment 24 (1996) 3 IHRR 261, para 4.

[16] There are a few exceptions. See Second Optional Protocol to the ICCPR, Art 2(1); ECHR, Art 57.

[17] HRC, General Comment 24, para 7 (emphasis added).

[18] HRC, General Comment 24, para 11.   [19] HRC, General Comment 24, para 11.

make a reservation to the effect that it does not consider itself bound by the obligation to submit periodic reports to its corresponding supervisory body.

This leaves very few areas where reservations to human rights treaties might be valid. The Human Rights Committee does give a few examples that would be considered acceptable, such as a reservation saying that communications can be heard by the Committee only after the entry into force of the ICCPR for the state party, or that communications cannot be examined if they are already being examined by a comparable international procedure. These reservations are procedural rather than substantive in nature. Even assuming a reservation is permitted, the Human Rights Committee has added a number of formal and substantive requirements to the type of reservations that can be made, for example: that they must be 'specific and transparent', cannot be 'general', and must 'refer to a particular provision'. Moreover, states should 'take into consideration the overall effect of a group of reservations', and avoid committing to treaties only to the extent that these conform with their domestic law.[20]

The European Court of Human Rights has also considered invalid a number of reservations that were 'too vague or broad for it to be possible to determine their exact meaning and scope.'[21] In *Loizidou v Turkey*, for example, it found that the 'special character of the Convention as an instrument of European public order' meant that Turkey's attempt to exclude the application of the ECHR to Northern Cyprus by a reservation was invalid.[22]

The grounds for such limitations to the ability to make reservations are easily understandable. International human rights bodies have sought to protect international treaties from crippling reservations that lead to 'a perpetual non-attainment of international human rights standards'[23] and protect beneficiaries from uncertainty about the exact scope of their rights. Thus, the use of reservations is tightly constrained by numerous rules which suggest that the object and purpose of the human rights treaty would be defeated by selective assumption of human rights obligations.

4.2 RESPONSIBILITY FOR ASSESSMENT

In a typical international law scenario, the invalidity of reservations will be raised by other states parties which presumably have an interest in doing so. However, one can see how the dependence on state objections to reservations is problematic for the protection of human rights. In the human rights context, states might be less likely to object to other states' reservations, for the simple reason that generally they are not impacted by them. States have occasionally manifested their rejection of other states' reservations, but this is a haphazard process. In fact, as the Human Rights Committee has pointed out, the pattern is so unclear that it is not safe to assume that a non-objecting state thinks that a particular reservation is acceptable.[24]

These key differences have led the Human Rights Committee to opine that 'the operation of the classic rules on reservations is inadequate for the [ICCPR]'.[25] Consequently, a new rule has emerged in the human rights treaty context whereby a purely consensual approach to reservations (reservations are accepted or not) has been replaced by an increasingly axiological one (reservations are valid or not). States are asked to act as the guardians of the integrity of human rights treaties and judge whether reservations are valid, rather than simply be the keepers of their own national interest. Moreover, human rights bodies, whether judicial or supervisory organs, have seen themselves as the defenders of the *ordre*

---

[20] HRC. General Comment 24, para 19.   [21] *Belilos v Switzerland* (1988) 10 EHRR 466, para 55.
[22] *Loizidou v Turkey* (1997) 23 EHRR 513, para 43.   [23] HRC, General Comment 24, para 19.
[24] HRC, General Comment 24, para 17.   [25] HRC, General Comment 24, para 17.

public of international human rights law and raised issues of invalid reservations before actual disputes arise. The particular interest that the international community has in the integrity of human rights treaties necessitates that reservations fall under a strong system of international supervision.

4.3 CONSEQUENCES

The consequences that flow from reservations are complex, particularly if reservations turn out to be invalid. This matter raises different problems for the treaty itself, the reserving state, and third states. There is a fundamental tension between, on the one hand, the desire to have as many states as possible ratify a treaty, thereby allowing it to enter into force as quickly as possible and in relation to as many parties as possible and, on the other hand, the risk of a treaty's integrity being compromised by too many reservations.

As regards the effects of reservations on the entire treaty, Article 20(2) VCLT provides that only where 'it appears from the limited number of the negotiating States and the object and purpose of a treaty that the application of the treaty in its entirety between all the parties is an essential condition of the consent of each one to be bound by the treaty' do all state parties to a treaty need to accept a reservation. This would be typical of treaties between very few parties. However, international human rights treaties are the exact opposite, since they are intended to become universal. Therefore, reservations do not have to be accepted by all states for a human rights treaty to enter into force. This explains why so many human rights treaties have entered into force despite considerable numbers of reservations.

The second question is what happens to reserving states. Under general international law, the position is that the reserving state becomes bound by the treaty if at least one other state accepts the reservation.[26] However, in the context of treaties of a humanitarian or human rights character, the ICJ has held that states can in fact become party to a treaty even if other state parties object to its reservation:

> The object and purpose of the Genocide Convention imply that it was the intention of the General Assembly and of the States which adopted it that as many States as possible should participate. The complete exclusion from the Convention of one or more States would not only restrict the scope of its application but would detract from the authority of the moral and humanitarian principles which are its basis. It is inconceivable that the contracting parties readily contemplated that an objection to a minor reservation should produce such a result.[27]

Not only is there an interest in states being bound as soon as possible notwithstanding the reservations of a few, but the specific nature of human rights treaties suggests that approval by other parties should really be seen as a secondary matter. This was further clarified by the Inter-American Court of Human Rights. The Inter-American Commission asked the Court for an advisory opinion on whether the American Convention on Human Rights (ACHR) would enter into force as soon as the requisite number of states had ratified it, or whether ratifications accompanied by reservations should be considered complete only when at least one state had accepted them (or, as the VCLT stipulates, all states parties had failed to object to them within a year of the ratification).[28] The Inter-American Court found that because of the special character of the ACHR as 'a multilateral legal instrument or framework enabling States to make binding unilateral commitments not to violate the human rights of individuals within their jurisdiction', it would enter into force regardless

---

[26] VCLT, Art 20(4)(c).   [27] *Reservations to the Genocide Convention*, para 24.
[28] VCLT, Art 20(4)(c).

of whether any other state accepted reservations appended to an instrument of ratification as 'no useful purpose would be served by such a delay'.[29] In other words, states became bound the moment they deposited their instrument of ratification, notwithstanding the fact that their reservations were not accepted and might even be invalid. This again underlines the strictly non-relational character of human rights treaties.

One of the problems created by this approach is that the actual validity of reservations will only be examined at a later date. This can create complex issues of retroactive application when a reservation turns out to have been invalid all along. A state that has ratified a treaty with a reservation may insist that it ratified the treaty only on the basis of such a reservation and that if the latter is then found to be invalid, it is either not bound by the provision to which the reservation relates or not bound by the treaty at all. The opposite stance is that invalid reservations are 'severable' from the commitment to be bound by a treaty so that the reservation can be 'quarantined' and the overall commitment to the treaty preserved.

This last proposition was illustrated in the *Loizidou* case. The European Court of Human Rights held that Turkey's reservation excluding its activities in Northern Cyprus from the supervision of the European Court was invalid. The Court was then required to ascertain whether Turkey's broader recognition of jurisdiction was nonetheless valid. Under normal international law rules, the tendency would be to consider that the whole consent to the treaty had been contaminated by the invalidity of the reservation. Against Turkey's arguments, however, the Court considered that the reservation could be severed from the recognition of jurisdiction, so that Turkey would still be considered to have accepted the compulsory jurisdiction of the European Court. This was all the more so since, the Court argued, Turkey must have known at the time that its reservation was invalid, especially in view of protests by several state parties.[30]

Finally, the situation of a state accepting another's reservation is perhaps the simplest. Under general international law, a state that agrees to another state's reservation is bound in its relations with the other state by that reservation.[31] However, that is not a very helpful way of thinking about human rights treaties, for which it should not make a difference to states' commitment to individuals within their jurisdiction whether other states have accepted their reservations. In particular, the fact that a state accepts another state's invalid reservation certainly does not make that reservation applicable between them. Similarly, a state that objects to another state's reservation, even on grounds of invalidity, cannot draw on this to then claim that it is not bound in its relations with the other state by the relevant provision, or that it is not bound at all by the relevant provision, or that it is not bound by the treaty at all. It should again make no difference for the entry into force of a human rights treaty that a state is objecting to a reservation, precisely because such a reservation cannot in any significant way be said to affect the interests of that state as they are normally understood in treaty law. For example, the UK could not say that it is not bound by the ECHR or its recognition of the European Court's jurisdiction simply because it objects to Turkey having limited its jurisdiction to its continental territory.

One can see from such examples how the application of normal principles of international law to human rights treaties is almost nonsensical. As the Human Rights Committee put it:

> Human rights treaties, and the [ICCPR] specifically, are not a web of inter-State exchanges of mutual obligations. They concern the endowment of individuals with rights. The principle of inter-State reciprocity has no place.[32]

---

[29] *Effect of Reservations*, para 33.   [30] *Loizidou*, para 96.
[31] VCLT, Art 20(4)(b).   [32] HRC, General Comment 24, para 17.

Therefore, a state is not and ought not to be released from its general obligation to abide by the relevant human rights treaties, merely because it disapproves of a reservation made by another state.

5 IMPLEMENTATION OF HUMAN RIGHTS OBLIGATIONS

Typically, under traditional international law, the manner in which an obligation is supposed to be discharged is not specified. States simply have to do what they commit themselves to do, and considerable discretion is left as to the means by which they do so. When it comes to human rights, this traditional *laissez-faire* approach will not do because of the broad and comprehensive character of the obligations involved and the need to make them meaningful for the human beings that stand to benefit from their implementation. International human rights law has thus come up with a complex concept of how obligations are to be discharged and a new vocabulary of obligations has emerged. Typically, states are supposed to 'respect and ensure rights to all individuals'.[33] This is a very broad obligation and in practice the UN human rights treaty bodies have adopted a more specific tripartite typology of how human rights obligations should be secured. According to that typology, states must 'respect', 'protect', and 'fulfil' human rights.

5.1 RESPECT

The duty to secure human rights is, perhaps first and foremost, a duty to 'respect' human rights. Thus, states have a negative obligation not to take any measures that result in a violation of a given right. They should not deliberately violate rights, either through their organs (for example, parliament or the executive) or through their agents (such as civil servants, the police, or the army). This obligation not to interfere with rights is perhaps the most classical one.

5.2 PROTECT

In addition, and this notion is becoming ever more important, states must 'protect' individuals from human rights violations.[34] This means that the state needs to proactively ensure that persons within its jurisdiction do not suffer from human rights violations at the hands of third parties or even broad phenomena such as preventable environmental catastrophes. This is much more akin to creating an environment in which rights are enjoyed. Of course, the state does not become liable for every adverse interference with individuals' rights by private actors. However, the state *is* liable for those failures that can be traced to its shortcomings in protecting individuals from others, for example because it has adopted a law that made the violation possible, or because it has failed to do something

---

[33] eg ICCPR, Art 2.

[34] This specific doctrinal meaning of the obligation to protect is very different and quite unrelated to the idea of the 'Responsibility to Protect', which has become quite popular in international circles, and which deals with state and international community responsibility to avert atrocities.

that would have prevented the violation from happening.[35] This is known as the indirect horizontal effect of human rights. States have been found liable for failing to protect demonstrators from third parties,[36] for failing to protect an individual from murder despite the fact that the police knew the victim's life had been threatened,[37] and, in cases of domestic violence, for failing to provide adequate structures or legal protection to abused women.[38] As the Inter-American Court of Human Rights put it in the landmark case of *Velásquez Rodríguez v Honduras*, which involved the forced disappearance by unidentified abductors of a student activist:

> An illegal act which violates human rights and which is initially not directly imputable to a State (for example, because it is the act of a private person or because the person responsible has not been identified) can lead to international responsibility of the State, not because of the act itself, but because of the lack of due diligence to prevent the violation or to respond to it as required by the [American] Convention. . . . [The state is liable when it] allows private persons or groups to act freely and with impunity to the detriment of the rights recognized by the Convention.[39]

The obligation to protect has been particularly instrumental in connecting states to violations of the rights of women. Violations that occur *a priori* in the private sphere (and were as a result traditionally neglected by human rights law) have thus been linked to the public sphere and state shortcomings.[40]

5.3 FULFIL

The obligation to 'respect' human rights is primarily a negative one (to not actively violate rights). Treaty bodies, however, have also long emphasized the existence of an obligation to 'fulfil' human rights, by which it is understood that states should take positive steps that have as a consequence the greater enjoyment of rights. Some civil and political rights, such as the right to vote, are meaningless if the state does nothing to implement them. Similarly, the right to be free from torture entails not only an obligation not to torture but also an obligation to adopt all types of concrete measures to prevent and sanction torture (for example, training of police or prison officers, rules on the non-admissibility of evidence obtained under torture, and so on).[41]

In formal terms, the obligation to fulfil involves an obligation on states to adopt appropriate laws that implement their international undertakings. This may involve incorporating the very rights protected by the international instrument into domestic law. However, treaty bodies, confronted with claims by states that rights were effectively protected simply because they were formally incorporated in the constitution, have insisted that the duty to secure human rights includes an obligation to adopt, not just legislative measures, but also 'judicial, administrative and educative and other appropriate measures',[42] and an obligation to organize the structure of the state apparatus in a way that ensures the full exercise of human rights.

---

[35] eg *X and Y v The Netherlands* (1986) 8 EHRR 235; *Young, James and Webster v UK* (1982) 4 EHRR 38. See also Chapter 6.   [36] *Plattform 'Ärzte für das Leben' v Austria* (1991) 13 EHRR 204.
[37] *Osman v UK* (2000) 29 EHRR 245; *William Eduardo Delgado Páez v Colombia*, CCPR/C/39/D/195/1985 (12 July 1990).   [38] *AT v Hungary* A/60/38 (Part I) Annex III (26 January 2005).
[39] *Velásquez Rodríguez v Honduras* (*Merits*), IACtHR Series C No 4 (29 July 1988), paras 172 and 176.
[40] See Chapter 16.   [41] See Chapter 9.
[42] HRC, General Comment 33, HRI/GEN/1/Rev.9 (Vol I) 243, para 7.

In particular, the obligation to fulfil entails provision of a remedy, whether judicial or administrative, to all victims of human rights violations. In the *Velásquez Rodríguez* case, the Inter-American Court of Human Rights insisted that:

> The State is obligated to investigate every situation involving a violation of the rights protected by the Convention. If the State apparatus acts in such a way that the violation goes unpunished and the victim's full enjoyment of such rights is not restored as soon as possible, the State has failed to comply with its duty to ensure the free and full exercise of those rights to the persons within its jurisdiction.[43]

Economic and social rights are the prime example of rights which entail a positive obligation to adopt specific measures and where 'not doing anything' is not an option. The obligation to fulfil has been understood in the context of the right to food as entailing both an obligation to *facilitate* individuals' ability to access resources and means to ensure their livelihood and a subsidiary obligation to *provide* them with adequate food whenever they are unable to enjoy the right to food 'for reasons beyond their control'.[44] At its most general, the obligation to fulfil is considered also to involve an obligation to *promote* human rights, which means that states should adopt policies that promote rights both domestically (for example, human rights education) and internationally (such as a foreign policy conducive to human rights).

In practice, the obligations to 'respect', 'protect', and 'fulfil' are closely interrelated and it may not always be easy to make a clear-cut distinction between these different facets of the overall obligation to comply with one's human rights obligations. Nevertheless, the typology is a helpful conceptual device to identify the various ways in which states can and must discharge their obligations that are specific to international human rights law.

6 VARYING DEGREES OF HUMAN RIGHTS OBLIGATIONS

Despite what is sometimes suggested, the vast majority of human rights are not absolute in the sense that they can never be limited. One of the only absolute rights is the right to be free from torture, which is absolute in the sense that no social goal or emergency can ever limit the categorical prohibition of torture. For the rest, there are two ways in which human rights can be limited. First, some treaty provisions explicitly provide circumstances in which the enjoyment of a right may be limited. These are known as limitations. Second, the acceptance of such limitations may in some human rights frameworks incorporate an element of pluralism and 'margin of appreciation.' Third, states have the possibility of derogating from some of their obligations in a time of emergency justifying exceptional measures.

6.1 LIMITATIONS

Although human rights stipulate certain forms of minimum treatment, the nature of this minimum treatment will vary somewhat. This is especially the case when human rights do not operate in an 'either/or' fashion (to be tortured or not to be tortured), but where the question is the scope of a right (for example, the degree of privacy to which one is entitled).

---

[43] *Velásquez Rodríguez*, para 176.
[44] CESCR, General Comment 12, HRI/GEN/1/Rev.9 (Vol I) 55, para 15.

Human rights obligations inevitably raise tensions between individual and social imperatives. To take an easy example, an individual who is imprisoned for having committed a crime following a fair trial cannot invoke a violation of his or her right not to be detained. It is understood that the right to liberty is limited by the exigencies of public order, as manifested through the operation of the criminal law. Moreover, it is primarily for the state to define the framework of collective life that constrains certain rights, in ways that other states will have little cause to complain about (unlike a normal international treaty situation based on exact reciprocity).

Limitations do not grant states the ability to abuse rights; they simply define the actual scope of rights. Rights are limited in a number of ways. Sometimes, because a right is crucial—and rights relating to integrity and security of the person are often considered to be—permitted limitations will be spelled out in detail. This is the case for the right to life (which is limited by the possibility of imposing the death penalty in some cases, killings in armed conflict situations, and the use of reasonable force by law enforcement agents)[45] or the right to liberty (which is limited by, for example, the possibility of being sentenced to imprisonment for a criminal offence, pursuant to a fair trial).[46]

Some instruments contain a general limitation clause. The Universal Declaration of Human Rights (UDHR), for example, proclaims that:

> In the exercise of his rights and freedoms, everyone shall be subject only to such limitations as are determined by law solely for the purpose of securing due recognition and respect for the rights and freedoms of others and of meeting the just requirements of morality, public order and the general welfare in a democratic society.[47]

A similar formulation is used for specific provisions of the ICCPR. For example, Article 12(3) ICCPR provides limitations to the right to liberty of movement, providing that the right 'shall not be subject to any restrictions except those which are provided by law, are necessary to protect national security, public order (*ordre public*), public health or morals or the rights and freedoms of others, and are consistent with the other rights recognized in the Covenant'.[48] The possibility of such limitations has been confirmed by international and domestic case law, but is typically subject to a tripartite test that ensures that the limitations are in conformity with human rights. Thus, limitations to rights have to be justified by the fact that they (1) are prescribed by law, (2) pursue a legitimate aim, and (3) are necessary in a democratic society.

6.1.1 Prescribed by law

The requirement that limitations be prescribed by law has been understood by the Inter-American Court to mean that they must be based on laws as instruments adopted by parliament, not merely that they are 'part of the Law'.[49] Given that limitations are those 'necessary in a democratic society', it is logical that they should be adopted by a legislative body rather than, for example, the executive. Nonetheless, it is accepted in the European context that the common law, for example, can constitute a sufficient basis for a rights limitation. What seems to matter is that limitations should either be democratically adopted or have a certain historical pedigree. The requirement that limitations be

---

[45] See Chapter 9.   [46] See Chapter 13.   [47] UDHR, Art 29(2).

[48] See also ICCPR, Art 19 (freedom of expression), Art 21 (peaceful assembly), and Art 22 (freedom of association).

[49] OC-6/86, *The Word 'Laws' in Article 30 of the American Convention on Human Rights*, IACtHR Series A No 6 (9 May 1986).

stipulated in law also guarantees a certain foreseeability of the law and the rights protected. The law should be:

> adequately accessible: the citizen must be able to have an indication that is adequate in the circumstances of the legal rules applicable to a given case. Secondly, a norm cannot be regarded as a 'law' unless it is it is formulated with sufficient precision to enable the citizen to regulate his conduct: he must be able—if need be with appropriate advice—to foresee, to a degree that is reasonable in the circumstances, the consequences which a given action may entail.[50]

Unfettered executive discretion, even if granted by the law, would not satisfy this requirement.[51]

6.1.2 Legitimate aim

According to the European Court of Human Rights, a legitimate aim must be a 'pressing social need'.[52] A state cannot overturn human rights simply for idiosyncratic policy preferences that are not themselves for the benefit of rights. Typically, pressing social needs are identified by human rights treaties themselves as grounds for limitations of rights that are prima facie valid. For example, the ICCPR mentions 'national security, public order (*ordre public*), public health or morals or the rights and freedoms of others'. These are then expanded through interpretation by human rights bodies. The protection of democracy, pluralism, or secularism have all been presented at various times as being legitimate goals. It is interesting that human rights law, which is often recognized as being against the state, is also very much about legitimizing a certain state role.

6.1.3 Necessary in a democratic society

The limitation has to be 'necessary'. It does not suffice simply to allege a desirable social policy and then adopt a measure that is in fact not truly connected to that goal. Many laws that criminalized homosexuality, for example, which were presented as in pursuance of the legitimate aim of maintaining public morals, were struck down because they were not related to that goal at all, especially since they stigmatized homosexuality in the private sphere.[53]

The necessity test also implies that the relevant measure must be proportionate to the goal sought. Proportionality involves a delicate equation evaluating the importance of the social aim, the importance of the right guaranteed, and the degree of encroachment. Certain rights are very inelastic to even the most important social goals. Others will be more responsive to limitations. For example, the right to freedom of assembly will be quite sensitive to states' invocation of public order or the need to protect the rights of others.

The onus to prove any limb of the test is typically on states, which cannot simply claim that they 'know better'. But by what standard are such limitations to be judged? After all, what is necessary for some might be seen as perfectly abusive by others. Several human rights instruments suggest that the key threshold is that of a 'democratic society'. In other words, limitations are justified on all the grounds that have just been introduced, if they conform to what would be considered necessary in a 'democratic society'. This is certainly a standard that can be criticized as vague (not to mention one that raises the problem of tensions between democracy and human rights), but at least such limitation clauses acknowledge that human rights are not simply about upholding absolutes but very often

---

[50] *Sunday Times v UK* (1979–80) 2 EHRR 245, para 49.
[51] *Hasan v Bulgaria* (2000) 24 EHRR 55.
[52] *Handyside v UK* (1979–80) 1 EHRR 737, para 48.
[53] *Dudgeon v UK* (1981) 4 EHRR 149.

about the complex exercise of balancing individual rights against legitimate social priorities. Human rights should be taken seriously, but the emphasis is on state justification, transparency, and accountability, in circumstances in which states may otherwise gladly invoke the priority of politics over rights.

6.2 THE MARGIN OF APPRECIATION

Whereas general international law obligations are typically not susceptible to fine-tuning by states, international human rights law has been at the forefront of efforts to develop a geographically and culturally plural notion of implementation. Although not uncontroversial, this is probably because in practice the implementation of human rights obligations requires significant adaptation to the historical, political, social, and cultural specificities of particular states. Particularly in the European context, there is no expectation of absolute uniform implementation. Instead, a certain minimum standard is to be achieved, whilst respecting the cultural, legal, and political specificity of each state. This is what the European Court of Human Rights describes as states having a 'margin of appreciation' in how they implement their obligations. As the European Court put it:

> the main purpose of the Convention is 'to lay down certain international standards to be observed by the Contracting States in their relations with persons under their jurisdiction'. This does not mean that absolute uniformity is required and, indeed, since the Contracting States remain free to choose the measures which they consider appropriate, the Court cannot be oblivious of the substantive or procedural features of their respective domestic laws.[54]

This is often related to the jurisdictional notion that 'the machinery of protection established by the Convention is subsidiary to the national systems safeguarding human rights'.[55] The European Court views the margin as 'go(ing) . . . hand in hand with a European supervision'.[56]

One rationale for the margin of appreciation is that states and domestic courts are better suited to assess local peculiarities, and that there is simply too much uncertainty about how human rights are to be implemented in practice for international supervision to exercise more than relatively minimal control. Issues of legitimacy also arise, as international bodies might provoke political backlash if they delve too deeply in matters that are seen as culturally specific.

Margin of appreciation reasoning has featured prominently in cases involving sexual minorities[57] and the place of religion in society,[58] to mention only some examples. The margin of appreciation involves an assessment of the degree of consensus (a minimum common denominator) about a certain practice across member states. In the absence of such consensus and, more importantly, in the presence of significant divisions, the European Court will hesitate to impose on a minority (let alone a majority) of states a particular understanding of rights. It is important to note that whether there is a margin of appreciation for a particular issue is something that can evolve over time. For example, states parties to the ECHR may have had a certain margin of appreciation 60 years ago when it came to criminalizing homosexuality, but the very same treaty is interpreted

---

[54] *Sunday Times*, para 61.   [55] *'Belgian Linguistics' Case* (1979–80) 1 EHRR 241.
[56] *Kjeldsen, Busk Madsen and Pedersen v Denmark* (1979–80) 1 EHRR 711, para 49.
[57] *Dudgeon; Frette v France* (2004) 38 EHRR 21; *Goodwin v UK* (2002) 35 EHRR 18.
[58] *Otto-Preminger-Institut v Austria* (1995) 19 EHRR 34; *Wingrove v UK* (1997) 24 EHRR 1, para 57; *'The Last Temptation of Christ' v Chile* (*Olmedo Bustos et al.*), IACtHR Series C No 73 (5 February 2001), para 64.

radically differently today given changes in the European consensus on the issue, so that criminalizing same-sex relations between consenting adults is now evidently a violation of several rights.

The idea of the margin of appreciation is not universally accepted beyond the European context. It has been criticized as leading to an excessively relativistic application of human rights that may even contain the seeds of the project's dissolution. The Human Rights Committee, in particular, has expressed skepticism about the notion.[59] Others, however, see it as an essential element of flexibility, adaptability, and pluralism among states that share a common goal but remain quite different in their approach as to how best implement it.[60]

6.3 DEROGATIONS

The law of state responsibility in general international law traditionally contemplates that a defence of necessity is available to states in limited circumstances precluding wrongfulness. However, international human rights treaties often have their own regime to deal with states of exception, known as the 'derogation' regime, which better takes into account the special character of human rights obligations.[61] Essentially, states are permitted to suspend some of their obligations under human rights treaties if a state of emergency requires them to do so. The consequence of recognizing states' power to derogate from human rights treaties in times of emergency is an increased regulation and supervision of such derogations by international organs. The regime applicable in situations of emergency is typically more constraining than for ordinary international law obligations.

First, a situation of public emergency under international human rights law needs to exist. It must be declared in advance, and its existence (and abrogation) notified to relevant international authorities (for example, the Secretary-General of the UN as the depository of the ICCPR and ICESCR).[62] A situation of public emergency can only be invoked where there exists a threat to 'the life of the nation' itself. This is clearly a high threshold, and such a threat cannot be inferred from 'every disturbance or catastrophe'. Not even an armed conflict will automatically justify the recognition of a public emergency.[63]

The European Court of Human Rights, for example, has described a public emergency under Article 15 ECHR as 'an exceptional situation of crisis or emergency which affects the whole population and constitutes a threat to the organized life of the community of which the State is composed.'[64] Adjudicators will look, as they did when the UK invoked a situation of public emergency following the attacks of 11 September 2001, at whether other similarly situated states deemed it necessary to invoke a situation of emergency. However, they often place much weight on the determinations of national governments who are the 'guardian of their own people's safety'.[65]

Second, the public emergency should be invoked only insofar and for as long as is strictly necessary to return to a situation of normalcy. Indeed, 'the restoration of a state of

---

[59] See HRC, General Comment 34, CCPR/C/GC/34 (12 September 2011), para 36.

[60] McGoldrick, 'A Defence of the Margin of Appreciation and An Argument for its Application by the Human Rights Committee' (2015) 65 *ICLQ* 21.

[61] eg ICCPR, Art 4; ECHR, Art 15; ACHR, Art 27. The ACHPR does not have a derogation regime. Other human rights treaties, such as UNCAT or CPED, do not have a derogation regime, but this is because they protect non-derogable rights.   [62] *Cyprus v Turkey* (1982) 4 EHRR 482, para 526.

[63] HRC, General Comment 29, HRI/GEN/1/Rev.9 (Vol I) 234, para 3.

[64] *Lawless v Ireland* (1979–80) 1 EHRR 15, para 28.

[65] *A and others v UK* (2009) 49 EHRR 29, para 180.

normalcy where full respect for the [ICCPR] can again be secured must be the predominant objective of a State party derogating from the Covenant'.[66] In other words, human rights can be suspended only in order for the state to be able to guarantee them as soon as the danger has passed, not to achieve something that is in itself alien to human rights. Derogations should specify their territorial[67] and temporal[68] reach, and can only be of an exceptional and temporary nature. A standard provision in several international human rights treaties, for example, is that emergencies should only be proclaimed 'to the extent strictly required by the exigencies of the situation'.

Third, situations of national emergency can only be invoked to suspend (at best) a limited set of so-called 'derogable' rights. For example, it may be legitimate for a state confronting an armed conflict or a major natural catastrophe to suspend the right to freedom of assembly or the right to vote. Conversely, there are a number of 'non-derogable' rights that can never be suspended. The list varies slightly from treaty to treaty, but the ICCPR mentions the following provisions: Articles 6 (life), 7 (torture), 8(1) and (2) (slavery), 11 (imprisonment for failure to fulfil a contractual obligation), 15 (*nullum crimen sine lege*), 16 (recognition as a person under the law), and 18 (freedom of thought, conscience, and religion). Derogation measures, furthermore, should not be inconsistent with states' other obligations under international law and should not involve discrimination solely on the ground of race, colour, sex, language, religion, or social origin. The former means that states cannot use derogations, for example, to violate international humanitarian law or commit crimes against humanity. Even in situations of emergency, moreover, states are to provide remedies, particularly judicial guarantees, to individuals whose rights may have been violated.

This intense regulation of situations of emergency is designed to ensure that exceptional situations are not maintained indefinitely, which can have a catastrophic impact on rights. The Human Rights Committee, for example, has frequently deplored that some states have been operating under states of emergency for decades, leading to situations in which rights can be easily trampled.[69]

7 REMEDIES FOR VIOLATIONS OF HUMAN RIGHTS OBLIGATIONS

A typical way in which international law obligations are enforced, traditionally, is through termination, suspension,[70] or even, under customary international law, counter-measures (that is, measures that would be otherwise unlawful) by the party that considers that it has suffered from an internationally wrongful act. This is appropriate in an inter-state world in which the dominant model is contractual and where states are really only bound to the extent that other parties respect their 'side of the bargain'. It is also a consequence of the fact that quite often enforcement bodies will not be available, so that each state has

---

[66] HRC, General Comment 29, para 1.

[67] eg As the European Court recognized in *Sakik and others v Turkey* (1998) 26 EHRR 662, the fact that Turkey had declared a state of emergency in Kurdistan did not mean that it was therefore in a similar state of exception in Northern Cyprus.

[68] This is particularly important in light of the tendency of states of emergency to prolong themselves far beyond what is strictly necessary. 'Sunset clauses', eg, should indicate the exact date or the occurrence of the event which will bring an end to the public emergency.

[69] eg HRC, Comments on Egypt, CCPR/C/79/Add.23 (1993).

[70] The possibility is anticipated by VCLT, Art 60.

to decide for itself whether obligations owed to it have been violated and whether one of these remedies is justified. This is what is sometimes known as the 'decentralized' enforcement of international law.

This is, of course, always problematic under classical international law, but it is arguably even more so when it comes to international human rights obligations. In fact, quite strikingly, Article 60 VCLT, which provides for the possibility of termination or suspension of a treaty, is said not to be applicable 'to provisions relating to the protection of the human person contained in treaties of a humanitarian character, in particular to provisions prohibiting any form of reprisals against persons protected by such treaties'.[71]

The idea is simple enough: whereas under general international law it is reasonable that a violating state suffer the consequences of its unwillingness or inability to respect its obligations, the same cannot be said if it is breaching its human rights obligations, which are not primarily secured for the benefit of other states. Several scenarios are conceivable. For example, in a context where state A violates the human rights of citizens of state B on its territory, one can imagine in theory that state B could cease to honour its human rights obligations vis-à-vis the citizens of state A. However, this would clearly run against the object and purpose of human rights treaties, the obligations of which are not primarily owed to other states parties.

Even more nonsensical is the possibility that state B would cease to respect its international human rights obligations vis-à-vis its own nationals as a counter-measure to state A not respecting its own obligations vis-à-vis persons within its jurisdiction. This would result in the state essentially punishing persons within its jurisdiction, and would have no effect on the offender state. It would be absurd from a human rights point of view.

Non-execution is thus clearly not an adequate remedy in the case of human rights violations. Because human rights obligations are primarily incurred by states vis-à-vis persons within their jurisdiction, the inter-state element in human rights enforcement has tended to recede.[72] Nevertheless, inter-state procedures do exist in the international human rights context and are sometimes used. In theory, nothing prevents states from bringing cases before the ICJ for violations of various international human rights instruments. They have certainly done so in relation to the Genocide Convention in the *Bosnia Genocide* case;[73] or the Convention on the Elimination of Racial Discrimination in the cases of *Georgia v Russia*[74] and *Ukraine v Russia*[75] or sometimes indirectly as in the cases brought by Germany and Mexico against the US concerning foreign nationals who had been sentenced to capital punishment following violations of the Vienna Convention on Consular Relations on the part of the US.[76] Several human rights instruments specifically envisage inter-state procedures, whether before regional courts or treaty bodies.[77]

Inter-state procedures provide evidence of the communal interest in the enforcement of a human rights guarantee. For example, the notion of *locus standi* (that is, standing to appear before a court or tribunal) has been adapted to fit the concerns of international

---

[71] VCLT, Art 60(5).   [72] See Chapters 19–23 for a detailed discussion.

[73] *Application of the Convention on the Prevention and Punishment of the Crime of Genocide (Bosnia and Herzegovina v Serbia and Montenegro)* [2007] ICJ Rep 43.

[74] *Application of the International Convention on the Elimination of All Forms of Racial Discrimination (Georgia v Russian Federation)* [2011] ICJ Rep 70.

[75] *Application of the International Convention for the Suppression of the Financing of Terrorism and of the International Convention on the Elimination of All Forms of Racial Discrimination (Ukraine v Russian Federation) (Request for the Indication of Provisional Measures: Order)* [2017] ICJ Rep.

[76] *Case Concerning the Vienna Convention on Consular Relations (Germany v United States of America) (Request for the Indication of Provisional Measures: Order)* [1999] ICJ Rep 9; *Avena and other Mexican Nationals (Mexico v United States of America)* [2004] ICJ Rep 12.   [77] eg ACHR, Art 44; ECHR, Art 24.

human rights law. Under traditional international law, the only subjects able to invoke a breach of an obligation are those that are directly its beneficiaries and, therefore, directly affected by its breach. Third parties do not normally have a general interest in the law's enforcement such that they could bring a sort of *actio popularis*. The ICJ famously considered that Liberia and Ethiopia did not have standing in the *South-West Africa* case to complain about violations of South Africa's trusteeship obligations in that territory because they could not adduce a violation of a specific interest.[78] However, because of the largely *erga omnes* character of human rights obligations, it seems that a third state *can* bring a case against a violating state even if none of its nationals were affected. It is assumed that states parties to human rights treaties are affected by a human rights violation committed by any state, even if it is against its own citizens.

This *erga omnes* nature of human rights obligations, incidentally, has implications not only for formal inter-state mechanisms but more generally for human rights foreign policy. By making human rights (regardless of where they may be violated) a matter of concern for all, the law profoundly redefines the notion of sovereignty and what constitutes the internal affairs of states. Normatively this should make it more difficult for states to claim that other states that criticize their human rights record are meddling in their internal affairs (although in practice and politically, of course, it may not be that difficult to make such claims).

However, it should be said that resort to inter-state human rights procedures has in practice been very much the exception. There have been fewer than two dozen inter-state procedures before the European Commission and Court of Human Rights, while no inter-state dispute regarding a violation of a human rights treaty obligation has been referred to a UN treaty body.

Instead, a number of important, innovative, *sui generis* mechanisms for enforcement have been pioneered in the international human rights field that emphasize the role of supranational institutions and jurisdictions. First are various mechanisms through which states are required to provide periodic reports to international committees, outlining how they have complied with their treaty obligations. These mechanisms are described in more detail in Chapters 19–23, but it is interesting to note here that they create a situation where states, in contrast to the tradition in international law, have to report on their behaviour even if there has been no dispute or litigation. This undeniably reflects the higher interest in preventing violations of human rights, rather than simply adjudicating upon them. Second, and this must surely count as international human rights' greatest innovation in terms of enforcement, many instruments create a right of petition for individuals before international bodies (or at least the possibility of such a right if it is recognized by state parties). This is inconceivable in the inter-state context where the possibility of individuals, or even significant non-state actors, intervening before the ICJ, for example, is never seriously entertained. There are relatively stringent conditions to appearing directly before international human rights bodies, but it is a remarkable characteristic of international human rights law that under certain conditions it allows individuals to directly sue their state at the international level.

8 WITHDRAWAL

In international law, withdrawal from a treaty under certain conditions is always an option, and is generally known as the possibility of 'denouncing' a treaty. This is consonant with the fact that general international law is not particularly concerned with the substantive content of obligations and, therefore, sees withdrawing from a particular set of obligations

---

[78] *South-West Africa Cases (Ethiopia v South Africa; Liberia v South Africa)* (Second Phase) [1966] ICJ Rep 6.

as not raising fundamental issues of principle. The situation is more complicated when it comes to human rights treaties. Withdrawals can have the effect of leaving populations legally vulnerable to violations, especially since supervisory machinery is often attached to substantive human rights commitments. The position of international human rights law on this matter is not entirely settled, but there appear to be two possibilities, depending on whether denunciation is explicitly anticipated by the relevant treaty.

Some international human rights instruments contain denunciation clauses. For example, Article 21 of the Convention on the Elimination of Racial Discrimination provides that '[a] State Party may denounce this Convention by written notification to the Secretary-General of the United Nations'. Similarly, the ECHR[79] and ACHR[80] also include denunciation clauses. It should be noted, nonetheless, that despite the existence of such provisions, straightforward withdrawal is quite unlikely.

Even though a state may do so for other alleged reasons, withdrawal from a human rights treaty is likely to be seen as an admission that a state is up to no good. At the time of writing, only three states have availed themselves successfully of the possibility of denouncing a human rights treaty, namely Greece, which denounced the ECHR from 1969 to 1974 following a military coup, Trinidad and Tobago, which denounced both the Optional Protocol to the ICCPR and the IACHR from 1998 to 1999 as a result of wanting to proceed in the execution of the death penalty without the oversight of the Inter-American Commission, and Venezuela which denounced the IACHR in 2013.

In none of these cases did the denunciations have retroactive effect and, therefore, these states could not escape liability for violations committed prior to withdrawal. Ironically, Venezuela's withdrawal may have been be an indirect consequence of an earlier failed attempt by Peru to withdraw from the contentious jurisdiction of the Inter-American Court, which the court dismissed as not anticipated by the IACHR. Neither Trinidad and Tobago nor Venezuela have withdrawn from the Organization of American States, which means that they still come under the Inter-American Commission's scrutiny in relation to the American Declaration of Human Rights.[81] As of 2017, Venezuela had nonetheless announced an intention to withdraw from the OAS, which is a technical possibility.

As regards human rights treaties that do not explicitly allow for denunciation, there is a view that denunciation is simply not an option. There is only one case to date of the issue being decided internationally, but it is an interesting and unusual one. In 1998, North Korea sought to withdraw entirely from the ICCPR, after becoming upset about the Human Rights Committee's criticism of its record. The question of whether this was possible was referred to the UN Secretary-General, as depository of the treaty, who promptly returned an opinion to the effect that a state could not withdraw from the ICCPR unless all other states agreed (an unlikely scenario). According to the Human Rights Committee's general comment on the issue, 'it is clear that the Covenant is not the type of treaty which, by its nature, implies a right of denunciation'.[82] Moreover, in what was quite a bold move, the Human Rights Committee went on to note that:

> the rights enshrined in the Covenant belong to the people living in the territory of the State party. The Human Rights Committee has consistently taken the view, as evidenced by its long-standing practice, that once the people are accorded the protection of the rights under the Covenant, such protection devolves with territory and continues to belong to them, notwithstanding change in government of the State party.[83]

---

[79] Art 58.   [80] Art 78.   [81] See Chapter 21.
[82] HRC, General Comment 26, HRI/GEN/1/Rev.9 (Vol 1) 222, para 3.
[83] HRC, General Comment 26, para 4.

In other words, and in striking contrast to general international law treaties, rights once recognized (rather than granted) cannot subsequently be withdrawn. This suggests a unique 'stickiness' to international human rights commitments, which cannot be undone even when states desire to do so formally. This has not prevented discussion about withdrawal from international human rights instruments in the UK for example. In somewhat similar fashion, there has been much talk of withdrawing from the Statute of the International Criminal Court although few states have made good on that threat and the Statute would continue to apply up to a year after the denunciation.

9 CONCLUSION

This chapter has presented some key ways in which international human rights obligations differ from mainstream international law obligations. Human rights obligations may allow for a degree of flexibility in their application, but they are also highly binding, regardless of how other state parties conform to their duties. The root of the tension lies in the fact that human rights are intrinsically different in nature and belong to a very different history than general international law. Although typically expressed through treaties, human rights obligations norms have a logic of their own.

It is testimony to the flexibility of international law that it has adapted itself to this new subject matter, in the process changing many rules and practices. In return, human rights law has also significantly shaped the evolution of public international law, and contributed to redefine it less as a project of coexistence between equal states, and more as a common effort to achieve certain universal minimal standards of treatment of the individual.

FURTHER READING

CAROZZA, 'Subsidiarity as a Structural Principle of International Human Rights Law' (2003) 97 *AJIL* 38.

CRAVEN, 'Legal Differentiation and the Concept of the Human Rights Treaty in International Law' (2000) 11 *EJIL* 489.

FOROWICZ, *The Reception of International Law in the European Court of Human Rights*. (Oxford University Press, 2010).

GARDBAUM, 'Human Rights as International Constitutional Rights' (2008) 19 *EJIL* 749.

GOODMAN, 'Human Rights Treaties, Invalid Reservations, and State Consent' (2002) 96 *AJIL* 531.

HUMAN RIGHTS COMMITTEE, General Comment 24, HRI/GEN/1/Rev.9 (Vol I) 210.

HUMAN RIGHTS COMMITTEE, General Comment 31, HRI/GEN/1/Rev.9 (Vol I) 243.

KAMMINGA and SCHEININ (eds), *The Impact of Human Rights Law on General International Law* (Oxford University Press, 2009).

KOJI, 'Emerging Hierarchy in International Human Rights and Beyond: From the Perspective of Non-Derogable Rights' (2001) 12 *EJIL* 917.

LIJNZAAD, *Reservations to UN-Human Rights Treaties: Ratify and Ruin?* (Martinus Nijhoff, 1995).

MAHONEY, 'Marvellous Richness of Diversity or Invidious Cultural Relativism' (1998) 19 *HRLJ* 1.

MCGOLDRICK, 'A Defence of the Margin of Appreciation and An Argument for its Application by the Human Rights Committee' (2015) 65 *ICLQ* 21.

MECKLED-GARCÍA and ÇALI (eds), *The Legalization of Human Rights: Multidisciplinary Perspectives on Human Rights and Human Rights Law* (Routledge, 2006).

MOWBRAY, 'The Creativity of the European Court of Human Rights' (2005) 5 *HRLR* 57.

MULLER, 'Limitations to and Derogations from Economic, Social and Cultural Rights' (2009) *HRLR* 557.

SHELTON, *Remedies in International Human Rights Law* (Oxford University Press, 2015).

WILDHABER, 'The European Convention on Human Rights and International Law' (2007) 56 *ICLQ* 217.

6

SCOPE OF APPLICATION

Sarah Joseph and Sam Dipnall

SUMMARY

A state is clearly not responsible for every act or omission which harms human rights, regardless of the perpetrator or the location. Therefore, it is necessary to examine the scope of application of a state's obligations under international human rights law. That is, when do human rights duties apply? This chapter first defines key concepts and identifies the duty-bearers and beneficiaries of human rights law. Then it explains the instances in which a state will be held responsible for the actions or omissions of particular persons or entities. Finally, it addresses the scope of the territorial application of a state's human rights duties.

1 INTRODUCTION

It is necessary to clarify some key concepts for the purposes of the discussion in this chapter: those of 'state responsibility' and 'jurisdiction'.

'State responsibility' refers to the circumstances in which a state will be held liable for a violation of its international obligations. For example, a state will be held to have breached international human rights law if an act or omission, which is wrongful under human rights law, is attributable to that state. The state will not be held in breach if the act or omission cannot be attributed to it.

The concept of 'jurisdiction' is very complex. It can refer, for example, to the circumstances in which a state is recognized under its own domestic law, or under international law, as having a right to prescribe and/or enforce its laws. In this chapter, it is used in a limited context to refer to a state's authority over a particular act or omission. The most obvious instance of such authority is when an act or omission is perpetrated by the state or its agents within the state's own territory. However, as seen below, a state's jurisdiction can extend to some acts and omissions perpetrated by non-state actors, as well as to some acts or omissions which occur outside its territory.

A state is not responsible under human rights law for every act or omission by any person that arises within its jurisdiction. However, a state's responsibility under human rights law is limited by its jurisdiction. That is, a state cannot be responsible for acts or omissions under human rights law that fall outside its jurisdiction.

2 WHO HAS HUMAN RIGHTS OBLIGATIONS?

States have duties under human rights treaties if they are party to them. Human rights treaties generally do not bind entities other than states. However, Article 43 Convention on the Rights of Persons with Disabilities provides for formal confirmation and accession by regional integration organizations and the European Union has so formally confirmed.[1] The ECHR also provides for accession by the European Union—a process which continues at the time of writing.[2]

Under customary international law, the principal duty-bearers of human rights obligations are again states. There are rare exceptions under customary international law where entities other than states have direct human rights obligations. Examples include the duties not to perpetrate genocide, certain war crimes, or crimes against humanity.[3] In this chapter, the focus is on the scope of application of a state's duties under human rights treaties.[4]

3 WHO HAS HUMAN RIGHTS?

As noted in Section 2, states generally have duties under international human rights law. To whom are these duties owed? That is, who is recognized as a person with human rights under international human rights law?

Individuals within a state's jurisdiction are generally recognized as having human rights. For example, Article 2(1) International Covenant on Civil and Political Rights (ICCPR) requires states parties to respect and ensure the human rights of 'all individuals' within their territory and jurisdiction.

3.1 NON-NATIONALS

One does not have to be a national of a state in order to be able to claim human rights against that state. Numerous international human rights decisions and judgments have confirmed that non-nationals have human rights.[5] In most instances, they enjoy civil and political rights to the same extent as nationals.[6] However, rights of political participation, such as those found in Article 25 ICCPR, including the right to vote and stand for election, may legitimately be restricted to citizens. Similarly, non-citizens do not have the same rights to enter or remain in a state as nationals,[7] though that is not to say that states have an absolute right under international human rights law to expel them. Due to their special vulnerability to deportation, non-nationals have unique procedural rights with regard to deportation under Article 13 ICCPR and similar provisions.

Under Article 2(3) International Covenant on Economic, Social and Cultural Rights (ICESCR), 'developing countries' are permitted to determine the extent to which they

---

[1] Formal Confirmation (23 December 2010). See <http://treaties.un.org/Pages/ViewDetails.aspx?src=TREATY&mtdsg_no=IV-15&chapter=4&lang=en>

[2] Council of Europe, *ECHR: Accession of the European Union*, available at <http://hub.coe.int/what-we-do/human-rights/eu-accession-to-the-convention>. This process has stalled somewhat following *Opinion 2/13 re Accession to the ECHR* [2015] 2 CMLR 21 from the Court of Justice of the European Union.

[3] See Joseph, *Corporations and Transnational Human Rights Litigation* (Hart, 2004) 48–9.

[4] See Chapter 28 for a discussion of the human rights duties of non-state actors.

[5] eg *Gueye v France*, CCPR/C/35/D/196/1985 (6 April 1989); *A v Australia*, CCPR/C/59/D/560/1993 (30 April 1997); *Adam v Czech Republic*, CCPR/C/57/D/586/1994 (25 July 1996); *Soering v UK* (1989) 11 EHRR 439.

[6] HRC, General Comment 15, HRI/GEN/1/Rev.9 (Vol 1) 189.

[7] See the interpretation of Art 12(4) ICCPR in *Nystrom v Australia* CCPR/C/102/D/1557/2007 (18 August 2011) and *Warsame v Canada* CCPR/C/102/D/1959/2010 (21 July 2011).

guarantee 'economic rights' to non-nationals, taking into account 'human rights and their national economy'. Economic rights have been defined by one commentator as those ICESCR rights 'that enable a person to earn a living or that relate to that process', that is, the employment rights in Articles 6 to 8 and perhaps Article 13(2)(e).[8] Article 2(3) has not been authoritatively interpreted by the Committee on Economic, Social and Cultural Rights. The Committee did not mention Article 2(3) in its General Comment 18 on the right to work,[9] nor in its General Comment 23 on the right to just and favourable conditions of work,[10] and it receives only the briefest of mentions and no explication in its General Comment 20 on non-discrimination.[11]

Hence, the extent of developing states' discretion under Article 2(3) ICESCR is unclear. Dankwa describes the provision as transitional, designed to permit post-colonial states to favour local people in employment to redress the balance in economies dominated by expatriot populations.[12] A report by the UN Special Rapporteur on the rights of non-citizens suggests that this 'exception to the general rule on equality' should be interpreted narrowly.[13]

3.2 THE UNBORN

Do human rights extend to the unborn? The American Convention on Human Rights (ACHR), in Article 4(1), explicitly contemplates life beginning from conception rather than birth, and thus seems to confer human rights on unborn children.[14] However, no successful complaint has ever been brought under that Convention in respect of an unborn child.

The European Court of Human Rights and the European Commission of Human Rights have found that a foetus is not a person protected by the right to life, and, in any case, its right would not automatically override the rights and interests of its mother. Accordingly, the European human rights bodies have found complaints brought on behalf of a foetus to be inadmissible.[15] They have also declined to decide whether the right to respect for private and family life extends to unborn children.[16] In *Queenan v Canada*, the Human Rights Committee found that a claim could not be brought on behalf of unborn children against the practice of abortion.[17]

3.3 ARTIFICIAL ENTITIES

Do artificial entities such as corporations and associations, including NGOs, have human rights? Corporations and associations have standing to make claims on their own behalf before the European Court of Human Rights. Examples include *Sunday Times v UK*,[18] a case concerning a media corporation's freedom of expression; *Refah*

---

[8] Dankwa, 'Working Paper on Article 2(3) of the International Covenant on Economic, Social and Cultural Rights' (1987) 9 *HRQ* 230, 240.

[9] CESCR, General Comment 18, HRI/GEN/1/Rev.9 (Vol 1) 139.

[10] CESCR, General Comment 23, E/C.12/GC/23 (27 April 2016).

[11] CESCR, General Comment 20, E/C.12/GC/20 (2 July 2009).   [12] Dankwa (1987), 246–9.

[13] Final report of the Special Rapporteur on the rights of non-citizens, E/CN.4/Sub.2/2003/23 (26 May 2003) para 19.

[14] The right to life in Art 4(1) applies 'in general, from the moment of conception': Case 2141, *The Baby Boy Case*, IACommHR Res 23/81 (6 March 1981).

[15] *Vo v France* (2005) 10 EHRR 12; *Paton v UK* (1981) 3 EHRR 408; *H v Norway* (1992) 73 DR 155.

[16] *A, B, C v Ireland* (2011) 53 EHRR 13.

[17] *Queenan v Canada*, CCPR/C/84/D/1379/2005 (23 August 2005). The HRC found the application of a prohibition on abortion to breach various rights in the ICCPR in *Huamán v Peru*, CCPR/C/85/D/1153/2003 (22 November 2005) and made similar findings concerning denial of a legal abortion in *L.M.R. v Argentina*, CCPR/C/101/D/1608/2007 (28 April 2011). See also *Mellet v Ireland*, CCPR/C/D/116/2324/2013 (17 November 2016).   [18] (1980) 2 EHRR 317.

Partisi (The Welfare Party) v Turkey,[19] a case concerning the rights of a political party; and *Sindicatul Pastorul cel Bun v Romania*,[20] a case concerning an application for registration of a trade union.

In contrast, the UN human rights treaties generally protect only individual rights. Though some rights can clearly be enjoyed in conjunction with other people, such as freedom of association in Article 22 ICCPR or minority rights in Article 27 ICCPR,[21] the only collective right recognized in the global treaty system is that of self-determination in Article 1 ICCPR and Article 1 ICESCR.[22] Corporations and other artificial entities do not have rights under the UN treaties,[23] though an organization can submit a complaint under the Convention on the Elimination of All Forms of Racial Discrimination as the representative of a group of individuals.[24]

Similarly, the Inter-American system is concerned with the rights of individuals,[25] though complaints may be submitted in respect of those rights by others, such as corporations or other artificial entities.[26] In an advisory opinion issued on 26 February 2016 in response to a request by Panama,[27] the Inter-American Court confirmed that only natural persons have human rights under the ACHR.[28]

However, restrictions on the rights of a corporation will, in some instances, inevitably impact severely on the rights of a person, such as a director or shareholder, such that that person may bring a claim of abuse of his or her own rights. *Singer v Canada* concerned a complaint under the ICCPR by one Alan Singer about Québec laws that banned businesses from advertising outdoors in a language other than French.[29] Canada responded that the real 'victim' of this limit to freedom of expression was Singer's company, Alan Singer Ltd, which owned the relevant business. The Human Rights Committee disagreed, noting that freedom of expression was 'inalienably linked to the person' and that person's 'freedom to impart information concerning his business in the language of his choice'.[30] It is likely that the Committee's decision was influenced by the fact that Singer's company was a small family business, such that breaches of its rights necessarily impacted on his enjoyment of those same rights. The same might not apply, for example, in regard to large listed companies.[31]

In contrast, other cases before the Human Rights Committee, such as *SM v Barbados*[32] and *Lamagna v Australia*,[33] which have concerned allegations of the unfair trial of small one-person companies, have been dismissed for want of personal jurisdiction.

---

[19] (2003) 37 EHRR 1.   [20] (2014) 58 EHRR 10.

[21] HRC, General Comment 31, HRI/GEN/1/Rev.9 (Vol 1) 243, para 9.   [22] See Chapter 18.

[23] *SM v Barbados*, CCPR/C/50/D/502/1992 (4 April 1994) (regarding a corporation); *JRT and the WG Party v Canada*, CCPR/C/18/D/104/1981 (6 April 1983) (regarding a political party); *Coordinamento v Italy*, CCPR/C/21/D/163/1984 (10 April 1984) (regarding a NGO), *Wallman v Austria*, CCPR/C/80/D/1002/2001 (29 April 2004) (regarding a partnership); *V.S. v Belarus*, CCPR/C/103/D/1749/2008 (21 November 2011) (regarding a religious organization).

[24] *Jewish Community of Oslo v Norway*, CERD/C/67/D/30/2003 (15 August 2005).

[25] ACHR, Art 2(1) clarifies that a person for the purposes of that Convention is a 'human being'.

[26] ACHR, Arts 1(2) and 44. See eg *Tabacalera Boqueron SA v Paraguay*, IACommHR Report 47/97 (16 October 1997), paras 29 and 35.

[27] OC-22/16, *Entitlement of Legal Entities to Hold Rights Under the Inter-American System of Human Rights*, IACtHR Series A No 22 (26 February 2016).

[28] See Mejia and Van Dalen, 'Do Human Rights Belong to Humans Exclusively?', *DPLF Justicia en Las Américas*, available at: <https://dplfblog.com/2016/10/27/do-human-rights-belong-to-humans-exclusively/>.

[29] CCPR/C/51/D/455/1991 (15 August 1994).

[30] CCPR/C/51/D/455/1991 (15 August 1994), para 11.2.

[31] Joseph and Castan, *The International Covenant on Civil and Political Rights: Cases, Materials, and Commentary* (OUP, 2013) 78.

[32] *SM v Barbados*, CCPR/C/50/D/502/1992 (4 April 1994) (regarding a corporation).

[33] CCPR/C/65/D/737/1997 (30 April 1999).

Emberland has criticized these decisions, particularly *Lamagna*, on the basis that the Committee adopted an overly formal approach to the issue at hand, leaving Ms Lamagna without any relevant human rights protection simply because she chose to use the corporate form to arrange her business affairs.[34] While Emberland does not recommend the conferral of rights on companies under the ICCPR, he recommends a less legalistic approach in the case of small businesses.

4 FOR WHICH ENTITIES IS A STATE RESPONSIBLE?

This section considers the responsibility of states under international human rights law for the acts of a person or entity. The key question is: when is an act or omission attributable to the state?

A state is clearly responsible under international human rights law for the actions of its organs, such as its executive, legislature, judiciary, and its bureaucracy.[35] Thus, breaches of human rights law may arise from actions taken by leaders, police officers, the army, judges, administrative officers, and so on. States remain responsible for the actions of their agents even when they act beyond their authority, as long as they are purportedly acting in an official capacity.[36]

Provincial government entities in a federal state are treated as emanations of the national government for the purposes of international human rights obligations. A federal division of powers is not deemed to alter a state's human rights obligations at all.[37] For example, Tasmanian anti-gay legislation gave rise to a breach of the ICCPR by Australia in *Toonen v Australia*,[38] even though the national government neither enacted nor approved of the impugned laws. Indeed, the national government of Canada has been found in breach of the ICCPR on numerous occasions due to provincial laws, even though it lacks, in some instances, the domestic constitutional power to alter those laws.[39]

Thus, states are clearly responsible for actions of their organs. But to what extent, if at all, are they responsible for the actions of other persons or entities such as private actors, international organizations, or other states?

4.1 PRIVATE ACTORS

Governments are not the only threat to human rights. The right of non-discrimination, for example, is a very limited right if it has no impact in the private sector. According to the International Law Commission's Articles on State Responsibility, a state is responsible for the acts of a private actor if that actor is acting in a governmental capacity, or under its direction and control, or where it adopts a person's actions as its own.[40] Such situations might arise, for example, when private contractors carry out governmental functions.

---

[34] Emberland, 'Corporate Veil in the Jurisprudence of the Human Rights Committee and the Inter-American Court and Commission of Human Rights' (2004) 4 *HRLR* 257, 272.

[35] HRC, General Comment 31, para 4. See also International Law Commission (ILC), Articles on Responsibility of States for Internationally Wrongful Acts, A/56/10, ch IV.E.1, Art 4.

[36] eg *Sarma v Sri Lanka*, CCPR/C/78/D/950/2000 (31 July 2003); see also ILC Articles, Art 7.

[37] eg ICCPR, Art 50.   [38] CCPR/C/50/D/488/1992 (4 April 1994).

[39] eg *Ballantyne et al. v Canada*, CCPR/C/47/D/385/1989 (5 May 1993); *Waldman v Canada*, CCPR/C/67/D/694/1996 (5 November 1999).

[40] ILC Articles, Arts 5, 8, and 11. The ILC is an expert group with a mandate under the UN Charter to develop and codify international law. The Articles were drafted over a number of decades, and were adopted in 2001. Most aspects of the Articles are recognized as customary international law.

Furthermore, the application of human rights within the private sphere is now well recognized in international human rights law.[41] Some human rights provisions, such as Article 20 ICCPR, explicitly require the regulation of private actors by the state.[42] The classical tripartite description of a state's human rights duties, that is, to respect, protect, and fulfil human rights, reveals a more general duty with regard to private actors. As part of a state's duty to *protect* a person's enjoyment of a human right, it must exercise due diligence by taking reasonable measures to prevent and punish actions by a private actor that prejudice the human rights of another. The Inter-American Court of Human Rights enunciated the duty in the following way in *Velasquez-Rodriguez v Honduras*:

> An illegal act which violates human rights and which is initially not directly imputable to a State (for example, because it is the act of a private person or because the person responsible has not been identified) can lead to international responsibility of the State, not because of the act itself, but because of the lack of due diligence to prevent the violation or to respond to it as required by the [American] Convention.[43]

The Human Rights Committee explained in General Comment 31:

> [T]he positive obligations on States Parties to ensure Covenant rights will only be fully discharged if individuals are protected by the State, not just against violations of Covenant rights by its agents, but also against acts committed by private persons or entities that would impair the enjoyment of Covenant rights in so far as they are amenable to application between private persons or entities. There may be circumstances in which a failure to ensure Covenant rights as required by article 2 would give rise to violations by States Parties of those rights, as a result of States Parties' permitting or failing to take appropriate measures or to exercise due diligence to prevent, punish, investigate or redress the harm caused by such acts by private persons or entities.[44]

In *Osman v UK*, the European Court of Human Rights confirmed that states have duties to do all that can reasonably be expected to prevent human rights abuses by private actors. The expectations upon a state increase if the state knows, or should know, that a person or entity poses a risk to another's enjoyment of human rights.[45]

The following are examples of this application of human rights within the private sphere. *A v UK* concerned a young boy who had been hit with a garden cane by his stepfather. The stepfather was acquitted of assault in the UK, where the court found he had merely engaged in 'reasonable chastisement'. The European Court found that the UK, in acquitting the stepfather in its courts, had failed properly to protect the boy's right to be free from inhuman and degrading treatment.[46] Various human rights bodies have held that states must take reasonable and effective measures to protect a person from domestic violence: failure to do so will result in violations of the rights of the person subjected to such violence, such as the right to life if the person is killed, or the right to be free from torture or other ill-treatment.[47] In *Lopez Ostra v Spain*, the European Court found that Spain had failed to take reasonable measures to prevent the spread of severe air pollution from a privately owned waste treatment plant, which breached the rights to privacy and

---

[41] See Chapter 5.
[42] See also Convention on the Elimination of All Forms of Discrimination Against Women (CEDAW) Arts 6 and 11; and Convention on the Elimination of All Forms of Racial Discrimination (ICERD) Art 5.
[43] IACtHR Series C No 4 (29 July 1988) para 172.   [44] HRC, General Comment 31, para 8.
[45] (2000) 29 EHRR 245, para 116.   [46] (1999) 27 EHRR 611, 624.
[47] eg *Opuz v Turkey* (2010) 50 EHRR 28; *AT v Hungary*, CEDAW/A/61/38/2006 (26 January 2005); *Goekce v Austria*, CEDAW/C/39/D/5/2005 (6 August 2007); *Yildirim v Austria*, CEDAW/C/39/D/6/2005 (6 August 2007). See also CEDAW, General Recommendation 19, HRI/GEN/1/Rev.9 (Vol II) 331.

family life of those who lived in the plant's vicinity.[48] Similarly, in *SERAC v Nigeria*, the African Commission on Human and Peoples' Rights found that Nigeria had failed to protect indigenous peoples in Ogoniland from harmful actions by an oil consortium, which breached the peoples' rights to health, property, housing, food, and freedom from forced deprivation of wealth and resources.[49] Finally, in *Krasovsky v Belarus*, the Human Rights Committee found the state in breach of the ICCPR due to its failure to properly investigate the disappearance of the victim, even though it had earlier failed to find that the disappearance was the work of state agents.[50]

4.2 INTERNATIONAL ORGANIZATIONS

To what extent, if at all, are states responsible for the actions of international organizations of which they are a member? *H v d P v Netherlands* concerned a complaint to the Human Rights Committee about the recruitment practices of the European Patent Office (EPO), an international organization of which the Netherlands was one of five member states.[51] The complaint was dismissed as it was aimed at the EPO and thus concerned issues beyond the jurisdiction of the Netherlands. However, the Committee has since stated that states are responsible for the actions of 'forces constituting a national contingent of a State party assigned to an international peace-keeping or peace-enforcement operation'.[52] One must, therefore, inquire as to when a state's personnel are its own and when they are the responsibility of an international organization.

The European Court of Human Rights, in the joined cases of *Behrami and Behrami v France* and *Saramati v France, Germany and Norway*, found that complaints against various European states that had contributed personnel to peacekeeping forces in Kosovo (KFOR) and to the UN interim administration in Kosovo (UNMIK), in respect of certain acts and omissions of KFOR and UNMIK, were inadmissible *ratione personae*.[53] The Court found that the activities of KFOR and UNMIK were attributable to the UN Security Council. It went on to find that it was not competent to review the actions of states parties in respect of actions taken by their personnel on behalf of the UN as part of KFOR and UNMIK.

The European Court distinguished *Behrami and Saramati* in its 2011 judgment in *Al-Jedda v UK*, which concerned the imprisonment of the applicant (a UK citizen) in Basrah between 2004 and 2007. The Court held that the situation in Iraq in 2004 was different from that in Kosovo in 1999 because the Security Council had 'effective control' and 'ultimate authority' in the latter situation but not the former.[54] It also held that, in the case of any ambiguity, Security Council resolutions ought to be interpreted compatibly with human rights, and it criticized the UK's interpretation of Resolution 1546 as authorizing the indefinite detention of terrorist suspects in Iraq.[55] The Court concluded that the UK was responsible under the ECHR for Mr Al-Jedda's detention, which violated his right to liberty under Article 5(1).

In *Jaloud v Netherlands*, the Netherlands was found to have jurisdiction over a fatal shooting at a checkpoint in Iraq in 2004, which was manned by its troops. The Netherlands had argued that the relevant area in Iraq, as well as the Dutch contingent, was under the operational command of the UK. Dutch jurisdiction was founded on the fact that the

---

[48] (1995) 20 EHRR 277.   [49] 155/96, 16th Activity Report of the ACommHPR (2002–2003).
[50] CCPR/C/104/D/1820/2008 (26 March 2012) paras 8.2 and 8.3.
[51] CCPR/C/29/D/217/1986 (8 April 1987).   [52] HRC, General Comment 31, para 10.
[53] (2007) 45 EHRR SE10.   [54] (2011) 53 EHRR 23, para 84.
[55] *Al-Jedda*, paras 102–6. See also *Al-Saadoon and Mufdhi v UK* (2011) 53 EHRR 9.

Netherlands retained full command of the relevant personnel.[56] As has been pointed out by Sari, this finding may effectively overturn *Behrami*, as individual states, even when contributing troops to multinational operations, always retain ultimate authority over their troops lest they 'cease to function as national military units'.[57] If so, the overturning is not explicit.

In *Blagojević v The Netherlands*, the European Court found that a suspect in the custody of the International Criminal Tribunal for the former Yugoslavia was not within the Netherlands' jurisdiction for the purposes of Article 1 EHCR, despite his physical presence in The Hague. The Court reasoned that the Tribunal was set up by the Security Council under Chapter VII of the UN Charter, and that its actions were attributable to the UN.[58] The Court also adverted to the fact that the legal provisions governing the Tribunal's operation provided appropriate human rights guarantees.[59]

Lambi Longa v The Netherlands concerned a witness for the defence of Thomas Lubanga Dyilo, the Congolese militia leader who was the first person to be convicted by the International Criminal Court (ICC). The applicant had been arrested in the Democratic Republic of the Congo (DRC) on charges related to the murders of UN personnel (which he denied). He claimed that the last valid detention order expired in 2007, yet he remained in detention in the DRC in 2011, when he was transferred to detention in The Hague to give evidence in the Lubanga trial. The applicant alleged before the European Court that he had been unlawfully detained by the Netherlands in breach of Article 5 ECHR. The Court held that the power to keep witnesses in custody was a 'necessary corollary' of the ICC's operations, and that (as in *Blagojević*) his physical presence in The Hague did not suffice to establish Dutch jurisdiction.[60] The applicant also claimed that the ICC's Rules of Procedure and Evidence failed to protect his human rights, but the Court rejected this argument.[61] *Blagojević* and *Lambi Longa* indicate that states parties to the ECHR will not be held responsible for those under the control of international organizations operating within their territory, so long as the organizations provide appropriate human rights guarantees to ensure against a 'legal vacuum'.

It appears that a state can be held responsible under human rights treaties for its own actions taken in order to implement a Security Council resolution and, by implication, other international obligations. In *Bosphorus v Ireland*, the European Court of Human Rights found a complaint regarding the seizure in Ireland of the applicant's leased aircraft to be admissible. The seizure took place pursuant to a ministerial decision that implemented an EC Council regulation which itself applied a Security Council resolution that had imposed sanctions on the Federal Republic of Yugoslavia. Ireland was bound under EC law to implement the regulation. Nevertheless, the impugned actions were deemed to be those of Ireland and the complaint was admissible. However, no violation (of the right to property) was ultimately found. The Court found that there was a presumption that actions taken to implement international obligations as a member of an international organization were compatible with the ECHR if the relevant organization provided equivalent or comparable protection of the rights recognized in the ECHR.[62] The presumption can be rebutted where protection of ECHR rights is 'manifestly deficient'. The presumption was not rebutted in *Bosphorus*.

---

[56] App no 47708/08, Judgment of 20 November 2014, paras 143 and 149.

[57] Sari, 'Jaloud v Netherlands: New Directions in Extra-Territorial Military Operations', *EJIL: Talk!*, available at: <http://www.ejiltalk.org/jaloud-v-netherlands-new-directions-in-extra-territorial-military-operations/>.

[58] App no 49032/07, Admissibility Decision of 9 June 2009, paras 31–46.

[59] App no 49032/07, Admissibility Decision of 9 June 2009, para 46.

[60] (2013) 56 EHRR SE1, paras 69–75.   [61] (2013) 56 EHRR SE1, paras 77–80.

[62] (2006) 42 EHRR 1, paras 155–6.

In contrast, in *Nada v Switzerland*, the European Court found that Swiss implementation of a Security Council resolution relating to al-Qaida and the Taliban violated a number of ECHR provisions.[63] The applicant, Nada, lived in a tiny Italian enclave surrounded by the Swiss canton of Ticino. From 2002 he was prevented from entering Switzerland (and thus leaving that enclave) for any purpose—including visiting his family or his Italian doctor—by a Federal Ordinance enacted in order to implement the Security Council resolution. In May 2005 the Swiss authorities determined that allegations against Nada of links with terrorism were unfounded, but refused to lift the travel ban, arguing that they could not do so until the Security Council removed Nada from the relevant sanctions list. The Security Council's Sanctions Committee did not remove Nada's name until September 2009. Switzerland claimed that it was not responsible for any violations of Nada's rights, as it was compelled to act as it did by the Security Council. The Court did not make a finding on the hierarchy of Switzerland's conflicting international obligations relating to compliance with the Security Council resolution and with the ECHR. Instead, it found that Switzerland had not done all it could, within the scope of discretion permitted to it by the Security Council, to protect Nada's rights. For example, it could have informed Italian authorities more quickly of its 2005 findings: after all Nada's name was removed from the UN Sanctions List quickly after Italy's request in 2009. It ultimately found that Switzerland had breached Articles 8 and 13 ECHR.[64] A similar decision was reached by the Human Rights Committee in *Sayadi and Vinck v Belgium*.[65]

In *Nada* and *Sayadi and Vinck*, the European Court and the Human Rights Committee found that the relevant Security Council resolution did not compel the rights abusive actions at issue. Hence, neither case addressed how a conflict between a Security Council resolution and human rights obligations would be resolved. *Bosphorus* goes further. It indicates that a state can be held responsible for human rights violations even if those violations are necessitated by its implementation of obligations to another international organization, though it benefits in this regard from a presumption of compatibility.

However, the Netherlands is not responsible for the actions of the many international courts located within its territory, according to *Blagojević* and *Lambi Longa*. Furthermore, *Behrami and Saramati* indicates that a state will not be held responsible for human rights violations by its personnel, such as its troops, if command of those people is given to an international body: those personnel are held to be beyond the jurisdiction of that particular state. Nevertheless, *Al-Jedda* shows that the context is important, and that a state cannot assume its responsibility has passed entirely to the international organization in every instance. Indeed, *Jaloud* may have implicitly overturned *Behrami and Saramati*, as that decision indicates it will be very difficult for a state to escape jurisdiction for the actions of its troops, even if part of a multinational force.

Thus, a state, which is a member of an international organization, is not per se responsible for the actions of that organization under international human rights law. Can a state be held responsible for its own actions within the organization, such as its votes, or even its decision to join a particular organization? The Committee on Economic, Social and Cultural Rights has stated, regarding the right to food, that states violate that right if they fail to take it into account 'when entering into agreements with other States or with international organisations'.[66] Therefore, for example, a state must take its ICESCR obligations

---

[63] (2013) 56 EHRR 18.   [64] (2013) 56 EHRR 18, paras 187–199.
[65] CCPR/C/94/D/1472/2006 (29 December 2008). See also Chapter 29.
[66] CESCR, General Comment 12, HRI/GEN/1/Rev.9 (Vol 1) 55, para 19. See also CESCR, General Comment 14, HRI/GEN/1/Rev.9 (Vol 1) 78, para 39.

into account when joining the World Trade Organization (WTO) or in entering into a free trade agreement with another state.[67] The Committee has also strongly implied that members of the Security Council must take ICESCR rights into account when imposing economic sanctions on a state.[68]

4.3 OTHER STATES

To what extent is a state responsible for the actions of another state? A state is responsible for those of its acts which expose a person to a real risk of a violation of his or her rights by another state, where that breach was reasonably foreseeable at the time of the relevant act. The classic situation where such issues arise is in the context of refoulement: where a state deports a person to another state in circumstances where 'the necessary and foreseeable consequence of the deportation would be a real risk of the killing or torture' of that person.[69] States are thus under a duty not to put individuals into such situations. This duty is explicit in Article 3 Convention against Torture and Other Cruel, Inhuman or Degrading Treatment or Punishment (UNCAT).

In *Soering v UK*, the European Court of Human Rights found that the extradition of Soering, a young man accused of murder, to the USA would amount to inhuman and degrading treatment contrary to Article 3 ECHR.[70] This was because the UK would have knowingly exposed Soering to a real possibility of experiencing the death row phenomenon, that is, a prolonged period of time on death row characterized by mounting anguish at the inevitable prospect of death.

Agiza v Sweden concerned the expulsion of a terrorist suspect, one Ahmed Hussein Agiza, from Sweden to Egypt.[71] He was transported to Egypt by US agents. Sweden was found to have violated Article 3 UNCAT by allowing Agiza to be transported from Sweden to Egypt where it could reasonably foresee that he was at risk of being tortured. Sweden also breached the prohibition on cruel, inhuman, and degrading treatment in Article 16 by handing Agiza over to US agents in Sweden, and apparently acquiescing in his inhuman and degrading treatment by US agents while he remained on Swedish soil prior to his removal to Egypt.[72] The Article 16 finding thus manifested a different type of responsibility of a state for the human rights violations of another state.

In *Othman (Abu Qatada) v UK*,[73] the European Court of Human Rights held that the UK could not legally deport the applicant, a terrorist suspect, to his country of nationality, Jordan, due to the risk that he would face an unfair trial there (contrary to the requirements of Article 6 ECHR). In particular, Abu Qatada alleged that some of the evidence likely to be used against him in Jordan had been obtained by torture. The UK conceded that he might not receive a fair trial, but denied that it would amount to a 'flagrant denial of justice'.[74] The European Court disagreed, finding that the real

---

[67] See generally Howse and Teitel, 'Beyond the Divide: The Covenant on Economic, Social and Cultural Rights and the World Trade Organization' (Occasional Paper No 30, Friedrich Ebert Stiftung, 2007), available at <http://library.fes.de/pdf-files/iez/global/04572.pdf/>.

[68] CESCR, General Comment 8, HRI/GEN/1/Rev.9 (Vol 1) 43, esp para 8. This statement also raises issues regarding the extraterritorial obligations of states, an issue which is discussed further in this chapter.

[69] *Pillai v Canada* CCPR/C/101/D/1763/2008 (25 March 2011), concurring opinion of Ms Keller, Ms Antoanella Motoc, Messrs Neuman and O'Flaherty, and Sir Nigel Rodley.   [70] (1989) 11 EHRR 439.

[71] CAT/C/34/D/233/2003 (24 May 2005).

[72] Agiza was stripped, blindfolded, and hooded for his flight to Egypt by US agents.

[73] (2012) 55 EHRR 1.

[74] The European Court had suggested in *Soering*, at para 113 that extradition would be precluded if a person foreseeably faced a 'flagrant denial of justice' in the receiving country.

risk of evidence obtained by torture being adduced at trial went to the 'very essence' of Article 6, and that the UK would itself breach its obligations by deporting Abu Qatada to face a trial which would be 'not only immoral and illegal, but also entirely unreliable in its outcome'.[75]

Until *Othman*, the case law from all international human rights tribunals had only established that a sending state's non-refoulement obligations protected prospective deportees from foreseeable violations of the right to life and the right to be free from torture and other cruel, inhuman, and degrading treatment in the receiving state. *Othman* extended the non-refoulement obligation under the ECHR to cases in which a 'flagrant denial of justice' was likely to occur in breach of fair trial guarantees.

In General Comment 31, the Human Rights Committee described the obligation not to deport as arising when deportation would give rise to a 'real risk of irreparable harm, such as that contemplated by Articles 6 and 7 of the Covenant'.[76] It seems doubtful that many other human rights violations can be characterized as 'irreparable'.[77] It is, however, assumed that the obligations are more extensive if the sending state somehow colludes with the receiving state in bringing about violations of those other rights.

5 WHERE DO HUMAN RIGHTS APPLY?

What is the territorial scope of a state's jurisdiction for the purposes of human rights law? Clearly, a state has jurisdiction over its own territory. For example, Article 2(1) ICCPR specifies the duties owed to individuals within a state's territory. What is the scope, if any, of a state's extraterritorial jurisdiction under human rights treaties?

Before moving on, it is important to set the limits of what is meant by 'extraterritorial jurisdiction'. Cases such as those concerning refoulement mentioned in Section 4.3 involve intra-territorial acts which generate extraterritorial consequences. They do not involve instances of extraterritorial jurisdiction. The actual breach by the sending state in such cases arises at the time of its intra-territorial act of expelling the person, rather than when (or even if) the receiving state perpetrates the anticipated human rights abuse (for example, an act of torture upon the deported person).

So, what about a state's jurisdiction outside its own territory? A state's obligations under the ICCPR are generally presumed to extend to its colonies unless it has made a contrary declaration at the time of ratification.[78] On the other hand, under Article 56 ECHR, a state must specifically extend the application of the Convention to its dependent territories.

The approaches to the extraterritorial application of rights adopted by various human rights bodies are discussed in the sections that follow.

---

[75] *Othman*, paras 265–7. The Court also stated that evidence obtained through other forms of ill-treatment (cruel, inhuman or degrading treatment or punishment) may also give rise to 'flagrant denials of justice', but found it unnecessary to decide the issue (para 267).

[76] HRC, General Comment 31, para 12.

[77] See, however, *R (Ullah) v Special Adjudicator* [2004] UKHL 26, where the UK House of Lords indicated that non-refoulement may apply to prevent exposure to very serious breaches of other rights, such as one's right to freedom of religion.

[78] The HRC's decision in *Kuok Koi v Portugal*, CCPR/C/73/D/925/2000 (8 February 2002) seems somewhat confused on the matter, but on balance favours this conclusion. See Joseph, 'Human Rights Committee: Recent Cases' (2002) 2 *HRLR* 287, 287–95. See also ICCPR, Art 1(3).

5.1 ECHR

Article 1 ECHR states that '[t]he High Contracting Parties shall secure to everyone within their jurisdiction the rights and freedoms' in the Convention. No territorial limit is expressed therein. The extraterritorial application of the ECHR in certain circumstances was confirmed in *Loizidou v Turkey*[79] and *Cyprus v Turkey*[80] where the acts of the authorities in Northern Cyprus were held to be within Turkey's jurisdiction due to the 'effective control' exercised over those authorities by Turkey. Similarly, the actions of the authorities in the Transdniestrian separatist region in Moldova were held in *Ilascu v Moldova and Russia* to be within Russia's jurisdiction, due to Russia's 'effective authority, or at the very least decisive influence' over those authorities, due to its 'military, economic, financial and political support'.[81] It seems that this threshold of 'effective authority' over Transdniestrian authorities is similar, or even slightly lower, than the requirement of 'effective control' over a territory in *Loizidou*.[82]

Banković et al. v Belgium et al. concerned a complaint about the actions of North Atlantic Treaty Organization (NATO) troops in bombing Radio Television Serbia in Belgrade during the airstrikes against the Federal Republic of Yugoslavia (FRY) in 1999. The complaint was issued against 17 European states that were members of NATO. The Grand Chamber of the European Court of Human Rights concluded that the complaint was inadmissible for want of territorial jurisdiction. Extraterritorial jurisdiction was limited to instances where a respondent state is in 'effective control' of a particular territory through, for example, military occupation. The firing of missiles was not enough to establish such a level of control. Furthermore, the Court went on to state that the ECHR was a regional treaty confined to a particular 'legal space (*espace juridique*)',[83] of which the FRY was not part. It stated: 'The Convention was not designed to be applied throughout the world, even in respect of the conduct of Contracting States'.[84] *Banković* thus seemed to close the door on claims under the ECHR with regard to the behaviour of contracting states outside the area of the Council of Europe.

However, the European Court has since retreated from this position. *Öcalan v Turkey*, decided soon after *Banković*, concerned the arrest of the leader of the Kurdistan Workers' Party (PKK), Abdullah Öcalan, by Turkish agents at Nairobi airport in Kenya and his blindfolded flight back to Turkey. The European Court found that Turkey had jurisdiction over the actions that took place at Nairobi airport and duly considered the complaint of unlawful detention in this regard.[85]

Issa v Turkey concerned an allegation of killings of captured shepherds by Turkish soldiers in northern Iraq. The applicants argued that that area was under the effective control of Turkish troops. On the issue of the Convention's 'legal space', the European Court stated that if the deceased had been under the effective control of Turkey at the relevant time, 'it would follow logically that they were within the jurisdiction of Turkey (and not that of Iraq, which is not a Contracting State and clearly does not fall within the legal space (*espace juridique*) of the Contracting States)'.[86] This argument renders the issue of 'legal space' irrelevant when a contracting state is in fact exercising 'effective control' over any area anywhere in the world.

---

[79] (1997) 23 EHRR 513.   [80] (2002) 35 EHRR 30.

[81] (2005) 40 EHRR 46, para 392. The court confirmed this line of reasoning in *Ivanţoc and Others v Moldova and Russia*, App no 23687/05, Judgment of 15 November 2011 and *Catan and Others v Moldova and Russia* (2013) 57 EHRR 4.

[82] Cerone, 'Human Dignity in the Line of Fire: The Application of International Human Rights Law during Armed Conflict, Occupation, and Peace Operations' (2006) 39 *Vanderbilt JTL* 1446, 1491.

[83] *Bankovic et al. v Belgium et al.* (2007) 44 EHRR SE5, para 80.   [84] *Bankovic*, para 80.

[85] (2005) 41 EHRR 45. Ultimately, that particular complaint was not upheld.

[86] (2005) 41 EHRR 27, para 74.

The Court also stated:

> [A] State may also be held accountable for violation of the Convention rights and free-
> doms of persons who are in the territory of another State but who are found to be under
> the former State's authority and control through its agents operating—whether lawfully or
> unlawfully—in the latter State …[87]

Thus, according to *Issa*, effective control can arise when a state's agents have effective
control over a person (or persons) rather than over a particular area. This represents
a considerable extension of the scope of extraterritorial jurisdiction recognized in
Banković.

Al-Skeini v United Kingdom concerned a claim of British responsibility for the deaths of
six Iraqi civilians at the hands of British troops in Iraq. Five of the deceased had allegedly
been killed by British forces in the streets of Basra, while the sixth was allegedly detained
and mistreated before dying in British custody at a military base in Basra. The European
Court held that all six victims had been within the UK's jurisdiction for the purposes of
Article 1 ECHR.[88] In doing so, it is arguable that it overturned most of the principles in
Bankovic. Frustratingly, it did not do so expressly.

Al-Skeini supports *Bankovic* in stating that extraterritorial jurisdiction is 'exceptional'.[89]
However, *Al-Skeini* moves away from the *espace juridique* concept which was so critical
in *Bankovic*. The European Court seemed to reinterpret the concept as meaning that the
ECHR does not 'govern the actions of States not Parties to it, nor does it purport to be
a means of requiring the Contracting States to impose Convention standards on other
States'.[90] Such a principle is uncontroversial and irrelevant on the facts in *Banković*—that
complaint was not against or about the behaviour of a non-party. In a remarkably unacknowledged obliteration of *Banković*, the Court went on to say that the principle 'does not
imply … that jurisdiction under Article 1 of the Convention can never exist outside the
territory covered by the Council of Europe Member States. The Court has not in its case-
law applied any such restriction'.[91]

In *Al Skeini*, the European Court identifies two separate bases for extraterritorial jurisdiction, that is where a 'State through its agents exercises control and authority over an
individual', and where a State 'exercises effective control of an area outside that national
territory'. Hence, extraterritorial jurisdiction under the ECHR is in fact as broad as indicated in *Issa*, and significantly broader than signalled in *Banković*.

Regarding the 'state agent authority and control' test, the European Court in *Al-Skeini*
found that it existed in three instances. First, it arose where the alleged violations arose
from the acts or omissions of diplomatic or consular agents operating abroad in accordance with international law.[92] A second instance arose where a person was in the 'physical power and control' of a state: all of the examples it gave with regard to this sub-category
either related to the person being in the custody of a state's agents outside its territory
(which explained *Öcalan* and *Issa*), or on a ship controlled by the relevant state.[93] A third
instance arose where a state was carrying out public functions, such as 'executive or judicial functions on the territory of another State'. In such a situation, 'the Contracting State
may be responsible for breaches of the Convention thereby incurred, as long as the acts
in question are attributable to it rather than to the territorial state'.[94] The Court went on
to base the jurisdictional link to all six deaths in this case on the UK's exercise of public
powers in the relevant part of Iraq.[95]

---

[87] *Issa*, para 71.   [88] (2011) 53 EHRR 18.   [89] *Al-Skeini*, para 131.
[90] *Al-Skeini*, para 141.   [91] *Al-Skeini*, para 142.   [92] *Al-Skein*, para 134.
[93] *Al-Skeini*, para 136.   [94] *Al-Skeini*, para 135.   [95] *Al-Skeini*, paras 143–150.

Al-Skeini was extensively discussed by the Court of Appeal of England and Wales in *Al-Saadoon v Secretary of State for Defence and Others* in late 2016.[96] The case concerned the scope of UK jurisdiction under the ECHR, and therefore the Human Rights Act, in respect of a number of alleged human rights abuses in Iraq perpetrated by UK soldiers. In *Al-Saadoon*, the parties agreed that the UK lacked effective control over any part of Iraq, so the test of effective control over territory was inapplicable. Hence, the jurisdictional claim was based on the exercise of UK control over the relevant person.[97] In particular, the Court of Appeal examined the scope of the sub-categories of that test identified in *Al-Skeini*, that is the exercise of 'public powers' and the exercise of 'physical power and control' (the exception regarding the actions of diplomatic and consular staff was not relevant on the facts).

Regarding 'public powers', the Court of Appeal clarified that the exercise of such is a question of 'the facts of control and the exercise of authority', rather than a question of whether a state of occupation has been formally recognized.[98] Hence, the UK could be, and was found to be, exercising public powers in parts of Iraq prior to the internationally recognized period of occupation, as well as in the post-occupation period.

The most important part of the *Al-Saadoon* decision lies in its discussion of the scope of the 'physical power and control' test. In particular, did it apply when a person was outside the physical custody of a state agent?[99] Could it, for example, apply to a person who was shot dead by a UK soldier without being under that soldier's prior control? If so, such a decision would eviscerate the final vestiges of *Bankovic*. The Court of Appeal did not go so far:

> I consider that in laying down this basis of extra-territorial jurisdiction [ie the 'physical power and control' exception], the Grand Chamber [in *Al-Skeini*] required a greater degree of power and control than that represented by the use of lethal or potentially lethal force alone. In other words, I believe that the intention of the Strasbourg court was to require that there be an element of control of the individual prior to the use of lethal force.[100]

The Court conceded that this rendered the test of 'physical power and control' to be 'inherently imprecise',[101] and subject to 'tenuous distinctions'.[102] Nevertheless, it was for the Strasbourg court to unambiguously extend the test (and therefore kill off *Bankovic*), rather than for the Court of Appeal.

Hence, *Al-Skeini*, as interpreted by the Court of Appeal in *Al-Saadoon*, confirms extra-territorial jurisdiction under the ECHR in the following circumstances: (a) where a state exercises effective control of territory; (b) where a state exercises public powers over the territory in which the relevant act or omission arises; (c) where the act or omission is that of a state's consular or diplomatic agent; and (d) where a state agent exercises *sufficient* physical power and control over a person. The use of only lethal or potentially lethal force alone does not suffice, whereas detaining a person does.

5.2 ACHR

Article 1(1) ACHR requires states to respect and ensure the rights of 'all persons subject to their jurisdiction', so, as with the ECHR, no territorial limit is expressed. In *Coard et al. v United States*, the Inter-American Commission on Human Rights found that the US exercised jurisdiction over persons in Grenada during its 1983 invasion for the purposes of the American Declaration of Human Rights.[103] The US is not a party to the ACHR and no jurisdictional clause is contained within the American Declaration. On the facts in *Coard*, it

---

[96] [2016] EWCA Civ 811.   [97] *Al-Saadoon*, para 24.   [98] *Al-Saadoon*, para 54.
[99] *Al-Saadoon*, para 4(1).   [100] *Al-Saadoon*, para 69.   [101] *Al-Saadoon*, para 70.
[102] *Al-Sadoon*, para 71.   [103] Case 10.951, IACommHR Report No 109/99 (29 September 1999).

does not seem debatable that the US had jurisdiction over the relevant persons. They were detained on a US military ship, and the US arguably had effective control over Grenada at the time.[104] Nevertheless, neither fact was explicitly referenced in the Commission's decision. It found that people could come within US jurisdiction through the actions of US agents, namely the US military in Grenada.

Alejandre v Cuba concerned the shooting down of unarmed civilian aircraft by Cuban aircraft.[105] The case again concerned findings under the American Declaration, as Cuba was not a party to the ACHR. The Inter-American Commission found that Cuba had jurisdiction over the four deceased occupants of the airplanes. The shootings took place in international airspace, and two of the deceased were not Cubans. The only potential basis for jurisdiction lay 'in the relationship between the agents of Cuba and the victims in the circumstances at the time of the incident'.[106] Indeed, the degree of control exercised over the victims seems analogous to that exercised by the NATO troops over the victims in *Bankovic*. It also goes beyond the degree of control recognized as grounding ECHR jurisdiction in *Al-Skeini*, as interpreted in *Al-Saadoon*.

The Inter-American Commission indicated that the ACHR had similar extraterritorial application to the American Declaration in *Saldano v Argentina*, stating that extraterritorial jurisdiction arose 'under certain circumstances for the acts and omissions of [state agents] which produce effects or are undertaken outside that State's own territory'.[107] Hence, the test adopted seems to be one of effective control over a person rather than effective control over the territory in which a violation takes place.

5.3 AFRICAN CHARTER ON HUMAN AND PEOPLES' RIGHTS

In its General Comment 3 on the right to life, the African Commission on Human and Peoples' Rights stated:

> A State shall respect the right to life of individuals outside its territory. A State also has certain obligations to protect the right to life of such individuals. The nature of these obligations depends for instance on the extent that the State has jurisdiction or otherwise exercises effective authority, power, or control over either the perpetrator or the victim (or the victim's rights), or exercises effective control over the territory on which the victim's rights are affected, or whether the State engages in conduct which could reasonably be foreseen to result in an unlawful deprivation of life.[108]

Hence, the African Commission seems to accept that extraterritorial jurisdiction arises in respect of a state's effective control of territory, perpetrator, or victim.[109]

5.4 ICCPR

The UN treaties are logically unaffected by any 'legal space' argument, given their global reach. Article 2(1) ICCPR requires states to respect and ensure ICCPR rights 'to all individuals within its territory *and* subject to its jurisdiction'.[110] Thus, the language of the ICCPR arguably limits a state's responsibility under the ICCPR to its territory. Nevertheless, the

---

[104] Cerone, 'The Application of Regional Human Rights Law Beyond Regional Frontiers: The Inter-American Commission on Human Rights and US Activities in Iraq', *ASIL Insights* (25 October 2005) 3.

[105] Case 11.589, IACommHR Report No 86/99 (29 September 1999).   [106] Cerone (2005), 4.

[107] IACommHR Report No 38/99 (11 March 1999) para 17.

[108] Adopted during the 57th Ordinary Session of the African Commission on Human and Peoples' Rights held from 4–18 November 2015, para 14.

[109] See also 227/99, *Democratic Republic of the Congo v Burundi, Rwanda, and Uganda*, 20th Activity Report of the ACommHPR (2006).   [110] Emphasis added.

Human Rights Committee has confirmed the extraterritorial impact of the ICCPR in a number of cases. The Committee (and other UN human rights treaty bodies) have confirmed Israel's responsibility for human rights abuses in the Occupied Territories,[111] and the same for the US regarding its detention camp in Guantánamo Bay in Cuba.[112] In numerous cases, such as *Montero v Uruguay*, states have been held responsible for the actions of their overseas consulates in unreasonably refusing to renew a passport.[113] In *Lopez Burgos v Uruguay*, Uruguay was held responsible for the kidnap in Argentina of a man by its agents.[114]

In General Comment 31, the Human Rights Committee described the extraterritorial impact of the ICCPR as follows:

[A] State party must respect and ensure the rights laid down in the Covenant to *anyone within the power or effective control* of that State Party, even if not situated within the territory of the State Party... ... This principle also applies to those within the power or effective control of the forces of a State Party acting outside its territory, regardless of the circumstances in which such power or effective control was obtained.[115]

Thus, the ICCPR applies extraterritorially where an affected person is under the effective control of a state's agents, rather than only where an affected person is within territory that is effectively controlled by a state. The focus of the Committee in defining the extent of jurisdiction seems to be on the state's relationship with the relevant impugned act and the person affected, rather than its relationship with the territory where a relevant act takes place.

Furthermore, it seems that jurisdiction under the ICCPR does extend to situations involving the 'mere' use of lethal or potentially lethal force. In Concluding Observations on the US, the HRC commented adversely on the use of drones for targeted killings, indicating that such killings were capable of breaching Article 6 ICCPR.[116]

The extent of a state's possible extraterritorial responsibilities was tested in *Munaf v Romania*.[117] The allegation in that case was that the Romanian embassy in Iraq wrongly released the complainant Munaf into the hands of the US embassy, where he was ultimately handed over to Iraqi authorities and charged with capital crimes. Ultimately, the claim of a breach of the right to life (and other rights) was not upheld, as Romania was found not to be in a position to have foreseen the events following its release of Munaf. However, the admissibility decision indicated that a state could, in principle, be held responsible for extraterritorial acts which facilitate the predictable abusive actions of another state (at least with regard to torture or killing).

In Concluding Observations on Germany in 2012, the Human Rights Committee expressed concern at 'German companies acting abroad allegedly in contravention of relevant human rights standards' (referring to complaints of forcible evictions in Uganda to make way for a coffee plantation owned by a German conglomerate) and made the following recommendation:

The State party is encouraged to set out clearly the expectation that all business enterprises domiciled in its territory and/or its jurisdiction respect human rights standards in

---

[111] eg HRC, Concluding Observations of the Human Rights Committee: Israel, CCPR/C/ISR/CO/3 (3 September 2010). See also *Legal Consequences of the Construction of a Wall in the Occupied Palestinian Territory* (Advisory Opinion) [2004] ICJ Rep 36.

[112] eg HRC, Concluding Observations: US, CCPR/C/USA/CO/3 (15 September 2006) paras 14–15.

[113] CCPR/C/18/D/106/1981 (31 March 1983).

[114] CCPR/C/13/D/52/1979 (29 July 1981). A similar decision arose in *Celiberti de Casariego v Uruguay*, CCPR/C/13/D/56/1979 (29 July 1981), concerning the kidnapping of a person from Brazil.

[115] HRC, General Comment 31, para 10 (emphasis added).

[116] CCPR/C/USA/CO/4 (23 April 2014), para 9.   [117] CCPR/C/96/D/1539/2006 (21 August 2009).

accordance with the Covenant throughout their operations. It is also encouraged to take appropriate measures to strengthen the remedies provided to protect people who have been victims of activities of such business enterprises operating abroad.[118]

Here, the HRC *encouraged* Germany to exert extraterritorial control over its private corporate citizens so as to constrain them from harming the human rights of people in other states. In 2015, the HRC's comments to Canada were stronger. It expressed concern over allegations of human rights abuses against Canadian mining companies operating abroad. It went on to state that Canada:

> *Should* (a) enhance the effectiveness of existing mechanisms to ensure that all Canadian corporations, in particular mining corporations, under its jurisdiction respect human rights standards when operating abroad; (b) consider establishing an independent mechanism with powers to investigate human rights abuses by such corporations abroad; (c) and develop a legal framework that affords legal remedies to people who have been victims of activities of such corporations operating abroad.[119]

This comment, clearly advancing the language of the 2012 observation on Germany, indicates that duties for home states to regulate the extraterritorial conduct of corporate nationals could be crystallizing under the ICCPR.

5.5 ICESCR

The extraterritorial scope of the ICESCR is more open to debate due to the current dearth of case law under that treaty. Furthermore, the ICESCR does not contain a provision relating to jurisdictional or territorial scope.[120] Article 2(1) does, however, say that states must progressively realize ICESCR rights through steps taken individually 'and through international assistance and cooperation'. Those words seem to imply that states should at least refrain from actions which harm those rights abroad, as such measures are decidedly non-cooperative.

The International Court of Justice confirmed in its advisory opinion on the *Legal Consequences of the Construction of a Wall in the Occupied Palestinian Territory* that states have duties under the ICESCR to 'territories over which a State party has sovereignty and to those over which that State exercises territorial jurisdiction'.[121] Ultimately, the Court found that Israel had violated a number of rights in the ICESCR by building part of its wall in the Occupied Territory and, for example, hindering access to educational facilities, places of employment, health services, agricultural land, and sources of water. In *Democratic Republic of Congo v Uganda* the International Court stated that states are responsible under international human rights treaties for acts done in the exercise of jurisdiction outside their territory, especially in occupied territories.[122] The *Wall* standard focused on territorial control (which Israel exercised over the West Bank), at least in respect of the ICESCR, while the *Congo* standard seemed to focus on extraterritorial acts with regard to all human rights treaties.

---

[118] Concluding Observations on Germany, CCPR/C/DEU/CO/6 (12 November 2012), para 16.

[119] Concluding Observations on Canada, CCPR/C/CAN/CO/6 (13 August 2015), para 6 (emphasis added).

[120] ICESCR-OP, Art 2 provides that communications may be received on behalf of people 'under the jurisdiction of a State party'.

[121] HRC, Concluding Observations of the Human Rights Committee: Israel, CCPR/C/ISR/CO/3 (3 September 2010), paras 111–13.

[122] *Armed Activities on the Territory of the Congo* (*Democratic Republic of the Congo v Uganda*) (Judgment, Merits) [2005] ICJ Rep 168, para 216.

Given that extraterritorial jurisdiction under the ICESCR exists, one may readily assume that states are required to *respect* ICESCR rights outside their borders, that is, to refrain from harming such rights. In fact, the most important aspects of a duty to respect may arise with regard to intra-territorial acts which have an extraterritorial effect, rather than with extraterritorial acts as such. For example, the adoption by a state of protectionist measures within its territory will often cause harm to the right to work of those in export industries outside its territory. Indeed, a state's intra-territorial acts are more likely to impact detrimentally (or beneficially) on economic, social, and cultural rights abroad than civil and political rights. The comparable analysis is arguably that of the refoulement cases, meaning that harm amounts to a breach of ICESCR obligations if a real risk of breach is reasonably foreseeable. On the other hand, the connection between the state and the expelled person is clearer than in the case of an external person who suffers economic harm, as the impugned act of refoulement initially occurs while the person is within the state's territory, and the act is clearly aimed at that person such as to cause harm to his or her rights. Therefore, the crucial jurisdictional issue in this context concerns the identification of circumstances when a state owes obligations to persons outside its territory such that it must avoid acts, whether occurring inside or outside its territory, that cause harm to their ICESCR rights. That is, the question may be more one of 'who has rights' rather than 'where has the impugned act occurred'.

The Committee on Economic, Social and Cultural Rights has indicated that states. parties also have duties to *protect* ICESCR rights in other states. For example, it stated in General Comment 15 on the right to water that states should take steps 'to prevent their own citizens and companies from violating the right to water of individuals and communities in other countries'.[123] On the other hand, the UN Special Representative on the issue of human rights and transnational corporations concluded that 'States are not [presently] generally required under international human rights law to regulate the extraterritorial activities of businesses domiciled in their territory and/or jurisdiction'.[124] Such a duty is easier to maintain if a state is actively facilitating its corporations' overseas activities, such as through the provision of export credits.

The most controversial aspect of potential extraterritorial duties under the ICESCR relates to *fulfilling* ICESCR rights in other states. Such a duty would imply that rich states are obliged to provide aid to assist poorer countries. Rich states predictably resist such a characterization of their ICESCR duties. Such a duty is more evident in the words of the Declaration on the Right to Development,[125] as well as the 2030 Agenda for Sustainable Development.[126] For its part, the Committee has indicated that states have a duty to assist other states to provide international assistance when they are in a position to do so.[127] On the other hand, the parameters of such a duty are difficult to determine. When, precisely, would state X have a duty to a person in state Y to take positive actions to fulfil his or her

---

[123] CESCR, General Comment 15, HRI/GEN/1/Rev.9 (Vol 1) 97, para 33. See also CESCR, General Comment 19, HRI/GEN/1/Rev.9 (Vol 1) 152, para 54. The Committee has reiterated this view in numerous Concluding Observations.

[124] See Report of the Special Representative of the Secretary-General on the issue of human rights and transnational corporations and other business enterprises: 'Guiding Principles on Business and Human Rights: Implementing the United Nations "Protect, Respect and Remedy" Framework', A/HRC/17/31 (21 March 2011), Principle 2. Compare with the text at page 126.

[125] Declaration on the Right to Development, esp Art 4.

[126] GA Res 70/1, Transforming Our World: The 2030 Agenda for Sustainable Development (21 October 2015).

[127] eg CESCR, General Comment 3, HRI/GEN/1/Rev.9 (Vol 1) 7, para 14; CESCR, General Comment 12, para 35; CESCR, General Comment 15, para 38.

rights? And when could that person's socio-economic deprivation be held to come within the responsibility of a particular external state?[128]

In September 2011, the Maastricht Principles on the Extraterritorial Obligations of States in the Area of Economic, Social and Cultural Rights (Principles) were adopted by a group of legal experts under the auspices of Maastricht University and the International Commission of Jurists. The preamble sets out the drafters' intention to address the actions of states in a globalized world which increasingly affect the economic, social, and cultural rights of individuals outside their borders. Principle 3 provides that '[a]ll States have obligations to respect, protect and fulfil human rights, including civil, cultural, economic, political and social rights, both within their territories and extraterritorially.' Principle 9 clarifies:

> A State has obligations to respect, protect and fulfil economic, social and cultural rights in any of the following:
>
> a) situations over which it exercises authority or effective control, whether or not such control is exercised in accordance with international law;
>
> b) situations over which State acts or omissions bring about foreseeable effects on the enjoyment of economic, social and cultural rights, whether within or outside its territory;
>
> c) situations in which the State, acting separately or jointly, whether through its executive, legislative or judicial branches, is in a position to exercise decisive influence or to take measures to realize economic, social and cultural rights extraterritorially, in accordance with international law.

The Principles also provide that states remain responsible for their own conduct even when they are acting as members of international organizations (Principle 15); that states must interpret and apply other international instruments (such as trade agreements) consistently with their human rights obligations (Principle 17); that states must refrain (and require non-state actors under their power to refrain) from actions which nullify or impair others' enjoyment of economic, social, and cultural rights (Principles 20 and 24); and that states must take steps to create an 'international enabling environment conducive to the universal fulfilment of economic, social and cultural rights' (Principle 29).[129] The Principles are not binding at international law, nor are they open for signature by states. The OHCHR describes such instruments as having 'an undeniable moral force' and providing 'practical guidance to States in their conduct.'[130] The Principles may also play a role in developing and crystallizing customary international law in the area, given they represent a statement by eminent experts of their opinion as to what that law is.

5.6 OVERALL ASSESSMENT

It seems that all major international human rights courts and tribunals accept that extraterritorial jurisdiction lies when a state has effective control of a foreign territory, and when it exercises control over the person whose rights have been allegedly abused. The scope of such 'personal' jurisdiction under the ECHR is probably narrower than under the other treaties.

---

[128] See Salomon, *Global Responsibility for Human Rights* (OUP, 2007) 184–93.

[129] De Schutter *et al.*, 'Commentary to the Maastricht Principles on Extraterritorial Obligations of States in the Area of Economic, Social and Cultural Rights' (2012) 34 *HRQ* 1084.

[130] See OHCHR, *International Law*, available at <http://www2.ohchr.org/english/law>.

Wilde has put forward a convincing argument that the focus on jurisdiction over a person, rather than territory, is the preferred determinant of establishing when a state has extraterritorial jurisdiction. He claims, correctly, that a territorial focus inevitably discriminates against non-nationals, as states are far more likely to be in control of territory populated by nationals. Furthermore, a solely territorial focus would permit states to dictate that their agents behave on foreign-controlled soil in a manner that is not permitted under human rights law at home. Finally, the territorial approach might regrettably generate legal vacuums where no human rights law applies.[131]

An issue arises as to the comprehensiveness of a state's extraterritorial human rights obligations. Within its territory, a state must respect, protect, and fulfil human rights. One might imagine that, extraterritorially, a sliding scale of duties applies according to the degree of control a state has over a particular situation.[132] For example, the detainees in Guantánamo Bay are under the total control of the US and, therefore, should be entitled to claim the full range of treaty rights against the US, regardless of their Cuban location. On the other hand, one might assume that Israel's human rights responsibilities in Gaza are not as comprehensive since its withdrawal from that territory. While Israel is obliged to refrain from measures which harm rights in Gaza, it seems unlikely that Israel retains the same obligation to fulfil the right to education in Gaza, where educational facilities are essentially controlled by Hamas, an entity that is hostile to Israel. Similarly, while the victim in *Montero v Uruguay* could claim the right to freedom of movement against the Uruguayan consulate in Germany with regard to a refusal to renew his passport, Montero could not claim that the consulate was required to take measures to protect the full range of his rights while he was in Germany. When jurisdiction is tied to an act with respect to a person, rather than effective control over territory, 'it would seem that the individual is within the jurisdiction of that state only for the purposes of that act',[133] with the relevant act in *Montero*, for example, being the refusal to renew the passport.

In *Banković*, the European Court of Human Rights denied that a state's obligations could 'be divided and tailored in accordance with the particular circumstances of the extra-territorial act in question'.[134] However, this 'all or nothing' approach seems unduly strict. There seems little difficulty, for example, in imposing a duty on states to respect human rights, and therefore refrain from actions which harm human rights outside their territory. On the other hand, the extent of extraterritorial positive obligations (to protect and fulfil) seems logically more dependent upon a greater degree of control over a situation.

Indeed, the European Court seemed to depart from its strict *Banković* position in *Ilascu*, with regard to the scope of Moldova's human rights responsibilities on the facts of that case. The complaint against Moldova in *Ilascu* concerned its jurisdiction over an area within its own territory, but where it plainly lacked control. Analogous situations include Cuba's responsibility for Guantánamo Bay and Cyprus's responsibility for Northern Cyprus. Does a state retain jurisdiction over such areas for human rights purposes? In *Ilascu*, the European Court conceded that Moldova did not have effective control over Transdniestria so the scope of its jurisdiction was reduced,[135] but it retained

---

[131] Wilde, 'Legal "Black hole"? Extraterritorial State action and international treaty law on civil and political rights' (2005) 26 *Michigan JIL* 1, 25–8. See also *Lopez Burgos*, including the concurring opinion of Mr Tomuschat.

[132] Wilde, 'Triggering State Obligations Extraterritorially: the Spatial Test in Certain Human Rights Treaties' (2007) 40 *Israel LR* 503, 524.   [133] Cerone (2006), 1497.

[134] *Bankovic et al. v Belgium et al.* (2007) 44 EHRR SE5, para 75.   [135] *Ilascu*, para 333.

'a positive obligation ... to take diplomatic, economic, judicial or other measures that [were] within its power to take ... to secure the rights guaranteed in the Convention'.[136] The concession that jurisdiction can be retained in a reduced form cut against the Court's 'all or nothing' approach in *Banković* that jurisdiction is not divisible.

In *Al-Skeini*, the European Court explicitly confirmed that its view had changed, stating:

> It is clear that, whenever the State through its agents exercises control and authority over an individual, and thus jurisdiction, the State is under an obligation under Article 1 to secure to that individual the rights and freedoms under Section 1 of the Convention that are relevant to the situation of that individual. In this sense, therefore, the Convention rights can be 'divided and tailored' (compare *Banković*, cited above, § 75).[137]

As noted by Milanovic, this finding is completely contradictory to *Bankovic*, so the Court was quite cheeky to ask us to 'compare' the findings.[138]

In *Al-Saadoon*, the Court of Appeal of England and Wales indicated that a state that exercises 'effective control' over an area outside its territory is in fact responsible 'for the entire range of substantive rights set out in the Convention and [relevant] additional Protocols'.[139] Hence, the notion of 'dividing and tailoring rights' has no application in cases of effective territorial control. It is relevant, according to *Al-Skeini*, when jurisdiction is grounded on the exercise of control over an individual.[140]

6 CONCLUSION

Generally, states owe human rights duties to individuals and groups within their jurisdiction. However, the extent of a state's jurisdiction for the purposes of its human rights treaty obligations is a complex and evolving concept. There would be gaping lacunae in human rights protection if a state's jurisdiction, and consequent responsibility, only arose in connection with its own acts and omissions within its own territory.

Therefore, human rights law has evolved to generate the concept of due diligence to ensure some accountability for human rights abuses in the private sphere. In contrast, the extent of state responsibility for the acts of international organizations is less clear.

The broader view of extraterritorial jurisdiction, which clearly prevails within the UN treaty bodies, the Inter-American bodies, and probably the International Court of Justice, holds that such jurisdiction arises when a state has effective control over the enjoyment of a particular right by an individual. This view has significant ramifications for the extraterritorial scope of the ICESCR, given the ubiquity of external economic impacts, and consequent effects on economic, social, and cultural rights, caused by state actions in today's interconnected global economy. The European Court seems to adopt a slightly narrower approach than other institutions after *Al-Skeini*, given that the exercise of 'mere' extraterritorial lethal force falls outside jurisdiction, though the scope of extraterritorial jurisdiction under the ECHR is now considerably larger than was decided in *Bankovic*.

---

[136] *Ilascu*, para 331. See also *Mozer v Republic of Moldova and Russia*, App no 11138/10, Judgment of 23 February 2016.   [137] See *Al-Skeini*, para 137.

[138] Milanovic, 'Al-Skeini and Al-Jedda in Strasbourg' (2012) 23 *EJIL* 121, 129.

[139] *Al-Saadoon*, para 34; see also *Al-Skeini*, paras 138–140.   [140] *Al-Skeini*, para. 137.

FURTHER READING

CERONE, 'Human Dignity in the Line of Fire: The Application of International Human Rights Law during Armed Conflict, Occupation, and Peace Operations' (2006) 39 *Vanderbilt JTL* 1446.

COOMANS and KAMMINGA (eds), *Extraterritorial Application of Human Rights* (Intersentia, 2004).

CRAVEN, 'The Violence of Dispossession: Extra-Territoriality and Economic, Social and Cultural Rights' in Baderin and McCorquodale (eds), *Economic, Social and Cultural Rights in Action* (Oxford University Press, 2007).

HATHAWAY *et al.*, 'Human Rights Abroad: When Do Human Rights Treaty Obligations Apply Extraterritorially?' (2011) 43 *Arizona State LJJ* 389.

INTERNATIONAL LAW COMMISSION, *Articles on Responsibility of States for Internationally Wrongful Acts*, A/56/10, ch IV.E.1.

KNOX, 'Horizontal Human Rights Law' (2008) 103 *AJIL* 1.

LANGFORD, SCHEININ, VANDENHOLE, and VAN GENUGTEN (eds), *Global Justice, State Duties* (Cambridge University Press, 2012).

MILANOVIC, *Extraterritorial Application of Human Rights Treaties: Law, Principles, and Policy* (Oxford University Press, 2011).

SALOMON, *Global Responsibility for Human Rights* (Oxford University Press, 2007).

SARI, 'Untangling Extra-Territorial Jurisdiction from International Responsibility in Jaloud v. Netherlands: Old Problem, New Solutions?' (2014) 53 *Military Law and the Law of War Review* 287.

SKOGLY, 'Extraterritoriality: Universal Human Rights without Universal Obligations?' in Joseph and McBeth (eds), *Research Handbook on International Human Rights* (Edward Elgar, 2010).

WILDE, 'The Extraterritorial Application of International Human Rights Law on Civil and Political Rights' in Rodley and Sheeran (eds), *Routledge Handbook on Human Rights* (Routledge, 2013).

PART III

SUBSTANTIVE RIGHTS

7

CATEGORIES OF RIGHTS

Theo van Boven

SUMMARY

This chapter seeks to identify different categories of human rights, but in doing so recognizes the indivisibility, interdependence, and interrelatedness of all human rights. A first categorization distinguishes civil and political rights from economic, social, and cultural rights. This distinction is, however, increasingly contested and should not disguise the mutual relationship between these rights as essential conditions for the life and well-being of the human person. A second distinction is that between the rights of individuals and the rights of collectivities, in particular indigenous peoples. Collective rights offer parameters for the effective enjoyment of individual rights. A third distinction is that between core rights and other rights, raising the issue of whether there is a ranking among human rights as to their fundamental nature. It is argued that basic substantive rights determining the life, survival, dignity, and worth of individuals and peoples may be considered as core rights. The chapter finally discusses the question of whether 'new human rights' are emerging. It advises that this question be approached with caution and that human rights should be understood in an inclusive and newly focused manner, encompassing hitherto marginalized and excluded groups and human beings.

1 INTRODUCTION

There is a certain uneasiness about classifying human rights in different categories. Leading UN documents state that all human rights are *indivisible*, *interdependent*, and *interrelated*. Whatever categories of human rights one may have in mind—civil, political, economic, social, or cultural rights; individual or collective rights; core rights or other rights—intersections bear out that all rights are interlinked and that categories or classifications correspond more to conceptual premises than to realities. The relative inadequacy of human rights categories and classifications becomes evident when the focus is on the human being whose enjoyment of rights and freedoms depends on prevailing conditions of freedom from fear and freedom from want. Domestic and international policies, insofar as they take into account the holistic nature of human rights, transcend human rights categorizations and classifications.

The comprehensive and holistic nature of human rights was recognized by US President Franklin D Roosevelt when, in his famous speech of 1941, he mentioned 'four essential freedoms' that must be guaranteed to all persons everywhere in the world: freedom of speech and expression, freedom of worship, freedom from want, and freedom from fear.[1] This forward-looking four freedoms message served as one of the sources of inspiration for the UN International Bill of Rights and continues to inspire policy-makers. For example, former UN Secretary-General Kofi Annan, in his landmark report *In Larger Freedom: Towards Development, Security and Human Rights for All*, drew extensively on the freedom from want and freedom from fear paradigm.[2] A major thrust thereof is that development, security, and human rights are not only interlinked, they also reinforce each other.[3] In order to attain larger freedom, human rights must be an integral part of development and security policies. Even though this chapter reviews various categories of human rights, this should neither distract from the indivisibility of all human rights, nor from their comprehensive and holistic nature.

2 CATEGORIES OF HUMAN RIGHTS

2.1 ECONOMIC, SOCIAL, CULTURAL RIGHTS/CIVIL, POLITICAL RIGHTS

Much attention has been given over the years to the distinction between, on the one hand, *economic, social, and cultural rights* (such as the rights to an adequate standard of living, education and work, dealt with in Chapters 10 and 12) and, on the other, *civil and political rights* (such as the rights to life and integrity of the person, the freedoms of thought, expression, association, and assembly, and the rights to liberty and a fair trial, dealt with in Chapters 9, 11, and 13).[4] There is indeed a significant difference between the two as far as the nature of states parties' obligations under the International Covenant on Economic, Social and Cultural Rights (ICESCR) and the International Covenant on Civil and Political Rights (ICCPR) are concerned. While Article 2 ICESCR provides for the *progressive realization* of economic, social, and cultural rights and acknowledges the constraints due to limits of available resources, the parallel Article 2 ICCPR prescribes the obligation to respect and ensure all civil and political rights as an *immediate* obligation. Accordingly, the Committee on Economic, Social and Cultural Rights has viewed the concept of progressive realization as a recognition that full realization of all economic, social, and cultural rights will generally not be achieved in a short period of time. Since progressive realization is an essential objective, not in the abstract but to the maximum of available resources, a question arises regarding how such an obligation of the state is to be interpreted in times of economic depression and shrinking resources as experienced at the end of the first decade of the twenty-first century. An essential bottom-line to be respected under all circumstances, even in times of shrinking resources, is that of non-discrimination, which the Committee termed 'an immediate and cross-cutting obligation in the [ICESCR].'[5]

Nevertheless, the Committee on Economic, Social and Cultural Rights has pointed out that, despite this difference, there are also significant similarities between the ICESCR and the ICCPR. In particular, the ICESCR imposes various obligations of *immediate effect*.[6] Thus, there are a number of provisions in the ICESCR that, as the Committee has pointed out in its General Comment 3, would seem to be capable of immediate application by

---

[1] Commager, *Documents of American History* (Crofts, 1946) 634.   [2] A/59/2005 (21 March 2005).

[3] See World Summit outcome document, GA Res 60/1 (24 October 2005) para 9.

[4] Van Boven, 'Distinguishing Criteria of Human Rights' in Vasak and Alston (eds), *The International Dimensions of Human Rights: Vol 1* (UNESCO/Greenwood Press 1982) 87.

[5] CESCR, General Comment 20, E/C.12/GC/20 (2009) para 7.

[6] CESCR, General Comment 3, HRI/GEN/1/(Vol 1) 7, para 1.

judicial and other organs in many domestic legal systems. Among these are the elimination of discrimination (Articles 2(2) and (3)), the right to form and join trade unions and to strike (Article 8), protection of children and young persons from economic and social exploitation (Article 10(3)), equal remuneration for work of equal value without distinction of any kind (Article 7(a)(i)), the provision of free and compulsory primary education for all (Article 13(2)(a)), the liberty of parents to choose schools for their children, other than those established by public authorities (Article 13(3)), and the liberty of individuals and bodies to establish and direct educational institutions which conform to certain minimum standards (Article 13(4)).[7]

In addition to the difference between obligations of immediate effect and progressive realization, it is quite common to advance further criteria to distinguish civil and political rights from economic and social rights by contrasting the concept of freedom rights with that of welfare rights or by referring to duties of the state not to intervene as opposed to duties to take positive measures. Such distinctions are helpful but do not apply across the board insofar as there is no strict dividing line between civil and political rights on the one hand and economic and social rights on the other.

While the status of civil and political rights as human rights is largely uncontested, this is less true for economic, social, and cultural rights.[8] The latter are sometimes referred to as 'aspirations' phrased in terms of rights but without legal enforceability. The media, many NGOs, public officials, as well as public opinion generally understand human rights in terms of the right to life, the abolition of the death penalty, the prohibition of torture, the right to privacy, freedom of information and expression, freedom of religion or belief, and the right to vote and to be elected. The rights to food, healthcare, housing, and employment are considered much less part of the human rights package. However, this perception of human rights overlooks the comprehensive nature of the Universal Declaration of Human Rights (UDHR) and notably its Article 28, which provides that everyone is entitled to a social and international order in which the rights and freedoms set forth in the Declaration can be fully realized. Over the years, as the human rights discourse became part of processes towards widening categories of entitlements and beneficiaries and linking human rights to the promotion of peace, security, and sustainable development, as well as preserving a healthy environment, a comprehensive human rights approach has evolved, encompassing the broad and interlinked scale of civil, political, economic, social, and cultural rights.

2.2 RIGHTS OF INDIVIDUALS/RIGHTS OF COLLECTIVITIES

The same process has also had an impact on another traditional categorization of human rights, namely the distinction between *rights of individuals* and *rights of collectivities*. In the frame of reference of the UDHR and the international covenants, with their emphasis on human dignity and the worth and uniqueness of every human being, the focus is on the rights of every individual person. Of course, in many ways individual human beings live and work in community and partnership with other human beings, in family and similar relations, in the exercise of religion or belief, in educational settings, and in forming and joining trade unions. Yet it is the individual person, while part of social or cultural relations of a community nature, who is the beneficiary of rights.

---

[7] CESCR, General Comment 3, paras 1 and 5.

[8] See Robinson, 'Advancing Economic, Social and Cultural Rights: The Way Forward' (2004) 26 *HRQ* 866; Roth, 'Defending Economic, Social and Cultural Rights: Practical Issues Faced by an International Human Rights Organization' (2004) 26 *HRQ* 63.

The same construction has been used, at least in the UN terminology, where rights of peoples and minority groups, addressed in Chapter 18, are involved. Minorities, as collectivities, are not referred to as beneficiaries of rights. This is so that any separatist ambitions that they may pursue in the states where they live are not legitimized. Accordingly, the relevant provision of the ICCPR, Article 27 reads: 'In those States in which ethnic, religious or linguistic minorities exist, *persons belonging to such minorities* shall not be denied the right, in community with other members of their group, to enjoy their own culture, to profess and practise their own religion, or to use their own language.'[9] This provision is phrased in very restrained terms and avoids, at least in theory, the recognition of collective rights. Similarly, the UN Declaration on the Rights of Persons Belonging to National or Ethnic, Religious and Linguistic Minorities (1992) cautiously and consistently refers to 'persons belonging to minorities', thereby focusing on individuals rather than collectivities.

A different approach, one that is more collectivist or peoples-oriented, is to be found in the UN Declaration on the Rights of Indigenous Peoples (2007). The text of this declaration was negotiated over a period of more than 20 years with considerable input from indigenous peoples themselves. In the preamble of the Declaration, the rights of individuals and the rights of collectivities are brought together in a dialectical fashion by 'recognizing and reaffirming that indigenous individuals are entitled without discrimination to all human rights recognized in international law and that indigenous peoples possess collective rights which are indispensable for their existence, well-being and integral development as peoples'.[10] Throughout the text of the Declaration, rights are attributed to indigenous peoples as well as to indigenous individuals, with the indigenous peoples as principal rights-holders and the express recognition of the right to self-determination as the cornerstone of their rights. Article 3 of the Declaration restates the wording of common Article 1 of the international covenants, applying it to the particular case of indigenous peoples: 'Indigenous peoples have the right to self-determination. By virtue of that right they freely determine their political status and freely pursue their economic, social and cultural development.' In many ways, the Declaration on the Rights of Indigenous Peoples brings together peoples' rights and individual rights in a spectrum of mutual relationship and reach. A good illustration of this is Article 7, which, echoing Article 3 UDHR, provides that 'indigenous individuals have the rights to life, physical and mental integrity, liberty and security of person', while at the same time making it clear, in language similar to the UN Declaration on the Right of Peoples to Peace (1984),[11] that 'indigenous peoples have the collective right to live in freedom, peace and security as distinct peoples'.

This collective dimension of the rights of peoples and populations, for present and future generations, recognizes that the realization and enjoyment of individual rights are conditioned by the attainment of peace, security, and development. The same notion is embodied in the right to self-determination, defined in terms of free determination of political status and free pursuance of economic, social, and cultural development. Peoples' right to self-determination is recognized as a leading and underlying principle for the enjoyment of civil, political, economic, social, and cultural rights and was therefore included in both international covenants as the first substantive provision. Against this background, the 1993 Vienna World Conference on Human Rights considered the denial of the right of self-determination as a violation of human rights.[12] Similarly, it is

---

[9] Emphasis added.   [10] GA Res 61/295 (13 September 2007) preamble.
[11] GA Res 39/11 (12 November 1984).
[12] Vienna Declaration and Programme of Action, A/CONF.157/23 (25 June 1993) para 2. See also Chapter 18.

significant that the UN Declaration on the Right to Development (1986) places the individual and collective aspects of this right in a mutual relationship and seeks to link the conditions of life of the human person with the welfare and well-being of peoples.[13] Thus, the right to development is defined as an inalienable human right with the proviso that equality of opportunity for development is a prerogative both of nations and of individuals who make up nations. Further, the Declaration states that 'the human person is the central subject of development and should be the active participant and beneficiary of the right to development'.[14]

2.3 ONE-DIMENSIONAL/COMPOSITE RIGHTS

As compared to rights such as freedom of expression or the right to a fair trial, the rights to self-determination and development, as well as the right to peace, are of a more complex nature. Therefore, they are often described as composite rights. The question may be asked what the legal significance of such rights is. While they condition the life and welfare of individual human beings, they are not rights inherent in the human person. Their realization depends on political, economic, social, and cultural policies deployed by national and international organs and institutions. These rights do not lend themselves to enforcement by legal authorities. Nevertheless, gross violations of the right to peace, the right to self-determination, or the right to development may, under given circumstances, incur state responsibility as well as civil responsibility of other major actors, or, if they amount to aggression, genocide, or crimes against humanity, even criminal responsibility of natural persons. While these rights primarily represent major policy objectives of a national and international order, their legal implications are not without significance and may be tested in political or judicial settings in case of their breach or gross denial.

A new instrument in the toolbox of composite rights is the Declaration on the Right to Peace, which was adopted by the UN General Assembly in December 2016. The Resolution was adopted by 131 votes in favour to 34 against and 19 abstentions, reflecting a North-South divide that also existed in respect of the right to self-determination and the right to development.[15] Arguments in favour of the Declaration were based on the maxim that 'peace and security, development and human rights are the pillars of the United Nations system and the foundations for collective security and well-being'[16] and on visions and goals reflected in the 2030 Agenda for Sustainable Development.[17] These were countered by arguments such as the lack of a legal basis for the right to peace in international law and the lack of consensus on the definition of this right. The text of the Declaration, which was the outcome of lengthy deliberations in the UN Human Rights Council, comes across as a curious combination of a long preamble of no less than 37 paragraphs and a minuscule operative part of five articles. Measured against the yardstick of ambitions and efforts constructively deployed by a broad civil society constituency and having regard to the creative work performed by the Advisory Committee of the UN Human Rights Council to spell out the right to peace into a normative framework with a series of guiding standards for the Declaration[18], the text appears rhetorically tempting but substantively wanting.

---

13 GA Res 41/128 (4 December 1986).
14 GA Res 41/128 (4 December 1986), Art 2(1).
15 GA Res 71/189 (19 December 2016).
16 GA Res 60/1 (24 October 2005).
17 GA Res 70/1 (25 September 2015).
18 See Villán Durán, *The Emerging Right to Peace: Its Legal Foundations* (Intersentia, 2014).

3 INTERDEPENDENCE AND INDIVISIBILITY OF ALL HUMAN RIGHTS

The previous section identified different categories of human rights: civil and political rights as compared to economic, social, and cultural rights; rights of individuals as compared to rights of collectives; one-dimensional rights as compared to rights of a composite nature. But it has also already been made clear that all these rights are intersected and interrelated. They condition each other, with the human person, as the UN Declaration on the Right to Development puts it, as 'the central subject' and 'beneficiary' of rights,[19] and, in the words of the preambles of the international covenants, with a focus on 'the ideal of free human beings enjoying freedom from fear and want'.

Against this background, the interdependence and indivisibility of all human rights, whether or not classified in various categories, has become a leading axiom in the international human rights discourse. A number of examples taken from UN instruments, statements, and practices can be advanced to underline this interdependence and indivisibility. The Proclamation of Teheran, adopted at the first world conference on human rights in 1968, stated that human rights and fundamental freedoms are indivisible.[20] The second world conference held in Vienna in 1993 stated with greater emphasis that '[a]ll human rights are universal, indivisible, and interdependent and interrelated'.[21] The outcome document of the 2005 World Summit reaffirmed this statement.[22] The General Assembly resolution of 2006 establishing the Human Rights Council again reaffirmed that 'all human rights are universal, indivisible, interrelated, interdependent and mutually reinforcing, and that all human rights must be treated in a fair and equal manner, on the same footing and with the same emphasis'.[23]

It may be argued that reiterating and reaffirming the same phrase does not necessarily make it a reality. Perhaps more convincing are the language and contents of specific legal instruments on non-discrimination and the rights of vulnerable persons and persons in need of special recognition and protection. Thus, the International Convention on the Elimination of All Forms of Racial Discrimination, the Convention on the Elimination of All Forms of Discrimination Against Women, the Convention on the Rights of the Child, the International Convention on the Protection of the Rights of All Migrant Workers and Members of Their Families, and the Convention on the Rights of Persons with Disabilities all recognize the full scope of human rights in a comprehensive interrelationship. Finally, as already noted, it can be argued that the UN Declaration on the Rights of Indigenous Peoples is in its scope and wording the most far-reaching illustration of the interdependence and interrelatedness of all human rights, be they economic, social, cultural, civil, or political rights; rights of individuals or collectivities; or composite rights such as the right to self-determination and the right to development.

In line with the interdependence and indivisibility of all human rights, a significant evolution has occurred over the years towards the *enhanced status of economic, social, and cultural rights*. Thus, UN supervisory mechanisms and procedures, including those relating to violations of human rights, have progressively brought economic, social, and cultural rights on a par with civil and political rights. Further, while initially, after the entry into force of the ICESCR, the UN Economic and Social Council was entrusted with general monitoring tasks, it soon became clear that it lacked the capacity and expertise to carry

---

[19] GA Res 41/128 (4 December 1986), Art 2(1).
[20] UN, *Compilation of International Instruments, Vol 1 (First Part)* (1993) 51–4, Art 13.
[21] Vienna Declaration and Programme of Action, A/CONF.157/23 (25 June 1993), para 5.
[22] GA Res 60/1 (24 October 2005), para 13.   [23] GA Res 60/251 (3 April 2006), preambular para 3.

out these tasks effectively. Therefore, the Council established a supervisory committee of independent experts, the Committee on Economic, Social and Cultural Rights, with similar tasks and responsibilities as the Human Rights Committee under the ICCPR. In 2008 the UN General Assembly adopted an Optional Protocol to the ICESCR, which provides for the right to petition by individuals or groups of individuals claiming to be victims of a violation of any of the rights set forth in the Covenant by a state party that has accepted the Optional Protocol. This legal instrument, which entered into force in 2013, can be considered as a counterpart to the previously established First Optional Protocol to the ICCPR. It helps to strengthen the legal protection of economic, social, and cultural rights by the development of case law which enhances, domestically and internationally, the justiciability of economic, social, and cultural rights. Although the Optional Protocol to the ICESCR was finally, after lengthy and protracted negotiations, adopted without a vote, it did not attract unreserved support of the entire UN membership. A number of states would have preferred an *à la carte* instrument which would expressly allow states to select the rights they would accept as falling under the operation of the Protocol. This view, however, did not prevail and the Protocol, therefore, covers all the rights included in the ICESCR.

The same tendency of rendering a more prominent status to economic, social, and cultural rights is also apparent in the system of special procedures developed under the former UN Commission on Human Rights and now operating under the authority of the Human Rights Council. These special procedures with geographic or thematic mandates were established to respond to gross and consistent patterns of human rights violations. They initially concentrated on violations of civil and political rights, notably enforced disappearances, extrajudicial, summary, and arbitrary executions, torture and ill-treatment, arbitrary arrests and detention, freedom of religion or belief, and freedom of opinion and expression.[24] Gradually, however, during the last decade of the twentieth century and in later years, civil and political rights mandates were complemented by mandates in the area of economic, social, and cultural rights, notably dealing with the right to adequate housing, the right to food, human rights and extreme poverty, the right to physical and mental health, the right to education, and the right to water. Other thematic mandates dealing with contemporary forms of racism, indigenous people, minority issues, the rights of migrants, the promotion of truth, justice, reparation, and guarantees of non-recurrence, and the protection against violence and discrimination based on sexual orientation and gender identity cover a whole range of human rights, not limited to civil and political rights or economic, social, and cultural rights.

A significant role in identifying and supporting the normative content of economic, social, and cultural rights was played by the Limburg Principles on the Implementation of the ICESCR, drawn up in 1986 by a group of experts.[25] The Limburg Principles were instrumental in helping to frame the conceptual work of the Committee on Economic, Social and Cultural Rights so as to clarify the obligations of states under the ICESCR, including their legal duties arising from violations of economic, social, and cultural rights. Ten years later, the Maastricht Guidelines on Violations of Economic, Social and Cultural Rights underscored the violations component by spelling out that violations can occur through both acts of commission and omissions by the state, and by providing guidance on states' responsibility for violations, the notion of victims, and remedies and other responses to violations.[26] More recently, the Maastricht Principles on Extraterritorial Obligations of States in the Area of Economic, Social and Cultural Rights were drawn up to clarify the content of extraterritorial state obligations to realize economic, social, and cultural rights.[27]

---

[24] See Limon and Piccone, *Human Rights Special Procedures* (Foreign Policy at Brookings & Universal Rights Group, 2014). [25] (1987) 9 *HRQ* 121. [26] (1998) 20 *HRQ* 691.
[27] (2011) 34 *HRQ* 1084.

The focus on violations is linked with the issue of the 'justiciability' of economic, so-cial, and cultural rights. Justiciability refers to the ability of an independent and impartial body to provide a remedy for individuals in case of a violation of a right.[28] The general comments by treaty bodies, notably the Committee on Economic, Social and Cultural Rights and the Committee on the Rights of the Child, have helped to define the content of economic, social, and cultural rights in view of their justiciability.[29] The Optional Protocol to the ICESCR will contribute to a broader acceptance of the notion of justiciability of economic, social, and cultural rights.

4 CORE RIGHTS

While the principle of interdependence and indivisibility of all human rights has become axiomatic and largely uncontested, the issue remains whether certain human rights rank higher than other rights because they are more essential for the preservation of human life and the upholding of human dignity and human welfare. For instance, there is little doubt that the right to life and the prohibition of torture, enshrined in Articles 2 and 5 UDHR, are more fundamental or basic than the right to rest and leisure, set out in Article 24. Widely-ratified human rights instruments and their interpretation by judicial and quasi-judicial human rights bodies clearly indicate that certain human rights represent or em-body core attributes of human life and human dignity, so that violations of these rights entail a special and imperative responsibility to prevent, to protect, and to remedy. The fol-lowing examples illustrate that in international human rights law certain rights and their protection rank particularly high on the scale of basic values of human life and existence and can thus be classified as core rights.[30]

Major human rights treaties, notably the ICCPR, the European Convention on Human Rights (ECHR), and the American Convention on Human Rights (ACHR), recognize a set of core rights from which no derogation is permitted, not even during times of public emergency. Thus, Article 4(2) ICCPR lists as non-derogable the right to life, the prohibition of torture or cruel, inhuman, or degrading treatment or punish-ment, the prohibition of slavery, the prohibition of imprisonment because of inability to fulfil a contractual obligation, the principle of legality in criminal law, the recogni-tion of everyone as a person before the law, and the freedom of thought, conscience, and religion. In its General Comment 29, the Human Rights Committee has analysed the implications of Article 4 in detail.[31] It notes that the enumeration of non-derogable provisions is related to, but not identical with, the question of whether certain human rights obligations have the nature of peremptory norms of international law (*jus cogens*) and recognizes that some of the non-derogable ICCPR rights also fall into that category, notably the right to life and the prohibition of torture or cruel, inhuman, or degrading treatment or punishment.

Core rights entail essential obligations on the part of states that have undertaken to respect, protect, and fulfil them. Such obligations are not limited to the field of civil and political rights but extend to economic, social, and cultural rights. Thus, the Committee on Economic, Social and Cultural Rights has stated in its General

---

[28] See Coomans (ed), *Justiciability of Economic and Social Rights; Experiences from Domestic Systems* (Intersentia, 2006).

[29] CESCR, General Comment 20. See further Committee on the Rights of the Child, General Comment 5, HRI/GEN/1/(Vol II) 421.

[30] See also Seiderman, *Hierarchy in International Law: The Human Rights Dimension* (Intersentia, 2001).

[31] HRC, General Comment 29, HRI/GEN/1/(Vol I) 234. See also Chapter 5.

Comment 3 that 'a minimum core obligation to ensure the satisfaction of, at the very least, minimum essential levels of each of the [ICESCR] rights is incumbent upon every State party'.[32] For example, a state party in which a significant number of individuals are deprived of essential foodstuffs, essential primary healthcare, basic shelter and housing, or the most basic forms of education would, according to the Committee, prima facie be failing to discharge its obligations under the Covenant. The formulation of these core obligations relating to basic conditions of human life corresponds to the phrase in common Article 1(2) of both international covenants concerning the right of all peoples to self-determination that 'in no case may a people be deprived of its own means of subsistence'. Consequently, basic subsistence rights which determine the life, the dignity, and the well-being of individuals and peoples should be considered as core rights.

Furthermore, with the development of international criminal law through standard-setting and national and international adjudication, violations of internationally protected basic human rights may amount to crimes under international law, with the corresponding duty of states to carry out an effective and prompt investigation and to prosecute and punish the perpetrators.[33] Another corresponding duty involves the provision of effective remedies to victims, including reparation for harm suffered. As the Human Rights Committee has stated in its General Comment 31, these obligations arise notably in relation to those violations of ICCPR provisions that are recognized as criminal under domestic or international law, such as torture, summary and arbitrary killing, and enforced disappearance.[34] When such violations of the Covenant are committed as part of a widespread or systematic attack on a civilian population, they are crimes against humanity under Article 7 Statute of the International Criminal Court.[35] While the violation of all human rights entails legal consequences in terms of effective remedies, the violation of core rights requires legal action so as to combat impunity and to make reparations. Moreover, the evolving practice of international human rights bodies, notably the European Court of Human Rights, the Inter-American Court of Human Rights, and the Human Rights Committee, makes it abundantly clear that in cases where core rights such as the right to life and the right to be free from torture or ill-treatment are at stake, urgent preventive action by way of provisional or interim measures are called for in order to avoid irreparable harm to persons.[36]

Finally, the newly evolving doctrine of the Responsibility to Protect, set out in the outcome document of the 2005 UN World Summit, attributes special responsibility to protect populations from genocide, war crimes, ethnic cleansing, and crimes against humanity. This responsibility rests primarily with individual states but may also require collective action, through the UN, should national authorities manifestly fail to protect their populations from such crimes.[37] The doctrine of the Responsibility to Protect represents a common *opinio juris* in theory but still needs affirmation and implementation in practice. However, what is important for present purposes is that it implies that core rights and core values pertaining to the very existence and survival of populations may, in situations where national authorities are failing to respect these rights and values, prevail over invocations of national sovereignty.

---

[32] CESCR, General Comment 3, para 10.   [33] See Chapter 26.

[34] HRC, General Comment 31, HRI/GEN/1/(Vol I) 243, para 18.

[35] HRC, General Comment 31, para 18.

[36] Rieter, *Preventing Irreparable Harm: Provisional Measures in International Human Rights Adjudication* (Intersentia, 2010).

[37] GA Res 60/1 (24 October 2005), paras 138–40. See further Evans, *The Responsibility to Protect: Ending Mass Atrocity Crimes Once and For All* (Brookings Institution Press, 2008).

5 NEW HUMAN RIGHTS?

It may be argued that the standard-setting or codification process of human rights was completed with the adoption and entry into force of the general and comprehensive human rights instruments, notably the international covenants and regional instruments such as the ECHR, the European Social Charter, the ACHR, and the ACHPR. However, while a broad corpus of internationally recognized standards has taken shape in these instruments, the standard-setting process did not stop but continued progressively in order to respond to widely felt needs to further define the normative scope of basic rights and principles and to provide more explicit protection for vulnerable and marginalized people.

Examples of the further elaboration of the normative scope of human rights include instruments relating to the abolition of the death penalty, the prohibition of torture or cruel, inhuman, or degrading treatment or punishment, and the elimination of discrimination on the grounds of race, religion, and gender. More explicit protection of specific groups of people is envisaged in instruments relating to the rights of women, children, migrant workers, persons with disabilities, persons subjected to enforced disappearance, and indigenous peoples. These instruments do not define new rights but re-define and re-conceptualize existing human rights in order to make them more explicit and more inclusive and to extend their reach to persons in need of special care, attention, and protection. This is a dynamic process that involves the shaping of the normative content of rights and basic principles such as the best interests of the child, the absolute prohibition of gender-based violence, and the relevance of the right to self-determination.

Human rights treaty bodies, as authoritative interpreters and custodians of treaty norms, have drawn up general comments and recommendations so as to further define or refine the scope and reach of the human rights norms already embodied in legal instruments. Do treaty bodies thereby create new human rights norms? This would not seem to be the purpose and task of treaty bodies. Rather, the purpose of general comments and recommendations is to clarify the normative scope of human rights. For instance, in its General Comment 15, the Committee on Economic, Social and Cultural Rights made it clear that there is a right to water, although such a right is not explicitly referred to in the ICESCR.[38] The Committee did not proclaim this right as a new human right, but defined it as emanating from, and indispensable for, the realization of the right to an adequate standard of living and as inextricably related to the rights to the highest attainable standard of health, adequate housing, and adequate food.[39] Similarly, the Committee on the Elimination of Racial Discrimination, in its General Recommendations on the rights of indigenous peoples, on discrimination against Roma, on descent-based discrimination, and on discrimination against non-citizens,[40] clearly set out the relevance and the applicability of the International Convention on the Elimination of All Forms of Racial Discrimination with respect to groups of marginalized and vulnerable people. It did this, not by the creation of new rights, but by explaining the normative content and the implications of the Convention in support of these groups.

In the human rights discourse and campaigns entertained by proponents of a rights-based strategy on behalf of marginalized and excluded groups, claims are often framed as being part of a 'struggle for new rights'.[41] The rights of children born of wartime

---

[38] See Chapter 10.   [39] CESCR, General Comment 15, HRI/GEN/1/(Vol I) 97, para 3.

[40] Committee on the Elimination of Racial Discrimination, General Recommendation XXIII, HRI/GEN/1/(Vol II) 285, General Recommendation XXVII, HRI/GEN/1/(Vol II) 289, General Recommendation XXIX, HRI/GEN/1/(Vol II) 296, General Recommendation XXX, HRI/GEN/1/(Vol II) 301.

[41] See in particular Bob (ed), *The International Struggle for New Human Rights* (University of Pennsylvania Press, 2009).

rape, Dalits, lesbian, gay, bisexual, transgender and intersex (LGBTI) people, mentally and physically disabled people, people living with HIV and AIDS, and other stigmatized minorities are advocated under this label. These campaigns have greatly contributed to awareness-building and the broadening and deepening of a rights-based approach in support of people who for a long time had been neglected and treated as outsiders or even outcasts. They constitute another step in the lengthy process from exclusion to inclusion, with due regard for the specific situation and the specific interests of the people concerned.

This newly developed reach of human rights has found expression in a series of new instruments and documents such as the Convention on the Rights of Persons with Disabilities, the General Recommendations of the Committee on the Elimination of Racial Discrimination on discrimination against Roma and descent-based discrimination, the General Recommendation of the Committee on the Elimination of Discrimination against Women on the avoidance of discrimination against women in national strategies for the prevention and control of AIDS, as well as the General Comment of the Committee on the Rights of the Child on HIV/AIDS and the rights of the child.[42] The Yogyakarta Principles on the Application of International Human Rights Law in Relation to Sexual Orientation and Gender Identity are a further example illustrating this new human rights focus.[43] While in all these instances the focus and scope of human rights is newly-defined and developed to underline their relevance and applicability to people hitherto neglected, ignored, or degraded, their basic thrust lies in the recognition that all people, without discrimination or exclusion, are entitled to the full benefit of all human rights, notably the right to be equal before the law and non-discrimination. It appears, therefore, that in these instances the term 'new human rights' is conceptually not called for. Instead, the better term might be 'newly focused human rights'. The concept of 'new human rights' should be approached with caution.

Attention may also be drawn to victims' rights in this context. Victims of gross human rights violations have been largely overlooked, both at the national and the international level. Only in recent decades, in particular in the context of transitional justice processes in societies scarred by serious crimes under international law, has there been a tangible movement towards the express recognition of victims' rights as a main condition for the attainment of reconciliation and justice.[44] This emphasis on victims' rights is duly reflected in the UN Basic Principles and Guidelines on the Right to a Remedy and Reparation to Victims of Gross Violations of International Human Rights Law and Serious Violations of International Humanitarian Law (2005) (Reparation Principles).[45] This instrument is not intended to define new victims' rights but to identify mechanisms, modalities, procedures, and methods for the implementation of victims' rights.[46] Another normative document of particular relevance to transitional justice situations is the Updated Set of Principles for the Protection and Promotion of Human Rights Through Actions to Combat Impunity (2005) (Impunity Principles).[47] This document provides for the right to know, the right to justice, and the right to reparation, and guarantees of non-recurrence. Under the right to know, the inalienable right to know the truth figures prominently. This right has a collective dimension. Every people has the right 'to know the truth about past events concerning the

---

[42] Committee on the Elimination of Racial Discrimination, General Recommendation XXVII; Committee on the Elimination of Discrimination against Women, General Recommendation 15, HRI/GEN/1/(Vol II) 327; Committee on the Rights of the Child, General Comment 3, HRI/GEN/1/(Vol II) 398.

[43] Available at: <http://www.yogyakartaprinciples.org/>. See Chapter 15.

[44] De Greiff, Report of the Special Rapporteur on the promotion of truth, justice, reparation and guarantees of non-recurrence, A/69/518 (14 October 2014).

[45] GA Res 60/147 (16 December 2005).   [46] GA Res 60/147, preambular para 7.

[47] E/CN.4/2005/102/Add.1, endorsed by UN Commission on Human Rights Res 2005/81 (21 April 2005).

perpetration of heinous crimes and about the circumstances and reasons that led . . . to the perpetration of those crimes'.[48] But the right to truth also includes the right of victims and their families 'to know the truth about the circumstances in which violations took place and, in the event of death or disappearance, about the victims' fate'.[49] In line with the Reparation Principles and Impunity Principles, the International Convention for the Protection of All Persons from Enforced Disappearance affirms the right of each victim to know the truth regarding the circumstances of the enforced disappearance, the progress and results of the investigation, and the fate of the disappeared person. Finally, it also spells out the right of victims to obtain reparation and prompt, fair, and adequate compensation.[50]

These normative developments raise the question of whether the right to know the truth, as a collective and individual right, qualifies as a 'new human right'. It may be argued in this connection that this right is a corollary of the freedom to seek, receive, and impart information and ideas of all kinds set out in Article 19(2) ICCPR. Technically speaking, this argument is correct, although it insufficiently appreciates the existential life and death dimensions that lie at the basis of the right to know the truth. Nevertheless, it can be argued that the right to know the truth is a basic principle that already forms part of existing human rights law. In fact, the International Convention for the Protection of All Persons from Enforced Disappearance gives support to this reasoning insofar as its preamble 'affirms' the right of any victim to know the truth.[51] Therefore, the right to know the truth should not be qualified as a 'new human right' as if it had only emerged recently. Such a classification would fail to do justice to efforts to seek and uncover the truth about many historical wrongs that still beleaguer past and present generations. Rather, there are good reasons to state, in consonance with the Impunity Principles, that there is an inalienable right to know the truth. This right is in need of recognition and renewed emphasis and is thus correctly affirmed in a legal document such as the International Convention for the Protection of All Persons from Enforced Disappearance.

6 CONCLUSION

All human rights are indivisible, interdependent, and interrelated. This chapter fully subscribes to this postulate, not as a method to put all rights in a melting-pot where they lose their own distinct character, but as a means to reinforce the validity and impact of all rights. Classifying human rights in various categories—civil, political, economic, social, and cultural; individual and collective; one-dimensional and composite—is not as such a reduction of the indivisibility, interdependence, and interrelatedness of human rights. Such classifications or categorizations are not meant to store human rights in watertight compartments. Their merit lies in their capacity to operationalize human rights, to make rights and responsibilities more specific and transparent, with corresponding claims and obligations.

Neither does the maxim of indivisibility, interdependence, and interrelatedness of all human rights stand in the way of the notion of core rights as distinct from other human rights. It is true that the notion of core rights presumes a ranking or hierarchy of human rights. Such ranking is inherent in essential rights and entails corresponding core obligations on the part of states and non-state actors. It runs across all human rights categories and classifications, with the right to life, the inviolability of the human person, and the very existence and subsistence of people as cornerstones.

---

[48] Impunity Principles, Principle 2.   [49] Impunity Principles, Principle 4.
[50] International Convention for the Protection of All Persons from Enforced Disappearance (CPED), Art 24.
[51] CPED, preambular para 8.

It is self-evident that human rights, in whatever manner they are classified or sub-divided, are the rights of individuals and collectivities. But it has been less obvious, under past and present policies and practices of exclusion and discrimination, that human rights are the inalienable rights of all members of the human family. The UDHR proclaimed human rights as the rights of all human beings and set into motion a major trend towards the inclusion of all people in human rights documents. It is in keeping with this trend to grant explicit recognition to people who had been, over the years and in many places if not everywhere, the subject of exclusion, discrimination, neglect, or treatment as inferi-ors. It was also in line with the same trend that the call was widely heard: women's rights are human rights, children's rights are human rights, indigenous rights are human rights, Roma rights are human rights, Dalits rights are human rights, and so on. International instruments with a specific focus on the human rights of particular categories of people were drawn up, most recently of persons with disabilities. Rather than labelling the rights of these persons as 'new human rights', they should be denominated as the rights of newly identified categories of people, as inclusive rights. In sum, categories of human rights are not abstract concepts. Human rights relate to all people, including categories of people who belong to the downtrodden, the disadvantaged, and the discarded in national and international society.

FURTHER READING

ALSTON, 'Conjuring up New Human Rights: A Proposal for Quality Control' (1984) 78 *AJIL* 607.

BOB (ed), *The International Struggle for New Human Rights* (University of Pennsylvania Press, 2009).

COOMANS (ed), *Justiciability of Economic and Social Rights: Experiences from Domestic Systems* (Intersentia, 2006).

DE GREIFF (ed), *The Handbook of Reparations* (Oxford University Press, 2006).

FERSTMAN, GOETZ, and STEPHENS (eds), *Reparations for Victims of Genocide, War Crimes and Crimes against Humanity: Systems in Place and Systems in the Making* (Martinus Nijhoff, 2009).

INTERNATIONAL COMMMISSION OF JURISTS, *Courts and the Legal Enforcement of Economic, Social and Cultural Rights* (Geneva, 2008).

MERON, 'On a Hierarchy of International Human Rights' (1986) 80 *AJIL* 1.

QUANE, 'A Further Dimension to the Interdependence and Indivisibility of Human Rights? Recent Developments Concerning the Rights of Indigenous Peoples' (2012) 25 *Harvard HRJ* 49.

SEIDERMAN, *Hierarchy in International Law: The Human Rights Dimension* (Intersentia, 2001).

SHELTON, *Remedies in International Human Rights Law* (Oxford University Press, 2015).

VANDENBOGAERDE and VANDENHOLE, 'The Optional Protocol to the International Covenant on Economic, Social and Cultural Rights: An *Ex Ante* Assessment of its Effectiveness in Light of the Drafting Process' (2010) 10 *HRLR* 207.

8

EQUALITY AND NON-DISCRIMINATION

Daniel Moeckli

SUMMARY

The international human rights system is founded on the idea that all human beings have the same set of fundamental rights. Accordingly, almost all general human rights instruments guarantee the right to equality and non-discrimination, and several specialized treaties provide protection against particular forms of discrimination. International human rights law prohibits discrimination in treatment (direct discrimination) as well as in outcome (indirect discrimination), regardless of whether it is intended or unintended. Yet it also acknowledges that it may sometimes be justified to classify people: differences in treatment or outcome are permissible as long as they pursue a legitimate aim in a proportionate manner. Indeed, the right to equality may *require* states to treat people differently in order to overcome historical patterns of disadvantage and achieve real equality.

1 INTRODUCTION

The notion that all human beings are equal and therefore deserve to be treated equally has a powerful intuitive appeal. It is one of the central ideals of the Enlightenment and at the heart of liberal theories of the state.[1] The US Declaration of Independence of 1776 famously proclaimed that 'all men are created equal', and today virtually every liberal democratic state guarantees equality in its constitution. The principle of equality and non-discrimination has gained a similarly important status in international law. It is included in the key human rights instruments and the Vienna Declaration and Programme of Action, adopted by the World Conference on Human Rights in 1993, describes it as 'a fundamental rule of international human rights law'.[2]

What this fundamental rule entails in practice, however, is difficult to establish. No two human beings are equal in the sense that they are identical. We might be able to say that two people are equal in respect of some measurable characteristic ('they both weigh 82 kilograms'), but they will always be different in some other respects (income, political opinion, and so on). In order to apply the principle of equality we first need to define the relevant

---

[1] See Chapter 1.   [2] A/CONF.157/23 (25 June 1993) para 15.

criterion in respect of which people should be judged to be alike or different. And even when two persons can be said to be alike, it might still be questionable whether they should always be treated equally. Furthermore, we need to decide what kind of equality we seek to achieve. Do we mean by equality that people should be treated identically? Or that they should be given the same opportunities? Or that they should be placed in the same position? Equality can be formulated in different ways, and deciding which concept of equality to use is not a question of logic but a political choice. In this sense, equality is an 'empty idea'[3]—it does not answer the questions of who are equals and what constitutes equal treatment. External values, not derivable from the concept of equality, are necessary to answer these questions.

The challenge, therefore, is to give substance to the abstract notion of equality by translating it into concrete legal formulations that make clear which forms of unequal treatment are legitimate because they are based on morally acceptable criteria and which ones are wrongful. This chapter explains how this challenge has been addressed in international human rights law.

Section 2 discusses what, in general terms, equality and non-discrimination can be interpreted to mean. Section 3 gives an overview of the different norms guaranteeing equality and non-discrimination in international human rights law. Section 4 explains the concepts of direct and indirect discrimination. Section 5 considers the requirements for a difference in treatment to be justified under international human rights law. Section 6 sets out the different sorts of obligations that the right to equality imposes on states, in particular their duty to take positive action to ensure everyone can enjoy this right.

2 THE MEANING OF EQUALITY AND NON-DISCRIMINATION

The terms 'equality' and 'non-discrimination' have often been used interchangeably and described as the positive and negative statement of the same principle: whereas the maxim of equality requires that equals be treated equally, the prohibition of discrimination precludes differential treatment on unreasonable grounds.[4] In recent years, however, there has been an increased emphasis on the positive formulation. This shift in terminology highlights that equality implies not only a negative obligation not to discriminate, but also a duty to recognize differences between people and to take positive action to achieve real equality.[5] Thus, whereas 'non-discrimination' corresponds to the more limited concept of *formal equality*, usage of the term 'equality' stresses the need for a more positive approach aimed at *substantive equality*.

2.1 FORMAL EQUALITY

Formal equality refers to Aristotle's classical maxim according to which equals must be treated equally or, more precisely, likes must be treated alike.[6] This notion of equality as consistency focuses on the process rather than the outcome: equality is achieved if individuals

---

[3] Westen, 'The Empty Idea of Equality' (1982) 95 *Harvard LR* 537.

[4] eg OC-4/84, *Proposed Amendments to the Naturalization Provisions of the Constitution of Costa Rica*, IACtHR Series A No 4 (1984), Separate Opinion of Rodolfo E Piza, J, para 10 ('it appears clear that the concepts of equality and non-discrimination are reciprocal, like the two faces of one same institution. Equality is the positive face of non-discrimination. Discrimination is the negative face of equality').

[5] See eg *Nachova v Bulgaria* (2006) 42 EHRR 43, para 145 (noting that 'the authorities must use all available means to combat racism and racist violence, thereby reinforcing democracy's vision of a society in which diversity is not perceived as a threat but as a source of enrichment').

[6] Aristotle, *The Nicomachean Ethics of Aristotle* (JM Dent, 1911) Book V3, paras 1131a–b.

in a comparable situation are treated equally, regardless of the result. The values underpinning formal equality are the liberal ideals of state neutrality and individualism, that is, the notion that the state should not give preference to any one group and that people should be treated exclusively on their individual merits and regardless of group membership.

However, as noted already, this idea of equality raises the question of when two cases can be said to be alike. It is inevitable that laws and government action classify persons into groups that are treated differently. Under a progressive taxation system, for example, people are treated differently according to their income. In states with a juvenile justice system, people are treated differently according to their age. These distinctions are generally seen as perfectly legitimate because they are based on morally acceptable grounds. Accordingly, at least in common language, the word 'discrimination' also has a neutral connotation ('to discriminate between right and wrong'). But which differences in treatment are legitimate and which ones are not? The principle that likes should be treated alike does not, by itself, answer this question.

There are a number of other problems with the concept of equality as consistency.[7] First, since it is not concerned with the outcome, it does not matter whether two parties are treated equally well or equally badly. Thus, it is compatible with this understanding of equality that a city closes all its swimming pools rather than open its 'whites only' pools to black people ('levelling down').[8] Second, inconsistent treatment can only be demonstrated if the complainant can find a comparably situated person who has been treated more favourably. Yet for a woman in a low-paid position, for instance, it may be difficult to find a man doing the same job. Third, treating people apparently consistently regardless of their differing backgrounds may have a disparate impact on particular groups. A law which, in the famous words of Anatole France, 'forbids the rich as well as the poor to sleep under bridges, to beg in the streets, and to steal bread' will in fact entrench inequality.[9]

2.2 SUBSTANTIVE EQUALITY

Proponents of a substantive conception of equality recognize that a merely formal notion of equality as procedural fairness can in fact perpetuate existing patterns of disadvantage. Drawing on values such as human dignity, distributive justice, and equal participation, they argue that equality must go beyond consistent treatment of likes. There are two main variants of substantive equality: equality of opportunity and equality of results.

According to the notion of equality of opportunity, true equality can only be achieved if people are not only treated equally but are also given the same opportunities. Like competitors in a race, everyone should be able to begin from the same starting point. Equality of opportunity requires the removal of barriers to the advancement of disadvantaged groups, such as upper age limits for employment that may disadvantage women with childcare responsibilities. According to a broader, substantive understanding of the concept, it may also require positive measures such as training. But equality of opportunity does not aim to achieve equality of outcome. Once the race has started, everyone is treated the same. Thus, while equality of opportunity is to some extent about redressing past discrimination, it also stresses individual merit.

Equality of results goes further than this and aims to achieve an equal distribution of social goods such as education, employment, healthcare, and political representation. It recognizes that removing barriers does not guarantee that disadvantaged groups will in fact be able to take advantage of available opportunities. Abolishing upper age limits, for

---

[7] See Fredman, *Discrimination Law* (OUP, 2011) 8–15.
[8] See *Palmer v Thompson* 403 US 217 (1971).   [9] France, *Le Lys Rouge* (Calmann-Lévy, 1894) ch 7.

example, does not, by itself, ensure that more women with childcare responsibilities will be able to apply for the respective jobs. Equality of results can be understood and achieved in different ways. In its strongest form, it explicitly aims to increase the representation of disadvantaged groups in educational institutions, employment, or public office through preferential treatment and quota systems.

These differing conceptions of equality find their reflection in different forms of legal regulation. Formal equality forms the conceptual basis of the requirement of equality before the law and prohibitions of direct discrimination, whereas prohibitions of indirect discrimination are supported by a substantive notion of equality (see Section 4 for the distinction between direct and indirect discrimination). 'Affirmative action' programmes (see Section 6) can be justified on the basis of a substantive notion of equality, but they are incompatible with a formal conception of equality as consistency. In any jurisdiction, a range of regulations that reflect different conceptions of equality will be found; no legal system relies exclusively on simply one approach to equality.

3 EQUALITY AND NON-DISCRIMINATION IN INTERNATIONAL LAW

The right to equality and non-discrimination gives concrete expression to the basic idea on which the whole international human rights system is founded: that all human beings, regardless of their status or membership of a particular group, are entitled to the same set of rights. Since it underlies all other human rights, equality is often described not only as a 'right' but also as a 'principle'. The foundational significance of equality is reflected in the fact that it is proclaimed in the very first article of the Universal Declaration of Human Rights (UDHR): 'All human beings are born free and equal in dignity and rights'.

This section first gives an overview of the different sources of the right to equality and non-discrimination in international law. Next, it considers the scope of these norms: do they guarantee equality and non-discrimination only in the context of other human rights or across the board? Finally, the prohibited grounds of distinction are explored: which groups are protected against discrimination?

3.1 SOURCES

Article 1(3) of the UN Charter makes it clear that one of the basic purposes of the UN is the promotion of the equal guarantee of human rights for all without any distinction. Numerous instruments aimed at the realization of this notion have been adopted under the auspices of the UN. The general human rights instruments guarantee the right to equality and non-discrimination in several of their provisions: the UDHR in Articles 1, 2(1), and 7; the International Covenant on Civil and Political Rights (ICCPR) in Articles 2, 3, and 26; and the International Covenant on Economic, Social and Cultural Rights (ICESCR) in Articles 2(2) and 3. As far as the specialized human rights treaties are concerned, at least three of them are specifically devoted to addressing certain forms of discrimination: the International Convention on the Elimination of All Forms of Racial Discrimination (ICERD), the Convention on the Elimination of All Forms of Discrimination Against Women (CEDAW), and the Convention on the Rights of Persons with Disabilities (CRPD). The Convention on the Rights of the Child (CRC) and the International Convention on the Protection of the Rights of All Migrant Workers and

Members of Their Families (ICRMW) at least partly pursue the same objective and contain explicit provisions on equality and non-discrimination.[10] The only international human rights treaties without explicit non-discrimination clauses are the Convention against Torture and Other Cruel, Inhuman or Degrading Treatment or Punishment (UNCAT) and the International Convention for the Protection of All Persons from Enforced Disappearance (CPED).

The right to equality and non-discrimination is also guaranteed by all major regional human rights instruments: the African Charter on Human and Peoples' Rights (ACHPR) (Articles 2, 3, 18(3)–(4), and 28), the American Convention on Human Rights (ACHR) (Articles 1 and 24), the American Declaration of the Rights and Duties of Man (Article II), the Arab Charter on Human Rights (Articles 2, 9, and 35), the ASEAN Human Rights Declaration (Articles 1, 2, 3, and 9), the European Convention on Human Rights (ECHR) (Article 14 and Protocol No 12), and the Charter of Fundamental Rights of the European Union (Articles 20, 21(1), and 23). In addition, the Inter-American Convention against All Forms of Discrimination and Intolerance provides protection against discrimination based on a long list of criteria, while several specialized regional treaties, such as the Protocol to the ACHPR on the Rights of Women in Africa, the Inter-American Convention against Racism, Racial Discrimination, and Related Forms of Intolerance, and the Inter-American Convention on the Elimination of All Forms of Discrimination against Persons with Disabilities, protect against particular forms of discrimination.

Finally, it is now widely acknowledged that, at the very least, the right to non-discrimination on the grounds of race, sex, and religion binds all states, irrespective of their ratification of human rights treaties, because it has become part of customary international law.[11] The Inter-American Court of Human Rights has gone further than this and held that also the guarantee against discrimination on other grounds, including language, political or other opinion, national, ethnic or social origin, nationality, age, economic situation, property, civil status, birth, or any other status, forms part of general international law and, indeed, is a norm of *jus cogens* that cannot be set aside by treaty or acquiescence.[12]

3.2 SCOPE: SUBORDINATE AND AUTONOMOUS NORMS

Non-discrimination provisions can be subdivided into subordinate and autonomous (or free-standing) norms. *Subordinate norms* prohibit discrimination only in the enjoyment of the rights and freedoms otherwise set forth in the respective instrument. An example of a subordinate norm is Article 2(1) ICCPR, which states:

> Each State Party to the present Covenant undertakes to respect and to ensure to all individuals within its territory and subject to its jurisdiction the rights recognized in the present Covenant, without distinction of any kind, such as race, colour, sex, language, religion, political or other opinion, national or social origin, property, birth or other status.

---

[10] CRC, Arts 2 and 28; ICRMW, Arts 1(1), 7, 18, 25, 27, 28, 30, 43, 45, 54, 55, and 70.

[11] For race, see eg *South-West Africa Cases (Second Phase)* [1966] ICJ Rep 6, 293 and 299–300 (Judge Tanaka, dissenting); *Barcelona Traction (Second Phase)* [1970] ICJ Rep 3, 32. For the other grounds, see Shaw, *International Law* (CUP, 2014) 208–9 and references cited there.

[12] OC/18, *Juridical Condition and Rights of the Undocumented Migrants*, IACtHR Series A No 18 (2003) paras 100–1 and 173.4.

Other subordinate norms include Article 2(1) UDHR, Article 2(2) ICESCR, Article 2(1) CRC, Article 7 ICRMW, Article 1 ACHR, Article 2 ACHPR, and Article 14 ECHR.[13] As the ECHR does not contain an autonomous norm in addition to its subordinate provision in Article 14, the jurisprudence of the European Court of Human Rights interpreting it is of particular importance. According to the European Court, in order to invoke Article 14, an applicant must show that the facts of the case fall 'within the ambit' of another substantive Convention right.[14] However, there is no need to show that there has been *a violation* of that Convention right. A measure that in itself is in conformity with the requirements of a given ECHR right, but is of a discriminatory nature, will violate that right *when read in conjunction with Article 14*. For example, it does not as such amount to a violation of Article 8 ECHR (the right to respect for family life) if a state fails to create a parental leave scheme. However, when a state does create such a scheme, then this is a matter falling within the ambit of Article 8, and there is a violation of that article read in conjunction with Article 14 if, without a legitimate reason, men are denied the right to parental leave while women are granted it.[15]

Article 7 UDHR, Article 26 ICCPR, Articles 2 and 5 ICERD, Article 24 ACHR, and Article 3 ACHPR, on the other hand, are *autonomous norms*: they guarantee non-discrimination not only in the context of other rights but in general. For example, Article 26 ICCPR provides:

> All persons are equal before the law and are entitled without any discrimination to the equal protection of the law. In this respect, the law shall prohibit any discrimination and guarantee to all persons equal and effective protection against discrimination on any ground such as race, colour, sex, language, religion, political or other opinion, national or social origin, property, birth or other status.

The UN Human Rights Committee elaborated on the scope of this provision in *Broeks v The Netherlands*.[16] Mrs Broeks had been denied unemployment benefits on the basis of legislation that provided that married women could only claim benefits if they could prove that they were 'breadwinners'—a requirement that did not apply to married men. The Netherlands argued that Mrs Broeks could not rely on Article 26 ICCPR as it could only be invoked in the sphere of civil and political rights; Mrs Broeks' complaint, however, re-lated to the right to social security, which was specifically provided for under the ICESCR. The Human Rights Committee rejected the government's argument, holding that it did not matter whether a particular subject matter is covered by the ICCPR or some other international instrument. It stressed that 'Article 26 does not merely duplicate the guar-antees already provided for in Article 2' but instead 'prohibits discrimination in law or in practice in any field regulated and protected by public authorities'.[17] The Committee confirmed this finding in its General Comment 18.[18] Thus, states parties to the ICCPR have a general obligation neither to enact legislation with a discriminatory content nor to apply laws in a discriminatory way.

As noted already, the ECHR only contains a subordinate non-discrimination guaran-tee. This gap is partially addressed by Protocol No 12 to the ECHR. The Protocol, which

---

[13] ECHR, Art 14 reads: 'The enjoyment of the rights and freedoms set forth in this Convention shall be secured without discrimination on any ground such as sex, race, colour, language, religion, political or other opinion, national or social origin, association with a national minority, property, birth or other status.'

[14] For a recent case see *Sousa Goucha v Portugal*, App no 70434/12, Judgment of 22 March 2016, para 57.

[15] *Konstantin Markin v Russia* (2013) 56 EHRR 8, para 130.

[16] CCPR/C/29/D/172/1984 (9 April 1987).   [17] *Broeks*, para 12.3.

[18] HRC, General Comment 18, HRI/GEN/1/Rev. 9 (Vol I) 195, para 12.

entered into force in 2005 but has not been widely ratified so far, contains a non-discrim-ination guarantee that is not limited to the enjoyment of Convention rights.[19] However, this guarantee is still narrower than the general right to equality before the law and equal protection of the law under Article 26 ICCPR in that it only applies to the enjoyment of rights set forth by (national) law.

3.3 PROHIBITED GROUNDS OF DISTINCTION

Which grounds of distinction are unacceptable and should, therefore, be prohibited? There is no straightforward answer to this question. Depending on one's moral and politi-cal views, any criterion may be regarded as either relevant or irrelevant. There is certainly broad consensus today that normally a person's inherent characteristics such as race, co-lour, or sex are not acceptable criteria for differential treatment. In addition, grounds such as membership of a particular group, holding certain beliefs, and national or social origin are outlawed by most human rights treaties. But as is evident from a comparison between the ICCPR, adopted in 1966, and the ICRMW, adopted in 1990, what is seen as unaccept-able can change over time: the ICRMW has considerably expanded the list of prohibited grounds by adding the criteria of conviction, ethnic origin, nationality, age, economic po-sition, and marital status. Today, further criteria, including disability[20] and sexual orienta-tion and gender identity,[21] would have to be added. In addition, discrimination may be intersectional, that is, based on a combination of characteristics that form an individual's identity rather than a single ground.[22] Intersectional discrimination often occurs based on sex in combination with one or more other grounds.[23]

Equality and non-discrimination norms vary widely in their approaches to defining the prohibited grounds of distinction. A first type of norm provides for a *general guarantee of equality*, without specifying any particular prohibited grounds. Article 24 ACHR, for in-stance, simply states: 'All persons are equal before the law. Consequently, they are entitled, without discrimination, to equal protection of the law.' Such norms leave it to the relevant body to decide which distinctions are acceptable and which ones are not.

A second category of norms uses a diametrically opposed approach: these norms con-tain an *exhaustive list* of prohibited grounds. The CEDAW, for instance, prohibits only distinctions based on 'sex' (Article 1), the ICERD those based on 'race, colour, descent, or national or ethnic origin' (Article 1(1)), and the CRPD those based on 'disability' (Articles 1 and 5). Article 2(2) ICESCR, Article 2(1) CRC, and Article 1 ACHR contain lists that are much longer but still fixed (in the case of the ICESCR, 'race, colour, sex, language, religion, political or other opinion, national or social origin, property, birth or other status').

Steering a middle course between these two extremes, there is a third category of norms which contain a list of prohibited grounds but one that is *open-ended*. For instance, Article 14 ECHR (as well as its Protocol No 12) prohibits 'discrimination on *any* ground *such as* sex, race, colour, language, religion, political or other opinion, national or social origin, as-sociation with a national minority, property, birth or other status'.[24] Similarly, Article 2(1)

---

[19] Protocol No 12 to the Convention for the Protection of Human Rights and Fundamental Freedoms, Art 1 ('(1) The enjoyment of any right set forth by law shall be secured without discrimination on any ground such as sex, race, colour, language, religion, political or other opinion, national or social origin, association with a national minority, property, birth or other status. (2) No one shall be discriminated against by any public authority on any ground such as those mentioned in paragraph 1').

[20] See CRPD.   [21] See Chapter 15.

[22] See Crenshaw, 'Mapping the Margins: Intersectionality, Identity Politics, and Violence Against Women of Color' (1991) 43 *Stanford LR* 1241.   [23] See Chapter 16.

[24] Emphasis added.

UDHR, Articles 1(1) and 7 ICRMW, and Article 2 ACHPR provide for non-discrimination 'without distinction of *any* kind, *such as* ... '.[25] As a consequence, even distinctions made on grounds that are not explicitly listed may engage these provisions. The European Court of Human Rights sometimes does not even find it necessary to state the particular ground of distinction involved when considering a case under Article 14 ECHR.[26]

The text of Article 26 ICCPR ('discrimination on *any* ground *such as* race, colour, sex, language, religion, political or other opinion, national or social origin, property, birth or other status')[27] suggests that this provision is also open-ended. Nevertheless, the Human Rights Committee has often been at pains to fit a particular distinction within one of the listed grounds, be it the specific ones or the broad rubric of 'other status'. Thus, it has found that the reference to 'sex' also includes 'sexual orientation'[28] and that 'other status' covers grounds such as nationality[29] and age.[30] But it has never clarified how it decides whether a difference in treatment comes within the reference to 'other status'. Its efforts to apply one of the listed grounds suggest that the Committee regards the list of Article 26 as exhaustive and it has accordingly stated that an applicant is required to show that the difference in treatment was based on one of the enumerated grounds.[31]

4 DIRECT AND INDIRECT DISCRIMINATION

At the heart of all non-discrimination norms is the formal equality requirement that likes should be treated alike. It is, therefore, clear that international human rights law prohibits direct discrimination (Section 4.1). But human rights bodies and courts have acknowledged that the requirement of consistent treatment is not sufficient to achieve true equality: not only discriminatory treatment but also a discriminatory outcome (indirect discrimination) is prohibited (Section 4.2). Finally, it is important to note that international human rights law prohibits both intended and unintended discrimination (Section 4.3).

Whether there has been a difference in treatment or result is the first question that a court needs to assess when considering a discrimination claim under international human rights law. Once a prima facie case of direct or indirect discrimination has been made out, the court must decide whether there is a justification for the difference in treatment or outcome. This second element of the test is discussed in Section 5.

4.1 DIRECT DISCRIMINATION

Direct discrimination occurs when a person, *on account of one or more of the prohibited grounds*, is treated less favourably than someone else in comparable circumstances. Thus, the complainant must show, first, that others have been treated better because they do not share the relevant characteristic or status and, second, that these others are in a comparable, or, in the terminology of the European Court of Human Rights, 'analogous'[32] or 'relevantly similar',[33] situation. In practice, international human rights bodies often tend

---

[25] Emphasis added.   [26] eg *Rasmussen v Denmark* (1984) 7 EHRR 371, para 34.
[27] Emphasis added.   [28] *Toonen v Australia*, CCPR/C/50/D/488/1992 (31 March 1994) para 8.7.
[29] *Gueye v France*, CCPR/C/35/D/196/1985 (3 April 1989) para 9.4.
[30] *Love et al. v Australia*, CCPR/C/77/D/983/2001 (28 April 2003) para 8.2.
[31] *Franz and Maria Deisl v Austria*, CCPR/C/81/D/1060/2002 (23 August 2004) para 10.5.
[32] *Lithgow v UK* (1986) 8 EHRR 329, para 177.   [33] *Fredin v Sweden* (1991) 13 EHRR 784, para 60.

to merge the comparability test with the test for whether there is an objective justification for the difference in treatment, explained in Section 5.

A classic example of direct discrimination is when members of a certain ethnic group are denied access to a public facility, such as a swimming pool, which is open to everyone else. But most cases of direct discrimination are not as straightforward as this. More often, direct discrimination occurs covertly: the 'discriminator' will not admit that the difference in treatment was based on a prohibited ground, making it difficult for the complainant to provide sufficient evidence. Furthermore, as explained already, it may not always be easy to identify a person who is in a comparable situation. How can a woman establish pay discrimination when there are hardly any men doing the same job?

4.2 INDIRECT DISCRIMINATION

Indirect discrimination occurs when a practice, rule, or requirement that is outwardly 'neutral', that is, not based on one of the prohibited grounds of distinction, has a disproportionate impact on particular groups defined by reference to one of these grounds. Thus, although there is no difference in treatment, due to structural biases, treating unequals equally leads to unequal results.

The concept of indirect discrimination has its origins in US and European Community (EC) law but has now also found its way into the jurisprudence of international and regional human rights bodies. The Human Rights Committee recognized the possibility of indirect discrimination, albeit without explicitly referring to the concept, for the first time in *Singh Bhinder v Canada*.[34] The case concerned a Sikh who was dismissed from his employment with the Canadian Railway because he refused to comply with a legal requirement that safety headgear be worn at work, as his religion required him to wear only a turban. The Committee found that the legislation may amount to de facto discrimination: although it was neutral in that it applied to all persons without distinction, it disproportionately affected persons of the Sikh religion. (There was nevertheless no violation of Article 26 ICCPR as the safety headgear requirement was based on reasonable and objective grounds.) But only much later, in *Althammer v Austria*, a case concerning the abolition of household benefits that affected retired persons to a greater extent than active employees, did the Committee expressly refer to the concept of 'indirect discrimination':

> The Committee recalls that a violation of article 26 can also result from the discriminatory effect of a rule or measure that is neutral at face value or without intent to discriminate. However, such indirect discrimination can only be said to be based on the grounds enumerated in Article 26 of the Covenant if the detrimental effects of a rule or decision exclusively or disproportionally affect persons having a particular race, colour, sex, language, religion, political or other opinion, national or social origin, property, birth or other status.[35]

Similarly, it was only in 2007 that the European Court of Human Rights, in its groundbreaking ruling in *DH and others v Czech Republic*, came up with an explicit definition of 'indirect discrimination'. Several Roma children had complained that the manner in which statutory rules governing assignment to schools were applied in practice resulted in the placement of a disproportionate number of Roma pupils in 'special schools' for children with 'mental deficiencies'. Referring to the definition of 'indirect discrimination' in EC law, the Grand Chamber of the European Court of Human Rights stated:

---

[34] CCPR/C/37/D/208/1986 (9 November 1989).
[35] CCPR/C/78/D/998/2001 (8 August 2003) para 10.2.

The Court has already accepted in previous cases that a difference in treatment may take the form of disproportionately prejudicial effects of a general policy or measure which, though couched in neutral terms, discriminates against a group ... In accordance with, for instance, Council Directives 97/80/EC and 2000/43/EC and the definition provided by ECRI [the European Commission against Racism and Intolerance], such a situation may amount to 'indirect discrimination', which does not necessarily require a discriminatory intent.[36]

The African Commission on Human and Peoples' Rights seems also to have recognized the concept of indirect discrimination when it found a violation of Articles 2 and 3 ACHPR in a case where legal remedies, even though guaranteed to everyone by law, were in practice 'only ... available to the wealthy and those that can afford the services of private counsel'.[37] The Inter-American Convention against All Forms of Discrimination and Intolerance 2013 contains, in Article 1(2), an explicit definition of 'indirect discrimination'.[38]

4.3 DISCRIMINATORY INTENTION

In some legal systems, such as in the USA, complainants need to show a discriminatory intention or purpose to establish discrimination.[39] There is no such requirement under international human rights law; the reason why someone has been treated less favourably is irrelevant.

That both intended and unintended discrimination are prohibited under international law is apparent from the explicit definitions of discrimination contained in some of the human rights treaties. ICERD defines discrimination as any distinction based on one of the listed grounds 'which has the purpose *or effect* of nullifying or impairing the recognition, enjoyment or exercise, on an equal footing, of human rights and fundamental freedoms'.[40] The CEDAW definition is almost identical.[41] The Human Rights Committee, in its General Comment on non-discrimination, has adopted the same definition for the purposes of the ICCPR[42] and has made it clear in its jurisprudence that discriminatory intention is not a necessary element of discrimination.[43] Equally, the European Court of Human Rights has indicated that discrimination under Article 14 ECHR may also relate to the *effects* of state measures.[44]

As is illustrated by the rulings in *Althammer* and *DH* described in Section 4.2, indirect discrimination is often equated with unintended discrimination. Conversely, it is normally assumed that where there is direct discrimination, there is a discriminatory intention. Although it is true that these concepts will often correlate, this is not always the case. There may be cases of direct discrimination—for example, the exclusion of pregnant women and mothers from certain types of work—where the intention is to protect the respective groups rather than to discriminate against them. On the other hand, a 'neutral' criterion such as a literacy test for job applicants may well be used as a pretext for excluding certain ethnic groups, amounting to intended indirect discrimination.

---

[36]   (2008) 47 EHRR 3, para 184.

[37]   241/2001, *Purohit and Moore v The Gambia*, 16th Activity Report (2002) paras 53–4.

[38]   Art 1(2) reads: 'Indirect discrimination shall be taken to occur, in any realm of public and private life, when a seemingly neutral provision, criterion, or practice has the capacity to entail a particular disadvantage for persons belonging to a specific group, or puts them at a disadvantage, unless said provision, criterion, or practice has some reasonable and legitimate objective or justification under international human rights law.'

[39]   The leading case is *Washington v Davis* 426 US 229 (1976).

[40]   Art 1(1) (emphasis added).   [41]   Art 1.   [42]   HRC, General Comment 18, para 7.

[43]   eg *Simunek et al. v The Czech Republic*, CCPR/C/54/D/516/1992 (19 July 1995) para 11.7; *Adam v The Czech Republic*, CCPR/C/57/D/586/1994 (23 July 1996) para 12.7.

[44]   *Oršuš v Croatia* (2011) 52 EHRR 7, para 150.

5 JUSTIFIED AND UNJUSTIFIED DISTINCTIONS

Once it is established that there has been a difference in treatment or outcome, the next question that needs to be answered is whether there is a justification for it. As explained already, it is to some extent inevitable that states classify people into different groups. The crucial question is whether there are objective and reasonable grounds for these distinctions. This section first explains the relevant test under international human rights law. Next, it explores what standard of review human rights bodies or courts apply to carry out this test. Finally, it considers matters concerning evidence and proof.

5.1 THE JUSTIFICATION TEST

The Human Rights Committee, in its General Comment on non-discrimination, has stressed that, for the purposes of the ICCPR, 'not every differentiation of treatment will constitute discrimination, if the criteria for such differentiation are reasonable and objective and if the aim is to achieve a purpose which is legitimate under the Covenant.'[45] But it is in the jurisprudence of the European Court of Human Rights that the criteria for distinguishing between justified and unjustified distinction have been most clearly articulated. The Court interpreted Article 14 ECHR for the first time in the *Belgian Linguistics Case* and has since repeatedly confirmed those conclusions:

> [T]he Court, following the principles which may be extracted from the legal practice of a large number of democratic states, holds that the principle of equality of treatment is violated if the distinction has no objective and reasonable justification. The existence of such a justification must be assessed in relation to the aim and effects of the measure under consideration, regard being had to the principles which normally prevail in democratic societies. A difference of treatment in the exercise of a right laid down in the Convention must not only pursue a legitimate aim: Article 14 is likewise violated when it is clearly established that there is no reasonable relationship of proportionality between the means employed and the aim sought to be realised.[46]

This two-limb test, requiring that any difference in treatment must (1) pursue a legitimate aim, and (2) be proportionate, is very similar to the test used in the context of other rights to assess the permissibility of limitations, described in Chapter 5. The test formulated by the European Court has been adopted, explicitly or implicitly, by most other human rights bodies. While the Human Rights Committee had originally failed to provide a clear and consistent explanation of what it means by 'reasonable and objective criteria', it later increasingly started to interpret these terms as requiring a legitimate aim and proportionality.[47] The Committee on the Elimination of Racial Discrimination and the Committee on Economic, Social and Cultural Rights have embraced the same approach,[48] as has the Inter-American Court of Human Rights.[49]

In terms of what exactly this test involves, its first limb will not usually be very difficult for states to meet: most distinctions can be argued to pursue some aim that qualifies as legitimate,

---

[45] HRC, General Comment 18, para 13.

[46] *Case Relating to Certain Aspects of the Laws on the Use of Languages in Education in Belgium (Belgian Linguistics Case) (No 2)* (1968) 1 EHRR 252, para 10.

[47] eg *Gillot v France*, A/57/40 (15 July 2002) para 13.2.

[48] CERD, Concluding observations: Australia, CERD/C/AUS/CO/14 (14 April 2005) para 24; CESCR, General Comment 20, E/C.12/GC/20, para 13.

[49] *Proposed Amendments to the Naturalization Provisions of the Political Constitution of Costa Rica*, paras 56–7.

for example the protection of public order or tailoring the education system to children's differing learning capabilities. More difficult to satisfy is the second element of the test, the proportionality requirement. This requirement reflects the basic notion that a fair balance ought to be struck between the interests of the community and respect for individual rights. A wide range of factors may need to be considered to assess proportionality, including the suitability of a distinction to achieve the aim pursued, the availability of alternative means, and the question of whether the disadvantage suffered by the affected individuals or groups is excessive in relation to the aim. Whilst this assessment inevitably turns on the specific facts of a given case, international human rights bodies have been consistent in their characterization of certain reasons as not sufficient to justify differential treatment; these include, among others, mere administrative inconvenience,[50] existence of a longstanding tradition,[51] general assumptions,[52] prevailing views in society,[53] stereotypes,[54] or convictions of the local population.[55]

5.2 STANDARD OF REVIEW

The stringency with which human rights courts or bodies review the existence of a justification will vary according to a number of factors.

Most importantly, certain grounds of distinction are generally regarded as inherently suspect and therefore require particularly strict scrutiny. The grounds attracting the greatest degree of attention and most likely to be declared unjustified are race, ethnicity, sex, and religion. That *race* is among these 'suspect classifications' is indicated by the general acceptance of the prohibition of racial discrimination as forming part of customary international law, the widespread ratification of the ICERD, and the finding of the European Commission of Human Rights, later endorsed by the Court, that 'a special importance should be attached to discrimination based on race' and that it may amount to degrading treatment.[56] The Inter-American Commission on Human Rights also applies a strict standard of scrutiny to distinctions based on race.[57] With regard to the related notion of *ethnicity*, the European Court has stressed that 'no difference in treatment which is based exclusively or to a decisive extent on a person's ethnic origin is capable of being objectively justified in a contemporary democratic society built on the principles of pluralism and respect for different cultures'.[58]

That distinctions based on *sex* are particularly suspect is underlined by the wealth of international treaties addressing the problem of sexual discrimination, including the CEDAW.[59] The Inter-American Commission has stated that distinctions based on sex 'necessarily give rise to heightened scrutiny'[60] and the European Court has observed that 'very weighty reasons would have to be advanced before a difference in treatment on the ground of sex could be regarded as compatible with the [ECHR]'.[61] Finally, the suspect nature of distinctions based on *religion* can be concluded from the unanimous adoption by the General Assembly of the Declaration on the Elimination of All Forms of Intolerance and Discrimination Based on Religion or Belief[62] and the European Court's finding that

---

[50] *Gueye v France*, para 9.5.
[51] *Müller and Engelhard v Namibia*, CCPR/C/74/D/919/2000 (26 March 2002) para 6.8.
[52] *Di Trizio v Switzerland*, App no 7186/09, Judgment of 2 February 2016, para 82.   [53] *Broeks*.
[54] *Konstantin Markin*, paras 141–3.   [55] *Inze v Austria* (1988) 10 EHRR 394, para 44.[56] *East African Asians v UK* (1973) 3 EHRR 76, paras 207–8; *Cyprus v Turkey* (2002) 35 EHRR 30, para 306.
[57] Case 11.625, *María Eugenia Morales de Sierra v Guatemala*, IACommHR Report No 4/01 (19 January 2001) para 36.   [58] *Timishev v Russia* (2007) 44 EHRR 37, para 58.
[59] See Chapter 16.   [60] *María Eugenia Morales de Sierra*, para 36.
[61] *Abdulaziz, Cabales and Balkandali v UK* (1985) 7 EHRR 471, para 78.
[62] GA Res 36/55 (25 November 1981).

'[n]otwithstanding any possible arguments to the contrary, a distinction based essentially on a difference in religion alone is not acceptable'.[63]

As far as other grounds of distinction are concerned, it is difficult to discern a consistent approach in international case law. The Human Rights Committee, for instance, has indicated that any distinction based on one of the grounds explicitly listed in Article 26 ICCPR 'places a heavy burden on the State party to explain the reason for the differentiation',[64] but that does not seem to mean that differential treatment on grounds other than race, sex, and religion are subject to the same intense scrutiny. The European Court, on the other hand, has suggested that also distinctions based on nationality,[65] illegitimacy,[66] and, more generally, membership of any 'particularly vulnerable group in society that has suffered considerable discrimination in the past' (such as people with HIV or a disability and members of sexual minorities) should be treated as inherently suspect.[67] Lists of suspect classifications are, in any event, not fixed but can change as international consensus on these matters develops. Given the recent emergence of new international norms against discrimination on grounds such as disability,[68] sexual orientation and gender identity,[69] and age,[70] it seems likely that these classifications will soon more widely be regarded as suspect.

Apart from the ground of distinction, the intensity of review may also depend on a number of other factors. For example, most courts and human rights bodies tend to apply a lenient standard as far as matters of social or economic policy are concerned,[71] whereas classifications affecting fundamental individual interests entail particularly strict scrutiny.[72] Furthermore, it will generally be more difficult for states to justify direct rather than indirect discrimination. The Declaration of Principles on Equality, an important but non-binding document signed by numerous human rights and equality experts, states that 'direct discrimination may be permitted only very exceptionally'.[73]

5.3 EVIDENCE AND PROOF

According to established human rights jurisprudence, it is up to the individual complaining of discrimination to establish a difference in treatment or outcome, the ground of distinction, and the existence of comparably situated groups. Having done so, the burden of proof shifts to the state to show that there is a justification for the distinction.[74]

In cases of alleged indirect discrimination, however, complainants may find it very difficult to prove that a neutral measure has a disproportionate impact on particular groups. Therefore, the European Court of Human Rights has held that less strict evidential rules should apply in these cases: 'statistics which appear on critical examination to be reliable

---

[63] *Hoffmann v Austria* (1993) 17 EHRR 293, para 36. See also *Vojnity v Hungary*, App no 29617/07, Judgment of 12 February 2013, para 36   [64] *Müller and Engelhard*, para 6.7.

[65] *Gaygusuz v Austria* (1996) 23 EHRR 364, para 42; *British Gurkha Welfare Society v UK*, App no 44818/11, Judgment of 15 September 2016, para 81.

[66] *Inze*, para 41; *Fabris v France* (2013) 57 EHRR 19, para 59.

[67] *Kiyutin v Russia* (2011) 53 EHRR 26, paras 63–4 and references cited there.   [68] See the CRPD.

[69] See Chapter 15.   [70] See UN Principles for Older Persons, GA Res 46/91 (16 December 1991).

[71] eg *Oulajin and Kaiss v The Netherlands*, CCPR/C/46/D/406/1990 and 426/1990 (23 October 1992), individual opinion submitted by Committee members Herndl, Müllerson, N'Diaye, and Sadi; *Hämäläinen v Finland*, App no 37359/09, Judgment of 16 July 2014, para 109 (stating that 'a wide margin is usually allowed to the State under the Convention when it comes to general measures of economic or social strategy').

[72] eg *Dudgeon v UK* (1981) 4 EHRR 149, para 52.

[73] Equal Rights Trust, Declaration of Principles on Equality, available at <http://www.equalrightstrust.org/content/declaration-principles-equality>, Principle 5.

[74] Declaration of Principles on Equality, Principle 21. For the ECHR, see *Timishev*, para 57.

and significant' may be sufficient prima facie evidence of indirect discrimination.[75] Thus, in *DH*, even though the statistical figures submitted by the applicants were contentious, the Court still thought that they revealed a dominant trend and thus accepted them as sufficient to establish a presumption of disproportionate numbers of Roma children being placed in 'special schools'. As a consequence, the burden of proof shifted to the government to show that there was a justification for the disparate impact of the legislation.[76]

DH demonstrates that statistical evidence may be of decisive importance to the outcome of cases of alleged indirect discrimination. Yet often the data required to establish a presumption that a measure has a discriminatory effect can, unlike in *DH*, only be collected by state authorities. The UN treaty bodies, therefore, regularly stress in their concluding observations that states have a duty to collect and analyse relevant statistical data, disaggregated by grounds of distinction.[77] Such a duty to gather information has also been included in the Declaration of Principles on Equality.[78]

6 POSITIVE ACTION

As with any other human right, the right to equality and non-discrimination entails state obligations of different types.[79] The *obligation to respect* requires states to refrain from any discriminatory action and to ensure that all their laws and practices comply with the right to non-discrimination. The *obligation to protect* imposes a duty on states to prevent discrimination by non-state actors. According to the consistent jurisprudence of the UN treaty bodies, this means that states must introduce comprehensive legislation prohibiting discrimination in fields such as employment, education, healthcare, housing, and the provision of goods and services. This conclusion is supported by various provisions in the respective human rights treaties themselves. Article 2(d) ICERD, for example, explicitly states that '[e]ach State Party shall prohibit and bring to an end, by all appropriate means, including legislation as required by circumstances, racial discrimination by any persons, group or organization'; CEDAW contains a parallel provision in Article 2(e); and most treaties are scattered with norms requiring states to prohibit particular actions of private parties that are discriminatory or may contribute to discrimination, such as racial hate speech (Article 20 ICCPR, Article 4 ICERD, Article 13(5) ACHR), trafficking in women and exploitation of prostitution of women (Article 6 CEDAW), or racial discrimination with regard to employment, housing, or education (Article 5(e) ICERD).

However, an exclusively prohibitory approach is severely limited in that it focuses on discrimination understood as individual, isolated events that can be remedied through penalizing the perpetrators and compensating the victims. In fact, discrimination is often the consequence of deeply embedded patterns of disadvantage and exclusion that can only be addressed through changes to social and institutional structures. Accordingly, it is now well established in international human rights law that it is not sufficient for states to have anti-discrimination legislation in place. Instead, they also have an *obligation to promote, guarantee, and secure* equality by taking proactive steps to eliminate structural patterns of disadvantage and to further social inclusion.[80] This obligation, often referred to as the duty

---

[75] *DH*, para 188.   [76] *DH*, paras 191–5.

[77] eg CEDAW Committee, Report on twenty-ninth session, A/58/38 (part II), para 134 (Brazil).

[78] Declaration of Principles on Equality, Principle 24.   [79] See Chapter 5.

[80] eg ICERD, Arts 2(1)(e), 2(2), and 7; CERD, General Recommendation XXIX, HRI/GEN/1/Rev. 9 (Vol II) 296, paras 5, 6, 8, 9, 17, 33–5; HRC, General Comment 4, HRI/GEN/1/Rev. 9 (Vol I) 175, para 2; HRC, General Comment 18, paras 5 and 10; CEDAW, Arts 3 and 5; Protocol to the African Charter on Human and Peoples' Rights on the Rights of Women in Africa, Arts 2(1)(d), 2(2), 3–24.

to take 'positive action', may cover a huge variety of legislative, administrative, and policy measures, ranging from the restructuring of institutions to the provision of 'reasonable accommodation'[81] for individuals in particular circumstances, from educational campaigns to the use of public procurement to promote equality, and from the 'mainstreaming'[82] of equality issues in public policy to encouraging participation of affected groups in relevant decision-making processes.

One important aspect of 'positive action' are 'affirmative action programmes' or, as they are generally called in international law, *special measures of protection*. These are 'measures … aimed specifically at correcting the position of members of a target group in one or more aspects of their social life, in order to obtain effective equality'.[83] In their strongest form, such special measures involve the preferential treatment of members of a previously disadvantaged group over others in the allocation of jobs, university places, and other benefits (often referred to as 'positive' or 'reverse discrimination'). For example, when two equally qualified persons apply for a job, priority is given to the female applicant, or a certain number of university places are reserved for racial minorities.

Although such preferential treatment is clearly incompatible with a formal notion of equality, international human rights law permits it, thus recognizing that it may be legitimate to prioritize the achievement of substantive equality over the requirement of consistent treatment. Article 1(4) ICERD, for example, provides:

> Special measures taken for the sole purpose of securing adequate advancement of certain racial or ethnic groups or individuals requiring such protection as may be necessary in order to ensure such groups or individuals equal enjoyment or exercise of human rights and fundamental freedoms shall not be deemed racial discrimination, provided, however, that such measures do not, as a consequence, lead to the maintenance of separate rights for different racial groups and that they shall not be continued after the objectives for which they were taken have been achieved.

CEDAW contains a similar provision in Article 4(1). For purposes of the ICCPR, the Human Rights Committee has made it clear that special measures are permissible as long as they meet the general justification test described in Section 5.1, that is, as long as they pursue a legitimate aim in a proportionate manner.[84] Proportionality in this context means, among other things, that the preferential treatment must be introduced for the benefit of genuinely disadvantaged groups, be temporary and cease once the objectives have been achieved, and not result in the maintenance of separate rights for different groups.

Not only does international human rights law permit but to some extent it even *requires* states to adopt special measures of protection. As the Human Rights Committee's General Comment on non-discrimination states:

> [T]he principle of equality sometimes requires States parties to take affirmative action in order to diminish or eliminate conditions which cause or help to perpetuate discrimination

---

[81] For a definition of 'reasonable accommodation', see CRPD, Art 2.

[82] For 'gender mainstreaming', that is, the integration of a gender perspective in all legislation and public policies, see Report of the Fourth World Conference on Women, A/Conf.177/20 (1995), strategic objective H.2. The Protocol to the African Charter on Human and Peoples' Rights on the Rights of Women in Africa contains, in Art 2(1)(c), an explicit obligation of gender mainstreaming. See further Chapter 16.

[83] Progress report on the concept and practice of affirmative action by the Special Rapporteur of the Sub-Commission on the Promotion and Protection of Human Rights, E/CN.4/Sub.2/2001/15 (26 June 2001) para 7.

[84] eg *Stalla Costa v Uruguay*, CCPR/C/30/D/198/1985 (9 July 1987) para 10; *Jacobs v Belgium*, CCPR/C/81/D/943/2000 (7 July 2004) para 9.5.

prohibited by the Covenant. For example, in a State where the general conditions of a certain part of the population prevent or impair their enjoyment of human rights, the State should take specific action to correct those conditions. Such action may involve granting for a time to the part of the population concerned certain preferential treatment in specific matters as compared with the rest of the population.[85]

That states may need to adopt special measures has also been highlighted by the Committee on Economic, Social and Cultural Rights.[86] As far as racial groups and women are concerned, the duty follows from Article 2(2) ICERD and Article 3 CEDAW, respectively. At the regional level, the Inter-American Court of Human Rights has observed that 'States are obliged to take affirmative action to reverse or change discriminatory situations that exist in their societies to the detriment of a specific group of persons',[87] and this obligation is now codified in the Inter-American Convention against All Forms of Discrimination and Intolerance.[88] The European Court has stressed that 'a failure to attempt to correct inequality through different treatment' may amount to a violation of the right to non-discrimination.[89]

7 CONCLUSION

The concept of equality and non-discrimination in international human rights law has evolved significantly since the adoption of the UDHR. Detailed legal standards have been drawn up and human rights bodies and courts have developed a rich jurisprudence, giving concrete substance to the notion of equality. Nevertheless, considerable gaps, inconsistencies, and uncertainties remain: the concept of indirect discrimination was developed in other jurisdictions and has only very recently been acknowledged by international human rights bodies; details of the justification test, such as the applicable standard of review and evidentiary rules, need further elaboration; and, as far as implementation at the national level is concerned, numerous states do not yet have comprehensive legislation to combat discrimination.

The most important challenge, however, is to ensure that every human being is in fact able to enjoy her or his right to equality. In a world in which the poorest 50 per cent collectively own less than one per cent of global wealth,[90] equal rights remain an unfulfilled promise for large sections of the population. Developments in international human rights law are evidence of a growing recognition that, while prohibitions of discrimination play a crucial role in achieving equality, states also have an obligation to proactively tackle structural patterns of disadvantage—in other words, formal and substantive approaches to equality need to be combined. One key component of such a proactive strategy must be to ensure that all people can participate on an equal basis in all areas of economic, social, and political life, including in the very decisions on how equality should be realized.

---

[85] HRC, General Comment 18, para 10.
[86] eg CESCR, General Comment 16, HRI/GEN/1/Rev. 9 (Vol I) 113, paras 15 and 35.
[87] *Juridical Condition and Rights of the Undocumented Migrants*, para 104.   [88] Art 5.
[89] *Stec and Others v UK* (2006) 43 EHRR 47, para 51.
[90] Credit Suisse Research Institute, Global Wealth Databook 2016, available at <https://www.credit-suisse.com/uk/en/about-us/research/research-institute/global-wealth-report.html>, 104.

FURTHER READING

ARNARDÓTTIR, Equality and Non-discrimination under the European Convention on Human Rights (Martinus Nijhoff, 2003).

ARNARDÓTTIR, 'The Differences that Make a Difference: Recent Developments on the Discrimination Grounds and the Margin of Appreciation under Article 14 of the European Convention on Human Rights' (2014) 14 *HRLR* 647.

BAYEFSKY, 'The Principle of Equality or Non-Discrimination in International Law' (1990) 11 *HRLJ* 1.

CHOUDHURY, 'Interpreting the Right to Equality under Article 26 of the International Covenant on Civil and Political Rights' [2003] *EHRLR* 24.

FREDMAN, *Discrimination Law* (Oxford University Press, 2nd edn, 2011).

FREDMAN, 'Emerging from the Shadows: Substantive Equality and Article 14 of the European Convention on Human Rights' (2016) 16 *HRLR* 273.

KHAITAN, *A Theory of Discrimination Law* (Oxford University Press, 2015).

LERNER, *Group Rights and Discrimination in International Law* (Martinus Nijhoff, 2003).

McCOLGAN, *Discrimination, Equality and the Law* (Hart, 2014).

MCKEAN, *Equality and Discrimination under International Law* (Clarendon Press, 1983).

USEFUL WEBSITES

UN Committee on the Elimination of Racial Discrimination (CERD): <http://www.ohchr.org/EN/HRBodies/CERD/Pages/CERDIndex.aspx/>

UN Committee on the Elimination of Discrimination against Women (CEDAW): <http://www.ohchr.org/EN/HRBodies/CEDAW/pages/cedawindex.aspx>

UN Committee on the Rights of Persons with Disabilities (CRPD): <http://www.ohchr.org/EN/HRBodies/CRPD/Pages/CRPDIndex.aspx>

European Commission Against Racism and Intolerance (ECRI): <http://www.coe.int/ecri>

Equal Rights Trust: <http://www.equalrightstrust.org>

9

INTEGRITY OF THE PERSON

Nigel S Rodley

SUMMARY

This chapter examines the right to be free from torture and cruel, inhuman, or degrading treatment or punishment and the right to life, arguably the core rights understood within the concept of integrity of the person. These rights also have a direct pedigree to the principle of respect for human dignity that is at the heart of the International Bill of Human Rights. The complex definitional issues of what constitutes torture and other ill-treatment are addressed, mainly in light of treaty definitions and case law of courts and other bodies charged with applying relevant treaties. The same approach is taken with respect to the right to life, where the central issues of the limits international law places on the death penalty and on the use of force by security forces and law enforcement officials are considered. Both rights are considered to be rules of customary international law and probably peremptory norms of international law (*jus cogens*).*

1 INTRODUCTION

1.1 RESPECT FOR HUMAN DIGNITY

Respect for human dignity is the one explicit underlying principle of the International Bill of Human Rights. It is invoked in the first preambular paragraph of the Universal Declaration of Human Rights (UDHR) and the second preambular paragraphs of both the International Covenant on Economic, Social and Cultural Rights (ICESCR) and the International Covenant on Civil and Political Rights (ICCPR).

The prohibition of torture and cruel, inhuman, or degrading treatment or punishment ('torture and ill-treatment') and the right to life both have an immediate link to the principle of human dignity. Thus, the African Charter on Human and Peoples' Rights (ACHPR) places the prohibition of torture and ill-treatment in its Article 5 that guarantees 'respect of the dignity inherent in a human being'. In a more limited way, the analogous Article 5 of the American Convention on Human Rights (ACHR), after stating the basic prohibition on torture and ill-treatment, provides that all persons deprived of liberty are to be 'treated with respect for the inherent dignity of the human person'. A similar requirement is found in Article 10(1) ICCPR. While this is separate from Article 7 ICCPR containing the prohibition of torture and ill-treatment, it has long been treated by the Human Rights

---

* This chapter was updated by Raffael Fasel.

Committee as intimately linked to Article 7.[1] With regard to the right to life, the first preambular paragraph of the Second Optional Protocol to the ICCPR (ICCPR-OP2), aimed at the abolition of the death penalty, affirms that abolition 'contributes to enhancement of human dignity'.

1.2 THE RIGHT TO INTEGRITY OF THE PERSON

The prohibition of torture and ill-treatment and the right to life are at the core of the notion of integrity of the person. Article 5 ACHR, for example, which guarantees the right to humane treatment, provides in its first paragraph: 'Every person has the right to have his physical, mental, and moral integrity respected.' The link between the right to humane treatment and personal integrity is established. The same is true for the link between the right to life and integrity of the person. Thus, Article 4 ACHPR stipulates the right of every human being 'to respect for his life and the integrity of his person'. Here the link is essential.

This chapter deals, first, with the right to be free from torture and ill-treatment (Section 2) and, then, with the right to life (Section 3).

2 THE RIGHT TO BE FREE FROM TORTURE AND ILL-TREATMENT

Article 5 UDHR provides: 'No one shall be subjected to torture or to cruel, inhuman or degrading treatment or punishment.' Verbally inspired by the prohibition of 'cruel and unusual punishments' in the English and American Bills of Rights, the direct stimulus for this provision was the Nazis' use of torture. Related vivid concerns included the use of harmful and painful medical experiments, such as those conducted by the notorious Dr Josef Mengele. This breadth of concern explains the expansive, non-technical language of the prohibition.

While torture had been legal under certain circumstances in Europe from at least Roman times, it had been abolished virtually everywhere by the end of the eighteenth century.[2] Its re-emergence in the heart of Europe in a post-Enlightenment world was a matter for shock and felt to be an aberration. Accordingly, after the prohibition's inclusion in the UDHR, it found its way uncontroversially, in almost identical language, into the ICCPR and the principal regional treaties.

That the use of torture may not have been such an aberration became clear in the 1970s when Amnesty International published a report documenting the practice of torture in many countries from all regions of the world and led a campaign on the issue. Demonstrably in response to this campaign, and a successor one in 1984–5,[3] the UN began sustained activities, first in the field of standard-setting, then in the area of developing an institutional response. There were also activities at the regional level to the same effect.

The product of the standard-setting is referred to in Section 2.1. The institutional output has included the creation of the mandate of the UN Special Rapporteur on the question

---

[1] HRC, General Comment 20, HRI/GEN/1/Rev.9 (Vol I) 200, para 2; General Comment 21, HRI/GEN/1/Rev.9 (Vol I) 202, para 3.

[2] Torture seems to have been alien to Islamic tradition from its beginnings, albeit not, in practice, to various governments claiming to apply Islamic law in their legal systems.

[3] See Amnesty International, *Report on Torture* (1973) and *Torture in the Eighties* (1984).

of torture, the establishment of the Committee against Torture under the UN Convention against Torture and Other Cruel, Inhuman or Degrading Treatment or Punishment (UNCAT), and a Subcommittee on the Prevention of Torture created by the Optional Protocol to UNCAT (UNCAT-OP). The latter was inspired by the work of the European Committee for the Prevention of Torture and Inhuman or Degrading Treatment or Punishment that was put in place by the European Convention of the same name adopted by the Council of Europe in 1987.

2.1 SOURCES

The right to be free from torture and ill-treatment is guaranteed by the general universal and regional human rights treaties: Articles 7 and 10 ICCPR, Article 3 European Convention on Human Rights (ECHR), Article 5 ACHR, and Article 5 ACHPR. In addition, a human rights treaty specifically designed to ensure protection of the right to be free from torture and ill-treatment has been adopted: UNCAT. Key UN 'soft law' sources include the Declaration on the Protection of All Persons from Being Subjected to Torture and Other Cruel, Inhuman or Degrading Treatment or Punishment (1975), the Code of Conduct for Law Enforcement Officials (1979), the Principles of Medical Ethics relevant to the Role of Health Personnel, particularly Physicians, in the Protection of Prisoners and Detainees against Torture and Other Cruel, Inhuman or Degrading Treatment or Punishment (1982), the Body of Principles for the Protection of All Persons under Any Form of Detention or Imprisonment (1988), the Principles on the Effective Investigation and Documentation of Torture and Other Cruel, Inhuman or Degrading Treatment or Punishment (Istanbul Principles) (2000), and the revised Standard Minimum Rules for the Treatment of Prisoners (Nelson Mandela Rules) (2015). There are also treaty provisions in the field of international humanitarian law that prohibit torture, cruel treatment, inhuman treatment, and humiliating and degrading treatment.[4] As with the human rights treaties, the terms are undefined. Finally, there is international criminal law, which covers, among other aspects, crimes against humanity and war crimes. Torture and other forms of ill-treatment may amount to war crimes and, when committed as part of a widespread or systematic attack against a civilian population, crimes against humanity. The case law of the International Criminal Tribunal for the former Yugoslavia and the International Criminal Tribunal for Rwanda, therefore, also provide helpful guidance in determining the normative content of the right to be free from torture and ill-treatment. Furthermore, the Rome Statute of the International Criminal Court (ICC Statute) has both codified crimes against humanity and war crimes and provided definitions for some components, including torture.[5]

2.2 LEGAL STATUS

There is no doubt that the prohibition of torture and other ill-treatment is a norm of customary international law. Relevant indications are: the fact that the rule is couched in absolute terms, brooking no exception (such as for public order or national security purposes, as allowed for in some rights, notably the freedoms covered in Chapter 11), not

---

[4] Geneva Convention I, Arts 12 and 50; Geneva Convention II, Arts 12 and 51; Geneva Convention III, Arts 17, 87, and 130; Geneva Convention IV, Arts 32 and 147; and Common Art 3 to all four Geneva Conventions, which is understood as reflecting the 'fundamental principles of international humanitarian law'. See Chapter 25.

[5] Arts 7 and 8. See Chapter 26.

even the spurious 'ticking bomb' situation;[6] the non-derogability of the rule even in time of war or other public emergency;[7] and the fact that states do not claim a right to torture. One might also look to the prohibition in international humanitarian law and its criminal nature under international criminal law.

It is also beyond peradventure that the prohibition of torture is a rule of *jus cogens*, a peremptory rule of international law which cannot be modified even by treaty.[8] It has been described as such by the International Court of Justice, as well as by the European Court of Human Rights, the Inter-American Court of Human Rights, the Human Rights Committee, the Committee against Torture, the International Criminal Tribunal for the former Yugoslavia, the International Law Commission, and the UK House of Lords.[9] It is worth noting that, not only has the influential American Law Institute long ago espoused this position, in its third Restatement of US Foreign Relations Law,[10] so has one of the controversial legal memoranda from the US Department of Justice that provided the basis for the temporary use of 'enhanced interrogation techniques' by US personnel of certain 'high value' detainees held in the context of the 'global war on terror'.[11] All that remains unsettled is whether the prohibition of other ill-treatment has the same status. The American Restatement makes no distinction. Most of the other sources cited focus on torture, without necessarily excluding other ill-treatment.

2.3 COMPONENTS

We have seen that the treaty prohibitions of torture and cruel, inhuman, or degrading treatment or punishment were drafted broadly with a view to avoiding an overly technical or narrow approach. Indeed, international bodies have found an extensive range of practices to fall foul of it. For instance, in the late 1960s and early 1970s the UK refused to admit British nationals being deported from Uganda, resulting in their 'shuttlecocking' between the two countries. In 1973, the (former) European Commission of Human Rights found the practice to violate Article 3 ECHR.[12] Another type of concern was highlighted when a team of UN Special Rapporteurs found that the widespread property destruction carried out by East Timorese paramilitaries in Dili engaged the prohibition of torture and ill-treatment.[13]

---

[6] This posits the extremely hypothetical situation that a person in custody knows where a bomb that would cause great loss of life has been placed and the aim is to locate it and prevent it from going off. In reality, the person's knowledge will be doubtful and the person will be able to prevaricate until the bomb goes off, even in the unlikely event that a 'specialist' interrogation team is available. A rare case that comes close to a 'ticking bomb' situation, but still deviates from it in significant respects, is the one of *Gäfgen v Germany* (2009) 48 EHRR 13.

[7] See case law listed below. See also *Chahal v UK* (1997) 23 EHRR 413; *Saadi v Italy* (2009) 49 EHRR 30.

[8] See Chapter 4.

[9] eg ICJ, *Questions relating to the Obligation to Prosecute or Extradite (Belgium v Senegal)* [2012] ICJ Rep 422, para 99; *Al-Adsani v UK* (2002) 34 EHRR 273, para 61; *Caesar v Trinidad and Tobago*, IACtHR Series C No 123 (11 March 2005); HRC, General Comment 29, HRI/GEN/1/Rev.9 (Vol I) 234, para 3; CAT, General Comment 2, HRI/GEN/1/Rev.9 (Vol I) 376, para 1; *Prosecutor v Furundzija* (1998), No 17–95–17/1, Trial Judgment, paras 153–7; International Law Commission, Draft Articles on State Responsibility, A/56/10, ch IV.E.2; *Regina v Bow Street Metropolitan Stipendiary Magistrate, ex parte Pinochet Ugarte (No 3)* [1999] UKHL 17.

[10] American Law Institute, Restatement of the Law: Restatement (Third) of the Foreign Relations Law of the United States, Vol II (1987) s 702.

[11] See Memorandum from Daniel P Levin to James B Comey (30 December 2004) 1 available at <https://www.aclu.org/files/torturefoia/released/082409/olcremand/2004olc96.pdf>.

[12] *East African Asians v UK* (1973) 3 EHRR 76.

[13] Joint report of the Special Rapporteurs on extrajudicial, summary or arbitrary executions, torture, and violence against women, A/54/660 (10 December 1999) paras 70–71. See also, for the Committee against Torture, *Hajrizi Dzemajl v Yugoslavia*, CAT/C/29/D/161/2000 (2 December 2002) and, for the European Court, *Ayder v Turkey*, App no 23656/94, Judgment of 8 January 2004, paras 104–11.

Nevertheless, the earliest case law, especially by the European Commission of Human Rights and the European Court of Human Rights, started to break down the prohibition into its component limbs, mostly in connection with cases dealing with prisoners.

2.3.1 Definition of 'torture' and 'cruel, inhuman, and degrading treatment or punishment'

In the *Greek Case*, arising out of treatment inflicted on political opponents by the military regime that seized power in Greece in 1967, the European Commission distinguished between various kinds of ill-treatment. In particular, it characterized *falanga* (beatings on the soles of the feet) as 'torture *and* inhuman treatment' while it considered some extremely severe beatings as 'torture *or* inhuman treatment'.[14]

The landmark case of *Ireland v UK* concerned the treatment by UK security forces of suspected Irish Republican Army (IRA) prisoners in Northern Ireland. Again the European Commission distinguished between treatment amounting to torture and other ill-treatment. While it assigned serious physical beatings to the category of inhuman treatment, it concluded that five special interrogation techniques amounted to torture. The five techniques were:

1) wall-standing: forcing the detainees to remain for periods of some hours in a 'stress position', spread-eagled against the wall, with their fingers put high above the head against the wall, the legs spread apart and the feet back, causing them to stand on their toes with the weight of the body mainly on the fingers;

2) hooding: putting a bag over the detainees' heads and, at least initially, keeping it there all the time except during interrogation;

3) subjection to noise: pending their interrogations, holding the detainees in a room where there was a continuous loud and hissing noise;

4) deprivation of sleep: pending their interrogations, depriving the detainees of sleep;

5) deprivation of food and drink: subjecting the detainees to a reduced diet.[15]

The European Court of Human Rights, however, decided in 1978 that these techniques should be considered as inhuman treatment rather than torture. It invoked the definition of torture found in the recently adopted UN Declaration against Torture (UNDAT). Article 1(2) UNDAT had defined torture as an aggravated and deliberate form of cruel, inhuman, or degrading treatment or punishment. For the European Court, the five techniques did not meet this criterion 'as so understood', the techniques being undeserving of the 'special stigma' of torture.[16] This was a controversial decision. After all, the definition of torture in the UNDAT had made clear that the pain or suffering inflicted did not have to be physical. It could also be *mental* pain or suffering. Many found it hard to understand what kind of mental pain or suffering might be required if the mixed mental *and* physical pain and suffering caused by interrogation techniques did not constitute torture.

The year 1984, also the title of George Orwell's futuristic novel which has his hero, Winston Smith, tortured by being in a room full of rats to which he was known to be phobic, brought us the UNCAT and its authoritative definition of torture. According to Article 1:

> For the purposes of this Convention, the term 'torture' means any act by which severe pain or suffering, whether physical or mental, is intentionally inflicted on a person for such purposes as obtaining from him or a third person information or a confession, punishing him for an act he or a third person has committed or is suspected of having committed, or

---

[14] *The Greek Case* (1969) 12 YB 468, 504 (emphases added).
[15] See *Ireland v UK* (1978) 2 EHRR 25, para 96.
[16] *Ireland v UK*, para 167.

intimidating or coercing him or a third person, or for any reason based on discrimination of any kind, when such pain or suffering is inflicted by or at the instigation of or with the consent or acquiescence of a public official or other person acting in an official capacity. It does not include pain or suffering arising only from, inherent in or incidental to lawful sanctions.

While the definition is formally only applicable to the states parties to the UNCAT and the Committee against Torture that monitors its implementation, it has proven to be the first port of call for most bodies seeking to identify practices of torture. The definition largely follows that of UNDAT, with one notable exception: it does not describe torture as an aggravated and deliberate form of inhuman treatment. The definition has three core elements:

1. pain or suffering that must be severe; it may be physical or mental;
2. it must be inflicted for a certain kind of purpose, that is, the sort of public purpose traditionally associated with torture; and
3. it must be inflicted by or under the aegis of public officialdom.

Each of these elements will be considered briefly. The first element, *severity of pain or suffering*, is common to most understandings of the term torture[17] and is found in the Article 7 ICC Statute definition of torture as a crime against humanity and in the definition of torture as a war crime in the Elements of Crimes adopted under the ICC Statute.[18] As indicated, there is no requirement for aggravation of pain or suffering. However, it should be noted that Article 16 UNCAT does make provision for cruel, inhuman, or degrading treatment or punishment that 'does not amount to torture'. This can lend itself to an interpretation that would reintroduce the idea of aggravation, but the better view is that it does not.

It is unclear to what extent the practice of the European Court of Human Rights may have been influenced by this evolution. Certainly, it has seen fit at least to attenuate the application of its distinction between torture and inhuman treatment. In the 1999 *Selmouni* case, it decided that the kind of serious beatings that had occurred in a number of cases, including *Ireland v UK*, and would earlier have been classified as inhuman treatment, would now be considered as torture. It invoked its doctrine of the ECHR as 'a living instrument' and argued that the definition of torture had to evolve with democratic society's understanding of the term.[19] It is probable that the European Court was also signalling that it would have been prepared to treat practices such as the five interrogation techniques similarly. The Court continues to distinguish torture from inhuman treatment that 'does not reach the level of severity' to constitute torture. However, it gives little away as to what is the criterion for inhuman treatment. Earlier, inhuman treatment had to be severe, thus requiring torture to be more than severe. It is possible that it may now require a certain level of seriousness of pain or suffering, but without rising to the level of 'severe', for treatment to be considered 'inhuman'. What is clear is that, after *Selmouni*, the European Court has brought down the threshold of pain or suffering required for a finding of torture.

The second element, *purpose*, was always part of European Commission and Court case law and it is found in all but one of the existing definitions of torture. Indeed, in the definition of torture as a war crime in the Elements of Crimes adopted under the ICC Statute, the only distinction between torture and inhuman (or cruel) treatment is the purposive element. However, there is one definition that omits the purposive element, namely that

---

[17] Inter-American Convention to Prevent and Punish Torture, Art 2 refers to 'physical or mental pain' without qualification.

[18] Elements of Crimes, Arts 8(2)(a)(ii)-1 and 8(2)(c)(i)-4.

[19] *Selmouni v France* (2000) 29 EHRR 403, para 101.

in Article 7 ICC Statute defining torture as a crime against humanity. This may be explained by the fact that crimes against humanity can be committed by unofficial groups, thus making the attribution of motivation more difficult than in respect of states or other officially constituted bodies. Also, unlike the other definitions, that of Article 7 is limited to persons in custody or under the control of the accused, thus implicitly assigning some public purposive context. The definition remains an unsatisfactory outlier. The approach taken by UNCAT and the ICC Elements of Crime, making purpose the key distinguishing factor between torture and cruel or inhuman treatment, may be the more satisfactory one.

Finally, as a third element, the UNCAT definition requires public *official responsibility* for the pain or suffering. This is not found in the ICC-related definitions. This is perhaps inevitable as crimes against humanity and war crimes are not necessarily committed by public officials in the sense of state officials. A party to an armed conflict may well not be a state. However, it must have sufficient elements of organization such as to endow it with the status of party to an armed conflict within the meaning of international humanitarian law. Similarly, a crime against humanity must also be committed in the context of an attack against a civilian population. This organizational dimension should be seen as substituting for the public official requirement, as is the case in respect of war crimes.

2.3.2 Specific practices

While most findings of torture have involved an accumulation of cruel acts, some specific practices have been found to be torture. We have already seen this in respect of the *falanga* and sustained beatings with instruments. Others include water suffocation,[20] 'Palestinian hanging' (tying a person's hands behind their back and suspending them in the air),[21] and rape.[22]

Since the suffering involved in torture can be physical or mental, it is clear that psychological torment, such as that to which Orwell subjected his fictional hero Winston Smith, may fall within the legal definition of torture. The classic example is the Human Rights Committee finding that the threat of amputation of a concert pianist's hands constituted torture.[23] Explicit and implicit threats of torture and death in circumstances where the threats were credible were found by the Inter-American Court of Human Rights to be torture.[24]

As far as other ill-treatment is concerned, it includes, first, any treatment that would amount to torture, but was not inflicted for a public purpose. Even since *Selmouni*, the European Court of Human Rights has found some beatings to be inhuman or degrading rather than torture. The reluctance to find torture may be attributable to the fact that in these cases there seem to be circumstances in which the facts, including the behaviour of the affected individual, are in doubt.[25] The unnecessary use of handcuffs or other physical restraints may, under certain circumstances, amount to prohibited ill-treatment,[26] as can unnecessary or oppressive strip-searching,[27] and displaying an alleged terrorist in prison garb.[28]

---

[20] *José Vicente and Amado Villafañe Chaparro v Colombia*, CCPR/C/60/D/612/1995 (14 June 1994). The case is evidently consistent with the proposition that 'waterboarding'—briefly authorized for use by US personnel in the reaction to the atrocities of 11 September 2001—is torture.

[21] *Aksoy v Turkey* (1997) 23 EHRR 553, para 64.

[22] Case 10.970, *Mejía v Peru*, IACommHR Report No 5/96 (1 March 1996) Annual Report 1995, 157, 186–7; *Case of the Miguel Castro-Castro Prison v Peru*, IACtHR Series C No 160 (25 November 2006) para 311; *Aydin v Turkey* (1998) 25 EHRR 251, para 86.

[23] *Estrella v Uruguay*, CCPR/C/18/D/74/1980 (23 March 1983) para 8.3.

[24] *Maritza Urrutia v Guatemala*, IACtHR Series C No 103 (27 November 2003) paras 91–5.

[25] eg *Egmez v Cyprus* (2002) 34 EHRR 29, paras 78–9.

[26] *Hénaf v France* (2005) 40 EHRR 44, paras 55–60.   [27] *Iwanczuk v Poland* (2004) 38 EHRR 8.

[28] *Loayza-Tamayo v Peru*, IACtHR Series C No 33 (17 September 1997) paras 46(d) and 58.

As far as persons in detention are concerned, they are at particular risk of ill-treatment during the *investigative phase* of detention, when the police or other detaining authority is seeking information of concern or a confession. This is because during this phase normal safeguards are not always respected. Thus, instead of detainees having prompt access to a lawyer and others from outside the place of detention, such as family members, or a medical practitioner, the detaining authority holds them at its sole mercy. This is generally called 'incommunicado detention'. Rules concerning the right to liberty aim at restricting this period of detention.[29] However, there is strong treaty body authority for the proposition that prolonged incommunicado detention in itself can violate the right of detainees to be treated with humanity and respect for their human dignity and the prohibition of torture and other ill-treatment.[30] Moreover, the UN Human Rights Council has clearly stated that prolonged incommunicado detention can amount to torture or other ill-treatment.[31] The Human Rights Committee has found that the US practice of capturing and detaining terrorist suspects in various parts of the world, as well as transferring them from place to place, violated the prohibition on torture and ill-treatment.[32] The European Court of Human Rights has gone as far as generally requiring assistance of a lawyer from the first police interview of a suspect.[33] The UN Special Rapporteur on torture has proposed the development of a universal protocol identifying a set of standards and procedural safeguards that ought to be applied to interviews during the investigative phase.[34]

The second phase of detention is the *remand phase*, the phase in which, typically, a judicial authority will order continued detention on criminal charges. As in this phase the detaining authority will usually be different from the investigating authority (the prison authorities rather than the police or security services), detainees are generally better protected from ill-treatment. However, even after being formally remanded in custody, people may remain in the hands of the police or other investigating authority. Therefore, human rights bodies tend to recommend that the period of pre-remand detention not exceed a very few days (typically not more than two or three)[35] and that places of remand be under an authority administratively separate from that responsible for the police or similar security agency.

The *post-conviction phase* raises two kinds of issue. The first is the conditions of detention, the second is the nature of the punishment.

As to the first, the fact that someone has been sentenced to a term of imprisonment does not mean that there are no limits to how the prisoner may then be treated. On the contrary, the basic principle is that conditions should be no more oppressive than those necessary to maintain the deprivation of liberty which is the object of the punishment.[36] Accordingly, standards have been developed to assist in this, notably the (revised) UN Standard Minimum Rules for the Treatment of Prisoners.[37] These cover such matters as avoidance of overcrowding, recreation, education and work, health care, limits to time

---

[29] See Chapter 13.

[30] *Aber v Algeria*, CCPR/C/90/D/1439/2005 (16 August 2007) para 7.3; HRC, General Comment 35, CCPR/C/GC/35, para 56; *Suárez-Rosero v Ecuador*, IACtHR Series C No 35 (12 November 1997) paras 90–91.

[31] Human Rights Council Res 8/8 (18 June 2008) para 7(c).

[32] Concluding observations: US, CCPR/C/USA/CO/3/Rev.1 (18 December 2006) paras 12 and 16.

[33] *Salduz v Turkey* (2008) 49 EHRR 421; compare *Ibrahim and others v UK*, App nos 50541/08, 50571/08, 50573/08, 40351/09, Judgment of 13 September 2016.

[34] Interim report of the Special Rapporteur on torture, A/71/298 (5 August 2016).

[35] eg Report of the Special Rapporteur on torture, E/CN.4/2003/68 (17 December 2002) para 26(g); CPT Standards, CPT/Inf/E (2002) I-Rev 2006, paras 40–6.

[36] eg UN Basic Principles for the Treatment of Prisoners, GA Res 45/111 (14 December 1990) para 5.

[37] See also General Comment 35. At the European level, the Council of Europe has adopted the European Prison Rules (2006).

spent confined in cells, and limits to disciplinary punishment. Not every breach of every rule will necessarily involve a violation of the prohibition of torture or ill-treatment or the right to treatment with respect for humanity and human dignity. However, the more serious or widespread the breach of the Rules, the more likely will be a finding of a violation of one of these human rights. Treaty bodies routinely invoke the Standard Minimum Rules in finding prison conditions to violate these rights.[38]

With regard to the second issue, the nature of the punishment, it will be recalled that the UNCAT definition of torture excludes 'lawful sanctions'. Does that mean that the prohibition of cruel, inhuman, and degrading *punishment* can only apply either to oppressive prison conditions or punishment inflicted extrajudicially, for example by the police? The answer has to be negative. There is extensive treaty body authority finding various forms of corporal punishment to violate the prohibition. The first was the 1978 *Tyrer* case in which the European Court of Human Rights found the infliction of a judicially ordered three strokes of the birch on a young person to be a degrading punishment violating Article 3 ECHR.[39] More recently, the Inter-American Court of Human Rights found the lashing of a naked adult strapped to a metal contraption, until he fainted, to be torture in violation of Article 5 ACHR.[40] The Human Rights Committee has long been clear in its rejection of corporal punishment as a violation of Article 7 ICCPR.[41] Similarly, the Human Rights Council has reminded governments that 'corporal punishment can amount to cruel, inhuman or degrading punishment or even to torture'.[42] This begs the question of the exclusion of lawful sanctions from the definition of torture. The proper understanding is that the exclusion refers to those sanctions that are lawful under both national *and* international law. Since it is widely accepted that corporal punishment at least amounts to cruel, inhuman, or degrading punishment, it does not qualify as a 'lawful sanction' and, accordingly, is not immunized against being categorized as torture.

2.4 TYPES OF OBLIGATION

The prohibition of torture is in formal terms primarily a negative obligation. The state is required to refrain from engaging in the practices concerned, either directly through its agents' acts or indirectly by its agents' omissions when there is a duty to act. However, the latter dimension already can be understood as an embryonic positive obligation. It arises to avoid the circumvention of the rule by simply blaming the acts on others (paramilitary groups, 'death squads', vigilantes, and so on), in circumstances in which the acts may well have been committed with 'a nod and a wink' from state authorities. Because such collusion is hard to prove, other positive obligations have been developed.

Thus, it is generally accepted that where there are grounds for believing that torture has taken place, there is an obligation on the state to initiate an effective investigation into the situation, typical elements of which are reflected in the Istanbul Principles. Moreover, not only should such an investigation be capable of sustaining a prosecution of those found to be responsible, there seems to be an obligation to initiate such prosecutions when the facts permit. Indeed, it is this very obligation that is increasingly seen as the basis for the impermissibility of granting amnesties to persons responsible for torture (and probably other ill-treatment).[43] The obligation to prosecute is reinforced by Article 7 UNCAT, which requires states parties to

---

[38] eg *Mukong v Cameroon*, CCPR/C/51/D/458/1991 (10 August 1994); *Greek Case*; *Dickson v UK* (2008) 46 EHRR 41, para 30 (note that the Court relied more heavily, as it generally does, on the European Prison Rules; see paras 31–6); *Raxcacó-Reyes v Guatemala*, IACtHR Series C No 133 (15 September 2005) paras 99–102.   [39] *Tyrer v UK* (1978) 2 EHRR 1.   [40] *Caesar*, paras 49(27) and (28).
[41] General Comment 20.   [42] Human Rights Council Res 8/8 (18 June 2008) para 7(a).
[43] eg HRC, General Comment 31, HRI/GEN/1/Rev.9 (Vol I) 243, para 18.

submit for prosecution the case of anyone in their jurisdiction against whom there is sufficient evidence of having committed torture, regardless of the jurisdiction in which the torture was committed and the nationality of the perpetrator (a form of universal jurisdiction). This applies unless the person is extradited to another state wishing to exercise jurisdiction. It was on this basis that in 1999 the UK House of Lords upheld the detention order made by a magistrate against former Chilean President Augusto Pinochet Ugarte, pending processing of an extradition request from Spain.[44] Similarly, the International Court of Justice found Senegal in breach of Article 7 UNCAT for failure either to prosecute or extradite former Chadian President Hissène Habré.[45] A further arguably positive obligation is to refrain from exposing a person to torture or ill-treatment by sending that person to a country where he or she faces a real risk of treatment in violation of the prohibition (*non-refoulement*). Interestingly, the case law began in cases involving the death penalty.[46] It was consolidated in the 1996 *Chahal v UK* case in which a Sikh former torture victim from India could not, according to the European Court of Human Rights, be returned to India even on national security grounds.[47] Requested by the UK to revisit the issue, especially in relation to terrorism cases, the Court in the 2008 case of *Saadi v Italy* resoundingly and unanimously reaffirmed its position.[48] This dimension of the prohibition is codified for states parties to UNCAT in its Article 3. It is to be noted that this provision applies to torture, but not expressly to other cruel, inhuman, or degrading treatment or punishment.

What the limits of positive obligations are is unclear. In principle, the question to be asked is: how far are the acts in question attributable to the state? But, once acts of omission rather than commission are in question and once we envisage an obligation to prevent torture and ill-treatment, it becomes hard to identify the borderlines of responsibility. As is reflected in the practice of the Human Rights Committee, the obligations may extend to action to prevent such phenomena as human trafficking and domestic violence.[49] It is not controversial that such obligations are ones of means, not of result, often known as 'due diligence'.[50] What means may be appropriate in any given situation, or what diligence is due, may well be far from evident. One factor that may be relevant in making any assessment is the extent to which the state may be said to have an interest in the perpetration or continuation of the harm suffered by the victims. The less the interest, the higher may be the threshold to attribute responsibility to the state.

2.5 RELATIONSHIP WITH OTHER HUMAN RIGHTS

There are various connections between the prohibition of torture and ill-treatment and other human rights. For example, one of the rules for a fair trial is that one may not be compelled to testify against oneself. Clearly, testimony coerced by prohibited ill-treatment would fall foul of that prohibition.[51] As already seen, rules relating to the right to liberty provide an essential guarantee against prohibited ill-treatment. Moreover, some forms of arbitrary detention such as prolonged detention may amount to a violation of the prohibition of ill-treatment. This will be especially true in respect of the most extreme form of detention, namely enforced disappearance.[52] In that case, among other rights, the right to life may also be engaged, as it evidently is when death occurs under torture.

---

[44] *Pinochet (No 3)*. See UNCAT, Arts 5–8.

[45] *Questions relating to the Obligation to Prosecute or Extradite*.

[46] *Amekrane v UK* (1973) 16 YB 356; *Soering v UK* (1989) 11 EHRR 439; *Ng v Canada*, CCPR/C/49/D/469/1991 (7 January 1994). See also HRC, General Comment 31, para 12.

[47] (1997) 23 EHRR 413.   [48] (2009) 49 EHRR 30.

[49] eg HRC, General Comment 28, HRI/GEN/1/Rev.9 (Vol I) 228, paras 11–12.

[50] eg *Velásquez-Rodriguez v Honduras*, IACtHR Series C No 4 (29 July 1988) para 172. See also Chapter 5.

[51] See Chapter 13.

[52] Declaration on the Protection of All Persons from Enforced Disappearance, GA Res 47/133 (18 December 1992), Art 1(2).

3 THE RIGHT TO LIFE

The right to life is dealt with very early and summarily in the UDHR. According to Article 3, '[e]veryone has the right to life, liberty and security of person'. There is no further reference to the right to life in the UDHR. This nevertheless leaves it as the first substantive right, after the Article 2 affirmation of the principle of non-discrimination. It was not further developed partly because of a lack of consensus as to what issues it covers, notably the death penalty.

The right to life has been considered the 'supreme human right'[53] and 'the fountain from which all human rights spring'.[54] On the other hand, treaty provisions giving effect to it are not couched in the same absolute language as those prohibiting torture. Typically, they will insist that 'no-one shall be arbitrarily deprived' of life. Indeed, it is not hard to think of circumstances in which states may be expected to sanction the taking of life. Warfare is the most obvious example and killings committed lawfully under international humanitarian law will not in principle be considered as violating the right to life. Law-enforcement personnel may also sometimes be required to take life, notably to protect the lives of others. And, of course, for centuries the death penalty, though now on the retreat, figured in most national legislation.

These considerations make the right to life a more complex concept than the prohibition of torture and ill-treatment. This in turn may help to explain why the right as a whole has not been the object of the same sustained campaigning and attention as that prohibition. Rather, work has focused on particular aspects, with the major emphasis being on the death penalty, as reflected in abolitionist protocols to general human rights treaties. Some 'soft law' instruments have been adopted, notably in relation to deprivation of life in law enforcement situations. Moreover, the second earliest thematic mechanism created by the UN Commission on Human Rights in 1982 was the mandate of Special Rapporteur on extrajudicial, summary, and arbitrary executions.

In practice, most of the case law concerns the central issues of deprivation of life by state authorities, either by the maintenance of law and public order or by recourse to the death penalty. This will, accordingly, be the principal focus of this section.

3.1 SOURCES

Article 6 ICCPR, Article 4 ACHR, and Article 4 ACHPR all guarantee the right not to be 'arbitrarily deprived of life'.[55] In contrast, Article 2 ECHR prohibits any intentional deprivation of life except for certain, listed purposes. In the practice of the bodies enforcing the ICCPR, the ACHR, and the ACHPR, those purposes would take the killing out of the designation of 'arbitrary'. All these articles make, in various ways, provision for the death penalty. The ICCPR-OP2, the Sixth and Thirteenth Protocols to the ECHR, and the Second Protocol to the ACHR all contemplate abolition of the death penalty. The main 'soft law' sources protecting the right to life are the UN Basic Principles on the Use of Force and Firearms by Law Enforcement Officials (1990), the UN Principles on the Effective Prevention and Investigation of Extra-legal, Arbitrary and Summary Executions (1989), and the UN Economic and Social Council's Safeguards Guaranteeing Protection of the Rights of Those Facing the Death Penalty (ECOSOC Safeguards) (1984).

---

[53] HRC, General Comment 6, HRI/GEN/1/Rev.9 (Vol I) 176, para 1.

[54] Report of the UN Special Rapporteur on summary and arbitrary executions, E/CN.4/1983/16 (31 January 1983) para 22.

[55] ACHPR, Art 4 reads: 'Human beings are inviolable. Every human being is entitled to respect for his life and the integrity of his person. No one may be arbitrarily deprived of this right.'

3.2 LEGAL STATUS

There can be little doubt that the right to life is a rule of customary international law, even if it has not received the same attention by way of treaty-making as the prohibition of torture. This is even suggested in the specific wording of the language of Article 6(1) ICCPR, which speaks of the 'inherent right to life'. Less certain is whether it is a rule of *jus cogens*. It has not had the same degree of case law so asserting as the prohibition of torture, but then the occasion has not arisen. It is true that the core content of the rule has not been defined with the same precision. Nevertheless, because of its importance, it is non-derogable in those treaties that contemplate derogations.[56] Murder, in the context of a widespread or systematic attack against a civilian population, is a crime against humanity and, together with wilful killing, a war crime. The prohibition of murder is treated as a *jus cogens* rule in the American Law Institute's Restatement of US Foreign Relations Law.[57] It cannot seriously be contested that this core content of the right is *jus cogens*, and the same must apply to the prohibition of the death penalty without basic fair trial standards; so, the prohibition of unnecessary and disproportionate killings deserves to fall into the same category. The Human Rights Committee's draft General Comment on the right to life characterizes Article 6 ICCPR as a peremptory norm of international law.[58]

3.3 SCOPE: BEGINNING AND END OF LIFE

When does life begin? In *Artavia Murillo et al. v Costa Rica*, the Inter-American Court of Human Rights had to decide whether in vitro fertilization is compatible with Article 4 ACHR, according to which the right to life of '[e]very person' is protected 'in general, from the moment of conception'. The Court found that 'conception' occurs only with the implantation of the embryo in the uterus and not at the moment of fertilization; hence, an embryo alone cannot be granted the status of a 'person'. Furthermore, the Court held that the protection of life under Article 4 ACHR is not absolute, but incremental according to the degree of development of the foetus.[59] Similarly, in its draft General Comment on the right to life, the Human Rights Committee has stated that, while states parties to the ICCPR may adopt legal restrictions on the ability of women to seek abortion, any such measures must not violate the right to life of pregnant mothers or the prohibition against exposing them to cruel, inhuman, and degrading treatment or punishment.[60]

Euthanasia and assisted suicide, both illegal in many states, but permitted in some, also raise questions. On the one hand, a genuine right (to life) cannot comfortably be considered to be not only an entitlement but also an obligation imposed on the right-holder. However, this did not deter the European Court of Human Rights from insisting that Article 2 ECHR does not comprehend a right to die.[61] Yet there is an issue of human dignity and possibly degrading treatment if one is denied the option of a longed-for death just because one is no longer physically capable of killing oneself. It is troubling that the European Court has refused to accept that denial of the right to needed assistance to commit suicide infringes Article 3.[62] On the other hand, the vulnerability of many people to improper influence means that the law should be very careful to contemplate any intentional third-party involvement in a deprivation of life.

---

[56] ICCPR, Art 4; ECHR, Art 15; ACHR, Art 27.

[57] American Law Institute, Restatement of the Law: Restatement (Third) of the Foreign Relations Law of the United States, Vol II (1987) s 702.

[58] HRC, Draft General Comment 36, CCPR/C/GC/R.36/Rev.2 (1 April 2015) para 65.

[59] IACtHR Series C No 257 (28 November 2012) paras 163–264.

[60] HRC, Draft General Comment 36, para 7.   [61] *Pretty v UK* (2002) 35 EHRR 1, paras 39–41.

[62] *Pretty*, paras 54–6. Compare the more nuanced approach in HRC, Concluding Observations: the Netherlands, CCPR/CO/72/NET (27 August 2001) para 5; CCPR/C/NLD/CO/4 (11 August 2009) para 7.

3.4 COMPONENTS

3.4.1 Protection against killings by security forces

Different bodies use different terms to describe unlawful killings by agents of public authority: 'extra-legal' or 'extrajudicial' 'killings' or 'executions'. Regardless of terminology, wherever there is intentional resort to outright killings of those considered undesirable, be they
street children, political opponents, or suspected organized criminals, this is clearly murder
by any definition and is at the core of the prohibition of arbitrary deprivation of life.

The central question is: what other killings fall into this category? Here, guidance may be
sought from the deprivations of life that, according to Article 2(2) ECHR, are not to be regarded as violations of the right to life, which include deprivations resulting 'from the use of
force which is no more than absolutely necessary: (a) in defence of any person from unlawful
violence; (b) in order to effect a lawful arrest or to prevent the escape of a person lawfully detained; (c) in action lawfully taken for the purpose of quelling a riot or insurrection.' It is generally accepted that law enforcement measures must conform to the principles of necessity
and proportionality. The ECHR limitation of force to the minimum necessary clearly meets
the *necessity* principle, requiring that the means used is no more than necessary to achieve
the objective. Less reassuringly, the text does not guarantee the test of *proportionality*; it does
not explicitly require the level of force to be no more than the harm to be avoided. Clearly,
the use of lethal force could be the only way to stop a pub brawl, or to prevent the escape of
someone imprisoned for contempt of court, but it would evidently be disproportionate.

The UN Basic Principles on the Use of Force and Firearms come to our assistance here.
Principle 9 reads:

> Law enforcement officials shall not use firearms against persons except in self-defence or defence
> of others against the imminent threat of death or serious injury, to prevent the perpetration of
> a particularly serious crime involving grave threat to life, to arrest a person presenting such a
> danger and resisting their authority, or to prevent his or her escape, and only when less extreme
> means are insufficient to achieve these objectives. In any event the intentional lethal use of
> firearms may only be made when strictly unavoidable in order to protect life.

It is clear from this text that the principle of proportionality is strictly drawn. Not only may *potentially* lethal force be used solely to protect life and limb from *imminent* threat, but *intentional*
lethal force may only be used to protect life. Principles 14 and 16 reaffirm this standard in respect
of dispersal of unlawful, violent assemblies, and avoidance of escape from custody, respectively.

The practice of treaty bodies is consistent with the Principles. An early example of the principle of necessity is found in the Human Rights Committee case of *Guerrero v Colombia*, where
the state was found to have violated Article 6 ICCPR as the police had waited in a location
inhabited by suspected terrorists and, on their arrival, shot them without making any attempt
to arrest them.[63] An even more stringent application of the principle is found in the case of
McCann and others v UK before the European Court of Human Rights. British security personnel summarily killed IRA members avowedly on 'mission' to detonate a bomb in a crowded
place in Gibraltar. The security personnel had been briefed to believe that the victims were
armed, that there was a bomb in their car, and that they could detonate it from a remote control
device on their person. In fact it turned out that they were not armed, there was no bomb in the
car, nor did they have a detonator. The Court found that the UK had violated Article 2 ECHR
by failing to take various planning measures that could have avoided the fatal outcome.[64]

---

[63] CCPR/C/15/D/45/1979 (31 March 1982). For reckless lethal attacks on premises violating the right to
life, see *Gül v Turkey* (2002) 34 EHRR 435, paras 79–83; *Zambrano Vélez and others v Ecuador*, IACtHR Series
C No 166 (4 July 2007) para 108.   [64] (1996) 21 EHRR 97.

The clearest example of the proportionality principle is found in the case of *Nachova and others v Bulgaria*. Invoking the UN Basic Principles, the European Court found that 'recourse to potentially deadly force cannot be considered as "absolutely necessary" where it is known that the person to be arrested poses no threat to life or limb and is not suspected of having committed a violent offence'.[65] More recently, in *Tagayeva and others v Russia*, the Court held that the indiscriminate use of heavy weaponry in order to break a siege involving a great number of vulnerable persons could not be regarded as absolutely necessary.[66] In these cases, the European Court is evidently using the language of necessity in Article 2 to embrace proportionality. In the case of *Detention Centre of Catia*, in which Venezuelan prison guards fired indiscriminately into prisoners they suspected of being involved in an escape, the Inter-American Court of Human Rights applied the principles of necessity and proportionality, finding that 'the actions of the security forces . . . were neither proportionate to the existing threat or danger, nor strictly necessary to keep the peace and order in the Detention Centre of Catia'.[67]

3.4.2 Protection against the death penalty

Inconsistent as it may seem, while international law apparently rules out corporal punishment as a cruel, inhuman, or degrading punishment—or even torture—it has not yet done so in respect of the death penalty. While the framers of the UDHR may have contemplated that at some time international law would reach that point, it had not then and still has not. This is because international law is not a system that operates by majority rule. State practice is a key element and as long as a substantial minority of states maintain the death penalty—especially states as influential as China, India, and the US—international law will have to reflect that reality.

All the human rights treaty norms guaranteeing the right to life, except Article 4 ACHPR, contemplate the possibility of the death penalty. Since any treaty provision has to be interpreted in the context of the treaty as a whole, this means that it is not possible to interpret the provisions on treatment of prisoners without reference to those on the right to life. The Human Rights Committee has indeed made the point that, but for the death penalty provisions of Article 6 ICCPR, it would find the death penalty to violate Article 7.[68]

Nevertheless, the last quarter of the twentieth century witnessed a trend towards abolition that is steady and sustained. The fact that the community of states was willing to adopt abolitionist protocols to human rights treaties makes it increasingly difficult for abolitionist states to deny that the death penalty is a human rights issue. Even before the adoption of the ICCPR-OP2, the Human Rights Committee had felt that the actual language of Article 6 preserving the death penalty permitted it to conclude that 'all measures of abolition should be considered as progress in the enjoyment of the right to life'.[69] Meanwhile, at the political level, the UN General Assembly long ago accepted that the objective should be 'progressive restriction' of the number of offences to which the punishment applies 'with a view to the desirability of abolishing this punishment in all countries'.[70] It now adopts a resolution biennially that calls on states that retain the death penalty to adopt moratoria on its use.[71]

As to the abolitionist protocols themselves, all but one envisage commitments that permit states to carve out an exception for wartime situations (few have done so in fact). The exception is Protocol 13 to the ECHR, adopted precisely to fill this gap left by Protocol 6. It is worth noting that, insofar as a commitment to adherence at least to Protocol 6 is a

---

[65] (2006) 42 EHRR 43, paras 71–4, 96, 107.

[66] App No 26562/07, Judgment of 13 April 2017, paras 600–10.

[67] *Montero-Aranguren and others (Detention Centre of Catia) v Venezuela*, IACtHR Series C No 150 (5 July 2006) paras 69–74.   [68] *Ng v Canada*, para 16.2.   [69] HRC, General Comment 6, para 6.

[70] GA Res 2857 (XXVI) (20 December 1971).   [71] eg GA Res 71/187 (19 December 2016).

condition of membership of the Council of Europe, the 47-country area of Europe, from the Atlantic to the Urals, is now effectively a death-penalty-free zone.[72]

If the death penalty as such remains a permissible exception to the right to life, it is clear that states do not have a free hand to resort to it at will. There is a range of far-reaching substantive, procedural, and personal limitations that have to be respected.

Substantive limitations

The most important substantive limitation is that of Article 6(2) ICCPR and Article 4(2) ACHR, requiring that imposition of the death penalty be limited to 'the most serious crimes'. The prohibition of arbitrary deprivation of the right to life of Article 4 ACHPR is to be understood at least as strictly as the ICCPR and ACHR provisions.[73] The first paragraph of the ECOSOC Safeguards endorses the notion of 'the most serious crimes'. Underlying these words is an implicit invocation of the principle of proportionality. The death penalty should not be disproportionate to the offence for which it is applicable.

The treaty provisions offer no definition of what elements would place a crime among the most serious. The ECOSOC Safeguards are helpful here. For them, the scope of the term 'should not go beyond intentional crimes with lethal or other extremely grave consequences'.[74] According to the African Commission on Human and Peoples' Rights, the term covers only 'crimes involving intentional killing'.[75] The Human Rights Committee has found a mandatory death penalty for armed robbery where death did *not* result to contravene Article 6(2) ICCPR.[76] It has subsequently also found the mandatory death penalty in all cases of murder to violate Article 6(1).[77] It is not clear whether it based this finding on the view that murder cases are not necessarily covered by Article 6(2) because they do not automatically meet the threshold of seriousness. This is the position taken by the Inter-American Court of Human Rights.[78] It is worth noting that the same court also found the 'simple crime of kidnapping' to fall outside the notion of 'most serious' and so a death penalty imposed for it violated Article 4 ACHR.[79]

Further substantive limitations following from Articles 6(2) and 15 ICCPR are that both the crime and the prescribed punishment must be non-retroactive, that is, provided by law at the time of the commission of the acts in question. In addition, under Article 4(2) ACHR, the death penalty may not be extended to crimes to which it does not 'presently' apply, while Article 4(3) ACHR prohibits reintroduction in states that have abolished it. It is also possible to interpret Article 6(2) ICCPR in the same way. Since it refers to 'countries which have not abolished the death penalty', it may be logical to infer that the possibility is not available to countries that *have* abolished the penalty.[80] Article 4(4) ACHR also prohibits the use of the death penalty for 'political offenses or related common crimes'.

---

[72] The Russian Federation, despite its commitment, has not yet ratified Protocol 6 but has implemented a formal moratorium. On 2 March 2010, the European Court of Human Rights concluded that the death penalty is no longer permitted, even under Article 2 ECHR. *Al-Saadoon and Mufdhi v UK* (2010) 51 EHRR 9.
[74] Para 1.
[73] ACommHPR, General Comment 3 (12 December 2015) para 24.
[75] ACommHPR, General Comment 3, para 24.
[76] *Lubuto v Zambia*, CCPR/C/55/D/390/1990/Rev.1 (30 June 1994) para 7.2.
[77] *Thompson v St Vincent and the Grenadines*, CCPR/C/70/D/806/1998 (18 October 2000) para 8.2.
[78] *Hilaire, Constantine, and Benjamin et al. v Trinidad and Tobago*, IACtHR Series C No 94 (21 June 2002) paras 106–8.
[79] *Raxcacó-Reyes*, paras 67–72.
[80] See also *Judge v Canada*, CCPR/C/78/D/829/1998 (20 October 2003) para 6.1 (holding that an abolitionist state that sends someone to another country to face the death penalty cannot benefit from the exception of Art 6(2) ICCPR for states that have not abolished the death penalty and so violates Art 6(1)).

Procedural limitations

The main procedural limitation is that the death penalty may only be imposed after a fair trial, as provided for under Article 14 ICCPR, including a right of appeal. While this is not stated in Article 6 ICCPR directly, Article 6(2) provides that the death penalty must not be contrary to the provisions of the Covenant. The General Assembly has called on all states to respect 'as a minimum' Articles 6, 14, and 15.[81] The Human Rights Committee has made clear its view that this means that, not only is Article 6 non-derogable, but so is Article 14 when it comes to the application of the death penalty.[82]

A few of the many examples of findings of a violation of Article 6 because of a violation of Article 14 in death penalty cases are: a trial in absentia ending in a death sentence in the absence of any effective attempt to notify the person accused;[83] a murder trial after the accused had pleaded guilty to manslaughter in a case involving the same incident;[84] deficient or non-existent legal representation;[85] and the failure to make a key witness available for cross-examination as well as the absence of additional witnesses.[86] The right of a foreign national to consular assistance may also fall within Article 14. This was the opinion of the Inter-American Court of Human Rights applying the comparable Article 4 ACHR and also referring to Article 14 ICCPR.[87]

Despite the absence of an explicit linkage in the ECHR and the ACHPR, the European Court of Human Rights and the African Commission on Human and Peoples' Rights have read the respective fair trial provisions together with the right to life provisions. So, in the case of Abdullah Öcalan, the leader of the Turkish PKK movement, the European Court held that implementation of the death penalty would be impermissible under Article 2 ECHR as he had not received a fair trial according to Article 6: Öcalan had been held in incommunicado detention for ten days, then allowed only two one-hour supervised meetings per week with his lawyers before his trial, which took place in a special security court that initially included a military judge.[88] Similarly, the African Commission found a violation of Article 4 ACHPR in respect of the execution of celebrated playwright Ken Saro-Wiwa after a summary trial for murder by a special court whose members were chosen by the executive and without right of appeal that involved multiple violations of the fair trial guarantee of Article 7.[89]

The right of appeal is explicitly guaranteed by Article 14(5) ICCPR, so its denial in death penalty cases is a violation not only of that provision but also of Article 6.[90] The ECOSOC Safeguards contain the same guarantee.[91] The right has to be effective, so both the trial court and an appeal court must provide a written judgment where that is a condition for further appeal.[92] In addition, Article 6(4) ICCPR and Article 4(6) ACHR require the

---

[81] GA Res 35/172 (15 December 1980); this was the first of several resolutions to the same effect.

[82] HRC, General Comment 29, para 15.

[83] *Mbenge et al. v Zaire*, CCPR/C/18/D/16/1977 (25 March 1983) paras 14(1)–(2) and 17.

[84] *Richards v Jamaica*, CCPR/C/59/D/535/1993/Rev.1 (29 April 1997) paras 7.2 and 7.5.

[85] eg *LaVende v Trinidad and Tobago*, CCPR/C/61/D/554/1993 (17 November 1997) para 5.8; *Aliev v Ukraine*, CCPR/C/78/D/781/1997 (7 August 2003) para 7.3; *Saidova v Tajikistan*, CCPR/C/81/D/964/2001 (8 July 2004) para 6.8; *Aliboeva v Tajikistan*, CCPR/C/85/D/985/2001 (18 October 2005) para 6.4.

[86] *Yuzepchuk v Belarus*, CCPR/C/112/D/1906/2009 (17 November 2014) paras 8.4, 8.6.

[87] Advisory Opinion OC-16/99, *The Right to Information on Consular Assistance in the Framework of Guarantees of the Due Process of Law*, IACtHR Series A No 16 (1 October 1999) paras 68–87.

[88] *Öcalan v Turkey* (2005) 41 EHRR 985, para 166.

[89] *International Pen et al. v Nigeria*, Communication nos 137/94, 154/96, and 161/97, 12th Activity Report of the ACommHPR (1998–1999).

[90] *Mansaraj et al. v Sierra Leone*, CCPR/C/72/D/841/1998 (16 July 2001) paras 5.6 and 6.2.

[91] Para 6.   [92] *Pratt and Morgan v Jamaica*, CCPR/C/35/D/210/1986 (6 April 1989) paras 13.5, 14(b).

possibility of submitting a clemency petition. The Human Rights Committee has found violations in cases where executions took place while appellate or clemency procedures were underway.[93]

A further procedural dimension is that the process in which the death penalty is carried out must cause the minimum possible suffering if it is not to violate the prohibition of ill-treatment. Thus, the Human Rights Committee held that execution by gas asphyxiation was incompatible with Article 7 ICCPR.[94] The method of execution is not the only relevant factor. The leading European Court of Human Rights case, *Soering v UK*, found that sending a young German man to face death row conditions in Virginia for six to eight years, when he could be tried in (abolitionist) Germany, would violate Article 3 ECHR.[95] Finally, where the death penalty is shrouded in secrecy, close family members of the executed person can be victims of inhuman treatment. This has been the case with the practice that was common in the former Soviet Union of treating the date of execution and place of burial as a state secret, thus causing an unacceptable 'state of uncertainty and mental distress' to family members.[96]

Personal limitations

The main personal limitation on the application of the death penalty is that, under Article 6(5) ICCPR, Article 4(5) ACHR, and Article 37 of the Convention on the Rights of the Child, it may not be imposed on persons under 18. The Human Rights Committee has found the very imposition of a death sentence on a person under 18 at the time of the offence to violate the ICCPR, despite later commutation of the sentence.[97]

According to Article 6(5) ICCPR, Article 4(5) ACHR, and paragraph 3 ECOSOC Safeguards, the death penalty may also not be carried out on pregnant women and, according to the ECOSOC Safeguards, recent mothers. The ECOSOC Safeguards also immunize 'persons who have become insane', and the Human Rights Committee has decided that the reading of a death warrant for the execution of a mentally incompetent person was a violation of Article 7 ICCPR.[98] Under Article 4(5) ACHR, states parties may not execute persons over 70 at the time of the offence.

3.5 TYPES OF OBLIGATION

As with the prohibition of torture and ill-treatment, the right not to be arbitrarily deprived of life is primarily a negative obligation. To the extent that there is no treaty obligation prohibiting the use of the death penalty, states are simply obliged to refrain from having recourse to it when not respecting the legal limitations that apply to it. Other deprivations of life involving the intentional killing of people by public authorities are to be avoided, if they do not meet the criteria of necessity or proportionality already considered here.

It is notable that three of the provisions guaranteeing the right to life (Article 6(1) ICCPR, Article 2(1) ECHR, and Article 4(1) ACHR) stipulate that the right 'shall be protected by law'. Such language has the connotation of positive obligation. It clearly lends itself to an interpretation, confirmed by practice, that states must investigate apparent unlawful killings. This is the thrust of the UN Principles on the Effective Prevention and Investigation

---

[93] *Ashby v Trinidad and Tobago*, CCPR/C/74/D/580/1994 (19 April 2002) para 10.8; *Chikunova v Uzbekistan*, CCPR/C/89/D/1043/2002 (16 March 2007) para 7.6.

[94] *Ng*, para 16.4.   [95] *Soering*, paras 106–11.

[96] *Lyashkevich v Belarus*, CCPR/C/77/D/887/1999 (24 April 2003) para 9.2.

[97] *Johnson, Clive v Jamaica*, CCPR/C/64/D/592/1994 (25 November 1998) para 10.3.

[98] *RS v Trinidad and Tobago*, CCPR/C/74/D/684/1996 (2 April 2002) para 7.2.

of Extra-legal, Arbitrary and Summary Executions. The Human Rights Committee has recently clarified that investigations have to meet the requirements of independence, impartiality, promptness, thoroughness, effectiveness, credibility, and transparency, and must provide an adequate remedy in case a violation is found.[99]

There have been numerous findings of state violations of the right to life because of the absence of an effective investigation, even when the killing could not be found on the evidence to be firmly attributable to the state. The European Court of Human Rights has found violations where the state was unable to show serious activity by investigating prosecutors,[100] or where the prosecutors confined themselves to interviewing the relevant security units involved without interviewing relevant non-official witnesses,[101] or where they made no effort to identify the unit responsible.[102] The UK coroners' inquest system was also found wanting in a series of Northern Ireland cases in which there was an alleged 'shoot-to-kill' policy by the security forces. This was because the inquiry could not compel the presence of police and other security force witnesses, could not make a finding of 'unlawful killing', and was neither prompt nor expeditious.[103]

In the case of *Amirov v Russian Federation*, the Human Rights Committee found a failure of effective investigation and so a violation of Article 6 ICCPR, where prosecutors opened and closed the investigation into the rape and murder of a woman in the Chechen Republic, numerous times, but without securing the testimony of federal agents who had seen the body at the time it was found.[104] The UN Principles and findings by treaty bodies are clear in understanding that there is an obligation on states to prosecute when an investigation determines that individuals are responsible for an unlawful killing. For example, the failure to do this was part of the violation of Article 6 ICCPR in *Amirov*.[105]

As with the prohibition of ill-treatment, exposing someone to the threat of a violation of the right to life is itself a violation of the prohibition or ill-treatment, as well as presumably of the right to life. The cases of *Soering* and *Ng* already discussed are the leading cases on the matter.[106]

There is also an evident obligation to protect people from death from third parties. But, as with the prohibition of torture, it is an obligation of means, not of result. The question will always be: did the state exercise 'due diligence' when apprised of circumstances that may have suggested that a person's life required protection? While finally not finding a violation, the European Court of Human Rights essentially followed this approach in respect of a schoolmaster who stalked a former student and then killed her. The Court held that the stalking itself did not suggest likely lethal consequences, but it was clear that if there had been evidence of impending harm, the state would have violated Article 2 ECHR.[107] Also, if it is difficult to justify rules permitting euthanasia and assisted suicide, it is because of the positive obligation on states to protect life and the need to avoid people being improperly influenced to seek or accept aid in terminating their lives.

---

[99] Draft General Comment 36, para 30.   [100] *Kaya v Turkey* (1999) 28 EHRR 1, paras 86–92.
[101] *Musayeva and others v Russia* (2008) 47 EHRR 25, para 162.
[102] *Khashiyev and Akayeva v Russia* (2006) 42 EHRR 20, para 158.
[103] *Jordan v UK* (2003) 37 EHRR 2, para 142; *Kelly and others v UK*, App no 30054/96, Judgment of 4 May 2001, para 136; *McKerr v UK* (2002) 34 EHRR 20, para 157; *Shanagan v UK*, App no 37715/97, Judgment of 4 May 2001, para 122.   [104] CCPR/C/95/D/1447/2006 (2 April 2009) para 11.4.
[105] CCPR/C/95/D/1447/2006 (2 April 2009) para 11.4.   [106] *Soering* and *Ng*.
[107] *Osman v UK* (1998) 29 EHRR 245, paras 121–2.

3.6 RELATIONSHIP WITH OTHER HUMAN RIGHTS

The links with the prohibition of torture and ill-treatment have already been discussed. An additional dimension here is the need even for the death penalty to avoid unnecessary suffering. The connection with the right to a fair trial is of central importance as regards the lawfulness (or otherwise) of the death penalty.

There is also a connection with the notion of security of person, as suggested by Article 3 UDHR. Although the European Court of Human Rights has not been willing to give content to the idea outside the context of deprivation of liberty, the Human Rights Committee has done so. For example, failure to give adequate protection to a person receiving death threats has been found to violate the Article 9 ICCPR guarantee of security of person.[108] To the uncertain extent that the right to life may be engaged in situations of economic and social deprivation, there is a connection with the corresponding economic and social rights.

4 CONCLUSION

The prohibition of torture and ill-treatment and the right to life are both situated by the language of the International Bill of Human Rights and other international instruments as directly based on the concept of human dignity, which inspires the whole corpus of human rights law, and as at the core of the right to personal integrity.

The understanding of the scope of the prohibition of torture and ill-treatment is capable of much elasticity and was indeed drafted in language intended to avoid rigid definitions of what might technically be called torture. Nevertheless, in the light of sustained attention to the problem of torture, notably of people deprived of liberty, there has been a focus on definitions of that concept, the UNCAT definition being the most influential. On the key issue of what the borderline may be between torture and other ill-treatment, this definition seems to avoid the approach of the European Court of Human Rights, according to which torture is seen as requiring even greater pain or suffering than that already required for the treatment to be considered inhuman. Rather, it is the purpose of the treatment (for example, obtaining information or confessions) that marks the treatment out as being torture or not. Also, the mental form of torture as exemplified by the Orwellian rats should not be downplayed. While a few states retain corporal punishment in their legislation and apply it in practice, the consistent view of human rights bodies has been to find such punishment to be cruel, inhuman, or degrading. Indeed, the Inter-American Court of Human Rights has found a manifestation of it to be torture.

As to the right to life, the aspects that have received most attention have been those relating to the limits on lethal force that can be used in the maintenance of law and public order and to the applicability of the death penalty. In the absence of authoritative definitions in treaties, international 'soft law' standards and the practice of human rights bodies have provided the principal guidance, especially in the area of recourse to lethal force. The crucial tests of whether a particular use of such force is lawful are those of necessity and proportionality. That is, the force must not only be the least harmful necessary to achieve a legitimate law enforcement objective, it must furthermore not exceed the harm to be avoided by its use. The right to life does not as yet rule out recourse to the death penalty. However, many states are parties to protocols to human rights treaties that prohibit the

---

[108] Compare *Delgado Páez v Colombia*, CCPR/C/39/D/195/1985 (12 July 1990) paras 5.5, 5.6, 6 with *Bozano v France* (1987) 9 EHRR 297, para 53.

death penalty. The other states are bound to respect a number of substantive limitations (notably, the death penalty must be used only for the most serious crimes), procedural limitations (notably, the rules concerning the rights to a fair trial, to appeal, and to seek clemency), and personal limitations (notably, the lower age limit of 18).

There is no serious doubting that the prohibition of torture is a rule of *jus cogens*. There is persuasive authority suggesting this also applies to other prohibited ill-treatment. While there is not as much explicit evidence in respect of the right to life (apart from with regard to outright official murder), the better view is that its status as 'the supreme human right' that, like the prohibition of torture and ill-treatment, is non-derogable must put it on a par with that prohibition.

FURTHER READING

Evans, 'Getting to Grips with Torture' (2002) 51 *ICLQ* 365.

Ginbar, *Why Not Torture Terrorists?: Moral, Practical, and Legal Aspects of the 'Ticking Bomb' Justification for Torture* (Oxford University Press, 2008).

Hood and Hoyle, *The Death Penalty: A Worldwide Perspective* (Oxford University Press, 2008).

Ingelse, *The UN Committee against Torture: An Assessment* (Kluwer Academic Publishers, 2001).

Kretzmer, 'Targeted Killing of Suspected Terrorists: Extra-Judicial Executions or Legitimate Means of Defence?' (2005) 16 *EJIL* 171.

Luban, *Torture, Power and Law* (Cambridge University Press, 2014).

Melzer, *Targeted Killing in International Law* (Oxford University Press, 2008).

Nowak, 'What Practices Constitute Torture?: US and UN Standards' (2006) 28 *HRQ* 809.

Nowak and McArthur, *The United Nations Convention Against Torture: A Commentary* (Oxford University Press, 2008).

Rodley, 'The Prohibition of Torture: Absolute Means Absolute' (2006) 34 *Denv J Int'l L & Pol'y* 145.

Rodley and Pollard, *The Treatment of Prisoners under International Law* (Oxford University Press, 2009).

Schabas, *The Abolition of the Death Penalty in International Law* (Cambridge University Press, 2002).

Schachter, 'Human Dignity as a Normative Concept' (1983) 77 *AJIL* 848.

Tiensuu, 'Whose Right to What Life?: Assisted Suicide and the Right to Life as a Fundamental Right' (2015) 15 *HRLR* 251.

Waldron, 'Is Dignity the Foundation of Human Rights?' in Cruft, Liao, and Renzo (eds), *Philosophical Foundations of Human Rights* (Oxford University Press, 2015).

Wicks, 'The Meaning of "Life": Dignity and the Right to Life in International Human Rights Treaties' (2012) 12 *HRLR* 199.

USEFUL WEBSITES

Association for the Prevention of Torture: <http://www.apt.ch>

Amnesty International: <http://www.amnesty.org>

European Committee for the Prevention of Torture and Inhuman or Degrading Treatment or Punishment: <http://www.cpt.coe.int/en/>

Convention Against Torture Initiative: <http://cti2024.org/>

Human Rights Watch: <http://www.hrw.org>

UN Special Rapporteur on Torture and Other Cruel, Inhuman or Degrading Treatment or Punishment:<http://www.ohchr.org/EN/Issues/Torture/SRTorture/Pages/SRTortureIndex.aspx>

UN Committee against Torture:<http://www.ohchr.org/EN/HRBodies/CAT/Pages/CATIndex.aspx>

UN Subcommittee on Prevention of Torture and other Cruel, Inhuman or Degrading Treatment or Punishment:<http://www.ohchr.org/EN/HRBodies/OPCAT/Pages/OPCATIndex.aspx>

10

ADEQUATE STANDARD OF LIVING

Asbjørn Eide

SUMMARY

This chapter considers the right to an adequate standard of living and its components, namely, the rights to food, housing, and health. These rights are, in whole or in part, contained in principal international human rights instruments, which impose an obligation on states parties to take a range of measures to ensure everyone can enjoy them. A particular challenge is to ensure the right to an adequate standard of living to those groups of people who have special needs or are particularly vulnerable. The chapter explores the relationship between the right to an adequate standard of living and other human rights and highlights the need for international action in the progressive implementation of the right.

1 INTRODUCTION

The right to an adequate standard of living was first introduced into international human rights law through the Universal Declaration of Human Rights (UDHR), Article 25(1) of which provides:

> Everyone has the right to a standard of living adequate for the health and well-being of himself and his family, including food, clothing, housing and medical care and necessary social services, and the right to security in the event of unemployment, sickness, disability, widowhood, old age or other lack of livelihood in circumstances beyond his control.

Among the main inspirations for this provision was US President Franklin D Roosevelt's 'Four Freedoms' address to Congress in 1941.[1] In that speech, Roosevelt referred to four fundamental human freedoms: freedom of speech, freedom of religion, *freedom from want*, and freedom from fear. The inspirational legacy of that speech is expressly recognized in the preamble to the UDHR:

> Whereas disregard and contempt for human rights have resulted in barbarous acts which have outraged the conscience of mankind, *and the advent of a world in which human beings*

---

[1] On the origin of Roosevelt's concern with freedom from want, see McGovern, *The Third Freedom: Ending Hunger in Our Time* (Simon & Schuster, 2001).

shall enjoy freedom of speech and belief and freedom from fear and want has been proclaimed as the highest aspiration of the common people.[2]

Article 25 UDHR can also be seen as an elaboration of Article 1 UDHR, which states that 'All human beings are born free and equal in dignity and rights. They are endowed with reason and conscience and should act towards one another in a spirit of brotherhood.' A life in dignity requires an adequate standard of living. Human rights are based on the assumption that individuals are not only rational but also have a social conscience, and are, therefore, concerned with the dignity of their fellow human beings. Such concern has to be put into practice through appropriate state implementation of human rights as public goods of society as a whole. The right to an adequate standard of living is also closely linked to Article 22 UDHR, which states that everyone has the right to social security and is entitled to realization of the economic, social, and cultural rights indispensable for their dignity and the free development of their personality.

This chapter starts, in Section 2, with an analysis of the meaning and key features of the right to an adequate standard of living. Section 3 examines the normative content of this right and its components, namely, the rights to food, housing, and health. The right to water is a necessary component of each of these rights, and is briefly addressed under the right to food. Section 4 explores the difficulties and special obligations in ensuring the right to an adequate standard of living for particular groups of people. Section 5 addresses the relationship between the right to an adequate standard of living and other human rights. Section 6 examines the question of progressive implementation of this right. Section 7 addresses the justiciability of the right to an adequate standard of living and the need for international action in its implementation.

2 MEANING AND FEATURES

Article 25 UDHR has been legally strengthened through subsequent guarantees of an adequate standard of living, including Articles 11 and 12 of the International Covenant on Economic, Social and Cultural Rights (ICESCR) and Article 27 of the Convention on the Rights of the Child (CRC). None of these instruments precisely define the term 'adequate standard of living', but it can to some extent be understood from the context. Article 25 UDHR refers to 'a standard of living adequate for the health and well-being of himself and of his family, including food, clothing, housing and medical care and necessary social services'. According to Article 11 ICESCR, an adequate standard of living includes 'adequate food, clothing and housing'. In addition, under Article 12 of the same covenant, states parties have recognized the right of everyone to the highest attainable standard of health. The standard of living guaranteed to every child by Article 27 CRC is one that is 'adequate for the child's physical, mental, spiritual, moral and social development'.

While the basic necessities referred to in these instruments include food, clothing, housing, and healthcare, an adequate standard of living requires more than simply these. Precisely how much more is required cannot be stated in general terms, but will depend on the conditions in the society concerned. The essential point is that everyone should be able, without shame and without unreasonable obstacles, to be a full participant in ordinary, everyday interaction with other people. In other words, everyone should be able to enjoy their basic needs under conditions of dignity. No one should have to live under conditions whereby the only way to satisfy their needs is by degrading or depriving themselves

---

[2] UDHR, second preambular para (emphasis added).

of their basic freedoms, such as through begging, prostitution, or bonded labour. In purely economic terms, an adequate standard of living implies a living above the poverty line of the society concerned, which according to the World Bank comprises two elements:

> The expenditure necessary to buy a minimum standard of nutrition and other basic necessities and a further amount that varies from country to country, reflecting the cost of participating in the everyday life of society.[3]

2.1 DUTIES OF THE INDIVIDUAL

The enjoyment of the right to an adequate standard of living depends on a combination of efforts by every adult individual to take care of her or his own needs and the needs of their children, together with measures taken by the state or public authorities to ensure everyone's enjoyment of that right. The obligations of the state are, therefore, to some extent, subsidiary to the efforts of the individual: *state* obligations come fully into play only when individuals cannot or do not manage by themselves to secure their own or their dependants' standard of living. The obligations of the *international community* are of an even more subsidiary nature, namely to encourage and assist states in implementing their obligations, to criticize them if they fail to do so, to abstain from harmful action that prevents other states from fulfilling their obligations, and to assist those states whose resources are too limited to fulfil their obligations under international human rights law.

Thus, individuals are expected, wherever possible through their own efforts and through the use of their own resources, to find ways to ensure the satisfaction of their needs. Use of one's resources presupposes that the person has resources that can be used—such as land, other capital or assets, and labour. Access to food and housing, for example, depends, first, on the assets held by the individual (ownership of land or capital) or her or his rights to common resources (for example, fishing grounds). Second, it depends on income from work (in the formal or informal sector, whether employed by others or self-employed). Third, it may depend on income in the form of social assistance or social security.

For most children, their standard of living depends primarily on that of their parents. If a child does not have parents or the parents fail to support the child, the state has an obligation to assist or provide. In many societies, women have been dependent on their family, or husband, for their standard of living. This was certainly not always the case—in the past, in many agricultural societies women were the main breadwinner. In modern post-industrial societies, women are now increasingly regaining their economic autonomy and becoming less dependent on the efforts of their husband, although in most societies the standard of living of families still depends on the joint effort of husband and wife. In pre-industrial society, the elderly were to a large extent taken care of by their offspring, just as they had taken care of their children. In many modern societies this is no longer practical, due in part to increased mobility. The standard of living of the elderly has, therefore, increasingly been secured through various forms of social security, such as old-age pensions.

2.2 STATE OBLIGATIONS

The nature of state obligations varies greatly, depending on the nature and level of its social development, the differences in the needs of individuals, the resources at the disposal of the state, and the different components of the right. In most societies there is a

---

[3] World Bank, *World Development Report 1990* (OUP, 1990) 26.

considerable difference between the role played by the state regarding the realization of the right to food or to housing, on the one hand, and the realization of the right to health, on the other hand. In economic terms, food and housing are mainly considered to be private goods which people are generally expected to obtain through their own efforts, whereas the right to health is widely associated with publicly organized healthcare as a public good and, therefore, a duty of the state. In spite of these differences, states do have obligations under international human rights law in regard to all these rights, although the content of the obligations varies from one to the other.[4]

Under the right to an adequate standard of living, states must, first, *respect* the individual's freedom to take the necessary action and use the necessary resources, alone or in association with others. It is in regard to the latter that collective or group rights become important: resources belonging to, or controlled by, a collective of persons, such as an indigenous population, must be respected if such a population is to satisfy its needs through their use. Similarly, the rights of peoples to exercise permanent sovereignty over their natural resources may be essential for them to be able, through their own collective efforts, to satisfy their needs.

Second, states have an obligation to *protect* individuals' freedom of choice and use of resources necessary to secure their basic needs. For example, states may be required to provide protection against fraud, unethical behaviour in trade and contractual relations, the marketing of dangerous products, and the dumping of hazardous waste. States are also obliged to protect against discrimination that directly or indirectly prevents particular groups of people from having access to food or housing. Generally, this is the most important aspect of the rights to food, housing, and water, requiring the state to act not as provider but as protector. This function is similar to the obligation of states to protect civil and political rights, such as the right to life or freedom from slavery, from violation by third parties.

Third, states have, when this is necessary, the obligation to *fulfil* everyone's right to an adequate standard of living—that is, to function as the provider. This may take two forms. First, states may have to *facilitate* people's access to resources and means to ensure their livelihood if they lack the opportunity to do so themselves. Second, states may have to directly *provide* the means and resources for the satisfaction of basic needs (in the form of direct aid or social security) to supplement the efforts of individuals. Extensive direct provision of resources may become necessary during periods of widespread unemployment (such as during a recession), sudden crises or disasters, or with regard to the disadvantaged, the elderly, or others who have been marginalized.

2.3 EQUALITY AND NON-DISCRIMINATION AS AN OVERARCHING PRINCIPLE

The duty of states to ensure equality and non-discrimination runs through all human rights instruments as a core principle and is essential to the enjoyment of economic, social, and cultural rights, including the right to an adequate standard of living. Article 2(2) ICESCR obliges states parties 'to guarantee that the rights enunciated in the present Covenant will be exercised without discrimination of any kind as to race, colour, sex, language, religion, political or other opinion, national or social origin, property, birth or other status'. More specifically, Article 3 requires states to ensure the equal right of men and women to enjoy all

---

[4] On the origins of the analysis that follows, see Eide, 'State Obligations Revisited' in Eide and Kracht (eds), *Food and Human Rights in Development, Vol I* (Intersentia, 2005) 137. See also Chapter 5.

Covenant rights. The obligations arising from the principle of equality and non-discrimination have been elaborated by the Committee on Economic, Social and Cultural Rights in its General Comment 20, adopted in May 2009.[5] The Committee has made it clear that states must eliminate formal and substantive, as well as direct and indirect, discrimination.[6] The Committee has also elaborated the meaning of equality and non-discrimination in the context of specific Covenant rights, including the rights to housing,[7] food,[8] health,[9] and water.[10]

3 NORMATIVE CONTENT

This section explains the different elements of the right to an adequate standard of living, namely the rights to food, housing, and health. The main legal sources and different components of each of these rights are considered and challenges to their realization set out. However, these rights should not be seen in isolation, but need to be seen in conjunction with other rights such as the rights to work, social security, and education and other rights that will be briefly touched upon in this chapter.

3.1 THE RIGHT TO FOOD

At the core of the right to an adequate standard of living is the right to food. While human beings do not live by bread alone, without food there is no life, and with the wrong food, life is shorter and more prone to ill-health. Access to adequate food and to food security has been a dominant concern in the evolution of civilizations and in the formation of states. Neglect or violation of the right to food is probably the most serious global human rights issue in terms of the number of people whose rights are not ensured. Nearly a billion people suffer from hunger and under-nutrition. For them, the right to food is the most important of all rights. Access to water is of crucial importance for the enjoyment of all the elements of the right to an adequate standard of living, including the right to food, and is therefore also briefly dealt with in this section.

3.1.1 Sources

The right to food set out in Article 25 UDHR is further elaborated in Article 11 ICESCR. While Article 11(1) recognizes everyone's right to adequate food, Article 11(2) obliges states parties to adopt more immediate and urgent steps to ensure 'the fundamental right of everyone to be free from hunger'. The right to food is also contained in other international human rights instruments, such as the CRC (Articles 24 and 27), and regional instruments such as in Article 12 of the Additional Protocol to the American Convention on Human Rights in the Area of Economic, Social and Cultural Rights ('Protocol of San Salvador'). While the African Charter on Human and Peoples' Rights (ACHPR) does not contain an express reference to the right to food, the African Commission on Human and Peoples' Rights, in its decision in *SERAC v Nigeria*, has suggested that the right is implicit in the ACHPR because it is inextricably linked to human dignity and is essential for the enjoyment of other rights.[11]

---

[5] CESCR, General Comment 20, E/C.12/GC/20 (2 July 2009).
[6] See Chapter 8 for an explanation of these concepts.
[7] CESCR, General Comment 4, HRI/GEN/1/Rev.9 (Vol I) 11; CESCR, General Comment 7, HRI/GEN/1/Rev.9 (Vol I) 38.   [8] CESCR, General Comment 12, HRI/GEN/1/Rev.9 (Vol I) 55.
[9] CESCR, General Comment 14, HRI/GEN/1/Rev.9 (Vol I) 78.
[10] CESCR, General Comment 15, HRI/GEN/1/Rev.9 (Vol I) 97.
[11] Communication No 155/96, 16th Activity Report of the ACommHPR (2002–2003).

3.1.2 Components and obligations

In its General Comment 12, the Committee on Economic, Social and Cultural Rights defined the right to food as follows: 'The right to adequate food is realized when every man, woman and child, alone or in community with others, has physical and economic access at all times to adequate food or means for its procurement'.[12] According to the Committee, 'adequate food' implies, first, 'the *availability* of food in a quantity and quality sufficient to satisfy the dietary needs of individuals, free from adverse substances, and acceptable within a given culture'.[13] *Availability* means that either people must be able to feed themselves directly from natural resources or well-functioning distribution and processing systems must exist; *dietary needs* implies that the diet as a whole contains all the necessary nutrients for physical and mental growth, development, and maintenance; *free from adverse substances* sets requirements for food safety; and *cultural or consumer acceptability* implies the need also to take into account perceived non nutrient-based values attached to food.[14] Second, the right to food requires 'the *accessibility* of such food in ways that are sustainable and that do not interfere with the enjoyment of other human rights',[15] encompassing both physical and economic accessibility.[16]

The legal obligations of states parties to the ICESCR under the right to food have been interpreted by the Committee in paragraph 15 of the same General Comment:

> The obligation to *respect* existing access to adequate food requires States parties not to take any measures that result in preventing such access. The obligation to *protect* requires measures by the State to ensure that enterprises or individuals do not deprive individuals of their access to adequate food. The obligation to *fulfil (facilitate)* means the State must pro-actively engage in activities intended to strengthen people's access to and utilization of resources and means to ensure their livelihood, including food security. Finally, whenever an individual or group is unable, for reasons beyond their control, to enjoy the right to adequate food by the means at their disposal, States have the obligation to *fulfil (provide)* that right directly. This obligation also applies for persons who are victims of natural or other disasters.[17]

The Committee has pointed out that some of the measures required from states are of a more immediate nature, while others are more long term in character.[18] The right to food is violated when a state fails to ensure the satisfaction of, at the very least, the minimum essential level required to be free from hunger. Resource constraints do not absolve the state from responsibility; it still has to show that every effort has been made to use all the resources at its disposal in an effort to satisfy, as a matter of priority, those minimum obligations.[19] Furthermore, any discrimination in access to food or to means and entitlements for its procurement constitutes a violation of Article 11 ICESCR.[20] The Committee has emphasized that violations can occur through the direct action of states or other entities insufficiently regulated by states. Non-state actors also have responsibilities in the realization of the right to food, and states should provide an environment that facilitates implementation of these responsibilities.[21]

---

[12] CESCR, General Comment 12, para 6.
[13] CESCR, General Comment 12, para 8 (emphasis added).
[14] CESCR, General Comment 12, paras 9–12.
[15] CESCR, General Comment 12, para 8 (emphasis added).
[16] CESCR, General Comment 12, para 13.
[17] Original emphases.   [18] CESCR, General Comment 12, para 16.
[19] CESCR, General Comment 12, para 17.   [20] CESCR, General Comment 12, para 18.
[21] CESCR, General Comment 12, paras 19–20.

3.1.3 The right to water

An adequate standard of living requires access to adequate water for personal and domestic use. While the right to water is not expressly mentioned in either Article 11 or Article 12 ICESCR, it is clearly implied. The availability and accessibility of safe and potable water throughout the day is essential for health. Water is required in producing, preparing, and consuming food. Water is necessary for personal hygiene and sanitation and is also, therefore, an integral part of the right to health.

As with the right to food, the Committee on Economic, Social and Cultural Rights has spelled out the different components of the right to adequate water in a General Comment, namely General Comment 15. According to the Committee, adequacy implies that the water supply for each person must be sufficient and continuous (*availability*), that water must be safe (*quality*), and that water and water facilities have to be within physical reach and affordable for all, without discrimination (*accessibility*).[22] The Committee has emphasized that the right to water includes freedoms, for example the right to be free from interferences such as disconnections or contamination of water supplies, as well as entitlements, such as the right to a system of water supply and management that provides equality of opportunity for people to enjoy the right to water.[23]

3.1.4 Realization

Extensive international attention has been paid to the right to food since the World Food Summit, held at the invitation of the Food and Agriculture Organization of the UN (FAO) in Rome in 1996. At that summit, governments from all parts of the world declared it unacceptable that more than 800 million people throughout the world, particularly in developing countries, did not have enough food to meet their basic nutritional needs. They recognized that this was not the result of a lack of food supplies, which in fact had increased substantially, but due to a lack of physical or economic *access* to food. Governments at the summit committed themselves to achieving food security for all and to an on-going effort to eradicate hunger in all countries, with an immediate view to reducing the number of undernourished people to half the 1996 level no later than the year 2015. Regrettably, this target was not met. The number of seriously undernourished persons was reduced only marginally—the figure at the end of 2015 was 795 million.[24] In relative terms, however, the figures are more encouraging. The world now feeds a much larger population than it did in 1996.[25] The problem is not an overall lack of food produced, but the inequality of access to it, together with enormous food waste.

Conditions differ widely between states, and, therefore, the most appropriate ways in which to implement the right to adequate food also vary considerably. Nevertheless, all states parties to the ICESCR and the CRC are obliged to take the measures required to ensure that everyone is free from hunger, and thereupon move as quickly as possible to a situation where everyone can enjoy their right to adequate food. In so doing, the different levels of state obligations discussed here should be applied, using the particular combination of measures warranted by the national situation.

---

[22] CESCR, General Comment 15, para 12.   [23] CESCR, General Comment 15, para 10.

[24] FAO, The State of Food Insecurity in the World 2015 (2015).

[25] Considering that the total world population has increased by 1.5 billion since 1996, the number of additional people now having access to sufficient food has increased by 700 million people. See FAO. The greatest reduction in hunger has been achieved in China since the 1990s. The greatest numbers of hungry people are now in Africa, South Asia, and North Korea. Technically, in terms of food production, it is feasible to extend the coverage of food to everyone in the world.

Therefore, every state should have, or should develop, a national strategy to implement the right to food. The first step in any such strategy should be to map the situation for different groups and regions within the country, taking into account the differences that might exist on the basis of gender, ethnicity, or race, and between rural and urban areas. Such mapping is necessary to identify those who are food-insecure and to develop appropriate responses to food insecurity. Having identified the groups that are food-insecure, the national strategy should create or recreate food security for those groups and for the population as a whole. When resource constraints emerge, measures should be undertaken to ensure, as a minimum, that vulnerable population groups and individuals do not face hunger. This should be achieved through social programmes, safety nets, and international assistance.

In the elaboration and implementation of national strategies for the right to food, people's informed participation is essential. Thus, states must ensure that particular conditions in different regions of the country are taken into account. Furthermore, attention must be given to all aspects of the food chain, from production to consumption. This includes paying attention to the processing of food in order to ensure food safety and the physical distribution of food in order to enable access for all. Finally, any national strategy should give particular attention to the need to prevent discrimination in access to food or resources for food.

In November 2004 the FAO Council adopted the 'Voluntary guidelines to support the progressive realization of the right to adequate food in the context of national food security'.[26] The objective of these guidelines, elaborated by an intergovernmental working group, is to provide practical guidance to states in the realization of the right to food. They are based on the legal standards mentioned already. The guidelines deal with general enabling conditions, but more importantly, they include a set of practical measures to be carried out. These include measures relating to access to resources and assets (labour, land, water, genetic resources for food and agriculture, and so on), food safety and consumer protection, nutrition policies, education and awareness-raising, national monitoring, and the setting of benchmarks for progressive realization.[27] The guidelines also underline the importance of ensuring that national human rights institutions address the realization of the right to food as part of their work.[28] Finally, they contain a section on international measures, which deals with international cooperation and unilateral measures, the role of the international community, international trade, external debt, international food aid, partnerships with NGOs, civil society organizations, and the private sector (corporations, enterprises).

3.2 THE RIGHT TO HOUSING

Second only to the enjoyment of the right to food, an adequate standard of living requires that everyone has a place to live—a physical space which provides personal and family security, basic infrastructure, satisfactory privacy, necessary warmth on cold days, and protection against heat on warm days.

3.2.1 Sources

The right to housing forms part of the guarantees set out in Article 25 UDHR and Article 11 ICESCR. Furthermore, it is either expressly referred to or implied in other international instruments such as the Convention on the Elimination of All Forms of Racial Discrimination (ICERD) (Article 5(e)(iii)), the CRC (Article 27), the Convention on the Elimination of All Forms of Discrimination Against Women (CEDAW) (Article 14(2)), and the Convention Relating to the Status of Refugees (Article 21). At the regional level, the right to housing is

---

[26] Available at <http://www.fao.org/docrep/meeting/009/y9825e/y9825e00.htm>.
[27] FAO Council, Guidelines 8–17.   [28] FAO Council, Guideline 18.

contained in the European Social Charter (Article 31). As with the right to food, the African Commission on Human and Peoples' Rights held in its decision in *SERAC v Nigeria* that, although there is no express reference to the right to housing in the ACHPR, the Charter must be interpreted to include such a right.[29]

3.2.2 Components and obligations

The Committee on Economic, Social and Cultural Rights has elaborated on the content of the right to housing in its General Comment 4.[30] In terms of the holders of the right, it has pointed out that the right applies to everyone. According to the Committee, the reference to 'himself and his family' in Article 11 ICESCR reflects traditional assumptions regarding gender roles and economic activity patterns, but cannot be read today as implying any limitations upon the applicability of the right to individuals or to female-headed households or collective groups. The concept of 'family' must, therefore, be understood in a wide sense and enjoyment of this right must not be subject to any form of discrimination.[31]

Adequate housing requires more than mere shelter in the sense of having a roof over one's head—it must be seen as the right to live somewhere in security, peace, and dignity. According to the Committee, the requirements for adequate housing are the following:

- *Legal security of tenure*: whatever the type of tenure, all persons should possess a degree of security of tenure which guarantees legal protection against forced eviction, harassment, and other threats.

- *Availability of services, materials, facilities, and infrastructure*: this includes safe drinking water, energy for cooking, heating and lighting, sanitation and washing facilities, means of food storage, refuse disposal, site drainage, and emergency services.

- *Affordability*: personal or household financial costs associated with housing should not be such that the attainment and satisfaction of other basic needs is threatened or compromised.

- *Habitability*: the housing must provide the inhabitants with adequate space and protection from cold, damp, heat, rain, wind, or other threats to health, structural hazards, and disease vectors.

- *Accessibility*: housing laws and policies must take into account the special needs of disadvantaged groups to ensure that such groups have full access to adequate housing resources.

- *Location*: adequate housing must be in a location which allows access to employment options, healthcare services, schools, childcare centres, and other social facilities.

- *Cultural adequacy*: the way housing is constructed, the building materials used, and the relevant policies must appropriately enable the expression of cultural identity and diversity of housing.[32]

In market economies, housing is generally considered to be a private good. However, the right to housing implies that the state has a duty to protect against discrimination in access to housing and to facilitate access to housing for all. To that extent, human rights makes housing a public good. That does not necessarily mean that states have an obligation to provide housing. Most people find their own way to obtain and secure their preferred place to live. As with other human rights, state obligations under the right to housing are a combination of passive and active duties. States have, first, a duty to *respect* the housing

---

[29] Communication No 155/96, 16th Activity Report of the ACommHPR (2002–2003).
[30] CESCR, General Comment 4.   [31] CESCR, General Comment 4, para 6.
[32] CESCR, General Comment 4, para 8.

found by people themselves by abstaining from forcible evictions and displacements. Second, they must *protect* the tenure of existing housing against interference or unjustified evictions by third parties and adopt and enforce the necessary regulations to ensure the necessary quality of housing. Third, they have an obligation through regulatory functions to *facilitate* the opportunity of everyone to find affordable housing. Fourth, in exceptional circumstances and in regard to particularly vulnerable groups, they have to *provide* necessary housing when individuals or groups cannot manage to do so themselves. State measures to implement the right to housing will, therefore, normally reflect a mixture of provisions regulating the private sector ('enabling strategies') and public or state-driven measures (public housing). In essence, the obligation on states is to demonstrate that they have done enough to realize the right for every individual in the shortest possible time, prioritizing for that purpose the use of available resources.[33]

3.2.3 Realization

The Committee on Economic, Social and Cultural Rights has pointed out that there remains a disturbingly large gap between the standards set out in Article 11(1) ICESCR and the situation prevailing in many parts of the world. This refers principally to developing countries, which confront major resource and other constraints, but there is also a significant and growing problem of homelessness and inadequate housing in some of the most economically developed societies. According to some UN estimates, there are over 100 million homeless persons worldwide and over 1 billion who are inadequately housed, with millions of homeless or inadequately housed persons located also in Europe and North America.

Besides homelessness, forced evictions (that is, evictions that are coercive or not carried out in accordance with pre-existing law) are the most severe violation of the right to housing. Forced evictions have been carried out against squatters, low-income renters, indigenous peoples, and other vulnerable groups with no or inadequate legal security of tenure. In its General Comment 7, the Committee on Economic, Social and Cultural Rights called for strict legislation to prevent unjustified evictions. Similarly, the Commission on Human Rights adopted a resolution in 2004 calling for a wide range of measures, including legislation, to prohibit forced evictions unless justified under strict limitations. It requested governments to eliminate the practice of forced evictions by 1) repealing existing plans involving, as well as any legislation allowing for, forced evictions, and 2) adopting and implementing legislation ensuring the right to security of tenure for all residents.[34]

No state party to the ICESCR is free of significant problems of one kind or another in relation to the right to housing. The Committee on Economic, Social and Cultural Rights has, therefore, expressed regret that many states do not acknowledge their difficulties in ensuring the right to adequate housing in their reports to the Committee.[35]

3.3 THE RIGHT TO HEALTH

The term 'right to health' can be misleading. There is no human right to be healthy. Due to genetics, risky behaviour, accidents, and other factors, it is not within the capacity of states to ensure that everyone lives a full and lengthy life. What is envisaged in international human rights law is that everyone shall have a right to the highest attainable standard of health—attainable both in terms of the individual's potential, the social and environmental

---

[33] CESCR, General Comment 4, para 14.
[34] CHR Res 2004/28, E/CN.4/RES/2004/28 (16 April 2004), para 2.
[35] CESCR, General Comment 4, para 4.

conditions affecting the health of the individual, and in terms of health services. For reasons of convenience, this chapter refers to the 'right to health', but this term should be understood in its proper sense of the right to the highest attainable standard of health.

3.3.1 Sources

The right to health is provided for in Article 25 UDHR. In the case of the ICESCR, it is contained in a separate, comprehensive provision (Article 12). Further human rights standards on the right to health include Article 12 CEDAW, Article 5(e)(iv) ICERD, Article 24 CRC, Article 11 of the European Social Charter, Article 10 of the Protocol of San Salvador, and Article 16 ACHPR.

3.3.2 Components and obligations

Under Article 12(1) ICESCR, states parties recognize the right of everyone to the enjoyment of the highest attainable standard of physical and mental health. The right to health extends to adequate healthcare, the underlying preconditions for health, and adequate fulfilment of the social determinants of health. Article 12(2) ICESCR sets out the main directions for state action in fulfilling this right. According to this provision, states must take steps for:

> (a) the provision for the reduction of the stillbirth-rate and of infant mortality and for the healthy development of the child; (b) the improvement of all aspects of environmental and industrial hygiene; (c) the prevention, treatment and control of epidemic, endemic, occupational and other diseases; (d) the creation of conditions which would assure to all medical service and medical attention in the event of sickness.

In its General Comment 14, the Committee on Economic, Social and Cultural Rights has specified that the right to health involves the following elements and state obligations:

- *Availability*: states must ensure that functioning public health and healthcare facilities, goods, and services are available in sufficient quantity. The precise nature of these facilities, goods, and services will vary depending on numerous factors, including the state party's level of development.

- *Accessibility*: health facilities, goods, and services have to be accessible to everyone. Accessibility has four overlapping dimensions: (1) non-discrimination; (2) physical accessibility; (3) economic accessibility (affordability); and (4) information accessibility (the right to seek, receive, and impart information and ideas concerning health issues).

- *Acceptability*: all health facilities, goods, and services must be respectful of medical ethics and culturally appropriate, sensitive to gender and lifecycle requirements, as well as being designed to respect confidentiality and improve the health status of those concerned.

- *Quality*: health facilities, goods, and services must be scientifically and medically appropriate and of good quality. This requires, inter alia, skilled medical personnel, scientifically approved and unexpired drugs, appropriate hospital equipment, safe and potable water, and adequate sanitation.[36]

The right to health requires states to adopt and implement measures ensuring the right of access to health facilities, goods, and services to all on a non-discriminatory basis, including to vulnerable or marginalized groups that otherwise might not have such access. This also requires the equitable distribution of all health facilities, which are often concentrated in the main urban areas, leaving rural and less important urban areas unattended.

---

[36] CESCR, General Comment 14, para 12.

As the Committee has pointed out, a state is in violation of its obligation to protect individuals' health if it fails to take all necessary measures to safeguard persons within its jurisdiction from infringements of the right to health by third parties. This may include omissions such as the failure to discourage production, marketing, and consumption of tobacco, narcotics, and other harmful substances; the failure to discourage the continued observance of harmful traditional medical or cultural practices; or the failure to enact or enforce laws to prevent the pollution of water, air, and soil by extractive and manufacturing industries.[37]

3.3.3 Realization

Realization of the right to health is closely linked to the realization of other economic and social rights. It is crucial that states ensure freedom from hunger and access for all to essential and sufficient food, which is nutritionally adequate and safe. The high level of child mortality, particularly in developing countries, is caused primarily by insufficient or inadequate food and unsafe and polluted water. Furthermore, realization of the right to health depends on access to basic shelter, housing, and sanitation, as well as an adequate supply of safe and potable water.

The Committee on Economic, Social and Cultural Rights has urged all states parties to adopt and implement a national public health strategy and plan of action, on the basis of epidemiological evidence, addressing the health concerns of the entire population. It has pointed out that the strategy and plan of action should be devised, and periodically reviewed, on the basis of a participatory and transparent process. They should include methods, such as right-to-health indicators and benchmarks, by which progress can be monitored, and should give particular attention to all vulnerable or marginalized groups. In addition, everyone should be ensured access to essential drugs as defined under the World Health Organization Action Programme on Essential Drugs.[38]

Of key importance is, finally, the task of ensuring reproductive, maternal (pre-natal as well as post-natal), and child healthcare. Maternal mortality is the leading cause of death among women and girls of reproductive age. It is estimated that half a million women and girls die annually from complications related to pregnancy and childbirth. If pregnancy-related injuries and disabilities are included, such as haemorrhage, infection, brain seizures, hypertension, anaemia, and obstetric fistulae, it is probable that tens of millions of women and girls are affected.

4 CATEGORIES AND GROUPS OF PEOPLE

Human rights, including the right to an adequate standard of living, should be equally applicable to everyone. In practice, however, it has proved necessary to pay special attention to the situation of some categories or groups of people, because they are vulnerable, have been neglected or marginalized, or have particular needs. It has been recognized that separate attention has to be given to the standard of living of different members of the family, including women and children. In addition, three particularly vulnerable groups of people will be discussed in this section: indigenous peoples, Dalits in South Asia, and the Roma in Europe.

4.1 WOMEN

International human rights bodies have recognized that women may face greater difficulties than men in securing an adequate standard of living. The Committee on Economic, Social and Cultural Rights has, therefore, urged states to include in their national strategies

---

[37] CESCR, General Comment 14, para 51. [38] CESCR, General Comment 14, para 43.

to implement the right to food guarantees of women's full and equal access to economic resources, including the right to inheritance and ownership of land and other property, credit, natural resources, and appropriate technology. Such strategies should also contain measures to respect and protect self-employment and work which provides adequate re-muneration to ensure a decent living for wage-earners and their families (as stipulated in Article 7(a)(ii) ICESCR).[39]

Healthcare is of particular importance for motherhood and childhood. Article 12 CEDAW requires states to 'take all appropriate measures to eliminate discrimination against women in the field of health care in order to ensure, on a basis of equality between men and women, access to health care services, including those related to family planning' and to ensure women have access to appropriate services in connection with pregnancy, confinement, and the post-natal period. The Committee on Economic, Social and Cultural Rights has underlined the need to develop and implement a comprehensive national strat-egy for promoting women's right to health to meet these requirements. It has pointed out that the realization of women's right to health requires the removal of all barriers inter-fering with access to health services, education, and information, including in the area of sexual and reproductive health. It has also emphasized the importance of preventive, promotional, and remedial action to shield women from the impact of harmful traditional cultural practices and norms that deny them their full reproductive rights.[40]

Article 14 CEDAW requires states to pay special attention to the particular problems faced by rural women. In particular, states must ensure such women have the right to adequate living conditions, particularly in relation to housing, sanitation, electricity and water supply, transport, and communications. Furthermore, they must be given the right to participate in the elaboration and implementation of development planning at all levels and to have access to adequate healthcare facilities, including information, counselling, and services in family planning.

4.2 CHILDREN

Article 27 CRC guarantees 'the right of every child to a standard of living adequate for the child's physical, mental, spiritual, moral and social development'. This involves adequate food, housing, nursing, and care. Article 27(2) provides that the parent(s) or others re-sponsible for the child have the primary responsibility to secure the conditions of living necessary for the child's development.

While ensuring the child's right to an adequate standard of living is the primary duty of parents, it is not exclusive. According to Article 27(3) CRC, states must take appropriate measures to assist parents to implement this right. If necessary, they have to provide mate-rial assistance and support programmes, particularly with regard to nutrition, clothing, and housing. In addition, many children grow up in single-parent households, or are orphaned or have parents that have absconded or neglect their duty, and, in such situations, where other relatives do not take it over, the state has a primary duty to ensure for the child an ad-equate standard of living through appropriate institutions or placement with foster parents.

Under the right to health, states have a duty to diminish infant and child mortality. Article 12(2)(a) ICESCR expressly requires states to make 'provision for the reduction of the stillbirth rate and of infant mortality and for the healthy development of the child'. Similar obligations are contained in Article 24(2)(a) CRC and flow from Article 6 CRC, which provides that every child has the inherent right to life and that states 'shall ensure to the maximum extent possible the survival and development of the child'. This obligation

---

[39] CESCR, General Comment 12, para 26.   [40] CESCR, General Comment 14, para 21.

may be understood as requiring measures to improve child and maternal health, sexual and reproductive health services, pre- and post-natal care, access to information, as well as to resources necessary to act on that information.

More generally, Article 24 CRC guarantees the right of the child to the enjoyment of the highest attainable standard of health and to facilities for the treatment of illness and rehabilitation of health. Thus, states must ensure that no child is deprived of his or her right of access to healthcare services. Furthermore, they have an obligation to ensure the provision of necessary medical assistance and healthcare to all children, combat disease and malnutrition, and develop preventive healthcare. The obligation of states parties to combat disease and malnutrition reflects the dominant problems facing children in many developing countries. A large number of children, particularly in the poorer sector of the population, die before the age of five, due to a combination of malnutrition, unsafe water and sanitation, and communicable diseases. The risks can be substantially reduced through readily available technology such as oral rehydration therapy and immunization against the common childhood diseases, but this alone is not enough. It is also essential to ensure provision of adequate nutritious food and clean drinking water.

4.3 INDIGENOUS PEOPLES

The indigenous peoples of the world are generally among the most impoverished.[41] Many of them are struggling to maintain and preserve their own culture. Since much of their land and resources has been taken away from them, the little that is left cannot provide them with enough to satisfy an adequate standard of living. While efforts to strengthen their rights have had some positive results in recent years, such as the adoption in 1989 of the ILO Convention on the Rights of Tribal and Indigenous Peoples (No 169) and in 2007 the adoption by the UN General Assembly of the Declaration on the Rights of Indigenous Peoples, they still suffer from severe deprivation. When they are displaced and live on 'welfare', their culture is undermined and the alien lifestyle leads to high degrees of alcoholism, suicide, and sometimes criminal behaviour. In line with the UN Declaration on the Rights of Indigenous Peoples, conditions must be established, including through recognition of their rights to land and natural resources which enable them to preserve their culture while sustaining a livelihood that ensures for them an adequate standard of living. This close link between rights to land and natural resources on the one hand and economic survival on the other hand has been highlighted by the Inter-American human rights bodies in a number of cases.[42] In the *Yakye Axa Indigenous Community* case, the Inter-American Court of Human Rights held that Paraguay had violated the rights of the members of that community to live a dignified existence, which follows from the right to life, by delaying the restitution of their ancestral lands and thus making it difficult for them to obtain food, clean water, adequate housing, and healthcare.[43]

The Committee on Economic, Social and Cultural Rights has repeatedly addressed the problems faced by indigenous peoples in its General Comments. It has drawn attention to the particular vulnerability of indigenous peoples whose ancestral land may be threatened. In several places corporations involved in oil or other mineral extraction have aggravated the situation of indigenous peoples, degraded their land, and caused their displacement.[44]

---

[41] For the definition of 'indigenous peoples', see Chapter 18.

[42] See Case 11.140, *Mary and Carrie Dann v United States*, IACommHR Report No 75/02 (27 December 2002); *Mayagna (Sumo) Awas Tingni Community v Nicaragua*, IACtHR Series C No 79 (31 August 2001); *Yakye Axa Indigenous Community v Paraguay*, IACtHR Series C No 125 (17 June 2005).

[43] *Yakye Axa Indigenous Community*, paras 164–8 and 176.   [44] CESCR, General Comment 12, para 13.

The Committee has also emphasized that as part of their obligations to protect people's resource base for food, states parties should take appropriate steps to ensure that activities of the private business sector are in conformity with the right to food.[45] With regard to the right to housing, it has pointed out that indigenous peoples are among those vulnerable groups who suffer most from evictions.[46] Finally, the Committee has called on states to take particular care to ensure that indigenous peoples and ethnic and linguistic minorities are not excluded from social security systems through direct or indirect discrimination, particularly through the imposition of unreasonable eligibility conditions or lack of adequate access to information.[47]

Indigenous peoples often live in remote areas with the lowest level of access to modern healthcare, and when they can reach healthcare stations there is often a poor understanding of, and respect for, their cultural requirements. The Committee has argued that indigenous peoples have the right to specific measures to improve their access to health services and care. Health services should be culturally appropriate and thus take into account traditional preventive care, healing practices, and medicines. States should provide resources for indigenous peoples to design, deliver, and control such services. The Committee has noted that, in indigenous communities, the health of the individual is often linked to the health of the society as a whole and has a collective dimension. Therefore, development-related activities that lead to the displacement of indigenous peoples, denying them their sources of nutrition and breaking their symbiotic relationship with their lands, have a deleterious effect on their health.[48]

4.4 DALITS IN SOUTH ASIA AND ROMA IN EUROPE

Many other minorities are subject to persistent discrimination, undermining their standard of living. These include the low-castes or Dalits in South Asia—particularly in India—who, as a result of social practices, are often marginalized, deprived of access to the means of adequate food and housing, and given access only to the lowest, most menial work. While such practices are generally prohibited under the respective national laws, enforcement of the law is often weak and segments of the police and other law enforcement agencies are themselves socialized in the same discriminatory attitudes that keep such practices alive. In its General Comment 20 of 2009, the Committee on Economic, Social and Cultural Rights pointed out that the prohibited ground of discrimination of 'birth' listed in Article 2(2) ICESCR also includes *descent*, especially on the basis of caste and analogous systems of inherited status. Therefore, states parties should take steps to prevent, prohibit, and eliminate discriminatory practices directed against members of descent-based communities and act against dissemination of ideas of superiority and inferiority on the basis of descent.[49]

A somewhat comparable situation exists in many parts of Europe, where the Roma and the Sinti are subject to widespread social discrimination, and where governments are unable fully to eradicate these practices. In 2012 the Commissioner for Human Rights of the Council of Europe presented a comprehensive report detailing extensive racially motivated violence against Roma and Travellers, police abuse of these groups, discrimination in access to adequate housing and to employment, denial of and discrimination by emergency medical health services and by health providers, exclusion from healthcare as a result of physical distance from healthcare facilities, and serious impediments to their

---

[45] CESCR, General Comment 12, para. 27.   [46] CESCR, General Comment 7, para 10.
[47] CESCR, General Comment 19, HRI/GEN/1/Rev.9 (Vol I) 152, para 35.
[48] CESCR, General Comment 14, para 27.   [49] CESCR, General Comment 20, para 26.

access to social security.[50] Multiple initiatives have been taken by the Council of Europe, the European Union, and by the Organization for Security and Cooperation in Europe (OSCE), but the persistent prejudices against, and exclusion of, the Roma and Sinti have made progress difficult.

5 RELATIONSHIP WITH OTHER HUMAN RIGHTS

As pointed out in the conclusions of the 1993 Vienna World Conference on Human Rights, '[a]ll human rights are universal, indivisible, interdependent and interrelated.'[51] It is easy to show that the right to an adequate standard of living is closely linked to other human rights. Most obviously, it is heavily dependent on the realization of other economic and social rights, such as the rights to work, education, and property. Of particular importance is the right to social security, dealt with in Section 5.1. Economic rights have a dual function, most clearly demonstrated in regard to the right to property. On the one hand, this right serves as a basis for entitlements which can ensure an adequate standard of living, while on the other hand it is a basis of independence and, therefore, freedom. Similarly, the right to work is also a basis of both independence (provided the work is freely chosen by the person concerned) and an adequate standard of living (provided that sufficient income is obtained from work).

The right to an adequate standard of living is also linked to cultural rights, which, according to Article 27 UDHR and Article 15 ICESCR, contain the following elements: the right to take part in cultural life, the right to enjoy the benefits of scientific progress and its applications, the right to benefit from the protection of the moral and material interests resulting from any scientific, literary, or artistic production of which the beneficiary is the author, and the freedom indispensable for scientific research and creative activity.[52] These rights intersect in several ways with the right to an adequate standard of living. To mention one example: the right to benefit from advances in scientific progress can be a basis for claiming a right of access to affordable new medicine, which may be crucial in treating diseases such as HIV and AIDS.

Finally, as explained in Section 5.2, the right to an adequate standard of living may also coincide or, on the other hand, clash with civil and political rights.

5.1 THE RIGHT TO SOCIAL SECURITY AND SOCIAL ASSISTANCE

The right to social security is essential when people are not able to secure an adequate standard of living themselves, particularly when they do not have the necessary property or are not able to work due to unemployment, old age, or disability. The drafters of the UDHR considered social security to be one of the core guarantees for the right of everyone to an adequate standard of living.

The general guarantee of an adequate standard of living set out in Article 25 UDHR includes 'the right to security in the event of unemployment, sickness, disability, widowhood, old age or other lack of livelihood in circumstances beyond his control'. But the UDHR also contains a separate guarantee of the right to social security that uses stronger terms. Article 22 states that '[e]veryone, as a member of society, has the right to social

---

[50] Commissioner for Human Rights of the Council of Europe, *Human Rights of Roma and Travellers in Europe* (Council of Europe Publications, 2012).

[51] Vienna Declaration and Programme of Action, A/CONF.157/23 (25 June 1993) para 5. See Chapter 7 and Eide, 'Interdependence and Indivisibility of Human Rights' in Donders and Volodin (eds), *Human Rights in Education, Science and Culture* (UNESCO Publishing/Ashgate, 2007). [52] See Chapter 14.

security'. The ICESCR, in Article 9, guarantees 'the right of everyone to social security, including social insurance', while Article 10 of the same covenant refers to social security within the context of the protection of the family, mothers, and children. CEDAW contains a range of social security guarantees relevant to women, including the right of women to social security, particularly in cases of retirement, unemployment, sickness, invalidity and old age, and other incapacity to work, as well as the right to paid leave (Article 11(1)(e)), the right to family benefits (Article 13(a)), and the right of rural women to benefit directly from social security programmes (Article 14(2)(c)). The CRC provides for the right of the child to benefit from social security, including social insurance (Article 26). The right to social security is also explicitly mentioned in regional human rights instruments, including the American Declaration of the Rights and Duties of Man (Article XVI), the Protocol of San Salvador (Article 9), and the European Social Charter (Articles 12, 13, and 14).

Social security must be distinguished from social assistance and charity. Charity is irrelevant in the present context, because it involves neither a right of the individual nor a duty imposed on the state. It is, therefore, not a human rights issue. Social assistance is often discretionary and, therefore, neither a right nor a duty, but in some states it is sufficiently well regulated in law and practice to make it conform to requirements of human rights law.

Measures to implement the right to social security as set out in Article 9 ICESCR can include contributory or non-contributory schemes, or a combination of the two. The Committee on Economic, Social and Cultural Rights, in its General Comment 19, has defined these two types of provision of social security benefits as follows. *Contributory* (or insurance-based) schemes, such as social insurance, which is expressly mentioned in Article 9, generally involve compulsory contributions from beneficiaries, employers, and, sometimes, the state, in conjunction with the payment of benefits and administrative expenses from a common fund. *Non-contributory* schemes include universal schemes, which provide the relevant benefit to everyone who experiences a particular risk or contingency, and targeted social assistance schemes, where benefits are received by those in a situation of need.

In recent years, an embryonic form of social security under the name of 'cash transfer programmes' has emerged, particularly in the least developed countries where the social security system has limited reach. These programmes, which provide payments in cash to individuals or households, are normally targeted at the poorest and most vulnerable sections of the population. The transfers may be in the form of non-contributory old-age pensions, disability grants, child support grants, widow's allowances, or household transfers to persons in extreme poverty. Some of these programmes are conditional, for example requiring that the supported children attend school. The former UN Independent Expert on the question of extreme poverty has recognized that these cash transfer programmes can assist states in fulfilling their human rights obligations. However, she has also pointed out that this requires that the programmes are fully integrated within broader social protection systems. Their legal and institutional frameworks must take into account the international and national standards regarding the right to social security.[53]

The Committee on Economic, Social and Cultural Rights has expressed its concern over the very low levels of access to social security. In 2008, it noted that about 80 per cent of the global population lacked access to formal social security, with 20 per cent living in extreme poverty. The Committee has emphasized that this denial of, or lack of access to, adequate social security has undermined the realization of many Covenant rights.[54] Conditions have improved since then, but there is still a long way to go.

---

[53] Report of the Independent Expert on the question of human rights and extreme poverty, A/HRC/11/9 (27 March 2009).

[54] CESCR, General Comment 19, paras 7 and 8.

5.2 CIVIL AND POLITICAL RIGHTS

Civil and political rights are essential in order to achieve the realization of an adequate standard of living. When rights to housing or food are unjustifiably denied, everyone, including the poor, must have effective access to remedies before independent courts or other institutions such as human rights commissions. In some parts of the world, civil and political rights have been extensively used to advance the realization of economic and social rights, including the right to an adequate standard of living.[55]

More specifically, torture and ill-treatment is not only a violation of core civil rights but also a violation of the right to health. Severe gaps in the realization of the right to health or the right to be free from hunger may lead, in turn, to violations of the right to life, which is a civil right. On the other hand, there can also be conflicts between these different categories of rights. To give just one example, while the state has an obligation under international human rights law to take measures to protect the right to health, such measures must comply with the rights of people who carry infectious diseases such as their rights to physical integrity, privacy, and liberty. In each specific case, the need to protect the health of the public at large has to be balanced against individual interests. Thus, the European Court of Human Rights has held that an individual can only be compulsorily isolated to prevent him or her from spreading the HIV virus *as a last resort*, that is, where less severe measures are insufficient to safeguard the public interest.[56]

6 PROGRESSIVE IMPLEMENTATION

It is obvious that the right of everyone to an adequate standard of living is still far from realized. Nearly 800 million people suffer from hunger and malnutrition. At least one billion, out of the total of 7.5 billion living on earth in 2017, have substandard housing or no housing at all. The problem of homelessness is growing also in 'rich' countries. There are enormous gaps between the standards set by international human rights law and the reality that many people face. This is also the case for many civil and political rights. Some may consider that human rights that are not applied in practice do not deserve the name 'rights'.

It has to be borne in mind that the UDHR was proclaimed as a 'common standard of achievement'.[57] All human rights set out in it, including the economic and social rights, must be realized through progressive measures to be taken both at the national and international level. Article 2 ICESCR envisages a progressive realization of the Covenant rights and acknowledges the constraints due to the limited available resources. However, it also imposes obligations which are of immediate effect. In particular, states parties must guarantee that the rights will be exercised without discrimination of any kind and must take immediate and progressive steps towards full realization of the relevant rights by all appropriate means, including particularly the adoption of legislative measures. The Committee on Economic, Social and Cultural Rights has pointed out that such steps should be deliberate, concrete, and targeted as clearly as possible towards meeting the obligations recognized in the Covenant.[58]

Full realization would require that human rights are given priority in development processes. Regrettably, this has often not been the case. Both at the national and international level, there are serious maldevelopments. The most pressing problem is the unregulated and misdirected process of globalization culminating in the financial crisis of 2008, which has led to a tremendous increase in inequality worldwide, particularly within states.

---

[55] See Chapter 7.   [56] *Enhorn v Sweden* (2005) 41 EHRR 633.
[57] UDHR, preambular para 8.   [58] CESCR, General Comment 3, HRI/GEN/1/Rev.9 (Vol I) 7, para 2.

Narrowly conceived economic growth can produce not only wealth but also poverty, unless development projects themselves are human rights-based.[59]

As previously explained, violations imputable to the state can occur either by direct action by the state and its agencies or by its failure to ensure rights. The Committee on Economic, Social and Cultural Rights has pointed out that in determining which actions or omissions amount to a violation, it is important to distinguish the inability of a state party to comply from its unwillingness to do so. Should, for instance, a state party argue that resource constraints make it impossible to provide access to food for those who are unable by themselves to secure such access, then it has to demonstrate that every effort has been made to use all the resources at its disposal in an effort to satisfy, as a matter of priority, its minimum obligations. A state claiming that it is unable to carry out its obligation for reasons beyond its control has the burden of proving that this is the case and that it has unsuccessfully sought to obtain international support to ensure the availability and accessibility of the necessary food. Furthermore, any discrimination in access to food, as well as to means and entitlements for its procurement, constitutes a violation of the ICESCR.[60]

7 THE IMPORTANCE OF INTERNATIONAL MONITORING AND RECOURSE PROCEDURES

Most states have some legislation relating to the rights to food, housing, and health. However, such legislation is often fragmented, does not guarantee them as proper entitlements, and is often weakly enforced or not enforced at all. International economic, social, and cultural rights constitute a comprehensive normative framework that should guide the content of national legislation in this area. In the absence of sufficient national legislation or its enforcement, the economic, social, and cultural rights contained in international instruments can play an important role for the individual. But are these rights justiciable? Behind this widely discussed question is a more fundamental one: what is the nature of international economic, social, and cultural rights?

The answer is not as difficult as is often thought. International human rights law serves two functions. First, it provides directive principles. Second, under some conditions, it provides subjective rights or genuine entitlements, provided national courts treat them as such. National courts have, to an increasing extent, enforced international guarantees of economic, social, and cultural rights.[61] This issue is further discussed in Chapter 24, so the discussion here will focus on the first issue.

The notion of directive principles is well-known from constitutional law. In India, for example, directive principles of state policy are contained in the constitution as guidelines to the central and state governments, to be considered when framing laws and policies. These provisions are not directly enforceable by any court, but they are considered to be fundamental principles of governance that must be applied by state authorities.[62] Similar principles are also found in other constitutions, such as that of Ireland, which focus on social justice and economic welfare. Such directive principles play an important role in the

---

[59] See further Eide, 'Human Rights-Based Development in the Age of Economic Globalization: Background and Prospects' in Andreassen and Marks (eds), *Development as a Human Right: Legal, Political, and Economic Dimensions* (Harvard UP, 2007) 220; Salomon, *Global Responsibility for Human Rights: World Poverty and the Development of International Law* (OUP, 2007). See also Chapter 30.

[60] CESCR, General Comment 12, paras 17 and 18.

[61] See Langford (ed), *Social Rights Jurisprudence: Emerging Trends in International and Comparative Law* (CUP, 2008).

[62] See further Chapter 24.

political process, but there are normally no national monitoring authorities supervising their implementation. In addition, they are often general and vague in their wording and, therefore, leave a wide margin for political disagreement concerning their implementation.

This is where international human rights law, and in particular guarantees of economic, social, and cultural rights, have an important additional value. International monitoring bodies can pursue a dialogue with each state on the optimal implementation of the directive principles and can elaborate and clarify the content of state obligations under international human rights standards. This is what the Committee on Economic, Social and Cultural Rights has done by issuing its General Comments, several of which concern the right to an adequate standard of living, and by adopting concluding observations and recommendations upon examination of state reports.

This monitoring through examination of state reports has been supplemented by a new procedure created by the Optional Protocol to the ICESCR, which was adopted in December 2008 and came into force in May 2013. Under the Optional Protocol, individuals who claim that their economic, social, and cultural rights have been violated can bring a complaint to the Committee after having exhausted available domestic remedies. This new procedure will undoubtedly add to the impact of economic, social, and cultural rights. Regrettably, the number of ratifications is still rather small (22 states parties in September 2017), but will hopefully grow as the procedure becomes better known. In any case, it will not reduce the importance of the monitoring process, which in some respects can produce more comprehensive effects than complaint procedures.[63]

In addition, the UN Human Rights Council and its predecessor, the Commission on Human Rights, have developed important thematic mechanisms to report on and promote the implementation of the right to an adequate standard of living. The reports by these Special Rapporteurs or Independent Experts play a very important role in advancing the enjoyment of the right to an adequate standard of living. There are Special Rapporteurs on the right to food, on the right to housing, on the right to health, on the right to water, and on the elimination of extreme poverty. All of these mechanisms perform important work in highlighting in their reports shortcomings and progress in the implementation of the right to an adequate standard of living in different parts of the world. Thereby, they make a significant contribution to the worldwide realization of this right.

8 CONCLUSION

Intended to promote and ensure freedom from want, the right to an adequate standard of living was given a central place in the proclamation of universal human rights from the very beginning in 1948. It has since been elaborated in international standards and clarified in detailed General Comments and practice. Several guidelines have been adopted for the implementation of the different components of an adequate standard of living, namely, the rights to food, water, housing, and health. The relevant international human rights standards serve both as directive principles and as subjective rights. While their main function has been as directive principles pursued through international monitoring and reporting, there is an emerging trend also to use them as subjective rights by adjudicative bodies.

Enormous gaps remain in the implementation of the right to an adequate standard of living. However, by adopting the 17 Sustainable Development Goals at the UN Summit

---

[63] See Langford, 'Closing the Gap?—An Introduction to the Optional Protocol to the International Covenant on Economic, Social and Cultural Rights' (2009) 27 *Nordic JHR* 1.

in 2015, the international community has now prioritized the need to ensure an adequate living standard for all. The three first-mentioned goals, to be achieved by 2030, are (1) to end poverty, (2) to achieve zero hunger, and (3) to ensure good health and well-being for all.[64] Obviously, realization of these goals must be combined with the achievement of the other 14 Sustainable Development Goals, but the fact that these three goals are listed first, highlights the importance given to the right of everyone to an adequate standard of living.

FURTHER READING

ALBUQUERQUE with ROAF, *On the Right Track: Good Practices in Realising the Rights to Water and Sanitation*, available at <http://www.ohchr.org/Documents/Issues/Water/BookonGoodPractices_en.pdf>.

CRAVEN, *The International Covenant on Economic, Social and Cultural Rights* (Oxford University Press, 2002).

DE SCHUTTER, 'The Right of Everyone to Enjoy the Benefits of Scientific Progress and the Right to Food: From Conflict to Complementarity' (2011) 33 *HRQ* 304.

EIDE and KRACHT (eds), *Food and Human Rights in Development: Volume I: Legal and Institutional Dimensions* (Intersentia, 2005).

EIDE and KRACHT (eds), *Food and Human Rights in Development: Volume II: Evolving Issues and Emerging Applications* (Intersentia, 2007).

EIDE, KRAUSE, and ROSAS (eds), *Economic, Social and Cultural Rights* (Martinus Nijhoff, 2001).

HEALTH AND HUMAN RIGHTS: AN INTERNATIONAL JOURNAL (Francois-Xavier Bagnaud Centre for Health and Human Rights).

KENT (ed), *Global Obligations for the Right to Food* (Rowman & Littlefield, 2008).

LANGFORD (ed), *Social Rights Jurisprudence* (Cambridge University Press, 2008).

LANGFORD *et al.* (eds), *Global Justice, State Duties: The Extraterritorial Scope of Economic, Social and Cultural Rights* (Cambridge University Press, 2013).

LECKIE (ed), *Housing, Land, and Property Restitution Rights of Refugees and Displaced Persons: Laws, Cases, and Materials* (Cambridge University Press, 2007).

SKOGLY, 'The Requirement of Using the "Maximum of Available Resources" for Human Rights Realisation: A Question of Quality as Well as Quantity?' (2012) 12 *HRLR* 393.

TOBIN, *The Right to Health in International Law* (Oxford University Press, 2012).

TOEBES, *The Right to Health as a Human Right in International Law* (Intersentia, 1999).

UNESCO, 'The Right to Water and Water Rights in a Changing World', available at <https://www.unesco.nl/sites/default/files/dossier/the_right_to_water_and_water_rights.pdf?download>

USEFUL WEBSITES

UN Committee on Economic, Social and Cultural Rights: <http://ohchr.org/en/hrbodies/cescr/pages/cescrindex.aspx>

UN Special Rapporteur on the right to food: <http://www.ohchr.org/EN/Issues/Food/Pages/FoodIndex.aspx>

UN Special Rapporteur on adequate housing as a component of the right to an adequate standard of living: <http://www.ohchr.org/EN/Issues/Housing/Pages/HousingIndex.aspx>

[64] GA Res 70/1 (25 September 2015). See Chapter 30.

UN Special Rapporteur on the right of everyone to the enjoyment of the highest attainable standard of physical and mental health <http://www.ohchr.org/EN/Issues/Health/Pages/SRRightHealthIndex.aspx>

UN Special Rapporteur on the human rights to safe drinking water and sanitation: <www.ohchr.org/EN/Issues/WaterAndSanitation/SRWater/Pages/SRWaterIndex.aspx>

UN Special Rapporteur on extreme poverty and human rights: <http://www.ohchr.org/EN/Issues/Poverty/Pages/SRExtremePovertyIndex.aspx>

European Committee of Social Rights: <http://www.coe.int/en/web/turin-european-social-charter/european-committee-of-social-rights>

11

THOUGHT, EXPRESSION, ASSOCIATION, AND ASSEMBLY

Dominic McGoldrick

SUMMARY

The four freedoms introduced in this chapter—thought, expression, association, and assembly—are interrelated and fundamental freedoms of the individual. They are essential for the exercise of many other rights. None are absolute in the sense that their exercise may never be restricted. International law provides the grounds on which each freedom may be required to be balanced against the rights of others or broader community interests. In the first instance it is national authorities that have to carry out the careful balancing act. But international law also offers principles to safeguard against abuse of restrictions by the state. Freedom of thought includes freedom of conscience, religion, or belief. Freedom of expression includes freedom of opinion and freedom of information. Media freedom is also protected in international human rights law as essential for the enjoyment of freedom of expression. Freedom of association concerns the right to establish autonomous organizations through which individuals pursue common interests together. The right of assembly protects non-violent, organized, temporary gatherings in public and private, both indoors and outdoors.

1 INTRODUCTION

1.1 FOUR FREEDOMS AND THEIR RELATIONSHIPS

The freedoms of thought, expression, association, and assembly, often described as fundamental freedoms, are closely related civil and political rights. The guarantee of each is necessary for the enjoyment of the other and indeed for the exercise of many human rights. Thus, freedom of expression is necessary if freedom of thought is to be exercised. In turn, freedom of expression has little meaning without the individual having freedom to think and have an opinion. The right to practise or to teach a religion includes the freedom to publish religious literature or broadcast religious programmes. If religious communities or denominations are to exist, their freedom of association is essential, as is their right to assemble for religious purposes. Freedom of expression is essential when people come together to pursue their interests through other associations, such as trade unions, political parties, or community groups. The European Court of Human Rights has defined one of the objectives of the freedom of association as the protection of opinions and the freedom to express them.[1] Freedom of expression is essential also to the freedom to assemble and the right to demonstrate over grievances. Thus, while each freedom is distinct in theory, in practice they are interrelated and interdependent.

The consecutive location of the freedoms in all international human rights texts, beginning with the Universal Declaration of Human Rights (UDHR), reflects their complementary nature. Article 18 UDHR proclaims freedom of thought, conscience, religion, or belief, Article 19 freedom of opinion and expression, and Article 20 the freedoms of association and assembly. Each of the freedoms is pivotal for the individual's right to democratic participation, a right proclaimed in Article 21 UDHR. Each freedom needs also to be understood as integrating the right to equality and non-discrimination in Article 2 UDHR. Denials of the freedoms often occur in the context of discriminatory policies directed at particular groups or minorities, for example religious or ethnic minorities.

Each freedom, as defined in international law, is expressed as a freedom of the individual but also has a collective dimension. Thus, Article 18 UDHR provides that freedom of thought, religion, or belief is to be enjoyed 'alone or in communion with others'. Freedom of expression includes not only the right of a speaker to communicate with others but the right of others to hear what the speaker has to say. By definition, the freedoms of association and assembly concern the collective activities of individuals.

1.2 LIMITATIONS

A common feature of these freedoms is that none is unconditional in the sense that its exercise by the individual or group cannot be limited by the state. International human rights standards set out the grounds of permitted limitation or restriction. Two categories of restriction are envisaged. First, the freedoms may legitimately be regulated by law to protect the rights and freedoms of others. Second, restriction may be justified for different public interest reasons, namely, public order, health, morality, or national security. The constant challenge arising in practice is how to strike a balance, which is acceptable in a democratic society, between the right to exercise the freedom, on the one hand, and the need to protect the rights of others and the public interest, on the other hand. The factual and legal contexts are always critical.[2] The European Court of Human Rights explicitly affords states a margin of appreciation in applying restrictions, albeit ultimately subject to European supervision.[3] Other international human rights bodies have not expressly adopted that doctrine—indeed the Human Rights Committee has explicitly rejected it, but in practice it may offer something similar.[4]

Most violations of these freedoms arise over patently unjustified restrictions by governments. The killing of journalists, prior censorship, censorship of the Internet, or the arbitrary banning of political movements or religious denominations occur with depressing frequency. But, even where these freedoms are broadly respected, difficult questions can arise over how to respond to direct conflict between the freedoms themselves or with other rights. In the case of the news media, for example, conflict arises on a daily basis between freedom of the press and the right to privacy. The tensions and misunderstandings which can arise between freedom of religion and freedom of expression were

---

[1] *Ouranio Toxo and Others v Greece* (2007) 45 EHRR 8, para 35.
[2] *Frumkin v Russia* (2016) 63 EHRR 18.   [3] See Chapter 5.
[4] McGoldrick, 'A Defence of the Margin of Appreciation and an Argument for its Application by the Human Rights Committee' (2016) 65 *ICLQ* 21.

vividly demonstrated in the worldwide controversy over the publication of cartoons of the Prophet Mohammad in a Danish newspaper in 2005.[5] Another contemporary example concerns the display of religious symbols or wearing of religious dress (see Section 2.4). In summary, a society which enjoys the freedoms under discussion is not one in which there are no restrictions on their exercise. It is rather one in which the boundaries of freedom are openly debated and democratically resolved under the rule of law.

Limitations will be discussed further as regards each freedom but some general principles applicable to all can be set out here:[6]

- *Legality*: any limitation on a freedom must be 'prescribed by' or be 'in accordance' with the 'law'. A restriction cannot be legitimate where it is the arbitrary whim of an official. The source of the national law may be a legislative or administrative measure, or a judicial ruling. The law must set out the ground of restriction in clear and precise terms so that it is both accessible and foreseeable.

- *Legitimate aim*: the interference or restriction must follow a legitimate purpose, that is, be based on one of the exhaustive grounds of limitation listed in the international standards which define the particular freedom.

- *Necessary in a democratic society*: the restrictions must correspond to a pressing social need, be justified by decisions that give relevant and sufficient reasoning, and be *proportionate* to the legitimate aim pursued. Any restrictive measure should be the minimum required to achieve the purpose of the limitation in a democratic society. States must choose the means that cause the least possible prejudice to the rights in question.

- *Presumption of freedom*: freedom is the rule, its limitation the exception. Restrictions are to be narrowly construed and convincingly justified.[7] Thus one should start with a strong presumption in favour of the freedom in question. The onus is on the authorities in the particular case to show that it is legitimate to restrict it. Blanket, indiscriminate restrictions will always be closely scrutinized. The situation is more complicated when two human rights have to be balanced. In such situations the rights may be of presumptively equal weight and an intensive factual and contextual analysis will be required.

The following sections consider, in turn, the right to freedom of thought (Section 2), freedom of expression (Section 3), freedom of association (Section 4), and freedom of assembly (Section 5). Each section explains the sources of the respective right, its scope, and the limitations that can be imposed on it.

2 FREEDOM OF THOUGHT, CONSCIENCE, AND RELIGION

2.1 SOURCES

This freedom is enshrined in Article 18 UDHR and in Article 18 of the International Covenant on Civil and Political Rights (ICCPR) as well as its Article 27 concerning the rights of minorities. It is also to be found in all regional human rights instruments.[8] The equality and non-discrimination provisions of the ICCPR (Articles 2, 3, and 26) and their

---

[5] eg *Ahmad and Abdol-Hamid v Denmark*, CCPR/C/92/D/1487/2006 (18 April 2008).

[6] See the analysis of Art 19(3) ICCPR, in Report of the Special Rapporteur on the Promotion and Protection of the Right to Freedom of Opinion and Expression, A/71/373 (6 September 2016). See also Chapter 5.

[7] *Sunday Times v UK* (1979) 2 EHRR 245, para 65.

[8] ECHR, Art 9; Protocol 1 to the ECHR, Art 2; CFREU, Art 10; ACHR, Art 12; ACHPR, Art 8; Arab Charter, Art 30; ASEAN Declaration, Art 22.

equivalents in the regional instruments are vital for the enjoyment of the freedom as they prohibit unjustified differential treatment on the basis of religion. In 1993 the Human Rights Committee adopted a General Comment on the scope and meaning of Article 18 ICCPR.[9] No international human rights treaty specifically devoted to freedom of thought, conscience, and religion has ever been adopted. However, an important Declaration was agreed by the UN General Assembly in 1981,[10] which provides the mandate of the Special Rapporteur on freedom of religion or belief, who is appointed by the UN Human Rights Council.[11]

2.2 SCOPE

Article 18 UDHR proclaims:

> Everyone has the right to freedom of thought, conscience and religion; this right includes freedom to change his religion or belief, and freedom, either alone or in community with others and in public or private, to manifest his religion or belief in teaching, practice, worship and observance.

The UDHR by its nature could not specify fully the substance of this freedom in international law. That came with the drafting of Article 18 ICCPR. The predominant focus of both texts is on freedom of religion. However, the scope of the right is wider. It protects freedom of thought, that is, the right of the individual to have independent thoughts, ideas, and beliefs. This includes, for instance, an individual's right not to have to accept a political ideology or a religion with which he or she disagrees. Freedom of conscience, the individual's moral sense of right and wrong, is also explicitly recognized and protected. One common instance, considered in Section 2.4, in which this freedom is invoked arises where a citizen refuses on grounds of conscience to undertake compulsory military service. Finally, Article 18(4) ICCPR offers specific safeguards against the indoctrination of children by the state. It establishes a duty on the state to respect the liberty of parents or guardians to determine the religious and moral education of their children in conformity with their own convictions. The child's right to freedom of thought, conscience, and religion is provided for in the Convention on the Rights of the Child (CRC) though it is accompanied by an obligation to respect the rights and duties of the parents and, when applicable, legal guardians, to provide direction to the child in the exercise of his or her right in a manner consistent with the evolving capacities of the child.[12]

2.3 FREEDOM OF RELIGION OR BELIEF

While freedom of religion is the central concern of Article 18 ICCPR, that provision speaks of 'religion or belief', thus underlining the intention of the drafters that all beliefs, including beliefs other than religious, are protected. The Human Rights Committee has confirmed this understanding in its General Comment: 'Article 18 protects theistic, non-theistic and atheistic beliefs, as well as the right not to profess any religion or belief.'[13]

There is no definition of religion offered in any international human rights instrument. It is probably impossible for states to agree a definition given the sheer diversity of religious ideas in the world. However, the significance of religion as one of the 'fundamental

---

[9] HRC, General Comment 22, HRI/GEN/1/Rev 9 (Vol I) 204.

[10] Declaration on the Elimination of All Forms of Intolerance and Discrimination Based on Religion or Belief, GA Res 36/55 (25 November 1981).

[11] HR Council Res 22/20 (12 April 2013). See Wiener, 'The Mandate of the Special Rapporteur on Freedom of Religion or Belief—Institutional, Procedural and Substantive Legal Issues' (2007) 2 *Religion and HR* 3.

[12] CRC, Arts 14(1) and (2). See Interim Report of the Special Rapporteur on Freedom of Religion or Belief, A/70/286 (5 August 2015).   [13] HRC, General Comment 22, para 2.

elements in [the] conception of life' for believers is recognized in international human rights law.[14] Freedom of religion is an individual right but has a collective aspect also. It means the right to hold spiritual beliefs and *to live by them*, whether in private or in public, alone or in community with others. The Human Rights Committee has stated that the term religion or belief is to be broadly construed. It is not limited to traditional religions.[15] New religions are as entitled to protection as old ones. But there are limits. For example, the Committee thought it inconceivable that the cultivation and worship of a narcotic drug could be a protected religion or belief under Article 18 ICCPR.[16]

2.3.1 Manifestation of religion

Article 18 ICCPR speaks of the right to manifest religion through 'worship, observance, practice and teaching'. The Human Rights Committee has offered guidance as to the wide range of activities encompassed by these words:

> The concept of *worship* extends to ritual and ceremonial acts giving direct expression to belief, as well as various practices integral to such acts, including the building of places of worship, the use of ritual formulae and objects, the display of symbols, and the observance of holidays and days of rest. The *observance and practice* of religion or belief may include not only ceremonial acts but also such customs as the observance of dietary regulations, the wearing of distinctive clothing or head coverings, participation in rituals associated with certain stages of life, and the use of a particular language customarily spoken by a group. In addition, the *practice and teaching* of religion or belief includes acts integral to the conduct by religious groups of their basic affairs, such as the freedom to choose their religious leaders, priests and teachers, the freedom to establish seminaries or religious schools and the freedom to prepare and distribute religious texts or publications.[17]

Practices that are merely *motivated* by religious belief are not protected. There must be an intimate connection between the act and the belief. The existence of a sufficiently close and direct nexus between the act and the underlying belief must be determined on the facts of each case but it is not necessary to establish that the individual acted in fulfilment of a duty mandated by the religion in question.[18] The freedom to manifest one's religion includes the right not to be obliged to disclose one's religion.[19]

2.3.2 Freedom to change religion or belief

It follows from the freedom of thought and conscience that one may decide to change one's beliefs. The individual's right to change or choose religious belief is contested particularly by the Islamic faith. In some Muslim majority countries conversion from Islam to another religion (but not the reverse) constitutes the offence of apostasy, which in some cases is punishable by death. Freedom to change a religion or belief is stated explicitly in Article 18 UDHR. However, reflecting Muslim sensitivities over the issue,[20] Article 18 ICCPR

---

[14] 1981 Declaration, preamble.   [15] HRC, General Comment 22, para 2.

[16] *MAB, WAT and JAYT v Canada*, CCPR/C/50/D570/1993 (25 April 1994). Compare, *Prince v South Africa*, CCPR/C/91/D/1474/2006 (14 November 2007).

[17] HRC, General Comment 22, para 4 (emphases added). See also Bielefeldt, Ghanea, and Wiener, *Freedom of Religion or Belief—An International Law Commentary* (OUP, 2016).

[18] *Eweida and Others v UK* (2013) 57 EHRR 8, para 82.   [19] *Işik v Turkey* (2015) 61 EHRR 6.

[20] Boyle, 'Freedom of Religion in International Law' in Rehman and Breau (eds), *Religion, Human Rights and International Law* (Brill, 2007) 37–40; Khaliq, 'Freedom of Religion and Belief in International Law: a Comparative Analysis', in Emon, Ellis, and Glahn (eds), *Islamic Law and International Human Rights Law* (OUP, 2012) 183–225.

speaks of 'freedom to have or to adopt a religion or belief of his choice'. Despite this difference of language, the Human Rights Committee has confirmed that Article 18 guarantees that anyone may replace a current religion with another religion or become an atheist.[21] States must respect this right by abolishing state-sanctioned punishments for conversion and ensuring that there are no administrative obstacles to changing religion. There is also a positive obligation to protect individuals from harassment or violence from third parties that arises as a consequence of conversion.

2.3.3 Proselytism

Article 18(2) ICCPR stipulates that there must be no coercion of the individual in the decision to either retain or change beliefs. Subject to this prohibition on forced conversion, the right to spread one's faith and to seek to persuade others to convert to it is protected as a manifestation of religion.[22] Proselytism or missionary activity by religious groups is, however, a controversial matter. Conversion from Islam is prohibited, and in India several states have passed anti-conversion laws aimed primarily at inhibiting conversion from Hinduism to Christianity. Some religious communities, inter-faith organizations, and NGOs have proposed various voluntary codes of conduct for religious conversion.[23]

2.3.4 Religion and the state

International human rights law does not require a separation between religion and the state. Such separation is to be found in the constitutional arrangements of many states, following the long-established examples of France and the US. But in other states the relationships range from fusion of state and religion to formal recognition in law of the majority faith. The sole principles on religion and the state that international human rights law insists upon are those of pluralism and non-discrimination. Thus, the existence of a state church should not entail the suppression of, or discrimination against, minority faiths or new religions.[24] It is the duty of the state to defend religious diversity in a democratic society, and to insist on the values of pluralism and tolerance should tensions arise from the coexistence of different faiths or beliefs.[25] The European Court of Human Rights has held that for democracy to function properly, the state must remain neutral and impartial in its relations with various religions, denominations, and beliefs.[26] The right to freedom of religion normally excludes any assessment by the state of the legitimacy of religious beliefs or their means of expression.[27] In states that require the registration of religions to give legal status to a denomination, neither the law nor its application should discriminate between religions by refusing, for example, to register some faiths while recognizing others.[28] All religions must have the freedom to establish communities or organizations and these should be autonomous in their

---

[21] HRC, General Comment 22, para 5.

[22] *Kokkinakis v Greece* (1994) 17 EHRR 397; *Sister Immaculate Joseph v Sri Lanka*, CCPR/C/85/D/1249/2004 (18 November 2005).

[23] See Richards, Svendsen, and Bless, 'Voluntary Codes of Conduct for Religious Persuasion: Effective Tools for Balancing Human Rights and Resolving Conflicts?' (2011) 6 *Religion and HR* 151; Report of the Special Rapporteur on Freedom of Religion or Belief, A/67/303 (13 August 2012).

[24] HRC, General Comment 22, para 9.

[25] *Serif v Greece* (1999) 31 EHRR 561; *Metropolitan Church of Bessarabia and others v Moldova* (2002) 35 EHRR 306.

[26] *Hasan and Chaush v Bulgaria* (2002) 34 EHRR 1339; *Magyar Keresztény Mennonita Egyház and Others v Hungary* (2015) 61 EHRR 23.   [27] *Hasan and Chaush*, para 78.

[28] *Metropolitan Church of Bessarabia.*

activities. Autonomy includes determining their own leadership without interference from the state.[29] Autonomy can also weigh heavily when balanced against individuals relying on other human rights against religious bodies.

While there may be exceptional cases,[30] the state has no general authority to decide whether or not a religion is legitimate. In *Moscow Branch of the Salvation Army v Russia*, the branch was refused registration by the city authorities. The authorities claimed that it was a paramilitary organization because of the word 'army' in its name and because its members wore uniforms and had ranks similar to those used in the military.[31] The branch complained to the European Court of Human Rights, which found a violation of its freedom of association in the context of the guarantee of freedom of religion. The Court emphasized that the guarantee of freedom of religion meant the state had no discretion to decide whether religious beliefs or the means used to manifest them were legitimate. It could not be credibly argued that the Salvation Army advocated the violent overthrow of the constitution or threatened the security of the state.

2.4 LIMITATIONS

2.4.1 *Forum internum* and *forum externum*

An important distinction is to be drawn between those dimensions of the freedom of re-ligion or belief which may be subject to limitation and those which may never be limited. Under Article 18(3) ICCPR it is the manifestation of the freedom of religion or belief in 'worship, observance, practice and teaching' (the *forum externum*) which may be lim-ited. The individual's freedom of thought, conscience, religion, or belief (*forum internum*), guaranteed in Article 18(1), must be respected by the state unconditionally, and that in-cludes the freedom to have or adopt a religion or belief of one's choice. Thus, no one may be compelled to reveal his or her thoughts or beliefs, for example by a requirement to swear a religious oath or to carry a religious affiliation in an identity card.[32]

2.4.2 Grounds of limitation

Manifestation of religious belief may be limited on the grounds set out in Article 18(3) ICCPR: 'public safety, order, health, or morals or the fundamental rights and freedoms of others'. National security, however, is not included as a permissible ground in the case of freedom of religion, whereas it is a permissible ground with the other freedoms. As explained already, any restriction applied on one of the permitted grounds must be pre-scribed by law and be necessary in a democratic society. Many cases ultimately turn on the proportionality of the particular restriction or its discriminatory application.

Religious clothing and symbols

A contemporary and complex issue regarding religious manifestation concerns regula-tion of the wearing of religious dress or symbols in public spaces, which amounts to an interference with the believer's freedom to express their religious beliefs or identity. For example, the injunction to women in the Koran of *Hijab* or modesty is the religious source of the headscarf or the *burka* worn by some Muslim women. International human rights bodies have taken different positions as to whether the wearing of the veil in public may be restricted by the state. They all agree that such restrictions are an interference

---

[29] *Hasan and Chaush*. It can also justify restrictions on access to justice. See *Nagy v Hungary*, App no 56665/09, Judgment of 14 September 2017.   [30] eg *MAB, WAT and JAYT*.   [31] (2006) 44 EHRR 912.
[32] HRC, General Comment 22, para 3; *Buscarini and Others v San Marino* (2000) 30 EHRR 208; *Alexandridis v Greece*, App no 19516/06, Judgment of 21 February 2008.

with the right to manifest religious belief but differ on whether such interferences can be justified.

If there is evidence that individuals present a threat to public order or that they have been involved in proselytism by exerting inappropriate pressure on passers-by, then a restriction on religious dress could be legitimate.[33] Greater regulation of the wearing of religious symbols in public may be permissible on the basis that state secularism or religious neutrality can take precedence over the right to manifest one's religion. A small number of states have banned any kind of face-covering in public. The ban is a general one but particularly impacts Muslim women who wear the *burqa* or the *niqab*. In *SAS v France* the European Court upheld such a ban on the basis that 'living together' was a legitimate dimension of 'the rights of others' that could justify limitations on freedom of religion.[34]

The Human Rights Committee found that the exclusion from a university in Uzbekistan of a practising Muslim student for wearing a headscarf interfered with her rights under Article 18 ICCPR.[35] The Committee held in line with its General Comment[36] that the freedom to manifest her religion encompasses the right to wear clothes or attire in public that was in conformity with her religion. In light of little evidence suggesting the restriction was justified, the Committee was also of the view that her exclusion from studies amounted to a violation of her right to be free from coercion in matters of religion under Article 18(2). In contrast, in *Leyla Sahin v Turkey*, the European Court of Human Rights upheld a similar Turkish regulation which prevented the applicant from continuing her medical studies at Istanbul University because she refused to remove her headscarf on religious grounds.[37] The majority of the judges considered that the interference with her religious freedom was justified in the interests of the rights and freedoms of others, which it linked to the Turkish constitutional principles of equality and secularism.[38]

Issues regarding regulation of religious dress are not limited to Islamic dress. In 2004 a French law banned the wearing of conspicuous religious symbols in state schools invoking the constitutional principle of secularism. The law prohibited not only the Islamic veil but also Jewish skullcaps, Sikh turbans, and Christian crosses. The European Court of Human Rights rejected complaints over this law brought by several Muslim girl pupils and Sikh boys over their expulsion from school. The children had worn substitute headwear, kerchiefs in the case of the girls and under-turbans in the case of the boys, which they refused to remove.[39] Noting that the pupils could still continue their schooling by correspondence courses, the Court found that the interference with their freedom to manifest their religion was justified and proportionate to the aims pursued, namely the rights and freedoms of others and public order. However, the Human Rights Committee took a different view in a communication based on similar facts, holding that expulsion could neither be considered necessary nor proportionate.[40] Where international human rights bodies take such different positions, states are put in a difficult position.[41]

---

[33] *Ahmet Arslan and Others v Turkey*, App no 41135/98, Judgment of 23 February 2010.

[34] (2015) 60 EHRR 11; followed in *Belkacemi and Oussar v Belgium*, App no 37798/13, *Dakir v Belgium*, App no 4619/12, Judgments of 11 July 2017. See Trispiotis, 'Two Interpretations of "Living Together" in European Human Rights Law' (2016) 58 *CLJ* 580.

[35] *Hudoyberganova v Uzbekistan*, CCPR/C/82/D/931/2000 (5 November 2004).

[36] See HRC, General Comment 22.   [37] (2007) 44 EHRR 5.

[38] Turkey has subsequently relaxed the restrictions on wearing headscarves.

[39] *Aktas v France, Bayrak v France, Gamaleddyn v France, Ghazal v France, J Singh v France, R Singh v France*, App nos 43563/08, 14308/08, 18527/08, 29134/08, 25463/08, and 27561/08, Admissibility Decision of 17 July 2009.   [40] *Singh v France*, CCPR/C/106/D/1852/2008 (4 February 2013).

[41] See McGoldrick (2016).

The Human Rights Committee has also held that a requirement for a Sikh man to appear bareheaded in an identity card photograph constitutes a continuing interference with his right to freedom of religion. The Committee noted that:

> even if the obligation to remove the turban for the identity photograph might be described as a one-time requirement, it would potentially interfere with the author's freedom of religion on a continuing basis because he would always appear without his religious head covering in the identity photograph and could therefore be compelled to remove his turban during identity checks.[42]

In some Muslim majority countries it is compulsory for all women to wear a veil, even if they are not Muslims. Such a requirement may also violate the freedom of religion. A human rights approach would argue that it should be for the individual to decide whether to wear religious dress or not. States should respect and seek to accommodate that choice.

Where restrictions upon religious dress in the workplace were imposed by a private company, the European Court has confirmed that the state still has a duty to ensure that a 'fair balance' is struck between the interests of the individual and those of the company.[43]

While religious clothing has been widely litigated, the presence of religious symbols (crucifixes) in Italian schools was challenged in *Lautsi v Italy*. The European Court of Human Rights held that there had been no violation of Article 2 (right to education) of Protocol No. 1, and that no separate issue arose under Article 9 ECHR.[44] It found in particular that the question of religious symbols in classrooms was, in principle, a matter falling within the margin of appreciation of the state—particularly as there was no European consensus as regards that question—provided that decisions in that area did not lead to a form of indoctrination.

Conscientious objection to military service

In a number of states, conscription laws require that male adult citizens (in the case of Israel females also) have a legal duty to undertake a period of military training or service. For some individuals such a duty conflicts with their conscience due to their religious or philosophical beliefs, and they assert the right to refuse to undertake military service. International human rights standards are evolving in the direction of accepting that such refusal is a manifestation of the individual's conscience and should be protected under the guarantee of freedom of thought, conscience, and religion. Indeed, the Human Rights Committee's interpretation of the right to conscientious objection to military service has evolved from not being protected at all to it being an absolute element of freedom of conscience under Article 18(1) which is not capable of limitation under Article 18(3) ICCPR.[45] States may, instead, require individuals to undertake alternative service. However, this service must not be punitive in nature. Rather, it must be a real service to the community and compatible with respect for human rights.[46] Similarly, the European Union Charter of Fundamental Rights and Freedoms (CFREU) recognizes a right to conscientious objection to military service.[47] All member states of the Council of Europe, except Turkey, have recognized such

---

[42] *Ranjit Singh v France*, CCPR/C/102/D/1876/2009 (27 September 2011) para 8.4.

[43] *Eweida and Others*.

[44] (2012) 54 EHRR 3. See McGoldrick, 'Religion in the European Public Square and in European Public Life' (2011) 11 *HRLR* 451.

[45] HRC, General Comment 22, para 11; *Yoon and Choi v Republic of Korea*, CCPR/C/88/D/1321–1322/2004 (23 January 2007); *Atasoy and Sartuk v Turkey* CCPR/C/104/D/1853–1854/2008 (29 March 2012). The right to conscientious objection to military service has been recognized also by other UN bodies. See CHR Res 1998/77 (22 April 1998); UN Working Group on Arbitrary Detention, Recommendation 2, E/CN.4/2001/14, paras 91–4; OHCHR, *Conscientious Objection to Military Service* (2012).

[46] *Jeong et al. v Republic of Korea*, CCPRC/C/101/D/1642–1741/2007 (24 March 2011).

[47] CFREU, Art 10.

a right. In *Bayatyan v Armenia*, the European Court of Human Rights relied upon this consensus when holding that opposition to military service, where it is motivated by a person's conscience or his deeply and genuinely held religious or other beliefs, constitutes a conviction or belief of sufficient cogency, seriousness, cohesion, and importance to attract the guarantees of Article 9 ECHR.[48] Thus compulsory military service can only be justified where convincing and compelling reasons suggest that there is a pressing social need for conscription. By contrast, the Inter-American Commission on Human Rights has declined to accept that obligatory military service may conflict with freedom of conscience.[49]

3 FREEDOM OF OPINION AND EXPRESSION

3.1 SOURCES

This freedom is contained in Article 19 UDHR and in Articles 19 and 20 ICCPR. Detailed and authoritative guidance on states' obligations under these provisions can be found in the Human Rights Committee's General Comment 34.[50] Similar but not identical formulations of the freedom can be found in the regional human rights instruments.[51] There are also important provisions in the International Convention on the Elimination of Racial Discrimination (ICERD), in particular Article 4, which concerns the prohibition of racist speech and organizations. The CRC recognizes the child's right to freedom of expression.[52] Since 1993 there exists the position of the Special Rapporteur on the promotion and protection of the right to freedom of opinion and expression, who is now appointed by the Human Rights Council.[53]

3.2 SCOPE

Freedom of expression has been described as the touchstone or cornerstone of all rights.[54] Not only is freedom of expression inseparable from freedom of thought, association, and assembly, it is essential for the enjoyment of many rights, including economic, social, and cultural rights. It is a vital freedom for individual development, the functioning of democracy, and modern economies.

Article 19 UDHR provides the foundation for the fuller definition of the freedom in the ICCPR:

> Everyone has the right to freedom of opinion and expression; this right includes freedom to hold opinions without interference and to seek, receive and impart information and ideas through any media and regardless of frontiers.

Although this text was drafted over 60 years ago, it powerfully expresses the ideal of freedom of speech in today's era of the Internet and other digital communication technologies. Freedom of expression is an individual right. It includes the freedom, without interference or penalty, to hold opinions. Freedom of expression also has its collective components.

---

[48] (2012) 54 EHRR 15.

[49] Case 12.219, *Cristián Daniel Sahli Vera et al. v Chile*, IACommHR Report No 43/05 (10 March 2005).

[50] HRC, General Comment 34, CCPR/C/GC/34 (12 September 2011).

[51] ECHR, Art 10; CFREU, Art 11; ACHR, Arts 13 and 14; ACHPR, Art 9; Arab Charter, Art 32; ASEAN Declaration, Art 23.   [52] Arts 12 and 13.

[53] HR Council Res 16/4 (8 April 2011).

[54] *Handyside v UK* (1976) 1 EHRR 737; *Compulsory Membership in an Association Prescribed by Law for the Practice of Journalism*, IACtHR Series A No 5 (13 November 1985).

Human beings communicate with others, not with themselves. The freedom includes the right to hear other views and to exchange ideas and information with others. It also includes the right to inform oneself, to be informed, and increasingly the right to access information. Hence the crucial importance of all media as means of communication.

3.2.1 Freedom of opinion

Article 19 ICCPR guarantees freedom of opinion as well as expression. Human beings have diverse and differing opinions on all kinds of subjects, including political and social affairs. Article 19(1) provides that everyone is entitled to hold such views without interference. No one can be forced to think in a particular way. Nor should anyone suffer prejudice, discrimination, or repression because of their views or opinions. The freedom to hold opinions may not be restricted. In the words of the Human Rights Committee: 'it is a right to which the Covenant admits no exception or restriction.'[55] In other words people may think what they like.

3.2.2 Freedom of expression

Article 19(2) ICCPR sets out the positive meaning of freedom of expression under international law. Its scope is extensive. The right is defined as including freedom to seek, receive, and impart information and ideas of all kinds. Freedom *to seek* includes active and investigative journalism in the public interest. Freedom *to receive* has been interpreted by the European Court of Human Rights as including the right of the public to be informed and the duty of the mass media to impart information to the public.[56] The freedom to *impart* extends to every kind of information and idea expressed through any media of choice, 'either orally, in writing or in print, [or] in the form of art'.[57] As the European Court has noted, the freedom 'is applicable not only to "information" or "ideas" that are favourably received or regarded as inoffensive or as a matter of indifference, but also to those that offend, shock or disturb the State or any sector of the population.'[58]

All forms of expression are protected. These include spoken and written language, satire, as well as art and images, including caricature and cartoons. The manner in which these are transmitted, that is through fictional and non-fictional books, newspapers, the Internet, leaflets, film, paintings, sculpture, song, and so on, is also protected.

The Internet

The Internet has become 'one of the principal means by which individuals exercise their right to freedom of expression and information; it provides essential tools for taking part in activities and discussions concerning political issues or matters of public interest.'[59] In 2011 a Joint Declaration on Freedom of Expression and the Internet was adopted by the UN Special Rapporteur on freedom of expression and Special Rapporteurs on freedom of expression from the Organization of American States, the Organization for Security and Cooperation in Europe, and the African Commission on Human and Peoples' Rights. The Declaration sets out that freedom of expression must apply to the Internet in the same way that it applies to any other media.[60] However, it has been recognized that the Internet is different from the printed press and poses greater risks for the enjoyment of the rights

---

[55] HRC, General Comment 34, para 9.
[56] *Thorgeir Thorgeirson v Iceland* (1992) 14 EHRR 843, para 63.   [57] ICCPR, Art 19(2).
[58] *Handyside*, para 49. See also *Ivcher-Bronstein v Peru*, IACtHR Series C No 74 (6 June 2001).
[59] *Yildirim v Turkey*, App no 3111/10, Judgment of 18 December 2012, para 54.
[60] Available at: <http://www.oas.org/en/iachr/expression/showarticle.asp?artID=848&lID=1>. See also, Report of the Special Rapporteur on the promotion and protection of the right to freedom of expression and opinion, A/HRC/17/27 (16 May 2011); HRC, General Comment 34, para 15.

THOUGHT, EXPRESSION, ASSOCIATION, AND ASSEMBLY   219

of others, particularly young people.[61] Duties and responsibilities are placed on the owners and controllers of Internet portals to exercise a degree of control over content. The duties and responsibilities will be heavier where economic interests of commercial organizations are involved and lighter if non-profit organizations are involved.[62]

There is a developing human right to access the Internet. Given the increasing importance of the Internet in daily lives, particularly in terms of participation, facilitating governmental transparency, and access to diverse sources of information, it is arguable that the positive obligations of states to promote and facilitate the right to freedom of expression must include facilitating access to the Internet.[63]

Freedom of expression is to be enjoyed 'without regards to frontiers', in other words it does not stop at the borders of the state. This clause was intended to outlaw forms of censorship such as the Cold War practice of radio jamming of foreign broadcast signals and extends in today's digital age, for example, to the blocking of access to the Internet or mobile phones. So, completely blocking access to the Internet during times of social unrest, as took place during the anti-government protests arising in various countries in the Arab world in 2011, known as the Arab Spring, or the blocking of content of particular websites, such as YouTube, Facebook, or Twitter, constitute interferences with the right.

3.2.3 Media freedom

There is no explicit recognition or protection offered to the press and other media in international human rights standards, although such is often to be found in national laws and constitutions. At the international level, the freedoms and responsibilities of the press have been developed from the guarantee of freedom of expression of the individual. The protection afforded under human rights standards to all media—modern mass electronic and print media and the new information communication technologies—is justified because of their role in making people's freedom of expression meaningful and their contribution to democratic life. All such means of communication provide access to news and to opportunities to exchange information and ideas. International and national standards on freedom of expression have largely been shaped by the struggle for journalistic and artistic independence against government licensing and censorship of media. That struggle continues in different parts of the world. Media freedom is thus inseparable in practice from the enjoyment of freedom of expression in society. The media has a watchdog role on the exercise of power in society, and free media facilitates political debate. As the European Court of Human Rights has put it:

> Freedom of the press affords the public one of the best means of discovering and forming an opinion of the ideas and attitudes of political leaders. In particular it gives politicians the opportunity to reflect and comment on the preoccupations of public opinion; it thus enables everyone to participate in the free political debate which is at the core of the concept of a democratic society.[64]

States must, therefore, protect journalists from threats, violence, or other acts of harassment that stop them from fulfilling this essential role.[65] Human rights bodies have adopted

---

[61] See *Editorial Board of Pravoye and Shtekel v Ukraine* (2014) 58 EHRR 28; *KU v Finland* (2009) 48 EHRR 52; (protection of minors); *Perrin v UK*, App no 5446/03, Admissibility Decision of 18 October 2005 (morals and the rights of others).

[62] *Delfi AS v Estonia* (2016) 62 EHRR 6; *Magyar Tartalomszolgáltatók Egyesülete and Index.hu Zrt v Hungary*, App no 22947/13, Judgment of 2 February 2016.

[63] See Report of the Special Rapporteur on the promotion and protection of the right to freedom of opinion and expression, A/66/290 (10 August 2011), paras 61–63; Tully, 'A Human Right to Access the Internet? Problems and Prospects' (2014) 14 *HRLR* 175.   [64] *Castells v Spain* (1992) 14 EHRR 445, para 43.

[65] HRC, General Comment 34, para 23; *Vélez Restrepo v Colombia* IACtHR Series C No 248 (3 September 2012) para 209.

an expansive definition of the term 'journalists', which includes: 'professional full-time reporters and analysts, as well as bloggers and others who engage in forms of self-publication in print, on the Internet or elsewhere'.[66] The duties and responsibilities on journalists include that they must investigate in a rigorous, objective, and balanced manner, although the methods of doing this may vary depending on the media in question.[67] However, journalistic freedom also includes possible recourse to a degree of exaggeration or even provocation. Concerning Internet discussion sites, the European Court has held that the limit of admissible criticism is broad where the comments are those of professional journalists who are well-known to the public and are commenting on matters of general interest.[68]

But media in all its forms is also a source of considerable power, including economic power. The international standards speak, therefore, of the media's duties and responsibilities.[69] Media regulation is necessary to ensure the effective protection of freedom of expression,[70] democratic accountability, and to guard against excessive concentration of ownership. Regulatory regimes, whether self-regulation or established by legislation, will differ according to different media because they impact these interests differently. Thus, public, private, or community broadcasting systems and the print or Internet media will often be subject to different regulatory codes which may be state or non-state based or a hybrid form. But all such regulatory systems should protect editorial freedom, promote plurality of the media, and operate independently of government.

3.2.4 Freedom of information laws

The most striking advance in the norms on freedom of expression over recent years has been the growth of laws implementing the right to access official information held by governments. Democracies, both new and old, have come to understand that transparency affords governments and public administration legitimacy in the eyes of the public. In all regions of the world, governments have established 'the right to know' through legislation. An 'access to information law' works on the principle of maximum disclosure: all official information should be made public as a matter of principle, unless there are legitimate reasons justifying non-disclosure. In 2009, the Council of Europe adopted the first international treaty on the subject: the Council of Europe Convention on Access to Official Documents.

In *Claude Reyes and others v Chile* the Inter-American Court of Human Rights became the first international tribunal to hold that there is a right to access information held by the government, derived from the guarantee of freedom of expression.[71] The case originated in a request for information made by three environmental activists about a controversial deforestation project, which was ignored by the government. The Human Rights Committee has confirmed that states must 'proactively put in the public domain Government information of public interest . . . [and] enact the necessary procedures, whereby one may gain access to information, such as by means for freedom of information legislation.'[72] However, the European Court of Human Rights has suggested that there is no positive obligation on the state to collect and disseminate information of its own

---

[66] HRC, General Comment 34, para 44; Report of the Special Rapporteur on the promotion and protection of the right to freedom of opinion and expression, A/HRC/20/17 (4 June 2012).

[67] *Delfi*, para 134.

[68] *Niskasaari and Otavamedia Oy v Finland*, App no 32297/10, Judgment of 23 June 2015, paras 9 and 54–59.

[69] On standards of responsible journalism see *De Carolis and France Televisions v France*, App no 29313/10, Judgment of 21 January 2016.   [70] See *Editorial Board of Pravoye Delo*.

[71] IACtHR Series C No 151 (19 September 2006). See also *Társaság a Szabadságjogokért v Hungary* (2011) 53 EHRR 3.

[72] HRC, General Comment 34, para 19. See also *Toktakunov v Kyrgyzstan*, CCPR//C/101/D/1470/2006 (28 March 2011).

motion.[73] The Court also indicated that Article 10 ECHR only obliges the government to impart information to an individual where access to the information is instrumental for the individual's exercise of his or her right to freedom of expression.

3.3 LIMITATIONS

If people may think what they like, they may not always say or write what they like. As opposed to freedom of opinion, freedom of expression is not an absolute right. Under Article 19(3) ICCPR its exercise carries with it 'special duties and responsibilities'. Such language acknowledges the power of the media, but also the justification of restriction where it is necessary to respect the rights or reputations of others, and where it is necessary on grounds of national security, public order, public health, or morals. It is possible to examine only some of these grounds here. But as discussed already, it is crucial how restrictions are applied because if wrongly or excessively invoked, they can have a 'chilling effect' on the freedom or even eliminate it.[74] For example, a ground such as national security in the context of counter-terrorism is often misapplied or abused to the detriment of freedom of expression.[75]

3.3.1 Privacy

One right which may clash with freedom of expression is privacy.[76] In *Von Hannover v Germany*, Princess Caroline of Monaco, who had campaigned for many years over paparazzi taking pictures for publication in European magazines of her and her children, complained to the European Court of Human Rights.[77] The Court found that her right to privacy was violated. There was no justification for the constant media intrusion into her private life. The public interest was not advanced since the photographs were published to satisfy public curiosity, not to contribute to public debate. The Court considered that the Princess, although a member of a royal family, exercised no official functions and was thus a private person. While public figures such as politicians and popular celebrities do have a right to private life, it is less extensive given that they are willingly in the public arena.[78] Therefore, when considering whether the correct balance has been struck between freedom of expression and privacy, regard should be had to the following issues: whether the expression contributes to a debate of general interest; how well-known the person concerned is; the nature of the activities that are the subject of the report and how they link to the role of the person concerned; the prior conduct of the person concerned; how the information was obtained and its veracity; the content, form, and consequences of publication; and finally the severity of the sanction imposed.[79]

3.3.2 Defamation

To publish a false statement about another which damages his or her reputation is a civil and often a criminal wrong. But the implementation of laws which impose liability for defamation can, and often do, undermine the freedom of the media to fulfil their function of informing the public and to comment critically on public affairs. Given the vital importance of free

---

[73] *Magyar Helsinki Bizottság v Hungary*, App no 18030/11, Judgment of 8 November 2016.

[74] *Baczkowski v Poland* (2009) 48 EHRR 19; *Fedotova v Russian Federation*, CCPR/C/106/D/1932/2010 (19 November 2012).

[75] HRC, General Comment 34, para 46. See also *The Johannesburg Principles On National Security, Freedom Of Expression And Access To Information* adopted by a group of NGO experts in 1996, available at: <https://www.article19.org/data/files/pdfs/standards/joburgprinciples.pdf>.   [76] ICCPR, Art 17.

[77] (2005) 40 EHRR 1.

[78] HRC, General Comment 34, para 38; *Axel Springer AG v Germany (No 2)*, App no 48311/10, Judgment of 18 July 2014.

[79] *Axel Springer AG v Germany* (2012) 55 EHRR 6, paras 89–95; *Von Hannover v Germany (No 2)* (2012) 55 EHRR 15.

media in a democracy, international human rights standards have been directed at ensuring that national laws on defamation are applied as narrowly as possible as regards 'political speech'. Robust criticism of the government or a politician should be tolerated in the interests of open debate on political issues. In *Lingens v Austria*, a journalist was convicted of criminal libel because he had accused a former Prime Minister of Austria of political opportunism and of using his influence to prevent an investigation of a political ally for Nazi crimes. The European Court of Human Rights found that Austrian law, which required Lingens to prove the truth of what were his opinions, operated as an excessive interference with press freedom.[80] There is an increasing trend towards the abolition of criminal penalties for defamatory statements based on the argument that civil remedies such as the payment of damages is a sufficient sanction and the threat of criminal prosecution has a chilling effect on freedom of expression. This approach has garnered the support of the Human Rights Committee.[81]

3.3.3 Hate speech

Control of the advocacy of violence, hatred, and discrimination against individuals or groups on the basis of their race, colour, ethnicity, religious beliefs, sexual orientation, or other status presents a challenge to all states. The Internet has added a global dimension to the availability of propaganda advocating violence or hatred of others. Article 20 ICCPR and Article 4 ICERD *oblige* states to criminalize speech that amounts to war propaganda or that advocates racial hatred. However, these limitations on expression must be compliant with Article 19(3) ICCPR and thus be provided by law and be the least restrictive means of achieving the relevant aim.[82] The use of speech to incite violence is a criminal offence in virtually all states. But to strike an acceptable balance between the right to freedom of expression and restraint on other forms of objectionable speech is in practice often difficult.[83] If the speech is regarded, in its context, as abusive, inciting, or justifying violence or armed resistance, condones terrorism, or is classed as 'hate speech', it may not be protected at all.[84] Alternatively it may be viewed as expression which states have considerable scope to restrict and restrain as necessary in a democratic society for the protection of the reputation and rights of others.[85]

Islamophobia, anti-Semitism, and Holocaust denial

The mere fact of defending *Sharia* (Islamic law), without calling for violence to introduce it, cannot be regarded as hate speech.[86] However, incitement to ethnic, racial, or religious hostility, hatred, and discrimination is not protected speech. A current concern is the widespread expression, particularly in Europe, of prejudice and hostility towards Muslims, sometimes termed Islamophobia. In 2001–2, a member of the British National Party displayed a large poster in his flat window with a photograph of the Twin Towers in flames with the caption 'Islam out of Britain—Protect the British People' and a symbol of a crescent and star in a prohibition sign. He was convicted of displaying hostility to a racial or religious group. His complaint to the European Court of Human Rights that his freedom of expression was infringed was dismissed.[87] The poster, the Court held,

---

[80] (1986) 8 EHRR 407. See also *Bodrozic v Serbia and Montenegro*, CCPR/C/85/D/1180/2003 (31 October 2005).

[81] HRC, General Comment 34, para 47; *Adonis v Philippines*, CCPR/C/103/D/1815/2008/Rev 1 (26 April 2012).

[82] *Rabbae, A.B.S and N.A. v Netherlands*, CCPR/C/117/D/2124/2011 (14 July 2016).

[83] See Report of the Special Rapporteur on the promotion and protection of the right to freedom of opinion and expression, A/67/357 (7 September 2012).

[84] See *Sürek (No 1) v Turkey*, App no 23927/94, Judgment of 8 July 1999 (encouraging violence and inciting hostility); *İ.A. v Turkey* (2007) 45 EHRR 30 (an abusive attack on the Prophet of Islam).

[85] *Vejdeland and Others v Sweden* (2014) 58 EHRR 15 (distributing homophobic leaflets).

[86] *Gunduz v Turkey* (2005) 41 EHRR 5.

[87] *Norwood v UK*, App no 23131/03, Admissibility Decision of 16 November 2004.

represented a vehement attack against Muslims linking the group as a whole with a grave act of terrorism.

Like Islamophobia, anti-Semitism is a widespread phenomenon, which frequently finds expression in Holocaust denial. Holocaust denial or negationism denies the Nazi genocide against Jews during the Second World War or seeks to minimize its true scale. Such speech is a criminal offence in several European states. A French historian, Robert Faurisson, in an interview with a magazine said it was his personal conviction that there were no homicidal gas chambers for the extermination of Jews in Nazi concentration camps. When convicted over these comments, he claimed before the Human Rights Committee that his freedom of expression had been violated. The Committee upheld the conviction as a justifiable interference with his freedom of expression under Article 19 ICCPR.[88] It was persuaded by the French government's argument that holocaust denial is the main vehicle of anti-Semitism in France.[89]

Disputing the existence of clearly established historical events, such as the Holocaust, does not constitute scientific or historical research.[90] However, debates surrounding historical events of a particularly serious nature should be able to take place freely as they are an integral part of freedom of expression to seek historical truth.[91] In *Perinçek v Switzerland*,[92] a Turkish politician was the subject of a criminal conviction for publicly expressing the view, in Switzerland, that the mass deportations and massacres suffered by the Armenians in the Ottoman Empire in 1915 and the following years had not amounted to genocide. The European Court held that there had been a violation of Article 10. It had not been necessary, in a democratic society, to subject Perinçek to a criminal penalty in order to protect the rights of the Armenian community. Perinçek's statements bore on a matter of public interest and did not amount to a call for hatred or intolerance.

By contrast, *M'Bala M'Bala v France*[93] concerned the conviction of M'Bala, a comedian with political activities, for public insults directed at persons of Jewish origin or faith. The European Court declared the application inadmissible, finding that under Article 17 ECHR (prohibition of abuse of rights), M'Bala was not entitled to the protection of Article 10. During the offending scene the performance in question could no longer be seen as entertainment but rather resembled a political meeting, which, under the pretext of comedy, promoted negationism and amounted to a degrading portrayal of Jewish deportation victims.

Blasphemy

Criticism of religion, as distinct from incitement to hatred of people because of their religious beliefs, is currently a highly contested freedom of expression issue at the international level. For example, the 1988 publication of *The Satanic Verses* by Salman Rushdie and the 2005 Danish cartoons that depicted the Prophet Mohammed were both considered to be 'insulting' to the Islamic faith.[94] Such incidences, amongst others, led to calls for a restriction on freedom of expression in order to suppress 'defamation of religions' and the Human Rights Council and General Assembly, led by Muslim majority states, have passed

---

[88] *Faurisson v France*, CCPR/C/58/D/550/1993 (8 November 1996).
[89] See also *Ross v Canada*, CCPR/C/70/D/736/1997 (18 October 2000); McGoldrick and O'Donnell, 'Hate-speech Laws: Consistency with National and International Human Rights Law' (1998) 18 *Legal Studies* 453.
[90] *Garaudy v France*, App no 65831/01, Admissibility Decision of 24 June 2003.
[91] *Dink v Turkey*, App nos 2668/07 and others, Judgment of 14 September 2010; *Kimel v Argentina*, IACtHR Series C No 177 (2 May 2008). [92] (2016) 63 EHRR 6.
[93] App no 25239/13, Admissibility Decision of 20 October 2015.
[94] Cox, 'Pourquoi Suis-Je Charlie? Blasphemy, Defamation of Religion, and the Nature of Offensive' Cartoons' (2015) 4 *Oxford J of L and Religion* 343.

resolutions supporting such an approach.[95] But others, mostly Western states, have rejected the need to protect religious institutions or doctrines from robust criticism, satire, or even ridicule. In 2011, the Human Rights Council moved away from the terminology of 'defamation of religion', returning to the idea of protecting believers from intolerance and violence.[96] This is a more convincing approach. Human rights law protects those individuals who have a religious belief rather than the religion itself. Therefore, blasphemy laws are, according to the Human Rights Committee, incompatible with the right to freedom of expression.[97] Nevertheless, a number of states still retain offences of blasphemy in their criminal codes[98] and the European Court of Human Rights has accepted the legitimacy of a prosecution for blasphemy where 'believers may legitimately [have felt] themselves to be the object of unwarranted and offensive attacks' and the punishment imposed was an 'insignificant fine'.[99]

4 FREEDOM OF ASSOCIATION

4.1 SOURCES

Freedom of association is proclaimed as an individual right in Article 20 UDHR and is included in both international covenants and regional instruments.[100] Article 22 ICCPR provides a general guarantee of freedom of association. It also includes the right to form and join trade unions, a right independently recognized in Article 23(4) UDHR. Article 8 of the International Covenant on Economic, Social and Cultural Rights (ICESCR) provides for the association rights of trade unions. Trade union rights are more fully protected in the international agreements of the International Labour Organization (ILO).[101] The ILO Committee on Freedom of Association, comprising an equal number of representatives of governments, employers, and unions, oversees the protection of trade union freedoms.[102]

4.2 SCOPE

Freedom of association is the freedom to pursue collective action. It protects the right of individuals to form associations for common purposes, free from government interference. It includes the right of the association independently to determine its membership, appoint officers, employ staff, and generally conduct its own affairs subject only to the law. While linked historically with trade unions, the freedom includes the freedom to establish and belong to political parties, which are vital for the functioning of democracy. But the right of the individual to establish and participate in all manner of civil society associations or voluntary organizations is equally part of this freedom. Article 16 ACHR speaks of the right to establish associations for 'ideological, religious, political, economic, labor, social, and cultural, sports, or other purposes'. This freedom is also of central importance to the activities of human rights defenders. The Declaration on Human Rights Defenders, passed by the UN General Assembly in 1999, affirms the right of human rights activists to

---

[95] eg GA Res 62/154 (6 March 2008); HR Council Res 7/36 (28 March 2008). See Langer, *Religious Offence and Human Rights: The Implications of Defamation of Religions* (CUP, 2014).

[96] HR Council Res 16/18 (12 April 2011).   [97] HRC, General Comment 34, para 48.

[98] Crouch, 'The Indonesian Blasphemy Case: Affirming the Legality of the Blasphemy Law' (2012) 1 Oxford J of L and Religion 514.   [99] *I.A. v Turkey* (2007) 45 EHRR 30, paras 29 and 32.

[100] ECHR, Art 11; CFREU, Art 12; ACHR, Art 16; ACHPR, Art 10; Arab Charter, Art 24.

[101] Freedom of Association and Protection of the Right to Organize Convention 1948 (No 87); Right to Organize and Collective Bargaining Convention 1949 (No 98).   [102] See also Chapter 12.

form, join, and participate in NGOs for the purpose of, inter alia, seeking and imparting information about human rights, discussing and developing new ideas on human rights, and advocating on issues of human rights.[103]

4.2.1 The right not to associate

The right to associate includes the negative freedom to choose not to belong to an association and not to be compelled to join one. The negative formulation of the right is included in the UDHR (Article 20(2)) but not in the ICCPR. The explanation for its absence concerns the status of collective bargaining agreements between trade unions and employers over the employment of union members only (closed shop agreements). For the same reason the right to freedom of association under Article 11 ECHR is also silent on the right not to associate. The European Court of Human Rights has approached compulsory union membership on a case-by-case basis. In *Young, James and Webster v UK*, the Court found that the dismissal of individuals employed prior to a closed shop agreement violated the right to freedom of association of the dismissed employees.[104] In *Sigurjonsson v Iceland*, the same Court examined an Icelandic law that made taxi drivers' licences contingent upon membership of a union.[105] The applicant had been licensed before the regulation came into force, had principled reasons for objecting to union membership, and lost his licence as a result of his refusal to join. The Court found that the government interest in this rule—facilitating the regulation of public transport—was relevant but not sufficient to justify the extreme consequence of non-membership of the union.

In *Gustafsson v Sweden* the applicant owned a restaurant. He was not a member of the restaurant employers association and was not bound by any collective agreement which the union representing restaurant workers had agreed with the association. Because he refused to enter into a substitute agreement recognizing the rights of his workers to collective bargaining, his business was placed under a boycott by the union. The applicant complained that the union's actions violated his negative freedom of association, which the state should have protected. The European Court noted the special role in Sweden of collective agreements in labour relations and held that there had not been a violation of the negative right of association.[106] By contrast, in *Sorensen and Rasmussen v Denmark*, compulsion to join a particular trade union was regarded as striking at the very substance of the right to freedom of association.[107] The Court noted that there was little support in the contracting states for the maintenance of closed-shop agreements and that several European instruments clearly indicate that their use in the labour market was not an indispensable tool for the effective enjoyment of trade union freedoms. These cases illustrate the tension which can arise between the individual and collective dimensions of the freedom of association.

4.2.2 The right to strike

The Human Rights Committee has held that the right to association in the ICCPR does not include a right to strike. In *JB et al. v Canada*, the Committee noted that ILO Convention No 87 had been interpreted to provide such a right and that the ICESCR includes the right to strike along with its recognition of trade union rights.[108] The Committee pointed out that 'each international treaty, including the [ICCPR] has a life of its own and must be interpreted in a fair and just manner'.[109] Having been drafted in parallel discussions, the

---

[103] GA Res 53/144 (8 March 1999).   [104] (1981) 4 EHRR 38.   [105] (1993) 16 EHRR 462.
[106] (1996) 22 EHRR 409.   [107] (2008) 46 EHRR 29.
[108] CCPR/C/28/D/118/1982 (18 July 1986). Five members dissented.
[109] *J.B. et al. v Canada*, CCPR/C/OP/1 (18 July 1986), para 6.2.

inclusion of the right to strike in the ICESCR without similar language in the ICCPR suggested that the right of association in that Covenant was not intended to protect the right to strike.

The European Court of Human Rights regards industrial action as a core aspect of trade union freedom. The taking of secondary industrial action, including strike action, by a trade union against one employer in order to further a dispute in which the union's members are engaged with another employer is also regarded as being covered by Article 11 ECHR.[110] However, states have been awarded a wide margin of appreciation when it comes to restricting secondary action.

4.3 LIMITATIONS

The Human Rights Committee addressed the type of activities that constitute an interference with the right of association in *Korneenko et al. v Belarus*.[111] In that case, the authorities stripped a human rights organization, 'Civil Initiatives', of its recognition because it had violated domestic regulations governing associations. Its official documentation was said to suffer from 'deficiencies' and it was accused of using equipment purchased with foreign grants for propaganda purposes. A domestic court ordered the dissolution of the group. The key determination for the Committee was whether the dissolution of the organization amounted to an interference with the right of association. The Committee held that the ICCPR protected all activities of an association. Dissolution of a group amounts to a severe interference with the freedom and must be strictly justified by reference to the grounds of limitation in Article 22(2). The government had failed to do this. Even if the NGO's documentation had been defective, the extreme step taken of dissolving it was a disproportionate response. The Committee found a violation.

Where domestic law requires registration of civic associations in order to obtain legal personality, a refusal or delay by the authorities in registration may constitute an interference with the freedom of association.[112] The European Court of Human Rights regards a refusal to register a political party as a drastic measure that can only be applied in the most serious cases where a party has not sought to pursue its aims by lawful and democratic means or its aims are incompatible with fundamental democratic principles.[113] The Inter-American Court of Human Rights has held that national requirements imposed on political parties to take part in elections must ensure that the members of indigenous and ethnic communities may participate in the electoral processes effectively and according to their traditions, practices, and customs.[114]

4.3.1 Banning political parties

Political parties are an essential form of association if democracy is to exist. Without an effective democracy, human rights cannot be guaranteed. Political parties thus must be guaranteed the fullest freedom of association and compelling reasons must be given for any interference with the freedom. That principle applies most particularly where political parties are banned or dissolved. Such measures will normally be considered disproportionate.

---

[110] *National Union of Rail, Maritime and Transport Workers v UK* (2015) 60 EHRR 10.
[111] CCPR/C/88/D/1274/2004 (10 November 2006).
[112] *Ismayilov v Azerbaijan*, App no 4439/04, Judgment of 17 January 2008.
[113] *Linkov v Czech Republic*, App no 10504/03, Judgment of 7 December 2006.
[114] *Yatama v Nicaragua*, IACtHR Series C No. 127 (23 June 2005). See also Report of the Special Rapporteur on the rights to freedom of peaceful assembly and of association, 'The exercise of the rights to freedom of peaceful assembly and of association in the context of elections', A/68/299 (7 August 2013).

In *Refah Partisi (the Welfare Party) and Others v Turkey*, the European Court of Human Rights upheld the decision of the Turkish Constitutional Court to disband the largest political party in the state.[115] The judgment sparked considerable controversy as at the time the Refah party was serving in a coalition government. Certain of its leaders were accused of advocating the introduction of *Sharia* in Turkey, and violating the secular principles of the Turkish Constitution. The Court recognized that closure constituted an extreme interference in the right of association, but concluded unanimously that it was justifiable. It noted that 'protection of public safety and the rights and freedoms of others and the prevention of crime might depend on safeguarding the principle of secularism'.[116] The Refah party was likely poised to be able to implement policies that could undermine the democratic and secular nature of Turkey and threaten the rights of others.[117]

The decision in *Refah* can be contrasted with an earlier Turkish case, *United Communist Party of Turkey and Others v Turkey*.[118] The Turkish Constitutional Court dissolved this political party on the basis that the party advocated class domination and threatened the territorial integrity of the state. The European Court found that the dissolution of the party was disproportionate. The party had not undertaken activities or adopted stances that would threaten the territorial integrity or national security of the state and the use of terminology that the state found offensive or threatening was not enough to justify the extreme step of its dissolution.

Thus, unless a party threatens the democratic nature of a state or its fundamental values and principles,[119] it cannot be suppressed, even if the party challenged the way the state was currently organized[120] or espoused offensive ideas. In *Ouranio Toxo and Others v Greece*,[121] a political party representing the Macedonian minority adopted a name that was deemed offensive to the majority Greek population. The government removed a sign with the party's name on it, claiming that the name—written in Macedonian—was specifically intended to elicit memories of a violent battle between the Greek and Macedonian people and exacerbated tensions in the region. The party replaced the sign. In response, citizens, including political leaders, attacked the headquarters of the party and destroyed its equipment. The Court determined that the removal of the sign constituted an arbitrary interference. Concerns over regional tensions did not justify removing the sign. The use of a minority language, regardless of its ability to inflame the sentiments of others, could not be said to constitute a threat to democratic society. The Court again noted the essential role played by political parties in democratic systems and emphasized the importance of political pluralism for democracy. It found that Article 11 ECHR had been violated by both the government's acts and its failure to protect the party's premises.

4.3.2 Additional limitations applicable to military and police

Article 22(2) ICCPR provides that members of the armed forces and of the police may be restricted by law in their exercise of the right of association. The provision, however, does not deny the right of military and police to freedom of association. It recognizes only that the state may regulate the exercise of that freedom. There are similar restrictions in the ECHR and the ACHR. Other state employees and civil servants have the right to form and join trade unions.[122]

---

[115] (2003) 37 EHRR 1.   [116] (2003) 37 EHRR 1, para 66.
[117] See also *Vona v Hungary*, App no 35943/10, Judgment of 9 July 2013.   [118] (1998) 26 EHRR 121.
[119] *Herri Batasune and Batasuna v Spain*, App nos 25803/04 and 25817/04, Judgment of 30 June 2009.
[120] *Party for a Democratic Society (DTP) and Others v Turkey*, App nos 3840/10 and others, Judgment of 12 January 2016.   [121] (2007) 45 EHRR 8.
[122] *Demir and Baykara v Turkey* (2009) 48 EHRR 54.

5 FREEDOM OF ASSEMBLY

5.1 SOURCES

The freedoms of assembly and association are contained in one provision in the UDHR and the ECHR,[123] and the Human Rights Council has created a single special procedure mandate for both rights.[124] The ICCPR (Article 21) and other regional instruments separate the rights.[125] While the rights of assembly and association are closely connected, they are distinct. They are both vital democratic freedoms that enable individuals to act collectively to promote their interests. Freedom of assembly is qualified as a right of 'peaceful assembly' or in the ACHR a right to 'peaceful assembly, without arms'. Specific types of assemblies, such as religious assemblies, are additionally protected by Article 18 ICCPR, as are private assemblies in one's home by Article 17 ICCPR.

5.2 SCOPE

The right of peaceful assembly protects non-violent, organized gatherings in public and private, both indoors and outdoors. A broad range of assemblies is encompassed, including political, economic, artistic, and social gatherings. The right entails the possibility of organizing and participating in a peaceful assembly, including the right to a stationary assembly (such as a picket) in a public location. The organizers of an assembly generally have the right to choose a location within sight and sound of their target audience.[126] The right also extends to counter-protests, though states have an obligation to ensure counter-demonstrators do not interfere with the initial demonstration.[127] Thus, states must not only abstain from interfering with the right, but are also required to take positive measures to protect peaceful assemblies. Although the right envisages temporary gatherings, it also protects mass political protests that may last for weeks or months.

The African Commission on Human and Peoples' Rights found that the convictions and executions of four indigenous Ogoni activists violated their right to life and also their right of assembly. The Nigerian government alleged that the activists were responsible for the deaths of four men following a rally for indigenous rights. The activists were not accused of perpetrating the deaths, but held responsible because their peaceful assembly 'incited' the killings. The Commission held that the executions were part of a widespread attempt to intimidate protestors and limit demonstrations.[128]

5.3 LIMITATIONS

Restrictions on peaceful assembly may be imposed under Article 21(2) ICCPR, provided these are prescribed by law and necessary in a democratic society in the interests of national security or public safety, public order, the protection of public health or morals, or the protection of the rights and freedoms of others. Outright banning of a demonstration may prove necessary, but

---

[123] UDHR, Art 20; ECHR, Art 11. See Salát, *The Right to Freedom of Assembly* (Bloomsbury, 2015).

[124] Special Rapporteur on the rights to freedom of peaceful assembly and of association. See HR Council Res 15/21 (6 October 2010).

[125] ACHR, Art 15; ACHPR, Art 11; ASEAN Declaration, Art 24.

[126] *Turchenyak et al. v Belarus*, CCPR/C/112/D/1948/2009 (19 January 2015).

[127] *Alekseev v Russian Federation*, CCPR/C/D/109/1873/2009 (2 December 2013); *Plattform 'Ärzte Für Das Leben' v Austria* (1988) 13 EHRR 204.

[128] 137/94, 149/94, 154/96, and 161/97, *International Pen, Constitutional Rights Project, Interights on behalf of Ken Saro-Wiwa Jr and Civil Liberties Organisation v Nigeria*, 12th Activity Report of the ACommHPR (1998–1999) paras 1–2, 106.

clearly requires the strongest justification. In *Öllinger v Austria*, the European Court of Human Rights held that the state's duty to protect the right of assembly as far as possible should have included considering alternatives to a total ban on a small counter-protest at a cemetery on All Saints Day where a commemoration was to take place for former SS soldiers.[129]

5.3.1 Prior notifications and permits

Regulation of demonstrations or gatherings through prior notification or issuing of a permit by the authorities before a march or public meeting can take place is compatible with the freedom to assemble.[130] In *Kivenmaa v Finland*, the Human Rights Committee accepted that a requirement to notify the police of an intended demonstration in a public place in Helsinki six hours before its commencement would be compatible with the permitted limitations laid down in Article 21 ICCPR.[131] Such administrative procedures enable other rights and interests to be balanced with the right to assemble, for example the freedom of movement of others, national security, public order, and the normal circulation of traffic. Undue delays or arbitrariness in the issuance of permits, however, can constitute a violation of the right. In *Turchenyak et al. v Belarus*, the Committee held that the *de facto* prohibition of an assembly in any public location in the entire city of Brest, with the exception of the Lokomotiv stadium, unduly limited the right to freedom of assembly.[132] In *Baczkowski v Poland*, the European Court of Human Rights heard a complaint over the mayor of Warsaw's refusal to authorize a march and different other public gatherings to protest over discrimination, including against homosexual people. The mayor had said publicly before considering the applications for permits that he would ban any public propaganda for homosexuality. The Court found, inter alia, that the mayor's refusal to permit the demonstrations constituted a discriminatory interference with the right to freedom of assembly.[133]

The dispersal of a spontaneous peaceful demonstration, one that occurs, for example, in response to an unexpected political event, solely because of the absence of prior notice may amount to a disproportionate restriction on freedom of peaceful assembly.[134] Similarly, arrest and conviction for participation in such a spontaneous demonstration may also be disproportionate. A balance is required and public authorities need to show a certain degree of tolerance towards peaceful gatherings which cause some disruption but do not endanger public order.[135] However, the police can disperse a demonstration where there was ample time to file notice of a public demonstration in advance but this was not done.[136] Should dispersal of a peaceful assembly take place through violent means, including the use of tear gas, this will not be proportionate.[137] Therefore, some of the military responses to the protests that took place during the Arab Spring were criticized because the protests were largely peaceful and the security forces had responded with excessive force.[138]

5.3.2 Repressive restrictions

Any restriction on assembly must be shown to be necessary in a democratic society. In *Oscar Elías Biscet et al. v Cuba*, the Inter-American Commission on Human Rights held

---

[129] (2008) 46 EHRR 38.   [130] *Coleman v Australia* CCPR/C/87/D/1157/2003 (10 August 2005).
[131] CCPR/C/50/D/412/1990 (9 June 1994).   [132] CCPR/C/112/D/1948/2009 (19 January 2015).
[133] (2009) 48 EHRR 19. See also *Alekseyev v Russia*, App nos 4916/07 25924/08 14599/09, Judgment of 21 October 2010.   [134] *Bukta and Others v Hungary* (2010) 51 EHRR 25
[135] *Oya Ataman v Turkey*, App no 74552/01, Judgment of 5 December 2006.
[136] *Éva Molnár v Hungary*, App no 10346/05, Judgment of 7 October 2008.
[137] Report of the Special Rapporteur on the rights to freedom of peaceful assembly and of association, A/HRC/20/27 (21 May 2012) paras 33–8.
[138] eg OHCHR Press Release, 'Tunisia: "Words must become reality, excessive use of force must end"—UN human rights experts' (14 January 2011).

that restrictions on the right of assembly are illegal if used solely to suppress the opposition.[139] The petitioners claimed they were arrested, detained, and intimidated because they discussed dissident publications at their weekly meetings. The Commission concluded that the convictions were an arbitrary restraint on freedom of assembly since their primary purpose was to constrain political opposition.

Even where an assembly is unauthorized, the penalties for participation must be justified and necessary. The Human Rights Committee has found a violation of Article 21 ICCPR where an individual had been refused a 'lawyer's licence' following the imposition of a fine for his participation in an unauthorized rally. Although the imposition of the fine was appropriate, it was not clear to the Committee how the non-issuance of the licence was necessary for the purposes of Article 21.[140]

6 CONCLUSION

In this chapter four freedoms—freedom of thought, expression, association, and assembly—were introduced. The freedoms were discussed along with the body of international human rights norms and jurisprudence, which have helped to define their scope since each was proclaimed in the UDHR in 1948. Each freedom was examined as a discrete freedom of the individual. But it was also noted that each has a collective component. All are interrelated and mutually reinforcing. The freedoms share the common feature that they are not unconditional entitlements. In practice their exercise needs balancing against the rights and freedoms of others and against certain public interest considerations, which are carefully and exhaustively set out in the international standards governing each freedom. A challenge common to all the freedoms is how to ensure that, where such restrictions are in principle necessary, they are implemented by the state in a proportionate manner. That requires a democratic society and one built on the rule of law. The freedoms are, in turn, part of the foundations of a democratic society. The right to dissent and to speak out, the freedom to come together with others in independent associations to promote common interests, and the freedom to demonstrate are all essential if a democratic society based on the participation of its members is to function successfully.

FURTHER READING

BARENDT, *Freedom of Speech* (Oxford University Press, 2nd edn, 2007).

BIELEFELDT, GHANEA, and WIENER (eds), *Freedom of Religion or Belief* (Oxford University Press, 2016).

CASADEVALL, MYJERT, and O'BOYLE (eds), *Freedom of Expression* (Wolf, 2012).

EVANS, *Freedom of Religion under the European Convention on Human Rights* (Oxford University Press, 2001).

EVANS, *Manual on the Wearing of Religious Symbols in Public Areas* (Council of Europe, 2009).

EVANS, PETKOFF, and RIVERS (eds), *The Changing Nature of Religious Rights Under International Law* (Oxford University Press, 2015).

FERRARI and PASTORELLI (eds), *The Burqa Affair Across Europe* (Ashgate, 2013).

---

[139] Cases 771/03 and 841/03, IACommHR Report No 57/04 (14 October 2004).
[140] *Gryb v Belarus*, CCPR/C/103/D/1316/2004 (26 October 2011).

GROSSMAN, 'Challenges to Freedom of Expression Within the Inter-American System: A Jurisprudential Analysis' (2012) 34 *HRQ* 361.

HARE and WEINSTEIN (eds), *Extreme Speech and Democracy* (Oxford University Press, 2009).

LANGER, *Religious Offence and Human Rights* (Cambridge University Press, 2014).

McDONAGH, 'The Right to Information in International Human Rights Law' (2013) 13 *HRLR* 25.

McGOLDRICK, 'Religious Symbols and State Regulation' (2017) 12 *Religion and Human Rights* (forthcoming).

McGONAGLE and DONDERS (eds), *The United Nations and Freedom of Expression and Information* (Cambridge University Press, 2015).

O'FLAHERTY, 'Freedom of Expression: Article 19 of the International Covenant on Civil and Political Rights and the Human Rights Committee's General Comment No 34' (2012) 12 *HRLR* 627.

REHMAN and BREAU (eds), *Religion, Human Rights and International Law: A Critical Examination of Islamic State Practices* (Brill, 2007).

SALÁT, *The Right to Freedom of Assembly* (Bloomsbury, 2015).

TEMPERMAN, *Religious Hatred and International Law* (Cambridge University Press, 2015).

VICKERS, *Religious Freedom, Religious Discrimination and the Workplace*, (Bloomsbury, 2nd edn, 2016).

OSCE, *Guidelines on Freedom of Peaceful Assembly*, available at: <http://www.osce.org/item/23835.html>.

OSCE, *Venice Commission Guidelines for Review of Legislation Pertaining to Religion or Belief*, available at: <http://www.osce.org/publications.odihr/2004/>.

USEFUL WEBSITES

International Labour Organization: <http://www.ilo.org>

On Freedom of Religion or Belief

Human Rights Without Frontiers: <http://www.hrwf.net/>

Forum 18: <http://www.forum18.org/>

On Freedom of Expression

Article 19: Global Campaign for Freedom of Expression: <http://www.article19.org/>

Amnesty International, Free Speech: <https://www.amnesty.org.uk/free-speech-freedom-expression-human-right>

On Freedom of Information

Access Info Europe: <http://www.access-info.org/>

Freedom Info.org: <http://www.freedominfo.org>

12

EDUCATION AND WORK

Fons Coomans

SUMMARY

This chapter focuses on the normative content of the right to education and the right to work. It discusses the sources of these rights under international human rights law and their main features and components. Both rights should be understood in terms of different entitlements and freedoms. The obligations resulting from each right are set out, demonstrating that states have both negative and positive obligations. Finally, the relationship of each right with other human rights is highlighted, thus illustrating that all human rights are interrelated and interdependent.

1 INTRODUCTION

This chapter discusses two human rights that belong to the category of economic, social, and cultural rights, namely the right to education and the right to work. It was long argued that this category of human rights is different from civil and political rights. The latter were said to be capable of immediate implementation, cost-free, and only entailing negative obligations (obligations not to interfere) for states. Economic, social, and cultural rights, on the other hand, were seen as subject to progressive realization, requiring financial resources, and entailing positive obligations (obligations to actively take measures). These differences were also said to imply that civil and political rights could be enforced by courts, whereas economic, social, and cultural rights were seen as non-justiciable, that is, not suitable for review by courts. This traditional view, which emphasized the inherent differences between the two categories of rights, dominated until the late 1980s. Gradually, however, this approach has given way to a view that stresses the unity, equality, and interdependence of all human rights.[1]

Section 2 deals with the right to education and Section 3 with the right to work and work-related rights. The chapter explains how the modern view of the nature of economic, social, and cultural rights can be applied to these rights. Each section first discusses the sources of the right under international human rights law, its main features, and components. Next, the obligations resulting from each right are discussed. Finally, the relationship of each right with other human rights is highlighted. Both rights are crucial for one's ability to live a life in dignity and develop one's personality.[2]

---

[1] See Chapter 7. [2] See UDHR, Art 22.

2 THE RIGHT TO EDUCATION

The right to education has been included in many constitutions and international treaties. States have agreed that illiteracy must be eliminated and that all children must attend school. However, there is a big gap between theory and reality. Worldwide there are still 60 million children of primary school age who do not have access to education. The right to education is crucial for a person's self-fulfilment and the development of society as a whole. This section explains what the right to education is and what states should do to make this key right a reality for those who lack access to education.

2.1 SOURCES

2.1.1 Universal instruments

Article 26 of the Universal Declaration of Human Rights (UDHR) has been the basis for further guarantees of the right to education in later human rights instruments. It provides for the three basic characteristics of the right to education, namely, recognition of the right to receive an education, a guarantee for the exercise of parental rights in matters of education, and a reference to the aims of education.

Article 26 UDHR was transformed into legally binding form through two provisions of the International Covenant on Economic, Social and Cultural Rights (ICESCR), which in comparison to other Covenant rights are rather detailed: Articles 13 and 14. The right to education laid down in Article 13 ICESCR is a universal right, granted to every person, regardless of age, language, social or ethnic origin, or other status. Article 13(1) lists the aims that education should achieve in society. Article 13(2) enumerates the different steps that states must take to achieve the full realization of the right to education, in particular the specific obligation to make education available and accessible in a non-discriminatory way. In performing this duty, states have a degree of discretion within the limits of the standards of Article 13 and the key provision of Article 2(1), which states:

> Each State Party to the present Covenant undertakes to take steps, individually and through international assistance and co-operation, especially economic and technical, to the maximum of its available resources, with a view to achieving progressively the full realization of the rights recognised in the present Covenant by all appropriate means, including particularly the adoption of legislative measures.

Article 14 deals with the implementation of primary education in states that have not yet realized this goal. It requires states to adopt a plan of action for the introduction of free and compulsory primary education. Article 13(3) and (4) guarantees the rights of parents in matters of education and the freedom to establish schools outside the public school system.

Other relevant universal instruments include the UN Educational, Scientific and Cultural Organization (UNESCO) Convention against Discrimination in Education, adopted in 1960, which aims to eliminate discrimination in education and promote equality of opportunity and treatment. The historical background of this Convention is the discrimination and segregation in education under the *apartheid* regime in South Africa. It remains relevant today as an important interpretation of the phenomenon of discrimination and exclusion in education. Article 10 of the Convention on the Elimination of All Forms of Discrimination Against Women (CEDAW) requires states to ensure that women have equal rights with men in the field of education. It lists a number of particular measures and goals, such as access to the same curricula and reduction in female student dropout rates. Article 28 of the Convention on the Rights of the Child (CRC) lists the measures that states must take progressively to realize this right. It includes one new element that is lacking in previous instruments, namely the obligation to ensure that school discipline is administered in a manner consistent with the child's dignity. This may be understood as a ban on applying corporal punishment in schools. Article 29(1) deals with the aims of education, while Article 29(2) guarantees the freedom of individuals and bodies to establish schools. Finally, Article 32(1) calls for protective measures against economic exploitation of children (child labour) which may interfere with the child's education.

2.1.2 Regional instruments

The right to education is also guaranteed by regional human rights instruments. In Europe, the relevant provision is Article 2 of the First Protocol to the European Convention on Human Rights (ECHR). This norm guarantees access to public educational institutions without discrimination and requires states to abstain from interference in the free exercise and free choice of education by pupils and parents. The European Commission and the European Court of Human Rights have interpreted this provision as requiring states only to maintain the level of educational services existing at a given time, without imposing an obligation to expand educational facilities or to increase funding for education.[3] Access to education within the context of labour and other professional activities is covered by the right to vocational training laid down in Article 10 of the European Social Charter (1961). Educational rights of national minorities are guaranteed by Articles 12 to 14 of the Council of Europe Framework Convention for the Protection of National Minorities (1995). Finally, the EU Charter of Fundamental Rights guarantees the right to education in Article 14. This provision contains the key elements of the ECHR and the European Social Charter relating to education, but it adds that the right to education includes the possibility of receiving free compulsory education (Article 14(2)). The latter element is also a key part of Article 13 ICESCR.

Article 17(1) of the African Charter on Human and Peoples' Rights (ACHPR) provides that '[e]very individual shall have the right to education'. The Charter does not elaborate on this brief and generally worded provision. However, the African Charter on the Rights and Welfare of the Child contains a detailed provision on the right to education in Article 11. It is modelled on other human rights instruments, in particular the ICESCR and the CRC. It also contains some elements that are relevant from an African perspective. These include a clause that education shall be directed to the preservation and strengthening of positive African morals, traditional values, and cultures, and to the promotion and achievements of African unity and solidarity (Article 11(2)(c) and (f)). Furthermore, Article 11(6) stipulates that states parties shall take all appropriate measures to ensure that children who become pregnant before completing their education shall have an opportunity to continue their education on the basis of their individual ability. This means that they should not be banned from attending school.

The Additional Protocol to the American Convention on Human Rights in the Area of Economic, Social and Cultural Rights (Protocol of San Salvador) deals with the right to education in Article 13. This provision is very similar to Article 13 ICESCR. It includes the rights to receive an education and to choose an education. What is special about this Protocol is that the complaints procedure of the American Convention on Human Rights (ACHR) applies to two of its provisions, namely certain trade union rights (Article 8a) and the right to education (Article 13). That means that there is a mechanism

---

[3] The ECtHR has interpreted the meaning and scope of Art 2 in a number of leading judgments: *Case relating to certain aspects of the laws on the use of languages in education in Belgium* (*Belgian Linguistics Case No 2*) (1968) 1 EHRR 252; *Kjeldsen, Busk Madsen and Pedersen v Denmark* (1976) 1 EHRR 711; *Campbell and Cosans v UK* (1982) 4 EHRR 293; *Leyla Sahin v Turkey* (2005) 44 EHRR 5; *Ponomaryov v Bulgaria* (2011) 59 EHRR 20.

open to individuals to enforce these rights where it is alleged that they 'are violated by action directly attributable to a State Party to this Protocol'.[4]

Article 41 of the Arab Charter on Human Rights, adopted in 2004, provides for the right to education and requires states to eradicate illiteracy. It contains references to free primary and fundamental education and the aims of education. However, it lacks a provision guaranteeing parental rights and the freedom to establish schools.

Finally, the non-binding Association of Southeast Asian Nations (ASEAN) Human Rights Declaration, adopted in November 2012, provides for the right to education in Article 31. Its structure and content are similar to other international provisions on the right to education.

From this overview, it becomes clear that Article 26 UDHR has been, and still is, a major source of inspiration for the drafting of universal and regional provisions on the right to education. However, subsequent developments, changing views, and regional particularities have been taken into account in more recent instruments.

2.2 FEATURES

Two aspects of the right to education as laid down in international documents can be identified. On the one hand, realization of the right to education demands an effort on the part of the state to make education available and accessible. It implies a positive state obligation. This may be defined as the *right to receive an education* or the *social dimension* of the right to education. On the other hand, there is the personal freedom of individuals to choose between state-organized and non-public education, which can be translated, for example, in parents' freedom to ensure their children's moral and religious education according to their own beliefs. From this stems the freedom of natural persons or legal entities to establish their own educational institutions. This is the *right to choose an education* or the *freedom dimension* of the right to education. It requires the state to follow a policy of non-interference in private matters. It implies a negative state obligation. Both aspects can be found in Articles 13 and 14 ICESCR. Article 13(2) and Article 14 cover the social dimension, while Article 13(3) and (4) embodies the freedom dimension.

In addition, the right to education has been explained by the Committee on Economic, Social and Cultural Rights and the UN Special Rapporteur on the right to education to include four interrelated features:

- *Availability*: functioning educational institutions and programmes have to be available in sufficient numbers, through a public educational system and allowing private parties to establish non-public schools.
- *Accessibility*: educational institutions and programmes have to be accessible to everyone, without discrimination on any ground, also implying physical and economic accessibility.
- *Acceptability*: the form and substance of education, including curricula and teaching methods, have to be relevant, culturally appropriate, of good quality, and in accordance with the best interests of the child; this includes a safe and healthy school environment.
- *Adaptability*: education has to be flexible, so that it can adapt to the needs of changing societies and communities and respond to the needs of students within their specific social and cultural context, including the evolving capacities of the child.[5]

---

[4] Protocol of San Salvador, Art 19(6).
[5] CESCR, General Comment 13, HRI/GEN/1/Rev.9 (Vol I) 63; Preliminary Report of the Special Rapporteur on the Right to Education, E/CN.4/1999/49 (13 January 1999) part II.

This '4-A' scheme is a useful device to analyse the content of the right to receive an education and the obligations of states parties resulting from it as well as to measure the level of its realization.

2.3 THE AIMS OF EDUCATION

Education can be used or abused to prepare children well or badly for life.[6] Education in Germany during the Nazi regime was an example of brainwashing children. Indeed, the formulation of the aims of education as contained in international human rights instruments reflects the need to avoid the horrors of the Second World War from recurring. This is clear from Article 26 UDHR, which provides that education should contribute to avoiding conflicts between nations, groups, and people by promoting understanding, tolerance, and friendship and the maintenance of peace. In addition, education must be directed to the full development of the human personality and to strengthening respect for human rights. By emphasizing the individual's sense of dignity and ability to participate in a free society, Article 13(1) ICESCR makes it clear that the interests of the individual should be central to education.

It is noteworthy that some instruments emphasize specific aims, such as the elimination of stereotyped concepts of the role of men and women at all levels and in all forms of education (Article 10(c) CEDAW) or the development of a child's personality, talents, and mental and physical abilities through education (Article 29(1)(a) CRC). The CRC also adds further goals for education, such as the development of respect for the natural environment and for people of indigenous origin. These common aims, laid down in a number of international instruments, reflect a 'broad universal consensus on the major aims and objectives of the right to education'.[7] They also constitute the foundation for education about human rights in schools worldwide.[8]

2.4 COMPONENTS

On the basis of treaty law, General Comments of the Committee on Economic, Social and Cultural Rights, and case law, the following four key components of the right to education can be identified.

2.4.1 Access to education on a non-discriminatory basis

The essence of the right to education is the right to access available educational facilities. In more concrete terms, this means the right of access to existing public educational institutions on a non-discriminatory basis.[9] This right is violated, for example, if people belonging to a specific ethnic, linguistic, or religious group have restricted access to existing public educational institutions, as is the case for Roma children in some European countries.[10] In addition, education provided by the state should be of the same quality for all groups. Girls, for example, should not be given education of an inferior quality compared to boys.[11] Another, extreme, example was the situation in Afghanistan where

---

[6] Tomasevski, *Education Denied* (Zed Books, 2003) 60.

[7] Nowak, 'The Right to Education' in Eide, Krause, and Rosas (eds), *Economic, Social and Cultural Rights* (Martinus Nijhoff, 2001) 251.

[8] eg UNESCO/OHCHR, Plan of Action: World Programme for Human Rights Education (2006).

[9] ICESCR, Arts 2(2) and 3; ICCPR, Art 26; CRC, Art 2.

[10] See *DH and Others v Czech Republic* (2009) 47 EHRR 3; Coomans, 'Discrimination and Stigmatisation Regarding Education: The Case of the Romani Children in the Czech Republic' in Willems (ed), *Developmental and Autonomy Rights of Children: Empowering Children, Caregivers and Communities* (Intersentia, 2002).

[11] UNESCO Convention Against Discrimination in Education, Art 1(1) and CEDAW, Art 10.

the Taliban regime banned girls and women from all types of educational institutions.[12] The case of the young Pakistani girl, Malala, who advocated for the right to education for girls and was shot in the head by the Taliban in 2012, shows that this right is still far from being accepted by everyone as a human right.[13] In some African countries, female students are forced to disclose a pregnancy and leave school once the pregnancy has been discovered. This practice was found to be discriminatory by the Botswana Court of Appeal.[14] Discriminatory treatment of an HIV-positive person in the school system was qualified as a violation of the right to education under the Protocol of San Salvador.[15]

2.4.2 The right to enjoy free and compulsory primary education

A second key component of the right to education is the right to enjoy primary education in one form or another, not necessarily in the form of traditional classroom teaching. Primary education is so fundamental for the development of a person's abilities that it can be rightfully defined as a minimum claim. Accordingly, the Supreme Court of India has held the right to (primary) education to be implicit in the right to life.[16] International human rights law does not define the term 'primary education', but guidelines have been developed by international organizations such as UNESCO.[17] Primary education relates to the first layer of a formal school system and usually begins between the ages of five and seven and lasts approximately six years, but in any case no fewer than four years.[18] Primary education includes the teaching of basic education or covering basic learning needs.

The term 'basic education' is frequently used, for example in outcome documents of international conferences such as the World Declaration on Education for All, but it is not part of international human rights law.[19] Basic education relates to the content of education rather than the form it takes (formal or non-formal schooling). Apart from a school and classroom system, basic education may be given in less traditional forms, such as village- or community-based, or in the open air. Usually, basic education is aimed at children within the framework of primary schooling. However, basic education is also relevant for other persons who lack basic knowledge and skills. This dimension is referred to as 'fundamental education' in Article 13(2)(d) ICESCR. The enjoyment of this right is not limited by age or gender; it extends to children, youth, and adults, including older persons; it is an integral component of adult education and life-long learning.[20]

The right to free and compulsory primary education also implies that no one, for example parents or employers, can withhold a child from attending primary education.[21] It is the only provision in the UDHR and the ICESCR in which the exercise of a right is linked to meeting an obligation, namely to attend primary education. States have an obligation

---

[12] Human Rights Watch, *1999 World Report*. See also Report of the UN Secretary-General on the situation of women and girls in Afghanistan, E/CN.4/Sub.2/2000/18 (21 July 2000).

[13] 'Pakistani girl shot over activism in Swat valley, claims Taliban', *The Guardian* (9 October 2012), available at: <http://www.guardian.co.uk/world/2012/oct/09/pakistan-girl-shot-activism-swat-taliban>.

[14] Quansah, 'Is the Right to Get Pregnant a Fundamental Right in Botswana?' (1995) 39 *J Afr L* 97.

[15] *Gonzales Lluy v Ecuador*, IACtHR Series C No 298 (1 September 2015).

[16] *Unni Krishnan and Others v State of AP and Others*, 1 SCC 645 (4 February 1993).

[17] UNESCO, Statistical Yearbook and Revised Recommendation concerning the Standardization of Educational Statistics (1978).

[18] Preliminary Report of the Special Rapporteur on the Right to Education, paras 75–9; Melchiorre, 'At what age? . . .' (2004) available at: <http://www.right-to-education.org>.

[19] Sustainable Development Goal No 4 aims to 'ensure inclusive and equitable quality education and promote lifelong learning opportunities for all'. GA Res 70/1, Transforming our world: the 2030 Agenda for Sustainable Development (21 October 2015). See further <http://www.un.org/sustainabledevelopment/education/>.

[20] CESCR, General Comment 13.

[21] See CESCR, General Comment 11, HRI/GEN/1/Rev.9 (Vol I) 52.

to protect this right from encroachments by third persons. According to Article 13(2)(a) ICESCR, primary education shall be compulsory. There is a worldwide trend to extend compulsory schooling beyond primary schooling. The rationale for a minimum length of compulsory schooling beyond 11 years of age is that it should last at least to the minimum age of employment.[22] Obviously it is not sufficient that primary education is compulsory by law. What is also necessary is a state inspection service to supervise and enforce this duty with respect to parents, schools, employers, and pupils themselves.

There are a number of factors that may influence actual attendance of children at school. These include inadequacy of school services, such as the distance between a student's home and the school, lack of transportation facilities, lack of running water and sanitation facilities at school, teaching in a language other than the child's mother tongue, and teaching materials and methods that do not fit in with the cultural background of children and their parents (adaptability of education). Other factors relate to the socio-economic and cultural status of parents, including their inability to pay for school attendance of their children, traditional attitudes regarding the education of girls, and loss of family income that a child attending classes would otherwise earn.

Article 13(2)(a) ICESCR also stipulates that primary education shall be free. The rationale behind this entitlement is that:

> children would not have to pay for their schooling or remain deprived of it when they cannot afford the cost. Children cannot wait to grow, hence their prioritized right to education in international human rights law. The damage of denied education while they are growing up cannot be retroactively remedied.[23]

The degree to which primary education is really free is determined by a number of direct and indirect costs, such as school fees, expenses for textbooks, extra lessons, meals at school canteens, school transport, school uniforms, medical expenses, and boarding fees. Another form of indirect cost for parents is taxation. Its effects upon the accessibility of education will depend upon the progressiveness of the tax system: do low income groups pay less, in absolute and relative terms, compared to high income groups?[24]

Primary education must be a priority when allocating resources, because it deals with the fundamental basis for a person's development and the development of society as a whole.[25] It is the responsibility of states to provide for primary education and maintain educational services. They cannot waive that responsibility by giving more room to the private sector or by stimulating public–private partnerships for the financing of the educational infrastructure. With respect to the right to education in the ECHR, the European Court of Human Rights has held that a state cannot absolve itself of responsibility by delegating its obligations to private school bodies.[26] UNICEF has emphasized that 'only the State . . . can pull together all the components into a coherent but flexible education system.'[27] The Committee on Economic, Social and Cultural Rights has stressed that 'Article 13 [ICESCR] regards States as having principal responsibility for the direct provision of education in most circumstances'[28] and that states have an immediate duty to provide primary

---

[22] See Progress report of the Special Rapporteur on the Right to Education, E/CN.4/2000/6 (1 February 2000) para 46 and Table 3. See also Melchiorre (2004).

[23] Report of the UN Special Rapporteur on the Right to Education, E/CN.4/2004/45 (15 January 2004) para 8.

[24] See background paper prepared by the Special Rapporteur on the Right to Education, E/C.12/1998/18 (30 November 1998) para 12.

[25] See CESCR, General Comment 13, para 51: 'States parties are obliged to prioritise the introduction of compulsory, free education.'   [26] *Costello-Roberts v UK* (1993) 19 EHRR 112.

[27] UNICEF, *The State of the World's Children 1999*, 63.   [28] CESCR, General Comment 13, para 48.

education for all.[29] Recently a number of governments of developing countries have begun to privatize educational services by allowing the private sector to set up fee-based commercial schools for primary and secondary education. This development has been criticized as contrary to the idea of education as a public good and the obligation of the state to make basic education available and equally accessible to all.[30] For those states that have not yet realized compulsory and free primary education, there is an 'unequivocal obligation' to adopt and implement a detailed plan of action as provided for in Article 14 ICESCR.[31] After a long delay, in 2009, India finally adopted an Act to implement the right to free and compulsory education for children of the age of six to fourteen years.[32]

2.4.3 Free choice of education

Yet another key component of the right to education is free choice of education without interference by the state or a third person, in particular, but not exclusively, with regard to religious or philosophical convictions. This component is violated when a state fails to respect the free choice of parents with regard to religious instruction of their children. Public education entails the danger of political goals, that is, the danger that the state will promote the most influential 'philosophy of life'.[33] Thus, a state must ensure an objective and pluralist curriculum and avoid indoctrination in this dominant philosophy.[34] However, in many states there is only limited, or no, opportunity to attend education of one's own choice: there may only be state-controlled education or, where available, private education is too expensive for parents. There is no obligation under international human rights law for states to provide financial support to private educational institutions. If they do, however, they must do so in a non-discriminatory way.[35]

2.4.4 The right to be educated in the language of one's own choice

A more controversial question is whether the right to be educated in the language of one's own choice is a key component of the right to education. In the *Belgian Linguistics* case, the European Court of Human Rights stated that 'the right to education would be meaningless if it did not imply, in favour of its beneficiaries, the right to be educated in the national language or in one of the national languages, as the case may be'.[36] This means that it is the state that determines whether a specific language is to be a national or official language as medium of instruction in education. In addition, the Strasbourg Court stressed that individuals cannot claim a right to state-funded education in the language of their own choice, thus rejecting claims of a positive state obligation in that regard.

On the other hand, a state must respect the freedom of individuals to teach, for instance, a minority language in schools established and directed by members of that minority. This does not imply, however, that a state must allow the use of this language as the only medium of instruction; this would be dependent on the educational policy of the state. As a minimum, states must not frustrate the right of members of national, ethnic, or linguistic minorities to be taught in their mother tongue at institutions outside the official system of public education, albeit they are not obliged to fund these institutions. This right of minorities is

---

[29] CESCR, General Comment 13, para 51.

[30] Protecting the right to education against commercialization, Report by the UN Special Rapporteur on the right to education, A/HRC/29/30 (10 June 2015).   [31] CESCR, General Comment 11, para 9.

[32] Act No 35 of 2009, *The Gazette of India* No 39, 27 August 2009.

[33] Compare ACHPR, Art 17(3): 'The promotion and protection of morals and traditional values recognized by the community shall be the duty of the State.'   [34] *Kjeldsen, Busk Madsen and Pedersen.*

[35] *Waldman v Canada*, CCPR/C/67/D/1996 (5 November 1999).

[36] *Kjeldsen, Busk Madsen and Pedersen*, para 3.

solidly established in international law.[37] It was a cornerstone of the minority protection system established under the auspices of the League of Nations after the First World War. Moreover, the right of minorities to establish educational institutions in which they are entitled to use their own language was characterized by the Permanent Court of International Justice in 1935 as 'suitable means for the preservation of their racial peculiarities, their traditions and their national characteristics'.[38] It is in this sense that the right to be educated in the language of one's own choice belongs to the key components of the right to education.

2.5 TYPES OF OBLIGATIONS

Obligations of states resulting from Articles 13 and 14 ICESCR may be derived from these treaty provisions themselves, Article 2(1) ICESCR, and General Comments 3, 11, and 13 of the Committee on Economic, Social and Cultural Rights. They may be divided into general obligations and specific obligations. *General obligations* include immediate obligations to prohibit discrimination in law and in fact, in the area of education, and to take steps to make primary education compulsory and free. Moreover, states are obliged not to take retrogressive measures, such as the introduction of school fees where previously education was free, and to protect the most vulnerable groups in society through special programs, such as schooling for street children. *Specific obligations* include obligations to draft, adopt, and implement a comprehensive national education strategy, to establish minimum standards for private educational institutions, to develop curricula that conform to the purposes of education, and to set up a school inspection system.

The typology of obligations introduced by the Committee on Economic, Social and Cultural Rights (obligations to respect, to protect, and to fulfil[39]) can be used to further define and refine the nature of states' obligations.

The obligation to *respect* the right to education requires states to abstain from interference. They must not prevent children from obtaining an education, for example by closing educational institutions in times of political tension without complying with the limitations clause of Article 4 ICESCR.[40] As a response to the July 2016 *coup d'état*, the Turkish government derogated from a number of human rights obligations under the ECHR,[41] including the right to education. It has closed approximately 1,000 private schools and 15 private universities and fired tens of thousands of teachers. Although this derogation may be lawful, the effects it has on the enjoyment of the right to education are disproportionate.[42] The obligation to respect can be characterized as an obligation of conduct: it requires the state to follow the specific course of action specified in the treaty provision.

The obligation to *protect* requires states to guarantee the exercise of the right to education in horizontal relations (between private groups or individuals). For example, they must protect against discrimination of students in obtaining access to non-public schools. Other examples of the obligation to protect are the adoption and enforcement of

---

[37] eg ICCPR, Art 27; Document of the Copenhagen Meeting of the Conference on the Human Dimension of the CSCE (1990) sections 32–4; Declaration on the Rights of Persons Belonging to National or Ethnic, Religious and Linguistic Minorities, Art 4; European Charter for Regional or Minority Languages, Art 8; Framework Convention for the Protection of National Minorities, Arts 12–14.

[38] *Minority Schools in Albania*, PCIJ, Advisory Opinion, Series A/B No 64 (1935) 17.

[39] See Chapter 5.   [40] CESCR, General Comment 13, para 59.

[41] See for the Turkish derogation statement: <https://wcd.coe.int/ViewDoc.jsp?p=&id=2436803&Site=C OE&BackColorInternet=F7F8FB&BackColorIntranet=F7F8FB&BackColorLogged=F7F8FB&direct=true>.

[42] Human Rights Watch, Turkey: Rights Protections Missing from Emergency Decree (26 July 2016), available at: <https://www.hrw.org/news/2016/07/26/turkey-rights-protections-missing-emergency-decree>.

legislation to combat child or bonded labour in private labour relations, or arrangements for monitoring and enforcing compulsory primary education.

The nature of the right to education is such that positive state action is needed to achieve the full realization of this right. In the view of the Committee on Economic, Social and Cultural Rights, 'it is clear that article 13 regards States as having principal responsibility for the direct provision of education in most circumstances'.[43] This statement can be seen as a confirmation of the obligation to *fulfil*. The obligation to fulfil requires states to make the various types of education available and accessible for all and to maintain that level of realization, which may involve a variety of measures. While it may be necessary to adopt legislation to provide a legal framework, the primary means of realizing the right to education are policy measures as well as financial and material support. It is clear that the embezzlement of public education funds will have a negative impact on the enjoyment of the right to education, because fewer resources will be available for the provision of education.[44] The obligation to fulfil implies that states have a substantial degree of latitude, depending also on the specific level of education and the wording of the respective treaty obligation. Therefore, the obligation to fulfil should be characterized as an obligation of result, leaving the choice of means to the state, providing the result achieved conforms to international standards.

Particular elements of the right to education give rise to *minimum core obligations* as defined by the Committee on Economic, Social and Cultural Rights in its General Comment on the nature of states parties' obligations.[45] Such obligations are not limited to cost-free (negative) obligations to respect but also include positive obligations to protect and to fulfil. Minimum core obligations emanating from the right to education apply irrespective of the availability of resources.[46] According to the Committee, the minimum core obligations with respect to the right to education include obligations:

> to ensure the right of access to public educational institutions and programs on a non-discriminatory basis; to ensure that education conforms to the objectives set out in article 13(1) [ICESCR]; to provide primary education for all in accordance with article 13(2)(a); to adopt and implement a national educational strategy which includes provision for secondary higher and fundamental education; and to ensure free choice of education without interference from the State or third parties, subject to conformity with 'minimum educational standards' (article 13(3) and (4)).[47]

It is obvious that for many states meeting these core obligations is a challenge from legal, policy, and financial points of view.

2.6 RELATIONSHIP WITH OTHER HUMAN RIGHTS

Education is a social good in that it creates opportunities and provides choices to people. In this sense, education is an end in itself. However, it is also a means to an end, because it helps to achieve economic growth, health, poverty reduction, personal development, and democracy. Therefore, the right to education should be characterized as an 'empowerment right'. Such a right 'provides the individual with control over the course of his or her life, and in particular, control over . . . the state'.[48] In other words, exercising an empowerment

---

[43] CESCR, General Comment 13, para 48.

[44] ECOWAS Community Court of Justice, *SERAP v Nigeria*, ECW/CCj/JUD/07/10 (30 November 2010), para 19.   [45] CESCR, General Comment 3, HRI/GEN/1/Rev.9 (Vol I) 7.

[46] 'Maastricht Guidelines on Violations of Economic, Social and Cultural Rights' (1998) 20 *HRQ* 691.

[47] CESCR, General Comment 13, para 57.

[48] Donnelly and Howard, 'Assessing National Human Rights Performance: A Theoretical Framework' (1988) 10 *HRQ* 214, 215.

right enables a person to experience the benefit of other rights: 'the key to social action in defense of rights . . . is an educated citizenry, able to spread its ideas and to organize in defense of rights'.[49] Education enables people to make a contribution to society as independent and emancipated citizens. Civil and political rights, such as freedom of expression, freedom of association, or the right to political participation only obtain substance and meaning when a person is educated. Galbraith has emphasized that 'education not only makes democracy possible; it also makes it essential. Education not only brings into existence a population with an understanding of the public tasks; it also creates their demand to be heard.'[50] In this sense, education is a threat to autocratic rule. Governments have used the education system for building nations, for instance through the introduction of a national language. Often this happened to the detriment of the languages and cultures of ethnic minorities and indigenous groups. For such groups, the right to education is an essential means to preserve and strengthen their cultural identity.

Education enhances social mobility: it helps people to escape from discrimination based on social status and to move up the social ladder. Moreover, education promotes the realization of other economic, social, and cultural rights, such as the right to work, the right to food, or the right to health: an educated person will have a greater chance of finding a job, will be better equipped to secure his or her own food supply, and is more aware of public health dangers. In general, education promotes the fulfilment of the right to an adequate standard of living; it provides people with access to the skills and knowledge for full membership of society. From the perspective of the rights of the child, education contributes to socializing children into understanding and accepting views different from their own. In other words, education unlocks the enjoyment of other human rights and contributes in an important way to the promotion of the essence of human rights, namely living in human dignity.

Finally, the right to education has a clear overlap with civil rights, such as freedom of religion and the right to privacy: the freedom of parents to determine the (religious) education of their children is not only part of the right to education but also of the freedom of religion[51] and is an issue belonging to people's private lives. Similarly, the right to education is linked to the freedom of association through the freedom to establish private educational institutions.

The interdependence of rights may also give rise to tensions and the need to weigh the different interests that are at stake. For example, a controversial issue is whether the state can prohibit the wearing of the headscarf in public educational institutions with a view to keeping the education system free from any religious expressions, or whether such a ban would violate the freedom of religion and expression of the student.[52]

In short, the right to education, through its links with other rights, accentuates the unity, indivisibility, and interdependence of all human rights.

3 THE RIGHT TO WORK AND WORK-RELATED RIGHTS

In the age of economic globalization, millions of workers in many parts of the world experience the flexibility of the world labour market on a daily basis. They may benefit from new jobs created as a result of foreign direct investment, or they may lose their job, because

---

[49] Donnelly and Howard (1988) 234–5.
[50] Galbraith, *The Good Society: The Humane Agenda* (Houghton Mifflin, 1996).
[51] See ICESCR, Art 13(3) and ICCPR, Art 18(4).   [52] See the case of *Leyla Sahin v Turkey*.

their employer fires them and moves the company to a country where labour is cheaper. Some countries rely on cheap labour and weak trade unions as a comparative advantage to attract foreign investments. As jobs move from one part of the world to another, so too do workers. Many migrant workers from developing countries try to find a living in rich countries by taking on work that is badly paid and often of an inferior status and quality. It is particularly in this type of situation that workers' rights come to the fore. These rights are meant to counter the negative consequences of economic globalization for labour, such as extreme forms of income inequality, exploitation of workers (including women, children, and migrant workers), and high levels of unemployment. The reaction of the international community to these consequences has been the call for social justice and decent work.[53] Workers' rights are crucial in this respect. They aim at protecting and promoting working conditions by laying down international minimum standards. The International Labour Organization (ILO) has played, and continues to play, a key role in setting, implementing, and monitoring these standards. This section of the chapter discusses the right to work and so-called 'work-related' rights, including, among others, the right to the enjoyment of just and favourable working conditions, the right to strike, and trade union rights.

3.1 SOURCES

3.1.1 Universal instruments

A discussion of the right to work and work-related rights should start with the origins of the ILO, which was established in 1919 after the First World War. From the preamble to its constitution it is clear that the achievement of social justice was considered to be crucial for the establishment of lasting peace between states. In addition, it was deemed important to improve labour conditions of workers in order to prevent social unrest, which could possibly result in social and political revolutions such as the one that took place in Russia in 1917.[54] Thus, governments at that time had a self-interest in improving labour conditions, although sentiments of justice and humanity were also mentioned as guiding concerns in the preamble. In this respect, it is interesting to note that in 1944 the ILO stated explicitly that 'labour is not a commodity'.[55] Hundreds of binding conventions and non-binding recommendations have been adopted within the framework of the ILO over the years. The tripartite structure of the organization provides a framework for representatives of governments, workers, and employers to discuss and agree on new rules. These are usually called international labour standards.

The early establishment of the ILO meant that it was far ahead in laying down work-related rights when the UN started its normative human rights activities after the Second World War. The ILO contributed actively to the drafting of both the UDHR and the ICESCR. Article 23 UDHR and Articles 6 to 8 ICESCR contain a number of elements that relate to the protection of the right to work, such as the free choice of work, equal pay for equal work, and trade union rights. Trade union rights are also part of the International Covenant on Civil and Political Rights (ICCPR), Article 22 of which recognizes the right to form and join trade unions. The ICCPR also provides for the prohibition of forced labour in Article 8(3). There are a number of further universal human rights instruments that deal with work-related rights. For example, Article 11 CEDAW lays down detailed obligations for states aimed at eliminating discrimination in the field of employment.

---

[53] See ILO Declaration on Social Justice for a Fair Globalization (2008).
[54] The text of the Constitution is available at: <http://www.ilo.org>.
[55] Declaration Concerning the Aims and Purposes of the International Labour Organization (Declaration of Philadelphia) (1944).

Article 32 CRC recognizes the right of children to be protected from economic exploitation and hazardous work. There is a clear link here with the elimination of child labour.
Article 10(3) ICESCR serves a similar purpose, adding that states 'should set age limits
below which the paid employment of child labour should be prohibited and punishable by
law'. Note the use of the permissive 'should' instead of the more mandatory 'shall'.

The work-related rights of migrant workers are of particular importance. The
International Convention on the Protection of the Rights of All Migrant Workers and
Members of their Families lays down a number of relevant rights. Its main feature is the
principle of non-discrimination with respect to rights granted to migrant workers and
members of their families (Article 7). This principle has been elaborated for matters of
employment and labour conditions in Article 25. However, Article 52 allows for restrictions that states of employment may impose on migrant workers' free choice of remunerated activities. Furthermore, the Convention contains a number of provisions that are
applicable to particular categories of migrant workers, such as frontier workers and sea-
sonal workers.[56] Some aspects of the Convention do not apply to migrant workers and
members of their families who are non-documented or in an irregular situation.[57]

The Convention on the Rights of Persons with Disabilities is based on the principles
of, among others, non-discrimination, full and effective participation and inclusion of
disabled people in society, and equality of opportunity (Article 3). As is made clear by
Article 27, these principles also apply to matters of work and employment. This means,
for example, that states have to prohibit discrimination on the basis of disability with
respect to conditions of recruitment for jobs and to promote employment opportunities
and career advancement for persons with disabilities in the labour market. Among numerous other positive obligations, states must also ensure that reasonable accommodation is
provided to persons with disabilities in the workplace.

3.1.2 Regional instruments

The European Social Charter (1961), the Additional Protocol to the European Social
Charter (1988), and the Revised European Social Charter (1996) all aim at protecting the
rights of workers. They extensively regulate various aspects of the right to work, employment conditions, vocational training, participation of workers in the determination of
labour issues, and access to social security, social assistance, and welfare services. The
Charter also identifies specific groups that need special protection, such as women, children, elderly persons, and migrant workers. The Charter does not recognize individual
rights that are directly enforceable against the state. Although rights language is used,
its provisions are framed as state obligations rather than individual rights. For example,
Article 1 Revised European Social Charter, dealing with the right to work, reads: 'With a
view to ensuring the effective exercise of the right to work, the Contracting Parties undertake . . . to accept as one of their primary aims and responsibilities the achievement
and maintenance of as high and stable a level of employment as possible, with a view to
the attainment of full employment.' The Charter of Fundamental Rights of the European
Union stipulates in Article 5 that no one shall be required to perform forced or compulsory labour. In addition, it contains a number of workers' rights, including protection in
the event of unjustified dismissal (Article 30) and the right of workers to information and
consultation (Article 27).

Article 15 ACHPR provides that every individual shall have the right to work under
equitable and satisfactory conditions and receive equal pay for equal work. Interestingly,

---

[56] CRPD, Arts 57–63.   [57] CRPD, Art 5.

the Charter also contains duties that are imposed on the individual, one of them being 'to work to the best of his abilities and competence' (Article 29(6)). Article 15 African Charter on the Rights and Welfare of the Child provides protection against child labour in similar terms to those of Article 32 CRC. Measures to protect children cover both the formal and informal sectors of employment.

In the Americas, the Protocol of San Salvador provides for the right to work in Article 6. Its wording is quite modern in that it refers to the notions of dignity and decency that have been essential features of recent debates about the right to work.[58] Article 7 lists a range of labour conditions that should be just, equitable, and satisfactory. Like Article 24 UDHR, it recognizes that workers have a right to rest, leisure, and paid holidays, and remuneration for national holidays (Article 7(h)).

In the Arab Charter on Human Rights, one comprehensive article deals with a number of aspects of the right to work. Article 34 provides that the right to work is a natural right of every citizen. It also requires states to provide, to the extent possible, a job for the largest number of those willing to work. The reference to 'those willing to work' is unique in the texts of human rights instruments. Article 34 also prescribes non-discriminatory treatment of men and women in matters of training, employment, job protection, and remuneration.

3.1.3 ILO conventions

Conventions adopted within the framework of the ILO are special conventions, because they deal with one or more particular labour issue(s). As the ILO has always stated, labour standards included in its conventions and recommendations are universal in nature. They are deliberately set low in order to achieve a worldwide reach, although more favourable national working conditions remain applicable.[59] The ILO conventions recognize that there are economic disparities between states and that these differences may have an impact on the way states implement their obligations.[60] What is decisive in the end is whether a state has complied with its treaty obligations. The conventions address a variety of issues relating to the right to work and work-related rights, and many of them have a long history. The first ILO convention, adopted in 1919, dealt with the regulation of hours of work in industrial plants,[61] while another early convention was designed to counter unemployment.[62] More recent conventions deal with the elimination of the worst forms of child labour, the safety and health of workers in mines, and the rights of domestic workers.[63]

3.2 FEATURES

The right to work has a number of special features. First of all, it is an aggregate right, that is, it includes a number of components, such as claims to employment, free choice of work, improvement of working conditions, and trade union rights. Furthermore, the nature of the right to work, understood as a claim to employment, is such that it is not possible to enforce it directly against the state. It is not a subjective right enforceable by courts. Most people are employed by private employers rather than the state. This means that the state must regulate, monitor, and enforce labour rules by laying down mechanisms that workers can use to enforce their rights against employers. Many labour standards thus apply in horizontal relationships between employers and employees. To implement the ILO conventions, states have to bring their domestic law and practice into conformity with the international standards and employers have to comply with the domestic law. The advantage of ILO standards

---

[58] Art 6(1) reads: 'Everyone has the right to work, which includes the opportunity to secure the means for living a dignified and decent existence by performing a freely elected or accepted lawful activity.'

[59] ILO Constitution, Art 19(8). [60] See also ILO Constitution, Art 19(3).

[61] Hours of Work (Industry) Convention 1919 (No 1). [62] Unemployment Convention 1919 (No 2).

[63] Convention No 182 (1999), Convention No 176 (1995), and Convention No 189 (2011) respectively.

is that they are specific and detailed, thus giving clear guidance to states as to how to implement them. Consequently, compared to other economic, social, and cultural rights, the right to work and work-related rights are well developed in terms of their normative content.

The detailed nature of ILO standards has helped to clarify the meaning of relevant provisions in human rights instruments. For example, Article 7(b) ICESCR mentions safe and healthy working conditions as a component of just and favourable conditions of work, without further explanation. ILO conventions and recommendations have been helpful in defining what this means for specific types of activity or categories of workers. For example, there is a convention on safety and health in the agricultural sector,[64] and a convention on the labour conditions of seafarers.[65] These detailed rules may be used by human rights supervisory bodies to explain the nature and scope of human rights obligations.

Traditionally, there was little cooperation and coordination between international labour circles, on the one hand, and the human rights movement, on the other hand. The ILO and trade unions paid little attention to the use of human rights language to promote their cause and human rights activists largely ignored labour rights issues in their campaigns.[66] This situation has changed gradually over time. The ILO has been devoting special attention to the role of human rights in achieving social justice. For example, in 2010 it adopted a Recommendation on HIV/AIDS and the World of Work, which is meant to give impetus to anti-discrimination policies at the workplace level.[67] For its part, the human rights community is focused increasingly on violations of workers' rights, which often result as a negative consequence of the globalization of production and trade. For example, Amnesty International has broadened its mandate to include economic, social, and cultural rights and has drawn attention to the abuse of rights of workers by multinational companies in the palm oil industry in Indonesia as a side-effect of uncontrolled business practices and economic growth.[68]

3.3 COMPONENTS

The right to work is composed of several key components. One of the most fundamental rights is the *freedom from slavery*, guaranteed by Article 8(1) ICCPR. Slavery is 'the status or condition of a person over whom any or all of the powers attaching to the right of ownership are exercised'.[69] Thus, a slave is unable to exercise the right of individual self-determination. Although slavery has been eradicated in many countries, it still exists in parts of Asia and Africa. For example, caste and ethnic status underpin the use of slavery in Niger, Mauritania, and Mali, where tens of thousands of people are ascribed slave status at birth and are then considered to be the property of their 'masters' who force them to work without pay.[70] In India many children work long hours in the cotton industry to pay off the debts of their parents. This is not freely chosen work, but bonded labour.

Forced or compulsory labour has also been banned under international human rights law. 'Forced or compulsory labour' is 'all work or service which is exacted from any person under the menace of any penalty and for which the said person has not offered himself

---

[64] Convention No 184 (2001).   [65] Maritime Labour Convention (2006).

[66] Leary, 'The Paradox of Workers' Rights as Human Rights' in Compa and Diamond (eds), *Human Rights, Labor Rights, and International Trade* (University of Pennsylvania Press, 1996) 22.

[67] ILO Recommendation 200 (2010).

[68] Amnesty International, The Great Palm Oil Scandal: Labour Abuses Behind Big Brand Names, available at: <https://www.amnesty.org/en/documents/asa21/5184/2016/en/>.

[69] Slavery Convention (1926), Art 1(1).

[70] See <http://www.antislavery.org> for more information on current forms of slavery.

voluntarily'.[71] In 1957, ILO member states agreed on new standards concerning the abolition of forced labour, committing themselves not to use forced labour as a means of political coercion or education or as a punishment for holding or expressing certain views; as a method of mobilizing and using labour for purposes of economic development; as a means of labour discipline; as a punishment for having participated in strikes; or as a means of racial, social, national, or religious discrimination.[72] The convention was directed against communist states that imposed forced labour in so-called labour camps for political opponents and states such as Rhodesia and South Africa that applied forced labour of black workers as part of their discriminatory laws and practice. Not all forms of 'compulsory' labour qualify as prohibited labour under international labour law and human rights law. Both the 1930 Forced Labour Convention and the ICCPR provide for exceptions, including compulsory military service and work required of persons in detention.[73] In 2016 an ILO Protocol to the Forced Labour Convention 1930 entered into force which is aimed at tackling forms of modern slavery. It, inter alia, requires employers to exercise due diligence to avoid modern forms of slavery in their business practices and supply chains.[74]

The counterpart of the prohibition of slavery and forced labour is the *freedom to work*, which means the right to free choice of work or occupation. Workers have a right, not a duty, to work. This right is codified in several human rights instruments, such as Article 6(1) ICESCR and Article 1(2) Revised European Social Charter. A current, controversial issue is the so-called *Kafala* (sponsorship) system applied in Qatar in the construction sector for employment of migrant workers. This system requires a 'No Objection Certificate' for workers from their employer if they want to change job or leave the country. In combination with mistreatment of migrant workers employed in the construction of stadiums and infrastructure for the 2022 FIFA World Cup tournament, this system of bonded labour has raised a great deal of international criticism because of the violation of the right to the free choice of work.[75]

Another key component of the right to work and work-related rights is the principle of *non-discrimination and equal treatment*, which is part of every human rights treaty. For example, Article 7(a)(i) ICESCR provides for 'equal remuneration for work of equal value without distinction of any kind, in particular women being guaranteed conditions of work not inferior to those enjoyed by men, with equal pay for equal work'. ILO standards lay down more specific rules and other grounds of discrimination that are prohibited.[76] Examples include trade union membership and action, marital status, pregnancy, and family responsibilities.

The right to work also includes the *right to seek work*, which implies that states must design, adopt, and implement active employment policies aimed at creating jobs and reducing unemployment. States are under a duty to act, not to succeed in providing everyone with a job. In some communist states, the right to work was constitutionally guaranteed and the authorities claimed that there was full employment, when in reality there was hidden unemployment. Today, the internationalization of economic processes has limited the role of governments to influence employment through national measures, but raising employment figures remain one of the major concerns.[77] The ILO has said that job creation for young people must be a priority in achieving inclusive and sustainable development.[78]

---

[71] See ILO Forced Labour Convention (No 29) (1930), Art 2(1).

[72] ILO Convention Concerning the Abolition of Forced Labour (No 105) (1957), Art 1.

[73] Forced Labour Convention (No 29), Art 2(2); ICCPR, Art 8(3).

[74] Protocol No 29 of 2014 to the Forced Labour Convention, 1930. See: <http://50forfreedom.org>.

[75] See the Complaint concerning non-observance by Qatar of Forced Labour Convention No 29 (1930) under Art 26 ILO Constitution, GB.326/INS/8 (Rev) (17 March 2016); Human Rights Watch, 'Qatar: Failing on Crucial Labor Reforms' (27 January 2016), available at: <https://www.hrw.org/news/2016/01/27/qatar-failing-crucial-labor-reforms>.

[76] See ILO Discrimination (Employment and Occupation) Convention (No 111) (1958).

[77] See ILO Employment Policy Convention (No 122) (1964) and Revised European Social Charter, Art 1(1).

[78] ILO, World Employment and Social Outlook for Youth 2016, available at: <http://www.ilo.org/global/research/global-reports/youth/2016/lang--en/index.htm>.

The right to work implies a right to, not just any kind of work but, *decent work*. Although there is no authoritative definition of 'decent work', this concept, which is at the heart of current ILO policies and programs, implies that work has to be of an acceptable quality in terms of conditions of work, feelings of value and satisfaction, relations between employer and employee, and remuneration.[79] The right to fair remuneration is protected by several human rights instruments.[80] It includes, inter alia, the right to equal pay for work of equal value. Fair remuneration is meant to guarantee to workers and their families a decent standard of living. The wage level is subject to a number of factors, such as the standard of living in a country, the type of work, and the situation on the labour market. For the European region, the European Committee on Social Rights has determined that the net minimum wage should amount to at least 60 per cent on the net national average wage.[81] Decency also implies that a certain minimum level of protection has to be met. For example, there is agreement that certain forms of child labour do not meet that standard, as is evidenced by the ILO Convention on the Worst Forms of Child Labour.[82] According to this convention, the worst forms of child labour include work which, by its nature or the circumstances in which it is carried out, is likely to harm the health, safety, or morals of children (Article 3(d)).

Other components of the right to work include the right to have access to free employment services in order to find a job as guaranteed by Article 1(3) Revised European Social Charter, and protection of employment security, that is, protection against unjustified dismissal. ILO Convention No 158 (1982) sets out reasons that cannot be invoked to justify a dismissal, such as union membership or the exercise of a right by a worker, such as maternity leave.

Finally, there are some instrumental rights, such as the freedom of association, the right to bargain collectively, and the right to strike that serve the purpose of promoting and protecting the right to work and work-related rights.

The critical importance of some fundamental work-related rights has been proclaimed and confirmed in a key Declaration adopted by all member states of the ILO in 1998. The Declaration on Fundamental Principles and Rights at Work establishes an obligation of member states, arising from the very fact of membership of the ILO, to respect, promote, and realize a number of *core principles and rights* laid down in ILO conventions. These include:

- freedom of association and effective recognition of the right to collective bargaining;
- elimination of all forms of forced or compulsory labour;
- effective abolition of child labour; and
- elimination of discrimination in respect of employment and occupation.

The significance of this Declaration lies in the fact that states agreed that they have these obligations even if they have not ratified the relevant conventions.[83] Furthermore, the

---

[79] For more information on ILO's decent work campaign see:<http://www.ilo.org/global/topics/decent-work/lang--en/index.htm>.

[80] eg ICESCR, Art 7(a)(i); Revised European Social Charter, Art 4; Protocol of San Salvador, Art 7(a); ACHPR, Art 15.

[81] Digest of the Case Law of the European Committee on Social Rights (2008) 43.

[82] ILO Convention No 182 (1999).

[83] ILO Declaration on Fundamental Principles and Rights at Work and Its Follow-Up (1998).

principles have universal reach and application, applying to all member states of the ILO with respect to both their domestic and international policies and practice. As a consequence, for example, importing and exporting states may not benefit from commodities produced through the use of forced labour or the worst forms of child labour.

3.4 OBLIGATIONS

Obligations resulting from the right to work and work-related rights can be derived from the treaty provisions themselves as well as the explanations given by the Committee on Economic, Social and Cultural Rights, for example in its General Comment 18. However, these obligations have been formulated in general terms, often making it difficult to monitor implementation.

As explained already, pursuant to Article 2(1) ICESCR, states must progressively realize the rights included in the ICESCR by taking appropriate measures, such as the adoption of legislation. Article 6(2) ICESCR lists a number of steps that states parties must take to achieve the full realization of the right to work, such as setting up vocational guidance and training programs. Some obligations are not subject to progressive realization, but have an immediate effect. One example is the obligation to guarantee that the right to work can be exercised 'without discrimination of any kind', as provided for in Article 2(2) ICESCR.

The Committee on Economic, Social and Cultural Rights has identified further obligations resulting from the right to work by using the typology of obligations 'to respect, to protect and to fulfil'.[84] These entail both negative obligations to abstain from interference and positive obligations to act. Under the obligation to *respect* the state must not, for example, apply forced or compulsory labour and must allow the establishment and functioning of trade unions. The obligation to *protect* requires states to lay down in domestic law standards for labour relations between private employers and employees (for example minimum wages, working hours, and occupational health and safety rules), to monitor compliance with the law, and to enforce it in case of infringement. In a globalized economy a key question is what role both home and host states can play through national legislation and policy in regulating and monitoring working conditions in subsidiaries of multinational companies, for example in the garment industry. Do companies give effect to their corporate social responsibility to respect and promote fair labour conditions through self-regulation and voluntary codes of conduct, or should soft law instruments persuade companies to adopt and implement a decent work approach?[85] Finally, the obligation to *fulfil* requires states, for instance, to develop an active employment policy to counter unemployment.

The Committee on Economic, Social and Cultural Rights has characterized some obligations as *minimum core obligations*, which must be realized under all circumstances. These include, for example, the obligation to ensure non-discrimination and equal opportunity in matters of employment, for instance with respect to the right of access to employment for women, migrants, and disabled people.[86] Another core obligation is the duty to abolish the worst forms of child labour pursuant to applicable ILO standards.

As far as the obligations arising from ILO conventions are concerned, two broad categories can be distinguished. First, some of the conventions entail immediate obligations for states. An example is the Equal Remuneration Convention (No 90) (1951), which stipulates in Article 2 that states shall ensure the application to all workers of the principle

---

[84] CESCR, General Comment 18, HRI/GEN/1/Rev.9 (Vol I) 139, paras 22–8.

[85] See for example the Draft OECD Due Diligence Guidance for Responsible Supply Chains in the Garment and Foodwear Sector (2015), available at:< https://www.oecd.org/daf/inv/mne/Due-Diligence-Guidance-Responsible-Supply-Chains-Textiles-Footwear.pdf>.

[86] CESCR, General Comment 18, HRI/GEN/1/Rev.9 (Vol I) 139, para 31.

of equal remuneration for men and women workers for work of equal value. States may use different methods to implement this principle, including national laws or regulations, legally established or recognized machinery for wage determination, or collective agreements between employers and workers. Other conventions, in contrast, contain obligations that are programmatic in nature, that is, they provide for programs of action that set general objectives for domestic policy. These conventions allow for policy freedom and discretion for authorities regarding how best to implement the standards. An example is the Human Resources Development Convention (No 142) (1975), which requires states to adopt and develop policies and programs of vocational guidance and vocational training.

3.5 RELATIONSHIP WITH OTHER HUMAN RIGHTS

The right to work and work-related rights are linked to the enjoyment of other human rights. They play a key role in facilitating the right to an adequate standard of living laid down in Article 25 UDHR and Article 11 ICESCR. When people earn money through work, they are in a much better position to get access to food, medical care, housing, and education. Income generated through work is instrumental in acquiring property, such as a house or land. In addition, decent work, not any kind of work, and just and favourable working conditions contribute to living in dignity. There are also links with the right to social security, that is, the right to access and maintain benefits in order to secure protection from a lack of work-related income, caused by illness, disability, maternity, employment injury, unemployment, old age, or death of a family member.[87] This right is thus complementary to the right to work and work-related rights. The right of children not to be subject to child labour is closely linked to the need to make the right to education a reality.[88]

There are also relationships with civil and political rights, such as the right to information concerning work-related issues, freedom of expression to speak out about abuses at the workplace, and freedom of association with regard to trade unions. Finally, the enjoyment of other rights has an impact on the enjoyment of the right to work. Workers who are well trained and in good health will probably find it easier to find a suitable job and will perform better. This relationship has been acknowledged in the Revised European Social Charter.[89]

Due to its different dimensions and its links to other work-related rights, the right to work is a composite and complex right. In practice, it is particularly relevant to the horizontal relationships between employers and employees. Similar to the right to education, it becomes clear with the right to work that all human rights are interrelated and interdependent. International human rights law is less developed with regard to the right to work than the international standards established within the framework of the ILO. The implementation of the right to work at the domestic level can benefit from the detailed rights and obligations laid down in ILO conventions. Similarly, it can be argued that ILO standards should be seen and applied as human rights norms, because they touch upon the protection of human dignity.

4 CONCLUSION

This chapter has demonstrated that both the right to education and the right to work are important for living a life in dignity. Both rights are critical for the development of society as a whole, but also for achieving self-fulfilment and 'moving up the social ladder'. Their

---

[87] CESCR, General Comment 19, HRI/GEN/1/Rev.9 (Vol I) 152, para 2. See also Chapter 10.
[88] See Worst Forms of Child Labour Convention (No 182) (1999), Art 7(2).
[89] Revised European Social Charter, Arts 10–13.

content, but also their realization, reflects the idea that all human rights are indivisible, interdependent, and interrelated. The modern approach to economic, social, and cultural rights emphasizes the importance of clarifying the normative content of each right by identifying its different dimensions, framed as entitlements and freedoms. These give rise to positive and negative obligations for states. It is a challenge for states to phrase, implement, and monitor their domestic policies in accordance with international standards. This is particularly so when implementation requires allocation of scarce (financial) resources in a period of economic recession. Human rights monitoring bodies, international organizations, and NGOs should be aware of these different dimensions when monitoring implementation of these rights by states.

FURTHER READING

ALSTON, 'Core Labour Standards and the Transformation of the International Labour Regime' (2004) 15 *EJIL* 457.

BEITER, *The Protection of the Right to Education by International Law* (Martinus Nijhoff, 2006).

BERLINER *et al.*, *Labour Standards in International Supply Chains* (Edward Elgar, 2015).

CHAPMAN and RUSSELL (eds), *Core Obligations: Building a Framework for Economic, Social and Cultural Rights* (Intersentia, 2002).

COOMANS, 'Justiciability of the Right to Education' (2009) 2 *Erasmus LR* 427.

EIDE, KRAUSE, and ROSAS (eds), *Economic, Social and Cultural Rights* (Martinus Nijhoff, 2001).

INTERIGHTS, 'Litigating the Right to Education in Africa' (2013) 17 *Interights Bulletin*, available at: <http://www.interights.org/document/259/index.html>.

KALANTRY, GETGEN, and KOH, 'Enhancing Enforcement of Economic, Social and Cultural Rights Using Indicators: A Focus on the Right to Education in the ICESCR' (2010) 32 *HRQ* 253.

MUNDLAK, 'The Right to Work: Linking Human Rights and Employment Policy' (2007) 146 *Intl Lab Rev* 189.

RODGERS, LEE, SWEPSTON, and VAN DALE, *The ILO and the Quest for Social Justice, 1919–2009* (International Labour Office, 2009).

SERVAIS, *International Labour Law* (Wolters Kluwer, 2014).

TOMASEVSKI, *Education Denied* (Zed Books, 2003).

USEFUL WEBSITES

ILO: <http://www.ilo.org>

UNESCO: <http://www.unesco.org>

International Network for Economic, Social & Cultural Rights: <http://www.escr-net.org>

Anti-Slavery International: <http://www.antislavery.org>

Right to Education Project: <http://www.right-to-education.org>

Center for Economic and Social Rights: <http://www.cesr.org>

13

DETENTION AND TRIAL

Sangeeta Shah

SUMMARY

This chapter investigates two rights: the right to liberty and the right to a fair trial. The right to liberty regulates powers of detention and provides safeguards against ill-treatment of detainees. The right to a fair trial sets out how court proceedings should be conducted and court systems organized. Both these rights establish extensive guarantees for individuals who are subjected to detention regimes or national justice systems, as well as specific guarantees for those suspected of having committed a criminal offence. These rights seek to prevent the arbitrary use of executive power and create a climate conducive to the realization of all human rights.

1 INTRODUCTION

When in detention, individuals are at their most vulnerable. They are at the complete mercy of their captors. Therefore detention powers should only be exercised when actually necessary. Similarly, the determination of disputes by judicial bodies subjects individuals to the authority of the state. Judicial proceedings must be conducted so that this authority is not exercised in an arbitrary manner. The rule of law can only be secured if trials are conducted fairly. Therefore, there is a need to regulate how individuals should be treated under national justice systems.

These concerns were recognized as early as 1215 in the Magna Carta, which gave certain individuals what can now be considered to be the origins of the rights to liberty and fair trial.[1] The rights to liberty and fair trial set out safeguards to ensure that notions of 'due process' are adhered to in the operation of regimes of detention, the investigation and prosecution of criminal charges, and the conduct of court proceedings. This chapter considers the content of the right to liberty, including freedom from arbitrary detention (Section 2), freedom from enforced disappearance (Section 3), and security of the person (Section 4), as well as the right to a fair trial (Section 5).

---

[1] The rights were only accorded to noblemen. See Chapter 1.

2 FREEDOM FROM ARBITRARY DETENTION

The ideal is that no one should be deprived of their liberty. However, there may be valid reasons for a state to assume custody of an individual. For example, it may be necessary to detain convicted criminals who pose a threat to the community. As such, traditionally, the main concern of human rights activists has been the capricious use of detention powers by oppressive governments in order to subdue their opponents. Beyond this, it is recognized that restrictions on liberty are permitted and may even be required. However, even where the grounds for detention may be justified, individuals in detention are susceptible to violations of their human rights. They are regularly 'forgotten'—left to languish in prisons or mental health facilities—or they may be subjected to torture or ill-treatment, either at the hands of their captors or by virtue of the conditions in which they are held.[2] Recognizing these concerns, human rights law provides an umbrella of protections that seek to prevent the arbitrary use of detention powers, provide timely remedies where arbitrary detention does take place, and provide safeguards to eradicate ill-treatment or 'disappearance' from instances of permitted detention. This section first surveys the sources of the right and then considers how these aims are realized.

2.1 SOURCES

Article 9 of the Universal Declaration of Human Rights (UDHR) provides that: 'No one shall be subjected to arbitrary arrest, detention or exile'. This pithy yet powerful provision was extended and its protections elaborated in Article 9 of the International Covenant on Civil and Political Rights (ICCPR). The Human Rights Committee has since adopted a detailed general comment on the right to liberty and security of the person[3] and the right has been guaranteed in other UN human rights treaties and declarations, including the Convention on the Protection of the Rights of Migrant Workers (Article 16), the Convention on the Rights of Persons with Disabilities (Article 14), and the Declaration on the Rights of Indigenous Peoples (Article 7). All regional human rights instruments also guarantee the right to liberty.[4] Freedom from arbitrary detention is a rule of customary international law[5] and the Human Rights Committee has claimed that this rule is peremptory in nature, that is, it is a *jus cogens* norm.[6]

There are a number of non-binding instruments that serve to elaborate upon the implications of the right, including the Revised UN Standard Minimum Rules for the Treatment of Prisoners (the Nelson Mandela Rules),[7] UN Body of Principles for the Protection of All Persons under Any Form of Detention or Imprisonment,[8] UN Basic Rules for the Treatment of Prisoners,[9] UN Rules for the Protection of Juveniles Deprived of their Liberty,[10] UN Rules for the Treatment of Women Prisoners and Non-Custodial Measures for Women Offenders,[11] the Council of Europe Minimum Rules for the Treatment of Prisoners,[12]

---

[2] See Chapter 9.

[3] HRC, General Comment 35, CCPR/C/GC/35 (16 December 2014), which replaces HRC, General Comment 8, HRI/GEN/1/Rev.9 (Vol I) 179.

[4] ECHR, Art 5; CFREU, Art 6; ADHR, Art I; ACHR, Art 7; ACHPR, Art 6; Arab Charter, Art 14.

[5] HRC, General Comment 24, HRI/GEN/1/Rev.9 (Vol I) 210, para 8. See also WGAD, Deliberation No 9, A/HRC/22/44 (24 December 2012).

[6] HRC, General Comment 29, HRI/GEN/1/Rev.9 (Vol I) 234, para 11.

[7] GA Res 70/175 (17 December 2015), revising ECOSOC Res 663C(XXIV) (31 July 1957).

[8] GA Res 43/173 (9 December 1988).   [9] GA Res 45/111 (14 December 1990).

[10] GA Res 45/113 (14 December 1990).   [11] GA Res 65/229 (16 March 2011).

[12] Committee of Ministers Res (73)5 (19 January 1973).

the Inter-American Commission of Human Rights' Principles and Best Practices on the Protection of Persons Deprived of Liberty in the Americas,[13] and the African Commission on Human and Peoples' Rights' Guidelines on the Conditions of Arrest, Police Custody and Pre-Trial Detention in Africa.[14]

Given the importance of the concerns regarding arbitrary detention, in 1991 the UN Commission on Human Rights created a Working Group on Arbitrary Detention (WGAD),[15] whose mandate has been renewed by the UN Human Rights Council.[16] The Working Group receives and investigates communications regarding possible cases of arbitrary detention by any member state of the UN. It also issues its own form of general comment—'deliberations'—on issues concerning arbitrary detention, which are an invaluable source of information.

2.2 SCOPE AND TYPES OF OBLIGATIONS

Although most issues concerning the right to liberty involve the arrest and detention of an individual in the context of criminal proceedings, the protections afforded by the right to liberty are not restricted to such situations.[17] For the Human Rights Committee, a deprivation of liberty exists when confinement takes place without the consent of the individual detained. Where individuals 'know that they are free to leave at any time, [they] are not being deprived of their liberty'.[18]

There are limits to the scope of right to liberty provisions. House arrest has been considered to be a deprivation of liberty,[19] while restrictions upon movement which confined an individual to his home during non-working hours was not a deprivation of liberty but a restriction upon the right to freedom of movement, which is protected by Article 12 ICCPR.[20] Similarly, restrictions upon movement within a state, a city, or even parts of a city are not deprivations of liberty, but rather freedom of movement concerns.[21]

Whilst it may seem obvious when an individual is in detention, there are difficult cases. In a controversial recent decision the WGAD held that Julian Assange's 'stay' in the Ecuadorian embassy in London following a claim for asylum was a deprivation of liberty. This was despite the fact that Assange could leave the embassy whenever he wished. Assange was subject to a European Arrest Warrant issued by Swedish authorities and had sought refuge in the embassy in order to avoid the execution of the warrant. Although the WGAD's reasons are unclear, it would appear that the UK and Swedish authorities' failure to recognize that Assange had been granted asylum by Ecuador, coupled with 'extensive surveillance by the British police during his stay in the Ecuadorian Embassy', led to the conclusion that this was a deprivation of liberty.[22]

---

[13] OEA/Ser/L/V/II.131 doc.26 (March 2008).

[14] (8 May 2014) available at: <http://www.achpr.org/files/instruments/guidelines_arrest_detention/guidelines_on_arrest_police_custody_detention.pdf>.

[15] CHR Res 1991/42 (5 March 1991).   [16] HR Council Res 15/18 (30 September 2010).

[17] HRC, General Comment 8, para 1. See also *Case Concerning Ahmadou Sadio Diallo (Republic of Guinea v Democratic Republic of the Congo)* [2010] ICJ Rep 639, para 77.

[18] HRC, General Comment 35, para 6.

[19] *Madani v Algeria*, CCPR/C/89/D/1172/2003 (21 June 2007); WGAD, Deliberation No 1, E/CN.4/1993/24 (12 January 1993).

[20] *Trijonis v Lithuania*, Application no 2333/02, Judgment of 17 March 2005.

[21] *Celepli v Sweden*, CCPR/C/51/D/456/91 (18 July 1994); *Karker v France*, CCPR/C/70/D/833/98 (26 October 2000).

[22] Opinion of the WGAD, A/HRC/WGAD/2015/54 (22 January 2016) para 88. For critique of the decision, see Happold, 'Julian Assange and the UN Working Group on Arbitrary Detention', *EJIL: Talk* (5 February 2016).

Crowd-control techniques may give rise to a deprivation of liberty, but it will depend on the context in which they are used. The European Court of Human Rights has held that the 'kettling'—or confinement—of persons inside a police cordon for up to seven hours did not constitute a deprivation of liberty when it took place in dangerous conditions that may have led to serious injury or damage.[23]

As a general proposition right to liberty provisions are concerned with narrow notions of detention involving the imposition of severe restrictions upon a person's physical being, where the intensity of the restriction depends on its duration, effects, and manner of implementation. However, this does not mean that short periods of detention are excluded. Detention for a period of 55 minutes has been held to engage Article 5, the arbitrary detention provision, of the European Convention on Human Rights (ECHR).[24]

The nature of the obligations corresponding to the right to liberty is primarily negative; that is, states should *respect* the right and not arbitrarily deprive an individual of their liberty. States must also *protect* the right. Where private actors undertake detention functions on behalf of the state, there is an obligation to ensure that all such instances of detention are compliant with the right to liberty. All other forms of detention by private actors, such as abduction and kidnapping, must be criminalized. The European Court of Human Rights has held that states have an obligation not to return an individual to a country where there is a 'real risk' that there may be a 'flagrant breach' of the right to liberty, such as indefinite or incommunicado detention for many years without the prospect of being brought to trial.[25] The Human Rights Committee has suggested that returning an individual in such circumstances may constitute inhuman treatment.[26] A clear violation of the positive obligations inherent in the right to liberty is state participation in extraordinary rendition processes, whereby the state detains an individual who is handed over to foreign officials outside of ordinary legal processes.[27] *Fulfilling* the right is essentially achieved through the establishment of procedural safeguards that are explicitly spelt out within the various international law provisions on liberty. These will be examined in Section 2.4.

2.3 PERMISSIBLE DEPRIVATIONS OF LIBERTY

Article 9(1) ICCPR acknowledges that states may legitimately restrict the right to liberty. It provides that: 'No one shall be subjected to arbitrary arrest or detention. No one shall be deprived of his liberty except on such grounds and in accordance with such procedures as are established by law.' Therefore, only where a deprivation of liberty is unlawful and/or arbitrary will it constitute a violation of Article 9(1). Other international treaties have similar provisions on arbitrary detention.[28] However, some grounds for detention are prohibited explicitly by international human rights law. If detention is solely on the basis of a disability or failure to fulfil a contractual obligation it will be unlawful.[29]

The ECHR sets out a more restrictive approach to detention. Rather than simply protecting individuals against illegal and/or arbitrary detention, Article 5(1) ECHR provides a list of grounds upon which detention is justified. These are:

1. execution of a sentence after conviction by a competent court;

2. non-compliance with a lawful court order or legal obligation;

---

[23] *Austin v UK* (2012) 55 EHRR 14.
[24] *Novotka v Slovakia*, App no 47244/99, Judgment of 4 November 2003.
[25] *Othman v UK* (2012) 55 EHRR 1; see also the Opinion of the WGAD, A/HRC/4/40 (9 January 2000), para 47.   [26] HRC, General Comment 35, para 57.
[27] *El-Masri v the Former Yugoslav Republic of Macedonia* (2013) 57 EHRR 25.
[28] eg ACHR, Art 7; ACHPR, Art 6.   [29] CRPD, Art 14(1)(b); ICCPR, Art 11.

3. reasonable suspicion of having committed an offence, to prevent flight having done so, or to prevent the commission of an offence where the ultimate aim is to bring the person before a competent court;

4. educational supervision in the case of minors;

5. prevention of the spread of infectious diseases;

6. where persons are of unsound mind, alcoholics, drug addicts, or vagrants; and

7. prevention of unauthorized entry into the state or where action is being taken with a view to deportation or extradition.

Detention on grounds other than those listed is not permissible under the ECHR in peace-time. However, the European Court of Human Rights has accepted that, in the context of an international armed conflict, international humanitarian law provides further bases for the detention of prisoners of war and civilians whose internment is necessary for impera-tive reasons of security.[30]

If the detention does not meet the specific Article 5(1) ground upon which it was justi-fied it will not be permitted. For example, in the wake of the attacks of 11 September 2001, a law was passed in the UK which authorized the detention of non-UK nationals who were suspected terrorists and could not be deported for fear that they may suffer torture abroad. The UK government justified these measures on the basis that they were immigra-tion measures and as such were permitted under Article 5(1)(f) ECHR. However, in *A and others v UK* the European Court of Human Rights disagreed, holding that the detention measures were not measures taken with a view to deportation as there was no prospect that the detained individuals could be removed from the UK. Therefore, the powers of detention were considered to be a violation of Article 5(1) ECHR.[31]

None of the grounds set out in Article 5(1) ECHR (or international humanitarian law) by itself is enough to justify detention. As with the other treaties, the detention must also be lawful and not arbitrary.

2.3.1 Legality

Any deprivation of liberty must be pursuant to domestic law. It must be both sanctioned by and in conformity with any procedural requirements set out in national legislation or an equivalent norm of common law. Such a law must be formulated with sufficient pre-cision to prevent arbitrary or overbroad application.[32] So, the involuntary detention of psychiatric patients in secure hospitals should only take place where there is a legal basis to do so, which clearly sets out the situations under which such detention will take place.[33] Similarly, where arrest warrants are mandatory and arrest takes place without one, a vio-lation of the right to liberty will be found.[34] For example, in an attempt to arrest former President Garcia, the Peruvian army arrested his wife and children. As the army lacked constitutional authority to arrest individuals and the arrests were not based upon a court order, the Inter-American Commission of Human Rights held that the arrests were unlaw-ful and thus in violation of the arbitrary detention provisions of the American Convention on Human Rights (ACHR).[35]

---

[30] *Hassan v UK*, App no 29750/09, Judgment of 16 September 2014. See Chapter 25.
[31] *A and others v UK* (2009) 49 EHRR 29.   [32] HRC, General Comment 35, paras 22–23.
[33] WGAD, Deliberation No 7, E/CN.4/2005/6 (1 December 2004).
[34] *Tibi v Ecuador*, IACtHR Series C No 114 (7 September 2004).
[35] *Garcia v Peru*, Case 11.006, IACommHR Report No 1/95.

2.3.2 Arbitrariness

Whether detention is arbitrary will depend upon considerations of 'inappropriateness, injustice and lack of predictability and due process of law' as well as 'elements of reasonableness, necessity and proportionality'.[36] Thus, detention is arbitrary when it takes place without a legal basis, as well as where 'it is not necessary in all the circumstances of the case'.[37]

In order to assess the *necessity* of detention measures, some form of proportionality assessment must take place. This assessment involves consideration of whether, *in the specific circumstances*, the detention regime is fit for the purported aim and whether there is a less invasive method of achieving that aim. So, the Human Rights Committee held that detention was a disproportionate punishment in *Fernando v Sri Lanka* where the author had been sentenced to one year of 'rigorous imprisonment' for contempt of court on the grounds of repeated applications to court, raising his voice, and refusing to apologize to the court. A fine would have sufficed.[38] The Australian policy of compulsory detention of asylum-seekers until their status has been determined has also been held to be disproportionate and thus arbitrary. The Human Rights Committee has held that although it is permissible to detain individuals requesting asylum for an initial period to record claims, confirm identity, and so on, detention beyond this period without good reasons that are specific to the individual, such as a risk of criminal behaviour, would be considered arbitrary.[39]

Where the detention of an individual would lead to a violation of another human right or is the result of a violation of another human right it may be considered arbitrary. As such violations of Article 9(1) ICCPR have been found when individuals were arrested for their political views in contravention of Article 19 ICCPR.[40] Similarly, detention on the basis of ethnic origin alone will be arbitrary.[41] Therefore, arrests on the basis of racial profiling, without further evidence, are prohibited.[42] Imprisonment after a grossly unfair trial will be considered arbitrary and the Human Rights Committee has held that a state will be in breach of its obligations if it gives effect, pursuant to an international prisoner transfer agreement, to a sentence imposed following a manifestly unfair trial.[43]

A detention that is legitimate at the outset may become arbitrary over time. This is because the rationale for detention may cease to be relevant. As a safeguard against this there is a right to *periodic* review of detention in certain circumstances. If the circumstances surrounding the detention have not changed, or the detention has only been for a short period of time, then there is no review requirement. For example, where a person is serving a sentence of detention as a punishment which has been imposed by a court of law, it is assumed that the court that imposed the sentence has reviewed the necessity of the detention. However, in cases of life imprisonment, or where there is a discretionary 'preventive' sentence of detention to be served after a mandatory 'tariff' or 'punitive' period, human rights bodies have clearly stated that there should be periodic reviews of the necessity of

---

[36] HRC, General Comment 35, para 12; Deliberation No 9, n 5.

[37] *A v Australia*, CCPR/C/59/D/560/93 (3 April 1997) para 9.2. See also *Garcia*, para 47.

[38] CCPR/C/83/D/1189/2003 (31 March 2005).

[39] *A v Australia; Baban v Australia*, CCPR/C/78/D/1014/2001 (6 August 2003). See also Report of the Special Rapporteur on the human rights of migrants, A/HRC/20/24 (2 April 2012), para 10.

[40] *Mukong v Cameroon*, CCPR/C/51/D/458/1991 (21 July 1994); *Kanana v Zaire*, CCPR/C/49/D/366/1989 (2 November 1993). See also 266/03, *Gunme v Cameroon*, 26th Activity Report of the ACommHPR (2009).

[41] 27/89, 46/91, 49/91, and 99/93, *Organisation Mondiale Contre La Torture v Rwanda*, 10th Activity Report of the ACommHPR (1997).

[42] CERD Committee, General Recommendation XXXI, HRI/GEN/1/Rev.9 (Vol II) 306, para 20.

[43] *Hicks v Australia*, CCPR/C/115/D/2005/2010 (19 February 2016).

the 'preventive' period of detention.[44] The key question is: does the detainee remain such a danger to society as to warrant continued detention? Furthermore, the European Court has held that the 'preventive' period of detention may become arbitrary if no reasonable effort is made to rehabilitate offenders and address the risks that they pose to society.[45] Similar principles apply to detention on grounds other than criminal conviction.

2.4 GUARANTEES TO THOSE DEPRIVED OF THEIR LIBERTY

Even if a state is justified in depriving someone of their liberty, its obligations regarding that individual do not end. Although states may legitimately restrict the enjoyment of some rights, such as freedom of expression, when necessary, the general position is that individuals do not lose their human rights as a consequence of detention. In addition to this general protection, there are a number of specific guarantees of treatment that must be accorded to detainees. Most of these are entitlements for those individuals who have been arrested or detained pursuant to a criminal charge, although some are safeguards of general application to all detainees. States should take into account specific vulnerabilities of individuals when fulfilling these guarantees to ensure their effective protection. So, the European Court of Human Rights has held that where individuals have been declared 'partially incapacitated' and placed in a psychiatric institution 'special procedural safeguards may be called for in order to protect the interests of persons who, on account of their mental disabilities, are not fully capable of acting for themselves.'[46]

2.4.1 Rights of all detainees

Right to be informed of reasons for detention

Article 9(2) ICCPR provides that '[a]nyone who is arrested shall be informed, at the time of arrest, of the reasons for his arrest.'[47] This elementary safeguard exists to ensure that individuals know why they are being detained, which serves both to reduce the distress of being incarcerated, as well as to allow detainees to challenge their detention. It applies to anyone who is in detention. The reasons for arrest must be communicated in a language that the detainee understands and must contain sufficiently detailed information to indicate why the individual is being incarcerated. The Human Rights Committee held that a violation of Article 9(2) ICCPR had occurred when individuals were told that they had breached state security, but no further details were given.[48] For this right to be effective for certain categories of detainees, such as those with certain mental disabilities or children, reasons for detention should be provided to an appropriate representative who can represent their interests.[49] Whilst the reasons for arrest must be communicated to the detainee 'immediately', exceptional delays will be permitted where they are kept to a minimum. For example, where overnight delays have occurred because of the need for an interpreter, this has been considered acceptable.[50]

Right to humane treatment

Article 10(1) ICCPR provides that all detainees must be 'treated with humanity and with respect for [their] inherent dignity.'[51] This fundamental protection has implications for the treatment of the individual as well as the conditions of detention. While most cases of

---

[44] HRC, General Comment 35, para 21. In the mental health context see *Stanev v Bulgaria* (2012) 55 EHRR 22.   [45] *James, Wells and Lee v UK* (2013) 56 EHRR 12.   [46] *Stanev*, para 170.

[47] See also, ECHR, Art 5(2) ECHR; ACHR, Art 7(4).

[48] *Ilombe and Shandwe v Democratic Republic of Congo*, CCPR/C/86/D/1177/2003 (17 March 2006).

[49] *Krasnova v Kyrgyzstan*, CCPR/C/101/D/1402/2005 (27 April 2010); *Z.H. v Hungary*, App no 28973/11, Judgment of 8 November 2012.   [50] *Hill and Hill v Spain*, CCPR/C/59/D/526/1993 (2 April 1997) para 12.2.

[51] See also ACHR, Art 5(2).

severe ill-treatment will be considered inhuman treatment or torture contrary to Article 7 ICCPR, Article 10(1) is triggered by attacks on dignity that do not reach the severity of suffering threshold required by Article 7 ICCPR.[52] States are obliged to protect all individuals from 'any hardship or constraint other than that resulting from the deprivation of liberty'.[53]

Fulfilment of a detainee's right to humane treatment is inextricably linked to the conditions of detention in which they are held. States must ensure that these conditions are adequate. Detention facilities must not be over-crowded and must provide satisfactory light, ventilation, bedding, sanitary facilities, food, and clothing, as well as access to appropriate medical care where necessary.[54] Although ensuring such minimum conditions may be financially expensive, the Human Rights Committee has emphasized that the 'fundamental nature of the right means that the application of this rule . . . cannot be dependent on the material resources available in the State Party'.[55] The Committee found a violation of Article 10(1) ICCPR in *Wanza v Trinidad and Tobago* where the author was detained in a windowless cell, ventilated by an 18 x 18 inch opening, for between 22 and 23 hours a day, whilst on weekends or holidays, when the number of prison staff was too low, he was not permitted to leave the cell at all.[56] A number of the recommendations and declarations adopted by the UN and regional bodies listed in Section 2.1 set out minimum standards of detention below which a violation would be found. There must be strict state regulation of *all* detention facilities, even where they are run by private organizations, to ensure that conditions of detention are appropriate. Furthermore, the Inter-American Commission has stressed that states must exercise overall effective control over prisons and prevent systems of self-government whereby prison life is governed by 'gangs' of prisoners. In such situations, the state is simply unable to protect the dignity of prisoners.[57]

Right to challenge the legality of detention

A further element of the guarantees against arbitrary detention is the right to bring habeas corpus proceedings; that is, detainees should have the opportunity to challenge the *legality* of their detention, and be released should it be considered unlawful.[58] This right of challenge aims to provide redress where incarceration is not necessary. Review of the legality of detention must be conducted by an independent court of law,[59] not by an administrative or executive body, and must take place without delay. In order for the right to be effective, detainees must have access to a lawyer, and individuals cannot be kept incommunicado.

Remedies for unlawful detention

Articles 9(4) and 9(5) ICCPR provide for two specific remedies where detention is found to be unlawful: release and compensation for pecuniary and non-pecuniary harm suffered. Similar rights are provided for in Article 10 ACHR and Article 5(5) ECHR, and the African Commission has confirmed that the ACHPR also requires such remedies.[60]

---

[52] See Chapter 9.

[53] HRC, General Comment 21, HRI/GEN/1/Rev.9 (Vol I) 202, para 3; *Vélez Loor v Panama*, IACtHR Series C No 218 (23 November 2010) para 198.

[54] See *Pacheco Teruel et al. v Honduras*, IACtHR Series C No 241 (27 April 2012).

[55] HRC, General Comment 21, para 4.   [56] CCPR/C/74/D/683/1996 (26 March 2002).

[57] IACommHR, *Report on the Human Rights of Persons Deprived of Liberty in the Americas* (OAS, 2011), para 14.

[58] ICCPR, Art 9(4); ECHR, Art 5(4); ACHR, Art 7(6). The ACommHPR has confirmed that this right is implicit in ACHPR, Art 7(1): *Constitutional Rights Project v Nigeria* (153/96), 13th Annual Activity Report (1999).

[59] On the meaning of 'independent court', see Section 5.3.2.   [60] *Constitutional Rights Project.*

National courts must have the power to order release and award compensation and such awards must be complied with in a timely fashion. In the case of *A and others v UK*, discussed in Section 2.3, the European Court found a violation of Article 5(5) ECHR. The individuals concerned had been released from detention as a result of a national court decision, but they had not been paid any compensation for the time they spent in unlawful detention.[61]

2.4.2 Rights of those detained on a criminal charge

In addition to those rights discussed already, human rights law provides specific protections to individuals who are detained pursuant to a criminal charge, or who have been arrested on the basis of a suspicion that they have committed a criminal offence. Prevention and punishment of crimes is one of the broadest bases upon which states may ground detention. The considerable powers of the state in these circumstances must be kept in check with mechanisms for accountability of law enforcement officers and safeguards for arrested persons.

Article 9(2) ICCPR provides that in the context of detention on the basis of a criminal charge, individuals should be informed promptly, in a language that they understand, of the criminal charges they face. The requirement of 'prompt' notification does not require notification at the moment of arrest; some delay is permitted: seven hours has been considered satisfactory,[62] whilst seven days has been considered too long.[63]

All individuals who are arrested pursuant to a criminal charge must be brought 'promptly before a judge or other officer authorized to exercise judicial power'.[64] This should be an automatic process and not one which is dependent upon a request by the arrested individual. The initial days of detention are often those when detainees are at their most vulnerable; the probability that torture or ill-treatment will occur is at its highest at this time. The aim of bringing a detainee before a judge is to ensure independent judicial supervision of the actions of law enforcement officers and to confirm the legal basis for detention. The judge or judicial officer should be empowered to order the release of detainees where detention is not appropriate. If they cannot do so, the protections provided by this right will be illusory. Furthermore, the judge or other officer should be 'independent, objective and impartial in relation to the issues dealt with'.[65] With regard to the requirement of 'promptness', the Human Rights Committee has stated that '48 hours is ordinarily sufficient to transport the individual and to prepare for the judicial hearing; any delay longer than 48 hours must remain absolutely exceptional and justified under the circumstances'.[66]

Protections afforded to those detained on a criminal charge continue beyond this first appearance before a judge. Article 9(3) ICCPR provides that such persons 'shall be entitled to trial within a reasonable time or to release' pending trial. Article 5(3) ECHR and Article 7 ACHR provide similar guarantees. The general rule is that individuals should not be kept in pre-trial detention unless it is really necessary to do so. Essentially these provisions provide a qualified right to release pending trial where exceptions are permitted 'to ensure the presence of the accused at the trial, to avert interference with witnesses and other evidence, or the commission of other offences'.[67] 'Public order', where the

---

[61]   *A and others v UK*.
[62]   *Fox, Campbell and Hartley v UK* (1991) 13 EHRR 157, para 42.
[63]   *Grant v Jamaica*, CCPR/C/56/D/597/1994 (22 March 1996) para 8.1.
[64]   ICCPR, Art 9(3); ECHR, Art 5(3). ACHR, Art 7(5) establishes that this is a right for *all* detainees and not just those detained on a criminal charge.   [65]   HRC, General Comment 35, para 32.
[66]   HRC, General Comment 35, para 33 [footnotes omitted].
[67]   *WBE v Netherlands*, CCPR/C/46/D/432/1990 (23 October 1992) para 6.3.

release of a suspected offender may give rise to a social disturbance,[68] and the 'personal safety of the suspect', where release of suspects may leave them vulnerable to attack, will also be relevant considerations.[69] The burden remains on the state to demonstrate that in the specific circumstances detention is necessary and proportionate. International human rights bodies have advocated the use of financial guarantees or the removal of travel papers and passports, rather than pre-trial detention, to secure the attendance of a suspect at trial.

Where individuals are held in pre-trial detention, as part of the right to humane treatment and in order to maintain the presumption of innocence, they should be kept segregated from convicted criminals (Article 10(2)(a) ICCPR). They are to be treated as innocent individuals until proven guilty of an offence. Article 10(2)(b) ICCPR also provides that '[a]ccused juveniles shall be separated from adults and brought as speedily as possible for adjudication'. Furthermore, where release is not possible, the trial of the accused must take place within a reasonable period of time. What is considered *reasonable* is a matter to be determined on a case-by-case basis, but factors that will be taken into account include: the complexity of the case, the conduct of the accused (have they delayed the proceedings with challenges or by subverting investigations), and the efficiency of national authorities. Of primary concern is 'whether the time that has elapsed, for whatever reason, before judgment is passed on the accused has at some stage exceeded a reasonable limit whereby imprisonment without conviction imposes a greater sacrifice than could, in the circumstances of the case, reasonably be expected of a person presumed innocent'.[70]

Finally, Article 10(3) ICCPR obliges states to ensure that detention following a conviction for a criminal offence is aimed at the reformation and social rehabilitation of offenders, not simply punishment. So, in *Kang v Republic of Korea*, the Human Rights Committee found a violation of this provision where the author had been held in solitary confinement for 13 years for failing to abandon his political views.[71]

2.4.3 Rights of foreign nationals

Foreign detainees are particularly vulnerable. They may have problems of participation in different and often disorientating legal systems, including a lack of knowledge of the official language of the host state. All foreign nationals who are 'arrested or committed to prison or to custody pending trial or . . . detained in any other manner' are entitled to access to a consular official from their home state.[72] Foreign detainees have the right to request that consular officials of their home state are notified of their arrest without delay and that all communications between the detainee and consular officials are forwarded without delay. All foreign detainees must be informed of these entitlements. These 'rights' have been confirmed by the International Court of Justice to apply in all cases of detention of foreign nationals.[73]

---

[68] *Letellier v France* (1992) 14 EHRR 83.

[69] *IA v France*, App No 28213/95, Judgment of 23 September 1998.

[70] *Wemhoff v Germany* (1979–80) 1 EHRR 55, para 5; Case 11.245, *Giménez v Argentina*, IACommHR Report No 12.96 (1 March 1996) para 83; *Case of the 'Juvenile Reeducation Institute' v Paraguay*, IACtHR Series C No 112 (2004).   [71] CCPR/C/78/D/878/1999 (15 July 2003).

[72] Vienna Convention on Consular Relations, Art 36(1); ICRMW, Art 16(7).

[73] *LaGrand (Germany v United States)* [2001] ICJ Rep 466; *Avena and other Mexican Nationals (Mexico v United States)* [2004] ICJ Rep 12; *Diallo*. Whilst the ICJ failed to confirm that the rights were human rights in these cases, the IACtHR has done so: see *Chaparro-Alvarez and Lapo-Iniguez v Ecuador*, IACtHR Series C No 170 (21 November 2007).

2.5 EMERGENCY DETENTION POWERS

The right to liberty has been the subject of many derogations by states from their human rights obligations.[74] Detention, particularly indefinite detention without charge, is often seen as an important tool by states to deal with emergencies. On a purely textual basis derogation from the right to liberty is permitted. However, any emergency deprivation of liberty measures must fulfil the requirements for a valid derogation, that is, the measures must be a necessary and proportionate response to the emergency faced. It would appear then that any such deprivations of liberty must not be arbitrary, and thus that the right to freedom from arbitrary detention is not derogable. Rather, it is the determination of what is arbitrary that changes when a state faces an emergency that threatens the life of the nation. So, in a time of armed conflict what constitutes an arbitrary detention will need to be determined by reference to the relevant rules of international humanitarian law.[75] Furthermore, the essential protections that the right to liberty affords serve to prevent violations of rights which are not derogable, such as freedom from torture and ill-treatment. Recognizing these further positive effects of the right to liberty, human rights bodies have stated that the procedural safeguards discussed already, including judicial oversight of arrests and the right to bring habeas corpus proceedings, must remain in place during times of emergency. For example, the Human Rights Committee has confirmed that '[i]t is inherent in the protection of rights explicitly recognized as non-derogable . . . that they must be secured by procedural guarantees, including, often, judicial guarantees' and so 'the right to take proceedings before a court to decide without delay on the lawfulness of detention must not be diminished by a State party's decision to derogate from the [ICCPR]'.[76] The Inter-American Court[77] and the European Court have made similar statements.[78]

3 ENFORCED DISAPPEARANCE

The most egregious violation of the right to liberty is an 'enforced disappearance', which comprises the secret deprivation of a person's liberty by state agents[79] who refuse to inform anyone of the arrest.[80] As such, at least insofar as the friends and family of the individual are concerned, the individual has effectively disappeared. The victim is removed from the protection of the law and cannot make use of the judicial safeguards described in Section 2. Such abductions often result in the death of the victim. A notorious recent example of enforced disappearance is the US Central Intelligence Agency's use of 'black sites' across the world to secretly detain individuals for prolonged periods of time in the context of the 'global war on terror'.[81] Enforced disappearance was used systematically in Latin America

---

[74] See Chapter 5.

[75] HRC, General Comment 35, paras 64–6; *Precautionary Measures in Guantanamo Bay, Cuba*, IACommHR (13 March 2002); *Hassan*, App no 29750/09.

[76] HRC, General Comment 29, paras 15–16; see also WGAD Deliberation No 9, para 47.

[77] OC-8/87, *Habeas Corpus in Emergency Situations*, IACtHR Series A No 8 (30 January 1987); OC-9/87, *Judicial Guarantees in States of Emergency*, IACtHR Series A No 9 (6 October 1987).

[78] *Brannigan and McBride v UK* (1994) 17 EHRR 539, para 62.

[79] The HRC has confirmed that an enforced disappearance can be at the hands of forces 'independent or hostile to a state party': *Hero v Bosnia*, CCPR//C/112/D/1966/2010 (27 November 2014).

[80] See CPED, Art 2; Inter-American Convention on Forced Disappearance of Persons, Art II; Rome Statute of the International Criminal Court, Art 7(2)(i); Working Group on Enforced or Involuntary Disappearances, General Comment on the definition of enforced disappearance, A/HRC/7/2 (10 January 2008).

[81] See Joint Study on Global Practices in Relation to Secret Detention in the Context of Countering Terrorism, A/HRC/13/42 (19 February 2010); Opinion of the WGAD 29/2006, A/HRC/4/40/Add.1 (September 2006); *El-Masri* (2013).

in the 1960s and 1970s, and given its experience of the practice, the OAS was the first international organization to adopt a treaty specifically directed at the eradication of the practice: the Inter-American Convention on Forced Disappearance of Persons 1994.

Each of the international human rights bodies has confirmed that enforced disappearance will constitute a violation of multiple human rights, including: the right to liberty, the right to humane conditions of detention, the right to recognition before the law, the right not to be tortured, and possibly the right to life.[82] Enforced disappearance may also result in violations of the prohibition of torture and ill-treatment in respect of the family members who are left worrying about the fate of abducted individuals.[83] The UN Convention for the Protection of All Persons against Enforced Disappearance has now confirmed that individuals have a 'free-standing' right not to be subjected to enforced disappearance.[84] Parties to the UN Convention or the Inter-American Convention are obliged to criminalize the practice of enforced disappearance and adopt further administrative and legal measures, in addition to those which exist to prevent arbitrary detention, to bring to an end the practice of 'secret detention'. The obligations to criminalize, investigate, and punish enforced disappearance have, according to the Inter-American Court of Human Rights, attained the status of *jus cogens*.[85]

4 SECURITY OF THE PERSON

Treaty provisions on the right to liberty invariably contain a reference to protection of the 'security of the person', which is concerned with freedom from injury. States are obliged to refrain from inflicting bodily injury on individuals, to investigate threats to the person from both state and non-state actors, and to provide protection for individuals where such threats are credible. Some human rights bodies have restricted the right to security of the person to those individuals who are threatened with arbitrary detention. In the *Garcia* case discussed in Section 2.3, the Inter-American Commission decided that there had been a violation of the right to personal security because Garcia was 'threatened with arbitrary and unlawful arrest'.[86] The Human Rights Committee, extending the protections beyond the detention context, has stated that '[i]t cannot be the case that, as a matter of law, States can ignore known threats to the life of persons under their jurisdiction, just because he or she is not arrested or otherwise detained'.[87] Therefore, it has found violations of the right to security where there was a failure to investigate credible death threats.[88]

5 THE RIGHT TO A FAIR TRIAL

The right to a fair trial is 'aimed at the proper administration of justice' and securing the rule of law.[89] Treaty provisions on fair trial establish a complex set of rules that cover two aspects of how the right is to be secured. First, there are rules specifying how court proceedings should be conducted. In general, fair trial guarantees are not primarily concerned

---

[82] *Sarma v Sri Lanka*, CCPR/C/78/D/950/2000 (16 July 2003); *Coronel v Columbia*, CCPR/C/76/D/778/1997 (24 October 2002); *Velásquez-Rodriguez v Honduras*, IACtHR Series C No 4 (29 July 1988); 24/97, *Mouvement Burkinabé des Droits de l'Homme et des Peuples v Burkina Faso*, 14th Activity Report of the ACommHPR (2001); *Kurt v Turkey* (1999) 27 EHRR 373; *Timurtas v Turkey* (2001) 33 EHRR 6.

[83] eg *Mojica v Dominican Republic*, CCPR/C/51/D/449/1991 (25 July 1994).

[84] CPED, Art 1.   [85] *Goiburu v Paraguay*, IACtHR Series C No 202 (22 September 2009).

[86] *Garcia v Peru*, 100.

[87] *Delgado Páez v Columbia*, CCPR/C/39/D/195/1985 (12 July 1990) para 5.5; see also General Comment 35, n 3, para 9.   [88] *Jayawardena v Sri Lanka*, CCPR/C/75/D/916/2000 (22 July 2002).

[89] HRC, General Comment 13, HRI/GEN/Rev.9 (Vol I) 184, para 1.

with the *outcome* of judicial proceedings, but rather the *process* by which that outcome is achieved. Fairness of outcome is not guaranteed. Second, there are structural rules regarding the organization of domestic court systems. Securing the right to a fair trial can require significant investment in the court system and many states fail to fulfil their obligations because of serious structural problems. Human rights law does not seek to impose a particular type of court system on states, but rather implements the principle that there should be a separation of powers between the executive and the judiciary.

5.1 SOURCES

Article 10 UDHR provides that '[e]veryone is entitled in full equality to a fair and public hearing by an independent and impartial tribunal, in the determination of his rights and obligations and of any criminal charge against him'. The UDHR also provides further, more specific, protections applicable when determining a criminal charge, in Article 11. The general and specific criminal protections are merged into one, extremely detailed, provision of the ICCPR: Article 14. Due to their importance, aspects of fair trial guarantees can be found in most of the UN human rights treaties, including: Article 40 of the Convention on the Rights of the Child (CRC), Article 18 of the Migrant Workers Convention, Article 5(a) of the Convention on the Elimination of Racial Discrimination (ICERD), Article 15 of the Convention against Torture (UNCAT), and Article 13 of the Convention on the Rights of Persons with Disabilities. All regional treaties guarantee the right to a fair trial.[90] Despite the sophisticated treaty provisions on the right to a fair trial, this is an area that has evolved by means of considerable elaboration by international human rights bodies.

The 'fundamental principles of fair trial' form part of customary international law and the Human Rights Committee considers them to be peremptory norms of international law.[91] Although not listed within derogation clauses, the Committee has held that such principles are non-derogable in times of emergency because they ensure that 'the principles of legality and the rule of law' are respected. These fundamental principles create safeguards for those norms that are explicitly listed as non-derogable, such as the right to life and the prohibition against torture.[92]

Particular aspects of the right to a fair trial are also elaborated upon in various declarations and guiding principles, including the Basic Principles on the Independence of the Judiciary,[93] the Basic Principles on the Role of Lawyers,[94] the UN Standard Minimum Rules for the Administration of Juvenile Justice,[95] and the UN Principles and Guidelines on Access to Legal Aid in Criminal Justice Systems.[96]

Not all prosecutions will take place nationally. International law imposes liability on individuals for international crimes,[97] and these crimes are sometimes tried at the international level. International criminal tribunals must ensure a fair trial of the accused and fair trial guarantees are provided in the relevant statutes and rules of procedure.[98]

---

[90] ECHR, Arts 6 and 7; ACHR, Arts 8 and 9; ACHPR, Art 7; Arab Charter, Arts 12, 13, 16, and 17; CFREU, Chapter VI. The protections in the ACHPR are augmented by the African Commission Principles and Guidelines on the Right to a Fair Trial and Legal Assistance in Africa, DOC/OS (XXX) 247 (2003).

[91] HRC, General Comment 29, para 11. Not all fair trial protections can be classified as such, see *Al-Dulimi v Switzerland*, App no 5809/09, Judgment of 21 June 2016, para 136.

[92] HRC, General Comment 29, para 15; see also HRC, General Comment 32, HRI/GEN/1/Rev.9 (Vol I) 248, para 6.   [93] GA Res 40/32 (29 November 1985) Annex.

[94] A/CONF.144/28/Rev.1 (1990), 118.   [95] GA Res 45/100 (14 December 1990) Annex.

[96] GA Res 67/187 (20 December 2012) Annex.   [97] See Chapter 26.

[98] eg Rome Statute of the International Criminal Court, Arts 55, 66, and 67. See McDermott, *Fairness in International Criminal Tribunals* (OUP, 2016).

These rules are based upon the protections found in Article 14 ICCPR and customary international law.

5.2 SCOPE AND TYPES OF OBLIGATIONS

Though concerns regarding the conduct of judicial proceedings have traditionally focused on how *criminal* trials should be conducted, the right to a fair trial extends beyond such trials to civil and certain administrative proceedings. Article 14(1) ICCPR provides that guarantees should apply to the determination of both rights and obligations in a 'suit at law' as well as criminal charges, while Article 6(1) ECHR refers to the determination of both criminal charges and 'civil rights and obligations'. What is meant by the terms 'suit at law' and 'civil rights and obligations' has been a difficult question to answer.

The Human Rights Committee has interpreted the term 'suit at law' widely:

> [T]he concept . . . is based on the nature of the right in question rather than on the status of one of the parties or the particular forum provided by domestic legal systems for the determination of particular rights. The concept encompasses (a) judicial procedures aimed at determining rights and obligations pertaining to the areas of contract, property and torts in the area of private law, as well as (b) equivalent notions in the area of administrative law such as the termination of employment of civil servants for other than disciplinary reasons, the determination of social security benefits or the pension rights of soldiers, or procedures regarding the use of public land or the taking of private property. In addition it may (c) cover other procedures which, however, must be assessed on a case by case basis in the light of the nature of the right in question.[99]

Similarly, Article 8(1) ACHR specifies that fair trial guarantees are to be accorded in all proceedings which involve 'the determination of . . . rights and obligations of a civil, labour, fiscal, or any other nature'. The case law of the European Court of Human Rights suggests that the reference to '*civil* rights and obligations' covers disputes between private parties, as well as disputes between the individual and the state which involve a pecuniary dimension.[100] Most importantly, for all the international bodies, the application of fair trial rights to a 'suit at law' or the determination of 'civil rights and obligations' does not depend on whether national law has provided that the issue should be determined by a court or another body.

Similarly, what constitutes a criminal charge is not restricted to what national law considers 'criminal' and thus punishable under the law. If this were the case, then states could avoid some of their human rights obligations by simply designating certain charges as something other than criminal. The idea of 'criminal charge' extends to those offences which are criminal in nature because they apply to the population at large and are accompanied by sanctions that 'must be regarded as penal because of their purpose, character or severity'.[101] The expulsion of aliens or disciplinary measures against soldiers, however, will not be considered 'criminal'. In the criminal context, the right to a fair trial is triggered at the moment official notification of a charge is given. Therefore, there may be some overlap with the protections granted by the right to liberty.

Fair trial norms oblige states to secure the right through a number of different guarantees. As stated already, these norms are very detailed in the treatment that individuals must experience in order to enjoy a fair trial. There are both negative obligations to *respect*

---

[99] HRC, General Comment 32, para 16 (footnotes omitted).
[100] Harris *et al.*, *Harris, O'Boyle and Warbrick: The Law of the European Convention on Human Rights* (OUP, 2014) 378–88.   [101] HRC, General Comment 32, para 15.

these guarantees by not interfering in their enjoyment and positive obligations to *fulfil* them through investment, monetary and otherwise, in the court system. States must also *protect* the rights. Although one might assume that justice is only administered by the state, there are instances where the state must protect fair trial rights from interference by other actors. For example, where states recognize religious courts or those based on customary law, they must ensure that these tribunals adhere to fair trial guarantees.[102] In addition, states must not transfer an individual to a jurisdiction where an individual may face a 'flagrant denial of justice', whereby there is a 'destruction of the very essence' of the right to a fair trial.[103]

5.3 GENERALLY APPLICABLE FAIR TRIAL GUARANTEES

What does the right to a fair trial entail? Article 14 ICCPR provides fair trial guarantees of general application that apply to all types of judicial proceedings (considered in this section) as well as detailed guarantees specific to criminal trials (considered in Section 5.4). The generally applicable guarantees are set out in Article 14(1) ICCPR, which provides, inter alia, that '[a]ll persons shall be equal before the courts and tribunals. . . . everyone shall be entitled to a fair and public hearing by a competent, independent and impartial tribunal established by law'.[104] The procedural aspects of a number of human rights obligations include recourse to judicial procedures and the general rights of due process will apply in these contexts. To take an example referred to already, Article 9(4) ICCPR provides that detainees have the right to have the legality of their detention determined by a court. Such review proceedings must be conducted according to the fundamental principles relating to a fair trial. Failure to do so will constitute violations of both Articles 9(4) and 14(1) ICCPR.

5.3.1 Equality before the courts

The right to equality before courts and tribunals is a specific application of the right to non-discrimination, contained in Article 26 ICCPR, to judicial proceedings.[105] It incorporates (1) the right of equal access to courts, and (2) the rights of all parties to proceedings to equality of arms and to be treated without discrimination.

Equal access

All human rights bodies have confirmed that there is a right to access courts of first instance to determine a criminal charge or rights and obligations in a suit at law. All individuals must have an equal chance to pursue their legal rights. '[A]ccess to administration of justice must be effectively guaranteed in all such cases to ensure that no individual is deprived, in procedural terms, of his/her right to claim justice'.[106]

Ensuring equal access to courts and tribunals involves substantial activity on the part of states. They must ensure that judicial systems are organized so that 'all individuals . . . who may find themselves in the territory or subject to [their] jurisdiction' can access the courts.[107] So there is a requirement of physical accessibility, both in terms of geography as well as for those with disabilities. But the right is not solely concerned with buildings. There also should be no legal impediments to accessing justice. For example, statutory provisions that only allow for husbands (and not wives) to bring proceedings regarding

---

[102] HRC, General Comment 32, para 24.
[103] *Othman*, para 260. See also *Soering v UK* (1989) 11 EHRR 439, para 113.
[104] See also ECHR, Art 6(1); ACHR, Art 8(1).   [105] See Chapter 8.
[106] HRC, General Comment 32, para 9.   [107] HRC, General Comment 32, para 9.

matrimonial property in the courts have been found to violate Article 14(1) ICCPR.[108] Access to courts and tribunals can be severely hampered if no legal assistance is available or only available at a prohibitively high cost. Article 14(3)(d) ICCPR obliges states to provide free legal aid in criminal cases where the interests of justice so demand and the individual concerned cannot afford to pay. Although there is no corresponding provision for civil proceedings, the Human Rights Committee has encouraged states 'to provide free legal aid . . . for individuals who do not have sufficient means to pay for it'.[109] Furthermore, where there are cultural practices or norms that exclude certain vulnerable groups from accessing justice, the state must make efforts to overcome these. For example, in Luxembourg free information is provided once a week for women on issues that might affect them, such as divorce and domestic violence, and how to access judicial help.[110]

However, states may restrict access to courts where such restrictions are based on law, can be justified on objective and reasonable grounds, and are not discriminatory.[111] A contentious restriction on access to justice is where claims of state immunity have barred judicial proceedings. *Al Adsani v UK* concerned a claim in tort that had been initiated before the courts in the UK regarding torture alleged to have been committed by the government of Kuwait. The Kuwaiti government relied upon the customary international law rule of state immunity, which provides that a state is immune from proceedings in foreign courts regarding certain official acts. This claim of immunity was upheld by the UK courts. The European Court of Human Rights held, by nine votes to eight, that restricting access to the courts by virtue of the rule of state immunity was permissible because it pursued the legitimate aim of 'complying with international law to promote comity and good relations between states through the respect of another's state sovereignty'.[112] Thus, applying the customary rule of state immunity to civil proceedings for torture did not violate the right to a fair trial.[113]

Equality of arms and treatment without discrimination

The right to equality before the courts also includes protections of equality of arms and treatment without discrimination. Equality of arms means that all parties should be provided with the same procedural rights unless there is an objective and reasonable justification not to do so and there is no significant disadvantage to either party. The essence of the guarantee is that each side should be given the opportunity to challenge all the arguments put forward by the other side.[114]

There should be no differential treatment of persons during court proceedings. Like cases should be treated alike unless there are objective and justifiable reasons not to do so. On this basis, the Human Rights Committee held in *Kavanagh v Ireland* that a situation where the Director of Public Prosecutions decided, with unfettered discretion, whether or not individuals accused of certain crimes would face a jury trial raised issues of equality before the law.[115] The treaties aimed at eradicating specific forms of discrimination, such as the ICERD and the Convention on the Elimination of All Forms of Discrimination

---

[108] *Ato del Avellanal v Peru*, CCPR/C/34/202/1986 (28 October 1988).

[109] HRC, General Comment 32, para 10. See also *Airey v Ireland* (1979–80) 2 EHRR 305; OC-11/90, *Exceptions to the Exhaustion of Domestic Remedies*, IACtHR Series A No 11 (10 August 1990) para 28.

[110] Report of the Special Rapporteur on the independence of judges and lawyers, A/HRC/17/30 (29 April 2011) para 75. [111] HRC, General Comment 32, para 9. [112] (2002) 34 EHRR 11, para 54.

[113] See also *Jones v UK* (2014) 59 EHRR 1; *Sechremelis v Greece*, CCPR/C/100/D/1507/2006 (30 November 2010). [114] HRC, General Comment 32, para 13.

[115] CCPR/C/71/D/819/1998 (4 April 2001). Although note that the majority found a violation of ICCPR, Art 26 and decided not to examine whether there had been a breach of Art 14(1).

Against Women (CEDAW), explicitly emphasize that there should not be distinction as to race, colour, national origin, heritage, or sex during court proceedings.[116] Distinction on these grounds can never be justified.

5.3.2 Hearing by a competent, independent, and impartial tribunal

The courts and tribunals before which claims are heard and criminal charges are determined must be 'competent, independent and impartial' and established pursuant to national law. Courts and tribunals are those institutions empowered to make legally binding decisions on the basis of the rules of law applicable within a state. Therefore, a panel which can make recommendations as to a particular course of action but not binding decisions, such as a parole board, will not be considered a *competent* court or tribunal for the purposes of fair trial provisions. The requirement that tribunals be *established by law* means that the basic rules on jurisdiction, organization, and membership of the court should be contained in legislation. This acts as a safeguard against executive abuse of court procedures.

The requirement of independence refers to the institutional setup of the courts. States are obliged to establish courts so that any form of interference with the activities of judges is thwarted. There are essentially two aspects to this. First, the courts should be fully independent of the executive and the parties to a dispute. Thus, courts should not take direction from government ministers or departments on how to decide a case.[117] Second, states must ensure that there are safeguards in place to preserve the independence of the judiciary, including 'clear procedures and objective criteria for the appointment, remuneration, tenure, promotion, suspension and dismissal of the judiciary and disciplinary sanctions taken against them'.[118] Providing such procedures and guarantees aims to remove the threat that justice may be subverted by appointing 'sympathetic' judges, corruption, or the removal of judges from their post. A clear violation of this principle, and thus breach of fair trial guarantees, was seen in *Lawyers for Human Rights v Swaziland* where the King assumed all judicial power, including the ability to remove judges as well as exercise judicial authority.[119] A recent attack on the independence of the judiciary has been seen in Turkey. Since the attempted coup in 2016, over 4,000 judges have been removed from office—with some being imprisoned—for their alleged links to those responsible for the uprising. This is likely to have a chilling effect on the activities of remaining judges, who may be less inclined to challenge government behaviour.

Related to the consideration of independence is the idea of *impartiality* of the courts. There are two aspects to this. First, judges of the court must be *subjectively* impartial. That is, they must act without any personal bias towards either party in a case. Judges must not harbour preconceptions about the action before them and should remain uninfluenced by the media and public perception. In general, there will be a presumption of subjective impartiality unless there is evidence to the contrary. The court should also be *objectively* impartial, so that the court and its judges must *appear* to the impartial observer to be free from bias. Justice must be seen to be done. For example, in *Piersack v Belgium* the presiding judge in the applicant's case had been the head of the public prosecutor's department during the investigation of the case. Although there was no evidence that the judge had knowledge of the investigation, the European Court of Human Rights held that he was not objectively impartial.[120] Where there is a perceived lack of independence and impartiality, people are wary of having recourse to justice systems and thus access to justice is affected.

---

[116] ICERD Art 5(a); CEDAW Art 15(2). See also General Recommendation XXXI.

[117] eg *Bahamonde v Equatorial Guinea*, CCPR/C/49/D/468/1991 (20 October 1993).

[118] HRC, General Comment 32, para 19. See also the UN Basic Principles on the Independence of the Judiciary; *Chocrón Chocrón v Venezuela*, IACtHR Series C No 227 (1 July 2011).

[119] 251/02, 18th Activity Report of the ACommHPR (2005).   [120] (1983) 5 EHRR 169.

Concerns have been expressed by international human rights bodies regarding the use of military courts to try civilians.[121] There are two grounds for such concerns. First, it is argued that military courts violate the principle of equality before the law because military trials deviate from the normal criminal trial procedures in a state, creating a distinction in the manner in which individuals are tried. The Human Rights Committee has stated that '[t]rials of civilians by military or special courts should be exceptional, i.e. limited to cases where the State party can show that resorting to such trials is necessary and justified by objective and serious reasons, and where with regard to the specific class of individuals and offences at issue the regular civilian courts are unable to undertake the trials'.[122]

The second concern is that military courts are not sufficiently impartial to fulfil the requirements of fair trial provisions. In the words of the African Commission:

> Withdrawing criminal procedure from the competence of the courts established within the judicial order and conferring [it] onto an extension of the executive necessarily compromises the impartiality of the courts. Independent of the qualities of the persons sitting in such jurisdictions, their very existence constitutes a violation of the principles of impartiality and independence of the judiciary.[123]

Thus, some have argued that military trials of civilians are, of themselves, a violation of the right to be tried by an independent and impartial court. There may even be concerns regarding impartiality where only one member of the court is a serving military officer while the others are civilians.[124]

The Human Rights Committee has held that a state must demonstrate that both these concerns have been adequately addressed for the military trial of a civilian to be compatible with Article 14 ICCPR.[125] If it can be shown that the military trial is necessary, has maintained impartiality, and has afforded the civilian a fair trial in procedural terms, then there will be no violation of Article 14(1) ICCPR. The procedural requirements of a fair trial are considered in Section 5.3.3.

5.3.3 Fair and public hearing

'Fair'

Fair trial guarantees explicitly provide for a right to a fair hearing in both civil and criminal proceedings.[126] The content of this right is ever-evolving as international human rights bodies consider new situations; however, there is a minimum core for criminal trials. The principle of fairness includes 'the absence of any direct or indirect influence, pressure or intimidation or intrusion from whatever side and for whatever motive'.[127] All judicial proceedings must adhere to this principle. Other aspects of a fair hearing include, inter alia, the right to equality of arms discussed already, the right of the accused to attend hearings, and the expeditious disposal of proceedings.

The right of the accused to attend hearings is based on the idea that individuals will wish to monitor proceedings concerning their interests. However, it is not an absolute guarantee. In criminal trials, a hearing in the absence of the defendant (*in absentia*) is generally not compatible with the idea of a fair hearing.[128] However, there are three exceptions to

---

[121] eg Report of the Special Rapporteur on the independence of judges and lawyers, A/68/285 (7 August 2013).
[122] HRC, General Comment 32, para 22 (footnotes omitted).
[123] 54/91, *Malawi African Association v Mauritania*, 13th Activity Report of the ACommHPR (2000) para 98. See also Case 11.084, *Salinas v Peru*, IACommHR Report No 27/94 (30 November 1994); *Durand and Ugarte v Peru*, IACtHR Series C No 68 (3 December 2001) para 125.
[124] *Incal v Turkey* (2000) 29 EHRR 449, paras 71–2.   [125] See *Madani*, para 8.7.
[126] ICCPR, Art 14(1); ECHR, Art 6(1); ACHR, Art 8(1).   [127] HRC, General Comment 32, para 25.
[128] *Maleki v Italy*, CCPR/C/66/D/699/1996 (15 June 1999).

this general position. First, an individual may waive his or her right to be at the trial. Second, where the authorities have tried diligently but failed to inform the accused of the trial date because, for example, he or she has moved away from their stated address, then there will be no violation of fair trial guarantees. Finally, there will be no violation if the accused aims to evade justice by not attending the trial. As regards civil proceedings, the right to be present at proceedings has been interpreted flexibly in accordance with different national legal systems. The presence of legal representatives may suffice. However, the European Commission of Human Rights stated that where 'the personal character and manner of life of the party concerned is directly relevant to the formation of the court's opinion', for example in child custody hearings, then there is a right to be present.[129]

A further aspect of the right to a fair trial is that there should be no excessive procedural delays in the resolution of a dispute. Delays call the effectiveness of the judicial system into question. Furthermore, a delay in determining a criminal charge will leave the defendant unsure of his or her fate and, although the guilt or innocence of the defendant is yet to be determined, public perceptions of guilt are often encouraged by long delays. Thus, there is a specific provision in the ICCPR (Article 14(3)(c)) that provides that everyone charged with a criminal offence should 'be tried without delay'. Although there is no comparable explicit protection in Article 14(1), the Human Rights Committee has interpreted the notion of 'fair hearing' to include the expeditious disposal of proceedings and so it is applicable to civil proceedings also.[130] The entire duration of proceedings, from the moment an individual is informed of a criminal charge or civil proceedings are initiated until a final appeal decision is made, is taken into account when deciding whether there has been undue delay. In addition, there may be a determination that the reasonable time guarantee has been violated for a particular stage of the judicial process. For example, a violation was found in *Pinkney v Canada* because appeals proceedings were delayed by nearly three years owing to the transcripts of the trial proceedings taking 29 months to prepare.[131] There is no absolute time limit within which judicial proceedings should take place. Instead, there are a number of considerations that need to be taken into account when assessing the reasonableness of a delay. These include: the length of each stage of the proceedings, the complexity of the legal issues at stake, the detrimental effects on the individual concerned caused by the delay, the availability of remedies to accelerate proceedings, and the outcome of any appeal proceedings.[132] Where delays to the administration of justice are caused by budgetary constraints, states must ensure that more resources are allocated to the judicial system. The Human Rights Committee has not accepted scarce financial resources as a valid excuse for a delay in the determination of criminal charges.[133] States are obliged to take appropriate measures to deal with temporary backlogs of cases.[134]

'Public'

Article 14(1) ICCPR also provides all individuals with a right to a public trial. Trials that are shrouded in secrecy are more likely to involve, or be perceived to involve, manipulation of the justice system in some states. Such trials have been used to suppress 'dissident' groups. There are two elements to this right. First, the trial itself should be conducted

---

[129]   *X v Sweden* (1959) 2 YB 354, 370.

[130]   *Fei v Columbia*, CCPR/C/53/D/514/1992 (4 April 1995). ACHR, Art 8(1) and ECHR, Art 6(1) explicitly provide this protection for both the determination of civil claims and criminal charges.

[131]   CCPR/C/14/D/27/1977 (29 October 1981).

[132]   *Deisl v Austria*, CCPR/C/81/D/1060/2002 (23 August 2004).

[133]   *Lubuto v Zambia*, CCPR/C/55/D/390/1990/Rev.1 (31 October 1995).

[134]   *Zimmermann v Switzerland* (1994) 6 EHRR 17.

publicly and orally. Information regarding upcoming court proceedings should be made readily available in good time and sufficient facilities should be provided in courtrooms to allow the press and other members of the public to observe the proceedings.[135] However, this aspect of the right is qualified and Article 14(1) contains an exhaustive list of situations where hearings can be conducted without public scrutiny: 'for reasons of public morals, public order (ordre public) or national security in a democratic society, or when the interest of the private lives of the parties so requires, or to the extent strictly necessary in the opinion of the court in special circumstances where publicity would prejudice the interests of justice'. The language of these restrictions implies that a condition of holding a trial without public scrutiny is that the principles of a democratic society must be upheld, so that questions of proportionality will come into play. Furthermore, for pre-trial proceedings or appellate proceedings based on purely written submissions, there is no need for public access.[136]

The second element to the right to a public trial provides that judgments should be made available to the public. Article 14(1) ICCPR provides that there may be exceptions to this rule where 'the interest of juvenile persons otherwise requires or the proceedings concern matrimonial disputes or the guardianship of children'.[137] In all other circumstances no restrictions to access to judgments are permitted. Even where the trial has been conducted without public scrutiny, the Human Rights Committee has stated that 'the judgment, including the essential findings, evidence and legal reasoning must be made public'.[138] The European Court of Human Rights has considered the finding of guilt or innocence in criminal cases by lay juries where no reasons for the final verdict are given. In order to avoid arbitrariness in the final decision, the Court held that it was necessary to ensure that a framework was established within which the verdict could stand. The use of procedural safeguards such as directions or guidance provided by the presiding judge to the jurors on the legal issues or evidence presented, and precise, unequivocal questions put to the jury by the judge, will provide such a framework.[139]

5.4 FAIR TRIAL GUARANTEES IN CRIMINAL PROCEEDINGS

A detailed account of what constitutes a fair criminal trial is to be found in most human rights treaty provisions on the right to a fair trial. In addition to the generally applicable principles discussed already, Article 14 ICCPR contains a further six paragraphs regarding the rights of defendants in criminal trials. Similar detailed guidance can be found in Article 6 ECHR, Article 8 ACHR, and the African Commission's Principles and Guidelines on the Right to a Fair Trial and Legal Assistance in Africa. The conduct of investigations often impacts upon criminal trials, and so to ensure that these rights are effective, they have been interpreted, where appropriate, to apply to the pre-trial phase as well.

5.4.1 Presumption of innocence

All treaty provisions on the right to a fair trial contain a guarantee of the right to be presumed innocent until proven guilty.[140] The Human Rights Committee has stated that this guarantee is one of the 'fundamental principles of fair trial' and constitutes a rule of

---

[135] *Marinich v Belarus*, CCPR/C/99/D/1502/2006 (19 August 2010).

[136] *Axen v Germany* (1984) 6 EHRR 195; *Helmers v Sweden* (1993) 15 EHRR 285.

[137] ECHR, Art 6(1) does not allow for any exceptions to this right, while the ACHR only provides this guarantee in the criminal context: see Art 8(5). No equivalent protections are set out in the ACHPR.

[138] HRC, General Comment 32, para 29.   [139] *Taxquet v Belgium* (2012) 54 EHRR 26.

[140] ICCPR, Art 14(2); ACHR, Art 8(2); ACHPR, Art 7(1)(b); ECHR, Art 6(2).

jus cogens.[141] This right applies from the moment that an individual is accused, even before a formal criminal charge is issued, until determination of the charge by the final appeal court. State authorities, including judges, must refrain from any conduct that would influence the outcome of a trial to the defendant's disadvantage. Declarations of the guilt of an individual before trial[142] and excessively long periods of pre-trial detention that affect perceptions of innocence will constitute violations of this right.[143] However, investigatory actions, such as fingerprinting, taking DNA samples, and searches of property, do not violate the presumption. As the presumption of innocence must be maintained at all times during the trial, the burden of proof rests upon the prosecution to prove guilt. If there is insufficient evidence, the court must decide in favour of the accused.

5.4.2 Freedom from self-incrimination

Closely related to the presumption of innocence is the right not to be compelled to incriminate oneself. This right is provided for in Article 14(3)(g) ICCPR as well as Articles 8(2)(g) and 8(3) ACHR, and has been read into what constitutes a fair trial for the purposes of Article 6(1) ECHR.[144] This right is 'to be understood in terms of the absence of any direct or indirect physical or undue psychological pressure from the investigating authorities on the accused, with a view to obtaining a confession of guilt'.[145]

Article 15 UNCAT prohibits the use of evidence obtained by torture 'in any proceedings, except against a person accused of torture as evidence that the statement was made', while the Human Rights Committee has gone further to state that any evidence arising from treatment contrary to Article 7 ICCPR, that is torture *or* inhuman or degrading treatment or punishment, must be excluded from evidence.[146] In fact, the UK House of Lords has held that even evidence obtained by a third party, who is not involved in the proceedings, by means of torture should not be admissible in court.[147] The African Commission has taken a strong position on this, assuming that any confession obtained during incommunicado detention has been obtained by coercion. It has held that 'where a confession is obtained in the absence of certain procedural guarantees against [torture or ill-treatment], it should not be admitted as evidence.'[148] However, disappointingly perhaps, the European Court of Human Rights has held that where evidence is secured as an *indirect* result of torture or ill-treatment—so-called 'fruit of the poisonous tree'—it may be admissible. In *Gäfgen v Germany*, the applicant was suspected of having kidnapped a young boy. He was threatened with torture in order to provide information regarding the boy's whereabouts. Although the confessions provided by the applicant following this threat were considered inadmissible, real evidence that had been found as a result of the confessions was admissible during the applicant's trial. The European Court held that as this evidence was not the only evidence pointing to guilt, its admissibility was not a violation of the right to a fair trial.[149]

Other instances of improper pressure will be decided on a case-by-case basis, examining whether the 'very essence of the right' not to incriminate oneself has been destroyed. So where adverse inferences are drawn in court from a suspect's silence during questioning, whether a violation has occurred will depend on whether there was other evidence pointing to guilt.[150]

---

[141] HRC, General Comment 29, para 11.

[142] See *Marinich*; *Allenet de Ribemont v France* (1995) 20 EHRR 557.

[143] eg *Cagas v Philippines*, CCPR/C/63/D/788/1997 (23 October 2001); *Chaparro-Álvarez*.

[144] eg *Saunders v UK* (1996) 23 EHRR 313.   [145] HRC, General Comment 32, para 41.

[146] HRC, General Comment 32, para 41. See also *Othman*, paras 263–7.

[147] *A v Secretary of State for Home Affairs* [2005] UKHL 71.

[148] 334/06, *Egyptian Initiative for Personal Rights and Interights v Egypt*, 29th Activity Report of the ACommHPR (2011) para 218.   [149] (2011) 52 EHRR 39.

[150] *John Murray v UK* (1996) 22 EHRR 29.

5.4.3 Right to be informed of the charge

Individuals accused of a criminal offence have the right to be informed of the charge that they are facing. This is in addition to the right of those detained to know the charge against them (see Section 2.4.1), and applies to an individual whether in detention or not from the moment he or she is formally charged or publicly named as an accused person.[151] This right, provided for in Article 14(3)(a) ICCPR, Article 7(4) ACHR, and Article 6(3)(a) ECHR, must be fulfilled promptly, without inexcusable delay. At the stage of being formally charged, suspects are entitled to be informed of the full details of the charge against them, including the type of offence and the elements upon which the accusation has been founded, in a language that they understand, so that they may begin to formulate a defence.

5.4.4 Right to an adequate defence

Beyond these protections are those that elaborate on the principle of equality of arms. So, for example, Article 14(3)(b) ICCPR provides that everyone is entitled 'to have adequate time and facilities for the preparation of his defence and to communicate with counsel of his own choosing'. Article 8(2)(c) ACHR, Article 7(1)(c) ACHPR, and Article 6(3)(b) ECHR contain similar provisions. What is considered adequate time will depend upon the nature and complexity of the case.

There are certain minimum levels of facilities, however, that must be accorded to all defendants for their defence to be effective. Explicitly provided for is the guarantee that defendants must be able to communicate with their counsel. In general, access to a lawyer should be facilitated when suspects are being questioned pre-trial. Access at this time serves to protect suspects from ill-treatment and coercion by the police, as well as to ensure that conditions conducive to a fair trial are fostered during questioning. However, the European Court of Human Rights has held that access to a lawyer may be delayed in the 'interrogation' period in some circumstances.[152]

Defendants must also be provided with all the materials that the prosecution is to use in court as well as any other material that may be exculpatory. Exculpatory evidence does not only include evidence that suggests innocence, but also material regarding the gathering of evidence which may show some impropriety. For example, where there is information that the evidence against the defendant has been obtained by torture, this should be transmitted to the defence. The materials must be presented so that the defendant *or* his counsel is able to understand them. Therefore, where the defendant requires translation of documents but his counsel does not, there is no obligation on the state to provide such translations.[153] The right to this information is not absolute however. In exceptional circumstances, for example where national security is at risk, a court may allow the prosecution to withhold disclosure of some evidence. This is only permitted where strictly necessary and where any difficulties to the defence from non-disclosure are counterbalanced in order to ensure that a fair trial takes place.[154]

There are other rights associated with aspects of an adequate defence guaranteed by international human rights law. Defendants have the right to be present at their trial and to defend themselves personally or to have counsel represent them.[155] Although the key principle is that individuals must be allowed to defend themselves, this right is not

---

[151] HRC, General Comment 32, para 31.
[152] *Ibrahim and others v UK*, App nos 50541/08, 50571/08, 50573/08 and 40351/09, Judgment of 13 September 2016.   [153] *Harward v Norway*, CCPR/C/51/D/451/1991 (16 August 1994).
[154] *Rowe v UK* (2000) 30 EHRR 1.
[155] ICCPR, Art 14(3)(d); ACHR, Art 8(2)(d); ACHPR, Art 7(1)(c); ECHR, Art 6(3)(c).

unlimited. If the interests of justice require a lawyer to represent the accused, then a lawyer may be assigned against the wishes of the accused. Such interests apply when an individual is charged with a serious offence but unable to act in his or her own interests, when the defendant is obstructing justice, or in order to prevent intimidation of witnesses if they are examined by the accused during the trial.[156] Any restriction on the choice of representation must be strictly proportionate to the serious purpose articulated.

Should the defendant require legal representation in order to exercise his or her defence but does not have the means to pay, states are obliged to provide legal aid where the interests of justice so require.[157] The seriousness of the offence and the possible punishment will be relevant to this consideration. Where 'deprivation of liberty is at stake, the interests of justice . . . call for legal representation'.[158] Similarly, free legal assistance should be given if the proceedings may result in the death penalty.[159] Legal aid may also be required where the personal circumstances of the defendant require it. For example, in *Quaranta v Switzerland* the European Court of Human Rights held that a young adult with a drug addiction from an underprivileged background was not capable of presenting his case in an adequate manner and should have been provided with legal assistance.[160]

The legal assistance provided must be effective. If the counsel provided is negligent in their duties, then the state will have breached its obligation. In *Myrie v Jamaica* the state-appointed counsel was absent from the courtroom for significant periods of the trial. The Inter-American Commission on Human Rights held that although the state cannot be held responsible for *all* deficiencies in state-provided legal assistance, it was required to 'intervene if a failure by legal aid counsel to provide effective representation is manifest or sufficiently brought to their attention'.[161] Furthermore, where court proceedings are conducted in a language which the defendant cannot understand, interpreter assistance must be offered free of charge.[162]

The right to an effective defence also includes the right of the defendant 'to examine, or have examined, the witnesses against him and to obtain the attendance and examination of witnesses on his behalf under the same conditions as witnesses against him'.[163] Essentially this secures the same powers for the defendant to compel witnesses to appear and cross-examine them as are granted to the prosecution. What is key is that the principle of fairness is upheld at all times. For example, in *Peart v Jamaica* the principal witness for the prosecution had made a written statement that indicated a person other than the defendant had committed the relevant crime.[164] However, the statement was not made available to the defence until after an appeal to the conviction had been rejected. The Human Rights Committee held that this was a serious obstruction of the defence in its cross-examination of the lead witness and thus precluded a fair trial of the defendant. Where cross-examination may lead to serious concerns for the safety of the witness, then restrictions upon the right to examine may be implemented. The interests of the defence must be balanced against those of a witness called to testify and so, in extreme cases, witnesses may remain anonymous. However, even where the witness remains anonymous to the public and the defendant, an effective examination of their testimony must still be facilitated. Where witnesses are completely absent from the trial, for example where they

---

[156] HRC, General Comment 32, para 37.
[157] ICCPR, Art 14(3)(d); ECHR, Art 6(3)(d); ACHR, Art 8(2)(e).
[158] *Benham v UK* (1996) 22 EHRR 293, para 61.   [159] HRC, General Comment 32, para 38.
[160] A 205 (1991).   [161] Case 12.417, IACommHR Report No 41/04 (12 October 2004) para 63.
[162] ICCPR, Art 14(3)(f); ACHR, Art 8(1)(a); ECHR, Art 6(3)(e).
[163] ICCPR, Art 14(3)(e). See also ACHR, Art 8(2)(f); ECHR, Art 6(3)(d).
[164] CCPR/C/54/D/464/1991 (24 July 1995).

have died during the course of the investigation, and a conviction is based 'solely or decisively' on their evidence, a violation of this right will be found unless 'there are sufficient counterbalancing factors in place, including measures that permit a fair and proper assessment of the reliability of that evidence to take place.'[165]

5.4.5 Right to review

Everyone convicted of a crime is entitled to have the conviction reviewed by a higher court in accordance with procedures set out in national law. This right is aimed at correcting miscarriages of justice, so higher courts are required to conduct an evaluation of the evidence presented at the trial and the conduct of the trial. This right is set out in Article 14(5) ICCPR and Article 8(2)(h) ACHR, while a more restrictive version of the right is to be found in Article 2 Protocol 7 ECHR. The African Commission on Human Rights confirmed in *Constitutional Rights Project v Nigeria* that this right is also protected by the ACHPR. The Commission criticized certain provisions of Nigerian law that precluded any judicial appeal of convictions for which the death penalty was imposed. It held that 'to foreclose any avenue of appeal to "competent national organs" in criminal cases bearing such penalties clearly violates Article 7(1)(a) of the African Charter, and increases the risk that severe violations may go unaddressed'.[166] Obviously all review proceedings must adhere to the principles of a fair trial discussed already.

Where a newly discovered fact shows conclusively that there has been a miscarriage of justice and hence a conviction is overturned or a pardon given, all affected individuals are entitled to compensation for the punishment already endured.[167] In *WJH v Netherlands* the author had been convicted of a number of offences but served no time in detention. Following a challenge to the conviction, the Dutch Supreme Court set aside the verdict and remitted the case back for consideration by a lower court, which acquitted him on procedural grounds. The Human Rights Committee rejected a claim that the Netherlands had violated its obligation to grant compensation for the initial conviction as 'the final decision in this case . . . acquitted the author, and since he did not suffer any punishment as a result of his earlier conviction'.[168] Therefore, miscarriages of justice must be distinguished from acquittals on appeal. It is only for miscarriages of justice that compensation is due.

5.4.6 *Ne bis in idem*

All major human rights treaties provide that the principle of *ne bis in idem* is applicable to all individuals who are charged with a criminal offence.[169] The principle essentially maintains that no person shall be tried twice for the same offence in the same jurisdiction. There are certain exceptions to this general rule. If there is evidence of newly discovered facts or there were serious defects in the earlier proceedings that affected the outcome of the case, the interests of justice may demand that cases should be reopened. Furthermore, individuals may be tried for the same offence in different jurisdictions. In the case of *AP v Italy* the author of the communication was convicted by a Swiss court of being involved in a kidnapping conspiracy which had taken place in Italy. Four years later, after the author had served his sentence, an Italian court convicted him of the same offence. The Human Rights Committee held that Article 14(7) ICCPR was not engaged in this case because it 'does not guarantee *ne bis in idem* with regard to the national jurisdiction of two or more States'.[170]

---

[165] *Al-Khawaja and Tahery v UK* (2012) 54 EHRR 23, para 147.
[166] 60/91, 8th Activity Report of the ACommHPR (1994–1995) 13.
[167] ICCPR, Art 14(6); ACHR, Art 10; ECHR Protocol No 7, Art 3.
[168] CCPR/C/45/D/408/1990 (22 July 1992).
[169] ICCPR, Art 14(7); ECHR Protocol No 7, Art 4; ACHR, Art 8(4); ACHPR, Art 7(2).
[170] CCPR/C/31/D/204/1986 (2 November 1987).

5.4.7 'No punishment without law'

The fundamental right of 'no punishment without law' is guaranteed by all human rights treaties and serves to protect individuals from being held guilty of criminal behaviour without adequate legal basis.[171] States may not derogate from this obligation in times of emergency. To mete out punishment without legal basis to do so is an obvious abuse of state power. Therefore, laws that are so vague that individuals cannot know how to regulate their actions in order to act in accordance with the law will constitute a violation of the right.

The right also includes the prohibition of retroactive legislation. This encompasses two guarantees. First, there should be no punishment for acts or omissions that 'did not constitute a criminal offence under national or international law' at the time of the offence (*nullum crimen sine lege*). Second, where harsher penalties are introduced after the commission of an offence, they may not be applied (*nulla poena sine lege*). There are two restrictions upon this aspect of the right. First, retroactive legislation will be permitted where the new law is more lenient than the old one. Second, legislation that is enacted to introduce criminal sanctions for international crimes, such as war crimes, can be applied retrospectively as long as the conduct was a crime under international law at the time of commission.[172]

5.4.8 Protection of juveniles

Juveniles, that is, those individuals who have not yet reached the age of majority, require special protection in criminal procedures. Recognition of this fact is set out in Article 40 CRC and Article 14(4) ICCPR. Underpinning both these provisions is the idea that children should be spared the stigma of being labelled criminals as far as possible and where offences are made out they should be met with educational rehabilitation rather than punitive measures. Thus, states should establish 'an appropriate criminal justice system, in order to ensure that juveniles are treated in a manner commensurate with their age' where measures such as mediation between the perpetrator and the victim are contemplated as an alternative to criminal trials.[173] Where criminal trials are held, juveniles should:

> be informed directly of the charges against them and, if appropriate, through their parents or legal guardians, be provided with appropriate assistance in the preparation and presentation of their defence; be tried as soon as possible in a fair hearing in the presence of legal counsel, other appropriate assistance and their parents or legal guardians, unless it is considered not to be in the best interest of the child, in particular taking into account their age or situation.[174]

6 CONCLUSION

Rights regarding the administration of justice are some of the oldest protections granted by law to individuals. Today, it is recognized that securing the rights to liberty and a fair trial is a necessary pre-requisite for the enjoyment of all other human rights. A substantial body of norms, guidelines, and jurisprudence regarding these rights has been developed to give more specific protections to all individuals. As criminal justice systems are often manipulated to the detriment of the enjoyment of human rights, a significant proportion

---

[171] ICCPR, Art 15; ACHR, Art 9; ACHPR, Art 7; ECHR, Art 7.
[172] ICCPR, Art 15(2); ECHR, Art 7(2). See *Kononov v Latvia* (2011) 52 EHRR 21.
[173] HRC, General Comment 32, paras 43 and 44.   [174] HRC, General Comment 32, para 42.

of the human rights framework for the administration of justice is devoted to this area. However, rights regarding the administration of justice are also concerned with issues such as the use of detention powers beyond the criminal justice context and the judicial resolution of civil disputes. Any failure to regulate these concerns is bound to raise questions about the credibility of a justice system.

FURTHER READING

AMNESTY INTERNATIONAL, *Fair Trial Manual* (Amnesty International, 2014).

CASSEL, 'International Human Rights Law and Security Detention' (2009) 40 *Case Western JIL* 383.

COOK, 'Preventive Detention—International Standards and the Protection of the Individual' in Frankowski and Shelton (eds), *Preventive Detention: A Comparative and International Law Perspective* (Martinus Nijhoff, 1992).

DÖRR, 'Detention, Arbitrary' in Wolfrum (ed), *Max Planck Encyclopaedia of International Law* (Oxford University Press, 2012).

DOSWALD-BECK and KOLB (eds), *Judicial Process and Human Rights: UN, European, American and African Systems: Texts and Summaries of International Case-Law* (Engel, 2004).

INTER-AMERICAN COMMISSION ON HUMAN RIGHTS, *Report on the Human Rights of Persons Deprived of Liberty in the Americas* (Organization of American States, 2011).

RODLEY and POLLARD, *The Treatment of Prisoners under International Law* (Oxford University Press, 2009) chs 8, 9, 11.

SCOVAZZI and CITRONI, *The Struggle Against Enforced Disappearance and the 2007 United Nations Convention* (Martinus Nijhoff, 2007).

TRECHSEL, 'Why Must Trials be Fair?' (1997) 31 *Israel LR* 94.

TRECHSEL, *Human Rights in Criminal Proceedings* (Oxford University Press, 2005).

UDOMBANA, 'The African Commission on Human and Peoples' Rights and the Development of Fair Trial Norms in Africa' (2006) 6 *African HRLJ* 299.

WEISSBRODT, *The Right to a Fair Trial: Articles 8, 10 and 11 of the Universal Declaration of Human Rights* (Martinus Nijhoff, 2001).

WEISSBRODT and MITCHELL, 'The United Nations Working Group on Arbitrary Detention: Procedures and Summary of Jurisprudence' (2016) 38 *HRQ* 655.

USEFUL WEBSITES

UN Working Group on arbitrary detention: <http://www.ohchr.org/EN/Issues/Detention/Pages/WGADIndex.aspx>

UN Special Representative on independence of the judiciary: <http://www2.ohchr.org/english/issues/judiciary/index.htm>

14

CULTURAL RIGHTS

Julie Ringelheim

SUMMARY

While cultural rights have long been neglected in human rights theory and practice, they are attracting growing attention today. This chapter examines the sources of this category of rights in international human rights law, describes their evolution, and highlights the major debates their interpretation has given rise to. It discusses more specifically the content and meaning of the right to take part in cultural life, the right to enjoy the benefits of scientific progress and its applications, and the rights of authors and inventors to the protection of their moral and material interests.

1 INTRODUCTION

A certain degree of fuzziness surrounds the notion of cultural rights. The source of the problem lies with the concept of culture itself. In the course of its history, the term 'culture' has been endowed with different meanings, each of which continues to coexist today.[1] First, at the time of the Enlightenment, that is, in the seventeenth and eighteenth centuries, the term culture began to be used in France in a metaphorical sense to mean the *cultivation of the mind* as well as the result of intellectual development, namely the knowledge of a person who is well versed in arts, letters, and science. During the nineteenth century, in an era of rising nationalism, the German term *Kultur* came to mean the intellectual and moral achievements of a whole nation. This new definition progressively permeated other languages. While in the earlier understanding culture was seen as an individual characteristic of universal relevance—the culture one could acquire was supposed to be common to the whole of mankind—this newer conception of culture was a collective phenomenon associated with a particular group. Yet, in both cases, the notion referred to a distinct set of social activities: it only included intellectual, artistic, or moral expressions, in other words 'the life of the mind', to the exclusion of material or technical aspects of social life. A third usage of the term emerged in the late nineteenth century in the nascent field of anthropology. Culture, in this context, was redefined as encompassing *all* manifestations of the social life of a given population.[2] This last understanding of the

---

[1] See Beneton, *Histoire de mots: Culture et civilisation* (Presses de la fondation nationale des sciences politiques, 1975).

[2] The British anthropologist Edward B. Tylor is widely considered as the first author to propose this new definition of culture in *Primitive Culture* (John Murray, 1871).

term spread during the twentieth century in common language. Thus conceived, culture became synonymous with the specific *way of life* of a community.

This plurality of meanings of the concept of culture presents a persistent challenge for the conceptualization of cultural rights.[3] The difficulty involved in defining the subject matter of this category of rights partly explains the often-noted fact that cultural rights have long been neglected.[4] But other factors have also contributed to this neglect. Culture is often seen as a luxury compared to more 'classic' human rights issues, such as the right to life or freedom from torture. Besides, the idea of recognizing a *right to culture* in the anthropological sense has been viewed by many as entailing the risk of legitimizing cultural practices that conflict with particular human rights, such as female genital mutilation.[5] Attitudes, however, seem to be changing. Since 2000, cultural rights have attracted increasing attention from human rights experts and international bodies. The decision of the UN Human Rights Council in 2009 to appoint an independent expert in the field of cultural rights is a sign of this rising interest.[6]

Among international treaties dealing with human rights, the International Covenant on Economic, Social, and Cultural Rights (ICESCR) is the only one to refer to *cultural rights* in its title. It is generally considered that cultural rights under this convention include the right to education (Articles 13 and 14) and the rights spelled out in Article 15. The latter provision is inspired by Article 27 of the Universal Declaration of Human Rights (UDHR) which lays down that everyone has 'the right freely to participate in the cultural life of the community, to enjoy the arts and to share in scientific advancement and its benefits' as well as 'the right to the protection of the moral and material interests resulting from any scientific, literary or artistic production of which he is the author.' Building upon this provision, Article 15(1) ICESCR recognizes three different rights: the right (1) to take part in cultural life; (2) to enjoy the benefits of scientific progress and its applications; and (3) to benefit from the protection of the moral and material interests resulting from any scientific, literary, or artistic production of which he or she is the author. Articles 15(2) to 15(4) provide additional clarifications as to what these rights require from states parties:

2. The steps to be taken by the States Parties to the present Covenant to achieve the full realization of this right shall include those necessary for the conservation, the development and the diffusion of science and culture.

3. The States Parties to the present Covenant undertake to respect the freedom indispensable for scientific research and creative activity.

4. The States Parties to the present Covenant recognize the benefits to be derived from the encouragement and development of international contacts and co-operation in the scientific and cultural fields.

Echoing this provision, the specialized UN human rights conventions—the International Convention on the Elimination of All Forms of Racial Discrimination (ICERD)

---

[3] McGoldrick, 'Culture, Cultures, and Cultural Rights', in Baderin and McCorquodale (eds), *Economic, Social and Cultural Rights in Action* (OUP, 2007) 447.

[4] Symonides, 'Cultural Rights: A Neglected Category of Human Rights' (1998) 158 *International Social Science J* 559; McGoldrick (2007), 447.

[5] Stamatopoulou, *Cultural Rights in International Law. Article 27 of the Universal Declaration of Human Rights and Beyond* (Martinus Nijhoff, 2007) 4–6.

[6] HR Council Res 10/23 (26 March 2009). In 2012, the Council conferred to the mandate holder the status of Special Rapporteur in the field of cultural rights: HR Council Res 19/6 (16 March 2012).

(Article 5(e)(iv)); the Convention on the Elimination of All Forms of Discrimination Against Women (CEDAW) (Article 13(c)); the Convention on the Rights of the Child (CRC) (Article 31(2)); the International Convention on the Protection of the Rights of All Migrant Workers and Members of their Families (ICRMW) (Article 43(1)(g)); and the Convention on the Rights of Persons with Disabilities (CPRD) (Article 30(1))— guarantee the right to participate in cultural life without discrimination of the specific categories of people they protect. At the regional level, the right to take part in the cultural or artistic life of the community is recognized in the American Declaration of the Rights and Duties of Man (Article 13), which preceded the UDHR, as well as in Article 14 of the Additional Protocol to the American Convention on Human Rights in the Area of Economic, Social and Cultural Rights. It is also proclaimed in the African Charter on Human and Peoples' Rights (Article 17(2)) as well as in the 2012 ASEAN Human Rights Declaration (Article 32). By contrast, the European Convention on Human Rights (ECHR) contains no similar provision, while the Revised European Social Charter only mentions an obligation for states to take measures to enable persons with disabilities to access cultural activities (Article 15(3)) and elderly persons to play an active part in cultural life (Article 23). The Inter-American Convention on Protecting the Human Rights of Older Persons (2015) guarantees more generally 'the right to culture' (Article 21).

In addition, in the human rights literature, it has become increasingly common to speak of *cultural rights* when referring to the special rights recognized to minorities and indigenous peoples in order to enable them to preserve their distinct identity.[7] International instruments relating to these groups, like Article 27 of the International Covenant on Civil and Political Rights (ICCPR), the ILO Convention No. 169 concerning Indigenous and Tribal Peoples in Independent Countries, or the Council of Europe Framework Convention on the Protection of National Minorities, do not explicitly label the rights they lay down as *cultural rights*. Yet, they contain numerous references to the notions of *culture, cultural identity*, or *cultural practices*. In particular, Article 27 ICCPR recognizes the right of persons belonging to minorities 'to enjoy their own culture'. The European Charter for Regional or Minority Languages includes an obligation for states to recognize the regional or minority languages 'as an expression of cultural wealth' (Article 7(1)(a)).[8] As we shall see, the evolution of the understanding of the right to take part in cultural life under Article 15 ICESCR has provided further support for this usage of the phrase *cultural rights*.

Since the right to education and the rights of minorities and indigenous peoples are dealt with in other chapters of this book,[9] this chapter focuses on the rights recognized in Article 27 UDHR and Article 15 ICESCR. One notion is central to these provisions, that of 'cultural life'. Section 2 traces the evolution of the interpretation of this concept. The three sections that follow analyse the content and scope of the three rights protected in these two articles: the right to take part in cultural life (Section 3), the right to science (Section 4), and the right of authors and inventors to the protection of their moral and material interests (Section 5).

---

[7] eg Stamatopoulou (2007); Francioni and Scheinin (eds), *Cultural Human Rights* (Martinus Nijhoff, 2008); Eide, 'Cultural Rights as Individual Human Rights', in Eide, Krause, and Rosas (eds), *Economic, Social and Cultural Rights. A Textbook* (Martinus Nijhoff, 2001) 289.

[8] See Mancini and de Witte, 'Language Rights as Cultural Rights: A European Perspective', in Francioni and Scheinin (2008) 247.   [9] See Chapters 12 and Chapter 18.

2 WHAT IS 'CULTURAL LIFE'?

The *travaux préparatoires* of the UDHR indicate that for its framers, the notion of 'cultural life' appearing in Article 27 meant intellectual and artistic activities.[10] More precisely, it was 'high culture' that they had in mind, that is, the traditional canons of literature, music, art, and so on.[11] The provision was primarily aimed at recognizing the right of the masses to access lofty cultural resources, which had so far been the privilege of an elite.[12]

With time, however, the interpretation of the term 'cultural life' used in Article 27 UDHR and Article 15 ICESCR has undergone a double evolution. First, the notion has been extended beyond *high culture* to include *popular* or *mass culture*. Second, it has been progressively acknowledged that the concept does not only refer to the idea of culture as intellectual and artistic expressions (culture as the *life of the mind*) but also covers culture in an anthropological sense (culture as a *way of life*).

2.1 FROM HIGH CULTURE TO POPULAR CULTURE

The work of the United Nations Educational, Scientific and Cultural Organisation (UNESCO) had an important influence on the evolution of the interpretation of 'culture' and 'cultural life' in the context of UN human rights instruments. Departing from the vision of the UDHR drafters, the UNESCO Recommendation on Participation by the People at Large in Cultural Life and their Contribution to It (1976) states that 'culture is not merely an accumulation of works and knowledge which an élite produces, collects and conserves in order to place it within the reach of all'.[13] Rather, it includes 'all forms of creativity and expression of groups or individuals'.[14] Thus:

> by participation in cultural life is meant the concrete opportunities guaranteed for all groups or individuals to express themselves freely, to communicate, act, and engage in creative activities with a view to the full development of their personalities, a harmonious life and the cultural progress of society.[15]

This text clearly asserts that cultural life is not restricted to high culture but also extends to non-elitist cultural expressions. This broader approach to cultural life was taken up by the Committee on Economic, Social and Cultural Rights. In the Revised Guidelines regarding the reports to be submitted by states under the ICESCR, adopted in 1991, the right to take part in cultural life is described as 'the right of everyone to take part in the cultural life *which he or she considers pertinent*' (emphasis added), including popular forms of culture such as cinema and traditional arts and crafts.[16] Under the current Guidelines, drafted in 2008, states are requested to provide information on the measures taken to promote popular participation in, and access to, concerts, theatre, cinema, and sport events, as well as information technologies such as the Internet.[17]

---

[10] Morsink, *The Universal Declaration of Human Rights: Origins, Drafting and Intent* (University of Pennsylvania Press, 1999) 217–19.

[11] O'Keefe, 'The Right to Take Part in Cultural Life under Article 15 of the ICESCR' (1998) 47 *ICLQ* 904, 905.

[12] O'Keefe (1998), 906; Donders, *Towards a Right to Cultural Identity?* (Intersentia, 2002) 141.

[13] Preamble, 5th recital, subpara (c).   [14] Para 3(a).

[15] Art 2(b). See also UNESCO Universal Declaration on Cultural Diversity (2001).

[16] Revised Guidelines regarding the form and contents of reports to be submitted by states parties under Arts 16 and 17 of the International Covenant on Economic, Social and Cultural Rights, E/1991/23, 88 at 108; O'Keefe (1998), 913–14.

[17] Revised Guidelines on treaty-specific documents to be submitted by States Parties under Articles 16 and 17 of the International Covenant on Economic, Social and Cultural Rights, E/C.12/2008/2, at 15.

2.2 FROM CULTURE AS THE LIFE OF THE MIND TO CULTURE AS A WAY OF LIFE

The second transformation affecting the concept of cultural life was more profound. The inclusion of popular cultural expressions within the notion of cultural life did not modify its basic nature: cultural life was still conceived as a specific sphere of activities within society, relating to creativity, imagination, and artistic or intellectual endeavours. By contrast, the endorsement of an anthropological conception of culture entailed a considerable expansion of its scope: this latter notion of culture basically embraces the whole way of life of a social group. It can encompass *any* social activity or expression that is specific to a given population: from art, language, or religion to techniques, economic activities, customs, laws, conception of the family, and so on. At the same time, the anthropological approach to culture focuses on traits which are *specific* to a given community. The right to culture in this latter sense becomes the right to one's *own* culture. It overlaps with minority protection and indigenous peoples' rights.

UNESCO had a leading role in this evolution. As early as 1982, the Mexico City Declaration on Cultural Policies defined culture as 'the whole complex of distinctive spiritual, material, intellectual and emotional features that characterize a society or social group', including 'not only the arts and letters, but also modes of life, the fundamental rights of the human beings, value systems, traditions and beliefs'.[18] The UNESCO Universal Declaration on Cultural Diversity (2001) embraces the same conception of culture.[19] A similar approach was progressively endorsed by the Committee on Economic, Social and Cultural Rights. During a day of general discussion on the right to take part in cultural life, organized by the Committee in 1992, various members declared that 'culture meant a way of life' and that taking part in cultural life 'embraced all the activities of the individual'.[20] The Committee's General Comment 21 on the right of everyone to take part in cultural life, adopted in 2009, confirms this evolution. Culture is described in it as 'encompassing all manifestations of human existence.'[21] For the purpose of Article 15 ICESCR, it includes:

> inter alia, ways of life, language, oral and written literature, music and song, non-verbal communication, religion or belief systems, rites and ceremonies, sport and games, methods of production or technology, natural and man-made environments, food, clothing and shelter and the arts, customs and traditions through which individuals, groups of individuals and communities express their humanity and the meaning they give to their existence, and build their world view representing their encounter with the external forces affecting their lives.[22]

This expansion of the concept of cultural life, while encouraged by many authors,[23] has been criticized by some.[24] Critics argue that the definition proposed in the General Comment is so broad that it is very difficult to identify specific individual entitlements and state obligations. Moreover, some fear that the emphasis now put in the context of Article 15 ICESCR on the protection of minorities and indigenous peoples, two subjects

---

[18] Para 6. See also *Our Creative Diversity: Report of the World Commission on Culture and Development* (UNESCO, 1995).   [19] Preamble, para 5.

[20] E/1993/22, para 213.   [21] E/C.12/GC/21 (21 December 2009), para 11.

[22] CESCR, General Comment 21, para 13.

[23] eg Stamatopoulou (2007); Eide (2001); Stavenhagen, 'Cultural Rights: A Social Science Perspective', in Eide, Krause, and Rosas (eds) (2001), 85.

[24] McGoldrick (2007), 450–1; Romainville, *Le droit à la culture, une réalité juridique: Le droit de participer à la vie culturelle en droit constitutionnel et international* (Bruylant, 2014) 355–70.

already covered by more specialized international instruments, risks reinforcing the traditional neglect affecting what initially was the main objective of this provision: promoting access to and participation of everyone, including the most disadvantaged, to culture in its artistic and intellectual sense.[25]

3 THE RIGHT TO TAKE PART IN CULTURAL LIFE

The Committee on Economic, Social and Cultural Rights has endeavoured to clarify the content, scope, and implications of the right to take part in cultural life protected by Article 15(1)(a) ICESCR in its General Comment 21. In line with the evolution described in Section 2, it attempts to do this on the basis of what can be termed a 'bi-dimensional' conception of culture, as meaning *both* the life of the mind and particular ways of life.

3.1 THE NORMATIVE CONTENT OF THE RIGHT TO TAKE PART IN CULTURAL LIFE

General Comment 21 distinguishes between three main components of the right to take part in cultural life.[26] First, *participation* in cultural life means the right to freely choose one's identity and engage in one's own cultural practices as well as to express oneself in the language of one's choice. Second, *access* to cultural life covers the right to know one's own culture and that of others through education and information, the right to follow a way of life associated with the use of cultural goods and resources such as land, water, biodiversity, language, or specific institutions, and the right to benefit from the cultural heritage and creations of others. Finally, *contribution* to cultural life refers to the right to be involved in creating the spiritual, material, intellectual, and emotional expressions of the community. This is supported by the right to take part in the elaboration and implementation of policies that have an impact on cultural rights.

The Committee on Economic, Social and Cultural Rights has applied the tripartite distinction—*respect*, *protect*, and *fulfil*[27]—to specify the corresponding obligations of state parties to the right to take part in cultural life. The obligation to *respect* requires states to refrain from interfering with the enjoyment of the right.[28] This entails a duty to guarantee various rights and freedoms inherent in the right to participate in culture: the right to freely choose one's own cultural identity; the freedom to create, which implies the abolition of censorship of cultural and artistic activities; freedom of expression in the language of one's choice; the right to access one's own cultural heritage and that of others; and the right to take part freely in decision-making processes that may have an impact on cultural rights. Freedom to create and to research is explicitly protected in Article 15(3) ICESCR, under which states must undertake 'to respect the freedom indispensable for scientific research and creative activity'. It can, moreover, be seen as a particular application of the right to freedom of expression.[29] The European Court of Human Rights has indeed acknowledged that freedom of expression under the ECHR covers freedom of artistic expression[30] as well as academic freedom.[31]

---

[25] Romainville (2014).   [26] CESCR, General Comment 21, para 15.   [27] See Chapter 5.
[28] CESCR, General Comment 21, para 49.   [29] See Chapter 11.
[30] *Müller and others v Switzerland* (1991) 13 EHRR 212, para 27.
[31] *Sorguç v Turkey*, App no 17089/03, Judgment of 23 June 2009, para 35. See more generally ECtHR, Research Division, *Cultural Rights in the Case-Law of the European Court of Human Rights* (Council of Europe, 2011). See also CFREU, Art 13, which recognizes artistic and academic freedom.

To meet their *obligation to protect*, states must take measures to prevent non-state actors from interfering in the exercise of the right. In addition, the Committee has linked four further sets of concerns to this obligation to protect.

First, states must protect cultural heritage in all its forms at all times, whether in time of war or peace and in case of natural disasters.[32] This echoes the numerous international treaties dealing with the preservation of cultural heritage.[33] To be sure, these conventions are not human rights instruments: their object is to secure the protection of cultural heritage, not to confer rights to individuals. Yet given that cultural heritage—whether tangible, intangible, or natural—includes resources that are indispensable to allow individuals to enjoy their cultural rights, its preservation is of major importance to make these rights effective.[34] It was initially in the context of armed conflicts that an international regime of protection was established.[35] Later on, other instruments have been adopted to organize the international protection of cultural heritage in time of peace.[36] Relevant instruments have also been adopted at the European level in the Council of Europe, notably the Framework Convention on the Value of Cultural Heritage for Society (2005). According to the UN Special Rapporteur in the field of cultural rights, the prohibition of acts of deliberate destruction of cultural heritage of major value for humanity, whether in time of war or peace, has now reached the level of customary international law.[37]

A second aspect of the obligation to protect is the protection of cultural heritage of all groups and communities in economic development and environmental policies.[38] The General Comment insists that 'particular attention should be paid to the adverse consequences of globalization, undue privatization of goods and services and deregulation on the right to participate in cultural life.'[39] It is often observed that economic globalization tends to favour cultural products and models of wealthier countries, resulting in the standardization of culture and marginalization of cultural expressions of poorer or smaller countries. The World Trade Organization (WTO) and international trade agreements concluded under its auspices have been criticized for undermining the ability of governments to maintain policies aimed at sustaining national cultural industries and creation.[40] This fear prompted the adoption of the UNESCO Convention on the Protection and Promotion of the Diversity of Cultural Expressions (2005), which aims 'to give recognition to the distinctive nature of cultural activities, goods and services as vehicles of identity,

---

[32] CESCR, General Comment 21, para 50(a).

[33] It can also be related to the duty incumbent upon states under ICESCR, Art 15(2) to take the necessary steps to ensure, *inter alia*, the conservation of culture.

[34] See Report of the independent expert in the field of cultural rights, A/HRC/17/38 (21 March 2011); Francioni, 'Culture, Heritage and Human Rights: An Introduction', in Francioni and Scheinin (2008), 1–17.

[35] Hague Conventions of 1899, Art 56, and 1907, Art 56; Protocol I Additional to the Geneva Conventions of 12 August 1949, and relating to the Protection of Victims of International Armed Conflicts, Art 53; Protocol II Additional to the Geneva Conventions of 12 August 1949, and relating to the Protection of Victims of Non-International Armed Conflicts, Art 16; Hague Convention for the Protection of Cultural Property in the Event of Armed Conflict 1954, Art 4; Rome Statute of the International Criminal Court 1998, Art 8(2).

[36] See, eg, Convention concerning the Protection of the World Cultural and Natural Heritage (1972), Convention on the Protection of the Underwater Cultural Heritage (2001), and Convention for the Safeguarding of Intangible Cultural Heritage (2003), all concluded under the framework of UNESCO.

[37] Report of the Special Rapporteur in the field of cultural rights, A/71/317 (9 August 2016) para 24. See also the UNESCO Declaration Concerning the Intentional Destruction of Cultural Heritage, adopted by the UNESCO General Conference, Paris, 17 October 2003.   [38] CESCR, General Comment 21, para 50(b).

[39] CESCR, General Comment 21, para 50(b).

[40] Morijn, 'The Place of Cultural Rights in the WTO System', in Francioni and Scheinin (2008) 285–316; Voon, *Cultural Products and the World Trade Organization* (CUP, 2007).

values and meaning' (Article 1(g)). Crucially, state parties 'reaffirm their sovereign rights to formulate and implement their cultural policies and to adopt measures to protect and promote the diversity of cultural expressions' (Article 5(1)). The Committee on Economic, Social and Cultural Rights' preoccupation, however, goes beyond the protection of states' national cultures in international trade: the General Comment stresses the need to protect in particular the cultural heritage of 'the most disadvantaged and marginalized individuals and groups' in economic development.[41] It thereby suggests that the protection of the right to take part in cultural life requires intervention by the state to regulate culture-related economic activities and support certain forms of cultural production with a view to ensuring that all groups and individuals, within their population, are able to maintain the cultural heritage they cherish.

A third dimension of the obligation to protect the right to take part in cultural life lies with the duty to defend the cultural productions of indigenous peoples, notably their traditional knowledge, natural medicines, folklore, and rituals. This includes protecting their lands and resources from illegal or unjust exploitation by state entities and private companies.[42] The Inter-American Court of Human Rights has established that when dealing with major development or investment plans that may have a profound impact on the traditional territory of an indigenous people, states must not only carry out prior consultation with this people, but also obtain their free, prior, and informed consent, in accordance with their traditions and customs.[43] This principle has also been endorsed by the Human Rights Committee in the context of Article 27 ICCPR.[44]

Finally, the Committee on Economic, Social and Cultural Rights also mentions, as part of the obligation to protect, the duty to prohibit discrimination based on cultural identity and incitement to discrimination, hostility, or violence on the basis of national, racial, or religious features.[45]

The *obligation to fulfil* entails a duty for states to take appropriate legislative, administrative, budgetary, judicial, and other measures necessary for the full realization of the right. This level of obligation includes an obligation to *facilitate* and *promote* the right as well as, in some circumstances, to *provide* conditions under which the right can be enjoyed:

- To *facilitate* the exercise of the right to participate in cultural life, states should establish and support public cultural institutions, develop adequate policies for the protection of cultural diversity, and grant assistance to individuals or organisations engaged in creative and scientific activities (artists, cultural associations, science academies, etc). They should also support minorities and other communities in their efforts to preserve their culture.[46]

- The obligation to *promote* requires states to ensure appropriate education and public awareness concerning the right to take part in cultural life, particularly in rural and deprived urban areas, as well as in relation to minorities and indigenous peoples.[47]

- Finally, states must *provide* individuals with the means necessary for the enjoyment of the right when, for reasons outside their control, they are unable to realize this

---

[41] CESCR, General Comment 21, para 50(b).   [42] CESCR, General Comment 21, para 50(c).

[43] *Case of the Saramaka People v Suriname*, IACtHR Series C No 172 (28 November 2007) para 137. In *Kichwa Indigenous People of Sarayuku v Ecuador*, IACtHR Series C No 245 (27 June 2012), the Court asserted that states' obligation to carry out prior consultation with indigenous communities on the exploitation of natural resources in their territory is a general principle of international law (para 164).

[44] HRC, General Comment 23, HRI/GEN/1/Rev.9 (Vol I) 207, para 7; *Angela Poma Poma v Peru*, CCPR/C/95/D/1457/2006 (27 March 2009) para 7.6.   [45] CESCR, General Comment 21, para 50(d).

[46] CESCR, General Comment 21, para 52.   [47] CESCR, General Comment 21, para 53.

right by themselves. The Committee ranks in this category the duty to preserve and restore cultural heritage; the duty to include cultural education, including history, literature, music, and teaching of other culture, in school curricula; and the obligation to guarantee access for all, including disadvantaged groups, to cultural institutions (museums, libraries, cinemas, theatres, etc.) and activities. Effective mechanisms should moreover be established to allow persons, individually, in association with others, or within a group, to participate effectively in decision-making processes.[48] The Inter-American Court of Human Rights has especially insisted on the duty of states to carry out prior consultation with indigenous communities on the exploitation of natural resources in their territory. It considers this obligation to be a general principle of international law.[49]

Among these elements, the Committee on Economic, Social and Cultural Rights identifies 'core obligations', that is, minimum essential levels of the right which all states must implement immediately, by contrast with other obligations that may be achieved progressively, depending on available resources. States must at least create and promote an environment within which people can participate in the culture of their choice. This entails the immediately applicable obligations to guarantee non-discrimination and gender equality in the enjoyment of the right to take part in cultural life; to respect the right of everyone to identify or not identify with one or more communities; to respect and protect the right of everyone to engage in their own cultural practices, while respecting human rights; to eliminate barriers or obstacles to people's access to their own culture or other cultures; and to allow and encourage the participation of members of minorities, indigenous peoples, or other communities in the design and implementation of laws and policies affecting them.[50]

3.2 GROUPS REQUIRING SPECIAL ATTENTION

For different reasons, certain groups require particular attention in the implementation of the right to take part in cultural life.

First of all, for some categories of people, special measures are needed to enable them to effectively access the cultural resources, activities, and infrastructures necessary for the enjoyment of this right. In the case of *persons with disabilities*, Article 30 CRPD requires steps to be taken to ensure access to cultural materials; television programmes, films, theatre, and other activities; and cultural infrastructures, such as theatres, museums, cinemas, libraries, tourist services, and, as far as possible, monuments and sites of national cultural importance. Moreover, their specific cultural and linguistic identity, including sign language, should be recognized.[51] The Committee on Economic, Social and Cultural Rights also emphasizes the need to pay particular attention to the promotion of cultural rights of *older persons*. It refers to the Vienna International Plan of Action on Aging (1982), which encourages governments to support programmes aimed at providing these persons with easier physical access to cultural institutions and calls for the development of programmes featuring older persons as teachers and transmitters of knowledge, culture, and spiritual

---

[48] CESCR, General Comment 21, para 54.

[49] *Kichwa Indigenous People of Sarayaku*, para 164. The HRC has also inferred from ICCPR, Art 27 a duty for states to take measures to ensure effective participation of indigenous peoples in decisions affecting their right to maintain a particular way of life associated with the use of land resources. See General Comment 23, para 7; *Angela Poma Poma*.   [50] CESCR, General Comment 21, para 55.

[51] CESCR, General Comment 21, paras 30–1.

values.[52] Additionally, the Committee expresses concern at the situation of *persons living in poverty* and urges states parties to take concrete measures to bring culture within the reach of all and ensure the full exercise of the right to enjoy and take part in cultural life by persons living in poverty.[53]

Minorities, indigenous peoples, and *migrants* are in a specific situation from the viewpoint of the right to take part in cultural life because they have a cultural heritage that differs from that of the majority. Accordingly, they are at risk of being subject to assimilation policies by the authorities. The Committee on Economic, Social and Cultural Rights insists that minorities should have the right to take part in the cultural life of the society at large as well as to conserve, promote, and develop their own culture.[54] In line with Article 31 ICRMW, it notes that the protection of cultural identities, language, religion, and folklore of migrants should receive particular attention.[55] In relation to indigenous peoples, the Committee considers that Article 15(1) ICESCR requires measures to be taken to protect their right to own, develop, control, and use their communal lands and resources as well as to act collectively to maintain and develop their cultural heritage, traditional knowledge, and cultural expressions.[56]

Finally, *women* and *children* must also be given special consideration. The Committee on Economic, Social and Cultural Rights highlights the duty of states to eliminate institutional and legal obstacles as well as those based on customs and traditions that prevent women from participating fully in cultural life, science, education, and research.[57] As for children, they 'play a fundamental role as the bearers and transmitters of cultural values from generation to generation.'[58] The right to take part in cultural life in their case is closely linked to the right to education. States should ensure that education is culturally appropriate, which means that it should enable children to develop their cultural identity and to learn about the culture of their own communities as well as of others.[59] Accordingly, school curricula for all children should respect the cultural specificities of minorities and indigenous peoples and incorporate their history, knowledge, cultural values, and aspirations.[60]

3.3 LIMITATIONS TO THE RIGHT

As with the other rights set out in the ICESCR, the right to take part in cultural life is not absolute. It may be subject to limitations. Such restrictions must, however, respect certain conditions: they must be determined by law, compatible with the nature of the right, and strictly necessary for the promotion of the general welfare in a democratic society.[61]

Of special concern here are cultural practices that conflict with certain human rights. The extension of the notion of 'cultural life' to culture in the anthropological sense has made this problem especially salient. Various practices anchored in cultural traditions are in tension with some human rights, in particular women's rights. The Committee on Economic, Social and Cultural Rights has emphasized in this regard that limitations to the right to take part in cultural life may be necessary to counter 'negative practices, including those

---

[52] CESCR, General Comment 21, para 28. See Inter-American Convention on Protecting the Human Rights of Older Persons, Art 21.   [53] CESCR, General Comment 21, paras 38–9.
[54] CESCR, General Comment 21, para 32.   [55] CESCR, General Comment 21, para 34.
[56] CESCR, General Comment 21, paras 36–7.
[57] CESCR, General Comment 21, para 25. See CEDAW, Art 2(f).
[58] CESCR, General Comment 21, para 26.   [59] CESCR, General Comment 21, para 26.
[60] CESCR, General Comment 21, para 27.
[61] ICESCR, Art 4. See CESCR, General Comment 21, para 19. See also Chapter 5.

attributed to customs and traditions, that infringe upon other human rights.'[62] In another part of General Comment 21, it goes even further and asserts that taking steps to combat customary or traditional practices harmful to the well-being of persons, such as female genital mutilation, would in fact be *required* by the right to take part in cultural life. Failing to do so would, according to the Committee, constitute a violation of this right insofar as such practices constitute barriers to the full exercise of the right by the affected persons.[63]

Interestingly, in some contexts, conflicts may arise between different aspects of the right to take part in cultural life. For instance, artistic freedom may in principle be limited by the prohibition of incitement to discrimination, hostility, and violence against an ethnic or religious group. Yet, evaluating whether a novel, song, or other work of art constitutes such form of incitement may raise arduous questions. As recognized by the European Court of Human Rights, it is important to take into account the particular nature of artistic expression, which can take metaphorical or satiric forms.[64] One must also be mindful of the risk that state authorities instrumentalize the accusation of incitement to hostility or violence to justify censorship of artistic creations that touch upon sensitive issues. In some states, in the name of combating incitement to religious hatred or protection of religious feelings of believers, penal sanctions are imposed on artists who mock or criticize religious doctrines.[65] But it is in the nature of art to challenge conventions, moral codes, and traditions. Artistic freedom must include the right to create works that 'offend, shock or disturb the State or any sector of the population', to use a famous quotation of the European Court of Human Rights.[66] This discussion reveals a potential tension between the two approaches to culture now brought together in the interpretation of the right to take part in cultural life. Artistic freedom, which pertains to culture understood as artistic and intellectual activities, has a distinctly individualist character: it includes the freedom of individual artists to question, subvert, or contest dominant social norms and identities. By contrast, the right to enjoy one's own culture in the anthropological sense has a communitarian and somewhat conservative connotation: it is primarily the right to preserve a community's traditions and way of life inherited from the past. Finding the right balance between these two dimensions of the right to take part in cultural life may not always be easy.

4 THE RIGHT TO SCIENCE

The right of everyone 'to enjoy the benefits of scientific progress and its applications', protected in Article 15(1)(b) ICESCR, has long been overlooked by human rights advocates and institutions.[67] It was largely perceived as vague and obscure. Yet it was rediscovered in the 1990s in the context of the controversies generated by the expansion of the international intellectual property regime.[68] Many argued that this latter development restricted the ability of the general public, and especially the most disadvantaged, to benefit from

---

[62] CESCR, General Comment 21, para 19.   [63] CESCR, General Comment 21, para 64.

[64] *Cultural Rights in the Case-Law of the European Court of Human Rights*, 5–7.

[65] The European Court has admitted that the protection of 'the right of citizens not to be insulted in their religious feelings' can constitute a legitimate aim for the purposes of ECHR, Art 10(2) (limitations to free speech): *Otto-Preminger-Institut v Austria* (1995) 19 EHRR 34, para 48. In its later case law it has, however, qualified this principle: see *Tatlav v Turkey*, App no 50692/99, Judgment of 2 May 1996; *Klein v Slovakia* (2010) 50 EHRR 15.   [66] *Handyside v UK* (1979–80) 1 EHRR 737, para 49.

[67] Chapman, 'Towards an Understanding of the Right to Enjoy the Benefits of Scientific Progress and Its Applications' (2009) 8 *Journal of HR* 1; Besson, 'Introduction' (2015) 4 *European JHR* 403.

[68] Plomer, 'The Human Rights Paradox: Intellectual Property Rights and Rights of Access to Science' (2013) 35 *HRQ* 143, 144.

scientific advancements, with a detrimental impact on the enjoyment of various rights (see Section 5). Against this background, the right provided for in Article 15(1)(b) started to attract more attention. Between 2007 and 2009, three expert meetings were convened by UNESCO, with the collaboration of academic institutions, resulting in the Venice Statement on the Right to Enjoy the Benefits of Scientific Progress and its Applications (2009), which attempts to clarify the normative content of this right. Moreover, the UN Special Rapporteur in the field of Cultural Rights published a report on the subject in 2012.[69] One important question is how to construe the notion of 'scientific progress' for the purpose of this provision.[70] The Venice Statement observes that a human rights-based approach 'requires that science and its applications are consistent with fundamental human rights principles such as non-discrimination, gender equality, accountability and participation, and that particular attention should be paid to the needs of disadvantaged and marginalized groups'.[71] Some authors further argue that 'scientific progress' in this context should mean discoveries and technologies that contribute to the enjoyment of human rights, including by the most disadvantaged.[72] Some technologies, however, can have both positive and negative effects on human development. The rise of environmental concerns epitomizes this problem: technologies which do improve immediate well-being of individuals by making their life more comfortable can have a negative impact on the environment and, therefore, jeopardize their living conditions in the long term. The implementation of the right under Article 15(1)(b) ICESCR is thus bound to raise dilemmas and controversies.

The obligations stemming from the right to benefit from scientific progress and its applications are potentially very wide. The obligation to *respect* entails that states should not interfere with the freedom of scientists to research, disseminate their results, and collaborate with other researchers across boundaries.[73] The obligation to *protect* requires states to safeguard people against harmful applications of scientific and technical progress.[74] Since 2008, the Committee on Economic, Social and Cultural Rights has asked states to indicate in their periodic reports the measures they have taken to prevent the use of scientific and technical progress for purposes that are contrary to the enjoyment of human dignity and human rights.[75] But the most distinctive contribution of Article 15(1)(b) certainly lies with the third level of obligation, namely the obligation to *fulfil* the right. This is interpreted as entailing a duty for states to take positive steps 'to ensure affordable access to the benefits of scientific progress and its applications for everyone, including disadvantaged and marginalized individuals and groups'.[76] It has been stressed that from a human rights perspective, science should be conceived as a public good rather than in service of profit.[77]

---

[69] The right to enjoy the benefits of scientific progress and its applications, A/HRC/20/26 (14 May 2012). In 2013, the High Commissioner for Human Rights organized a seminar aimed at improving the conceptual clarity of this right (A/HRC/26/19).

[70] Eide (2001), 296.   [71] Para 12(b).

[72] De Schutter, 'The Right of Everyone to Enjoy the Benefits of Scientific Progress and the Right to Food: From Conflict to Complementarity' (2011) 33 *HRQ* 304, 309; Chapman (2009), 11.

[73] Chapman (2009), 18; UN Special Rapporteur in the field of Cultural Rights (2012), paras 39–41. See also ICESCR, Arts 15(3) and (4).

[74] Venice Statement, para 15. See also the Declaration on the Use of Scientific and Technological Progress, UNGA Res 3384 (XXX) (1975), Arts 2 and 8.   [75] Revised Guidelines, para 70(b).

[76] Revised Guidelines, para 70(a); Venice Statement, para 16(2); UN Special Rapporteur in the field of Cultural Rights (2012), paras 26–38.

[77] Shaver, 'The Right to Science: Ensuring that Everyone Benefits from Scientific and Technological Progress' (2015) 4 *European JHR* 411, 417; Besson, 'Science without Borders and the Boundaries of Human Rights:

The importance of science and technology for the realization of certain rights is already highlighted in two other provisions of the ICESCR. Under Article 11(2)(a), states must, in order to achieve the right to food:

> improve methods of production, conservation and distribution of food by making full use of technical and scientific knowledge, by disseminating knowledge of the principles of nutrition and by developing or reforming agrarian systems in such a way as to achieve the most efficient development and utilization of natural resources.

The right to health commands 'the creation of conditions which would assure to all medical service and medical attention in the event of sickness' (Article 12(2)(d)). But promoting access to scientific innovations may be important for the realization of various other rights, such as the right to an adequate standard of living, to education, or to water.[78]

There is, however, an important limit to this obligation: Article 2 ICESCR requires states to act only *to the maximum of their available resources* to realize the rights recognized in the Covenant. Hence, states cannot be obliged to provide access to technologies that are disproportionately costly compared to their financial means.[79]

Beside the issue of cost, the will to ensure affordable access to the benefits of scientific progress and its applications may clash with intellectual property rules. This points towards a wider debate, which is at the core of current discussions on Article 15(1)(c) ICESCR, that of the relationship between intellectual property and human rights law.

5 THE RIGHTS OF AUTHORS AND INVENTORS

While the right to take part in cultural life and the right to science concern the whole population, the third right recognized in Article 15 ICESCR concerns a specific category of persons, namely scientists, writers, and artists. Similarly to Article 27(2) UDHR, Article 15(1)(c) ICESCR provides that everyone has the right to 'the protection of the moral and material interests resulting from any scientific, literary or artistic production of which he is the author.' The insertion of this clause in the UDHR generated vociferous debates during the drafting process. Introduced at the insistence of the French delegation, Article 27(2) was strongly opposed by several delegations, including those of the UK and the US, who contested that intellectual property was a basic human right. Chile pointed out the potential conflict between the protection of intellectual work and freedom of access to literary, artistic, or scientific output. Nevertheless, a majority of states voted in favour of this right.[80]

5.1 HUMAN RIGHTS AND INTELLECTUAL PROPERTY

A crucial question raised by the right under Article 15(1)(c) ICESCR is that of its relationship with intellectual property law, which has been developed largely outside the human rights framework, through domestic legislation, bilateral agreements, and multilateral treaties.[81] Broadly stated, this body of law aims to safeguard the producers of intellectual goods or services by granting them certain time-limited rights that allow them to prohibit

---

Who Owes the Human Right to Science?' (2015) 4 *European JHR* 462; UN Special Rapporteur in the field of Cultural Rights (2012), para 65.   [78] Venice Statement, para 12(d).

[79] Eide (2001), 296.   [80] Morsink (1999), 219–22 and Plomer (2013), 171–5.

[81] eg the Paris Convention for the Protection of Industrial Property (1883, last revised 1967); the Berne Convention for the Protection of Literary and Artistic Works (1886, last revised 1971); and the International Convention for the Protection of Performers, Producers of Phonograms and Broadcasting Organizations (1961).

or authorize the use of those productions by others and to draw financial reward from such use.[82] Whereas *copyright* relates to literary and artistic creations (such as books and other writings, music, paintings, or films) and technology-based works like computer programs and electronic databases, *industrial property* covers the protection of inventions through patents, as well as trademark and industrial design protection. Importantly, a patent holder may benefit from a right of exclusion: once a patent has been granted in a certain country, the patentee can exclude others from making, using, or selling the protected invention in that country.[83] In all national systems, however, there are some exceptions and limitations to intellectual property rights.

While human rights and intellectual property rights have long developed in relative isolation from each other, this changed radically with the adoption of the Trade Related Aspects of Intellectual Property Rights (TRIPS) agreement by the WTO in 1994. TRIPS had the effect of imposing high minimum standards of intellectual property on all WTO member states, including on developing countries where copyright and patent laws were, at that time, absent or very limited. This generated intense criticism. It was observed that strict intellectual property models were likely to significantly disadvantage less developed countries by increasing the costs of development, in a context where industrialized countries hold the overwhelming majority of the patents registered worldwide. Furthermore, it was realized that intellectual property norms could hamper the achievement of various human rights, in particular the rights to health and to food.[84] A number of UN human rights institutions expressed serious concerns about this development. In 2000, the Sub-Commission on the Promotion and Protection of Human Rights adopted Resolution 2000/7 on 'Intellectual Property Rights and Human Rights', stating that 'actual or potential conflicts exist between the implementation of the TRIPS Agreement and the realisation of economic, social and cultural rights'.[85] The following year, the UN High Commissioner for Human Rights drafted a report on the impact of TRIPS on human rights, focusing on the right to health.[86] Also in 2001, the Committee on Economic, Social and Cultural Rights adopted a statement on 'Human rights and intellectual property'.[87] All these documents insisted on the primacy of human rights obligations over TRIPS and called upon states to ensure that intellectual property regulations correspond with international human rights law.

The tensions between intellectual property rules and human rights are especially acute in the case of the right to health. The standard justification for the intellectual property system is that it creates an incentive for innovation, including in the pharmaceutical field. Yet, whereas affordability of medicines is a central component of the right to health, medical patents result in higher prices for drugs, which restrict access for the poor. The problem became particularly salient in relation to the HIV and AIDS pandemic that predominantly affects the populations of developing countries. Additionally, because it links innovation

---

[82] World Intellectual Property Organization (WIPO), *Introduction to Intellectual Property: Theory and Practice* (Kluwer, 1997) 3.

[83] WIPO, *Understanding Industrial Property*, WIPO Publication No. 895(E), 7–8.

[84] Chapman, 'The Human Rights Implications of Intellectual Property Protection' (2002) 5 *Journal of International Economic Law* 861; Cullet, 'Human Rights and Intellectual Property Protection in the TRIPS Era' (2007) 29 HRQ 404; Plomer (2013); Helfer and Austin, *Human Rights and Intellectual Property: Mapping the Global Interference* (CUP, 2011).   [85] E/CN.4/Sub.2/2000/7 (17 August 2000).

[86] The Impact of the Agreement on Trade-Related Aspects of Intellectual Property Rights on Human Rights, Report of the High Commissioner, E/CN.4/Sub.2/2001/13 (27 June 2001).

[87] 'Human Rights and Intellectual Property: Statement by the Committee on Economic, Social and Cultural Rights', Follow-up to the day of general discussion on Article 15(1)(c), 26 November 2001, E/C.12/2001/15 (14 December 2001).

to commercial motivation, the system of intellectual property entails that research is directed first and foremost towards 'profitable' diseases, namely diseases that are prevalent in rich countries, where the return is likely to be the greater.[88]

The impact of intellectual property on the right to food has also become a source of major concern. In order to encourage innovation in agriculture, intellectual property has been extended to new plant varieties in the form of patents and plant breeders' rights. As a result, a few agricultural corporations have acquired virtual monopolies on the genome of important crops, enabling them to set prices at levels far exceeding actual costs. In consequence, poor farmers experience difficulties in accessing seeds and production resources. This situation, moreover, can lead to higher prices for food, making it less affordable for the poorest.[89]

Another crucial debate concerns the protection of traditional knowledge (relating to medicine, agriculture, etc.) and artistic creations of indigenous communities. These intellectual goods rarely qualify for intellectual property protection because they are usually considered by the community to belong to the whole group, whereas intellectual property rules presuppose a single owner. Accordingly, such knowledge and creations are considered to be part of the public domain, which makes them available for exploitation and appropriation by third parties. This leads to a situation called 'biopiracy', 'whereby traditional knowledge is expropriated and patented by outsiders without the indigenous sources receiving any benefit'.[90] In an effort to counter this phenomenon, Article 31(1) of the UN Declaration on the Rights of Indigenous Peoples recognizes the right of indigenous peoples 'to maintain, control, protect and develop their intellectual property over [their] cultural heritage, traditional knowledge, and traditional expressions'.

5.2 THE CONTENT AND LIMITATIONS OF THE RIGHT UNDER ARTICLE 15(1)(c) ICESCR

Against the backdrop of these controversies, in 2005 the Committee on Economic, Social and Cultural Rights issued a General Comment on the right protected in Article 15(1)(c). At the outset, the Committee asserts that this right 'does not necessarily coincide with what is referred to as intellectual property rights under national legislation or international agreements.'[91] The right to benefit from the protection of the moral and material interests resulting from any scientific, literary, or artistic production of which she is the author is a *human right*, which derives from the inherent dignity and worth of all persons, while intellectual property rights are first and foremost *means* by which states seek to advance societal interests, namely to 'provide incentive for inventiveness and creativity, encourage the dissemination of creative and innovative productions, as well as the development of cultural identities, and preserve the integrity of scientific, literary and artistic productions for the benefit of society as a whole.'[92] The right under Article 15(1)(c) is essentially aimed at safeguarding the personal link between authors and their creations and allowing them to enjoy an adequate standard of living, whereas intellectual property regimes 'primarily protect business and corporate interests and investments.'[93]

The Committee thus distinguishes the right under Article 15(1)(c) from intellectual property rights. Yet the approach developed in the General Comment denotes a

---

[88] Report of the High Commissioner (2001), para 38.   [89] De Schutter (2011).
[90] Chapman (2002) 872–3.
[91] CESCR, General Comment 17, HRI/GEN/1/Rev.9 (Vol I) 123, para 2. By contrast with ICESCR, Art 15(1)(c), CFREU, Art 17(2) explicitly protects intellectual property.
[92] CESCR, General Comment 17, para 1.   [93] CESCR, General Comment 17, para 2.

conceptual framework that 'is still largely influenced by existing intellectual property rights frameworks.'[94] According to the Committee, the 'moral interests' referred to in the provision include the right of authors to be recognized as the creators of their intellectual productions and to object to any distortion, mutilation, or modification which would be prejudicial to their honour and reputation.[95] The protection of 'material interests' is meant to allow authors to enjoy an adequate standard of living.[96] Among the obligations imposed on states lies the duty to 'prevent the unauthorized use of scientific, literary and artistic productions that are easily accessible or reproducible through modern communication and reproduction technologies.' This may be achieved 'by establishing systems of collective administration of authors' rights or by adopting legislation requiring users to inform authors of any use made of their productions and to remunerate them adequately.'[97]

Furthermore, the Committee asserts that states should take action to effectively protect the interests of indigenous peoples in relation to their intellectual productions, which are often expressions of their cultural heritage and traditional knowledge.[98] As seen already, a similar obligation has also been derived by the Committee from the right to take part in cultural life, which in its view entails a duty to defend the cultural productions of indigenous peoples, including their traditional knowledge and natural medicines, against unjust exploitation by state entities or private companies.[99]

The rights of authors, scientists, and inventors can be subject to limitations provided they are compatible with the essential aims of the right, namely protecting their personal link with their creation and allowing them to enjoy an adequate standard of living.[100] Significantly, the Committee calls for an adequate balance to be struck between state obligations under Article 15(1)(c) and under the other provisions of the Covenant:

> In striking this balance, the private interests of authors should not be unduly favoured and the public interest in enjoying broad access to their productions should be given due consideration. States parties should therefore ensure that their legal or other regimes for the protection of the moral and material interests resulting from one's scientific, literary or artistic productions constitute no impediment to their ability to comply with their core obligations in relation to the rights to food, health and education, as well as to take part in cultural life and to enjoy the benefits of scientific progress and its applications, or any other right enshrined in the Covenant.[101]

In particular, states parties 'have a duty to prevent unreasonably high costs for access to essential medicines, plant seeds or other means of food production, or for schoolbooks and learning materials, from undermining the rights of large segments of the population to health, food and education.'[102]

Importantly, the Committee insists that the right to the protection of the moral and material interests resulting from the production of which one is the author is intrinsically linked to the other rights recognized in Article 15, the right of everyone to take part in cultural life, the right to enjoy the benefits of scientific progress and its applications as well as the right to artistic and academic freedom. The relationship between these rights 'is at the same time mutually reinforcing and reciprocally limitative.'[103] The Committee

---

[94] Cullet (2007) 422.
[95] CESCR, General Comment 17, para 13.
[96] CESCR, General Comment 17, para 15.
[97] CESCR, General Comment 17, para 31.
[98] CESCR, General Comment 17, para 32.
[99] CESCR, General Comment 21, para 50(c).
[100] CESCR, General Comment 17, para 23.
[101] CESCR, General Comment 17, para 35.
[102] CESCR, General Comment 17, para 35.
[103] CESCR, General Comment 17, para 4.

thereby calls for a holistic interpretation of Article 15 ICESCR, implying the search for a fair equilibrium between the rights of authors and inventors to the protection of their private interests and the right of the public to access culture and science.[104]

6 CONCLUSION

The cultural rights recognized in Article 27 UDHR and Article 15 ICESCR have tradition-ally been neglected in human rights theory and practice. Today, however, these rights are attracting growing attention. They prove to be particularly relevant to some crucial debates of our time, such as how to protect local cultures in the face of economic globalization; how to safeguard indigenous peoples', minorities', and migrants' rights to preserve their cultural heritage; how to ensure access for all to essential scientific advancements; or how to prevent intellectual property rules from hindering the enjoyment of human rights. Nonetheless, many interpretive questions remain. Two issues in particular are likely to continue to gen-erate discussions in the years to come. One is how to develop an effective protection of cultural life given the very broad conception that has been endorsed by the Committee on Economic, Social and Cultural Rights, as including both culture as intellectual and artistic expressions and culture in the anthropological sense. A second critical question is how to find the right balance between the different components of Article 15 ICESCR, in particular the right of authors and inventors to the protection of their interests, on the one hand, and, on the other hand, the right of everyone to access culture and science.

FURTHER READING

BESSON, 'Science without Borders and the Boundaries of Human Rights: Who Owes the Human Right to Science?' (2015) 4 *European JHR* 462.

CULLET, 'Human Rights and Intellectual Property Protection in the TRIPS Era' (2007) 29 *HRQ* 404.

DONDERS, *Towards a Right to Cultural Identity?* (Intersentia, 2002).

EIDE, 'Cultural Rights as Individual Human Rights', in Eide, Krause, and Rosas (eds), *Economic, Social and Cultural Rights: A Textbook* (Martinus Nijhoff, 2001) 289.

FRANCIONI and SCHEININ (eds), *Cultural Human Rights* (Martinus Nijhoff, 2008).

HELFER and AUSTIN, *Human Rights and Intellectual Property: Mapping the Global*

Interference (Cambridge University Press, 2011).

MCGOLDRICK, 'Culture, Cultures, and Cultural Rights', in Baderin and McCorquodale (eds), *Economic, Social and Cultural Rights in Action* (Oxford University Press, 2007) 447.

PLOMER, 'The Human Rights Paradox: Intellectual Property Rights and Rights of Access to Science' (2013) 35 *HRQ* 143.

SHAVER, 'The Right to Science: Ensuring that Everyone Benefits from Scientific and Technological Progress' (2015) 4 *European JHR* 411.

STAMATOPOULOU, *Cultural Rights in International Law: Article 27 of the Universal Declaration of Human Rights and Beyond* (Martinus Nijhoff, 2007).

---

[104] See the two reports of the UN Special Rapporteur in the field of cultural rights: Copyright policy and the right to science and culture, A/HRC/28/57 (24 December 2014); Patent policy and the right to science and culture, A/70/279 (4 August 2015).

THORNBERRY, 'Cultural Rights and Universality of Human Rights', Contribution to the Day of General Discussion on 'The right to take part in cultural life' organized by the UN Committee on Economic, Social and Cultural Rights (9 May 2008).

VRDOLJAK (ed), *The Cultural Dimension of Human Rights* (Oxford University Press, 2013).

USEFUL WEBSITES

UN Committee on Economic, Social and Cultural Rights: <http://www2.ohchr.org/english/bodies/cescr/>

Day of General Discussion on 'The right to take part in cultural life', UN Committee on Economic, Social and Cultural Rights, 9 May 2008 (including background papers from experts): <http://www.ohchr.org/EN/HRBodies/CESCR/Pages/DiscussionMay2008.aspx>

UN Special Rapporteur in the field of cultural rights: <http://www.ohchr.org/EN/Issues/CulturalRights/Pages/SRCulturalRightsIndex.aspx>

Venice Statement on the Right to Enjoy the Benefits of Scientific Progress and its Applications: <https://www.aaas.org/sites/default/files/VeniceStatement_July2009.pdf>

15

SEXUAL ORIENTATION AND GENDER IDENTITY

Michael O'Flaherty

SUMMARY

Worldwide, people are subject to persistent human rights violations because of their actual or perceived sexual orientation and gender identity. The range of violations demonstrates that the members of sexual minorities are highly vulnerable to human rights abuse. This chapter assesses the forms of their vulnerability and identifies the applicable international human rights law. It will be seen that the jurisprudence focuses on issues of non-discrimination and privacy and that important human rights protections can also be derived from the range of other civil, political, economic, social, and cultural human rights of general application. The chapter concludes with an examination of an exercise in the clarification of the application of human rights law concerning issues of sexual orientation and gender identity, the Yogyakarta Principles.*

1 INTRODUCTION

Typically, to be different to the majority in any society is to be vulnerable to prejudice, discrimination, and even attack. The greater the difference, the greater the risk. The story of the human rights movement is replete with moments defined by the identification of such vulnerable minorities and efforts to protect them. Thus, today, treaties address the situation of ethnic, racial, indigenous, religious, and other communities. However, the protection afforded by international law is by no means confined to groups whose protection has been the explicit focus of treaties. International human rights treaty law has proved itself to be flexible in addressing the plight of groups whose vulnerability may not have been in the minds of the treaty drafters. One of the most vibrant contemporary human rights debates concerns the extent to which international law offers protection to members of what are sometimes termed 'sexual minorities'.

A wide range of terms are used to describe the diverse members of sexual minorities, such as homosexuals, bisexuals, gays, lesbians, transsexuals, transgender, and inter-sex. Other terms, such as 'queer', can be considered pejorative in some contexts and acceptable in others. The variety of designations and usages, as well as the manner in which some of them have changed over time, can give rise to confusion when seeking to identify applicable provisions of human rights law. With this in mind, recent discourse on the

* The views in this chapter are solely those of the author and its content does not necessarily represent the views or positions of the European Union Fundamental Rights Agency.

application of human rights law has tended to cluster issues around two categorizations: 'sexual orientation' and 'gender identity'. An authoritative document that we will consider in this chapter, the Yogyakarta Principles,[1] describes 'sexual orientation' as 'each person's capacity for profound emotional, affectional and sexual attraction to, and intimate sexual relations with, individuals of a different gender or the same gender or more than one gender'.[2] 'Gender identity' is described as:

> each person's deeply felt internal and individual experience of gender, which may or may not correspond with the sex assigned at birth, including the personal sense of the body (which may involve, if freely chosen, modification of bodily appearance or function by medical, surgical or other means) and other expressions of gender, including dress, speech and mannerisms.[3]

Of course, these definitions are no more than intellectual constructs and, as such, can be subject to criticism. However, they have some force in that they tend to reflect the contexts in which affected people experience discrimination, exclusion, and attack in many societies. They also—and this is especially the case with regard to 'sexual orientation'—are grounded in the jurisprudence of human rights courts and treaty-monitoring bodies. To the extent possible, this chapter will employ these terms.[4]

2 FORMS OF VULNERABILITY

Before we examine the extent of applicable human rights law, it is important to take account of the situation in which people of diverse sexual orientations and gender identities find themselves. Even the briefest of global surveys demonstrates a remarkable degree of vulnerability and abuse.[5] As of May 2015, eight states maintained the death penalty for consensual same-sex practices,[6] and reports are commonplace of persons who are killed because of their sexual orientation or gender identity. Perpetrators often go unpunished. Persons with diverse gender identities are particularly likely to be targeted for violence. They are 'often subjected to violence in order to "punish" them for transgressing gender barriers or for challenging predominant conceptions of gender roles',[7] and transgender youth have been described as 'among the most vulnerable and marginalized young people in society'.[8] Violations directed against lesbians because of their sex are often inseparable from violations directed against them because of their sexual orientation. For example, there are accounts of multiple rape of a lesbian arranged by her family in an attempt to

---

[1] The Yogyakarta Principles on the Application of International Human Rights Law in Relation to Sexual Orientation and Gender Identity (2007), available at: <http://www.yogyakartaprinciples.org>.

[2] Yogyakarta Principles, preamble.   [3] Yogyakarta Principles, preamble.

[4] For a general discussion of this usage and its implications, see Hamzic, 'The Case of "Queer Muslims": Sexual Orientation and Gender Identity in International Human Rights Law and Muslim Legal and Social Ethos' (2011) 11 *HRLR* 237.

[5] For an extensive review of the forms of vulnerability, see O'Flaherty and Fisher, 'Sexual Orientation, Gender Identity and International Human Rights Law: Contextualising the Yogyakarta Principles' (2008) 8 *HRLR* 207.

[6] Report of the Office of the UN High Commissioner for Human Rights on discrimination and violence against individuals based on their sexual orientation and gender identity, A/HRC/29/23 (4 May 2015) para 46.

[7] Report of the Special Rapporteur on the question of torture and other cruel, inhuman or degrading treatment or punishment, A/56/156 (3 July 2001) para 17.

[8] Report of the Special Rapporteur on the sale of children, child prostitution and child pornography, E/CN.4/2004/9 (5 January 2004) para 123.

'cure' her of her homosexuality.[9] Same-sex sexual relations between consenting adults constitute a criminal offence in some 75 states. Some states apply laws against 'public scandals', 'immorality', or 'indecent behaviour' to punish people for looking, dressing, or behaving differently from what are considered to be the social norms.

Serious problems have also been identified regarding the enjoyment of economic, social, and cultural rights. For example, people have been denied employment or employment-related benefits or have faced dismissal because of their sexual orientation or gender identity. In the context of the right to adequate housing, lesbian and transgender women are reported to be at a high risk of homelessness; discrimination based on sexual orientation or gender identity when renting accommodation has been experienced both by individuals and same-sex couples; and children have been thrown out of the family home by their families upon learning of their sexual orientation or gender identity. Transgender persons often face obstacles in seeking access to gender-appropriate services at homeless shelters. Materials referencing issues of sexual orientation and gender identity have been banned from school curricula; student groups addressing sexual orientation and gender identity issues have been prohibited; students have faced high levels of bullying and harassment because of their actual or perceived sexual orientation or gender identity; and, in some cases, young persons who express same-sex affection have been expelled from school. In some countries, laws have prohibited the 'promotion of homosexuality' in schools. Numerous health-related human rights violations based on sexual orientation and gender identity have been documented. People have been forcibly confined in medical institutions, subjected to 'aversion therapy', including electroshock treatment, and inter-sex people have been subjected to involuntary surgeries in an attempt to 'correct' their genitals.

The plight in which people of diverse sexual orientations and gender identities find themselves is well summarized in a comment by an Indonesian human rights expert, Siti Musdah Mulia:

> I realise that compared to other minority groups, LGBT [Lesbian, Gay, Bisexual, and Transgender] people suffer more stigmas, stereotypes and discriminatory treatment, and even ruthless exploitation. The majority community (in Indonesia) still considers homosexuality as illicit, often as unmentionable.[10]

3 REVIEW OF LAW AND JURISPRUDENCE

There are no specific references to issues related to sexual orientation or gender identity in the global human rights treaties. At the regional level, explicit references are confined to the prohibition of discrimination in recently adopted, thematically focused treaties.[11] The UN human rights treaty-monitoring bodies and the European Court of Human Rights have, however, developed a significant body of jurisprudence on the topics while the Inter-American Court of Human Rights issued its first, and wide-ranging, judgment on issues of sexual orientation in 2012.[12] The findings tend to be clustered in three groups: protection

---

[9] Report of the Special Rapporteur on violence against women, its causes and consequences, E/CN.4/2002/83 (31 January 2002) para 102.

[10] Musdah Mulia, 'Promoting LGBT Rights through Islamic Humanism' (1–6 June 2008).

[11] Charter of Fundamental Rights of the European Union (2000); Council of Europe Convention on the Protection of Children against Sexual Exploitation and Sexual Abuse (2007); Council of Europe Convention on Preventing and Combating Violence Against Women and Domestic Violence (2011); Inter-American Convention against All Forms of Discrimination and Intolerance (2013); Inter-American Convention on Protecting the Human Rights of Older Persons (2015).

[12] *Atala Riffo and daughters v Chile (Merits)*, IACtHR Series C No 239 (24 February 2012).

of privacy rights, combating of discrimination, and ensuring other general human rights protection to all, regardless of sexual orientation or gender identity. We will look at each of these in turn.

3.1 PROTECTION OF PRIVACY RIGHTS

The European Convention on Human Rights (ECHR), in Article 8, the American Convention on Human Rights (ACHR), in Article 11, and the International Covenant on Civil and Political Rights (ICCPR), in Article 17, contain provisions for the protection of an individual's privacy. These reflect a perception of the drafters that there is an autonomous zone within which a person may live a personal life and make choices without interference. While the scope and the limits of that private space are impossible to chart outside the context of specific cases, it is acknowledged that 'respect for private life must also comprise to a certain degree the right to establish and develop relationships with other human beings'.[13]

The first successful international human rights cases on issues of sexual orientation were brought under the ECHR and invoked the privacy argument with regard to same-sex sexual activity. In *Dudgeon v UK*[14] and *Norris v Ireland*,[15] the criminalization of such practices was deemed a violation of Article 8 ECHR. In *Modinos v Cyprus*, the European Court, taking account that many of the prohibitions were not actually enforced in practice, held that even a 'consistent policy' of not bringing prosecutions under the law was no substitute for full repeal.[16] Privacy arguments were also successful regarding a ban on recruitment to the military of homosexuals: *Smith and Grady v UK*[17] and *Lustig-Prean and Beckett v UK*.[18] The European Court has also invoked privacy rights to identify a right of same-sex civil partnership in the cases of *Vallianatos and Others v Greece*[19] and *Oliari and Others v Italy*.[20] The Inter-American Court of Human Rights, in its first finding of sexual orientation-related violations of the ACHR, identified a violation of the right to privacy in the case of the loss of parenting rights on the part of a woman, divorced from the father of her children, who was living with a same-sex partner.[21]

The European Court of Human Rights has recognized privacy protection with regard to issues of gender identity. The approach of the Court reflects a perception that privacy protection may extend to the choices one makes regarding one's own choice of gender identity or expression. Interestingly, the cases are not about any effort of states to prohibit forms of gender identity choices. Instead, they address the positive obligation on the state to take the administrative actions, such as amending identity documents, which are necessary for the affected individuals to live in their changed gender identity. In *Goodwin v UK*[22] and *I v UK*,[23] the European Court reversed a long line of previous case law and held that the UK's refusal to change the legal identities of two transsexual women constituted a violation of Article 8 ECHR. In *Van Kuck v Germany*, the Court considered the case of a transsexual woman whose health-insurance company had denied her reimbursement for costs associated with sex-reassignment surgery. It found a violation of Article 8, holding that the German courts had failed to respect 'the applicant's freedom to define herself as a female person, one of the most basic essentials of self-determination'.[24] In *L v Lithuania*,

---

[13] *Niemietz v Germany* (1993) 16 EHRR 97, para 29.   [14] (1982) 4 EHRR 149.
[15] (1988) 13 EHRR 186.   [16] (1993) 16 EHRR 485.   [17] (1999) 29 EHRR 493.
[18] (1999) 29 EHRR 548.   [19] (2014) 59 EHRR 12.
[20] Application Nos 18766/11 and 36030/11, Judgment of 21 July 2015.
[21] *Atala Riffo and daughters.*   [22] (2002) 35 EHRR 447.   [23] (2002) 35 EHRR 18.
[24] (2003) 37 EHRR 51, para 73.

the Court considered that the state was required to legislate for the provision of full gender-reassignment surgery whereby a person in the 'limbo' of partial reassignment could complete the process and be registered with the new gender identity.[25]

The Human Rights Committee, in the communication *Toonen v Australia*, adopted the approach of the European Court of Human Rights and considered that a criminal prohibition on same-sex sexual activity, even if unenforced, constituted an unreasonable interference with Mr Toonen's privacy under Article 17 ICCPR.[26] It is sometimes suggested that *Toonen* turns on its facts in the particular context of a state that cherishes diversity and that the findings might have been very different in the case of, for example, an Islamic state with a dominant moral code that rejected homosexual acts.[27] This view ascribes to the Human Rights Committee a doctrine of margin of appreciation such as that to be found in the practice of the European Court of Human Rights.[28] In 2011, in its General Comment 34 on Article 19 ICCPR, the Committee repudiated such a doctrine in its practice. It also stated that morals may only be invoked to restrict rights where such morals are, inter alia, non-discriminatory in effect and compatible with the universality of human rights.[29]

The Human Rights Committee has not considered relevant applications of the right to privacy other than with regard to criminalization. This, in itself, does not tell us anything about the position of the Committee, since it can only develop case-specific jurisprudence on the basis of the complaints that are submitted to it. In this regard it is notable to observe that the Human Rights Committee seems now to be exploring the range of applications of a privacy approach in the context of its review of periodic reports submitted by states parties to the ICCPR. For instance, in 2015, it invoked the privacy provision of the ICCPR in expressing concern regarding the restrictive requirements for legal recognition of gender reassignment in the Republic of Korea.[30]

3.2 DISCRIMINATION

As we have seen, people of diverse sexual orientations and gender identities are subject to multiple forms of discrimination. It is not surprising, then, that a considerable body of practice has developed in the work of the international human rights treaty bodies. The Committee on Economic, Social and Cultural Rights has addressed sexual orientation-related discrimination in its General Comments. In General Comments 18, on the right to work,[31] 15, on the right to water,[32] and 14, on the right to the highest attainable standard of health,[33] it has indicated that the International Covenant on Economic, Social and Cultural Rights (ICESCR) proscribes any discrimination on the basis of, inter alia, sex and sexual orientation, 'that has the intention or effect of nullifying or impairing the equal enjoyment or exercise of [the right at issue]'. The Committee has consistently based this prohibition on the terms of the anti-discrimination provision—Article 2(2) ICESCR—which prohibits discrimination on a variety of specified grounds as well as one termed 'other status'. In 2009, the Committee adopted a General Comment on non-discrimination specifying that, '"other status" as recognised in article 2(2) includes sexual orientation.

---

[25] (2008) 46 EHRR 22.   [26] CCPR/C/50/D/488/1992 (4 April 1994).

[27] Cowell and Millon, 'Decriminalization of Sexual Orientation Through the Universal Periodic Review' (2012) 12 *HRLR* 341.

[28] See Chapter 5.

[29] HRC, General Comment 34, CCPR/C/GC/34 (12 September 2011), paras 32 and 36.

[30] HRC, Concluding observations on the fourth periodic report of the Republic of Korea, CCPR/C/KOR/CO/4 (3 December 2015).   [31] CESCR, General Comment 18, HRI/GEN/1/Rev.9 (Vol I) 139.

[32] CESCR, General Comment 15, HRI/GEN/1/Rev.9 (Vol I) 97.

[33] CESCR, General Comment 14, HRI/GEN/1/Rev.9 (Vol I) 78.

States parties should ensure that a person's sexual orientation is not a barrier to realising Covenant rights.'[34] The Committee, in its General Comments, also invokes the provision addressing the equal rights of men and women, Article 3 ICESCR, as a basis for its prohibition of sexual orientation-related discrimination.[35]

Other treaty bodies have adopted similar positions in their General Comments. The Committee on the Rights of the Child, in its General Comment 4, stated that:

> [s]tate parties have the obligation to ensure that all human beings below 18 enjoy all the rights set forth in the Convention [on the Rights of the Child] without discrimination (art. 2), including with regard to 'race, colour, sex, language, religion, political or other opinion, national, ethnic or social origin, property, disability, birth or other status.' These grounds also cover [inter alia] sexual orientation.[36]

In 2010, the Committee on the Elimination of Discrimination Against Women (CEDAW Committee) issued two General Recommendations—one on the rights of older women and the other on the core obligations of states—in which it recognized that sexual orientation and gender identity are prohibited grounds of discrimination against women.[37]

The treaty bodies frequently raise issues of sexual orientation and gender-identity-related discrimination when considering periodic reports of states parties. The Committee on Economic, Social and Cultural Rights did so regarding 7 of the 23 states considered in 2014, and the Committee on the Rights of the Child regarding 5 of the 16 states considered in the same period. In each case, the Committees expressed concern in their 'concluding observations'. Given the non-binding and flexible nature of these treaty body outputs, they are not always a useful indicator of formal obligations under the treaty. However, where the treaty body expresses concern about a specific practice, we can surmise that serious issues arise under the treaty. Examples include the Committee on Economic, Social and Cultural Rights' regret, in 2005, that Hong Kong's anti-discrimination legislation failed to cover sexual orientation-related discrimination,[38] and its concern, in 2000, that Kyrgyzstan classified lesbianism as a sexual offence in its penal code.[39] The CEDAW Committee, on a number of occasions, has criticized states for discrimination on the basis of sexual orientation. For example, it too addressed the situation in Kyrgyzstan and recommended that 'lesbianism be reconceptualised as a sexual orientation and that penalties for its practice be abolished'.[40]

Issues of sexual orientation-related discrimination have received extensive attention in the work of the Human Rights Committee. In *Toonen*, the Committee said that 'the reference to "sex" in articles 2, paragraph 1, and 26 is to be taken as including sexual orientation'. The Committee accordingly considered that sexual orientation-related discrimination is a suspect category in terms of the enjoyment of ICCPR rights (Article 2) and, more generally, for equality before and equal protection of the law (Article 26).[41] A small number of individual cases have illustrated the Human Rights Committee's approach. In *Young v Australia*[42]

---

[34] CESCR, General Comment 20, E/C.12/GC/20 (10 June 2009) para 32.

[35] eg CESCR, General Comment 18, para 12(b)(i).

[36] CRC Committee, General Comment 4, HRI/GEN/1/Rev.9 (Vol II) 410, para 6.

[37] CEDAW Committee, General Recommendation 27, CEDAW/C/2010/47/GC (16 December 2010); CEDAW Committee, General Recommendation 28, CEDAW/C/2010/47/GC.2 (16 December 2010).

[38] CESCR, Concluding Observations: People's Republic of China (including Hong Kong and Macau), E/C.12/1/Add.107 (13 May 2005) para 78.

[39] CESCR, Concluding Observations: Kyrgyzstan, E/C.12/1/Add.49 (1 September 2000) para 17.

[40] CEDAW Committee, Concluding Observations: Kyrgyzstan, A/54/38 (5 February 1999) para 128.

[41] On equality and non-discrimination, see Chapter 8.

[42] CCPR/C/78/D/941/2000 (6 August 2003).

and *X v Colombia*,[43] the Committee was of the view that distinctions made in law between same-sex partners who were excluded from pension benefits, and unmarried heterosexual partners who were granted such benefits, constituted violations of the ICCPR. However, not every case has been successful. In *Joslin v New Zealand*, the differential treatment under taxation regulations of same-sex unmarried couples (for whom marriage was not available in law) and heterosexual married couples was considered not to constitute a violation of Article 26 ICCPR. And yet, an individual concurring opinion of two members observed that 'the Committee's jurisprudence supports the position that such differentiation may very well, depending on the circumstances of a concrete case, amount to prohibited discrimination.'[44]

The Human Rights Committee frequently raises the issue of discrimination on the basis of sexual orientation and/or gender identity in its consideration of periodic reports. During 2014, it did so regarding 14 of the 18 states under review and, for example, criticized many states for the criminalization of homosexual sexual relations and the failure to incorporate sexual orientation into anti-discrimination legal frameworks. It also expressed concern regarding unequal ages of consent for sexual activity, failure to prohibit education-related discrimination, and lack of education programmes to combat discriminatory attitudes.

The European Court of Human Rights has generated a substantial body of jurisprudence concerning discrimination both on the grounds of sexual orientation and gender identity. In *Salgueiro da Silva Mouta v Portugal*, it held that a judge's denial of child custody to a homosexual father on the ground of his sexual orientation was discriminatory.[45] The Inter-American Court adopted a similar line of reasoning in *Atala Riffo and daughters v Chile*.[46] In *Karner v Austria*, the European Court considered that the failure of Austria to permit a homosexual man to continue occupying his deceased partner's flat was discriminatory, since this entitlement, available to family members under Austrian law, did not apply to same-sex partners. Austria claimed that excluding homosexuals aimed to protect 'the family in the traditional sense', but the Court considered that it had not demonstrated how the exclusion was necessary to that aim.[47] In *L and V v Austria*[48] and *SL v Austria*,[49] the Court considered that Austria's differing age of consent for heterosexual and homosexual relations was discriminatory. As the Court put it, the differing age 'embodied a predisposed bias on the part of a heterosexual majority against a homosexual minority', which could not 'amount to sufficient justification for the differential treatment any more than similar negative attitudes towards those of a different race, origin or colour'.

One area of discrimination in which the European Court was slow to find a violation of the Convention concerned the adoption of children. In the case of *Frette v France*, a homosexual man complained regarding a refusal to allow him to adopt a child for reasons of his sexual orientation.[50] The Court found against him, referring to the fast-evolving and very diverse practice across Europe, as well as the conflicting views of experts as to what would be in the best interests of the child. The decision in *Frette* is unsatisfactory. It posits false dilemmas such as a supposed tension between the rights of the man and the child. There is no such tension. The tension is between the rights of homosexual and heterosexual prospective adoptive parents, with the best interests of the child as the overarching consideration. Issues such as these were handled in a better manner in *EB v France*. In that case, the Court, while maintaining the paramount principle of the best interests of the child, held that, 'in rejecting the applicant's application for authorisation to adopt, the domestic

---

[43] CCPR/C/89/D/1361/2005 (14 May 2007).

[44] CCPR/C/75/D/902/1999 (30 July 2002).   [45] (1999) 31 EHRR 1055.

[46] IACtHR Series C No 239 (24 February 2012).   [47] (2003) 38 EHRR 24.

[48] (2003) 36 EHRR 55.   [49] (2003) 37 EHRR 39.   [50] (2003) 38 EHRR 21.

authorities made a distinction based on considerations regarding her sexual orientation, a distinction which is not acceptable under the Convention.'[51] In the later case of *X v Austria*, the Court held that a prohibition of the adoption of the child of a same-sex partner was in violation of the Convention since Austria extended such an entitlement to partners in different-sex relationships.[52] Also at the European level, the European Committee of Social Rights, the monitoring body for the European Social Charter, has interpreted the terms 'sex' and 'other' among the prohibited forms of discrimination to include discrimination on the grounds of sexual orientation.[53]

Overall, we can consider that the regional courts and the treaty bodies have mapped out an extensive range of areas and contexts in which sexual orientation and gender-identity-related discrimination is prohibited. Furthermore, as we will see in Section 3.3, it can also be assumed that the protections apply for the non-discriminatory enjoyment of *all* human rights.

3.3 GENERAL HUMAN RIGHTS PROTECTION

The international monitoring bodies are increasingly addressing issues of the entitlement of people of diverse sexual orientations and gender identities to benefit from the protection of other human rights of general application. The European Court of Human Rights, in *Alekseyev v Russia*, ruled that a municipal ban on LGBT Pride marches violated various provisions of the ECHR, including Article 11 on freedom of assembly.[54] The Human Rights Committee, in *Fedotova v Russian Federation*, held that the prevention of a display of posters that declared, 'Homosexuality is normal' and 'I am proud of my homosexuality' near a secondary school building constituted a violation of the protester's right to freedom of expression. The Committee observed that the protester had 'not made any public actions aimed at involving minors in any particular sexual activity or at advocating any particular sexual orientation. Instead, she was giving expression to her sexual identity and seeking understanding for it.'[55]

The Human Rights Committee, in 2014, adopted a General Comment on the right of liberty and security of the person (Article 9 ICCPR). It stated that the right benefited 'everyone' with that term embracing lesbian, gay, bisexual, and transgender persons.[56] The Committee and the other treaty bodies, as we have seen above, have also generated significant practice in the context of the review of periodic reports of states parties. The Human Rights Committee has expressed concern to specific states regarding violent crimes perpetrated against persons of minority sexual orientation, including by law enforcement officials; the failure to address such crime in legislation on hate crime; the frequent failure of states to investigate such acts; and the need for training of law enforcement and judicial officials in order to sensitize them to the rights of sexual minorities.[57] The Committee on the Rights of the Child has expressed concern that homosexual and transsexual young people often do not have access to the appropriate information, support, and necessary protection to enable them to live their sexual orientation.[58] On a number of occasions, the Committee against Torture has expressed concern about the torture of homosexuals and regarding complaints of threats and attacks against sexual minorities and transgender activists.[59]

---

[51] (2008) 47 EHRR 21, para 96.   [52] (2013) 57 EHRR 14.

[53] European Committee of Social Rights, Conclusions concerning Albania: Article 1(2) (30 June 2006), *Conclusions 2006—Volume 1* (2006) 28.

[54] Application nos 4916/07, 25924/08, and 14599/09, Judgment of 21 October 2010.

[55] CCPR/C/106/D/1932/2010 (30 November 2012) para 10.7.

[56] HRC, General Comment 35, CCPR/C/GC/35 (16 December 2014) para 3.

[57] eg HRC, Concluding Observations: United States of America, CCPR/C/USA/CO/3/Rev.1 (18 December 2006) para 25.

[58] eg CRC Committee, Concluding Observations: Russian Federation, CRC/C/RUS/CO/4–5 (31 January 2014) paras 24–25.   [59] eg *JK v Canada*, CAT/C/56/D/562/2013 (10 February 2016).

The reports of the 'special procedures' of the Human Rights Council constitute a particularly valuable repository of examples of the application for people of diverse sexual orientations and gender identities of general human rights protections, as well as of the principle of non-discrimination. The Council's Working Group on Arbitrary Detention has frequently invoked *Toonen* as a basis for its finding of arbitrary detention of homosexuals.[60] A former Independent Expert on the situation of human rights defenders was assiduous in condemning attacks on members of sexual minorities.[61] She drew attention to such human rights violations as summary execution; torture; arbitrary detention; unreasonable impediments to freedom of expression, movement, and association; and participation in public life.

A number of the 'special procedures' have drawn attention to the intersectional nature of many human rights violations, where already vulnerable people face heightened risk when promoting the rights of people of diverse sexual orientations and gender identities. For example, the Independent Expert on minority issues has referred to the multiple forms of exclusion of members of minority communities, based on aspects of their identities and personal realities such as sexual orientation or gender expression that challenge social or cultural norms.[62]

Some of the 'special procedures' that address economic, social, and cultural rights have indicated the extent to which violations of these rights are at issue for people of diverse sexual orientations and gender identities. The work of a former Special Rapporteur on the right to health is particularly notable. In 2004, he observed that:

> fundamental human rights principles, as well as existing human rights norms, lead ineluctably to the recognition of sexual rights as human rights. Sexual rights include the right of all persons to express their sexual orientation, with due regard for the well-being and rights of others, without fear of persecution, denial of liberty or social interference.[63]

A former Special Rapporteur on education has identified a right to comprehensive sexual education.[64]

A broad range of human rights are also increasingly engaged at the regional level. The Council of Europe Commissioner for Human Rights often refers to violations.[65] Country reports and follow-up reports of the Inter-American Commission on Human Rights comment on such violations as 'social-cleansing' (killing) of homosexuals and the treatment of lesbian prisoners.[66] The UN and regional level examples clearly reinforce the assertion that human rights of general application may not be constrained on the basis of sexual orientation or gender identity.

But how does one distinguish rights of general application from those that are intended only to benefit a certain category of people? The answer to this question will usually be straightforward. For instance, the ICCPR limits the right to participate in political life to citizens. The question arises though of when a generally stated human right is limited in terms of who may benefit. For our purposes, the issue concerns when a right exclusively addresses the situation and choices of what we might term sexual majorities. This is the context for one of the most

---

[60] McGoldrick, 'The Development and Status of Sexual Orientation Discrimination under International Human Rights Law' (2016) 16 *HRLR* 613, 628 n 108.

[61] Report of the Special Representative of the Secretary-General on human rights defenders, E/CN.4/2006/95/Add.1 (22 March 2006).

[62] Report of the Independent Expert on minority issues, E/CN.4/2006/74 (6 January 2006).

[63] Report of the Special Rapporteur on the right of everyone to the enjoyment of the highest attainable standard of physical and mental health, E/CN.4/2004/49 (16 February 2004) para 54.

[64] Report of the Special Rapporteur on the Right to Education, A/65/162 (23 July 2010).

[65] Discrimination on grounds of sexual orientation and gender identity in Europe, Report of the Council of Europe Commissioner for Human Rights (June 2011).

[66] Annual Report of the Inter-American Commission on Human Rights 2006, ch IIIC(1).

[67] (2011) 53 EHRR 20, para 61.

topical contemporary debates concerning the rights of sexual minorities: whether international human rights law recognizes a right of same-sex marriage or of same-sex family life.

The Human Rights Committee, in *Joslin*, was unequivocal on the matter of same-sex marriage. It contended that the right to marriage (Article 24(2) ICCPR) refers to a right of a man and a woman and that same-sex marriage is thereby excluded from the protection of the Covenant. The position of the European Court of Human Rights is more nuanced. In its 2010 judgment in *Schalk and Kopf v Austria*, it observed that, '[it] would no longer consider that the right to marry enshrined in Article 12 must in all circumstances be limited to marriage between two persons of the opposite sex'. However, in the case before it, it concluded that the diversity of practice across states parties to the European Convention was such that the matter of same-sex marriage 'is left to regulation by the national law'.[67] In a judgment delivered in 2012, the Court also felt it necessary to state, *obiter*, that the Convention does not require states to grant access to marriage to same-sex couples.[68] The Court confirmed these views in the 2015 case of *Oliari and Others v Italy*.[69]

It will be interesting to observe the extent to which a right of same-sex marriage may emerge over time from the jurisprudence and practice of the international courts and treaty bodies, taking account of such considerations as the observations of the European Court of Human Rights regarding changing circumstances within societies, an evolution in national law and jurisprudence (such as the US Supreme Court finding in the 2015 case of *Obergefell*)[70] and the academic criticism leveled at the Human Rights Committee's findings in *Joslin*.[71]

When we turn to the related but distinct issue of the identification of the family in international human rights law, we may observe that the UN and regional human rights monitoring bodies are moving, albeit haltingly, towards recognition of the existence of and rights pertaining to same-sex unmarried families. Article 23(1) ICCPR states the fundamental importance of the family and its entitlement to protection by the state, without reference to the form of family under consideration. Only in Article 23(2) do we find reference to the right of men and women to marry and found families. It is not necessarily the case that Article 23(2) restricts the meaning of the word 'family' in Article 23(1). And the Human Rights Committee, in *Young* and in *X*,[72] has criticized state practices that impede same-sex couples from benefiting from family-related benefits, such as transfer of pension entitlements. These cases, however, only addressed issues of inequality before the law (Article 26 ICCPR) and, in *X*, in a dissenting opinion of two members, it was observed that 'a couple of the same sex does not constitute a family within the meaning of the Covenant and cannot claim benefits that are based on a conception of the family as comprising individuals of different sexes'.[73]

It is the regional courts that are providing the clearest guidance. Reference has already been made to the approach of the European Court of Human Rights to same-sex civil partnerships. The Court, also in *Schalk and Kopf v Austria*, reversed previous findings[74] whereby, 'a cohabiting same-sex couple living in a stable de facto partnership, falls within the notion of "family life," just as the relationship of a different-sex couple in the same situation would'.[75] The Inter-American Court of Human Rights adopted similar reasoning in the *Atala Riffo and daughters* case.[76]

---

[68] *Gas and Dubois v France*, Application No 25951/07, Judgment of 15 March 2012, para 66.

[69] Application nos 18766/11 and 36030/11, Judgment of 21 July 2015.

[70] *Obergefell v Hodges* 576 US (2015).

[71] Gerber, Tay, and Sifris, 'Marriage: A Human Right for All?' (2014) 36 *Sydney LR* 643.

[72] CCPR/C/78/D/941/2000 (6 August 2003) and CCPR/C/89/D/1361/2005 (14 May 2007).

[73] CCPR/C/89/D/1361/2005 (14 May 2007), separate opinion of Mr Abdelfattah Amor and Mr Ahmed Tawfik Khalil. [74] (2011) 53 EHRR 20.

[75] (2011) 53 EHRR 20, para 94. See also, *P.B. and J.S. v Austria* (2012) 55 EHRR 31.

[76] IACtHR Series C No 239 (24 February 2012).

One final uncertainty may be observed concerning the reach of human rights law to address abuses related to sexual orientation or gender identity. It remains unclear how far a human rights approach can go in terms of the regulation of practices of non-state actors.[77] This issue is of obvious importance since so many of the forms of abusive behaviour are to be found outside the state sector, such as in the workplace, privately owned housing, religious communities, and so forth.

4 LEGAL INITIATIVES TO BRIDGE THE GAP BETWEEN LAW AND PRACTICE

This chapter's review of the law has shown the long reach of international human rights standards as regards the particular situation of people of diverse sexual orientations and gender identities. Fundamental principles, such as those of non-discrimination and of the universal application of general human rights standards, have been strongly affirmed. However, as has also been demonstrated, the courts, the treaty bodies, and the independent experts, limited as they are by the facts before them or their various mandates, have only indicated the actual application of these principles to a limited number of circumstances.

As a result, a certain degree of legal uncertainty persists. That uncertainty is compounded by the terminological confusion, referred to already, which is to be found throughout the case law, comments of treaty bodies, and reports of special procedures. In particular, issues of gender identity have been little understood, with, for instance, some special procedures and states referencing transsexuality as a 'sexual orientation', and others frankly acknowledging that they do not understand the term.

There has been a significant initiative to address the uncertainty regarding the reach of the law (and the terminological confusion). In 2007, a group of 29 international human rights experts produced a text known as the Yogyakarta Principles on the application of international human rights law in relation to sexual orientation and gender identity.[78] This document has a tripartite function.[79] In the first place, it constitutes a 'mapping' of the experiences of human rights violations experienced by people of diverse sexual orientations and gender identities. Second, the application of international human rights law to such experiences is articulated. Finally, the Principles spell out the nature of the obligation on states for implementation of each of the human rights.

The Principles have no binding force. They are neither a treaty nor the finding of a judicial or quasi-judicial body. Nevertheless, they carry the authority of their expert authors and have been considered by many states and experts to constitute a careful articulation of the state of existing law.[80] Accordingly, they bear examination in some detail. Each principle comprises a statement of the law, its application to a given situation, and an indication of the nature of the state's duty to implement the legal obligation. Principles 1 to 3 address the principles of the universality of human rights and their application to all persons without discrimination, as well as the right of all people to recognition before the law. The experts placed these elements at the beginning of the text in order to recall the fundamental significance of the universality of human rights and the scale and extent of discrimination against people because of their actual or perceived sexual orientation or gender identity, as well as the manner in which they are often rendered invisible within society and its legal structures. Principles 4 to 11 deal with the fundamental rights to life, freedom from violence

---

[77] See Chapter 28.   [78] Yogyakarta Principles.
[79] Address of the Rapporteur, launch event of the Principles (March 2007).
[80] O'Flaherty and Fisher (2008).

and torture, privacy, access to justice, and freedom from arbitrary detention. Principles 12 to 18 address non-discriminatory enjoyment of economic, social, and cultural rights, including accommodation, employment, social security, health, and education. Principles 19 to 21 concern the importance of the freedom to express oneself, one's identity, and one's sexuality, without state interference, based on sexual orientation or gender identity, including the rights to participate peaceably in public assemblies and events and otherwise associate in community with others. Principles 22 and 23 address the right to seek asylum from persecution based on sexual orientation or gender identity. Principles 24 to 26 deal with the rights to participate in family life, public affairs, and the cultural life of the community, without discrimination based on sexual orientation or gender identity. Principle 27 recognizes the right to defend and promote human rights without discrimination based on sexual orientation and gender identity, and the obligation of states to ensure the protection of human rights defenders. Principles 28 and 29 affirm the importance of holding rights violators accountable, and of ensuring redress for those whose rights are violated.

A notable feature of the principles is the manner in which they spell out in some detail the legal obligations of the state with regard to each of the rights that are affirmed. A general typology for the obligations can be observed. States must: (1) take all necessary legislative, administrative, and other measures to eradicate impugned practices; (2) take protection measures for those at risk; (3) ensure accountability of perpetrators and redress for victims; and (4) promote a human rights culture by means of education, training, and public awareness raising. Also, in the document's preamble, as we have already observed, the experts proposed the definition of the terms 'sexual orientation' and 'gender identity'. These formulations, drawing on their wide usage within academic writing and advocacy communities, establish a personal scope of application for the Principles. The preface also includes references that acknowledge the imperfections of the text and the need to keep its contents under review with a view to future reformulations that would take account of legal changes as well as developing understandings of the situation of people of diverse sexual orientations and gender identities.

5 CONCLUSION

This chapter has assessed the actual human rights situation of people of diverse sexual orientations and gender identities worldwide as well as the extent of the application to them of international human rights law. The gap between law and practice has been highlighted and a major initiative to address that gap, the Yogyakarta Principles, has been discussed. These Principles are presented as a form of *aide-mémoire* that indicates the contemporary state of the law and presents it in an integrated and coherent manner.

Also pertinent for this area of the law are the relevant national and international politics. It is of particular utility to study the practice in such international diplomatic fora as the UN Human Rights Council and the General Assembly. For instance, it will be of interest to examine and assess the debates at the Human Rights Council and the General Assembly surrounding the establishment in 2016 of a new 'special procedure' in the form of an independent expert on protection against violence and discrimination based on sexual orientation and gender identity.[81] That initiative emerged from a context of longstanding contestation. For instance, when, in 2012, the UN High Commissioner for

---

[81] Meeting Summary, 'Council establishes mandate on protection against violence and discrimination based on sexual orientation and gender identity' (30 June 2016), available at: <http://www.unog.ch/unog/website/news_media.nsf/(httpNewsByYear_en)/F3DCF8000D6489F6C1257FE200621CD5?OpenDocument>.

Human Rights tabled an unprecedented report on violence and discrimination based on sexual orientation and gender identity,[82] Pakistan's representative, speaking on behalf of the Organization of Islamic Cooperation, denounced the discussion and questioned the concept of sexual orientation.[83] Four years earlier, a statement in support of full protection of human rights for persons of diverse sexual orientations and gender identities was proclaimed at the General Assembly on behalf of 66 states (the authors of which acknowledged the extent to which its contents were informed by the Yogyakarta Principles).[84] In a form of response, what is sometimes described as the 'counter-statement' was delivered on behalf of 57 other states.[85] These patterns of diplomatic practice recall the extent to which the subject area is highly controversial and in a state of political flux. We are thus precluded from drawing any firm conclusions as to prospects for better enforcement of the law or its further development. We can no more than observe that with regard to the plight of many members of sexual minorities, the universal enjoyment of human rights remains an elusive and distant goal.

FURTHER READING

EUROPEAN AGENCY FOR FUNDAMENTAL RIGHTS, EU LGBT Survey (Publications Office of the European Union, 2014).

McGOLDRICK, 'The Development and Status of Sexual Orientation Discrimination under International Human Rights Law' (2016) 16 *HRLR* 613.

O'FLAHERTY and FISHER, 'Sexual Orientation, Gender Identity and International Human Rights Law: Contextualising the Yogyakarta Principles' (2008) 8 *HRLR* 207.

O'FLAHERTY, 'The Yogyakarta Principles at Ten' (2015) 33 *NJHR* 280.

Report of the Office of the United Nations High Commissioner for Human Rights on discrimination and violence against individuals based on their sexual orientation and gender identity, A/HRC/29/23 (4 May 2015).

USEFUL WEBSITES

International Commission of Jurists: <http://www.icj.org>

Human Rights Watch: <http://www.hrw.org/en/category/topic/lgbt-rights>

International Lesbian, Gay, Bisexual, Trans and Intersex Association: <http://www.ilga.org>

ARC International: <http://www.arc-international.net>

[82] A/HRC/19/41 (17 November 2011). The debate at the Human Rights Council is summarized at: <http://www.ohchr.org/Documents/Issues/Discrimination/LGBT/SummaryHRC19Panel.pdf>.

[83] Available at: <http://www.ohchr.org/en/NewsEvents/Pages/DisplayNews.aspx?NewsID=11920&LangID=E>.

[84] Statement of Argentina (18 December 2008) video-archived (at 2 hours, 25 mins), available at: <http://www.un.org/webcast/ga.html>.

[85] Statement of Syria (18 December 2008), video-archived (at 2 hours, 32 mins), available at: <http://www.un.org/webcast/ga.html>.

16

WOMEN'S RIGHTS

Dianne Otto

SUMMARY

International human rights law prohibits discrimination against women in their enjoyment of all human rights and fundamental freedoms. While non-discrimination is an essential component to the realization of women's rights, its comparative approach measures women's equality against men's enjoyment of rights, reinforcing gender dualism and the masculinity of the universal subject of human rights law whose rights are fully promoted and explicitly protected. To the extent that violations experienced exclusively or primarily by women are expressly recognized in the founding human rights instruments, they are treated as a sub-category of the universal and often formulated as 'protective' measures rather than as human rights. There have been many efforts to address the resulting marginalization of women's rights, including the adoption of the Convention on the Elimination of All Forms of Discrimination Against Women and the strategy of gender mainstreaming in the application of general human rights instruments. While these efforts have been successful in many respects, there are continuing conceptual and practical problems, including, not only the limitations of anti-discrimination law and dualistic conceptions of gender, but the danger that specific recognition of women's rights violations may simply reproduce women's secondary status. Recent attention to discrimination based on 'gender identity' opens new, although contested, opportunities for feminist change.

1 INTRODUCTION

In 1945, the UN Charter recognized the principle that human rights and fundamental freedoms should be enjoyed by everyone 'without distinction as to . . . sex'.[1] Since then, international human rights instruments have repeatedly affirmed that women and men must equally enjoy the human rights they enumerate, without discrimination on the ground of sex.[2] The new era of universal human rights promised women, for the first time in international law, the full recognition of their humanity, marking a decisive break with the longstanding legal representation of women as lacking full legal and civil capacity.

---

[1] UN Charter, Art 1(4).
[2] See eg Universal Declaration of Human Rights (UDHR), Art 2; International Covenant on Civil and Political Rights (ICCPR), Arts 2(2) and 3; International Covenant on Economic, Social and Cultural Rights (ICESCR), Arts 2(1) and 3.

Significantly, the promise of equality also extended to the private realm of the family.[3] Women were no longer to be treated as the dependants of men, or as the property of their fathers or husbands.

Yet there has been widespread resistance to taking these obligations seriously, as evidenced by the many sweeping reservations to the Convention on the Elimination of All Forms of Discrimination Against Women (CEDAW). This convention was adopted in 1979 to draw specific attention to the entrenched nature of women's inequality and the need for significant affirmative measures to address it. Unashamedly, some of the reservations to CEDAW challenge the very idea of women's equality with men.[4] Further, as UN women's human rights experts warned in 2017, in a Statement to the Human Rights Council on International Women's Day: 'Not only is the advancement of women taking a very long time and full equality far from a global reality, but today women's hard fought achievements face the risk of reversal . . . by an alliance of conservative political ideologies and religious traditionalism'.[5] Hard-won advances towards the recognition of women's rights have also been threatened in the name of thwarting international terrorism.[6]

The grim reality is that women fare considerably worse than men on almost every indicator of social well-being, despite the assumption by all states of at least some international legal obligations to promote their equal enjoyment of human rights, and despite many good intentions. Everywhere, despite women's increasing participation in the workforce, their average wage is considerably less than that of men and they are concentrated in precarious work in the formal and informal sectors. Furthermore, many women do not receive any remuneration for work in family enterprises and have unequal access to social security assistance.[7] Violence against women and girls continues to be pervasive, and its prevalence may even be increasing due to new forms created by the Internet and other communications technology, endangering women's lives in both public and private spheres.[8] The World Health Organization estimates that every day 830 women and girls die of preventable complications related to pregnancy and childbirth.[9] Women's inequality is still widely regarded as 'natural' and as prescribed by religious teachings and cultural traditions.

Yet, although lack of political will presents a significant barrier to the realization of women's rights and equality, it is not the only problem. International human rights law itself presents some obstacles. As Douzinas has observed, human rights 'construct humans', rather than the reverse, and it follows that '[a] human being is someone who can successfully claim rights'.[10] This recognition presents a conundrum for women's human rights

---

[3] UDHR, Art 16(1). See further ICCPR, Art 23(4).

[4] Clark, 'The Vienna Convention Reservations Regime and the Convention on Discrimination Against Women' (1991) 85 *AJIL* 281; Cook, 'Reservations to the Convention on the Elimination of All Forms of Discrimination Against Women' (1990) 30 *Virginia JIL* 643. On reservations to human rights treaties generally, see Chapter 5.

[5] International Women's Day Statement by United Nations Women's Human Rights Experts, 34th Session of the Human Rights Council, 7 March 2017.

[6] Report of the Special Rapporteur on the promotion and protection of human rights and fundamental freedoms while countering terrorism, Part III, 'A gender perspective on countering terrorism', A/64/211 (3 August 2009) paras 18–53.

[7] Razari et al. *Gendered Impacts of Globalization—Employment and Social Protection*, UNSRID Research Paper 2012–13 (March 2012).

[8] Report of the Special Rapporteur on violence against women, its causes and consequences, A/HRC/32/42 (19 April 2016) para 5.

[9] World Health Organization, 'Maternal Mortality Fact Sheet' (updated November 2016).

[10] Douzinas, 'The End(s) of Human Rights' (2002) 26 *Melbourne ULR* 445, 457.

advocates because, in crafting laws that respond to the gendered realities of women's lives, there is the risk of reconstituting gender stereotypes through reproducing those realities, rather than challenging them. At the same time, 'special' measures designed to address women's specific injuries and disadvantage continue to affirm the maleness of the universal subject of human rights law, as men need no special enumeration of their gender-specific injuries.[11] Charlesworth has called this the 'paradox of feminism'; whether women's rights are best protected through general norms that treat women the same as men, or through specific norms applicable only to women.[12] Ultimately, the paradox forces us to ask hard questions about how women's inclusion as full subjects of the universal regime of human rights law might be achieved. One such question is whether the recognition of gendered harms suffered by everyone because of their gender identity, including men, women, trans and other genders, would help to shift the harmful dualistic gender stereotypes that continue to reside in the idea of the universal human being.

This chapter critically examines the many efforts to achieve women's full inclusion in international human rights law. Section 2 describes the treatment of women in international law prior to the adoption of the UN Charter, in order to highlight the significance of the subsequent shift to the promotion of women's equality. The importance of the non-discrimination approach favoured by the drafters of the founding human rights instruments is recognized, while some of its limitations are highlighted. Section 3 examines the innovative approach taken in CEDAW, whereby the drafters hoped to address the problems attending the concept of non-discrimination by promoting a strong version of women's substantive equality. Yet while CEDAW fostered a better understanding of the measures that may be necessary to achieve women's equal enjoyment of human rights, it also reinforced the marginalization of women's rights practically and conceptually, and institutionalized the idea that gender is a duality that always works to women's disadvantage. The other human rights treaty bodies tacitly used the existence of the CEDAW Committee as an excuse to continue their neglect of women's rights, and different administrative arrangements helped to 'ghettoise' both the CEDAW Committee and its work. To tackle this marginalization, a new strategy of 'gender mainstreaming' was adopted during the 1990s, which sought to reinterpret mainstream human rights to be inclusive of women's experiences. This strategy is examined in Section 4. The chapter concludes, in Section 5, by drawing attention to some continuing obstacles presented by the law itself, which prevent women from successfully claiming and enjoying human rights, and suggests that addressing the gendered harms experienced by men and other gender identities has the potential to complement and strengthen efforts to realize women's equal enjoyment of human rights.

2 A NEW ERA OF NON-DISCRIMINATION ON THE GROUND OF SEX AND EQUALITY WITH MEN

While the UN Charter was the first international treaty to promote women's equality with men, it was not the first time that women were constituted as a category in international law. This section will briefly describe how women appeared in earlier international legal texts before examining how women's rights were recognized by the foundational human

---

[11] Otto, 'Lost in Translation: Re-Scripting the Sexed Subject of International Human Rights Law' in Orford (ed), *International Law and Its Others* (CUP, 2006) 318.

[12] Charlesworth, 'Not Waving but Drowning: Gender Mainstreaming and Human Rights in the United Nations' (2005) 18 *HHRJ* 1.

rights instruments. While the idea of women's equality with men was a radical and visionary development, of great importance to women (and men), this approach failed to acknowledge the specificity of many human rights violations suffered exclusively or predominantly by women and therefore failed to construct them as fully human.

2.1 THE POSITION PRIOR TO 1945

Before 1945, international law had taken a paternalistic or 'protective' approach to women, treating them as the property, extension, or dependants of men, as primarily mothers and wives, and as incapable of full autonomy and agency.[13] Women were valued for their premarital chastity, their prioritization of motherhood and domesticity, and their acceptance of the heterosexual family hierarchy and the paternal protection of the state and its laws. The laws of war, for example, required an occupying power to respect 'family honour and rights', treating women as part of (male) family property and reputation, to be protected by the law.[14] Early international labour conventions prohibited women from certain types of work, such as night work and mining, on the basis that this interfered with their domestic and reproductive responsibilities.[15] Anti-trafficking conventions made women's consent to working in the sex industry irrelevant, thereby treating all sex workers as victims, needing rescue and rehabilitation.[16] None of these conventions constructed women as rights-bearers. Instead, women were granted 'protections', sometimes in the form of 'privileged' treatment, because of their socially ascribed secondary status.

2.2 THE UDHR AND THE INTERNATIONAL COVENANTS

Following the Second World War, the shift from protectionism to universal human rights promised to recognize women as fully human, for the first time, by granting them the same human rights as men. The primary means for achieving women's equality, adopted by the drafters of the UDHR, was to prohibit discrimination based on sex in the enjoyment of universal rights and freedoms which, notably, does not single women out as the disadvantaged gender group.[17] The decision not to recognize rights that were specific to women's experiences was deliberately made on the basis that this would compromise the idea of the 'universality' of rights and wrongly emphasize women's difference from men rather than their common humanity.[18]

---

[13] Hevener, 'International Law and the Status of Women: An Analysis of International Legal Instruments Related to the Treatment of Women' (1978) 1 *Harvard Women's LJ* 131, 133–40.

[14] See Convention Respecting the Laws and Customs of War on Land 1899 (Hague Convention II), Art 46; and Convention Respecting the Laws and Customs of War on Land 1907 (Hague Convention IV), Art 46.

[15] eg International Labour Organization, Maternity Protection Convention 1919 (Convention 3); International Labour Organization, Convention Concerning Night Work of Women Employed in Industry 1919 (Convention 4); International Labour Organization, Convention Concerning the Employment of Women on Underground Work in Mines of All Kinds 1935 (Convention 45).

[16] International Agreement for the Suppression of the White Slave Traffic 1904; International Convention for the Suppression of White Slave Traffic 1910; International Convention for the Suppression of the Traffic in Women and Children 1921; Convention for the Suppression of the Traffic in Women of Full Age 1933. See further, Doezema, 'Loose Women or Lost Women? The Re-Emergence of the Myth of White Slavery in the Contemporary Discourses of Trafficking in Women' (2000) 18 *Gender Issues* 23, 24.

[17] UDHR, Art 2. This type of non-discrimination provision is described as a 'subordinate norm' because it prohibits discrimination only with respect to the rights and freedoms set out in the instrument.

[18] Morsink, 'Women's Rights in the Universal Declaration' (1991) 13 *HRQ* 229. For a critical analysis see Bequaert Holmes, 'A Feminist Analysis of the Universal Declaration of Human Rights' in Gould (ed), *Beyond Dominance: New Perspectives on Women and Philosophy* (Rowman & Allanheld, 1983) 250.

In transforming the UDHR into legally binding instruments, the International Covenant on Economic, Social and Cultural Rights (ICESCR) and the International Covenant on Civil and Political Rights (ICCPR) followed suit, relying largely on the prohibition of sex discrimination in the enjoyment of the rights they enumerated to achieve women's equality.[19] As the Covenants did not define 'discrimination' or 'equality', many states parties interpreted their obligations narrowly, to require formal, but not substantive, equality.[20] However, an additional provision was included as Article 3 common to both Covenants, which required states parties to ensure 'the equal right of men and women to the enjoyment of all . . . [rights] set forth in the present Covenant', indicating that particular attention must be paid to achieving gender equality and, by the use of the term 'enjoyment', signifying that substantive equality was the goal, although states parties were slow to embrace this interpretation.

The obligation to ensure that women equally enjoy the same rights as men was a very significant step forward for women. States parties are required to treat women and men alike when they are in a comparable situation. Think, for example, of the importance to women of the universal franchise, the freedom to move and to express their opinions to the same extent as men, of equal pay, and access to education on the same basis as men. In addition, the unprecedented acknowledgement that women and men 'are entitled to equal rights as to marriage, during marriage and at its dissolution',[21] broke through the tradition in liberal legal thinking that exempted the private sphere from legal scrutiny.[22] This provision opened the way for challenging the public–private dichotomy that has kept human rights violations experienced by women in the 'private' realm of the family hidden and delivered impunity to perpetrators. However, as would soon become apparent, this development was in tension with states' responsibilities to protect the institution of the family and the right to privacy as also set out in the UDHR and ICCPR.[23] For Third World women in particular, the issue of private actors violating their rights is not only a concern within their extended family networks, but also an issue of the unregulated activities of global private actors, such as transnational corporations and banks.[24] Many global economic actors exploit local resources and labour, with highly gendered effects, compounding the difficulties that poor states have in complying with their human rights obligations. Yet the 'private' conduct of the marketplace is not directly regulated by human rights law.

Despite these shortcomings, the prohibition of sex discrimination left little doubt that the differences between women and men, which had previously been treated as immutable and used to justify women's inequality, were to be understood as socially constructed and therefore amenable to change. Thus international human rights law had the potential to challenge the 'naturalness' of discriminatory beliefs and gendered practices, and to assist in the task of changing harmful stereotypes of both 'women' and 'men', as well as other gender identities.

While ground-breaking in many respects, the preferred method of realizing women's full legal subjectivity by promoting their equal and non-discriminatory enjoyment of human rights soon proved to be problematic, both conceptually and in practice. Conceptually,

---

[19] ICESCR, Art 2(2); ICCPR, Art 2(1).   [20] See Chapter 8.

[21] UDHR, Art 16(1); ICCPR, Art 23(4).

[22] Romany, 'State Responsibility Goes Private: A Feminist Critique of the Public/Private Distinction in International Human Rights Law' in Cook (ed), *Human Rights of Women: National and International Perspectives* (University of Pennsylvania Press, 1994) 85.

[23] UDHR, Arts 12 and 16(3); ICCPR, Arts 17(1) and 23(1).

[24] Oloka-Onyango and Tamale, '"The Personal is Political" or Why Women's Rights are Indeed Human Rights: An African Perspective on International Feminism' (1995) 17 *HRQ* 691, 702.

non-discrimination was interpreted as a formal (*de jure*) rather than substantive (*de facto*) obligation, despite common Article 3 in the Covenants. Treating women in the same way as men works well when women's and men's experiences of human rights violations are directly comparable, as in the first communication concerning sex discrimination considered by the Human Rights Committee. The communication was brought by a group of Mauritian women, complaining that legislation discriminated against women because it granted automatic residency to the foreign wives of Mauritian men but denied automatic residency to the foreign husbands of Mauritian women.[25] On these facts, the Human Rights Committee easily found that the legislation made an 'adverse distinction based on sex' because it negatively affected married women's enjoyment of ICCPR rights related to privacy and family life, as compared to married men.[26]

However, a comparison with the rights that men enjoy does not help in situations where women's experiences are substantially different from men's, as in the case of work. Rights recognized by the ICESCR that protect the right to work assume a male model of formal employment, which makes women's unremunerated work in the family and their poorly remunerated work in the informal sector invisible.[27] This approach also fails to take account of women's often interrupted patterns of paid work, the problem of gender segregation in the workforce, and the need for maternity leave, childcare provision, and a radical change in the distribution of domestic and caring responsibilities. A further problem with the comparative approach of equality and non-discrimination is that, when the Covenants do explicitly refer to women's different experience, international law's discursive heritage of treating women protectively tends to re-emerge, as in the requirement that states parties ensure 'special protection' (rather than rights) for mothers for a period before and after childbirth.[28] The result is that when women are included in the Covenants by reference to the gendered specificities of their lives, they are treated as needing 'special' treatment. This approach constructs women's experience as non-universal and has the effect of buttressing the masculinity of the universal subject. The ICESCR also describes the right of everyone to an adequate standard of living 'for himself [sic] and his family',[29] breathing life into the erroneous stereotype that all women are dependent on male household breadwinners, although the Committee on Economic, Social and Cultural Rights has since strongly repudiated this interpretation.[30]

In practice, drawing formal comparisons between women and men proved to be a limited means of promoting women's substantive equality. The narrow focus of a comparison does not take account of the need to redress the institutionalized history of discrimination and disadvantage that often affects women's ability to exercise their rights in the same way as men, for example by ensuring they have the information, autonomy, and freedom of movement to exercise their right to vote. A formal comparison also ignores the need to create enabling circumstances that will make women's equal enjoyment of rights possible, which may involve changing deeply embedded social and cultural attitudes that stigmatize or punish women for exercising their rights.

The limitations of relying on the prohibition of sex discrimination to do all the work of ensuring that women fully enjoy universal human rights and fundamental freedoms was

---

[25] *Aumeeruddy-Cziffra et al. v Mauritius*, CCPR/C/12/D/35/1978 (9 April 1981).

[26] *Aumeeruddy-Cziffra*, paras 9.2(b)2(i)8 and 9.2(b)2(ii)4.

[27] ICESCR, Arts 6, 7, and 8. See further, Promoting Women's Enjoyment of their Economic and Social Rights: Expert Group Meeting, EGM/WESR/1997/Report (1–4 December 1997) paras 46–8.

[28] ICESCR, Art 10(2).   [29] ICESCR, Art 11(1).

[30] CESCR, General Comment 4, HRI/GEN/1/Rev.9 (Vol I) 11, para 6.

soon apparent.[31] In addition to interpreting equality as a formal rather than substantive obligation, women's human rights violations were rarely addressed by human rights treaty bodies in the early years of their operation. This was because the comparative standard of non-discrimination did not force them to rethink their own gendered frameworks, and human rights NGOs were preoccupied with addressing Cold War violations experienced by men in the public sphere, such as the freedom of political expression and the release of political prisoners, which blinded them to what was happening to women, even where they too were political prisoners.

3 THE SUBSTANTIVE EQUALITY APPROACH OF CEDAW

Growing dissatisfaction with women's marginalization within the general framework and implementation of international human rights law led to the adoption of CEDAW by the UN General Assembly in 1979. Although CEDAW takes the same general approach as the Covenants by promoting non-discrimination, it is concerned specifically with discrimination against *women* and the promotion of women's equality with men, advancing a strong form of women's substantive equality as the international norm. This section discusses the positive features of the approach taken by CEDAW and then examines some of its limitations. It begins with a discussion of three strategies adopted by CEDAW to promote a robust understanding of women's equality: the adoption of a comprehensive definition of discrimination against women; the promotion of the use of temporary and permanent 'special measures'; and the requirement that states parties tackle the causes of women's inequality by promoting social change relating to both women and men in all spheres of life, including in families.

3.1 TOWARDS A ROBUST UNDERSTANDING OF EQUALITY

The first step towards advancing women's substantive equality is the provision of a comprehensive definition of 'discrimination against women' in Article 1 CEDAW:

> [it] shall mean any distinction, exclusion or restriction made on the basis of sex which has the effect or purpose of impairing or nullifying the recognition, enjoyment or exercise by women, irrespective of their marital status, on a basis of equality of men and women, of human rights and fundamental freedoms in the political, economic, social, cultural, civil or any other field.

This definition covers a wide range of conduct and, importantly, prohibits discriminatory treatment (direct discrimination) as well as discriminatory outcome (indirect discrimination), and intended (purposive) discrimination as well as unintended discrimination (discrimination in effect). Both 'sex' and 'marital status' are specified as prohibited grounds of discrimination against women, and it should further be noted that other provisions in CEDAW (for example Article 11(2) in the field of employment) also prohibit discrimination on the grounds of 'pregnancy' and 'maternity'.

The definition specifically promotes substantive equality by requiring that women must be able to 'enjoy' or 'exercise' their human rights and fundamental freedoms, and makes it clear that the prohibition of discrimination against women applies to all fields of life,

---

[31] Petersen, 'Whose Rights? A Critique of the "Givens" in Human Rights Discourse' (1990) 15 *Alternatives* 303.

not only the public sphere. Indeed, the application of CEDAW to private actors, including individuals and organizations, is made explicit in many instances in the text.[32] The CEDAW Committee, which monitors its implementation, has specified that states parties have the obligation to act with 'due diligence' to ensure that private actors do not violate the Convention.[33] The Committee has also clarified many of the other obligations required by its substantive approach to women's equality in its interpretations of CEDAW, helping to constitute a more gender-inclusive subject of human rights law. For example, the Committee has urged states parties to adopt criteria in the determination of equal pay that facilitate the comparison of the *value* of the work usually done by women with the *value* of those more highly paid jobs usually done by men,[34] and to implement health measures that address 'the distinctive features and factors that differ for women in comparison with men'.[35]

The second way that CEDAW promotes women's substantive equality is by making it clear that non-identical treatment aimed at addressing women's specific experiences of disadvantage may be necessary to achieve women's equality. CEDAW distinguishes between temporary and permanent measures. Article 4(1) promotes the use of 'special temporary measures' (also known as 'affirmative action', 'positive action', or 'reverse discrimination'), which are directed towards 'accelerating de facto equality between women and men' by remedying the effects of past or present discrimination against women and promoting the structural, social, and cultural changes necessary to support the realization of women's substantive equality.[36] Such discriminatory measures are not prohibited, as long as they do not entail 'the maintenance of unequal or separate standards' for women and men and are discontinued when their objectives have been achieved. Thus 'temporary' measures may result in the application of the measures for a sustained period of time, until their objectives have been realized.[37] Some specific references to temporary special measures can be found in CEDAW's substantive provisions, such as measures in the field of education that increase women's functional literacy (Article 10(c)) and reduce the drop-out rates of female students (Article 10(f)). On many occasions the CEDAW Committee has advocated special temporary measures, such as the adoption of quotas to promote gender balance in political bodies.[38]

CEDAW also supports permanent 'special measures' to ensure that non-identical treatment of women, due to their biological differences from men, is not considered discriminatory and does not work to their disadvantage. Article 4(2) makes it clear that measures 'aimed at protecting maternity' are not discriminatory, and this point is reinforced by other more specific provisions including measures safeguarding women's reproductive capacities in the field of employment (Article 11(1)(f)) and measures that provide women with 'appropriate' reproductive health services (Article 12(2)). Recognizing that these provisions have a 'protective' orientation, the CEDAW Committee has emphasized that the term 'special', when used in the context of CEDAW, breaks with the past paternalistic usage of the term to indicate that a group suffering discrimination is weak or vulnerable, and refers instead to measures designed to serve a specific human rights goal.[39] However, in practice, avoiding protective responses to women's specificities is a continuing challenge.

---

[32] eg CEDAW, Arts 2(e), 2(f), 3, 5, and 6.
[33] CEDAW Committee, General Recommendation 19, HRI/GEN/1/Rev.9 (Vol II) 331, para 9.
[34] CEDAW Committee, General Recommendation 13, HRI/GEN/1/Rev.9 (Vol II) 325, para 2.
[35] CEDAW Committee, General Recommendation 24, HRI/GEN/1/Rev.9 (Vol II) 358, para 12.
[36] See further CEDAW Committee, General Recommendation 25, HRI/GEN/1/Rev.9 (Vol II) 365.
[37] CEDAW Committee, General Recommendation 25, para 20.
[38] CEDAW Committee, General Recommendation 23, HRI/GEN/1/Rev.9 (Vol II) 347, para 29.
[39] CEDAW Committee, General Recommendation 25, para 21.

The third way that CEDAW promotes women's substantive equality is by requiring that states parties address the underlying causes of women's inequality. As mentioned, religious teachings and cultural practices have often been (mis)used to reinforce dominant beliefs about women's secondary status, generating systemic discrimination against women, which may be perceived as 'natural'. To tackle systemic discrimination, Article 5(a) requires states parties to work towards 'the elimination of prejudices and customary and all other practices which are based on the idea of the inferiority or the superiority of either of the sexes or on stereotyped roles for men and women'. This obligation is echoed in other provisions, such as the requirement that gender stereotypes be removed from school programmes and textbooks (Article 10(c)) and the deeming of legal instruments to be null and void if they restrict the legal capacity of women (Article 15(3)). Article 5(b) builds further on states parties' social change obligations by requiring that they promote change in sex-stereotyped attitudes and practices in families, including by 'recognition of the common responsibility [of women and men] in the upbringing and development of their children'. Some specific aspects of this obligation are also spelled out in other provisions, such as the requirement to establish a network of childcare services 'to enable parents to combine family obligations with work responsibilities and participation in public life' (Article 11(2)(c)), and access to 'information and advice on family planning' that will help to ensure the health and well-being of families (Article 10(h)). Unfortunately, CEDAW takes a consistently negative view of social, religious, and cultural traditions, yet it must be remembered that they can also lend valuable support to realizing women's equality.[40]

3.2 LIMITATIONS OF THE CEDAW APPROACH

The approach taken by CEDAW also has some limitations, four of which will be highlighted: its dualistic conception of gender and associated reliance on a comparison with men; the lack of reference to violence against women; its assumption of normative married heterosexuality; and the very limited acknowledgement of multiple and intersectional forms of discrimination. The CEDAW Committee has ameliorated many of these problems by treating CEDAW as a dynamic instrument that must be read in light of changing circumstances, and progressively interpreting its provisions in Concluding Observations to states parties' periodic reports and in General Recommendations. However, it is difficult for these efforts to completely overcome the limitations in the CEDAW text without supporting interpretations from other human rights bodies and good faith implementation by states parties. Also, the Committee has been cautious in addressing lesbian issues[41] and almost completely silent about transgendered discrimination,[42] despite the obligation to modify gender stereotypes and fixed parental roles which should enable it to support everyone's right to express their gender identity in the way they choose.[43]

---

[40] Nyamu-Musembi, 'Are Local Norms and Practices Fences or Pathways? The Example of Women's Property Rights' in An-Na'im (ed), *Cultural Transformation and Human Rights in Africa* (Zed Books, 2002) 126; Obiora, 'Feminism, Globalization, and Culture: After Beijing' (1997) 4 *Glob Legal Stud J* 355.

[41] Roseman and Miller, 'Normalizing Sex and its Discontents: Establishing Sexual Rights in International Law' (2011) 34 *Harvard J L & Gender* 313, 353; Otto, 'Between Pleasure and Danger: Lesbian Human Rights' [2014] *EHRLR* 618, 626.

[42] Otto, 'Queering Gender [Identity] in International Law' (2015) 33 *NJHR* 299, 307.

[43] Holtmaat, 'The CEDAW: a Holistic Approach to Women's Equality and Freedom' in Hellum and Aasen (eds), *Women's Human Rights: CEDAW in International, Regional and National Law* (CUP, 2013) 95, 115–6.

The first limitation is that CEDAW relies fundamentally on a comparison between women and men. This is problematic for at least two reasons. First, it does not allow women to claim rights that men do not enjoy, except as 'special measures'. Consider the example of access to information, advice, and services related to family planning (Articles 10(h) and 12(1)) and the right to 'decide freely and responsibly [sic] on the number and spacing of their children' (Article 16(1)(e)), which are all to be enjoyed 'on a basis of equality of men and women'. This leaves little room, if any, for the recognition of women's specific, stand-alone reproductive rights, including abortion rights, unless they qualify as 'measures protecting maternity' (Article 4(2)). By contrast, the 2003 Protocol on the Rights of Women in Africa (African Protocol) recognizes women's autonomous right to sexual and reproductive health, including the right to control their own fertility, to decide on the number and spacing of children, to choose any method of contraception, and to have family planning education.[44]

CEDAW's primary reliance on comparing women with similarly situated men is also problematic because it does not recognize gender identities that do not conform to the duality of male/female and does not address discrimination between different groups of women.[45] For example, denying unmarried women access to reproductive technologies that are available to married women is prohibited by CEDAW only if unmarried men (the relevant comparator) are able to access the technology. The comparison does not adequately recognize women's interests because men have very different needs for reproductive assistance, and it renders lesbians and transwomen invisible. Only if the comparator is a married woman, can unmarried women (including single women and women in de facto lesbian relationships) claim discrimination on the basis of marital status. The reproductive rights of transwomen, transmen (especially if they are able to conceive), and other gender identities remains unclear, whether married or not.

A second limitation of CEDAW is its lack of reference to violence against women. This is a silence that can be explained by the reliance on a comparative model, because gendered violence does not affect men in the same way as women (which is not to deny that men may also experience gendered violence). The failure in CEDAW to make specific reference to rights associated with security of the person suggests that, at the time of drafting, the prevalence of violence against women, especially in the private sphere, was unknown or simply accepted as the norm. Much has changed since then. The General Assembly adopted the Declaration on the Elimination of Violence Against Women in 1993, recognizing that gendered violence is 'one of the crucial social mechanisms by which women are forced into a subordinate position compared with men'.[46] In 1994, the Commission on Human Rights (now the Human Rights Council) established the mandate of the Special Rapporteur on violence against women, its causes and consequences, which continues today.[47] In 1992, the CEDAW Committee pre-empted these developments by adopting General Recommendation 19, which interpreted gender-based violence as a form of 'discrimination against women' that is prohibited by CEDAW. Thus, violence 'directed against a woman because she is a woman or that affects women disproportionately' breaches specific CEDAW provisions, even though the provisions do not expressly make reference to violence.[48] This approach has been applied in the jurisprudence of the CEDAW Committee under its Optional Protocol procedure,

---

[44] African Protocol, Art 14(1).

[45] An exception to this rule is CEDAW, Art 14 concerning 'rural women'.

[46] Declaration on the Elimination of Violence Against Women, GA Res 48/104 (20 December 1993).

[47] Commission on Human Rights Res 1994/45 (4 March 1994), Chap XI, E/CN.4/1994/132. See further: <http://www.ohchr.org/EN/Issues/Women/SRWomen/Pages/SRWomenIndex.aspx>.

[48] CEDAW Committee, General Recommendation 19, paras 1 and 6.

which has found violations of states obligations to eliminate discrimination against women in family relations (Article 16) where states parties have not acted positively, with due diligence, to protect complainants from domestic violence.[49] The Committee continues to grapple with the issue of violence against women. General Recommendation 19 was updated on 14 July 2017 by General Recommendation 35 (CEDAW/C/GC/35).

Addressing violence against women as a human rights violation has been further expounded in three regional human rights instruments. The first, the 1994 Inter-American Convention on the Prevention, Punishment and Eradication of Violence Against Women (Inter-American Convention) defines violence against women broadly as 'any act or conduct, based on gender, which causes death or physical, sexual or psychological harm or suffering to women, whether in the public or the private sphere'.[50] Importantly, this definition does not confine violence against women to a form of sex discrimination, but recognizes that it may constitute a human rights violation in itself, without the need for a male comparator. States parties must adopt a wide range of positive measures to eliminate such violence, including by applying 'due diligence' to 'prevent, investigate and impose penalties'.[51] The African Protocol develops the definition of violence against women further by including acts which 'cause *or could cause* [women] physical, sexual, psychological, and *economic harm*', threats, and all such acts during armed conflict.[52] Violence against women is specifically recognized as a violation of the right to dignity,[53] the rights to life, integrity, and security of the person,[54] and the right to be protected from harmful practices.[55] The particular vulnerability of asylum-seeking and internally displaced women, and elderly and disabled women, is also acknowledged.[56] The third regional instrument is the Council of Europe's Convention on Preventing and Combating Violence Against Women and Domestic Violence 2011, which identifies women's empowerment and economic independence among its aims, reflecting a conscious effort to counter protective responses.[57] These regional developments update CEDAW obligations, overcoming some of their textual limitations.

A third limitation of CEDAW is that, like the Covenants, women's experience of 'family life' is assumed to be married and heterosexual (Article 16(1)) except when it comes to rights as a parent in matters relating to children, which are to be enjoyed regardless of marital status (Article 16(1)(d)). One result of the emphasis on 'marriage' and the equal rights of 'spouses' is that the diversity of family forms within which women live, including customary and de facto heterosexual and same-sex partnerships, is rendered invisible. Consequently, the text ignores human rights violations that take place within different family formations, like the unequal sharing of income and assets in a customary marriage or violence in a lesbian relationship, and fails to protect women's equal rights when a non-marital relationship breaks down. The CEDAW Committee has gone some way towards rectifying this problem by acknowledging that various forms of the family exist by using the terminology of 'spouse or partner',[58] and by insisting that women and men be treated equally in families, whatever form they take.[59] However, the Committee has never engaged proactively with issues of same-sex partnerships or families, and has only made reference to them on the rare occasions that states parties themselves have provided information about developments in their

---

[49] *AT v Hungary*, A/60/38, Annex III (26 January 2005); *Goekce v Austria*, CEDAW/C/39/D/5/2005 (6 August 2007); *Yildrim v Austria*, CEDAW/C/39/D/6/2005 (1 October 2007); *VK v Bulgaria*, CEDAW/C/49/D/20/2008 (27 September 2011); *Jallow v Bulgaria*, CEDAW/C/52/D/32/2011 (28 August 2012).

[50] Inter-American Convention, Art 1.   [51] Inter-American Convention, Art 7(b).

[52] African Protocol, Art 1(j) (emphases added).   [53] African Protocol, Art 3(4).

[54] African Protocol, Art 4.   [55] African Protocol, Art 5(d).

[56] African Protocol, Arts 11(3), 22(b), and 23(b).

[57] Council of Europe Convention, Arts 6, 12(6), and 18(3).

[58] See eg CEDAW Committee, General Recommendation 21, HRI/GEN/1/Rev.9 (Vol II) 337, para 22.

[59] CEDAW Committee, General Recommendation 21, paras 13, 18, 29, 33, and 39.

periodic reports.[60] Another repercussion of CEDAW's normative focus on heterosexual marriage is that women's sexuality is reduced to issues of procreation, with reference to family planning and the spacing of children. This means that CEDAW also fails to address the discrimination that many women face for expressing their sexuality outside marriage, whether in committed relationships, in pursuit of sexual pleasure, as lovers of other women, or as sex workers.

The fourth limitation is that CEDAW largely treats 'women' as a homogeneous group who share the same experience of discrimination. Yet sex discrimination can intersect with other forms of discrimination and create experiences of discrimination that are not fully comprehended by the concept of sex discrimination. This has been called 'compound' or 'intersectional' discrimination,[61] and its most extreme forms are experienced by the most disadvantaged groups of women. While CEDAW acknowledges some limited differences between women, on the basis of maternity for example, and age in respect of child marriage, there is only one significant exception to the general pattern of assumed homogeneity. Article 14 requires that states parties 'take into account the specific problems faced by rural women and the significant roles which rural women play in the economic survival of their families',[62] and many of the rights it goes on to enumerate do not rely on a comparison with men. This usefully enables the CEDAW Committee to draw comparisons between rural and urban women, and the Committee has interpreted 'rural' very broadly in many of its Concluding Observations in order to discuss intersectional forms of discrimination faced by women, on the basis of age, ethnicity, caste, and indigeneity.[63] The CEDAW Committee has also drawn attention to 'multiple' or 'double' discrimination faced by specific groups of women in the context of Article 5(a), which requires modification of social and cultural attitudes and practices that are inconsistent with women's equality.[64] Further, a number of General Recommendations emphasize CEDAW's application to specific groups of women,[65] and others have stressed that special attention must be paid to the needs of women belonging to 'vulnerable' and 'disadvantaged' groups.[66] In a very positive development, the CEDAW Committee has started to draw attention to intersectional discrimination in its jurisprudence under the Optional Protocol,[67] after failing to acknowledge intersectionality in four of its first five cases which concerned immigrant or minority women.[68]

As with violence against women, the more recent regional women's rights instruments fill some of the gaps in CEDAW. The Inter-American Convention requires states parties

---

[60] See, eg, Concluding Observations on Chile, CEDAW/C/CHL/CO/5–6 (12 November 2012) para 46, where it is 'noted' that 'a bill on de facto unions, which includes same-sex relationships, is before the Senate'.

[61] Crenshaw, 'Demarginalizing the Intersection of Race and Sex: A Black Feminist Critique of Anti-Discrimination Doctrine, Feminist Theory and Antiracist Politics' [1989] *U Chi LF* 139.

[62] There is also a reference to 'rural women' in CEDAW, Art 10(a) about vocational guidance and access to studies.

[63] See eg India, A/54/38 (1 February 2000) paras 51–3; China, A/54/38 (3 February 1999) para 294.

[64] See eg Sweden, A/56/38 (31 July 2001) para 356.

[65] eg CEDAW Committee, General Recommendation 18, HRI/GEN/1/Rev.9 (Vol II) 330 (disabled women); General Recommendation 26, CEDAW/C/2009/WP.1/R (5 December 2008) (women migrant workers); General Recommendation 27, CEDAW/C/GC/27 (16 December 2010) (older women); and General Recommendation 34, CEDAW/C/GC/34 (7 March 2016) (rural women).

[66] CEDAW Committee, General Recommendation 24, HRI/GEN/1/Rev.9 (Vol II) 358, para 6 (health needs of refugee and internally displaced women, women with physical or mental disabilities, amongst others).

[67] See *Teixeira v Brazil*, CEDAW/C/49/D/17/2008 (27 September 2011) para 7.7; *Kell v Canada*, CEDAW/C/51/D/19/2008 (27 April 2012) para 10.2.

[68] See *Nguyen v The Netherlands*, A/61/38 (14 August 2006) Annex VIII; *Szijjarto v Hungary*, A/61/36 (14 August 2006) Annex VIII; *Goekce*; *Yildrim*.

to adopt measures that take 'special account' of women whose vulnerability to violence is compounded by such factors as their 'race or ethnic background', their 'status as migrants, refugees or displaced persons . . . while pregnant or . . . disabled, of minor age, elderly, socio-economically disadvantaged, affected by armed conflict or deprived of their freedom'.[69] The African Protocol has provisions that address the rights of asylum-seeking and internally displaced women, elderly women, and women with disabilities, and also recognizes specific rights that must be enjoyed by widows[70] and 'women in distress', which includes poor women, women heads of families, pregnant or nursing women, and women in detention.[71] Both instruments recognize women's diversity more fully than CEDAW, and draw attention to the need to address the compound effects of multiple forms of discrimination.

There is little doubt that the almost universal ratification of CEDAW, the work of the CEDAW Committee, and the efforts of many women's rights and human rights NGOs[72] have advanced the project of making international human rights law more gender inclusive. However, the adoption of a specialist women's rights treaty also, in many respects, reinforced women's marginalization. The high number of reservations to CEDAW, particularly those that defeat its object and purpose, undermines the idea that women's rights are as universal as 'men's'. Rather than prompting the other human rights treaty committees to take women's rights more seriously, the existence of CEDAW tended to have the opposite effect of reinforcing their marginalization.[73] While a specific convention focusing on women's equality was necessary to address women's marginalization in international human rights law, it was plainly not sufficient.

4 MAINSTREAMING WOMEN'S HUMAN RIGHTS

Another major effort to advance the prospects of women successfully claiming their human rights sought to refocus attention on the general human rights instruments by promoting 'gender mainstreaming'.[74] The strategy was adopted by the 1993 Vienna World Conference on Human Rights and reaffirmed by the 1995 Beijing World Conference on Women. These developments prompted the chairpersons of the human rights treaty bodies to commit to fully integrating gender perspectives into their working methods.[75] This led eventually to the adoption of General Comments by four treaty bodies, which aim to comprehensively incorporate women's experience of human rights violations into the coverage of their respective treaty texts. This section examines each of these General Comments, noting the diversity of thinking about how to achieve gender mainstreaming that emerges. It also highlights the tenacity of protective representations of women, especially in the context of addressing gendered violence, and concludes that women are not yet constructed as fully human by international human rights law.

---

[69] Inter-American Convention, Art 9.   [70] African Protocol, Art 20.

[71] African Protocol, Art 24.

[72] Dairiam, 'From Global to Local: The Involvement of NGOs' in Schopp-Schilling (ed), *The Circle of Empowerment: Twenty-Five Years of the UN Committee on the Elimination of Discrimination Against Women* (Feminist Press, 2007) 313.

[73] Byrnes, 'The "Other" Human Rights Treaty Body: The Work of the Committee on the Elimination of Discrimination Against Women' (1989) 14 *Yale JIL* 1; Reanda, 'Human Rights and Women's Wrongs: the United Nations Approach' (1981) 3 *HRQ* 11.

[74] Bunch, 'Women's Rights as Human Rights: Towards a Re-Vision of Human Rights' (1990) 12 *HRQ* 486; Kouvo, *Making Just Rights? Mainstreaming Women's Human Rights and a Gender Perspective* (Iustus Forlag, 2004).

[75] Report of the Sixth Meeting of Persons Chairing the Human Rights Treaty Bodies, A/50/505 (4 October 1995) para 34(a)–(f).

4.1 RE-IMAGINING THE UNIVERSAL SUBJECT: THE APPROACH OF THE HUMAN RIGHTS COMMITTEE

The Human Rights Committee led the way in 2000 with the adoption of General Comment 28 on equality between men and women.[76] The General Comment works through each of the ICCPR rights, bringing women-specific violations into the mainstream by re-imagining the subject of the ICCPR as a woman. For example, it is recognized that the right to life (Article 6) may be violated if women have no option but to resort to backyard abortions or if they are living in extreme poverty,[77] and the right to be free from torture and other cruel, inhuman, and degrading treatment (Article 7) may be violated if a state party fails to protect women from domestic violence.[78] The General Comment clearly promotes women's equality as a substantive concept and accepts that different treatment of women and men may be necessary to achieve equality. The result is an ambitious and creative 'feminization' of ICCPR rights.[79]

However, some of the problems associated with seeking to include women by reference to their 'difference' are also evident. The extensive cataloguing of women's specific injuries and disadvantages, particularly the emphasis on violence, invites protective responses. Indeed, the frequent use of the language of 'protection' is disquieting.[80] It revives the historically conditioned tendency to slide into protective measures when thinking about women as 'victims' of gendered and sexual violence, working against legal responses that empower women as full legal subjects. This tendency is compounded by the failure of the General Comment to identify any gendered human rights abuses that may be specific to men, such as military conscription.

4.2 ANALYSING THE RELATIONSHIP BETWEEN GENDER AND RACIAL DISCRIMINATION: THE APPROACH OF THE COMMITTEE ON THE ELIMINATION OF RACIAL DISCRIMINATION

The Committee on the Elimination of Racial Discrimination, which monitors implementation of the International Convention on the Elimination of All Forms of Racial Discrimination (ICERD), was initially resistant to the idea of gender mainstreaming.[81] After intensive lobbying by women's groups, the Committee changed its mind and General Recommendation XXV on the 'gender-related dimensions of racial discrimination' was adopted in 2000.[82] In contrast to the Human Rights Committee's approach, which identified the gender issues associated with each of the substantive rights recognized by the ICCPR, the ICERD Committee elaborates a methodology for analysing the relationship between gender and racial discrimination, with the aim of developing 'a more systematic and consistent approach', in conjunction with states parties.[83] The method requires particular consideration of gender in: (1) the form and manifestation of racial discrimination; (2) the circumstances in which it occurs; (3) its consequences; and (4) the availability and accessibility of remedies.[84]

---

[76] HRC, General Comment 28, HRI/GEN/1/Rev.9 (Vol I) 228.

[77] HRC, General Comment 28, para 10.   [78] HRC, General Comment 28, para 11.

[79] See further, Otto, ' "Gender Comment": Why Does the UN Committee on Economic, Social and Cultural Rights Need a General Comment on Women?' (2002) 14 *Can J Women & L* 1.

[80] HRC, General Comment 28, paras 8, 10, 11, 12, 16, and 22.

[81] Crooms, 'Indivisible Rights and Intersectional Identities or, "What Do Women's Human Rights Have to Do with the Race Convention?" ' (1997) 40 *Howard LJ* 619; Gallagher, 'Ending Marginalisation: Strategies for Incorporating Women into the UN Human Rights System' (1997) 19 *HRQ* 283.

[82] CERD, General Recommendation XXV, HRI/GEN/1/Rev.9 (Vol II) 287.

[83] CERD, General Recommendation XXV, para 3.   [84] CERD, General Recommendation XXV, para 5.

This approach opens the way to a deeper understanding of the structural dimensions of the intersection of race and gender discrimination and how they work together to intensify women's inequality. The methodology is very flexible, allowing for diverse and shifting conceptions of race, which, like gender, is understood as socially constructed. However, similar to General Comment 28, the few examples of intersectional discrimination provided are concerned with addressing violence against women,[85] which also runs the risk of eliciting protective responses. While General Recommendation XXV is notable for its use of the language of 'gender' rather than 'women', it is not at all clear that it is intended to recognize that men, as well as women, may suffer from discrimination in which race and gender intersect.

4.3 ADDRESSING THE INEQUALITY OF BOTH WOMEN AND MEN: THE APPROACH OF THE COMMITTEE ON ECONOMIC, SOCIAL AND CULTURAL RIGHTS

A fuller conception of 'gender' mainstreaming is evident in General Comment 16, adopted in 2005 by the Committee on Economic, Social and Cultural Rights.[86] The approach taken is similar to General Comment 28 of the Human Rights Committee in the attention given to identifying the gender dimensions of each of the rights enumerated in the ICESCR and the emphasis on addressing gendered violence. However, its distinctiveness lies in its identification of men, as well as women, as potentially suffering sex discrimination and inequality in the enjoyment of ICESCR rights. For example, with respect to the right to social security, states parties are expected to guarantee 'adequate maternity leave for women, paternity leave for men, and parental leave for both men and women'.[87] General Comment 16 also recognizes that victims of domestic violence are 'primarily women', thereby acknowledging that men too may be victims.[88] This position would be highly controversial if it was used as a means to deny the general reality of women's inequality vis-à-vis men. However, it has the potential to support a radical move towards recognizing men's gendered human rights abuses, as well as women's, which would help to eliminate protective approaches to women and underline the importance of changing the way 'men' are stereotyped in the process of realizing 'women's' equality.

4.4 RECOGNIZING GENDER AS A KEY FACTOR: THE APPROACH OF THE COMMITTEE AGAINST TORTURE

In 2008, the Committee against Torture adopted a General Comment on implementation obligations, which makes some important observations about the gender dimensions of the Convention Against Torture (UNCAT), conceiving gender mainstreaming even more inclusively.[89] General Comment 2 emphasizes that special attention must be given to protecting marginalized groups or individuals who are 'especially at risk of torture', including those who may be at risk because of '[race,] gender, sexual orientation, transgender identity . . . or any other status or adverse distinction'.[90] States parties are requested to provide additional information in their periodic reports about the implementation of UNCAT with respect to women, keeping in mind that 'gender is a key factor' that can intersect with other characteristics of a person to make them more vulnerable to torture or ill-treatment.[91] The Committee notes that women are particularly at risk in contexts

---

[85] CERD, General Recommendation XXV, para 2.   [86] HRI/GEN/1/Rev.9 (Vol I) 113.
[87] CESCR, General Comment 16, para 26.   [88] CESCR, General Comment 16, para 27.
[89] CAT, General Comment 2, HRI/GEN/1/Rev.9 (Vol II) 376.
[90] CAT, General Comment 2, para 21.   [91] CAT, General Comment 2, para 22.

that include 'deprivation of liberty, medical treatment, particularly involving reproductive decisions, and violence by private actors in communities and homes'.[92] The Committee observes that men too may be subject to gendered violations of UNCAT, 'such as rape or sexual violence and abuse', and, further, that men and boys, as well as women and girls, may be subject to violations 'on the basis of their actual or perceived non-conformity with socially determined gender roles'.[93] This approach opens the way for the Committee to identify the specificity of human rights violations that are experienced solely or primarily by both women and men, as well as by the full range of gender non-conformists. This approach is in keeping with the definition of gender identity adopted by the Yogyakarta Principles on the Application of International Human Rights Law in relation to Sexual Orientation and Gender Identity, which makes it clear that *everyone* has a gender identity which can give rise to multiple forms of gender discrimination.[94]

While all the General Comments aimed at gender mainstreaming promote women's equal enjoyment of human rights in a substantive sense, taking their lead from CEDAW, they also reinterpret mainstream human rights to be more inclusive of women's experience. These reinterpretations alleviate the need to compare women's experience with that of men's by reconstructing the universal standard itself, so that it is more gender-inclusive. Yet only the Committee Against Torture breaks with the tradition of gender duality. This creates a foothold for more complex and dynamic understandings of the operation of gender hierarchies in human rights law and practice, which has the potential to strengthen the struggle for women's rights by more fully making them an issue of the mainstream.

5 CONCLUSION

The history of women's rights in international human rights law reveals a conundrum: how to insist on the recognition of women's specific human rights abuses without reproducing women's secondary status and encouraging protective responses. While every effort to more fully recognize women's rights in the development, interpretation, and implementation of international human rights law has met with some success, these efforts have also highlighted new challenges. While anti-discrimination law can be a very powerful means of promoting women's enjoyment of human rights, the comparative standard that it relies upon presents quandaries about how best to frame, measure, and realize women's substantive equality, which have yet to be resolved. While recognizing gendered violence as a violation of women's human rights has been a massive achievement, the historical pull towards embracing protective responses highlights the challenge of promoting, instead, a rights-based response that takes women's sexual injuries seriously while also respecting women's sexual agency. While the need to take account of other forms of discrimination that intersect with or compound discrimination against women is increasingly acknowledged, there remain many conceptual and practical problems about how to make such discrimination legally cognizable. Finally, while gender mainstreaming has led to radical reinterpretations of mainstream human rights obligations, emphasizing the interdependence of ideas about 'men' and 'women' and the realization that women's equality depends on challenging accepted wisdom about dominant masculinities, it has also highlighted the dilemma of how fully to embrace 'gender' as a socially constructed category and include the whole range of gender identities in its coverage. We need new thinking about legal

---

[92] CAT, General Comment 2, para 22.   [93] CAT, General Comment 2, para 22.
[94] Yogyakarta Principles on the Application of International Human Rights Law in relation to Sexual Orientation and Gender Identity (2007). See further Chapter 15.

representations of gender that challenges the dualistic and naturalized gender stereotypes that underpin the panoply of gendered human rights abuses, before it will be possible for international human rights law to recognize women as fully human.

FURTHER READING

ANDERSON, 'Violence Against Women: State Responsibilities in International Human Rights Law to Address Harmful "Masculinities"' (2008) 26 *NQHR* 173.

BANDA, *Women, Law and Human Rights: An African Perspective* (Hart Publishing, 2005).

COOK and CUSACK, *Gender Stereotyping: Transnational Legal Perspectives* (University of Pennsylvania Press, 2009).

HELLUM and AASEN (eds), *Women's Human Rights: CEDAW in International, Regional and National Law* (Cambridge University Press, 2013).

KAPUR, 'The Tragedy of Victimization Rhetoric: Resurrecting the "Native" Subject in International/Post-Colonial Feminist Legal Politics' (2002) 15 *HHRJ* 1.

MERRY, *The Seductions of Quantification: Measuring Human Rights, Gender Violence and Sex Trafficking* (University of Chicago Press, 2016).

MILLER, 'Sexuality, Violence against Women, and Human Rights: Women Make Demands and Ladies Get Protection' (2004) 7 *Health and HR* 16.

OTTO, 'Queering Gender [Identity] in International Law' (2015) 33 *NJHR* 299.

OTTO (ed), *Gender Issues and Human Rights, Vols I-III* (Elgar, 2013).

VAN LEEUWEN, *Women's Rights are Human Rights—The Practice of the UN Human Rights Committee and the Committee on Economic, Social and Cultural Rights* (Intersentia, 2009).

USEFUL WEBSITES

CEDAW materials (OHCHR):<http://www2.ohchr.org/english/bodies/cedaw/index.htm>

United Nations Entity for Gender Equality and the Empowerment of Women (UN Women): <http://www.un.org/womenwatch/daw/daw/index.html>

Women Watch (UN Inter-Agency Network on Women and Gender Equality): <http://www.un.org/womenwatch/>

International Women's Rights Action Watch (IWRAW): <http://www1.umn.edu/humanrts/iwraw/>

IWRAW Asia-Pacific (IWRAW-AP): <https://www.iwraw-ap.org/>

17

CHILDREN'S RIGHTS

Geraldine Van Bueren

SUMMARY

The UN Convention on the Rights of the Child 1989 (CRC) transforms traditional human rights protections by recognizing that children should not be the object of paternalistic protection; rather they are capable of being active rights-holders who participate in decisions concerning their well-being. This is achieved by recognition of certain principles that allow for a child-centred approach to human rights. These include: the principle of non-discrimination; the best interests of the child; the right to life, survival and development; the right to be heard; and the principle of the evolving capacities of the child. The CRC contains protections of civil and political rights alongside economic, social, and cultural rights, and addresses the situation of children in both times of peace as well as armed conflict. The extensive range of protections afforded by the CRC can be viewed through the functional framework of 4Ps: protection, prevention, provision, and participation. The CRC has stimulated the adoption of a wide range of international and regional legal instruments regarding children's rights, which recognize the importance of a child-centred approach to human rights. At the same time, international law has faced new challenges regarding the balance that ought to be maintained between children's rights, parental rights and duties, and the duties of the state.

1 INTRODUCTION

Human rights treaties are the embodiment of hope and the UN Convention on the Rights of the Child 1989 (CRC), as the primary international children's rights treaty, is no exception. Although originally envisioned as a legally binding repetition[1] of what would have been by the 1980s an unambitious international instrument—the UN Declaration of the Rights of the Child 1959[2]—the final text is one of the most wide-ranging human rights treaties and has radically challenged many prevailing conceptions surrounding childhood. The CRC seeks to provide protection for children of the full range of human rights: civil, political, economic, social, and cultural. Unusually for a human rights treaty, it addresses both human rights guarantees in times of peace, as well as the treatment of children in

---

[1] Poland's original draft proposal reiterated the provisions of the Declaration.
[2] GA Res 1386 (XIV) (1959). The Declaration built on those rights that had been recognized in the League of Nations Declaration of the Rights of the Child 1924.

situations of armed conflict.[3] The CRC also outlines protections for children facing particular situations, such as the refugee child,[4] as well as providing binding safeguards for adoption procedures.[5] The CRC establishes an expert treaty body—the Committee on the Rights of the Child (CRC Committee)—composed of 18 independent experts, which is to monitor state compliance with obligations under the Convention.[6]

It could be argued that there was, and is, no need for a separate treaty on children's rights. The majority of the provisions in the international bill of rights—that is, the Universal Declaration of Human Rights, the International Covenant on Economic, Social and Cultural Rights 1966 (ICESCR), and the International Covenant on Civil and Political Rights 1966 (ICCPR)—seek to protect 'everyone'. However, prior to the adoption of the CRC, children were generally invisible within the United Nations (UN) or were passive objects of concern for international law. Thus children were viewed frequently as only victims and not capable of being participants in their own destinies. With the adoption of the CRC, there is recognition that a child-centred approach to the protection of human rights is required.

The protections and mechanisms for the enforcement of the CRC have been expanded upon in three Optional Protocols: the Optional Protocol to the Convention on the Rights of the Child on the sale of children, child prostitution and child pornography 2000, the Optional Protocol to the Convention on the Rights of the Child on the involvement of children in armed conflict 2000, and the Optional Protocol to the Convention on the Rights of the Child on a communications procedure 2011. In addition to these three Optional Protocols, the CRC has provided a template for a myriad of detailed international instruments on child criminal justice,[7] inter-country adoption,[8] and a major regional treaty on children's rights: the African Charter on the Rights and Welfare of the Child 1990 (African Children's Charter). The CRC has been recognized by the Inter-American Court of Human Rights as forming, together with regional human rights treaties, 'part of a very comprehensive international *corpus juris* for the protection of the child' that assists regional (and arguably national) courts in interpreting the content of regional human rights law in relation to children.[9]

The CRC has been ratified by all states with the exception of the US,[10] and this almost comprehensive global adoption is frequently and justifiably celebrated by civil society. However, this near universality also raises significant challenges, including overcoming cynicism with the slow progress of implementation in particular areas such as the protection of child refugees and children in armed conflict. Nonetheless, even if the CRC and subsequent child-focused international and regional instruments have achieved nothing else, they have radically transformed the responsibilities of the UN, regional bodies, and states toward children and changed what had been a shifting state-by-state definition of who is a child into a globally accepted definition.

This chapter begins with a consideration of the international legal definition of the 'child' (Section 2). It proceeds by examining basic principles underlying the international law on the rights of the child and how one of these principles—the universally recognized principle of 'best interests'—has been transformed (Section 3). The international law of

---

[3] CRC, Art 38.   [4] CRC, Art 22.   [5] CRC, Art 21.   [6] CRC, Art 43. See Chapter 19.

[7] eg UN Guidelines for Action on Children in the Criminal Justice System, ECOSOC Res 1997/30 (1997).

[8] eg Hague Convention on the Protection of Children in Intercountry Adoption 1993.

[9] *Case of the 'Street Children' (Villagrán-Morales et al.) v Guatemala* (Merits) IACtHR Series C No 63 (19 November 1999) para 194.

[10] The US signed the CRC following a deathbed request by the then Secretary-General of UNICEF to Hillary Clinton during the presidency of her husband, Bill Clinton. Ratification is yet to take place.

the rights of the child can be divided into 4Ps: prevention, provision, protection, and participation and these are explored in Section 4. Finally, the chapter examines the protection of children's rights at the regional level (Section 5).

2 THE INTERNATIONAL LEGAL
DEFINITION OF CHILDHOOD

The CRC defines a child as 'every human being below the age of eighteen years unless under the law applicable to the child, majority is attained earlier'.[11] There is no indication in the CRC regarding the point at which childhood commences. The only reference to the beginning of childhood is found in the Preamble to the CRC, which provides that 'the child, by reason of his physical and mental immaturity, needs special safeguards and care, including appropriate legal protection, before as well as after birth'. This repeats the corresponding preambular paragraph of the UN Declaration of the Rights of the Child. The mere repetition of a preambular paragraph does not of itself change its non-binding status into binding law. The omission was the only solution for achieving a global treaty on children's rights. Hence, for those states that permit abortion no legislative change is required and for those states, including many in Latin America as well as the Holy See, for whom life begins at conception, the treaty was acceptable. To have accepted any other approach would also have placed the CRC in direct contradiction to another human rights treaty, the American Convention on Human Rights 1969 (ACHR), Article 4(1) of which provides that the right to life is protected '*in general*, from the moment of conception'.[12] In light of the omission from the CRC, some states (for example the UK) have explicitly indicated that the Convention is applicable only after a live birth, whilst others (for example Argentina) have indicated that it applies to the foetus.[13]

Before the adoption of the CRC, because of the lack of a globally agreed definition of childhood, much of the focus of UN human rights bodies had been on younger children. Under the CRC childhood ends at the age of 18 *or* the age of majority in a particular state as dictated by national law. However, the CRC Committee, which monitors implementation of the CRC, has sought to raise standards. It has called for the periodic reports of states parties to include material on the protections afforded to all children until they reach the age of 18, whether or not the age of majority is attained before this.[14] This has not attracted significant opposition from states parties. The Committee has also criticized national criminal justice legislation which treats children aged 17 as adults.[15] This focus on the rights of older children has led to the recent adoption of a General Comment on the implementation of the rights of the child during

---

[11] CRC, Art 1.

[12] Emphasis added. See Case 2141, *The Baby Boy Case*, IACommHR Res 23/81 (6 March 1981), Annual Report 1980–1. See also Chapter 6.

[13] See Declarations and Reservations to the CRC, available at: <https://treaties.un.org/pages/ViewDetails.aspx?src=TREATY&mtdsg_no=IV-11&chapter=4&clang=_en>

[14] CRC Committee, Treaty-specific guidelines regarding the form and content of periodic reports to be submitted by States parties under article 44, paragraph 1(b), of the Convention on the Rights of the Child, CRC/C/58/Rev.3 (3 March 2015) para 22.

[15] eg CRC Committee, Concluding Observations: United Kingdom of Great Britain and Northern Ireland, CRC/C/GBR/CO/5 (12 July 2016) para 79. See also CRC Committee, General Comment 10 on children's rights in juvenile justice, CRC/C/GC/10 (25 April 2007) paras 36–39.

adolescence.[16] The African Union has explicitly enshrined the higher standard in the African Children's Charter. In that instrument, childhood extends to 18 without any reference to the age of majority. Therefore, states parties are prohibited from recruiting soldiers under the age of 18.[17]

3 GENERAL PRINCIPLES

Early on in its work, the CRC Committee identified four provisions of the Convention as enshrining 'general principles' that are particularly necessary for the enjoyment of the rights in the CRC.[18] These are the principle of non-discrimination;[19] the principle that the best interests of the child should be a primary consideration in all actions concerning children;[20] the right to life, survival, and development;[21] and the right to be heard.[22] Cognizance of and respect for these general principles is necessary in order to ensure a child-centred approach to the protection of all the rights listed in the CRC. A further principle—the evolving capacity of the child[23]—is an important innovation in the CRC that facilitates this child-centred approach. This section will introduce these principles.

3.1 NON-DISCRIMINATION

Article 2 CRC enshrines the principle of non-discrimination. Often the reason for the violation of a child's rights is age. Consider, for example, that in some states it is considered lawful for schools to use corporal punishment as a method of discipline; the use of such force would be unlawful if used against an adult.[24] Some differences in treatment on the basis of age are of course justifiable. However, not all will be.[25]

Discrimination does not only occur on the basis of age; it also occurs between different groups of children. Discrimination on grounds of gender[26] or disability[27] are obvious examples and Article 2 provides an open-ended list of grounds upon which unjustified distinction is prohibited. Furthermore, it provides protection for a child from discrimination not only on grounds related to the child's status, but also on grounds related to the status of the child's parents. The CRC Committee has stated that the principle of non-discrimination does not only require a prohibition of unjustified differential treatment, but also requires 'states to actively identify individual children and groups of children the recognition and realization of whose rights may demand special measures'.[28]

3.2 THE BEST INTERESTS OF THE CHILD

Article 3(1) of the CRC provides that the best interests of the child shall be 'a primary consideration' in all actions concerning children. Whilst the principle of acting in the best interests of the child predates the adoption of the CRC, this long-established exercise of

---

[16] CRC Committee, General Comment 20, CRC/C/GC/20 (6 December 2016).
[17] African Children's Charter, Arts 2 and 22.
[18] CRC Committee, General Comment 5, HRI/GEN/1/Rev.9 (Vol II), 421.   [19] CRC, Art 2.
[20] CRC, Art 3(1).   [21] CRC, Art 6.   [22] CRC, Art 12.   [23] CRC, Art 5.
[24] CRC Committee, General Comment 8, CRC/C/GC/8 (2 March 2007).   [25] See Chapter 8.
[26] See CRC Committee, Day of General Discussion on the Girl Child, CRC/C/38 (27 January 1999).
[27] See CRC, Art 23; CRC Committee, General Comment 9, CRC/C/GC/9 (27 February 2007).
[28] CRC Committee, General Comment 5, para 12.

adult power on behalf of children has now been transformed into a more dynamic, participatory, and child-centred principle. As the CRC Committee has stated, the principle 'is aimed at ensuring both the full and effective enjoyment of all the rights recognised in the [CRC] and the holistic development of the child.'[29] Governments, administrative bodies, and regional and national courts ought now to apply the principle of best interests in a manner that is consistent with each of the rights of the child, and in particular, must give due regard to the child's right to participate in decisions, which affects both the child as an individual and children as a group. The principle has a reinforcing legal effect. Not only ought the application of the best interests principle not violate one of the rights of the child, but also the very exercise of best interests ought to reinforce and strengthen each of the rights of children.

The CRC Committee has asserted that the child's best interests is a 'threefold concept': a substantive right, an interpretative principle, and a rule of procedure.[30] A child has the *right* that his or her best interests will be a primary consideration for decision-makers. Consideration of best interests is not discretionary; it is compulsory. As an *interpretative principle*, it provides that where a legal provision is open to different interpretations, that which most effectively serves the best interests of the child should be chosen. Finally, the *procedural* aspect of best interests requires an assessment of the impact of a decision on a child or group of children, as well as provision of an explicit account of how best interests has been considered in the decision-making process.

Defining 'best interests' is by no means an easy task. In its General Comment on best interests, the CRC Committee has stated that the concept is 'complex', 'flexible', and 'adaptable'. 'It should be adjusted and defined on an individual basis, according to the specific situation of the child or children concerned, taking into consideration their personal context, situation and needs.'[31] One clear feature though is that an action will never be in the best interests of a child where it is contrary to the rights of the child. Beyond this point of certainty, the CRC Committee has provided a non-exhaustive list of factors to be taken into account when assessing a child's best interests. These include: the child's views (to be obtained in accordance with Article 12 CRC, see Section 3.4); the child's identity; preservation of the family environment and maintaining relations; care, protection, and safety of the child; situations of vulnerability; the child's right to health; and the child's right to education.[32] Taking into account these factors as appropriate to the particular context ensures a rights-based approach to identifying the best interests of the child.

Article 3(1) CRC provides that 'the best interests of the child shall be a *primary* consideration'. Therefore the best interests of the child do not have absolute priority over the interests of others, such as those of parents seeking a divorce, when there is a conflict. However, as a primary consideration, the best interests of the child have 'high priority' and should not be lost among the many considerations to be taken into account when making a decision. A contrast can be made between the Article 3(1) direction and Article 21 CRC, which provides that in states parties that permit adoption, 'the best interests of the child shall be the *paramount* consideration'. In the circumstances of adoption, the best interests of the child are the determining factor in any decision. No other interest can prevail.

As part of one of the most widely ratified human rights treaties, the principle appears to have garnered significant support. Reservations to the CRC have tended to endorse

---

[29] CRC Committee, General Comment 14, CRC/C/GC/14 (29 May 2013).
[30] CRC Committee, General Comment 14, para 6.
[31] CRC Committee, General Comment 14, para 32.
[32] CRC Committee, General Comment 14, paras 52–79.

the principle rather than reject it.[33] Thus, it is arguable that the principle that in every action concerning a child, the best interests of the child is a primary, although not the sole, consideration, has attained the status of customary international law.[34] The best interests principle therefore offers significant potential for protecting children's rights in three particular situations: by providing protection for children of those rights protected by treaties that have not been ratified the state; by requiring respect for those rights in treaties to which reservations have been attached; and as an interpretative principle to be applied to those treaties which do not enshrine expressly the best interests of the child, such as the European Convention on Human Rights (ECHR).[35]

3.3 THE RIGHT TO LIFE, SURVIVAL, AND DEVELOPMENT

Without life, all human rights are meaningless. Article 6 CRC, which protects the right to life, survival, and development of the child, is therefore a fundamental provision of the Convention and constitutes a guiding principle when considering how other rights in the CRC should be implemented. The right goes beyond 'survival', that is avoidance of death, to encompass 'development' of the child, which is to be considered 'holistically' so as to encompass 'the child's physical, mental, spiritual, moral, psychological and social development'.[36] Therefore, when implementing the CRC, states should be mindful to create 'an environment which enables all children . . . to grow up in a healthy and protected manner, free from fear and want, and to develop their personality, talents and mental and physical abilities to their fullest potential'.[37]

3.4 THE RIGHT TO BE HEARD

Article 12(1) CRC provides that 'states parties shall assure to the child who is capable of forming . . . views the right to express those views freely in all matters affecting the child, the views of the child being given due weight in accordance with the age and maturity of the child', and Article 12(2) provides particular protection for this in the context of judicial and administrative proceedings affecting the child. This 'right to be heard' acknowledges that children are not passive objects about which decisions by benevolent actors are made. Rather, children should *participate* in the decision-making process. This requires a dynamic approach to participation. States should not restrict themselves to deciding whether a child, or group of children, is competent to express views but should go further and 'ensure conditions for expressing views that account for the child's individual and social situation and an environment in which the child feels respected and secure when freely expressing her or his opinions.'[38] Whilst it is recognized that it may not be possible for a child to participate in all aspects of the decision, respecting the right of the child to participate implies that a decision may need to be broken down into

---

[33] eg the reservations entered by Germany, Luxembourg, and Singapore. See Declarations and Reservations to the CRC.

[34] It is suggested that the principle may even be considered a *jus cogens* norm: see Van Bueren, 'Committee on the Rights of the Child' in Langford (ed), *Social Rights Jurisprudence: Emerging Trends in International and Comparative Law* (CUP, 2008) 569, 575–7.

[35] See further Van Bueren, 'The Separation of Powers and the International Legal Status of the Best Interests of the Child in Assisting Domestic Courts to Protect Children's Economic and Social Rights', in Collins *et al.* (eds), *Rights of the Child: Proceedings of the International Conference* (Ottawa, 2007) 240.

[36] CRC Committee, General Comment 5, para 12.

[37] Nowak, *Commentary on the United Nations Convention on the Rights of the Child, Article 6* (Brill, 2005) 2.

[38] CRC Committee, General Comment 12, CRC/C/GC/12 (20 July 2009) para 23.

those elements that are appropriate for the child to participate in and those that are not. Simply listening to the views of children is not enough; the views must be given serious consideration.

This right has also been incorporated into the procedural mechanisms established to oversee states parties' compliance with their obligations. The CRC Committee has encouraged states parties not only to consult with children when compiling their state reports but also to include children in their delegation.[39]

The creation of child-specific international complaint mechanisms gives further effect to this principle. The Optional Protocol to the CRC on a communications procedure was adopted in 2011 and entered into force in April 2014.[40] The CRC Committee has begun receiving individual communications, delivering its first admissibility decision in June 2015.[41] This mechanism was presaged by the mechanism established by the African Children's Charter, which permits any person, group, or NGO recognized by the African Union to petition the African Committee of Experts on the Rights and Welfare of the Child in relation to alleged violations of that Charter.[42]

3.5 THE EVOLVING CAPACITY OF THE CHILD

In addition to the 'general principles' considered above, one further principle enunciated in the CRC should be examined: the 'evolving capacity of the child'. Article 5 CRC provides:

> states parties shall respect the responsibilities, rights and duties of parents, or where applicable, the members of the extended family or community as provided by local custom, legal guardians or other persons legally responsible for the child, to provide, in a manner consistent with the evolving capacities of the child, appropriate direction and guidance in the exercise of the rights recognized in the present Convention.

Whilst acknowledging that children may require assistance to exercise their rights, this provision recognizes that the need for such assistance will vary according to the 'evolving capacities of the child'. The CRC is the first instrument to recognize that childhood is not an immutable concept, and that there are differences between the needs of, for example, a 17 year old child, a 5 year old child, and a 6 month old child. Developing levels of maturity will affect a child's capacity to exercise their rights. Maturity is not just related to age; it may differ across states or even regions within the state because of life experiences. Therefore a dynamic case-by-case assessment as to the child's capacity and a rejection of any presumptions of immaturity is required when considering how children's rights can be enjoyed. The principle of evolving capacity of the child requires recognition that as a child's capacities develop he or she should be granted increasing autonomy in the exercise of rights. The CRC Committee has recommended that as a child attains more experience, direction and guidance become advice and later an exchange of views on an equal footing.[43]

---

[39] CRC Committee, Working methods for the participation of children in the reporting process of the Committee on the Rights of the Child, CRC/C/66/2 (16 October 2003).

[40] See de Beco, 'The Optional Protocol to the Convention on the Rights of the Child on a Communications Procedure: Good News?' (2013) 13 *HRLR* 367.

[41] *Abdul-Hamid Aziz v Spain* CRC/C/69/D/1/2014 (4 June 2015).

[42] African Children's Charter, Art 44. See, eg, *Dalia Lotfy on behalf of Ahmed Bassiouni v Egypt* 008/Com/001/2016 (31 March 2016).   [43] CRC Committee, General Comment 12, para 84.

4 THE 4PS: PROTECTION, PREVENTION, PROVISION, AND PARTICIPATION

Rather than focusing on the arbitrary and restrictive division of human rights into civil and political and economic, social, and cultural, the extensive range of children's rights found in the CRC can be divided into a functional framework known as the '4Ps': namely, protection, prevention, provision, and participation.[44] This framework is useful as an indication of the scope of rights protection afforded by the CRC.

4.1 PROTECTION

Protection refers to protection from discrimination and all forms of harm and exploitation,[45] including protection from all forms of child abuse, neglect, exploitation, and cruelty,[46] the right to special protection in times of armed conflict,[47] and protection from abuse in the criminal justice system.[48]

The CRC extends traditional legal protections for children. For example, Article 6(5) ICCPR prohibits the death penalty for actions committed by children below the age of 18, whereas Article 37(a) CRC prohibits both the death penalty and the imposition of a sentence of life imprisonment without the possibility of release. Given that these prohibitions are included in the provision that prohibits torture and ill-treatment, it is clear that to impose a sentence of life imprisonment without possibility for release on a child is so egregious as to constitute torture or inhuman punishment.

Articles 37 and 40 CRC protect the rights of the child in justice systems and focus on creating a juvenile justice system that serves the best interests of the child. Arrest, detention, and imprisonment of the child should only be used as a matter of last resort and for the shortest appropriate period of time. The UN Rules for the Protection of Juveniles Deprived of their Liberty 1990[49] provide a valuable framework to which the CRC Committee draws states parties' attention. These Rules, originally drafted by NGOs and submitted to the Criminal Justice Branch of the UN,[50] place the emphasis of child detention not on security but on the best interests of the child. They prohibit the carrying of weapons by detention staff[51] and punishments for children, which may be acceptable for adults, such as solitary confinement.[52] Article 40 CRC sets out fair trial guarantees for (alleged) child offenders. However, it also obliges states to consider alternatives to formal justice systems. Wherever appropriate and desirable, states parties should seek measures other than judicial proceedings for child offenders, whilst ensuring that the human rights of the child, and associated legal safeguards, are fully respected. Greater details of the rights of children in the criminal justice system are found in the UN Standard Minimum Rules for the Administration of Juvenile Justice 1985 (the Beijing Rules).[53] However, the CRC standards take precedence where there is a clash with the Beijing Rules.

---

[44] Some authors refer to the 3P's framework wherein 'protection' includes 'prevention'.

[45] Note that in this context 'protection' is distinct from 'protect' in the tripartite typology of state obligations (see Chapter 5).   [46] CRC, Arts 19, 34, and 36.   [47] CRC, Art 38.

[48] CRC, Arts 37 and 40.   [49] GA Res 45/113 (14 December 1990).

[50] The drafting of the Rules is an example of how a lack of budgetary provision within the UN can be turned to the advantage of human rights advocates. The lack of budget meant that the Rules were drafted over several weekends by NGOs in Geneva and sent to the UN Criminal Justice Branch, which in turn sent them to states for adoption. The author was one of the drafters of the UN Rules for Juveniles Deprived of their Liberty.

[51] UN Rules for the Protection of Juveniles Deprived of their Liberty, Rule 65.

[52] UN Rules for the Protection of Juveniles Deprived of their Liberty, Rule 67.

[53] GA Res 40/33 (29 November 1985).

Two of the three Optional Protocols (OPs) to the CRC focus on expanding the protection entitlements of children. Article 38 CRC is a reflection of attempts made during the drafting of the Convention to prohibit the involvement of children in armed conflict both directly and indirectly. It provides that states parties are not to recruit children under the age of 15 into the armed forces and that they shall take all 'feasible measures' to ensure that children under the age of 15 do not take a direct part in hostilities. Furthermore, states shall 'endeavour' to give priority to older children when recruiting children under the age of 18 (and above the age of 15). These protections have been augmented by the Optional Protocol to the Convention on the Rights of the Child on the involvement of children in armed conflict 2000.[54] Children under the age of 18 are not to be compulsorily recruited into the armed forces, and where they genuinely volunteer (with parental consent), a state party is to take 'all feasible measures' to ensure that they do not take a direct part in hostilities.[55] The Optional Protocol to the Convention on the Rights of the Child on the sale of children, child prostitution and child pornography 2000 similarly raises the standards established by Articles 34 and 35 CRC regarding the rights of children who have been victims of trafficking and sexual exploitation[56] and in the establishment of jurisdiction over the offences and extradition.[57]

4.2 PREVENTION

Closely linked to *protection* is *prevention*, which refers to prevention of harm to children. Whilst there are significant overlaps, a distinction is made between the two categories because regrettably it is still the case that much of the work of international human rights bodies is post-violation rather than seeking to prevent violations. Prevention requires that systems are in place to protect children from abuse.

The CRC Committee has laid much stress on prevention, particularly in relation to violence against children. Article 19 CRC obliges states parties to take all appropriate measures to prevent violence against children. States parties must ensure that measures have been taken by all levels of society to protect the child from all forms of physical and mental violence. In its General Comment on violence against children, the Committee has recommended that primary prevention is conducted through public health, education, and social services and that states parties need to create a systematic and transparent budgeting system in order to make the best use of allocated resources for child protection, including prevention.[58] The Committee has also called for increased state reporting on the measures for the prevention of violence, awareness-raising activities, and the promotion of positive, non-violent relationships.[59] The idea is to ensure a holistic, rather than fragmented, approach to preventing violence against children. Where measures fail to prevent such violence, states parties are obliged to respond in a child-centred manner whereby the basic principles of the Convention are respected.[60]

One of the more contested areas of children's rights is the physical punishment of children. As Bitensky observes, '[i]t is telling that as historically oppressed people have liberated themselves from being legally categorized as the property of others, such liberation

---

[54] See Coomaraswamy, 'The Optional Protocol to the Convention on the Rights of the Child on the Involvement of Children in Armed Conflict—Towards Universal Ratification' (2010) 18 *Intl J Child R* 535.

[55] OP Armed Conflict, Arts 1, 2, 3(3). Under Art 4(1), non-state armed groups are prohibited from recruiting, or using in hostilities, children under the age of 18.

[56] OP Sale of Children, Art 8.   [57] OP Sale of Children, Arts 4 and 5.

[58] CRC Committee, General Comment 13, CRC/C/GC/13 (18 April 2011), paras 3(g), 42(iv), 46–47.

[59] CRC Committee, General Comment 13, para 9.

[60] CRC Committee, General Comment 13, paras 49–58.

typically has brought in its wake legal protection from physical chastisement'.[61] Although the *travaux préparatoires* of the CRC make clear that a number of states did not interpret Article 19 as prohibiting physical punishment within the family, the Committee has interpreted Article 19 as requiring states parties to ban *all* forms of physical punishment, including that which takes place within the family.[62] This approach has clearly had a positive effect. An increasing number of states have abolished all forms of physical punishment of children and there is widespread support that this is in the best interests of children.

4.3 PROVISION

Provision refers to provision of assistance, including the resources, skills, and other requirements necessary for the survival and full development of the child. It encompasses a wide range of rights from education;[63] to leisure, play, and culture;[64] and to special protection and assistance for children who cannot be looked after by their own family.[65] Many of these rights were recognized in early international children's rights instruments, including both the 1924 and 1959 Declarations of the Rights of the Child, and can be found in the ICESCR. The CRC enshrines these rights from a child-centred perspective. For example, the duty on states parties to provide for the right to education found in Article 13 ICESCR is extended by Article 29 CRC to include entitling children to receive education which develops the child's full potential and respect for human rights, and which is aimed at educating children in a spirit of peace, tolerance, and equality of the sexes. These rights recognize that children require assistance from adults. However, in line with the general principles of the CRC, provision of such assistance should be in the best interests of children, taking into account their views and capacity to exercise their rights independently.

Provision also includes newer rights for children, such as the right of a child victim of a rights violation to physical and psychological recovery and social reintegration in an environment which fosters the health, self-respect, and dignity of the child.[66] Special consideration is also given to children who are particularly vulnerable, such as those seeking refugee status and those who are disabled.[67] In the case of the latter group, states should provide, on application, assistance 'designed to ensure that the disabled child has effective access to education, training, health care services, rehabilitation services, preparation for employment and recreation opportunities in a manner conducive to the child's achieving the fullest possible social integration and individual development, including his or her cultural and spiritual development'.[68]

4.4 PARTICIPATION

The fourth P, *participation*, is regarded as the most challenging and to some the most radical. It requires recognition that children are entitled to the freedom to express opinions and to have a say in matters affecting their political, social, economic, cultural, and religious life. Participation rights include the rights to hold beliefs[69] and express opinions[70] and for those opinions to be heard,[71] as well as the rights to information[72] and freedom of

---

[61] Bitensky, 'Spare the Rod, Embrace our Humanity: Toward a New Legal Regime Prohibiting Corporal Punishment of Children' (1998) 31 *University of Michigan J of L Reform* 440.

[62] CRC Committee, General Comment 8.   [63] CRC, Art 29.   [64] CRC, Art 31.

[65] CRC, Art 20. See also Polonko, Lombardo, and Bolling, 'Law Reform, Child Maltreatment and the UN Convention on the Rights of the Child' (2016) 24 *Intl J Child R* 30.   [66] CRC, Art 39.

[67] CRC, Arts 22 and 23.   [68] CRC, Art 23(3).   [69] CRC, Art 14.   [70] CRC, Art 13.

[71] CRC, Art 12.

[72] CRC, Art 17. See CRC Committee, Day of General Discussion: The Child and the Media, CRC/C/15/Add.65 (7 October 1996), paras 242–57.

association.[73] Participation is also facilitated by the obligation under Article 42 CRC for states parties to 'make the principles and provisions of the Convention widely known, by appropriate and active means, to adults and children alike'. Recognition of the rights that facilitate participation signals that children are considered to have (now, or in the future) the necessary capacity and competence to exercise them.

As we have seen (Section 3.4), Article 12 CRC affords a child the right to express his or her views on all matters affecting the child. The weight given to a child's opinion will depend upon the age and maturity of the child. Even though children's views and opinions are still not always recognized and heard, theoretically this right remains of great importance to the development of children's rights.[74] Therefore, this right has been recognized as a general principle of the CRC.[75]

There is also a standalone right to freedom of expression provided for in Article 13 CRC. This is a right to receive and share information, through any media of the child's choice, including orally, in writing or through art. Read together with Article 12, the full potential of a child's right to freedom of expression through non-traditional forms of media is yet to be fully explored. It could, if implemented fully, have a transformative effect in relation to a wide range of proceedings from policy consultations to judicial proceedings. There is currently an over-reliance on written and oral communications in these settings. However, a child may not be able to express their views through written word but may be able to communicate through drawings or music. There is significant potential for increasing child participation in decision-making.

The right to freedom of thought, conscience, and religion stipulated in Article 14 CRC has attracted numerous reservations and interpretative declarations. Many of these have related to 'choice' of religion. In some religions, such as Islam, it is a matter of divine law that children follow their parents' religion; children do not make a choice. The text of Article 14 is unclear on choice of religion (stating only that '[t]he states parties shall respect the right of the child to freedom of thought, conscience and religion'). Some states have affirmed that the CRC does protect freedom of choice of religion (for example, Belgium and the Netherlands); others have entered a reservation to the Convention such that they do not recognize any right of the child to choose their religion (for example, Jordan and Iraq); whilst others have suggested that Article 14 does not give a child the right to choose their religion (for example, United Arab Emirates). Where it is recognized that a child can adopt a religion of their choice, states parties are under a duty to 'respect the rights and duties of the parents . . . to provide direction to the child in the exercise of his or her right in a manner consistent with the evolving capacities of the child'.[76] Therefore as a child matures, parental direction on religion should decrease.

5 REGIONAL PROTECTION OF CHILDREN'S RIGHTS

Children's rights are also protected by regional human rights instruments and institutions. This section will consider these regional protections and discuss whether they expand or limit the protections afforded by the CRC.

---

[73] CRC, Art 15.

[74] Krappmann, 'The Weight of the Child's View (Article 12 of the Convention on the Rights of the Child)' (2010) 18 *Intl J Child R* 501, 510.

[75] Lucker-Babel, 'The Right of the Child to Express Views and to Be Heard: An Attempt to Interpret Article 12 of the UN Convention on the Rights of the Child' (1995) 3 *Intl J Child R* 391.

[76] CRC, Art 14(2).

5.1 AFRICA

The situation of most African children is 'critical due to the unique factors of their socio-economic, cultural, traditional, and developmental circumstances, natural disasters, armed conflicts, exploitation, and hunger'.[77] Whilst the same can be said of other continents such as Asia, the African Union has responded to this pressing concern by adopting the African Charter on the Rights and Welfare of the Child 1990. By including both rights and welfare in its title, the African Children's Charter underlines the fact that both welfare *and* rights are necessary for a child and they are mutually reinforcing. As with the concept of 'best interests', a child's welfare must be interpreted and applied within the context of rights, so that the adult exercise of discretion implicit in welfare does not violate any of the rights of the child. The advantage of the African Children's Charter is that it is a *regional* children's rights treaty, which means that it may appear more accessible and less distant than the CRC.

The African Children's Charter appears to raise the standard of best interests as a general principle to above that found in the CRC. Article 4 provides that the best interests of the child are not *a* primary consideration but '*the* primary consideration in all action concerning children'.[78] There is express provision that the child's best interests take priority over all other considerations, and, unlike the CRC, this includes decisions concerning other family members. There is also a greater focus on specific groups of vulnerable children in relation to their right to education than is found in either the CRC or the ICESCR. For example, Article 11(3)(e) African Children's Charter requires states to take 'special measures in respect of female, gifted and disadvantaged children, to ensure equal access to education for all sections of the community'.

Perhaps unsurprisingly, the African Children's Charter repeats the articulation of responsibilities of the child towards the family set out in Article 29 of the African Charter on Human and Peoples' Rights (ACHPR). This unwelcome repetition is set out in Article 31 African Children's Charter, which assigns responsibilities to every child 'to work for the cohesion of the family, to respect his parents, superiors and elders at all times and to assist them in case of need' and 'to preserve and strengthen African cultural values'. The responsibility to assist in case of need is also found in another regional instrument: Article 30 of the American Declaration on the Rights and Duties of Man. However, the repetition of the duty to respect parents, superiors, and elders 'at all times' is clearly inappropriate towards abusive parents and other exploitative adults and could go against the best interests of the child.[79] Whilst it is true that some responsibilities by children may be beneficial to their lives and enhance their sense of dignity, a similar provision was not included in the CRC to avoid any possible taint of conditionality: that is, the enjoyment by children of their rights is not dependent upon them exercising their responsibilities.

There are a number of omissions from the African Children's Charter. Firstly, there is no specific reference to 'child-headed' households. These are households where children take on parenting roles because of the premature death of their parents and any responsible adults, often as a result of HIV/AIDS. This creates particular problems not only in terms of the burdens which interfere with all children's rights, particularly leisure and education, but also because specific legislation needs to be adopted by states, so that child-headed

---

[77] African Children's Charter, Preamble. See Muyilla, *African Values and Problems of Rights of the Child: A Search for Explanations* (Danish Institute of Human Rights, 2006).   [78] Emphasis added.

[79] Van Bueren, *The International Law on the Rights of the Child* (Martinus Nijhoff, 1998) 76.

households are made eligible to receive a wide range of state support on behalf of their families. This omission in both the African Children's Charter, as well as the CRC, is due to the lack of awareness at the time of the drafting about HIV/AIDS and the resultant impacts.[80]

The second omission is in relation to the child's right to freedom of expression.[81] Once again, the restrictive approach taken in the ACHPR is replicated. Article 7 African Children's Charter provides that '[e]very child who is capable of communicating his or her own views shall be assured the rights to express his opinions freely in all matters and to disseminate his opinions subject to such restrictions as are prescribed by laws.' This open-ended restriction is at odds with Article 13(2) CRC, which provides that restrictions on freedom of expression are only permitted for reasons related to the rights and reputations of others, protection of national security or public order, or public health or morals. However, given that the African Committee of Experts on the Rights and Welfare of the Child can take 'inspiration' from the CRC,[82] in practical terms this ought not to lead to a lowering of standards from those set out in the CRC.

5.2 THE AMERICAS

Although the Organization of American States (OAS) lacks a specific children's rights treaty, there is a provision within the ACHR devoted to the protection of children. Article 19 ACHR provides that '[e]very minor child has the right to the measures of protection required by his condition as a minor on the part of his family, society, and the state.' The Inter-American Court of Human Rights has developed a significant jurisprudence on children's rights. In addition, the Inter-American Commission on Human Rights has established a Rapporteurship on the Rights of the Child, which is mandated to promote the rights of children and adolescents in the OAS.[83]

The Inter-American Court has adopted two major advisory opinions on the rights of the child: *Juridical status and human rights of the child*[84] and *Rights and guarantees of children in the context of migration and/or in need of special measures of protection*.[85] In both these opinions the Inter-American Court stressed that the CRC is to give content and scope to the obligations imposed by Article 19 ACHR.[86] In its opinion on the *Rights and guarantees of children in the context of migration and/or in need of special measures of protection* the Court applied the guiding principles of the CRC (namely, non-discrimination, the best interests of the child, the right to life, survival, and development, and the right to be heard) when considering the measures of protection required to make the rights of the child under Article 19 effective.[87] In particular, the Court was keen to emphasize the need for a contextualized approach to the best interests of the child assessment and it confirmed that in immigration and asylum proceedings the affected child has the right to be heard and that his or her views will be adequately taken into account.[88]

---

[80] The CRC Committee adopted a General Comment on the issue in 2003. See CRC Committee, General Comment 3, HIV/AIDS and the rights of the child, CRC/GC/2003/1.

[81] Krappmann (2010), 510.   [82] African Children's Charter, Art 46.

[83] See: <http://www.oas.org/en/iachr/children/default.asp>.

[84] OC-17/02, IACtHR Series A No 17 (28 August 2002).

[85] OC-21/14, IACtHR Series A No 21 (19 August 2014).

[86] *Juridical status and human rights of the child*, para 24; *Rights and Guarantees in the context of migration*, para 57.   [87] *Rights and Guarantees in the context of migration*, para 69.

[88] *Rights and Guarantees in the context of migration*, para 70.

The first contentious judgment from the Inter-American Court regarding children's rights was the *Case of the 'Street Children' (Villagrán-Morales et al.) v Guatemala*, which concerned the widespread murder of children living and working on the streets in Guatemala City.[89] The Inter-American Court conceptualized this as a double violation, because in addition to violating the children's rights to life and physical integrity, Guatemala had failed to 'prevent them from living in misery, thus depriving them of the minimum conditions for a dignified life and preventing them from the "full and harmonious development of their personality"'.[90] Significantly, the Inter-American Court did not restrict this duty to children living and working on the streets but applied it to all children who are 'at risk'.[91] The Inter-American Court held that Guatemala had violated a number of the children's rights under the ACHR[92] and had breached various obligations under the Inter-American Convention to Prevent and Punish Torture.[93] In particular, Guatemala had failed to adopt special measures to protect and assist children, and instead tolerated their arbitrary arrest, torture, and eventual murder as part of a larger practice of violence against street children. The Inter-American Court looked to the CRC to help interpret the obligations that Guatemala had under Article 19 ACHR in relation to children living and working on the streets.

The reparation ordered by the Inter-American Court was both wide-ranging and progressive. The Court ordered compensation to the victims' families, the investigation and prosecution of the perpetrators, and the building of a school with a plaque commemorating the murder of the children, so that the children's lives were not taken in vain. The Court also recognized that children who live and work on the streets not only come within the protected category of childhood but also ought to be protected as an additional identifiable social group, whose way of living is distinct as a result of other human rights violations. The implication is that children living and working on the streets ought to be prioritized by states as requiring additional protection and not be at the tail end of resource allocation.

The Inter-American Court's judgments have also focused on many politically contentious issues concerning children's rights. For example, in the case of *Yean and Bosico v Dominican Republic*, two girls aged 10 months and 12 years old respectively were refused birth certificates because they failed an onerous 11-point nationality test.[94] The Inter-American Court concluded that the test was too difficult and discriminated against Dominicans of Haitian descent. The Court also held that the denial of nationality deprived the children of a juridical personality, which violated their right to dignity. The initial refusal by the Dominican Republic to provide the two children with birth certificates resulted in a violation of their right to a name, as they could not publicly identify with their parental chosen names. The older girl had been denied admittance to schooling because of the lack of documentation, amounting to a violation of the special protection rights to which all children are entitled. In relation to the girls' families, the Court held that there had been a violation of their right to personal integrity because of the distress the families suffered fearing their deportation.

In addition to compensation and the establishment of a non-discriminatory system of birth registration, the Inter-American Court also ordered that the Dominican Republic issue, within six months of the judgment, a public act of recognition and responsibility and a guarantee of free access to primary education to children regardless of their

---

89 *Street Children.*   90 *Street Children*, para 191.
91 *Street Children*, para 191.
92 Including those rights protected by ACHR, Arts 4, 5(1), 5 (2), 8, 19, and 25.
93 Inter-American Convention to Prevent and Punish Torture, Arts 1, 6, and 8.
94 IACtHR Series C No 156 (8 September 2005).

heritage or origin. In 2005 the Dominican Ministry of Foreign Affairs pronounced the judgment 'unacceptable' and this was followed by a formal rejection of the judgment by the Senate of the Dominican Republic in October of that year. The case is an illustration of how children's rights can go to the core of the perceived identity of the state and how an often overlooked instrumental children's right, the right to birth registration, in particular contexts can be politically challenging to implement even after a regional human rights court ruling.

5.3 EUROPE

Within the Council of Europe there is currently very little prospect of a specific wide-ranging children's rights treaty.[95] Whilst there is the European Convention on the Exercise of Children's Rights 1996, this is a relatively narrow treaty providing for measures that aim to promote the rights of children, in particular in family proceedings, before judicial authorities.

The two principal human rights organs of the Council of Europe, the European Court of Human Rights (European Court) and the European Committee of Social Rights (ECSR) have both considered issues relating to children's rights, such as the physical punishment of children. For example, *Association for the Protection of All Children (APPROACH) v France* concerned Article 17 of the Revised European Social Charter, which guarantees the right of children to appropriate social, legal, and economic protection.[96] In that case, the ECSR confirmed that compliance with Article 17 required that 'domestic law must prohibit and penalize all forms of violence against children that is acts or behavior likely to affect the physical integrity, dignity, development or psychological well-being of children. The relevant provisions must be sufficiently clear, binding and precise, so as to preclude the courts from refusing to apply them to violence against children. Moreover, states must act with due diligence to ensure that such violence is eliminated in practice.'[97]

In its case law the European Court has repeatedly invoked the 'best interests of the child', often by reference to the CRC.[98] The Court has often found that states have violated the ECHR regarding protection, prevention, and provision aspects of children's rights. Less frequent are judgments that find states to have breached their obligations by failing to respect the child's right to participation. One rare example is *Gülcü v Turkey*.[99] In that case, the European Court found that Turkey had violated the right of assembly and association by sentencing a child aged 15 to a total of seven years and six months imprisonment for participating in an unauthorized demonstration and belonging to an illegal organization. The Court ruled that although the applicant had also been convicted of stone-throwing during the demonstration, the sentence and conditions of imprisonment were dispropor-tionate to the offences for a child.

However, the European Court has not always recognized the value of a child's partici-pation in decision-making processes. In the case of *Raw v France*,[100] the European Court

---

[95] Although in 1979 the Parliamentary Assembly of the Council of Europe recommended the adoption of a 'European Charter on the Rights of the Child', this was never implemented.

[96] Complaint no 92/2013, Decision of 3 November 2014.

[97] *APPROACH*, para 36. See also *World Organisation against Torture (OMCT) v Portugal*, Complaint No 34/2006, Decision of 5 December 2006.

[98] eg *Paradiso and Campanelli v Italy*, Application No 25358/12, Judgment of 24 January 2017; *Blokhin v Russia*, Application No 47152/06, Judgment of 23 March 2016.

[99] Application No 17526/10, Judgment of 19 January 2016.

[100] Application No 10131/11, Judgment of 7 March 2013.

decided that France had violated the right to family life when refusing to order the return of children to their mother in the UK, despite the children, aged 12 and 10, expressing the view that they did not want to return to their mother. The French authorities had held that it would be in the best interests of the children to remain in France with their father. The European Court found that the obligations regarding custody and return under the Hague Convention on the Civil Aspects of International Child Abduction 1980 should prevail over the views of the children and the decision by the French authorities based on a best interests assessment. The European Court's rigid adherence to the Hague Convention suggests a departure from the importance accorded by the CRC to the participation of children in return proceedings affecting them.[101]

In respect of protection, one of the most significant cases involving children and the criminal justice system before the European Court was *T & V v UK*.[102] The European Court held that to try two children aged 10 years old as adults for murder violated their right to a fair trial. The Court was of the view that the applicants' age prevented them from fully understanding the nature of the charges against them, and thus they were unable to participate in their defence as they would have been able to had they been adults.

The European Court has extensively interpreted the positive obligations of the state when considering protection of the child, particularly regarding sexual offences against children. In *C.A.S. and C.S. v Romania*,[103] the Court found that Romania had violated the right to be free from inhuman and degrading treatment and the right to family life in its failure to investigate and prosecute in a timely fashion an adult for the rape of a seven-year-old boy. The breach of ECHR obligations also included the failure to provide counselling for the child after the rape was reported. This ruling was despite the fact that the accused rapist was acquitted when he was finally brought to court.

Perhaps the most far-reaching of the cases involving the state duty to protect children from sexual offences was the ruling by the Grand Chamber of the European Court in *O'Keeffe v Ireland*.[104] The Court ruled, by a majority of 11 to 6, that Ireland had breached the right to be free from inhuman and degrading treatment when it failed to protect a nine-year-old child from repeated sexual abuse while she was in the care of the Catholic Church. The Court also ruled that Ireland was in breach of its obligation to provide a remedy in law for the person who had been subjected to the assaults, and who had brought her application to the Court after becoming an adult. Overall, the European Court has been receptive to complaints that states parties have failed to protect children. Whilst the need to protect is clearest when children are in the care of a state body, it also extends to protecting children from abuse in the private sector.

6 CONCLUSION

Children's rights have developed as a 'Go-Stop-Go' policy. The world's first general human rights declaration—the Declaration of the Rights of the Child 1924—was focused on children. Although not legally binding per se, it had consequences in practical terms. For example, in France a copy was hung in every classroom. However, gradually children

---

101 See also *X v Latvia* (2014) 59 EHRR 3.
102 (2000) 30 EHRR 121.
103 (2015) 60 EHRR 18.
104 (2014) 59 EHRR 15.

began to disappear from the international legal agenda with only a second slightly broader declaration, the UN Declaration of the Rights of the Child 1959, and minimal protection in the two UN Covenants and regional treaties. The International Year of the Child in 1979 was never intended to kick-start a quiet revolution, but the drafting of the CRC and its subsequent ratification by all but one state radically transformed children from passive invisible beings into contributory active citizens of the world. Many of the elements of the CRC have been implemented in regional treaties and incorporated in national constitutions.

It would be easy to become cynical and conclude that governments ignore international children's rights when they choose. However, that would be an over-simplification. The CRC was never intended to be a quick universal panacea for all violations of children's rights. The international human rights instruments on children have achieved much. Most importantly, there is now widespread acceptance of the concept of children's rights; they are no longer a radical innovation. The creation of specific child-centred regional and international complaints mechanisms; the successful bringing of complaints by children from a wide range of states; the acceptance by the majority of states that child criminal justice is no longer only of domestic concern; the creation and enhancement of child safety mechanisms; and the creation of mechanisms by which children can participate in national, regional, and international policy decisions all demonstrate this.

Despite setbacks, we remain in the second 'Go' phase. This needs to continue. Innovative ways of working with children on the protection of their rights need to be developed to ensure that governments are held to account.[105]

FURTHER READING

ARCHARD, *Children: Rights and Childhood* (Routledge, 2015).

CRC Committee, General Comment 14 on the right of the child to have his or her best interests taken as a primary consideration, CRC/C/GC/14 (29 May 2013).

DETRICK, *A Commentary on the United Nations of the Convention on the Rights of the Child* (Martinus Nijhoff, 1999).

FREEMAN, *Commentary on the United Nations Convention on the Rights of the Child, Article 3: The Best Interests of the Child* (Brill, 2007).

INVERNIZZI and WILLIAMS (eds), *The Human Rights of Children: From Vision to Implementation* (Routledge, 2016).

KILKELLY, 'The Best of Both Worlds for Children's Rights? Interpreting the European Convention on Human Rights in the Light of the UN Convention on the Rights of the Child' (2001) HRQ 311.

LANSDOWN, *The Evolving Capacities of the Child* (UNICEF, 2005).

NOLAN and KILKELLY, 'Children's Rights under Regional Human Rights Law—A Tale of Harmonisation' in Buckley, Donald, and Leach (eds), *Towards Convergence in International Human Rights Law: Approaches of Regional and International Systems* (Brill, 2016) 296.

PARKES, *Children and International Human Rights Law* (Routledge, 2013).

SLOTH-NIELSEN (ed), *Children's Rights in Africa: A Legal Perspective* (Ashgate, 2008).

VAN BUEREN, *The International Law on the Rights of the Child* (Martinus Nijhoff, 1998).

VAN BUEREN, *Child Rights in Europe* (Council of Europe, 2007).

[105] The author is grateful to Nicole Lieberman for research assistance with this chapter.

USEFUL WEBSITES

African Committee of Experts on the Rights and Welfare of the Child: <http://www.acerwc.org/>

Child Rights Connect: <http://www.childrightsconnect.org>

Child Rights International Network (CRIN): <www.crin.org>

CRC materials (OHCHR): <http://www.ohchr.org/EN/HRBodies/CRC/Pages/CRCIndex.aspx>

OHCHR Compilation of Thematic Reports on Rights of the Child: <http://www.ohchr.org/EN/Issues/Children/ThematicReports/Pages/ThematicreportsonchildrenIndex.aspx>

18

GROUP RIGHTS

Robert McCorquodale

SUMMARY

This chapter concerns the human rights of three particular groups: peoples with the right of self-determination, minorities, and indigenous peoples. The right of self-determination is a right that protects a group as a group entity in regard to their political participation, as well as their control over their economic, social, and cultural activity as a group. It is a right that applies to 'peoples' in all states and can be exercised in many ways, with most exercises of the right today being within the boundaries of a state. The right cannot be limited by the rights of others and by the general interests of the international community except in restricted circumstances. Rights of minorities can be seen as both individual and group rights, and have been the subject of increasing international human rights protection in recent years, as have the rights of indigenous peoples.

1 INTRODUCTION

1.1 GROUP RIGHTS

Most of the discussion in this book, and the focus of many of its chapters, is about the human rights of individual human beings. This is not surprising, as the historical and conceptual bases of human rights generally developed from considerations concerning the dignity and oppression of individuals, and almost all national constitutional and legislative protections of human rights have been drafted to protect the rights of individuals. Similarly, the vast majority of human rights protected in international and regional treaties, such as the right to life, the right to an adequate standard of living, the right to education, and the right to freedom of thought, protect the rights of individual human beings.

However, human rights are not limited to those of individual human beings. As long as each individual is a part of one or many groups, an individual's identities, histories, and engagements are affected by belonging to groups and by the communities within which they live. Human rights can be understood in terms of the need to protect the dignity and physical integrity of a group (or a 'people'), as well as its civil, cultural, economic, political, and social engagement. As human rights should reflect lived realities, it is necessary to see them as more than about individuals. After all, most societies accord an importance to communities, collectives, and families, and humans possess a general communal quality. International human rights law is conceived and exercised within the context of communities, with rights being limited (in all except a few instances) by the rights of others and the general interests of the relevant community.[1]

Yet in a number of situations it is a group of individuals who are discriminated against or oppressed because of the fact that they belong to a group or they have a group identity and sense of human dignity that is dependent on them belonging to a group. For example, the prohibition on genocide is a human right premised on the need to protect a group as a group from actions against its physical integrity and not only to protect the individual's right to life. Similarly, many indigenous communities have an identity that is dependent on them being a group rather than being a selection of individuals. Therefore, group rights (sometimes called 'collective rights') are intended to protect a group (for example, a people) from discrimination and oppression *as a group*.

1.2 GROUP RIGHTS V RIGHTS OF INDIVIDUALS

Many individual human rights do have the effect of protecting a group. For example, the right of freedom of assembly, the right to join a trade union, and the right of freedom of religion all enable groups to gather, have protection, and express their thoughts. Yet each of these rights is an individual right under international human rights law. It is an individual right exercised in concert with other individual human rights but it can only be held and claimed by an individual human being. While there is now some case law that enables legal entities, such as religious institutions and corporations, to bring claims on behalf of individuals (and perhaps even in their own right),[2] these remain individual rights that may lead indirectly to the protection of a group. They are not rights that directly protect a group as a group.

The UN Human Rights Committee considered the difference between group rights and individual rights when considering the right of self-determination (which is a group right), stating that:

> The right of self-determination is of particular importance because its realization is *an essential condition* for the effective guarantee and observance of individual human rights and for the promotion and strengthening of those rights. It is for that reason that States set forth the right of self-determination in a provision of positive law in both Covenants [the International Covenant on Civil and Political Rights and the International Covenant on Economic, Social and Cultural Rights] and placed this provision as article 1 apart from and before all of the other rights in the two Covenants.[3]

In making this statement, the Human Rights Committee both recognized the difference between group rights and individual rights, and acknowledged that when groups are subject to oppression as a group and their rights are not able to be exercised, then the individuals within those groups are also not able to exercise their individual rights. The Committee made the difference even clearer when it took the view that a group who brought a complaint under the Optional Protocol to the International Covenant on Civil and Political Rights (ICCPR-OP1) alleging a breach of the right of self-determination could not do so because the specific terms of the ICCPR-OP1 only enabled complaints by 'individuals'.[4]

---

[1] Limitations on human rights are discussed in Chapter 5.

[2] eg *Autronic AG v Switzerland* (1990) 12 EHRR 485; *Singer v Canada*, CCPR/C/51/D/455/1991 (8 April 1993); and 155/96, *Social and Economic Rights Action Center and the Center for Economic and Social Rights (SERAC) v Nigeria*, 15th Activity Report of the ACommHPR (2001).

[3] HRC, General Comment 12, HRI/GEN/1/Rev.9 (Vol I) 183, para 1 (emphasis added).

[4] *Ominayak and the Lubicon Lake Band v Canada*, A/45/40 (Vol II) Annex IX, 1, para 32.1.

While there is some criticism of the Committee taking this stance, other international human rights treaties do not tend to contain the restriction that only individuals are able to bring a complaint. For example, the Optional Protocol to the International Covenant on Economic, Social and Cultural Rights (ICESCR) allows for complaints by groups concerning the rights protected by the ICESCR, which includes the right of self-determination.

1.3 RELEVANCE OF GROUP RIGHTS

While there are a range of group rights, such as the prohibition on genocide, the right to development, and the right to a clean environment, a specific focus of this chapter is on the right of self-determination (sometimes called the right *to* self-determination). This is because the right of self-determination is protected under the International Covenant on Civil and Political Rights (ICCPR) and the ICESCR, it has been considered in case law and other jurisprudence, and it has wide and significant impacts across the international community, as will be shown.

The rights of minorities have similar wide and significant impacts, as there are minorities in every state. While these rights have often been seen as within the compass of individual rights, it will be shown that they are also now considered as group rights. One type of collective that has been especially affected by the development of peoples and minorities rights is indigenous peoples, and so they are also considered in this chapter.

The acknowledgment that peoples, minorities, and indigenous groups have human rights, and that their rights should be protected in international law, has taken a long time. They are still not fully understood and respected. However, they are important human rights that affect the whole of the international community. With the reality that almost every state in the world has some current or potential issue connected with group rights, it is important that these rights are understood, respected, and applied appropriately.

2 THE RIGHT OF SELF-DETERMINATION

2.1 CONCEPT

Claims have been made for centuries about matters that could now be seen in terms of self-determination, with some writers tracing it as far back as the early stages of the institution of government. However, the use of self-determination in an international legal context primarily developed during the immediate post-First World War period, with US President Wilson stating that, '[P]eoples may now be dominated and governed only by their own consent. "Self-determination" is not a mere phrase. It is an imperative principle of action, which statesmen will henceforth ignore at their peril.'[5]

At about the same time Marxist thought on national liberation took root in the USSR. The combined effect of these ideas (and others) was that self-determination, despite its vague content and the sense to which it could be applied to a range of situations, became an accepted term of use in international relations. Then in 1945 the UN Charter proclaimed

---

[5] Wilson, *War Aims of Germany and Austria* (1918), reproduced in Baker, Dodd, and Leach (eds), *The Public Papers of Woodrow Wilson: War and Peace* (Harper and Brothers, 1927) 177 at 182. Wilson was supported by the British Prime Minister, Lloyd George, who declared that one reason for the UK entering the First World War had been the 'principle of self-determination' and that future territorial questions should be resolved by respecting 'the consent of the governed': address to the Trade Union Conference, 5 January 1918, reported in *The New York Times Current History* (New York) 270.

that one of the purposes of the UN was 'respect for the principle of equal rights and self-determination of peoples'.[6]

Since that time, through resolutions of the Security Council and the General Assembly, in decisions and opinions of the International Court of Justice (ICJ), in treaties, and in state practice—some of which will be referred to in this chapter—the idea of self-determination of peoples has been restated, reinforced, and reinvigorated. It has also been used in diverse contexts, not least because 'couching political goals in the language of legal entitlement has an undisputed rhetorical appeal',[7] and has become part of international law.

2.2 DEFINITIONS

Despite the general acceptance that self-determination is part of international law, it was not until the conclusion of the two international human rights Covenants that it was accepted that self-determination was a human right and that some form of legal definition was provided. Article 1 ICCPR and ICESCR provides:

1. All peoples have the right of self-determination. By virtue of that right they freely determine their political status and freely pursue their economic, social and cultural development.

2. All peoples may, for their own ends, freely dispose of their natural wealth and resources without prejudice to any obligations arising out of international economic co-operation, based upon the principle of mutual benefit, and international law. In no case may a people be deprived of its means of subsistence.

3. The States Parties to the present Covenant, including those having responsibility for the administration of Non-Self-Governing and Trust Territories, shall promote the realization of the right of self-determination, and shall respect that right, in conformity with the provisions of the Charter of the United Nations.

The definition in Article 1(1) is largely repeated in all the subsequent international and regional human rights treaties and documents that contain a right of self-determination, although the African Charter on Human and Peoples' Rights (ACHPR) elaborates on it slightly.[8]

Yet this definition does not clarify all aspects of the right. While it is evident that it is a right that is relevant in political contexts, it is also applicable in economic, social, and cultural contexts, with, for example, Article 1(2) of the Covenants dealing with a particular economic manifestation of the right and Article 55 UN Charter referring to economic and social aspects of the right. It is also a right of peoples as distinct from individuals, although the lack of further clarification as to who are the 'peoples' who have the right, has been a major stumbling block for many diplomats and writers.

---

[6] UN Charter, Art 1(2).

[7] Drew, 'Self-Determination, Population Transfer and the Middle-East Peace Accords' in Bowen (ed), *Human Rights, Self-Determination and Political Change in the Occupied Palestinian Territories* (Martinus Nijhoff, 1997) 127.

[8] ACHPR, Art 20 provides:

1. All peoples shall have the right to existence. They shall have the unquestionable and inalienable right to self-determination. They shall freely determine their political status and shall pursue their economic and social development according to the policy they have freely chosen.

2. Colonized or oppressed peoples shall have the right to free themselves from the bonds of domination by resorting to any means recognized by the international community.

3. All peoples shall have the right to the assistance of the States parties to the present Charter in their liberation struggle against foreign domination, be it political, economic or cultural.

There have been many attempts to establish a definition of 'peoples'.[9] The definition often referred to is that of an influential group of UNESCO experts:

A people for the [purposes of the] rights of people in international law, including the right to self-determination, has the following characteristics:

(a) A group of individual human beings who enjoy some or all of the following common features:

    (i) A common historical tradition;

    (ii) Racial or ethnic identity;

    (iii) Cultural homogeneity;

    (iv) Linguistic unity;

    (v) Religious or ideological affinity;

    (vi) Territorial connection;

    (vii) Common economic life.

(b) The group must be of a certain number who need not be large (e.g. the people of micro States) but must be more than a mere association of individuals within a State.

(c) The group as a whole must have the will to be identified as a people or the consciousness of being a people—allowing that groups or some members of such groups, though sharing the foregoing characteristics, may not have the will or consciousness.

(d) Possibly the group must have institutions or other means of expressing its common characteristics and will for identity.[10]

This definition appears to be an 'objective' one that can be applied to all relevant groups around the world, by providing some criteria that should be met for a 'people' to be established. However, an objective definition is impossible—and is likely to reinforce a developed-world, colonial, male construct of a 'people'[11]—and there would be few groups who have been universally accepted as peoples having the right of self-determination (including some of those who are in former colonies) who would meet all these criteria. This impossibility is acknowledged in paragraph (c) of the definition given here, where a 'subjective' criterion is included. This is because a key aspect of 'self' is self-identification, where the group identifies themselves consciously as a 'people'. This is an essential part of the definition of a 'people', not least because 'nations and peoples, like genetic populations, are recent, contingent and have been formed and reformed constantly throughout history',[12] often due to the oppression that they have received or to attain certain ends.[13]

In fact, in many situations, it is evident who are the 'peoples' with the right of self-determination. This can be because the relevant national constitution, legislation, or practice indicates this. There is also, as will be shown in Section 3, universal acceptance that the right

---

[9] eg Kiwanuka, 'The Meaning of "People" in the African Charter of Human and Peoples' Rights' (1988) 82 *AJIL* 80.

[10] Final Report and Recommendations of an International Meeting of Experts on the Further Study of the Concept of the Right of People for UNESCO, SNS–89/CONF.602/7 (22 February 1990). For a similar definition, see International Commission of Jurists, *Events in East Pakistan* (International Commission of Jurists, 1972) 49.

[11] See Charlesworth, Chinkin, and Wright, 'Feminist Approaches to International Law' (1991) 85 *AJIL* 613; Gaete, 'Postmodernism and Human Rights: Some Insidious Questions' [1991] *Law and Critique* 149.

[12] Kamenka, 'Human Rights, Peoples' Rights' in Crawford (ed), *The Rights of Peoples* (Clarendon Press, 1988) 127 at 133. See also Allott, 'The Nation as Mind Politic' (1992) 24 *NYUJILP* 1361.

[13] Chinkin and Wright, 'Hunger Trap: Women, Food and Self-Determination' (1993) 14 *Michigan JIL* 262, 306, propose that 'food, shelter, clean water, a healthy environment, peace and a stable existence must be the first priorities in how we define or "determine" the "self" of both individuals and groups, instead of the present definitions, which are based on masculinist goals of political and economic aggrandizement and aggressive territoriality'.

of self-determination applies to all peoples in colonial territories, as well as significant state practice that applies it beyond the colonial context. Consistent oppressive action by those in power over another group may also indicate an acceptance of the group as a 'people', not least because it may be a catalyst for the self-identification of the group as a people with the right of self-determination. External recognition by a state or group of states can be very useful for the group (such as the recognition by many states of the Palestinian people) but it is not conclusive of the group being a people for the purposes of the right of self-determination.

Indeed, if such external state recognition was conclusive it would allow the possibility of the existence of a human right (as distinct from the ability of a human right to be exercised) being dependent on the whims of governments. Above all, dependence on the government for the existence of a right would undermine the concept of a human right as being, for example, inherent in human dignity.[14]

Therefore, it is necessary to adopt a very flexible definition as to who are a 'people'. A definition is required that is broad and inclusive, not decided by states alone or imposed on a group, and is adaptable to the many circumstances that exist worldwide. The definition must respect the self-identification of a group as a people. There would need to be some territorial nexus for a 'people' with a right of self-determination. Yet a 'people' can include just a part of a population in a state and it can include groups that live across state territorial boundaries (which reflect the fact that in reality there is no 'nation-state'). It would include all those who are subject to 'alien subjugation, domination and exploitation'.[15]

If a broad and adaptable definition is adopted, then the focus on the right of self-determination under international human rights law is in relation to how and when the right can be exercised. As with all human rights, the concept of the right itself (being to protect the human dignity of the group as a group) cannot be dependent on governments or political considerations alone. Further, a broad definition of the possessors of this human right is consistent with the need to protect as many people as possible from violations of human rights by a state, considering both the inequality of power between a state and its inhabitants and the non-reciprocal nature of human rights treaties. Such a broad definition would then be consistent with the approach to other human rights in this book.

3 THE APPLICATION OF THE RIGHT OF SELF-DETERMINATION

3.1 COLONIAL CONTEXT

From the earliest time that the UN focused on self-determination as part of international law, it applied it to colonial territories. In 1960 self-determination was considered in the context of 'the necessity of bringing to a speedy and unconditional end colonialism in all its forms and manifestations'.[16] Article 1(3) ICCPR and ICESCR makes express reference to the special responsibility of colonial powers in regard to the right of self-determination:

> The States Parties to the present Covenant, including those having responsibility for the administration of Non-Self-Governing and Trust Territories, shall promote the realization of the right of self-determination, and shall respect that right, in conformity with the provisions of the Charter of the United Nations.[17]

---

[14] See Chapter 2.
[15] Declaration on Independence for Colonial Countries and Peoples, GA Res 1514 (XV) (14 December 1960).
[16] Declaration on Independence for Colonial Countries and Peoples, preamble.
[17] The special responsibility of colonial powers in regard to self-government of Non-Self-Governing Territories is also stated in UN Charter, Art 73.

The term 'Non-Self-Governing Territories' refers to the list of territories held by the UN that was meant to designate which were colonial territories. While this list was never comprehensive (especially as it was possible for states unilaterally to remove territories from the list), the term was a recognized UN abbreviation for colonial territories or colonies.

The ICJ has consistently held that the right of self-determination applies to all peoples in all colonial territories. In its *Namibia Opinion*, concerning the illegal presence of South Africa in Namibia, the Court's view was:

> [T]he subsequent development of international law in regard to non-self-governing territories, as enshrined in the Charter of the United Nations, made the principle of self-determination applicable to all of them. . . . The ultimate objective of the sacred trust was the self-determination and independence of the peoples concerned.[18]

This position was confirmed by the ICJ in the *Western Sahara Case*, with Judge Dillard stating that '[t]he pronouncements of the Court thus indicate, in my view, that a norm of international law has emerged applicable to the decolonisation of those non-self-governing territories which are under the aegis of the United Nations'.[19]

State practice confirms that the right of self-determination applies to all peoples in colonial territories. This is evident not only from the vast number of colonial territories that have exercised their right of self-determination to become new states, but also because of the acceptance by the colonial powers that they have a legal obligation to allow this exercise. Some writers have concluded from this consistent state practice, *opinio juris*, and lack of any denial by states that the right of self-determination of colonial peoples is now a matter of *jus cogens*.[20]

3.2 OUTSIDE THE COLONIAL CONTEXT

State practice shows that the right of self-determination has definitely been applied outside the colonial context. For example, when East and West Germany were united into one state in 1990, it was expressly stated in a treaty signed by four of the five permanent members of the UN that this was done as part of the exercise of the right of self-determination by the German people.[21] The right of self-determination was also referred to in the context of the dissolution of the USSR and Yugoslavia,[22] internally within states, and the ICJ confirmed that the right of self-determination applies to the Palestinian people in its *Advisory Opinion on the Wall*.[23]

The ICJ has gone further and has declared that the right of self-determination is 'one of the essential principles of contemporary international law' and has 'an *erga omnes* character'.[24] By having an *erga omnes* character it means that there is an obligation on *all states* to protect

---

[18] *Legal Consequences for States of the Continued Presence of South Africa in Namibia (South West Africa) notwithstanding Security Council Resolution 276 (1970)* [1971] ICJ Rep 16, para 52.

[19] *Western Sahara Case* [1975] ICJ Rep 12, per Judge Dillard at 121, and see Majority Opinion, paras 54–5.

[20] eg Cassese, *Self-Determination of Peoples: A Legal Appraisal* (CUP, 1995) 140; Crawford, *The International Law Commission's Articles on State Responsibility: Introduction, Text and Commentaries* (CUP, 2002) in relation to Art 41; Saul, 'The Normative Status of Self-Determination in International Law: A Formula for Uncertainty in the Scope and Content of the Right?' (2011) 11 *HRLR* 609. See Chapter 4 for an explanation of *jus cogens*.

[21] Treaty on the Final Settlement With Respect to Germany (1990) 29 *ILM* 1186.

[22] eg the terms of the European Community's Declaration on Yugoslavia and its Declaration on the Guidelines on Recognition of New States in Eastern Europe and the Soviet Union (16 December 1991), (1992) 31 *ILM* 1486.

[23] *Legal Consequences of the Construction of a Wall in the Occupied Palestinian Territory* (Advisory Opinion) [2004] ICJ Rep 136, paras 118 and 122.

[24] *East Timor Case (Portugal v Australia)* [1995] ICJ Rep 90, para 29. The HRC also requires all states parties to the ICCPR to report on their protection of the right of self-determination: General Comment 12, para 3.

and respect the right of self-determination. This makes clear that it is not only an obligation on colonial powers and so the right applies to peoples beyond the colonial context.

Indeed, since 1960 the right of self-determination has not been expressed in any international or regional instrument solely in the context of colonial territories but as a right of 'all peoples'. This is seen in the Declaration on Principles of International Law 1970 (which is often considered as being an internationally agreed clarification of the principles of the UN Charter) which provides:

> [All States should bear] in mind that subjection of peoples to alien subjugation, domination and exploitation constitutes a violation of the principle [of equal rights and self-determination of peoples], as well as a denial of fundamental human rights, and is contrary to the Charter of the United Nations.[25]

In fact, even the Declaration on Independence of Colonial Countries and Peoples 1960 dealt with colonialism 'in all its forms and manifestations'. The forms and manifestations of colonialism relevant to the application of the right of self-determination are about the oppressive *nature* of the administrative power over a people and not simply about the physical distance of the administering colonial power from the colonial territory. Hence, where a group or groups in a state administer power in such a way that there is 'subjugation, domination and exploitation' of another group that oppresses, demeans, and undermines the dignity of that group, then the right of self-determination may apply to the latter group. Therefore, the right of self-determination applies to any peoples in any territory (including non-colonial territories) who are subjected to 'alien subjugation, domination and exploitation'. Indeed, it would be contrary to the concept of a human right if the right of self-determination could only be exercised once (such as by a colonial territory) and then not again. All peoples in all states have the right of self-determination.

4 THE EXERCISE OF THE RIGHT OF SELF-DETERMINATION

4.1 EXTERNAL AND INTERNAL SELF-DETERMINATION

Under international human rights law, there is a concentrated focus on the *exercise* of a human right. This is usually because a particular issue has arisen due to an alleged restriction on the exercise of a right by a state. Similarly, the exercise of the right of self-determination is a crucial aspect in understanding the right.

The Declaration on Principles of International Law sets out the principal methods as to how the right of self-determination can be exercised. It provides that:

> The establishment of a sovereign and independent State, the free association or integration with an independent State or the emergence into any other political status freely determined by a people constitute modes of implementing the right of self-determination by that people.

While the vast majority of peoples in colonial territories exercised their right of self-determination by independence, this was not the only method of exercise that was either available or used. For example, the British and the Italian Somaliland colonies joined into one state of Somalia, part of the British colony of Cameroon merged with the French

---

[25] GA Res 2625(XXV) (1970) Annex.

colony of Cameroun to form the new state of Cameroon and the remaining part joined with the existing state of Nigeria, and Palau and a number of other Pacific Ocean islands formed a free association with the USA (that is, they had general self-government but their foreign affairs and defence were controlled by the USA).

In non-colonial situations, a range of exercises of the right of self-determination have occurred. While many have been by independence, such as Bangladesh from Pakistan and Montenegro from its union with Serbia, others have been by merger (for example, the two Yemens), or by free association (for example, Bougainville with Papua New Guinea). Some have occurred after prolonged armed conflict, such as Eritrea's independence from Ethiopia in 1993, or a period of international territorial administration, such as in Kosovo. In the latter instance, the Kosovo Assembly issued, on 17 February 2008, a unilateral declaration of independence from Serbia. A large number of states, including the UK and USA, recognized Kosovo as an independent state, while other states, including Serbia and Russia, rejected this independence on the grounds that it was contrary to international law. The ICJ was asked by the UN General Assembly to give its opinion. In the *Advisory Opinion on Kosovo*, the majority of the ICJ held:

> Whether, outside the context of non-self-governing territories and peoples subject to alien subjugation, domination and exploitation, the international law of self-determination confers upon part of the population of an existing State a right to separate from that State is, however, a subject on which radically different views were expressed . . . Similar differences existed regarding whether international law provides for a right of "remedial secession" and, if so, in what circumstances . . . The Court considers that it is not necessary to resolve these questions in the present case. The General Assembly has requested the Court's opinion only on whether or not the declaration of independence is in accordance with international law . . . [T]he Court considers that general international law contains no applicable prohibition of declarations of independence. Accordingly, it concludes that the declaration of independence of 17 February 2008 did not violate general international law.[26]

This avoidance by the Court in deciding these issues has been, rightly, strongly criticized. Judge Simma took the view that:

> the Court could have delivered a more intellectually satisfying Opinion, and one with greater relevance as regards the international legal order as it has evolved into its present form, had it not interpreted the scope of the question so restrictively. To treat these questions more extensively would have demonstrated the Court's awareness of the present architecture of international law.[27]

In these types of situation there has been a change in the international relationships between the peoples exercising their right of self-determination and the original state/colonial power, as well as with other states and international actors. So these are considered exercises of *external* self-determination.

Yet, self-determination can also be exercised by *internal* means, where there is a change in the internal relationships and administrations within a state but no change in the external relationships. The Declaration on Principles of International Law expresses internal self-determination as being where 'a government [is] representing the whole people

---

[26] *Accordance with International Law of the Unilateral Declaration of Independence in Respect of Kosovo,* (Advisory Opinion) [2010] ICJ Reports, paras 82–4.

[27] Kosovo Advisory Opinion, Declaration of Judge Simma, para 7. See also, for example, Hannum, 'The Advisory Opinion on Kosovo: An Opportunity Lost, or a Poisoned Chalice Refused?' (2011) 24 *Leiden JIL* 155.

belonging to the territory without distinction as to race, creed or colour'. The Canadian Supreme Court considered that internal self-determination in relation to the peoples of the province of Québec enabled the 'residents of the province freely [to] make political choices and pursue economic, social and cultural development within Québec, across Canada, and throughout the world. The population of Québec is [and should be] equitably represented in legislative, executive and judicial institutions.'[28]

Accordingly, there are a range of internal exercises of the right of self-determination. For example, outside the colonial context there has been devolution of some legislative powers to Scotland and Wales in the UK, control over cultural, linguistic, and other matters within the Swiss cantons, and a form of federalism in Bosnia-Herzegovina and Iraq. These methods are often called forms of autonomy or governance. In many instances, the method of exercise has been by agreement with the government for significant autonomy within a state, such as Mindanao in the Philippines, and the northern regions of Mali.[29]

What is shown by all these examples is that there are many possible exercises by peoples of their right of self-determination. While independence—called 'secession' when it is from an existing independent state—is often seen as the only option in non-colonial contexts, it is but *one option* of very many forms of exercise, and not normally the first option lawfully able to be exercised under international law. The Supreme Court of Canada made this clear when it stated that:

> The recognized sources of international law establish that the right to self-determination of a people is normally fulfilled through internal self-determination—a people's pursuit of its political, economic, social and cultural development within a framework of an existing state. A right to external self-determination (which in this case potentially takes the form of the assertion of a right to unilateral secession) arises in only the most extreme of cases and, even then, under carefully defined circumstances.[30]

What the court is indicating is that, in most instances outside the colonial context, independence will not be considered to be the legitimate first step in the exercise of the right of self-determination. However, should other methods of exercise, such as internal self-determination, be made impossible due to the actions of the state, and if there is increased oppression of the group as a group, then it may be argued that, in those limited circumstances, the people could exercise their right of self-determination by seeking independence as a last resort.[31]

In any event, there must be flexibility in the forms of exercise of the right of self-determination (and there are also limitations on the exercise—see Section 5). In many instances, the exercise will be dependent on the particular context and the resolution of a dispute. For example, the Badinter Commission which was established by the European Community (now European Union) to clarify the legal position during the dissolution of Yugoslavia, held that:

> In the Committee's view one possible consequence of [the right of self-determination] might be for the members of the Serbian population in Bosnia-Herzegovina and Croatia to be recognized under agreements between the Republics as having the nationality of their choice, with all the rights and obligations which that entails with respect to the states concerned.[32]

---

[28] *Reference Re Secession of Québec* [1998] 2 SCR 217, (1998) 37 ILM 1342, para 136.

[29] For details of these and other exercises, see Weller, 'Settling Self-Determination Conflicts: Recent Developments' (2009) 20 *EJIL* 111.   [30] *Reference Re Secession of Québec*, para 126.

[31] See *Aaland Islands Opinion*, International Committee of Jurists (1920) LNOJ Spec Supp 3; *Loizidou v Turkey* (1997) 23 EHRR 513, per Judges Wildhaber and Ryssdal.

[32] Badinter Commission, Opinion 2, (1992) 31 ILM 1495, para 3.

This suggestion of different nationalities and sovereign powers within one state is a possibility that should be explored. It could also operate across states, as has happened to some extent with the peace agreements concerning Northern Ireland, where both the British and Irish governments were involved in the key negotiations and both signed the various agreements, even though Northern Ireland is entirely within the UK. While such solutions challenge traditional notions of sovereignty, they acknowledge the breadth of impact of the right of self-determination and seek to provide effective means to exercise the right as fully as possible.

4.2 PROCEDURES FOR EXERCISING THE RIGHT OF SELF-DETERMINATION

The exercise of the right of self-determination must be by the people themselves. The ICJ confirmed this when it emphasized 'that the application of the right of self-determination requires a free and genuine expression of the will of the peoples concerned'.[33] In most instances the will of the people can be determined by a popular consultation, such as by referendum or elections. For example, the Badinter Commission decided that the will of the peoples in Bosnia-Herzegovina had to be ascertained, possibly by a referendum carried out under international supervision.[34]

However, there may be exceptional circumstances where there is no consultation, such as where the position is clear in all the circumstances. For example, during the dissolution of the USSR few referenda were held. Yet consultations can be manipulated. When Indonesia sought to integrate West Papua, which had been under a separate Dutch colonial administration from the rest of Indonesia, just a few indigenous leaders were asked their views as to whether they would accept Indonesian control and, probably under military threats, agreed to accept this control. Similarly, the people of Hong Kong were not fully consulted about the transfer of sovereignty of that separate, distinctive region to China. Even if the geopolitical situation is one where the choices of the people may be limited, they must be able to make a free and genuine decision on a clear question, which is their own decision and is not imposed by governments or others. In ensuring that the genuine will of the people is clear, it is important that the views of all within the group, including those of women and minorities, are heard and listened to equally.

In regard to the majority needed at a popular consultation, it should be at least 50 per cent plus one. Yet, it is not clear if this should be the majority of all people eligible to vote, the majority of people who do vote, or if it should be both or some other majority. The decision on the necessary majority and form of public consultation is important, especially as the numbers voting can be affected by a boycott (for example, by smaller groups who may seek a different exercise of their right of self-determination) or other circumstances. The practice during the dissolution of Yugoslavia varied considerably. In Bosnia-Herzegovina, it was assumed that 50 per cent plus one was sufficient and a boycott by the Serbian population (who comprised over 30 per cent of the population) did not affect the result, with over 60 per cent of all those eligible to vote casting their votes in favour of independence. In Montenegro the EU stated that there had to be a majority of 55 per cent of votes cast and there had to be a participation of at least 50 per cent plus one of those eligible to vote. This required majority was probably based on the opinion polls suggesting that approximately half of the population supported independence while a relatively large share of the population strongly opposed it.[35] When there was a

---

[33] *Western Sahara*, para 55.   [34] Badinter Commission, Opinion 4, (1992) 31 ILM 1495, para 4.
[35] See Vidmar, *Democratic Statehood in International Law* (Hart, 2013).

referendum in 2011 as to whether South Sudan should secede, the relevant national law required three steps: at least 60 per cent of registered voters casting their votes; if this 60 per cent was not achieved, then the referendum was to be repeated; and the result had to be one that secured 50 per cent plus 1 of the total number of votes cast. In the end, there were significantly more than 60 per cent of voters casting their vote, with over 95 per cent in favour of independence.

The actual voters in the referendum may not always be easy to decide. This is seen in the debate over which people to include in a referendum on Western Sahara, being primarily whether those who could vote were limited to those who were living in Western Sahara at the time of the ICJ opinion or if the referendum could include those (mainly Moroccans) who have moved there since.[36] Further, even if a majority of the people choose to exercise their right of self-determination by seeking secession from a state, this will not automatically lead to that result (though it may give a strong mandate to a people in their consultations with the relevant government), as there can be limitations on the exercise of the right of self-determination.

5 LIMITATIONS ON THE EXERCISE OF THE RIGHT OF SELF-DETERMINATION

5.1 RIGHTS OF OTHERS

Almost all human rights (with the exception of absolute rights such as the prohibition on torture) have limitations on their exercise. These limitations are to protect the rights of others or the general interests of the society (such as public order and public health). The right of self-determination is a human right and, because it is not an absolute right, it has limitations on its exercise. These are limitations on the ability of the peoples with the right to exercise that right fully and legitimately under international law.

In relation to the limitation in regard to the rights of others, each of the two international human rights Covenants provides:

> Nothing in the present Covenant may be interpreted as implying for any State, group or person any right to engage in any activity or perform any act aimed at the destruction of any of the rights and freedoms recognized herein or at their limitation to a greater extent than is provided for in the present Covenant.[37]

This limitation applies to the right of self-determination. Therefore, where there is another people with the right of self-determination within the state or region or a people who are few in number with the right of self-determination within a larger population (as with most colonial territories), then the right is limited in its exercise in order to take into account the right of the other people. As shown in other chapters, this right is limited only to the extent to which it enables all rights to be exercised as fully as possible in the circumstances.

An example of the operation of this limitation is found in the decision of the Canadian Supreme Court concerning the potential secession (through the exercise of the right of self-determination) of the people of the province of Québec. The Court noted that the rights of the indigenous ('aboriginal') peoples in the province were also affected:

> We . . . acknowledg[e] the importance of the submissions made to us respecting the rights and concerns of aboriginal peoples in the event of a unilateral secession, as well as the appropriate means of defining the boundaries of a seceding Québec with particular regard

---

[36] *Western Sahara.*   [37] ICESCR and ICCPR, Art 5(1).

to the northern lands occupied largely by aboriginal peoples. However, the concern of aboriginal peoples is precipitated by the asserted right of Québec to unilateral secession. In light of our finding that there is no such right applicable to the population of Québec, either under the Constitution of Canada or at international law, but that on the contrary a clear democratic expression of support for secession would lead under the Constitution to negotiations in which aboriginal interests would be taken into account, it becomes unnecessary to explore further the concerns of the aboriginal peoples in this Reference.[38]

The Court not only acknowledged the rights of the indigenous peoples in this passage but also the human rights and constitutional rights of other parts of Canada. It determined that, even if there had been a clear majority of the people of Québec who wished to secede, they could not do so without negotiations with the other parts of Canada. However, this does not necessarily give a permanent veto power to the other parts of Canada, as the internal right of self-determination of the people of Québec must not be so restricted.

5.2 TERRITORIAL INTEGRITY

The limitation on the exercise of the external right of self-determination that is most often asserted by governments is 'territorial integrity'. This is a claim that asserts that the state itself should not be divided up and is broadly based on the general interests of international peace and security. This limitation on the right of self-determination was expressed in the Declaration on Principles of International Law:

> Nothing in the foregoing paragraph [recognizing the right of self-determination] shall be construed as authorizing or encouraging any action which would dismember or impair, totally or in part, the territorial integrity or political unity of sovereign and independent States conducting themselves in compliance with the principle of equal rights and self-determination of peoples as described above and thus possessed of a government representing the whole people belonging to the territory without distinction as to race, creed or colour.

This is an important potential limitation on the exercise of the right. However, it is only a justifiable limitation in certain situations, namely when an exercise of external self-determination (such as independence) is being sought and when a state is 'possessed of a government representing the whole people belonging to the territory without distinction as to race, creed or colour'. In other words, it can only be a legally justifiable limitation on the exercise of the right of external self-determination when a state is *already* enabling full internal self-determination for those people.

A particular aspect of this limitation on the exercise of the right of self-determination is the international legal principle of *uti possidetis juris*. This principle provides that states emerging from colonial administrative control must accept the pre-existing colonial boundaries. Its purpose is to achieve stability of territorial boundaries and to maintain international peace and security. This was made clear by a Chamber of the ICJ:

> The maintenance of the territorial *status quo* in Africa is often seen as the wisest course, to preserve what has been achieved by peoples who have struggled for their independence, and to avoid a disruption which would deprive the continent of the gains achieved by much sacrifice. The essential requirement of stability in order to survive, to develop and gradually to consolidate their independence in all fields, induced African states judiciously to consent to the respecting of colonial frontiers.[39]

---

[38] *Reference Re Secession of Québec*, para 139.
[39] *Frontier Dispute Case (Burkina Faso v Mali)* [1986] ICJ Rep 554 (Chamber of the ICJ), para 25.

While this has been uniformly accepted as a principle applicable solely to colonial territories, it was surprisingly applied by the Badinter Commission to the former Yugoslavia.[40] This latter application was probably incorrect, as it confused historically established boundaries with colonial boundaries (as the former will not have resulted from colonial determinations). There is some scope for considering that historically established boundaries (as was the case in much of the former Yugoslavia and the USSR) may be accepted as *prima facie* the appropriate territorial boundaries on independence even in non-colonial contexts, unless there are agreements to the contrary.

The principle of *uti possidetis juris* may appear to be a sound one in terms of preserving international peace and security at the time of independence. However, it has not prevented many boundary disputes.[41] This is mainly because many of these boundaries were created to preserve the interests of the colonial states and were not related to natural or cultural boundaries understood by the peoples on the ground. As one of the architects of these boundary determinations said at the time:

> We have been engaged . . . in drawing lines upon maps where no white man's feet have ever trod; we have been giving away mountains and rivers and lakes to each other, but we have only been hindered by the small impediment that we never knew exactly where those mountains and rivers and lakes were.[42]

The ICJ recognized these problems when it stated that '*uti possidetis juris* is essentially a retrospective principle, investing as international boundaries administrative limits intended originally for quite other purposes'.[43] It could be argued that adoption of the principle today gives legitimacy to political or diplomatic actions purely on the basis that those actions occurred during the colonial era and were made without taking the views of the people on the territory into account.[44]

Therefore, the principle of *uti possidetis juris* is of questionable legitimacy as a limitation on the right of self-determination. It should only apply, if at all, in (the now very few) situations of decolonization or, perhaps, where the states involved in a dispute expressly choose to use a colonial boundary as relevant evidence for a boundary delimitation.[45]

5.3 OTHER LIMITATIONS

There are two other potential limitations on the exercise of the right of self-determination that are often raised: competing claims over the relevant territory by states; and the use of force. It is not uncommon for there to be a situation where more than one state asserts sovereignty over a territory where there are people with a right of self-determination. The ICJ recognized this situation in the *East Timor Case*, where it accepted that Portugal, as the colonial power, and Indonesia, as the occupying power, had forms of jurisdiction over the same territory, as did the people of East Timor, who had the right of self-determination.[46] In many instances, a state will assert that an early treaty enables it to

---

[40] Badinter Commission, Opinion 2, para 1.

[41] See Craven, *The Decolonization of International Law* (OUP, 2007). While Sudan accepted the secession of South Sudan, there were still disputes over the territorial boundary. See Vidmar, 'South Sudan and the International Legal Framework Governing the Emergence and Delimitation of New States' (2012) 47 *Texas ILJ* 541; and Derso, 'International Law and the Self-Determination of South Sudan' (2012) Institute for Security Studies Paper No 231.

[42] Lord Salisbury, speaking in 1890, as quoted in the Separate Opinion of Judge Ajibola, in *Territorial Dispute (Libya v Chad)* [1994] ICJ Rep 6, 53.

[43] *Land, Island and Maritime Dispute (El Salvador v Honduras)* [1992] ICJ Rep 355, 388.

[44] See *Frontier Dispute (Burkina Faso v Niger)* [2013] ICJ Rep, Declaration of Judge Bennouna.

[45] *Frontier Dispute (Burkina Faso v Niger)*, Judgment, para 63.

[46] *East Timor (Portugal v Australia)* [1995] ICJ Rep 90, para 32.

gain sovereignty (as did China in relation to Hong Kong and as Spain does in relation to Gibraltar), notwithstanding the wishes of the people of that territory. This situation was considered in the *Western Sahara Case*:

> [T]he consultation of the people of a territory awaiting decolonization is an inescapable imperative . . .. Thus even if integration of territory was demanded by an interested State, as in this case, it could not be had without ascertaining the freely expressed will of the people—the very *sine qua non* of all decolonization.[47]

Therefore, even where there may be a lawful competing claim by another state over a particular territory, the peoples on that territory still have a right of self-determination that they must be able to exercise.

In relation to the use of force, it is not uncommon that the peoples seeking to exercise their right of self-determination use force and have force used against them. The general position appears to be that set out in the Declaration on Principles of International Law:

> Every State has the duty to refrain from any forcible action which deprives peoples referred to above in the elaboration of the present principle of their right to self-determination and freedom and independence. In their actions against and resistance to such forcible action in pursuit of the exercise of their right to self-determination, such peoples are entitled to seek and to receive support in accordance with the purposes and principles of the Charter of the United Nations.

This makes clear that a state cannot use force (arguably at least not disproportionate force) to prevent the exercise of the right of self-determination (which was one basis of criticism about Serbia's actions during the dissolution of Yugoslavia). The people themselves are entitled to support from other states when forcible action occurs against them as a people. That support must be in accordance with the purpose and principles of the UN Charter, so occupation by one state to 'support' a people's right of self-determination in another state would not be lawful. This was one of the criticisms of the Russian actions to support Abkhazia and South Ossetia in Georgia, as well as of Russia's role in the Crimea in 2014.[48] Significantly, when Additional Protocol I to the Geneva Conventions 1949 was agreed in 1977, its protection extended to wars of national liberation, being 'armed conflicts which peoples are fighting against colonial domination and alien occupation and against racist regimes in the exercise of their right of self-determination.'[49] The restrictions on the use of force against peoples seeking to exercise the right of self-determination do not seem to restrict the peoples themselves using force to assert their right of self-determination, such as the people of Eritrea, though other human rights issues may then arise as their force cannot infringe the human rights of others, such as minorities.

6 MINORITIES

6.1 DEFINING 'MINORITIES'

Article 27 ICCPR and the Declaration on the Rights of Persons Belonging to National or Ethnic, Religious and Linguistic Minorities (Declaration on Minority Rights) provide protections for those who are 'ethnic, religious or linguistic' minorities. The Special

---

[47] *Western Sahara Case*, per Judge Nagendra Singh, 81.

[48] Report of the Independent International Fact-Finding Mission on the Conflict in Georgia (30 September 2009); see *Georgia v Russia* (2012) 54 EHRR SE10, Annex 1.

[49] Protocol Additional to the Geneva Conventions of 12 August 1949, and Relating to the Protection of Victims of International Armed Conflicts (Protocol I), Art 1(4).

Rapporteur of the UN Sub-Commission on Prevention of Discrimination and Protection of Minorities determined that:

> [Minorities are groups who are] numerically inferior to the rest of the population of a State, in a nondominant position, whose members—being nationals of the State—possess ethnic, religious, or linguistic characteristics differing from those of the rest of the population and show, if only implicitly, a sense of solidarity, directed towards preserving their culture, traditions, religion or language.[50]

However, there are other minorities who may be excluded from this definition, and it is not clear how minorities are determined.[51] Indeed:

> [t]he difficulty in arriving at a widely acceptable definition lies in the variety of situations in which minorities live. Some live together in well-defined areas, separated from the dominant part of the population. Others are scattered throughout the country. Some minorities have a strong sense of collective identity and recorded history; others retain only a fragmented notion of their common heritage.[52]

Therefore, any determination as to the existence of a minority must take into account objective elements, such as shared ethnicity, language, or religion, and subjective considerations, such as the self-identification by individuals as members of a minority. Despite the lack of a clear definition, human rights supervisory bodies continue to protect effectively the rights of minorities.[53]

While the Declaration on Minority Rights (see Section 6.2) is devoted to national, ethnic, religious, and linguistic minorities, it is also important to combat multiple discrimination and to address situations where a person belonging to a national, ethnic, religious, or linguistic minority is also discriminated against on other grounds such as gender, disability, or sexual orientation. Similarly, it is important to keep in mind that, in many states, minorities are often found to be among the most marginalized groups in society and severely affected by, for example, pandemic diseases, and in general have limited access to health services. Undoubtedly, the state-focused nature of the international human rights legal system means that it is largely minorities within a state as a whole who are protected by this right.

6.2 RIGHTS OF MINORITIES

At the same time that self-determination was being developed as part of international law, rights relating to minorities were being set out in treaties. At the Paris Peace Conference in 1919 after the First World War a number of treaties were drafted to protect minorities in the new states being created, as a condition for settlement of territorial boundaries.[54] The obligations to protect minorities under these treaties largely related to giving minorities some autonomy.

---

[50] Capotorti, UN Special Rapporteur, Study on the Rights of Persons Belonging to Ethnic, Religious and Linguistic Minorities, E/CN.4/Sub.2/384/Rev.1 (1979), para 242.

[51] For example, the ECtHR has noted that, as a result of their turbulent history and constant uprooting, the Roma people have become a specific type of disadvantaged and vulnerable minority, and require special protection: see *Koky and Others v Romania*, Application No 13642/03, Judgment of 12 June 2012.

[52] OHCHR, *Minority Rights: International Standards and Guidance for Implementation* (2010) 2.

[53] See *Koky and others*.

[54] See Macklem, 'Minority Rights in International Law' (2008) 6 *IJConL* 531; Berman, 'But the Alternative is Despair: European Nationalism and the Modernist Renewal of International Law' (1992–3) 106 *Harvard LR* 1792.

However, significant development of minority rights did not occur until the adoption of Article 27 ICCPR, which provides:

> In those States in which ethnic, religious or linguistic minorities exist, persons belonging to such minorities shall not be denied the right, in community with the other members of their group, to enjoy their own culture, to profess and practice their own religion, or to use their own language.

Subsequently, the Declaration on Minority Rights was adopted by the General Assembly in 1992.[55] The Declaration provides guidance about the development of law in this area—as do some regional treaties in this field.[56] There is now probably a customary international law obligation on all states to protect the rights of minorities.[57] Indeed, the Human Rights Committee has asserted that 'provisions in the Covenant that represent customary international law (and a fortiori when they have the character of peremptory norms) may not be the subject of reservations. Accordingly, a State may not reserve the right to ... deny to minorities the right to enjoy their own culture, profess their own religion, or use their own language.'[58]

6.3 EXERCISE OF MINORITY RIGHTS

The types of rights for which minorities have protection are, as Article 27 ICCPR provides, 'to enjoy their own culture, to profess and practice their own religion, or to use their own language'. The Declaration on Minority Rights adds to these: the rights to participate in cultural, religious, social, economic, and public life; to participate in decisions on the national and, where appropriate, regional level; and to associate with other members of their group and with persons belonging to other minorities.

In some instances the exercise of minority rights does raise issues of conflict between the individual and the group. In the case of *Lovelace*,[59] the claim by a divorced indigenous Canadian to return to the indigenous land was upheld by the Human Rights Committee despite Canadian law (intending to protect the indigenous minority) precluding her from so doing. However, a Swedish law that protected the identity of the Sami minority as a whole by revoking the reindeer husbandry rights of those who pursued more lucrative work was held to be valid despite the consequent restriction imposed on the individual Sami.[60] The Human Rights Committee's view was that 'a restriction upon the right of an individual member of a minority must be shown to have a reasonable and objective justification and to be necessary for the continued viability and welfare of the minority as a whole'.[61] Therefore, there are times when the minority rights protection of an individual will be limited by the

---

[55] A/RES/47/135/Annex (18 December 1993).

[56] European Charter for Regional and Minority Languages; Framework Convention for the Protection of National Minorities; Document of the Copenhagen Meeting of the Conference on the Human Dimension of the Conference (now Organization) for Security and Co-operation in Europe, para 35; and Establishment of the OSCE High Commissioner on National Minorities, Helsinki Summit of Heads of State, 9–10 July 1992. In addition, protections of the rights of minorities were contained in the EC documents regarding the dissolution of the former Yugoslavia and the former USSR, and were applied by the Badinter Commission: EC's Declaration on Yugoslavia and its Declaration on the Guidelines on Recognition of New States in Eastern Europe and the Soviet Union (16 December 1991).

[57] Badinter Commission, Opinion 2, para 2.

[58] HRC General Comment 24, HRI/GEN/1/Rev.9 (Vol 1) 210, para 8. See Chapter 14 on Cultural Rights.

[59] *Sandra Lovelace v Canada*, A/36/40 at 166 (1981).

[60] *Ivan Kitok v Sweden*, CCPR/C/33/D/197/1985 (27 July 1988); *Handölsdalen Sami Village and others v Sweden* App no 39013/04, Judgment of 30 March 2010; Report of the UN Special Rapporteur James Anaya, The situation of the Sami peoples in the Sápmi region of Norway, Sweden and Finland, A/HRC/18/XX/Add.Y (2011).

[61] *Ivan Kitok*, para 15.

broader interest of the group as a whole. These examples also show that indigenous peoples may be able to assert their human rights through the use of minority rights protections.[62]

6.4 INDIVIDUAL V GROUP RIGHTS

The concept of human rights of minorities embodies both the protection of the rights of individuals who are part of a minority group and of the minority group as a group, according minorities a collective right to enjoy the common traits of their group. There are two views as to how these rights should be approached. The individual rights approach to minority rights argues that such rights must be vested in, and be exercised by, the individual members claiming affiliation with the minority group rather than the minority group itself. In contrast, the group rights approach recognizes that the collective qualities that the minority possess, such as their group culture and their group language (being an inherent part of their human dignity), distinguishes them from the majority and so requires them to be protected as a group. However, it should be noted that, under both approaches, who is a minority may change over time and location, and this makes the right somewhat contingent on historical circumstances, which is unusual for a human right.[63]

It is clear that Article 27 ICCPR is solely an individual right for those who are part of a minority. For example, the Human Rights Committee has rejected group claims based on Article 1 (right of self-determination), as discussed already, but accepted the same claim under Article 27 as long as it was argued as an individual right.[64] However, there is a good argument that where 'national' minorities are concerned then treating the right as a group right is the appropriate approach. Indeed, it is strongly argued that minorities can form a 'people' for the purposes of the right of self-determination, especially as the definitions for each group are very similar, the right of self-determination is now more commonly exercised by internal means, and many minorities use the language of self-determination.[65] For example, the Badinter Commission considered that the shared ethnic, religious, and linguistic background of Serbians from Bosnia-Herzegovina and Croatia with Serbians in Serbia did not prevent them from being a 'people' for the purposes of the right of self-determination even though they had specific minority rights protection as well.[66] While the exercise by a minority of their right of self-determination may be limited to internal self-determination, in that minority groups would usually seek to exercise their right by enabling some degree of autonomy over matters of relevance to their culture, language, religion, or ethnic identity, it does not mean that they do not possess a right of self-determination.

7 INDIGENOUS PEOPLES

7.1 DEFINING 'INDIGENOUS PEOPLES'

There are significant similarities between minorities and indigenous peoples. Indigenous peoples have also been in a non-dominant position, and their cultures, languages, and religious traditions are normally different from the majority in the societies in which they live. International law has tended to recognize and protect indigenous rights separately.

---

[62] It has been argued that the UN approach has been to accommodate the rights of indigenous peoples but to seek assimilation of minorities more generally: Kymlicka, 'The Internationalization of Minority Rights' (2008) 6 *IJConL* 5.   [63] See Macklem (2008).

[64] *Ominayak and the Lubicon Lake Band*, 27.

[65] Thornberry, *International Law and the Rights of Minorities* (OUP, 1991).

[66] Badinter Commission, Opinion 2.

For example, the ILO adopted in 1957 and 1989 two treaties, ILO Convention No. 107 concerning Indigenous and Tribal Populations and ILO Convention No. 169 concerning Indigenous and Tribal Peoples, which apply to members of 'semi-tribal or tribal populations', 'tribal peoples', and 'groups regarded as indigenous', with specific characteristics.

However, no definition of 'indigenous peoples' has unanimously been adopted by the international community. Since the importance of maintaining their distinct identities and characteristics under the self-identification principle was accepted, the idea of a formal definition has deliberately been rejected.[67] Nevertheless, the recognition and protection of the rights of indigenous peoples under international law has not depended on a formal definition, and their main characteristics have been outlined widely in different instruments. The UN Working Group on Indigenous Populations listed the relevant factors to the understanding of the concept of 'indigenous', which have also been taken into account by international organizations and legal experts:

(a) Priority in time, with respect to the occupation and use of a specific territory;

(b) The voluntary perpetuation of cultural distinctiveness, which may include the aspects of language, social organization, religion and spiritual values, modes of production, laws and institutions;

(c) Self-identification, as well as recognition by other groups, or by State authorities, as a distinct collectivity; and

(d) An experience of subjugation, marginalization, dispossession, exclusion or discrimination, whether or not these conditions persist.[68]

These still remain the main elements of definitions of indigenous peoples.

7.2 THE RIGHTS OF INDIGENOUS PEOPLES

The main concern in relation to indigenous peoples has been the preservation of their views and traditions as a group:

> Under the basic principles of universality, equality and non-discrimination, indigenous peoples are entitled to the full range of rights established under international law. However, indigenous peoples, as collectivities, have distinct and unique cultures and world views, and their current needs may differ from those of the mainstream population. Their equal worth and dignity can only be assured through the recognition and protection of not only their individual rights, but also their collective rights as distinct groups. It is when these rights are asserted collectively that they can be realized in a meaningful way. This has led to the development of a separate body of international instruments for the recognition and protection of the rights of indigenous peoples.[69]

Thus, indigenous peoples are entitled to the full range of individual human rights, including protection from discrimination, rights in relation to children, and cultural rights, as well as the rights of the indigenous peoples as a group.

---

[67] See Workshop on data collection and disaggregation for Indigenous Peoples, 'The Concept of Indigenous Peoples, Background prepared by the Secretariat of the Permanent Forum on Indigenous Issues', PFII/2004/WS.1/3 (2004).

[68] Working Group on Indigenous Populations, Working paper by the Chairperson-Rapporteur, Mrs. Erica-Irene A Daes, on the concept of 'indigenous people', E/CN.4/Sub.2/AC.4/1996/2 (1996).

[69] UN Development Group, Guidelines on Indigenous Peoples Issues (2008) at 6.

The ILO Conventions remain the only international binding instruments that specifically provide a detailed list of rights and obligations of states in respect of indigenous peoples. The ILO Convention No. 107 covered a wide range of issues, such as traditionally occupied lands; social, economic, and cultural development; recruitment and conditions of employment; and social security and health. However, it had an integrationist approach that was gradually seen as outdated and so was modified by the ILO Convention No. 169, on the basis of the recognition of, and respect for, ethnic and cultural diversity of indigenous peoples as permanent societies. ILO Convention No. 169 acknowledges the rights of indigenous peoples to identity (in relation to the recognition of their legal capacity or juridical status), territory, autonomy, participation in the political and social national life, physical welfare, and cultural integrity.

The UN Declaration on the Rights of Indigenous Peoples 2007 represents the most comprehensive response to the issue of indigenous peoples at the universal level. The Declaration proclaims:

Article 1

Indigenous peoples have the right to the full enjoyment, as a collective or as individuals, of all human rights and fundamental freedoms as recognized in the Charter of the United Nations, the Universal Declaration of Human Rights and international human rights law.

Article 3

Indigenous peoples have the right to self-determination. By virtue of that right they freely determine their political status and freely pursue their economic, social and cultural development.

Article 4

Indigenous peoples, in exercising their right to self-determination, have the right to autonomy or self-government in matters relating to their internal and local affairs, as well as ways and means for financing their autonomous functions.

Its provisions are compatible with ILO Convention No. 169, although it does not provide a mechanism to monitor its implementation and it does not have a legally binding character. Nonetheless, the Declaration has been influential and its provisions have been reflected in some national laws,[70] and in the decisions of the Inter-American Court of Human Rights.[71] It is, therefore, clear that there is a general consensus, based on acceptance of the UN Declaration and other state practice, that indigenous peoples have the right to self-determination.

In relation to other group rights of indigenous peoples, the Inter-American Court of Human Rights has accepted a right to collective property, noting the existence of a special relationship between the indigenous peoples and their traditional lands and resources:

Among indigenous peoples there exists a communitarian tradition related to a form of collective land tenure, inasmuch as land is not owned by individuals but by the group and the community . . . [T]he protection of the territories of indigenous and tribal peoples also stems from the need to guarantee the security and continuity of their control and use of natural resources, which in turn allows them to maintain their lifestyle . . . This connection

---

[70] Impacts on national law include Bolivia incorporating the Declaration into its Constitution on 7 November 2007 (adopted as Bolivian National Law 3760 on the Rights of Indigenous Peoples) and the Belize Supreme Court deciding that the property provisions of the Declaration embodied 'general principles of international law' that had the same force as a treaty: *Aurelio Cal and the Maya Village of Santa Cruz v Attorney General of Belize; and Manuel Coy and Maya Village of Conejo v Attorney General of Belize*, (Consolidated) Claim Nos 171 and 17 (18 October 2007).

[71] *Kichwa Indigenous People of Sarayaku v Ecuador*, IACtHR Series C No 245 (27 June 2012) para 217.

between territory and natural resources that indigenous and tribal peoples have tradition-ally maintained, one that is necessary for their physical and cultural survival and the development and continuation of their worldview, must be protected under Article 21 of the Convention so that they can continue living their traditional lifestyle, and so that their cultural identity, social structure, economic system, customs, beliefs and traditions are respected, guaranteed and protected by States.[72]

The Court has also developed a system of reparations that are applicable in the cases of violations of indigenous peoples' rights.[73]

7.3 EXERCISE OF INDIGENOUS PEOPLES' RIGHTS

The exercise of indigenous peoples' rights follows similar patterns to those seen with regard to the right of self-determination and minority rights, with the same diversity of means of exercise. In addition, there is a specific right of consultation that is considered to be essential for protecting indigenous peoples, which finds its origins in the right of self-determination and has been recognized as a general international law obligation.

Because of their particular economic and social characteristics, including their vulnerable situation, indigenous peoples have the right to be consulted about decisions affecting their land. The Inter-American Court of Human Rights has stated:

> The Court has established that in order to ensure the effective participation of the members of an indigenous community or people in development or investment plans within their territory, the State has the obligation to consult the said community in an active and informed manner, in accordance with its customs and traditions, within the framework of continuing communication between the parties. Furthermore, the consultations must be undertaken in good faith, using culturally-appropriate procedures and must be aimed at reaching an agreement. In addition, the people or community must be consulted in accordance with their own traditions, during the early stages of the development or investment plan, and not only when it is necessary to obtain the community's approval, if appropriate. The State must also ensure that the members of the people or the community are aware of the potential benefits and risks so they can decide whether to accept the proposed development or investment plan. Finally, the consultation must take into account the traditional decision-making practices of the people or community. Failure to comply with this obligation, or engaging in consultations without observing their essential characteristics, entails the State's international responsibility.[74]

This is a broad obligation on states and is reflective of the breadth of impact on indigenous peoples of the activities of states and of other actors, such as corporations.[75]

The importance of the obligation on states to consult indigenous peoples prior to engaging in development, extraction, or investment plans is highlighted by its codification in the national laws of various states such as Bolivia (Article 30(II)(15) of the Bolivian Constitution) and Chile (Article 34 of Indigenous Law No. 19 253 of 1993). Yet the broader lack of recognition of consultation with indigenous peoples in other states continues to constitute a barrier to the effective protection of indigenous rights.

---

[72] *Kichwa Indigenous People of Sarayaku*, paras 145–6.

[73] eg *Saramaka People v Suriname*, IACtHR Series C No 172 (28 November 2007). See also Antkowiak, 'A Dark Side of Virtue: The Inter-American Court and Reparations for Indigenous Peoples' (2014) 25 *Duke J Intl & Comp L* 2

[74] *Kichwa Indigenous People of Sarayaku*, para 177. This is also recognized in the ILO Convention No. 169, Art 6.

[75] See Chapter 28.

8 CONCLUSION

Human rights are not only in relation to rights of individual human beings; they can also protect a group as a group. One of these group rights is the right of self-determination. This right applies to a wide range of peoples, not just those in colonial territories and not just those recognized by some states as having the right. It is a right of all peoples in all territories. This right can be limited in its exercise due to others' rights (such as others' right of self-determination) and where the general interests of the relevant society is legitimately applied. In the exercise of this right, there are many alternatives, such as internal control over the people's own cultural affairs, with independence now being difficult to justify legally in the first instance in most contexts. Both indigenous groups and minorities can assert a right of self-determination. There are also individual minority rights protected under international human rights law, which encompass cultural, ethnic, linguistic, religious, and national minorities, and indigenous peoples have both individual and group rights. In exercising these individual rights, the collective rights of the group as a group will need to be taken into account.

With the right of self-determination, minority rights, and the rights of indigenous peoples, the intention is to enable the rights-holders to determine their political, economic, social, and cultural destiny as they wish, while not overriding the legitimate interests of others affected. These rights developed once it was generally accepted that the traditional approach to international law and to the determination of boundaries had a severe consequence on some groups.

These group rights are, therefore, a reflection of the changing of values in the international community away from a state-based and solely state-interested, system towards a more flexible system. Indeed, the reason behind many of the claims relating to the right of self-determination, and those in relation to minority and indigenous rights, is that the state-based international legal order has failed to respond appropriately and justly to the legitimate aspirations of peoples.

FURTHER READING

ALSTON (ed), Peoples' Rights (Oxford University Press, 2001).

ANAYA, Indigenous Peoples in International Law (Oxford University Press, 2005).

CASSESE, Self-Determination of Peoples: A Legal Reappraisal (Cambridge University Press, 1995).

CHINKIN and WRIGHT, 'Hunger Trap: Women, Food and Self-Determination' (1993) 14 Michigan JIL 262.

CRAWFORD (ed), The Rights of Peoples (Oxford University Press, 1988).

ENGLE, 'On Fragile Architecture: The UN Declaration on the Rights of Indigenous Peoples in the Context of Human Rights' (2011) 22 EJIL 141.

FRENCH (ed), Statehood and Self-Determination: Reconciling Tradition and Modernity in International Law (Cambridge University Press, 2013).

GHANEA and XANTHAKI (eds), Minorities, Peoples and Self-Determination: Essays in Honour of Patrick Thornberry (Martinus Nijhoff, 2005).

KLABBERS, 'The Right to Be Taken Seriously: Self-Determination in International Law' (2006) 28 HRQ 186.

KYMLICKA, 'The Internationalization of Minority Rights' (2008) 6 IJConL 1.

LENNOX and SHORT (eds), Handbook of Indigenous Peoples' Rights (Routledge, 2016).

MCCORQUODALE (ed), *Self-Determination in International Law* (Ashgate, 2000).

PAVKOVIĆ and RADAN (eds), *The Ashgate Research Companion to Secession* (Ashgate, 2011).

SAUL, 'The Normative Status of Self-Determination in International Law: A Formula for Uncertainty in the Scope and Content of the Right?' (2011) 11 *HRLR* 609.

SHELTON, 'Self-Determination in Regional Human Rights Law: From Kosovo to Cameroon' (2011) 105 *AJIL* 60.

WILDE, 'Self-Determination, Secession, and Dispute Settlement after the Kosovo Advisory Opinion' (2011) *Leiden JIL* 149.

XANTHAKI, 'Indigenous Rights in International Law over the Last 10 Years and Future Developments' (2009) 10 *Melbourne JIL* 27.

PART IV

PROTECTION

19

UNITED NATIONS

Jane Connors

SUMMARY

According to its Charter, the promotion and protection of human rights is one of the principal purposes of the United Nations (UN). This chapter considers the work of the UN in the field of human rights. Particular attention is given to the Human Rights Council and the treaty bodies that consider progress in the implementation of UN human rights treaties. The role of the High Commissioner for Human Rights and Office of the High Commissioner for Human Rights is briefly described, as is that of the General Assembly, Security Council, Secretary-General, and International Court of Justice.

1 INTRODUCTION

Human rights have pervaded political discourse since 1945. The massive affront to human dignity of the Second World War and the need to prevent the recurrence of these horrors prompted the codification, at the international level, of human rights and fundamental freedoms. Thus, Article 1 UN Charter identifies 'promoting and encouraging respect for human rights and for fundamental freedoms for all without distinction as to race, sex, language or religion' as one of the principal purposes of the UN.

The Universal Declaration of Human Rights (UDHR), adopted on 10 December 1948, was the first step taken by the UN towards that objective. In 1948 most governments recognized the UDHR, but insisted that its provisions were not legally binding. Since then, human rights and fundamental freedoms have been codified in hundreds of universal, regional, and sub-regional, binding and non-binding, instruments. At the level of the UN, this process is still in progress, but the main challenge is implementation of existing standards at the national level. Another challenge is to enhance the effectiveness and the visibility of the UN mechanisms in the field of human rights.

This chapter introduces the work of the UN in the field of human rights. It shows the progress that has been made, particularly since the adoption of the Vienna Declaration and Programme of Action (VDPA) by the World Conference on Human Rights in 1993.[1] This document reaffirms the commitment of all states to fulfil their obligations to promote universal respect for, observance, and protection of human rights and fundamental freedoms for all in accordance with the UN Charter, human rights instruments, and international

---

[1] A/CONF.157/23 (25 June 1993).

law. It makes clear that all human rights are universal, indivisible, interdependent, and interrelated, and although the significance of national and regional particularities and various historical, cultural, and religious backgrounds must be borne in mind, it is the duty of states, regardless of their political, economic, and cultural systems, to promote and protect all human rights and fundamental freedoms.

2 THE HUMAN RIGHTS COUNCIL

The preamble to the UN Charter reaffirms 'faith in fundamental human rights, in the dignity and worth of the human person, [and] in the equal rights of men and women'. Article 1 UN Charter identifies respect for human rights as one of the purposes of the organization. To realize this purpose, Article 55 provides that the UN shall promote universal respect for, and observance of, human rights and fundamental freedoms for all without distinction as to race, sex, language, or religion, whilst Article 56 commits member states to take both joint and separate action in cooperation with the UN to achieve these goals. The UN has established bodies, known as 'Charter-based' bodies, to fulfil these functions. These include the Commission on Human Rights and its replacement from 2006: the Human Rights Council.

2.1 1946–2006: FROM THE COMMISSION ON HUMAN RIGHTS TO THE HUMAN RIGHTS COUNCIL

In 1946 the UN Economic and Social Council (ECOSOC), one of the principal organs of the UN, created the Commission on Human Rights. For 60 years, the Commission, composed of 53 representatives of UN member states, performed countless activities aimed at the protection and promotion of human rights. It made important contributions to human rights standard-setting, including drafting the UDHR, and other human rights treaties. The Commission also developed UN institutional capacity to promote and protect the full range of human rights. It developed working methods and procedures, creating a Sub-Commission on the Promotion and Protection of Human Rights to prepare thematic studies, and provided a forum for human rights discourse in which it allowed civil society to participate to an extent not known in other parts of the UN system. Through the establishment and operation of its special procedures system, consisting of experts mandated to investigate particular human rights issues or human rights violations in specific countries, and a confidential mechanism for individuals to report consistent patterns of gross and systematic violations of human rights in a country, the Commission helped to improve the human rights situation of many individuals in many countries.

Despite these achievements, the Commission became increasingly subject to criticism, with particular attention focused on the politicization of its work. In 2005, in a report on UN reform, former Secretary-General Kofi Annan described the Commission to be:

> undermined by its declining credibility and professionalism . . . States have sought membership of the Commission not to strengthen human rights but to protect themselves against criticism or to criticize others. As a result, a credibility deficit has developed, which casts a shadow on the reputation of the United Nations system as a whole.[2]

The Secretary-General's critique set the stage for the replacement of the Commission by a new body: the Human Rights Council. His call for reform was underpinned by the

---

[2] In Larger Freedom: Towards Development, Security and Human Rights for All, Report of the Secretary-General, A/59/2005 (21 March 2005) para 182.

assumption that the system should move from 'standard-setting'—that is, the negotiation of new instruments—to implementation. The Secretary-General proposed the creation of a smaller Human Rights Council, which would be a standing body. Importantly, he suggested that the Human Rights Council should function as a 'chamber of peer review' and that its principal task would be the evaluation of the fulfilment by *all* states of *all* their human rights obligations.[3]

Substantive negotiations on the establishment of the Human Rights Council began in May 2005, and on 15 March 2006, the General Assembly adopted Resolution 60/251 establishing the Human Rights Council. The Resolution was adopted by 170 states voting in favour, four against, and three abstentions. The Commission was abolished on 16 June 2006, and the first meeting of the Council was convened on 19 June 2006.

2.2 COMPOSITION, WORKING METHODS, AND MANDATE

The Human Rights Council is composed of 47 members. All UN member states are eligible for membership, not only those with a good human rights track record or that have ratified the majority of international human rights instruments and cooperate with their respective mechanisms. Members are elected in a secret ballot by a simple majority vote of the members of the GA. When electing members, the 'contribution of candidates to the promotion and protection of human rights and their voluntary pledges and commitments made thereto' should be taken into account.[4] The vast majority of candidates submits written pledges and commitments. These include promises of better cooperation with the UN human rights treaty bodies, standing invitations to special procedures mandate holders, ratification of international instruments, and promises of action at the national level.[5]

All Council members must uphold the highest standards in the promotion and protection of human rights, fully cooperate with the Council, and be reviewed under the Council's review mechanism during their membership. There is no formal mechanism to hold members to account, but a member that has committed gross and systematic violations of human rights may be suspended by the General Assembly by a two-thirds majority of its members present and voting. Despite calls from civil society and others over the years that the General Assembly suspend several members, including high-profile demands in 2016 in relation to Burundi and Saudi Arabia,[6] this procedure has been invoked once only. This was in March 2011, when the General Assembly, acting on a recommendation of the Human Rights Council, agreed by consensus to suspend the membership of the Libyan Arab Jamahiriya.[7] The suspension, described by some delegations during the Assembly debate as unprecedented and not to be used lightly, was reversed by the General Assembly in November 2011, on the recommendation of the Human Rights Council.[8]

---

[3] In Larger Freedom, Addendum 1, paras 6–8.

[4] Civil society organizations often comment on candidate countries; eg, Human Rights Watch protested against the Asian Group's endorsement of the candidature of the Syrian Arab Republic in 2011; and in 2016, 87 NGOs signed a letter requesting member states to consider carefully whether the Russian Federation's actions in Syria were compatible with the principles and aims of the HR Council. The Syrian Arab Republic withdrew its candidature and the Russian Federation was not elected.

[5] These are available on the elections and appointments webpage of the GA: <http://www.un.org/en/ga/71/meetings/elections/hrc>.

[6] Joint NGO Letter, 'Suspension of Burundi from Human Rights Council', 26 October 2016, available at: <https://www.hrw.org/news/2016/10/26/joint-ngo-letter-suspension-burundi-human-rights-council>; Amnesty International, Joint Public Statement, 'Suspend Saudi Arabia from the UN Human Rights Council', 29 June 2016, AI Index: MDE 23/4345/2016.

[7] GA Res 65/265 (1 March 2011).

[8] GA Res 66/11 (18 November 2011).

Council membership is broken down into regional groupings. The African and Asian groups are allocated 13 seats each. Eight seats are reserved for the Latin American and Caribbean group, six for the Eastern European group, and seven for the Western European and Others group. Members serve for a period of three years and are not eligible for imme-diate re-election after two consecutive terms. Non-governmental organizations (NGOs) may participate in the Human Rights Council as observers if they have been granted con-sultative status with the ECOSOC.[9] Similarly, national human rights institutions (NHRIs) that are fully compliant with the Paris Principles may participate in Council meetings.[10]

The Human Rights Council meets regularly throughout the year, convening at least three annual sessions. There must be at least ten weeks of scheduled sessions to allow the Council to adopt a comprehensive approach to human rights and respond effectively to human rights situations as they develop. Special sessions, lasting one or two days at a time, may also be scheduled at the request of a Council member that has garnered the support of at least one-third of the Council's membership.

GA Resolution 60/251 establishes the Council as a subsidiary organ of the General Assembly, and requires it to report to the Assembly annually. It also spells out the Council's principal duties. These include: promote universal respect for the protection of all human rights and fundamental freedoms for all; address and make recommenda-tions on situations of violations of human rights, including gross and systematic viola-tions; promote effective coordination and mainstreaming of human rights in the UN system; help prevent human rights violations through advisory services, technical assis-tance and capacity-building in consultation and with the consent of the states concerned; serve as a forum for dialogue on thematic issues; make recommendations to the General Assembly on developing new human rights standards; help prevent human rights viola-tions through dialogue and cooperation; respond promptly to human rights emergencies; and support the work of the UN High Commissioner for Human Rights and his/her office. The Council is to work in close cooperation with governments, regional organiza-tions, NHRIs, and NGOs. In addition, the resolution stipulates that the Council shall un-dertake a 'universal periodic review' (UPR), based on objective and reliable information, of the fulfilment by each state of its human rights obligations and commitments in a way that ensures universality of coverage and equal treatment. In fulfilling its mandate, the Council's work should be based on the principles of *universality, impartiality, objectivity, non-selectivity, constructive international dialogue*, and *cooperation*.

2.3 UNIVERSAL PERIODIC REVIEW

The universal periodic review (UPR) mechanism was conceived as a form of 'peer review' of UN member states' action to fulfil their human rights obligations, as well as a means of identifying areas in which help and advice are required. The performance of states is measured against the relevant standards in the UN Charter, the UDHR, the UN human rights treaties to which the state is a party, and voluntary commitments and pledges made by the state in the field of human rights.

GA Resolution 60/251 left the modalities of the UPR procedure for the Council to work out. The Council's 'institution-building period' began in June 2006 and ended in June 2007. During this period, the Council negotiated and agreed its rules, working methods, and tools, including the way UPR is to be conducted. On 18 June 2007, the Human

---

[9] ECOSOC Res 1996/31 (25 July 1996) sets out the principles to be applied by the ECOSOC Committee on NGOs when considering whether NGOs should be accorded consultative status.

[10] See Chapter 24 for a discussion of NHRIs and the Paris Principles.

Rights Council adopted Resolution 5/1.[11] The framework of the UPR mechanism and its processes are set out in the annex to this resolution, and subsequent Council resolutions and decisions regarding the Council and the UPR.[12] States have now undergone two UPR cycles. The first began in April 2008 and was completed in October 2011; the second began in June 2012 and was completed in March 2017. The third cycle commenced on 1 May 2017.

Each of the 193 UN member states is reviewed once every four-and-a-half years. Forty-two states are reviewed per year during three annual two-week sessions, with 14 states reviewed each session. The review is conducted by a UPR Working Group, consisting of all members of the Council, chaired by its President. Three Council members, each from a different regional group and drawn by lot, known as the 'troika', facilitate each review. Reviews are based on three documents, which address implementation of recommendations accepted in previous cycles of the UPR and the development of the human rights situation in the state under review.[13] These are:

(1) The *National report* is prepared by the state under review. This report should not exceed 20 pages, and it should include developments since the previous review, details of human rights achievements, best practices, challenges and constraints in relation to implementation of accepted recommendations from earlier reviews, key priorities for the state, expectations in terms of capacity-building, and requests, if any, for technical assistance. In preparing their reports, states are encouraged to adopt a broad consultative process with relevant stakeholders, such as local NGOs and NHRIs.

(2) The *Compilation of UN information* gathers together relevant recommendations, observations, and comments on the state made since the last review by the UN treaty bodies, special procedures mandate holders, as well as summaries of other relevant UN documents. The report is produced by the Office of the High Commissioner for Human Rights (OHCHR) and should not exceed ten pages.

(3) The *Summary of stakeholders' information* is also prepared by the OHCHR and should not be longer than ten pages. It compiles additional 'credible and reliable' country information from relevant stakeholders such as NGOs, NHRIs, academic sources, and regional organizations. The contribution of NHRIs that are fully compliant with the Paris Principles are summarized in a separate section of this report. Stakeholders are encouraged to include information on follow-up to the preceding review in their submissions.

The review itself consists of a three-and-a half hour interactive dialogue between the state under review and the UPR Working Group. All Council members and observers can participate in the dialogue, but interventions are subject to strict time-limits. Advance questions may be transmitted by members and observers at least ten working days before the review and are relayed by the troika to the state. After the review, the troika submits an 'outcome report', which is prepared with the assistance of the UPR secretariat and the involvement of the state under review for adoption by the UPR Working Group. The outcome report summarizes the dialogue, recommendations made by the Working Group on how to improve human rights protection within the state, the state's responses to these recommendations, including those that it accepts at this initial stage and its voluntary commitments. The state under review has an opportunity to react to any recommendations and may 'accept' or 'note', but not 'reject', them. In practice, states have not always complied with this directive,

---

[11] HR Council Res 5/1 (18 June 2007).
[12] See HR Council Dec 6/102 (27 September 2007); HR Council Res 16/2 (25 March 2011); HR Council Dec 17/119 (19 July 2011).   [13] HR Council Dec 17/119.

with many submitting responses such as 'partially accepted', 'accepted in principle', 'already implemented'. The outcome report that is adopted by the Working Group, accompanied by an addendum that records the state's position on all the recommendations, is submitted to the next ordinary session of the Human Rights Council, where one hour is allowed for its discussion. Twenty minutes is allotted to the state under review to make a statement. If the NHRI of that state is fully compliant with the Paris Principles, it is entitled to intervene immediately after the state's statement. Thereafter, all member states, observers, NGOs, and other stakeholders may comment. At the end of this discussion a final outcome report, containing the accepted and noted recommendations, is adopted. This report serves as the basis for the state's subsequent review.

In 2007, the Secretary-General characterized the UPR as a mechanism with 'great potential to promote and protect human rights in the darkest corners of the world'.[14] The first two cycles have been judged by most to be extremely positive. All UN member states have participated,[15] proving it be truly universal. The majority fielded representatives of a very high level and engaged in a constructive and open fashion. In preparation for their reviews, many states created processes to allow for internal review across governmental bodies and between government and civil society. NHRIs, civil society organizations, UN entities, and development actors engaged with the mechanism, as did individuals on the ground, with many watching the proceedings via webcast. In particular, civil society organizations have used the UPR as a means to coordinate with one another, including by formulating joint submissions in advance of the review and following up on recommendations. They have also found the mechanism to provide a non-confrontational and constructive framework for state engagement which can lead to positive change on the ground.[16] Over 56,000 recommendations were made over the first two cycles, covering a broad range of human rights issues, with follow-up to these providing a means to initiate or strengthen human rights dialogue and cooperation at national, regional, and global levels.[17] States have made specific commitments in relation to human rights issues at various stages of the review, while many have adopted the practice, encouraged by the Council, of submitting voluntary mid-term reports on implementation of recommendations.[18]

Experience of UPR shows that it is largely complementary to, and not in competition with, the procedures of the UN treaty bodies (see Section 3). During UPR sessions, states are frequently quizzed about their follow-up to treaty body recommendations, and the final outcome documents regularly contain concrete recommendations to this effect. Treaty bodies often raise the commitments made by states parties under the UPR process in their proceedings. Cooperation with treaty bodies, including submission of reports, as well as ratifications of human rights treaties and withdrawal of reservations to treaties, often increases before a review or as a result of recommendations.

---

[14] Secretary-General's video message to the opening of the fourth Council session (12 March 2007), available at: <http://www.un.org/webcast/unhrc/archive.asp?go=004>.

[15] Israel decided not to participate in its second review in early 2013, leading the Council to adopt a decision on the non-cooperation of a state under review (A/HRC/OM/71, 28 January 2013). In May 2013, the President reported to the Council on the steps he had taken in this context, and in October Israel participated in its review, albeit expressing strong reservations.

[16] Brown, 'The Universal Periodic Review and Human Rights Progress: A Case Study from Australia' *Human Rights Monitor* (International Service for Human Rights, June 2016) 23; UPR Info, 'The Butterfly Effect: Spreading Good Practices of UPR Information' (2016).

[17] UPR Info maintains a comprehensive database of UPR recommendations and voluntary pledges, available at: <http://www.upr-info.org/database/>.

[18] See: <http://www.ohchr.org/EN/HRBodies/UPR/Pages/UPRImplementation.aspx>.

Nevertheless, UPR is not without its critics. Concerns have been expressed that some states avoid negative UPR assessments by ensuring that friendly governments praise their human rights record and ignore their shortcomings. Thus, the outcome of the review may not address human rights violations that are occurring within the state. In addition, the response of the state under review to recommendations may not be clear. The proliferation of recommendations has also raised concern, as has the fact that some may be repetitive. Some suggest that far fewer recommendations address economic, social, and cultural rights than civil and political rights, thereby undermining UPR's objective of promoting the universality, interdependence, indivisibility, and interrelatedness of all human rights.[19] Others raise the issue that some recommendations are so vague as to be unimplementable. In December 2015, the incoming Human Rights Council President expressed the view that the UPR mechanism could be made more efficient and effective and called for a collective effort towards that end. However, it is unlikely that there will be any major changes to the UPR process.[20]

Follow-up to and implementation of UPR recommendations are indicators of whether the mechanism meaningfully promotes and protects human rights or whether it constitutes 'ritualism'—that is, a non-substantive cyclical exercise.[21] One study reports positively that slightly over two-thirds of the recommendations made during the first cycle had been accepted by the state under review, with acceptance rates increasing over the cycle.[22] An analysis of NGO mid-term assessments of implementation of first-cycle recommendations by 165 states indicates that 48 per cent of recommendations had generated action.[23] Another study suggests that the second cycle has seen the same level of acceptance of recommendations as the first cycle, although the majority of these have been couched in 'soft' language, rather than specific and measurable terms.[24]

Implementation of recommendations is primarily for the state itself, but states are encouraged to conduct broad consultations with all stakeholders in this process. A voluntary fund exists to assist the least-developed and small-island developing states implement UPR recommendations.[25] The OHCHR, other UN entities, regional organizations, parliaments, and civil society actors, including NHRIs, have invested significant energy into UPR follow-up.[26]

2.4 RESPONSES TO URGENT SITUATIONS

When responding to serious human rights situations, the Human Rights Council can convene for special sessions or hold urgent debates during regular sessions. Since June 2006, the Council has held 26 special sessions. This should be contrasted with the Commission on Human Rights, which between May 1990, when ECOSOC authorized it to hold such

---

[19] Saiz, 'The UPR and Economic, Social and Cultural Rights: A Skewed Agenda?' *Human Rights Monitor* (International Service for Human Rights, June 2016) 12.

[20] Gujadhur and Limon, 'Towards the Third Cycle of the UPR: Stick or Twist? Lessons Learnt from the First Ten Years of the Universal Periodic Review' (2016), 42–47, available at: <http://www.universal-rights.org>.

[21] Charlesworth and Larking (eds), *Human Rights and the Universal Periodic Review: Rituals and Ritualism* (CUP, 2014).   [22] UPR Info, 'Universal Periodic Review: On the Road to Implementation' (2012).

[23] UPR Info, 'Beyond Promises: the Impact of UPR on the Ground' (2014).

[24] McMahon and Johnson, *Evolution Not Revolution: The First Two Cycles of the UN Human Rights Council Universal Periodic Review Mechanism* (Friedrich Ebert Stiftung, 2016). See also Gujadhur and Limon (2016).

[25] HR Council Res 6/17 (28 September 2007). This resolution also creates a trust fund to assist states with their participation in the UPR.

[26] eg, OHCHR, *National Mechanisms for Reporting and Follow-up: A Practical Guide to Effective State Engagement with International Human Rights Mechanisms*, HR/PUB/16/1 (2016); OHCHR, *National Mechanisms for Reporting and Follow-up: Study of State Engagement with International Human Rights Mechanisms*, HR/PUB/16/1/Add.1 (2016).

sessions,[27] and its replacement by the Council in June 2006, convened only five. Two of the Council's special sessions have had a thematic focus (the effects of the global economic crisis and the world food crisis), one has focused on the attacks and abuses committed by Boko Haram across the African continent, and the balance has addressed urgent human rights situations in countries. Six have related to the human rights situation in the Israeli Occupied Territory, one to Israeli military operations, and five to the situation in the Syrian Arab Republic. The other sessions have concerned the human rights situation in Burundi, the Central African Republic, Côte d'Ivoire, Darfur (Sudan), the Democratic Republic of Congo, Haiti, Iraq, the Libyan Arab Jamahiriya, Myanmar, Sri Lanka, and South Sudan. The Council has also convened three urgent debates during its regular sessions: one in relation to Israel and two on Syria.

The outcomes of special sessions or urgent debates have included the creation of, or deployment of existing, expert fact-finding missions,[28] which sometimes include the relevant Special Rapporteur;[29] the creation of independent international commissions of inquiry[30] and requests for existing commissions to commence special inquiries;[31] the appointment of an independent expert;[32] requests for existing special procedures to urgently investigate a particular situation;[33] and requests for the High Commissioner or OHCHR to report on the situation or issue.[34]

In response to less urgent situations within countries, the Council can also create commissions of inquiry during its regular sessions,[35] commissions on human rights,[36] or mandate the High Commissioner to report on human rights concerns in individual countries,[37] including in relation to technical assistance and capacity building provided by OHCHR.[38] OHCHR investigations can also be established by the Council.[39] The Council is also able to create a special procedure to address a country situation (see Section 2.5). However, resolutions establishing such procedures, fact-finding missions, commissions of inquiry and similar mechanisms,[40] are unlikely to be adopted by consensus unless the country concerned is willing to agree to the mandate's creation and expresses its willingness to cooperate with the mechanism. When they are adopted without the state's cooperation, the mechanism is usually refused access to the state concerned. Where the country expresses willingness to cooperate, the scope of the mandate will be primarily technical assistance and capacity building.

Whether the Council will address a country situation depends on the willingness of its membership. The operation of regional groups and alliances assumes particular

---

[27] ECOSOC Res 1990/48 (25 May 1990).

[28] eg, Israeli military attacks against the Occupied Gaza Strip (2009); Israeli attacks against the humanitarian boat convoy (2010); Syria (2011); Iraq (2014); Burundi (2015).

[29] eg, situation in Occupied Palestinian Territories (2006).

[30] eg, situation in Lebanon caused by Israeli military operations (2006); Israeli military incursions in the Occupied Palestinian Territory, including northern Gaza and Beit Hanoun (2006); Darfur (2006); Syria (2011); ensuring respect for international law in the Occupied Palestinian Territory, including East Jerusalem (2014).

[31] eg, Aleppo, Syria (2016).   [32] eg, Central African Republic (2014).

[33] eg, Democratic Republic of Congo (2008).

[34] eg, Israeli military attacks in the Occupied Palestinian Territory (2008); Democratic Republic of Congo (2008); Côte d'Ivoire (2010); Boko Haram (2015).

[35] eg, Democratic Peoples' Republic of Korea (2013); Eritrea (2014); Burundi (2016).

[36] eg, regarding South Sudan (2016).

[37] eg, promoting reconciliation and accountability in Sri Lanka (2013); Northern Mali (2013).

[38] eg, Afghanistan (2013); Guinea (2013).   [39] eg, Sri Lanka (2014); Libya (2015).

[40] These investigatory mechanisms may also be created by the Security Council, the General Assembly, the Secretary-General, and the High Commissioner for Human Rights. See: <libraryresources.unog.ch/factfinding>.

importance here and it should be noted that, given the composition of the Council, the African and Asian groups have an automatic majority in Council decision-making. There have been charges that the Human Rights Council is selective and politically biased. Some point to the existence of the standing Council agenda item 7 on the human rights situation in Palestine and other occupied Arab territories and the fact that developing states with difficult human rights situations have largely escaped such scrutiny as evidence to support their claims. It is worth noting that no special session, special procedure, nor similar mechanism has been put forward regarding Western states. Proposals to examine a particular country situation are often opposed on the basis that 'cooperative' approaches to human rights should be used—that is, approaches with which the state concerned consents. Clearly, this is the preferred way forward, but workable only where the state has a true desire to improve human rights enjoyment. Some delegations also argue that UPR is the ideal mechanism to address country situations, as it is based on state cooperation. However the fact that it addresses individual states only periodically makes it unsuitable for urgent and chronic human rights concerns.

2.5 SPECIAL PROCEDURES

The creation of the special procedures mechanisms was one of the major achievements of the Commission on Human Rights. From the establishment of the first special procedures mandate in 1980—the Working Group on Enforced and Involuntary Disappearances—to the end of the Commission's final session, the special procedures system evolved remarkably.[41] These mechanisms, consisting of independent experts who work *pro bono*—either individually or as part of a five-member working group—address country-specific situations or thematic issues that concern all states. GA Resolution 60/251 mandated the Human Rights Council to review and, where necessary, rationalize and improve all mandates and mechanisms of the former Commission 'in order to maintain a system of special procedures' within one year of its first session. Any decision to discontinue, merge, or streamline mandates must be guided by the need to enhance human rights protection and promotion.

Seven country-specific mandates have been discontinued since 2006, although one was re-established in 2012,[42] and a further six have been created.[43] Thirteen thematic mandates have been added. At the beginning of August 2017, there were a total of 56 special procedures mandates: 12 on country situations;[44] 12 focusing on civil and political rights;[45] ten in the area of economic, social, and cultural rights;[46] and 15 mandates that focus on

---

[41] See, Nolan, Freedman, and Murphy (eds), *The United Nations Special Procedures System* (Brill/Martinus Nijhoff, 2016).

[42] The mandates on Belarus, Burundi, Cuba, the Democratic Republic of the Congo, and Liberia were discontinued; the Belarus mandate was re-established in 2012.

[43] Mandates relating to Central African Republic, Côte d'Ivoire (discontinued in June 2017), Eritrea, Iran, Mali, and Syria (who will only take up his functions after the relevant Commission of Inquiry on that country has finished its work).

[44] Belarus, Cambodia, Central African Republic, Democratic Peoples' Republic of Korea, Eritrea, Iran, Mali, Myanmar, Occupied Palestinian Territories, Somalia, Sudan, and Syria.

[45] Counter-terrorism, freedom of expression and opinion, freedom of religion, human rights defenders, independence of judges and lawyers, peaceful assembly and association, privacy, racism, summary executions, torture, Working Group on Arbitrary Detention, and the Working Group on Enforced and Involuntary Disappearances.

[46] Cultural rights, education, environment, extreme poverty, food, foreign debt, hazardous substances, health, housing, and safe drinking water and sanitation.

specific groups.[47] The remaining mandates are: business and human rights; the negative impact of unilateral coercive measures on the enjoyment of human rights; promotion of a democratic and equitable international order; promotion of truth, justice, reparation and guarantees of non-recurrence; right to development; human rights and international solidarity; and the Working Group on African Descent.

Mandate holders are experts in their respective fields. They are selected on the basis of technical criteria developed by the Human Rights Council.[48] A five-member Consultative Group, comprising ambassadors from each of the five regional group who serve in their personal capacity, conducts a selection process including an interview, and then proposes a shortlist of experts for vacant mandates to the Council President. After broad consultation among Council members, the President puts forward a candidate for each vacancy for the Council's approval, along with an explanation if the proposal differs from that of the Consultative Group. Throughout the process consideration is given to gender balance, equitable geographic distribution, and representation of different legal systems.

Each mandate holder serves in his or her personal capacity and independently. They should not hold a decision-making position in government or any other body that may result in a conflict of interest. He or she must also respect the principle of non-accumulation of human rights functions. Thematic mandate holders may serve up to two three-year consecutive terms, and country mandate holders usually serve six one-year consecutive terms; the maximum consecutive term for both types of mandate holders in the same function is six years.[49] While the denomination of experts varies ('Special Rapporteur', 'Independent Expert', or 'member of working group'), their status is equal. They benefit from such diplomatic privileges and immunities as are required for the discharge of their duties.[50]

Since 1993, mandate holders have met annually for one week to discuss themes of common interest and harmonization of working methods. During these meetings they also interact with the High Commissioner for Human Rights, the Bureau of the Human Rights Council, and others. Their manual of operations was adopted and revised in the context of such a meeting.[51] A Coordination Committee of special procedures, comprising six mandate holders, was established in 2005 to represent the system, including by making statements on its behalf. This Committee meets regularly to discuss issues pertinent to the special procedures system, including with states and civil society.

All mandate holders conduct *country visits*. Currently, 118 UN member states and one observer state have extended 'standing invitations', and so, in principle, any thematic special procedure may visit these states. However, in all circumstances a visit must be agreed with the state concerned, and some that have issued standing invitations have not consented to a visit when requested. Where other states are concerned, a specific invitation must be extended. Before the start of a visit, its terms of reference are negotiated and agreed by the mandate holder and the government. During visits, mandate holders meet with relevant stakeholders and visit facilities relevant to their mandate. Before they leave, they debrief

---

[47] The Working Group on discrimination against women in law and in practice; enjoyment of human rights by persons with albinism; indigenous peoples; internally displaced persons; elimination of discrimination against persons affected by leprosy and their family members; migrants; minorities; older persons; protection against violence and discrimination based on sexual orientation and gender identity; rights of persons with disabilities; sale of children; slavery; trafficking; violence against women; and the Working Group on Mercenaries.

[48] See HR Council Res 5/1, Annex; HR Council Dec 6/102.

[49] Presidential Statement of the Human Rights Council on terms of office of special procedures mandate holders, A/HRC/8/PRST/2 (18 June 2008).

[50] Regulations Governing the Status, Basic Rights and Duties of Officials other than Secretariat Officials, and Experts on Mission, ST/SGB/2002/9 (18 June 2002).

[51] Manual of Operations of the Special Procedures of the Human Rights Council (August 2008).

the authorities and the media on their (preliminary) findings and conclusions. A report on the visit, including conclusions and recommendations, is subsequently transmitted to the Human Rights Council, annexing any comments from the state. The report is presented during the Council's annual interactive debate on the mandate. During 2016 mandate holders carried out 96 visits to 65 states and territories.[52]

Most mandate holders examine *complaints* from individuals, human rights defenders, or other interested persons regarding alleged human rights violations that fall within the area(s) of their mandate. The OHCHR channels these to the relevant mandate holders for action. 'Letters of allegation' are addressed to governments requesting clarification of the allegation. Where alleged violations are time-sensitive (imminent loss of life, life-threatening situations, ongoing or imminent damage of a severe nature) 'urgent appeals' are dispatched. Mandate holders also transmit 'other letters' that address non-state actors and thematic issues. In 2016, mandate holders sent 526 communications to 119 states and 23 non-state actors, with 455 being transmitted jointly by two or more mandates. A report containing communications transmitted, and any replies received, is submitted to each session of the Human Rights Council. Two special procedures have developed sophisticated working practices and adopt reasoned opinions in response to complaints. The Working Group on Enforced and Involuntary Disappearances receives reports of alleged disappearance, which it seeks to clarify. Since its establishment in 1980, it has transmitted over 55,000 cases to states, of which approximately 44,000 in respect of 91 states remain under active consideration.[53] The Working Group on Arbitrary Detention adopts opinions on complaints regarding arbitrary arrest and detention. This Working Group was established in 1991, and, to date, has adopted over 900 opinions.[54]

Some mandate holders *develop authoritative opinions and standards*, thus contributing to the progressive development of international law. For example, the special procedure on internally displaced persons formulated Guiding Principles on Internal Displacement;[55] the former Special Representative of the Secretary-General on human rights and transnational corporations and other business enterprises developed Guiding Principles on Business and Human Rights;[56] and the Independent Expert on the effects of foreign debt prepared Guiding Principles on Foreign Debt and Human Rights.[57] Others adopt 'deliberations' or general comments on specific themes.[58] Thematic mandate holders often research a specific theme, either at the request of the Human Rights Council or on their own initiative, and whilst all present annual thematic reports to the Council, the majority also do so to the General Assembly. Similarly, country mandate holders report annually to the Council, and many to the General Assembly. Questionnaires are often transmitted to states, NGOs, and other stakeholders and meetings convened to elicit comprehensive, up-to-date information. At the end of their tenure, some mandate holders present a report which analyses the global human rights situation as regards their mandate.[59] They frequently organize, in conjunction with the OHCHR, governments, and NGOs, seminars or consultations which contribute to the analysis of human rights issues. Some special rapporteurs submit amicus briefs to international, regional, or national courts on issues related to their mandate.

---

[52] Report on the twenty-third annual meeting held in June 2016, A/HRC/34/34 (31 January 2017) Annex 1.
[53] Report of the Working Group on Enforced or Involuntary Disappearances, A/HRC/33/51 (28 July 2016) para 5. [54] See: <http://www.ohchr.org/EN/Issues/Detention/Pages/OpinionsadoptedbytheWGAD.aspx>.
[55] E/CN.4/1998/53/Add.2 (11 February 1998). [56] A/HRC/17/31 (21 March 2011).
[57] A/HRC/20/23 (10 April 2011).
[58] eg, Working Group on Arbitrary Detention, Deliberation No. 9, A/HRC/22/44 (24 December 2012) 16–25.
[59] eg, Special Rapporteur on the independence of judges and lawyers, Review and assessment of the main issues addressed over six years of mandate, A/70/263 (3 August 2015).

Mandate holders also *raise awareness of human rights concerns* by releasing joint or individual press statements and engaging in regular contact with the media, especially during country visits and Human Rights Council or General Assembly sessions. Attendance at activities and meetings organized by states, NGOs, or academic institutions is used to raise awareness about their mandates, create and develop partnerships, and learn about new developments. An increasing number of mandate holders also follow up on communications and visits with further communications, reports, visits, public statements, and consultations, in order to accelerate implementation of their recommendations.[60]

The Human Rights Council adopted a Code of Conduct for Special Procedures Mandate Holders in June 2007, which is designed to 'enhance the effectiveness of the system by defining the standards of ethical behaviour and professional conduct that special procedures mandate-holders . . . shall observe whilst discharging their mandates'.[61] The Code sets out general principles on the conduct, status, and prerogatives of mandate holders, and regulations on sources of information, communications, relations with states, and field visits. On occasion, states have used the Code in statements during Council sessions or correspondence with mandate holders, the Secretary-General, High Commissioner, or the Council President to found allegations that individual mandate holders have acted improperly, often with a view to restricting their activities, and even to dismiss individual experts.[62] In June 2008 the Council adopted Presidential Statement 8/2, which provides that the President will convey any information of persistent non-compliance by a mandate holder with the Code, especially prior to the mandate holder's renewal, to the Council for consideration and action as appropriate. A year later, the Council adopted Resolution 11/11, which notes that it is incumbent on mandate holders to exercise their functions with full respect for, and strict observance of, their mandates set out in the relevant Council resolutions and full compliance with the Code. It also requests the OHCHR to assist special procedures mandate holders in this regard.[63]

While the Code of Conduct was being negotiated, proposals were made for a body to oversee its implementation, but these were unsuccessful. Instead, in 2008, the special procedures' Coordination Committee adopted an 'Internal Advisory Procedure' (IAP) to review practices and working methods. The IAP includes a mechanism, facilitated by the Coordination Committee, to deal confidentially with issues that arise in the practices and working methods of the mandate holders. In early 2010, Philip Alston, then the Special Rapporteur on extrajudicial, summary, or arbitrary executions, suggested the creation of a committee to deal with complaints by governments and others of non-compliance with the Code by mandate holders and governments in a way that would protect mandate holders' independence and integrity, yet hold them accountable.[64] This proposal was rejected by other mandate holders, many states, and most civil society actors. Several states introduced this idea in a somewhat different form during the review of the Council that took place in 2011 (see Section 2.8) but it was not adopted. A similar idea, and elements for a draft Human Rights Council resolution on the implementation of the code of conduct,

---

[60] Report on the twenty-third annual meeting, Annex IX.

[61] HR Council Res 5/2 (18 June 2007).

[62] See Baldwin-Pask and Scannella, 'The Unfinished Business of a Special Procedures System' in Bassiouni and Shabas (eds), *New Challenges for the UN Human Rights Machinery: What Future for the UN Treaty Body System and the Human Rights Council Procedures* (Intersentia, 2011) 439, 463–70.

[63] HR Council Res 11/11 (18 June 2009).

[64] His proposals are outlined in Alston, 'Hobbling the Monitors: Should UN Human Rights Monitors be Accountable?' (2011) 52 *Harvard ILJ* 563.

was put forward in 2015 by another mandate holder.[65] This is unlikely to be the last time that such a suggestion is made.

Reference to the Code of Conduct by states in their interactions with special procedures is now less frequent. However, mandate holders still face criticism, including in relation to funding of their activities through non-UN sources that is alleged to affect their impartiality.[66] Cooperation by some states with special procedures remains weak. States' conduct towards mandate holders can also be inappropriate, leading one state, France, to propose the introduction of a code of conduct for states themselves. This proposal was not taken up.

Successive UN Secretaries-General have described the special procedures as the 'eyes and ears' of the Human Rights Council. One commentator has labelled them 'catalysts for human rights', and argues that they play a critical role in shaping international human rights norms, shedding light on how states comply with these, as well as influencing government behaviour for the benefit of millions of people.[67] Mandate holders have generated positive changes in many countries, and these changes have been facilitated by their expertise, the quality of their recommendations, and the openness of some states to cooperate. However, the full potential of the special procedures remains untapped, in particular in relation to their capacity to provide early warning of potential human rights violations. The impact of their activities is negatively affected by lack of state cooperation, inadequate resources, and, as in the case of all human rights mechanisms, weak follow-up.

2.6 COMPLAINT PROCEDURE

The Council complaint procedure is based on the '1503 procedure' created by ECOSOC in May 1970, which was implemented by the Commission on Human Rights.[68] This confidential procedure, the oldest human rights complaint mechanism in the UN system, was concerned with patterns of gross violations of human rights rather than individual cases. Similarly, the Council complaint procedure is concerned with identifying 'consistent patterns of gross and reliably attested violations of all human rights and all fundamental freedoms occurring in any part of the world and under any circumstances'.[69]

A complaint alleging a pattern of violation can be transmitted by a person, or group, claiming to be the victims of violations of human rights, or by any person or group of persons, including NGOs, who have direct and reliable knowledge of the alleged violations. Complaints will be considered inadmissible if they have manifestly political motivations or are inconsistent with the purposes of the UN. All complaints must give a factual description of the alleged violation and an indication of the rights violated. The language used must not be abusive, although such a complaint may be considered if it meets the other admissibility criteria after deletion of the abusive elements. Complaints should not be based solely on media reports. Domestic remedies should be exhausted before a complaint is submitted, unless it appears that such remedies would be ineffective or unreasonably prolonged, and situations being dealt with by a special procedure or other UN or regional human rights complaints mechanism will not be considered.

---

[65] Jazairy, 'In Defence of Special Procedures of the Human Rights Council: An Alternative Narrative from the South', *Ibn Khaldun Research Paper No 3* (Geneva Centre for Human Rights Advancement and Global Dialogue, 2015).

[66] Connors, 'Special Procedures: Independence and Impartiality', in Nolan, Freedman, and Murphy (2016), 52, 75–83.

[67] Piccone, *Catalysts for Change: How the UN's Independent Experts Promote Human Rights* (Brookings Institution Press, 2012), viii.

[68] ECOSOC Res 1503 (XLVII) (27 May 1970).   [69] HR Council Res 5/1, Annex, para 85.

Complaints do not go directly to the Human Rights Council. Rather, they are pre-screened by the OHCHR and two Council working groups: the Working Group on Communications (WGC) and the Working Group on Situations (WGS). Both working groups are composed of five members, each representing one of the five regional groups. WGC members are designated by the Human Rights Advisory Committee (see Section 2.7) from amongst its members, while the WGS is appointed by the regional groups of the member states of the Council. Complaints are pre-screened by the Chairperson of the WGC with the OHCHR. At this point those communications that are manifestly ill-founded or anonymous are dismissed. Those considered admissible are transmitted to the state concerned for observations. Complaints and state replies are examined by the WGC, which transmits cases it considers admissible, including its recommendations on the case, to the WGS. The WGS may dismiss a case or keep it under review until its subsequent session, requesting further information from the state. The WGS also prepares a report for a closed session of the Human Rights Council plenary, including recommendations for action, usually in the form of a draft decision or resolution. Proceedings in both working groups are confidential. They are conducted on the basis of written materials alone, with neither governments nor complainants appearing before them. Unlike the '1503 procedure', both the author of the communication and the state are informed of the status of the proceedings at key stages as well as the final outcome.

Although the value of the complaint procedure has been questioned, it is often resorted to. The OHCHR receives between 11,000 and 15,000 communications annually. This is probably due to the fact that unlike the treaty-based complaint procedures, which depend on the acceptance of the state concerned (see Section 3.4), complaints can concern any country. Increasing numbers of situations have been referred to the Council by the WGS since 2011, and although most situations have been discontinued,[70] the impact of the complaint procedure should not be underrated. It is well-placed to serve as an early warning mechanism. The confidential nature of the procedure may also encourage states, most of which respond to the communications submitted to them, to take remedial action in order to avoid public scrutiny. In some cases the Council has recommended the provision of technical assistance to states subject to communications.[71] Notably, in September 2012, the Council decided to discontinue the review of complaints alleging widespread violations of human rights in Eritrea under the complaints procedure in order to consider the matter publicly in the context of the appointment of a Special Rapporteur on human rights in Eritrea.[72] The Council also decided to transmit the documentation received under the complaint procedure to the Special Rapporteur and invite her to investigate those allegations and report back.

2.7 HUMAN RIGHTS COUNCIL ADVISORY COMMITTEE

The Human Rights Council Advisory Committee is set up to operate as a 'think-tank' for the Council.[73] Consisting of 18 independent and impartial experts, the Advisory Committee replaced the 26-member Sub-Commission on the Promotion and Protection of Human Rights of the Commission on Human Rights. Committee members are elected by the Human Rights Council by secret ballot from a list of candidates who fulfil the requirements for nomination, which include high moral standing and recognized competence and expertise in the field of

---

[70] For a list of situations referred to the Human Rights Council under the complaint procedure between its creation and October 2014, see: <http://www.ohchr.org/Documents/HRBodies/ComplaintProcedure/SituationsConsideredUnderComplaintsProcedures.pdf>. No further cases have been referred to the Council for action.

[71] eg, re Democratic Republic of the Congo, A/HRC/18/2 (18 November 2011) para 210; and Iraq, A/HRC/19/2 (16 August 2012) para 324; and A/HRC/20/2 (3 August 2012) para 212.

[72] HR Council Res 21/1 (27 September 2012).   [73] HR Council Res 5/1, paras 65–84.

human rights.[74] All members must be independent and impartial, so those who hold decision-making positions in governments or any other entity that might give rise to a conflict of interest are excluded. The geographic distribution of experts is: African states: five; Asian states: five; Eastern European states: two; Latin American and Caribbean states: three; and Western European and other states: three. All UN member states may propose and endorse candidates from their own region. They should consult their NHRIs and civil society organizations in the process, and include the names of those supporting their candidates. Members serve for a period of three years and are eligible for consecutive re-election once. They may not accumulate other human rights functions during their tenure.

The Advisory Committee convenes two annual sessions, for a maximum of ten days per year. Additional sessions may be scheduled with the approval of the Council. An annual report of the Committee's activities is submitted to the Council's September session and an interactive dialogue with the Committee's Chairperson is conducted during this session.

The role of the Advisory Committee is to provide expertise to the Council in the manner and form it requests, mainly through studies and research-based advice. Unlike its predecessor, the Sub-Commission, the Advisory Committee may not adopt resolutions or decisions, nor may it examine and decide on specific country situations. Expertise may only be provided to the Council on its request and under its guidance. However, the Committee may make proposals to the Council for the incremental enhancement of procedural efficiency, and research proposals within the scope of the thematic work of the Human Rights Council. The Advisory Committee's activity is to be implementation-oriented and it is to engage with states, NHRIs, NGOs, and other civil society stakeholders. Council members and observers, UN specialized agencies, other intergovernmental institutions, academics, and NGOs may participate in the work of the Advisory Committee.[75]

The Advisory Committee's studies are usually produced by drafting groups of members drawn from regional groups, which seek comments and advice from stakeholders through questionnaires. The output of the drafting groups is discussed and revised in the Committee. Since its first session in August 2008, the Advisory Committee has prepared a draft declaration on human rights education and training,[76] a draft set of principles and guidelines for the elimination of discrimination against persons affected by leprosy and their family members,[77] a draft declaration on the right to peace,[78] and a draft declaration on the rights of peasants and other people working in rural areas.[79] It has addressed subjects including missing persons, the protection of civilians in armed conflicts, the promotion of a democratic and equitable international order, human rights and international solidarity, aspects of the right to food, and promoting human rights and fundamental freedoms through a better understanding of traditional values of humankind. The Committee has worked at the Council's request on the human rights of elderly people, international cooperation on human rights, human rights and terrorist hostage-taking, and promotion of the human rights of the urban poor. It also works to mainstream a gender perspective and the human rights of persons with disabilities into its work.

Despite these important contributions, the fact that the Advisory Committee cannot initiate its own work or adopt resolutions or decisions has circumscribed its capacity to

---

[74] HR Council Dec 6/102.

[75] eg, the Advisory Committee has created a network of 'Academic Friends' who work pro bono.

[76] A/HRC/AC/4/4 (10 February 2010). The Declaration was adopted by GA Res 66/137 (19 December 2011).

[77] A/HRC/AC/5/2 (3 June 2010). The Guidelines were welcomed by the General Assembly: GA Res 65/251 (21 December 2010).

[78] A/HRC/20/31 (16 April 2012), Annex. The HRC has since adopted the Declaration on the Right to Peace, HR Council Res 32/28 (1 July 2016).   [79] A/HRC/19/75 (24 February 2012), Annex.

provide the Council with expertise. The Council's 'guidelines' on the way its requests to the Advisory Committee should be addressed are also prescriptive, thus affecting the way this expertise can be provided. The Advisory Committee now puts forward priority proposals for the consideration of the Council, accompanied by detailed concept papers. It is important for the Committee to devise ways to strengthen its influence. These could include working with other mechanisms and in different frameworks, and perhaps convening panels or expert group meetings during its sessions. Committee members have valuable expertise, and while some states consider that the Committee's work replicates that of other bodies or goes beyond its mandate, the Council should explore ways to maximize its potential.

2.8 REVIEW AND OTHER DISCUSSIONS

GA Resolution 60/251 provided that the Human Rights Council would review its work and functioning five years after its establishment and report to the General Assembly. In turn, the General Assembly was to review the status of the Council. The outcome of the five-year review of the Council's work and functioning was adopted on 25 March 2011.[80] The review focused on five issues: the UPR; the special procedures; the Human Rights Council Advisory Committee, and the Council's complaint procedure; the agenda and framework for the programme of work; and methods of work and rules of procedure.

A myriad of proposals was put forward during review discussions, but few changes were actually agreed. Many states expressed dissatisfaction with the outcome, and the US disassociated itself from it. A group of influential NGOs described the result as a 'vital opportunity to strengthen the Council's work and functioning . . . squandered.'[81] These reactions related predominantly to the fact that proposals for a mechanism to improve the Council's responsiveness to emergency and chronic human rights situations could not gain consensus.

Nonetheless, the outcome includes some important elements. For example, the role of NHRIs that are fully compliant with the Paris Principles in the UPR and with regard to special procedures was strengthened. Procedures for the selection and appointment of special procedures mandate holders were enhanced. States were urged to cooperate with and assist special procedures by responding in a timely manner to requests for information and visits. Technical measures to streamline the work of the Council, including a voluntary yearly calendar of resolutions, were encouraged. A task force on accessibility of persons with disabilities to the Council and its mechanisms and the use of information technology, including video-conferencing or video-messaging to enhance participation of all stakeholders, was established.

Importantly, the outcome highlighted the issue of reprisals against individuals and groups who cooperate, or have cooperated, with the UN or its representatives and mechanisms in the field of human rights. States were urged to prevent and ensure adequate protection against such acts. Since the adoption of the review document, cross-regional statements on reprisals are now made by states during Council sessions and discussions have been held on ways to prevent reprisals.[82] During 2012, the President of the Council raised allegations of reprisals in Council sessions and with relevant delegations. Her successors have been similarly vigilant. The Coordination Committee of Special Procedures also have a framework for dealing with intimidation and reprisals.[83]

---

[80] HR Council Res 16/21 (25 March 2011).

[81] Joint NGO Statement on the review of the Council's status by the General Assembly, IOR 41/006/2011, available at: <https://www.amnesty.org/en/documents/ior41/006/2011/en/>.

[82] eg, A/HRC/22/34 (17 December 2012).

[83] See: <www.ohchr.org/EN/HRBodies/SP/Pages/Actsofintimidationandreprisal.aspx>.

Disappointment was also expressed at the result of the General Assembly's review of the status of the Council. The Council remains a subsidiary body of the General Assembly. However this is to be reconsidered before 2026.[84] Some states and many NGOs had hoped that the General Assembly review would lead to an enhanced election process for membership to the Council, perhaps by including a means by which the pledges put forward by states presenting their candidatures would be reviewed publicly. They had also hoped that 'open slates' for elections might be required. However, none of these proposals was adopted.

Despite being labelled by several NGOs as 'technical and bureaucratic', a number of changes was introduced that make a practical difference to the work of the Council. The Council's annual report now covers the period from 1 October to 30 September, allowing the outcome of all of its sessions in any one year to be considered by the General Assembly that year. Its sessions are aligned to the calendar year, rather than starting in June as before; and the President of the Council presents its annual report to the Assembly's plenary and Third Committee, with the latter engaging in an interactive dialogue on the report. Importantly, the need to provide adequate financing to fund unforeseen and extraordinary expenses resulting from resolutions and decisions of the Council was recognized. These had been met previously by the OHCHR diverting funds from other activities.

While no formal review of the Council has taken place since 2011, many initiatives directed at improving its efficiency, effectiveness, and working culture and realizing its full potential have been proposed. In 2015 the annual Glion Human Rights Dialogue[85] was focused on improving the relevance and strengthening the impact of the Human Rights Council as it reached its tenth anniversary. Recent Council presidents have prioritized efficiency and effectiveness, and many civil society organizations have presented proposals aimed at strengthening implementation and impact.[86] Ideas will continue to be exchanged, but, just as in the case of the review, it is likely that any adjustments to the 'institution-building package' will be very modest.

2.9 CONCLUSION

Early in its life, several observers and NGOs criticized, or even dismissed outright, the activities of the Human Rights Council. They pointed to the fact that numerous states with questionable human rights records were members of the Council and that most of its special sessions unfairly 'targeted' Israel, whilst other serious country situations, such as that in Zimbabwe, had not been scrutinized, let alone criticized. With the Council now in its 11th year, these issues remain.[87] Despite these concerns, assessment of this increasingly active body's performance is generally positive. Experience of the UPR mechanism has been extremely positive, and the future of the special procedures system appears secure.

The Council has proved itself to be willing to address critical country situations through special sessions, urgent debates, and other formats, such as enhanced interactive debates and inter-sessional discussions.[88] Indeed, in April 2011, it was the first UN

---

[84] GA Res 65/281 (17 June 2011).

[85] See: <http://www.universal-rights.org/the-glion-human-rights-dialogue/>.

[86] eg, Joint Civil Society Paper, Strengthening the Council at 10 (April 2016) available at: <http://www.ishr.ch/sites/default/files/article/files/hrc10_joint_paper_final.pdf>.

[87] See Piccone, 'Ten Years Later: The Status of the UN Human Rights Council', Testimony prepared for the Tom Lantos Human Rights Commission of the US Congress (17 May 2016), 2–3, available at: <https://www.brookings.edu/testimonies/ten-years-later-the-status-of-the-u-n-human-rights-council/>.

[88] Piccone and McMillen, 'Country-Specific Scrutiny at the United Nations Human Rights Council: More than Meets the Eye' (May 2016), available at: <https://www.brookings.edu/research/country-specific-scrutiny-at-the-united-nations-human-rights-council-more-than-meets-the-eye/>.

intergovernmental body to address the profound human rights concerns in Syria. Its attention to this situation has been sustained: it has adopted strong resolutions, created a Country Rapporteur, and a Commission of Inquiry. It has been equally strong in relation to other countries, such as Burundi, Eritrea, and the Democratic People's Republic of Korea. The Council has continued to establish country-specific special procedures mandates. It has also adopted resolutions to support countries, encouraging accountability measures through technical assistance, as well as facilitating cooperation and capacity-building.

The Council has made progress on thematic issues also. The UN's first resolution on human rights, sexual orientation, and gender identity was adopted by the Council in July 2011,[89] and it created an Independent Expert on protection against violence and discrimination based on sexual orientation and gender identity in 2016.[90] Progress has been made on women's rights, the safety of journalists, human rights and climate change, and the rights of persons with disabilities. In March 2011, the Council adopted, by consensus, a ground-breaking resolution on freedom of religion or belief, which dropped references to 'defamation of religions' and provides a comprehensive road map for coordinated national and international efforts to ensure that freedom of religion or belief is not undermined.[91] It has been swift to adopt new human rights instruments, such as the International Convention for the Protection of all Persons from Enforced Disappearance, the Optional Protocol to the ICESCR, and the third Optional Protocol to the Convention on the Rights of the Child.

The Council has sought to achieve universal participation of states in its deliberations through the Voluntary Trust Fund to support the participation of Least Developed Countries and Small Island Developing States. However, the Council's workload often results in three or four three-hour meetings daily. This has significant resource implications. It also compromises the capacity of delegations, especially those which are small, to engage meaningfully with the work of the Council. Established practices for the participation of NGOs in the work of the Council have been maintained and the role of NHRIs strengthened. The Council has also grappled with concerns relating to shrinking civil society space in relation to its work and generally. Thousands of NGO representatives participate at each session, whilst hundreds of side events are convened by states and civil society. The Council's presidency and bureau have been assiduous in addressing reprisals against, and intimidation of, those who collaborate with the Council or its mechanisms or seek to do so.

Inevitably, differences of opinion exist among the members of the Council. The challenge is to avoid polarization and divisiveness. During 2016, strong divisions appeared in relation to the creation of a special procedure mandate on protection against violence and discrimination based on sexual orientation and gender identity. Following difficult substantive and procedural discussions, involving 11 amendments, the relevant resolution was adopted with 23 members in favour, 18 against, and 6 abstentions.[92] Thereafter, the African Group member of the Consultative Group recused himself from the process of preparing the shortlist of candidates for the mandate.[93] Following the mandate holder's appointment, the Russian Federation and the Organization of Islamic Cooperation (except Albania) made clear that they would not cooperate with the special procedure. This series of events raised the issue of the Council's relationship with the General Assembly. A resolution was tabled in the Third Committee of the General Assembly, on behalf of the African Group, seeking to defer consideration of the resolution creating the Independent Expert despite the fact that the mandate holder had

---

[89] HR Council Res 17/19 (14 July 2011).   [90] HR Council Res 32/2 (30 June 2016).
[91] HR Council Res 17/13 (24 March 2011).   [92] HR Council Res 32/2 (30 June 2016).
[93] Letter of Ambassador HE Mr Amr Ramadan (29 July 2016).

already taken up his functions. The initiative was defeated.[94] The African Group's successive efforts to reintroduce its proposal and deny funding for the mandate were also unsuccessful. At this stage, the mandate and the activities of the mandate holder appear secure. However, the broader issues of the General Assembly's institutional relationship with the Human Rights Council and its prerogative to review the Council's work remain.

In 2013, the General Assembly decided to defer consideration of a Council resolution that called on the Secretary-General to nominate a focal point on reprisals.[95] To date, the General Assembly has not considered the resolution and its status remains unclear. The possibility that challenges to outcomes agreed by the Council being raised at the General Assembly will not be removed unless the Council is established as a principal body of the UN. To do so would contribute significantly to the recognition of human rights as a pillar, along with development and peace and security, of the UN.[96] This will be considered in the next review of the Council's status.[97]

3 THE TREATY-BASED BODIES

When the UDHR was adopted in December 1948, there was broad agreement that the rights it enshrined should be spelled out in treaties that would be binding on those states which ratified, acceded, or succeeded to them. The year 1965 saw the adoption of the International Convention on the Elimination of Racial Discrimination (ICERD) by the General Assembly, while the ICCPR and the ICESCR were adopted in 1966. Since then, a further six 'core' UN human rights treaties have been adopted, as have substantive and procedural protocols, most under the auspices of the Commission on Human Rights and the Human Rights Council. All UN member states have ratified at least one of the core human rights treaties, and the majority has ratified over four. While it is often argued that no further human rights standard-setting activities are required and that new instruments would duplicate rather than complement those which exist, new instruments have been proposed on topics such as the human rights of older persons,[98] the regulation of private military and security companies,[99] and the activities of transnational corporations and other business enterprises.[100]

Where the core human rights treaties are concerned, a body composed of between 10 and 23 independent experts—a 'human rights treaty body'—examines the progress made by states parties in the implementation of the treaty guarantees (see Table 19.1 for an overview of UN treaty bodies). A 25-member treaty body also implements the mandates created by the Optional Protocol to the Convention against Torture. Treaty body experts are elected at biennial meetings of states parties to the instruments on the basis of their expertise in human rights.[101] Although they are nominated by states parties, experts are independent and not subject to instruction from any state. Each expert works *pro-bono* and is not an employee of the UN. The treaty bodies hold two or three regular sessions of two to four weeks' duration per year, in Geneva.

[94] Report of the Third Committee, A/71/479 (5 December 2016).

[95] HR Council Res 24/24 (27 September 2013).

[96] See Rucker, 'Repositioning the Human Rights Council as a principal organ of the UN', *Human Rights Monitor*, 58–59.   [97] GA Res 65/281, para 3.

[98] GA Res 65/182 (21 December 2010).   [99] HR Council Res 15/26 (7 October 2010).

[100] HR Council Res 26/9 (26 June 2014).

[101] The exception is the Committee on Economic, Social and Cultural Rights, established by ECOSOC Res 1985/17 (28 May 1985), whose members are elected by ECOSOC member states. Unlike other treaty bodies, membership is subject to strict regional distribution. The General Assembly has recommended that consideration be given to replacing this procedure with elections by states parties to the ICESCR, while preserving the requirements set out by ECOSOC: GA Res 68/268 (21 April 2014), para 11.

Table 19.1 Overview of the UN treaty bodies

Instrument	Treaty body	Number of states parties
International Convention on the Elimination of Racial Discrimination (ICERD)	Committee on the Elimination of Racial Discrimination (18 members)	178
International Covenant on Civil and Political Rights (ICCPR)	Human Rights Committee (18 members)	169
First Optional Protocol to the ICCPR (ICCPR-OP1)	Human Rights Committee	116
Second Optional Protocol to the ICCPR on the Abolition of the Death Penalty (ICCPR-OP2)	Human Rights Committee	85
International Covenant on Economic, Social and Cultural Rights (ICESCR)	Committee on Economic, Social and Cultural Rights (18 members)	165
Optional Protocol to the ICESCR (ICESCR-OP)	Committee on Economic, Social and Cultural Rights	22
Convention against Torture and Other Forms of Cruel, Inhuman and Degrading Treatment (UNCAT)	Committee against Torture (10 members)	162
Optional Protocol to UNCAT (UNCAT-OP)	Subcommittee on Prevention of Torture (25 members)	84
Convention on the Elimination of All Forms of Discrimination against Women (CEDAW)	Committee on the Elimination of Discrimination against Women (23 members)	189
Optional Protocol to CEDAW (CEDAW-OP)	Committee on the Elimination of Discrimination against Women	109
Convention on the Rights of the Child (CRC)	Committee on the Rights of the Child (18 members)	196
Optional Protocol on Sale of Children, Child Prostitution and Child Pornography	Committee on the Rights of the Child	173
Optional Protocol on Children in Armed Conflict	Committee on the Rights of the Child	167
Optional Protocol to the Convention on the Rights of the Child on a Communications Procedure	Committee on the Rights of the Child	35
International Convention on the Rights of Migrant Workers and their Families (ICRMW)	Committee on the Rights of Migrant Workers (14 members)	51
Convention on the Rights of Persons with Disabilities (CRPD)	Committee on the Rights of Persons with Disabilities (18 members)	175
Optional Protocol to the CRPD (CRPD-OP)	Committee on the Rights of Persons with Disabilities	91
International Convention for the Protection of all Persons from Enforced Disappearance (CPED)	Committee on Enforced Disappearances (10 members)	57

Each treaty body overseeing a core treaty is invested with various tools to assist states parties' implementation of their treaty obligations. These include: consideration of state reports, the issuance of general comments, the conduct of inquiries, and individual communication procedures.[102]

3.1 STATE REPORTING

States parties to each core UN human rights treaty undertake to report regularly on their implementation of the treaty.[103] Initial reports must generally be submitted to the relevant treaty body within one year of the treaty entering into force for the state concerned. Thereafter, periodic reports[104] are due in accordance with the provisions of the treaty or the established practice of the treaty body concerned; periodicity varies from two to five years.

All treaty bodies have issued detailed reporting guidelines on the form and content of initial and periodic reports.[105] In general, states are to submit a 'Treaty Specific Document' setting out the legal, administrative, and judicial measures taken to give effect to the treaty provisions and any difficulties encountered in implementing the rights. States are also to submit a 'Common Core Document' to all the treaty bodies to which they report, which sets out the general domestic legal and constitutional framework for the protection of human rights and information on implementation of substantive treaty provisions which are common to all, or several, treaties.[106]

State reports are prepared at the national level, usually under the direction of a lead ministry or an inter-ministerial committee. As noted in relation to UPR, the UN High Commissioner for Human Rights encourages systematization of the preparation of reports through the establishment of a national reporting and coordination mechanism to facilitate national consultations and follow-up.[107] Preparation of the report offers states parties the opportunity to undertake a comprehensive review of measures they have taken to harmonize national laws and policies with provisions of the relevant international human rights instrument; monitor the progress made in the enjoyment of the rights in the treaties; identify shortcomings and problems with the domestic implementation; and evaluate future needs. Reporting guidelines urge states to provide concrete examples of treaty implementation, and not focus exclusively on the constitutional and legal framework.

Once submitted, the report is translated into the three working languages of the committee concerned and scheduled for examination. There is usually a delay in the consideration of the report as most treaty bodies have many reports awaiting examination.[108] Normally one or two sessions prior to the session at which it will consider the state report, the treaty

---

[102] GA Res 68/268.

[103] See OHCHR Report on the working methods of the human rights treaty bodies relating to the state party reporting process, HRI/ICM/2011/4 (23 May 2011).

[104] CPED, Art 29 only requires a report on implementation two years after the entry into force for the state concerned. However, the Committee on the Rights of Persons with Disabilities may request further information on implementation.

[105] These can be found on the webpages of each treaty body at: <http://www.ohchr.org>. See Compilation of Guidelines on the Form and Content of Reports to be Submitted by States Parties to the International Human Rights Treaties, HRI/GEN/2/Rev.6 (3 June 2009).

[106] States are encouraged to review their common core documents as appropriate: GA Res 68/268, para 3; Report of the Chairs of the human rights treaty bodies on their twenty-eight meeting, A/71/270 (2 August 2016) para 91.

[107] eg, OHCHR, *National Mechanisms for Reporting and Follow-up: A Practical Guide to Effective State Engagement with International Human Rights Mechanisms*, HR/PUB/16/1 (2016); OHCHR, *National Mechanisms for Reporting and Follow-up: Study of State Engagement with International Human Rights Mechanisms*, HR/PUB/16/1/Add.1 (2016).

[108] See Status of the Human Rights Treaty Body System, A/71/118 (18 July 2016) paras 29–35 and Annex VIII, for an indication of the backlog of reports awaiting review on 31 December 2015.

body will adopt a 'list of issues' based on all available information, including that provided by entities other than the state such as NGOs and NHRIs, which is sent to the state party. In replying to this list, the state party may update the information contained in its report or provide additional information. In 2007, the Committee against Torture adopted an optional reporting procedure, whereby if the state agrees, the Committee prepares lists of issues *prior* to the submission of the state report that are based on all available information, and the response, together with the common core document, constitutes the state's periodic report. The General Assembly has encouraged the treaty bodies to offer this 'simplified reporting procedure' to states parties.[109] All treaty bodies now invite states to use this approach with respect to *periodic* reports, and the Committee on the Elimination of Racial Discrimination and the Committee against Torture offer this option to states with long overdue *initial* reports.[110]

Consideration of reports takes place in public session, in the presence of a delegation of the state party. To date, at least one state party has appeared before a committee using video-conferencing facilities. Treaty body members aim to engage the delegation in a constructive dialogue on how the guarantees in the relevant instrument can be respected better. After the public consideration, treaty bodies adopt 'concluding observations'. These identify progress in implementation since the last report and remaining concerns. Each concern is matched by a specific recommendation or practical advice designed to give the state suggestions on further steps to improve implementation. There is a clear correlation between the substance of the treaty body–state dialogue and the substance and specificity of the recommendations in concluding observations, which should be short, targeted, specific, pragmatic, and as implementable as possible, so that the state party may follow-up.[111]

All the treaty bodies with the competence to review state reports require information on implementation of previous recommendations in the next periodic report, and most assess the progress made by the state party against the concerns and recommendations they have identified. The Human Rights Committee, the Committee against Torture, the Committee on the Elimination of Racial Discrimination, the Committee on the Elimination of Discrimination against Women, the Committee on the Rights of Persons with Disabilities, and the Committee on Enforced Disappearances have developed procedures for follow-up to their concluding observations. These committees generally invite states to report back within one or two years on all follow-up action. Most have appointed a Special Rapporteur(s) or Coordinator(s) for follow-up who is/are in regular contact with states parties. Where follow-up information is deficient or not forthcoming despite reminders, this mechanism can organize meetings with government representatives to survey possible follow-up action and urge the state party to implement the committee's recommendations. Some of the treaty bodies that have developed follow-up procedures grade states on progress made and most report on the status of follow-up in a chapter of their annual reports to the General Assembly and on their webpages.

An important feature of the reporting process is the contribution that various stakeholders make. All treaty bodies have emphasized the importance of cooperation with NGOs, whether national or international, and the positive role NGOs can play at the domestic level in follow-up activities. In addition, most treaty bodies have instituted formal

---

[109] GA Res 68/268, para 1.

[110] Status of Human Rights Treaty Body System, Annex XIV. The advantages of the simplified reporting procedure are outlined in: Simplified Reporting Procedure, HRI/MC/2014/4 (14 April 2014).

[111] See GA Res 68/268, para 6. See also Report of the Chairs of the human rights treaty bodies on their twenty-sixth meeting, A/69/285 (11 August 2014) Annex II.

mechanisms for consultations with NGOs.[112] NGOs often submit 'alternative', 'parallel', or 'shadow' reports to treaty bodies, which analyse and often challenge the content of the state party's report. Many treaty body members rely on NGO information when preparing their dialogue with the state party, or during the questioning of state delegations. Treaty bodies also receive information from NHRIs, and some have adopted guidelines for these institutions.[113] Specialized agencies and other entities of the UN system, including UN Country Teams (UNCTs), also provide information.

Reporting to the treaty bodies can be a challenge for states parties, particularly those that have ratified most or all of the core instruments. Many states face a serious reporting backlog. The reports of some states are more than a decade overdue, and some may have never submitted a report.[114] This has prompted the treaty bodies to coordinate and streamline their procedures and discuss options for reform. States that experience difficulties with the reporting procedures may solicit technical assistance from the OHCHR, which has conducted many reporting workshops for states often in partnership with other organizations and/or NGOs.

Where states fail to submit reports despite repeated reminders, the relevant treaty body may initiate a process, sometimes referred to as the 'review procedure', for consideration of the state's implementation efforts in the absence of a report. The state party is notified of the intention of the treaty body to proceed with a review in the absence of a report. Should the state party submit a report at this time, or indicate that one will be submitted, the review procedure is suspended. Where no such response is received, the treaty body may formulate a list of issues and questions for the state party and invite a state delegation to attend a nominated session. Concluding observations are formulated on the basis of the dialogue with the state party and other information. Although states are actively encouraged to send a delegation, where no response is received the review will proceed in the absence of the state party. Examination of the state's performance by the treaty body takes place in public session on the basis of existing information from relevant stakeholders and the concluding observations adopted are communicated to the state concerned. The review procedure is used in exceptional cases only, although since October 2010 the Human Rights Committee has examined at least one state party per session in this way. In most cases, notification by a committee that it intends to consider a state in the absence of a report results in the state agreeing to present the overdue report within an agreed deadline.

3.2 GENERAL COMMENTS

All treaty bodies, with the exception of the Sub-Committee for the Prevention of Torture, issue 'general comments'. In the case of the Committee on the Elimination of Racial Discrimination and the Committee on the Elimination of Discrimination against Women these are termed 'general recommendations'. These documents are to be adopted through a consultative and transparent process.[115] The comments or recommendations, which may

---

[112] See *Working with the United Nations Human Rights Programme: A Handbook for Civil Society* (2008), available at: <http://www.ohchr.org/EN/AboutUs/Pages/CivilSociety.aspx>.

[113] See 'Engagement of NHRIs with the UN Human Rights Treaty Bodies: An Overview of Procedures and Practices' (May 2016), available at: <http://www.ohchr.org/EN/HRBodies/AnnualMeeting/Pages/MeetingChairpersons.aspx>

[114] See Status of Human Rights Treaty Body System, Annex II for information on reporting compliance. See also: Timely, late and non-reporting by States parties to the human rights treaty bodies, HRI/MC/2016/2 (22 March 2016).

[115] Report of the Chairs of the human rights treaty bodies on their twenty-seventh meeting, A/70/302 (7 August 2015) para 91.

be formulated jointly by one or more committees,[116] are adopted by consensus and provide authoritative guidance on the general treaty obligations of states parties or set out how the treaty body interprets the scope of the substantive provisions of their treaty. Thus, they offer helpful interpretative guidance to states and other stakeholders. General comments and recommendations frequently deal with wider thematic or cross-cutting issues, such as the role of NHRIs, the obligations of states during states of emergency, violence against women, or gender-related dimensions of racial discrimination. While not legally binding, these comments are often invoked by states and complainants in reporting and complaints procedures, and, increasingly, by international, regional, and national courts in their judgments.[117]

3.3 INQUIRIES

The Committee against Torture, the Committee on the Elimination of Discrimination against Women, the Committee on Economic, Social and Cultural Rights, the Committee on the Rights of Persons with Disabilities, and the Committee on the Rights of the Child may initiate inquiries upon receipt of reliable, well-founded indications of serious, grave, or systematic violations of the respective conventions by a state party. Inquiries may only be conducted in relation to states that have recognized the competence of the relevant committee to conduct them. The inquiry procedures are confidential and the cooperation of the state party is required throughout. Once a state has consented to an inquiry, the relevant committee may urgently designate one or several members to undertake a confidential inquiry and report back. Where this is warranted and the state consents, this may include a visit to the state. The findings of the members are examined by the whole committee and transmitted to the state party with appropriate recommendations. Confidentiality is the hallmark of the inquiry procedure, but findings are usually disclosed in some form after dialogue with the state party at the end of each inquiry. The Committee against Torture has conducted inquiries on Brazil, Egypt, Lebanon, Mexico, Nepal, Peru, Sri Lanka, Turkey, and the former Yugoslavia; the Committee on the Elimination of Discrimination against Women has conducted inquiries on Canada, Mexico, and the Philippines; and the Committee on the Rights of Persons with Disabilities has conducted an inquiry on the UK.

A similar inquiry procedure is created by Article 33 CPED, which allows the Committee on Enforced Disappearance to request that one or more of its members visit a state party where it receives reliable information indicating a serious violation of the Convention. States parties do not have to have recognized the competence of the Committee for it to request a visit, although consultation with the state and agreement are required before the visit, as is collaboration in respect of its modalities and conduct. In addition to the inquiry procedure, the Committee has two other innovative methods of dealing with urgent or severe violations of the CPED. First, it may request urgent action that a disappeared person be sought and found. By March 2017, 368 urgent actions had been registered. Second, having sought information from the state concerned, the Committee may bring

---

[116] eg, Joint General Recommendation 31 of the Committee on the Elimination of Discrimination against Women/General Comment 18 of the Committee on the Rights of the Child on harmful practices, CEDAW/C/GC/31-CRC/C/GC/18 (14 November 2014).

[117] eg, *Advisory Opinion relating to the Administrative Tribunal of the International Labour Organization on a complaint filed against the International Fund for Agricultural Development* [2012] ICJ Rep 10; *Case Concerning Ahmadou Sadio Diallo (Republic of Guinea v Democratic Republic of Congo)* [2010] ICJ Rep 639; *Secretary of Security v Sakthevel Prabakar* [2005] 1 HKLRD 289 (Hong Kong Court of Final Appeal); *Vishaka v State of Rajasthan* (1997) 6 SCC 241 (Supreme Court of India).

well-founded indications that enforced disappearance is being practised on a widespread or systematic basis by a state party to the attention of the General Assembly through the Secretary-General.[118]

The UNCAT-OP creates a novel preventative inquiry mechanism. It establishes a system of complementary regular visits to places of detention conducted by both independent international and national bodies. UNCAT-OP's two-pillar approach relies on an international body, the Subcommittee on Prevention of Torture, and 'national preventive mechanisms' (NPMs)—national bodies which must be established by each state party within one year of entry into force of the UNCAT-OP for the relevant state. NPMs should have unrestricted access to all places of detention and all relevant information about the treatment and conditions of detention of individuals deprived of liberty. In order to discharge its mandate to advise states on national mechanisms and supervise their work, the Subcommittee should have the same level of unrestricted access as the NPMs. Since the beginning of its activities in 2007, the Subcommittee has conducted over 50 visits, including regular visits to states parties, follow-up visits, and visits to advise NPMs.

3.4 COMPLAINTS PROCEDURES

The ability to claim that human rights have been violated is an important part of the protection mechanisms of the UN human rights treaties. The ICCPR-OP1, ICESCR-OP, UNCAT, ICERD, ICRMW, CPED, and CRC-OP3 provide for a state party to complain to the relevant treaty body that another state party is not fulfilling its treaty obligations where both states concerned have accepted this competence.[119] These are known as inter-state complaints mechanisms. To date there have been no inter-state complaints to treaty bodies. Instead, attention has been focused on mechanisms for individuals to complain that their rights under a particular treaty have been violated by a state party.

All but one of the treaty bodies that support the core treaties implement optional individual complaints procedures. These procedures allow individuals to complain that a state party has violated its obligations under the relevant treaty or substantive protocols to that treaty. As these are optional mechanisms, states must accept the competence of the relevant committee to receive individual complaints. Only the Committee on Migrant Workers cannot yet receive such communications. The ICRMW provides for such a procedure, but it has not been accepted by the required number of states for the Committee to start receiving communications.[120]

The procedure for the examination of individual complaints is generally characterized as 'quasi-judicial'. It is written and confidential; oral hearings are rare. Complaints are pre-screened as to their compatibility with the provisions of the relevant treaty and fulfilment of basic admissibility requirements by the OHCHR. Complainants do not need to be supported by legal representation, but this is advisable; however there is no UN system of legal aid to help with this. Complaints may be brought by third parties on behalf of individuals provided they have given their written consent or are unable to do so.

A treaty body member designated as Special Rapporteur for New Communications, or a Working Group, decides on the registration of complaints and issues instructions on how to proceed with new cases. Once formally registered, the complaint is normally transmitted to the respondent state party for observations. Deadlines for observations vary, but

---

[118] CPED, Arts 30 and 34.
[119] ICCPR, Art 41; ICESCR-OP, Art 10; UNCAT, Art 21; ICERD, Arts 12–13, ICRMW, Art 76; CPED, Art 32; CRC-OP3, Art 12.
[120] 10 acceptances are required before this procedure can start functioning; see ICRMW, Art 77(8).

states generally have six months to submit observations on both the admissibility and merits of a communication. As the treaty bodies are careful to apply the principle of equality of arms, the state party's observations are sent to the complainant for comments. If a state party fails to respond to a complaint, the relevant treaty body usually bases its assessment of the situation on the facts as submitted by the complainant, provided they are properly substantiated. A state party may request that the treaty body examine the admissibility of the communication separately from the merits should it believe that the communication is inadmissible. The state must set out the reasons for its view. In such circumstances the complainant is given the opportunity to respond to the claims of inadmissibility and it is then for the treaty body to decide whether to consider the admissibility and merits of the communication separately.

Treaty bodies may issue interim measures of protection in situations of particular urgency, which require immediate action to prevent irreparable harm to the complainant. These are often issued in death penalty, life-threatening, and deportation or extradition cases.[121] The vast majority of states parties complies with such requests. The Human Rights Committee and the Committee against Torture also issue requests for 'provisional measures of protection'. Such requests differ from interim measures as they indicate explicitly that they may be reviewed, at the request of the state, in light of information and comments received from it and further comments, if any, from the complainant. Treaty bodies regard compliance with interim measures requests as inherent in a state party's treaty obligations and any failure to comply with them a serious breach thereof.[122]

Decisions on admissibility are adopted either at the level of the Committee plenary or by a working group. The Committees examine a number of admissibility criteria.[123] First, the complainant must show that he or she is a 'victim' of a violation of provisions of the instrument he or she invokes. The complainant must be personally affected by the impugned state action. General claims by groups or an individual not affected by the alleged violation ('actio popularis') are not permissible.

Second, the complaint must relate to events which occurred *after* the entry into force of the complaint mechanism for the state party concerned (admissibility *ratione temporis*), unless these produce effects after the entry into force which constitute a violation of the relevant treaty.

Third, the complaint must relate to rights that are actually protected by the instrument invoked by the complainant (admissibility *ratione materiae*).

Fourth, the same matter must not have been examined by the treaty body concerned or by another international investigation or settlement procedure, such as the European Court of Human Rights, the Inter-American Court of Human Rights, or the African Commission on Human and Peoples' Rights, or be undergoing examination by such a procedure. In regard to ICCPR-OP1 and CPED, only those cases that are being examined by such a procedure *at the same time* as the communication to the UN treaty body will be excluded. Most European states parties have entered a reservation to the ICCPR-OP1 to the effect that once the European Court of Human Rights has disposed of a complaint, it cannot subsequently be considered by the Human Rights Committee.[124]

---

[121] HRC, Rules of Procedure, Rule 92; CAT, Rules of Procedure, Rule 108(1); CERD, Rules of Procedure, Rule 94(3). Explicit powers to request interim measures are included in the CEDAW-OP, CRPD-OP, CPED, ICESCR-OP, and CRC-OP3.

[122] eg, *Piandiong v The Philippines*, CCPR/C/70/D/869/1999 (19 October 2000) para 5.2.

[123] These admissibility criteria are set out in the ICCPR-OP1; CERD, Art 14; UNCAT, Art 22; CEDAW-OP; CPRD-OP; CPED, Art 31; CRC-OP3, Art 7; ICESCR-OP, Art.3.

[124] See Phuong, 'The Relationship Between the European Court of Human Rights and the Human Rights Committee: Has the "Same Matter" Already Been "Examined"?' (2007) 7 *HRLR* 385.

Fifth, the complainant must have exhausted all available domestic remedies. This means that, in principle, the highest court of the state party concerned must have considered and dismissed the case before a treaty body may consider it. The rule does not apply if the pursuit of domestic remedies has been 'unreasonably prolonged'. This is an assessment that must be made on a case-by-case basis. Such remedies must not only be available but also *effective*, thereby offering a reasonable prospect of actual redress.

Complaints that do not fulfil these criteria will be declared inadmissible and such decisions are final.[125] Those complaints declared admissible are referred to the state party for observations on the merits, if such observations have not already been given. Once provided and the complainant has been given a reasonable opportunity to comment on these observations, or the deadline for submission has expired, the treaty body will examine the merits of the case.

The CESCR-OP and CRC-OP3 provide that their respective committees shall make available their good offices to the parties with a view to reaching a friendly settlement of the matter of the communication. An agreement on a friendly settlement terminates consideration of the communication.

Treaty bodies generally adopt decisions on complaints—called 'views' or 'opinions'—by consensus. The decisions include measures to be taken by the state if a violation is found. Often those experts who do not share the opinion of the majority append individual (dissenting or concurring) opinions to the final decisions. This does not in any way undermine the authority of the decision.

One, if not the principal, weakness of the treaty body complaints procedures is that the final merits decisions are not strictly speaking legally binding and thus cannot be enforced. However, in its General Comment 33, the Human Rights Committee stated that although its views are non-binding they 'exhibit some important characteristics of a judicial decision'.[126] Furthermore, the Committee stated that its views are an authoritative interpretation of the ICCPR by a body entrusted by states parties to give such interpretations, and, as such, the principle of good faith to treaty obligations requires that states cooperate with the Committee and inform it of action taken to implement its views. In order to strengthen the legal value of their decisions, the treaty bodies have Special Rapporteurs mandated to consider state follow-up on views. These Rapporteurs monitor how states parties respond to the recommendations for a remedy and other measures to be taken following the finding of a violation. It is normally expected that states will submit follow-up information within a few months of a decision. The Special Rapporteurs are in regular contact with states parties and the annual reports of the treaty bodies to the General Assembly include a chapter in which state party follow-up to views is detailed. All follow-up information provided by the parties to a case is, in principle, public.[127]

It is difficult to categorize state party follow-up. Many states parties pay compensation to victims, even though some observe they do so not as a matter of legal obligation but *ex gratia*. Others have released individuals detained or imprisoned arbitrarily, or commuted death sentences. Others either do not provide follow-up information or challenge the findings of the treaty body concerned. 'Enabling legislation'—that is, legislation that makes decisions of treaty bodies enforceable at the national level—is rare. However, the fact that all treaty bodies which decide complaints have instituted and largely synchronized follow-up mechanisms has improved the level of compliance with recommendations.

---

[125] ICESCR-OP provides that the CESCR may decline to consider a communication if it does not reveal that the alleged victim has suffered a 'clear disadvantage', unless the Committee considers that the communication raises a serious issue of general importance.

[126] HRC, General Comment 33, CCPR/C/GC/33 (5 November 2008) para 11.

[127] Follow-up to Decisions, HRI/ICM/2009/7 (11 November 2009) para 5.

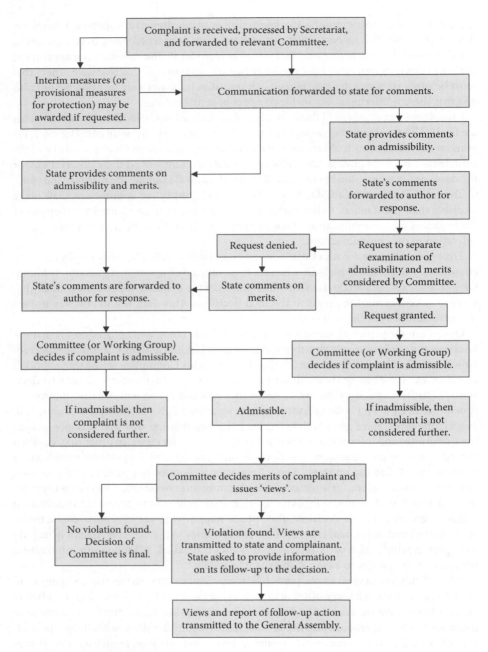

Figure 19.1 Individual complaints procedures

For many years, the treaty bodies developed their jurisprudence under the complaints procedures in what could be called 'splendid isolation' from that of regional human rights mechanisms or national tribunals. This raised the spectre of conflicting interpretations of substantively very similar, if not identical, provisions of international or regional human rights instruments. One such example is the different treatment of the 'death row phenomenon' under the ICCPR and the European Convention on Human Rights by the Human

Rights Committee and the European Court of Human Rights.[128] More recently, comparative analyses of jurisprudence prepared by the OHCHR have helped treaty bodies to keep abreast of relevant developments in regional and national tribunals. This has led to a welcome 'cross-fertilization' of human rights jurisprudence. The treaty bodies now take into account the relevant jurisprudence of regional courts and national tribunals when seized of complex or novel legal issues. Conversely, the regional mechanisms (for example, the European Court of Human Rights and the Inter-American Court of Human Rights)[129] and some national tribunals now regularly rely on, or cite, treaty body jurisprudence. This contributes to the emergence of substantively consistent and truly universal human rights jurisprudence.

3.5 TREATY BODY COORDINATION, HARMONIZATION, REFORM, AND STRENGTHENING

The treaty bodies have continuously sought to improve their effectiveness by streamlining and harmonizing their working methods and practices. Even so, differences remain in areas such as the treatment of NGO information, the preparation of lists of issues, or the procedure for the examination of reports. Many states parties complain of such procedural differences and urge further harmonization.

The treaty body chairpersons assemble annually, usually in Geneva, to discuss issues of common concern, working methods, common approaches to thematic issues, and so on, with a view to enhancing the effectiveness of the treaty body system as a whole. These meetings have also been held in Brussels, Addis Ababa, New York, and Costa Rica in order to bring the treaty bodies closer to the site of implementation and strengthen links among international and regional mechanisms and institutions and stakeholders.

Harmonization of the human rights treaty body system has been an issue since the first meeting of chairpersons over 30 years ago. It has been the subject of many UN reports, as well as academic commentary, and gained greater prominence as the number of treaty bodies has grown and the number of states party to the treaties has increased, leading to an over-stretched system. In 2002, the UN Secretary-General identified modernization of the UN treaty system as a crucial element in the UN goal to promote and protect human rights. He called on the treaty bodies to craft a more coordinated approach to their activities by standardizing their reporting requirements and allowing states parties to produce a *single report* summarizing their compliance with the full range of treaties to which they are a party.[130] The idea of a single report did not gain favour with the treaty bodies and other stakeholders, but the treaty bodies were amenable to standardizing their reporting requirements. In 2005, Louise Arbour, then the High Commissioner for Human Rights made a far-reaching proposal for treaty body reform when she called for discussions on proposals for a unified treaty system and the replacement of the existing treaty bodies by a single, unified, standing treaty body.[131] The OHCHR prepared a detailed concept paper,

---

[128] Compare *Soering v UK* (1989) 11 EHRR 439 and *Barrett and Sutcliffe v Jamaica*, CCPR/C/44/D/270 and 271/1998 (30 March 1992).

[129] eg *González (Claudia) et al.* ('Cotton Field') v Mexico, IACtHR Series C No 205 (16 November 2009); *Opuz v Turkey* (2010) 50 EHRR 28.

[130] Strengthening of the United Nations: An Agenda for Further Change, A/57/387 (9 September 2002) paras 52–4.

[131] Plan of Action submitted by the High Commissioner for Human Rights. Annex to 'In Larger Freedom: Towards Development, Security and Human Rights for All', Report of the Secretary-General, A/59/2005/Add.3 (26 May 2006).

which was discussed widely.[132] A majority of stakeholders—many states parties, most treaty bodies and experts, and numerous NGOs—was wary of the proposal. Many pointed out that the establishment of such a body would jeopardize and eventually undermine the specificity of the core human rights instruments and their respective treaty bodies. Others considered that the creation of a single body merging all treaty body activities was premature and politically unrealistic, but that some form of unification, such as a single body for examination of complaints, might be feasible.

Successive High Commissioners have not pursued this proposal. In 2009, the High Commissioner Navi Pillay launched a process of reflection on ways to strengthen the treaty body system based on the premise that the legal parameters of the treaties should not be altered. Around 20 consultations involving states, treaty body experts, UN entities, NHRIs, academics, and civil society were organized by OHCHR. Whilst there was broad support for this multi-stakeholder process, in 2011 some states expressed the view that states must play the primary role in any discussions relating to the treaty body system. As a result, in early 2012, the General Assembly adopted a resolution requesting its President to launch an inter-governmental process on strengthening and enhancing the effective functioning of the human rights treaty body system.[133] In June 2012, the High Commissioner published a report setting out her vision for the future of the system.[134] In July 2012, the intergovernmental process was initiated, culminating in April 2014 with the adoption of General Assembly Resolution 68/268 on strengthening and enhancing the effective functioning of the human rights treaty body system.[135]

General Assembly Resolution 68/268 is long and detailed. It reaffirms the independence of the treaty bodies and their members, whilst encouraging the treaty bodies to align their methodology and harmonize their working methods. However, in this process attention must be paid to the views of states and no new obligations for states should be created. To this end, the treaty bodies are encouraged to enhance the role of their chairpersons in relation to procedural matters. Strengthened interaction between states parties and the chairpersons during their annual meetings is encouraged so that these meetings constitute a forum where all issues, including those related to the independence and impartiality of treaty bodies, can be raised constructively. Strategies for enhancing efficiency are promoted. These include: combining overdue reports to eliminate the backlog of outstanding reporting obligations; establishing word limits for documents produced by states parties, other stakeholders, and the treaty bodies themselves; and limiting treaty body working languages and translation of summary records. In order to enhance accessibility and visibility of the treaty bodies, they are encouraged to webcast their public meetings and the Secretary-General is requested to make the system accessible to persons with disabilities to ensure their full and effective participation. To enable wider participation in the state reporting process, the OHCHR is requested to facilitate via videoconferencing the participation of members of its delegations not present in Geneva. States are encouraged to provide voluntary funds to facilitate the engagement of states parties, particularly those without representation in Geneva, with the treaty body system. Recommendations are

---

[132] Concept Paper on the High Commissioner's Proposal for a Unified Standing Treaty Body, HRI/MC/2006/CRP.1 (14 March 2006).

[133] GA Res 66/254 (23 February 2012). The resolution was introduced by Russia and adopted with 85 states voting in favour, none against, and 66 abstaining.

[134] UN Reform: Measures and Proposals, A/66/960 (26 June 2012).

[135] GA Res 68/268. See Broecker and O'Flaherty, 'The Outcome of the General Assembly's Treaty Body Strengthening Process: An Important Milestone on a Longer Journey', Universal Rights Group Policy Brief (June 2014).

made to sustain and strengthen the independence and impartiality of treaty body members, and all acts of intimidation and reprisals against individuals and groups contributing to the work of human rights treaty bodies are condemned. At the heart of the resolution, however, is the increased meeting time allocated to the human rights treaty bodies, determined on the basis of a formula based on their workload in 2014, to be reviewed biennially. This is mirrored by a capacity-building programme, including the deployment of dedicated officers in the OHCHR's regional offices, designed to support states parties to implement their treaty obligations.

Full implementation of General Assembly Resolution 68/268 began on 1 January 2015. The Secretary-General is to report on progress made to the General Assembly on a biennial basis. The General Assembly will review the state of the human rights treaty body system in 2020, including the measures taken in line with Resolution 68/268 to ensure their sustainability, and, if appropriate, to decide on further action to strengthen and enhance the effective functioning of the system.

3.6 CONCLUSION

The activities of the human rights treaty bodies have developed greatly in terms of scope and sophistication. The reporting procedures are being increasingly harmonized to assist states parties with multiple reporting obligations, whilst the quality, specificity, and usability of concluding observations has gradually improved, making it possible for states parties to follow-up on recommendations meaningfully. Follow-up procedures have helped to keep those states parties that display little or no political will to implement treaty body recommendations engaged. In terms of individual complaints, the jurisprudence emanating from such procedures has improved substantively and qualitatively over the years. A very positive development has been the increasing 'cross fertilization' of human rights jurisprudence. Follow-up to decisions of the treaty bodies has also improved, with increasing numbers of states granting appropriate remedies following a finding of a violation.

Despite these achievements, the treaty bodies must continue to respond to the challenges they face. First, the state reporting procedures must be harmonized further and simplified to prompt *all* states parties to meet their reporting obligations and reduce the large number of overdue reports. Second, the backlog of pending individual complaints that apply to some treaty bodies must be reduced. While the quality of decisions has improved, decision-making is slow and cumbersome. There is also scope for distilling good practice in the jurisprudence of treaty bodies regarding remedies.[136] The non-binding nature of treaty body decisions remains a concern. Although it is currently politically unrealistic to call for treaty amendments that would make all final decisions under the treaty-based complaints procedures legally binding and executable, follow-up procedures that strengthen the domestic implementation of decisions should be developed further. Finally, endeavours pursuant to General Assembly Resolution 68/268, and in line with High Commissioner Pillay's report, that aim to create holistic and harmonized functioning of the treaty body system should continue. This is all the more necessary given the likely adoption of new treaties and establishment of attendant mechanisms and the lack of appetite for rationalizing existing treaty bodies.[137]

In the long term, harmonization of working methods and capacity-building of states will not address the challenges posed by the existence of nine human rights treaty bodies

---

[136] See A/71/270, paras 35–37.

[137] eg, pursuant to CPED, Art 27, a Conference of States parties was convened on 19 December 2016 to consider whether to transfer the Committee on Enforced Disappearances' functions to another treaty body. It decided to continue the Committee's operation.

enjoying similar competence, and another exercising a preventive function, whose treaties enjoy wide acceptance. These challenges can be met only if appropriate and realistic financial and human resources are allocated to the system or if it undergoes profound structural change. It is to be hoped that innovative proposals to secure the system's future, which do not weaken its protection for individuals, will emerge during the lead-up to the General Assembly's review of the system in 2020.

4 THE OFFICE OF THE UN HIGH COMMISSIONER FOR HUMAN RIGHTS

From the adoption of the UDHR the international community sought to establish a body within the UN that could support implementation of human rights obligations by countries at the national level and effectively deal with human rights violations. Suggestions for the creation of a UN High Commissioner for Human Rights were advanced as early as 1947 and in the mid-1960s Costa Rica made a concrete proposal, but for political reasons it was dropped.[138]

The 1993 World Conference on Human Rights reactivated discussions about the institution and mandate of a High Commissioner for Human Rights, and called on the General Assembly to 'begin, as a matter of priority, consideration of the question of the establishment of a High Commissioner for Human Rights'.[139] The General Assembly reacted swiftly, establishing a working group on the issue, and, on 20 December 1993, General Assembly Resolution 48/141, which created the post of High Commissioner for Human Rights and set out its mandate, was adopted without a vote. The High Commissioner is appointed by the Secretary-General and approved by the General Assembly, and serves for a four year term, which is renewable once. The first UN High Commissioner for Human Rights, José Ayala Lasso from Ecuador, took office in April 1994. Since then there have been five High Commissioners.[140]

The High Commissioner has the responsibility of promoting and protecting the effective enjoyment by all of all human rights. In order to carry out this mandate, he or she is to liaise with competent UN bodies and issue recommendations on how to improve promotion and protection of human rights, as well as rationalize and strengthen the UN human rights machinery. The High Commissioner should also coordinate UN education and public human rights information programmes. States should be helped to realize their human rights obligations by providing advisory, technical, and financial services, and engaging governments in dialogue aimed at improving human rights protection. As well as enhancing international cooperation for the promotion of human rights, the High Commissioner should play an active role in removing current obstacles to the full realization of all human rights and in preventing the continuation of human rights violations throughout the world. Finally, the High Commissioner is to promote the realization of the right to development. The High Commissioner reports annually to the Human Rights Council and the General Assembly on his or her activities and those of his or her office—the OHCHR.

The High Commissioner's extensive mandate is fulfilled through the OHCHR, which is a department of the UN Secretariat. The OHCHR has developed greatly in terms of the

---

[138] Clapham, 'Creating the High Commissioner for Human Rights: The Outside Story' (1994) 5 *EJIL* 556.

[139] VDPA, para 18.

[140] Mary Robinson (Ireland); Sergio Vieira de Mello (Brazil); Louise Arbour (Canada); Navanethem Pillay (South Africa); Zeid Ra'ad al Hussein (Jordan). Bertrand G. Ramcharan (Guyana) was Acting High Commissioner from August 2003 to June 2004.

scope of its activities, the mandates it supports and services, and the human and financial resources made available to it. The headquarters of the OHCHR are located in Geneva, with an office in New York. In addition, the OHCHR has staff based in around 70 countries as part of regional offices, country offices, human rights components of UN peace operations, and UN country teams.

The work of the OHCHR focuses on three broad areas: human rights standard-setting, human rights monitoring, and supporting human rights implementation at the country level. Within these three areas, it provides expertise and substantive (research and analysis) and technical support to the UN human rights bodies described earlier and contributes to the monitoring of human rights situations and implementation of human rights standards at the national level. More specifically at the national level, the OHCHR provides technical expertise and capacity development on the ground, including in relation to laws, policies, and institutions. It also provides support to NHRIs, civil society, and individuals and groups in their advocacy and efforts to claim their rights, including through human rights education and information. The OHCHR responds to human rights emergencies with rapid deployments, and provides guidance regarding follow-up to UPR, treaty body, and special procedures mandate holders' recommendations. It administers 13 voluntary funds, many of which support the victims of human rights abuses.[141] The OHCHR also supports the High Commissioner in his or her role as the global human rights conscience and advocate. Since 2014, the OHCHR has pursued six thematic priorities in its work, which reflect leading human rights challenges. These are: strengthening human rights mechanisms; enhancing equality and countering discrimination; combating impunity and strengthening accountability and the rule of law; integrating human rights in development and the economic sphere; widening the democratic society space; and early warning and protection of human rights in situations of conflict, violence, and insecurity.[142]

The 1986 UN Declaration on the Right to Development[143] and the 2030 Agenda for Sustainable Development, which is based on the 2015 Sustainable Development Goals (SDGs),[144] have manifold implications for the work of the OHCHR. Development issues cut across much of the work of the OHCHR, and it was keen to ensure that the SDGs were grounded in human rights principles and standards. The OHCHR provides expertise and field support in the areas of the right to development, poverty and aid policy issues, human rights indicators, human trafficking, anti-corruption policies, globalization, and trade. The work programme of the OHCHR in this area is largely defined by reference to decisions of the General Assembly and the Human Rights Council, and the work and recommendations of the latter's Open-Ended Working Group on the Right to Development. The OHCHR provides support to UN country teams and human rights field presences in respect of the SDGs and works on development policy and programming issues under the auspices of the UN Development Group.

Much of the work of the OHCHR now takes place in the field and there has been an identifiable shift of emphasis away from headquarters. The importance of work in the field cannot be underestimated. For example, the genocide in Rwanda in 1994, which had been predicted by NGOs and development agencies on the ground, highlighted the need for the establishment of preventive mechanisms, of which human rights field presences were seen

---

[141] eg the UN Voluntary Fund for the Victims of Torture and the UN Voluntary Trust Fund on Contemporary Forms of Slavery.

[142] OHCHR Management Plan, 2014–2017—Working for your rights, available at: <http://www2.ohchr.org/english/ohchrreport2014_2017/omp_web_version/index.html>.

[143] GA Res 41/128 (4 December 1986).

[144] GA Res 70/1 (25 September 2015). The SDGs supersede the Millennium Development Goals.

as part and parcel. The first High Commissioner made the creation of field presences a priority, and a field office in Rwanda was set up in 1994. Since then the OHCHR has taken numerous policy decisions designed to 'operationalize' its activities and create and strengthen field presences—whether country-specific, regional, or part of peacekeeping missions—throughout the world. By the end of 2016 the OHCHR ran or supported 60 field presences.

The decision to create a field presence is taken in consultation with the relevant government, taking into consideration the domestic human rights situation, security and political considerations, human and financial resources, administrative arrangements, and the scope of activities to be undertaken (whether monitoring and/or technical cooperation activities). The OHCHR country and stand-alone offices are established on the basis of a standard agreement between OHCHR and the host government that delineates the activities of the field presence: generally, human rights observation, technical cooperation activities, and public reporting. However, some field presences are restricted to technical cooperation only. Regional offices and centres are also established on the basis of an agreement with the host governments and in consultation with other countries in the region, and these focus on cross-cutting regional human rights concerns and assisting governments in their interaction with human rights mechanisms. Several regional human rights centres, such as those in Cambodia, Cameroon, and Doha, have been created by the General Assembly, and their mandates are set out in their constituent resolutions. Similarly, where there is a human rights component to a Security Council peacekeeping, special political, or peacebuilding mission, such as in Mali, Libya, and South Sudan, the mandate is governed by the resolution creating the mission. Finally, human rights advisers in UN country teams assist and support the integration of human rights into programming activities, and seek to build the human rights capacity of national stakeholders. Reports on the work of field presences are regularly presented to the Human Rights Council for consideration and possible action.

The variety and complexity of field presences have grown beyond expectation since 1994. While some stand-alone field presences are tiny and closely associated with the local UN country team, other field offices, for example in Cambodia and Colombia, are staffed by numerous human rights officers recruited both internationally and locally. Where larger country offices are actively engaged in monitoring human rights violations and regular reporting thereon, relations with the host state's authorities can become strained. Sometimes the re-negotiation with the relevant government of the agreement for the field presence may become a politically difficult exercise that requires the personal involvement of the High Commissioner.

The 2005 World Summit recognized that human rights, peace and security, and development were the pillars of the UN system, and resolved to strengthen the OHCHR through the doubling of its regular budget resources over five years.[145] Yet only 3.5 per cent of the total UN regular budget is allocated to OHCHR and much of its activities are funded by voluntary contributions. On average, approximately 40 per cent of OHCHR's funding needs are covered by the UN regular budget. The remaining funds are made up of voluntary funding from states and other donors. In general, extra-budgetary resources support work not covered by the regular budget, the majority of which is activities in the field. Voluntary contributions also assist the financing of implementation of mandates established by intergovernmental bodies, as frequently the regular budget allocation for these is insufficient.[146] The dependence on voluntary contributions may be problematic because the OHCHR consistently relies on the contributions of major donors to implement

---

[145] GA Res 60/1 (24 October 2005) para 124.
[146] OHCHR Report 2016, 77–82, available at: <http://www2.ohchr.org/english/OHCHRreport2016/>.

essential activities and, thus, these will be affected in times of economic downturn when there is a funding shortfall. Indeed, such shortfalls have forced the OHCHR to cut posts and activities in the past, and an appeal for funds has been launched annually since 2013. Furthermore, although the High Commissioner strongly encourages unearmarked financing, major donor countries may be tempted to peg sizeable voluntary contributions to achieve some political leverage over the content of programmes, or influence staffing policy. This is a preoccupation voiced by some states, in particular non-donors.[147] However, unless states are prepared to allocate the full resource requirements needed to support the activities of the UN human rights programme, the OHCHR will require voluntary contributions to fund its essential work.

5 HUMAN RIGHTS ACTIVITIES IN OTHER PARTS OF THE UN

In his first report on the renewal of the UN system published in 1997, former Secretary-General Kofi Annan advocated for the integration of human rights into the activities of other UN Departments and specialized agencies.[148] This is known as 'mainstreaming' human rights and much progress has been made. General Assembly Resolution 60/251 tasks the Human Rights Council with an important role in promoting the effective coordination and mainstreaming of human rights within the UN system, and it convenes an annual discussion with heads of UN entities on this theme. Increased integration of human rights standards and principles, including the right to development, into UN system policies relating to development, humanitarian action, peace and security, and economic and social issues is one of the OHCHR's global expected accomplishments, and much of the work of the OHCHR entails provision of guidance, policy advice, and technical support to implement the mainstreaming imperative. In addition, the OHCHR and other relevant UN entities have agreed a policy on human rights in UN peace operations and political missions that provides guidance on how human rights are to be integrated into these activities.

In May 2008, the Secretary-General issued a policy decision reaffirming the centrality of human rights in the development work of the UN. The Human Rights Working Group of the UN Development Group (UNDG), funded through a multi-donor trust fund, was established in response to this.[149] The Working Group is made up of 18 UN agencies, funds, and programmes and is chaired by the OHCHR and a senior representative of another UNDG entity. Its work focuses on three pillars: serving as the primary forum to ensure policy coherence on human rights mainstreaming; supporting the UNDG to make system-wide human rights expertise available to national development actors; and supporting the UN development system in respect of Human Rights up Front (Section 5.3).[150]

The OHCHR provides guidance, policy advice, and technical support in respect of the mainstreaming of human rights. This has influenced the approach of the main UN organs in the area of human rights, including the General Assembly, Security Council (SC), Secretary-General, and International Court of Justice (ICJ). These will be discussed below.

---

[147] JIU/REP/2014/7 (2014). The Secretary-General's response to the report is contained in A/70/68/Add.1.
[148] Renewing the United Nations: A Programme for Reform, A/51/950 (14 July 1997) paras 78 and 79.
[149] See <http://hrbaportal.org/human-rights-mainstreaming-mechanism>.
[150] See: UNDG-Human-Rights-Working-Group-TORs-5Dec2014.pdf, available at: <https://undg.org/>.

5.1 GENERAL ASSEMBLY

The General Assembly, the UN's principal deliberative organ composed of all member states, is regularly seized of human rights issues. Article 13 UN Charter provides that the General Assembly 'shall initiate studies and make recommendations for the purpose of . . . assisting in the realization of human rights and fundamental freedoms for all without distinction as to race, sex, language, or religion'. It is generally the Third Committee of the General Assembly, responsible for social, humanitarian, and cultural issues, which reviews human rights issues. The Third Committee receives and discusses the Human Rights Council's annual report (which is also considered by the General Assembly plenary); reports from the Council's special procedures; the annual report of the High Commissioner for Human Rights; annual reports of the treaty bodies; and reports on human rights issues considered by the Secretary-General. This Committee also negotiates and adopts resolutions on thematic human rights issues and country situations, some of which overlap with those of the Human Rights Council.[151]

The plenary General Assembly adopts human rights-related declarations or resolutions, such as on the right to development,[152] or on the outcome of the Human Rights Council's review of its work and functioning.[153] It formally adopts new instruments in the field of human rights that have been adopted by the Council or other UN bodies. The General Assembly also discusses and endorses the results and outcome documents of international or world conferences dealing with human rights, such as the World Conference against Racism, Racial Discrimination, Xenophobia and Related Intolerance, held in Durban in 2001, and the Durban Review Conference, held in Geneva in 2009. Human rights instruments are also elaborated in ad hoc working groups of the General Assembly, while human rights considerations are also taken up during its High-level Meetings, for example the 2005 World Summit, the 2012 High-level Meeting on the Rule of Law, and the 2016 Summit for Refugees and Migrants. The General Assembly is also able to create commissions of inquiry and other mechanisms which, inter alia, address human rights concerns,[154] as may its special sessions and emergency special sessions. In December 2016, in response to the absence of Security Council action to ensure accountability for international crimes committed in Syria the General Assembly used its powers to establish a mechanism to assist in the investigation and prosecution of those responsible for the most serious crimes under international law committed in that country since March 2011.[155]

5.2 SECURITY COUNCIL

The Security Council, the 15-member UN body with primary responsibility for the maintenance of international peace and security, has increasingly recognized the importance of the enjoyment of human rights for the fulfilment of its mandate.[156] However, although it has often characterized massive human rights violations as threats to international peace and its discussions and resolutions regarding situations

---

[151] Universal Rights Group, 'The Human Rights Council as a Subsidiary Organ: Evaluating its relationships with the General Assembly and UN Security Council' (2016), 5–6.

[152] GA Res 41/128 (4 December 1986).   [153] GA Res 65/281 (17 June 2011).

[154] GA Res 65/281.

[155] GA Res 71/248 (21 December 2016); Implementation of the resolution establishing the International, Impartial and Independent Mechanism to Assist in the Investigation and Prosecution of Persons Responsible for the Most Serious Crimes under International Law Committed in the Syrian Arab Republic since March 2011, A/71/755 (19 January 2017).

[156] Security Council Report, Human Rights and the Security Council—An Evolving Role (January 2016).

in countries or regions, such as Afghanistan, the Democratic People's Republic of Korea, the Democratic Republic of Congo, Haiti, Mali, Myanmar, the Middle East, including the Occupied Palestinian Territories, South Sudan, and Syria, frequently address human rights concerns, its first debate on human rights and prevention of armed conflict did not take place until 18 April 2017.[157] The Security Council also addresses several thematic issues with human rights dimensions. These include women, peace and security,[158] protection of civilians,[159] children and armed conflict,[160] sexual violence in armed conflict,[161] and trafficking in persons in conflict situations.[162] It has established a working group on children and armed conflict, made up of its 15 members, which examines reports of monitoring and reporting mechanisms in countries of concern, makes recommendations, and monitors grave abuses of children that may occur in an armed conflict.[163] The Security Council has created mechanisms which touch on human rights issues. Thus, Security Council Resolution 1888 established a Special Representative of the Secretary-General on sexual violence in conflict who is empowered to report countries suspected to be responsible for such violence to the Security Council.[164] In addition, peacekeeping, or special political and peace-building support missions, increasingly have human rights promotion and protection as part of their mandates. In January 2016 there were 15 human rights components of such missions. The Security Council also conducts missions to the field during which human rights issues may be raised. Finally, it has responded to impunity for massive human rights violations by establishing ad hoc international tribunals for the Former Yugoslavia and Rwanda[165] and exercising its capacity to refer situations to the Prosecutor of the International Criminal Court in respect of Darfur[166] and Libya.[167] Its failure to refer Syria has led some critics to suggest that it fails to use this power consistently. The Security Council may mandate the establishment of commissions of inquiry, and several of these have required investigations into human rights violations.[168]

The High Commissioner for Human Rights and OHCHR senior staff regularly engage in open debates with the Security Council on protection of civilians and in formal meetings or informal consultations on country situations. Under the 'Arria formula',[169] which allows the Security Council to meet informally with non-members of the Council outside the Security Council Consultation Room, members of Human Rights Council commissions of inquiry, special procedures, and human rights components of peace operations have also provided human rights briefings that inform the work of the Security Council or its subsidiary bodies.[170] There is more frequent reference in the Security Council to

---

[157] This was convened by the US presidency: S/PV.7926; The Non-Aligned Movement transmitted a communique to the presidency expressing its concern that the debate represented an attempt by the SC to expand its mandate beyond areas which do not pose a threat to international peace and security: S/2017/335, Annex.

[158] SC Res 1325 (31 October 2000); SC Res 2122 (18 October 2013); SC Res 2242 (13 October 2015).

[159] SC Res 1265 (17 September 1999); SC Res 1674 (28 April 2006); SC Res 1894 (11 November 2009).

[160] S/PRST/1998/18 (29 June 1998).

[161] SC Res 1820 (19 June 2008), SC Res 1888 (30 September 2009); SC Res 1889 (5 October 2009); SC Res 1960 (16 December 2010); SC Res 2106 (24 June 2013); SC Res 2272 (11 March 2016).

[162] SC Res 2331 (20 December 2016).

[163] SC Res 1612 (26 July 2005); SC Res 1882 (4 August 2009).   [164] SC Res 1888.

[165] This Tribunal closed on 31 December 2015; its residual tasks are undertaken by the UN Mechanism for International Criminal Tribunals established by SC Res 1966 (22 December 2010).

[166] SC Res 1593 (31 March 2005).   [167] SC Res 1970 (26 February 2011). See Chapter 26.

[168] Cote d'Ivoire, S/PRST/2004/17 (25 May 2004); Darfur, SC Res 1564 (18 September 2004); Central African Republic, SC Res 2013 (5 December 2013).

[169] Named after former Permanent Representative to the UN of Venezuela and Security Council President, Diego Arria.

[170] Breen, 'Revitalizing the United Nations Human Rights Special Procedures Mechanisms as a Means of Achieving and Maintaining International Peace and Security' (2008) 12 *Max Planck YB of UN Law* 177.

Human Rights Council resolutions or its mechanisms, and vice versa, and the same country situations are sometimes considered by both.[171] Some Human Rights Council resolutions have requested that its reports be transmitted to the Security Council,[172] while such reports have sometimes been provided to it at the written request of particular members.[173]

This increased integration of human rights in the Security Council's work, however, has tended to be *ad hoc*. In order to encourage a more systematic approach, Switzerland launched an appeal on 13 June 2016 to put human rights at the heart of conflict prevention. The appeal, which has been endorsed by 90 states, calls on states to foster and enhance communication and exchanges between the Human Rights Council and the rest of the UN system, and in particular the Security Council.[174] Perhaps this appeal will encourage the Security Council to accelerate its efforts to mainstream human rights.

5.3 SECRETARY-GENERAL

The Secretary-General of the UN is the 'chief administrative officer' of the organization and is appointed by the General Assembly upon the recommendation of the Security Council.[175] The role of the Secretary-General is rather loosely defined in the UN Charter, and each holder of the post has defined their role in different ways. Most importantly, the Secretary-General is to uphold the values and authority of the UN in all his or her work.

The Secretary-General from 1 January 2007 to 31 December 2016, Ban Ki Moon, frequently recalled the 2005 Summit's acknowledgment that peace and security, development, and human rights are the pillars of the UN system and are interlinked and mutually reinforcing. He reaffirmed the central role of human rights in the work of the UN in his Five-year Action Agenda in 2012 and in his final Human Rights Day message underlined the fact that upholding human rights is in the interests of all, as it advances well-being for every individual, stability for every society, and harmony for our interconnected world.

Throughout his tenure, Secretary-General Ban regularly addressed the Human Rights Council and took up a range of human rights concerns, including discrimination and violence against women, reprisals against human rights advocates, the death penalty, and discrimination and violence based on sexual orientation and gender identity in this and other fora.[176] In addition, in 2011, he instituted a human rights due diligence policy, which provides guidance to those UN entities that support non-UN security forces. The policy sets out the measures UN entities must take to exercise 'due diligence' to ensure that UN support is not provided to non-UN security forces where there are substantial grounds for believing there is a real risk that they may commit grave violations of international humanitarian, human rights, or refugee law. The policy also sets out steps to be taken where grave violations are committed by such forces.[177] In 2012, a policy was adopted on human rights screening of UN personnel.[178]

The Secretary-General also routinely focused on human rights violations in country situations. For example, in 2010, with the agreement of the President of Sri Lanka, he

---

[171] Universal Rights Group, 'The Human Rights Council as a Subsidiary Organ: evaluating its relationships with the UN General Assembly and the UN Security Council' (2016), 9–10.

[172] eg HRC Res 28/20 (27 March 2015); HRC Res 30/10 (1 October 2015), in relation to the Commission of Inquiry on Syria.   [173] Security Council Report, 6.

[174] See: <https://www.admin.ch/gov/en/start/documentation/media-releases.msg-id-62152.html>.

[175] UN Charter, Art 97.

[176] Secretary-General Ban Ki-Moon, 'Remarks to the Human Rights Council,' 10 September 2012, available at: <http://www.un.org/apps/news/infocus/sgspeeches/statments_full.asp?statID=1643>.

[177] A/67/775–S/2013/110, Annex.

[178] UN Policy Committee Decision 2012/18, available at: <http://hdl.handle.net/11176/387395>.

established a Panel of Experts to advise him on the issue of accountability with regard to alleged violations of international human rights and humanitarian law during the final stages of the conflict on Sri Lanka. A second Panel was established to consider the response of the UN in this context, which reported to the Secretary-General on 14 November 2012. This Panel highlighted the UN's 'systemic failure' in Sri Lanka.[179] In response, the Secretary-General launched the Human Rights up Front (HRuF) initiative in 2013, and in 2014 issued an internal Human Rights up Front Action Plan, which contains more than 60 actions directed at coordination of early warning and crisis response, exchange of information among UN entities and support for UN country teams.[180] HRuF, described by Secretary-General Ban as a major effort to achieve existing prevention mandates through cultural and operational change and engagement with member states,[181] calls for collective responsibility across the whole UN system to prevent serious human rights violations, identifying risks of human rights violations at an early stage, ensuring that the whole range of UN mandates and mechanisms respond, and that senior officials on the ground are supported and backed by UN Headquarters.[182]

The Secretary-General chairs the UN system Chief Executives Board for Coordination, composed of the Executive Heads of all UN specialized agencies, funds, and programmes as well as of the World Bank, International Monetary Fund, International Atomic Energy Agency, and the World Trade Organization (WTO). The Chief Executives Board regularly discusses human rights issues, as do two of its subsidiary bodies: the High-level Committee on Programmes and the UNDG.

The 'good offices' of the Secretary-General helped address and resolve human rights violations affecting particular individuals or groups. These are reserved for politically sensitive and high visibility cases. Secretary-General Ban appointed special envoys or representatives for such cases, and directed them to broker a solution or compromise. The Secretary-General is also able to designate representatives to address particular themes. For example, in 2016 he announced that Andrew Gilmour, Assistant Secretary-General for Human Rights, would lead UN system efforts to stop intimidation of and reprisals against those cooperating with the UN in the field of human rights.

The ninth Secretary-General, António Guterres, took office on 1 January 2017. When taking the oath of office, he paid tribute to Secretary-General Ban for putting human rights at the heart of the UN's work, and referred to human rights, with sustainable development and peace, as pillars of the UN. He emphasized that it was critical to establish human rights as a fundamental value which should be defended above all, and that civil, political, economic, social, and cultural rights should be enjoyed by all, including minorities of all genders, without discrimination.[183] It remains to be seen how Secretary-General Guterres operationalizes these ideas, but these comments and more recent statements suggest a real commitment to human rights.

---

[179] Secretary-General Ban Ki-Moon, 'Statement on the Internal Review Panel Report on Sri Lanka', 14 November 2012, available at: <https://www.un.org/sg/en/content/ban-ki-moon/human-rights-front-initiative>.

[180] UNDG, 'Rights up Front, detailed Action Plan', January 2014, available at: <https://undg.org/wp-content/uploads/2015/02/Detailed-Plan-of-Action-Rights-up-Front>.

[181] Letter dated 24 December 2015 from the Secretary-General addressed to the President of the General Assembly, A/70/656 (6 January 2016). Other documents can be found at: <http://un.org/sg/en/content/ban-ki-moon/human-rights-up-front-initiative>.

[182] See Kurtz, 'With Courage and Coherence, the Human Rights up Front Initiative of the United Nations', Global Public Policy Paper (July 2015).

[183] 'Secretary-General-designate António Guterres' remarks to the General Assembly on taking the oath of office' (12 December 2016), available at: <https://www.un.org/sg/en/content/sg/speeches/2016-12-12/secretary-general-designate-ant%C3%B3nio-guterres-oath-office-speech>.

5.4 INTERNATIONAL COURT OF JUSTICE

The role of the International Court of Justice, the principal judicial organ of the UN, is to settle legal disputes submitted to it by states and hand down advisory opinions on legal questions referred to it by authorized UN organs and specialized agencies. Individuals cannot bring cases to the Court. Recent judgments and advisory opinions have drawn on the provisions of the principal UN human rights instruments and pronouncements of the UN human rights treaty bodies. Judgments or advisory opinions may clarify the interpretation of provisions of international human rights instruments, or spell out the legal obligations of states under these instruments.[184] Some human rights treaties provide that inter-state disputes relating to the interpretation or application of the treaty concerned may be referred to the ICJ, usually after certain preconditions are fulfilled.[185] One such dispute led the Court to spell out the obligations of states parties to UNCAT to prosecute alleged perpetrators of torture or extradite them to another country with jurisdiction to prosecute.[186] Furthermore, the ICJ has developed an increasingly human rights sensitive jurisprudence.[187] This may be attributable, in part, to the fact that several of the ICJ's judges, past or present, were members of the human rights treaty bodies, special procedures of the Commission on Human Rights, or its Sub-Commission, or judges in regional human rights courts prior to their election to the ICJ.[188]

6 CONCLUSION

The UN human rights protection system has grown in ways that could hardly have been predicted at the time of the adoption of the UDHR. It is now a multi-tiered and sophisticated system with numerous international human rights instruments and monitoring mechanisms, supported by a sizeable and increasingly operational OHCHR.

The growth of the UN human rights protection system has contributed to an improvement in the human rights situation in many countries and many thematic areas. So has the mainstreaming of human rights into other UN programmes, notably UN development, peace, and security activities. The UN's human rights work is now highly visible, particularly as a result of social media. This ensures dissemination of knowledge of international human rights standards and mechanisms. National level implementation of recommendations and decisions of treaty bodies, special procedures, the UPR, and the Human Rights Council improves steadily, even though there remains considerable room for the improvement of existing follow-up mechanisms, coordination amongst them, as well as identification of good practices.

---

[184] eg *Legal Consequences of the Construction of a Wall in the Occupied Palestinian Territory* [2004] ICJ Rep 136; *Ahmadou Sadio Diallo*. See Ghandhi, 'Human Rights and the International Court of Justice: The *Ahmadou Sadio Diallo* Case' (2011) 11 *HRLR* 527.

[185] eg ICERD, Art 22; CEDAW, Art 29; CAT, Art 30; CMW, Art 29; CED, Art 42.

[186] *Questions relating to the Obligation to Prosecute or Extradite (Belgium v Senegal)* [2012] ICJ Rep.

[187] ILA International Human Rights Law Committee Interim Report, 'International Human Rights and the International Court of Justice' (2014), available at: <http://www.ila-hq.org/en/committees/index.cfm/cid/1027>; Rodley, 'The International Court of Justice and Human Rights Treaty Bodies' in Adenas and Bjorge (eds), *Farewell to Fragmentation* (CUP, 2015) 87.

[188] eg Judge Al-Khasawneh, Judge Rosalyn Higgins, Judge Thomas Buergenthal, Judge Bruno Simma, Judge Peter Kooijmans, and Judge Antônio Cançade Trindade.

Regardless of the budgetary constraints facing the UN and its human rights programme, demands for its support are unlikely to decrease, particularly as the Human Rights Council steps up efforts to address critical human rights issues, and other UN bodies, including the Security Council, and development mechanisms mainstream human rights into their work. Major challenges will be: ensuring genuine dialogue on all issues in the Human Rights Council and avoiding politicization of its work; resolving the division of labour between the Human Rights Council and the General Assembly; exploiting the full potential of the special procedures mandates; further harmonization of the procedures of the treaty bodies and treaty body strengthening; coordinated follow-up to, and encouraging implementation of, human rights mechanisms' recommendations; and the consolidation of the field presences of the OHCHR, especially through the establishment of regional and subregional offices in those parts of the world with currently limited or no OHCHR presence. If all these challenges are addressed and resolved, the UN human rights programme will fulfil its role of assisting to secure the protection of human rights where it matters most: at the national and grassroots levels.

FURTHER READING

ALSTON, 'Hobbling the Monitors: Should UN Human Rights Monitors be Accountable?' (2011) 52 *Harvard ILJ* 563.

BASSIOUNI and SCHABAS, *New Challenges for the UN Human Rights Machinery (What Future for the UN Treaty Body System and Human Rights Council Procedures?)* (Intersentia, 2011).

EGAN, *The UN Human Rights Treaty System: Law and Procedure* (Bloomsbury Professional, 2011).

FREEDMAN, *The United Nations Human Rights Council: A Critique and Early Assessment* (Routledge, 2013).

FREEDMAN, *Failing to Protect: The UN and Politicisation of Human Rights* (Hurst and Company, 2014).

GAER and BROECKER, *The United Nations High Commissioner for Human Rights: Conscience for the World* (Martinus Nijhoff, 2014).

HOPGOOD, *The Endtimes of Human Rights* (Cornell University Press, 2013).

INTERNATIONAL JOURNAL OF HUMAN RIGHTS, Special Issue, 'The Role of the Special Rapporteurs of the United Nations Human Rights Council in the Development and Promotion of International Human Rights Norms' (2011) 15 *IJHR*.

KELLER and ULFSTEIN, *UN Human Rights Treaty Bodies: Law and Legitimacy* (Cambridge University Press, 2012).

MAHONY and NASH, *Influence on the Ground: Understanding and Strengthening the protection impact of United Nations Human Rights Field Presences* (Fieldview Solutions, 2012).

ORGANIZATION INTERNATIONALE DE LA FRANCOPHONIE, *Practical Guide, Universal Periodic Review* (Organization Internationale de la Francophonie, 2013).

PICCONE, *Catalysts for Change, How the UN's Independent Experts Promote Human Rights* (Brookings Institution Press, 2012).

POSNER, *The Twilight of Human Rights Law* (Oxford University Press, 2014).

SIMMA, 'Mainstreaming Human Rights: The Contribution of the International Court of Justice' (2012) 3 *Journal of International Dispute Settlement* 7.

WENAWESER and COCKAYNE, 'Justice for Syria? The International, Impartial and Independent Mechanism and the Emergence of the UN General Assembly in the Realm of International Criminal Justice' (2017) *JICJ* 1.

USEFUL WEBSITES

UPR-Info: <http://www.upr-info.org>

United Nations: <http://www.un.org>

Office of the High Commissioner for Human Rights: <http://www.ohchr.org>

Universal Human Rights Index: <http://www.universalhumanrightsindex.org>

Universal Rights Group: <https//www.universal-rights.org>

International Court of Justice: <http://www.icj-cij.org>

20

REGIONAL PROTECTION

Başak Çalı

SUMMARY

The co-existence of regional and global protections of human rights has been a core feature of international human rights law since the end of the Second World War. Regional human rights systems contribute to both the development of global human rights norms and their application and enforcement in regional contexts. At the same time, regional human rights regimes may undermine or stand in conflict with global norms. Whilst the experience of the well-established regional protection systems in the Americas, Europe, and Africa point to the bolstering of global norms by these systems, the more contemporary or newly emerging regional human rights systems created under the auspices of the League of Arab States and the Association of Southeast Asian Nations raise the question of whether regional human rights initiatives undermine global norms. Regional human rights systems that have independent interpretive organs and provide access to individuals have been successful in navigating potential tensions between regional and universal protection of human rights and offer a model for the newly emerging systems.

1 INTRODUCTION

The study of regional protections of human rights offers us an important lens through which to evaluate the scope, institutionalization, interpretation, and enforcement of international human rights law. Regional protection of human rights is used here to refer to both the human rights standards adopted and the institutions created by particular regional organizations.[1]

A key strength of regional protection of human rights is its potential to act as a conduit in making global human rights local. The proximity of regional systems to domestic legal and political contexts protects regional human rights from the criticism that human rights regimes are the imposition of the values of powerful western states on the rest of the world. This enables human rights law to move beyond 'the West and the rest' rhetoric. The regional

---

[1] The term 'regional human rights systems' is used in this chapter to cover organizations that may be cross-regional in a geographical sense, such as the League of Arab Nations, or sub-regional, as is the case with the Association of Southeast Asian Nations. Whilst an important advance for ensuring that actions taken by EU institutions and member states pursuant to EU law, the EU Charter of Fundamental Rights will not be considered in this chapter. For discussion of this instrument, see Chapter 22.

protection of human rights is also an important avenue to make local human rights concerns global. Human rights laws and interpretations developed in one regional system often travel to the United Nations (UN) as well as to other regional systems.

Regional systems are also important for the enforcement of international human rights norms. Forging consensus on legally binding, independent monitoring mechanisms and remedies has seen more success regionally than globally. This is because the interests of states within regions are more aligned with each other than is the case with the states within the UN. It is no surprise that human rights courts are a distinct institutional feature of regional protection of human rights and are present in Africa, the Americas, and Europe, whilst an initiative to establish a regional court under the auspices of the League of Arab States is also underway. The regional protection of human rights thus has an important added value in the reinforcement, development, and enforcement of human rights.

However, there are also downsides to development of human rights norms at the regional level. Firstly, regional human rights norms may not always reinforce those norms developed at the UN level. Instead, regional human rights law may develop in ways that openly conflict with global human rights norms. This may happen in the form of both regional soft law and hard law. The 1990 Cairo Declaration on Human Rights in Islam (Cairo Declaration)[2] and the 1993 Bangkok Declaration on Human Rights[3] are soft law instances of this conflict. Both texts promote an alternative approach to human rights to that promoted by the Universal Declaration of Human Rights (UDHR). There are also doubts as to whether the more recent 2004 Arab Charter on Human Rights (Arab Charter),[4] the 2012 Association of Southeast Asian Nations Declaration on Human Rights (ASEAN Declaration),[5] and the 2015 Human Rights Declaration of the Cooperation Council for the Arab States of the Gulf (GCC Declaration)[6] are compatible with the standards enshrined in UN human rights law and well-established regional human rights law from the Americas, Europe, and Africa.

Secondly, regional human rights bodies may interpret similar provisions of human rights law differently from UN human rights bodies or from each other. Research shows that UN, African, American, and European human rights bodies are all guided by the principle of 'effective protection of human rights' when interpreting their constitutive documents.[7] However, comparative regional human rights scholarship also shows that there are notable divergences when regional and global bodies interpret specific and similar treaty provisions.[8] Interpretations of human rights law by regional bodies, therefore, may be at odds with interpretations of UN bodies.[9] Thus, the proliferation of human rights standards and their interpretations across regions and the UN raises the question: what counts as healthy human rights law pluralism across regional systems and the global human rights regime of the UN?

---

[2] A/CONF.157/PC/62/Add.18 (1993).   [3] A/CONF.157/PC/59 (1993), 3.

[4] (2005) 12 IHRR 893. See Rishmawi, 'Arab Charter on Human Rights and the League of Arab States: An Update' (2010) 10 *HRLR* 169.

[5] Available at: <http://asean.org/asean-human-rights-declaration/>. See Doyle, 'The ASEAN Human Rights Declaration and the Implications of Recent Southeast Asian Initiatives in Human Rights Institution Building and Standard Setting' (2014) 63 *ICLQ* 67.

[6] Available at: <http://www.gcc-sg.org/en-us/CognitiveSources/DigitalLibrary/Lists/DigitalLibrary/Human%20Rights/1453192982.pdf.>

[7] Çalı, 'Human Rights Treaties: Specialised Rules for Treaty Interpretation' in Hollis (ed), *The Law of Treaties* (OUP, 2012) 525.

[8] See, eg, Dembour, *When Humans Become Migrants: Study of the European Court of Human Rights with an Inter-American Counterpoint* (OUP, 2015).

[9] See, eg, the differing approaches taken by the ECtHR and the HRC to restrictions on religious dress, discussed in Chapter 11.

Regional human rights law and systems, therefore, have the dual potential of bolstering international human rights law and its enforcement and destabilizing the universal premise of international human rights law. When human rights regionalism bolsters international human rights law it enables effective internalization of human rights law in domestic contexts and allows states in a given region to develop a common human rights law culture through mutual and comparative learning. For this reason, regional protection of human rights finds strong support within the UN system. The Office of the High Commissioner for Human Rights has affirmed that '[r]egional human rights systems, consisting of regional instruments and mechanisms, play an important role in the promotion and protection of human rights. Regional human rights instruments (e.g. treaties, conventions, declarations) help to localise international human rights norms and standards, reflecting the particular human rights concerns of the region.'[10] However, when operating as a destabilizing force, regional protection of human rights may cause international human rights law to fragment, thereby sending mixed signals to victims of human rights violations about the prospects of successful international remedies regionally and internationally. In turn, this may create confusion amongst non-governmental organizations (NGOs), communities, and individuals about international human rights law and may undermine efforts for the promotion and protection of human rights domestically.

This chapter will first map the regional human rights treaties and declarations in different parts of the world and compare their scope with the International Bill of Rights, composed of the UDHR, the International Covenant on Civil and Political Rights (ICCPR), and the International Covenant on Economic Social and Cultural Rights (ICESCR) (Section 2). In Section 3 the regional human rights institutions will be discussed. In Section 4 the interpretive tools adopted by regional human rights bodies will be considered. Section 5 provides an assessment of the advantages and disadvantages of regional human rights protection and concludes with a discussion of the future prospects for interaction between regional and UN human rights institutions, in particular, in light of the recent developments that have been undertaken by the League of Arab States and the Association of Southeast Asian Nations (ASEAN).

2 THE DEVELOPMENT OF HUMAN RIGHTS NORMS AT REGIONAL AND UN LEVELS

From its very inception regional protection of human rights has developed in a continuous interaction with the global protection of human rights at the UN. This interaction, however, has taken on a particular flavour in each regional system. Some regional human rights norms have been precursors to the global development of norms and have played a significant role in making local human rights issues global through the conduit of regional human rights systems. Others have either expanded or subtracted from the list of rights recognized in UN human rights treaties, while still others have been articulations of resistance to the global development of human rights norms at the UN.

The emergence of regional human rights norms marginally predates the emergence of human rights within the UN system. Adopted on 10 December 1948, the UDHR is often regarded as the beginning of the recognition of a catalogue of human rights for international concern.[11] However, this history actually begins in April

---

[10] See: <http://bangkok.ohchr.org/programme/regional-systems.aspx>.   [11] See Chapter 1.

of the same year with the world's first international human rights declaration: the American Declaration on the Rights and Duties of Man (ADHR). In this instrument Latin American nations, including 20 of the 51 original member states of the UN, recognized a catalogue of civil, political, economic, social, and cultural rights and highlighted the importance of democratic regimes for the protection of these rights. The focus on economic, social, and cultural rights in the ADHR was important for their inclusion in the UDHR just a few months later,[12] whilst the right to an effective remedy in the UDHR is based on the Latin American doctrine of *amparo*.[13] The ADHR was also the first international declaration to recognize duties alongside rights and this too is replicated in the UDHR.[14] Conversely, developments in the UN human rights system influenced the regional development of human rights in the Americas. For example, the 'progressive realization' standard for economic, social, and cultural rights introduced in the ICESCR was adopted three years later for the 1969 American Convention on Human Rights (ACHR).[15]

The 1950 European Convention on Human Rights (ECHR), in its preamble, recognizes the importance of the UDHR providing an explicit link between regional and global protection of human rights. The ECHR, however, is a text that offers its own regional perspective on what it takes to protect human rights regionally in the aftermath of the spread of totalitarian and fascist regimes in Europe. The ECHR is limited to the catalogue of civil and political rights recognized in the UDHR. It, therefore, acts as a precursor to the codification of civil and political rights and economic, social, and cultural rights in separate treaties at the UN level (that is, the ICCPR and the ICESCR). The 1961 European Social Charter, revised in 1996, sets out protections for economic and social rights in Europe. Uniquely, the European Social Charter allows states to choose how many social rights provisions they are willing to accept when ratifying the Charter.

Owing to its concern with combating fascism and totalitarianism in Europe, the ECHR includes specific protections on the abuse of rights[16] and a prohibition on the use of restrictions for rights for purposes that are not provided for in the Convention.[17] There is an emphasis on the primacy of democracy as the only political regime compatible with the protection of human rights in Europe.[18] However, unlike its regional and global soft law predecessors, it does not recognize a standalone right of non-discrimination. This was addressed by the adoption of Protocol No 12 to the ECHR in 2000.[19] Other protocols have also added to the protections afforded by the ECHR over time. For example, the Council of Europe became a death penalty-free zone with the adoption and entry into force of Protocol Nos 6 and 13.

The African Charter on Human and Peoples' Rights (ACHPR) was adopted in 1981, 33 years after the adoption of the UDHR. This comparative delay in the emergence of regional human rights protection in Africa is best put down to the more pressing priorities of decolonization and state-building in Africa in the post-World War II era.[20] Despite these other concerns, between 1948 and the 1980s the newly-independent African states were active human rights norm-setters within the UN. They were instrumental in the negotiations concerning the first UN human rights treaty: the 1965 International Convention on

[12] Morsink, *The Universal Declaration of Human Rights: Origins, Drafting, and Intent* (University of Pennsylvania Press 1999) 130–34.

[13] See Glendon, 'The Forgotten Crucible: The Latin American Influence on the Human Rights Idea' (2003) 16 *Harvard HRJ* 27, 31.   [14] UDHR, Art 29.

[15] See ICESCR, Art 2 and ACHR, Art 26.   [16] ECHR, Art 17.   [17] ECHR, Art 18.

[18] See Chapter 22. See also Moravcsik, 'The Origins of Human Rights Regimes: Democratic Delegation in Postwar Europe' (2000) 54 *International Organization* 217.

[19] Ten states are party to Protocol No 12.   [20] See Chapter 23.

the Elimination of All Forms of Racial Discrimination. Borne out of the anti-apartheid campaign at the UN, this treaty was ratified with no reservations by a significant number of newly decolonized African states in the 1970s.[21]

The ACHPR both follows the International Bill of Rights and expands it. It is a hybrid treaty that encompasses civil, political, economic, social, and cultural rights. Significantly, the ACHPR has the most comprehensive list of collective rights of all regional human rights treaties. Echoing Common Article 1 of the ICCPR and the ICESCR, it recognizes the right of peoples to self-determination. The ACHPR further recognizes, as collective rights enjoyed by peoples, the right to the free disposal of wealth and natural resources, the right to economic, social, and cultural development, the right to national and international peace and security, and the right to a general satisfactory environment.[22] The ACHPR is unique amongst its regional and global counterparts in its recognition of the rights of peoples to the equal enjoyment of the common heritage of mankind. The Charter also goes beyond the ADHR in detailing individual duties to the family, society, the state, and the international African community.[23]

The 1990 Cairo Declaration and the 2004 Arab Charter, representing the efforts of cross-regional groups (the Organisation of the Islamic Conference (OIC) and the League of Arab States), offer a different approach to the interactions between regional and global human rights systems.

Whilst the American, European, and African human rights instruments approve the universality of human rights in general terms, but offer different lists of rights, the Cairo Declaration offers an alternative normative basis for rights grounded in Islamic Shariah. The Cairo Declaration pronounces its purpose to be 'general guidance for Member States [of the OIC] in the field of human rights'.[24] There is no reference to the UDHR in the preamble or operative part of the text. This is therefore the first cross-regional human rights declaration that does not offer fidelity (even in symbolic terms) to the UDHR. The Cairo Declaration, however, proceeds to offer a mixture of civil, political, economic, and social rights. Yet, the central feature of the Declaration is its subjection of the interpretation of all its provisions to Islamic Shariah.[25] So, freedom from inhuman and degrading punishment, equality between men and women, and freedom of expression, to name a few rights, are only protected to the extent they are compatible with Shariah. In this respect, the Cairo Declaration reflects the reservations based on Shariah made by Islamic states to various UN human rights treaties[26] and presents a direct textual departure from the protections afforded by these treaties.[27]

The Arab Charter was initially pronounced by the League of Arab States in 1994 and was revised in 2004. It is regarded as a text that seeks to reconcile the Cairo Declaration with global developments in international human rights law at the time of its drafting. The Arab Charter follows the UDHR tradition of recognizing civil, political, economic, social, and cultural rights and adopts the holistic language of the 1993 Vienna Declaration and Programme of Action by recognizing that all human rights are 'universal, indivisible, interdependent and interrelated'.[28] It further reflects the contemporary concerns of the time of its drafting with specific provisions for the rights of victims of human trafficking[29] and

---

[21] eg, Cameroon (1971), Central African Republic (1971), Chad (1979), Democratic Republic of Congo (1976), and Ethiopia (1976).   [22] ACHPR, Arts 21–24.

[23] ACHPR, Arts 27–29. See Mutua, 'The Banjul Charter and the African Cultural Fingerprint: an Evaluation of the Language of Duties' (1995) 35 *VaJIL* 339.   [24] Cairo Declaration, preamble.

[25] Cairo Declaration, Art 24.

[26] See Abiad, *Sharia, Muslim States and International Human Rights Treaty Obligations: A Comparative Study* (BIICL, 2008).   [27] See, Mayer, *Islam and Human Rights: Tradition and Politics.* (Westview, 2012).

[28] Arab Charter, Art 4.   [29] Arab Charter, Art 10.

the rights of persons with disabilities.[30] Similar to the ACHPR, it recognizes the right to development, but as a right of individuals, and not of peoples.[31]

However, some provisions of the Arab Charter are narrower in scope than the International Bill of Rights. These provisions reflect the Cairo Declaration approach concerning the primacy of Shariah law over international human rights law. The Arab Charter prohibits torture and cruel, degrading, humiliating, or inhuman treatment, but not punishment.[32] Article 3(3) of the Arab Charter echoes the Cairo Declaration, providing that '[m]en and women are equal in respect of human dignity, rights and obligations within the framework of the positive discrimination established in favour of women by Islamic Shariah, other divine laws and by applicable laws and legal instruments'. Article 7 permits the imposition of the death penalty against children below 18 years of age if provided for in national law.

The Arab Charter further reflects the political economy considerations of some of the Arab states, in particular the Gulf Cooperation Council states, with large migrant populations. These states have been subjected to sustained criticism from the UN human rights treaty bodies for their treatment of migrant workers and their families.[33] Some economic and social rights, such as the right to work, the right to free basic health care, and the right to free education at the primary and basic levels, are only granted to citizens and not all persons under the jurisdiction of the state.[34]

A more contemporary regional human rights initiative is the 2012 ASEAN Human Rights Declaration. The ASEAN Declaration is a soft law document, and thus is not legally binding on the member states of ASEAN.[35] The ASEAN Declaration is, similar to its precursors. It takes a hybrid approach to regional protection of human rights. It borrows from UN human rights treaties and from other regional human rights instruments, whilst aiming to create a text that reflects the characteristics of the Southeast Asian region. Similar to the UDHR, the ASEAN Declaration includes civil, political, economic, social, and cultural rights. It also expands on existing protections at the UN level. For example, provisions regarding protection from slavery and servitude explicitly include protection from smuggling and trafficking of persons and the trafficking of human organs.[36] The ASEAN Declaration synthesizes all the UN human rights treaties dedicated to vulnerable groups when it instructs specific attention to be paid to the rights of women, children, persons with disabilities, migrant workers, and marginalized groups.[37] It also goes beyond existing UN treaties with its requirement to pay special attention to the rights of the elderly.[38] There is a specific prohibition on the economic and social exploitation of children.[39] The ASEAN Declaration further connects with a number of regional trends in Africa and the Americas. Similar to the ACHPR, it recognizes collective rights, namely the right to development and the right to peace,[40] and also places emphasis both on the human rights and the duties of individuals to their communities, similar to the American and African texts.[41]

---

[30] Arab Charter, Art 40.   [31] Arab Charter, Art 37.   [32] Arab Charter, Art 8.
[33] Çalı, Ghanea, and Jones, 'Big Promises, Small Gains: Domestic Effects of Human Rights Treaty Ratification in the Member States of the Gulf Cooperation Council' (2016) 38 *HRQ* 21.
[34] Arab Charter, Arts 34, 39(1), and 41(2).
[35] Renshaw, 'The ASEAN Human Rights Declaration 2012' (2013) 13 *HRLR* 557, 558, has suggested that the ASEAN Declaration may be seen as a precursor to a formal treaty in the region in the same way that the UDHR preceded the ICCPR and ICESCR and the ADHR preceded the ACHR.   [36] ASEAN Declaration, Art 23.
[37] ASEAN Declaration, Art 4.   [38] ASEAN Declaration, Art 4.
[39] ASEAN Declaration, Art 27(3).
[40] ASEAN Declaration, Arts 35–37 (right to development) and Art 38 (right to peace).
[41] ASEAN Declaration, Art 6.

Despite evidence showing that the ASEAN Declaration is in sync with both regional and global developments, there are a number of important omissions. It does not enshrine the right to freedom of association or the right to change religion. Nor does it contain a right to rest and leisure, including reasonable limitation of working hours and periodic holidays with pay. Unlike its counterpart in Africa, there is no recognition of the right to self-determination and, despite the 2008 UN Declaration on the Rights of Indigenous Peoples that predates the ASEAN Declaration and the emerging indigenous rights jurisprudence in other regions, there is no recognition of the rights of indigenous peoples.[42]

The textual convergences and divergences amongst regional human rights instruments and UN instruments point to the multifaceted interaction between regionalism and universalism in international human rights law-making. Regional human rights texts perform diverse functions ranging from confirming universal standards and developing and expanding the human rights norms enshrined in the UDHR, UN treaties and soft law to shortening the list of human rights in UN human rights treaties and creating an alternative paradigm of regional human rights that may potentially, or openly, be in conflict with UN human rights law.

Each of these differences between the regions and the UN, as well as between the regions themselves, point to the importance of independent and authoritative human rights institutions. Such institutions can calibrate the differences and tensions between global and regional human rights texts into a more harmonious interpretive enterprise, which is both respectful of regional contexts but remains true to the universal ideal of human rights law and its dynamic evolution.

3 REGIONAL HUMAN RIGHTS INSTITUTIONS

Regional human rights systems contain important novelties in the institutional protection of human rights. Significantly, alongside inter-governmental institutions for the promotion of human rights, regional human rights systems exhibit a preference for the judicial protection of human rights based on the right of individuals to complain to independent, supranational, judicial, or quasi-judicial institutions. The regional human rights court and commission model for the enforcement of regional human rights treaties, which was first developed in Europe (the European system had a commission until its reform in 1998),[43] has been replicated in the Americas and Africa. In the Arab region the League of Arab States has also agreed to establish an Arab Court for Human Rights, showing support for the trend of judicial protection of human rights at the regional level.[44] To date, this model has not, however, been followed by the ASEAN, where the institutional protection model pursued is inter-governmental.

Whilst regional human rights regimes in the well-established European, American, and African systems are based on the right to individual petition, there are differences with respect to how this model is implemented. Europe stands out as the only region where the ratification of the regional human rights treaty (the ECHR) and acceptance of the compulsory jurisdiction of its human rights court (the European Court of Human Rights) are required to be a member of the regional organization (the Council of Europe). Both the Americas and Africa have 'opt-in' systems for access to regional human rights courts by individuals. Unlike the European system, each retains a dual structure of a

---

[42] Meijknecht and de Vries, 'Is There a Place for Minorities' and Indigenous Peoples' Rights within ASEAN?: Asian Values, ASEAN Values and the Protection of Southeast Asian Minorities and Indigenous Peoples' (2010) 17 *Int J on Minority and Group Rights* 75.   [43] See Chapter 22.

[44] Ministerial Council of League of Arab States Res 7990 (7 September 2014).

human rights commission and a court. The human rights commissions, alongside their mandates to promote human rights, can receive complaints from individuals and pronounce on individual cases. In both systems the commissions also have the task of referring cases to the respective court, if states have agreed to its jurisdiction.[45] In the African system, member states of the African Union can also accept the direct jurisdiction of the African Court on Human and Peoples' Rights (thus not requiring referral by the African Commission) by making a declaration under Article 34(6) of the Protocol to the African Charter on Human and Peoples' Rights on the Establishment of the African Court on Human and Peoples' Rights.[46]

The human rights regime established by the League of Arab States broadly reflects the regional trends in favour of independent human rights monitoring bodies, although it also incorporates inter-governmental features. The Arab Permanent Committee on Human Rights (also referred to in some literature as the Arab Commission on Human Rights, or the Arab Standing Committee for Human Rights) is the main inter-governmental organ in charge of the protection of human rights within the Arab League system. It meets twice a year. There are no subsidiary independent bodies that inform its work, for example, akin to UN human rights special rapporteurs reporting to the UN Human Rights Council. The Committee does not address country specific or thematic situations. Its mandate covers establishing cooperation among member states in the field of human rights; formulating an Arab position on human rights issues that are under discussion at the regional and international levels; preparing draft human rights treaties and providing recommendations on any issues related to human rights that is referred to the Permanent Committee by the Council or the Arab League General Secretariat or any of the member states.[47]

The Arab Human Rights Committee—the treaty body established by the Arab Charter—became operational in 2009. Established under Article 45(1) Arab Charter, the Committee is composed of seven independent experts who should be 'highly experienced and competent in the Committee's field of work'.[48] Members are nominated by states and chosen by secret ballot. The Committee monitors compliance with the Arab Charter through scrutiny of periodic state reports. This system is similar to that of the UN human rights treaty bodies; the Arab Human Rights Committee is expected to receive regular reports from states as well as NGOs and issue concluding observations and recommendations to states under review.[49] These recommendations are only available in Arabic. Unlike the UN treaty monitoring system, this committee can only receive information from NGOs registered in the state under review. This leaves out international NGOs as well as domestic NGOs not recognized in their countries of origin.[50] The monitoring work undertaken by the Arab Human Rights Committee under the Charter does not inform the work of the inter-governmental Arab Permanent Committee on Human Rights.

---

[45] Inter-American Commission Rules of Procedure, Art 45; Protocol to the African Charter on Human and Peoples' Rights on the Establishment of the African Court on Human and Peoples' Rights, Art 5(a). See Chapters 21 and 23.
[46] See Chapter 23.
[47] Rishmawi, *The League of Arab States Human Rights Standards and Mechanisms Towards Further Civil Society Engagement A Manual for Practitioners* (Open Society Foundations and Cairo Institute for Human Rights Studies, 2015).
[48] Arab Charter, Art 45(2).
[49] See Chapter 19.
[50] See International Commission on Jurists, 'An Arab Court for Human Rights: A Flawed Statute for an Ineffective Court' (2015), available at: <https://www.icj.org/arab-court-of-human-rights-comprehensive-amendments-required-before-ratification-new-report/#!lightbox/0/>.

The Statute of the Arab Court for Human Rights, if ratified by the required number of statets, will see the establishment of a sub-regional human rights court.[51] The Statute of the Arab Court establishes an opt-in mechanism to recognize the jurisdiction of the Court for member states of the Arab League.[52] Upon its establishment, the Court will have jurisdiction to hear complaints from states and NGOs , where states have agreed to this in advance, regarding the Arab Charter or any other human rights treaty concluded under the auspices of the Arab League ratified by the respondent state.[53] Victims of violations will not have direct access to the Court. When operational, the Court will sit in Manama, Bahrain.

Recent efforts towards human rights institution building in the Arab region have attracted criticisms from NGOs. A central criticism mounted against the Arab Human Rights Committee and the Statute of the Arab Court has been the failure of these institutions to reflect best practices concerning the independence and impartiality of the members of the Committee and, the proposed Court.[54] For example, it has been noted that despite the requirement for 'independent' experts to be nominated to the Committee, the guidelines remain general and, to date, no further guidance has been provided on the nomination or election procedures of Committee members.[55] Furthermore, experience in the human rights field is a preferred, but not a mandatory, qualification for proposed candidates.[56] The Statute of the Arab Court makes no reference to gender balance considerations in the composition of the Court.

ASEAN has an Inter-governmental Commission on Human Rights (AICHR), which is composed of government representatives. It was established in 2009, three years before the adoption of the ASEAN Declaration. A guiding principle in the work of the AICHR is 'non-interference' in the internal affairs of ASEAN member states.[57] The AICHR does not have a mandate to investigate country-specific situations. Its mandate is focused on the promotion of human rights through enhancing public awareness of human rights, encouraging ASEAN states to ratify international human rights treaties, and promoting the implementation of ASEAN human rights instruments.[58] There have been calls to revise the terms of reference of AICHR to explicitly include a protection mandate, including access for individuals to the Commission. However, to date, these have remained unanswered.

There have been a number of academic proposals to establish a world court for human rights.[59] These proposals have been clearly influenced by the establishment of three regional human rights courts. Whilst regional human rights courts have contributed significantly to the body of international human rights law, the limits of reaching consensus on human rights institutions at the global level is a, possibly insurmountable, obstacle for the establishment of a world human rights court. Furthermore, whilst the judicial model of human rights protection is a trend in the regional protection systems, the preference, with the exception of Europe, is for optional oversight by human rights courts.

4 CONVERGENCE AND DIVERGENCE IN REGIONAL HUMAN RIGHTS PROTECTION

Regional human rights commissions and courts have produced a vast body of case law that displays two important characteristics. First, the regional institutions in the Americas, Europe, and Africa all interpret human rights instruments using the 'living

---

[51] According to Art 33, the Statute of the Arab Court will enter into force following seven ratifications. To date, no state has ratified the Statute.   [52] Statute of the Arab Court, Art 30.
[53] Statute of the Arab Court, Art 16.   [54] See International Commission on Jurists (2015).
[55] Rishmawi (2010), 173   [56] Statute of the Arab Court, Art 7.
[57] Terms of Reference of the AICHR, Art 2(1)(b).   [58] Terms of Reference of the AICHR, Section 4.
[59] eg Nowak, 'The Need for a World Court for Human Rights' (2007) 7 *HRLR* 251.

instrument' doctrine and give priority to the effective interpretation of the rights of individuals over the sovereign rights of states. Second, regional human rights systems do not treat their domain of interpretation as a closed circuit, but interpret provisions of their constituent treaties in the light of UN human rights treaty standards. Despite these two important interpretive convergences, regional human rights systems diverge on one important interpretive issue: whether domestic authorities, by virtue of their continuous contact with their local population, should enjoy a 'margin of appreciation' in the interpretation of the scope of human rights. The development of new regional and sub-regional systems raises the question of whether over time these systems will follow the established trends of convergence and divergence in the regional interpretations of human rights and if so, to what extent.

4.1 EFFECTIVE AND HARMONIOUS INTERPRETATION

The regional systems in the Americas, Europe, and Africa have adopted effective interpretation in favour of individuals rather than sovereign states as the central canon of interpreting human rights treaties.[60] A corollary of this is the interpretation of human rights treaties as 'living instruments', allowing their interpretation to be responsive to changing social, political, and moral developments in contemporary societies.[61] Regional human rights courts and commissions also tend to approach the interpretation of human rights-based duties of states in a consistent manner. They all acknowledge that human rights come with procedural and substantive positive obligations that are to be determined in the light of the human right and the context at stake.[62] Given that the canon of effective interpretation is also a central feature within the UN human rights system, the interpretation of rights is conducive to convergence not only across regions, but also between regional and UN human rights systems. However, differences in the interpretation of substantive norms still remain.[63]

Due to the lack of individual complaints mechanisms within the Arab and the ASEAN human rights systems, it is not yet possible to establish whether these two new systems will simply follow the principle of effective interpretation of human rights and the 'living instrument' doctrine at the expense of pro-sovereignty arguments. The human rights texts in both regions offer sources that would allow for effective interpretation. But opting for effective interpretation would require clearly demarcating what the references to Shariah in the text would mean under dynamic interpretation of human rights in the case of the Arab Charter and clarifying how the reference to the primacy of state interests can be balanced in favour of the individuals in the ASEAN Declaration. Harmonious interpretation in the case of new regional systems is not beyond reach, but requires the creation of independent institutions and, through them, regional doctrines to ensure harmonization.

Established regional bodies have positioned their treaties within the broader universe of international human rights law. In the case of the European system, this has come about by adopting a systemic interpretation of ECHR obligations in the light of the broader context of international human rights law.[64] In the case of the Inter-American system, Article 29 ACHR was interpreted to bring UN human rights law to bear on regional human rights

---

[60] See Çalı (2012).   [61] eg *Rantsev v Cyprus and Russia* (2010) 51 EHRR 1.
[62] See Chapter 5.
[63] Buckley, Donald, and Leach (eds), *Towards Convergence in International Human Rights Law: Approaches of Regional and International Systems* (Brill, 2016).
[64] eg *Golder v UK* (1979–80) 1 EHRR 524.

law.[65] In Africa, the African Court of Human and Peoples' Rights is obliged to apply the ACHPR and any human rights treaties that have been ratified by the state concerned.[66]

When it comes to the newer regional human rights systems, treaty texts also provide some scope for locating the regional treaties within the broader context of international human rights law. Under Article 43 Arab Charter there is an explicit requirement that the rights under the Charter cannot be interpreted in a manner that would impair the rights guaranteed under those international and regional human rights instruments, which the states parties have ratified. This provision directs all interpretations of the Arab Charter to be in harmony with states' UN human rights treaty obligations. Noting that some Arab states have entered general blanket reservations to human rights treaties such as the Convention on the Elimination of Discrimination against Women and the Convention on the Rights of the Child, this provision places important responsibilities on the shoulders of the Arab Human Rights Committee and a future Arab Human Rights Court to develop doctrines of harmonious interpretation. A crucial limitation to the harmonizing effect of Article 43, however, may be the lack of ratifications of the ICCPR and the ICESCR by states parties to the Arab Charter.[67] In the case of the ASEAN, the recognition that all human rights are interdependent and interrelated offers a jurisprudential base to consider the rights in the ASEAN Declaration within the broader context of international human rights law.[68] Conversely, the general limitation clause in Article 8 may undermine states' commitments under UN human rights treaties. In the absence of interpretive judicial organs focusing on specific cases, however, the potential and pitfalls in the Arab and ASEAN regimes remain hypothetical.

4.2 THE MARGIN OF APPRECIATION IN THE REGIONAL HUMAN RIGHTS SYSTEMS

An unsettled issue in the regional human rights systems is the role to be accorded to the margin of appreciation doctrine in the interpretation of regional texts.[69] Should regional bodies exercise deference to state authorities in view of their better position with respect to facts, social forces, culture, and political traditions?

The margin of appreciation was initially developed as a judge-made doctrine in the European human rights system. When it enters into force, Protocol 15 to the ECHR will add a direct reference to the concepts of subsidiarity and the margin of appreciation in the preamble to the Convention. The uses of the margin of appreciation doctrine in Europe are diverse and have many faces.[70] It has been employed in order to provide deference to executive, legislative, and judicial authorities when interpreting the scope of rights and restrictions to rights. When the European Court of Human Rights does not find a European consensus on a contested matter, it may offer states a wide margin of appreciation.[71] The margin, however, also depends on the nature of the right.[72] States do not enjoy a margin in cases of absolute rights[73] (for example, prohibition of torture) and have a narrow margin

---

[65] eg *Claude-Reyes et al. v Chile,* IACtHR Series C No 151 (19 September 2006) para 76.

[66] Protocol to the African Charter on Human and Peoples' Rights on the Establishment of the African Court on Human and Peoples' Rights, Art 7.

[67] As of December 2016, Saudi Arabia, Qatar, United Arab Emirates, and Oman have not ratified the ICCPR or the ICESCR.   [68] ASEAN Declaration, Art 7.

[69] See Chapter 5 for discussion of the margin of appreciation.

[70] See Spielmann, 'Allowing the Right Margin: The European Court of Human Rights and the National Margin of Appreciation Doctrine: Waiver or Subsidiarity of European Review?' (2012) 14 *CYELS* 381.

[71] *Pretty v UK* (2002) 35 EHRR 1.

[72] *Eon v France*, App no 26118/10, Judgment of 14 March 2013.

[73] *Saadi v Italy* (2009) 49 EHRR 30.

with respect to interpretation of rights that are essential to the healthy functioning of a democratic regime (for example, freedom of political expression). The European Court also affords a wide margin of appreciation to domestic courts in the assessment of facts, interpretation of domestic law and when courts responsibly balance competing rights.[74] Recently, the European Court has also recognized that national parliaments that carry out a careful balancing of competing rights when legislating may enjoy a margin of appreciation.[75]

The margin of appreciation does not have a formal textual place in the jurisprudence of the Inter-American and the African systems. It has also not been adopted as a formal doctrine by these regional systems. The UN human rights treaty bodies also do not formally embrace the concept.[76] This may be explained with the preferences of these institutions to set uniform human rights standards in their domains of jurisdiction and their lack of trust in domestic judiciaries or parliaments to adequately balance rights with competing rights or interests.

The text of the Arab Charter also does not formally incorporate a margin of appreciation doctrine. The Arab Charter, however, indicates that Charter rights may be limited by domestic laws, without specifying an autonomous standard to review such laws. This may lead to an endorsement of a margin of appreciation in favour of national legislatures.[77] A similar argument may be also made with respect to allowances made for Shariah law in the Charter. As Shariah law is interpreted differently in different national contexts, a margin of appreciation doctrine may be necessary to accommodate the diversity of the application of Shariah law.[78] The Arab Court, when established, however, may also choose to reject developing a margin of appreciation doctrine and instead opt for developing sub-regional standards across all rights for states under its jurisdiction.

In the case of the ASEAN Declaration, giving states some form of margin of appreciation is recognized as a general principle. Whilst the Declaration recognizes that human rights are interdependent, interrelated, and universal, it further states that 'the realization of human rights must be considered in the regional and national context bearing in mind different political, economic, legal, social, cultural, historical and religious backgrounds.'[79] This provision may be read both as celebrating the diversity in different societies and tailoring human rights protections in the light of this diversity, but it may also be used as an excuse not to protect vulnerable and marginalized groups due to the preferences of majorities.

In the case of both the Arab and the ASEAN human rights systems, whether the textual openness to a doctrine of national margin of appreciation translates into its actual use is an open-ended question. It will depend on the institutional preferences of the regional mechanisms. Given the current lack of a right of individual petition in both systems, it is difficult to foresee whether these institutions will interpret their founding texts in broad deference to domestic laws and domestic courts across the full spectrum of rights. From a regional institutional perspective, given that the Arab and the ASEAN regions face difficulties in terms of a lack of independent judiciaries as part of democratic constitutional regimes, insisting on a broad margin of appreciation doctrine may undermine the protection of human rights in these regions and lead to differentiated standards of protection between the regional and the UN systems.

---

[74] *Van Hannover (No 2) v Germany* (2012) 55 EHRR 15.   [75] *SAS v France* (2015) 60 EHRR 11.

[76] See McGoldrick, 'A Defence of the Margin of Appreciation and an Argument for its Application by the Human Rights Committee' (2016) 65 *ICLQ* 21.

[77] eg Arab Charter, Art 30.

[78] See reference made to Shariah law in Arab Charter, Art 3(3) on ensuring gender equality.

[79] ASEAN Declaration, Art 7.

The Arab and ASEAN texts incorporate provisions that show both awareness of the existing global human rights system and point to the need to take into account regional particularities. The experience of the more established regional human rights systems shows that interpretation of human rights texts is able to reconcile apparent tensions in regional treaty texts through paying attention to their 'living instrument' nature and by offering doctrines that mediate between public interests and rights, such as proportionality. The established systems have also seen updates through additional protocols and new treaties. In the light of these dynamics, it will be interesting to see how the Arab and ASEAN systems will evolve institutionally and, whether they can evolve towards harmonious interpretation rather than conflict with UN human rights treaties.

5 CONCLUSION

This chapter has laid out the important advantages and disadvantages of human rights regionalism within the context of the recent proliferation of regional human rights systems. A central advantage of human rights regionalism is the ability of the regional human rights systems to bring international human rights law closer to home and national and regional experiences closer to international human rights law. Whilst the universality of human rights is an important premise, human rights violations take different forms in different political, legal, social, and cultural contexts. It is, therefore, no surprise that the Inter-American human rights system has been central in the promotion of the rights of indigenous peoples,[80] whilst this concern has been largely absent in the European system. Even though the regional context of human rights violations matters, it is also the case that regions are transient legal spaces and may have more in common than it may initially seem. The indigenous peoples' rights case law of the Inter-American system, for example, has found significant echoes in the case law of the African Commission.[81] In the same vein, regional human rights developments have subsequently led to the adoption of universal standards. For example, the 2006 International Convention for the Protection of All Persons from Enforced Disappearance followed the adoption of the 1994 Inter-American Convention on Forced Disappearance of Persons.

The dynamics of reinforcing and contextualizing human rights standards in regional human rights systems, however, largely depends on the existence of strong and independent regional human rights institutions, both judicial and quasi-judicial, and broad access of individuals and NGOs to the regional human rights systems. Contextualization of human rights is successful to the extent that individuals of the region can access human rights systems and receive an independent and impartial assessment of their cases. Individual access to human rights systems, a key contribution to human rights law by regional systems, has been deemed crucial to the health of the international human rights law project as a whole. Eight out of the nine core UN human rights treaty bodies have individual petition systems in force to which states can opt in.[82] Seen from this perspective, the current reluctance in the ASEAN system to allow for a right of individual petition falls below both regional and UN standards.

---

[80] Shelton, 'The Inter-American Human Rights Law of Indigenous Peoples' (2013) 35 *U Haw LRev* 937.

[81] 276/2003, *Centre for Minority Rights Development (Kenya) and Minority Rights Group (on behalf of Endorois Welfare Council) v Kenya*, 27th Activity Report of the ACommHPR (2009); (2009) AHRLR 75.

[82] The right of individual petition under the ICRMW will become effective when 10 states have accepted the competence of the Committee on the Rights of Migrant Workers to receive individual communications; see ICRMW, Art 77(8).

Furthermore, developments in the League of Arab States and ASEAN show that human rights regionalization carries the potential to fragment human rights norms by offering conflicting and potentially lower standards of protection than at the level of the UN. Furthermore, the existence of the systems in these regions may reduce the pressure to ratify UN human rights treaties (or withdraw reservations from them) and therefore lead to the emergence of autonomous regional human rights systems.

Divergence in the interpretation of norms amongst different institutions is an inevitable feature of international human rights law with its multiple sources. It is, however, crucial that regional human rights systems display openness to international human rights law, instead of developing as autonomous closed systems. A key purpose of international human rights law and institutions, be they global or regional, has been to make national legal systems more open and responsive to human rights concerns. The experience from the Americas, Europe, and Africa has shown that regional human rights interpreters have been resourceful in reconciling regional differences with the universal premise of human rights law. Whether the human rights institutions in the Arab League and the ASEAN will evolve into independent institutions offering more meaningful access to individuals and civil society, and in turn, produce similar outcomes remains to be seen.

FURTHER READING

BAIK, *Emerging Regional Human Rights Systems in Asia* (Cambridge University Press, 2012).

BUCKLEY, DONALD, and LEACH (eds), *Towards Convergence in International Human Rights Law: Approaches of Regional and International Systems* (Brill, 2016).

ÇALI, MADSEN, and VILJOEN (eds), 'Symposium: Comparative Regional Human Rights: Defining a Research Agenda' (2018) 16 *ICON*.

MATTAR, 'Article 43 of the Arab Charter on Human Rights: Reconciling National, Regional, and International Standards' (2013) 26 *Harvard HRJ* 91.

RENSHAW, 'The ASEAN Human Rights Declaration 2012' (2013) 13 *HRLR* 557.

SHELTON and CAROZZA, *Regional Protection of Human Rights* (Oxford University Press, 2013).

VILJOEN, 'The Relevance of the Inter-American Human Rights System for Africa' (1999) 11 *African JICL* 659.

USEFUL WEBSITES

Arab Human Rights Committee (in Arabic): <http://www.lasportal.org/ar/humanrights/Committee/Pages/default.aspx>

ASEAN Inter-Governmental Commission on Human Rights: <http://aichr.org>

OHCHR: An Overview of Regional Human Rights Systems: <http://bangkok.ohchr.org/programme/regional-systems.aspx>

21

THE AMERICAS

Thomas M Antkowiak

SUMMARY

The Inter-American human rights system was created by the Organization of American States (OAS), an international organization comprised of all independent states in the Western hemisphere. The OAS has adopted several human rights treaties and legal instruments; the two central ones are the American Declaration of the Rights and Duties of Man and the American Convention on Human Rights. The supervisory institutions in the Inter-American system are the Inter-American Commission on Human Rights (the Commission) and the Inter-American Court of Human Rights (the Court). The Commission and the Court consider individual complaints of human rights abuse. In addition, the Commission conducts country and thematic studies, and the Court has advisory jurisdiction to assist the American states in complying with their global human rights obligations. Together, the Commission and the Court have made key contributions to the protection of human rights in the Americas; moreover, their jurisprudence has become increasingly influential on other international human rights institutions.

1 INTRODUCTION

Several governments of the Americas have progressed from the brutal dictatorships of the 1970s and 1980s to the democracies of today. Yet numerous states in the region struggle with impunity from that dark era, as well as confront many contemporary human rights challenges, such as rampant discrimination, poverty, and repression of freedom of speech. In this way, it is essential that victims of human rights abuse can turn to the Inter-American human rights system to safeguard their rights when their national legal systems fail them.

Human rights protection in the Americas is governed by the Organization of American States (OAS), an international organization comprised of the independent states of the Western hemisphere. In 1962, Cuba was excluded from participating in the OAS because it had adopted a Marxist-Leninist form of government. The OAS General Assembly lifted the suspension in 2009, although Cuba has not yet chosen to engage with the organization.

The OAS has adopted several human rights treaties and legal instruments. The most influential of these are the American Declaration of the Rights and Duties of Man (American Declaration) and the American Convention on Human Rights (ACHR). The two supervisory bodies, the Inter-American Commission and the Inter-American Court, have distinct but complementary functions and powers in promoting and safeguarding human rights in the Americas. A primary role for both organs is the processing of individual complaints that allege state responsibility for the violation of protected human rights. All individual petitions must first be filed with the Commission. Once proceedings have concluded at the Commission, under certain circumstances cases may be submitted to the Court.

The cases initially referred to the Inter-American Court involved gross and systematic human rights violations including forced disappearances, torture, and extra-judicial executions. The Court has handed down pioneering judgments, starting with its case law on state responsibility for forced disappearances.[1] Over the years, the Court's jurisprudence has expanded to encompass many of the rights protected by the ACHR. The Court has issued landmark decisions on amnesty laws, the redress of victims, and the rights of children, women, indigenous peoples, and migrants, among various other subjects.

Although the Commission and Court have served numerous victims—and potential victims—across the region, they have also faced their share of challenges. Like many human rights institutions, the Inter-American system suffers from inadequate funding. In addition, from 2011 to 2013, the Commission came under intense scrutiny from various states, and the resulting changes to the Commission's procedures have, in some respects, weakened its authority.[2] Furthermore, commentators have recently asserted that 'the Court's assessment of potential rights violations and reparations has become less transparent and rigorous, and, at the same time, more deferential to States'.[3]

2 HISTORICAL OVERVIEW

The OAS was established in 1948, when the sovereign states of the Americas adopted the Charter of the Organization of American States (OAS Charter). The OAS Charter is the constituent treaty that sets out the organization's legal framework. It is binding on all OAS member states. The purposes of the OAS include strengthening peace and security, promoting and consolidating representative democracy, and eradicating extreme poverty. One of the basic principles of the OAS Charter affirms that fundamental rights belong to every human being without distinction as to race, nationality, creed, or gender.[4]

The 1948 conference that approved the OAS Charter also adopted the American Declaration on the Rights and Duties of Man. This declaration, adopted months before the Universal Declaration of Human Rights, proclaims numerous civil, political, economic, social, and cultural rights. In addition, it specifies corresponding duties owed by individuals to society and the state, such as the duties to vote, pay taxes, work, obey the law, and care for minor children and parents. The Inter-American Court and Commission have both held that the American Declaration stands as an important source of legal obligations for OAS member states.[5]

---

[1] *Velásquez Rodríguez v Honduras* (Merits), IACtHR Series C No 4 (29 July 1988).

[2] A major concern involves modifications to the Commission's procedure on precautionary measures, making the process slower and more cumbersome. See IACommHR Res 1/2013, 'Reform of the Rules of Procedure, Policies and Practices' (2013).

[3] Antkowiak and Gonza, *The American Convention on Human Rights: Essential Rights* (OUP, 2017), 2.

[4] OAS Charter, Art 3(l).

[5] OC-10/89, *Interpretation of the American Declaration of the Rights and Duties of Man within the Framework of Article 64 of the American Convention on Human Rights*, IACtHR Series A No 4 (14 July 1989) paras 35–45; and Case 9647, *Roach and Pinkerton v US*, IACommHR Res 3/87 (22 September 1987) paras 46–9.

The Protocol of Buenos Aires, adopted in 1967, amended the OAS Charter to incorporate the Inter-American Commission as a principal organ of the OAS. Under the Charter, the Commission's primary function is to 'promote the observance and protection of human rights and to serve as a consultative organ of the Organization in these matters'.[6] At that time, no binding OAS human rights treaty was in effect in the Americas. In 1969 the American Convention on Human Rights was adopted. The Convention sets forth 23 civil and political rights that states parties pledge to respect and ensure. One provision, Article 26, explicitly addresses economic, social, and cultural rights.

The OAS has adopted two Protocols to the ACHR: the Additional Protocol in the Area of Economic, Social and Cultural Rights, also referred to as the 'Protocol of San Salvador', which entered into force in 1999; and the Protocol to Abolish the Death Penalty, which entered into force in 1991. Additional OAS treaties in force include: the Inter-American Convention on Forced Disappearance of Persons; the Inter-American Convention to Prevent and Punish Torture; the Inter-American Convention on the Prevention, Punishment and Eradication of Violence against Women, also known as the 'Convention of Belém Do Pará'; and the Inter-American Convention on the Elimination of All Forms of Discrimination against Persons with Disabilities. Two more recent treaties, the Inter-American Convention Against Racism, Racial Discrimination, and Related Forms of Intolerance and the Inter-American Convention Against All Forms of Discrimination and Intolerance, have not yet entered into force.

The Inter-American system has also adopted other human rights instruments. The most significant of these include the Inter-American Declaration of Principles on Freedom of Expression; the Principles and Best Practices on the Protection of Persons Deprived of Liberty in the Americas; the Social Charter of the Americas; and the American Declaration on the Rights of Indigenous Peoples.

The OAS, like the Council of Europe, has affirmed its commitment to the democratic political system, adopting the Inter-American Democratic Charter in 2001. The OAS Charter, for its part, recognizes that representative democracy is essential for stability, peace, development, and the protection of human rights. In 2009, the OAS General Assembly relied on the Inter-American Democratic Charter when it temporarily suspended Honduras from OAS participation after a coup d'état that deposed the constitutionally-elected president.[7] The Inter-American Court also has affirmed that a democratic form of government is vital for the protection of human rights.[8]

3 AMERICAN CONVENTION ON HUMAN RIGHTS

Twenty-two of the 35 OAS member states are states parties to the ACHR. The treaty has not been ratified by Canada, the United States, Belize, and some Caribbean nations. After ratifying the Convention, Trinidad and Tobago later denounced it in 1998; Venezuela did the same in 2012. Denunciations become effective one year from the date of communication.[9]

States parties undertake to respect and ensure the human rights specified in the ACHR to all persons who are subject to their jurisdiction.[10] Jurisdiction, under international human rights law, is not limited to a state's physical territory; rather, it includes all areas over which a state exercises effective authority and control.[11] As explained by the Inter-American Commission,

---

[6] OAS Charter, Art 106. The Commission was created by a resolution of the Fifth Meeting of Consultation of Ministers of Foreign Affairs in Santiago, Chile in 1959.

[7] OAS Press Release, 'OAS Suspends Membership of Honduras', 5 July 2009.

[8] OC-6/86, *The Word 'Laws' in Article 30 of the American Convention on Human Rights*, IACtHR Series A No 6 (9 May 1986) para 35.   [9] ACHR, Art 78.   [10] ACHR, Art 1(1).   [11] See Chapter 6.

the Guántanamo detainees, although outside the physical territory of the US, are 'wholly within the authority and control of the United States government'.[12] Therefore, the US can be held responsible for human rights abuses taking place there. States parties also agree to give legal effect to the rights and freedoms set forth in the ACHR at the domestic level.[13] In this way, various American states have incorporated international human rights standards in their laws and constitutions, and have established means to comply with the judgments of the Inter-American Court.

The rights and freedoms protected by the ACHR include the rights to life, equality, humane treatment, personal liberty, due process, privacy, property, assembly, and political participation. The Convention also contains the freedoms of thought and expression, conscience and religion, association, movement and residence, as well as prohibitions on slavery and *ex post facto* laws. Rights of the family and of the child are likewise recognized.

The ACHR establishes two supervisory institutions: the Inter-American Commission and the Inter-American Court. The first and foremost authorities to deal with claims of human rights abuse are national authorities. Only when there are defects in the domestic system or its efforts are not effective can the case be referred to the Commission and the Court. Of course, such individual complaint systems suffer limitations. For example, many victims lack knowledge of the Inter-American system or the financial means to access it. Also, in some situations, victims and their families fear retaliation if they litigate before the system. Consequently, the ACHR allows parties who are unrelated to victims to file petitions.[14] Any person or non-governmental entity legally recognized in an OAS member state may submit a petition to the Commission denouncing human rights violations.

4 INTER-AMERICAN COMMISSION ON HUMAN RIGHTS

The Inter-American Commission plays a dual role in the Inter-American human rights system. The Commission was created as a principal OAS institution under the OAS Charter, and it was also established as an organ for the protection of human rights under the ACHR. Under the Charter, the Commission has authority to oversee the human rights obligations of all OAS member states.[15]

If a complaint is filed against a state that has not ratified the ACHR, the Commission will focus on whether the state violated the rights in the American Declaration. For those states that have ratified or acceded to the ACHR, however, the Commission determines whether there has been a violation of that treaty. In this way, OAS states have somewhat distinct human rights obligations depending on their ratification of the ACHR, its protocols, and the other regional treaties mentioned above.

4.1 STRUCTURE AND COMPOSITION

The Inter-American Commission is composed of seven commissioners who are elected by secret ballot of all OAS member states at the OAS General Assembly. They are elected to four-year terms and may be re-elected once. Commissioners do not serve as representatives

---

[12] 'Guántanamo Bay Precautionary Measures Communication of March 12, 2002 from IACHR President Juan E Méndez to US Secretary of State Colin Powell' (2002) 96 *AJIL* 730. See Tittemore, 'Guantanamo Bay and The Precautionary Measures Of The Inter-American Commission On Human Rights: A Case For International Oversight In The Struggle Against Terrorism' (2006) 6 *HRLR* 378.

[13] ACHR, Art 2.   [14] ACHR, Art 44.   [15] OAS Charter, Art 106.

of states. They must be nationals of OAS member states, and no two commissioners may be nationals of the same state. Members of the Commission must be 'persons of high moral character and recognized competence in human rights'.[16] The Commission is located at the OAS headquarters in Washington, DC. It is in session only on a part-time basis, but the Commission's Secretariat, composed of lawyers and human rights specialists, functions on a full-time basis.

4.2 INDIVIDUAL COMPLAINTS PROCEDURES

A primary function of the Commission is the examination of individual petitions denouncing human rights violations in the Americas. Complaints to the Inter-American system must first be filed and processed by the Inter-American Commission. Except in the case of urgent provisional measures, the Commission must complete its proceedings before a case may be referred to the Inter-American Court. In 2015, the Commission received 2,164 individual petitions against 26 OAS member states.[17] The Commission takes an average of six and a half years to process a petition from its initial submission to providing a decision on the merits (and possible referral to the Inter-American Court).[18]

Human rights petitions to the Commission must meet criteria of admissibility. A petition must state facts that tend to establish a violation of a guaranteed right. Also, a petition must show that the petitioner has pursued and exhausted all remedies under national law when that is possible; that the petition was lodged within six months of the notification of a final judgment in the domestic court; that the subject of the petition is not pending in another international proceeding; and that the petition contains basic information such as the name, nationality, and domicile of the person who lodged the petition.[19] If the petition lacks the required content, the Commission may ask the petitioner to furnish additional information. When the complaint is determined to be prima facie admissible, in that it satisfies the formal requirements of admissibility, the Commission will forward the pertinent aspects of it to the state. The Commission then forwards the relevant parts of the government's response to the petitioner, along with a request for observations. If there is no state response, the Commission may treat the petitioner's allegations as presumptively true. States today generally respond to Commission requests for information.

After the Commission has made a formal decision that a petition is admissible, it will consider the merits of the case. It may hold hearings to receive evidence. Occasionally, with the prior permission of the respondent state, and if the Commissioners consider it to be necessary, the Commission may carry out an on-site investigation in the state where the violations allegedly occurred.[20]

Starting early in the process, the Commission will attempt to bring about a settlement between the petitioner and the state. The settlement procedure is an important tool in the Inter-American system to resolve a case more expeditiously. Settlements have included generous reparations packages for victims of human rights violations.[21] In the event that

---

[16] ACHR, Arts 34–7.

[17] Annual Report of the Inter-American Commission on Human Rights 2015, 64.

[18] Dulitzky, 'Too Little, Too Late: The Pace of Adjudication of The Inter-American Commission on Human Rights' (2013) 35 *Loyola J Int'l & Comp LR* 131, 136.

[19] ACHR, Art 46(1). *Velásquez Rodríguez*, para 61.   [20] IACommHR Rules of Procedure, Art 39.

[21] See IACommHR, Impact of the Friendly Settlement Procedure, OEA/Ser.L/V/II.Doc.45/13 (2013); Laparra Martínez and family: Mexico, Report on Friendly Settlement, OEA/Ser.L/V/II.157 (2016).

the parties reach an agreement, the Commission will adopt a report, transmit it to the parties, and publish it.

In most cases, petitioners and states do not reach a settlement. In such instances, after consideration of the merits, if the Commission finds that the state has violated rights, it will recommend reparations. If the state does not follow these recommendations, and it has accepted the jurisdiction of the Inter-American Court, the Commission's Rules of Procedure provide for the referral of the case to the Court 'unless there is a reasoned decision by an absolute majority of the members of the Commission to the contrary'.[22] Among other factors, the Commission considers the view of the petitioner and the potential impact of an eventual Court decision. The Commission sends to the Court, on average, about a dozen cases per year.[23]

In addition to authorizing individuals to file complaints of human rights abuses, the ACHR also permits inter-state complaints. States parties to the Convention may accept the competence of the Inter-American Commission to receive and examine communications in which one state alleges that another state party has violated individual human rights.[24] Inter-state complaints require reciprocity; both states must have made declarations accepting the competence of the Commission to examine state-to-state complaints. To date, very few such complaints have been filed.[25]

4.3 OTHER ROLES OF THE COMMISSION

The Commission can also issue 'precautionary measures' to address 'serious and urgent situations presenting a risk of irreparable harm.'[26] It has used precautionary measures to protect the rights of both individuals and groups. Further, the Commission studies and reports on human rights in a broader context. The Commission may prepare a country study when there are alarming reports about the human rights situation in a member state. Country reports and the publicity they generate have contributed to the downfall of military dictatorships and the eventual democratization of states in the Americas. For example, during the 'dirty war' in Argentina, when thousands of people were forcibly disappeared by the government, the Inter-American Commission made an official visit to that nation. It met with government officials and also heard testimony from victims and their families. Thousands of people waited in the streets to testify before the Commission or to support those who did. Some commentators credit its visit as one factor in the collapse of the ruling junta.[27]

The Commission also has published numerous thematic studies concerning specific rights and vulnerable populations throughout the hemisphere. Commissioners serve as rapporteurs who analyse and report on the rights of migrants, LGBTI persons, human rights defenders, persons of African descent, detainees, indigenous peoples, women, and children. The Commission also has a Special Rapporteur for Freedom of Expression, and a Unit on Economic, Social and Cultural Rights.

---

[22] IACommHR Rules of Procedure, Art 45.

[23] See Inter-American Commission on Human Rights, 'Statistics', available at: <http://www.oas.org/en/iachr/multimedia/statistics/statistics.html> (describing last 10 years).

[24] ACHR, Art 45(1).

[25] See Inter-State Case 01/06, *Nicaragua v Costa Rica*, IACommHR Report No 11/07 (8 March 2007); Inter-State Case IP-02, *Ecuador v Colombia*, IACommHR Report No 112/10 (21 October 2010).

[26] IACommHR Rules of Procedure, Art 25(1).

[27] Weissbrodt and Bartolomei, 'The Effectiveness of International Human Rights Pressures: The Case of Argentina, 1976–1983' (1991) 75 *Minn LR* 1009.

5 INTER-AMERICAN COURT OF HUMAN RIGHTS

The Inter-American Court of Human Rights is the sole judicial organ of the OAS. The Court was created in 1979 following the entry into force of the American Convention. The ACHR authorizes the Court to adjudicate contentious cases, issue advisory opinions, and order states to take provisional measures to protect persons or groups who are in grave and imminent danger. A state is subject to the jurisdiction of the Court if it has ratified the ACHR and explicitly accepted the Court's contentious jurisdiction. This jurisdiction authorizes the Court to adjudicate cases of alleged violations of human rights enumerated by the Convention and various specialized Inter-American treaties. Currently, 20 states parties to the ACHR have accepted the Court's contentious jurisdiction.

5.1 STRUCTURE AND COMPOSITION

The Court is composed of seven judges who are elected to a six-year term by a vote of the states parties to the Convention. Judges may be re-elected for one additional term, and they continue to hear cases that they have begun to hear and that are still pending when their terms expire. The judges are elected by secret ballot by an absolute majority of the states parties to the ACHR. A state party may nominate an individual who is a national from any OAS member state, not only from those states that have ratified the ACHR and accepted the jurisdiction of the Court. Thus, Judge Thomas Buergenthal, a US national nominated by Costa Rica, was one of the initial judges elected to the Court, even though the United States has not ratified the ACHR.

No two judges may be nationals of the same state. Judges are to be chosen from 'jurists of the highest moral authority' who are recognized for their competence in human rights law and who possess the qualifications to be a judge in the state of the nominee's nationality. The judges serve in their individual capacities and do not represent the states that nominate them. Judges may not hold other positions incompatible with their responsibilities on the Court, such as serving as officers of international organizations or as high-ranking government officials who are under the control of the executive branch. Although the Court previously allowed the respondent state to appoint an ad hoc judge in certain circumstances, this practice has been changed. In 2009 the Court issued an advisory opinion deciding that ad hoc judges are now permitted only in inter-state cases.[28] Even sitting judges who are nationals of the respondent state are not permitted to participate in individual cases.[29]

The Inter-American Court sits on a part-time basis and decides cases in plenary session. In addition to its six regular sessions, the Court held two special sessions in 2015. In that year, it issued 18 judgments and supervised compliance with its reparations orders in 154 contentious cases.

The Court is located in San José, Costa Rica, where it often holds its regular sessions. Yet at a state's invitation and with the agreement of the majority of the judges, the Court may convene in any OAS member state. In recent years, it has held sessions in over 15 nations. When holding sessions away from Costa Rica, the judges will often meet with government officials and civil society. In this way, the Court brings its important work to the attention of the public. The Court has a small but full-time secretariat of attorneys and other staff. The Court's official languages are Spanish, English, Portuguese, and French.

---

[28] OC-20/09, *Article 55 of the American Convention on Human Rights*, Series A No 20 (29 September 2009).
[29] IACtHR, Rules of Procedure approved by the Court (24 November 2009), Art 19.

5.2 CONTENTIOUS CASES

Under the ACHR, only the Commission and states parties have authority to refer cases to the Inter-American Court. This referral may take place only after the Commission has completed its proceedings. The state may make preliminary objections to the case's admissibility or to the Court's jurisdiction. If a state does not submit preliminary objections, or the case is not dismissed at the preliminary objections stage, the Court will address the merits of the case.

At the merits stage of the proceedings, the Court considers written briefs, affidavits from witnesses, other documentary evidence, and often holds public hearings to take oral testimony from witnesses and experts. Oral proceedings are not mandated in the Inter-American system. In response to an increasing caseload, the Inter-American Court has attempted to limit the number of days scheduled for public hearings and the number of witnesses testifying at the hearings. In this way, it often accepts sworn declarations or affidavits in place of live testimony. Still, public hearings are essential to develop a full factual record, to provide petitioners an opportunity to engage the Court, and to attract media attention that will increase public understanding of the case and the far-reaching problems it represents.[30]

The petitioner's role before the Court has steadily expanded, and the Commission's role has been reduced. Although the ACHR specifies that the Commission must appear before the Court in all cases, the Commission no longer represents the alleged victim, who has full standing before the Court once the case has been submitted. At all stages of the Court's proceedings, the victims are represented by their own attorneys. If the alleged victims do not have legal representation, the Court may appoint Inter-American public defenders to represent them.[31] During hearings, judges may question any witness or party.

After the proceedings the judges hold private deliberations, which remain confidential. The Court's judgments are binding on the parties to the case and cannot be appealed. However, the Court can interpret a judgment at the request of one of the parties to the case if there is disagreement as to the meaning or scope of the judgment. The average duration of Court proceedings, from the presentation of the case to the final judgment, is approximately 22 months.[32] Even when the state has accepted responsibility for rights violations, the Court's judgment should fully set out the proven facts and legal conclusions to establish an authoritative record of the events. This record vindicates victims and supports human rights advocates in their efforts to obtain justice and impact public opinion.

5.3 COURT-ORDERED REPARATIONS AND STATE COMPLIANCE

When the Inter-American Court determines that the respondent state is liable for a rights violation, or the state voluntarily accepts responsibility for a violation, the Court orders the state to provide reparations to the victim. One of the Court's greatest contributions to international human rights law is its expansive, victim-centred reparations.[33] The Court has directed remedies toward individuals, communities, and whole societies.

---

[30] See generally Cavallaro and Brewer, 'Reevaluating Regional Human Rights Litigation in the Twenty-First Century: The Case of the Inter-American Court' (2008) 102 *AJIL* 768.

[31] IACtHR, Rules of Procedure, Art 37. The Court and the Inter-American Association of Public Defenders signed an Agreement of Understanding on 25 September 2009 to provide free legal assistance to alleged victims who lack economic resources or legal representation before the Court. See IACtHR Press Release 15-09 (29 September 2009).   [32] Annual Report of the Inter-American Court 2015, 50.

[33] Antkowiak, 'An Emerging Mandate for International Courts: Victim-Centered Remedies and Restorative Justice' (2011) 47 *Stanford JIL* 279.

Financial compensation was the traditional type of reparation when the state was held liable for a human rights violation, and it remains one aspect of reparations in the Inter-American system. The ACHR requires that 'fair compensation be paid to the injured party'.[34] Monetary compensation may cover loss of earnings, property taken or destroyed,

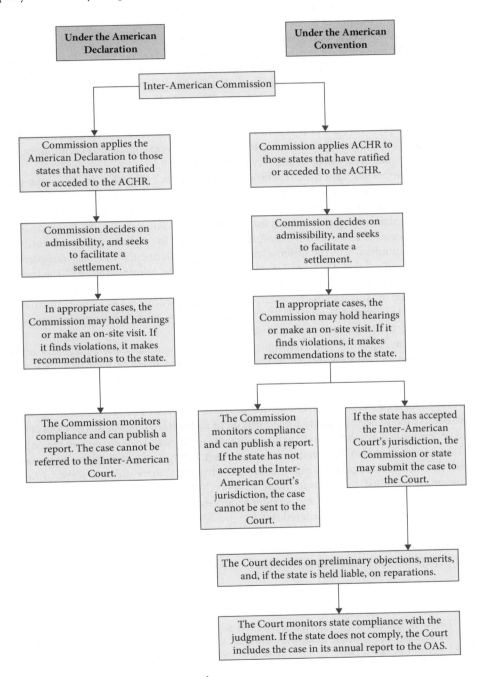

Figure 21.1 Individual petitions procedure

[34] ACHR, Art 63(1).

and payment for moral damages for emotional harm to the victim. Overall, states have complied respectably with Court-ordered financial compensation awards, although payments are sometimes delayed beyond the period specified by the Court. The state also must reimburse successful litigants for their costs and expenses. Financial compensation alone is not sufficient, however, for those who have suffered human rights abuses. As stated by the mother of a victim who had been executed by the Venezuelan military, '[m]y son was not a cow. I don't want money. What I want is justice.'[35]

The ACHR provision on reparations, Article 63, authorizes the Court 'to rule that the injured party be ensured the enjoyment of his right or freedom that was violated'. The Court drew on this aspect of its authority when it ordered Peru to release Maria Elena Loayza Tamayo, a university professor who had been wrongfully imprisoned in Peru for several years.[36] Peru obeyed the Court's order and released Loayza Tamayo. However, not all states comply with all Court reparations orders. For instance, Paraguayan lawmakers voted against the return of ancestral lands to the Yakye Axa indigenous community, despite a Court judgment ordering delivery of the territory.[37]

Another important aspect of reparations under the ACHR is that the 'consequences of the measure or situation that constituted the breach of such right or freedom be remedied'.[38] Pursuant to this authority, the Court has ordered that states amend or repeal domestic legislation, and even reform their constitutions. For instance, the Court ordered Chile to implement all necessary measures to guarantee the right to access information. Chile fully complied with the order when its President signed the Law on Transparency of Public Functions and Access to Information of the State Administration.[39] The legislation was enacted in response to the Court's judgment in *Claude Reyes v Chile*, in which an environmental organization had requested the Chilean government to release information regarding a deforestation project.[40] This transparency law limits government corruption by enhancing public access to information.

Further, the Argentine Supreme Court struck down national amnesty legislation that protected human rights abusers, citing the Inter-American Court's decision in *Barrios Altos v Peru*.[41] In *Barrios Altos*, the Court declared that two Peruvian amnesty laws promulgated by the government of President Alberto Fujimori were incompatible with the ACHR and thus without legal effect.[42] This influential judgment and related Inter-American jurisprudence have led to accountability for the crimes of authoritarian regimes. The Court's varied orders for legislative reform have paved the way for society-wide changes in the region.

The Court may also find that a domestic court ruling was not made in accordance with the ACHR's due process guarantees. Following the Court's order in *Raxcacó Reyes*, Guatemala annulled the victim's death sentence.[43] Guatemala also complied with the Court's instructions in the *Fermín Ramírez* judgment and held a new trial.[44]

In addition, the Court has ordered states to provide: human rights training to the armed forces and police, medical and psychological treatment, scholarships, and funds for community development programmes. Many remedies show creativity and engagement with victim populations. In the *Kawas Fernández v Honduras* case, concerning the murder of an

---

[35] See Krsticevic, 'Conference on Reparations in the Inter-American System: A Comparative Approach' (2007) 56 *AmUniv LR* 1418, 1420–1.

[36] *Loayza Tamayo v Peru*, IACtHR Series C No 33 (17 September 1997).

[37] See Amnesty International, 'Paraguayan Congress Risks Lives of 90 Indigenous Families' (28 June 2009).   [38] ACHR, Art 63(1).   [39] Inter-American Court Annual Report 2008, 26.

[40] IACtHR Series C No 151 (19 September 2006).

[41] Corte Suprema de Justicia [CSJN], 14/6/2005, 'Case of Julio Hector Simon/recurso de hecho', No. 17.768 (Arg).

[42] IACtHR Series C No 75 (14 March 2001).   [43] Inter-American Court Annual Report 2008, 18.

[44] Inter-American Court Annual Report 2008, 17.

environmental activist, the Court ordered, among other measures, that the state conduct a national campaign to educate the public about how environmental activists have contributed to the defence of human rights.[45]

In the interest of general deterrence, and in an attempt to clear the names of victims who have often been maligned by states, the Court generally orders the partial publication of its judgments. The Court also may order the state to undertake public acts and ceremonies, so that society will learn the truth about the facts underlying the case. After the *Myrna Mack* judgment, Guatemala implemented a key aspect of the Court's reparations order by holding a public event to accept responsibility for the murder of the social activist. The President of Guatemala spoke at the ceremony and hundreds attended—including high-ranking officers of the state's security forces.[46] In several cases, top state officials have apologized to victims following the Court's instructions; such apologies have even occurred during the Court's public hearings. Related actions taken by states in compliance with Court-ordered reparations include naming streets or schools after victims or building memorials.

To combat impunity, the Court regularly mandates that states investigate human rights violations and identify, prosecute, and punish those responsible. The obligation persists until the state has complied with this duty. However, these orders are rarely fulfilled to the Court's satisfaction, as they often require significant government commitment and resources to prosecute divisive cases.

The Inter-American system lacks an effective political mechanism to enforce state compliance with its orders and judgments. The ACHR provides that if a state has not complied with orders of the Inter-American Court, the Court should inform the OAS General Assembly in its annual reports and make pertinent recommendations regarding the state. Unfortunately, the General Assembly lacks the political will to impose sanctions on states that fail to comply with their human rights obligations. For its part, the Court has developed a robust procedure by which it regularly supervises compliance with its judgments. However, the resources of the part-time Court have been stretched thin: at the end of 2015, it was monitoring state compliance in 154 cases. The Court holds hearings to promote and facilitate compliance; it also raises public awareness by providing compliance information on its website.

5.4 INTERIM MEASURES

The ACHR authorizes the Inter-American Commission and the Court to act quickly in urgent situations. 'In cases of extreme gravity and urgency, and when necessary to avoid irreparable damage to persons', the Convention allows the Court to adopt binding provisional measures.[47] The Commission may request that the Court take such measures even when the case is not yet on the Court's docket, such as when the persons to be protected are petitioners or witnesses before the Commission. In addition, the Commission is able to directly request that states take non-binding precautionary measures in emergency situations.

A common circumstance warranting provisional measures involves endangered witnesses. The Commission and Court also frequently issue precautionary or provisional measures to protect human rights activists, journalists, and news organizations. These

---

[45] (Merits, Reparations and Costs), IACtHR Series C No 196 (3 April 2009), operative para 14.
[46] See Krsticevic (2007), 1420–1.   [47] ACHR, Art 63(2).
[48] See *Case of Gloria Giralt de García Prieto et al.* (Provisional Measures), IACtHR (26 September 2006); *Matter of Mery Naranjo et al.* (Provisional Measures), IACtHR (31 January 2008); *Matter of the Forensic Anthropology Foundation regarding Guatemala* (Provisional Measures), IACtHR (21 April 2006).

persons and organizations who report on human rights abuses or official corruption are subject to reprisals and may require special protection.[48]

Initially, the Inter-American Court restricted provisional measures to individually-identified persons. The Court subsequently changed its criteria, stating that potential beneficiaries must be identifiable but not necessarily named individually.[49] In this way, entire communities have been granted protection. For example, the 1,200 members of a 'peace community', which attempted to maintain its neutrality in the midst of the Colombian armed conflict, were identifiable as those living in the community.[50] Forty-seven members of the community had been killed in the nine-month period before provisional measures were ordered.

The Court has also required provisional measures to safeguard prison populations where overcrowding, abusive guards, and other inhuman detention conditions resulted in violent outbreaks and the death and injury of inmates. Provisional measures in such cases often consist of orders to reduce overcrowding, implement more safety measures, provide adequate medical care, separate convicted prisoners from detainees awaiting trial, and otherwise adapt the facilities to international standards.[51]

In 2015, the Court held two public hearings on provisional measures and issued 22 orders; several Court orders continued or expanded protective measures, while provisional measures were ended in two cases. Five requests for protective action were denied. In most cases, the Court orders the state to consult with the beneficiaries to determine what measures would be most effective in the circumstances. Although they offer mostly temporary solutions and may be issued only after unfortunate delays, provisional and precautionary measures provide a crucial tool to rights advocates in the Inter-American human rights system.

5.5 ADVISORY JURISDICTION

An OAS member state or institution may request that the Inter-American Court issue an advisory opinion. An advisory opinion constitutes an authoritative explanation of a legal provision or issue, in order to help states understand and comply with their international human rights obligations. Requests to the Court may concern interpretations of certain rights or procedures established in the ACHR or in other treaties.

For example, in the *Right to Information on Consular Assistance within the Framework of the Guarantees of Legal Due Process*, Mexico asked the Court to explain the parameters of the right to consular assistance, as established by the Vienna Convention on Consular Relations.[52] The question arose because Mexican nationals, who had not been granted the opportunity to confer with a Mexican consulate, had been sentenced to death in the US. The Inter-American Court affirmed, among other points, that the Vienna Convention required that host states inform detained foreign nationals of their right to consular assistance.[53] Subsequently, the US State Department distributed a handbook to law enforcement authorities throughout the country advising them of this key right.

---

[49] *'Juvenile Reeducation Institute' v Paraguay*, IACtHR Series C No 112 (2 September 2004) para 108.

[50] *Peace Community of San José de Apartadó (Colombia)* (Provisional Measures), IACtHR (24 November 2000). See also *Miskitu Indigenous People of the North Caribbean Coast (Nicaragua)* (Provisional Measures), IACtHR (23 November 2016).

[51] See *The Matter of the Monagas Detention Center ('La Pica') (Venezuela)* (Provisional Measures), IACtHR (3 July 2007); *The Matter of the Children and Adolescents Deprived of Liberty in the 'Tatuapé Complex' of the CASA Foundation (Brazil)* (Provisional Measures), IACtHR (3 July 2007).

[52] OC-16/99, *The Right to Information on Consular Assistance in the Framework of the Guarantees of Due Process of Law*, IACtHR Series A No 16 (1 October 1999).   [53] *The Right to Information*, para 82.

At the request of a member state, the Court may also issue an advisory opinion on the compatibility of the state's laws with international human rights treaties. To illustrate, the Costa Rican government asked the Court whether a proposed amendment to its constitution was in accordance with the ACHR and with Costa Rica's other international human rights obligations. The amendment would have allowed foreign women who married Costa Rican nationals to become naturalized Costa Rican citizens, but would not have provided the same opportunity for foreign men. The Inter-American Court determined that, although states have the general authority to regulate nationality, they may not violate superior norms such as the right to equality and freedom from discrimination.[54] Following the Court's opinion in *Proposed Amendments to the Naturalization Provisions of the Costa Rican Constitution*, Costa Rica's Supreme Court held that the law on the naturalization of spouses could not discriminate on the basis of gender.[55]

Advisory opinions grant the Court opportunities to shape the development of international law. In the *Proposed Amendments* opinion, the Court went beyond the questions asked and asserted that not all differences in treatment violate equality principles—only those that lack 'objective and reasonable justification'.[56] As a result, preferential treatment such as affirmative action may be necessary for vulnerable sectors of the population. States have continued to consult the Court on important transnational issues, such as the legal consequences of major development projects and the parameters of asylum.[57]

6 CHALLENGES TO THE INTER-AMERICAN SYSTEM

The Inter-American human rights system currently faces various financial, political, and jurisprudential challenges. The Inter-American Commission and the Inter-American Court have constantly lacked sufficient funds. In 2016, the Commission's budget problems approached crisis levels.[58] The increasing numbers of petitions, contentious cases, and requests for urgent measures overburden the two institutions. Underfunding results in fewer staff attorneys, sessions, and hearings, as well as greater delays for petitioners. The situation calls for a permanent Commission and Court, but the OAS General Assembly has not supported this solution.[59]

For some years, the Commission and the Court have had to rely on voluntary contributions to supplement their modest budgets. A percentage of these voluntary contributions come from OAS member states, which are subject to the jurisdiction of the Court and Commission. Such contributions, particularly those from states that are defending cases before the Inter-American system, can compromise the system's integrity. Of course, inadequate financial resources also impede victim access to the Inter-American system.

---

[54] OC-4/84, *Proposed Amendments to the Naturalization Provisions of the Constitution of Costa Rica*, IACtHR Series A No 4 (19 January 1984).

[55] Exp 2965-S-91, Voto 3435–92, *Ricardo Fliman Wargraft v Director y el Jefe de la Sección de Opciones a Naturalizaciones*, Constitutional Chamber of the Supreme Court of Justice of Costa Rica (11 November 1992).

[56] *Proposed Amendments*, para 56.

[57] See IACtHR, Request for Advisory Opinions, available at: <http://www.corteidh.or.cr/cf/Jurisprudencia2/solicitud_opiniones_consultivas.cfm?lang=en>.

[58] See IACommHR, 'Severe Financial Crisis of the IACHR Leads to Suspension of Hearings and Imminent Layoff of Nearly Half Its Staff', Press Release No 69/16 (2016).

[59] See OAS General Assembly, 'Strengthening of human rights systems pursuant to the mandates arising from the Summit of the Americas', OEA/Ser.P, AG/doc 5006/09 (4 June 2009).

In 2009, however, this problem was addressed to some extent when the OAS Permanent Council created the Legal Assistance Fund to help petitioners finance legal proceedings before the Inter-American Commission and Court.[60]

In 2011, a group of states started a movement to 'reform' the Inter-American Commission, an initiative that many perceived to be an attack on the institution's independence and powers.[61] Following the Commission's calls for Brazil to stop construction on a large power plant endangering indigenous communities, that state withdrew its OAS ambassador and stopped paying dues to the OAS.[62] Not long afterward, the OAS Permanent Council issued numerous recommendations, several of which aimed to restrict the Commission's mandate and activities.[63] Resulting changes to the Commission's procedures have, in some respects, weakened its authority.[64]

Beyond political and financial matters, the Inter-American system faces jurisprudential challenges. Despite its enduring calls for a *pro homine*, or victim-centred, interpretation of the ACHR, the Court has weakened some Convention protections in recent years.[65] Showing excessive deference to states, the Court has occasionally refused to find torture and other violations to personal integrity, failed to criticize defective national laws, and upheld significant constraints on the freedom of speech, to cite only a few examples.[66]

In this way, the states, and even the judges and commissioners of the Inter-American system, must re-commit to the region's fundamental human rights principles. The ACHR must be upheld among states parties, and must be ratified by those nations that have yet to do so. A broad acceptance of the Inter-American Court's jurisdiction is also important. States, moreover, must improve their compliance with the Court's judgments and the Commission's recommendations.[67] In an era of widespread nationalism, xenophobia, and discrimination, these objectives will be difficult to attain. Nevertheless, the Inter-American system has shown that it can prevail in volatile times; its leadership is needed now as much as ever before.

7 CONCLUSION

While there is much progress still to be made, the Inter-American system has greatly contributed to the protection of human rights in the region. Initially, it was feared that states would withdraw from the ACHR and the Inter-American Court's jurisdiction if they were

---

[60] It is essential that states repay the Fund if it is to remain solvent. In 2012, of the 13 cases that benefitted from access to the Fund, only one state, El Salvador, paid the amount ordered. Inter-American Court Annual Report 2012, 81.

[61] See Martin and Rodríguez Pinzón, 'Strengthening or Straining the Inter-American System on Human Rights' in Haeck, Ruiz-Chiriboga, and Burbano Herrera (eds), *The Inter-American Court of Human Rights: Theory and Practice, Present and Future* (Intersentia, 2015).

[62] Case 382/10, *Indigenous Communities of the Xingu River Basin (Brazil)* (Precautionary Measures), IA-CommHR (1 April 2011).

[63] Report of the Special Working Group to Reflect on the Workings of the Inter-American Commission on Human Rights with a View to Strengthening the Inter-American Human Rights System for Consideration by the Permanent Council, GT/SIDH 13/11 rev. 2 (13 December 2011).

[64] A major concern involves modifications to the Commission's procedure on precautionary measures, making the process slower and more cumbersome. See IACommHR Res 1/2013, 'Reform of the Rules of Procedure, Policies and Practices' (2013).   [65] Antkowiak and Gonza (2017), 2.

[66] Antkowiak and Gonza (2017), 18–26.

[67] For example, in 2017 the Argentine Supreme Court unfortunately decided that the Inter-American Court lacked the authority to revoke a national court judgment. National Supreme Court of Justice, *Ministerio de Relaciones Exteriores y Culto s/informe sentencia dictada en el caso 'Fontevecchia y D'Amico vs. Argentina' por la Corte Interamericana de Derechos Humanos*, 14 February 2017.

held liable for rights violations and ordered to provide reparations to victims. Although both Trinidad and Tobago and Venezuela have denounced the ACHR, most states have kept their commitments to the system.[68]

Even before a final judgment, states now accept responsibility in almost half of the contentious cases referred to the Inter-American Court. In response to Court-ordered reparations, states have paid monetary compensation to numerous victims and reformed national legislation, including the repeal of objectionable amnesty laws. States have apologized to victims in high-profile ceremonies, provided medical and psychological rehabilitation, reversed wrongful convictions, cleared criminal records, and trained national security forces in human rights.[69] However, the Court has generally not been satisfied by official efforts to investigate and prosecute perpetrators of rights abuse.

The jurisprudence of the Inter-American human rights system has proven increasingly influential on other human rights institutions. The Inter-American system was the first regional system to confront, on a regular basis, serious and systematic violations such as forced disappearances, extra-judicial killings, and torture. The European human rights system has increasingly needed to address such abuses, and has referred to Inter-American case law.[70] The Inter-American Court's extensive jurisprudence on indigenous rights, forced displacement, and military attacks on civilians, among other topics, is particularly relevant for the African Commission and Court of Human and Peoples' Rights.[71] Finally, the impact of the Inter-American system has also extended to various UN human rights institutions.[72] As its jurisprudence expands and its stature rises, the Inter-American system's influence will continue to grow across the globe.

FURTHER READING

ANTKOWIAK and GONZA, *The American Convention on Human Rights: Essential Rights* (Oxford University Press, 2017).

ANTKOWIAK, 'An Emerging Mandate for International Courts: Victim-Centered Remedies and Restorative Justice' (2011) 47 *Stanford JIL* 279.

BURGORGUE and ÚBEDA DE TORRES, *The Inter-American Court of Human Rights: Case-Law and Commentary* (Oxford University Press, 2011).

CAVALLARO and BREWER, 'Reevaluating Regional Human Rights Litigation in the Twenty-First Century: The Case of the Inter-American Court' (2008) 102 *AJIL* 768.

FAÚNDEZ LEDESMA, *The Inter-American System for the Protection of Human Rights: Institutional and Procedural Aspects* (Inter-American Institute of Human Rights, 2007).

GARCÍA RAMÍREZ, 'The Relationship between Inter-American Jurisdiction and States (National Systems): Some Pertinent Questions' (2015) 5 *Notre Dame JI & Comp L* 115.

GROSSMAN, 'The Inter-American System of Human Rights: Challenges for the Future' (2008) 83 *Indiana LJ* 1267.

---

[68] Peru once attempted to withdraw from the Court's jurisdiction without denouncing the Convention, but a subsequent government administration announced full commitment to the Court.

[69] See Antkowiak (2011), 292–303. [70] eg *Silih v Slovenia* (2009) 49 EHRR 37.

[71] eg *Centre for Minority Rights Development (Kenya) and Minority Rights Group International on behalf of Endorois Welfare Council v Kenya*, 27th Activity Report of the ACommHPR (2009); (2009) AHRLR 75.

[72] eg Report of the Special Rapporteur on the situation of human rights and fundamental freedoms of indigenous people, James Anaya, A/HRC/15/37 (2010), para 75; Committee on Economic, Social and Cultural Rights, Concluding Observations on the third periodic report of Ecuador, E/C.12/ECU/CO/3 (30 November 2012) para 9 (urging Ecuador to comply with the orders of the IACtHR).

HAECK, RUIZ-CHIRIBOGA, and BURBANO HERRERA (eds), *The Inter-American Court of Human Rights: Theory and Practice, Present and Future* (Intersentia, 2015).

HUNEEUS, 'Courts Resisting Courts: Lessons from the Inter-American Court's Struggle to Enforce Human Rights' (2011) 44 *Cornell ILJ* 493.

KRSTICEVIC, 'Conference on Reparations in the Inter-American System: A Comparative Approach' (2007) 56 *AmUniv LR* 1418.

MEDINA, *The American Convention on Human Rights: Crucial Rights and their Theory and Practice* (Intersentia, 2014).

NEUMAN, 'Import, Export, and Regional Consent in the Inter-American Court of Human Rights' (2008) 19 *EJIL* 101.

PASQUALUCCI, *The Practice and Procedure of the Inter-American Court of Human Rights* (Cambridge University Press, 2013).

PASQUALUCCI, The Advisory Practice of the Inter-American Court of Human Rights: Contributing to the Evolution of International Human Rights Law' (2002) 38 *Stanford JIL* 241.

SHELTON and CAROZZA, *Regional Protection of Human Rights* (Oxford University Press, 2013).

USEFUL WEBSITES

Inter-American Commission on Human Rights: <http://www.oas.org/en/iachr>
Inter-American Court of Human Rights: <http://www.corteidh.or.cr/>

22

EUROPE

Steven Greer

SUMMARY

In addition to current trends and challenges, this chapter considers the origins, historical development, key characteristics, and principal achievements of Europe's two pre-eminent transnational organizations for the legal protection of human rights, the Council of Europe and the European Union (EU). The Council of Europe's most significant institution, the European Court of Human Rights (ECtHR), is universally celebrated by human rights scholars and activists as the world's most successful international human rights tribunal. Yet its purpose, efficacy, and authority remain in dispute. Similarly, the EU's relatively recent but rapidly developing interest in human rights has been widely welcomed. Yet it also suffers from flaws, particularly a lack of coherence and consistency. An interdependent, but uncertain, future seems to lie ahead for both organizations. However, the debate about the form this should, and is likely to take, has only just begun.

1 INTRODUCTION

For two conflicting reasons Europe occupies a central and unique place in the history of international human rights law. First, it is, together with the United States, the birthplace of the now global processes of political, social, legal, and economic modernization which embody, amongst other things, liberalization, democratization, marketization, and internationalization. Second, and paradoxically, it was also the site of the Holocaust and a crucial theatre for the twentieth century's two world wars, events that together constituted or precipitated the most systematic and serious violations of human rights the world has ever seen.

In the second half of the twentieth century, this positive and negative heritage not only inspired and laid the foundations for international human rights law itself; it also led to increasing convergence in European political, constitutional, legal, and economic systems around a common institutional model formally defined by democracy, human rights, the rule of law, and the democratically regulated market. These processes now operate on three principal and overlapping dimensions: European states, the Council of Europe, and the EU. While this chapter is devoted to the last two of these, it should be recognized that other international institutions with a human rights brief, including the United Nations, are also active across the continent. However, only the Council of Europe and the EU have legislative and/or judicial functions, essential for the development of a distinctive European human rights law.

2 THE ORGANIZATION FOR SECURITY AND COOPERATION IN EUROPE

We should begin by noting that, in addition to the Council of Europe and the EU, the most prominent pan-European intergovernmental organization with a human rights brief is the 57-member Organization for Security and Cooperation in Europe (OSCE), the largest regional security organization in the world.[1] Participating states from Europe, Central Asia, and North America have equal status and take politically, but not legally, binding decisions on a consensual basis. The OSCE was established in December 1994 as a more permanent post-Cold War version of the Conference on Security and Cooperation in Europe (CSCE), created in the early 1970s as an ad hoc multilateral forum for dialogue and negotiation between East and West during the thaw in the Cold War known as 'détente'. Its main achievements were the Helsinki Final Act, signed on 1 August 1975—which included key commitments on political, military, economic, environmental, and human rights issues, central to the so-called 'Helsinki process'—and the Decalogue, ten fundamental principles governing the behaviour of states towards each other and their own citizens.

At its inception the OSCE was intended to assist in the management of the post-Cold War transition in Europe. Today its main functions cover the three core 'dimensions' of security: the politico-military; the economic and environmental; and the human. Within these fields the OSCE's activities range across traditional security issues such as conflict prevention, to fostering economic development, ensuring the sustainable use of natural resources, and promoting full respect for human rights and fundamental freedoms. Its four specialist human rights-related agencies are: the Office for Democratic Institutions and Human Rights (ODIHR), active in election observation, democratic development, and the promotion of human rights, tolerance, non-discrimination, and the rule of law; the Office of the Special Representative and Coordinator for Combating Trafficking in Human Beings, which supports the development and implementation of anti-trafficking policies; the Representative on Freedom of the Media, who provides early warning on violations of freedom of expression and promotes full compliance with OSCE press freedom commitments; and the High Commissioner on National Minorities, who seeks to identify and to resolve ethnic tensions which might endanger peace, stability, or friendly relations between participating states.

3 THE COUNCIL OF EUROPE

The Council of Europe was founded in Strasbourg in 1949 by ten West European liberal democracies as one of several Cold War initiatives to promote interdependence, common identity, and collective security.[2] Its main achievements, and the principal focus of this chapter, were and remain the European Convention on Human Rights (ECHR), which, amongst other things, established the European Court of Human Rights (ECtHR). The Council of Europe has also been responsible for over 200 other treaties on a wide range of issues, three of the most important of which—the European Social Charter, the European Convention for the Prevention of Torture and Inhuman or Degrading Treatment or Punishment, and the European Framework Convention for the Protection of National Minorities—are considered in Section 3.3. But first, the Council's origins and key institutions will be reviewed.

---

[1] Galbreath, *The Organization for Security and Co-operation in Europe* (Routledge, 2007).
[2] Royer, *The Council of Europe* (Council of Europe, 2010).

3.1 ORIGINS

At the core of the political history of Europe in the nineteenth and twentieth centuries is the story of the formation of nation-states and their struggles between competing conceptions of themselves—liberal or authoritarian—and their battles with each other. By the end of the twentieth century three main lessons, both for human rights and for international peace, had become clear. First, competitive European nationalism, unrestrained by effective international institutions, is likely to result in massively destructive international armed conflict. Second, the attempt after the First World War to protect national minorities and to secure European peace by establishing a collective complaints procedure to the League of Nations had failed.[3] Third, liberal democracies with regulated capitalist economies committed to the rule of law and constitutional rights are essential not only for national prosperity and justice but also for international peace.

Therefore, as the Second World War drew to a close, proposals for increased European collaboration were debated by the Western allies including the United States. Towards the end of 1948 the governments of Belgium, France, and the United Kingdom agreed to establish a Council of Europe and invited Denmark, Ireland, Italy, Norway, and Sweden to participate in the negotiations. Luxembourg and the Netherlands joined later. At its foundation, the Council had four main objectives: to contribute to the prevention of another war between West European states; to provide a statement of common values contrasting sharply with Soviet-style communism, hence the almost exclusive emphasis on civil and political rights in the ECHR; to re-enforce a sense of common identity and purpose should the Cold War become an active armed conflict; and to establish an early-warning device by which a drift towards authoritarianism in any member state could be detected and dealt with by complaints from other states to an independent transnational judicial tribunal. This early-warning function was also itself inextricably linked to the prevention of war, since the slide towards the Second World War indicated that the rise of authoritarian regimes in Europe made the peace and security of the continent more precarious. The Council of Europe's founding statute contains several core principles. Certain unspecified 'spiritual and moral values'—'the cumulative influence of Greek philosophy, Roman law, the Western Christian Church, the humanism of the Renaissance and the French Revolution'[4]—are said to constitute the 'common heritage' of the signatory states, to be the 'true source of individual freedom, political liberty and the rule of law', and to form the 'basis of all genuine democracy'. 'Closer unity' between like-minded European states is also deemed to be required in order to implement these principles and to promote 'economic and social progress'.[5]

3.2 KEY INSTITUTIONS

In addition to the ECtHR, considered in Section 4, the Council of Europe's key institutions are the Committee of Ministers, the Parliamentary Assembly, the Secretariat, the European Commissioner for Human Rights, the Congress of Regional and Local Authorities, and the Conference of International Non-Governmental Organizations.

The Committee of Ministers—the executive and formal policy and treaty-making body which also supervises execution of judgments of the ECtHR—consists of the foreign

---

[3] See Chapter 1.
[4] Robertson, *The Council of Europe: Its Structure, Functions and Achievements* (Stevens & Sons, 1961) 2.
[5] Statute of the Council of Europe, preamble.

ministers of member states who usually meet in Strasbourg once a year at ministerial level for a day or two half-days. Their Deputy Permanent Representatives also meet once a week in plenary session and several times a week in subsidiary groups.

The Parliamentary Assembly of the Council of Europe (PACE) has 324 members (plus a further 324 substitutes) elected on a proportional basis by, and from, national parliaments. It meets four times a year in Strasbourg's Palais de l'Europe, which it shares with the European Parliament, the parliamentary body of the EU. PACE's chief functions are to make recommendations, to pass resolutions, and to express opinions about, and to monitor state compliance with, Council of Europe policy. It also appoints the European Commissioner for Human Rights, the Secretary-General and Deputy Secretary-General of the Council of Europe, and selects judges for the ECtHR from the lists of three candidates presented by each member state. It has no legislative powers.

The Secretary-General presides over the Secretariat, the Council of Europe's bureaucracy, and also has some formal responsibilities with respect to the ECHR. The post of European Commissioner for Human Rights—not to be confused with the now defunct European Commission of Human Rights (see Section 4.2)—was created in the Secretariat by a resolution of the Committee of Ministers in 2000 to promote education and awareness of human rights in member states, including collaborating with national and international human rights institutions and ombudsmen, identifying human rights shortcomings in national law and practice, and promoting effective observance of all Council of Europe human rights instruments. As part of the general monitoring responsibility the Commissioner can also receive individual complaints but can neither adjudicate nor present them before any national or international court. ECHR Protocol No 14 enables the Commissioner to submit written comments to the ECtHR and to take part in Chamber and Grand Chamber hearings on his own initiative. By March 2017 there had been 14 interventions of this kind.[6]

Drawn from local and regional representatives, the principal function of the 324-member Congress of Local and Regional Authorities (plus a further 324 substitutes) is to advise the Committee of Ministers, PACE, and member states on a wide range of local and regional issues. The 400 or so NGOs with participatory status at the Council of Europe meet four times a year at the Conference of International Non-Governmental Organizations, an official Council of Europe institution, constituting civil society's contribution to the Council of Europe's 'quadrilogue' with the Committee of Ministers, PACE, and the Congress of Local and Regional Authorities.

It is unclear whether the Council of Europe could be said to have an overall human rights policy beyond the general one of drafting treaties and other documents and promoting state compliance with them. Nor is it clear which institution is most influential in policy formation. Some insiders claim policy is initiated by states, others that it originates in the various committees of the Secretariat, while still others believe the goals and agendas of particular individuals are central. However, it is widely acknowledged that integration and coordination between the activities of the Council's many different agencies and institutions could be improved. While some insiders consider that PACE has the greatest legitimacy regarding the formation of human rights policy—particularly as it consists of members of national legislatures—others believe that, when it comes to identifying priorities, the European Commissioner for Human Rights has more.[7]

---

[6] European Commissioner for Human Rights, 'Third Party Interventions by the Commissioner for Human Rights', available at: <https://www.coe.int/en/web/commissioner/third-party-interventions>.

[7] Information for this paragraph was collected in July 2007 from interviews with some key Council of Europe officials in Strasbourg, generously funded by a Nuffield Foundation Social Sciences Small Grant.

3.3 KEY INSTRUMENTS

As already indicated, while the ECHR, considered in Section 4, is the Council of Europe's principal achievement, three of its many other treaties—the European Social Charter, the European Convention for the Prevention of Torture and Inhuman or Degrading Treatment or Punishment, and the European Framework Convention for the Protection of National Minorities—also warrant brief discussion.

Among other differences between the ECHR and the European Social Charter 1961 (revised in 1996),[8] several are particularly worthy of note. First, the ECHR contains mostly civil and political rights whereas the Charter contains a catalogue of social and economic rights, including those relating to housing, health, education, and work. Second, accession to the Charter, unlike the Convention, is not a condition of Council of Europe membership. To date, 43 of the Council's 47 states have signed and ratified the original Charter, the revised version, or both. Third, states can choose not to accede to certain nominated Charter provisions. Fourth, while the ECHR applies to all persons within the jurisdiction of member states, the Charter only applies to citizens of states parties and to their nationals lawfully resident or working regularly within the territory of the state concerned. Fifth, the Charter has no judicial institutions or processes, nor, sixth, a right of individual complaint. Compliance is instead monitored in two ways by the 15 independent and impartial expert members of the European Committee of Social Rights (ECSR). Under the reporting procedure the ECSR publishes its 'conclusions' every year based on annual state self-assessment reports. If the Committee of Ministers is dissatisfied with a state's response, guided by a Governmental Committee comprising representatives of Charter states and observers from European employers' organizations and trade unions, it can make appropriate resolutions and recommendations. Second, under a complaints procedure provided by an optional protocol adopted in 1995, ratified or acceded to by 15 states parties so far, the ECSR can also make decisions on applications—119 from 1998 to 2015[9]—received from employers' organizations, trade unions, and NGOs, which in turn may provide the basis for recommendations by the Committee of Ministers. Levels of compliance with both reporting and complaints processes are difficult to determine. Benelhocine claims that states generally respond positively to findings of violation including amending legislation if necessary.[10] However, as De Schutter and Sant'Ana point out, it is 'patently clear that findings of non-compliance can be ignored by the State with little cost'.[11]

The European Convention for the Prevention of Torture and Inhuman or Degrading Treatment or Punishment 1987 (ECPT), amended in 2002, aims to 'strengthen by non-judicial means of a preventive nature',[12] the right of everyone detained by a public authority in a member state not to be subjected to torture or to inhuman or degrading treatment or punishment. It seeks to do so by providing an enforcement regime based on unannounced visits to places of detention, particularly those holding vulnerable people, by delegations from the 47 independent and impartial expert member European Committee for the Prevention of Torture and Inhuman or Degrading Treatment or Punishment, one per state party to the ECPT.[13] The Committee is obliged to inform states of its intention to visit, but not of the precise locations chosen for inspection. While all states are subject to periodic missions every

---

[8] See Dörr, 'European Social Charter', in Schmahl and Breuer (eds), *The Council of Europe: Its Law and Policies* (OUP, 2017); Benelhocine, *The European Social Charter* (Council of Europe, 2012); Harris and Darcy, *The European Social Charter* (Transnational, 2000).

[9] ECSR, *Activity Report 2015* (Council of Europe, 2016) 13.   [10] Benelhocine (2012), 26 and 52.

[11] De Schutter and Sant'ana, 'The European Committee of Social Rights (the ECSR)', in de Beco (ed), *Human Rights Monitoring Mechanisms of the Council of Europe* (Routledge, 2012) 90.   [12] ECPT, preamble.

[13] Chetwynd, 'The European Committee for the Prevention of Torture (CPT)' in Kleinsorge (ed), *Council of Europe (CoE)* (Wolters Kluwer, 2015).

four to six years, the Committee can, at its own discretion, visit on an ad hoc basis and make 'rapid reaction interventions', typically if prompted by concerns expressed by individuals, groups, or other state parties that ill-treatment is a problem in the state concerned. Since the purpose of visits is to initiate constructive dialogue with states, missions end with the delegation conveying preliminary impressions to officials in the expectation of a response to the subsequent report. Although formally confidential, publication of reports has become the rule rather than the exception. If, following 'high level talks', a state fails to cooperate or to improve defects in compliance with the ECPT to which its attention has been drawn, the Committee can 'make a public statement'. Up to July 2017 this had happened only eight times—with respect to Russia (three times), Turkey (twice), and Greece, Belgium, and Bulgaria (once each).[14] Confidential reports are also submitted to the Committee of Ministers and follow-up visits can assess progress. Now a condition of Council of Europe membership, the ECPT has been signed and ratified by every member state. Collectively the Committee's recommendations form 'part of a dynamic corpus of standards'.[15] However, although these and the Committee's other activities have influenced states and affected other standard-setting instruments, such as the European Prison Rules, it is not clear if the ECPT has had any significant direct impact on the prevention of torture or the ill-treatment of detainees.[16]

Prompted in the 1990s by the 'shock of interethnic violence that afflicted Eastern Europe with the unfreezing of the Cold War', the Framework Convention for the Protection of National Minorities 1995 marks a departure from the Council of Europe's commitment to individual rather than collective rights.[17] The term 'Framework' indicates that the principles in question are not directly applicable in national legal systems but require implementation through legislation and national public policy. The Framework Convention aims to ensure that states respect the rights of national minorities and facilitate the protection and development of their culture and identity, including by combating discrimination, promoting equality, guaranteeing certain freedoms in relation to access to the media, minority languages, and education, and encouraging participation by national minorities in public life. The Committee of Ministers monitors national compliance with the assistance of an appointed Advisory Committee, of between 12 and 18 independent and impartial experts,[18] which examines the reports states are required to submit at five-yearly intervals or when the Committee of Ministers so requests. Countries may also be visited and meetings held with state officials. Although the Advisory Committee does not deal with individual complaints, it may, nevertheless, receive information from individuals and other sources such as NGOs. In the light of the Advisory Committee's opinion, the Committee of Ministers makes its final decision ('conclusion') concerning implementation by any state party. Where appropriate, it may also make recommendations. Conclusions, recommendations, the Advisory Committee's opinions, and any comments by the state concerned are made public. By 2017 the Framework Convention had been signed and ratified by 39 of the Council of Europe's 47 member states. Assessing the effectiveness of the Framework Convention is next to impossible, not least because of its programmatic nature and because the term 'national minority' is not formally defined.

---

[14] Available at: <http://www.coe.int/en/web/cpt/public-statements>.

[15] Kicker, 'The European Committee for the Prevention of Torture and Inhuman or Degrading Treatment or Punishment (the CPT)' in de Beco (2012), 52, 63 (n 56).   [16] Kicker (2012), 52–3, 62–3, 65.

[17] Verstichel et al. (eds), *The Framework Convention for the Protection of National Minorities* (Intersentia, 2008); Oeter, 'Conventions on the Protection of National Minorities', in Schmahl and Breuer (2017); Weller (ed), *The Rights of Minorities: A Commentary on the European Framework Convention for the Protection of National Minorities* (OUP, 2005) vii.

[18] de Beco and Lantschner, 'The Advisory Committee on the Framework Convention for the Protection of National Minorities (the ACFC)' in de Beco (2012).

4 THE EUROPEAN CONVENTION ON HUMAN RIGHTS

The Convention for the Protection of Human Rights and Fundamental Freedoms (more commonly known as the 'European Convention on Human Rights' or 'ECHR') was drafted by the Council of Europe in 1950 and entered into force in 1953. Its ratification has been a condition of membership of the Council of Europe since the beginning. The Convention's central objective is to provide an independent judicial process at Strasbourg which can authoritatively determine whether a Convention right has been violated by a given member state. This section considers the substantive rights the Convention contains, reviews the establishment and development of its key institutions and processes, describes the current inter-state and individual applications processes, discusses the resolution of complaints by friendly settlement and adjudication of the merits, and finally outlines how the Committee of Ministers supervises the execution of the Court's judgments.

4.1 SUBSTANTIVE RIGHTS

The ECHR is similar in content to other international and national instruments dealing with civil and political rights, particularly the International Covenant on Civil and Political Rights. Article 1 requires member states 'to secure to everyone within their jurisdiction' the rights and freedoms the Convention contains. Articles 2 to 13 provide the rights: to life; not to be subjected to torture or to inhuman or degrading treatment or punishment; not to be held in slavery or servitude or to be required to perform forced or compulsory labour; to freedom from arbitrary arrest and detention; to a fair trial; not to be punished without law; to respect for private and family life, home, and correspondence; to freedom of thought, conscience, and religion; to freedom of expression; to freedom of assembly and association; to marry and to found a family; and to an effective national remedy for the violation of a Convention right. Article 14 states that the enjoyment of any Convention right shall be secured without discrimination on any ground such as sex, race, colour, language, religion, political or other opinion, national or social origin, association with a national minority, property, birth, or other status. Article 15 enables all but a handful of rights to be suspended 'in time of war or other public emergency threatening the life of the nation', provided such 'derogations' are 'strictly required by the exigencies of the situation' and are not incompatible with the state's other international legal obligations. Article 16 provides that nothing in Articles 10, 11, and 14 shall be regarded as preventing restrictions on the political activities of aliens. Article 17 prohibits the ECHR from being interpreted to imply a right to engage in any activity, or to perform any act, aimed at the destruction of any Convention right or freedom, or its limitation to a greater extent than the Convention itself permits. Article 18 limits restrictions upon rights to purposes the ECHR itself expressly provides.

Sixteen subsequent protocols have either added further rights or reformed procedure and/or institutions. The former are optional and usually come into effect when the formalities have been completed by a specified number of states. Protocol No 1, for example, contains rights to education, the peaceful enjoyment of possessions, and free elections, while Protocol No 4 provides the right not to be imprisoned for debt, the right to freedom of movement, the right of nationals not to be expelled from the state to which they belong, and the right of aliens not to be collectively expelled. Protocol No 6 abolishes the death penalty except in time of war. Protocol No 7 contains procedural safeguards regarding the expulsion of aliens, the right of appeal in criminal proceedings, the right to compensation for wrongful conviction, the right not to be tried or punished twice in the same state for the same offence, as well as the equal right of spouses under the law. Protocol No 12 outlaws discrimination in relation to any right 'set forth by law', in contrast with Article 14 ECHR which prohibits discrimination only with respect to Convention rights. Protocol No 13 outlaws the death penalty even in time of war. Once a universal procedural protocol comes into effect, its provisions are seamlessly incorporated into the revised text of the Convention and it loses its separate identity. Protocols 14–16 are discussed in the following section.

4.2 INSTITUTIONAL AND PROCEDURAL BACKGROUND

At its inception it was agreed that the Convention's main *modus operandi* would be complaints brought by states against each other (the 'inter-state' process). Some members also chose to permit individual applications before this became compulsory in 1998. The ECHR was at first, therefore, much more clearly about protecting the democratic integrity of member states through the medium of human rights, and promoting international co-operation between them, than it was about providing individuals with redress for human rights violations by national public authorities.

When it was first established, the Convention system had three main institutions. The European Commission of Human Rights was the first port of call for both state and individual applicants. It ascertained the facts, determined if the admissibility criteria were satisfied, and explored the possibility of friendly settlement. If this could not be secured, the Commission expressed a non-binding opinion concerning whether or not the Convention had been violated. Then, providing the jurisdiction of the ECtHR—the second institution which began operating in 1959—had been accepted by the state or states concerned, the case could be referred by the Commission, the respondent state, or the state of which the applicant was a national—but not by individual applicants themselves—to the Court for a legally binding decision. The Committee of Ministers, the third institution, also decided cases over which the ECtHR did not have jurisdiction and those the Commission did not refer to the Court. Both the Commission and the ECtHR were then staffed by part-time judges.

For most of its first 30 years the ECHR had very little impact on victims of human rights abuses and was almost entirely ignored by lawyers, politicians, jurists, and other commentators. Only 800 or so individual applications were received by the Strasbourg institutions per year. But from the mid-1980s onwards things began to change dramatically. First, it became clear that inter-state complaints—about two dozen in the Convention's entire history[19]—were largely a dead letter, not least because litigation is a hostile act in most circumstances and, therefore, not an ideal vehicle for cultivating international interdependence. Second, in sharp contrast, the rate of individual applications began to rise steeply, reaching crisis proportions by the late 1990s and between 2000 and 2016 inclusive, a total of 741,100 individual complaints were formally received ('allocated to a judicial formation'), an annual average of 43,594.[20]

The exponential rise in the individual application rate since the late 1990s was due partly to the third significant change: the huge expansion in the number of Council of Europe states, from a mere ten in 1950 to 46 by the end of the 1990s to 47 with a combined population of 820 million—including all former communist states of Central and Eastern Europe except Belarus—by the beginning of the 21st century. A fourth change, and also a key factor in the rising application rate, is the fact that the ECHR is now much better known by lawyers and by the general public throughout Europe than hitherto.

---

[19] Committee of Ministers, Protocol No 14 to the Convention for the Protection of Human Rights and Fundamental Freedoms, Amending the Control System of the Convention, Explanatory Report (12 May 2004) para 11.

[20] ECtHR, *Analysis of Statistics 2016*, 7, available at: <http://www.echr.coe.int/Documents/Stats_analysis_2016_ENG.pdf>.

In response to the mushrooming application rate, the judicial process was reformed by Protocol No 11, effective from 1 November 1998. The European Commission of Human Rights was abolished and the restructured Court became a professional full-time institution with responsibility for the formal receipt of complaints, ascertaining the facts, deciding if the admissibility criteria were satisfied, seeking friendly settlement, delivering legally binding judgments, and issuing advisory opinions at the request of the Committee of Ministers.[21] Protocol No 11 also stripped the Committee of Ministers of its power to settle cases on the merits, a responsibility deemed incompatible with the now enhanced judicial character of the complaints processes. The role of the Committee of Ministers is limited now to supervising the execution of the Court's judgments. Both the right of individual petition and acceding to the Court's jurisdiction also became compulsory, although by the 1990s each had already been voluntarily endorsed by all member states.

However, by 2000, Protocol No 11 was already officially recognized as inadequate, not least because the consequences of the post-communist enlargement had not been adequately anticipated. In May 2004 another modest reform package, Protocol No 14, was unanimously approved by all states parties. The most significant changes were to the applications and enforcement of judgments processes (see Section 4.3). But by early 2005 it was becoming increasingly doubtful if these would make much difference to the rising tide of complaints. So, in May 2005, a Group of Wise Persons was appointed to make further proposals. However, their report, made public in November 2006, contained nothing substantially new, largely recycled ideas already rejected in the course of the Protocol No 14 debate, and assumed that the new protocol would soon come into effect.[22] But in December 2006 the Russian parliament refused to ratify it, ostensibly because of objections to admissibility decisions being made by 'single-judge formations'. The Council of Europe, therefore, provided an interim set of optional measures, Protocol No 14bis, intended to apply to the other 46 states. In the meantime, the Registry began to take a more robust approach to the receipt of petitions, including by providing an online admissibility checklist and by adhering more strictly to time limits.[23] The ECtHR also sought to manage its workload by prioritizing applications according to their seriousness and urgency. However, following its unexpected ratification by the Russian parliament in January 2010, Protocol No 14 came into effect for all 47 Council of Europe states on 1 June that year.

But this did not, by any means, conclude the debate about reform. However, rather than address the more challenging, controversial, and fundamental issues of purpose and function, various proposals for further micro-bureaucratic changes were considered by the Council of Europe at a series of High Level Conferences on the Future of the ECtHR held in Interlaken in 2010, Izmir in 2011, Brighton in 2012, and Brussels in 2015. A 15th Protocol was opened for signature on 24 June 2013. When it comes into effect this will require candidates for appointment to the ECtHR to be under the age of 65 when the three-person lists are requested by PACE, abolish the right of parties to veto relinquishment of litigation to the Grand Chamber, shorten from six to four months the time limit within which applications to the Court must be made from the last decision by the national legal system on the matter, include a reference to subsidiarity, the margin of appreciation, and Strasbourg's supervisory jurisdiction in the preamble to the Convention, and remove the requirement from Article 35(3)(b) ECHR

---

[21] To date, the Committee of Ministers has made three requests for advisory opinions and the Court has delivered two: see ECtHR, *Annual Report 2011*, 13, available at: <http://echr.coe.int/Documents/Annual_report_2011_ENG.pdf>. These figures have been confirmed by Court officials to the author as accurate up to the end of 2015.

[22] Report of the Group of Wise Persons to the Committee of Ministers, Cm(2006)203 (15 November 2006).

[23] Cameron, 'The Court and the Member States: Procedural Aspects' in Føllesdal, Peters, and Ulfstein (eds), *Constituting Europe: the ECtHR in a National, European and Global Context* (CUP, 2013) 28–9.

that an application must have been 'duly considered by a domestic tribunal' before it can be rejected as inadmissible on the grounds that the applicant has suffered 'no significant disadvantage'. A further optional protocol, No 16—which permits national courts to request, in ongoing litigation, discretionary, non-binding advisory opinions from the Grand Chamber regarding matters of principle relating to the interpretation and application of Convention rights—was adopted by the Committee of Ministers on 10 July 2013 and opened for signature on 2 October 2013.

4.3 COMPLAINTS PROCEDURES

4.3.1 Inter-state applications

The inter-state applications process is set out in Figure 22.1. Although very infrequently used, and less than a resounding success in correcting alleged violations, it is not yet totally moribund and can have considerable symbolic significance.[24] For example, in 2009 and 2011 respectively, complaints made by Georgia against Russia—the former concerning multiple alleged violations of the Convention rights of Georgians living in the Russian Federation and the latter connected with the armed conflict between the two states in 2008—were ruled admissible by the Court.[25] Ukraine has also lodged four applications against Russia concerning events in Crimea and eastern Ukraine, one of which was struck off the Court's list on 1 September 2015 when the Ukrainian government decided to no longer pursue it.[26] On 15 September 2016, Slovenia also petitioned the Court alleging violations of the rights to fair trial, to peaceful enjoyment of possessions, and to an effective remedy on the part of the Croatian courts and executive with respect to the attempted recovery of debts from Croatian companies by a Slovenian bank following the disintegration of the former Yugoslavia.[27]

Under the inter-state process an applicant state lodges a complaint against a respondent state with the Registry, which can initiate the friendly settlement procedure at any stage of the proceedings (see Section 4.4.1). Having received an application, the Registry informs the President of the ECtHR who notifies the respondent state and allocates the complaint to one of the Court's five Sections. A seven-judge Chamber, including the judges elected with respect to applicant and respondent states and capable of being reduced to five by the Committee of Ministers at the Court's request, is then convened to consider admissibility. The requirements are much less exacting than those for individual petitions. The ECHR must have been binding on all state parties to the litigation, and applicable to the persons concerned within the jurisdiction of the respondent state at the material time and place. Except where the allegation concerns judicial proceedings or an ongoing administrative practice, all domestic remedies must have been exhausted. The application must also be deposited with the Court within a period of six months (four months when Protocol No 15 takes effect) from the date on which the final decision on the relevant subject matter was taken in the respondent state's legal system. While a formal prima facie case is not required, inter-state applications will be rejected as inadmissible if the allegations concerned are wholly unsubstantiated. The processes of friendly settlement, judgment of the merits, and the roles of the Court's Grand Chamber and the Committee of Ministers are substantially the same as under the individual applications process as amended by Protocol No 14 (see Sections 4.4 and 4.5).

---

[24] Greer, *The European Convention on Human Rights: Achievements, Problems and Prospects* (CUP, 2006) 24–8.
[25] *Georgia v Russia (No 1)* (2011) 52 EHRR SE14; *Georgia v Russia (No 2)* (2012) 54 EHRR SE10.
[26] ECtHR Press Release, ECHR 296 (2015) (1 October 2015).
[27] ECtHR Press Release, ECHR 340 (2016) (20 October 2016).

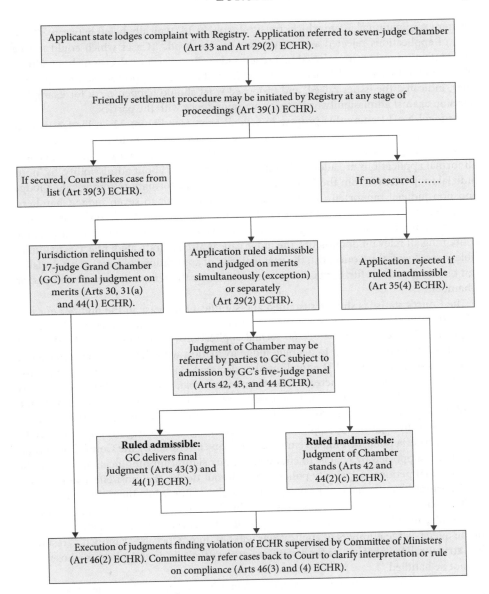

Figure 22.1 The inter-state applications process

4.3.2 Individual applications

Under Protocol No 11 the management of formal applications was the responsibility of a Judge Rapporteur assisted by a Registry case-processing lawyer. The Judge Rapporteur examined and prepared the file, including requiring documents and further particulars from the parties, and channeled the complaint for an admissibility decision—together with proposals about its disposal—either to a three-judge committee, if it appeared to be clearly inadmissible, or to a Chamber of seven judges if its inadmissibility was not so clear. Under Article 28 ECHR a committee could, and still can, unanimously declare an application inadmissible, or strike it off the list, 'where such decision can be taken without further examination',[28] a fate which, pre-Protocol No 14, typically befell between 80 and 90% of applications rejected as inadmissible or struck off.[29] Cases which could not be settled unanimously were referred to a seven-judge Chamber for a decision about admissibility and judgment on the merits. A report from the Judge Rapporteur summarized the facts, indicated the issues raised, and proposed what should happen next, for example a decision against admissibility or further correspondence with the parties.

Protocol No 14 alters this process in several ways (see Figure 22.2). First, it is now possible for the friendly settlement procedure (see Section 4.4.1) to be initiated by the Registry at any stage of the proceedings and not just post-admissibility as before. Second, all formal applications are allocated, initially for a decision about admissibility, by 'non-judicial rapporteurs' from the Registry to: a 'single judge formation' comprising a judge and non-judicial rapporteur, to three-judge committees, or to seven-judge Chambers. The judge elected with respect to a particular state is not permitted to sit on a single-judge formation hearing applications against that state. While the rapporteur manages the file containing all relevant documents, the judge can, as already indicated, reject as inadmissible, or strike off the Court's list, the vast majority of applications (where such a decision can be taken without further examination), and direct the remainder to a committee or Chamber.

The Court's statistics show a sustained and significant increase in the number of cases rejected at the filtering stage since the single judge procedure came into effect. For example, in 2012, 48,350 of the 65,150 formal applications, deemed likely to be declared inadmissible, were allocated to a single judge formation with the remainder referred to Chambers or committees.[30] The total number declared inadmissible or struck off the list (86,201) constituted a 70% increase from the previous year, while those disposed of in this manner by single judge formations increased by 74%.[31] In 2009 the Court amended Rule 41 of the Rules of Court requiring it to 'have regard to the importance and urgency of the issues' raised by a particular application, distinguishing seven categories by reference to specified criteria published in November 2010.[32] Given refusals by the Council of Europe and states, supported by NGOs, to countenance any significant modification to the right of individual petition, a 'priority policy' was, without doubt, the most effective response the Court itself could make to its burgeoning caseload. But, while the right to individual petition has, in fact, been formally preserved by these developments, it has nevertheless been undermined by them. As a consequence of having been sent indefinitely to the back of the queue, 'large numbers of applications will not, in practice, be examined',[33] resulting in 'a structural denial of justice for certain categories of meritorious applicants whose cases cannot be handled'.[34]

From the late-1990s to the mid-2010s, the escalating application rate also created a huge backlog in complaints awaiting decisions on admissibility and judgments on the merits. But by the end

---

[28] ECHR, Art 28(1)(a).

[29] Report of the Evaluation Group to the Committee of Ministers on the European Court of Human Rights, EG Court 1 (2001) (27 September 2001), para 28.

[30] ECtHR, *Analysis of Statistics 2012*, para A, available at: <http://www.echr.coe.int/Documents/Stats_analysis_2012_ENG.pdf>. [31] *Analysis of Statistics 2012*, para C.2.

[32] ECtHR, The Court's Priority Policy, available at: <http://www.echr.coe.int/Documents/Priority_policy_ENG.pdf>.

[33] Cameron (2013), 43. [34] Mahoney, 'The European Court of Human Rights and its Ever-Growing Caseload: Preserving the Mission of the Court While Ensuring the Viability of the Individual Petition' in Flogaitis, Zwart, and Fraser (eds), *The European Court of Human Rights and its Discontents: Turning Criticism into Strength* (Edward Elgar, 2013), 26.

Figure 22.2 The individual applications process

of 2015, Protocol No 14, the priority policy, and the stricter approach to the receipt of complaints, at last seemed to be reducing the scale of this problem. In 2014 the number of applications allocated to a judicial formation fell from an all-time high of 65,800 the previous year, to 56,200, dropping further in 2015 to 40,600, while the backlog of those awaiting a decision also declined, from an historic peak of 151,600 in 2011, to 69,900 in 2014 and to 64,850 in 2015.[35] Between November 1998 and December 2010 only 3.8% of applications allocated to a judicial formation were declared admissible.[36] But between 2000 and 2016 inclusive this figure had increased to just under 14%.[37] However, although it is too early to say whether they constitute merely a temporary blip or the beginning of a new phase, the figures for 2016 also show significant reversals in some of these trends. For example, by the end of 2016, the number of applications allocated to a judicial formation rose to 53,500.[38] Of a total caseload of 79,750 applications, 1.1% were classified as urgent (Category I), 0.4% concerned issues capable of impacting upon the effectiveness of the Convention system or raised important questions of general interest (Category II), 23.6% prima facie gave rise to issues under Articles 2, 3, 4, or 5(1) ECHR as their main complaint ('core rights', Category III), 26.5% were potentially well founded on other provisions (Category IV), 43.6% were repetitive and had already been dealt with in a pilot or leading judgment (Category V), and 4.8% gave rise to a problem of admissibility (Category VI) or were manifestly inadmissible (Category VII).[39] Of those cases pending by the end of January 2017, 30,500 were repetitive, almost 11,500 were 'priority' (Categories I–III),[40] and some 21,000, which according to the ECtHR's Annual Report 2016 constitute 'the greatest weight' on the Court's docket, were neither clearly inadmissible nor repetitive.[41] The Court has itself declared that, although more priority applications are being processed and adjudicated than before, 'this will not be sufficient' for 'substantial inroads' to be made 'into the backlog of Chamber cases', and that further reflection on 'new working methods and approaches to further streamline the proceedings for different categories of applications' will be required.[42]

Protocol No 14 preserves the existing admissibility tests and adds a new one. As before, individual applications can be ruled inadmissible if the applicant was not a victim of a Convention violation, redress has not been sought through the national legal system as far as it could have been ('exhaustion of domestic remedies'), more than six months have elapsed between the last national decision on the matter and formal application to Strasbourg (to be reduced to four by Article 4 Protocol No 15), the complaint is substantially the same as one already examined, it is incompatible with the Convention, it is an abuse of process, and/or is 'manifestly ill-founded', that is, patently has no hope of being settled in the applicant's favour. Protocol No 14 also enables the Court to reject as inadmissible complaints by applicants where no significant disadvantage has been suffered, provided the issue has been 'duly considered' by a domestic tribunal and there are no other human rights reasons for admitting it.[43] Until 2012 this test could only be applied by Chambers and the Grand Chamber, and in 2015 only 0.1% of the cases declared inadmissible were disposed of in this manner.[44] As already indicated, the 'duly considered' requirement will be abolished when Protocol No 15 comes into effect.[45]

---

[35] *Analysis of Statistics 2016*, 7.

[36] ECtHR, *Annual Report 2010*, 155, available at: <http://www.echr.coe.int/NR/rdonlyres/F2735259-F638–4E83–82DF-AAC7E934A1D6/0/2010_Rapport_Annuel_EN.pdf>

[37] *Analysis of Statistics 2016*, 7 and 9.   [38] *Analysis of Statistics 2016*, 7.

[39] *Analysis of Statistics 2016*, 9; The Court's Priority Policy.

[40] ECtHR, *Annual Report 2016*, 18, available at: <http://echr.coe.int/Documents/Annual_report_2016_ENG.pdf>.   [41] *Annual Report 2016*, 13–14.

[42] *Analysis of Statistics 2016*, 5; Annual Report 2016, 19.

[43] ECHR, Art 35(3)(b). See Greer, 'The New Admissibility Criterion', in Besson (ed), *The European Court of Human Rights after Protocol 14: Preliminary Assessment and Perspectives* (Schulthess, 2011).

[44] Information provided to the author by an official at the ECtHR on 2 March 2016.

[45] Protocol No 15, Art 5.

Under Protocol No 14, unanimous committees of three judges are now able simultaneously to settle admissibility and the merits of those applications which, according to well-established Convention case law, disclose clear-cut violations. A three-judge committee may include the judge elected with respect to the respondent state, particularly when the exhaustion of domestic remedies is at issue. While states may contest recourse to the committee procedure, they cannot veto it.

Protocol No 14 also preserves the Court's power to strike an application off its list if the applicant does not intend to pursue it, the matter has been resolved (for example, by friendly settlement), or where, for any other reason, further examination is no longer considered necessary. Legal aid is available for individual applicants lacking sufficient means.

4.4 RESOLUTION OF COMPLAINTS

All admissible inter-state and individual applications—provided they have not been struck off or settled summarily by three-judge committees—are resolved either by friendly settlement or full adjudication of the merits.

4.4.1 Friendly settlement

The ECtHR (in practice the Registry) can facilitate and advise about the terms of friendly settlement, which is open to the parties on the basis of respect for human rights at any stage of the proceedings. In individual cases friendly settlements typically involve offers of money by the respondent state, some other benefit (for example, a residence permit the applicant claims to have been deprived of by the alleged violation), and sometimes an undertaking to make legislative or policy changes. Between 1959 and 2016 friendly settlement/striking out judgments accounted for only 5.6% of the total number of judgments (1,094 out of 19,570).[46]

4.4.2 Adjudication on the merits

Most admissible applications not resolved by friendly settlement, struck off for other reasons, or settled by committees simultaneously with the decision on admissibility, are judged on the merits by Chambers of seven judges. However, subject to the consent of the parties (a requirement to be abolished when Article 3 Protocol No 15 comes into effect), a Chamber may relinquish jurisdiction to a Grand Chamber of 17 judges where the application raises a serious question affecting the interpretation of the ECHR or where there is a prospect of a departure from previous case law. However, this is extremely rare.[47] Between 1959 and 1999 fewer than 1,000 judgments were rendered.[48] Yet, by the end of 2016, the figure had risen to a total of 19,570.[49] Between 2000 and 2016 the Court delivered an annual average of 1,092 judgments, including 695 in 2000, the year with the fewest within this timeframe, and 1,625 in 2009, the year with the most.[50] 84% of judgments and 92% of cases judged on the merits result in a finding of at least one violation.[51] Only a handful of provisions are

---

[46] ECtHR, Violations by Article and by States 1959–2016, available at: <http://www.echr.coe.int/Documents/Stats_violation_1959_2016_ENG.pdf>.

[47] See, for example, Mowbray, 'An Examination of the Work of the Grand Chamber of the European Court of Human Rights' [2007] PL 507, 509.

[48] ECtHR, *Annual Report 2011*, 12.

[49] Violations by Article and by States 1959–2016.

[50] *Analysis of Statistics 2016*, 10.

[51] ECtHR, Overview 1959–2016 ECHR, 3, available at: <http://www.echr.coe.int/Documents/Overview_19592016_ENG.pdf>. Judgments on the merits refers to 'Judgments finding at least one violation' plus 'Judgments finding no violation', Violations by Article and by State 1959–2016.

regularly found to have been breached. From 1959–2016 over 84% of violations concerned only five provisions: the right to fair trial under Article 6 (40.32%, 21.34% of which concerned length of proceedings), the right to liberty and security under Article 5 (12.86%), the right to peaceful enjoyment of possessions under Article 1 of Protocol No 1 (11.93%), the right not to be tortured, etc under Article 3 (10.71%), the right to an effective remedy under Article 13 (8.39%), the right to respect for private and family life under Article 8 (4.69%), and the right to life under Article 2 (4.58%).[52] Third, only a small minority of states dominate the Court's docket and are repeatedly in receipt of adverse judgments. By the end of 2016, for example, 85.7% of pending applications were against ten countries (percentage in brackets)—Ukraine (22.8), Turkey (15.8), Hungary (11.2), Russia (9.8), Romania (9.3), Italy (7.8), Georgia (2.6), Poland (2.3), Azerbaijan (2.1), and Armenia (2.0).[53] Between 1959 and 2016, 53% of findings of at least one violation involved only five states: Turkey (2,889), Italy (1,791), Russia (1,834), Romania (1,147), and Ukraine (1,106).[54]

Judgments on the merits—which rely mostly on written submissions from the parties but in certain cases also upon oral public hearings—are drafted by a Judge Rapporteur, assisted by the judge elected in respect of the respondent state or, in some cases by a drafting committee, and put to a vote of all judges sitting on the particular panel. Typically they contain summaries of the facts, the history of the dispute including a review of relevant domestic law, the arguments presented by the parties, relevant provisions of the ECHR, the Court's reasoned verdict, a concise statement of the substantive result, plus concurring and dissenting opinions if any.

In urgent cases, where serious consequences, such as death or torture could ensue before the matter is finally resolved, a Chamber may 'indicate to the parties any interim measure which it considers should be adopted'.[55] Since the Grand Chamber's judgment in *Mamatkulov and Askarov v Turkey*,[56] the Court regards these as binding on respondent states with, in most cases, failure to comply constituting a violation of the obligation under Article 34 ECHR not to hinder the right of individual application. Although breaches are uncommon, interim applications have, however, led to a huge surge in the application rate—mostly in cases involving imminent expulsion or extradition—from an annual average of about 100 until 2006 to an annual average of 1,892 between 2014–16, of which 506 (8.9%) were granted.[57]

In judging the merits, the primary issue the Court has to consider is whether, on the evidence presented, the respondent state has violated the ECHR. This involves interpreting the alleged misconduct in context and determining what the sparse and abstract statements of the relevant rights mean. While a handful of Convention rights are subject to no express exceptions and cannot be suspended under Article 15 (the 'derogation provision'), the remainder are subject to various express limitations and can also be suspended under Article 15. The Court also applies a dozen or so 'principles of interpretation' not found in the text of the Convention itself but identified and developed in the process of litigation over the years.[58] These are rooted in the 'teleological principle', derived from Articles 31

---

[52] Overview 1959–2016 ECHR, 6. See Greer and Wylde, 'Has the European Court of Human Rights Become a "small claims tribunal" and Why, If At All, Does It Matter?' [2017] *EHRLR* 146 (at 154, line 13 should read 'only a handful of provisions regularly feature in judgments' not 'are regularly been found to have been breached').   [53] *Analysis of Statistics 2016*, 8.

[54] Violations by Article and by States 1959–2016.

[55] Rules of Court, rule 39. See also Harby, 'The Changing Nature of Interim Measures before the European Court of Human Rights' [2010] *EHRLR* 73.   [56] (2005) 41 EHRR 25.

[57] ECtHR, Rule 39 requests granted and refused in 2014, 2015 and 2016 by respondent state, available at: <http://www.echr.coe.int/Documents/Stats_understanding_ENG.pdf>; Zwart, 'More Human Rights than Court: Why the Legitimacy of the European Court of Human Rights is in Need of Repair and How it Can be Done', in Flogaitis *et al.* (2013), 94–5.   [58] See Greer (2006), ch 4.

to 33 of the Vienna Convention on the Law of Treaties, which requires the text of international treaties to be interpreted in good faith according to the ordinary meaning of their terms in context—unless any special meaning was intended by the parties—and in the light of the overall object and purpose of the agreement in question. But, unlike most international treaties which are merely reciprocal agreements between states, the ECHR is a 'constitutional instrument of European public order in the field of human rights', which creates a 'network of mutual bilateral undertakings ... [and] ... objective obligations'.[59] The principle of effective protection of individual rights holds that, given the primary function of the ECHR, rights should be interpreted broadly and exceptions narrowly. This is linked to the principle of non-abuse of rights and limitations, which prohibits states and others from undermining rights by abusing either the rights themselves or their limitations. However, the principles of implied rights and implied limitations allow some scope for extensions to rights, and also inherent but not extensive limitations, to be read into the text. The principle of positive obligations permits the Court to interpret the ECHR so as to impose obligations upon states actively to protect Convention rights, and not merely the negative obligation to avoid violating them.

Armed with the principle of autonomous interpretation the Court can define some of the Convention's key terms in order to prevent states conveniently re-defining their way around their obligations, for instance, by re-designating crimes as mere 'administrative infractions'. Similarly, the principle of evolutive, or dynamic, interpretation enables outmoded conceptions of how terms in the Convention were originally understood to be abandoned when significant, durable, and—according to the principle of commonality—pan-European changes in the climate of European public opinion have occurred, for example that homosexuality and transsexualism are aspects of private life requiring respect from public authorities.[60] The twin principles of subsidiarity and supervision (expressly incorporated in the preamble to the Convention by Article 1 Protocol No 15) indicate that the role of the Court is subordinate to that of member states and is limited to determining whether the Convention has been violated rather than acting as final court of appeal or fourth instance.

The principle of proportionality limits interference with Convention rights to that which is least intrusive in pursuit of a legitimate objective, while the closely related doctrine of the margin of appreciation (expressly incorporated into the preamble by Article 1 Protocol No 15), refers to the room for manoeuvre the Strasbourg institutions are prepared to accord national authorities in fulfilling their Convention obligations. Pervasive in the ECHR are the closely related principles of legality, the rule of law, and procedural fairness—which seek to subject the exercise of public power to effective, formal legal constraints in order to avoid arbitrariness—and the principle of democracy, which assumes that human rights flourish best in the context of democratic political institutions and a tolerant social climate.

While the Court generally seeks to remain faithful to its own previous decisions, these are not formally binding, nor is there much doctrinal exposition as in the common law tradition. Most judgments, therefore, amount to little more than decisions on the facts where the precise circumstances of the dispute are held to constitute, or not to constitute, a violation of the ECHR but which establish little of general application beyond. Moreover, because the Court considers itself less well placed than national authorities to prescribe what should be done, adverse judgments typically declare only that the ECHR has been breached. Where this is the case, an award of compensation, though not automatic, is now the norm. Excluding claims under Article 1 Protocol No 1 (which reflect the value of the property involved) and

---

[59] *Ireland v UK* (1980) 2 EHRR 25, para 239; *Austria v Italy* (1961) YB 116, 138. [60] See Chapter 15.

other outliers, the average compensation per applicant is in the region of €8,300,[61] tending to confirm that the Court has become a 'human rights small claims tribunal' rather than a 'tribunal of principle', to which, some argue, it should instead aspire.[62]

However, over the past decade or so, and primarily to stem floods of similar complaints, the Court has shown greater willingness in several 'pilot judgments', to indicate the type of remedial action required from states found in breach. For example, in *Broniowski v Poland* the Grand Chamber held that the applicant's right to the peaceful enjoyment of possessions under Article 1 Protocol No 1 had been violated by the expropriation of his property coupled with the payment of inadequate compensation, adding that, since the violation 'originated in a widespread problem which resulted from a malfunctioning of Polish legislation and administrative practice ... which has affected and remains capable of affecting a large number of persons',[63] appropriate measures should be introduced to secure an adequate right of compensation or redress, not simply for the particular applicant, but for all similar claimants.[64] Subsequent applications complaining of violations deriving from the same source could, therefore, be directed back to the Polish authorities to settle according to the terms of the *Broniowski* judgment without the Court having to reconsider the merits afresh in each instance. Research has shown that, while pilot judgments have been 'relatively successful' in some contexts, they have been less so in others.[65]

A Chamber's verdict, whether unanimous or by majority, usually disposes of the matter. However, exceptional cases may be referred by one or more of the parties to a Grand Chamber of 17 judges within three months of the original judgment. Technically, such referrals are not 'appeals' but 're-hearings' and are conditional upon approval by the Grand Chamber's five-judge 'admissibility' panel, which is obliged to accede to them where the case raises 'a serious question affecting the interpretation or application of the Convention or the Protocols thereto, or a serious issue of general importance'.[66] References to the Grand Chamber are not common, the vast majority fail to cross the admissibility threshold, and about half of those which are reconsidered confirm the original verdict.[67] Judgments of Chambers become final under three circumstances: when the parties declare they will not request a reference to the Grand Chamber, three months after the date of judgment if a reference to the Grand Chamber has not been made, or where there has been a reference to the Grand Chamber but the five-judge panel has rejected it.

4.5 SUPERVISION OF THE EXECUTION OF JUDGMENTS

Supervision of the execution of judgments against respondent states is the responsibility of the Committee of Ministers, which considers whether the obligation under Article 46(1) ECHR, to 'abide by the final judgment of the Court', has been discharged. Since this is a matter for negotiation, the respondent state effectively participates in supervising enforcement against itself. Judgments, including those involving friendly settlement, are referred to the Committee of Ministers by the Directorate General of Human Rights and Rule of Law and are entered on the agendas of special quarterly human rights meetings. Not surprisingly, the Court's workload problems have also been mirrored in the enforcement

---

[61] Greer and Wylde (2017), 153.

[62] See, eg, Greer and Wildhaber, 'Revisiting the Debate about "Constitutionalising" the European Court of Human Rights' (2012) 12 *HRLR* 655, 686.   [63] (2005) 40 EHRR 495, para 189.

[64] (2005) 40 EHRR 495, para 200.

[65] Leach *et al.*, *Responding to Systematic Human Rights Violations: An Analysis of 'Pilot Judgments' of the European Court of Human Rights and their Impact at National Level* (Intersentia, 2010) 178.

[66] ECHR, Art 43(2).   [67] See, for example, Mowbray (2007), 512, 513, and 518.

process with 9,941 cases pending at the end of 2015.[68] Of these 8,448 (85%) were repetitive—applications raising complaints already condemned in the specific respondent state stemming mostly from the absence of effective local remedies including difficulties with the enforcement of domestic court judgments.[69]

In the past the Committee's view about what constituted sufficient evidence of execution varied from case to case with little apparent rationale.[70] But more convincing evidence that the source of the violation has been effectively tackled is now said to be required.[71] When satisfied that any compensation has been paid—which happened within the deadline in 81% of cases between 2001 and 2015[72]—and that any other necessary measures have been introduced, the Committee of Ministers publicly certifies that its responsibilities under Article 46(2) ECHR have been discharged. This process can take years, for example over eight-and-a-half in the notoriously protracted case of *Marckx v Belgium*, which involved discrimination between legitimate and illegitimate children in the law of affiliation.[73] States may find it difficult to correct the systemic source of a violation for various reasons including: lack of clarity in the Court's judgment, political problems, the daunting scale of the reforms required, managing complex legislative procedures, budgetary issues, adverse public opinion, the possible impact of compliance on obligations deriving from other institutions, and bureaucratic inertia.[74]

Under Articles 46(2) and 46(3) ECHR the Court may be involved in the supervision of the execution of its own judgments in two ways, each activated by a two-thirds majority vote of the Committee of Ministers. First, where execution is hindered by problems in determining what the judgment means, the Court may be called upon to provide further clarification. Second, the Committee can refer cases back to the Grand Chamber where doubts have arisen about the respondent state's compliance with the original judgment. But there is no prospect under these arrangements of re-opening the original verdict or of financial penalties. Up to the end of 2015 neither procedure had been used.[75]

At the end of the supervision of the execution of judgments process, there is very little the Council of Europe can do with a state persistently in violation, short of suspending its voting rights on the Committee or expelling it from the Council of Europe altogether, each of which is likely to prove counterproductive in all but the most extreme circumstances.

5 THE EUROPEAN UNION

For European integrationists, the Council of Europe was a missed opportunity and a bitter disappointment. Jean Monnet, the French Planning Commissioner, regarded it as 'entirely valueless' and President de Gaulle found it 'simply ridiculous'.[76] The French Foreign

---

[68] Committee of Ministers, Supervision of the Execution of Judgments and Decisions of the European Court of Human Rights: 10th Annual Report of the Committee of Ministers 2016, 47, available at: <https://rm.coe.int/168062fe2d>. [69] Supervision of the Execution of Judgments, 47; Cameron (2013), 39–42.

[70] Tomkins, 'The Committee of Ministers: Its Roles under the European Convention on Human Rights' [1995] *EHRLR* 49, 59–60; Klerk, 'Supervision of the Execution of the Judgments of the European Court of Human Rights—The Committee of Ministers' Role under Article 54 of the European Convention on Human Rights' (1998) 45 *Netherlands ILR* 65, 77–8.

[71] Lambert-Abdelgawad, *The Execution of Judgments of the European Court of Human Rights* (Council of Europe Publishing, 2008) 37–8. [72] Supervision of the Execution of Judgments, 80, Table D.3a.

[73] Tomkins (1995), 61.

[74] Steering Committee for Human Rights (CDDH), Guaranteeing the long-term effectiveness of the control system of the European Convention on Human Rights—Addendum to the final report containing CDDH proposals (long version) (9 April 2003) 34.

[75] Information provided to the author by officials at the ECtHR.

[76] Simpson, *Human Rights and the End of Empire—Britain and the Genesis of the European Convention* (OUP, 2001) 646.

Minister, Robert Schuman, therefore, proposed a European Coal and Steel Community (founded by six Council of Europe states in 1951), to integrate the French and German coal and steel industries in order to provide a stronger impediment to another Franco–German war. In 1957, the same six states developed this idea further by creating a common market, the European Economic Community (EEC). In 1965 the merger of the EEC with the European Coal and Steel Community, and the European Atomic Energy Community (also founded in 1957), created the European Communities (EC). Further developments in 1992 transformed the EC into the 12-member European Union (EU). Retaining the distinctive identity of the EC as the 'First Pillar', the EU added a 'Second Pillar' (a Common Foreign and Security Policy), and a 'Third Pillar' (Justice and Home Affairs) embracing such issues as asylum and immigration, drugs, judicial cooperation on civil and criminal justice, and police cooperation on terrorism and international crime. The 'three pillars' were, however, abandoned on 1 December 2009 when, under the Treaty of Lisbon, the EU acquired a consolidated legal personality. By 2013, new members, mostly from the former communist bloc, brought the number of EU states to 28, over half that of the Council of Europe.

For much of its 40-year history the EEC/EC showed little overt interest in human rights. This was largely for three reasons. First, although the ideals of democracy, human rights, and the rule of law were always regarded as important and desirable, human rights were not initially seen as a priority for European economic integration. Second, it was, in any case, assumed that they were adequately addressed by the Council of Europe and the ECHR to which all members of the EEC/EC, but not the EEC/EC itself, also belonged. Third, the judicial organs of the EEC/EC in Luxembourg—the Court of Justice (also referred to as the European Court of Justice or ECJ), the General Court, and the Tribunal, known collectively since the Treaty of Lisbon as the Court of Justice of the European Union (CJEU)—generally interpreted EEC/EU law as it applied to member states, although not to the institutions of the Union itself, in accordance with the ECHR and the jurisprudence of the Strasbourg institutions.

However, for several reasons, towards the end of the twentieth century, the profile of human rights increased in the EU, albeit in an ad hoc rather than systematic manner. First, it became clear that the success of European integration hinged upon the supremacy of Community/EU law. A rebellion threatened since the late 1960s by national constitutional courts, fearing the risks this posed to national constitutional rights, increasingly compelled the ECJ/CJEU to articulate its own fundamental rights jurisprudence. Second, the EU began to require respect for human rights as a condition of entering into formal trading and other relationships with non-EU states. It, therefore, became increasingly difficult for it not to have a developed human rights policy for its own internal affairs. Third, human rights are inextricably interwoven with issues which arose under the Third Pillar, now the Area of Freedom, Security and Justice. Fourth, in the late 1990s, the provision of a formal human rights document, and more effective human rights monitoring arrangements, were seen as offering a solution to the EU's 'legitimacy crisis' caused by the widening gap between the élite-led deepening and widening European integration, on the one hand, and the needs and less ambitious aspirations of Europe's citizens, on the other.

Fifth, Protocol No 14 to the ECHR enables the EU to become a party to the Convention,[77] while Article 6(2) of the Consolidated Version of the Treaty on European Union requires the EU to accede to the ECHR. In the summer of 2010 the Steering Committee on Human Rights and the European Commission were given a mandate by, respectively, the Council of Europe's Committee of Ministers and the EU, to negotiate a treaty enabling the EU to

---

[77] Art 59(2), ECHR; Eckes, 'EU Accession to the ECHR: Between Autonomy and Adaptation' (2013) 76 *MLR* 254.

become a party to the ECHR but not a member of the Council of Europe. A Draft Accession Agreement was concluded and made public on 5 April 2013.[78] Yet, in spite of having been closely involved in the discussions, on 18 December 2014, the ECJ ruled that, in the terms proposed, accession was beyond the powers granted the EU by its foundational treaties.[79] Particular concern was expressed about the risk that accession would effectively subordinate the ECJ to the ECtHR with respect to Convention rights, compromise the transfer of sovereignty by member states to the EU, and undermine the effectiveness, autonomy, and unity of EU law. Therefore, unless its foundational treaties are amended—a very remote prospect—accession to the ECHR will remain a formal treaty obligation which the EU is legally incapable of discharging.[80]

5.1 HUMAN RIGHTS AND THE COURT OF JUSTICE OF THE EUROPEAN UNION

The EU operates on the basis that 'fundamental rights form an integral part of the general principles of [its] law', and that 'respect for human rights is … a condition of the lawfulness' of Community/Union acts.[81] In theory, therefore, violations of fundamental rights can be litigated before the CJEU by EU institutions against each other, by member states against each other, by the Commission against member states, by individuals and subnational organizations with legal personality against EU institutions, and, through preliminary references from national courts in ongoing litigation, by individuals and subnational organizations with legal personality against member states. However, in practice it is rare for any of this to happen. In principle, individuals can complain to the CJEU about a violation of their fundamental rights by EU institutions in one of two ways. First, under Article 263 of the Consolidated Version of the Treaty on the Functioning of the European Union, 'any natural or legal person' can initiate proceedings for review of the legality of acts of EU institutions against 'an act addressed' to, or which is 'of direct and individual concern', to them. But this is a very difficult test to satisfy since the ECJ/CJEU has interpreted it to mean that the applicant has been affected 'by reason of certain attributes which are peculiar to them or by reason of circumstances in which they are differentiated from all other persons'.[82] The second route is more indirect. Under Article 267, a national court may ask the CJEU for a preliminary ruling on whether EU law, including that relating to fundamental rights, has been violated. But this is not available to litigants 'as a matter of right'.[83] Although neither of these routes requires an 'exhaustion of domestic remedies' as under the ECHR, each, nevertheless, is likely to be expensive and protracted. It is hardly surprising, therefore, that the CJEU has heard few human rights complaints from individual applicants and that judicial review in Luxembourg has led to the annulment of

---

[78] Council of Europe, Fifth negotiation meeting between the CDDH ad hoc negotiation group and the European Commission on the accession of the European Union to the European Convention on Human Rights, Final Report to the CDDH, Appendix 1, 47+1(2013)008rev2 (10 June 2012).

[79] *Opinion 2/13 re Accession to the ECHR* [2015] 2 CMLR 21; Odermatt, 'A Giant Step Backwards? Opinion 2/13 on the EU's Accession to the European Convention on Human Rights' (2015) 47 *NYUJILP* 783.

[80] Groussot, Lorenz, and Petursson, 'The Paradox of Human Rights Protection in Europe: Two Courts, One Goal?', in Arnardóttir and Buyse (eds), *Shifting Centres of Gravity in Human Rights Protection: Rethinking Relations between the ECHR, EU and National Legal Orders* (Routledge, 2016) 19–25; Björgvinsson, 'The Role of the European Court of Human Rights in the Changing European Human Rights Architecture', in Arnardóttir and Buyse (2016), 31–5.

[81] *Opinion 2/94 on Accession by the Community to the ECHR* [1996] ECR I-1759, paras 33 and 34.

[82] Case 25/62, *Plaumann & Co v Commission* [1963] ECR 95, 107.

[83] Case C-50/00 P, *Unión de Pequeños Agricultores v Council* [2002] ECR I-6677, para 42.

only a handful of EU measures on human rights grounds.[84] Finally, the jurisdiction of the CJEU over actions of EU institutions and member states is limited. Although activities under the Area of Freedom, Security and Justice are included, the CJEU has no jurisdiction at all in relation to the EU's common foreign and security policy, where human rights issues might also arise.

5.2 THE CHARTER OF FUNDAMENTAL RIGHTS

The Treaty of Nice 2001 both inaugurated the process of providing the EU with more formal constitutional foundations and provided its first formal statement of rights, the Charter of Fundamental Rights (CFREU), which collects together, in a single document, rights which the EU has already recognized in various other disparate sources.[85] However, it was not until the Treaty of Lisbon 2009 that the CFREU became legally binding on member states, subject to exemptions granted to the UK and Poland by Protocol No 30.

The CFREU differs from the ECHR in five principal ways. First, it includes rights contained in the ECHR but not in precisely the same terms. For example, Article 6 CFREU provides the right to liberty and security of the person in a single clause—'everyone has the right to liberty and security of the person'—while Article 5 ECHR has no less than five clauses, one of which has six further sub-clauses (12 elements in total) for the same right. Article 52(3) CFREU requires the meaning and scope of rights found in both the Charter and ECHR to be interpreted in the same way as those found in the latter. But, as the Council of Europe's Steering Committee for Human Rights put it, 'experience tends to show that it is difficult to avoid contradictions where two differently worded texts on the same subject-matter are interpreted by two different courts'.[86] However, this does not yet appear to have happened in any CJEU case.

Second, the ECHR is largely confined to civil and political rights. The CFREU, on the other hand, also includes a wide range of social, economic, cultural, and citizenship rights, similar to those found in the European Social Charter discussed in Section 3.3.

Third, the ECHR provides different limitation clauses for each right. Article 52 CFREU, on the other hand, sets out general limitations on all substantive Charter rights in the following terms. They must be provided for by law, respect the essence of the rights and freedoms in question, and be subject to the principle of proportionality. They must also be necessary and genuinely meet objectives of the general interest recognized by the EU or protect the rights and freedoms of others. Charter rights deriving from EU Treaties must also be exercised under the conditions and within the limits defined by those treaties.

The fourth difference between the ECHR and the CFREU is that the former generally binds member states in any and all of their activities, while, according to Article 51(1), in addition to the EU, the CFREU applies to member states only as far as the formulation and implementation of EU law are concerned.

Finally, since the CFREU does not provide any additional right of individual petition, the only recourse to the CJEU open to individual litigants for a breach of a Charter right remains the existing limited ones described in Section 5.1. However, even before it acquired formal legal status, the CFREU was already being used as a point of reference by national

---

[84] Douglas-Scott, 'The European Union and Human Rights After the Treaty of Lisbon' (2011) 11 *HRLR* 645, 679–80.

[85] Douglas-Scott (2011), 650–8; see also Defeis, 'Human Rights, the European Union, and the Treaty Route: From Maastricht to Lisbon' (2012) 35 *Fordham Int'l LJ* 1207.

[86] Steering Committee for Human Rights (CDDH), Study of Technical and Legal Issues of a Possible EC/EU Accession to the European Convention on Human Rights, DG-II(2002)006 [CDDH(2002)010 Addendum 2] (25–28 June 2002), para 80.

courts and by EU institutions, including the CJEU. It now operates as the primary source for human rights in the EU which has become 'one of the most significant areas of EU law'.[87]

5.3 THE FUNDAMENTAL RIGHTS AGENCY AND THE COMMISSIONER FOR JUSTICE, FUNDAMENTAL RIGHTS AND CITIZENSHIP

Developing an idea first approved in 2003, in June 2005 the EU formally proposed to expand the remit of its European Centre on Racism and Xenophobia to create a Fundamental Rights Agency (FRA), which came into operation on 1 January 2007.[88] Using the Charter as its main point of reference, attempting to avoid overlap with the Council of Europe, and networking with national institutions, the FRA is intended to discharge the following functions: to be an independent centre of expertise on fundamental rights issues through data collection, analysis, and networking; to provide relevant EU institutions and bodies, plus member states, with assistance and expertise when implementing EU law relating to fundamental rights; and to advise Union institutions and member states on how best to prepare and implement fundamental rights-related Union legislation. However, the FRA has no power to examine individual complaints, to issue regulations, or to carry out 'normative monitoring' for the purposes of Article 7 EU Treaty. In 2010 the European Commission's Justice, Freedom and Security portfolio was divided between the new posts of Commissioner for Justice, Fundamental Rights and Citizenship, and Commissioner for Home Affairs, each with responsibility for policy development in their respective fields.

6 CONCLUSION

There can be little doubt that the European nation-state remains the most important arena for the legal protection of human rights. Assuming civil peace, a distribution of resources which is at least not gravely inequitable, and effectively regulated markets, human rights are most likely to be secured by genuinely democratic and rights-sensitive national legislative and executive institutions, independent, professional, and rights-aware national judiciaries, and by the provision of national justiciable constitutional rights.

The main human rights-related functions of both the Council of Europe and the EU are, therefore, to contribute to the preservation and protection of these elements where they have already firmly taken root, and to attempt to encourage their development where this is not yet the case. Their core achievements in the human rights field lie principally in the successful institutionalization of their respective missions in both political and legal spheres. In turn, this has contributed significantly to securing minimum standards across the continent, albeit not evenly or un-problematically. While the central trends are their expansion and their increasing complexity and interpenetration, the key challenges concern how this could, and should, be properly understood and coherently, legitimately, and effectively managed, particularly given that over the past half-decade or so the authority and legitimacy of both the ECtHR and the EU have each been called into question by rising rights-and-Euro-scepticism and by more militant forms of populist, exclusionary nationalism, driven especially by post-2008 economic austerity, jihadi terrorism, mass migration, and disillusionment with multiculturalism. As the twenty-first century progresses, these and other issues invite debate about which analytical model(s) might provide the best insights, and which pan-European institutional, procedural, and normative

---

[87] Douglas-Scott (2011), 645.
[88] See Sokhi-Bulley, 'The Fundamental Rights Agency of the European Union: A New Panopticism' (2011) 11 *HRLR* 683.

framework(s) the most attractive solutions, particularly with respect to two clusters of questions representing the flip sides of the same coin: to what extent are the autonomy, separate identity, and divergence of the Council of Europe and the EU likely to be preserved, or is more integration, interdependence, convergence, and harmonization likely? And, to what extent, are the alternatives they present desirable?[89]

FURTHER READING

ARNARDÓTTIR and BUYSE (eds), *Shifting Centres of Gravity in Human Rights Protection: Rethinking Relations Between the ECHR, EU and National Legal Orders* (Routledge, 2016).

BATES, *The Evolution of the European Convention on Human Rights: From Its Inception to the Creation of a Permanent Court of Human Rights* (Oxford University Press, 2010).

CHRISTOFFERSEN and MADSEN (eds), *The European Court of Human Rights between Law and Politics* (Oxford University Press, 2011).

DZEHTSIAROU et al. (eds), *Human Rights in Europe: The Influence, Overlaps and Contradictions of the EU and the ECHR* (Routledge, 2014).

FØLLESDAL et al. (eds), *Constituting Europe: The European Court of Human Rights in a National, European and Global Context* (Cambridge University Press, 2013).

GREER, GERARDS, and SLOWE, *Human Rights in the Council of Europe and the European Union: Achievements, Trends and Challenges* (Cambridge University Press, 2017).

GREER and WILDHABER, 'Revisiting the Debate about "Constitutionalising" the European Court of Human Rights' (2012) 12 *HRLR* 655.

GRABENWARTER (ed), *The European Convention on Human Rights: A Commentary* (Hart, 2013).

HARRIS et al., *Harris, O'Boyle and Warbrick: Law of the European Convention on Human Rights* (Oxford University Press, 2014).

TORRES PÉREZ, *Conflicts of Rights in the European Union: A Theory of Supranational Adjudication* (Oxford University Press, 2009).

SCHMAHL AND BREUER (eds), *The Council of Europe: Its Law and Policies* (Oxford University Press, 2017).

USEFUL WEBSITES

Council of Europe: **<http://www.coe.int/>**

European Court of Human Rights: **<http://www.echr.coe.int/echr>**

European Commissioner for Human Rights: **<http://www.coe.int/t/commissioner>**

European Union: **<http://europa.eu/>**

EU Charter of Fundamental Rights: **<http://ec.europa.eu/justice_home/unit/charte/index_en.html>**

European Union Agency for Fundamental Rights: **<http://www.fra.europa.eu/fra>**

Court of Justice of the European Union: **<http://curia.europa.eu/>**

Organization for Security and Cooperation in Europe: **<http://www.osce.org/>**

---

[89] These and other issues are explored in Greer, Gerards, and Slowe, *Human Rights in the Council of Europe and the European Union: Achievements, Trends and Challenges* (CUP, 2017).

23

AFRICA

Christof Heyns and Magnus Killander

SUMMARY

The extent to which human rights is protected at the national level in Africa is monitored not only by the UN system but also through an extensive framework of regional instruments adopted by the African Union and its predecessor, the Organization of African Unity, as well as sub-regional organizations such as the Economic Community of West African States, the East African Community, and the Southern African Development Community. The African Commission on Human and Peoples' Rights, established by the African Charter on Human and Peoples' Rights 1981, and operating under the auspices of the African Union, remains the main human rights body of the continent. The African Court on Human and Peoples' Rights has been established to complement the work of the Commission.

1 INTRODUCTION

The African continent of today is characterized, inter alia, by the coexistence of traditional and modern strands of society. As is the case in traditional societies across the world, recognition of values such as human dignity, a prohibition of harm to others, and the ideals of benevolent governance may be found in many African societies—the same norms that underlie much of the modern notion of human rights. However, the idea of enforcement of these norms is typically not well developed in traditional societies. To the extent that people may be considered to be the bearers of human rights in such societies, these rights are rights in the weak sense of the word—the corresponding duty they impose is at best a moral or an aspirational one. There are few effective channels for actions against abusive leaders or governments.

While there is an increasing recognition of human rights in Africa not only in the weak but also in the strong sense of the word, where enforcement is possible, the continent is still facing a myriad of challenges to the full realization of the human rights of its people. This is despite widespread formal commitment to human rights across the continent in the form of bills of rights, establishment of national human rights institutions, declarations by intergovernmental organizations, and the establishment of a regional human rights system. Poverty and human rights violations go hand in hand in Africa, as is the case in other parts of the world.[1] However, the situation is particularly pronounced in Africa in view of the high general levels of poverty.

[1] See Chapter 30.

This chapter examines the role played by African regional intergovernmental organizations, in particular the African Union, in the realization of human rights. The focus is on the African Charter on Human and Peoples' Rights (ACHPR or Charter) and the main organs, the African Commission on Human and Peoples' Rights (African Commission) and the African Court on Human and Peoples' Rights (African Court), which have been established to ensure its implementation.

2 HISTORICAL OVERVIEW

The Charter of the Organization of African Unity (OAU Charter), adopted in 1963, made few references to human rights. However, the Charter did set the task for the new organization of enforcing human rights norms by recognizing the goal of bringing an end to colonialism and apartheid in Africa. In the late 1970s, in the wake of the mass murders of the regimes of, for example, Idi Amin in Uganda, the OAU started to pay some attention to the human rights situation in its member states.

In 1978 President Jawara of The Gambia made the following statement before the UN General Assembly:

> With the attainment of self-determination and independence, it would be ironic indeed if the freedom gained from the defeat of colonialism should ... be denied our people by our own leaders. After centuries of a deliberate policy of dehumanisation, subjugation, and oppression, the minimum our people expect and must have is the full enjoyment of their political, economic, social, and cultural rights ... It should be the duty of all of us to ... ensure that ... the people enjoy ... their civil and political rights.[2]

Over the following years President Jawara, one of the few democratically elected leaders in Africa at the time, played a leading role in the development of the ACHPR, which is also known as the Banjul Charter, after the capital of The Gambia. The OAU Assembly adopted the ACHPR in 1981 and it entered into force in 1986. In 1987 the OAU Assembly elected the 11 members of the African Commission on Human and Peoples' Rights. The Commission recommended that, to guard its independence, the Secretariat of the Commission should not be located at the headquarters of the OAU in Addis Ababa, Ethiopia. A year later, the OAU Assembly decided that the Secretariat of the Commission should be located in Banjul. Ironically, The Gambia would soon afterwards become one of the most repressive societies on the African continent, and an ill-placed host to the Commission.

With democratic elections in South Africa in April 1994, the OAU had finally succeeded in its main objective of the liberation of Africa from colonialism and apartheid. It was felt that the OAU was in need of transformation and in 2000 the OAU Assembly adopted the Constitutive Act of the African Union (AU). The AU was launched in Durban, South Africa, in 2002. The headquarters of the AU remain in Addis Ababa, Ethiopia.

The main principles of the OAU were sovereign equality and 'non-interference in the internal affairs of states'.[3] These principles have been retained in the AU Constitutive Act. However, it is noticeable that a number of new objectives have been added in the Act. These include the objective to 'promote and protect human and peoples' rights in accordance with the ACHPR and other relevant human rights instruments'.[4] In addition to the

---

[2] Alhaji Sir Dawda Kairaba Jawara, Statement at the 33rd session of the UN General Assembly, 22 September 1978, quoted in Touray, *The Gambia and the World—A History of the Foreign Policy of Africa's Smallest State 1965–1995* (Institut für Afrika-Kunde, 2000) 161.   [3] OAU Charter, Art 3.

[4] AU Constitutive Act, Art 3.

commitments set out in the Constitutive Act, the AU established a new institutional framework with a mandate that includes the realization of human rights. The new institutions include the African Court on Human and Peoples' Rights, the Pan-African Parliament, the Peace and Security Council, the New Partnership for Africa's Development, and the African Peer Review Mechanism.

There are no entry requirements in terms of human rights practices for states to join the AU, and all the members of the OAU became members of the AU without scrutiny of their human rights records. However, there is at least a theoretical possibility that violations of human rights may lead to suspension from the AU and other sanctions.[5] AU inaction in the face of gross human rights violations in, for example Burundi, Eritrea, Sudan, and Zimbabwe, however, illustrates that the principle of non-interference still dominates. In fact the AU has only used its power to sanction member states after military coups. A sitting head of state runs little risk of being castigated by his peers in respect of how much he (few African heads of state have been women) has manipulated an election to stay in power. Many current African presidents first came to power through military coups. Most of them have then tried to legitimize their rule through elections. However, sometimes the people manage to oust such leaders as happened with President Compaoré of Burkina Faso in 2014 and President Jammeh of The Gambia in early 2017.

Concern over human rights in Africa by intergovernmental organizations is of course not limited to the AU. The UN plays a major role through treaty bodies, special procedures, field presences, and so on. Impunity is being addressed, among others, through the work of the International Criminal Court (ICC).[6] However, it should be noted that many African governments view the ICC as having focused too much on Africa and interfered in domestic politics through indicting African leaders such as the President of Sudan.

Sub-regional African intergovernmental organizations have taken an increased interest in human rights. The AU has recognized eight Regional Economic Communities (RECs) as building blocks towards an African Economic Community.[7] The most active of these in the field of human rights is the Economic Community of West African States (ECOWAS).[8] The ECOWAS Community Court of Justice can hear complaints about human rights violations in member states without the requirement of exhaustion of local remedies. Among its case law can be mentioned cases dealing with arbitrary detention in The Gambia and slavery in Niger.[9] The East African Court of Justice (EACJ) does not have explicit jurisdiction to deal with complaints of human rights violations, but has nevertheless dealt with human rights issues that were considered to constitute violations of the East African Community treaty.[10]

The Tribunal of the Southern African Development Community (SADC) followed the same approach, but, in a step which does not auger well for the protection of human rights through courts in Africa, this tribunal was dissolved by the SADC Summit in 2012 following its finding of human rights violations in Zimbabwe.[11]

---

[5] AU Constitutive Act, Art 23.   [6] See Chapter 26.   [7] Assembly/AU/Dec.112 (VII) (July 2006).

[8] On the human rights mandate of the RECs, see Viljoen, *International Human Rights Law in Africa* (OUP, 2012) 469.

[9] *Manneh v The Gambia*, ECW/CCJ/JUD/03/08 (5 June 2008); (2008) AHRLR 171; *Koraou v Niger*, ECW/CCJ/JUD/06/08 (27 October 2008); (2008) AHRLR 182.

[10] *Katabazi and Others v Secretary General of the East African Community and Another* [2007] EACJ 3, (2007) AHRLR 119 (EAC 2007); *Campbell (Pvt) Ltd and others v Zimbabwe* [2007] SADCT 1 (28 November 2008); (2008) AHRLR 199.

[11] Final communiqué of the 32nd Summit of the SADC Heads of State and Government, Maputo, Mozambique (18 August 2012) para 24.

Some RECs have also been active in human rights standard-setting. For example a SADC Protocol on Gender and Development was adopted in 2008.

At the domestic level, all 55 member states of the AU have written constitutions which recognize human rights.[12]

3 THE AFRICAN CHARTER AND OTHER RELEVANT TREATIES

The ACHPR has been ratified by 54 member states of the AU. Morocco is yet to ratify.

3.1 NORMS RECOGNIZED IN THE AFRICAN CHARTER

The ACHPR goes further than the primary regional human rights conventions of Europe and the Americas in recognizing, in one treaty, not only civil and political rights, but also some economic, social, and cultural rights and not only individual rights but also peoples' rights. The Charter also provides for duties.

A number of shortcomings in respect of the provisions concerning civil and political rights in the ACHPR when compared to other international instruments can be noted. For example, the right to privacy and the right against forced labour are not explicitly mentioned in the Charter. Fair trial rights and the right of political participation are provided for in less detail than in other human rights treaties. However, the African Commission has, in resolutions and in its decisions on cases, interpreted the Charter in line with established international practice. Thus, the ACHPR has been interpreted to encompass some of the rights or aspects of rights not explicitly included. For example, the content of the fair trial rights in the ACHPR has been expounded by the Commission in its detailed Principles and Guidelines on the Right to a Fair Trial and Legal Assistance in Africa adopted in 2003.[13]

The inclusion in the ACHPR of socio-economic rights alongside civil and political rights emphasizes the indivisibility of human rights and the importance of development issues, which are obviously important matters in the African context. At the same time it should be noted that a modest number of socio-economic rights are explicitly included in the Charter. It only recognizes 'a right to work under equitable and satisfactory conditions' (Article 15), a right to health (Article 16), and a right to education (Article 17). Among rights not explicitly included are the rights to food, water, social security, and housing. The socio-economic rights in the ACHPR have generally received scant attention from the African Commission, but in its 2001 decision in *SERAC v Nigeria* the Commission dealt extensively with the issue.[14] In this case, which dealt with gross human rights violations in the oil-rich Ogoniland region of Nigeria, the Commission deduced an implicit right to 'housing or shelter' in the ACHPR from the provisions on health, property, and family life in the Charter. Similarly, a right to food was read into the right to dignity. It should also be noted that the Commission in 2004 established a Working Group on Economic, Social, and Cultural Rights and in 2011 adopted elaborate Principles and Guidelines on Economic, Social, and Cultural Rights.[15]

---

[12] Heyns and Kaguongo, 'Constitutional Human Rights Law in Africa' (2006) 22 *S African JHR* 673.

[13] DOC/OS(XXX)247 (May 2003).

[14] 155/96, 15th Activity Report of the ACommHPR (2001–2002); (2001) AHRLR 60.

[15] Available at: <http://www.achpr.org/files/instruments/economic-social-cultural/achpr_instr_guide_draft_esc_rights_eng.pdf>.

Peoples' rights, on the other hand, are more fully developed in the ACHPR than in the UN covenants which set out only a right to self-determination. According to the Charter, all 'peoples' have a right to be equal (Article 19); to existence and self-determination (Article 20); to freely dispose of their wealth and natural resources (Article 21); to economic, social, and cultural development (Article 22); to peace and security (Article 23); and to a satisfactory environment (Article 24). Clearly, part of the motivation for the recognition of 'peoples' rights' lies in the fact that, historically, entire 'peoples' in Africa have been colonized and otherwise exploited. 'Peoples' can thus refer to the whole population of the country. For example, the African Commission has held that a military coup constituted not only a violation of the right to political participation in Article 13, but also violated the right to self-determination in Article 20.[16] Peoples' rights may also be exercised by a part of the population of a state 'bound together by their historical, traditional, racial, ethnic, cultural, linguistic, religious, ideological, geographical, economic identities and affinities, or other bonds'.[17]

At the same time there is little room for secession to be found in the Charter. In *Katangese Peoples' Congress v Zaire* the claimant requested that the African Commission recognize the independence of the Katanga province in the then Zaire (now Democratic Republic of the Congo). The Commission held:

> In the absence of concrete evidence of violations of human rights to the point that the territorial integrity of Zaire should be called to question and in the absence of evidence that the people of Katanga are denied the right to participate in government as guaranteed by article 13(1) of the African Charter, the Commission holds the view that Katanga is obliged to exercise a variant of self-determination that is compatible with the sovereignty and territorial integrity of Zaire.[18]

The Commission upheld this position in a case against Cameroon in which it held that grievances of the Anglophone part of Cameroon against the dominant Francophone part should not be 'resolved through secession but through a comprehensive national dialogue'.[19]

In *SERAC v Nigeria*, discussed earlier, the African Commission found the Nigerian government guilty of violating Article 21 ACHPR by giving 'the green light to private actors, and the oil companies in particular, to devastatingly affect the well-being of the Ogonis'.[20] In this case, the Commission also found a violation of the right to a satisfactory environment in Article 24 ACHPR. The *Endorois* case, decided in 2009, dealt with the rights of indigenous people in Kenya. Among other violations, the Commission found that Kenya had violated the right to economic, social, and cultural development (Article 22) of the Endorois people.[21]

3.2 DUTIES AND LIMITATIONS

Articles 27, 28, and 29 ACHPR provide for individual duties towards the community. These range from duties towards the family, such as the maintenance of parents 'in case of need', to duties towards the state. The African Commission has not pronounced itself

---

[16] 147/95 and 149/96, *Jawara v The Gambia*, 13th Activity Report of the ACommHPR (1999–2000); (2000) AHRLR 107, para 73.

[17] 266/03, *Gunme and Others v Cameroon*, 26th Activity Report of the ACommHPR (2009), (2009) AHRLR 9, para 171.

[18] 75/92, 8th Activity Report of the ACommHPR (1994–1995); (2000) AHRLR 72, para 6.

[19] *Gunme*, para 203.   [20] *SERAC*, para 58.

[21] 276/2003, *Centre for Minority Rights Development (Kenya) and Minority Rights Group International on behalf of Endorois Welfare Council v Kenya*, 27th Activity Report of the ACommHPR (2009); (2009) AHRLR 75.

on the content of these duties except for its application of Article 27(2) ('the rights and freedoms of each individual shall be exercised with due regard to the rights of others, collective security, morality and common interest') as a general limitation clause.

Article 9(2) provides that '[e]very individual shall have the right to express and disseminate his opinions within the law'. As phrased, the right seems to recognize the right in question only to the extent that it is not infringed upon by national law. Freedom of conscience and religion in Article 8, freedom of association in Article 10, freedom of assembly in Article 11, and freedom of movement in Article 12 are apparently similarly restricted. This type of limitation is often referred to as a claw-back clause—what is given with the one hand is taken away with the other.[22] However, the African Commission has held that provisions in the ACHPR that allow rights to be limited 'in accordance with law', should be understood to require such limitations to be provided by domestic legal provisions that comply with the standards set by Article 27(2) and with international human rights law standards.[23]

3.3 PROTECTION OF WOMEN, CHILDREN, AND VULNERABLE GROUPS

Article 18(2) ACHPR places a duty on the state to assist the family as 'the custodian of morals and traditional values recognized by the community'. However, such values may not discriminate as this would violate the general prohibition of discrimination in Article 2 and the specific prohibition of discrimination against women in Article 18(3), which also provides for the protection of the rights of women and children 'as stipulated in international declarations and conventions'. Article 18(4) provides for 'special measures of protection' for the aged and disabled.

The OAU Assembly adopted the African Charter on the Rights and Welfare of the Child (Children's Charter) in 1990. The Children's Charter can be seen as a regional response to the UN Convention on the Rights of the Child (CRC), adopted less than a year before the African treaty. The Children's Charter provides some increased protection compared to the CRC, including further protections for child soldiers, as well as protections against child marriages and for internally displaced children. Unlike the CRC, the Children's Charter also provides for duties for children.[24]

A Committee on the Rights and Welfare of the Child (separate, thus, from the African Commission on Human and Peoples' Rights) was established under the Children's Charter. The 11 members of the Committee were elected in July 2001 and the first meeting of the Committee was held in 2002. States have to report to the Committee within two years of the entry into force of the convention for the state party concerned and every three years thereafter. However, despite the fact that the Committee was established in 2001, it only began to consider the reports it had received in 2008.[25] Apart from state reporting, the Children's Charter also provides for a communication procedure. The Committee does not have its own secretariat, and is serviced by the Department for Social Affairs at the AU Commission in Addis Ababa. The Committee has considered a number of state reports and in 2011 handed down its first decision with regard to a communication dealing with

---

[22] See Chapter 5.
[23] 105/93, 128/94, 130/94 and 152/96, *Media Rights Agenda and Others v Nigeria*, 12th Annual Activity Report of the ACommHPR (1998); (2000) AHRLR 200, paras 64–71.   [24] Viljoen (2012), 393–4.
[25] Mezmur and Sloth-Nielsen, 'An Ice-Breaker: State Party Reports and the 11th session of the African Committee of Experts on the Rights and Welfare of the Child' (2008) 8 *African HRLJ* 596.

the right to nationality of Nubian children in Kenya.[26] This has been followed by decisions against Uganda and Senegal.[27]

In 2003, the AU Assembly adopted the Protocol to the African Charter on Human and Peoples' Rights on the Rights of Women (Women's Protocol). As a protocol to the African Charter it expands and extends the protection of the rights of women already recognized therein. Through its 24 substantive provisions the Women's Protocol provides much more comprehensive protection than the UN Convention on the Elimination of All Forms of Discrimination against Women (CEDAW). For example, the Women's Protocol includes provisions on domestic violence, trafficking, elimination of harmful practices, reproductive rights, HIV/AIDS, and inheritance and protection of elderly women.

During the drafting of the Protocol, there were many controversial issues, including the question of polygamy which is recognized and practised in many African countries. For example, South African President Zuma has four wives, and King Mswati III of Swaziland, one of the world's last absolute monarchs, at the time of writing had 15 wives. The CEDAW Committee has held that polygamy violates the right to equality in marriage.[28] In a clear attempt to strike a compromise, Article 6(c) Women's Protocol provides that 'monogamy is encouraged as the preferred form of marriage and that the rights of women in marriage and family, including in polygamous marital relationships are promoted and protected'. The African Commission and the African Court are responsible for monitoring the implementation of the Women's Protocol.

The OAU Convention Governing the Specific Aspects of Refugee Problems in Africa was adopted in 1969 and can thus be seen as the first African human rights treaty. The convention was a response to the 1967 UN Protocol Relating to the Status of Refugees, which extended the application of the UN Refugee Convention to the whole world. The African Convention includes a broader definition of 'refugee' than the UN Convention, extending the protection to those seeking refuge because of 'external aggression, occupation, foreign domination or events seriously disturbing public order'.[29]

The AU has adopted a number of treaties of relevance to human rights in recent years such as the Convention on Preventing and Combating Corruption, the African Youth Charter, the African Charter on Democracy, Elections and Governance, and the AU Convention for the Protection and Assistance of Internally Displaced Persons in Africa.

4 THE PROTECTIVE MECHANISMS

4.1 THE AFRICAN COMMISSION

4.1.1 Structure and composition

Article 30 ACHPR provides for the establishment of the African Commission on Human and Peoples' Rights. The African Commission was established in 1987 following the entry into force of the Charter in 1986. According to Article 45 ACHPR, the mandate of the Commission includes promoting human rights through research, dissemination of

[26] 002/09, *IHRDA and Open Society Justice Initiative (OSJI) (on behalf of children of Nubian descent in Kenya) v Kenya* (22 March 2011).

[27] 001/05, *Michelo Hansungule and others (on behalf of children in Northern Uganda) v Uganda* (15 April 2013); 001/12, *The Centre for Human Rights (University of Pretoria) and La Rencontre Africaine pour la Defense Des Droits de l'homme (Senegal) v Senegal* (15 April 2014).

[28] CEDAW Committee, General Recommendation 21, HRI/GEN/1/Rev.9 (Vol II) 337, para 14.

[29] OAU Convention Governing the Specific Aspects of the Refugee Problem in Africa, Art I(2).

information, and cooperation with other human rights bodies. The Commission also has a mandate to interpret the provisions of the Charter and consider complaints against a state alleging that it has violated the ACHPR. The Commission has also been given the mandate to consider state reports on implementation of the Charter. Although this is not explicitly provided for in the Charter, the Commission also accepts and considers communications or complaints lodged by individuals.

The African Commission consists of 11 Commissioners who serve in their individual capacities and are nominated by states parties to the Charter and elected by the AU Assembly. The independence of the Commission has sometimes been questioned as a number of civil servants and ambassadors have served on it. However, in a *note verbale* to the member states in April 2005 the AU Commission provided guidelines that excluded senior civil servants and diplomatic representatives from being elected.[30] These guidelines have been followed with regard to new appointments to the Commission. The Commission meets twice a year in regular sessions for a period of up to two weeks, alternating its meetings between its headquarters in Banjul and other African capitals.

4.1.2 The complaints procedure

Both states and individuals may bring complaints to the African Commission alleging violations of the ACHPR by states parties. The inter-state complaint procedure by which one state brings a complaint about an alleged human rights violation by another state is not often used. Only one such case has been decided by the Commission. In *Democratic Republic of the Congo v Burundi, Rwanda and Uganda*,[31] the Commission held that the three respondent states had violated a number of individual and peoples' rights during the presence of their armed forces on Congolese territory.

Articles 55, 56, 57, and 58 ACHPR deal with 'other communications', that is, communications not submitted by a state. As indicated above, while the Charter is silent on who can bring such communications, the Commission has in its practice accepted complaints from individuals as well as from NGOs. From the case law of the Commission it is clear that the complainant does not need to be a victim or a family member of a victim.[32]

Article 56 ACHPR lists the admissibility criteria. These include that communications should indicate the author, be compatible with the Charter, not be written in disparaging or insulting language, not be based exclusively on media reports, be submitted within reasonable time, and not deal with a situation which has already been settled. In practice, the most important criterion for admissibility is the exhaustion of local remedies. The Commission has stated that for a case not to be admissible, local remedies must be available, effective, sufficient, and not unduly prolonged.[33] In *Purohit and Another v The Gambia*, a case dealing with detention in a mental health institution, the Commission gave a potentially far-reaching decision on the exhaustion of local remedies when it held that:

> [t]he category of people being represented in the present communication are likely to be people picked up from the streets or people from poor backgrounds and as such it cannot be said that the remedies available in terms of the Constitution are realistic remedies for them in the absence of legal aid services.[34]

---

[30] BC/OLC/66/VolXVIII (5 April 2005).
[31] 227/99, 20th Activity Report of the ACommHPR (2006); (2003) AHRLR 19.
[32] *SERAC*, para 49.   [33] *Jawara*, paras 28–40.
[34] 241/01, *Purohit and Another v The Gambia*, 16th Activity Report of the ACommHPR (2002–2003); (2003) AHRLR 96, para 37.

Figure 23.1 The African Charter communications procedure

The criterion of submission within reasonable time has become increasingly important as the Commission has narrowed its definition of what constitutes reasonable time so as, in many cases, to effectively apply the six-month rule originally inscribed in the European and American Conventions.

When a complaint is lodged, the state in question is asked to respond in writing to the allegations against it. If it does not respond, and the admissibility criteria are met, the Commission proceeds on the basis of the facts as provided by the complainant. If a state has responded, the Commission gives the complainant an opportunity to respond to the arguments by the state. The communication is then scheduled for a hearing at one of the sessions of the Commission. The complainant and respondent state are invited to make presentations at the hearing which is not public.

If the Commission finds a violation, it may make recommendations. These may include that continuing violations should stop (for example, prisoners be released), or specific laws be amended or repealed. However, often the recommendations are rather vague, and the state party is merely urged to 'take all necessary steps to comply with its obligations under the Charter'.

The ACHPR does not contain a provision on interim or provisional measures. However, the Rules of Procedure of the Commission grant the Commission the power to grant provisional measures. The Commission has used provisional measures in a number of cases, for example when an execution has been imminent, although this has often been without success. The Commission has held that a breach of provisional measures constitutes a violation of Article 1 ACHPR.

The Commission has handed down approximately 200 decisions on communications since it was established in 1987 (including cases that were declared inadmissible or discontinued due to withdrawal or loss of contact with the complainant). The individual complaints procedure is thus not used as frequently as would have been expected on a continent with the type of human rights problems that Africa experiences. This could, to some extent, be attributed to a lack of awareness about the system. Even where there is awareness, however, there is often not much faith that the system will make a difference, given the emphasis on the continent on state sovereignty and the dismissive approach which is often taken in respect of human rights.

The Commission's recommendations are often vague and there is no system of follow-up to its recommendations. While the Commission sometimes recommends compensation to the complainant, it has generally not decided on the amount to award. However, this practice has changed in some recent cases.[35] It is also noticeable that, despite the relatively low number of cases, the Commission often takes more than five years to decide a case.

4.1.3 Consideration of state reports

Unique amongst the regional human rights systems, the ACHPR contains a state reporting procedure modelled on those of the UN human rights treaties. Each state party is required to submit a report every two years on its efforts to comply with the ACHPR. Reporting has been very tardy, and some states have never submitted a report. Reporting under the Charter requires the state to measure its legislation, policies, and practices against the norms of the ACHPR ('introspection'). This introspection is followed by 'inspection' by the African Commission in which it measures the performance of the state in question against the Charter. The objective is to facilitate a 'constructive dialogue' between the Commission and the states. The dialogue takes place at the public sessions of the African Commission.

NGOs are allowed to submit shadow or alternative reports, but the impact of this avenue is diminished by the lack of access of NGOs to the state reports to which they are supposed to respond. However, recently the Commission has begun to publish the state reports for the upcoming session on its website. Since 2001 the Commission has adopted concluding observations after considering the reports.

4.1.4 Special Rapporteurs and working groups

The system of special procedures of the Commission, again loosely similar in nature to those of the UN, is a further unique feature among regional human rights systems. The Commission has appointed a number of Special Rapporteurs to deal with thematic human rights issues. The Special Rapporteurs are always appointed from within the ranks of the members of the Commission. The Commission has also appointed working groups, some of which include members who are not Commissioners.

In the mid-1990s the Commission adopted the first Special Rapporteur mandates: the Special Rapporteur on extrajudicial, summary or arbitrary executions; the Special Rapporteur on prisons and conditions of detention; and the Special Rapporteur on the rights of women. The position of Special Rapporteur on extrajudicial, summary or arbitrary executions has been defunct since 2001, though the mandate of the Working Group

---

[35] eg 323/06, *Egyptian Initiative for Personal Rights and Interights v Egypt*, 31st Activity Report of the ACommHPR (2011); (2011) AHRLR 90, para 275.

on the Death Penalty was expanded in 2012, and it is now known as the Working Group on the Death Penalty and Extra-Judicial, Summary or Arbitrary Killings in Africa. The Commission has more recently appointed Special Rapporteurs on freedom of expression and access to information; refugees and internally displaced persons; and human rights defenders. The Commission has also established a committee to monitor the implementation of the Guidelines and Measures for the Prohibition and Prevention of Torture, Cruel, Inhuman or Degrading Treatment or Punishment in Africa (Robben Island Guidelines); and Working Groups on Indigenous People or Communities; Economic, Social and Cultural Rights; the Death Penalty; and the Rights of Older Persons and Persons with Disabilities in Africa.[36]

The Special Rapporteurs and Working Groups follow developments in the area covered by their mandate and engage with NGOs. They may issue press releases or write letters to governments when they receive reliable information about violations of the ACHPR. The Special Rapporteurs also undertake on-site visits and produce reports with recommendations to governments. Special procedures also take the lead in developing normative instruments such as the Model Law on Access to Information, developed under the auspices of the Special Rapporteur on Freedom of Expression and Access to Information;[37] and General Comment 3 on the Right to Life, developed by the Working Group on the Death Penalty and Extra-Judicial, Summary or Arbitrary Killings in Africa.[38]

4.1.5 On-site visits

The Commission has conducted a number of on-site visits or missions. These can be divided into protective and promotional missions. Protective missions may be linked to a case under consideration by the Commission or to a situation of massive violations of human rights. Promotional missions help to give the Commission an understanding of the human rights situation in a country through meetings with governments and NGO representatives. They are often aimed at spreading knowledge about the Commission and its work. The missions are generally conducted by one or two members of the Commission, sometimes the Special Rapporteur on a specific issue, together with a legal officer from the Secretariat. Mission reports are adopted by the Commission as a whole at its sessions. Many reports have never been published, in print or on the internet, which diminishes their impact.

4.1.6 Resolutions

The African Commission has adopted resolutions on a number of human rights issues in Africa. In addition to country-specific and other more ad hoc resolutions, it has adopted resolutions on topics such as fair trial; freedom of association; human and peoples' rights education; humanitarian law; contemporary forms of slavery; antipersonnel mines; prisons in Africa; the independence of the judiciary; the electoral process and participatory governance; the International Criminal Court; the death penalty; torture; HIV/AIDS; maternal mortality; and freedom of expression. The Commission, in turn, has relied on these resolutions in its case law. Some of the resolutions, for example the Principles and Guidelines on the Right to a Fair Trial and Legal Assistance in Africa, are quite elaborate and can be seen as regional equivalents of the general comments adopted by the UN treaty bodies. The Commission has also taken the lead on issues that remain deeply divisive on the African continent such as, for example, through the adoption in 2014 of the Resolution

---

[36] Final communiqué of the 45th ordinary session of the ACommHPR held in Banjul, The Gambia, 13–27 May 2009, para 31.   [37] Available at: <http://www.achpr.org/instruments/access-information/>.
[38] Available at: <http://www.achpr.org/instruments/general-comments-right-to-life/>.

on Protection against Violence and other Human Rights Violations against Persons on the basis of their real or imputed Sexual Orientation or Gender Identity.[39]

4.1.7 Relationship with NGOs

NGOs have often been instrumental in bringing cases to the African Commission and in supporting its work in general. NGOs submit shadow reports, propose agenda items at the outset of Commission sessions, and provide logistical and other support to the Commission, for example by placing interns at the Commission and providing support to the Special Rapporteurs and missions of the Commission. NGO workshops are arranged prior to Commission sessions, and many NGOs participate actively in the public sessions of the Commission. NGOs also collaborate with the Commission in developing resolutions and new normative instruments. NGOs that wish actively to engage with the Commission need to apply for observer status, which to date has been granted to more than 400 African and international NGOs.[40]

4.1.8 Interaction with AU political bodies

The activity reports of the Commission, which reflect the decisions, resolutions, and other acts of the African Commission, are submitted after the Commission's meetings to the AU summit, which is held twice a year. The activity report must be adopted by the AU Assembly before it can be published. Controversy arose in 2004 when Zimbabwe managed to delay the publication of a case against it due to lack of consultation by the Commission. At around the same time there was debate over the publication of country-specific resolutions.[41] For a few years the AU Assembly and Executive Council reverted to their previous practice of serving as a rubber stamp for the Activity Report of the Commission before there was renewed controversy over the contents of a report leading to a delay in publication. The principle that the very people in charge of the institutions whose human rights practices are at stake—the heads of state—take the final decision on publicity, undermines the legitimacy of the system. This is not to deny that constructive engagement by the AU political organs could be used to put pressure on states to comply with the decisions of the Commission. The relationship between the African Commission and the AU Executive Council came in to focus in 2015 when the African Commission granted observer status to the Coalition for African Lesbians. In a response reflecting the homophobic nature of many African governments, the Executive Council called on the African Commission to review its decision and revise its guidelines for granting observer status to NGOs.[42]

4.2 THE AFRICAN COURT ON HUMAN AND PEOPLES' RIGHTS

4.2.1 Background

The only monitoring mechanism included in the ACHPR is the African Commission. In 1994, the OAU Assembly adopted a resolution requesting the Secretary-General of the OAU to convene a Meeting of Experts to consider the establishment of an African Court on Human and Peoples' Rights. The decision to strengthen the regional human rights system with the establishment of a court should be seen in the context of the increased focus

---

[40] Final communiqué of the 45th ordinary session, para 23.

[39] Available at: <http://www.achpr.org/sessions/55th/resolutions/275>.

[41] Killander, 'Confidentiality v Publicity: Interpreting Article 59 of the African Charter on Human and Peoples' Rights' (2006) 6 *AHRLJ* 572.

[42] Decision on the 38th activity report of the African Commission on Human and Peoples' Rights, EX.CL/Dec.887(XXVII) (June 2015).

on human rights both in Africa and worldwide in the early 1990s. The Protocol on the African Court on Human and Peoples' Rights was adopted in Addis Ababa, Ethiopia, in 1998 (Protocol on the African Court). The Protocol entered into force in January 2004. By the end of 2016, 30 states had ratified the Protocol. The seat of the court is in Arusha, Tanzania.

The AU Assembly decided at its summit in July 2004 that the African Human Rights Court must be merged with the African Court of Justice. The reason behind the merger was seemingly a need to rationalize the AU structures. The Court of Justice is one of the organs of the AU provided for in the Constitutive Act but it has not been established. It was meant to function as a court adjudicating disputes arising from the increasing integration of the member states of the AU. In July 2008 the AU Assembly adopted the Protocol on the Statute of the African Court of Justice and Human Rights. This Protocol envisages that the new court will replace the current African Human Rights Court, and that the new court will have one human rights section and one general affairs section. This Protocol has not yet entered into force.

In 2014, however, the plans for the future changed again. The Assembly adopted the Malabo Protocol, which is aimed at giving the Court jurisdiction over international crimes. However, by the end of 2016 no state had ratified the Protocol. The Malabo Protocol, if it enters into force, will give the African Human Rights Court jurisdiction over international crimes covered by the ICC, such as genocide, crimes against humanity, and war crimes, but also over crimes such as corruption, unconstitutional change of government, and terrorism. In a major and controversial departure from the position in the ICC Statute, the Malabo Protocol provides for immunity for heads of state and senior state officials.

4.2.2 Composition

The African Court on Human and Peoples' Rights, as it currently exists, 'complements' the protective mandate of the African Commission under the Charter. The court consists of 11 judges nominated by states parties to the Protocol, and elected by the Assembly. Only the president holds a full-time appointment. The Protocol on the African Court provides that the judges are appointed in their individual capacities, and that their independence is guaranteed. Special provision is made in Article 18 Protocol on the African Court that '[t]he position of judge of the Court is incompatible with any activity that might interfere with the independence or impartiality of such a judge'. A judge will not be allowed to sit in a case if that judge is a national of a state which is a party to the case. The first judges were elected by the Assembly in January 2006. Until recently the Court had nine male judges and two female judges. However, in July 2016 the AU Executive Council elected the only two female candidates nominated for the four vacancies on the Court. Two more female judges were elected in January 2017 leaving the Court with six male and five female members.

4.2.3 Procedure

In the majority of cases the Commission will take a case to the African Court if it has found a violation and has established that the state has not complied with its recommendations. Individuals and those who act on their behalf will be able to take cases directly to the African Court only in respect of those states that have made an additional declaration in terms of Article 34(6) Protocol on the African Court specifically authorizing them to do so. Seven states (Benin, Burkina Faso, Cote d'Ivoire, Ghana, Malawi, Mali, and Tanzania) have made such a declaration. Rwanda has recently withdrawn its declaration. This opt-in process for direct access to the Court will remain the same under the merged court. The Court may also deliver advisory opinions at the request of the AU, any of its organs, or any 'African organisation recognised by the [AU]'.[43] The Court has handed down a number of merits judgments and separate judgments on reparations. The Court may adopt provisional measures in cases of 'extreme gravity and urgency' when 'irreparable harm to persons' would otherwise ensue and has done so in a few cases.[44] Most of the merits judgments have been against two of the states that have made the Article 34(6) declaration, Burkina Faso and Tanzania.

In respect of the Court's findings, the Protocol on the African Court determines that '[i]f the Court finds that there has been a violation of a human or peoples' right, it shall make appropriate orders to remedy the violation, including the payment of fair compensation or reparation'.[45] The Protocol provides that the Council of Ministers (now the AU Executive Council) shall monitor the execution of the judgments of the Court.[46]

4.3 THE AU MAIN ORGANS AND HUMAN RIGHTS

4.3.1 Overview

The African human rights system is not limited to the African Commission, the African Court, and the Children's Committee. The AU also has the following main organs: the Assembly of Heads of State and Government, the Executive Council, the Permanent Representative Committee, the Pan-African Parliament, the African Court of Justice, the AU Commission (which replaced the OAU Secretariat), Specialised Technical Committees, the Economic, Social and Cultural Council, financial institutions, and the Peace and Security Council. A number of these organs have human rights mandates.

4.3.2 Pan-African Parliament

The Pan-African Parliament (PAP) shall 'ensure the full participation of African peoples in the development and economic integration of the continent'. One of the Parliament's objectives is to '[p]romote the principles of human and peoples' rights and democracy in Africa'.[47] The PAP has held sessions twice a year since its inception in 2004. Each state party to the Protocol establishing the Parliament sends five national parliamentarians to the PAP, which is based in Midrand, South Africa. Currently the powers of the Parliament are purely consultative and advisory. In the implementation of its human rights mandate, the PAP has sent fact-finding missions to, for example, Darfur, and election observation missions to many AU member states. The PAP electoral observation mission to the Zimbabwe presidential election in 2008 concluded that the elections had not been free and fair. In contrast, the AU Assembly avoided criticizing the election. This episode is symptomatic of the general lack of impact of the PAP.

4.3.3 The Economic, Social and Cultural Council

The Economic, Social and Cultural Council (ECOSOCC) is an advisory organ made up of representatives nominated by civil society organizations of member states. One of ECOSOCC's objectives is to '[p]romote and defend a culture of good governance, democratic principles and institutions, popular participation, human rights and freedoms as well as social justice'. The statutes of ECOSOCC were adopted by the AU Assembly in July 2004. Since then, ECOSOCC has been busy establishing its structures rather than

---

[43] Protocol on the African Court, Art 4(1). It is unclear whether 'African organisations' include NGOs or is simply a reference to the RECs. The merged court will have advisory jurisdiction only at the request of AU organs. [44] Protocol on the African Court, Art 27(2).

[45] Protocol on the African Court, Art 27(1). [46] Protocol on the African Court, Art 29(2).

[47] Protocol to the Constitutive Act of the African Union relating to the Pan-African Parliament, Art 3(c).

establishing itself as a voice of civil society engaging with and putting issues such as human rights on the AU agenda.

4.3.4 Peace and Security Council

The attempts to develop mechanisms to deal with conflict in Africa are by their very nature also of importance in trying to prevent massive human rights violations. The Protocol on the Peace and Security Council (PSC), adopted in 2002, entered into force in 2003. The PSC has a rotating membership of representatives of 15 AU member states. The criteria for membership include 'respect for constitutional governance . . . as well as the rule of law and human rights'. Article 4 PSC Protocol provides that the Council shall be guided by the AU Constitutive Act, the UN Charter, and the Universal Declaration of Human Rights. The Protocol further provides that one of the Council's objectives is to 'promote and encourage democratic practices, good governance and the rule of law, protect human rights and fundamental freedoms, respect for the sanctity of human life and international humanitarian law, as part of efforts for preventing conflicts'.

Article 19 PSC Protocol provides that the PSC 'shall seek close cooperation with the African Commission'. Nonetheless, from the activity reports of the Commission and the communiqués of the PSC, it appears that the two organs have not often collaborated, despite references to PSC resolutions in the Commission's country-specific resolutions. It should also be noted that the PSC in 2015 requested the African Commission to undertake a fact-finding mission to Burundi.[48]

4.4 THE AFRICAN PEER REVIEW MECHANISM

The Declaration on Democracy, Political, Economic and Corporate Governance (Governance Declaration) was adopted at the final OAU Assembly in Durban in 2002. The Governance Declaration provided for the establishment of an African Peer Review Mechanism (APRM) 'to promote adherence to and fulfilment of the commitments' in the Declaration.

The APRM grew out of the New Partnership for Africa's Development (NEPAD), adopted by the AU in 2001 as the development framework for the Union. The secretariats of the APRM and NEPAD are based in Midrand, South Africa. The highest decision-making body in the APRM is the APRM Forum consisting of the heads of state and government of the participating states. A panel of eminent persons with seven members oversees the review process and a member of this panel is chosen to lead the review team on its country mission.

The APRM process consists of a self-evaluation by the state that has signed up to be reviewed and a review by an international review team. The outcome of the process is a national Programme of Action with time-bound action points to redress identified shortcomings.

The international review process consists of five stages. First, a background study is carried out by the secretariat assisted by consultants. This stage also includes a support mission to the country that will be reviewed. In the second stage, a review team led by one of the eminent persons visits the country for discussions with all stakeholders, after which the team prepares its report (third stage). A number of partner institutions and independent consultants participate in the review mission and assist in the preparation of the report. The fourth stage consists of the submission of the report to the APRM Forum

---

[48] AU Peace and Security Council's communiqué PSC/PR/COMM.(DLI), 17 October 2015.

and the discussion among peers. The fifth stage is the publication of the report and further discussion in other AU institutions such as the Pan-African Parliament. After concluding the reviews, participating states submit annual reports to the Forum on the implementation of the Programme of Action.

The APRM is voluntary and 36 of the AU's 55 member states have as of September 2017 signed the Memorandum of Understanding which forms the legal basis for the review. Of these, less than half had reached the fourth stage of the process and there have been few country review missions in recent years, illustrating a lack of commitment to the APRM.

The APRM integrates the political level of the AU in a way that other parts of the African human rights system have not done. However, African leaders have not shown a great interest in criticizing their peers. Hence, there are reasons to be sceptical about whether 'peer pressure' will be employed in the process and whether the provisions on sanctions as a last resort against a recalcitrant state will ever be used. However, to focus solely on the pressure exercised at this level would be to underestimate the process as a whole.

There has not been much cooperation between the APRM and the African Commission on Human and Peoples' Rights, which is unfortunate. For example, despite the relevance of the APRM for the realization of human rights, no member of the African Commission has participated in a country review mission. The documents guiding the APRM process are cumbersome and repetitive and do not sufficiently address human rights.

5 CONCLUSION

Human rights protection in Africa clearly has a long way to go, and the mechanisms for their protection have been criticized by many commentators. All too often human rights violations are merely endured or it is left to those whose rights are infringed to seek their own redress, resulting in more violations. At the same time, the progress that has been made and the role of the official recognition of the concept of human rights on all levels on the continent—the regional, sub-regional, and the national—have to be recognized as steps in the right direction. By and large, the standards have been set and the foundations for the enforcement mechanisms have been laid.

The challenge remains primarily one of political will and implementation—not only of the human rights standards and systems, but also of those policies aimed at addressing the root causes of human rights violations, such as poverty.

FURTHER READING

AYENI (ed), *The Impact of the African Charter and the Maputo Protocol in Selected African States* (Pretoria University Law Press, 2016).

EBOBRAH, 'Litigating Human Rights before Sub-Regional Courts in Africa: Prospects and Challenges' (2009) 17 *African JCIL* 79.

EBOBRAH, 'Towards a Positive Application of Complementarity in the African Human Rights System: Issues of Functions and Relations' (2011) 22 *EJIL* 663.

EVANS and MURRAY (eds), *The African Charter on Human and Peoples' Rights: The System in Practice, 1986–2006* (Cambridge University Press, 2008).

HEYNS (ed), *Human Rights Law in Africa* (Martinus Nijhoff, 2004).

HEYNS and KILLANDER (eds), *Compendium of Key Human Rights Documents of the African Union* (Pretoria University Law Press, 2016).

HEYNS and KILLANDER, 'The African Regional Human Rights System' in Gómez Isa and de Feyter (eds), *International Human Rights Law in a Global Context* (University of Deusto, 2009).

KILLANDER, 'The African Peer Review Mechanism and Human Rights: The First Reviews and the Way Forward' (2008) 30 *HRQ* 41.

KILLANDER, 'African Human Rights Law in Theory and Practice' in Joseph and McBeth (eds), *Research Handbook on International Human Rights Law* (Edward Elgar, 2010).

KILLANDER, 'Human Rights Developments in the African Union During 2014' (2015) 15 *AHRLJ* 537.

KILLANDER, 'Human Rights Developments in the African Union During 2015' (2016) 16 *AHRLJ* 532.

KUFUOR, *The African Human Rights System: Origin and Evolution* (Palgrave Macmillan, 2010).

MURRAY and LONG, *The Implementation of the Findings of the African Commission on Human and People's Rights* (Cambridge University Press, 2015).

OUGUERGOUZ, *The African Charter on Human and Peoples' Rights: A Comprehensive Agenda for Human Rights* (Kluwer Law International, 2003).

SSENYONJO (ed), *The African Regional Human Rights System* (Martinus Nijhoff Publishers, 2012).

VILJOEN, *International Human Rights Law in Africa* (Oxford University Press, 2012).

VILJOEN, 'Human Rights in Africa: Normative, Institutional and Functional Complementarity and Distinctiveness' (2011) 18 *SAJIA* 191.

VILJOEN and LOUW, 'State Compliance with the Recommendations of the African Commission on Human and Peoples' Rights, 1993–2004' (2007) 101 *AJIL* 1.

USEFUL WEBSITES

African Commission on Human and Peoples' Rights: <http://www.achpr.org>

African Committee on the Rights and Welfare of the Child: <http://acerwc.org/>

African Court on Human and Peoples' Rights: <http://www.african-court.org/en/>

African Human Rights Case Law Analyser: <http://caselaw.ihrda.org/>

African Union: <http://www.africa-union.org>

Centre for Human Rights, University of Pretoria: <http://www.chr.up.ac.za>

24

WITHIN THE STATE

Andrew Byrnes and Catherine Renshaw

SUMMARY

This chapter outlines the role and responsibility of the state for promoting and protecting human rights. The chapter first details the state's obligation to implement internationally guaranteed human rights and describes the different processes by which customary international law norms and international human rights treaties become part of domestic law. The chapter then discusses the principal domestic legal sources of protection of human rights: constitutional and legislative provisions as well as the common law. Finally, the discussion turns to some of the key institutions within the state that have a role in the protection and promotion of human rights: the courts, the executive, the legislature, ombudsmen, and national human rights institutions.

1 INTRODUCTION

The primacy of the state in the protection and fulfilment of internationally guaranteed human rights is the fundamental starting point of international human rights law. In the words of former UN High Commissioner for Human Rights, Louise Arbour: 'States remain the primary actors, the key conduits through which human rights must be realised. The obligation to respect and enforce human rights rests on states.'[1] As explained in Chapters 4 to 6, states are bound by human rights treaties and customary international law to ensure respect for, and the full enjoyment of, human rights of those persons subject to their jurisdiction. States carry out these obligations through a combination of legislative, institutional, judicial, administrative, financial, and other types of measures. Precisely which measures are used will depend on the specific treaty provision or customary international law obligation, and the political structure and practices of the state concerned. The touchstone for implementation of human rights obligations is ultimately a substantive one—not merely whether necessary laws, institutions, and procedures are in place, but whether they ensure that persons within the state's jurisdiction in fact enjoy the rights guaranteed.

This chapter considers the various methods of protection of human rights at the national level, with a particular focus on legal protections and institutions with a specific rights mandate. Whether those individuals subject to the jurisdiction of the state enjoy human

---

[1] Statement by Ms Louise Arbour, UN High Commissioner for Human Rights, on the opening of the 61st Session of the Commission on Human Rights (Geneva, 14 March 2005).

rights in reality depends on a range of factors, including the nature and content of substantive human rights protections applicable within the domestic system, the role of political and legal institutions in the implementation and enforcement of rights, the resources available to ensure the fulfilment of rights, the availability of remedies for violations of rights, the role of the media and other independent commentators, and the perception of the importance of rights among the members of the community and on the national political agenda.

Section 2 deals with *substantive* protections—the nature, status, and scope of human rights protections under national law. These include the incorporation or other use of international human rights norms in domestic law, constitutional guarantees of rights, human rights legislation, protection under the general law, including the concept of the rule of law, and the common law. Section 3 deals with *institutional* protections of human rights. It briefly outlines the types of institutions which commonly play a role in the implementation, monitoring, and protection of human rights, including the courts, the executive, the legislature, as well as mechanisms such as ombudsmen and national human rights institutions.

2 SUBSTANTIVE PROTECTIONS

A fundamental aspect of ensuring the fulfilment of human rights is their formal legal protection under national law. A state party to an international human rights treaty is in general not required to directly implement the provisions of the treaty into domestic law. What is required is that the protection and fulfilment of the rights guaranteed by the treaty are secured through domestic law and practice. While the level of domestic protection should not fall short of the international obligation, national law and practice may provide more generous protection.

There are a number of forms that legal protection of human rights may take in domestic legal systems, including:

1. the incorporation of treaty or customary international law protections into domestic law;
2. constitutional guarantees of human rights;
3. legislative protection of human rights, whether in the form of general human rights legislation or subject-specific legislation; and
4. protection of human rights through the common law in common law jurisdictions.

In addition to human rights-specific protection, human rights can also be protected by laws in particular sectors which provide remedies for violations. Examples include defamation laws as protection of the right to privacy; landlord and tenant laws as protection of the right to property and the right to adequate housing; and criminal procedure laws as protection of the rights of the accused and of victims of crimes. The positive obligation of the state to fulfil human rights may also be embodied in legislative frameworks, which give effect to rights and, in turn, may provide individual or group remedies for failure to ensure the enjoyment of these rights. Examples include legislation on education giving effect to the right to education; public housing legislation to ensure the right to adequate housing; and food safety and consumer protection laws as protection of the rights to life, health, and an adequate standard of living.

Underpinning all these is the protection afforded by concepts such as the rule of law, the *Rechtsstaatsprinzip*, or the principle of legality—essentially the principle that the exercise of the power of the state must be referable to a positive grant of constitutionally derived power and be subject to review and restraint by independent courts. Procedures such as the writ of habeas corpus in common law jurisdictions and the comparable *amparo* or *tutela* in some civil law jurisdictions are examples of remedies for violations of the principle of legality. The protection afforded by systems of administrative law also complements direct rights protection under domestic law (for example, the presumption that a statute does not authorize the making of regulations that infringe on fundamental rights and the resulting invalidity of infringing regulations).

2.1 INCORPORATION OF INTERNATIONAL HUMAN RIGHTS NORMS INTO DOMESTIC LAW

Human rights treaties[2]—and to a lesser extent customary international law rules—can provide significant protection when they are incorporated into domestic law and are capable of being invoked before judicial, administrative, or other authorities. A person may be able to rely on each of these types of international law norms in a domestic legal system to challenge alleged violations of rights, though treaty-based norms are of greater practical importance. The extent of protection they afford depends in large part on their status in national law. Discussions of the place of international law in domestic legal systems often distinguish between *monist* systems, in which international law norms form part of domestic law without the need for legislative transformation, and *dualist* systems, according to which international and national law are two different systems, and rules of international law must be adopted or transformed by legislative enactment before they form part of the domestic legal order. In relation to customary international law rules, most legal systems have monist elements: these rules are automatically received into domestic law, though the effect of that reception varies considerably. When it comes to treaties, the variety of constitutional arrangements does not reflect a simplistic monist/dualist dichotomy.[3]

2.1.1 Customary international law

In some legal systems, in particular most common law jurisdictions, customary international law is accepted as 'part of the law of the land' or as 'a relevant source of law'. However, this is generally only to the extent that the applicable rule of customary international law is not inconsistent with binding judicial precedent or a legislative rule.

Under most monist systems, including most civil law systems, customary international law forms part of domestic law, its hierarchical status depending on the particular constitutional arrangements. In many civil law systems, constitutional provisions explicitly provide that customary international law rules form part of national law. In others, such as Argentina, no specific provision exists, but customary international law has been recognized by courts as part of the domestic legal order.[4] Customary international law rules may have a constitutional status, an enhanced statutory status (so that they prevail over all statutes, both prior and subsequent), or the same status as an ordinary statute. For example, Article 25

---

[2] Other treaties or international instruments may also contain human rights protections, but our focus is on human rights treaties. Furthermore, we do not address the example of the Charter of Fundamental Rights and Freedoms of the European Union, which has an impact on the law of member states of the EU.

[3] See generally European Commission for Democracy through Law (Venice Commission), *Report on the implementation of international human rights treaties in domestic law and the role of courts, adopted by the Venice Commission at its 100th plenary session (Rome, 10–11 October 2014)*, CDL-AD(2014)036.

[4] Vinuesa, 'Direct Applicability of Human Rights Conventions within the Internal Legal Order: The Situation in Argentina' in Conforti and Francioni (eds), *Enforcing International Human Rights in Domestic Courts* (Martinus Nijhoff, 1997) 149, 159–60.

Basic Law of the Federal Republic of Germany provides: 'The general rules of public international law shall be an integral part of federal law. They shall take precedence over the laws and shall directly create rights and duties for the inhabitants of the federal territory.' This provision has the effect that rules of customary international law are part of federal law and prevail over federal statutes and the laws of the *Bundesländer* (the federal states).

2.1.2 Human rights treaties in monist jurisdictions

The extent to which persons can rely on human rights treaties as part of domestic law will depend on the place of those treaties in the national legal system and on whether the treaty or specific provisions of it, even when part of domestic law, are *directly applicable*. In this regard, it is common to contrast monist and dualist states. Yet this classification conceals a range of constitutional arrangements that defy such an easy categorization.

In some states, ratification of, or accession to, a treaty—the formal indication of a state's intention to be bound by that treaty as a matter of international law—triggers the incorporation of the treaty into the domestic legal system. This may simply follow ratification by the executive, as a result of an express or implied constitutional or statutory rule governing reception of treaties. In other cases, prior legislative approval of the ratification may be required before the treaty is received as part of domestic law. For example, under the US Constitution, the President must receive the advice and consent of two-thirds of the Senate before the USA can ratify the treaty at the international level and before it can become the 'supreme law of the land'. In other states, there are constitutional requirements that the legislature approve by ordinary law the international ratification of a treaty before it can become part of domestic law. In a sense, all these models are 'monist' in that, once the required steps are taken, the provisions of the treaty become part of domestic law.

Under other systems, the usual practice is to adopt a law 'ratifying' a specific treaty (rather than relying on a general rule of reception that applies to all treaties), as a result of which the treaty then becomes part of the domestic legal system. 'Ratifying' is used here in the sense of formal legislative approval at the national level and is different from the act of ratification which takes effect on the international plane, indicating the state's consent to be bound by the treaty.

Civil law jurisdictions with systems under which treaties become part of national law by one of the aforementioned routes include Brazil, Egypt, France, Japan, Mexico, Namibia, the Netherlands, the Russian Federation, and Switzerland. For example, Article 93 Netherlands Constitution provides: 'Provisions of treaties and of resolutions by international institutions which may be binding on all persons by virtue of their contents shall become binding after they have been published.' A number of common law states, such as Cyprus and Nepal, have also adopted such an approach.[5]

Another mechanism for reception of treaties as domestic law in a particular area—sometimes known as 'sector monism'—is a legislative provision providing that international treaties prevail over the provisions of existing legislation in that area should an inconsistency arise. For example, Section 15 Finnish Criminal Code provides:

> If an international treaty binding on Finland or another statute or regulation that is internationally binding on Finland in some event restricts the scope of application of the criminal law of Finland, such a restriction applies as agreed. The provisions in this chapter notwithstanding, the restrictions on the scope of application of Finnish law based on generally recognised rules of international law also apply.[6]

---

[5] Constitution of Cyprus, Art 169(3) and Nepal Treaty Act 2047 [1990], Art 9(1).

[6] See also Norwegian Criminal Procedure Act, s 4 and Civil Procedure Law of the People's Republic of China, Art 238.

In some states, ratified treaties generally, or a specific treaty, are given constitutional status. For example, in Austria, the European Convention on Human Rights (ECHR) has constitutional status, as do human rights treaties in a number of Latin American states (for example, Argentina).[7] In other states treaties may be given supra-constitutional status. For example, in the Netherlands treaties that conflict with the Constitution may be approved by a two-thirds parliamentary majority and will then prevail over provisions of the Constitution.[8] In still other states the status may be less than constitutional but superior to other laws, whether pre-existing or subsequent. For example, Article 7(1) Constitution of Costa Rica provides: 'Public treaties, international agreements and concordats duly approved by the Legislative Assembly shall have a higher authority than the laws upon their enactment or from the day that they designate.'

In most other states, including the USA, the provisions of the treaty will be given effect as ordinary national laws, prevailing over existing inconsistent laws but subject to being overridden by subsequent national laws. In federal systems in which treaties become part of the law of the land with the status of a federal legislative norm, they will prevail over both prior and subsequent state or provincial legislation and federal subordinate legislation. Germany and the USA are examples: directly applicable treaties prevail over inconsistent laws of the *Bundesländer* or of the constituent states of the USA, respectively.

Even if a treaty forms part of national law, there are additional requirements before it may be relied on directly as a source of rights by an individual. In particular, it must be 'directly applicable' or 'self-executing'.[9] Whether a treaty or a specific provision is directly applicable depends on a number of factors, including the intention of the drafters of the treaty (whether or not they intended that detailed implementing legislation would be required) and the nature of the treaty provision (in particular whether it is sufficiently precise to be applied directly or whether it is vague and general such that it requires further implementing legislation to give it content). It is possible for some provisions of a treaty to be considered directly applicable while others are not. For example, the Swiss Federal Supreme Court has held that Articles 7(1) and 12 Convention on the Rights of the Child (CRC) (rights of the child to registration on birth, a name, a nationality, and to know his or her parents; right of the child to be heard in proceedings) are directly applicable, while other provisions such as Articles 23 and 26 (right of disabled children to enjoy a full and decent life; right of the child to benefit from social security) are not.[10] Courts of certain states have come to the same conclusion in relation to the UN Convention on the Rights of Persons with Disabilities (CRPD)[11] and the International Covenant on Economic, Social and Cultural Rights (ICESCR).[12]

Treaties incorporated into domestic law can provide important protection of human rights, either on their own or as a complement to constitutional protections of rights. For example, in most member states of the Council of Europe the ECHR forms part of domestic law directly and can be invoked before the courts and other authorities. The courts of states parties to the ECHR regularly invoke its provisions as a direct source of rights or to inform their interpretation of constitutionally guaranteed

---

[7] Constitution of Argentina, Art 75(22).   [8] Constitution of the Netherlands, Art 91(3).

[9] See Kaiser, 'Treaties, Direct Applicability' in *Max Planck Encyclopedia of Public International Law*, available at: <http://www.mpepil.com>.

[10] *Bundesamt für Sozialversicherungen v K*, 8C_295/2008 (22 November 2008) para 4.2.

[11] Complaint procedure, B 1 KR 78/11 B (10 May 2012) ILDC 2095 (German Federal Social Court) (finding that some provisions of the CRPD are directly applicable while others are not).

[12] eg *Campodónico de Beviacqua, Ana Carina c/Ministerio de Salud y Acción Social Secretaría de Programas de Salud y Banco de Drogas Neoplásicas* (24 October 2000) (Supreme Court of Argentina).

rights. The same is true of the courts of many member states of the Organization of American States, for which the American Convention on Human Rights (ACHR) and other treaties are part of the domestic legal order, occasionally with constitutional status. UN and other regional human rights treaties as well as International Labour Organization (ILO) conventions may also provide protection not otherwise available under domestic law.

There are many examples of cases in which treaties have been successfully invoked before national courts. For example, in a case before the French Conseil d'État, a resident of France who had brought her four-year-old child to live with her without seeking official permission challenged an administrative decision to expel the child, on the ground that the expulsion would be contrary to the CRC. The Conseil d'État held that treaties could be directly relied on to challenge administrative action, found that the decision to separate the child from her mother would undermine the child's best interests contrary to Article 3 CRC, and annulled the decision.[13] Another example is the decision of the Supreme Court of Argentina in the *Campodónico de Beviacqua* case, in which a challenge had been brought against a governmental decision to stop providing medication to a child who suffered from a severe immunological condition and who was dependent on the drug. The Court held that the right to health in the ICESCR and the Constitution of Argentina required the government to continue to provide the drug to the child.[14]

National courts have rarely had difficulty in finding most *civil and political rights* guarantees directly applicable. For example, the Dutch and Bulgarian courts have held the right to be tried without undue delay (Article 14(3)(c) International Covenant on Civil and Political Rights (ICCPR)) to be directly applicable,[15] as have the Belgian courts in relation to the right to be informed of the nature of the charges for which one has been arrested (Article 14(3)(a) ICCPR)[16] and the right to free assistance of an interpreter (Article 14(3)(f) ICCPR).[17]

The courts of many states have also directly enforced a wide variety of treaty provisions relating to *economic and social rights*, be it in direct reliance on a treaty such as the ICESCR or an ILO convention as the primary norm, as a parallel source to a national law, or as an interpretive guide to national constitutional or legislative provisions. Other courts have not been so ready to find economic and social rights directly applicable, particularly where reliance is placed on the ICESCR. This reluctance has arisen not only from concern about the nature and justiciability of individual economic and social rights, but in particular from the terms of the ICESCR, under which states parties undertake to realize the rights guaranteed 'progressively'.[18] For example, in a case involving a challenge to an increase in university fees to be paid by students on the ground that it was inconsistent with Article 13(2)(c) ICESCR, the Swiss Federal Supreme Court held that in general the rights guaranteed by the ICESCR are not directly applicable. Rather than creating justiciable rights

---

[13] Conseil d'État, Section, *Mlle Cinar* (22 September 1997), available at International Labour Organization, *Use of International Law by Domestic Courts: Compendium of Court Decisions* (December 2007) Case No 56: <http://compendium.itcilo.org/en>.

[14] *Campodónico de Beviacqua, Ana Carina c/Ministerio de Salud y Acción Social Secretaría de Programas de Salud y Banco de Drogas Neoplásicas* (24 October 2000).

[15] eg Court of Appeal of Arnhem, *Public Prosecutor v X* (1980) 11 *Netherlands YB IL* 301; Bulgarian Supreme Court of Cassation, *Encheva v Pazardzhik District Investigation Service*, Judgment No. 719, Civil Case No. 2397/2001 (16 July 2002) ILDC 613.

[16] Cour de Cassation, *Pasikrisie belge*, 1984, I, 524 (17 January 1984) cited in Maresceau, 'Belgium' in Jacobs and Roberts (eds), *The Effect of Treaties in Domestic Law* (Sweet & Maxwell, 1987) 1, 18.

[17] Cour de Cassation, *Pasikrisie belge*, 1985, I, 239 (16 October 1984) cited in Maresceau (1987), 18.

[18] See Chapter 7.

that an individual could invoke before the national courts, the treaty addressed the legislator—which was obliged to transform the obligations into detailed domestic law—and did not itself provide a sufficiently precise standard that could be applied by a national court.[19]

This approach seems to be based on an understanding of the obligations under the Covenant that does not reflect more recent analysis or international and national jurisprudence. The work of the Committee on Economic, Social and Cultural Rights, in particular, has pointed out the directly applicable aspects of many of the rights in the ICESCR.[20] Other courts (in particular, but not only, in Latin America) have found that the 'progressive implementation' obligation under the ICESCR is no bar to finding that provisions of the ICESCR are directly applicable. For example, in *Mariela Viceconte v Estado Nacional (Ministerio de Salud y Ministerio de Economía de la Nación)*, a case involving a claim based on Article 12(2)(c) ICESCR in relation to the government's failure to arrange the production of a vaccine against Argentinean haemorrhagic fever, the Federal Administrative Court of Appeals of Argentina found a violation of the ICESCR and ordered the state to arrange for production of the vaccine.[21]

2.1.3 Human rights treaties in dualist jurisdictions

In systems which are dualist, the executive act of ratifying a treaty does not bring the treaty directly into domestic law. Rather, the treaty must be adopted by some authoritative legislative act (a statute, delegated or secondary legislation, or a decree) in order to be directly invoked before national courts. This reflects the principle that the law of the land should only be changed by acts of the legislature and not by executive acts alone. Most jurisdictions with a common law heritage follow this approach, including many members of the Commonwealth such as Australia, Canada, India, New Zealand, Nigeria, Tanzania, and the UK, as well as jurisdictions such as Ireland and the Hong Kong Special Administrative Region of China. A number of civil law states, such as Denmark, Norway, and Sweden, also have such systems.

In many such jurisdictions the legislative enactment of a human rights treaty as a whole into domestic law is relatively rare. Examples include the UK Human Rights Act 1998, the Irish European Convention on Human Rights Act 2003, the Nigerian African Charter on Human and Peoples' Rights (Ratification and Enforcement) Act 1983, and the Hong Kong Bill of Rights Ordinance 1991. The more common practice is either to fulfil the substantive treaty obligations by way of enactment of laws that are consistent with the treaty (sometimes drawing on its terms) or to enact specific parts of the treaty as directly enforceable national law. Thus, it is not the treaty provision itself that can be directly invoked as part of domestic law but the national legislative provisions that have transformed it into domestic law.

2.1.4 The relevance of unincorporated human rights treaties

Even in jurisdictions in which treaties do not form part of domestic law unless they have been specifically incorporated, or where an incorporated treaty provision is not directly applicable or self-executing, human rights treaty provisions may still have an impact on judicial and executive decision-making and on the legislative process. In many states, courts have adopted approaches that allow unincorporated treaties to be taken into

---

[19] *Verband Studierender an der Universität Zürich et al. v Regierungsrat des Kantons Zürich*, BGE 120 Ia 1 (11 February 1994), para 5c; *A und B v Regierungsrat des Kantons Zürich*, BGE 126 I 240 (22 September 2000) ILDC 350.   [20] See Chapters 10 and 12.
[21] No 31.777/96, judgment of 2 June 1998, available at: <http://www.escr-net.org/caselaw/>.

account. In the context of common law dualist systems, the 1988 Bangalore Principles on the Domestic Application of International Human Rights Norms and subsequent reaffirmations of them by many judges have underlined the possibility, and responsibility, of courts to draw on international law standards when there is uncertainty or a gap in domestic law. Principle 7 Bangalore Principles states that:

> it is within the proper nature of the judicial process and well-established judicial functions for national courts to have regard to international obligations which a country undertakes—whether or not they have been incorporated into domestic law—for the purpose of removing ambiguity or uncertainty from national constitutions, legislation or common law.

There are a number of ways in which unincorporated treaties (as well as customary international law standards) have been used in this indirect way. These include: presumptions that, where reasonably possible, legislation or constitutional provisions should be interpreted in a manner consistent with a state's obligations under international human rights law;[22] requirements for decision-makers to take into account a relevant unincorporated treaty in the exercise of administrative discretion;[23] creation of a legitimate expectation that decision-makers will apply the provisions of a treaty;[24] taking an unincorporated treaty into account in the development of the common law where the common law is unclear;[25] or drawing on such a treaty to identify the demands of public policy.

These possibilities are not confined to states with a common law system. Most legal systems adopt the principle of statutory interpretation that the legislature is presumed not to have legislated in a manner inconsistent with the state's international obligations. International norms may also be drawn on in determining the content of national conceptions of public policy or *ordre public*.

2.2 CONSTITUTIONAL GUARANTEES OF HUMAN RIGHTS

2.2.1 Development of constitutional rights

Constitutional guarantees of human rights can be found today in the overwhelming majority of national constitutions, though the scope and efficacy of these guarantees vary widely. Most constitutions set out to describe (and to limit) the power of those who govern and the way in which power is exercised, by protecting individual rights against the potentially intrusive power of the state and preventing the oppression of minorities or those without power through majoritarian political processes. As political documents often drafted in the wake of oppression, revolution, and the arrival of new political orders, national constitutions frequently embody the desire of their drafters to distinguish the new order from the old. The rights of those marginalized under past systems of law, for example indigenous peoples or women, are often explicitly protected in new constitutions. At the same time, new constitutions are sometimes seen as a bulwark against the exercise of power by the incoming governments of states newly independent of their colonial masters. In some cases, constitutions may also provide protection against the violation of rights by non-state actors.

---

[22] eg *Vishaka v State of Rajasthan* [1997] INSC 665, (1997) 6 SCC 241 (Supreme Court of India).

[23] eg *R v Director of Immigration, ex parte Simon Yin Xiang-jiang & Others* (1994) 4 HKPLR 264 (Hong Kong Court of Appeal).

[24] eg *Minister for Immigration & Ethnic Affairs v Teoh* [1995] HCA 20, (1995) 183 CLR 273 (High Court of Australia).   [25] eg *Mabo v Queensland (No 2)* (1992) 175 CLR 1, 42 (High Court of Australia).

The different emphasis placed on rights in various national constitutions reflects, to a significant extent, the issues which preoccupied the nation at the period in history during which the constitution was drafted. The Spanish Constitution, for example, drafted after 36 years of Franco's dictatorship, grants rights of association but is careful to note that 'secret and paramilitary associations are prohibited' (Article 22). Fiji's 1997 Constitution, drafted in the wake of two racially motivated coups d'état (and abrogated by the military in 2009), declared the right to freedom from discrimination, but was careful to preserve as lawful positive or affirmative measures to assist indigenous Fijians and Rotumans, perceived to have been disadvantaged under the former political order.

2.2.2 Content of constitutional rights

Typically, constitutionally-protected rights address three principal concerns. First, they protect the right to choose political representatives. Second, they restrain the state from unduly interfering with individual liberties and property. Third, they place a duty on the state to assist the individual or group to realize their potential ('pursue happiness') through the opportunity to pursue economic, social, and cultural rights. Rights protected in modern constitutions have been influenced by international human rights instruments, above all the Universal Declaration of Human Rights (UDHR), the ICCPR, and the ICESCR. Many national courts draw on such instruments to interpret constitutional guarantees, sometimes as a matter of interpretive practice, in other cases in accordance with a constitutional stipulation such as that contained in Article 10(2) Constitution of Spain that '[p]rovisions relating to the fundamental rights and liberties recognized by the Constitution shall be construed in conformity with the Universal Declaration of Human Rights and international treaties and agreements thereon ratified by Spain'.

Most constitutions protect political rights (such as universal suffrage and the right to vote by secret ballot) and civil rights (such as freedom from torture, freedom from unreasonable searches and seizures, freedom of expression, and equality before the law). Economic, social, and cultural rights are less commonly found in constitutions and, where present, are often couched only in aspirational terms, as a duty on the part of the state to 'promote' certain rights rather than to 'guarantee' them. For example, the Indian Constitution places economic, social, and cultural rights in a separate section to civil and political rights and describes them as 'Directive Principles of State Policy'.[26] The Constitution provides that these principles 'shall not be enforceable in any court' but are nevertheless 'fundamental in the governance of the country and it shall be the duty of the state to apply these principles in making laws'. Judicial interpretation of constitutional rights has often functioned to expand the substantive content of rights. The US Constitution, for example, does not explicitly mention a right to privacy, but the US Supreme Court has derived such a right from other provisions of the Constitution, extending it into areas which include personal autonomy over reproductive decisions. In *Roe v Wade* it famously held that the right protected a woman's decision to terminate her pregnancy in certain circumstances.[27] The Indian courts, constrained from directly enforcing economic, social, and cultural rights, have by interpretation expanded the content of (justiciable) civil and political rights to encompass economic, social, and cultural rights. For example, the obligation on the state to provide free and compulsory education (a 'Directive Principle of State Policy' only),

---

[26] The model was Art 45 of the Constitution of Ireland, and the same approach has been adopted in the constitutions of Bangladesh, Nepal, Pakistan, and Sri Lanka.   [27] 410 US 113 (1973).

was held by the Indian Supreme Court to be a 'fundamental right' guaranteed by the right to life and hence justiciable.[28] The right to life in Article 21 of the Constitution has been held to include the rights to live with dignity, to livelihood, and to health.[29] In a similar vein, the Supreme Court of Pakistan has held that the right to life in the Constitution of Pakistan includes the right to a healthy environment.[30]

The South African Constitution provides a leading modern example of constitutional guarantees of wide-ranging economic and social rights that are subject to review by the courts. The rights guaranteed in the Bill of Rights include the right to adequate housing, the right to healthcare services, and rights to sufficient food, water, social security, and education. The obligation of the state is in general 'to take reasonable legislative and other measures, within its available resources, to achieve the progressive realisation' of the rights, but there are also unqualified guarantees against arbitrary eviction and refusal of emergency medical treatment. In a series of important cases relating to a number of these constitutional guarantees, the South African courts have developed a standard for assessing whether particular legislation and government policy is reasonable.[31]

Many modern constitutions set out the permissible limitations that may be imposed on the exercise of protected rights, often drawing on the framework contained in international treaties. Generally, the state must demonstrate that any restriction is adopted in pursuit of a legitimate aim (for example, 'to protect the rights and freedoms of others', to ensure 'national security', or to protect 'public order'), is provided for by law, and is a reasonable and proportionate restriction on the exercise of the right. Even where limitations are not expressly provided for in the text of a constitution, courts frequently imply similar limitations when adjudicating on the meaning and scope of a particular right.

2.3 LEGISLATIVE PROTECTION OF HUMAN RIGHTS

2.3.1 Legislative bills of rights

Fundamental rights protections are not always entrenched constitutionally. They can also be adopted by governments as ordinary pieces of legislation, with the same status as any other act of parliament. Important recent examples of such legislation include the New Zealand Bill of Rights Act 1990, the UK Human Rights Act 1998, and Israel's Basic Law: Human Dignity and Liberty 1992.[32] An earlier version of a statutory bill of rights was the Canadian Bill of Rights of 1960, which was largely ineffectual and was ultimately superseded by constitutional protection in the form of the Canadian Charter of Rights and Freedoms 1982. The decisions in these jurisdictions to adopt legislative bills of rights rather than constitutional ones reflect a variety of factors: the difficulty of achieving constitutional change due to complex amendment procedures; concerns

---

[28] *Unni Krishnan JP v State of Andhra Pradesh* [1993] INSC 60, (1993) 1 SCC 645.

[29] *Francis Coralie Mullin v The Administrator, Union of Territory Delhi* [1981] INSC 12, (1981) 2 SCR 516, 529. See Muralidhar, 'India: The Expectations and Challenges of Judicial Enforcement of Social Rights' in Langford (ed), *Social Rights Jurisprudence: Emerging Trends in International and Comparative Law* (CUP, 2008) 102, 103.   [30] *Shehla Zia v WAPDA*, PLD 1994 SC 693.

[31] See Motala and Ramaphosa, *Constitutional Law: Analysis and Cases* (OUP, 2002) 389–413; and Liebenberg, *Socio-Economic Rights: Adjudication Under a Transformative Constitution* (Juta, 2010).

[32] In addition to constitutional guarantees of fundamental rights, Ireland has also adopted a legislative bill of rights (the European Convention on Human Rights Act 2003). There are also a number of sub-national legislative bills of rights based on the ICCPR, eg the Human Rights Act 2004 of the Australian Capital Territory and the Victorian Charter of Human Rights and Responsibilities 2006.

about the impact that a constitutional bill of rights may have on the process of representative democracy (in particular perceptions that it involves the transfer to the judiciary of responsibility for decisions that are properly made by elected legislatures); concerns about freezing rights in constitutional form; and what is politically possible in a given context.[33]

These legislative bills of rights commonly focus on the protection of civil and political rights, with limited inclusion of social, economic, and cultural rights (although the UK Human Rights Act includes protection of the right to property and the right to education). They usually provide that legislation is to be interpreted so far as possible to conform to the rights guaranteed. If this is not possible, the courts are not empowered to strike down the legislation, but may make a 'declaration of incompatibility', which invites parliament to reconsider the legislation. Recent examples of such bills of rights—sometimes described as 'parliamentary' or 'dialogue' bills of rights—have the goal of developing a 'culture of human rights' in government and the legislature. They aim to achieve this by requiring executive certification that bills are consistent (or not) with human rights, and in some cases by establishing parliamentary procedures for close scrutiny of bills and other aspects of government policy in light of human rights standards, combined with a procedure for the legislature to revisit its policy decisions following an adverse finding by a court in the form of a declaration of incompatibility. The Joint Committee on Human Rights of the UK Parliament is a leading example of the possibilities for enhanced legislative scrutiny of human rights issues developed as a result of the new wave of 'parliamentary'/'dialogue' bills of rights.[34]

There are two obvious weaknesses to legislative protection of rights. The first is that legislation is capable of being repealed or amended by a later act of the legislature. The second is that parliament is able to pass legislation that is directly inconsistent with the legislative bill of rights and this later, inconsistent, legislation will prevail. However, in practice, courts, as well as legislators, have tended to view legislative bills of rights as having a status different from that of a normal piece of legislation—a quasi-constitutional or enhanced status. For example, the New Zealand courts have treated the New Zealand Bill of Rights Act as 'not entrenched but not an ordinary Statute either'.[35] In formal terms, however, these statutes are still subject to repeal or overriding just as any other ordinary statute.

2.3.2 Legislative protection of human rights through other means

Legislative protection of human rights is not confined to bills of rights or general human rights statutes. In many jurisdictions there exists extensive legislative protection of rights, particularly in fields such as discrimination, privacy, or labour rights. For example, many states have enacted legislation that prohibits discrimination on the grounds of race or ethnic origin, sex, pregnancy, marital status, sexual orientation, disability, and other grounds. Sometimes these laws take the form of a statute that covers one such ground or closely related grounds, as with the Australian Racial Discrimination Act 1975 (Cth) and Sex Discrimination Act 1984 (Cth), both of which give effect in part to relevant

---

[33] Gardbaum, *The New Commonwealth Model of Constitutionalism: Theory and Practice* (CUP, 2013); Gearty, *On Fantasy Island: Britain, Europe, and Human Rights* (OUP, 2016).

[34] For the Joint Committee's work, see: <http://www.parliament.uk/business/committees/committees-a-z/joint-select/human-rights-committee/>. See also Hiebert and Kelly, Parliamentary Bills of Rights: The Experiences of New Zealand and the United Kingdom (CUP, 2015); and Hunt, Hooper, and Yowell (eds), *Parliaments and Human Rights: Redressing the Democratic Deficit* (Hart, 2015).

[35] *Herewini v Ministry of Transport* (1992) 9 CRNZ 307, 326 (Fisher J).

international treaties.[36] Or they take the form of a general anti-discrimination statute that covers multiple grounds of discrimination. Other legislation of this sort may combine prohibitions of discrimination in certain areas with programmatic and institutional measures, as is the case with the Indian Persons with Disabilities (Equal Opportunities, Protection of Rights and Full Participation) Act 1995. In many cases such legislation is accompanied by the establishment of institutions that have an implementation or monitoring role, which may have responsibility for resolving complaints of violations. Examples include the Dutch Equal Treatment Commission, the British Equality and Human Rights Commission, and the various Scandinavian Equality Ombudsmen.

2.4 COMMON LAW PROTECTION OF HUMAN RIGHTS

For states with a common law heritage, the common law (judicial decisions determining the rights of persons in particular cases brought before the courts) contains principles that can provide significant protection against encroachment on human rights by the state. However, common law rules and presumptions must give way to a clear expression of legislative intent to displace or override them. The common law can operate to protect human rights in three key respects. First, it is a repository of rights developed in case law by judges. Second, the law-making function of judges enables them to apply principles of international human rights law when they interpret legislation or apply the common law in cases that come before them. A state's international obligations under treaties such as the ICCPR and the ICESCR are relevant to judicial approaches to statutory interpretation. Third, judges in some jurisdictions have found that the common law can operate to protect civil and political rights that exist in free and democratic societies, such as the right to freedom of communication. The same is true of many civil law jurisdictions in which human rights values may inform the interpretation and application of public policy and the concept of *ordre public*.

The common law approach to interpreting legislation (as indeed the approach in many civil law jurisdictions) proceeds on the basis of the 'basic principle that Parliament did not intend to invade fundamental rights, freedoms and immunities'.[37] Thus, there are (rebuttable) presumptions that parliament did not intend to retrospectively change rights, infringe personal liberty, alter criminal law practices based on the principle of a fair trial, exclude the right to claim self-incrimination, authorize the commission of a tort, or interfere with the course of justice.[38] As with all such rules or presumptions, these protections can be overridden by a legislature that is intent on doing so, and there are many examples of this occurring, in areas as diverse as counter-terrorism legislation and mental health legislation. Even long-established protections in the criminal process are not immune from being cut back, as is evidenced, for example, by recent efforts, some of which have been successful, to introduce limitations to the protection against 'double jeopardy' in criminal cases, the principle that an individual should not be in jeopardy of punishment by the state twice for the same offence.[39]

---

[36] The International Convention on the Elimination of All Forms of Racial Discrimiation 1965 and the Convention on the Elimination of All Forms of Discrimination against Women 1979.

[37] Spigelman, 'The Common Law Bill of Rights' in Spigelman, *Statutory Interpretation and Human Rights* (University of Queensland Press, 2008) 3, 24.

[38] Spigelman (2008), 26–9.

[39] See McNamara, 'Rolling Back an Established Right: "Reforming" the Rule against Double Jeopardy' in McNamara, *Human Rights Controversies: The Impact of Legal Form* (Taylor & Francis, 2007) 37–98.

3 INSTITUTIONAL PROTECTIONS

All the organs of the state have a responsibility for observing and promoting human rights in their respective spheres of responsibility. Institutions that play an important role in the monitoring and enforcement of human rights include the courts, the legislature, and the executive as well as a range of further bodies, which may or may not have a specific human rights mandate, including ombudsmen and national human rights institutions.

3.1 THE COURTS

As is apparent from Section 2, domestic courts may play an important role in protecting human rights through applying human rights guarantees contained in international or national law, interpreting legislation in a human rights-sensitive manner, and developing the common law. Courts with general jurisdiction will have the potential to protect human rights within the area of law they administer (for example, administrative, criminal, or civil law). In some jurisdictions there may be specialized courts or administrative tribunals with a human rights jurisdiction—most frequently seen in the area of anti-discrimination law or industrial law.[40] In those states that guarantee human rights at the constitutional level, courts may protect human rights through constitutional review.

Under some legal systems, courts have the power to review the constitutionality of laws enacted by the legislature. The early and well-known example of the US Supreme Court in *Marbury v Madison* (1803), in which that court held it had the power to review the constitutionality of legislation, has influenced arrangements in many states. Constitutional review may take place before *any* court in some systems such as Australia, Canada, India, and the USA. In others, including Germany and Indonesia, the jurisdiction to review constitutionality may be vested in a constitutional court, the exclusive function of which is that of constitutional review. In yet others, such as South Africa, there may be a shared constitutional jurisdiction among the courts of general jurisdiction and a constitutional court, with the latter having the final say.

Some jurisdictions will permit a challenge to the constitutionality of a law to be launched only *after* that law has been enacted (Australia, Canada, Malaysia, and the USA), while others provide for constitutional review only *before* a law is enacted or commences operation (Sri Lanka and, until 2008, France).[41] In these latter jurisdictions, the courts often also have the power to review the constitutionality or legality of executive acts, even if they cannot rule on the constitutionality of enacted laws. Some jurisdictions will limit constitutional challenges to cases in which an individual can show a particular interest in the case, while others also allow members of parliament, political parties, or state organs to seek rulings on constitutionality in the abstract (as with the *abstrakte Normenkontrolle* jurisdiction of the German Federal Constitutional Court).[42]

The scope and effectiveness of constitutional protection of rights by courts will depend on the courts' independence and their perception of their role as defenders of rights and place in the constitutional division of powers, as well as the extent of access

---

[40] eg the Norwegian Equality Tribunal and the Administrative and Equal Opportunity Division of the New South Wales Civil and Administrative Tribunal.

[41] As the result of the passage of the *Constitutional Law on the Modernization of the Institutions of the Fifth Republic* of 23 July 2008, the Conseil Constitutionnel has a limited role of review of constitutionality of laws, when matters are referred to it by other courts.

[42] Steinberger, *Models of Constitutional Jurisdiction* (Council of Europe Press, 1993).

to court in practice and the respect for court decisions shown by the government and the legislature.

3.2 THE EXECUTIVE

The role of the executive in protecting human rights is also critical. The executive should have procedures in place to ensure that it takes into account both its positive and negative obligations in relation to human rights when deciding on its policy priorities and in assessing the appropriateness of its approach to implementing them. Many states have detailed assessment procedures for ensuring that draft laws are consistent with human rights, both within the bureaucracy and also when proposals are put to cabinet for approval (for example, through requirements in cabinet procedures that the human rights implications of draft legislation be clearly identified).

3.3 THE LEGISLATURE

Legislatures also have an important role to play, both as guarantors of human rights through enactment of legislation and also as monitors of proposals put before them. The means by which legislatures carry out human rights monitoring vary widely.[43] Some legislatures have established a legislative committee with a specific human rights mandate to review legislative proposals (and sometimes other aspects of government policy and conduct) for human rights consistency. The UK Joint Committee on Human Rights is one such example. The Australian Parliamentary Joint Committee on Human Rights, established in 2012,[44] is another. This body has the function of scrutinizing all new legislative proposals and existing legislation in light of the seven principal UN human rights treaties to which Australia is party. Other legislatures have established scrutiny of bills committees that have the responsibility to identify and draw to the attention of the legislature whether legislative proposals 'trespass unduly on personal rights and liberties' or violate a range of other standards.[45] Yet other legislatures may consider human rights issues in other substantive legislative committees, for example ones focusing on legal and constitutional affairs, foreign affairs and trade, or home affairs.

In some states, the role of ensuring that legislation conforms to the constitution may reside exclusively in the legislature instead of the courts. In China, for example, the Standing Committee of the National People's Congress has the power to issue formal, binding opinions on the interpretation of the Constitution. Furthermore, as noted already, in some of the systems with constitutional judicial review, members of parliament are authorized to seek rulings on the constitutionality of proposed legislation before its enactment or entry into force.

3.4 OTHER BODIES

There are many other types of national institutions that can contribute to the protection and enjoyment of human rights. Some of these may have an explicit human rights mandate, while others do not. Examples of institutions that do not necessarily have a specific human rights

[43] Inter-Parliamentary Union, PARLINE Database: Parliamentary Human Rights Bodies, available at: <http://www.ipu.org/parline-e/Instance-hr.asp>.

[44] The Committee is established by the Human Rights (Parliamentary Scrutiny) Act 2011 (Cth). See <http://www.aph.gov.au/Parliamentary_Business/Committees/Joint/Human_Rights>. For further examples of national experiences, see Hunt et al. (2015).

[45] eg the Australian Senate's Standing Committee on Scrutiny of Bills. See <http://www.aph.gov.au/Parliamentary_Business/Committees/Senate/Scrutiny_of_Bills>.

mandate but that may nonetheless protect human rights in fact include ombudsmen, parliamentary commissioners for administration (who may be entrusted with the task of monitoring public administration and responding to complaints of maladministration), public advocates, inspectors of prisons, data protection mechanisms, and telecommunications and broadcasting regulatory authorities. Institutions with a specific human rights mandate may include human rights commissions, equality bodies, ombudsmen with a specific human rights mandate, and public bodies or offices with responsibility for overseeing government.

3.4.1 Ombudsmen

The institution of the ombudsman has its roots in Scandinavia but has been taken up in many states.[46] While the original ombudsman institution developed in Sweden, its Norwegian and Danish variants have been particularly influential. The traditional model of an ombudsman has been an independent institution that is established by and answerable to parliament, with the power to consider complaints and conduct investigations on its own initiative, and to make recommendations to government rather than to adopt binding decisions. In terms of mandate, there are two main models of ombudsman (though some ombudsmen are hybrids of the two): the classical ombudsman and the human rights ombudsman.[47] More than 170 classical or hybrid ombudsman institutions have been established at local and national government levels across the world.

Classical ombudsmen have jurisdiction to oversee government administration and to consider complaints of unfair, unjust, or poor administration. Such bodies are an important means of ensuring that citizens have an affordable and accessible avenue of complaining about administrative conduct. They do not generally have an explicit human rights mandate, but their actions may assist complainants in realizing their rights (for instance, a fair hearing by a government decision-maker or the granting of a social security benefit) and ensuring that constitutional and other legal guarantees of human rights are observed. In some cases, classical ombudsmen make explicit use of international and national human rights norms in their work. The institution of the classical ombudsman is to be found in all regions of the world.[48]

Human rights ombudsmen, on the other hand, have an explicit human rights mandate (and possibly a general maladministration mandate). This may be a specialized mandate focusing on specific human right issues. For example, the Norwegian Gender Equality Ombud had a specific role under the Gender Equality Act, while in Sweden there were until 2009 four Ombuds working in the area of equality and non-discrimination (the Ombudsman against Ethnic Discrimination, the Ombudsman against Discrimination on Grounds of Sexual Orientation, the Equal Opportunities Ombudsman, and the Children's Ombudsman)—these have now been replaced with one Equality Ombudsman with jurisdiction over all these issues. Similarly, a number of states have children's ombudsmen or commissioners. Alternatively, the mandate may be a more general human rights mandate, in which case the ombudsman institution may be very similar to a national human rights institution in its coverage.

---

[46] See generally Reif, *The Ombudsman, Good Governance and the International Human Rights System* (Martinus Nijhoff, 2004); Gregory and Giddings (eds), *Righting Wrongs: The Ombudsman in Six Continents* (IOS Press, 2000); Hossain, Besselink, Selassie, and Völker (eds), *Human Rights Commissions and Ombudsman Offices: National Experiences Throughout the World* (Kluwer, 2000).

[47] Reif (2004), 8–9.

[48] Examples include the Swedish Parliamentary Ombudsmen (Riksdagens ombudsmän), the UK's Parliamentary Commissioner for Administration (and similar institutions in many Commonwealth jurisdictions), the Australian Commonwealth Ombudsman, and the institution of the Defensor del Pueblo that is to be found in Spain and many Latin American states. See generally Reif (2004), 187–92.

Both classical and human rights ombudsmen can provide substantive protection for human rights, by explicitly applying and enforcing domestic and international human rights norms, or by applying standards of good administration without express reference to human rights norms.[49]

3.4.2 National human rights institutions

In the past thirty years, national human rights institutions (NHRIs) have become increasingly significant actors in promoting and protecting human rights within the state. These institutions, established by constitution or legislation, carry out dual functions in relation to the state. Their first role is to work with government in attempting to ensure that legislation complies with the state's international human rights obligations or constitutional guarantees, to educate government officials about human rights, and to advise government about the human rights implications of government action. Their second role is to critique government action that violates human rights and to provide remedies—be it through conciliation or adjudication—to individuals whose rights have been violated. The first role requires NHRIs to be able to work closely and effectively with government. The second role requires them to be staunchly independent of government. The experience of NHRIs suggests that the balance between the two roles is sometimes a difficult one to achieve.[50]

Nonetheless, NHRIs have been and continue to be established in all regions of the world, in very different political circumstances. One of the key factors driving their establishment is recognition that remedies for breaches of international human rights provided at the international level (for example, by the UN treaty-based bodies empowered to receive individual complaints) are inaccessible to most people. For reasons of access and affordability, remedies must be provided at the national level.

Recognizing that some states may attempt to establish NHRIs as mere human rights 'window-dressing', in 1993 the UN General Assembly adopted the Paris Principles, a set of standards aimed at ensuring the independence and effectiveness of NHRIs.[51] The Paris Principles provide guidelines as to the composition of NHRIs (requiring that they be representative of the pluralism in society) and the appointment of commission members (requiring that they have a clearly defined term of appointment and transparent procedures for appointment and dismissal). They further require NHRIs to be given competence to promote and protect human rights and as broad a mandate as possible, which is to be clearly anchored in a constitutional or legislative text. In addition, they provide that NHRIs should be empowered to:

- make recommendations and report to government on matters concerning human rights (including in relation to legislative or administrative provisions and any situation of human rights violations they decide to take up);
- promote conformity of national laws and practices with international human rights standards;
- encourage ratification of international human rights treaties and implementation of international standards;

---

[49] Reif (2004), 103–12, provides an overview of the ways in which both classical ombudsmen and human rights ombudsmen can use domestic and international human rights norms in their work.

[50] See Smith, 'The Unique Position of National Human Rights Institutions: A Mixed Blessing' (2006) 28 HRQ 904.

[51] Principles Relating to the Status and Functions of National Institutions for the Promotion and Protection of Human Rights, GA Res 48/134, Annex (1993). See de Beco and Murray, *A Commentary on the Paris Principles on National Human Rights Institutions* (CUP, 2015).

- contribute to reporting procedures under international instruments;
- assist in the formulation and execution of human rights teaching and research and increase public awareness through information and education; and
- cooperate with the UN, regional institutions, and national institutions of other states.

As well as these functions, many NHRIs have 'quasi-judicial' powers, such as the power to compel production of documents and giving of evidence, powers of investigation, and the power to conciliate complaints. Some NHRIs refer complaints to appropriate authorities for investigation or institution of legal proceedings. Where this is the case, NHRIs often possess the power to appear in courts and tribunals as *amicus curiae* in order to bring relevant principles of human rights law to the attention of the court. Many NHRIs also have the power to undertake public inquiries into human rights issues. Public inquiries have proved an effective way for NHRIs, with limited resources and subjected to multiple demands, to make a significant impact in certain areas. The publicity attached to these inquiries and the fact that they are undertaken by an organ within the state often make it politically difficult for governments to ignore their findings and recommendations.[52]

Despite their location within the state and their susceptibility to lack of independence from the government, NHRIs have the potential to be effective actors in strengthening human rights protection. Their ability to pursue issues and hold inquiries of their own accord sets them apart from the courts, which must wait for rights-relevant cases to be brought before them in order that they can make determinations that support the development of human rights law.

4 CONCLUSION

Securing the enjoyment of human rights within the state is a complex process, involving the interaction between substantive norms of human rights and their status in the domestic legal system, the availability and effectiveness of a range of institutions (including those with a specific human rights mandate), the legitimacy of human rights discourse among political leaders and the community, and the level of stability in a given society. All measures for the domestic protection of human rights rely for their efficacy on the allocation by the state of sufficient resources. The provision of legal aid and funding for public interest litigation, a judiciary, a legal profession, and a community educated in human rights are all essential to the realization of human rights.

FURTHER READING

ALSTON (ed), *Promoting Human Rights Through Bills of Rights: Comparative Perspectives* (Clarendon Press, 1999).

CARVER, 'A New Answer to an Old Question: National Human Rights Institutions and the Domestication of International Law' (2010) 10 *HRLR* 1.

---

[52] Brodie, *Not Something Our Nation Can Ignore—Addressing Systemic Human Rights Violations: The Impact of National Inquiries Conducted by National Human Rights Institutions in the Asia Pacific* (Brill, forthcoming).

CONFORTI and FRANCIONI (eds), *Enforcing International Human Rights in Domestic Courts* (Martinus Nijhoff, 1997).

EUROPEAN COMMISSION FOR DEMOCRACY THROUGH LAW (VENICE COMMISSION), *Report on the implementation of international human rights treaties in domestic law and the role of courts, adopted by the Venice Commission at its 100th plenary session (Rome, 10–11 October 2014)*, CDL-AD (2014).

FATIMA, *Using International Law in Domestic Courts* (Hart, 2005).

FENWICK, *Fenwick on Civil Liberties and Human Rights* (Routledge, 2017).

GARGARELLA, DOMINGO, and ROUX (eds), *Courts and Social Transformation in New Democracies: An Institutional Voice for the Poor?* (Ashgate, 2006).

GOODMAN and PEGRAM (eds), *Human Rights, State Compliance, and Social Change: Assessing National Human Rights Institutions* (Cambridge University Press, 2012).

HOSSAIN, BESSELINK, SELASSIE, and VÖLKER (eds), *Human Rights Commissions and Ombudsman Offices: National Experiences Throughout the World* (Kluwer, 2000).

HUNT, HOOPER, and YOWELL (eds), *Parliaments and Human Rights: Redressing the Democratic Deficit* (Hart, 2015).

JAYAWICKRAMA, *The Judicial Application of Human Rights Law: National, Regional and International Jurisprudence* (Cambridge University Press, 2002).

LANGFORD (ed), *Social Rights Jurisprudence: Emerging Trends in International and Comparative Law* (Cambridge University Press, 2008).

SIMMONS, *Mobilizing for Human Rights: International Law in Domestic Politics* (Cambridge University Press, 2009).

USEFUL WEBSITES

Asia Pacific Forum of National Human Rights Institutions: <http://www.asiapacificforum.net/>

Global Alliance of National Human Rights Institutions: <http://nhri.ohchr.org/EN/Pages/default.aspx>

International Labour Organization, *Compendium of Court Decisions: International Labour Standards for Judges, Lawyers and Legal Educators*: <http://compendium.itcilo.org/en>

Inter-Parliamentary Union, *PARLINE Database: Parliamentary Human Rights Bodies*: <http://www.ipu.org/parline-e/Instance-hr.asp>

Oxford Reports on International Law in Domestic Courts: <http://www.oxfordlawreports.com/home>

Venice Commission of the Council of Europe, *CODICES, the Infobase on Constitutional Case-Law of the Venice Commission*: <http://www.codices.coe.int/NXT/gateway.dll?f=templates&fn=default.htm>

World Court International Case Law Database: <http://www.worldcourts.com/>

World Legal Information Institute (database of national and international case law): <http://www.worldlii.org/>

PART V

LINKAGES

25

INTERNATIONAL HUMANITARIAN LAW

Sandesh Sivakumaran

SUMMARY

International humanitarian law is concerned with the regulation of armed conflict. It is closely related to international human rights law. Although the two come from different historical backgrounds, they have common values, primarily those of respect for, and dignity of, the human person. International human rights law does not cease to apply in time of armed conflict. The continued applicability of international human rights law provides added value to the regulation of armed conflict but also creates difficulties. Given the applicability of both international human rights law and international humanitarian law in time of armed conflict, it is important to discern the relationship between them.

1 INTRODUCTION

The principal body of international law that applies in time of armed conflict is international humanitarian law. International humanitarian law seeks to balance the violence inherent in an armed conflict with the dictates of humanity. It protects the civilian population from the ravages of conflict and establishes limitations on the means and methods of combat. International human rights law does not cease to apply in situations of armed conflict. Rather, it continues to apply alongside international humanitarian law. This continued applicability complements international humanitarian law and offers distinct advantages as far as the protection of the human person is concerned. It also poses some difficulties, not least identifying the exact relationship between the two bodies of law.

Section 2 considers the nature of international humanitarian law and identifies some of its cardinal principles and key rules. Section 3 explores the similarities and differences between international humanitarian law and international human rights law, comparing and contrasting their historical origins and conceptual approaches.

Given that international humanitarian law applies in situations of armed conflict, whether there is a need for international human rights law also to apply is the subject of Section 4. As these two bodies of law coexist, it is crucial to ascertain the relationship between them. Accordingly, this forms the subject of Section 5. Section 6 considers some of the difficulties with the application of international human rights law in time of armed conflict.

2 WHAT IS INTERNATIONAL HUMANITARIAN LAW?

The principal body of law that applies in time of armed conflict operates under different names: international humanitarian law, the law of war, or the law of armed conflict. It is the body of law which seeks to balance the violence inherent in armed conflict with the dictates of humanity. It belies the idea that 'when the guns go off the law becomes silent'. It is, simply put, 'the last lifeline, when nothing else stands between mankind and a relapse into savagery'.[1]

International humanitarian law is comprised of treaties—principally, the Hague Regulations of 1899 and 1907, the Geneva Conventions of 1949, and the Protocols Additional to the Geneva Conventions of 1977 (Additional Protocols)—and customary international law.[2] Different rules govern international armed conflicts (generally fought between two or more states),[3] situations of belligerent occupation (the placing of territory under the authority of a hostile army), and non-international armed conflicts (fought between a state and a non-state armed group or between two or more armed groups). There is an abundance of treaty law, which regulates international armed conflicts and belligerent occupations, but relatively few treaty rules which regulate non-international armed conflicts. Principal amongst the latter are Article 3, common to all four Geneva Conventions of 1949, and Additional Protocol II. Non-international armed conflicts do benefit from detailed regulation at the level of customary international law but even this is not to quite the same extent as international armed conflicts. This is because states viewed, and to some degree continue to view, non-international armed conflicts as matters of domestic concern.

The cardinal principles of international humanitarian law are those of distinction and unnecessary suffering.[4] The principle of distinction requires that combatants (or fighters, in the language of non-international armed conflict) be distinguished from civilians, and civilian objects be distinguished from military objectives. The principle of unnecessary suffering prohibits the use of means (weapons) and methods (tactics) of warfare that are of a nature to cause suffering or injury beyond that which is required for its military purpose. Underlying these principles are the fundamental tenets of humanity, military necessity, and chivalry.

The key provisions of international humanitarian law seek to afford a measure of protection to civilians and persons *hors de combat* (literally 'outside of combat'; primarily military personnel who abstain from hostile acts due to sickness, injury, detention, or other cause) and to place certain restrictions on the means and methods of warfare. Ideas of military necessity are imbued in the provisions and, as such, a state cannot justify a violation of the rules by claiming that it was militarily necessary. The rules of international humanitarian law are tailored for an exceptional situation, namely armed conflict. Accordingly, there is no possibility of derogating from them on the basis of strategic expedience or necessity.

---

[1] Quentin-Baxter, 'Human Rights and Humanitarian Law—Confluence or Conflict?' (1985) 9 *Australian YIL* 94, 103.

[2] For a useful list of treaties see: <http://www.icrc.org/ihl.nsf/INTRO?OpenView>. For the ICRC's list of customary international humanitarian law rules see: <https://ihl-databases.icrc.org/customary-ihl/eng/docs/v1_rul>. The ICRC's list of customary international humanitarian law rules is not binding, but it is persuasive evidence of the state of the law.

[3] Pursuant to the Protocol Additional to the Geneva Conventions of 12 August 1949, and relating to the Protection of Victims of International Armed Conflicts 1977 (Additional Protocol I), Art 1(4), wars of national liberation, which are fought between states and national liberation movements are also international armed conflicts.

[4] *Legality of the Threat or Use of Nuclear Weapons, Advisory Opinion* [1996] ICJ Rep 226, para 78.

Let us consider some of the key rules.

Protections afforded to civilians and persons hors de combat: the guiding principle is that of humane treatment. This guarantee encompasses such prohibitions as violence to life and person, outrages upon personal dignity, the taking of hostages, collective punishments, slavery, and forcible displacement.[5] Special protections are in place for particular categories of persons including the wounded and sick, medical and religious personnel, women, and children.[6]

Targeting: the civilian population and civilian objects shall not be made the object of attack.[7] Indiscriminate attacks are similarly prohibited.[8] Equally forbidden are attacks that would violate the principle of proportionality, namely if the attack may be expected to cause incidental loss of civilian life, injury to civilians, or damage to civilian objects, 'which would be excessive in relation to the concrete and direct military advantage anticipated'.[9] In the event that an attack takes place, all feasible precautions must be taken to avoid injury to civilians and damage to civilian objects.[10]

Means and methods of combat: the means of injuring the enemy are not unlimited. Some weapons are specifically prohibited, such as poison, biological and bacteriological weapons, gas, and other chemical weapons.[11] Weapons that are indiscriminate by nature or are of a nature to cause unnecessary suffering are similarly prohibited.[12] Equally, the methods of combat are not unlimited. For example, it is prohibited to order that there shall be no survivors, to kill those who have expressed a desire to surrender, and to make improper use of flags and uniforms.[13]

3 DIFFERENT APPROACHES; SHARED VALUES

International humanitarian law is sometimes described as the human rights law of armed conflict. Such a description is misleading as, although the two bodies of law share some of the same purposes, they are historically different, operate in different ways, and remain distinct.

International human rights law flourished in the immediate aftermath of the Second World War, with the adoption of the Universal Declaration of Human Rights (UDHR). It has since been followed by the International Covenant on Civil and Political Rights (ICCPR) and the International Covenant on Economic, Social and Cultural Rights as well as numerous treaties, declarations, and the like. International humanitarian law's first flourish took place in the 1860s with the conclusion of the Instructions for the Government of

---

[5] eg Additional Protocol I, Art 75; Protocol Additional to the Geneva Conventions of 12 August 1949, and relating to the Protection of Victims of Non-International Armed Conflicts 1977 (Additional Protocol II), Art 4; Customary International Humanitarian Law (CIHL), Rules 87–105.

[6] eg Convention (I) for the Amelioration of the Condition of the Wounded and Sick in Armed Forces in the Field (1949) (First Geneva Convention), Arts 12–15, 24–32; Additional Protocol I, Arts 10, 15, 76, 77; Additional Protocol II, Arts 7–9; CIHL, Rules 109–11, 25–30, 134–8.

[7] Additional Protocol I, Arts 51(2), 52(1); Additional Protocol II, Art 13(2) (the civilian population); CIHL, Rules 1 and 7.   [8] Additional Protocol I, Art 51(4); CIHL, Rule 11.

[9] Additional Protocol I, Art 51(5)(b); CIHL, Rule 14.

[10] Additional Protocol I, Art 57; CIHL, Rules 15–24.

[11] eg Geneva Protocol for the Prohibition of the Use in War of Asphyxiating, Poisonous or Other Gases, and of Bacteriological Methods of Warfare (1925); Convention on the Prohibition of the Development, Production and Stockpiling of Bacteriological (Biological) and Toxin Weapons and on Their Destruction (1972); Convention on the Prohibition of the Development, Production, Stockpiling and Use of Chemical Weapons and on Their Destruction (1993); CIHL, Rules 72–6.

[12] Additional Protocol I, Art 35(2); CIHL, Rules 70–1.

[13] Additional Protocol I, Arts 40, 41, 39; CIHL, Rules 46, 58–63.

Armies of the United States in the Field (Lieber Code) (1863), the Geneva Convention for the Amelioration of the Condition of the Wounded in Armies in the Field (1864), and the St Petersburg Declaration Renouncing the Use, in Time of War, of Explosive Projectiles Under 400 Grammes Weight (1868).

At a conceptual level, international humanitarian law applies between two or more competing factions (states and/or armed groups). International human rights law, on the other hand, principally regulates the relationship between the state and the individual. International humanitarian law operates on the basis of equality of obligation of the parties to the conflict; while the fundamental premise of international human rights law is the unequal relationship between the governor and the governed.

More markedly, the two sets of rules differ in their substance. The right not to be arbitrarily deprived of one's life, for example, is fundamental to human rights law.[14] It is the supreme right on which all others are built. International humanitarian law, by contrast, accepts the killing of combatants and fighters as inherent in an armed conflict and tolerates the killing of civilians in certain circumstances. For example, a military objective must not be attacked if the attack 'may be expected to cause incidental loss of civilian life, injury to civilians, damage to civilian objects, or a combination thereof, which would be excessive in relation to the concrete and direct military advantage anticipated'.[15] Accordingly, incidental civilian casualties are tolerated provided they are not excessive in comparison with the anticipated military advantage. Thus, the rules of international humanitarian law, humanitarian though they may be, take as their starting point the combatant's privilege, namely a license to kill. This is fundamentally different to human rights law.

Given these differences, there was relatively little interaction between the two bodies of law in the period immediately after 1945. Some of the most important instruments of both fields were adopted at around the same time: the UDHR was adopted in 1948 and the four Geneva Conventions in 1949. Yet few persons participated in the drafting of both sets of instruments and the impact of the one on the other was minimal. Whilst international human rights law largely developed within the United Nations (UN) system, international humanitarian law developed outside, primarily through its guardian, the International Committee of the Red Cross (ICRC). Historically, the ICRC was wary of associating itself with the, politicized, UN; while the UN, having outlawed the threat or use of force in its Charter, was concerned about considering the law that applies during armed conflict lest it be thought that such outlawry was doomed from the outset.[16]

It took until 1968 and the International Conference on Human Rights in Tehran for the two bodies of law to come into close contact with one another. During that Conference, convened by the UN in the International Year for Human Rights, a resolution was adopted that called on all states to ratify the international humanitarian law treaties then in existence and requested the General Assembly to invite the Secretary-General to prepare a study on various aspects of international humanitarian law.[17]

Since the Tehran Conference, there has been greater interaction between international human rights and humanitarian law. International human rights law has influenced

---

[14] See Chapter 9.   [15] Additional Protocol I, Art 51(5)(b); CIHL, Rule 14.

[16] Such was the concern that the International Law Commission—tasked by the UN General Assembly with codifying and progressively developing international law—felt unable to place the revision of the law of armed conflict on its work agenda despite the urgent need for its revision as evidenced by the Second World War. See *1949 Yearbook of the International Law Commission* (UN, 1956) 281, para 18.

[17] 'Human Rights in Armed Conflicts', Res XXIII of the International Conference on Human Rights, Tehran (12 May 1968), reprinted in Schindler and Toman (eds), *The Laws of Armed Conflicts* (Martinus Nihoff, 2004) 347; GA Res 2444 (XXIII) (19 December 1968).

international humanitarian law and vice versa. The fundamental guarantees of the 1977 Additional Protocols prohibiting murder, torture, and the like are a reflection of international human rights law and are inspired by that body of law.[18] The 1989 Convention on the Rights of the Child (CRC)—a human rights instrument—requires states parties to 'respect and to ensure respect for rules of international humanitarian law applicable to them in armed conflicts which are relevant to the child'.[19] The Optional Protocol thereto on the Involvement of Children in Armed Conflict, unusually for a human rights instrument, refers to armed groups, namely that they 'should not, under any circumstances, recruit or use in hostilities persons under the age of 18 years'.[20]

The mutual influence of the two sets of rules and the closer association between the organizations working with them is, in many respects, unsurprising given that they share similar goals, namely respect for, and dignity of, the human person. The idea of human dignity is at the very heart of international human rights law, human rights being derived from the 'inherent dignity of the human person'.[21] In international humanitarian law, the prohibition on 'outrages upon personal dignity' is based on this idea of human dignity.[22] It is also infused throughout that body of law. The Martens clause, for example, a residual clause contained in most international humanitarian law instruments, provides that 'in cases not covered by the law in force, the human person remains under the protection of the principles of humanity and the dictates of the public conscience'.[23]

4 REASONS FOR THE APPLICATION OF HUMAN RIGHTS LAW IN ARMED CONFLICT

Given that a body of international law—international humanitarian law—is designed to regulate armed conflict, it is legitimate to ask whether there is need for another body of international law—international human rights law—also to apply. There are a number of reasons to suggest that there is.

4.1 NON-APPLICABILITY OF INTERNATIONAL HUMANITARIAN LAW

It has been remarked that, 'the first line of defense against international humanitarian law is to deny that it applies at all'.[24] International humanitarian law presupposes the existence of an armed conflict; a declared war, which is nowadays rare; or occupation of territory, which usually, though not always, results from an armed conflict. An armed conflict, in turn, exists 'whenever there is a resort to armed force between States or protracted armed violence between governmental authorities and organized armed groups or between such groups within a State'.[25] In order to deny the applicability of international humanitarian law, states sometimes contest the very existence of an armed conflict. This has been the approach, for example, of the Russian government in respect of the situation in Chechnya (1999–2009).

---

[18] Additional Protocol I, Art 75; Additional Protocol II, Art 4.   [19] CRC, Art 38(1).

[20] Optional Protocol to the Convention on the Rights of the Child on the Involvement of Children in Armed Conflict, Art 4(1).   [21] ICCPR, preamble; ICESCR, preamble.

[22] eg Common Art 3(1)(c).   [23] eg Additional Protocol II, preamble.

[24] Baxter, 'Some Existing Problems of Humanitarian Law' (1975) 14 *Military Law and the Law of War Review* 297, 298.

[25] *Prosecutor v Tadić*, Decision on the Defence Motion for Interlocutory Appeal on Jurisdiction, IT-94-1-AR72, 2 October 1995, para 70.

Events may be characterized as internal tensions or disturbances ('troubles' or 'riots'), or the non-state armed group may be characterized by the government as criminals or terrorists (as was the case with the National Transitional Council (NTC) of Libya (2011) and the Free Syrian Army (2012–)), with the implication that an armed conflict is not taking place.

One of the key difficulties in this area is that no single, authoritative body is mandated to determine issues such as the existence of an armed conflict, the characterization of that conflict as international or non-international, or whether territory is occupied. These questions, and others, are left to the state and the armed group for their own determinations; yet such determinations will hardly be undertaken in a neutral manner. The views of third states, the ICRC, and UN bodies may be influential, though, ultimately, they will not be determinative in the application of international humanitarian law by the parties. The pronouncements of international courts and tribunals—like the International Criminal Tribunal for the former Yugoslavia or the International Criminal Court (ICC)—will be authoritative but they are likely to be handed down some years after the conflict in question commenced.

Given the uncertainty surrounding the existence of an armed conflict and the denial of the applicability of international humanitarian law, there is a very real need for a body of international law to be applicable at all times. International human rights law, thus, has an important role to play. A state may derogate from certain provisions of international human rights law, but states derogate only infrequently and certain provisions are non-derogable.[26] The difference in starting point between international human rights law and international humanitarian law reveals the potential importance of the former. The default presumption for international human rights law is that it applies, and for international humanitarian law that it does not. International humanitarian law does not apply until an armed conflict takes place.[27] By contrast, international human rights law applies unless and until the state derogates from it and continues to apply subject to the limited extent of the derogation.

Even with the applicability of international human rights law, there has been some concern over a potential lacuna in the international legal regulation of internal tensions and disturbances. International humanitarian law would not be applicable to such a situation given that the violence falls short of an armed conflict. Certain provisions of international human rights law would not be applicable were the state to consider the tensions a grave public emergency and derogate from some of its obligations. In light of such a potential lacuna, a group of experts has drafted a 'Declaration of Minimum Humanitarian Standards' outlining the fundamental standards of humanity applicable regardless of the situation,[28] but this has not garnered the full support of states.

4.2 GENERALLY HIGHER STANDARDS OF PROTECTION

In many respects, human rights law offers a higher standard of protection for the human person than international humanitarian law. For example, although a duty to investigate the loss of life does not appear in the text of the principal human rights treaties, it has been read into certain provisions of human rights law. The European Court of Human Rights has held that the obligation to protect the right to life, coupled with a state's general duty to secure Convention rights pursuant to Article 1 of the European Convention on Human

---

[26] See Chapter 5.

[27] Certain provisions are applicable in peace time, such as dissemination of the Geneva Conventions and Additional Protocols (Additional Protocol I, Art 83(1); Additional Protocol II, Art 19). However, the bulk of the law is not.

[28] Report of the Secretary-General prepared pursuant to Commission Resolution 1995/29, E/CN.4/1996/80 (28 November 1995), Annex.

Rights (ECHR), implies that 'there should be some form of effective official investigation when individuals have been killed as a result of the use of force'.[29] Other bodies have taken a similar position.[30] The investigation is required to be prompt, thorough, and effective and should be undertaken by an independent and impartial body.[31] An investigation seeks to avoid the creation of a climate of impunity, which so often provides the setting for further violations. The obligation to investigate does not cease just because the loss of life occurred during a military operation: 'neither the prevalence of violent armed clashes nor the high incidence of fatalities can displace the obligation'.[32]

The general obligation to investigate the loss of life does not, as yet, form part of the corpus of international humanitarian law. In certain specified situations—such as in the case of deaths of prisoners of war,[33] and in response to allegations of war crimes[34]—a duty to investigate exists, but no general duty to investigate the loss of life can be identified. This is because of the different contexts in which the requirement to investigate operates. In peacetime, it is exceptional for an individual to be killed at the hands of the state; whereas in time of conflict, it is unexceptional, indeed it is in the nature of conflict. Nonetheless, there are cogent reasons as to why international humanitarian law *should* contain a somewhat broader duty to investigate and it seems to be moving in this direction. Notably, the Israeli Supreme Court has said that a 'thorough investigation' is to be performed in the event that a civilian suspected of taking an active part in hostilities is attacked.[35] Until such time as international humanitarian law does contain such a duty, international human rights law fills the gap, but must do so in a manner that appreciates the different contexts of armed conflict and peace.[36]

4.3 ENFORCEMENT MECHANISMS

One of the principal means of enforcing international humanitarian law is the prosecution of individuals for breach of that law. Prosecution may take place at the domestic level and, particularly with the advent of the ICC, at the international level.[37] Prosecution is not a remedy for all the world's ills: the ICC is of limited jurisdiction while domestic prosecutions are few and far between.

In addition to prosecutions, there are various non-judicial means by which to enforce international humanitarian law. The International Humanitarian Fact-Finding Commission is competent to inquire into any factual allegations of grave breaches and serious violations of the Geneva Conventions or Additional Protocol I.[38] The ICRC is the pre-eminent organization working in the field of international humanitarian law and seeks to protect and assist those affected by armed conflict.[39] The ICRC operates on the basis of confidentiality, which allows it to gain access

---

[29] *Isayeva v Russia* (2005) 41 EHRR 38, para 209.

[30] *Myrna Mack Chang v Guatemala*, IACtHR Series C No 101 (25 November 2003) para 157; 74/92, *Commission Nationale des Droits de l'Homme et des Libertés v Chad*, 9th Activity Report of the ACommHPR (1995) para 22.

[31] eg HRC, General Comment 31, HRI/GEN/I/Rev.9 (Vol I) 243, para 15; *Isayeva*, paras 209–14.

[32] *Kaya v Turkey* (1999) 28 EHRR 1, paras 87 and 91.

[33] Geneva Convention Relative to the Treatment of Prisoners of War of August 12, 1949 (Third Geneva Convention), Art 121.   [34] CIHL, Rule 158.

[35] *The Public Committee Against Torture in Israel v The Government of Israel*, HCJ 769/02 (2006) para 40.

[36] See *The Public Commission to Examine the Maritime Incident of 31 May 2010, The Turkel Commission, Second Report, Israel's Mechanisms for Examining and Investigating Complaints and Claims of Violations of the Laws of Armed Conflict According to International Law* (February 2013) 118–46.

[37] See Chapter 26.   [38] Additional Protocol I, Art 90. See: <http://www.ihffc.org>.

[39] See: <http://www.icrc.org>.

to people and places despite such access being denied to other organizations, but this also usually prevents it from publicizing violations.

Belligerent reprisals are another means by which to enforce the law. A belligerent reprisal is 'an act in breach of a rule of the law of armed conflict, directed by one belligerent party against the other with a view to inducing the latter party to stop violating that or another rule of this branch of international law'.[40] Were the act not undertaken with this purpose in mind, it would be unlawful. Certain actions cannot be carried out even as a belligerent reprisal, for example, attacking the wounded and sick or prisoners of war;[41] and actions that are not prohibited as a belligerent reprisal are limited by a number of restrictions, such as that they be a matter of last resort.[42] Nonetheless, belligerent reprisals remain controversial given that they are not directed at the perpetrators of the initial violation and could lead to an escalation of the violence.

There are many more enforcement mechanisms in the human rights field.[43] Individuals may institute proceedings before a regional human rights court or commission, or a UN human rights treaty body that has a mandate to hear the complaint.[44] One state may file a complaint against another state before an empowered institution. UN human rights treaty bodies scrutinize reports submitted by states parties to the core human rights treaties on the measures they have taken to give effect to the treaty rights. The Human Rights Council periodically reviews the human rights record of all member states of the UN. Special Rapporteurs of the Human Rights Council conduct fact-finding missions, prepare reports, and respond to individual complaints.[45] Numerous national and international NGOs monitor human rights violations and 'name and shame' governments. The applicability of human rights law to situations of armed conflict is useful, then, for its enforcement mechanisms.

If human rights law is being applied with the primary aim of using its enforcement mechanisms, an alternative approach would be to bypass the applicable law and use the human rights enforcement mechanisms to monitor not just human rights law but also humanitarian law. For a time, the Inter-American Commission on Human Rights did just this, applying international humanitarian law directly to several matters before it. In the *Abella* case, for example, the Inter-American Commission characterized violence at the *La Tablada* military base in Argentina as an armed conflict and proceeded to assess the events against the standards of international humanitarian law.[46] However, such an approach raises issues of lack of expertise and overstepping of mandates. For the latter reason, the Inter-American Court of Human Rights held that neither it nor the Commission had the competence to apply directly international humanitarian law.[47] Rather, it could use international humanitarian law in its interpretation of the American Convention on Human Rights.[48] Despite some criticism on the part of certain states, UN entities—the Special Rapporteur on extrajudicial, summary or arbitrary executions and the Working Group on Arbitrary Detention, to name but two—continue to apply and enforce international humanitarian law.[49]

---

[40] Kalshoven, 'Belligerent Reprisals Revisited' (1990) 21 *NYIL* 43, 44.

[41] First Geneva Convention, Art 46; Third Geneva Convention, Art 13.

[42] *Prosecutor v Kupreškić et al.*, Judgment, IT-95–16-T, 14 January 2000, para 535.

[43] See the chapters in Part IV.

[44] eg the European Court of Human Rights, the Inter-American Commission on Human Rights, and the UN Human Rights Committee.   [45] See Chapter 19.

[46] Case 11.137, *Abella v Argentina*, IACommHR Report No 55/97 (18 November 1997), paras 156, 176–89.

[47] *Las Palmeras v Colombia*, IACtHR Series C No 67 (4 February 2000) paras 32–4.

[48] *Bámaca-Velásquez v Guatemala*, IACtHR Series C No 70 (25 November 2000) para 209.

[49] eg Report of the Special Rapporteur on extrajudicial, summary or arbitrary executions, A/HRC/23/47 (9 April 2013) paras 63–74; Report of the Working Group on Arbitrary Detention, E/CN.4/2003/8 (16 December 2002) paras 61–4.

An alternative approach would be to enhance the enforcement mechanisms of international humanitarian law, but this has had little success to date. Even a relatively modest proposal by Switzerland and the ICRC in 2015 to establish 'an effective, voluntary, and non-politicized institutional forum … for States to meet regularly in order to exchange views on issues related to strengthening respect for IHL, based on dialogue and cooperation'[50] did not meet with the approval of all states and remains under consideration.[51]

5 THE RELATIONSHIP BETWEEN THE TWO BODIES OF LAW

That international human rights law applies in armed conflict is, today, beyond question. This is clear from the human rights treaties themselves. The ICCPR, for example, provides that a state party to the ICCPR may derogate from certain of its obligations '[i]n time of public emergency which threatens the life of the nation', a situation that includes armed conflict.[52] Other, non-derogable, obligations continue to bind the state. A number of human rights treaties—the African Charter on Human and Peoples' Rights for one—do not contain derogation clauses. In respect of these treaties, no derogation is permitted and the full set of obligations remains applicable.[53] As the International Court of Justice (ICJ) put it:

> [T]he protection offered by human rights conventions does not cease in case of armed conflict, save through the effect of provisions for derogation of the kind to be found in Article 4 of the International Covenant on Civil and Political Rights.[54]

The applicability of international human rights law to situations of armed conflict is also acknowledged by international humanitarian law treaties. The rules in Additional Protocol I relating to the treatment of persons in the power of a party to the conflict, for example, are described as being additional to 'other applicable rules of international law relating to the protection of fundamental human rights during international armed conflict'.[55] In the context of non-international armed conflict, the preamble to Additional Protocol II recalls that 'international instruments relating to human rights offer a basic protection to the human person'.[56] Influential international law and human rights bodies such as the ICJ, the International Law Commission, and the Human Rights Committee have confirmed that international human rights law continues to apply in time of armed conflict.[57]

Far more difficult—and still unsettled—is the precise relationship between international human rights law and international humanitarian law. The most authoritative, though

---

[50] 32nd International Conference of the Red Cross and Red Crescent, Geneva, Switzerland, 8–10 December 2015, Strengthening compliance with international humanitarian law: Draft resolution & Concluding report (Geneva, October 2015) 4.

[51] 32nd International Conference of the Red Cross and Red Crescent, Geneva, Switzerland, 8–10 December 2015, Strengthening compliance with international humanitarian law: Resolution.

[52] ICCPR, Art 4, ECHR, Art 15, and ACHR, Art 27 specifically mention 'war'.

[53] *Commission Nationale des Droits de l'Homme et des Libertés*, para 21.

[54] *Legal Consequences of the Construction of a Wall in the Occupied Palestinian Territory* (Advisory Opinion) [2004] ICJ Rep 136, para 106. This was reiterated by the ICJ a few years later, in *Armed Activities on the Territory of the Congo* (*Democratic Republic of the Congo v Uganda*) [2005] ICJ Rep 168, para 216.

[55] Additional Protocol I, Art 72.   [56] Additional Protocol II, preamble.

[57] *Nuclear Weapons*, para 25; Fragmentation of International Law: Difficulties arising from the Diversification and Expansion of International Law, Report of the Study Group of the International Law Commission, A/CN.4/L.682 (4 April 2006) para 104; HRC, General Comment 31, para 11.

ultimately inconclusive, statement on point is the pronouncement of the ICJ in its *Wall* advisory opinion. In that case, the ICJ was asked by the General Assembly to pronounce on the 'legal consequences arising from the construction of the wall being built by Israel, the occupying Power, in the Occupied Palestinian Territory . . . considering the rules and principles of international law'.[58] The rules and principles of international law in question included international human rights law and international humanitarian law. Accordingly, the ICJ had to consider the relationship between them. On this, the ICJ opined that:

> As regards the relationship between international humanitarian and human rights law, there are . . . three possible situations: some rights may be exclusively matters of international humanitarian law; others may be exclusively matters of human rights law; yet others may be matters of both these branches of international law.[59]

It is worth exploring this statement in more detail.[60]

5.1 RIGHTS EXCLUSIVELY MATTERS OF INTERNATIONAL HUMANITARIAN LAW

It is only natural that international humanitarian law contains rights that are not to be found in international human rights law, because the former body of law was designed specifically for situations of armed conflict. The structure of some of the rules is also specific to the situation at hand. Consider, for example, occupied territory. International humanitarian law contains a detailed set of rules relating to the law of belligerent occupation. That body of law strikes a delicate balance between the rights of the occupied, the occupying power, and the displaced sovereign. The rules relating to the requisitioning of property are a case in point. As regards 'public buildings, real estate, forests, and agricultural estates belonging to the hostile State, and situated in the occupied country', the occupying power is the usufruct, being able to use and enjoy but not damage or alter them. The occupying power can take into its possession certain property belonging to the sovereign 'which may be used for military operations' but requisitions from the general population are prohibited 'except for the needs of the army of occupation'.[61] These rules reflect the competing interests of the different actors—the occupied, the occupying power, and the displaced sovereign. This tripartite relationship does not map neatly onto classical international human rights law, which largely regulates the relationship between the state and the individual. Accordingly, many of the features of the law of belligerent occupation are not replicated in international human rights law.

5.2 RIGHTS EXCLUSIVELY MATTERS OF INTERNATIONAL HUMAN RIGHTS LAW

Equally, there are rights grounded in international human rights law that are nowhere to be found in international humanitarian law. The right not to be imprisoned on the ground of inability to fulfil a contractual obligation and the right to recognition as a person before the law are rights featured in the ICCPR from which there may be no derogation.[62]

---

[58] *Wall*, para 1.   [59] *Wall*, para 106. This, too, was reiterated in *DRC v Uganda*, para 216.
[60] See Dinstein, 'Human Rights in Armed Conflict: International Humanitarian Law' in Meron (ed), *Human Rights in International Law* (Clarendon Press, 1985) 345.
[61] Regulations respecting the Laws and Customs of War on Land, annexed to Convention (IV) respecting the Laws and Customs of War on Land, The Hague, 1907, Arts 55, 53, and 52 respectively.
[62] ICCPR, Arts 11 and 16.

International humanitarian law contains no equivalent provisions. The American Convention on Human Rights lists as non-derogable the rights of the family and the right to a name.[63] Again, there are no equivalent rules in international humanitarian law as these are matters that tend not to be particularly pronounced in situations of armed conflict.

5.3 RIGHTS MATTERS OF BOTH INTERNATIONAL HUMAN RIGHTS LAW AND INTERNATIONAL HUMANITARIAN LAW

In the majority of situations, both international human rights law and international humanitarian law will contain rules on the same subject and these rules will not always be identical. There have been two principal approaches to dealing with such situations. The first approach has been to use the *lex specialis* principle. The second approach has been to use Article 31(3)(c) of the Vienna Convention on the Law of Treaties.

5.3.1 *Lex specialis*

The *lex specialis* principle provides that the more specific rule takes precedence over the more general rule.[64] There are two variants of the *lex specialis* principle. The first applies in the event of a conflict between two norms. In this situation, the specific rule *modifies* the general rule to the extent of the inconsistency between them. The general rule does not fall away. It remains in the background and applicable to the extent that it does not conflict with the specific rule. The second variant applies when one norm is of greater specificity than the other norm, or is more tailored to the particular circumstances at hand, but there is no inconsistency between them. Here, the two are read together and the more specific rule is but an *application* of the more general rule. Although it may be useful to distinguish between these variants, a firm distinction between modification and application is difficult to draw and somewhat artificial.

5.3.1.1 *Lex specialis* as modification

The first variant of the *lex specialis* principle is the modification of the general rule by the specific rule to the extent of any inconsistency between them. Recall our example of the right to life in international human rights law. The ICCPR protects against the arbitrary deprivation of life. This begs the question of when a deprivation of life is considered arbitrary. Does the use of nuclear weapons in armed conflict, for example, constitute an arbitrary deprivation of life? The ICJ has considered this issue and indicated that:

> In principle, the right not arbitrarily to be deprived of one's life applies also in hostilities. The test of what is an arbitrary deprivation of life, however, then falls to be determined by the applicable *lex specialis*, namely, the law applicable in armed conflict which is designed to regulate the conduct of hostilities. Thus, whether a particular loss of life, through the use of a certain weapon in warfare, is to be considered an arbitrary deprivation of life contrary to Article 6 of the Covenant [ICCPR], can only be decided by reference to the law applicable in armed conflict and not deduced from the terms of the Covenant itself.[65]

In this instance, the relevant rules of international humanitarian law constituted the *leges speciales* and therefore trumped, to the extent of the inconsistency, the equivalent rule

---

[63] ACHR, Arts 17 and 18.
[64] See Fragmentation of International Law, paras 56–122. For a critical assessment of the *lex specialis* principle in this context, see Milanovic, 'The Lost Origins of Lex Specialis: Rethinking the Relationship between Human Rights and International Humanitarian Law', in Ohlin (ed), *Theoretical Boundaries of Armed Conflict and Human Rights* (CUP, 2016).   [65] *Nuclear Weapons*, para 25.

found in international human rights law. For example, an attack resulting in the loss of life, which was undertaken in accordance with the international humanitarian law rules on targeting, would not be considered a violation of the right to life, even if it did not comply with the human rights law requirement that the use of lethal force be a last resort.

It is important to note that the passage from the *Nuclear Weapons* opinion cited above cannot be read as holding, as is sometimes thought, that the *body* of international humanitarian law always constitutes the *lex specialis*. The ICJ was considering one particular right—the right to life—and one particular aspect of that right—its compatibility with the use of nuclear weapons.[66] It does not follow that the entire body of international human rights law is the *lex generalis* and the full corpus of international humanitarian law the *lex specialis*. Generalizations cannot be made at the level of the overarching body; it comes down to an analysis of the individual rule. Competing rules have to be identified and the specificity between them ascertained. Should the relevant rule of international human rights law contain the more specific rule, it would modify the general rule of international humanitarian law to the extent of the inconsistency between them.

The conflict set out in this example is readily resolvable because of the word 'arbitrary'. The term 'arbitrary' serves as a hook to which the relevant rules of international humanitarian law can latch on. Sometimes, however, it is more difficult to resolve conflicts of norms.[67] Consider the example of internment, that is, preventive detention ordered by the executive without criminal charge being brought against the individual being detained.[68] International humanitarian law allows for internment in certain situations.[69] For its part, Article 5(1) ECHR provides for the right to liberty and security of the person, subject to certain listed exceptions, of which internment is not one. A conflict, thus, exists between the humanitarian law norms, which allow for internment, and the human rights law norm, which does not. In *Al-Jedda*, the European Court of Human Rights took the view that, as international humanitarian law contains a power to intern rather than an obligation to do so, whereas the ECHR contains an obligation to respect the liberty of the person, a state can observe both sets of rules by not interning.[70] However, if this amounted to a *de facto* prohibition of internment in situations in which the ECHR is applicable, it would be unrealistic.

5.3.1.2 *Lex specialis* as application

The second variation of the *lex specialis* principle is the application of the more specific rule as a detailed or tailored version of the general rule. In this situation, there is no conflict between the two rules and the two are to be read together.

Consider the right to a fair trial in the context of non-international armed conflict. The ICCPR provides for a lengthy list of fair trial guarantees.[71] For its part, Article 3, common to the four Geneva Conventions, requires the provision of 'judicial guarantees

---

[66] In the *Wall* advisory opinion, the ICJ did refer to taking into consideration international humanitarian law 'as *lex specialis*' (para 106). However, when the ICJ reproduced the passage in *DRC v Uganda*, the relevant sentence was omitted (para 216).

[67] Some take the view that certain norm conflicts are unresolvable: Milanovic, 'A Norm Conflict Perspective on the Relationship between International Humanitarian Law and Human Rights Law' (2010) 14 *JCSL* 459, 474–6.

[68] ICRC, *Commentary on the Additional Protocols of 8 June 1977 to the Geneva Conventions of 12 August 1949* (ICRC/Martinus Nijhoff, 1987) para 3063.

[69] Geneva Convention relative to the Protection of Civilian Persons in Time of War of August 12, 1949, Art 42 ('if the security of the Detaining Power makes it absolutely necessary'), Art 78 ('for imperative reasons of security'); Third Geneva Convention, Art 21 (prisoners of war).

[70] *Al-Jedda v UK* (2011) 53 EHRR 23, para 107.   [71] ICCPR, Arts 14–15. See Chapter 13.

which are recognized as indispensable by civilized peoples'. No list of the required guarantees is provided. Additional Protocol II does contain such a list but that list is not self-contained. Rather, it refers to 'all necessary rights and means of defence'.[72] In order to interpret that clause, it is necessary to turn to the relevant rules of international human rights law, which form the *leges speciales* on point. The point here is that there is no conflict between the relevant rules of international human rights law and international humanitarian law. One contains a detailed body of regulation; the other, somewhat vague standards. In order to give content to the general rule, it is necessary to have regard to its more specific counterpart.

However, care needs to be taken when importing ideas from one body of law into another, as they may be appropriate in one context but not in another. Some modification may be required in order to render the idea being transferred suitable to the body of law in which it now finds itself. As the International Criminal Tribunal for the former Yugoslavia has had occasion to observe, 'notions developed in the field of human rights can be transposed in international humanitarian law only if they take into consideration the specificities of the latter body of law'.[73]

For example, the use of torture is prohibited in both international human rights law and international humanitarian law. Torture is subject to a detailed definition in international human rights law; in international humanitarian law it is undefined. The international human rights law definition provides that torture is:

> any act by which severe pain or suffering, whether physical or mental, is intentionally inflicted on a person for such purposes as obtaining from him or a third person information or a confession, punishing him for an act he or a third person has committed or is suspected of having committed, or intimidating or coercing him or a third person, or for any reason based on discrimination of any kind, when such pain or suffering is inflicted by or at the instigation of or with the consent or acquiescence of a public official or other person acting in an official capacity. It does not include pain or suffering arising only from, inherent in or incidental to lawful sanctions.[74]

Given that the term 'torture' is undefined in international humanitarian law, at first sight, this ready-made definition looks useful. Closer inspection, however, reveals a problem. The definition requires 'a public official or other person acting in an official capacity'. Armed groups fighting in non-international armed conflicts are generally not considered public officials or persons acting in an official capacity. Does this mean members of armed groups are not covered by the prohibition on torture? Clearly it could not be so. This particular aspect of the definition has been considered inapplicable for the purposes of the definition of torture under international humanitarian law.[75]

5.3.2 Taking into account any relevant rules of international law

The second approach to addressing the relationship between human rights law and international humanitarian law is to take one into account when interpreting the other. It is thus similar to the second variation of the *lex specialis* principle (Section 5.3.1.2), but there is no need to inquire into which is the special rule and which is the general rule. Article 31(3) of the Vienna Convention on the Law of Treaties provides that, in interpreting a treaty, '[t]here shall be taken into account, together with the context: ... (c) Any relevant rules of international law applicable in the relations between the parties.'

---

[72] Additional Protocol II, Art 6(2)(a).
[73] *Prosecutor v Kunarac et al.*, Judgment, IT-96–23-T, 22 February 2001, para 471.
[74] UN Convention against Torture, Art 1(1).   [75] *Kunarac*, para 496.

In the *Hassan* case, the European Court of Human Rights held that it needed to take into account the context and provisions of international humanitarian law when interpreting Article 5(1) ECHR.[76] It found that '[b]y reason of the co-existence of the safeguards provided by international humanitarian law and by the Convention in time of armed conflict, the grounds of permitted deprivation of liberty set out in subparagraphs (a) to (f) of that provision should be accommodated, as far as possible, with the taking of prisoners of war and the detention of civilians who pose a risk to security under the Third and Fourth Geneva Conventions.'[77] An additional permissible ground for detention was thus read into Article 5(1) ECHR, namely where the detention was consistent with the Third or Fourth Geneva Conventions.[78] The Court noted that, in order to preclude a violation of Article 5(1), the deprivation of liberty must be lawful, that is to say, it must 'comply with the rules of international humanitarian law' and 'it should be in keeping with the fundamental purpose of Article 5 § 1, which is to protect the individual from arbitrariness.'[79]

The European Court also took international humanitarian law into account when interpreting the procedural safeguards in Article 5(4) ECHR. It noted that, in an international armed conflict, it might not be practical for the legality of the detention to be determined by an independent 'court' as required by Article 5(4) ECHR. However, in order for a state party to comply with its obligations under Article 5(4), the 'competent body' that reviews the detention (the language used in Art 78 of the Fourth Geneva Convention) 'should provide sufficient guarantees of impartiality and fair procedure to protect against arbitrariness.'[80] In setting out the procedural safeguards required, the Court thus relaxed the general ECHR standard by not requiring review by a court, while raising the standard required by international humanitarian law.

5.4 AN ALTERNATIVE APPROACH: REGULATION THROUGH APPLICATION OF INTERNATIONAL HUMAN RIGHTS LAW

In recent years, an alternative approach has been suggested, that of a human rights-based law of armed conflict. Although primarily a construct of scholars, the European Court of Human Rights has adopted what may be termed a human rights approach to non-international armed conflict in certain cases, regulating the conduct of hostilities through the application of human rights law not international humanitarian law.[81] The case of *Isayeva v Russia* is the leading case on point. That case concerned an aerial attack on a village just outside Grozny, Chechnya, as rebels were passing through it in retreat from the besieged Grozny. The applicant's son and other family members were killed by a bomb during the attack. In considering whether there was a violation of the right to life, the European Court held that '[a]ny use of force must be no more than "absolutely necessary" for the achievement of one or more of the purposes set out in' the ECHR and 'strictly proportionate to the achievement of the permitted aims'.[82] The European Court, thus, applied rules of human rights law to events arising out of a non-international armed conflict even though the relevant humanitarian law on point differs.

---

[76] *Hassan v UK*, App no 29750/09, Judgment of 16 September 2014, para 103. This argument was not put to the Court in *Al-Jedda*.   [77] *Hassan*, para 104.

[78] In the UK Supreme Court case of *Abd Ali Hammed Al-Waheed v Ministry of Defence; Serdar Mohammed v Ministry of Defence* [2017] UKSC 2, this was read by the majority as extending to detention in a non-international armed conflict that was authorized by a resolution of the UN Security Council.

[79] *Hassan*, para 105.   [80] *Hassan*, para 106.

[81] *Isayeva*. See Abresch, 'A Human Rights Law of Internal Armed Conflict: The European Court of Human Rights in Chechnya' (2005) 16 *EJIL* 741.   [82] *Isayeva*, para 173.

In international humanitarian law, civilians must not be made the object of attacks; but it is not unlawful to target combatants, fighters, or persons taking a direct part in hostilities for such time as they do so. The ECHR, on the other hand, provides for the right to life but goes on to provide that deprivation of life shall not constitute a violation 'when it results from the use of force which is no more than absolutely necessary' in certain specified situations (in defence of a person, lawful arrest or detention, or to quell a riot).[83] This rule applies to combatants, fighters, and civilians alike, such that only force that is 'absolutely necessary' may be directed even against a fighter. The exact consequences of this rule are yet to be seen but the implication is that lethal force may not be used against a fighter in situations in which it is feasible to arrest him.[84] Accordingly, to kill a fighter when it would have been possible to capture him may be a violation of human rights law. This is an important divergence from the position under international humanitarian law and it reflects the different starting points of the two bodies of law.

It should not be assumed from this that human rights law always affords greater protections than international humanitarian law. In certain instances, the reverse is true. For example, expanding bullets are permitted to be used in peace time, but their use is prohibited during armed conflicts.[85]

6 DIFFICULTIES WITH THE APPLICATION OF INTERNATIONAL HUMAN RIGHTS LAW TO ARMED CONFLICT

The application of human rights law to armed conflict gives rise to a number of difficulties.

6.1 ASYMMETRICAL OBLIGATIONS BETWEEN THE PARTIES

Human rights are traditionally considered to govern the relationship between the state and the individual. The state is the holder of the obligation and the individual the beneficiary of the right. As discussed above, in non-international armed conflicts—and the vast majority of conflicts in the world today are of such a character—the conflict is fought between a state and an armed group or between armed groups. Injecting human rights standards into the equation may be, then, to impose additional obligations for one side (the state) but not the other (the non-state armed group). This inequality of obligation does not bode well for compliance: one party to the conflict may not be willing to abide by obligations that are not binding on the other. Once parties start to violate their obligations, there is the danger that, all too quickly, things will spiral out of control.

An alternative approach would be to impose human rights obligations on both parties to the conflict, that is to say, on armed groups as well as states. This has the advantage of equality of obligation, but it represents a shift in the conceptualization of human rights. There is certainly movement in this direction, with UN special procedures and commissions of inquiry taking the view that armed groups that control territory must respect human rights,[86] but it is too early to reach a definitive conclusion.

---

[83] ECHR, Art 2.
[84] See *de Guerrero v Colombia*, CCPR/C/15/D/45/1979 (31 March 1982), paras 13.2–13.3.
[85] Hague Declaration concerning Expanding Bullets, 1899; CIHL, Rule 77.   [86] See Chapter 28.

The imposition of human rights obligations on armed groups presupposes that such groups have the capacity to implement their obligations. This cannot be taken for granted, with certain human rights standards going beyond the reach of many armed groups. Further work will need to be undertaken to determine the extent to which armed groups have human rights obligations. A possible division might be between armed groups that exercise control over people and/or territory and those that do not, and there may be a possible distinction between negative and positive obligations.[87] However, even this shift might face opposition from certain states, unhappy with the state-like treatment being accorded to armed groups and any legitimacy that this is perceived to afford them.

6.2 DIFFERENTIAL OBLIGATIONS WITHIN A COALITION

Large-scale international armed conflicts, such as the early years of the recent armed conflicts in Afghanistan and Iraq, often involve coalitions of states. They may also involve regional military alliances, such as the North Atlantic Treaty Organization (NATO) or the Economic Community of West African States Monitoring Group (ECOMOG). The same is true of some non-international armed conflicts. In such situations, several states fight alongside one another. Simplicity dictates that they would be bound by the same legal rules. Yet, states—even close allies—are not party to the same human rights treaties. Those that are may have entered reservations to particular provisions or have different understandings of the same rule. In addition, states outside a particular regional grouping would not be party to the regional human rights treaty to which other members of the coalition or alliance are bound. These differing obligations pose difficult questions. For example, can troops from state A, which is party to the ECHR, lawfully transfer an individual in their custody to state B, which is not party to the ECHR, if that individual may face the death penalty in state B? This was at issue in the *Al-Saadoon* case before the ECtHR.[88] In that case, Al-Saadoon and Mufdhi, who were being held by UK troops in Iraq, were transferred to the Iraqi authorities for trial. The transfer was undertaken pursuant to a treaty concluded between the UK and Iraq. However, the European Court held that the transfer violated the UK's obligations under the ECHR and Protocol No 13 due to the real risk that the individuals would be sentenced to death. The case is a good example of the difficulties that arise when different parties to a conflict are bound by different treaty obligations.

6.3 SPHERE OF APPLICABILITY: THE EXTRATERRITORIAL APPLICATION OF HUMAN RIGHTS TREATIES

States frequently fight outside their territorial boundaries. They do so as a matter of course in international armed conflicts; they also do so when they intervene on behalf of one side or another in an otherwise non-international armed conflict. The question that this raises is whether, when a state acts outside its own territory, it continues to be bound by its human rights obligations.

Many human rights treaties do not contain a provision delimiting their territorial application. In respect of these treaties, the presumption is that they have extraterritorial effect.[89] Other treaties contain a clause to the effect that a state party is under an obligation

---

[87] See Clapham, *Human Rights Obligations of Non-State Actors* (OUP, 2006) ch 7; Murray, *Human Rights Obligations of Non-State Armed Groups* (Hart, 2016); Fortin, *The Accountability of Armed Groups under Human Rights Law* (OUP, 2017).

[88] *Al-Saadoon and Mufdhi v UK* (2010) 51 EHRR 9.

[89] *Application of the International Convention on the Elimination of All Forms of Racial Discrimination* (*Georgia v Russian Federation*), Provisional Measures Order [2008] ICJ Rep, para 109.

'to respect and to ensure to all individuals within its territory and subject to its jurisdiction the rights recognized' therein.[90] The 'and' is to be read disjunctively such that the obligation arises in respect of those individuals 'within its territory' and, in addition, those individuals 'subject to its jurisdiction'.[91] The question remains as to the meaning of the term 'jurisdiction'. On this, there is varied authority.[92]

The Human Rights Committee has indicated that 'a State party must respect and ensure the rights laid down in the [ICCPR] to anyone within the power or effective control of that State Party, even if not situated within the territory of the State Party'.[93] In the *Al-Skeini* case, the European Court of Human Rights held that jurisdiction for the purposes of the ECHR is primarily territorial. The Court went on to hold that certain extra-territorial acts of a state may constitute an exercise of its jurisdiction. This includes where state agents operate outside the state's territorial borders and exercise control over individuals, and where a state exercises effective control over an area outside its territory.[94]

The point here is that when a state engages in an armed conflict that takes place abroad, it is not always going to be bound by its human rights obligations. Thus, before we get to the stage of ascertaining the relationship between international human rights law and international humanitarian law, we first have to answer the question of whether international human rights law is even applicable.

7 CONCLUSION

International human rights law applies in time of armed conflict. This much is clear. Although existing alongside international humanitarian law, there is good reason for its application, not least the mechanisms for its enforcement. It is generally accepted that 'some rights may be exclusively matters of international humanitarian law; others may be exclusively matters of human rights law; yet others may be matters of both these branches of international law'. However, difficulties with the precise relationship between human rights law and humanitarian law remain. Despite this uncertainty, cognizance should be taken of the fundamental shift in the issue. The question is no longer *whether* international human rights law applies in time of armed conflict but *how* it applies. This movement from applicability to application is a significant one and is reflective of a more general trend towards what has been described as the 'humanization of international humanitarian law'.[95]

FURTHER READING

ABRESCH, 'A Human Rights Law of Internal Armed Conflict: The European Court of Human Rights in Chechnya' (2005) 16 *EJIL* 741.

BEN-NAFTALI (ed), *International Humanitarian Law and International Human Rights Law* (Oxford University Press, 2011).

DOSWALD-BECK and VITÉ, 'International Humanitarian Law and Human Rights Law' (1993) 293 *IRRC* 94.

DROEGE, The Interplay between International Humanitarian Law and International Human Rights Law in Situations of Armed Conflict' (2007) 40 *Israel LR* 310.

---

[90] This is the language of ICCPR, Art 2.　　[91] See *Wall*, para 111; *DRC v Uganda*, para 216.
[92] See Chapter 6.　　[93] HRC, General Comment 31, para 10.
[94] *Al-Skeini and Others v UK* (2011) 53 EHRR 18, paras 130–40.
[95] See Meron, 'The Humanization of Humanitarian Law' (2000) 94 *AJIL* 239.

KRIEGER, 'A Conflict of Norms: The Relationship between Humanitarian Law and Human Rights Law in the ICRC Customary Study' (2006) 11 *JCSL* 265.

LUBELL, 'Challenges in Applying Human Rights Law to Armed Conflict' (2005) 87 *IRRC* 737.

MERON, 'The Humanization of Humanitarian Law' (2000) 90 *AJIL* 239.

MILANOVIC, 'A Norm Conflict Perspective on the Relationship between International Humanitarian Law and Human Rights Law' (2010) 14 *JSCL* 459.

MILANOVIC, 'The Lost Origins of *Lex Specialis*: Rethinking the Relationship between Human Rights and International Humanitarian Law', in Ohlin (ed), *Theoretical Boundaries of Armed Conflict and Human Rights* (Cambridge University Press, 2016) 78.

PROVOST, *International Human Rights and Humanitarian Law* (Cambridge University Press, 2002).

USEFUL WEBSITES

International Committee of the Red Cross: **<http://www.icrc.org>**

The Rule of Law in Armed Conflict: **<http://www.rulac.org>**

26

INTERNATIONAL CRIMINAL LAW

Robert Cryer

SUMMARY

There are many links between human rights and international criminal law, and many human rights lawyers and activists are conversant with international criminal law. This chapter seeks to introduce the ideas behind international criminal law, the crimes themselves, and the interplay of those crimes with human rights law. It then looks to the main examples of prosecutions of international crimes and the non-prosecutorial options that have been adopted. It concludes with an analysis of the merits and demerits of using international criminal law to protect human rights.

1 INTRODUCTION

International criminal law[1] has a great deal in common with international human rights law. Both are, at least in part, of post-Second World War vintage, as they were part of the response to, and attempted safeguard against, depredations of the type that characterized the Nazi era. Also both, unlike the bulk of international law, attempt to deal more or less directly with individuals. Broadly speaking, if international human rights law deals with the rights that are granted to individuals, international criminal law deals with their duties, and what can be done when they are breached.[2]

The underlying idea of the parts of international criminal law that are of relevance to human rights is that certain conduct is seen as so unacceptable that it is not simply a matter of domestic jurisdiction, but something of concern to all. However, the level of consensus on this differs amongst the various forms of conduct that are of interest to international criminal law, and as such, two different tracks have developed within international criminal law.

---

[1] The term itself is a controversial one, with various different meanings. Here it will be used primarily to cover those crimes directly criminalized by international law. See Cryer, Friman, Robinson, and Wilmshurst, *An Introduction to International Criminal Law and Procedure* (CUP, 2014) ch 1.

[2] For a classic discussion of this see Lauterpacht, 'The Subjects of the Law of Nations Part I' (1947) 63 *LQR* 439; Lauterpacht, 'The Subjects of the Law of Nations Part II' (1948) 64 *LQR* 97.

The first is direct international criminalization (international crimes in the narrow sense). These are crimes that are directly created by international law and are covered by the famous pronouncement of the Nuremberg International Military Tribunal (IMT) that:

> Individuals have international duties which transcend the national obligations of obedience imposed by the individual State … [C]rimes against international law are committed by men, not by abstract entities, and only by punishing individuals who commit such crimes can the provisions of international law be enforced.[3]

Such international crimes may be prosecuted by international courts without reference to domestic law and, with the possible exception of the crime of aggression, by any state in the world on the basis of universal jurisdiction, as a matter of international law.[4] Only four crimes can currently claim this status: genocide, crimes against humanity, war crimes, and aggression. It is also possible that individual acts of torture or terrorism that do not otherwise fall under the definition of one of these four crimes may be added to this list; some commentators are of the view that they are already directly criminalized by international law,[5] a view that has been adopted about terrorism by one 'internationalized' court.[6] However, there is no agreement that they are, and the better view is that they are not (at least yet).

The second way of involving international law in criminalization occurs when so-called 'transnational crimes' are created.[7] Such crimes involve treaty-based regimes that require states to create crimes within their domestic legal order and require states either to prosecute those who are found on their territory and who are suspected of such offences, or to extradite them to a state willing to prosecute them.[8] Here, therefore, the obligation is on states rather than on individuals directly.

There are a large number of treaties of this sort. To the extent to which the conduct described in those treaties overlaps with human rights norms, they can be seen as part of human rights protection. The UN Convention against Torture and the International Convention for the Protection of all Persons from Enforced Disappearance are two examples of such treaties. However, not all transnational crimes are relevant to human rights. The law relating, for example, to cutting undersea cables contained in the Convention for the Protection of Submarine Cables, whilst important, especially in the internet era, probably does not have any direct human rights implications. These treaties, whether relevant to human rights or not, do not create crimes in and of themselves. The *locus* of the criminal liability for the individual is the domestic, rather than the international, legal order.[9] They will not be covered in depth here.

---

[3] Nuremberg IMT, 'Judgment and Sentence' (1947) 41 *AJIL* 172, 221, 223.

[4] See Cryer, Friman, Robinson, and Wilmshurst (2014), ch 3.

[5] Cassese *et al.*, *Cassese's International Criminal Law* (OUP, 2013) chs 7–8.

[6] Special Tribunal for Lebanon (STL), Interlocutory Decision on the Applicable Law: Terrorism, Conspiracy, Homicide, Perpetration, Cumulative Charging, STL-11–01–17 *bis*, 16 February 2011. See Saul, 'Legislating from a Radical Hague: The United Nations Special Tribunal for Lebanon Invents an International Crime of Transnational Terrorism' (2011) 24 *LJIL* 677. At least one domestic court has relied upon the STL decision: *R v Gul* [2012] EWCA 280, paras 33–5.

[7] See Boister, *An Introduction to Transnational Criminal Law* (OUP, 2012).

[8] See *Questions Relating to the Obligation to Extradite or Prosecute (Belgium v Senegal)* [2012] ICJ Rep 422.

[9] Although the International Convention for the Protection of All Persons from Enforced Disappearance, Art 5, accepts that such conduct may amount to an international crime in the relevant context.

2 HUMAN RIGHTS LAW AND INTERNATIONAL CRIMES

The overlaps between human rights and international criminal law occur both in their substantive norms and underlying philosophies.[10] There are some questions regarding whether human rights and international criminal law are as coherent as many say. Robinson, for example, notes that:

Many of the prohibitions of ICL [international criminal law] are drawn from, and similar to, prohibitions in human rights and humanitarian law. Faced with familiar-looking provisions, ICL practitioners often assume that the ICL norms are coextensive with their human rights or humanitarian law counterparts, and uncritically transplant concepts and jurisprudence from other domains to flesh out their content. Such assumptions overlook the fact that these bodies of law have different purposes and consequences and thus entail different philosophical commitments.[11]

It is true that human rights law and international criminal law are not identical, but nor are they utterly separate, and international criminal tribunals have relied on human rights jurisprudence quite heavily, particularly in their early practice.[12] Human rights courts have also drawn upon the work of international criminal tribunals,[13] and, to varying extents, taken on a supervisory role in relation to national prosecutions of international crimes.[14] A useful inter-judicial dialogue can serve to improve both areas of law where human rights lawyers and international criminal lawyers are mindful of the context in which the bodies of law apply and their separate nature.

As stated in Section 1, there are four international crimes in the sense used here: genocide, crimes against humanity, war crimes, and aggression. This section explains the overlaps between the substantive crimes and human rights law.

2.1 GENOCIDE

Genocide was created as a separate international crime in the 1940s. The term was coined by Raphaël Lemkin in his classic work, *Axis Rule in Occupied Europe*.[15] Although the term was mentioned in the indictment at Nuremberg, it was not prosecuted separately there (the Holocaust being prosecuted as war crimes and/or crimes against humanity). In 1946, however, the UN General Assembly, in Resolution 96(I) stated that:

Genocide is a denial of the right of existence of entire human groups,…such denial of the right of existence shocks the conscience of mankind, results in great losses to humanity

---

[10] Gasser, 'The Changing Relationship Between International Criminal Law, Human Rights Law and Humanitarian Law', in Doria *et al.* (eds), *The Legal Regime of the International Criminal Court: Essays in Honour of Professor Igor Blischenko* (Kluwer, 2009) 1111; Teitel, *Humanity's Law* (OUP, 2011).

[11] Robinson, 'The Identity Crisis of International Criminal Law' (2008) 21 *LJIL* 925, 946.

[12] See Cryer, 'The Interplay of International Human Rights and International Humanitarian Law: The Approach of the ICTY' (2009) 14 *JCSL* 511; Symposium, 'The Influence of the European Court of Human Rights on International Criminal Law' (2011) 9 *JICJ* 571.

[13] eg *Jorgić v Germany* (2008) 47 EHRR 6; *Vasiliaukas v Lithuania*, Application No 35343/05, Judgment of 20 October 2015.

[14] Huneeus, 'International Criminal Law by Other Means: The Quasi-Criminal Jurisdiction of the Human Rights Courts' (2013) 107 *AJIL* 1; *Vasiliaukas*. [15] (Carnegie Endowment, 1944).

in the form of cultural and other contributions represented by these human groups, and is contrary to moral law and to the spirit and aims of the United Nations.... The General Assembly, therefore ... affirms that genocide is a crime under international law.

Genocide 'is a crime simultaneously directed against individual victims, the group to which they belong, and human diversity'.[16] The drafting of the Convention on the Prevention and Punishment of the Crime of Genocide (Genocide Convention) was completed in 1948. Article I Genocide Convention confirms that 'genocide . . . is a crime under international law.' As early as 1951, the year the Convention came into force, the International Court of Justice (ICJ) stated that 'the principles underlying the Convention are principles which are recognized by civilized nations as binding on States, even without any conventional obligation.'[17] The ICJ has more recently declared that the prohibition of genocide is 'assuredly' an example of a norm having reached *jus cogens* status.[18] The term has considerable political weight, and its application to particular circumstances is legally and politically significant, and contentious.[19]

2.1.1 Definition

Article II Genocide Convention contains the classic definition of genocide, which is:

[A]ny of the following acts committed with intent to destroy, in whole or in part, a national, ethnical, racial or religious group, as such:

(a) Killing members of the group;

(b) Causing serious bodily or mental harm to members of the group;

(c) Deliberately inflicting on the group conditions of life calculated to bring about its physical destruction in whole or in part;

(d) Imposing measures intended to prevent births within the group;

(e) Forcibly transferring children of the group to another group.

This definition was repeated in the Statutes of the International Criminal Tribunal for the former Yugoslavia (ICTY) and the International Criminal Tribunal for Rwanda (ICTR),[20] and, despite some attempts to 'fix' the definition during the drafting of the Statute of the International Criminal Court (ICC), is essentially repeated in Article 6 of that Statute.[21] Like all crimes, genocide is made up of an external element (the conduct element) and an internal element (the mental element).

2.1.2 External element

There is a common theme between all the underlying acts of genocide except, perhaps, the forcible transfer of children. This is that the acts are related to physical, not cultural, destruction of the group. When the Genocide Convention was being drafted, there were those who

---

[16] Cryer, Friman, Robinson, and Wilmshurst (2014), 205.

[17] *Reservations to the Convention on the Prevention and Punishment of the Crime of Genocide* (Advisory Opinion) [1951] ICJ Rep 15, 23.

[18] *Case Concerning Armed Activities on the Territory of the Congo* (New Application: 2002) (*DRC v Rwanda*) [2006] ICJ Rep 6, para 64.

[19] Luban, 'Calling Genocide by Its Rightful Name: Lemkin's Word, Darfur, and the UN Report' (2006–7) 7 *Chicago JIL* 303.   [20] ICTY Statute, Art 4; ICTR Statute, Art 2.

[21] See von Hebel and Robinson, 'Crimes Within the Jurisdiction of the Court' in Lee (ed), *The International Criminal Court: The Making of the Rome Statute, Issues, Negotiations, Results* (Kluwer, 1999) 79, 89.

suggested that 'cultural genocide' should be included, but this was rejected. There have been attempts to revive this notion. However, they were not accepted by the ICTY,[22] or the ICJ.[23]

The physical acts of genocide have clear overlaps with human rights law. Killing and inflicting serious bodily or mental harm (which can include sexual offences)[24] and deliberately inflicting conditions of life calculated to bring about a group's physical destruction raise fairly clear human rights issues. These types of acts can amount to a violation of civil and political rights. In certain circumstances, they can also amount to a violation of economic, social, and cultural rights, such as the right to health and the right to food. This is particularly true of inflicting conditions of life calculated to bring about the destruction of a group.[25] Imposing measures intended to prevent births within the group would certainly implicate issues of private, home, and family life, as well as likely being inhuman and degrading. The same is true of the transfer of children.

2.1.3 Protected groups

The Genocide Convention expressly limits itself to protecting 'national, ethnical, racial and religious' groups. In General Assembly Resolution 96(I), other groups, such as political and social groups, were included. However, they were not included in the Convention. Some argue that the definition of genocide should be expanded to cover political killings, or that the customary international law definition of genocide already includes political killings. There are understandable reasons for this.[26] However, crimes against humanity cover political killings, and it is questionable whether political groups are equivalent to the national, ethnic, racial, and religious groups to which they are sometimes equated, as there is a permanence and immutability about those groups that does not apply to political groups.[27] That said, the relationship between national and political groups may be both complex and controversial.[28]

Determining the existence and membership of groups is not always as simple as the Genocide Convention might imply.[29] This has caused interpretative problems, for example whether the terms 'national, ethnical, racial or religious' are to be interpreted separately or together. The ICTR, in its first major case, *Akayesu*, tried to define each of the terms separately. This led to problems. On such an interpretation it was difficult to see the Hutus and Tutsis as different groups, yet they clearly saw themselves as different.[30] More recently, and more authoritatively, the ICTY, after a detailed review of the relevant materials held that:

---

[22] *Prosecutor v Krstić*, Judgment, IT-98–33-T, 2 August 2001, para 580 and (on appeal) Judgment, IT-98–33-A, 19 April 2004, para 25.

[23] *Case Concerning Application of the Convention on the Prevention and Punishment of the Crime of Genocide (Bosnia and Herzegovina v Serbia and Montenegro)* [2007] ICJ Rep 43, para 344.

[24] eg *Prosecutor v Akayesu*, Judgment, IT-96–4-T, 2 September 1998, para 731.

[25] The Elements of Crimes for the ICC state that 'the term "conditions of life" may include, but is not necessarily restricted to, deliberate deprivation of resources indispensable for survival, such as food or medical services, or systematic expulsion from homes'. Elements of Crimes, Art 6(c), Element 4, fn 4, ICC/ASP/1/3.

[26] Van Schaack, 'The Crime of Political Genocide: Repairing the Genocide Convention's Blind Spot' (1997) 106 *Yale LJ* 2259; Nersessian, *Genocide and Political Groups* (OUP, 2010).

[27] There was an attempt to read the convention as protecting all 'stable and permanent groups' in the *Akayesu* case, but this was a clear misreading of the Convention and its *travaux préparatoires*. See Cryer, Friman, Robinson, and Wilmshurst (2014), 169–71.

[28] *Vasiliaukas*, paras 182–6.

[29] Equally, there are times when the issue is relatively clear, one example being the Yadizi religious minority in Syria, who have almost certainly been subject to genocide by ISIS/Daesh. See Cryer, 'International Criminal Law and Daesh', available at: <https://blog.oup.com/2016/04/international-criminal-law-and-daesh/>.

[30] *Akayesu*, paras 511–15. It was this that led the ICTR Trial Chamber to claim that the Genocide Convention protected all 'stable and permanent' groups.

The preparatory work of the Convention shows that setting out such a list was designed more to describe a single phenomenon, roughly corresponding to what was recognised, before the second world war, as 'national minorities', rather than to refer to several distinct prototypes of human groups. To attempt to differentiate each of the named groups on the basis of scientifically objective criteria would thus be inconsistent with the object and purpose of the Convention.[31]

This is the preferable approach given the difficulty of determining groups precisely.[32] The question of perceived difference (as, for example, in the 'Arab'/'African' divide in Darfur) has led to the adoption of a test that relies on the reality of the distinction in the eyes of the relevant population. If such a group is considered to exist in the relevant cultural context, then the perception of the perpetrator that the victim is a member of that group suffices for them to be considered a member for the purposes of genocide.[33]

2.1.4 The context of genocide

Some take the view that genocide, of its essence, requires a plan or policy.[34] The ICTY has taken the view that there could, in theory, be a 'lone *génocidaire*' acting outside any plan;[35] a finding that has been criticized.[36] The drafters of the ICC Statute took a middle path, creating guidance for the ICC to the effect that '[t]he conduct took place in the context of a manifest pattern of similar conduct directed against that group or was conduct that could itself effect such destruction'.[37] There are two aspects to this. Fulfilling either suffices for genocide. The first is that there are other people undertaking similar acts against the relevant group, although not necessarily with genocidal intent.[38] The second was designed to cover an example such as where one person obtained a nuclear weapon and used it against a protected group.[39] The ICC has upheld the applicability of this element of the crime,[40] but the ICTY has held that it does not reflect customary international law and , irrespective of the merits or otherwise of the element, is only , as a matter of current general international law, applicable directly before the ICC.[41]

2.1.5 Internal element

Genocide is distinguished from other crimes by its particular mental element. The perpetrator must act with the intent 'to destroy, in whole or in part, a national, ethnical, racial or religious group, as such'. This is not simply a discriminatory intent, it is an eliminationist one. The Tribunals have taken a fairly strong line on this and so many charges relating to 'ethnic cleansing' in the former Yugoslavia have failed, as it was not proved that the policy was to destroy the respective groups, rather than to discriminate against them and remove them from particular areas.[42] There are difficulties involved in determining what amounts to a group and how large the 'part' of the group has to be for this aspect of the crime,

---

[31] *Krstić* Trial Chamber, para 556.

[32] Although see Wilson, *Writing History in International Criminal Trials* (CUP, 2011) ch 7.

[33] eg *Prosecutor v Semanza*, Judgment, ICTR-97–20-T, 15 May 2003, para 317.

[34] Vest, 'A Structure-Based Concept of Genocidal Intent' (2007) 5 *JICJ* 781.

[35] *Prosecutor v Jelesić*, Judgment, IT-95–10-A, 5 July 2001, para 48.

[36] Schabas, 'The Jelesić Case and the *Mens Rea* of the Crime of Genocide' (2001) 14 *LJIL* 125.

[37] eg Elements of Crimes, Art 6(1)(a), Element 4.

[38] Oosterveld, 'Context of Genocide' in Lee et al. (eds), *The International Criminal Court: Elements of Crimes and Rules of Procedure and Evidence* (Transnational, 2001) 44, 47–8.

[39] Oosterveld (2001), 46.

[40] *Prosecutor v al Bashir*, Decision on the Prosecution's Application for a Warrant of Arrest Against Omar al-Bashir, Pre-Trial Chamber 1, ICC-02/05–01/09, 4 March 2009, paras 126–8.

[41] *Prosecutor v Krstić*, Judgment, IT-98–33-A, 19 April 2004, para 224.

[42] See also *Bosnian Genocide*, para 190.

although the ICTY, ICJ, and ICC all agree that it must be 'substantial'.[43] This can include a part of the group, which is considered emblematic of the group, such as its leadership, even if that part is not numerically large.[44]

2.2 CRIMES AGAINST HUMANITY

The second set of international crimes are crimes against humanity. These were first prosecuted before the Nuremberg IMT, where they were defined, in Article 6(c), as:

> murder, extermination, enslavement, deportation, and other inhumane acts committed against any civilian population, before or during the war; or persecutions on political, racial or religious grounds in execution of or in connection with any crime within the jurisdiction of the Tribunal, whether or not in violation of the domestic law of the country where perpetrated.

The most widely ratified treaty-based definition of crimes against humanity is that in Article 7 ICC Statute. This reads:

1. For the purpose of this Statute, 'crime against humanity' means any of the following acts when committed as part of a widespread or systematic attack directed against any civilian population, with knowledge of the attack:

   (a) Murder;

   (b) Extermination;

   (c) Enslavement;

   (d) Deportation or forcible transfer of population;

   (e) Imprisonment or other severe deprivation of physical liberty in violation of fundamental rules of international law;

   (f) Torture;

   (g) Rape, sexual slavery, enforced prostitution, forced pregnancy, enforced sterilization, or any other form of sexual violence of comparable gravity;

   (h) Persecution against any identifiable group or collectivity on political, racial, national, ethnic, cultural, religious, gender . . . or other grounds that are universally recognized as impermissible under international law, in connection with any act referred to in this paragraph or any crime within the jurisdiction of the Court;

   (i) Enforced disappearance of persons;

   (j) The crime of apartheid;

   (k) Other inhumane acts of a similar character intentionally causing great suffering, or serious injury to body or to mental or physical health.[45]

Contrary to the Nuremberg definition, crimes against humanity do not need to be linked to an armed conflict and are, therefore, committable in peacetime.[46] There are, in essence, two types of crimes against humanity: 'murder-type' crimes against humanity and 'persecutive' crimes against humanity.[47] Broadly speaking, the latter consist of all crimes against

---

[43] *Bosnian Genocide*, para 198; *al Bashir*, para 146. [44] *Krstić*, para 12.

[45] Although it must be noted that this definition is not necessarily entirely reflective of customary international law on the point.

[46] Ratner, Abrams, and Bischoff, *Accountability for Human Rights Atrocities in International Law: Beyond the Nuremberg Legacy* (OUP, 2011) 52–9.

[47] Schwelb, 'Crimes Against Humanity' (1946) 23 *BYIL* 178, 190 (although Schwelb (rightly) rejects most of the legal differences between them; as will be seen, only the *mens rea* really differs).

humanity that are covered by Article 7(1)(h) while the former consist of all the others in Article 7(1). Both types have clear human rights implications.

2.2.1 Context: widespread or systematic attack

Although acts that come within the purview of crimes against humanity, at least when undertaken by state actors, are almost always violations of human rights law, they must have an additional contextual element to amount to an international crime. They must be committed against the backdrop of, and have a nexus to, a widespread or systematic attack against the civilian population. The terms have been most authoritatively defined by the ICTY: '[w]idespread refers to the large-scale nature of the attack and the number of victims, while the phrase "systematic" refers to the organized nature of the acts of violence and the improbability of their random occurrence'.[48] The ICC appears to agree with the ICTY on this.[49] The attack does not have to be a military attack.[50]

2.2.2 Context: policy

It can be argued that the requirement that crimes against humanity be widespread or systematic also implies a separate requirement: that there was a policy to commit these acts. That position was rejected as a matter of customary law by the ICTY in the *Kunarac* case.[51] However, the requirement is clearly present in the ICC Statute.[52] The debate in relation to the ICC has concentrated on what type of 'organization' can have such a policy.[53] The relationship between this and the human rights obligations of non-state actors is an issue that has not yet been fully determined.

2.2.3 External element

The physical acts that, when committed in context, amount to crimes against humanity all raise clear human rights issues. Torture and disappearances, for example, are both the subject of separate human rights/transnational criminal law treaties. Similarly, murder and deprivation of liberty in violation of fundamental standards of international law are clear violations of human rights.[54] The most detailed discussion of the interrelationship has occurred with respect to 'persecutive' crimes against humanity. The Appeals Chamber of the ICTY has defined such crimes as:

[A]n act or omission which:

1. discriminates in fact and which denies or infringes upon a fundamental right laid down in international customary or treaty law (the *actus reus*); and

2. was carried out deliberately with the intention to discriminate ....[55]

---

[48] *Prosecutor v Kunarac, Kovać and Vuković*, Judgment, IT-96–23/1-A, 12 June 2002, para 94.

[49] *al Bashir*, para 81.   [50] *Kunarac*, para 86.   [51] *Kunarac*, para 98.

[52] ICC Statute, Art 7(2)(a) defines 'attack against any civilian population' as being 'a course of conduct involving the multiple commission of acts referred to in paragraph 1 against any civilian population, pursuant to or in furtherance of a State or organizational policy to commit such attack'.

[53] Werle and Burghardt, 'Do Crimes Against Humanity Require the Participation of a State or "State-Like" Organization?' (2012) 10 *JICJ* 1151; Kress, 'On the Outer Limits of Crimes against Humanity: The Concept of Organization within the Policy Requirement: Some Reflections on the March 2010 ICC Kenya Decision' (2010) 23 *LJIL* 855.

[54] On the overlap in relation to enslavement, see *Prosecutor v Kunarac, Kovać and Vuković*, Judgment, IT-96–23-T, 22 February 2001, paras 518 ff.

[55] *Prosecutor v Blaskić*, Judgment, IT-95–14-A, 29 July 2004, para 131.

The ICTY has been careful, however, not to indicate a complete overlap between crimes against humanity and human rights law, opining that cases from human rights and refugee law 'cannot provide a basis for individual criminal responsibility. It would be contrary to the principle of legality to convict someone of persecution based on a definition found in international refugee law or human rights law'[56] as they were created for different purposes. However, it used human rights instruments to assist with the task of defining 'persecution'.[57] As one ICTY Trial Chamber has said, '[i]n practice, not every denial of a fundamental human right will be serious enough to constitute a crime against humanity.'[58] On the other hand, the ICTY has determined that violations of socio-economic rights, such as the right to employment and medical care, can form the basis of persecutive crimes against humanity.[59]

The fact that words can, in some circumstances, be part of the conduct element of 'persecutive' crimes against humanity has led to some discussion in the ICTR. In the *RTLM* Appeal, which related to a radio station that incited genocidal violence, the majority said that:

[H]ate speech targeting a population on the basis of ethnicity, or any other discriminatory ground, violates the right to respect for the dignity of the members of the targeted group as human beings, and therefore constitutes 'actual discrimination'...it is not necessary that every individual act underlying the crime of persecution should be of a gravity corresponding to other crimes against humanity: ... It is the cumulative effect of all the underlying acts of the crime of persecution which must reach a level of gravity equivalent to that for other crimes against humanity.[60]

Judge Meron, however, argued that the majority did not take sufficient account of freedom of expression.[61]

Turning to the ICC, the drafters of the Elements of Crimes were concerned that crimes against humanity (in particular, but not only, persecutions and 'other inhuman acts') could be used to criminalize all human rights violations. Therefore, they included a statement in those elements designed to limit that possibility:

Since article 7 pertains to international criminal law, its provisions ... must be strictly construed, taking into account that crimes against humanity as defined in article 7 are among the most serious crimes of concern to the international community as a whole, warrant and entail individual criminal responsibility, and require conduct which is impermissible under generally applicable international law, as recognized by the principal legal systems of the world.[62]

This was included specifically at the behest of a small number of states that felt their existing practices might amount to crimes against humanity and reflects the fact that the Elements of Crimes are the outcome of negotiated compromises.

---

[56] *Prosecutor v Kupreškić, Kupreškić, Kupreškić, Papić and Šantić*, Judgment, IT-95–16-T, 14 January 2000, para 589.

[57] *Kupreškić*, para 621. Although see *Prosecutor v Stakić*, Judgment, IT-97–24-T, 31 July 2003, para 721, which is more sceptical of the use of such instruments.

[58] *Prosecutor v Krajišnik*, Judgment, IT-00–39-T, 27 September 2006, para 735. This has been accepted by the ICTY Appeals Chamber. See eg *Prosecutor v Brđanin*, Judgment, IT-99–36-A, 3 April 2007, para 296.

[59] *Brđanin*, paras 292–7.

[60] *Prosecutor v Nahimana, Barayagwiza and Ngeze*, Judgment, ICTR-99–52-A, 28 November 2007, paras 986–7.   [61] *Nahimana*, Separate and Partially Dissenting Opinion of Judge Meron, paras 5–16.

[62] Elements of Crimes, Introduction to Elements for Art 7.

2.2.4 Internal element

The internal element of the crime is, first, that the person had the mental element required for the underlying crime (murder etc). In addition they have to have knowledge of the broader context in which their crimes are committed, that is, that their actions took place in the context of a widespread or systematic attack on the civilian population. In the Appeal in *Tadić* it was said that:

> The acts of the accused must comprise part of a pattern of widespread or systematic crimes directed against a civilian population and ... the accused must have *known* that his acts fit into such a pattern [but it is not required that the conduct be undertaken for public, rather than personal reasons].[63]

In contrast to the ICTY Statute, the ICTR Statute explicitly requires a discriminatory intent.[64] Although some thought this to be a part of the ICTY definition, it is now accepted that it is not a part of the customary prohibition of crimes against humanity, not least because the ICC Statute does not reflect such a condition. There is one exception: for 'persecutive' crimes against humanity the perpetrator must have a discriminatory, although not necessarily persecutory, intention.[65]

2.3 WAR CRIMES

War crimes are the oldest of the international crimes. They are serious violations of international humanitarian law, for which there is individual criminal responsibility. The relationship between humanitarian law and human rights law, and the main norms humanitarian law contains, are covered in Chapter 25. Suffice it to say here that war crimes can only be committed in times of armed conflict and need to be related to the conflict.

Humanitarian law (and, thus its subgenre, war crimes law) is often split into 'Geneva' and 'Hague' law, the former dealing with the protection of those not taking part in a conflict and the latter dealing with targeting and weapon use. The two categories are not clear at the boundaries, but this still provides a useful way of dividing the area. The basic norms of 'Geneva' law can be found in Common Article 3 Geneva Conventions. This is a distillation of the four Geneva Conventions of 1949, and is now considered applicable to all armed conflicts.[66] It reads (in part):

> [E]ach Party to the conflict shall be bound to apply, as a minimum, the following provisions:
>
> (1) Persons taking no active part in the hostilities, including members of armed forces who have laid down their arms and those placed *hors de combat* by sickness, wounds, detention, or any other cause, shall in all circumstances be treated humanely, without any adverse distinction founded on race, colour, religion or faith, sex, birth or wealth, or any other similar criteria. To this end, the following acts are and shall remain prohibited at any time and in any place whatsoever with respect to the above-mentioned persons:
>
>   (a) violence to life and person, in particular murder of all kinds, mutilation, cruel treatment and torture;
>
>   (b) taking of hostages;
>
>   (c) outrages upon personal dignity, in particular humiliating and degrading treatment;

---

[63] *Prosecutor v Tadić*, Judgment, IT-94-1-A, 15 July 1999, para 248.   [64] ICTR Statute, Art 3.

[65] *Blaškić* Appeal, paras 164–5.

[66] Different law applies in international and non-international armed conflicts, although there is increasing overlap between them.

(d) the passing of sentences and the carrying out of executions without previous judgment pronounced by a regularly constituted court, affording all the judicial guarantees which are recognized as indispensable by civilized peoples.

The human rights implications of much of this are clear. Torture and humiliating and
degrading treatment are also prohibited by international human rights law, although the
definition may not be quite the same. Murder, at least by state officials, and fair trial rights
are also familiar to human rights law. Given the overlaps, it is unsurprising that many
human rights advocates refer to humanitarian law.

Many human rights lawyers are less comfortable with 'Hague' law. This law has some
principles with which few would quarrel, such as that of unnecessary suffering, and the
banning of poison, gas, and biological weapons. However, the law of war crimes (and
humanitarian law), despite prohibiting direct attacks on civilians, permits proportionate
incidental civilian deaths ('collateral damage') that are the result of an attack on lawful
military targets. Many in the human rights community are uncomfortable with this, and
the possibility of differing interpretations between human rights lawyers and military officials is something that the ICTY has accepted:

> The answers to these questions [on proportionality] are not simple. It may be necessary to
> resolve them on a case by case basis, and the answers may differ depending on the back-
> ground and values of the decision maker. It is unlikely that a human rights lawyer and an
> experienced combat commander would assign the same relative values to military advan-
> tage and to injury to non-combatants.[67]

It is controversial whose views ought to prevail here.

Of course, not all murders and the like that occur in wartime are war crimes. People
still get involved in, for example, brawls during armed conflicts. That does not mean they
are war crimes. Therefore, for activity (or, in relevant circumstances, inactivity) to amount
to a war crime there has to be some nexus between the conflict and the conduct. As the
ICTY has said, 'what distinguishes a war crime from a purely domestic offence is that a
war crime is shaped by and dependent upon the environment—the armed conflict—in
which it was committed',[68] which meant that:

> The armed conflict need not have been causal to the commission of the crime, but the
> existence of an armed conflict must, at a minimum, have played a substantial part in the
> perpetrator's ability to commit it, his decision to commit it, the manner in which it was
> committed or the purpose for which it was committed.[69]

This aspect of war crimes law is also present in the Elements of Crimes for the ICC, although the definition is slightly different.[70]

2.4 AGGRESSION

Aggression is sometimes described as the 'supreme international crime'[71] (although others would reserve this moniker for genocide), and it is probably also the most controversial. It was prosecuted before the Nuremberg and Tokyo IMTs, as well as a number of
national tribunals after the Second World War, but at no point in those proceedings was

---

[67] Final Report to the Prosecutor by the Committee Established to Review the NATO Bombing Campaign
Against the Federal Republic of Yugoslavia, para 50, available at: <http://www.icty.org/sid/10052#IVA64d>.
[68] *Kunarac*, para 58.   [69] *Kunarac*, paras 58–9.
[70] Elements of Crimes, Introduction and eg Elements for Art 8(2)(a)(i), 4–5.
[71] Nuremberg Judgment, 186.

a definition authoritatively set down. It took the General Assembly until 1974 to draft a definition of the concept (though not necessarily the crime) of aggression.[72] The only international criminal tribunal after the Nuremberg and Tokyo IMTs to have jurisdiction over aggression is the ICC. Article 5(1) ICC Statute provides that aggression is a crime within the jurisdiction of the Court, but Article 5(2) requires, for the ICC to exercise that jurisdiction, that the Statute be amended to include a definition of the crime.[73]

This was not thought likely at the time, but, in 2010 the Review Conference of the ICC Statute (in Kampala, Uganda) adopted an amendment to that Statute containing a definition. However it is not yet in force. The definition provides that aggression is 'the planning, preparation, initiation or execution, by a person in a position effectively to exercise control over or to direct the political or military action of a State, of an act of aggression which, by its character, gravity and scale, constitutes a manifest violation of the Charter of the United Nations.'[74] Although achieving a definition at all is a major development in international criminal law, aspects of the definition, as well as the jurisdiction of the ICC over this crime, remain complex and controversial.[75]

Although the Nuremberg IMT asserted that aggression differed from other international crimes 'in that it contained within itself the accumulated evil of the whole',[76] the relationship of aggression to human rights is perhaps the least clear of the international crimes. The criminalization of aggression can be seen as contributing to the right to peace (to the extent that the right exists separately to other human rights),[77] or at least operating in tandem to it. That said, the negotiations in Kampala were not based on the right to peace, nor was there much, if any, talk of it there, and many human rights NGOs remain ambivalent about the crime, in particular its relationship to humanitarian intervention.[78]

3 PROSECUTIONS: INTERNATIONAL AND NATIONAL

Prosecutions are often, and not necessarily inaccurately, thought to be important from the point of view of human rights protection. For example, in the *Velasquez-Rodriguez* case, the Inter-American Court of Human Rights held that the failure to investigate the disappearance of the applicant's son and punish those responsible was part of the violation of his right to life.[79] In the European system, a failure to undertake a proper investigation into a death can be a violation of the right to life.[80] It is increasingly, albeit controversially, thought that, in the circumstances of international crimes, the rights of the victims include a right to see those who have committed such crimes prosecuted. This is probably a little in advance of the current state of international law, but such views have gained considerable ground in the last decade, especially with respect to high-ranking offenders.[81]

---

[72] GA Res 3314 (1974).

[73] See Schabas, *An Introduction to the International Criminal Court* (OUP, 2017) 31–139.

[74] RC/Res.6 (Article 8bis). This Article also contains a number of examples drawn from GA Res 3314.

[75] See the special issue 'After Kampala, Aggression' (2012) 10 *JICJ* 1–288; Kreβ and Barriga (eds), *Crime of Aggression Library: The Crime of Aggression Vols I and II* (CUP, 2017).

[76] Nuremberg Judgment, 186.

[77] Tehindrazanarivelo and Kolb, 'Peace, Right to, International Protection' in Wolfrum (ed), *The Max Planck Encyclopaedia of Public International Law* (OUP, 2012) Vol VIII, 153, 155, Schabas, 'Aggression and International Human Rights Law' in Kreβ and Barriga (eds), 351. See also Chapter 7.

[78] Schabas, 357–60.   [79] *Velasquez-Rodriguez v Honduras*, IACtHR Series C No 4 (29 July 1988).

[80] *McCann v UK* (1995) 21 EHRR 67, para 161.

[81] *Prosecutor v Kondewa*, Decision on Lack of Jurisdiction/Abuse of Process: Amnesty Provided by the Lomé Accord, SCSL-2004–14-AR72(E) 25 May 2004, Separate Opinion of Robertson J, para 48.

There is a long, although not always illustrious, history of the prosecution of war crimes, both at the national and international level. There were initially plans to try German war criminals by the Allies after the First World War.[82] However, these floundered and only a small number of those defendants were tried in Leipzig, Germany, in proceedings considered strongly skewed towards the defence.[83]

Probably the most well-known prosecutions of the twentieth century occurred after the Second World War, when the Nuremberg and Tokyo IMTs were set up to try the major Axis war criminals in both spheres of that conflict. It is possible to trace the beginnings of modern international criminal law to the Nuremberg IMT, which tried Nazi leaders for war crimes, crimes against humanity, and aggression. The latter charge caused the most controversy, on the basis that the offence probably did not exist in international law at the time. However, it is questionable whether international law contained an absolute prohibition of retroactive criminal legislation at the time and later instruments such as the European Convention on Human Rights (ECHR) and the International Covenant on Civil and Political Rights (ICCPR) contain savings clauses that were in part designed to avoid the implication that the Nuremberg Charter violated human rights. For example, Article 15 ICCPR provides both that '[n]o one shall be held guilty of any criminal offence on account of any act or omission which did not constitute a criminal offence under national or *international* law at the time when it was committed' and that 'nothing in this article shall prejudice the trial and punishment of any person for any act or omission which, at the time when it was committed, was criminal according to the general principles of law recognized by the community of nations'.[84]

Overall, the general view of the Nuremberg IMT has been quite positive, in part because the President of the Tribunal, Sir Geoffrey Lawrence, exercised a firm but fair hand over the proceedings.[85] History has not been so kind to the Tokyo IMT, the fair trial standards of which have, in particular, been singled out for criticism.[86] There were also large numbers of domestic trials in countries occupied during the Second World War.

During the Cold War there was little movement on a permanent international criminal court, and national prosecutions for international crimes, such as that of Adolf Eichmann in Jerusalem in 1960,[87] were the exception rather than the rule. Change came about in 1993, when the Security Council created the ICTY. It did so in Resolution 837, using an innovative interpretation of its powers under Chapter VII UN Charter.[88] It acted similarly in 1994 to create the ICTR in Resolution 955. Both had their difficulties in the beginning and had slow starts, particularly in the absence of cooperation from a number of states. However, the picture slowly brightened, and both tribunals, despite some criticism of their approaches to fair trial,[89] and some controversies over their interpretations of the law,[90] have prosecuted a number of high-ranking leaders and

---

[82] Treaty of Versailles, Arts 227–9.

[83] See eg Bass, *Stay the Hand of Vengeance* (Princeton UP, 2000) ch 3.

[84] Emphasis added. See Gallant, *The Principle of Legality in International and Comparative Law* (CUP, 2008) ch 4b.

[85] Tusa and Tusa, *The Nuremberg Trial* (BBC Books, 1995) 112.

[86] See generally Boister and Cryer, *The Tokyo International Military Tribunal: A Reappraisal* (OUP, 2008).

[87] *A-G of Israel v Eichmann* (1968) 36 ILR 18.

[88] See *Prosecutor v Tadić*, Decision on the Defence Interlocutory Appeal on Jurisdiction, IT-94-1-AR72, 2 October 1995, paras 34–5.

[89] McDermott, 'Rights in Reverse: A Critical Analysis of Fair Trial Rights Under International Criminal Law', in Schabas, McDermott, and Hayes (eds), *The Ashgate Research Companion to International Criminal Law: Critical Perspectives* (Ashgate, 2013) 165.

[90] eg Sadat, 'Can the ICTY Šainović and Perišić Cases Be Reconciled?' (2014) 108 *AJIL* 475.

catalysed the development of international criminal law more generally. The ICTR has now closed and, as at April 2017, the ICTY was in its last days. Their functions have been (for the ICTR) or are being (for the ICTY) replaced by 'residual mechanisms' to deal with issues such as parole and commutation of sentence.[91] The era of *ad hoc* tribunals has now probably entered its closing phases.

The largest development in international prosecution of international crimes was the creation of the ICC, the Statute of which was drafted in Rome in 1998.[92] Despite opposition from some states (most notably, but not limited to, the US) the Statute entered into force in 2002. It currently has 124 states parties. The ICC, although permanent, does not have jurisdiction over all international crimes. It can prosecute war crimes, crimes against humanity, genocide, and, in the future, aggression,[93] but only in relation to crimes committed by nationals of states parties or on their territories.[94] The only exception to this is if the Security Council refers a situation to the Court. The Security Council has done this twice, in Resolutions 1593 and 1970, which referred the situation in Darfur, Sudan, and Libya, respectively to the ICC.

The jurisdiction of the ICC, unlike that of the ICTY and ICTR, is intended to be 'complementary' to that of states. In other words, the ICC can act only if states are 'unwilling or unable genuinely' to prosecute the offences themselves.[95] The precise meaning of these terms is the subject of some controversy and litigation before the Court.[96].

The principle of complementarity is meant to reflect the primary role of national jurisdictions in prosecuting international crimes. It is true that states may assert universal jurisdiction over genocide, war crimes, and crimes against humanity (the position on aggression is less certain).[97] Indeed, in some circumstances, in particular for grave breaches of the Geneva Conventions, they are obliged to do so. In practice, however, the states of nationality of perpetrators tend to be unwilling to prosecute, and territorial states are often also unwilling or unable to prosecute offenders themselves. In spite of something of an upturn in prosecution by third states, they often prefer to remain inactive. The prosecutions that have occurred tend to be of suspects from conflicts where there is already a practical consensus on the necessity of prosecuting suspects.[98] Other prosecutions have proved controversial.[99]

The fact that the ICC has concentrated, rightly or otherwise, largely on African states has caused some, including at times the African Union and its members, to criticize the

---

[91] See SC Res 1966 (2010), Annex I: Statute of the International Residual Mechanism for Criminal Tribunals; 'Symposium' (2011) 9 *JICJ* 787–837.

[92] There is also the significant development of 'internationalized' courts such as the Special Court for Sierra Leone (which has completed its work and is now closed), the Extraordinary Chambers for Prosecuting the Khmer Rouge in Cambodia, and the Special Tribunal for Lebanon. See Cryer, Friman, Robinson, and Wilmshurst (2014), ch 9.

[93] ICC Statute, Arts 5(1)(2) and 8*bis*.

[94] ICC Statute, Art 12. The crime of aggression is more complex. See Article 15*bis*.

[95] ICC Statute, Art 17.

[96] eg *Prosecutor v Katanga and Ngudjolo*, Judgment on the Appeal of Mr Germain Katanga against the Oral Decision of Trial Chamber II of 12 June 2009 on the Admissibility of the Case, ICC-01/04–01/07–1497, 25 September 2009. See generally Stahn and el Zeidy (eds), *The International Criminal Court and Complementarity, Vols I and II* (CUP, 2012).

[97] Cryer, Friman, Robinson, and Wilmshurst (2014), 50–62.

[98] Langer, 'The Diplomacy of Universal Jurisdiction: The Political Branches and the Transnational Prosecution of International Crimes' (2001) 105 *AJIL* 1.

[99] Van der Wilt, 'Universal Jurisdiction under Attack: an Assessment of African Misgivings towards International Criminal Justice as Administered by Western States' (2011) 9 *JICJ* 1043.

Court, and indeed to threaten to leave.[100] However, others have leapt to the ICC's defence on point, and only one State (Burundi) has an extant declaration of withdrawal, which is due to enter into force in mid-October 2017.[101] Furthermore, the Prosecutor is also investigating the situation in Georgia,[102] although whether this blunts the criticism is a matter of conjecture.

In the African context, in 2014, the African Union adopted the Malabo Protocol, which would give the African Court on Human and People's Rights criminal jurisdiction over international crimes and certain transnational crimes, including terrorism, piracy, and mercenarism.[103] It will enter into force when it has been ratified by 15 states. As of 2017, however, its future remains uncertain.

4 NON-PROSECUTORIAL OPTIONS

There are ways of dealing with international crimes other than by prosecution. The legality of some of them has come under fire recently, from human rights groups in particular, but there is probably still room for them to play at least a complementary role for some offenders. In addition, prosecution is not a panacea for all of the consequences of international crimes and human rights violations.

4.1 AMNESTIES

Amnesties are probably the most controversial option that does not involve prosecutions. Indeed, they prevent them. There are serious arguments about the lawfulness of amnesties under international law, both where there are treaties that create obligations to prosecute, for example the Geneva Conventions for grave breaches and the Genocide Convention for that crime, and under human rights law. In the former case, it is clear that a duty to prosecute is violated by a domestic law preventing prosecution.[104] With regard to human rights law, there are significant arguments that amnesties, certainly unconditional ones, are contrary to various human rights obligations such as the duty to investigate losses of life attributable to the state and the right of access to courts.[105] However, it is by no means clear that amnesties are always unlawful. It is true that the Inter-American Court of Human Rights has taken a strong line against amnesties, observing that:

> This Court considers that all amnesty provisions, provisions on prescription and the establishment of measures designed to eliminate responsibility are inadmissible, because they are intended to prevent the investigation and punishment of those responsible for serious human rights violations such as torture, extrajudicial, summary or arbitrary execution and

---

[100] BBC News, 'African Union Backs Mass Withdrawal from International Criminal Court' available at: <http://www.bbc.co.uk/news/world-africa-38826073>.

[101] Ambos, 'Expanding the Focus of the "African Criminal Court"' 'in Schabas *et al.*, 499.

[102] *Situation in Georgia*: Decision on the Prosecutor's Request to Authorization of an Investigation, ICC 01/15 (27 January 2016).

[103] Protocol on Amendments to the Statute of the African Court of Human and People's Rights, Article 14, available at: <https://www.au.int/web/sites/default/files/treaties/7804-treaty-0045_-_protocol_on_amendments_to_the_protocol_on_the_statute_of_the_african_court_of_justice_and_human_rights_e.pdf>.

[104] Although on traditional principles of international law an amnesty in one state would not prevent another state from prosecuting.

[105] Orentlicher, 'Settling Accounts: The Duty to Prosecute Human Rights Violations of a Former Regime' (1991) 100 *Yale LJ* 2537.

forced disappearance, all of them prohibited because they violate non-derogable rights recognized by international human rights law.[106]

Some take the view that this case has determined a more generally applicable norm against amnesties in international law,[107] but this may be stretching that court's jurisprudence a little too far. Other tribunals have not been as assertive.[108] The position was best summed up by the Special Court for Sierra Leone when it said that:

> [T]hat there is a crystallising international norm that a government cannot grant amnesty for serious violations of crimes under international law is amply supported by materials placed before the Court [but the view] that it has crystallised may not be entirely correct … it is accepted that such a norm is developing under international law.[109]

The merits of amnesties are hotly contested, with some claiming that they foster reconciliation and others saying they often allow powerful perpetrators, literally, to get away with murder, and create a culture of impunity that will only encourage future violations.

4.2 TRUTH AND RECONCILIATION COMMISSIONS

Amnesties can be accompanied by truth and reconciliation commissions and, where they are, there is often more sympathy for the relevant amnesty. This was the case for the South African system, which was set up in the aftermath of apartheid. In South Africa, a failure to fully inform the Truth and Reconciliation Commission of the crimes committed could lead to a refusal of amnesty and indeed did in some cases.[110] The merits and demerits of truth and reconciliation commissions are hotly contested. Some see them as providing the groundwork for later reconciliation; others do not feel that there can be a shared state-authorized truth. Much depends on the composition, mandate, and functioning of such bodies.[111] It is sometimes suggested that lustration—that is, the collective removal of people from their jobs—is an appropriate method of dealing with international crimes, but any collective measure is likely to be questionable on human rights grounds, especially the right to have rights and duties adjudicated at law.[112]

5 CONCLUSION

There is much to be said for using international criminal law to vindicate human rights. For example, as the Nuremberg IMT implied in its famous statement referenced in Section 1,[113] using criminal law actually brings home to high-level leaders that they personally

---

[106] *Barrios Altos Case* (*Chumbipuma Aguierre et al. v Peru*) IACtHR Series C No 75 (2001) para 41.

[107] Laplante, 'Outlawing Amnesty: The Return of Criminal Justice to Transitional Justice Schemes' (2008–2009) 48 *Virginia JIL* 915.

[108] See generally Seibert-Fohr, *Prosecuting Serious Human Rights Violations* (OUP, 2009).

[109] *Prosecutor v Kallon and Kamara*, Decision on Challenge to Jurisdiction: Lomé Amnesty Accord, SCSL-2004–15-AR72(E) and SCSL-2004–16-AR72(E), 13 March 2004, para 82. Although see Akhavan, 'Whither National Courts? The Rome Statute's Missing Half: Towards An Express and Enforceable Obligation For the National Repression of International Crimes' (2010) 8 *JICJ* 1245.

[110] Prosecutions have not been notable by their successes though. See Bubenzer, *Post-TRC Prosecutions in South Africa* (Martinus Nijhoff, 2009).   [111] Hayner, *Unspeakable Truths* (Routledge, 2011)

[112] ICCPR, Art 14; *Casanovas v France*, CCPR/C/51/D/441/1990 (26 July 1994).   [113] Text at n 3.

rather than only the impersonal state, will bear the consequences of their decisions. There is also the possibility that civil human rights claims will not provide for a sufficient sense of justice for the victims.[114] Another advantage that has been suggested is the possibility that victims will find testimony cathartic, although this is controversial.[115] Furthermore, it is at least arguable that subjecting facts to forensic scrutiny can later prevent denial of those atrocities.[116] However, whether prosecutions can have a significant deterrent effect on the commission of later human rights violations is a matter which is more the subject of, often sceptical, speculation rather than scientific proof.[117]

Perhaps the shadow side of this is that prosecutions for international crimes are, for a variety of reasons, selective, and so not all of those who commit such crimes can be prosecuted. Indeed, as has been noted here, not all human rights violations are also international crimes, although most international crimes would amount to human rights violations when committed by states. Furthermore, when prosecuting international crimes, it is important to remember that prosecutions for international crimes can also, themselves, involve violations of human rights, as the trial of former Iraqi president Saddam Hussein showed.[118] That said, international criminal law can, and often does, walk hand in hand with human rights law and practice.

FURTHER READING

BASSIOUNI (ed), *International Criminal Law Vols I-III* (Martinus Nijhoff, 2008).

CASSESE et al., *Cassese's International Criminal Law* (Oxford University Press, 2013).

CASSESE et al. (eds), *The Oxford Companion to International Criminal Justice* (Oxford University Press, 2009).

CRYER, FRIMAN, ROBINSON, and WILMSHURST, *An Introduction to International Criminal Law and Procedure* (Cambridge University Press, 3rd ed., 2014).

GUILFOYLE, *International Criminal Law* (Oxford University Press, 2016).

HUNEEUS, 'International Criminal Law by Other Means: The Quasi-Criminal Jurisdiction of the Human Rights Courts' (2013) 107 *AJIL* 1.

SCHABAS, *The International Criminal Court: A Commentary on the Rome Statute* (Oxford University Press, 2nd ed., 2016).

SCHABAS, *An Introduction to the International Criminal Court* (Cambridge University Press, 5th ed., 2017).

STAHN (ed), *The Law and Practice of the International Criminal Court* (Oxford University Press, 2015).

WERLE and JESSBERGER, *Principles of International Criminal Law* (Oxford University Press, 2014).

---

[114] Although for the argument that this represents only one understanding of justice, see Clarke, *Fictions of Justice: The International Criminal Court and the Challenge of Legal Pluralism in Sub-Saharan Africa* (CUP, 2009).

[115] Stover, *The Witnesses* (Penn State Press, 2007).

[116] Cohen, *States of Denial: Knowing About Atrocities and Suffering* (Polity, 2001).

[117] Although see Cryer, 'The Role of International Criminal Prosecutions in Increasing Compliance with International Humanitarian Law in Contemporary African Conflicts', in Krieger (ed), *Inducing Compliance with International Humanitarian Law: Lessons from the African Great Lakes Region* (CUP, 2015) 188.

[118] Bhuta, 'Fatal Errors: The Trial and Appeal Judgments in the *Dujail* case' (2008) 6 *JICJ* 39.

USEFUL WEBSITES

International Criminal Tribunal for the former Yugoslavia: <http://www.icty.org/>

International Criminal Tribunal for Rwanda: <http://unictr.unmict.org/>

International Criminal Court: <http://www.icc-cpi.int/>

United Nations Mechanism for International Criminal Tribunals: <http://www.unmict.org/en>

27

INTERNATIONAL REFUGEE LAW

Alice Edwards

SUMMARY

International refugee law is concerned with the status and standards of treatment of refugees. The two legal regimes of international human rights law and international refugee law emerged from the same historical background of the Second World War, in which millions of persons were displaced as a result of conflict and persecution. The two regimes are, thus, closely related yet also distinct. International human rights law informs and reinforces international refugee law and the rights of refugees. At the same time, the specific rights provided by international refugee law, based on the special character of refugees, remain the primary source of their protection.

1 INTRODUCTION

The primary sources of the rights of refugees are found in the instruments and customary norms making up international refugee law, centring on the 1951 Convention relating to the Status of Refugees (Refugee Convention). International refugee law defines who is and is not a refugee and specifies the range of rights to which they are entitled. In recognition of the special character of refugees, as persons who are outside their country of origin or nationality and are at risk of persecution, the Refugee Convention was drafted to capture the specific rights and needs of refugees and the obligations on host states—in substitute of their own governments— to provide protection to such persons. International human rights law, in contrast, is a set of rights that are applicable to all persons, generally regardless of their immigration or other status. As such, international refugee law and international human rights law operate in parallel, with many similar provisions and safeguards. This simultaneous application of the two regimes poses some problems in determining which rights apply to refugees in which circumstances. This can only be resolved at the level of the individual right, rather than at the level of the regime. Such resolutions must be subject to the guiding ethos that the higher standard ought to prevail, in recognition of the inherent dignity of refugees and the aim of the Refugee Convention to ensure refugees the widest possible exercise of their fundamental rights.[1]

---

[1] Refugee Convention, preamble and Art 5.

Section 2 explains the purpose and scope of international refugee law. Section 3 identifies the five fundamental elements of the Refugee Convention, and also explains other important parameters of international refugee law more broadly. Section 4 explores the relationship between the two bodies of law at the macro-level, while Sections 5–8 deal with specific aspects of refugee law—namely, the definition of a refugee, the prohibition of *refoulement* especially in situations at sea, refugee rights, and the ending of refugee status and solutions—and analyse how international human rights law informs them.

2 WHAT IS INTERNATIONAL REFUGEE LAW?

International refugee law is the body of law that regulates the status and rights of refugees and the securing of long-term solutions to their situation. Its purpose is to ensure that refugees who are outside their countries of origin or nationality receive protection of their basic rights, which they no longer enjoy from their own governments.

International refugee law is made up of treaties and customary international law, centring on the Refugee Convention and the 1967 Protocol relating to the Status of Refugees (1967 Protocol), as well as regional refugee and other protection instruments. In terms of customary international law, from among the range of rights contained in the Refugee Convention, only the prohibition on *refoulement*,[2] or return to countries of origin where the refugee faces a threat to their life or freedom, has crystallized into a customary norm.[3]

While the Refugee Convention and the 1967 Protocol are the principal treaties at the global level, and are widely ratified, a number of regional refugee instruments also exist. These are: the Organization of African Unity's (now African Union) 1969 Convention governing the Specific Aspects of Refugee Problems in Africa (OAU Refugee Convention), the Cartagena Declaration on Refugees,[4] and the European Union's *asylum acquis*, the latter being composed of a series of directives and regulations inter alia on refugee and subsidiary protection,[5] reception, and asylum procedures.

Refugee law is informed by international human rights law, which also forms an integral part of the regime. The Refugee Convention is a human rights treaty in the sense that it codifies the rights that refugees are to enjoy and the correlative obligations on states to respect, protect, and fulfil those rights. It is, though, distinct from the main human rights treaties as it is a specific regime for the protection of a specific class of human being, namely refugees. The protections of international human rights law supplement the refugee regime in multiple ways, as detailed in this chapter.

---

[2] Art 33.

[3] See, in particular, Declaration of States Parties to the 1951 Convention and or Its 1967 Protocol relating to the Status of Refugees, HCR/MMSP/2001/09 (16 January 2002), para 4.

[4] Adopted by the Colloquium on the International Protection of Refugees in Central America, Mexico and Panama, 22 November 1984.

[5] 'Subsidiary protection' covers persons who have reasons for being outside their country of origin owing to a real risk of serious harm arising from '(a) the death penalty or execution; (b) torture or inhuman or degrading treatment or punishment; or (c) serious and individual threat to a civilian's life or person by reason of indiscriminate violence in situations of international or internal armed conflict.' They are entitled to the rights and benefits outlined in the EU Directive 2011/95/EU of the European Parliament and of the Council of 13 December 2011 on standards for the qualification of third-country nationals or stateless persons as beneficiaries of international protection, for a uniform status for refugees or for persons eligible for subsidiary protection, and for the content of the protection granted (recast), 20 December 2011, OJ L 337, 9–26, Arts 2 and 15.

The mandate and functions of the UN High Commissioner for Refugees (UNHCR) also comprise part of international refugee law. UNHCR is a global humanitarian and non-political organization with the specific mandate granted by the UN General Assembly to provide international protection to refugees and, together with governments, to seek solutions to the situation of refugees. Part of this mandate includes supervising the application of international conventions for the protection of refugees.[6] It does this through a range of measures including producing authoritative legal and policy guidelines and positions, intervening as *amicus curiae* before international and national courts, engaging in diplomatic interventions with governments, and monitoring states' implementation of their treaty obligations. In turn, states parties to the Refugee Convention and/or 1967 Protocol are required to cooperate with UNHCR in the exercise of its functions and to inform it of any laws or regulations enacted relating to refugees.[7]

3 FUNDAMENTAL ELEMENTS OF INTERNATIONAL REFUGEE LAW

International refugee law is premised on the human right 'to seek and enjoy in other countries asylum from persecution' found in Article 14(1) of the Universal Declaration of Human Rights (UDHR). Although it has often been argued by states that there is no obligation 'to grant' asylum under the Refugee Convention, because it does not contain such an explicit obligation, this is an outdated view. It is clear that the purpose of the Refugee Convention is precisely to provide sanctuary to persons defined as refugees and in the form outlined in the Convention; the choice for states rests only in the domestic form that such sanctuary takes.

The Refugee Convention can be broken down into five fundamental elements. First, the Refugee Convention *defines* a refugee as anyone who 'is outside their country of origin owing to a well-founded fear of being persecuted for reasons of race, religion, nationality, membership of a particular social group or political opinion.'[8] Although the definition was originally limited to refugees fleeing events in Europe (or elsewhere, via declaration)[9] prior to 1 January 1951, the 1967 Protocol 'amended' the Convention to allow states to lift both these geographical and temporal caveats, turning the Convention into a truly universal treaty.[10] The regional instruments expand this definition to cover groups of persons in flight from events such as armed conflict, massive or systematic human rights violations, or serious disturbances of public order.[11]

The Refugee Convention definition does not apply to persons for whom there are serious reasons to believe they have committed acts which exclude them from refugee protection, such as war crimes, crimes against humanity, or serious ordinary crimes.[12]

Palestinian refugees are also not in principle covered by the Refugee Convention, being instead protected and assisted by the international community via a special regime under the auspices of the UN Relief and Works Agency for Palestine Refugees in

---

[6] Statute of the Office of the United Nations High Commissioner for Refugees, GA Res 428(V), A/RES/428(V) (14 December 1950), para 8(1).

[7] Refugee Convention, Arts 35 and 36; 1967 Protocol, Art II.   [8] Art 1(A)(2).   [9] Art 1(B).

[10] 1967 Protocol, Art I.

[11] OAU Refugee Convention, Art 1(2); Cartagena Declaration on Refugees, Art 3.

[12] Refugee Convention, Art 1F.

the Near East (UNRWA), which operates in Gaza, the West Bank, Jordan, Lebanon, and Syria.[13] Palestinian refugees may, however, benefit from refugee status under the Refugee Convention automatically when the protection or assistance of UNRWA has ceased. Such protection or assistance may be considered ceased, for example, if the Palestinian refugee is outside UNRWA's areas of operation and is unable to re-avail him- or herself of that protection or assistance for reasons beyond his or her control.[14]

Second, the *principle of non-discrimination* provides that refugees and asylum-seekers who are protected by the Convention shall enjoy their rights without distinction except where any distinction can be objectively justified. This is captured in Article 3 of the Convention, which requires that all refugees shall enjoy Convention rights regardless of 'race, religion or country of origin'.

Third, *the principle of non-refoulement* protects refugees from return to threats to life or freedom (discussed in Section 6).

Fourth, there is a *guarantee of non-penalization* of asylum-seekers and refugees who show 'good cause' for illegal entry or stay.[15] Penalties in this sense include both criminal and administrative penalties such as fines or detention. Noting that persons in flight are rarely able to satisfy immigration entry requirements, the Conference of Plenipotentiaries to the Refugee Convention observed that 'good cause' would include fleeing persecution, but there could be other good causes for why a refugee would need to enter a country without official authorization, such as for reasons of family unity.[16]

The fifth fundamental principle is that refugees are to enjoy the *widest possible exercise of their fundamental rights*.[17] Articles 3 to 34 Refugee Convention contain a number of rights and entitlements for refugees (discussed in Section 7), while Article 2 notes that refugees are subject to the laws and regulations of the host country and they have a duty to respect them.

In addition to the five fundamental elements of the Refugee Convention, a further key principle of refugee law is that of *finding solutions for refugees* (discussed in Section 8).

Unlike some human rights treaties, the Refugee Convention does not contain a general derogation clause permitting rights to be suspended in a state of emergency.[18] However, the Convention permits—via Article 9—derogation in respect of 'particular persons' who pose a threat to national security 'in times of war or other exceptional circumstances.' This means that particular persons who pose a threat to national security may be subject to security measures, such as restrictions on their freedom of movement, internment or confiscation of property. The suspension of their rights may continue until refugee status is granted, or, even after refugee status is granted, where it is considered necessary in the individual's circumstances. Article 8 ensures, however, that such security measures are not applied to refugees solely on the basis of their nationality.[19]

---

[13] Refugee Convention, Art 1D.

[14] Case C-364/11, *Abed El Karem El Kott v Bevándorlási és Állampolgársági Hivatal* [2013] All ER (EC) 1176.

[15] Refugee Convention, Art 31(1).

[16] Refugee Convention, Art 31; Goodwin-Gill, 'Article 31 of the 1951 Convention Relating to the Status of Refugees: Non-Penalization, Detention, and Protection', in Feller, Türk, and Nicholson (eds), *Refugee Protection in International Law* (CUP, 2003) 185.

[17] Refugee Convention, preamble.

[18] On derogations see Chapter 5.

[19] For more on derogation and the 1951 Convention, see Davy, 'Article 8: Exemption from Exceptional Measures', in Zimmerman (ed), *The 1951 Convention relating to the Status of Refugees and its 1967 Protocol: A Commentary* (OUP, 2011) 755; Davy, 'Article 9: Provisional Measures', in Zimmerman, 781. On the application of derogation in mass influx situations, see Edwards, 'Temporary Protection, Derogation and the 1951 Refugee Convention' (2012) 13 *Melbourne JIL* 1.

4 RELATIONSHIP BETWEEN THE TWO BODIES OF LAW

Borne of the evils of the Second World War, in which millions of Jews and others were subjected to persecution forcing them to seek safety across international frontiers, both modern refugee law and human rights law share common roots. However, each body of law responds to different, albeit related, problems: human rights law aims to ensure that such events will never happen again by creating a global regime of fundamental rights, whilst refugee law responds to the displacement of persons caused when such rights are violated. The regimes are, thus, complementary yet distinct.

The Refugee Convention is a human rights instrument of a particular scope—protecting the rights of a specific category of person, the refugee. Post-dating the UDHR, but predating the main human rights treaties, the preambular paragraphs of the Refugee Convention recall the UN Charter, the UDHR, and 'the principle that human beings shall enjoy fundamental rights'. Coupled with Article 5, which provides that '[n]othing in this Convention shall be deemed to impair any rights and benefits granted by a Contracting State to refugees apart from this Convention', the Refugee Convention is the floor but not the ceiling for the rights of refugees. Accordingly, it is necessary to consider those developments in human rights law that are applicable to refugees.

Although states were adamant that the International Covenant on Civil and Political Rights (ICCPR) should not contain a right to asylum equivalent to Article 14 UDHR, the right to seek and enjoy asylum from persecution is implicit in the very existence of the Refugee Convention. The European Court of Human Rights appears to have adopted this view in its judgment in the case of *MSS v Belgium and Greece*: 'Belgium and Greece have ratified the *1951 Geneva Convention relating to the Status of Refugees* . . . which defines the circumstances in which a State *must grant* refugee status to those who request it, as well as the rights and duties of such persons.'[20] Moreover, at the regional level, the right to asylum has been located squarely within human rights instruments,[21] and is also explicit in the OAU Refugee Convention.[22]

The application of human rights instruments to refugees has been consistently recognized by the UN General Assembly, which has called inter alia on states to respect the rights of refugees.[23] Human rights treaty bodies have also dealt with refugee issues.[24] In fact, refugees and asylum-seekers are increasingly resorting to human rights mechanisms in the absence of an individual complaints procedure under the Refugee Convention.[25] Furthermore, the Executive Committee of the High Commissioner for Refugees' Programme has consistently 'reiterate[d] . . . the obligation to treat asylum-seekers and

---

[20] (2011) 53 EHRR 28, 263 [emphasis added].

[21] American Declaration on the Rights and Duties of Man, Art XXVII; American Convention on Human Rights, Art 22(7); African Charter on Human and Peoples' Rights, Art 12(3); European Union Charter of Fundamental Rights, Art 18. [22] OAU Refugee Convention, Art 2.

[23] eg UNHCR, Thematic Compilation of General Assembly and ECOSOC Resolutions (December 2015), available at: <http://www.unhcr.org/53b2c42c9.pdf>.

[24] eg Committee on the Rights of the Child, General Comment No 6 on the Treatment of Unaccompanied and Separated Children outside their Country of Origin, HRI/GEN/1/Rev.9 (Vol II) 441; Committee on the Elimination of All Forms of Discrimination against Women, General Recommendation No 32 on the Gender-related Dimensions of Refugee Status, Asylum, Nationality and Statelessness of Women, CEDAW/C/GC/32 (14 November 2014).

[25] Edwards, 'Peter Pan's Fairies and Genie Bottles: The UN Human Rights Treaty Bodies and Supervision of the 1951 Convention', in Simeon (ed), *The UNHCR and the Supervision of International Refugee Law* (CUP, 2013) 159.

refugees in accordance with applicable human rights and refugee law standards as set out in relevant international instruments'.[26]

International human rights law thus intersects with refugee law in at least three main ways:

- refugees include those fleeing their countries of origin or nationality on account of serious human rights violations;
- international refugee law is a rights-granting instrument, which is informed by human rights standards; and,
- at the same time, as human beings refugees are also entitled to benefit from the general human rights regime as far as it applies.

Goodwin-Gill and McAdam have noted that '[r]efugee [l]aw is an incomplete legal regime of protection, imperfectly covering what ought to be a situation of exception.'[27] International human rights law can, thus, usefully serve to fill gaps in the refugee protection architecture. At the same time, as noted by Hathaway, the rights in the Refugee Convention in a number of ways go beyond those available in international human rights law, at least as far as the human rights regime applies to non-nationals. Hathaway refers, in particular, to the detailed set of socio-economic rights provided to refugees in the Refugee Convention (see Section 7).[28]

The only exception to the generally held view that the Refugee Convention, while being a human rights instrument, is the primary tool of refugee protection is that of Chetail. He claims that human rights law should be the primary source of refugee rights, rather than the inverse, asserting that human rights law has broadly eclipsed the protections in the Refugee Convention.[29] Chetail's article, although thought-provoking, only focuses on the positive aspects of human rights law, in other words, where it strengthens refugee rights in the Refugee Convention. Some of the shortcomings in human rights law are ignored, such as the limitations on economic rights to non-nationals in the International Covenant on Economic, Social and Cultural Rights (ICESCR), which would not be permitted under the Refugee Convention.[30] Likewise, he downplays the many rights that are tailored to the specific circumstances of refugees in the Refugee Convention, which do not find expression in human rights instruments.[31]

Apart from filling gaps, developments in international human rights law have also had a bearing on the understanding of key terms in the Refugee Convention, in particular the definition of a refugee.

---

[26] Executive Committee Conclusion No 82 (XLVIII) on 'Safeguarding Asylum' (1997), para (d)(vi). See also, Conclusion No 19 (XXXI) on 'Temporary Refuge' (1980), para (e); Conclusion No 22 (XXXII) on 'Protection of Asylum Seekers in Situations of Large-Scale Influx' (1981), para B; Conclusion No 36 (XXXVI) on 'General [Matters]' (1985), para (f).

[27] Goodwin-Gill and McAdam, *The Refugee in International Law* (OUP, 2007) 1.

[28] Hathaway, *The Rights of Refugees under International Law* (CUP, 2005) eg 93–95, 121–123.

[29] Chetail, 'Are Refugee Rights Human Rights? An Unorthodox Questioning of the Relations between Refugee Law and Human Rights Law', in Rubio-Marin (ed), *Migrations and Human Rights* (OUP, 2014).

[30] See Edwards, 'Human Rights, Refugees and the Right to "Enjoy" Asylum' (2005) 17 *IJRL* 297, which looks at two specific rights—the right to work and the right to family life or unity—and acknowledges that human rights law can fill the gaps in the Refugee Convention.

[31] These rights include exemption from usual requirements as to length of stay in enjoyment of rights (Art 6), continuity of lawful residence (Art 10), refugee seamen (Art 11), movable and immovable property (Art 13), recognition of foreign diplomas (Art 19), welfare rights (Arts 20 to 24), special administrative assistance (Art 25), travel documents (Art 28), exemption from fiscal charges (Art 29), transfer of assets (Art 30), non-penalization for illegal entry or stay (Art 31), and naturalization (Art 34).

5 HUMAN RIGHTS AND REFUGEE STATUS

As already noted, a Convention refugee is someone who is outside their country of origin owing to a fear of persecution on account of one or more of five grounds. The definition of a refugee in Article 1A(2) Refugee Convention is the subject of volumes of court judgments and legal treatises. The two pivotal aspects of the definition are (i) persecution, and (ii) the grounds or reasons for that persecution.

Persecution is generally understood to include, at a minimum, threats to life or freedom.[32] The term covers serious human rights violations, such as torture, arbitrary detention, arbitrary prosecution, and other 'serious harm'.[33] Not every human rights violation is a form of persecution however. The drafters intended international protection to be made available only to victims of those violations considered to be sufficiently serious to satisfy the threshold of persecution. As a regime predicated on the absence or loss of state protection, such that sanctuary in another country is activated, the regime of refugee law is not appropriate to respond to all human rights violations. Rather, human rights violations that are not sufficiently serious to evidence a fracturing of protection between the individual and his or her state should be dealt with instead under national laws and redress mechanisms.

While human rights law is an important source of defining forms of persecution, rigid reliance on it to understand the terms in the refugee definition should be avoided. This is because not all known forms of persecution have been codified in human rights instruments yet; and the means and methods of persecution are limited only by human imagination. A further reason against tying the definition too closely to human rights law is that doing so can add an additional legal layer of proof to the granting of status. It is worth noting in this regard that there is no explicit human rights violation of persecution in any of the main international human rights conventions.

As not all human rights violations have yet been codified as such, 'serious harm' has been used as a 'catch-all'. Before the mid-1990s, for example, sexual and gender-based violence (SGBV) against women and girls was not considered an issue for human rights law, and as of today, there is no explicit universal treaty prohibition on the subject. Yet clearly SGBV is serious harm, and has been increasingly recognized as both a human rights violation and a form of persecution.[34] Keeping the definition of persecution open allows the regime to accommodate both new human rights violations of sufficient severity as well as serious harms that are not yet viewed as human rights violations but which threaten one's life or freedom and are, thus, persecutory. Serious violations of the laws of war could also amount to persecution, drawing on international humanitarian law.[35]

What about discrimination? Is discrimination persecution? While the grounds of persecution import discrimination as an integral part of the refugee definition, being subjected

---

[32] Refugee Convention, Art 33; UNHCR, *Handbook on Procedures and Criteria for Determining Refugee Status* (UNHCR, 1979, reissued 2011) para 51.   [33] UNHCR Handbook.

[34] eg *Islam (A.P.) v Secretary of State for the Home Department; R v Immigration Appeal Tribunal and Another, Ex Parte Shah (A.P.)* [1999] 2 WLR 1015; *Minister for Immigration and Multicultural Affairs v Khawar* [2002] HCA 14. Both cases accepted that domestic violence constituted a form of persecution in the context of Pakistan because of the absence of state protection.

[35] See UNHCR, Guidelines on International Protection No 12: Claims to refugee status related to situations of armed conflict and violence under Article 1A(2) of the 1951 Convention and/or 1967 Protocol relating to the Status of Refugees, HCR/GIP/16/12 (2 December 2016), 14–15. On international humanitarian law, see Chapter 25.

to discrimination per se is not sufficient for refugee status. The exception is cumulative forms of discrimination that lead to intolerable hardship. Lesser forms of discrimination— while clearly being human rights violations—are not persecution.[36]

The second pivotal aspect of the Convention definition are the 'grounds' on which an individual is at risk of being persecuted, namely 'race, religion, nationality, membership of a particular social group or political opinion'. These are clearly reminiscent of the proscribed grounds of discrimination in international law but are more limited. The ICCPR provisions on non-discrimination (Articles 2 and 26), for example, have an extensive list of proscribed grounds, including discrimination on account of 'other status'.[37] The Refugee Convention definition, in contrast, is limited to the five specific grounds. The most flexible, albeit least understood, ground is that of 'membership of a particular social group'. Added at the last moment during the Conference of Plenipotentiaries that drafted the Convention, there is no drafting history to draw from to inform its meaning. As a consequence, courts have adopted two distinct, yet similar, tests.

The first, based on the ordinary meaning of the phrase, asks whether someone is perceived in society at large as a member of a social group. This approach is linked to human rights but in a less obvious way than the second approach.[38] The second approach, in identifying that the five Convention grounds are united by each being a 'protected characteristic', draws on human rights concepts such as human dignity to explain who is to be protected.[39] Through the social group ground, the scope of refugee protection has been expanded to slowly become more aligned with other proscribed grounds of discrimination under international human rights law, and cases that have been successful under the 'membership of a particular social group' ground have included those based on age, gender, sexual orientation, and family membership, as well as those involving child soldiers and victims of trafficking.[40] Notably economic or social standing has not yet been widely accepted as a ground for refugee status.[41]

---

[36] UNHCR Handbook, paras 54–5.

[37] 'Other status' has, for example, been used by the Human Rights Committee to deal with discrimination against refugees, asylum-seekers, or stateless persons; all statuses that are not listed explicitly: HRC, General Comment No 31, HRI/GEN/1/Rev.9 (Vol I) 243, paras 10 and 12.

[38] Examples of this approach include: *Applicant A v Minister for Immigration and Ethnic Affairs* (1997) 190 CLR 225 (rejecting that being parents wishing to have more than one child in contravention of China's one child policy constitutes a social group); compared with *Chen Shi Hai v The Minister for Immigration and Multicultural Affairs* [2000] HCA 19 (accepting that 'black children' or children born outside of China's one child policy were a social group because of the distinct treatment and discrimination faced by such children).

[39] The 'protected characteristics' test was elaborated in *Matter of Acosta*, A-24159781, US Board of Immigration Appeals, 1 March 1985, para 11: 'member of a group of persons, all of whom share a common, immutable characteristic, i.e., a characteristic that either is beyond the power of the individual members of the group to change or is so fundamental to their identities or consciences that it ought not be required to be changed'; and *Canada (Attorney General) v Ward* [1993] 2 SCR 689: 'In distilling the contents of the head of "particular social group", account should be taken of the general underlying themes of the defence of human rights and anti-discrimination that form the basis for the international refugee protection initiative. A good working rule for the meaning of "particular social group" provides that this basis of persecution consists of three categories: (1) groups defined by an innate, unchangeable characteristic; (2) groups whose members voluntarily associate for reasons so fundamental to their human dignity that they should not be forced to forsake the association; and (3) groups associated by a former voluntary status, unalterable due to its historical permanence.'

[40] *Islam; Khawar; Secretary of State for the Home Department (Respondent) v K (FC) (Appellant); Fornah (FC) (Appellant) v Secretary of State for the Home Department (Respondent)* [2006] UKHL 46.

[41] See Foster, *International Refugee Law and Socio-Economic Rights: Refuge from Deprivation* (CUP, 2007).

6 REFUGEE *NON-REFOULEMENT* AND HUMAN RIGHTS

Concerned with the protection of refugees from persecution at the hands of their own governments, the cardinal provision in the Refugee Convention is Article 33—the 'refugee *non-refoulement*' clause. As already noted, states have accepted that *non-refoulement* of refugees is a norm of customary international law.[42] Article 33 has two parts: Article 33(1) protects a refugee from expulsion or return 'in any manner whatsoever' to where he or she would face threats to his or her life or freedom on account of race, religion, nationality, membership of a particular social group, or political opinion; Article 33(2) permits a number of exceptions to the prohibition.

The obligation in Article 33(1) applies to all refugees, including those who have been recognized as such as well as to asylum-seekers whose status has not yet been determined. It includes not only direct *refoulement* where a refugee is sent home directly, but also indirect or 'chain *refoulement*', that is, where the refugee is returned to an interim country despite the fact that it is reasonably foreseeable that that state is likely to return him or her to their country of origin. Refugee *non-refoulement* also applies to rejection at the frontiers of states. Although this appears to conflict with the general principle in international law that states have the right to control the entry of non-nationals into their territory and their stay therein, allowing states to reject asylum-seekers at the border, or closing their borders in the event of a mass influx of asylum-seekers, would render meaningless the refugee *non-refoulement* obligation. In other words, Article 33 is an exception to the general discretion of states in respect of immigration control.

Given the overlap between the refugee *non-refoulement* norm and the prohibition on return under international human rights law to torture or other forms of inhuman or degrading treatment,[43] human rights law and regional human rights courts have helped strengthen and reaffirm the prohibition of *refoulement* for asylum-seekers and refugees. In the case of *Hirsi v Italy*, for example, the European Court of Human Rights determined that the Italian practice of 'push backs' in the Mediterranean Sea to Libya—that is, the turning back of boats carrying asylum-seekers and migrants (in this case including 11 Somali and 13 Eritrean nationals)—was unlawful and in violation of its obligations under Article 3 ECHR—the prohibition on *refoulement* to torture—because, despite credible information of risks of torture and ill-treatment in Libya, the Italian government continued to carry out its policy. While the Court did not rule on whether the 'push backs' also violated Article 33 Refugee Convention, the Court did cite the provision as part of the applicable legal framework, and further took note of the fact that Libya is not a party to the Refugee Convention in assessing Italy's liability.[44] Reinforcing *Hirsi*, in another case, the Court found against Italy for intercepting Afghan asylum-seekers at Adriatic ports and pushing them back to Greece where they risked being *refouled* indirectly to Afghanistan, in violation of the prohibition on collective expulsion in violation of Article 4 of Protocol 4 to the ECHR. The judgment was based on the fact that the individuals in question were not afforded an opportunity to complain of their transfer to Greece, nor were the details of some of their identities recorded.[45]

Likewise, the Inter-American Commission on Human Rights, having been asked to give an opinion on the interception by the US of boats carrying Haitian asylum-seekers,

---

[42] Declaration of States Parties to the 1951 Convention and or Its 1967 Protocol relating to the Status of Refugees, HCR/MMSP/2001/09 (16 January 2002) para 4.   [43] See Chapter 6.

[44] *Hirsi Jamaa and Others v Italy*, App no 27765/09, Judgment of 23 February 2012.

[45] *Sharifi and Others v Italy and Greece*, App no 16643/09, Judgment of 21 October 2014. Compare, *Khlaifia and Others v Italy*, App no 16483/12, Judgment of 15 December 2016, where the collective expulsion argument failed on the basis of the facts.

decided that the US practices interfered with the Haitians' right to seek asylum in other countries (that is, countries other than the US in the region) and, in pushing them back to their country of origin, violated a number of rights set out in the American Declaration on Human Rights.[46] Although the petitioners raised Article 33 Refugee Convention as part of their submissions, the Commission stated that it lacked jurisdiction to assess the US' compliance with it.[47] Notably, the US Supreme Court had earlier ruled that the Refugee Convention obligation of *non-refoulement* did not extend to the Haitian 'boat people' on the high seas as they were not considered within the jurisdiction of the US.[48] This remains the position of the US regarding interception of asylum-seekers on the high seas.

The jurisdictional question was also raised in the UK House of Lords' *Roma Rights* case. The Law Lords held that the principle of refugee *non-refoulement* did not apply to persons of Roma ethnicity who had been prevented by UK officials in the Czech Republic from boarding a plane to the UK where they wished to seek asylum. The House of Lords relied in part on the fact that the individuals had not yet left their country of nationality and so were not 'outside' it in order to be treated as refugees and for the obligations under the Refugee Convention to become activated.[49] The case was not pursued to the European Court, but it would be interesting to see how such a case would be decided today in light of *Hirsi v Italy*.

Similar questions have arisen before the Australian courts, such as the important case involving a Sri Lankan plaintiff and 156 other passengers who had been making their way to Australia from India when they were intercepted by the Australian navy.[50] The Court found that the Australian authorities had the statutory power to detain them during their removal from Australia's contiguous zone in the Indian Ocean to a safe place outside Australia, namely India. Separate majority opinions were issued in this case, with varying views expressed on the *refoulement* question; among those, French CJ held that the power to remove them to a 'safe' place outside Australia embraced risks assessments akin to those in the Refugee Convention and the UN Convention against Torture; while others argued that as no facts had been presented as to those risks, the issue would not be addressed.[51]

In sum, the position at international law on the scope of refugee *non-refoulement* under Article 33(1) Refugee Convention, especially as it concerns actions taken on the high seas, is unsettled, in part because of the lack of case law dealing with the Refugee Convention directly. Nonetheless, the most recent case law of the European Court of Human Rights in recognizing obligations of *non-refoulement* to asylum-seekers and refugees, albeit under the ECHR, helps to understand the limits and obligations in the parallel principle in the Refugee Convention. It is interesting to note that the UNHCR intervened as *amicus curiae* in several of the cases, applying a mixture of Refugee Convention and human rights arguments.[52]

---

[46] Case 10.675, *The Haitian Centre for Human Rights et al. v United States*, IACommHR Report No 51/96 (13 March 1997).   [47] *The Haitian Centre*, para 76.

[48] Chris Sale, Acting Commissioner, Immigration and Naturalization Service, et al. v Haitian Centers Council Inc., et al. (1993) 509 US 155.

[49] *R v Immigration Officer at Prague Airport and Another, Ex parte European Roma Rights Centre and Others* [2004] UKHL 55.

[50] *CPCF v Minister for Immigration and Border Protection and Another* [2015] HCA 1.

[51] *CPCF*, per French CJ, para. 12.

[52] See UN High Commissioner for Refugees, Submission by the Office of the United Nations High Commissioner for Refugees in the case of *Hirsi and Others v. Italy*, March 2010, available at: <http://www.unhcr.org/refworld/docid/4b97778d2.html>; UN High Commissioner for Refugees, *The European Roma Rights Center and Others (Appellants) v. (1) The Immigration Officer at Prague Airport, (2) The Secretary of State for the Home Department (Respondents), and the Office of the United Nations High Commissioner for Refugees (Intervener). Skeleton Argument on Behalf of the Intervener (UNHCR)*, 30 January 2003, available at: <http://www.refworld.org/docid/3e5ba6d45.html>; *UNHCR Submissions in the High Court of Australia in the case of CPCF v Minister for Immigration and Border Protection and the Commonwealth of Australia*, 15 September 2014, NO S169 OF 2014, available at: <http://www.refworld.org/docid/54169e8e4.html>.

Article 33(2) is an exception to Article 33(1) in that it permits the lawful *refoulement* of refugees in two limited cases: in respect of refugees for 'whom there are reasonable grounds for regarding as a danger to the security of the country' as well as those 'who, having been convicted by a final judgment of a particularly serious crime, [constitute] a danger to the community of that country'. Despite these exceptions, Article 33(2) has been rendered largely irrelevant by developments in international human rights law, where *non-refoulement* to certain violations such as torture, are considered absolute, without exception and with no derogation.[53] At the regional level, it is also the case that Article II OAU Refugee Convention does not contain the national security exception and, thus, in Africa, the exceptions to *refoulement* do not apply. So while Article 33(2) has historical significance, states that rely on this exception are likely to be found in violation of their other obligations, and particularly those under international human rights law.

There are, thus, two main distinctions between refugee *non-refoulement* and human rights *non-refoulement*:

- The scope of the protection: in refugee law, *refugees* are protected against return to threats to life or freedom, or other serious human rights violations or serious harm amounting to persecution; in human rights law, *all individuals* are protected against return to a range of rights violations, the scope of which is still undergoing development. At a minimum, human rights law prohibits return to torture or other forms of inhuman or degrading treatment; Article 33 Refugee Convention permits entry to seek asylum.

- The exceptions to *non-refoulement*: the Refugee Convention permits lawful *refoulement* in specific circumstances, whereas human rights *non-refoulement* to certain risks (such as torture) is absolute. The latter has rendered the exceptions in Article 33(2) Refugee Convention largely irrelevant.

7 THE PROTECTIONS ACCORDED TO REFUGEES

The Refugee Convention contains a range of rights to which refugees are entitled. Articles 3 to 34 list a range of civil rights—such as freedom of religion (Article 3), property rights (Articles 13 and 14), freedom of association (Article 15), and access to courts (Article 16), as well as economic, social, and cultural rights—such as employment rights (Articles 17 to 19) and welfare, social security, and education rights (Articles 20 to 24). The 'structure of entitlement' in the Convention has two specific layers.

First, not all rights are immediately applicable; rather their applicability is dependent upon the length of stay in the territory ('attachment'). There are four general categories of attachment, namely 'simple presence', 'lawful presence', 'lawful residence', and 'habitual residence'.[54] Very few rights included in the Refugee Convention explicitly apply to asylum-seekers, that is, those who have not yet been determined to be refugees. Articles 31 (non-penalization) and 33 (*non-refoulement*) are two such provisions. It is, however, arguable that all those provisions without an indicated level of attachment also apply to asylum-seekers, such as the right to education for children (Article 22), based on the argument that refugee status is declaratory rather than determinative—that is, determining a person to be a refugee does not *make* him or her a refugee, but rather such determination simply *recognizes* that he or she is a refugee (and, in most cases, was a refugee at the time of entry to the territory).[55] This concept is important given the time lag between an application for refugee status and the final determination of that application.

---

[53] eg, *Chahal v UK* (1997) 23 EHRR 413; *Soering v UK* (1989) 11 EHRR 439.
[54] Goodwin-Gill and McAdam (2007), 524–8.   [55] UNHCR Handbook, para 28.

The second structure of entitlement is that the rights are to be enjoyed on an equivalent basis to three types of legal persons: nationals, 'most favoured nationals' (that is, the standards applicable to the most favoured foreigners, such as permanent residents or particular nationalities benefiting from preferred treatment under regional arrangements, such as EU or ECOWAS nationals), or 'aliens generally' (that is, other non-nationals). In fact, the Refugee Convention is an elaborate mixture of rights, and one needs to analyse carefully each right in question to determine its full and proper scope.

Given that the Refugee Convention is a treaty that is dedicated to setting the standards of treatment of refugees, how is it that recourse to human rights law is permitted as a matter of international law? And why is it needed at all?

In response to the first question, there are two main arguments for importing human rights standards into refugee law. First, Article 5 Refugee Convention, already mentioned, stresses that '[n]othing in this Convention shall be deemed to impair any rights and benefits granted by a Contracting State to refugees apart from this Convention'. The *travaux préparatoires* relating to Article 5 indicate that it was inserted as an attempt to safeguard more generous practices of some states that had been assumed voluntarily.[56] A modern reading of the provision would incorporate new obligations assumed under international law as applicable to refugees, unless specific reservations were made to those treaties.

The second argument is that human rights treaties are applicable to 'everyone' and to 'all human beings' and are in only very few instances 'category-specific' (eg citizens' rights to political participation in Article 25 ICCPR). As such, they apply to refugees as human beings per se. The main exception is in respect of economic rights: Article 2(3) ICESCR allows developing countries—where 86 per cent of the world's refugees are hosted[57]—to make an exception with respect to extending economic rights to non-nationals, subject to some safeguards.[58]

Moving to the question of why recourse to human rights law is needed, the answer is that the Refugee Convention, despite having an extensive list of rights, many of which do not find expression in human rights law, does not deal with all the issues facing refugees. While it could be argued that certain rights were omitted because refugees were not meant to benefit from them, this does not make sense across the board. For example, the prohibition on torture is not contained in the Refugee Convention but it would never be suggested that refugees could be tortured. In fact, human rights law is regularly used to fill gaps in the refugee protection architecture. There is considerable jurisprudence explaining how various human rights provisions apply to refugees.[59] Further, refugees are regularly sheltered in many states that are not parties to the Refugee Convention and where human rights standards apply. In fact four of the top six refugee hosting countries are not party to the Refugee Convention, or maintain geographical limits on its application.[60]

---

[56] *The Refugee Convention, 1951: The Travaux Preparatoires Analysed with a Commentary by Dr Paul Weis*, 37, available at: <http://www.unhcr.org/4ca34be29.html>. See also, Skordas, 'Article 5', in Zimmerman (2011), 669.

[57] UNHCR, *Global Trends 2015*, available at: <http://www.unhcr.org/statistics/unhcrstats/576408cd7/unhcr-global-trends-2015.html>.

[58] See Edwards, Human Rights (2005), for an exploration of how this operates in respect of the right to work.

[59] Edwards, Human Rights (2005).

[60] Pakistan, Lebanon, and Jordan are not parties to the Refugee Convention; Turkey, the largest host, maintains the geographical limit: *Global Trends 2015*.

8 THE END OF REFUGEE STATUS AND
SOLUTIONS FOR REFUGEES

Neither UNHCR's Statute, which calls on UNHCR to find, together with governments, solutions for refugees, nor the Refugee Convention, intended for refugee status to be lifelong. As an anomaly to normal citizen–state relations, the reattachment to a state—either through repatriation to one's country of origin, local integration/naturalization in the country of asylum, or resettlement to a third country—is considered to bring about the end of refugee status.

The Refugee Convention stipulates both individual and general conditions under which refugee status formally comes to an end. Article 1C(1)–(4) outlines the circumstances in which individual action triggers the cessation of status, such as voluntary re-establishment in one's country of origin. Through Article 1C(5)–(6), by contrast, refugee status ceases where fundamental and durable changes in the country of origin indicate that protection is no longer needed. This is known as general cessation.[61] The prevailing general human rights conditions in the country of origin form part of the general cessation assessment. General cessation has been recommended 29 times on a group basis between 1973 and 2015.[62]

Of the three traditional durable solutions, the Refugee Convention is oriented towards 'assimilation and naturalization' in the country of asylum (Article 34), also called local integration. This is the most common solution for refugees in industrialized countries, where permanent residency and later citizenship are made available to refugees usually within three to five years of being granted refugee status. Commonly, access to citizenship is on more favourable terms than other migrants in recognition of refugees' loss of state protection. However, granting residency or citizenship is not an obligation and realizing this goal has become increasingly elusive in other parts of the world. As such, the international community has developed different strategies to find 'solutions' for refugees.

The repatriation of refugees to their countries of origin on a voluntary basis when conditions permit is considered by most states to be the preferred option for many large-scale refugee situations. Historic examples of voluntary repatriation include the 300,000 Cambodian refugees repatriated from Thailand in time for national elections in 1993, the more than 5.7 million Afghan refugees who have returned voluntarily to Afghanistan since 2001, and the 155,000 Liberians who returned home from Guinea in 2012. However, as armed conflicts continue and oppressive regimes remain in place, there has been a significant decline in repatriation rates. In 2015, UNHCR reported that just over 200,000 refugees returned to their country of origin.[63]

---

[61] UNHCR, Guidelines on International Protection: Cessation of Refugee Status under Article 1C(5) and (6) of the 1951 Convention relating to the Status of Refugees (The 'Ceased Circumstances' Clauses), HCR/GIP/03/03 (10 February 2003). There are exceptions to cessation for those with a continuing need for international protection or owing to compelling reasons of previous persecution cannot be expected to return: see [19]–[21]. See also, *Minister for Immigration and Multicultural and Indigenous Affairs v QAAH of 2004* (2006) 231 CLR 1, 53.

[62] Siddiqui, 'Reviewing the Application of the Cessation Clause of the *1951 Refugee Convention relating to the Status of Refugees* in Africa', Working Paper No 76, Refugee Studies Centre, University of Oxford (August 2011), Annex 1, at 52. Siddiqui counted 25 cessation declarations from 1973–2008. Added to this, general cessation was recommended in 2012 for Angolan and Liberian refugees; and in 2013 for pre-1999 Rwandan refugees, although it remains subject to the variable implementation by host governments, and some blocks by the Rwandan government. In 2014, UNHCR recommended starting the cessation process for the 1990s refugees from Croatia.   [63] *Global Trends 2015.*

Resettlement to third countries, whereby refugees are relocated as both a protection and burden-sharing measure, has been a modern response offered by some states. Prior to the current Syria crisis, 27 countries offered approximately 80,000 resettlement places annually, with by far the largest number of resettlement places being allocated by traditionally known 'immigration countries' such as the US, Australia, and Canada. As a protection response, resettlement works to remove vulnerable refugees from countries where they remain at risk. Resettlement has also been used to unlock protracted refugee situations or to respond to large-scale crises.

The current Syria crisis and in particular the large-scale arrivals of refugees into Europe by sea has seen a sizeable increase in both the number of countries offering resettlement or humanitarian admission, sometimes limited to Syrian refugees (in 2015, a total of 33 countries did so), and an increase in the number of refugees admitted for resettlement (in 2015, 107,000).[64]

In recent years some consideration has been paid to other pathways to comprehensive, durable solutions, namely helping refugees to access safe and regulated migration options for work and study purposes.[65] Refugees have long made use of increased global mobility, albeit not always indicating their international protection needs when applying for visas. This 'new' approach has multiple benefits: it would give refugees opportunities to lawfully 'migrate out' of situations where they may not enjoy the right to work, or where conditions do not permit self-sufficiency or other prospects for a decent life, and it has the potential to reduce pressure on host countries and thereby keep borders open. At the same time, some of the well-known consequences of the draw of resettlement, such as incentivizing movements to countries with large resettlement operations and thereby over-burdening them, may also repeat for countries processing migration opportunities. Further, as has been the experience of Germany with its light-touch humanitarian admission programme for Syrian refugees, it is likely that a large number of migrating refugees would apply for asylum immediately upon arrival in the states to which they migrate, especially if their migrant visas are considered not to provide adequate protection.

Finding durable solutions for refugees is not straightforward, and goes well beyond legal provisions. In fact, identifying durable solutions for refugees generally requires political solutions to the many intractable and cyclical conflicts that cause refugee flight in the first place.

9 CONCLUSION

Refugee rights are human rights. The Refugee Convention and regional refugee instruments are human rights instruments in so far as they grant rights to refugees. They are also refugee-specific instruments, which were designed to reflect the particular circumstances of refugees, such circumstances not being as easily reflected in the main human rights instruments. Sharing as background a history of persecution and oppression, human rights law sets the standards against which states' behaviour towards those within their jurisdiction are to be judged, while the Refugee Convention was intended to ensure protection of persons who could no longer obtain the protection of their own states. The two regimes are, therefore, distinct and, at the same time, mutually reinforcing.

---

[64] *Global Trends 2015.*
[65] See GA Res 71/1, New York Declaration for Refugees and Migrants (3 October 2016), paras 77, 79.

FURTHER READING

ANKER, 'Refugee law, Gender, and the Human Rights Paradigm' (2002) 15 *Harvard HRJ* 133.

EDWARDS and FERSTMAN (eds), *Human Security and Non-Citizens: Law, Policy and International Affairs* (Cambridge University Press, 2010).

FELLER, TÜRK, and NICHOLSON (eds), *Refugee Protection in International Law: UNHCR's Global Consultations on International Protection* (Cambridge University Press, 2003).

LAMBERT (ed), *International Refugee Law* (Ashgate, 2010).

MUSALO, 'Claims for Protection Based on Religion or Belief: Analysis and Proposed Conclusions' (2004) 16 *IJRL* 165.

PLENDER and MOLE, 'Beyond the Geneva Convention: Constructing a *de facto* right of asylum from international human rights instruments', in Nicholson and Twomey (eds), *Refugee Rights and Realities* (Cambridge University Press, 1999).

SHACKNOVE, 'Who is a refugee?' (1985) 95 *Ethics* 274.

TÜRK, EDWARDS, and WOUTERS (eds), *In Flight from Conflict and Violence: UNHCR's Consultations on Refugee Status and Other Forms of International Protection* (Cambridge University Press, 2017).

WEISSBRODT, *The Human Rights of Non-Citizens* (Oxford University Press, 2008), chs 5 and 7.

ZIMMERMAN (ed), *Commentary on the 1951 Convention relating to the Status of Refugees* (Oxford University Press, 2011).

USEFUL WEBSITES

Forced Migration Online: <http://www.forcedmigration.org/>

Refworld: <http://www.refworld.org/>

The Refugee Law Reader: <http://www.refugeelawreader.org/>

RefLaw: <http://www.reflaw.org/>

Center for Gender and Refugee Studies: <http://cgrs.uchastings.edu/>

PART VI

CHALLENGES

28

NON-STATE ACTORS

Andrew Clapham

SUMMARY

It is increasingly recognized that human rights law has to address the challenge posed by non-state actors. This chapter starts with a reflection on how the term 'non-state actor' is used and why it is appropriate to look at the impact of non-state actors on the enjoyment of human rights. It then recalls the positive obligations of states to protect those within their jurisdiction from abuses by non-state actors and how states provide for redress at the national level. In the next part, it considers the human rights obligations of different non-state actors: international organizations, corporations, and armed non-state actors. The chapter argues that we should meet the following challenges: extending and translating certain norms so that they clearly denote the obligations of non-state actors; creating and adapting specific institutions to ensure greater accountability for the activities of non-state actors; and adjusting our assumptions about who are the duty-bearers in the human rights regime.

1 INTRODUCTION

Even though the term 'non-state actor' can be defined quite simply as any entity that is not a state, it deserves some explanation. In some contexts the term is used to refer to benign civil society groups working for human rights—and it has become commonplace (even a cliché) to refer to the need to 'involve non-state actors in the conversation'. In other contexts, however, the term is understood to refer to some very 'uncivil' groups determined to resort to violence and even acquire weapons of mass destruction. Depending on the context, international law provides that states are either obliged to punish non-state actors or, alternatively, obliged to cooperate with them.[1] So the expression non-state actor can conjure up different entities in different contexts, but different non-state actors will have different obligations. For example an armed group may have an obligation not to recruit children, while the European Union (EU) may have detailed specific obligations under the Convention on the Rights of Persons with Disabilities.

---

[1] See eg AU Convention for the Protection and Assistance of Internally Displaced Persons in Africa (2009), Art 1; SC Res 1540 (28 April 2004); Cotonou Agreement between the Members of the African, Caribbean and Pacific Group of States and the European Community and its Member States (2000), Art 6.

Like states, non-state actors are seen as embodying the paradox that their capacity to violate contains within it the potential for protection. In this way, non-state actors can be the 'source and target of pressure at the same time'.[2]

But even if we admit that the expression 'non-state actor' means different things in different contexts, and that all such actors have the potential both to violate and to promote a variety of human rights, there is another problem we need to address. The problem is that the human rights regime has developed along state-centric lines. Human rights treaties were mainly written by states as sets of obligations for themselves. The accompanying monitoring mechanisms that provide for state accountability are based on traditional rules of state responsibility. To adjust this system, and to revise the assumptions that have grown up around it, tends to trigger considerable resistance from states and international lawyers.

Why would lawyers and governments want to exclude non-state actors from the state-centric regime of international law in general, and human rights law in particular? There are a number of reasons. First, with regard to armed opposition groups (also sometimes characterized as 'terrorists'), it is argued that suggesting such groups have human rights obligations under international law is a sort of recognition which in turn could enhance their legitimacy. Second, in some circumstances, governments may be wary of allowing international organizations or corporations to assume state-like features by taking on international obligations, such as those relating to human rights. This has been the case, for example, with regard to the attitude of some governments towards the EU playing a greater role as the bearer of human rights obligations or towards developing regimes to cover the human rights obligations of private security companies. Third, corporations and international financial institutions such as the World Bank and the International Monetary Fund are usually not keen to take on a raft of responsibilities that they see as properly the responsibilities of states. With regard to international financial institutions, Philip Alston, the Special Rapporteur on Extreme Poverty and Human Rights, has identified an additional fear from within: an institution like the World Bank could be asked to become a global enforcer, some sort of 'human rights cop'.[3] This, of course, is far from what civil society is asking for when it appeals for the World Bank to respect human rights and adopt a human rights policy.[4] In the imagined extension of all human rights obligations to corporations, there is an additional perceived danger of undermining or diluting the responsibilities of states. For example, in 2006, John Ruggie, the UN Secretary-General's Special Representative on business and human rights, advised the UN Commission on Human Rights that: 'Corporations are not democratic public interest institutions and ... making them, in effect, co-equal duty bearers for the broad spectrum of human rights ... may undermine efforts to build indigenous social capacity and to make governments more responsible to their own citizenry.'[5]

We have, then, broadly speaking, two perceived problems: a 'legitimacy' problem and a 'dilution' problem. These problems can be quite easily overcome. We can remind ourselves that armed opposition groups and their members are increasingly accused of violations of international humanitarian law and even convicted of war crimes. Highlighting violations of these obligations ought to be seen as *de-legitimizing* rather than recognizing some sort

---

[2] Arat, 'Looking beyond the State But Not Ignoring It', in Andreopoulos, Arat, and Juvilier (eds), *Non-State Actors in the Human Rights Universe* (Kumarian Press, 2006) 8.

[3] Report of the Special Rapporteur on Extreme Poverty and Human Rights, A/70/274 (4 August 2015) esp paras 34–48.

[4] van Genugten, *The World Bank Group, the IMF and Human Rights: A Contextualized Way Forward* (Intersentia, 2015).

[5] Interim Report of the Special Representative of the Secretary-General on the Issue of Human Rights and Transnational Corporations and Other Business Enterprises, E/CN.4/2006/97 (22 February 2006) para 68.

of enhanced international status. The problem of legitimizing armed groups evaporates if we decouple human rights from the idea that human rights supposedly emerge from an essential link between governments and their citizens. When we see human rights as rights rather than self-imposed governmental duties, and when we envisage the rights project as founded on better protection for human dignity rather than privileges granted by states, we can start to see how we might imagine human rights obligations for non-state actors. Rather than concentrating on abstract questions of legitimacy, we can take a more sentimental approach and imagine ourselves in the shoes of a victim. From the victim's perspective, the inhuman and degrading treatment is an assault on dignity whether it is suffered at the hands of a policeman, a rebel commander, or a private security company.

With regards to dilution, we can suggest that corporations, international financial institutions, and development agencies have to respect human rights in ways that complement the responsibilities of states, rather than replacing state obligations. We can admit that, as we come to realize that international organizations and private security companies now have the *de facto* power to detain and use force, we should provide a normative framework that protects the individuals with whom they come into contact. The fact that this does not fit easily with a history of human rights that emphasizes the social contract with a government, should not distract us from the urgency of the task.

Moreover, the most promising theoretical basis for human rights obligations for non-state actors is to remind ourselves that the foundational basis of human rights is best explained as rights which belong to the individual in recognition of each person's inherent dignity. The implication is that these natural rights should be respected by everyone and every entity. We should recall that the Universal Declaration of Human Rights is written as a proclamation of rights; the actual obligations of states were not agreed upon at that time. The word 'state' hardly appears in the Declaration. Furthermore, if we leave aside the treaty regimes, with their state-centred monitoring mechanisms, and concentrate on general principles or customary international law,[6] it becomes apparent that even though the jurisdictional clauses of the treaty bodies preclude complaints against non-state actors, the substantive norms themselves might easily be adapted to apply to non-state actors.

Before turning to the actual state of human rights law, let us look at five dynamics that have implications for the development of human rights obligations for non-state actors.

2 THE CHALLENGE OF NON-STATE ACTORS: GLOBALIZATION, PRIVATIZATION, FRAGMENTATION, FEMINIZATION, AND CRIMINALIZATION

The *globalization* of the world economy and means of communication have highlighted the power of large corporations and their limited accountability in law for human rights abuses.[7] There exist today increased possibilities for enterprises to outsource different links in the manufacturing chain, by relying on subcontractors all over the world. In addition, competition between states to attract foreign direct investment has sometimes resulted

---

[6] Chinkin is clear that 'Rules of customary international law … may be held to bind non-state actors that cannot be parties to treaties.' See Chapter 4, Section 4, page 72.

[7] eg Amnesty International, *Undermining Freedom of Expression in China: The Role of Yahoo!, Microsoft and Google* (2006).

in pressure on labour rights, in particular in the garment sector and in special export-processing zones, with minimal regulation or control over employer practices. Despite some recent national initiatives aimed at goods produced in violation of basic rights,[8] the global picture remains stark for the workers involved.

In separate developments, foreign companies working in the extractive industry have had to resort to special security arrangements in the host state. This practice has led to serious questions about violence at the hands of public and private security guards in this context and to the imposition of a human rights based normative framework.[9] It has also led to initiatives to generate due diligence obligations on companies with regards to their supply chains.[10]

In a first phase, emphasis was put on the state's duty to protect individuals from such non-state actors. This is sometimes referred to as a duty of due diligence or a positive obligation. However, this approach has considerable limits. Imagine a situation with a host state's institutions failing and a break down not only in law and order but also in the rule of law itself. A corporation is called in. By definition, the host state is no longer able to fulfill its positive obligations, and, in practice, it is hard to argue that any other state is responsible for all the acts of this corporation. In the real world, there are hardly any effective remedies against a host state for failure to exercise due diligence over massive foreign chemical or extractive industries operating with little regard for the health of those being affected. In each case, to rely on the states concerned to protect people from such abuses has been unworkable. Accordingly, a second approach has been suggested, namely that corporate activity should be directly dealt with by national legal tools such as tort or contract law. Transnational activity, with links to multiple jurisdictions, ought to make it easy to find an accountability mechanism; but the opposite is the case.[11] Globalization reminds us that corporate actors have the possibility to operate from multiple jurisdictions, which will not necessarily ensure that they are held accountable for human rights abuses anywhere. It also reminds us that governments competing for investment have shown little inclination to develop accountability for corporate abuses either at home or abroad.

The *privatization* of sectors such as television, health, education, prisons, water, communications, security forces, and military training has forced us to think again about the applicability of human rights law to the private sector. Many assume that something which is privatized remains subject to human rights law as the concept of human rights is related to so-called 'public functions'. But this assumption is not borne out in practice.

First, the whole point of privatization is to remove certain activity from the state-run sphere, increasing flexibility and usually diminishing accountability. The usual consequence is that the protections that have developed with regard to state activity no longer apply and, although in theory new private remedies should apply, such remedies tend

---

[8] In the UK, the Modern Slavery Act (2015) is aimed at human trafficking slavery, servitude, and forced or compulsory labour. See also the Bangladesh Accord, which is 'an independent, legally binding agreement between brands and trade unions designed to work towards a safe and healthy Bangladeshi Ready-Made Garment Industry', available at: <http://bangladeshaccord.org/>.

[9] eg Voluntary Principles on Security and Human Rights (2000); Jerbi, *The International Code of Conduct for Private Security Service Providers: Academy Briefing 4*, (Geneva Academy of International Humanitarian Law and Human Rights, 2013).

[10] *OECD Due Diligence Guidance for Responsible Supply Chains of Minerals from Conflict-Affected and High-Risk Areas* (3rd ed, 2016). See also the sectoral initiatives, for example, with regard to diamonds (the Kimberley Process) and those listed in OECD, *Gold Industry and Sector Initiatives for the Responsible Sourcing of Minerals* (2014).

[11] See McCorquodale, *Survey of the Provision in the United Kingdom of Access to Remedies for Victims of Human Rights Harms* (BIICL, 2015); Solé et al, *Human Rights in European Business: A Practical Handbook for Civil Society Organisations and Human Rights Defenders* (Tragona Centre for Environmental Law Studies, 2016).

not to include human rights protection in name. The same act therefore gets relabelled. What was once a human rights violation becomes a civil wrong, a tort, or a breach of contract.

Second, the new entity which has taken on the former responsibilities of the state has something that the state did not have. The new non-state entity may have competing human rights which can be enforced or weighed against anyone claiming their rights against this non-state actor. So, for example, the owners and managers of a private shopping mall dominating a town centre will be able to claim respect for the enjoyment of their private property when protestors claim freedom of expression and assembly in that privatized space.[12]

The *fragmentation* of the power in a state may occur not only by the rise of powerful corporate actors but also through the emergence of armed groups or even through delegated authority or power to international organizations. The exercise of power by armed groups has in recent times led to particular scrutiny from the international community. The demands go beyond international humanitarian law and individual responsibility under international criminal law. As we shall see in this chapter, Commissions of Inquiry and the Special Rapporteurs of the UN Human Rights Council now report on human rights violations by all sides during civil strife, and the state/non-state actor boundary may be difficult to patrol as state influence over such groups waxes and wanes. Worries about recognition may be giving way to concern over ensuring scrutiny and accountability. The so-called 'Islamic State' is obviously not a state and yet the UN Human Rights Council has dedicated a resolution to that entity and condemned 'in the strongest possible terms the systematic violations and abuses of human rights ... resulting from the terrorist acts committed by the so-called Islamic State'.[13]

Under this heading of fragmentation, we should also mention the assumption of state-like tasks carried out by the UN or other inter-governmental organizations. Such tasks could even include territorial administration (Kosovo and East Timor are perhaps exceptional examples) or simply *de facto* control over people (NATO and the African Union have both developed detention policies with regard to their peace operations). Such 'hands on' work by international organizations has led to new developments with regard to the applicability of human rights law not only to the UN but also to other international organizations. The cholera crisis in Haiti has forced the UN to think not only about issues of responsibility but also liability and accountability towards those harmed.[14]

Although various obstacles may remain when human rights claims are brought against international organizations in national courts, where there is no equivalent legal protection or alternative means to achieve redress, some national courts have started to prioritize human rights over claims for immunity from international organizations.[15]

---

[12] *Appleby v UK* (2003) 37 EHRR 38. Whether or not a non-state actor is able to claim rights under the ECHR or should be considered a governmental organization is a complex question. See Williams, 'Strasbourg's Public-Private Divide and the British Bill of Rights' [2015] *EHRLR* 617.

[13] HR Council Res S-22/1 (1 September 2014).

[14] See Report of the Special Rapporteur on Extreme Poverty and Human Rights, Philip Alston, A/71/367 (26 August 2016).

[15] eg, in Argentina, the constitutional right of access to court has been given priority over the immunity of international organizations. See Reinisch (ed), *The Privileges and Immunities of International Organizations in Domestic Courts* (OUP, 2013). For examples of national courts prioritizing the right of access to a court under the ECHR over the claim of functional immunity by an international organization, see Reinisch, 'Privileges and Immunities', in Klabbers and Wallendahl (eds), *Research Handbook on the Law of International Organizations* (Edward Elgar, 2011) 143–6.

In evoking *feminization* we are highlighting that the developments surrounding the international human rights of women have led to a complete reappraisal of the way in which the public/private divide has been constructed to delimit human rights law. Some treaties now specifically require the state to take action to protect women in the 'private sphere' or to guarantee women's rights in public and private life.[16] International obligations and commitments have been reconfigured through the prism of due diligence, to ensure that they cover daily harm to women and not only a narrow range of concerns of men. The feminization of human rights has shifted the emphasis to issues of violence against women, certain unfair labour practices, sexual exploitation, trafficking, and 'traditional practices' such as 'honour' killings. Moreover, the idea that sexual violence at the hands of armed non-state armed groups actors is somehow outside the scope of the study of human rights today seems absurd, not to say offensive. In particular, the sexual violence at the core of some of the activities of the so-called 'Islamic State' has to be tackled head on and not as an aspect of the failure of the relevant states.[17]

Lastly, when we consider *criminalization* in the international legal sphere, we have to recognize a radical development which we can trace back in part to the Nuremberg moment when international law was clearly accepted as binding entities that were not states. In the Nuremberg Judgment, in 1946, it was declared that international law could bypass the state and fix directly on individuals.[18] Today it is more and more likely that international criminal law will become primarily concerned with non-state individuals as opposed to state officials. The Statute of the International Criminal Court provides that its jurisdiction can be triggered by a state party that refers a situation in which relevant crimes appear to have been committed.[19] Several states have referred their own situations to the court. In nearly all situations—Uganda, Central African Republic, the Democratic Republic of the Congo, Mali, and Gabon—the government concerned may be cooperating with the Court in order to see non-state actors tried before the Court. Thus, the first trials before the International Criminal Court (ICC) have veered towards prosecuting crimes committed by rebel leaders rather than crimes committed by state actors.[20] To the extent that any new Criminal Chamber of the African Court of Justice and Human Rights will prosecute individuals under its statute, it is already clear that there will be more obstacles to prosecuting state officials than there will be for prosecutions against non-state individuals.[21]

Similarly, the only prosecution in the UK for the international crime of torture concerned an Afghan, non-state, warlord who had been fighting the government.[22] Attempts to prosecute state actors are met with a variety of obstacles, including reliance on the international law of state immunity.[23] Although this migration of international law from state actors to non-state actors has mostly been observed at the level of individual criminal responsibility, there is no convincing conceptual reason why international law should not

---

[16] See Chapter 16.

[17] Bangura, 'Faith in Islam & Faith in Women: Why Gender Justice is Key to an Islam Without Extremes' (International Crisis Group, 2015).

[18] Scharf, *Customary International Law in Times of Fundamental Change: Grotian Moments* (CUP, 2013).

[19] Art 14.   [20] See Chapter 26.

[21] Protocol on Amendments to the Protocol on the Statute of the African Court of Justice and Human Rights (2014), Art 46A bis, provides that '[n]o charges shall be commenced or continued before the Court against any serving Head of State or Government, or anybody acting or entitled to act in such capacity, or other senior state officials based on their functions, during their tenure of office.'

[22] *R v Zardad*, Central Criminal Court (7 April 2004). See Clapham, *Human Rights Obligations of Non-State Actors* (OUP, 2007) 342–3.

[23] eg *The Queen on the application of Freedom and Justice Party and others v Secretary of State for Foreign and Commonwealth Affairs and others* [2016] EWHC 2010 (Admin).

be extended to cover corporate actors and rebel groups as such. We will return below to the increasing prospect of criminal prosecutions of corporations for violations of international law.

3 THE LEGAL FRAMEWORK

3.1 HUMAN RIGHTS TREATIES AND THE STATE'S POSITIVE OBLIGATIONS

All human rights treaties have been held to contain positive obligations that oblige states to protect those within their jurisdiction from harms committed by non-state actors.[24] Different treaty bodies and international courts have addressed the extent of these obligations in different contexts. The Human Rights Committee has stated in relation to the International Covenant on Civil and Political Rights (ICCPR) that:

> the positive obligations on States Parties to ensure Covenant rights will only be fully discharged if individuals are protected by the State, not just against violations of Covenant rights by its agents, but also against acts committed by private persons or entities that would impair the enjoyment of Covenant rights in so far as they are amenable to application between private persons or entities. There may be circumstances in which a failure to ensure Covenant rights as required by article 2 [ICCPR] would give rise to violations by States Parties of those rights, as a result of States Parties' permitting or failing to take appropriate measures or to exercise due diligence to prevent, punish, investigate or redress the harm caused by such acts by private persons or entities.[25]

Although several UN human rights treaty bodies have tended to concentrate on the obligations of states parties to the treaties, rather than explaining what is actually expected of the non-state actors themselves, a new direction may be emerging, as evidenced by General Comment 16 of the UN Committee on the Rights of the Child, which recognized that:

> duties and responsibilities to respect the rights of children extend in practice beyond the State and State-controlled services and institutions and apply to private actors and business enterprises. Therefore, all businesses must meet their responsibilities regarding children's rights and States must ensure they do so. In addition, business enterprises should not undermine the States' ability to meet their obligations towards children under the Convention and the Optional Protocols thereto.[26]

There is a rich vein of case law that allows us to determine the extent to which it is reasonable to expect states, not only to punish, but also to prevent, non-state actors from interfering with the enjoyment of human rights under human rights treaties.[27] There are a number of possibilities through which states may give effect to their positive obligation to protect individuals from harms committed by non-state actors.

---

[24] See Chapter 5.   [25] HRC, General Comment 31, HRI/GEN/1/Rev.9 (Vol 1) 243.

[26] CRC, General Comment 16, State obligations regarding the impact of the business sector on children's rights, CRC/C/GC/16 (17 April 2013) para 8.

[27] eg *X and Y v The Netherlands* (1985) 8 EHRR 235; *Velásquez Rodríguez v Honduras*, IACtHR Series C No 4 (29 July 1988); 204/97, *Mouvement Burkinabé des Droits de l'Homme et des Peuples v Burkina Faso*, 14th Activity Report of the ACommHPR (2001). See generally Clapham (2007), chs 8 and 9; Nolan, 'Addressing Economic and Social Rights Violations by Non-state Actors through the Role of the State: A Comparison of Regional Approaches to the "Obligation to Protect"' (2009) 9 *HRLR* 225.

3.2 NATIONAL LAW

First, some states may give effect to certain international human rights by simply incorporating treaty rights and obligations into their national legal orders. In some situations this may mean that the human rights obligation applies to certain non-state actors even in the absence of special legislation.[28] Recent judgments from the Court of Appeal of England and Wales have gone so far as to apply human rights, such as the right to a remedy, found in the EU Charter of Fundamental Rights in a 'horizontal way' against entities not party to the EU treaties in ways which displace the provisions of a UK Act of Parliament.[29] The extent to which these fundamental rights can continue to be applied directly in the UK courts against non-state actors will depend on any successful appeals to the Supreme Court and on the terms of 'Brexit'. The prospect that more and more EU fundamental rights will come to apply directly and horizontally (ie against non-state actors) through the national legal orders of the other 27 EU member states is nevertheless very real.[30]

A second possibility is that the jurisdiction in question allows for human rights claims against private entities in its constitution (such as South Africa) or has some legislation that is applied to facilitate human rights claims against non-state actors. The cases litigated under the US Alien Tort Statute (ATS, also known as the Alien Tort Claims Act) may prove significant in this context. The ATS confers upon US federal district courts original jurisdiction over 'any civil action by an alien for a tort only, committed in violation of the law of nations' wherever it may have taken place.[31] US courts have been gradually refining the list of violations of the 'law of nations' that will be justiciable in this context. Rulings have determined that genocide, slave trading, slavery, forced labour, and war crimes are actionable even in the absence of any connection to the state.[32] In addition, according to the *Kadic v Karadzic* judgment, where rape, torture, and summary execution are committed, these crimes 'are actionable under the Alien Tort Act, without regard to state action, to the extent they were committed in pursuit of genocide or war crimes'.[33] In fact, even though US courts, including the Supreme Court, have determined that violations of the 'law of nations' under the ATS must be those that are 'specific, universal and obligatory' and have suggested that its drafters probably had in mind a narrow set of violations such as piracy or an assault on an ambassador, the list is not exhaustive, as international law continues to evolve.[34]

In the 2013 case of *Kiobel v Royal Dutch Petroleum*, the US Supreme Court avoided the question as to whether or not a corporation could be a defendant in a case concerning a violation of the 'law of nations'. Instead, it focused on the presumption against extraterritorial application of legislation and required that claims demonstrate a nexus with the US.[35] The issue may yet come again before the Supreme Court as different Circuits in the

---

[28] eg the situation in the Netherlands: Jägers and van der Heijden, 'Corporate Human Rights Violations: the Feasibility of Civil Recourse in the Netherlands' (2008) 33 *Brooklyn JIL* 834, 856. For more examples see Oliver and Fedtke (eds), *Human Rights and the Private Sphere* (Routledge-Cavendish, 2007).

[29] See *Benkharbouche v Sudanese Embassy* [2015] EWCA Civ 33; *Google v Vidal Hall* [2015] EWCA Civ 311.

[30] Frantziou, 'The Horizontal Effect of the Charter of Fundamental Rights of the EU: Rediscovering the Reasons for Horizontality' (2015) 21 *ELJ* 657.

[31] 28 USC § 1350.

[32] *Wiwa v Royal Dutch Shell Petroleum (Shell)*, Case 96 civ 8386 (KMV), Opinion and Order of 28 February 2002, 39. See also *Doe I v Unocal Corporation* (2002) 395 F 3d 932, paras 3 ff.

[33] *Kadic v Karadzic* (1995) 70 F 3d 232, 243–4.

[34] *Sosa v Alvarez-Machain et al.* (2004) 542 US 692, 732 and 734–7.

[35] *Kiobel v Royal Dutch Petroleum* (2013) 569 US 108.

US Federal Court system have been split on whether the law of nations can attach to corporate defendants under this Statute. As explained in 2015 by the Second Circuit there is 'a growing consensus among our sister circuits that the ATS allows for corporate liability. To date, the other circuits to have considered the issue have all determined that corporate liability is possible under the ATS.'[36] It has also become clear from the 2011 *amicus* brief by the United States that, at least in the view of the US Government, international norms defined with sufficient specificity can apply to corporations.[37]

A third possibility is that the incorporating legislation for the human rights treaty addresses the issue of non-state actors explicitly. This is the case for the Human Rights Act 1998 in the UK. Section 6, entitled 'Acts of public authorities', provides that 'it is unlawful for a public authority to act in a way which is incompatible with a Convention [ECHR] right'. A 'public authority' includes, in subsection (3)(b), 'any person certain of whose functions are functions of a public nature', but that '[i]n relation to a particular act, a person is not a public authority by virtue only of subsection (3)(b) if the nature of the act is private.' So a non-state actor with functions of a public nature carrying out acts that are not of a private nature has human rights obligations under the Act. Interpreting this conundrum has given rise to a rich stream of case law and has split what was then called the Appellate Committee of the House of Lords (today the Supreme Court) in the context of a complaint against a residential care home,[38] and led to new legislation.[39]

Stepping back from the detailed statutory interpretations in these cases, the question of whether to apply human rights to non-state actors has forced judges to reflect on the foundational rationale for human rights—to protect individual dignity—and admit that it does not matter from which side of the public/private divide the harm comes. At this point we find that opinions divide, not only on whether certain functions such as education, healthcare, restaurants, rented accommodation, social housing, shopping malls, telephone services, residential care for the elderly, detention, and security are 'obviously' public functions, but also on the question of how much power should judges have to interpret such 'new' obligations for private actors. Our answer depends in part on our approach to human rights: must they be granted through the authoritative process of law-making? Or are they inherent in the individual, generated from a basic obligation on us all to protect human dignity and autonomy?

In a case brought by Naomi Campbell against Mirror Group Newspapers for a breach of her privacy in respect of publication of a photograph of her leaving Narcotics Anonymous, the issue arose as to the weight (if any) to be given to her right to privacy as opposed to the freedom of expression and information claims made by the newspaper. In the past, such a

---

[36] In re *Arab Bank, PLC Alien Tort Statute Litigation*, 808 F.3d 144, 156 (2nd Cir. 2015) the Court then references the following: '*Doe I v. Nestle USA, Inc.*, 766 F.3d 1013, 1022 (9th Cir. 2014); *Doe VIII v. Exxon Mobil Corp.*, 654 F.3d 11, 57 (D.C. Cir. 2011), *vacated on other grounds*, 527 F. App'x 7 (D.C. Cir. 2013); *Flomo v. Firestone Nat. Rubber Co.*, 643 F.3d 1013, 1021 (7th Cir. 2011); *Romero v. Drummond Co.*, 552 F.3d 1303, 1315 (11th Cir. 2008); *see also Al Shimari v. CACI Premier Tech., Inc.*, 758 F.3d 516, 530–31 (4th Cir. 2014). *Beanal v. Freeport-McMoran, Inc.*, 197 F.3d 161, 163 (5th Cir. 1999).'

[37] 'At the present time, the United States is not aware of any international-law norm of the sort identified in Sosa that distinguishes between natural and juridical persons. Corporations (or agents acting on their behalf) can violate those norms just as natural persons can.' Brief for the United States, *Kiobel*, No. 10–1491 (U.S. filed Dec. 21, 2011) 7.

[38] *YL (by her litigation friend the Official Solicitor) (FC) (Appellant) v Birmingham City Council and others (Respondents)* [2007] UKHL 27.

[39] See Social Care Act 2009, s 145; Care Act 2014, s 73. See also Dickson, *Human Rights and the United Kingdom Supreme Court* (OUP, 2013) 85–8.

claim might have been seen as having nothing to do with human rights due to the absence of a state actor. Today, the expectations are different. Lord Hoffmann reflected this in his speech:

> What human rights law has done is to identify private information as something worth protecting as an aspect of human autonomy and dignity. And this recognition has raised inescapably the question of why it should be worth protecting against the state but not against a private person. There may of course be justifications for the publication of private information by private persons which would not be available to the state—I have particularly in mind the position of the media, to which I shall return in a moment—but I can see no logical ground for saying that a person should have less protection against a private individual than he would have against the state for the publication of personal information for which there is no justification. Nor, it appears, have any of the other judges who have considered the matter.[40]

Lastly, in other jurisdictions, legislation and the constitution have been *interpreted* to cover human rights claims brought against non-state actors. We can find a pervasive percolation of human rights values into judicial reasoning and constitutional interpretation, in ways that indirectly apply human rights obligations to non-state actors.[41]

4 THE OBLIGATIONS OF INTERNATIONAL ORGANIZATIONS

A traditional starting point for the assertion that international organizations have international obligations is the International Court of Justice's statement that international organizations are subject to 'general rules of international law'.[42] As Christian Tomuschat points out:

> Substantively, international organizations may be characterized as common agencies operated by States for the fulfilment of certain common tasks. Now, if States acting individually have been subjected to certain rules thought to be indispensable for maintaining orderly relations within the international community, there is no justification for exempting international organizations from the scope *ratione personae* of such rules.[43]

Many would agree with Tomuschat that, even if states can limit the powers of the organization they create, they 'cannot thereby shield their creation from becoming liable towards other subjects of international law on account of [their] activities'.[44] This reasoning has been reflected in the approach of the European Court of Human Rights and some national courts when individuals claimed a denial of their human rights due to the immunity accorded to international organizations in national courts.[45]

---

[40] *Campbell v MGN Limited* [2004] UKHL 22, para 50.

[41] See Gardbaum, 'The "Horizontal Effect" of Constitutional Rights' (2003) 102 *Michigan LRev* 387; Barak, 'Constitutional Human Rights and Private Law' in Friedmann and Barak-Erez (eds), *Human Rights in Private Law* (Hart Publishing, 2001) 13; Tushnet, 'The Issue of State Action/Horizontal Effect in Comparative Constitutional Law' (2003) 1 *Intl J Const L* 79; Hughes, *Human Dignity and Fundamental Rights in South Africa and Ireland* (Pretoria University Law Press, 2014).

[42] *Interpretation of the Agreement of 25 March 1951 Between the WHO and Egypt* [1980] ICJ Rep 73, 89–90.

[43] Tomuschat, 'International Law: Ensuring the Survival of Mankind on the Eve of a New Century: General Course on Public International Law' (1999) 281 *RdC* 9, 34–5.   [44] Tomuschat, 129–30.

[45] *Waite and Kennedy v Germany* (2000) 30 EHRR 261, para 67; Reinisch, 'Privileges and Immunities' in Klabbers and Wallendahl (eds), *Research Handbook on the Law of International Organizations* (Edward Elgar, 2011) 132.

Given that international organizations can have human rights obligations,[46] two questions arise. Firstly, where do these obligations come from? And, second, how do we build accountability mechanisms that would help to influence their behaviour and provide redress for victims? To answer the first question would take us way beyond the scope of this chapter. However, many might agree with the conclusions of Faix that 'inasmuch as human rights can be considered to form general principles of international law and international customary rules, they can be considered relevant sources of international obligations of international organisations, subject to the implications of specialty.'[47]

One option to ensure clear content and accountability is to ensure that human rights treaties allow for international organizations to become contracting parties. This is currently the case for both the Convention on the Rights of Persons with Disabilities and its Optional Protocol. The Convention explains that it allows for 'regional integration organizations' to become parties where those organizations are 'constituted by sovereign States of a given region, to which its member States have transferred competence in respect of matters governed by this Convention.'[48] The EU formally confirmed in 2011 its participation in the treaty regime and declared the extent of its competence with respect to matters governed by the Convention.

In the same way, Protocol No 14 ECHR allows for the EU to become a party to the European Convention and its Protocols so that complaints could eventually be brought against the Union before the European Court of Human Rights. These formal solutions are however riven with complications at the political and technical levels.[49] Accordingly, the way forward is more likely to revolve around international organizations detailing their own human rights obligations and attendant monitoring. In turn, the existing human rights mechanisms are adapting to include recommendations to the relevant international organizations. For example, General Comments prepared by the Committee on Economic, Social and Cultural Rights on topics such as the right to health, the right to food, the right to water, and the right to work now include the duty of states to protect individuals from non-state actors that might infringe on the enjoyment of these rights. The Committee also has a chapter at the end of its General Comments entitled 'Obligations of Actors Other than State Parties'. This includes, for example, in the context of the right to work, recommendations for 'individuals, local communities, trade unions, civil society and private sector organisations'.[50] Special attention is given to 'private enterprises—national and multinational'. The respective General Comment goes on to address the role of 'the ILO [International Labour Organization] and the other specialized agencies of the United Nations, the World Bank, regional development banks, the International Monetary Fund, the World Trade Organization and other relevant bodies within the United Nations system'.

---

[46] The Institutions of the EU are bound to respect the rights in the Charter of Fundamental Rights of the European Union, as well as aspects of international human rights law. See Douglas-Scott, 'The European Union and Human Rights after the Treaty of Lisbon' (2011) 11 *HRLR* 645; Ahmed and de Jesús Butler, 'The European Union and Human Rights: An International Law Perspective' (2006) 17 *EJIL* 771.

[47] Faix, 'Binding International Organisations to Human Rights Obligations—Some Underlying Questions' in Šturma and Baez (eds), *International and Internal Mechanisms of Fundamental Rights Effectiveness* (RW&W, 2015) 51–2; Faix, 'Are International Organisations Bound by International Human Rights Obligations?' (2014) 5 *Czech YB of Public and Private International Law* 267. [48] Arts 42–4.

[49] For the draft agreement on accession, see Fifth Negotiation Meeting between the CDDH and Ad Hoc Negotiation Group and the European Commission on the Accession of the European Union to the European Convention on Human Rights: Final report to CDDH, 47+1(2013) 008. The European Court of Justice has however concluded that the agreement on accession is not compatible with the Treaty on European Union and its Protocol 8: *Opinion 2/13 re Accession to the ECHR* [2015] 2 CMLR 21.

[50] CESCR, General Comment 18, HRI/GEN/1/Rev.9 (Vol I) 243.

5 CORPORATE SOCIAL RESPONSIBILITY AND THE MOVE TOWARDS ACCOUNTABILITY

Some businesses have expressed human rights commitments out of a sense of corporate social responsibility. This can stem from a desire to: protect reputation; reduce risk of disruption through strikes, protests, and boycotts; enhance their attractiveness for future and current employees; and because it is the 'right thing to do'. Major companies now have human rights policies as a matter of course and few now claim openly (as they used to do) that 'human rights are none of our business'. Several factors have led to greater attention being paid to the human rights implications of corporate activity.

First, studies and mechanisms being developed by international organizations such as the UN, the ILO, and the Organisation for Economic Co-operation and Development (OECD) are reinforcing the notion that companies have international responsibilities. Worthy of particular mention are the multiple studies produced by the Special Representative of the UN Secretary-General, John Ruggie, and the possibility of complaining to an OECD National Contact Point that a company has failed to respect human rights.[51]

In 2005, the UN appointed John Ruggie to identify and clarify the relevant human rights standards for corporate responsibility and accountability. In 2011, the resulting Guiding Principles on Business and Human Rights were endorsed by the Human Rights Council; they rest on a protect, respect, and remedy framework with three pillars:

- the state duty to *protect* against human rights abuses by third parties, including business enterprises, through appropriate policies, regulation, and adjudication;

- an independent corporate responsibility to *respect* human rights, which means that business enterprises should act with due diligence to avoid infringing on the rights of others and address adverse impacts with which they are involved;

- the need for greater access by victims to effective *remedy*, both judicial and non-judicial.

In Ruggie's words: 'Simply put: states must protect; companies must respect; and those who are harmed must have redress.'[52]

Paragraph 12 of the Guiding Principles states:

The responsibility of business enterprises to respect human rights refers to internationally recognized human rights understood, at a minimum, as those expressed in the International Bill of Human Rights and the principles concerning fundamental rights set out in the International Labour Organization's Declaration on Fundamental Principles and Rights at Work.

However, the imperative that companies have responsibilities and 'must respect human rights' is conceived in this context as a moral (rather than legal) demand. The Commentary to the Guiding Principles suggests that legal obligations are found elsewhere: '[t]he responsibility of business enterprises to respect human rights is distinct from issues of legal liability and enforcement, which remain defined largely by national law provisions in relevant jurisdictions.'[53] Although these Guiding Principles have led to

---

[51] OECD, *OECD Guidelines for Multinational Enterprises 2011 Edition* (OECD, 2011); but see Daniel et al., *Remedy Remains Rare: An Analysis of 15 Years of NCP Cases and Their Contribution to Improve Access to Remedy for Victims of Corporate Misconduct* (OECD Watch, 2015).

[52] Ruggie, *Just Business: Multinational Corporations and Human Rights* (W.W. Norton, 2013) xx-xxi.

[53] A/HRC/17/31 (21 March 2011) 14.

multiple initiatives aimed at changing the policies of governments and business,[54] civil society organizations (joined by some states) consider that there needs to be a more robust international legal framework ensuring not just a moral sense of responsibility on the part of companies but concrete forms of legal accountability that go beyond action plans and reporting obligations.

Second, in response to this dissatisfaction, a UN governmental working group was established in 2014 'to elaborate an internationally legally binding instrument to regulate, in international human rights law, the activities of transnational corporations and other business enterprises'.[55] Civil society and leading scholars have presented various proposals for consideration, covering a wide spectrum of options. They range from a treaty which would create obligations for states to provide legal remedies under national law for corporate non-compliance with human rights obligations, through to additionally defining the obligations for corporations both under criminal law and civil law, right up to proposals for a world court of human rights which could hear cases against corporations.[56]

Third, human rights compliance is increasingly factored into investment decisions, in particular by funds which advertise an ethical investment dimension. Perhaps the most well-known process in this respect is the Norwegian Council on Ethics for the Government Pension Fund Global. Under Section 3 of the Council's Guidelines, companies may be put under observation or be excluded if there is an unacceptable risk that the company contributes to or is responsible for:

a) serious or systematic human rights violations, such as murder, torture, deprivation of liberty, forced labour and the worst forms of child labour

b) serious violations of the rights of individuals in situations of war or conflict

c) severe environmental damage

d) acts or omissions that on an aggregate company level lead to unacceptable greenhouse gas emissions

e) gross corruption

f) other particularly serious violations of fundamental ethical norms.[57]

Fourth, and lastly, the assumption that international criminal law only applies to individuals has been seriously challenged. There have been three recent developments in this regard.

The first is a new treaty, adopted by the African Union in 2014, which adds a criminal chamber to the African Court of Justice and Human Rights and does so in a way that makes clear that corporations can be prosecuted for certain international crimes in this

---

[54] For the national action plans, available at: <http://www.ohchr.org/EN/Issues/Business/Pages/NationalActionPlans.aspx>. For OHCHR guidance on implementing the 'access to remedy for victims of business-related human rights abuse', see A/HRC/32/19 (10 May 2016), A/HRC/32/19/Add.1 (12 May 2016), and the companion document 'Illustrative examples for guidance to improve corporate accountability and access to judicial remedy for business-related human rights abuse' (5 July 2016), available at: <http://www.ohchr.org/EN/Issues/Business/Pages/OHCHRstudyondomesticlawremedies.aspx>.

[55] HR Council Res 26/9 (26 June 2014).

[56] See eg Bilchitz, 'The Necessity for a Business and Human Rights Treaty' (2016) 1 *Business and Human Rights Journal* 203; ESCR-Net and FIDH, *Ten Key Proposals for the Treaty* (ESCR-Net, 2016); Nowak and Kozma, *A World Court of Human Rights—Consolidated Statute and Commentary* (Neuer Wissenschaftlicher Verlag, 2010) esp Art 4 and Commentary, 33–4.

[57] Listings of which companies have been excluded or put under observation, are available at: <https://www.nbim.no/en/responsibility/exclusion-of-companies/>. See generally Hebb *et al.* (eds) *The Routledge Handbook of Responsible Investment* (Routledge, 2016).

new Chamber.[58] For the members of the African Union at least there is now no doubt as to the applicability of international criminal law to corporations.

Whether or not the new Criminal Chamber is quickly established, we are now a step closer to designing procedures for *national* prosecutions of corporations for international crimes. As this new international jurisdiction will be complementary to national jurisdictions, in the same way that the ICC allows for inadmissibility of certain cases that are properly pursued at the national level, national legislation will likely be drafted to ensure that cases against corporations can be prosecuted at the national level. This will have to go beyond the existing legislation related to the ICC, not only because of the new possibility of corporate criminal responsibility, but also because the list of crimes has been considerably extended, including for example the following: The crime of unconstitutional change of government; piracy; terrorism; mercenarism; corruption; money laundering; trafficking in persons; trafficking in drugs; trafficking in hazardous wastes; illicit exploitation of natural resources; and an expansion of the list of war crimes.

We have thus come a long way from the assumption that international legal principles do not apply to corporations, or that if they do this would be limited to 'certain war crimes and crimes against humanity'.[59] Some might dismiss this development as 'a regional anomaly', but companies operating in Africa, regardless of nationality, will have to consider that they could in the future be prosecuted for these crimes and that their behaviour will be judged against these norms. In sum, we now have an international treaty, adopted by states, that assumes or creates international obligations for corporations, and proposes that they be held accountable for any violations of these obligations in courts of law nationally and at the international (regional) level.

The second development relates to the Special Tribunal for Lebanon. On 2 October 2014, the Appeals Panel ruled that a corporation could be prosecuted for contempt of court before this international criminal tribunal. The Panel drew two interesting conclusions, the first with regard to human rights law and the second with regard to criminal law. Having reviewed developments in human rights law, in particular at the UN Human Rights Council and the UN Human Rights Committee, the Panel concluded that 'that the current international standards on human rights allow for interpreting the term "person" to include legal entities for the purposes of Rule 60 *bis* [on contempt]'.[60] With regard to criminal law, it examined a number of developments at the national level as well as treaties that refer to corporate criminal responsibility, and concluded that 'corporate criminal liability is on the verge of attaining, at the very least, the status of a general principle of law applicable under international law'.[61]

The third development relates to crimes against humanity. The Drafting Committee of the International Law Commission (ILC) provisionally adopted a text in 2016 which confirmed that corporations can commit crimes against humanity. In the context of the ILC's Draft Articles on Crimes Against Humanity the following text was adopted:

> Subject to the provisions of its national law, each State shall take measures, where appropriate, to establish the liability of legal persons for the offences referred to in this draft

---

[58] Protocol on Amendments, Art 46, entitled 'Corporate Criminal Liability', provides in (C)(1) that, '[f]or the purpose of this Statute, the Court shall have jurisdiction over legal persons, with the exception of States'.

[59] Interim report of the Special Representative of the Secretary-General, para 60.

[60] *New TV Karma Mohamed Tahsin Al Khayat*, Decision on Interlocutory Appeal Concerning Personal Jurisdiction in Contempt proceedings, STL-14–05/PT/AP/AR126.1 (2 October 2014) para 60. This ruling has since been rejected by the Contempt Judge in a related proceeding: STL-14–06/PT/CJ, 6 November 2014.

[61] *New TV Karma Mohamed Tahsin Al Khayat*, para 67.

article. Subject to the legal principles of the State, such liability of legal persons may be criminal, civil or administrative.[62]

6 ARMED NON-STATE ACTORS

According to the International Committee of the Red Cross (ICRC), it is 'undisputed' that the core international humanitarian law rules, such as those found in Common Article 3 of the 1949 Geneva Conventions, apply to the non-state party to a non-international armed conflict.[63] Nevertheless there is an apparent problem with the application of human rights law to such armed groups. We might suggest that this could be for two main reasons. First, because in contrast to international humanitarian law, human rights law is seen by some as specifically designed for states as human rights treaties only rarely address non-state armed groups.[64] Second, there is a perception that engaging with rebel groups on human rights issues lends them a certain legitimacy. This is in part related to the first issue: by claiming that a group has violated human rights, one is implying that they are a state-like entity because it is presumed that only states have human rights obligations.

Both these apparent obstacles are, it is submitted, being eroded. The human rights monitoring mechanisms are starting to include reporting on non-state armed groups in their range of activities. Although several commentators have insisted in the past that only states have human rights obligations in this context,[65] and that non-state actors are exclusively bound by international humanitarian law, this is being challenged in direct and indirect ways. One challenge comes in the form of increasing demands by different international entities that armed groups respect human rights. These demands can come in the form of Security Council Resolutions, in the reports of the various truth commissions (such as those in Guatemala and Sierra Leone) which detail the human rights violations committed by non-state actors, or in the findings of commissions of inquiry and other expert panels.

Before we look at the exact terms of these inroads to the traditional approach, let us pause to consider some of the theoretical issues.[66] How can a treaty or indeed custom bind any entity which has not consented to be bound? The development of international criminal law has made it clear that international law is capable of binding entities other than states and their creations (international organizations). In the past, it was sometimes

---

[62] Draft article 6, paragraph 7, provisionally adopted by the Drafting Committee, A/CN.4/L.892 (26 May 2017).

[63] ICRC, *Commentary to the First Geneva Convention* (CUP, 2016) para 508. See also para 505 ('it is today accepted that common Article 3 is binding on non-State armed groups, both as treaty and customary law'); *Military and Paramilitary Activities in and against Nicaragua (Nicaragua v USA)* [1986] ICJ Rep 14, para 219; *Prosecutor v Sam Hinga Norman*, Decision on Preliminary Motion Based on Lack of Jurisdiction (Child Recruitment), SCSL-2004–14-AR72(E) (31 May 2004) para 22.

[64] One exception being the Optional Protocol to the CRC on the involvement of children in armed conflict. See later for an application in the case of Syria.

[65] Moir, *The Law of Internal Armed Conflict* (CUP, 2002) 194; Zegveld, *Accountability of Armed Opposition Groups in International Law* (CUP, 2002) 53.

[66] For a discussion of some of the theories that have been proposed to justify the application of human rights law to armed groups, see Sivakumaran, *The Law of Non-International Armed Conflict* (OUP, 2012) 95–100; Murray, 'How International Humanitarian Law Treaties Bind Non-State Armed Group' (2014) 20 *JCSL* 101; Clapham, 'Focusing on Armed Non-State Actors', in Clapham and Gaeta (eds), *The Oxford Handbook of International Law in Armed Conflict* (OUP, 2014) 766.

suggested that this is because states create obligations for their nationals through the ratification of treaties, but it is clear that the obligations under international criminal law, inside and outside armed conflict, extend beyond the nationals of states parties. If states can create obligations on third parties for the purposes of prosecution, why can this not happen for non-criminal responsibility?

The next doctrinal obstacle is the idea that human rights law is inherently incapable of creating legal obligations for non-state actors. This is often said to be because of how human rights law is traditionally conceived. As already suggested, the same commentators that have assertively argued that international humanitarian law (IHL) is incontestably binding on non-state actors, deny the applicability of international human rights law (IHRL) in this context.

> IHL applies to all parties to the conflict, including (in the case of a non-international armed conflict) non-state organised armed groups. On the other hand, IHRL traditionally only applies to states and significant controversy exists as to whether, and if so, to what extent, non-state armed groups incur IHRL obligations. The ICRC's position is that non-state armed groups generally do not have IHRL obligations as a matter of law, subject to the exception where a non-state armed group's *de facto* responsibilities can be recognised by virtue of its *de facto* capacity to act like a state government.[67]

But this exception is in the end not really admitted to be a proper legal exception, as Breitegger explains later in the same article:

> This review shows that there is no consensus among states and experts that non-state armed groups incur legal obligations under IHRL. However, there is an enhanced recognition that where non-state armed groups as entities have the semblance of state authority and exercise *de facto* authority over a population, they are expected to respond positively to the moral rather than legal expectations of the international community to respect IHRL.[68]

If we drill down a little and consider the theoretical justifications for applying international humanitarian law to armed groups, we find that there is nothing that would exclude human rights law from applying to the same groups. Sivakumaran has helpfully grouped these theoretical justifications under seven headings which he says together 'explain how non-state parties to [non-international armed conflicts] are bound by IHL.'[69] They include:

- ratification by the state;
- domestic law;
- the binding nature of treaties on third parties;
- consent of the armed group to be bound by Common Article 3;
- claims of the armed group to represent the state;
- the armed group's exercising state-like functions; and
- on the basis of customary international law.

The doctrinal debates surrounding the suitability of these routes for providing a convincing legal argument are carefully explained by Sivakumaran and need not detain us here. It seems to the present author that each of these routes is potentially capable of providing a rationale for

---

[67] Breitegger, 'The Legal Framework Applicable to Insecurity and Violence Affecting the Delivery of Health Care in Armed Conflicts and Other Emergencies' (2013) 96 *IRRC* 83, 88.

[68] Breitegger (2013), 103. The author also clarifies at 89, that 'the terminology used by the ICRC is "responsibilities" and thus falls short of recognising legally binding obligations.'

[69] 'The Addressees of Common Article 3', in Clapham, Gaeta, and Sassòli (eds), *The 1949 Geneva Conventions: A Commentary* (OUP, 2015) 417.

armed groups being bound by international human rights law and not just international humanitarian law. Let us turn to some practical applications of human rights obligations to armed non-state actors: first, the work of the Security Council with regard to children's rights; second, the work of the UN special mechanisms/ad hoc inquiries; and third, the work of NGOs.

6.1 THE UN SECURITY COUNCIL'S WORK ON CHILDREN AND ARMED CONFLICT

The UN's work on children and armed conflict has led to an innovative approach which details violations by parties to armed conflicts, both states and non-state actors. Reports by the UN Secretary-General to the Security Council on certain situations list the actual parties concerned and whether they are involved in any of six 'grave violations':

(1) Killing or maiming of children.

(2) Recruiting or using child soldiers.

(3) Attacks against schools or hospitals.

(4) Rape or other grave sexual violence against children.

(5) Abduction of children.

(6) Denial of humanitarian access for children.

The UN Secretary-General's initial report explains that these violations are based on international norms, commitments that have been made by the parties to the conflict, national laws, and peace agreements.[70] Subsequent reports on various country situations have detailed the 'grave violations of children's rights' committed by the non-state actors concerned.[71] These reports dedicate as much, if not more, space to the violations committed by the non-state actors as they do to addressing the states concerned. The mechanism vis-à-vis the non-state actors works not only through naming and shaming, but by encouraging the armed groups to submit an 'action plan' to the Security Council. In this way, the groups can eventually be removed from the list of violators. The Security Council also has in mind that it could adopt:

> country-specific resolutions, targeted and graduated measures, such as, inter alia, a ban on the export and supply of small arms and light weapons and of other military equipment and on military assistance, against parties to situations of armed conflict which are on the Security Council's agenda and are in violation of applicable international law relating to the rights and protection of children in armed conflict.[72]

Although the focus started with the recruitment of child soldiers, the Security Council has requested the Secretary-General to include in his reports 'those parties to armed conflict that engage, in contravention of applicable international law', in the grave violations (1)-(5) listed at the start of this section.[73] Each year the Secretary-General lists those entities that are engaged in grave violations separating out the violations and highlighting those which can be considered 'persistent perpetrators', namely those who have appeared on the list for five years.[74] Even if the reports refer in general terms to the rules of international

---

[70] Report of the Secretary-General on Children and Armed Conflict, S/2005/72 (9 February 2005).

[71] See eg Report of the Secretary-General on Children and Armed Conflict, S/2009/158 (26 March 2009).

[72] SC Res 1612 (26 July 2005) para 9.

[73] SC Res 1882 (4 August 2009); SC Res 1998 (12 July 2011); SC Res 2225 (18 June 2015).

[74] See eg Children and Armed Conflict: Report of the Secretary-General, A/70/836-S/2016/360 (20 April 2016), which lists around 30 persistent perpetrators from Afghanistan, Central African Republic, Colombia, the Democratic Republic of the Congo, Iraq, Myanmar, Philippines, Somalia, South Sudan, Sudan, Syria, and Yemen.

law that are actually being violated, the prospect of follow-up sanctions by the Security Council is premised on the idea that these groups have violated international law and not simply a set of moral or political imperatives.

This activity is complemented by the Special Representative of the Secretary-General on children and armed conflict whose work not only feeds into the reports to the Security Council but also relies on country visits, engagement with non-state actors, and facilitation of commitments by those armed groups. Let us look, however, at the work of the UN special procedures and ad hoc inquiries more generally.

6.2 UN SPECIAL PROCEDURES AND AD HOC INQUIRIES

UN special procedures and ad hoc inquiries have taken different approaches to the issue of human rights obligation of non-state armed groups.

The former UN Special Rapporteur on extrajudicial, summary or arbitrary executions, Philip Alston, grappled with the question of the human rights obligations of non-state armed groups in the context of his 2006 report on Sri Lanka. He noted that, '[a]s a non-State actor, the LTTE [Liberation Tigers of Tamil Eelam] does not have legal obligations under ICCPR, but it remains subject to the demand of the international community, first expressed in the Universal Declaration of Human Rights, that every organ of society respect and promote human rights'.[75] Alston went on to include specific human rights recommendations addressed to the non-state actor concerned.[76] A similar approach was applied in the joint 2006 report on Lebanon and Israel by a group of four Special Rapporteurs.[77] By contrast, a 2008 report of the UN High Commissioner for Human Rights with regard to Hamas, simply recalled 'that non-State actors that exercise government-like functions and control over a territory are obliged to respect human rights norms when their conduct affects the human rights of the individuals under their control'.[78]

More recently, in 2012, the Commission of Inquiry on Syria applied a limited set of human rights obligations to the armed non-state actors. The Commission stated with regard to the Free Syrian Army (FSA) that:

> [A]t a minimum, human rights obligations constituting peremptory international law (*ius cogens*) bind States, individuals and non-State collective entities, including armed groups. Acts violating *ius cogens*—for instance, torture or enforced disappearances—can never be justified.[79]

---

[75] Report of the Special Rapporteur on extrajudicial, summary or arbitrary executions, Philip Alston, Mission to Sri Lanka, E/CN.4/2006/53/Add.5 (27 March 2006) para 25.

[76] Report on Mission to Sri Lanka, para 85. See also the letter addressed directly to the LTTE concerning prevention of killings, lack of investigations, and the application of the death penalty: 'Allegation letter sent 21 November 2005', E/CN.4/53/Add.1 (27 March 2006) 320.

[77] Report of the Special Rapporteur on extrajudicial, summary or arbitrary executions; the Special Rapporteur on the right of everyone to the enjoyment of the highest attainable standard of physical and mental health; the Representative of the Secretary-General on human rights of internally displaced persons; and the Special Rapporteur on adequate housing as a component of the right to an adequate standard of living, A/HRC/2/7 (2 October 2006) para 19.

[78] Human Rights Situation in Palestine and other Occupied Arab Territories, HRC/8/17, (6 June 2008) para 9.

[79] Report of the Independent International Commission of Inquiry on the Syrian Arab Republic, A/HRC/19/69 (22 February 2012) paras 106–7. See also the approach of the Report of the International Commission of Inquiry to investigate all Alleged Violations of International Human Rights Law in the Libyan Arab Jamahiriya, A/HRC/17/44 (1 June 2011).

In 2013, the Commission went further in the context of enforced disappearances and stated: '[a]lthough anti-Government armed groups are per se not a party to the Convention [for the Protection of All Persons from Enforced Disappearance], their actions may be assessed against customary international legal principles, and they are subject to criminal liability for enforced disappearance amounting to a crime against humanity.'[80] Using the expression 'customary legal principles' suggests a set of human rights principles that do not necessarily have to be proven as customary international rules developed specifically for non-state actors, but rather fundamental standards that ought to apply to all actors in all circumstances.

For its part, the Panel of Experts appointed by the UN Secretary-General to report on accountability in Sri Lanka explained their approach as follows:

> With respect to the LTTE, although non-state actors cannot formally become party to a human rights treaty, it is now increasingly accepted that non-state groups exercising *de facto* control over a part of a State's territory must respect fundamental human rights of persons in that territory. Various organs of the United Nations, including the Security Council, have repeatedly demanded that such actors respect human rights law. Although the Panel recognizes that there remains some difference of views on the subject among international actors, it proceeds on the assumption that, at a minimum, the LTTE was bound to respect the most basic human rights of persons within its power, including the rights to life and physical security and integrity of the person, and freedom from torture and cruel, inhuman or degrading treatment and punishment.[81]

Perhaps the clearest list of obligations is set out in the context of the 2014 UN report on South Sudan:

> The most basic human rights obligations, in particular those emanating from peremptory international law (*ius cogens*) bind both the State and armed opposition groups in times of peace and during armed conflict. In particular, international human rights law requires States, armed groups and others to respect the prohibitions of extrajudicial killing, maiming, torture, cruel inhuman or degrading treatment or punishment, enforced disappearance, rape, other conflict related sexual violence, sexual and other forms of slavery, the recruitment and use of children in hostilities, arbitrary detention as well as of any violations that amount to war crimes, crimes against humanity, or genocide.[82]

The 2013 UN report by Thomas Hammarberg on human rights in Transnistria, under the preliminary heading 'legal obligations', considers that the starting point is 'customary international law obligating *de facto* authorities to uphold the most fundamental human rights norms.'[83] The right to freedom of religion or belief has also arisen with regard to conscientious objection from military service in territories controlled by *de facto* regimes (non-state actors) in places such as Transnistria (Moldova) and the Turkish Republic of Northern Cyprus.[84] In the latter situation Heiner Bielefeldt, the Special Rapporteur

---

[80] Report of the Independent International Commission of Inquiry on the Syrian Arab Republic, A/HRC/22/59 (5 February 2013) para 85.

[81] Report of the Secretary-General's Panel of Experts on Accountability in Sri Lanka (31 March 2011) para 188.

[82] United Nations Mission in the Republic of South Sudan (UNMISS), Conflict in South Sudan: A Human Rights Report (8 May 2014) para 18.

[83] Report on Human Rights in the Transnistrian Region of the Republic of Moldova (14 February 2013) 4.

[84] Bielefeldt, Ghanea, and Wiener, *Freedom of Religion or Belief: An International Law Commentary* (OUP, 2016) 286–8.

on Freedom of Religion or Belief, called for 'strict compliance with article 18(3) of the International Covenant on Civil and Political Rights and article 1(3) of the 1981 Declaration' on the Elimination of All Forms of Intolerance and of Discrimination Based on Religion or Belief.[85]

Although findings that human rights treaties have been violated usually refer to states, we can see here the application of treaty law to non-state actors. An even more precise example is provided by the Commission of Inquiry on Syria, which concluded in 2013 that '[a]nti-Government armed groups are also responsible for using children under the age of 18 in hostilities in violation of the CRC-OPAC [Optional Protocol to the Convention on the Rights of the Child], which by its terms applies to non-State actors.' The summary also makes the same point: 'Both Government-affiliated militia and anti-Government armed groups were found to have violated the Optional Protocol to the Convention on the Rights of the Child on the involvement of children in armed conflict, to which the Syrian Arab Republic is a party.'[86] The complexity of the situation of detainees in Libya forced the Office of the High Commissioner, in 2016, to abandon any pretense of separate regimes or vocabulary:

> In the present report the term 'detention' and its variants ('detainee', 'detention facilities') is intended to reflect deprivation of liberty by both State and armed groups in view of the complex factual situation in Libya, in particular given that armed groups remain in control of many facilities, and that many armed groups were theoretically brought under the purview of the Ministries of the Interior, Defence or Justice during integration processes carried out after 2011. The term 'conflict-related detainee' is used as a reference to persons detained as a result of the conflicts in Libya in 2011 or 2014 and 2015.[87]

On the basis of these reports and resolutions, we might conclude that the more recent practice of the UN Human Rights Council, relevant UN experts, and the Office of the High Commissioner is to investigate and condemn violations of human rights by *de facto* regimes and armed groups in more or less the same terms as those used for states. In some situations, with dozens of armed groups all in positions of control over people, various groups may or may not be operating under the control or auspices of the state on any one day. As research in other social sciences demonstrates, the idea that there is at all times a clear bright line between state and non-state groups is fallacious. In some contexts armed groups can be better described as 'spin offs' from the state rather than non-state actors, and those same groups may at various stages take on functions that the state chooses not to entrust to its own forces.[88]

We might also conclude that, even if the approach at one stage may have been to confine the application of human rights law to those politically organized groups that had effective control over territory and persons, the challenge of reporting on groups such as the Lord's Resistance Army, Boko Haram, or the hundreds of groups in Syria and Libya, means that we may have to admit that it is no longer possible always to ground the application of human rights law in 'territorial control'.[89] In fact, there is no real reason to ground human

---

[85] Report of the Special Rapporteur on freedom of religion or belief, Heiner Bielefeldt, Addendum, Mission to Cyprus, A/HRC/22/51/Add.1 (24 December 2012) para 82.

[86] Report of the Commission of Inquiry on Syria, para 44 and p 2.

[87] Investigation by the Office of the United Nations High Commissioner for Human Rights on Libya, A/HRC/31/CRP.3 (23 February 2016) para 130. At para 30, the High Commissioner notes that, 'Libya does not have a straightforward delineation of State security forces and opposition forces. Instead, it has a complex set of armed actors, with varying degrees of association with the State and each other.'

[88] Schlichte, 'With the State against the State? The Formation of Armed Groups', in Krause (ed), *Armed groups and Contemporary Conflicts: Challenging the Weberian State* (Routledge, 2010).

[89] See also Report of the Special Rapporteur on freedom of religion or belief, Heiner Bielefeldt, A/HRC/28/66 (29 December 2014), paras 54–5.

rights obligations in issues of territory and in this way we could avoid the problematic issues of sovereignty and loss of governmental control. Human rights obligations should flow from the fact that the group has control over *people* and duties towards those they are affecting. This would better mirror the approaches in international humanitarian law and international criminal law.[90]

6.3 NON-GOVERNMENTAL REPORTING AND ENGAGING WITH ARMED NON-STATE ACTORS

Engagement with armed groups is not limited to UN human rights mechanisms. NGOs increasingly engage with armed groups and denounce human rights abuses committed by them. Such reporting may go beyond concerns about killings, torture, and detention, and cover all sorts of human rights violations, including for example denial of freedom of association,[91] or failure to ensure fair trials.[92] Most recently it has become clear that attention might now turn to the procedural safeguards an armed group should offer to its detainees who wish to challenge their detention.[93]

The NGO Geneva Call has engaged armed non-state actors[94] in 'Deeds of Commitment' regarding a 'total ban on anti-personnel mines and for cooperation in mine action', 'the protection of children from the effects of armed conflict', and 'the prohibition of sexual violence in situations of armed conflict and towards the elimination of gender discrimination.'[95] Having negotiated the signature of the Deed, Geneva Call receives the armed non-state actors' regular reports, monitors compliance with the Deed, and, in the context of land mines, helps arrange mine action including demining and destruction of stocks. It is worth inquiring at this point what might be the incentives for a non-state actor to bind itself to such a Deed or indeed to develop their own codes of conduct dealing with human rights issues.[96]

First, rebel groups realize the advantages of being seen to abide by international norms in the context of moves towards peace negotiations. Second, it is much easier to criticize governments and their armed forces for committing international crimes if the group has policies in place to avoid and punish such crimes. Third, factions may be able to distinguish themselves from other armed groups and thus 'get ahead' in terms of dialogue with the government or other actors. Lastly, in some circumstances, entering into such commitments will facilitate access to assistance from the international community, for example in the form of mine clearance.

---

[90] Apart from the specific case of 1977 Additional Protocol II, the law of non-international armed conflict applies when the non-state armed group is organized and there is an intense level of violence. The armed group need not exercise territorial control. The Rome Statute of the ICC does not include any reference to control of territory with regard to the threshold of violence for war crimes in non-international armed conflict. See Statute, Article 8(2)(d) and (f).

[91] Amnesty International, 'Yemen: Huthi armed group must end crackdown on human rights defenders and NGOs' MDE 31/2931/2015.

[92] Human Rights Watch, *'Being Neutral is Our Biggest Crime': Government, Vigilante, and Naxalite Abuses in India's Chhattisgarh State* (2008) 98; Human Rights Watch, *Syria: End Opposition Use of Torture, Executions* (2012).

[93] Clapham, 'Detention by Armed Groups under International Law' (2017) 93 *International Law Studies* 1.

[94] 'Geneva Call focuses on organized armed entities involved in internal armed conflicts that are primarily motivated by political goals, operate outside State control and therefore lack legal capacity to become party to relevant international treaties. These include armed groups, *de facto* governing authorities and non- or partially internationally recognized States.' See: <http://genevacall.org/who-we-are/faqs/#faq-1>.

[95] See: <http://genevacall.org/>.

[96] See Bangerter, *Internal Control: Codes of Conduct within Insurgent Armed Groups* (Small Arms Survey, 2012).

Such explicit recognition of specific obligations by the groups themselves helps to transform the debate about the human rights obligations of non-state actors. If armed groups are prepared to take on such obligations, arguments about their non-applicability under international law lose much of their force. States may fear the legitimacy that such commitments seem to imply, and international lawyers may choose to accord them no value, but from a victim's perspective such commitments may indeed be worth more than the paper they are written on.

7 CONCLUSION

This chapter suggests three challenges posed by non-state actors. First, there is a need to find ways to translate existing norms to create appropriate obligations for non-state actors. This work has started in that it is now clear that individual non-state actors will be prosecuted for certain international crimes. Furthermore, corporations and armed groups are increasingly expected to respect not only international criminal law but human rights obligations as well. The second challenge concerns the development of monitoring and accountability. As we have seen, while the jurisdictional state-centric limits of the traditional human rights courts and bodies remain, the UN and NGOs have developed their own ways of monitoring non-state actors. Lastly, it is suggested that a further challenge is to question our own assumptions about what it means to talk about human rights and who has human rights obligations. It is hoped that those readers who have reached this point may be starting to meet this last challenge.

FURTHER READING

CONSTANTINEIDES, 'Human Rights Obligations and Accountability of Armed Opposition Groups: The Practice of the UN Security Council' (2010) 4 *HR and International Legal Discourse* 89.

DE SCHUTTER, 'Towards a New Treaty on Business and Human Rights' (2015) 1 *Business and Human Rights Journal* 41.

FORTIN, *The Accountability of Armed Groups under Human Rights Law* (Oxford University Press, 2017).

HESSBRUEGGE, *Personal Self-Defense in International Law*, (Oxford University Press, 2017) esp Ch 6.

KAHANA and SCOLNICOV (eds), *Boundaries of State, Boundaries of Rights: Human Rights, Private Actors, and Positive Obligations* (Cambridge University Press, 2016).

MCBETH, *International Economic Actors and Human Rights* (Routledge, 2010).

MASTORODIMOS, *Armed Non-State Actors in International Humanitarian and Human Rights Law: Foundation and Framework of Obligations, and Rules on Accountability* (Ashgate, 2016).

MURRAY, *Human Rights Obligations of Non-State Armed Groups* (Hart, 2016).

NOWAK and JANUSZEWSKI, 'Non-State Actors and Human Rights', in Noortmann, Reinisch, and Ryngaert (eds), *Non-State Actors in International Law* (Hart, 2015).

NOWAK, *Human Rights or Global Capitalism: The Limits of Privatization* (University of Pennsylvania Press, 2017).

PETERS, *Beyond Human Rights: The Legal Status of the Individual in International Law*, (Cambridge University Press, 2016).

RODLEY, 'Non-state Actors and Human Rights', in Sheeran and Rodley (eds), *Routledge Handbook of International Human Rights Law* (Routledge, 2013).

THOMAS, *Public Rights, Private Relations* (Oxford University Press, 2015).

ZIEGLER, *Human Rights and Private Law: Privacy as Autonomy* (Hart, 2007).

USEFUL WEBSITES

Business and Human Rights Resource Centre: <http://www.business-humanrights.org/Home>

CORE : <http://corporate-responsibility.org/>

European Human Rights in Business: <http://humanrightsinbusiness.eu/>

Geneva Call: <http://www.genevacall.org/>

International Corporate Accountability Roundtable: <http://icar.ngo>

OECD Watch: <http://oecdwatch.org/>

29

TERRORISM

Martin Scheinin

SUMMARY

Terrorism, and measures to combat terrorism, pose major challenges to the international protection of human rights. Those challenges relate to both the substance of human rights norms and their scope of application. While the focus of attention has been on a number of specific human rights and the rights of those who are suspected of involvement in terrorism, everyone's human rights are, to a lesser or greater extent, affected by counter-terrorism measures. Acts of terrorism, in turn, constitute a serious form of crime and often result in the destruction of human rights.

1 INTRODUCTION

Particularly in the era after the atrocious terrorist attacks in the USA on 11 September 2001 (9/11), several waves of counter-terrorism measures have been introduced. Typically, this has occurred in the aftermath of recent terrorist incidents that have not reached the magnitude of 9/11 but still serve as tragic reminders that the threat of terrorism is real. While human rights are not always absolute, and public security may form a legitimate ground for introducing certain limitations, it would be a mistake to conclude that security generally trumps human rights. A more nuanced legal analysis is required in order to respond to the challenges of complying with human rights while at the same time effectively combating terrorism. Those challenges appear not only at the level of domestic law, where increased security has often been the justification for measures that restrict human rights. At the international level, the UN Security Council has identified international terrorism as a threat to peace and security, and resorted to its far-reaching powers under Chapter VII of the UN Charter. Shortly after 9/11 it adopted Resolution 1373, imposing a whole set of legally binding counter-terrorism obligations upon states, and established a new subsidiary body, the Counter-Terrorism Committee (CTC).[1] Another subsidiary body, the 1267 Sanctions Committee, administers a regime of listing individuals and entities for targeted sanctions for their association with al-Qaida or ISIS/ISIL/Daʻesh.[2]

---

[1] SC Res 1373 (28 September 2001).

[2] By way of SC Resolutions 1988 and 1989 (17 June 2011), the earlier combined al-Qaida and Taliban sanctions regime was split into two separate mechanisms. Resolution 1989 came to constitute the basis for listing individuals or entities associated with al-Qaida by the 1267 Sanctions Committee. On 17 December 2015, the SC adopted Resolution 2253, which expands the listing criteria to include individuals and entities supporting the Islamic State in Iraq and the Levant (ISIL).

Section 2 addresses the question of whether terrorism constitutes a violation of human rights, or whether the notion of human rights violations can only be applied to action by states. Section 3 deals with challenges to the applicability of human rights law in the fight against terrorism, particularly since 9/11. Section 4 focuses on the notion of terrorism and in particular the risks created to human rights protection by vague or over-inclusive definitions of terrorism. The main section of the chapter, Section 5, deals with some of the major challenges posed by counter-terrorism measures to substantive human rights protections. While all human rights are affected by global waves of new counter-terrorism laws and measures, some human rights have been at the forefront. Section 6 addresses the issue of listing of terrorists by the UN, which poses a challenge of an institutional nature. Is the Security Council bound by international human rights standards, and how can the sanctions resulting from its listing of terrorists be made subject to judicial or other independent review? The final section, Section 7, suggests that the unprecedented post-9/11 wave of counter-terrorism laws and measures that infringed upon human rights was unique and that, despite new terrorist incidents, governments and intergovernmental organizations must avoid overreacting and recognize that full compliance with human rights in the fight against terrorism is not only morally and legally correct but in the long term also the most effective way of combating terrorism.

2 IS TERRORISM A VIOLATION OF HUMAN RIGHTS?

Human rights are usually seen as vertical norms between the state and a private beneficiary, in most cases an individual person. However, changes in the world order, often referred to as globalization, have resulted in an awareness of the existence of other public and private actors that are equally as powerful as states in their capacity directly to affect the enjoyment of human rights.[3] Terrorism is one such challenge emanating from non-state actors. It is generally defined as deadly or otherwise serious violence against 'civilians', that is, members of the general population or a segment of it, for the purpose of spreading fear amongst the population, or to compel the authorities to do, or refrain from doing, something. Acts of terrorism adversely affect several human rights, including the right to life, the right to physical integrity, the right to health, the right to property, in cases of hostage-taking the right to liberty, and so on. Terrorism has, therefore, been rightly described as the destruction, or the antithesis, of human rights.

However, this does not necessarily mean that terrorist acts amount to a *violation* of human rights. Resolutions adopted by intergovernmental organizations in response to the threat of terrorism apply different approaches to the issue of whether the perpetrators of acts of terrorism may be described as violating human rights. Variation in the wording of such resolutions reflects different doctrinal and political positions on the question of whether only states may commit human rights violations, or whether such violations can also be attributed to non-state actors. For example, the 2005 resolution of the then UN Commission on Human Rights that originally created the mandate of the Special Rapporteur on human rights and counter-terrorism referred in its preamble to acts, methods, and practices of terrorism being 'aimed at the destruction of human rights', while deploring the occurrence of human rights 'violations'—by states—in the context of their fight against terrorism.[4] However, the same Commission on Human Rights had on other occasions adopted resolutions that speak of human rights 'violations' committed by

---

[3] See Chapter 28.   [4] CHR Res 2005/80 (21 April 2005).

terrorists.[5] The current Special Rapporteur (at the time of writing) on human rights and counter-terrorism has taken the view that the word 'violations' should be used with regard to terrorists themselves.[6]

Although the general public may feel perplexed by such inconsistencies and by the insistence of many human rights experts to reserve the notion of human rights violations to states alone, there is, in the view of the present author, good reason for maintaining the distinction between terrorism as *destruction* of human rights and a more straightforward reference to human rights *violations* by states, at least for the time being. The legally binding normative framework of human rights law is established in human rights treaties. Those treaties are clearly based on human beings as their beneficiaries and states parties as bearers of the corresponding obligations. Even where human rights norms have evolved to the status of customary law, their substance addresses the relationship between a state and an individual and it is not self-evident that such customary norms would, with the same content, be binding upon other actors beyond states. Further, all monitoring mechanisms under human rights treaties are geared towards making *states* accountable for human rights violations. When human rights treaty bodies find a human rights violation, this represents the end result of the application of the treaty in a concrete case or situation and includes an attribution of state responsibility for a breach of its obligations. Under other, non-treaty-based procedures, such as the special procedures of the Human Rights Council, a finding of a human rights violation entails a pronouncement that a state has acted in breach of its obligations under international human rights law.

No similar treaty-based or other monitoring mechanisms generally exist in respect of *non-state* actors. Hence, even assuming that the notion of human rights violations could meaningfully be applied in respect of terrorists, there are no human rights mechanisms through which the actors in question could be made accountable. To a limited extent, the development of international criminal law has come to serve as a substitute for the inability of human rights mechanisms to address the destruction of human rights by non-state actors. For instance, many of the crimes for which an individual can be prosecuted and punished under the 1998 Rome Statute of the International Criminal Court have a direct destructive effect on the enjoyment of human rights. In some instances, the Rome Statute may be applicable in respect of specific acts of terrorism.[7] In addition, several international conventions and protocols address particular forms of terrorism—such as hostage-taking, or hijacking of an airplane—and require states parties to criminalize the acts in question.[8]

---

[5] eg CHR Res 2004/44 (19 April 2004). In the preamble, the Commission expresses serious concern 'at the gross violations of human rights perpetrated by terrorists'.

[6] See Report of the Special Rapporteur on human rights and counter-terrorism (Ben Emmerson), A/HRC/20/14 (4 June 2012) para 12: 'Some still argue that terrorists, rebels and other belligerents cannot commit violations of international human rights law unless the degree of organization, territorial control and State recognition involved in a conflict situation has escalated to the level of a full-blown insurgency or internal armed conflict. However, it is a central tenet of international human rights law that it must keep pace with a changing world. Some of the gravest violations of human rights are nowadays committed by, or on behalf of, non-State actors operating in conflict situations of one kind or another, including by domestic and international terrorist networks. If international human rights law is to keep pace with these changes, the victims of acts of terrorism must now be recognized as victims of grave violations of international human rights law' (footnotes omitted).

[7] eg Rome Statute of the International Criminal Court, Art 7(1) (listing eg torture and disappearance as crimes against humanity).

[8] For a summary of the 19 major conventions and protocols dealing with terrorism, see: <http://www.un.org/en/counterterrorism/legal-instruments.shtml>.

If, in the future, a mechanism such as a World Court of Human Rights,[9] with jurisdiction over both states and non-state actors, was established, then it will make more sense to speak about terrorist organizations being responsible for human rights *violations*. Without such a mechanism, there is no forum in which, and no procedure through which, to establish a violation and attribute it to a particular non-state actor.

3 APPLICABILITY OF HUMAN RIGHTS LAW IN THE FIGHT AGAINST TERRORISM

The applicability of human rights law to the fight against terrorism has been challenged in two ways. First, some states have argued that this fight amounts to an armed conflict or that it justifies the proclamation of a state of emergency and, therefore, makes it possible to derogate from certain human rights. Second, some states have argued that international human rights law does not apply to counter-terrorism measures taken outside the state's own territory.

3.1 TIMES OF ARMED CONFLICT OR EMERGENCY

Some governments have sought to justify their unilateral exceptions to international human rights norms by referring to a 'war' against terrorism, which triggers the application of international humanitarian law.[10] Such a position is usually factually incorrect, since acts of terrorism on their own constitute neither an international armed conflict between two or more states, nor a non-international armed conflict between a state and a non-state actor capable of conducting armed hostilities. Instead, terrorism should primarily be seen as a serious form of crime and fought within a law-enforcement paradigm. Therefore, the full applicability of human rights law as the proper legal framework for the rights of terrorist suspects or other persons affected by counter-terrorism measures should be the point of departure.

It is possible, however, that for a limited period of time and in respect of a specific geographic area non-state actors referred to as 'terrorists' may be engaged in an armed conflict. The prime example is Afghanistan in late 2001, when members of al-Qaida were engaged in an armed conflict against the USA, siding with the local Taliban that constituted the de facto government of Afghanistan.[11] But even in such rare circumstances human rights law remains applicable, although it may need to be interpreted in the light of more specific rules contained in international humanitarian law.[12]

Major terrorist attacks, or another situation in which a terrorist organization manages to destabilize public order in a state, may constitute a threat to 'the life of the nation' in the sense of the derogation clauses contained in many human rights treaties. Consequently, a state may officially proclaim a state of emergency and introduce measures that derogate from certain human rights.[13] For instance, declaring a curfew for a city, introducing checkpoints on major roads, restrictions on mass demonstrations, and closer inspection of

---

[9] Kozma, Nowak, and Scheinin, *A World Court of Human Rights—Consolidated Statute and Commentary* (Neuer Wissenschaftlicher Verlag, 2010).

[10] For international humanitarian law and its relationship with human rights law, see Chapter 25.

[11] See Report of the Special Rapporteur on human rights and counter-terrorism, A/HRC/6/17/Add.3 (22 November 2007) in particular para 9.

[12] Report of the Special Rapporteur, para 7. See Chapter 25.   [13] See Chapter 5.

postal packages may, within the exigencies of the situation, constitute lawful derogations in respect of the normal scope of freedom of movement, the right to peaceful assembly, and the right to privacy as guaranteed by the International Covenant on Civil and Political Rights (ICCPR). Such measures must be temporary and their aim must be the restoration of normalcy, including the protection of human rights.

As has been elaborated by the Human Rights Committee in its General Comment on states of emergency, the power of a state to derogate from some provisions of the ICCPR does not mean a power to suspend completely the application of these provisions. Rather, any derogation is subject to the requirements of necessity and proportionality. Not only must there be full respect for non-derogable human rights, but also the rights that are subject to derogation must remain protected as far as possible and they may include non-derogable dimensions.[14]

Since the November 2015 terrorist attacks in Paris, France has maintained and periodically renewed a state of emergency and notified both the Council of Europe and the UN that it will derogate from, respectively, the ECHR and the ICCPR.[15] Under both treaties the derogations are problematic as they are quite generic and do not explain the actual measures undertaken.

3.2 EXTRATERRITORIAL APPLICABILITY OF HUMAN RIGHTS LAW

A separate, but in practice often simultaneously presented, challenge to the applicability of human rights in the counter-terrorism context is the argument that human rights obligations are territorial in scope, limited to a state's own territory where it exercises full jurisdiction. For example, governments may establish detention centres abroad and argue that constitutional guarantees or human rights treaties do not apply there.

While this argument has some support in the text of Article 2(1) ICCPR,[16] consistent practice by the Human Rights Committee demonstrates that a state must comply with the Covenant wherever it factually exercises powers that affect the enjoyment of the rights enshrined in the ICCPR.[17] Thus, even if that provision were to be taken as excluding an obligation to 'legislate' for other countries or their population,[18] this cannot form a justification to engage extraterritorially in outright human rights violations such as arbitrary detention, torture, or other cruel, inhuman, or degrading treatment.[19]

In summary, human rights law continues to apply during situations of armed conflict or a state of emergency, and it applies also to a state's conduct abroad. Closer analysis may be needed as to how the norms of human rights law and international humanitarian

---

[14] HRC, General Comment 29, HRI/GEN/1/Rev.9 (Vol 1) 234 (27 May 2008). See also Chapter 5.

[15] At the time of writing, the derogations had been extended until 1 November 2017, see <http://www.coe.int/en/web/conventions/search-on-treaties/-/conventions/treaty/005/declarations> and <https://treaties.un.org/doc/Publication/CN/2017/CN.408.2017-Eng.pdf>.

[16] ICCPR, Art 2(1) provides: 'Each State Party to the present Covenant undertakes to respect and to ensure to all individuals within its territory and subject to its jurisdiction the rights recognized in the present Covenant'.

[17] eg *Lopez Burgos v Uruguay*, CCPR/C/13/D/52/1979 (29 July 1981); *Gueye et al. v France*, CCPR/C/35/D/196/1985 (6 April 1989); HRC, Concluding observations: Israel, CCPR/C/79/Add.93 (18 August 1998); HRC, Concluding observations: Israel, CCPR/CO/78/ISR (21 August 2003); HRC, General Comment 31, HRI/GEN/1/Rev.9 (Vol I) 243 (27 May 2008) para 10. See further Chapter 6.

[18] This was the expression used in 1950 by the US representative, Mrs Eleanor Roosevelt, in the drafting of the ICCPR. See Third Periodic Report of the USA to the HRC, CCPR/C/USA/3 (28 November 2005) annex I.

[19] Report of the Special Rapporteur on human rights and counter-terrorism, A/HRC/6/17/Add.3 (22 November 2007) para 8.

law inform the proper interpretation of each other during times of armed conflict, what derogations from certain human rights norms may be permitted as necessary and proportionate within the exigencies of a state of emergency, and what the exact scope of a state's human rights obligations is when its agents are operating outside its own territory. These considerations, however, do not change the basic rule that human rights law continues to apply in any of these circumstances.

4 THE NOTION OF TERRORISM AND ITS MISUSE

'One man's freedom fighter is another man's terrorist', attributed to the British author Gerald Seymour, is an oft-heard and somewhat cynical reference to the degree of opportunism employed when using the word 'terrorism'. Although the UN has adopted a whole series of international treaties related to specific forms of terrorism, such as hostage-taking, nuclear terrorism, or terrorist bombings,[20] work towards a comprehensive convention against terrorism is still underway and not very likely to yield results soon. Governments have not been able to agree on a definition of terrorism. Differing views persist, inter alia, with regard to whether states can commit acts of terrorism and whether the quest for self-determination precludes an act from being a form of terrorism.

Particularly in the aftermath of 9/11, governments have increasingly resorted to vague and broad definitions of terrorism. While this may have been triggered partly by a desire to respond to an unspecific threat, all too often governments intended to target individuals or groups that do not deserve to be labelled as terrorist, such as political opposition groups, radical trade unions, vocal but non-violent separatist movements, indigenous peoples, religious minorities, or even human rights defenders. At least for a while, the global consensus about the imperative of combating terrorism was so compelling that authoritarian governments could get away with their repressive practices whenever they renamed their opponents as 'terrorists'.

Of particular concern to the international protection of human rights is that in the aftermath of 9/11, and in the absence of a universal and comprehensive definition of the term, repeated calls by the international community, including the Security Council, for action to combat terrorism could be understood as leaving it to individual states to define what is meant by 'terrorism'. This aggravates the potential for unintended human rights abuses and even the deliberate misuse of the term. There is a clear risk that the international community's use of the term 'terrorism', without defining it, results in the unintentional international legitimization of conduct undertaken by oppressive regimes, through delivering the message that the international community wants strong action against terrorism, however defined. Besides situations where some states resort to the deliberate misuse of the term, there is reason for concern about the more frequent adoption in domestic anti-terrorism legislation of terminology that is not properly confined to the countering of terrorism.[21]

---

[20] For a summary of the 19 major conventions and protocols dealing with terrorism, see: <http://www.un.org/en/counterterrorism/legal-instruments.shtml>.

[21] eg Reports of the Special Rapporteur on human rights and counter-terrorism, A/HRC/4/26/Add.2 (16 November 2006) paras 11–18; A/HRC/4/26/Add.3 (14 December 2006) paras 12–17; A/HRC/6/17/Add.2 (7 November 2007) paras 23–4; A/HRC/10/3/Add.2 (16 December 2008) paras 6–14; A/HRC/16/51 (22 December 2010). The last-mentioned report was the final report by the current author as the first Special Rapporteur on human rights and counter-terrorism, identifying ten areas of best practice in the fight against terrorism, including a model national law definition of terrorism (para 28).

Legal definitions of terrorism should refer to the methods used, not the underlying aim. What transforms political or ideological aspirations into terrorism is the decision by one or more morally responsible individuals to employ the morally inexcusable tactics of deadly or otherwise serious violence against 'civilians', that is, innocent bystanders. With the qualification that hostage-taking entails a threat of serious violence and should, therefore, be included in the definition, terrorism and terrorist crimes should always be defined so that such violence forms a mandatory element of the definition.[22]

Amongst Security Council resolutions calling for action against terrorism, Resolution 1566 comes closest to defining terrorism by including the following three cumulative conditions:

(1) acts, including against civilians, committed with the intention of causing death or serious bodily injury, or the taking of hostages; and

(2) irrespective of whether motivated by considerations of a political, philosophical, ideological, racial, ethnic, religious, or other similar nature, also committed for the purpose of provoking a state of terror in the general public or in a group of persons or particular persons, intimidating a population, or compelling a government or an international organization to do or to abstain from doing any act; and

(3) such acts constituting offences within the scope of and as defined in the international conventions and protocols relating to terrorism.[23]

As to the third cumulative element, that only acts constituting offences within existing terrorism-related conventions may fall under the terrorism definition, there is a qualification to be made. Where a state is responding to an international call to suppress terrorism, this third cumulative element is essential in determining what type of conduct is to be suppressed. However, states may feel compelled to implement additional counter-terrorism measures according to regional or domestic threats. Where there is evidence that a state must respond to domestic or regional terrorist threats it may, therefore, have genuine reasons to proscribe acts that fall outside the scope of offences under the existing universal terrorism-related conventions.

However, any national definitions of crimes must meet the requirement of legality, enshrined in the non-derogable provision of Article 15 ICCPR. In the absence of an internationally agreed definition of terrorism, this provision has come to serve, together with the prohibition against discrimination, as the basis for a checklist for the conformity of definitions of terrorism or terrorist crimes with human rights. Besides the obvious element of a prohibition against the retroactive application of the criminal law, Article 15 ICCPR also includes the requirements of *nullum crimen sine lege* (all elements of a crime must be defined by the law), *nulla poena sine lege* (all punishments must be defined by the law), accessibility (the law must be publicly available), precision (the line between permitted and prohibited conduct must be clear), and foreseeability (the law must enable an individual to anticipate the consequences of his or her conduct). The safest way to secure compliance with these requirements is to base any definitions of terrorist crimes on an exhaustive list of already defined serious violent crimes. Criminalization of terrorist intent as such, or circular definitions that refer back to the word 'terror', or definitions that generally cover crimes against the state, regularly fail the test under Article 15 ICCPR.

---

[22] Report of the Special Rapporteur on counter-terrorism and human rights, E/CN.4/2006/98 (28 December 2005).

[23] SC Res 1566 (8 October 2004) para 3. For the view that customary international law contains a norm defining the international crime of terrorism, at least in peacetime, see, Special Tribunal for Lebanon, Interlocutory Decision on the Applicable Law, STL-11–01/1 (16 February 2011), in particular para 85.

5 SUBSTANTIVE CHALLENGES TO HUMAN RIGHTS LAW IN THE FIGHT AGAINST TERRORISM

Governments have often felt tempted to depart from ordinary laws, normal procedures, or the fundamental rights of the individual when confronted with acts of terrorism or the threat of them. Since 9/11, unprecedented waves of special legislation or special powers have emerged all over the world, and practically all human rights have been under attack or 'reconsideration'. While most human rights are not absolute but allow for some limitations to protect public security, in many cases governments have gone beyond these permissible limitations, resulting in human rights violations. This section gives an overview of some of the most frequent areas of problematic practices.

As a graphic illustration of the effects of counter-terrorism measures upon human rights, reference can be made to a pyramid. At its top, a relatively small number of individuals—in many cases real or suspected terrorists—are subjected not only, and perhaps not at all, to lawful trial and prosecution but to grave human rights violations, such as torture or extrajudicial execution. At the bottom of the pyramid, all members of society are confronted with new interferences with some of their human rights because of counter-terrorism legislation. Typically, everyone's right to privacy is affected by new rules on interception of communications, databases and data retention, and exchange of personal information across borders.[24] Between the top and the base of the pyramid, certain groups of individuals are affected more than the average citizen by counter-terrorism measures, and many of these interferences easily escalate into violations of human rights law.[25] Immigrants or ethnic or religious minorities are often targeted by counter-terrorism measures affecting a broad range of human rights. Persons fleeing persecution in their own country are confronted with tighter controls of international borders in the name of countering terrorism, effectively preventing them from exercising their human right to leave their own country.[26] Even human rights defenders may find themselves targeted, as associations, public gatherings, and fundraising are subject to tighter control by the authorities.

By using the metaphor of a pyramid it is made clear that the perception that insistence on the importance of human rights in the fight against terrorism would seek to defend the terrorists is wrong. Everyone's human rights are affected to a lesser or greater degree by counter-terrorism measures, and keeping all counter-terrorism legislation under careful public scrutiny is the best way to ensure that measures justified as targeting the 'real terrorists' do not result in the erosion of human rights in general.

5.1 FREEDOM FROM TORTURE AND CRUEL, INHUMAN, OR DEGRADING TREATMENT

The prohibition against torture or any other form of cruel, inhuman, or degrading treatment or punishment is an absolute human right that allows for no exception, even during times of emergency.[27] Accordingly, it is very rare that states would actually legislate to

---

[24] See Report of the Special Rapporteur on human rights and counter-terrorism, A/HRC/13/37 (28 December 2009). Since the revelations by Edward Snowden in 2013, there is much wider attention to the right to privacy than before, including at the UN level.

[25] For an assessment of the gender impact of counter-terrorism, see Report of the Special Rapporteur on human rights and counter-terrorism, A/64/211 (3 August 2009).

[26] See Report of the Special Rapporteur on human rights and counter-terrorism, A/62/263 (15 August 2007).

[27] UNCAT, Arts 1 and 2(2); ICCPR, Arts 7 and 4(2). See also Chapter 9.

allow for torture. Proposals of legalized forms of torture, such as courts being empowered to issue 'torture warrants' in order to administer lawful torture in a 'ticking-bomb scenario' (which assumes that the police have captured a terrorist who refuses to reveal the location of a time bomb that will soon detonate and kill thousands of innocent people), have remained hypothetical.[28] Furthermore, governments will normally deny that extra-legal torture is used by their law enforcement or intelligence agencies or military forces. Nevertheless, the practice of subjecting terrorist suspects or their presumed associates to torture or related practices became widespread after 9/11 and many long-term patterns of using torture against terrorist suspects were also revealed.[29]

There are various ways in which many governments have ended up compromising the absolute prohibition against torture. First, denial of the extraterritorial applicability of the Convention against Torture (UNCAT) and the ICCPR has been used as an argument by the USA to cover the engagement in torture of military forces or intelligence agencies abroad. Second, some states, such as the UK, have relied on information obtained by torture 'for operational purposes' and various forms of cooperation with states that practise torture to circumvent existing rules about torture. Third, by using notions such as 'enhanced interrogation techniques' (USA) or 'moderate physical pressure' (Israel) some governments have tried to shift the barrier between what is prohibited and what is permitted. Fourth, some governments have tried to relax the standard for sending a person to another country under the risk of torture or other ill-treatment, by proposing the replacement of an absolute prohibition in situations of 'real risk' with a 'balancing test', a 'more likely than not' standard, or shifting the responsibility to the receiving state through the use of diplomatic assurances.[30] Finally, there has been a lack of investigation and accountability in cases where allegations of torture of terrorist suspects were made. In Spain, for instance, the authorities have maintained that allegations of ill-treatment are standard operating methods of terrorist organizations and, therefore, prima facie unfounded.

In a report dealing with the role of intelligence agencies and their oversight bodies in countering terrorism, the Special Rapporteur on human rights and counter-terrorism applied the principles of state responsibility and concluded that any form of collusion in torture or other prohibited treatment by intelligence agencies amounts to a human rights violation.[31]

5.2 RIGHT TO LIBERTY AND RIGHT TO A FAIR TRIAL

In the counter-terrorism context, practices breaching the prohibition against torture are often coupled with, and shielded by, secret or arbitrary detention and the denial of a fair trial. The right to liberty of the person and the right to a fair trial are guaranteed, respectively, by Articles 9 and 14 ICCPR.[32] Resort by governments to emergency powers while

---

[28] For a critique of a broad interpretation of what constitutes a 'ticking bomb' scenario, see Report of the Special Rapporteur on human rights and counter-terrorism, A/HRC/6/17/Add.4 (16 November 2007) paras 20–1.

[29] eg Amnesty International, Saudi Arabia: Assaulting Human Rights in the Name of Counter-Terrorism (22 July 2009).

[30] While many states, including Canada and the USA, demonstrate elements of this trend, the most systematic effort towards 'reconsidering' the rule of *non-refoulement* was made by the UK and several other states in *Saadi v Italy* (2009) 49 EHRR 30. The Grand Chamber of the European Court of Human Rights maintained its position that the rule is absolute.

[31] Report of the Special Rapporteur on human rights and counter-terrorism, A/HRC/10/3 (4 February 2009).   [32] See Chapter 13.

countering terrorism constitutes a major challenge to these guarantees, as neither of these provisions is on the list of non-derogable rights contained in Article 4(2) ICCPR. Only the requirement of legality in the field of criminal law of Article 15 ICCPR, including the principles of *nullum crimen sine lege* and the prohibition of retroactive criminal laws, is explicitly listed as non-derogable. However, in its General Comments on states of emergency and the right to a fair trial, the Human Rights Committee has clarified that the rights to liberty and a fair trial nevertheless include dimensions from which there can never be derogation.[33] Arbitrary detention and denial of court review over any form of detention are prohibited at all times. The fundamental principles of fair trial, including the presumption of innocence and the requirement that only a court can order a criminal punishment, must equally be respected during a state of emergency.

As a consequence, laws and practices that are applied in the name of combating terrorism may be in violation of the rights to liberty and a fair trial. Secret or unacknowledged detention automatically violates the prohibition against arbitrary detention and in some cases also amounts to prohibited disappearance of the person.[34] Even narrowly crafted provisions on *incommunicado* detention, or on delays in effective court review over the lawfulness of detention, easily result in breaches of Article 9 ICCPR. This risk can be demonstrated by a reference to Spain, which despite international criticism continues to apply a regime of *incommunicado* detention, denying terrorist suspects contact with a freely chosen lawyer during the initial period of detention. Instead, detainees are represented by a state-appointed lawyer whom they will usually not meet. The compatibility of such a regime with international human rights law is doubtful and will depend on the merits of the reasons given for denying freely chosen legal representation and the ability of the appointed lawyer to independently and effectively protect the rights of the detainee, including against any form of torture or other prohibited treatment.[35]

The US detention facility at Guantánamo Bay has become a notorious symbol of practices of long-term detention of terrorist suspects without trial. Many other states continue also to detain terrorist suspects or their presumed associates without trial or even any criminal charges. Hence, the first fundamental dimension of the right to a fair trial, access to a court, is denied and as a consequence the persons concerned cannot exercise any of their fair trial rights. Some governments, including the US administration, have referred to the war paradigm as the framework for their counter-terrorism measures, seeking to justify long-term detention without trial as long as the 'war on terror' or 'war against al-Qaida' continues. Under a law-enforcement paradigm that treats terrorism as a serious crime, however, it is evident that the purpose of detaining terrorist suspects must be the investigation of their alleged crimes in preparation of a criminal trial.

Even in countries in which terrorist suspects *are* brought before a court for trial, there may be serious deviations from international human rights standards. Through special legislation, terrorism cases may be dealt with by military or special courts. The trying of civilians by a military court as such is problematic under the right to a fair trial. Moreover, outright violations of Article 14 ICCPR may result from the lack of independence and impartiality of the judges of a military or special court and from undue interference by

---

[33] HRC, General Comment 29, in particular paras 12–16; HRC, General Comment 32, HRI/GEN/1/Rev.9 (Vol 1) 248 (27 May 2008) in particular para 6; HRC, General Comment 35, CCPR/C/GC/35 (16 December 2014) paras 65–67.

[34] See International Convention for the Protection of All Persons from Enforced Disappearance, Art 2.

[35] See Report of the Special Rapporteur on counter-terrorism and human rights, A/HRC/10/3/Add.2 (16 December 2008).

the executive in deciding that a case will be tried by a military or special court, in the worst cases even after acquittal by an ordinary court. In addition, trials before military or special courts may involve restrictions on the rights of the defence, including in respect of secret evidence, denial of full communication between client and counsel, and breaches of the principle of equality of arms, for instance through restrictions on access by the defence to exculpatory evidence. As to the last-mentioned example, terrorist trials often involve a huge amount of primary material such as transcripts of intercepted telephone calls. If only the prosecution has access to the full records and if it presents to the court only a carefully selected sample, this may result in bias against the defence who may wish to contest the value of the excerpts as evidence by putting them into a broader context. However, this may only be possible if access to exculpatory evidence not presented by the prosecution to the court is provided to the defence, under terms that allow its proper examination.

A general solution to the challenges related to the detention and trial of terrorist suspects can be identified in the 'principle of normalcy'. Terrorism should be treated as a serious form of crime, which is subject to ordinary laws on criminal procedure and dealt with by ordinary courts. This is a recommended course of action for avoiding the temptation to engage in practices that violate international human rights law.[36]

5.3 RIGHT TO NON-DISCRIMINATION

As demonstrated by the pyramid metaphor referred to at the beginning of Section 5, not everyone's human rights are equally affected by counter-terrorism measures. An alarming trend in the post-9/11 era has been the increased use of 'terrorist profiling' as a significant component of states' counter-terrorism efforts.[37] Profiling has been applied, for instance, in the context of data-mining initiatives, that is, searches of personal data sets according to presumed characteristics of suspects. But it also occurs in less explicit forms. For example, law-enforcement agents often rely on sets of physical characteristics when deciding whom to stop and search for counter-terrorism purposes. Even when there are no explicit instructions to target specific groups, stop-and-search powers may disproportionately affect persons of a certain ethnic or religious appearance.

When law-enforcement agents use broad profiles that reflect unexamined generalizations, their practices may constitute disproportionate interferences with human rights. In particular, profiling based on stereotypical assumptions that persons of a certain 'race', national or ethnic origin, or religion are particularly likely to be involved in terrorism may lead to practices that are incompatible with the principle of non-discrimination. Such profiling is also ineffective. An illustrative case is the so-called *Rasterfahndung* programme, initiated by the German authorities in the wake of 9/11 to identify terrorist 'sleepers'. The German police forces collected personal records of several million individuals from public and private databases. The criteria for the search included: being male, age 18–40, current or former student, Muslim denomination, and a link through birth or nationality to one of several specified countries with a predominantly Muslim population. Approximately 32,000 persons were identified as potential terrorist sleepers and more closely examined.

---

[36] For a systematic assessment of the right to a fair trial in the context of countering terrorism, see Report of the Special Rapporteur on counter-terrorism and human rights, A/63/223 (6 August 2008). For the 'principle of normalcy' as one element of best practice in countering terrorism, see Report of the Special Rapporteur on counter-terrorism and human rights, A/HRC/16/51 (22 December 2010) paras 17–21.

[37] Report of the Special Rapporteur on human rights and counter-terrorism, A/HRC/4/26 (29 January 2007).

In none of these cases did the *Rasterfahndung* lead to bringing criminal charges for terrorism-related offences. The programme was eventually found to be unconstitutional by the German Constitutional Court.[38]

In the UK, police forces have relied on profiles based on a person's ethnic and/or religious appearance when conducting stops, document checks, or searches for counter-terrorism purposes. Accordingly, stops and searches under section 44 of the Terrorism Act 2000, which authorized the police in designated areas to stop and search people without having to show reasonable suspicion, have been shown disproportionately to affect ethnic minorities, in particular Asian and black persons.[39]

At worst, terrorist profiling is not only legally and morally wrong and ineffective, it may even be counterproductive. Terrorist organizations can easily evade the profiles employed by the authorities and adjust their tactics accordingly, for instance when recruiting suicide bombers and choosing them for a mission. Profiling may also have negative effects on the targeted minorities. Their stigmatization may result in a feeling of alienation and end up facilitating recruitment to terrorism from within the group.

The Special Rapporteur on human rights and counter-terrorism has, therefore, recommended abandonment of profiling based on group characteristics and its replacement with a combination of universal controls affecting everyone equally, genuinely random searches coupled with proper monitoring to secure that they do not transform into unregulated de facto targeting of specific groups, and profiling based on individual conduct instead of group membership.[40]

5.4 OTHER HUMAN RIGHTS

The examples given in Section 5.3 all relate to well-known and widely discussed human rights impacts of counter-terrorism measures. However, it is important to understand that all human rights are affected, to a greater or lesser extent, and in respect of a smaller or larger group of individuals, by counter-terrorism measures.

An under-explored issue relates to the effect of counter-terrorism measures upon economic, social, and cultural rights.[41] While the equal status, indivisibility, and interdependence of all human rights has been broadly acknowledged,[42] the discourse on human rights and counter-terrorism has tended to focus on civil and political rights. Even among the UN human rights treaty bodies, the Human Rights Committee and the Committee against Torture have been much more systematic than the other treaty bodies in questioning and assessing states' compliance with human rights while countering terrorism. The Committee on Economic, Social and Cultural Rights has very rarely given attention to counter-terrorism measures.

A prime example that demonstrates the need for a systematic assessment is the construction of a wall or barrier into the Occupied Palestinian Territory (OPT) by Israel, the occupying power. Explained as a security measure against the risk of suicide terrorists trying to enter Israel or to attack Israeli settlements inside the OPT, the wall or barrier has resulted not only in the construction of a major physical barrier between Israel and the

---

[38] Bundesverfassungsgericht, 1 BvR 518/02, 4 April 2006.

[39] Report of the Special Rapporteur on human rights and counter-terrorism, A/HRC/4/26 (29 January 2007) para 37. With regard to more recent years, see eg Home Office, *Operation of Police Powers under TA 2000 and Subsequent Legislation* (March 2016) Table S.02 and equivalent tables from previous years,

[40] Report of the Special Rapporteur, paras 83–9.

[41] See Report of the Special Rapporteur on human rights and counter-terrorism, A/HRC/6/17 (21 November 2007).   [42] See Chapter 7.

OPT but also in a whole architecture of associated obstacles, barriers, walls, checkpoints, and so on within the OPT.[43] As a consequence, Palestinian individuals find their everyday life devastated through multiple forms of hardship, many of which are directly related to their enjoyment of economic, social, and cultural rights. For instance, access to hospitals, schools, water resources, olive groves, and other places of work are all adversely affected and in many cases to a degree that amounts to a violation of, respectively, the rights to health, education, water, an adequate standard of living, and work. In its advisory opinion on the Israeli wall, the International Court of Justice concluded that Israel was in breach of international law, including of the International Covenant on Economic, Social and Cultural Rights, through the construction of the wall.[44]

The case of the Israeli wall illustrates that economic, social, and cultural rights must also be taken into account when societies design their security infrastructure, including their measures against terrorism. But economic, social, and cultural rights also have another important role in ensuring responses to terrorism conform to human rights. Violations of human rights in general have been identified in the UN Global Counter-Terrorism Strategy as one of the conditions conducive to the spread of terrorism.[45] Amongst the other identified conducive conditions there are many that have direct links with economic, social, and cultural rights. Hence, long-term work for the promotion of the full enjoyment of economic, social, and cultural rights can be seen as an important element in building societies without terrorism.[46]

6 AN INSTITUTIONAL CHALLENGE: TERRORIST LISTING BY THE SECURITY COUNCIL

While states are responsible for many violations of human rights in the name of countering terrorism, the listing of terrorist individuals or entities is one of the rare occasions where the UN itself engages in action that has a direct effect upon individuals. Therefore, the question of the UN's compliance with human rights arises.[47]

In Resolution 1373, the Security Council identified the terrorist attacks of 9/11, 'like any act of international terrorism', as a threat to international peace and security. Acting under Chapter VII of the UN Charter, it imposed upon all member states a range of legally binding obligations to counter terrorism, including an obligation to report on their measures to a new body, the CTC. This Committee is composed of the diplomatic representatives of the 15 states that at any given time serve as members of the Security Council.

Despite its fundamental role in UN action against terrorism, Resolution 1373 did not result in the blacklisting of terrorists by the UN. The UN is not involved in any general listing of terrorists. Instead, the listing system in place is based on the earlier Security Council Resolution 1267 of 1999 and is today limited to individuals or entities belonging

---

[43] See Report of the Special Rapporteur on human rights and counter-terrorism, A/HRC/6/17/Add.4 (16 November 2007).

[44] *Legal Consequences of the Construction of a Wall in the Occupied Palestinian Territories* (Advisory Opinion) [2004] ICJ Rep 136, para 116.   [45] GA Res 60/288 (20 September 2006).

[46] For a broader discussion on the role of economic, social, and cultural rights in the context of countering terrorism, see the Report of the Special Rapporteur on human rights and counter-terrorism, A/HRC/6/17 (21 November 2007).

[47] See Report of the Special Rapporteur on human rights and counter-terrorism, A/65/258 (6 August 2010). See also Chapter 28.

to or associated with al-Qaida or ISIS/ISIL/Daesh. The list is maintained by a separate Security Council committee, the 1267 Sanctions Committee, and it includes over 250 individuals and 75 entities.[48] As Resolution 1267 was also adopted under Chapter VII of the UN Charter, the implementation of the resolution and the listing decisions by the 1267 Committee are often perceived by states as Charter obligations that under Article 103 UN Charter trump competing treaty obligations, including those emanating from human rights treaties. Article 103 proclaims the primacy of Charter obligations over any other agreement to which a state is party. As a consequence, many governments take the view that national authorities enjoy no discretion whatsoever in implementing the sanctions but must without hesitation freeze the assets, and prevent international travel, of any person put on the 1267 terrorist list. Some governments, as well as many scholars and human rights experts, however, argue that as long as there is no effective independent review of listing and delisting decisions at the UN level, member states must secure such review in respect of their own measures implementing the UN-imposed sanctions.[49]

Against this background it is natural that there is persistent concern that the Security Council itself must comply with human rights when listing or delisting persons. Several rounds of improvement have already been made, including Security Council Resolution 1822 of 2008, which introduced a duty to inform the person of the reasons for his or her placement on the list, as well as a mandatory two-year review by the 1267 Committee of all the entries in the list. However, these piecemeal improvements did not remedy the main shortcomings of the 1267 listing procedure.

In October 2008, the Human Rights Committee concluded that Belgium had violated Articles 17 (right to privacy) and 12 (freedom of movement) ICCPR in respect of a Belgian couple, because it had initiated their listing as terrorists by the 1267 Committee, and was subsequently unable to have them delisted even though no case had been proven against them.[50] On 20 July 2009, the 1267 Committee finally removed the couple from its list. This decision by the 1267 Committee is indicative of a broader acknowledgement that there is a need for judicial or other independent review of terrorist listing. Although Belgium was unable to reach a delisting decision earlier, it managed to obtain consensus within the 1267 Committee, after the Human Rights Committee had concluded that because it initiated the listing, Belgium was responsible for a human rights violation. The subsequent decision to delist these individuals can be seen as a recognition of the Committee's possibility to conduct indirect quasi-judicial review over the consequences of the listing by the Security Council, as long as a state that has ratified the Optional Protocol to the ICCPR can be shown to have had a strong enough role in initiating (or implementing) the listing.

Further reforms have been introduced through subsequent Security Council Resolutions.[51] Yet listing decisions are still taken by a political body composed of diplomatic representatives of the 15 member states of the Security Council. States do not

---

[48] See list established and maintained by the 1267 Committee with respect to individuals, groups, undertakings and other entities associated with ISIL (Daesh) or Al-Qaida, available at: <https://www.un.org/sc/suborg/en/sanctions/1267/aq_sanctions_list>.

[49] See Report of the Special Rapporteur on human rights and counter-terrorism, A/61/267 (16 August 2006) in particular para 39. See also *Nada v Switzerland* (2013) 56 EHRR 18, in particular para 212 (where the Court 'further finds that there was nothing in the Security Council resolutions to prevent the Swiss authorities from introducing mechanisms to verify the measures taken at national level pursuant to those resolutions') and *Al-Dulimi and Montana Management Inc. v Switzerland*, App no 5809/08, Judgment of 21 June 2016.

[50] *Sayadi and Vinck v Belgium*, CCPR/C/94/D/1472/2006 (29 December 2008).

[51] See in particular SC Res 1989 (17 June 2011) and SC Res 2083 (17 December 2012). The latest resolution is SC Res 2253 (17 December 2015).

necessarily disclose any real evidence for a listing proposal even to each other but may be acting on the basis of secret intelligence information, even if a 'statement of case' is nowadays required.[52] An independent delisting Ombudsperson acts upon requests by listed individuals or entities and may recommend delisting.[53] Remarkably, the delisting recommendation by the Ombudsperson becomes a decision to delist by default, unless either the 1267 Committee by consensus decides to retain the listing or any member state of the Security Council refers the case to the full Security Council where normal voting rules apply, so that delisting will require a qualified majority and can be blocked by any of the five permanent members.[54] Independently of delisting requests sent to the Ombudsperson, the 1267 Committee will review every entry on the list every three years.[55]

Despite the gradual improvements towards transparency and adequate procedure, the terrorist listing procedure of the 1267 Committee fails to meet the requirements of a 'fair and clear procedure', a notion used to describe the level of procedural guarantees that one can expect an intergovernmental organization to deliver, not to speak of full compliance with the right to a fair trial, as would be required if a state were to impose criminal sanctions. Hence, calls for judicial review, either of the listing itself at the UN level or of the implementation of the sanctions at the national (or EU) level, are still vocal.

Important indications of this broad trend of calling for judicial review are the *Kadi* ruling by the European Court of Justice, quashing EU-level implementation of sanctions imposed by the 1267 Committee due to insufficient procedural guarantees,[56] the subsequent *Nada* ruling by the European Court of Human Rights,[57] and a UN General Assembly resolution adopted in 2008, urging states 'while ensuring full compliance with their international obligations', to include 'adequate human rights guarantees' in their national procedures for the listing of terrorist individuals and entities.[58] This statement should be seen as an appeal to states to implement UN-imposed sanctions against terrorists not blindly but subject to adequate human rights guarantees. Equally importantly, since 2008 the Security Council itself has repeatedly acknowledged that the UN should comply with human rights when listing individuals.[59]

7 CONCLUSION: WILL THE PENDULUM BE SWINGING BACK AND FORTH?

The terrorist acts of 9/11 led to the worst backlash in the international protection of human rights since the inclusion of the notion of human rights in the UN Charter, in the aftermath of the Second World War. In this sense, terrorism can be seen as the antithesis

---

[52] SC Res 2083 (17 December 2012), para 11.   [53] SC Res 2083, para 19.

[54] SC Res 2083, para 21.   [55] SC Res 2083, para 42.

[56] Joined Cases C-402/05 P and C-415/05 P, *Kadi and Al Barakaat International Foundation v Council of the European Union* [2008] ECR I-6351. The 1267 Committee decided on 5 October 2012 to delist Mr Kadi, after he had been subject to a travel ban and assets freeze for 11 years. In a new ruling of 18 July 2013, the European Court of Justice affirmed the rationale of its own earlier judgment.   [57] (2013) 56 EHRR 18.

[58] GA Res 63/185 (3 March 2009) para 19. The resolution has been reaffirmed several times.

[59] See SC Res 1822 (30 June 2008) ('Reaffirming the need to combat by all means, in accordance with the Charter of the United Nations and international law, including applicable international human rights, refugee, and humanitarian law, threats to international peace and security caused by terrorist acts, stressing in this regard the important role the United Nations plays in leading and coordinating this effort').

of human rights. Still, one needs to remember that what constituted the backlash was the reaction and overreaction by governments that introduced a whole wave of retrogressive measures in respect of human rights in the aftermath of 9/11. Furthermore, the terrorist attacks were more a triggering cause than a structural one. Many of the human-rights-hostile practices employed by governments in the name of countering terrorism existed prior to 2001 in some parts of the world, albeit that those practices have now become much more widespread.

Two things have been disheartening in the backlash. First, the ease with which governments that were known as champions of the international concern for human rights changed course and became generators of legal arguments and doctrines that seek to deny the applicability or substantive contents of human rights law when they engage in measures against terrorism. Such constructions try to turn the clock back by 70 years, to times when human rights were not yet recognized as a matter of concern for the international community. Even worse, some Western governments, such as the G.W. Bush administration of the USA, appeared at times to try to turn the clock back by 200 years, to times before Immanuel Kant, by reducing a human person to a mere means, instead of treating every individual always as an end. Mass murderers are recognized as an end in the traditional criminal law system, which aims at establishing the facts, the culpability of the person, and the punishment. But suspected terrorists—or even persons only suspected of knowing something of relevance—are reduced to a means when they are tortured to extract information, without any intention to bring them before a court for their possible crimes. Whether a government itself tortures or whether it is complicit in creating an international industry of torture for the production of intelligence information does not matter.

The second disheartening development is that even if the damage to human rights triggered by the terrorist acts of 9/11 was acknowledged and the process of repairs started, any new incidents of terrorism tend to cause the pendulum to swing back again. For instance, in the USA, important steps have been taken to depart from earlier human-rights-hostile practices, but those lessons learned are not necessarily permanent. Within the UN Security Council and other important engines of counter-terrorism measures, it was gradually understood that violating human rights in the name of countering terrorism is not only wrong in legal and moral terms but also counterproductive for any effective strategy against terrorism, as respect for, and promotion of, human rights are acknowledged as important elements in building societies without terrorism. Still, also at the UN level a further terrorist attack may trigger a response that reverses what was gradually achieved towards better respect for the rule of law.[60]

The main lesson from the more than 15 years since 9/11 is that human rights voices matter, as public warnings, as constructive critiques, and as a strategic perspective to a successful fight against terrorism. That said, every silver lining has its cloud, in this case meaning that there are no permanent victories, as any new act of terrorism will easily trigger responses that are incompatible with human rights.

---

[60] Reference is made to the hasty and unanimous adoption of SC Res 2178 (24 September 2015) on foreign terrorist fighters. For the current author's critique of the resolution, see <https://www.justsecurity.org/15407/post-911-panic-security-council-resolution-foreign-terrorist-fighters-scheinin/>.

FURTHER READING

CAMERON, 'UN Targeted Sanctions, Legal Safeguards and the European Convention on Human Rights' (2003) 72 *NJIL* 159.

DOSWALD-BECK, *Human Rights in Times of Conflict and Terrorism* (Oxford University Press, 2011).

DUFFY, *The 'War on Terror' and the Framework of International Law* (Cambridge University Press, 2005).

FARER, *Confronting Global Terrorism and American Neo-Conservativism: The Framework of a Liberal Grand Strategy* (Oxford University Press, 2008).

INTERNATIONAL COMMISSION OF JURISTS, *Assessing Damage, Urging Action: Report of the Eminent Jurists Panel on Terrorism, Counter-terrorism and Human Rights* (Geneva, 2009).

JENKINS, HENRIKSEN and JACOBSEN (eds), *The Long Decade: How 9/11 Has Changed the Law* (Oxford University Press, 2013).

MOECKLI, *Human Rights and Non-discrimination in the 'War on Terror'* (Oxford University Press, 2008).

SAUL, *Defining Terrorism in International Law* (Oxford University Press, 2006).

SAUL (ed), *Research Handbook on International Law and Terrorism* (Edward Elgar Publishing, 2014).

UNITED NATIONS, Reports by the UN Special Rapporteur on the promotion and protection of human rights and fundamental freedoms while countering terrorism.

USEFUL WEBSITES

Reports by the UN Special Rapporteur on human rights and counter-terrorism: <http://www.ohchr.org/EN/Issues/Terrorism/Pages/Annual.aspx>

UN website on countering terrorism: <http://www.un.org/en/counterterrorism/index.shtml>

Website on prevention of terrorism by the UN Office on Drugs and Crime: <http://www.unodc.org/unodc/en/terrorism/index.html>

30

POVERTY

Stephen P Marks

SUMMARY

This chapter addresses the challenge posed by poverty to the protection of human rights. Human rights define the entitlements considered necessary for a life of dignity in society, including the right to an adequate standard of living, that is, the right to be free from poverty. At this high level of abstraction, the elimination of poverty and realization of human rights are similar in that both clarify what needs to be done so that all human beings enjoy minimal standards of a decent existence. The context for this inquiry is the consensus regarding the imperative of poverty reduction and human rights realization, and the contested interpretations of the relationship between the two. This context will be set out first, followed by a discussion of how international discourses on human rights and poverty diverge and, finally, how they converge.

1 INTRODUCTION

Human rights have emerged in national and international legal systems as a means of enhancing the lives of people in a position to claim their rights. But what do these rights mean for the one-fifth of humanity who live in misery and lack the basic necessities in terms of income, health, education, food, and employment? Without a minimal level of social and economic status, the extremely poor might be expected to see human rights as a luxury beyond their reach. For them the elimination of poverty is likely to be perceived as the highest priority in the human rights struggle.

There are deep political and even ideological issues involved in the relationship between the elimination of poverty and the struggle for human rights. It has been argued that 'the present global institutional order is foreseeably associated with such massive incidence of avoidable severe poverty, its (uncompensated) imposition manifests an on-going human rights violation—arguably the largest such violation ever committed in human history'.[1] Others would rely on the self-correcting and wealth-generating power of markets, such

---

[1] Pogge, 'Severe Poverty as a Human Rights Violation' in Pogge (ed), *Freedom from Poverty as a Human Right: Who Owes What to the Very Poor?* (OUP, 2007) 52. See also Pogge, 'Are We Violating the Human Rights of the World's Poor' (2011) 14 *Yale HR and Development LJ* 1; Pogge, 'Are We Violating the Human Rights of the World's Poor? Responses to Four Critics' (2014) 17 *Yale HR and Development LJ* 74.

as those who claim that most of the credit for the success in recent decades in reducing poverty 'must go to capitalism and free trade, for they enable economies to grow—and it was growth, principally that has eased destitution'.[2] Others have argued that the development of a middle class who exercise economic freedoms under competitive capitalism without state interference should come first and then political freedom and democracy will follow. A survey of attitudes of lower and middle class people in 13 countries confirms the hypothesis that '[e]conomic well-being is linked with support for democracy'[3] and '[m]iddle-class respondents often assign a higher priority to free speech than do those in the lower income group'.[4] Although it may appear tautological, the survey found that 'lower-income respondents were more likely than their wealthier fellow citizens to prioritize avoiding hunger and poverty'.[5] Are the poor indifferent to human rights beyond the economic and social rights that enhance their economic well-being? Is the way out of poverty to provide economic freedoms under competitive capitalism and thus favour the classes that benefit most from economic growth on the assumption that it is on those classes that the affirmation of human rights must rely and that a rising tide (middle- and upper-class income) lifts all boats (including the poor)? Or is it the responsibility of the state to redistribute wealth so as to eliminate poverty and guarantee all human rights—including economic and social rights—to all, including the poor?

This chapter addresses the relationship between human rights and models of development in response to these questions. If, as the classical liberal model might suggest, human rights are a luxury that comes to people who have risen out of poverty, then it is likely to be limited to what Karl Marx called 'bourgeois freedoms'—those that protect the interests of the middle class and the rich against those of the poor.[6] The first challenge regarding the relationship between poverty and human rights is, therefore, to explore whether, and to what extent, human rights is a regime that is hostile to the interests of the poor. Such would be the case if a narrow interpretation of human rights consisting exclusively of negative freedoms (civil and political rights) were used, rather than the nearly universally accepted understanding of human rights as integrating civil, cultural, economic, political, and social rights.[7] In other words, if human rights were limited to those rights that protect the interests and wealth of people with resources, then the poor would rightfully be suspicious of them.

While the narrow understanding may still have proponents today (as will be seen), the more widely accepted understanding of human rights is that they not only embrace economic, social, and cultural dimensions but also empower the poor in their struggle against the obstacles to their liberation from misery. As the former Secretary-General of Amnesty International put it, '[h]uman rights are claims that the weak advance to hold the powerful accountable, and that is why poverty is first and foremost about rights'.[8] From this

---

[2] 'Towards the End of Poverty', *The Economist* (1 June 2013) 11.

[3] Pew Global Attitudes Project, *The Global Middle Class: Views on Democracy, Religion, Values, and Life Satisfaction in Emerging Nations* (Pew Research Center, 2009) 2. The countries in the study were Argentina, Brazil, Bulgaria, Chile, Egypt, India, Malaysia, Mexico, Poland, Russia, South Africa, Ukraine, and Venezuela. A World Bank study questions some of the methods of this study: Lopez-Calva, Rigolini, and Torche, 'Is There Such Thing as Middle Class Values? Class Differences, Values and Political Orientations in Latin America', World Bank Policy Research Working Paper 5874 (November 2011) 4.

[4] *The Global Middle Class*, 14.   [5] *The Global Middle Class*, 15.

[6] *Marx & Engels Collected Works—Vol. 3* (International Publishers, 1975) 164. ('None of the so-called rights of man, therefore, goes beyond the egoistic individual, beyond the individual as a member of bourgeois society, withdrawn into his private interests and separated from the community.')

[7] The equal importance to these categories of rights was reaffirmed in the Vienna Declaration and Programme of Action, A/CONF.157/23 (25 June 1993) para 5; World Summit outcome document, GA Res 60/1 (24 October 2005) para 9. See Marks, 'The Past and Future of the Separation of Human Rights into Categories' (2009) 24 *Maryland JIL* 208.

[8] Khan, *The Unheard Truth: Poverty and Human Rights* (WW Norton, 2009) 21.

perspective—and this is the real challenge raised by this chapter—poverty is a human rights issue in terms of ends and means. The *end* of human rights is to ensure for all—rich and poor—equal rights, including those called 'economic, social, and cultural rights', among which is, in the words of Article 25 of the Universal Declaration of Human Rights (UDHR), the right of everyone 'to a standard of living adequate for the health and well-being of himself and of his family, including food, clothing, housing and medical care and necessary social services, and the right to security in the event of unemployment, sickness, disability, widowhood, old age or other lack of livelihood in circumstances beyond his control.' The *means* of human rights—awareness by rights-holders through learning and accountability of duty-bearers through laws, policies, and enforcement mechanisms—provide anti-poverty campaigns tools for mobilization and action. Unless and until these ends and means guide popular awareness and the functioning of institutions, poverty will pose a serious challenge to the protection, and perhaps the very concept, of human rights.

2 POVERTY, HUMAN RIGHTS, AND SOCIAL JUSTICE

At the outset, it is necessary to define the meaning of 'poverty' and explore its relationship to human rights and social justice.

2.1 POVERTY AND HUMAN RIGHTS

Development practitioners and scholars distinguish between extreme (or absolute) poverty and relative poverty. Extreme poverty is measured by economists as the number of people living on an income below a certain threshold, called the 'poverty headcount ratio' and set by the World Bank in 2015 at US$1.90 per day, in 2011 PPP (Purchasing Power Parity) terms. This threshold is the average of the national poverty lines in the poorest 15 countries. According to 2016 estimates, this number declined from 1.851 billion people (35 per cent of the world population) in 1990 to 767 million (10.7 per cent) in 2013. The World Bank estimates that 'global extreme poverty continues to fall rapidly', considering that 'around 100 million people moved out of extreme poverty from 2012 to 2013, and since 1990, nearly 1.1 billion people have escaped extreme poverty'.[9]

The World Bank Group President Jim Yong Kim announced in April 2013 that '[w]e are at an auspicious moment in history when the successes of past decades and an increasingly favourable economic outlook combine to give developing countries a chance—for the first time ever—to end extreme poverty within a generation.'[10] Thus, according to Kim, this goal can be reached by 2030 if sustained high growth is maintained in South Asia and Sub-Saharan Africa, inequality is curbed primarily through job creation, and potential new food, fuel, or financial crises and climatic disasters are averted or mitigated. The idea of ending poverty by 2030 has been supported by economists[11] and was formally adopted as part of the UN 2030 Agenda for Sustainable Development in 2015 as Sustainable Development Goal No 1: 'By 2030, eradicate extreme poverty for all people everywhere'.[12]

---

[9] World Bank, 'Poverty', available at: <http://povertydata.worldbank.org/poverty/home>.

[10] World Bank, 'World Bank Group President Calls for a World Free of Poverty', Press Release (2 April 2013).

[11] eg Towards the end of poverty, 22–4.

[12] GA Res 70/1 (25 September 2015). Although the wording of SDG 1 adds 'currently measured as people living on less than $1.25 a day,' the World Bank is using the updated international poverty line of US$1.90 a day per person. World Bank, *World Development Indicators 2016*, 1, available at: <http://dx.doi.org/10.1596/978-1-4648-0683-4>.

While absolute poverty lines set a floor such as the current threshold of US$1.90 used by the World Bank, relative poverty lines measure, for example, the bottom 10 per cent of the income distribution or a certain fraction of median income, such as the 40th percentile. The Human Poverty Index ranks countries according to an index of several factors, which differ between developing and developed countries. While calculating the number of people living on extremely low income is a convenient way of identifying poverty, it is widely acknowledged that the definition of poverty is broader than income data. As the Nobel prize-winning economist Amartya Sen put it, '[the] identification of poverty with low income is well established, but there is, by now, quite a substantial literature on its inadequacies'.[13] In addition to low income, Sen identifies four types of contingencies that determine variations in the impact of poverty: individual physical characteristics, environmental conditions, social conditions, and behavioural expectations within the community.[14] These characteristics vary by individual, family, and society such that a given level of income may result in one person living in poverty in terms of their capability to lead a life they value, compared to another with the same income but whose 'functionings' (the term used by Sen for what you actually do) provide a higher level of happiness or well-being. In sum, 'real poverty (in terms of capability deprivation) can easily be much more intense than we can deduce from income data'.[15]

Building on this challenge to monetary income as a sufficient measure of poverty, several alternative tools of measurement have been proposed, such as the *World Happiness Report* (first published in 2012), which 'provides a broader indicator of human welfare than do measures of income, poverty, health, education, and good government viewed separately'.[16] Another is the UN Development Programme's (UNDP) *Human Development Report*, launched in 1990 and containing, since 2009, a Human Development Index (HDI), followed in 2010 by an Inequality-adjusted Human Development Index (IHDI), as well as the Multidimensional Poverty Index (MPI), developed in cooperation with the Oxford Poverty and Human Development Initiative (OPHI).[17] The MPI uses the same three dimensions as the HDI (health, education, and standard of living). However, instead of life expectancy at birth as the indicator of health, mean years and expected years of schooling as the indicator of education, and gross national income per capita as the indicator of standard of living, the MPI uses ten indicators covering, respectively, nutrition and child mortality; years of schooling and school attendance; and a combination of access to electricity, drinking water, and improved sanitation, use of cooking fuel, floor of the home, and assets relating to information, mobility, and livelihood.[18] The MPI thus defines the poor as those suffering deprivations which poor households typically face. According to UNDP, in 2015 'almost 1.5 billion people in the 101 developing countries covered by the MPI—about 29 percent of their population—live in multidimensional poverty—that is, with at least 33 percent of the indicators reflecting acute deprivation in health, education and standard of living'.[19]

---

[13] Sen, *The Idea of Justice* (Allen Lane, 2009) 254.   [14] Sen (2009), 255–6.   [15] Sen (2009), 256.

[16] Helliwell, Layard, and Sachs (eds), *World Happiness Report 2016 Update*, Introduction, available at: <http://worldhappiness.report/wp-content/uploads/sites/2/2016/03/HR-V1_web.pdf>.

[17] OPHI, Global Multidimensional Poverty Index, available at: <http://www.ophi.org.uk/multidimensional-poverty-index/>.

[18] UNDP, *Human Development Report 2015: Work for Human Development*, Technical Notes, 9, available at: <http://hdr.undp.org/sites/default/files/hdr2015_technical_notes.pdf>.

[19] UNDP, MPI, available at: <http://hdr.undp.org/en/content/multidimensional-poverty-index-mpi>. See also UNDP, 'Human Development Report 2016' (2016) 54. The total population living in poverty is sometimes called 'the bottom billion': Collier, *The Bottom Billion: Why the Poorest Countries Are Failing and What Can Be Done About It* (OUP, 2008).

UN human rights bodies, in particular the Committee on Economic, Social and Cultural Rights, share the critique of an income-based definition of poverty. In its statement on poverty, the Committee endorsed a 'multi-dimensional understanding of poverty', which reflects the indivisible and interdependent nature of all human rights' and defined poverty 'as a human condition characterized by sustained or chronic deprivation of the resources, capabilities, choices, security and power necessary for the enjoyment of an adequate standard of living'.[20]

Whether measured in relative or absolute terms or in terms of capabilities, the problem of global poverty is staggering in its magnitude and affects both developing and developed countries. It has attracted the attention of the human rights community for decades, if not centuries. For Jean-Jacques Rousseau it was 'plainly contrary to the law of nature . . . that the privileged few should gorge themselves with superfluities, while the starving multitude are in want of the bare necessities of life'.[21]

In preparation for the adoption in 1948 of the UDHR, the UN Educational, Scientific and Cultural Organization (UNESCO) convened a Committee on the Philosophical Principles of the Rights of Man to reflect on an eventual declaration of human rights, which stated, 'one group of rights is essentially connected with the provision of means of subsistence, through [one's] own efforts or, where they are insufficient, through the resources of society'.[22] In 1968, on the occasion of the twentieth anniversary of the UDHR, the International Conference on Human Rights proclaimed that '[t]he widening gap between the economically developed and developing countries impedes the realization of human rights in the international community'.[23] Thus, the basic idea that poverty and underdevelopment are human rights concerns has been part of the rhetoric of human rights since the founding of the contemporary human rights movement and even before. The UN High Commissioner for Human Rights declared in 1998 that extreme poverty was the worst violation of human rights.[24] The issue had already been raised by the Commission on Human Rights, which in 1990 requested its Sub-Commission to consider the relationship between human rights and poverty.[25] The Sub-Commission appointed a Special Rapporteur on human rights and extreme poverty, whose report was published in 1996.[26] In a related development, the High Commissioner published in 2001 a document setting out basic principles of a human rights approach to: (1) the process of formulating a poverty reduction strategy; (2) determining the content of a poverty reduction strategy; and (3) guiding the monitoring and accountability aspects of poverty reduction strategies.[27]

A mandate of Independent Expert on extreme poverty and human rights was created in 1998. The second mandate-holder, Arjun Sengupta, in 2008 defined extreme poverty as

---

[20] CESCR, Statement on Poverty and the ICESCR, E/C.12/2001/10 (10 May 2001) para 8.

[21] Rousseau, *The Social Contract and Discourses* (DGH Cole tr, 1782, Campbell, 1973) 117.

[22] UNESCO, *Human Rights: Comments and Interpretations. A Symposium Convened by UNESCO*, UNESCO/PHS/3 (rev) (25 July 1948), Appendix II, 11. The published version of the work of the Committee appears in Maritain, *Universal Declaration of Human Rights: Comments and Interpretations* (UNESCO, 1949).

[23] Proclamation of Teheran, Final Act of the International Conference on Human Rights, Teheran, A/CONF.32/41, 3 (13 May 1968) para 12.

[24] 'I am often asked what is the most serious form of human rights violations in the world today, and my reply is consistent: extreme poverty.' UNDP, *Poverty Reduction and Human Rights: A Practice Note* (UNDP, 2003) iv.   [25] CHR, Human Rights and Extreme Poverty, E/CN.4/Res/1990/15 (23 February 1990) 5.

[26] Leandro Despouy, *The Realization of Economic, Social and Cultural Rights: Final report on human rights and extreme poverty, submitted by the Special Rapporteur*, UN Doc E/CN.4/Sub.2/1996/13 (28 June 1996).

[27] Hunt, Nowak, and Osmani, *Draft Guidelines: A Human Rights Approach to Poverty Reduction Strategies* (OHCHR, 2002). See also Hunt, Nowak, and Osmani, *Human Rights and Poverty Reduction Strategies: Human Rights and Poverty Reduction: A Conceptual Framework* (OHCHR, 2003).

'people suffering from income poverty (being below an agreed level of minimum disposable income or expenditure required for leading a sustainable life) and people suffering from human development poverty (without access to, or availability of, certain basic goods and services to make it possible for them to lead a meaningful life) as well as people in social exclusion (without basic security to lead an adequate social existence, dependent on the structure of social relationships)'.[28]

In preparing the guiding principles on extreme poverty and human rights, the third Independent Expert on extreme poverty and human rights, Magdalena Sepúlveda Carmona, adopted the 2001 definition of the Committee on Economic, Social and Cultural Rights quoted earlier[29] for poverty and Sengupta's 2008 definition of extreme poverty. She added that:

> Persons living in poverty are confronted by the most severe obstacles—physical, economic, cultural and social—to accessing their rights and entitlements. . . . Persons experiencing extreme poverty live in a vicious cycle of powerlessness, stigmatization, discrimination, exclusion and material deprivation, which all mutually reinforce one another.[30]

With these definitions of poverty as related to human rights, we now turn to the relationship between human rights and social justice.

2.2 SOCIAL JUSTICE AND HUMAN RIGHTS

A definitional issue that should be clarified is the overlap and distinction between human rights and 'social justice'. While social justice is part of the vocabulary of both development and human rights, the focus of much of the social justice movement is to challenge unjust structures (structural violence); support communities of poor, vulnerable, and marginalized people, using methodologies of community development and empowerment; and challenge the processes of international economic integration ('globalization') by which the rich get richer and the poor get poorer. A human rights approach to addressing poverty may well find merit in such approaches but would focus more on an accountability framework for pursuing social justice and refer to explicit human rights norms rather than a broad appeal to notions of redistributive or egalitarian justice.

In one sense, human rights is narrower than the general commitment to social justice in that it is based on specific norms agreed upon as enforceable human rights of individuals and groups rather than on structural reform of societies. It is at the same time more general insofar as it protects rights for all, not just the poor. Therefore, social justice, which has various definitions, is used here in its focus on reducing inequalities and eliminating poverty, whereas human rights is concerned with poverty among other problems that affect people's capacity to lead meaningful lives.

3 DIVERGENCE OF POVERTY REDUCTION AND HUMAN RIGHTS AGENDAS

To a certain extent, the divergence in perspective between the human rights and poverty reduction discourses can be explained by the dominance of law, political science, and philosophy among those who theorize about and develop policies on human rights and the

---

[28] Report of the independent expert on the question of human rights and extreme poverty, A/HRC/7/15 (28 February 2008) para 31.

[29] CESCR, Statement on Poverty and the ICESCR.

[30] Final draft of the guiding principles on extreme poverty and human rights, submitted by the Special Rapporteur on extreme poverty and human rights, A/HRC/21/39 (18 July 2012) para 4.

dominance of economics and planning among those who theorize about and develop poverty reduction strategies. Some of these divergent ways of thinking are explored in Section 3.1, which examines how economists think about poverty and human rights. Section 3.2 analyses the thinking of governors of central banks and ministers of finance.

3.1 RESISTANCE TO HUMAN RIGHTS DISCOURSE IN ECONOMIC THINKING

Economists and economic decision-makers only rarely invoke human rights concepts, although many are open to related notions. Some economists tend to consider their professional role as value-neutral, offering the tools of analysis to be applied to policies set by others. Other economists address moral dimensions of economic issues, but avoid human rights language. Jeffrey Sachs proposed to end extreme poverty by 2025 through a nine-step programme that he places in the historical trajectory of the ending of slavery, colonialism, segregation, and apartheid. Although all of these were human rights movements, he does not call them that.[31] He does not explicitly make the link between the human rights causes of the past and the current cause of poverty elimination.

Economists often apply notions of minimum standards, transparency, participation, and the like in the context of development policy, without relating them to a human rights framework. Thus, in the economics literature on international trade, there has been much discussion about appropriate mechanisms to promote labour standards, including addressing child labour in developing countries.[32] Likewise, the literature on public services has highlighted how a lack of transparency, insufficient accountability, and corrupt government officials will increase social wastage and distort economic and service delivery outcomes.[33] Other research has focused on matters of 'process', correlating economic performance with democracy and the rule of law.[34]

These analyses are illustrative of the divergence between human rights and economic thinking insofar as the authors grapple with many of the same concerns as are used in human rights (fairness, accountability, transparency, labour standards, child labour, democracy, rule of law) without reference to the relevant standards contained in international human rights instruments. Nobel prize-winning economist Joseph Stiglitz, in his influential book *Making Globalization Work*, contrasted how at the national level 'we argue for and against different policies on the basis of whether they are just, whether they hurt the poor, whether their burden falls disproportionately on those less well off', whereas in the international arena, 'not only do we fail to do the analysis, we almost never argue for a policy on the basis of fairness'.[35] He does allude in his conclusion to the UDHR but only as something the founding fathers of the USA would be pleased with, rather than as the inaugural document to a rather extensive set of international instruments relevant to reducing what he calls the 'gap between economic and political globalization'.[36]

Furthermore, there are many points of tension between mainstream economic thinking and human rights-centred approaches when it comes to defining development goals or implementing anti-poverty policy. One such point of tension is that growth-oriented

---

[31] Sachs, *The End of Poverty: Economic Possibilities for Our Time* (Penguin Press, 2005) 360–8.

[32] eg Edmonds, 'Child Labor' in Schultz and Strauss (eds), *Handbook of Development Economics—Volume 4* (Elsevier, 2007) 3609.

[33] eg Rose-Ackerman (ed), *International Handbook on the Economics of Corruption* (Edward Elgar, 2007).

[34] eg Rigobon and Rodrik, *Rule of Law, Democracy, Openness and Income: Estimating the Interrelationships* (Kennedy School of Government, Harvard University, 2004); World Bank, *World Development Report 2017: Governance and the Law* (2017).

[35] Stiglitz, *Making Globalization Work* (WW Norton, 2006) 278.   [36] Stiglitz (2009), 292.

economic analysis tends to disregard the impact of income on the realization of such human rights as the rights to health, education, and cultural and political freedoms. Economic analysis and policy interventions are fundamentally about making *choices* among alternatives in a world of limited resources. In contrast, the language of human rights (and associated *obligations* towards bearers of rights) appears less forgiving about choices and options. Rights language tends to be used by economists when it enhances, rather than limits, choices. As Sen has said:

> In economics the concept of rights is often invoked . . . however . . . [n]o intrinsic importance is attached to the existence or fulfilment of rights, and they have been judged by their ability to achieve good consequences, among which the fulfilment of rights have not figured.[37]

The current Special Rapporteur on extreme poverty and human rights, Philip Alston, underscored the divergence of perspective in his 2015 report on the World Bank. He described the Bank as, for most purposes, 'a human rights-free zone' that is 'unable to engage meaningfully with the international human rights framework'.[38] A recent example is the World Bank's *World Development Report 2017* which is devoted to governance and the rule of law. Human rights are mentioned as one of many experiences with the law but not as part of the Bank's approach to ending poverty, as Alston argued it should be.[39] The report is premised on the idea, expressed by the Bank's president in his foreword, that '[w]ithout paying greater attention to stronger governance, the World Bank Group's goals of ending extreme poverty and boosting shared prosperity, as well as the transformational vision of the United Nations' broader Sustainable Development Goals, will be out of reach'.[40]

Another point of tension between human rights and economic thinking is that, even when the importance of goals other than that of economic growth is recognized in economic analysis, there is a temptation to consider civil and political rights as optional goods that can await a sufficient level of economic growth. The holistic human rights approach would not accept such a trade-off. Economic literature has come down on both sides of this issue. There are scholarly articles, both theoretical and empirical, which suggest that priority attention to political rights, for instance, can make a positive contribution to economic growth.[41] Others suggest that economic growth is more likely to pave the way for institutional, including political, development—and that prioritizing political freedom may not be the best strategy for developing countries to pursue economic growth.[42] There seems to be little doubt that the enjoyment of political freedoms is positively related to economic growth and that rising living standards foster democratic freedoms, while declining living standards subvert them. However, as Benjamin Friedman has said:

> That there is usually more freedom in countries with higher per capita incomes does not by itself reveal whether having a high income leads a society to value and therefore provide these freedoms, or whether having widespread rights and liberties enables a country to achieve a higher level of income—in other words, whether a high material standard of living fosters freedom, or freedom facilitates economic success.[43]

---

[37] Sen, *On Ethics and Economics* (Blackwell, 1988) 49.

[38] Report of the Special Rapporteur on extreme poverty and human rights, A/70/274 (4 August 2015) para 68.   [39] World Bank (2017).

[40] World Bank (2017), xiii.

[41] eg Kaufmann, 'Human Rights, Governance, and Development: An Empirical Perspective' (2006) 8 *Development Outreach* 15, 15–20 and references cited therein.

[42] eg Glaeser *et al.*, *Do Institutions Cause Growth?* (National Bureau of Economic Research, 2004).

[43] Friedman, *The Moral Consequences of Economic Growth* (Alfred A Knopf, 2005) 314.

The more interesting question is how adherence to human rights principles can instrumentally contribute to the effectiveness of economic policy interventions, including those aimed at growth and efficiency.

Thus, there is no simple answer to the question of how economists think about poverty and human rights. Some attempt to be value-neutral; some favour eliminating poverty through redistribution; some apply the concept of development as freedom; but most favour raising the condition of the poor through market-based growth. The latter group tends to dominate in high-level decision-making among central bankers and treasury departments.

3.2 THE PERSPECTIVE OF CENTRAL BANKS AND MINISTRIES OF FINANCE

The divergence between human rights and poverty reduction agendas is perhaps best illustrated by the Group of Twenty (G20).[44] Founded in 1999, it claims to represent around two-thirds of the world's population and 80 per cent of world gross domestic product.[45] It describes itself as 'the premier forum for international cooperation on the most important issues of the global economic and financial agenda',[46] which do not include human rights. The G20 finance ministers and central bank governors meet once a year. Typical of their approach is the Statement on Global Development Issues adopted at their meeting in China in 2005. Neither 'human rights' nor 'human development' is mentioned in that document and 'good governance' is only mentioned in relation to sound economic policies and accountability. The statement does say, 'we are committed to strengthening the dialogue on varying development philosophies, strategies, and policies, from which all countries can benefit'.[47] Human rights did not fare any better at the meeting in South Africa in 2007, the final communiqué of which makes no mention of 'human rights' or even 'right', and the word 'human' is never attached to development (it is used once in 'human capital').

Following the 2008 financial crisis, the G20 began meeting at the summit level of heads of state and government. The G20 acknowledged 'the human dimension to the crisis', as it was called in the Global Plan for Recovery and Reform adopted by the Second G20 Leaders' Summit in London in 2009. Once again, there was no reference to 'human development' or 'human rights', only the rather feeble commitment 'to support those affected by the crisis by creating employment opportunities and through income support measures.'[48] The Pittsburgh Summit the same year expressed the underlying philosophy of the summit: 'the only sure foundation for sustainable globalisation and rising prosperity for all is an open world economy based on market principles, effective regulation, and strong global institutions'.[49] Critiquing the London communiqué of the G20, two human rights scholars noted:

---

[44] The members of the G20 are the finance ministers and central bank governors of 19 states: Argentina, Australia, Brazil, Canada, China, France, Germany, India, Indonesia, Italy, Japan, Mexico, Russia, Saudi Arabia, South Africa, South Korea, Turkey, UK, and USA, along with the European Union. Senior officials of the International Monetary Fund (IMF) and the World Bank participate in G20 meetings.

[45] See <https://www.g20.org/Webs/G20/EN/G20/Participants/participants_node.html>.

[46] See <https://www.g20foundation.org/g20/>.

[47] G20 Statement on Global Development Issues (Xianghe, Hebei, China, 2005) para 3, available at: <http://www.g20.utoronto.ca/2005/2005development.html>.

[48] The Global Plan for Recovery and Reform (London, 2009), para 26, available at: <http://www.g20.utoronto.ca/2009/2009communique0402.html>.

[49] G20 Leaders Statement: The Pittsburgh Summit (Pittsburgh, 2009), paras 34 and 38, available at: <http://www.g20.utoronto.ca/2009/2009communique0925.html>.

The crisis, its human impact, and the proposed solutions are also issues of international human rights law—and in particular of state obligations to take collective action to create a global economic system amenable to the fulfilment of basic rights to subsistence, security, and freedom.[50]

The focus on growth continued, including under the Russian presidency in 2013, which organized the agenda around 'three overarching priorities, aimed at starting the new cycle of economic growth: [g]rowth through quality jobs and investment; [g]rowth through trust and transparency; [g]rowth through effective regulation.'[51] In contrast, a group of independent researchers called Civil 20 prepared, for the 2013 St Petersburg summit, 'an independent analysis and proposals for a dialogue between a wide range of stakeholders and the G20 governors on the G20 concerted policies and actions to improve economic equality within their countries and beyond.'[52] In its report, Civil 20 included among the 'Common Principles and Policies for All' the following: 'good governance and basic human rights, specifically, universal access to the rule of law, anti-corruption, anti-tax evasion, and equal access to essential food, water, health care and rights of movement for citizens within the country.'[53]

Subsequent G20 summits, such as Brisbane, Australia, in 2014; Antalya, Turkey, in 2015; and Hangzhou, China, in 2016, have followed the trend of a strong focus on growth with vague references to equality and sustainability and no direct mention of human rights or human development. The Brisbane communiqué alluded to 'poverty elimination' but in the context of reducing the global average cost of transferring remittances.[54] When human rights is mentioned, the reference is ambiguous. For example, the Hangzhou Communiqué states that 'we will reinforce the G20's efforts to enhance international cooperation against corruption, while fully respecting international law, human rights and the rule of law as well as the sovereignty of each country.'[55] In the G20 Leaders Declaration, adopted in Hamburg, Germany, in July 2017, contrary to previous summits, human rights is mentioned five times, twice in relation to sustainable global supply chains (para. 7), once in relation to national action plans on business and human rights and elimination of child labour, forced labour, human trafficking and all forms of modern slavery (para. 8), once in relation to displacement and migration (para. 39), and once in relation 'to protecting the human rights of all persons regardless of their status' (para. 42).

A similar focus on growth and markets as the solution to poverty characterizes the pronouncements of eight highly industrialized nations (France, Germany, Italy, the UK, Japan, the USA, Canada, and Russia) known as the G8, or the G7 after suspension of Russia in 2014. Although it is committed 'to achieve strong, sustainable, balanced and inclusive growth', the G7 also refers to its 'shared values of freedom and democracy, peace, security, the rule of law, and respect for human rights.'[57]

---

[50] Fukuda-Parr and Salomon, 'A Human Rights Analysis of the G20 Communique: Recent Awareness of the "Human Cost" Is Not Quite Enough,' Carnegie Council online, available at: <http://www.carnegiecouncil.org/publications/ethics_online/0033.html>.

[51] Priorities of Russia's G20 presidency in 2013, available at: <http://en.g20russia.ru/docs/g20_russia/priorities.html>.

[52] G20 Research Group at the University of Toronto and the International Organizations and International Cooperation Institute of the National Research University Higher School of Economics, *Sustained and Balanced Growth Requires Equitable Policies, Draft Report*, available at: <https://www.hse.ru/data/2013/05/14/1299928420/Equality%20Report%20final.pdf>.   [53] G20 Research Group, 28.

[54] G20 Leaders'Communiqué: Brisbane Summit (Brisbane, 2014), para 11, available at: <http://www.g20australia.org/sites/default/files/g20_resources/library/brisbane_g20_leaders_summit_communique.pdf>.

[55] G20 Leaders'Communiqué: Hangzhou Summit (Hangzhou, 2016), para 22, available at: <https://www.g20.org/Content/DE/_Anlagen/G7_G20/2016-09-04-g20-kommunique-en.pdf?__blob=publicationFile&v=1>.

[56] <https://www.g20.org/Content/EN/_Anlagen/G20/G20-leaders-declaration.pdf?_blob=publicationFile&v=7>.

[57] G7 Taormina Leaders' Communiqué, Taormina Summit (Taormina, Italy, 2017), available at: <http://www.consilium.europa.eu/en/press/press-releases/2017/05/27-g7-leaders-communique/>.

These pronouncements of the G20 and the G7 illustrate an ambiguity regarding human rights and poverty. The confrontation is not between the morally indignant voices of the poor against a band of greedy capitalists meeting in some boardroom in Washington or London. Many in the anti-globalization movement do indeed claim to speak for the poor, but so do the representatives of the G20 governments, which include India and China, as well as Argentina, Mexico, South Africa, and the European Union. These are not the forces of evil against the forces of good. They are the principal actors in the global economy and they send contradictory messages about the proposition that human rights have anything to do with poverty. It is little wonder, therefore, that human rights do not figure prominently among the approaches to poverty in vogue in policy pronouncements on the international financing of development. The critique by the human rights community of the G20 approach is found, among others, in the work of 'RightingFinance', which noted in 2011 that 'human rights considerations have no place in their discussions or statements' but that 'their actions have significant impacts on the realization and enjoyment of human rights, and the members of the G20 are Nation-states that cannot disregard their human rights obligations in any forum, including multilateral economic institutions.'[58] RightingFinance has continued to address the human rights shortcomings of a wide range of international finance issues, including national development banks, vulture funds, private-market financed infrastructure, financing for development, and tax policy.[59]

However, the situation is changing progressively as human rights specialists learn more about the economic analyses of poverty and development economists learn about the compatibility of their goals with those of human rights and the instrumental value of human rights for poverty reduction. These trends have opened the space—still fairly restricted—for the convergence of human rights and poverty reduction agendas.

4 CONVERGENCE OF POVERTY REDUCTION AND HUMAN RIGHTS AGENDAS

Section 3 illustrated several ways in which human rights concerns diverge from those of development and poverty reduction. This section addresses the convergence—or at least the trends that demonstrate mutually reinforcing relations—between human rights and anti-poverty agendas, beginning in Section 4.1 with some economic thinking that is congruent with human rights and continuing in Section 4.2 with policies to combat poverty using human rights tools.

4.1 TRENDS IN ECONOMIC THINKING CONGRUENT WITH HUMAN RIGHTS

Apart from the economic studies referred to already, which deal with fairness, transparency, and participation, there is another strand of development economics that acknowledges human rights as providing goals for development: the development ethics movement. The International Development Ethics Association (IDEA), for example, defines its members as 'a cross-cultural group of philosophers, social scientists, and practitioners who apply ethical reflection to global development goals and strategies and to North/South relations'. They advocate a normative approach to development-based theories 'that appeal to social justice, human rights, basic needs, and theological understandings of the

---

[58] Rightingfinance, 'The Group of 20, Financial Regulation and Human Rights', available at: <http://www.rightingfinance.org/?p=97>.

[59] See the publications available at: <http://www.rightingfinance.org/?cat=9>.

human condition'.[60] In 1989, IDEA adopted the Mérida Declaration, which enumerates among their guiding ethical principles 'the absolute respect for the dignity of the human person, regardless of gender, ethnic group, social class, religion, age or nationality'.[61] Leading development economists, such as David A Crocker, Paul Streeten, and especially Denis Goulet, spearheaded this movement. Human rights and poverty are central to their concerns, although human rights as such is rarely an operative concept in their work.

Another major exception to the divergence between human rights and economic thinking is the 'human development and capabilities' approach, theorized primarily by Amartya Sen and Martha Nussbaum. This approach has been embraced by UNDP's *Human Development Report* and is promoted by an association of academics and practitioners called the Human Development and Capability Association (HDCA). The openness to human rights of this perspective is due to the centrality of the concept of development as freedom and expanding choices. In the words of the *Human Development Report*:

> Human development shares a common vision with human rights. The goal is human freedom. And in pursuing capabilities and realizing rights, this freedom is vital. People must be free to exercise their choices and to participate in decision-making that affects their lives. Human development and human rights are mutually reinforcing, helping to secure the well-being and dignity of all people, building self-respect and the respect of others.[62]

A third example is William Easterly, an economist who is quite explicit in attributing the failure of many poverty-reduction projects to the failure of economists to break out of their technocratic straightjackets and to apply human rights. '[P]overty is really about a shortage of rights', he writes.[63] For him, 'the poor should have the same rights as the rich.'[64]

Among government economists, the farther one moves from trade, finance, and treasury departments of governments, including in their multilateral settings of the WTO and the G20, and the closer one gets to bilateral and multilateral fora for addressing poverty, the more relevant human rights considerations become. This continuum runs from the G20 to the World Bank Group and regional development banks to broad-based deliberative bodies (such as the global conferences and summits, and the UN Economic and Social Council), to development aid agencies and programmes (such as the UK Department for International Development (DFID) and UNDP), to UN human rights bodies (such as the Human Rights Council and the Third Committee of the General Assembly), to human rights treaty regimes and special procedures. To illustrate the gap, compare the various G20 communiqués discussed in Section 3.2, representing one end of this continuum, with the statement of the Committee on Economic, Social and Cultural Rights on poverty, cited in Section 2.1, representing the other end. In that statement, the Committee regretted 'that the human rights dimensions of poverty eradication policies rarely receive the attention they deserve. This neglect is especially regrettable because a human rights approach to poverty can reinforce anti-poverty strategies and make them more effective.'[65]

The World Conference on Human Rights, in its 1993 Vienna Declaration, stated that '[t]he existence of widespread extreme poverty inhibits the full and effective enjoyment

---

[60] See: <http://developmentethics.org/about-2/what-is-development-ethics/>.

[61] See: <http://developmentethics.org/announcements/declarations-2/>.

[62] UNDP, *Human Development Report 2001*, 9. See also Reddy, 'Economics and Human Rights: A Non-Conversation' (2011) 12 *J Human Development and Capabilities* 64.

[63] Easterly, *The Tyranny of Experts: Economists, Dictators, and the Forgotten Rights of the Poor* (Basic Books, 2013) 7.   [64] Easterly (2013), 340.

[65] CESCR, Statement on Poverty and the ICESCR, para 2.

of human rights; its immediate alleviation and eventual elimination must remain a high priority for the international community'.[66] It further affirmed:

> [E]xtreme poverty and social exclusion constitute a violation of human dignity and . . . urgent steps are necessary to achieve better knowledge of extreme poverty and its causes, including those related to the problem of development, in order to promote the human rights of the poorest, and to put an end to extreme poverty and social exclusion and to promote the enjoyment of the fruits of social progress. It is essential for States to foster participation by the poorest people in the decision-making process by the community in which they live, the promotion of human rights and efforts to combat extreme poverty.[67]

The test of this commitment to a human rights-based approach (HRBA) to poverty reduction is the extent to which it has been translated into the policies and practices of development.

4.2 HUMAN RIGHTS APPROACHES IN DEVELOPMENT POLICIES AND PRACTICES

Human rights have become part of the international development agenda, including poverty reduction, through the introduction of human rights approaches into UN development cooperation, poverty reduction strategies, the 2030 Development Agenda and bilateral development programmes. Each of these is examined in this section, before turning to the most systematic approach to integrating poverty and human rights, namely by considering development itself as a human right.

4.2.1 UN development cooperation

In 2003, representatives from across the UN defined a Common Understanding on a Human Rights-based Approach to Development Cooperation.[68] This document became a standard reference for translating normative human rights commitments of member states into development cooperation policies and projects of UN agencies, funds, and programmes. In his report Strengthening of the United Nations: An Agenda for Further Change, the UN Secretary-General called human rights 'a bedrock requirement for the realization of the Charter's vision of a just and peaceful world'. He listed, among 36 actions to realize this vision, Action 2 designed to strengthen human rights, which integrated human rights into humanitarian, development, and peacekeeping work throughout the UN system.[69] Until 2009, this programme supported over 60 UN country teams and their national partners in capacity-building to integrate human rights into their work,[70] including by issuing the UN Common Learning Package on HRBA.[71] In late 2009, the UN Development Group Human Rights Mainstreaming Mechanism (UNDG-HRM) replaced Action 2 with the overarching objective 'to further institutionalize human rights mainstreaming efforts in the UN development system and to strengthen system-wide coherence'.[72] The mechanism included a UN Practitioners Portal on Human Rights

---

[66] Vienna Declaration, para 14.   [67] Vienna Declaration, para 25.

[68] UNDG, 'The Human Rights Based Approach to Development Cooperation: Towards a Common Understanding Among UN Agencies' (7 May 2003), available at: <http://www.unescobkk.org/fileadmin/user_upload/appeal/human_rights/UN_Common_understanding_RBA.pdf>.

[69] Strengthening of the United Nations: An Agenda for Further Change, A/57/387 (9 September 2002) paras 45–51.

[70] Report of the UN High Commissioner for Human Rights, A/64/36 (6 August 2009) para 93.

[71] Available at: <http://hrbaportal.org/common-learning-package-on-hrba>.

[72] UNDG, UNDG Human Rights Mainstreaming Mechanism Summary of the Operational Plan 2011–2013 (18 October 2011) 2.

Based Approaches to Programming (HRBAP)[73] and a Multi-Partner Human Rights Mainstreaming Trust Fund.[74] UNDG-HRM was replaced in January 2015 by the UN Development Group's Human Rights Working Group (UNDG-HRWG), consisting of 18 agencies of the UN system, which continues 'to integrate human rights in the UN's development work'.[75]

4.2.2 Poverty reduction strategies

After the Asian financial crisis in the 1990s, there was a rethinking in the World Bank and the IMF of their earlier policies of structural adjustment, sometimes taking into account the human rights impact of such policies, but mostly to avoid social impacts that reduce the productivity of workers and the stability of regimes. Health and education are frequently cited as having suffered the most from structural adjustment programmes. In 1999, the IMF and the World Bank launched the Poverty Reduction Strategy process, involving 'a comprehensive country-based strategy for poverty reduction'. The process was initially linked to debt reduction, but was delinked in 2015.[76]

In a concept note, the High Commissioner for Human Rights drew the World Bank's attention to the value of 'linking a Poverty Reduction Strategy to a universal normative framework and State obligations emanating from the human rights instruments' and sustaining it 'with enhanced accountability of the relevant stake-holders'.[77] These concepts were reflected in the 'Guiding Principles on extreme poverty and human rights', adopted by the Human Rights Council in September 2012.[78] They are designed for policy-makers and other actors to align public policies with international law and the objective of poverty reduction.

4.2.3 Human rights in the 2030 Development Agenda

Following the commitments made by heads of state at the Millennium Summit in 2000, all governments and international institutions set specific targets for poverty reduction in the Millennium Development Goals (MDGs). While these goals served to guide development planning, they tended to ignore commitments made by states to human rights and the rule of law. The High Commissioner for Human Rights drew attention to the relationship between the MDGs and human rights by disseminating charts on the intersection of human rights treaty obligations and the MDGs and an exhaustive analysis of how human rights can contribute to the MDGs.[79] Similarly, the UNDP published a primer called *Human Rights and the Millennium Development Goals: Making the Link*,[80] and various national development agencies published their own human rights approaches to MDGs.[81]

---

[73] More information available at: <http://hrbaportal.org>.

[74] Available at: <http://mptf.undp.org/factsheet/fund/HRM00>.

[75] UNDG-HRWG, Terms of Reference (5 December 2014), available at: <https://undg.org/wp-content/uploads/2016/08/UNDG-Human-Rights-Working-Group-TORs-5Dec2014.pdf>.

[76] IMF Factsheet, available at: <http://www.imf.org/external/np/exr/facts/prsp.htm>.

[77] OHCHR, Comments on the Concept Note. Joint World Bank and IMF Report on Poverty Reduction Strategy Papers—Progress in Implementation 2005 PRS Review, available at: <http://siteresources.worldbank.org/INTPRS1/Resources/PRSP-Review/un_ohchr.pdf>.

[78] HR Council Res 21/11 (27 September 2012).

[79] OHCHR, *Claiming the MDGs: A Human Rights Approach* (2008).

[80] UNDP, *Human Rights and the Millennium Development Goals: Making the Link* (Oslo Governance Centre, 2007).

[81] eg the Swedish International Development Agency (available at: <http://www.sida.se/English?About-us/Organization/Policy/>); the UK's DFID (available at: <https://www.gov.uk/government/organisations/department-for-international-development/about>); the US MCC (<http://www.mcc.gov/pages/about>); Canada's CIDA (available at: <http://www.acdi-cida.gc.ca/acdi-cida/acdi-cida.nsf/en/JUD-13173118-GPM>); and Denmark's DANIDA (available at: <http://um.dk/en/danida-en/goals/mdg/>).

As the 2015 end-date for the MDGs approached, insightful reflections on human rights and the MDGs—and, therefore, on human rights and poverty—focused on integrating human rights more meaningfully into the post-2015 development agenda.[82] The 2012 UN Conference on Sustainable Development (Rio+20) affirmed 'the importance of . . . respect for all human rights, including the right to development and the right to an adequate standard of living'[83] along with eight other references to human rights. The UN Secretary General appointed a High-Level Panel of Eminent Persons on the Post-2015 Development Agenda,[84] and a UN System Task Team recommended a 'vision for the future that rests on the core values of human rights, equality and sustainability'.[85]

The final report of the High-Level Panel was not based on the Task Team's core values, but rather on 'five big, transformative shifts', including, as part of the first shift 'Leave no one behind', ensuring 'that no person—regardless of ethnicity, gender, geography, disability, race or other status—is denied universal human rights and basic economic opportunities'.[86] Occasional human rights-related observations appear in other 'shifts',[87] including the following statement: 'We envision a world where the principles of equity, sustainability, solidarity, respect for human rights and shared responsibilities in accordance with respective capabilities, has been brought to life by our common action.'[88] The language becomes more directly relevant to a human rights-based approach to poverty reduction in Annex II, which affirms that the rights in the UDHR 'form the foundations of human development.'[89]

Sakiko Fukuda-Parr remarked that the MDGs 'do not reflect the meaning of poverty as an affront to human dignity in the human rights and capabilities perspective'.[90] A similar position was taken by OHCHR official and scholar Mac Darrow, who proposed that the 'international human rights framework can serve a vital purpose in helping to ensure that the negotiations towards 2015 focus on legitimate *ends* of human development, corresponding to internationally agreed upon human rights norms, rather than context-specific and contested *means*'.[91] Many NGOs, such as Human Rights Watch and the Centre for Economic and Social Rights, pushed the human rights focus.[92] A joint statement, endorsed by 19 leading human rights organizations in 2013, called for human rights to be placed at the core of the new development agenda.[93]

The final product that emerged was Resolution 70/1, adopted by the General Assembly on 25 September 2015, with the title 'Transforming our world: the 2030 Agenda for

---

[82] Darrow, 'Millennium Development Goals: Milestones or Millstones—Human Rights Priorities for the Post-2015 Development Agenda' (2012) 15 *Yale HR and Development LJ* 55.

[83] GA Res 66/288 (27 July 2012) Annex, para 8.

[84] Terms of Reference for the High-Level Panel of Eminent Persons on the Post-2015 Development Agenda, available at: <https://www.un.org/sg/sites/www.un.org.sg/files/documents/management/ToRpost2015.pdf>.

[85] UN, *Realizing the Future We Want For All: Report to the Secretary-General* (June 2012) i.

[86] High-Level Panel of Eminent Persons on the Post-2015 Development Agenda, *A New Global Partnership: Eradicate Poverty and Transform Economies Through Sustainable Development: The Report of the High-Level Panel of Eminent Persons on the Post-2015 Development Agenda* (UN, 2013) Executive Summary and 7.

[87] eg *A New Global Partnership*, Executive Summary, 9 and 18.

[88] *A New Global Partnership*, 27.   [89] *A New Global Partnership*, 50.

[90] Fukuda-Parr, 'Recapturing the Narrative of International Development', UN Research Institute for Social Development Research Paper No. 2012–5 (July 2012) 6.   [91] Darrow (2012), 105.

[92] Human Rights Watch, 'Letter to the High-level Panel of Eminent Persons on the Post-2015 Development Agenda' (24 March 2013), available at: <http://www.hrw.org/news/2013/03/24/letter-high-level-panel-eminent-persons-post-2015-development-agenda>; Centre for Economic and Social Rights and OHCHR, *Who Will Be Accountable? Human Rights and the Post-2015 Development Agenda* (UN, 2013).

[93] 'New development goals must have human rights at their core' (6 May 2013), available at: <http://www.rightingfinance.org/?p=402>.

Sustainable Development' and consisting of a Preamble and a Declaration, enumerating the 17 goals and 169 targets.[94] From the human rights perspective, the 2030 Agenda is certainly an advance over the MDGs, beginning with the affirmation in the preamble that the Sustainable Development Goals (SDGs) 'seek to build on the Millennium Development Goals and complete what they did not achieve. They seek to realize the human rights of all.'[95] The Declaration contains several strong paragraphs affirming the importance of human rights in the post-2015 development agenda, such as this one:

> 19. We reaffirm the importance of the Universal Declaration of Human Rights, as well as other international instruments relating to human rights and international law. We emphasize the responsibilities of all States, in conformity with the Charter of the United Nations, to respect, protect and promote human rights and fundamental freedoms for all, without distinction of any kind as to race, colour, sex, language, religion, political or other opinion, national or social origin, property, birth, disability or other status.[96]

That paragraph was taken verbatim from the Rio+20 Declaration as a diplomatic compromise in response to concerns of certain delegations to avoid broader anti-discrimination language that might imply recognition of LGBT rights.[97] Specific additional references are found in numerous other paragraphs, as well as in the paragraph outlining the follow-up and review processes, which 'will be people-centred, gender-sensitive, respect human rights and have a particular focus on the poorest, most vulnerable and those furthest behind'.[98]

Compared to the MDGs, which make no reference to human rights, the SDGs contain 14 references to human rights. In its position paper on the 2030 Agenda, the OHCHR concluded:

> Despite some gaps from a human rights perspective, the new Agenda goes far beyond the MDGs in encompassing issues related [sic] not only economic, social and cultural rights but also civil and political rights and the right to development. With its universal applicability and its importance in shaping development priorities, the 2030 Agenda will open up new avenues to integrate human rights into global and national policies in both developed and developing countries over the next 15 years. However, a strong accountability architecture must be established at national, regional and global levels. Indicators should be grounded in human rights and data should be disaggregated as far as possible according to the grounds of discrimination prohibited under human rights law. People should be empowered to hold their governments accountable for meeting the new Goals.[99]

Implementation of the SDGs will be monitored by the High Level Political Forum on Sustainable Development (HLPF), a UN platform meeting annually under the auspices of the Economic and Social Council, and every four years under the auspices of the General Assembly. Indicators have been prepared by the Inter-Agency and Expert Group on SDG Indicators (IAEG-SDGs) and agreed upon by the UN Statistical Commission in March 2017.[100] The Center for Economic and Social Rights commented that 'the new development agenda could be an important vehicle for human rights fulfilment', adding that to do

---

[94] GA Res 70/1, paras 54 ff.   [95] GA Res 70/1, Preamble.   [96] GA Res 70/1, para 19.

[97] CESR, 'Strong commitments in final SDG text, despite sordid final compromises', available at <http://cesr.org/strong-commitments-final-sdg-text-despite-sordid-final-compromises>.

[98] GA Res 70/1, para 74. See also paras. 3, 8, and 10, 20, 29, 35, and 67.

[99] OHCHR, Transforming Our World: Human Rights in the 2030 Agenda for Sustainable Development, available at: <http://www.ohchr.org/Documents/Issues/MDGs/Post2015/TransformingOurWorld.pdf>.

[100] Report of the Inter-Agency and Expert Group on Sustainable Development Goal Indicators, E/CN.3/2017/2 (15 December 2016) Annex III.

so 'the indicators will also need to be human rights-aligned'.[101] For this purpose, it has published a policy brief, enumerating human rights-based criteria for indicator selection.[102]

Additional reflection on the human rights strengths and weaknesses of the SDGs is found in the work of the Reflection Group on the 2030 Agenda for Sustainable Development. Its 2016 report found 'severe obstacles to the implementation of the 2030 Agenda and overcoming them is a prerequisite for achieving the SDGs and fulfilling the commitments made to human rights and sustainability'.[103] The report made numerous critical observations and recommendations about the potential for a more human rights-focused approach to the SDGs.

4.2.4 Bilateral development cooperation

The trend of national development agencies to adopt human rights approaches has been studied by the Organisation for Economic Co-operation and Development (OECD) and the World Bank, as part of the effort of the World Bank Nordic Trust Fund (NTF), which was created in 2008 'to help develop an informed view among Bank staff on how human rights relate to the Bank's core work'.[104] That study is premised on the proposition that 'human rights offer a coherent normative framework that can guide development assistance'.[105] The advantages identified by the study relate to adaptability to different political and cultural environments, the potential for operationalizing human rights principles, relevance to good governance and meaningful participation, poverty reduction, and aid effectiveness.[106] Examples of bilateral policies and programmes applying a HRBA to development are found in Sweden, the UK, Germany, Austria, Australia, Canada, the Netherlands, the USA, Switzerland, New Zealand, Norway, and Ireland.[107]

Efforts to integrate human rights have been less successful in relation to the Paris Declaration on Aid Effectiveness, adopted in 2005 by ministers or senior officials of some 85 developed and developing countries and heads of 20 bilateral and multilateral development agencies. The Declaration seeks to reform the delivery of aid and outlines the five overarching principles of ownership, alignment, harmonization, managing for development results, and mutual accountability, with agreed upon indicators, targets, timetables, and processes to monitor implementation. Each of these principles has been examined critically from the human rights perspective in a paper commissioned by the OECD from the Overseas Development Institute, which argues for using human rights to broaden the scope and content of the Paris Declaration commitments and indicators on mutual accountability.[108] Although human rights are not mentioned in the Paris Declaration, they are referred to twice in the Accra Agenda for Action, adopted by the Third High-Level Forum on Aid Effectiveness, held in Accra, Ghana, in 2008. The Agenda states that 'gender equality, respect for human rights, and environmental sustainability are cornerstones for achieving enduring impact on the lives and potential of poor women, men, and children. It is vital that all our policies address these issues in a more systematic and coherent way'.[109]

---

[101] CESR, The Measure of Progress: How Human Rights Should Inform SDG Indicators (October 2015), available at: <http://www.cesr.org/measure-of-progress>.   [102] CESR (2015).

[103] *Spotlight on Sustainable Development 2016: Report by the Reflection Group on the 2030 Agenda for Sustainable Development* (2016) 12.

[104] OECD and World Bank, *Integrating Human Rights into Development: Donor Approaches, Experiences, and Challenges* (World Bank, 2016) 16.   [105] OECD and World Bank (2016), 26.

[106] OECD and World Bank (2016), xxiii-xxv.   [107] OECD and World Bank (2016), 107–13.

[108] Foresti, Booth, and O'Neil, *Aid Effectiveness and Human Rights: Strengthening the Implementation of the Paris Declaration* (Overseas Development Institute, 2006).

[109] The Accra High Level Forum (HLF3) and the Accra Agenda for Action, para 3, available at: <http://www.oecd.org/dac/effectiveness/theaccrahighlevelforumhlf3andtheaccraagendaforaction.htm>.

The Fourth High Level Forum on Aid Effectiveness, held in 2011 in Busan, Republic of Korea, adopted the Busan Partnership for Effective Development Cooperation, which refers to 'our agreed international commitments on human rights, decent work, gender equality, environmental sustainability and disability'[110] and to rights-based approaches of civil society organizations, which 'play a vital role in enabling people to claim their rights,'[111] but does not add to the human rights content of the Accra Agenda for Action. It called for a 'new, inclusive and representative Global Partnership for Effective Development Co-operation [GPEDC] to support and ensure accountability for the implementation of commitments at the political level'.[112] This GPEDC has since convened two high level meetings, 2014 in Mexico City and 2016 in Nairobi. At the Nairobi meeting—the first high level meeting since the 2030 Development Agenda was adopted—the GPEDC did not go beyond reiterating 'agreed international commitments on environmental sustainability, human rights, decent work, gender equality and the elimination of all forms of discrimination'.[113] In contrast, civil society partners participating in Nairobi committed to 'respect and promote human rights and social justice' and 'to develop and implement strategies, activities and practices that promote individual and collective human rights, including the right to development'.[114]

4.2.5 The right to development

One of the greatest challenges for an economic approach to poverty is to accept the proposition that development itself—essentially an economic process—can be regarded as a human right—an essentially legal and governance concept. The challenge from the beginning has been to translate the hopeful but ambiguous language of the UN Declaration on the Right to Development (1986)[115] into concepts that are meaningful to economists and useful to the rethinking of the development process and poverty reduction strategies. The Declaration does not address poverty as such, although elimination of poverty is implicit in concepts such as 'constant improvement of well-being', 'eliminating obstacles to development', and 'access to basic resources, education, health services, food, housing, employment and the fair distribution of income'. The chapter on poverty in the exhaustive OHCHR publication *Realizing the Right to Development* 'examines the connection between development processes and poverty through the lens of the right to development'.[116] The author recalls the High Commissioner's statement on the 25th anniversary of the Declaration that '[i]t's not an act of nature that leaves more than 1 billion people around the world locked in the jaws of poverty. It's a result of the denial of their fundamental human right to development'.[117] The General Assembly has regularly made the connection between poverty and this right, including recognizing 'that eradicating poverty in all its forms and dimensions, including extreme poverty, is one of the critical elements in the promotion and realization of the right to development'.[118]

Most developing states use the right to development to voice their concerns about the negative impact of certain aspects of international trade, unequal access to technology,

[110] Fourth High Level Forum on Aid Effectiveness, para 11, available at: <http://www.oecd.org/dac/effectiveness/fourthhighlevelforumonaideffectiveness.htm>.

[111] Fourth High Level Forum on Aid Effectiveness, para 22.

[112] Fourth High Level Forum on Aid Effectiveness, para 36.

[113] Nairobi Outcome Document (1 December 2016) para 4, available at: <http://effectivecooperation.org/wp-content/uploads/2016/12/Global-Partnership-Nairobi-Outcome-Document-FINAL-1-December-2016.pdf>.

[114] Nairobi Outcome Documen, para 67(c).

[115] GA Res 41/128 (4 December 1986).

[116] Hadiprayitno, 'Poverty' in OHCHR, *Realizing the Right to Development* (OHCHR, 2013) 137.

[117] Hadiprayitno (2013), 139.   [118] GA Res 71/192 (19 December 2016) preamble.

and the crushing debt burden; they favour the idea of an international convention to establish binding obligations to realize the right to development. In contrast, most donor states see the right to development as a way of improving the governance and rule-of-law performance of recipient states, without the need for new binding legal obligations.

The real test is whether the right to development can help define a middle ground between these two contrasting positions, on which consensus can be sustained and practical outcomes achieved. The High-Level Task Force on the implementation of the right to development (which functioned under Human Rights Council resolutions from 2004 to 2010) attempted to bridge this gap between political posturing and practical policy in its report to the Working Group on the Right to Development in 2010. It defined the right to development as 'the right of peoples and individuals to the constant improvement of their well-being and to a national and global enabling environment conducive to just, equitable, participatory and human-centred development respectful of all human rights'.[119] The Task Force proposed three components or attributes, which not only clarify the meaning of the right, but specify how it can be instrumental in responding to poverty. The three attributes correspond to the concepts of policy, process, and outcome. The *policy* defined in attribute 1 is a 'comprehensive and human-centred development policy'. Attribute 2, focused on *process*, refers to 'participatory human rights processes', that is, processes that conform to rules and principles of human rights, participation, accountability, and transparency. Attribute 3 makes clear that the *outcome* of action to realize the right to development is 'social justice in development' in terms of fair distribution of the benefits and burdens of development. The Task Force also provided criteria, sub-criteria, and indicators to further specify what is expected of national and international development policy and practice conducive to poverty elimination and realization of the right to development.

Since the Task Force submitted its consolidated findings, the Working Group has collected comments and views by governments, groups of governments, and regional groups, as well as by others[120] and the Human Rights Council has called for the Working Group to 'further consider, revise and refine the draft criteria and operational sub-criteria'[121] and 'once considered, revised and endorsed by the Working Group', they 'should be used, as appropriate, in the elaboration of a comprehensive and coherent set of standards for the implementation of the right to development'.[122] Also in 2016, the General Assembly instructed the Working Group to 'finalize consideration of the criteria and operational subcriteria, preferably no later than the nineteenth session of the Working Group [2018]', and appointed a Special Rapporteur on the right to development.[123] It is unclear whether this appointment, the standards drafted by the chair-rapporteur[124] and the instructions to the Working Group will advance the effort since 2010 to move the right to development from political rhetoric to development practice in ways that reduce the structural causes of poverty.

Responsibility for the right to development is complicated by the fact that states have not translated their commitment to this right into decision-making in their international partnerships aimed at poverty reduction and, without an explicit mandate, it is unlikely that national and international policies and programmes will incorporate the right to development. Most poverty reduction strategies are based on political and legal commitments with clear incentives to comply with standards and procedures, often resulting in

---

[119] A/HRC/15/WG.2/TF/2.Add.2 (2 February 2010) Annex.   [120] A/HRC/WG.2/13/CRP.1 and 2.
[121] HRC Res 21/32 (28 September 2012) para 8.   [122] HRC Res 21/32, para 9(b).
[123] HRC Res 33/14 (29 September 2016) paras 13 and 14, welcomed by GA Res 71/192 (19 December 2016) para. 16. The current mandate holder is Mr Saad Alfarargi (Egypt).
[124] Report of the Chair-Rapporteur of the Working Group on the Right to Development, Standards for the implementation of the right to development, A/HRC/WG.2/17/2 (16 March 2016).

targeted funding or debt forgiveness. The right to development has no such incentives or a legally-binding commitment, and prospects for an international treaty are dim. The right to development is guaranteed in two regional human rights treaties, namely in Article 22 of the African Charter on Human and Peoples' Rights and Article 37 of the Arab Charter on Human Rights. However, none of the institutions that monitor implementation of these treaties had taken any significant steps to hold states parties accountable according to these provisions until the African Commission on Human and Peoples' Rights issued its landmark decision concerning the violation of the right to development as a result of an eviction of an indigenous group from a wildlife reserve in Kenya.[125] Article 22 of the African Charter was also found to have been violated by the Republic of Sudan as a result of attacks and forced displacement of the Darfurian people.[126] Beyond those cases, there has been virtually no legal accountability for the right to development.

The politics of the right to development is largely a matter of balancing the national and international dimensions of this right, since each dimension reflects the preference of different groups of states. In theory and in the wording of the Declaration, both are complementary rather than conflicting. The greatest challenge in bringing the right to development into the realm of practice is for all states to embrace the indivisibility and interdependence of 'all the aspects of the right to development' as set forth in Article 9 of the Declaration and to agree to development agendas consistent with the affirmation in Article 4 that, 'as a complement to the efforts of developing countries, effective international co-operation is essential in providing these countries with appropriate means and facilities to foster their comprehensive development'. The right to development has so far proved to be too broad in scope and too demanding in terms of structural change to be a significant factor in the practice of poverty reduction. It remains, nevertheless, the most systematic human rights framework for addressing issues of poverty at the normative level.

5 CONCLUSION

There are two reasons why those who favour the growth model of development resist what they see as the well-intentioned but misguided intrusion of human rights into pro-poor development work. The first is the conviction that economic progress suffers as a result of advancing human rights before a sufficient level of prosperity has been reached. However, the examples of countries that developed rapidly under conditions of human rights deprivation and that liberalized later (for example, Brazil, Chile, South Korea, and Taiwan) are far too complex to be probative, and counter-examples can be found, such as Costa Rica, Ghana, India, Senegal, and Thailand, that did not impose systematic human right deprivation as the price of economic development. The second is that those who have primary responsibility over the economy—ministers of finance and planning, corporate executives, shareholders, and many academic economists—often assume that human rights are merely matters of legal disputes or strident claims of the political opposition to the government which they represent or with which they cooperate.

However, in response to the challenges posed at the beginning of this chapter, there are compelling reasons why human rights are both definitional of and instrumental to anti-poverty objectives. The definitional component is the common purpose of both human

---

[125] 276/03, *Centre for Minority Rights Development (Kenya) and Minority Rights Group International on behalf of Endorois Welfare Council v Kenya*, 27th Activity Report of the ACommHPR (2009).

[126] 279/03–296/05, *Sudan Human Rights Organisation & Centre on Housing Rights and Evictions (COHRE) v Sudan*, 28th Activity Report of the ACommHPR (2010).

rights and development, which specialists in both fields usually articulate in terms of human welfare. The instrumental component is the relationship between human rights and forms of empowerment that make anti-poverty measures sustainable and equitable.

A powerful justification for human rights in the anti-poverty agenda relates to the proposition that human rights define the same objective as pro-poor development, for which human development is a convenient proxy. From the capability perspective, both human development and human rights increase freedom. From the utilitarian perspective, both enhance human well-being. However, the similarity is diminished if development is defined merely in terms of growth in production and consumption of goods and services, which is the case in particular of the G20 process discussed in Section 3. Growth is desirable but not as an end in itself; it is a means towards various possible ends. If the end is the enrichment of the few at the expense of the many and of the planet, then it will not help the poor. If it is a means toward sustainable and equitable development, then it must be governed so as to reach that end. Another way of understanding the relationship between the means and ends of development is to recall that '[e]conomic growth is often promoted as a means to alleviate poverty; yet even when growth does materialize, its benefits are unevenly distributed and rarely accrue to the poor.'[127]

Thus, the first step in clarifying in practical terms the meaning of poverty in the context of human rights is to note that pro-poor human development, like human rights, is a process that enables choices by all people to lead a life they value and, thus, enhances their well-being. Human rights are also about creating an environment in which people can develop their full potential and lead creative lives by, in the words of the UDHR, assuring 'the dignity and worth of the human person' and promoting 'social progress and better standards of life in larger freedom'.[128] The ultimate objective of both human development and human rights is, therefore, well-being as understood in both fields. The greatest obstacle to those choices is poverty, which is both capability deprivation and a measure of the denial of human rights.

The economic empowerment of people to be subjects rather than objects of their own history, to know, claim, and realize the full range of their human rights is both morally desirable and the principal means to realize what Article 28 UDHR refers to as the right to 'a social and international order in which the rights and freedoms set forth in this Declaration can be fully realized'. The combats against poverty and for human rights come together in the vision of such a social and international order.

FURTHER READING

ALSTON and ROBINSON (eds), *Human Rights and Development: Toward Mutual Reinforcement* (Oxford University Press, 2005).

ANDREASSEN and MARKS (eds), *Development as a Human Right: Legal, Political and Economic Dimensions* (Intersentia, 2010).

COLLIER, *The Bottom Billion: Why the Poorest Countries Are Failing and What Can Be Done About It* (Oxford University Press, 2007).

DARROW, 'The Millennium Development Goals: Milestones or Millstones? Human Rights Priorities for the Post-2015 Development' (2012) 15 *Yale HR and Development LJ* 55.

---

[127] Millen, Irwin, and Yong Kim, 'Conclusion: Pessimism of the Intellect, Optimism of the Will', in Yong Kim *et al.* (eds), *Dying for Growth: Global Inequality and the Health of the Poor* (Common Courage Press, 2000) 383.   [128] UDHR, preambular para 5.

FERRAZ, 'Poverty and Human Rights' (2008) 28 *OJLS* 585.

GAISBAUER, SCHWEIGER, and SEDMAK (eds), *Ethical Issues in Poverty Alleviation* (Springer, 2016).

GAURI and GLOPPEN, 'Human Rights-Based Approaches to Development: Concepts, Evidence, and Policy' (2012) 44 *Polity* 485.

GREADY and VANDENHOLE (eds), *Human Rights and Development in the New Millennium: Towards a Theory of Change* (Routledge, 2014).

HUNT, NOWAK, and OSMANI, *Human Rights and Poverty Reduction Strategies: Human Rights and Poverty Reduction: A Conceptual Framework* (OHCHR, 2003).

KHAN, *The Unheard Truth: Poverty and Human Rights* (WW Norton, 2009).

LANGFORD, SUMNER, and YAMIN, *Millennium Development Goals and Human Rights: Past, Present and Future* (Cambridge University Press, 2013).

OSMANI, 'Poverty and Human Rights: Building on the Capability Approach' (2005) 6 *J of Human Development* 205.

OHCHR, *Claiming the MDGs: A Human Rights Approach* (UN, 2008).

OHCHR, *Realizing the Right to Development: Essays in Commemoration of 25 Years of the United Nations Declaration on the Right to Development* (UN, 2013).

POGGE, *World Poverty and Human Rights* (Polity Press, 2008).

SALOMON, *Global Responsibility for Human Rights: World Poverty and the Development of International Law* (Oxford University Press, 2007).

SEN, *Development as Freedom* (Alfred A Knopf, 2000).

SEN, 'Human Rights and Capabilities' (2005) 6 *J of Human Development* 151.

UVIN, *Human Rights and Development* (Kumarian Press, 2004).

VIZARD, *Poverty and Human Rights: Sen's 'Capability Perspective' Explored* (Oxford University Press, 2006).

USEFUL WEBSITES

Special Rapporteur on extreme poverty and human rights: <http://www.ohchr.org/EN/Issues/Poverty/Pages/SRExtremePovertyIndex.aspx>

International Network for Economic, Social and Cultural Rights: <http://www.escr-net.org/>

World Bank: <http://www.worldbank.org/>

Oxfam International: <http://www.oxfam.org>

United Nations, SDGs-Poverty: <http://www.un.org/sustainabledevelopment/poverty/>

Centre for Economic and Social Rights: <http://www.cesr.org>

INDEX

Introductory Note

References such as '178–9' indicate (not necessarily continuous) discussion of a topic across a range of pages. Wherever possible in the case of topics with many references, these have either been divided into sub-topics or only the most significant discussions of the topic are listed. Because the entire work is about 'human rights', the use of this term (and certain others which occur constantly throughout the book) as an entry point has been restricted. Information will be found under the corresponding detailed topics.